RECUEIL DES COURS

429 (2023)

L'Académie de droit international de La Haye

honorée du prix Wateler de la Paix (1936, 1950), du prix Félix Houphouët-Boigny pour la recherche de la paix (1992), de l'ordre du Rio Branco, Brésil (1999), et de la médaille de l'Institut royal d'études européennes, Espagne (2000)

The Hague Academy of International Law

awarded the Wateler Peace Prize (1936, 1950), the Félix Houphouët-Boigny Peace Prize (1992), the Order of Rio Branco, Brazil (1999), and the Medal of the Royal Institute of European Studies, Spain (2000)

ISBN 978-90-04-54462-8

Printed by/Imprimé par Triangle Bleu, 59600 Maubeuge, France

ACADÉMIE DE DROIT INTERNATIONAL

FONDÉE EN 1923 AVEC LE CONCOURS DE LA
DOTATION CARNEGIE POUR LA PAIX INTERNATIONALE

RECUEIL DES COURS

COLLECTED COURSES OF THE HAGUE ACADEMY OF INTERNATIONAL LAW

2023

Tome 429 de la collection

BRILL | NIJHOFF

Leiden/Boston

COMPOSITION DU CURATORIUM
DE L'ACADÉMIE DE DROIT INTERNATIONAL DE LA HAYE

PRÉSIDENT

MEMBRES

SECRÉTAIRE GÉNÉRAL
DE L'ACADÉMIE DE DROIT INTERNATIONAL DE LA HAYE

ACADÉMIE DE DROIT INTERNATIONAL DE LA HAYE

— FONDÉE EN 1923 AVEC LE CONCOURS DE LA DOTATION CARNEGIE —

HONORÉE DU PRIX WATELER DE LA PAIX (1936, 1950), DU PRIX FÉLIX HOUPHOUËT-BOIGNY POUR LA RECHERCHE DE LA PAIX (1992), DE L'ORDRE DU RIO BRANCO, BRÉSIL (1999), ET DE LA MÉDAILLE DE L'INSTITUT ROYAL D'ÉTUDES EUROPÉENNES, ESPAGNE (2000)

L'Académie constitue un centre d'études et d'enseignement du droit international public et privé, et des sciences connexes. Son but est de faciliter l'examen approfondi et impartial des problèmes se rattachant aux rapports juridiques internationaux.

L'enseignement de l'Académie est principalement donné au Palais de la Paix, à La Haye, par des personnalités de différents États. Il porte sur le droit international, sous ses aspects théoriques et pratiques, et sur la jurisprudence internationale. La durée de ses deux principales sessions est en été de six semaines s'étendant sur les mois de juillet et d'août, et partagée en deux périodes, consacrées l'une au droit international public, l'autre aux relations privées internationales, et, en hiver, de trois semaines, consacrée en janvier au droit international. L'enseignement est dispensé en français ou en anglais, avec traduction simultanée dans l'autre langue. Les sessions de l'Académie se déroulent sous l'autorité du Secrétaire général.

L'enseignement de l'Académie est conçu dans un esprit à la fois pratique et hautement scientifique. Nettement différencié des enseignements similaires des universités et écoles nationales, il s'adresse à tous ceux qui possèdent déjà des notions de droit international et ont, par intérêt professionnel ou curiosité d'esprit, le désir de se perfectionner dans cette science.

Il n'existe pas de cadre permanent de professeurs à l'Académie. Le Curatorium, qui est le corps chargé de la direction scientifique de l'institution, et qui se compose de dix-huit membres appartenant statutairement à des nationalités différentes, adresse chaque année, en toute liberté, ses invitations aux personnes qu'il estime qualifiées pour donner un cours ou une conférence à l'Académie. Les personnes ayant donné des cours à l'Académie ne sont donc aucunement fondées à s'intituler professeur de ou à l'Académie de droit international de La Haye.

L'Académie décerne un diplôme à ceux des auditeurs qui, réunissant les qualifications spéciales exigées par le règlement en vigueur, auront subi avec succès des épreuves d'examen devant le jury de la session à laquelle ils se sont inscrits. Elle délivre en outre aux auditeurs un certificat attestant l'assiduité aux cours de l'Académie à la fin de la session suivie.

Toute personne désirant suivre l'enseignement de l'Académie doit faire parvenir par voie électronique au secrétariat de l'Académie, au Palais de la Paix, à La Haye, un formulaire d'inscription dûment rempli. L'Académie perçoit des droits d'inscription fixés par le Conseil d'administration de l'Académie.

Un programme de bourses d'études permettant d'assister aux cours d'été ou d'hiver est institué auprès de l'Académie. Le mode d'attribution de ces bourses fait l'objet d'un règlement disponible sur le site Internet de l'Académie.

Tous les cours professés à l'Académie durant les sessions d'été et d'hiver font, en principe, l'objet d'une publication dans le *Recueil des cours de l'Académie de droit international de La Haye*, ainsi que sur une plateforme Internet, dans la langue dans laquelle ils ont été professés. Certains cours sont également publiés ou réédités dans des collections spéciales.

THE HAGUE ACADEMY OF INTERNATIONAL LAW

— FOUNDED IN 1923 WITH THE SUPPORT OF THE CARNEGIE ENDOWMENT —

AWARDED THE WATELER PEACE PRIZE (1936, 1950), THE FÉLIX HOUPHOUËT-BOIGNY PEACE PRIZE (1992), THE ORDER OF RIO BRANCO, BRAZIL (1999), AND THE MEDAL OF THE ROYAL INSTITUTE OF EUROPEAN STUDIES, SPAIN (2000)

The Academy is an institution devoted to the study and teaching of Public and Private International Law and related fields. Its mission is to further the thorough and impartial examination of issues arising from international legal relations.

The courses of the Academy are dispensed principally at the Peace Palace in The Hague by personalities from different States. They deal with the theoretical and practical aspects of international law, including international jurisprudence. The duration of its two main sessions is, in Summer, of six weeks in July and August, divided into two periods of three weeks each, one devoted to Public International Law and the other to Private International Law, and, in Winter, of three weeks, in January, devoted to international law. They are taught in either English or in French, with simultaneous interpretation into the other language. The Secretary-General is responsible for managing the sessions of the Academy.

The education offered by the Academy is designed to be both practical and highly academically advanced. Clearly distinct from the teachings provided in national universities and law schools, it is intended for those who already possess some notion of international law and who, out of professional interest or intellectual curiosity, desire to deepen their knowledge in this field.

There is no permanent teaching staff at the Academy. The Curatorium, which is the body entrusted with the scientific management of the institution, and which consists of eighteen members of different nationalities, invites each year, in its unfettered discretion, whomsoever it deems best qualified to dispense a course or give a lecture at the Academy. It follows that no one who has lectured at the Academy is entitled to style himself or herself Professor of or at The Hague Academy of International Law.

The Academy awards a Diploma to those attendees who possess special qualifications as set out in the regulations, after having successfully passed examinations before the Jury of the session in which they are registered. It also delivers a certificate of attendance to registered attendees at the end of the session.

Anyone wishing to attend the courses at the Academy must send a completed electronic registration form to the Secretariat of the Academy at the Peace Palace in The Hague. The registration fee for each session of courses is fixed by the Administrative Board of the Academy.

The Academy manages a programme of scholarships to allocate at its discretion to attendees at the Summer and Winter Courses. The regulations governing scholarships are published on the website of the Academy.

All courses taught at the Academy during the Summer and Winter Courses are, in principle, published in the *Collected Courses of The Hague Academy of International Law*, which also exist in electronic format, in the language in which they were delivered. Some courses are also published or reissued in special collections.

GENERAL TABLE OF CONTENT

PRIVATE (AND PUBLIC) INTERNATIONAL LAW IN INVESTMENT ARBITRATION

by

JOSÉ ANTONIO MORENO RODRÍGUEZ

J. A. MORENO RODRÍGUEZ

TABLE OF CONTENTS

BIOGRAPHICAL NOTE

José Antonio Moreno Rodríguez was born on 14 November 1966, in Asunción, Paraguay. He studied at the National University of Asunción (1990, Law Degree; 1995, Doctor in Law *summa cum laude*) and at Harvard University (1993, LLM, thesis supervised by Professor Emeritus Arthur Taylor von Mehren).

Dr Moreno Rodríguez is a Founding Partner of Altra Legal, and is President of the Centro de Estudios de Derecho, Economía y Política (CEDEP), co-organizing the International Academy of Comparative Law General Congress (2022) and the Hague Academy External Programme (2023).

He is a member of the Arbitration Court of the International Chamber of Commerce (ICC), the Permanent Court of Arbitration (PCA), the International Centre for Settlement of Investment Disputes (ICSID) Panel of Arbitrators and the Court of Arbitration for Sport (CAS) in the general and football lists. He acts regularly as an arbitrator before these bodies.

Dr Moreno Rodríguez is the President of the Inter-American Juridical Committee of the Organization of American States (OAS), Rapporteur of its Guide on the Law Applicable to International Commercial Contracts in the Americas (2019) and Rapporteur of its future Guide on the Applicable Law to Investment Arbitration.

He is also a member of the UNIDROIT Governing Council and Chair of the UNIDROIT Working Group on the topic of Agricultural Land Investment Contracts.

Dr Moreno Rodríguez was a delegate at the Thirty-Ninth Session of the United Nations Commission on International Trade Law (UNCITRAL, 2006), at which the amendments to the Model Law on International Commercial Arbitration were approved. He was also a delegate before the OAS for the VII Inter-American Specialized Conference on Private International Law (CIDIP VII), the expert of the Working Group on the Hague Principles on Choice of Law in International Commercial Contracts (2010-2015), acted as a representative before the Special Commission of the Hague Conference on Private International Law, where he led the drafting of the instrument on the applicable law to international contracts, and authored and introduced to the legislature Paraguay's pioneering Law 5395/2015 ("Regarding the Applicable Law to International Contracts").

Dr Moreno Rodríguez has been a Professor at Heidelberg University in the International Law, Investments and Trade LL.M program and a Visiting Professor at Paris Pantheón-Assas University, among other institutions. He continues to teach undergraduate and graduate courses in Paraguay and lectures at numerous conferences on dispute resolution and international commercial and financial law.

Dr Moreno Rodríguez is the former President and Secretary-General of the American Association of Private International Law (ASADIP), former President of the Instituto Paraguayo de Derecho Bancario (IPDBS) and the former *ad honorem* Legal Advisor to the Ministry of Foreign Affairs of Paraguay in matters of public international law related to the National Boundary Commission. He is the recipient of the Rosalba Medal, awarded by the Secretariat of the Permanent Tribunal of Revision of the MERCOSUR, for his work on international law.

PRINCIPAL PUBLICATIONS

Books

Choice of Law in International Commercial Contracts: Global Perspectives on the Hague Principles [regional editor], Oxford, Oxford University Press, 2021.
Use of the UNIDROIT Principles to Interpret and Supplement Domestic Contract Law [co-editor with A. Garro] (*Ius Comparatum*: Global Studies in Comparative Law, Vol. 51), Cham, Springer, 2021.
Arbitraje Comercial y de Inversiones, Asunción, Intercontinental / CEDEP, 2019.
La Compraventa Internacional y la CISG [co-editor with A. Garro], Asunción, Intercontinental / CEDEP, 2019.
Curso de Contratos, 2nd ed., Asunción, Intercontinental / CEDEP, 2017.
Código Civil de la República del Paraguay, Comentado [co-editor], 3rd. ed., Asunción, La Ley Paraguaya, 2017.
Contratos Internacionales [co-editor with D. Fernández Arroyo] (Biblioteca de Derecho de la Globalización), Washington, DC, ASADIP / OAS, 2015.
Derecho aplicable y arbitraje, Bogotá, Universidad del Rosario, 2013; Lima, Thomson Reuters, 2013; Asunción, Intercontinental / CEDEP, 2013; Madrid, Thomson Reuters, 2014; Curitiba, Direito Aplicável / Arbitragem, Juruá Editora, 2015.
Curso de Hechos y Actos Jurídicos, Asunción, Intercontinental / CEDEP, 2016.
Libro homenaje a Roberto Ruíz Díaz Labrano [co-editor with D. Fernández Arroyo], Asunción, CEDEP, 2013.
Curso de Contratos, 2nd ed., Asunción, Intercontinental / CEDEP, 2017.
Arbitraje en el Paraguay, Asunción, Intercontinental / CEDEP, 2011.
Contratos [collective work], Asunción, Intercontinental / CEDEP, 2011.
Derecho Societario y Concursal Panamericano [co-editor with D. Roque Vítolo], Buenos Aires, Legis Argentina / CEDEP, 2013.
Contratación y Arbitraje: Contribuciones recientes, Asunción, CEDEP, 2010.
¿Cómo se codifica hoy el derecho comercial internacional? [co-editor with J. Basedow and D. P. Fernández Arroyo], Asunción, Thomson Reuters / CEDEP, 2010.
Técnica Legislativa y su Relación con los Procesos Mundiales y Regionales de Elaboración Normativa [editor, 2 vols.], special issue, *Revista Jurídica La Ley Paraguaya* (2008).
Protección al Consumidor en América – los Trabajos de la CIDIP (OEA) [co-editor with D. Fernández Arroyo], Asunción, La Ley Paraguaya, 2007.
Suplemento sobre Derecho Informático [editor], Asunción, La Ley Paraguaya, 2007.
Dos tesis sobre contratos, Asunción, Intercontinental, 2007.
Temas de Contratación Internacional, Inversiones y Arbitraje, Asunción, Catena Editores / CEDEP, 2006.
Legislación Bursátil y Fiduciaria [co-author with V. H. Dejesús Chena and J. I. Godoy Giménez], Asunción, Intercontinental, 2005.
Arbitraje y Mediación [editor], Asunción, Intercontinental, 2003.
Cláusulas Abusivas en los Contratos, Asunción, Intercontinental, 1999.
Teoría de la Causa, Asunción, Intercontinental, 1996.
Derecho Bancario [co-author], Asunción, La Ley Paraguaya (editions 1995, 1999, 2001).
Curso de Derecho Civil, Hechos y Actos Jurídicos, Asunción, Intercontinental, 1991 (reissued 1995, 1999, 2001, 2004, 2008).

Book chapters

"El derecho no estatal en la nueva ley uruguaya de Derecho Internacional Privado" [co-author with E. Florio de León], in E. Vescovi (ed.), *Comentarios a la Nueva Ley General de Derecho Internacional Privado (No. 19.920 del 17 de noviembre de 2020)*, Montevideo, Ediciones Idea, 2022, pp. 145-161.

"Paraguay", in L. Mistelis, L. Shore and H. Smit (eds.), *World Arbitration Reporter (WAR)*, 2nd ed., New York, Juris, 2021, Vol. 1A, para. 1-33.
"Paraguayan Perspectives on the Hague Principles", in D. Girsberger, T. Kadner Graziano and J. L. Neels (eds.), *Choice of Law in International Commercial Contracts: Global Perspectives on the Hague Principles*, Oxford, Oxford University Press, 2021, pp. 1089-1103.
"The OAS Guide and the Hague Principles", in D. Girsberger, T. K. Graziano and J. L. Neels (eds.), *Choice of Law in International Commercial Contracts: Global Perspectives on the Hague Principles*, Oxford, Oxford University Press, 2021, pp. 931-950.
"Perspectives on the Hague Principles in International Commercial Arbitration" [co-author with L. Gama and D. Girsberger], in D. Girsberger, T. Kadner Graziano and J. L. Neels (eds.), *Choice of Law in International Commercial Contracts: Global Perspectives on the Hague Principles*, Oxford, Oxford University Press, 2021, pp. 200-234.
"Advocating Party Autonomy in Private International Law: The 2015 Choice of Law Principles", in T. John, R. Gulati and B. Kohler (eds.), *The Elgar Companion to the Hague Conference on Private International Law*, Cheltenham, Edward Elgar, 2020, pp. 349-358.
"The CISG in Paraguay", in I. de Aguilar Vieira and G. Cerqueira (eds.), *La Convention de Vienne en Amérique : 40e anniversaire de la Convention des Nations unies sur les contrats de vente internationale de marchandises / The Vienna Convention in America: 40th Anniversary of the United Nations Convention on Contracts for the International Sale of Goods*, Paris, Société de législation comparée, 2020, pp. 251-270.
"Paraguay: La Reforma del Sistema de Garantías Mobiliarias" [co-author with L. E. Cazal Zaldívar], in D. M. Bovio (ed.), *Ley Modelo Interamericana sobre Garantías Mobiliarias: Su Implementación*, Madrid, Marcial Pons, 2020, pp. 253-265.
"The New OAS Guide on International Contracts", in C. Benicke and S. Huber (eds.), *National, International, Transnational: Harmonischer Dreiklang im Recht, zum 70, Festschrift für Herbert Kronke, Geburtstag*, Bielefeld, Verlag Ernst / Werner Gieseking, 2020, pp. 399-413.
"El rol pionero de los Tratados de Montevideo para. la codificación del derecho de la contratación internacional en el mundo", in C. F. de Aguirre and G. A. Lorenzo Idiarte (eds.), *Legado y futuro de sus soluciones en el concierto internacional actual: 130 Aniversario de los Tratados de Montevideo de 1889*, Montevideo, Fundación de Cultura Universitaria, 2019, pp. 165-180.
"Régimen Jurídico de las Inversiones Extranjeras en el Paraguay, en Tratado de Inversiones Extranjeras y Arbitraje de Inversiones", in C. Esplugues Mota (ed.), *Tratado de Inversiones Extranjeras y Arbitraje de Inversiones en Iberoamérica*, Valencia, Tirant lo Blanch, 2019, pp. 553-589.
"La efectividad del Arbitraje Comercial Internacional como mecanismo de solución de controversias", in F. E. Zenedin Glitz (eds.), *Questões de Direito Internacional: pessoa, comércio e procedimento II*, Paraná, JML Editora, 2018, pp. 145-162.
"Paraguay", in *Encyclopedia of Private International Law*, Vol. 3: *National Reports A-Z*, Cheltenham, Edward Elgar, 2017, pp. 2397-2410.
"Interpretation and Application of the New York Convention in Paraguay", in G. A. Bermann (ed.), *Recognition and Enforcement of Foreign Arbitral Awards: The Interpretation and Application of the New York Convention by National Courts*, Cham, Springer, 2017, pp. 743-751.
"El Derecho No Estatal en la Nueva Ley Paraguaya de Contratos Internacionales", in S. Godoy (ed.), *Compendio de Derecho Administrativo Presidencial*, Asunción, Thomson Reuters, 2017, pp. 111-130.
"The New Paraguayan Law on International Contracts: Back to the Past?", in *Eppur si muove: The Age of Uniform Law – Essays in Honour of Michael Joachim Bonell*

to Celebrate His 70th Birthday, Vol. 2, Rome, UNIDROIT, 2016, pp. 1146-1178.
"El Derecho No Estatal en la Nueva Ley Paraguaya de Contratos Internacionales", in A. Do Amaral Júnior and L. Klein Vieira (eds.), *El Derecho Internacional Privado y sus Desafíos en la Actualidad*, Bogotá, Grupo Editorial Ibañez, 2016, pp. 277-302.
"El arbitraje como servicio y el derecho internacional privado", in J. A. Moreno Rodríguez and C. Lima Marques (eds.), *Los servicios en el derecho internacional privado*, Asunción, ASADIP, 2014, pp. 261-280.
"El Derecho no Estatal en la Contratación Latinoamericana Actual", in L. Olavo Baptista, L. Ramina and T. Scheila Friedrich (eds.), *Direito Internacional Contemporáneo*, Curitiba, Juruá Editora, 2014, pp. 375-391.
"Autonomía contractual transfronteriza en el Paraguay: ¡Habemus jurisprudencia!", in *Derecho internacional privado y Derecho de la integración, Libro homenaje a Roberto Ruíz Díaz Labrano*, Asunción, CEDEP, 2013, pp. 373-386.
"Comentario al artículo 35", in P. Perales Viscasillas and I. Torterola (eds.), *Nuevo Reglamento de Arbitraje de la CNUDMI 2010, Anotado y Comentado*, Buenos Aires, Editorial Legis, 2011, pp. 353-384.
"Arbitraje Comercial Internacional en el Paraguay: Marco Legal y Jurisprudencial", in C. Conejero *et al.* (eds.), *El Arbitraje Comercial Internacional en Iberoamérica, Marco legal y jurisprudencial*, Madrid, La Ley / Wolters Kluwer, 2011, pp. 619-648.
"Los contratos de la Haya: ¿ancla al pasado o puente al futuro?", in J. Basedow, J. A. Moreno Rodríguez and D. P. Fernández Arroyo (eds.), *¿Cómo se codifica hoy el derecho comercial internacional?*, Asunción, Thomson Reuters / CEDEP, 2010, pp. 245-339.
"Autonomía de la voluntad en el Derecho internacional privado paraguayo", in D. P. Fernández Arroyo and J. A. Moreno Rodríguez (eds.), *Derecho internacional privado – derecho de la libertad y el respeto mutuo – Ensayos a la Memoria de Tatiana B. de Maekelt*, Asunción, CEDEP, 2010, pp. 409-451.
"Orden Público y Arbitraje: Algunos Pronunciamientos Recientes y Llamativos en Europa y el Mercosur", in J. Oviedo Albán (ed.), *Derecho Comercial en el Siglo XXI*, Bogotá, Editorial Temis, 2008.
"Paraguay", in C. Esplugues Mota, D. Hargaín and G. Palao Moreno (eds.), *Derecho de los Contratos Internacionales en Latinoamérica, Portugal y España*, Madrid, Edisofer, 2008, pp. 563-615.
"La Responsabilidad Civil en la Contratación Pública", in P. A. Sandoval Diez (ed.), *Vademécum sobre las Responsabilidades Jurídicas en el Proceso de las Contrataciones Públicas*, Asunción, Arandura Editorial, 2008.
"Orden público y arbitraje: algunos pronunciamientos recientes y llamativos en Europa y el MERCOSUR", in J. Oviedo Albán (ed.), *Derecho comercial en el siglo XXI*, Bogotá, Editorial Tamis, 2008, pp. 199-242.
"La Interpretación del Contrato dentro del Nuevo Escenario Internacional", in C. A. Soto (ed.), *Tratado de la Interpretación del Contrato en América Latina*, Lima, Editorial Grijley, 2007, pp. 1411-1450.
"Paraguay", in *International Mergers & Acquisitions Law*, Aspartore Books, 2006, pp. 483-499.
"Ramiro Rodríguez Alcalá, Silencioso Artífice del Código Civil Patrio", in A. T. Solís (ed.), *Derecho Privado Paraguayo: estudios por los 20 años del Código Civil*, Asunción, La Ley, 2007, pp. 15-39.
"Paraguay's New Arbitration Law: A Bridge Out of the Island", in T. Carbonneau (ed.), Penn State University Press, 2006.
"Régimen jurídico del comercio exterior" [co-author with G. Palao Moreno], in C. Esplugues Mota and D. Hargaín (eds.), *Derecho del comercio internacional: Mercosur-Unión Europea*, Madrid, Editorial Reus; Montevideo, Editorial B de F, 2005, pp. 77-140.
"Compraventa internacional de mercaderías: La convención de Viena de 1980 sobre compraventa internacional de mercaderías" [co-author with C. Esplugues Mota

and I. de Aguilar Vieira], in C. Esplugues Mota and D. Hargaín (eds.), *Derecho del comercio internacional: Mercosur-Unión Europea*, Madrid, Editorial Reus; Montevideo, Editorial B de F, 2005, pp. 345-397.

"La contratación internacional: Régimen general" [co-author with C. Esplugues Mota], in C. Esplugues Mota and D. Hargaín (eds.), *Derecho del comercio internacional: Mercosur-Unión Europea*, Madrid, Editorial Reus; Montevideo, Editorial B de F, 2005, pp. 281-344.

"Causa y Consideration en la forma del contrato: estado actual en el derecho comparado", in A. A. Alterini and N. L. Nicolau (eds.), *El Derecho privado ante la internacionalidad, la integración y la globalización. Homenaje al profesor Miguel Á. Ciuro Caldani*, Asunción, La Ley, 2005, pp. 401-421.

"El futuro de la codificación del derecho contractual en el Mercosur: un ensayo en perspectiva", in G. M. Dora Martinic and R. M. Tapia (eds.), *Sesquicentenario del Código Civil de Andrés Bello, Pasado, Presente y Futuro de la Codificación*, Vol. 2, Santiago, Lexis Nexis, 2005, pp. 1143-1174.

"Los Principios UNIDROIT de derecho contractual", in *Arbitraje y Mediación*, Asunción, Intercontinental, 2003, pp. 277-299.

Journal articles

"La nueva guía de la Organización de Estados Americanos y el derecho aplicable a los contratos internacionales", *Revista Española de Derecho Internacional*, Vol. 73 (2021), Parte I in No. 1, pp. 187-206 and Parte II in No. 2, pp. 261-284.

"El Arbitraje como Servicio y el Derecho Internacional Privado", *Boletim 106 da Sociedade Brasileira de Direito Internacional* (2019), pp. 97-113.

"Más allá de la Convención de México y los Principios de la Haya: ¿Qué sigue para. las Américas?", *Derecho Internacional Privado y de la Integración Eldial.com*, supplement 24/ May 2018, eds. S. L. Feldstein de Cárdenas (2018).

"El Arbitraje Internacional y la Nueva Ley Paraguaya de Contratos Internacionales", *Revista de Derecho Comercial y de las Obligaciones de la Argentina*, Vol 290 (2018), pp. 609-629.

"El Arbitraje Internacional y La Nueva Ley Paraguaya de Contratos Internacionales", *Lima Arbitration*, Vol. 3 (2017), pp. 96-123.

"Principios de La Haya: ¡Al fin una solución universal para. problemas de derecho aplicable a la contratación internacional!", *Revista de Derecho Privado y Comunitario de la Argentina*, Vol. 3 (2017), pp. 495-542.

"The Hague Principles and the New Paraguayan Law on International Contracts: Potential Influence on Legal Reform in the Americas and Abroad", *Global Forum on Private International Law* (2017), pp. 203-214.

"The Hague Principles, the OAS Guide and the New Paraguayan Law on International Contracts", *Curso de Derecho Internacional*, Vol. 44 (2017), pp. 155-154.

"La efectividad del arbitraje comercial internacional como mecanismo de solución de controversias", *Revista Foro de Derecho Mercantil* (2017), pp. 99-127.

"El Derecho no Estatal en la nueva ley paraguaya de contratos internacionales", *Revista Foro Derecho Mercantil*, No. 50 (2016), pp. 93-114.

"Prólogo", *Revista Secretaría del Tribunal Permanente de Revisión*, No. 8 (2016), pp. 9-11.

"A arbitragem internacional e a nova lei paraguaia de contratos internacionais", *Revista de la Secretaría del Tribunal Permanente de Revisión*, No. 7 (2016), pp. 97-126.

"Debate sobre el Derecho No Estatal y la Lex Mercatoria", *Arbitraje Internacional de Forseti*, No. 2 (2014), pp. 73-97.

"Debate sobre el Derecho No Estatal y la Lex Mercatoria", *Revista Jurídica de la U. Católica de Asunción*, Vol. 23 (2014), pp. 35-68.

"Derecho Aplicable a la Contratación y el Arbitraje Internacional", *Revista Ecuatoriana de Arbitraje*, Vol. 3 (2012), pp. 491-518.

"Los Principios de la Haya y el Derecho No Estatal en el Arbitraje Comercial Internacional", *Revista Jurídica de la UNICURITIBA*, Vol. 2. N. 29 (2012), pp.30-62.

"Reflexiones emergentes de la Convención de México para. la elaboración del futuro instrumento de La Haya en materia de contratación internacional" [co-author with

M. Albornoz], *Revista Electrónica El Dial, Suplemento de Derecho Internacional Privado y de la Integración*, No. 58 (2011).
"Contracts and Non-State Law in Latin America", *Uniform Law Review*, new series, Vol. 16 (2011), pp. 877-889.
"Reflections on the Mexico Convention in the Context of the Preparation of the Future Hague Instrument on International Contracts" [co-author with M. Albornoz], *Journal of Private International Law*, Vol. 7, No. 3 (2011), pp. 491-526.
"La Convención más trascendente en la historia del Derecho Privado", in D.P. Fernández Arroyo and N. González Martín (eds.), *Tendencias y Relaciones del Derecho Internacional Privado Americano Actual* (2010), pp. 381-415.
"Derecho Aplicable a la Contratación y el Arbitraje Internacional", *Revista Jurídica Universidad Católica de Asunción* (2011), pp. 893-923.
"La Convención más trascendente en la historia del Derecho Privado", *Revista Jurídica La Ley Paraguaya*, No. 32 (2009), pp. 273-294.
"La Responsabilidad Civil dentro del Nuevo Escenario Internacional", Responsabilidad Civil, Daños y Perjuicios", *División de Investigación, Legislación y Publicaciones*, Centro Internacional de Estudios Judiciales, Corte Suprema de Justicia, e Intercontinental Editora, Asunción (2008), pp. 107-140.
"La Responsabilidad Civil dentro del Nuevo Escenario Internacional", *Revista Jurídica La Ley Paraguaya* (2008), pp. 885-901.
"Orden Público y Arbitraje: Algunos llamativos pronunciamientos recientes en Europa y el Mercosur", *Revista Foro de Derecho Mercantil*, No. 20 (2008), pp. 139-180.
"Orden Público y Arbitraje: Algunos llamativos pronunciamientos recientes en Europa y el Mercosur", *Revista Electrónica Lima Arbitration* (2007), pp. 63-105.
"Orden Público y Arbitraje: Algunos Llamativos Pronunciamientos Recientes en el MERCOSUR y la Unión Europea", *Revista Jurídica La Ley Paraguaya* (2007), pp. 679-699.
"Homogeneización del Derecho Contractual en Europa y el Mercosur (1)", *Revista de la Facultad de Derecho de la Universidad Nacional de Asunción* (2006), pp. 325-344.
"El régimen jurídico de las inversiones extranjeras en el Paraguay", *DeCITA: direito do comércio internacional / derecho del comercio internacional*, D. P. Fernández Arroyo, A. Dreyzin de Klor and L. Otávio Pimentel (eds.), No. 3 (2005), pp. 240-269.
"Los Principios Contractuales de UNIDROIT: ¿Un Mero Ejercicio Académico de Juristas Notables?", *Revista Foro de Derecho Mercantil*, Vol. 9 (2005), pp. 31-55.
"Regulación del derecho procesal civil internacional en el Paraguay" [co-author with M. E. Moreno Rodríguez], *DeCITA: direito do comércio internacional / derecho del comercio internacional*, D. P. Fernández Arroyo, A. Dreyzin de Klor and L. Otávio Pimentel (eds.), No. 3 (2005), pp. 660-674.
"Derecho aplicable, orden público y el régimen arbitral paraguayo", *Revista Brasileira de Arbitragem*, No. 3 (2004), pp. 83-112.
"Esfuerzos Mundiales de Homogeneización del Derecho Mercantil Internacional", *Revista de la Facultad de Derecho de la Universidad Nacional de Asunción* (2005), pp. 175-200.
"Régimen Jurídico Bursátil Apuntes Introductorios", *Revista de la Facultad de Derecho de la Universidad Católica de Asunción*, No. 11 (2002), pp. 262-270.
"Nueva Lex Mercatoria: ¿Fantasma creado por profesores de La Sorbona?", *Revista de Derecho Mercantil Internacional*, Vol. 1 (2003), pp. 95-124.
"Reforma del Mercado de Valores en el Paraguay, Reflexiones, Apuntes y Sugerencias", *Revista Jurídica de la Facultad de Derecho de la Universidad Nacional de Asunción* (2001), pp. 391-398.
"Cláusulas Contractuales Abusivas en el Derecho Paraguayo", *Revista de Derecho Comparado, Cláusulas Abusivas*, No. 2 (2000), pp. 131-170.
"El Arbitraje y los Contratos con Cláusulas Predispuestas", *Publicación de la Cámara Nacional de Comercio de Uruguay, Centro de Conciliación y Arbitraje*, Centro de Arbitraje Internacional para. el MERCOSUR (2000).
"Técnica Legislativa: Apuntes, Reflexiones y Sugerencias", *Revista Jurídica de la Facultad de Ciencias Jurídicas y Diplomáticas*, Universidad Católica de Asunción (1998), pp. 211-220.
"Limitación de Elección de Directores en el Régimen Bursátil Paraguayo", *Revista Jurídica La Ley* (1994), pp. 81-82.

PRINCIPAL ABBREVIATIONS

AANZFTA	Agreement Establishing the ASEAN-Australia-New Zealand Free Trade Area
ABA	American Bar Association
ACIA	ASEAN Comprehensive Investment Agreement
ACICA	Australian Centre for International Commercial Arbitration
ADR	alternative dispute resolution
ALI	American Law Institute
ALIC	UNIDROIT/IFAD Legal Guide on Agricultural Land Investment Contracts
AMU	Arab Maghreb Union
APEC	Asia-Pacific Economic Cooperation
APPIL	Asian Principles of Private International Law
ASADIP	American Association of Private International Law
ASEAN	Association of Southeast Asian Nations
BIT	bilateral investment treaty
CAFTA	Central America Free Trade Agreement
CAFTA-DR	Dominican Republic-Central America Free Trade Agreement
Cape Town Convention	Convention of 16 November 2001 on International Interests in Convention Mobile Equipment
CAPPIL	Commission on the Asian Principles of Private International Law
CAS	Court of Arbitration for Sport
CCIA Agreement	COMESA Common Investment Agreement
CCJA	Common Court of Justice and Arbitration [OHADA]
CEN-SAD	Community of Sahel-Saharan States
CETA	Comprehensive Economic and Trade Agreement [between Canada and the European Union]
CIDIP	The Inter-American Specialized Conferences on Private International Law
CIETAC	China International Economic and Trade Arbitration Commission
CISG / Vienna Sales Convention	Convention on Contracts for the International Sale of Goods [United Nations]
CJEU	Court of Justice of the European Union
CJI	Inter-American Juridical Committee [OAS]
COMESA	Common Market for Eastern and Southern Africa
CPTPP	Comprehensive and Progressive Agreement for Trans-Pacific Partnership
CRCICA	Cairo Regional Centre for International Commercial Arbitration
DCFR	Draft Common Frame of Reference
DFC	US International Development Finance Corporation
DFI	direct foreign investment
DIAC	Dubai International Arbitration Centre
DIL	Department of International Law [OAS]
DIS	German Arbitration Institute

DSB	dispute settlement body
EAC	East African Community
ECCAS	Economic Community of Central African States
ECCJ	Community Court of Justice of ECOWAS
ECGLC	Economic Community of the Great Lakes Countries
ECJ	European Court of Justice
ECOWAS	Economic Community of West African States
ECOWIC	ECOWAS Common Investment Code
ECT	Energy Charter Treaty
EEC	European Economic Community
EFTA	European Free Trade Association
EGPIL/GEDIP	European Group of Private International Law
EU	European Union
EVFTA	EU-Vietnam Free Trade Agreement
FCN	Friendship, Commerce and Navigation
FET	fair and equitable treatment
FIDIC	International Federation of Consulting Engineers
FPS	full protection and security
FTA	free trade agreement
GAFTA	Grain and Feed Trade Association
GATS	General Agreement on Trade in Services
GATT	General Agreement on Tariffs and Trade
Hague Conference / HCCH	Hague Conference on Private International Law
Hague Principles	Hague Principles on Choice of Law in International Contracts
HKIAC	Hong Kong International Arbitration Centre
IACAC	Inter-American Commercial Arbitration Commission
IBA	International Bar Association
IBRD	International Bank for Reconstruction and Development
ICC	International Chamber of Commerce
ICC Rules	ICC Arbitration Rules
ICCA	International Council for Commercial Arbitration
ICDR	International Centre for Dispute Resolution
ICJ	International Court of Justice
ICSID	International Centre for Settlement of Investment Disputes
ICSID Convention	Convention on the Settlement of Investment Disputes Between States and Nationals of Other States
IDA	International Development Association
IFC	International Finance Corporation
IFAD	International Fund for Agricultural Development
IGAD	Inter-Governmental Authority on Development
IIA	international investment agreement
IIL	Institute of International Law
IISD	International Institute of Sustainable Development
ILA	International Law Association
ILC	International Law Commission [United Nations]
IMF	International Monetary Fund
IOC	Indian Ocean Commission

IPRs	Intellectual Property Rights
ISDS	investor-State dispute settlement
ITC	International Trade Centre
LCIA	London Court of International Arbitration
LINDB	Introductory Law to the Norms of Brazilian Law
MAC Protocol	Protocol to the Convention on International Interests in Mobile Equipment on Matters specific to Mining, Agricultural and Construction Equipment
MAI	multilateral agreement on investment
MERCOSUR	Common Market of the Southern Cone
Mexico Convention	Inter-American Convention on the Law Applicable to International Contracts
MFN	most-favored-nation clause
MIGA	Multilateral Investment Guarantee Agency
MRU	Mano River Union
MST	minimum standard of treatment
NAFTA	North American Free Trade Agreement
NAI	Netherlands Arbitration Institute
New York Convention	The Convention on the Recognition and Enforcement of Foreign Arbitral Awards
NT	national treatment
OAS	Organization of American States
OAS Guide	OAS Guide on the Applicable Law to International Commercial Contracts in the Americas
OECD	Organisation for Economic Co-operation and Development
OHADA	Organization for the Harmonization of Business Law in Africa
OHADAC	Organization for the Harmonization of Business Law in the Caribbean
OPIC	Overseas Private Investment Corporation [United States]
PAIC	Pan-African Investment Code [African Union]
PCA	Permanent Court of Arbitration
PCA Rules	PCA Arbitration Rules
PCIJ	Permanent Court of International Justice
PECL	Principles of European Contract Law
PIL	private international law
Porter Convention	Convention of the Peaceful Resolution of International Disputes
RCEP	Regional Comprehensive Economic Partnership
REC	regional economic community
Rome I	Regulation on the Law Applicable to Contractual Obligations [European Union]
Rome II	Regulation on the Law Applicable to Non-Contractual Obligations [European Union]
SACU	Southern African Customs Union
SADC	Southern Africa Development Community
SCC	Stockholm Chamber of Commerce
SIAC	Singapore International Arbitration Centre
TFEU	Treaty on the Functioning of the European Union
TIPs	Treaties with Investment Provisions
TPP	Trans-Pacific Partnership

Transjus	ASADIP Principles on Transnational Access to Justice
Treaty of Asunción	Treaty Establishing a Common Market between the Argentine Republic, the Federal Republic of Brazil, the Republic of Paraguay and the Eastern Republic of Uruguay
TRIMS	Agreement on Trade-Related Investment Measures
TRIPS	Agreement on Trade-Related Aspects of Intellectual Property Law
TTIP	Transatlantic Trade and Investment Partnership
UCC	Uniform Commercial Code
UCP	Uniform Customs and Practice for Documentary Credits
UEMOA	West African Economic and Monetary Union
UIA	Union Internationale des Avocats
UN	United Nations
UNCC	United Nations Compensation Commission
UNCITRAL	United Nations Commission on International Trade Law
UNCITRAL Model Law	United Nations Commission on International Trade Law Model Law on International Commercial Arbitration (1985), with amendments as adopted in 2006
UNCITRAL Rules	UNCITRAL Arbitration Rules
UNCTAD	United Nations Conference on Trade and Development
UNIDROIT	United Nations International Institute for the Unification of Private Law
UNIDROIT Principles / UPICC	UNIDROIT Principles of International Commercial Contracts
USMCA	United States-Mexico-Canada Agreement
VCLT	Vienna Convention on the Law of Treaties
VIAC	Vienna International Arbitral Centre
WIPO	World Intellectual Property Organization
WTO	World Trade Organization

ACKNOWLEDGMENTS

Agatha Brandão de Oliveira provided magnificent assistance in preparing the Hague Academy lectures and in providing the general editing for this written contribution, with the valuable help of José Antonio Moreno Bendlin. Eleanor Dennis and Clarke Ries also assisted wonderfully in the editing of this manuscript. A special thanks also to those others involved in the many stages of the research and editing process, particularly Lucía Cazal, Luis Serrano, Felicita Argaña, Belén Moreno Bendlin, Regina Moreno Bendlin, Gabriela Melgarejo, Ruth Schneiderman, Rafael Silva, Ramiro Moreno Bendlin, Antonella Salgueiro and Gabriella Prado.

A special thanks to Professor Diego Fernández Arroyo for the honor of proposing my name for consideration by the Hague Academy Curatorium to lecture on the topic of this book.

Renowned scholars and legal experts were kind enough to read in whole or in part drafts of this book. I would like to thank David Stewart, Stanimir Alexandrov, Franco Ferrari, Jean Michel Arrighi, Soterios Loizou, Hans van Loon, Daniel Girsberger, Alejandro Garro, Alvaro Galindo, Fernando Cantuarias, Pedro Mendoza, Francisco Amallo, Pablo Parrilla, Nicolas Caffo, Facundo Pérez-Aznar, Ana Toubiana, Fabian Villeda, Fernando Ayala, Juan Ignacio Stampalija, Margie-Lys Jaime, Priscila Pereira de Andrade, Analía González, Mercedes Albornoz, Marta Pertegás, Christian Sommer, Jean Ho, and many others for their valuable comments and generous words of praise and encouragement.

The responsibility for the final text is, of course, entirely mine.

CHAPTER I

INTRODUCTION

A. Preliminary remarks

The resolution of international investment disputes through arbitration demands a multidisciplinary approach. The mechanism of international investment arbitration developed within public international law as one of its oldest and most central disciplines. In recent decades, much attention has been paid to the astonishing evolution of the field. By contrast, the relationship between international investment arbitration and private international law (including private law in general) has received relatively little consideration.

For this reason, the title of this book may be misleading if understood to mean that private international law currently occupies a relevant space in mainstream investment arbitration scholarship and practice [1]. From the outset, it must be clear that it does not. Should it? One of the central messages of this work is that it must.

Private international law, particularly after a significant rethinking and reshaping in recent decades, provides valuable tools for better handling several classes of investment claims. The same can be said of private law in general, which has been influential in the emergence, shaping and evolution of public international law. Closer attention to these developments and their implications for international investment arbitration is useful to achieve clarity about highly contested related issues. The timeless words of Wilfred Jenks are instructive in this regard:

> "By instinct and training the legal mind accepts the discipline of established ideas; it lacks the philosophic impulse perpetually to re-examine the foundations of accepted modes of thought and, perhaps partly because of the immense burden which keeping track of the development of the law by traditional processes represents, it frequently tends to shirk the intellectual effort involved in the

1. The original title of this work was "Private International Law and Investment Arbitration". Since the public aspect is repeatedly mentioned herein, I finally decided to add "(and Public)" to the title, which is still preceded by the word "Private".

constant assimilation of new sources of knowledge and ideas from beyond the established frontiers of the law." [2]

B. Scope of this book

Recent decades have ushered in profound changes in the fields of private international law, international arbitration and foreign investment.

Private international law has experienced profound shifts, ranging from restructuring its theoretical foundations to changes in its regulation and everyday practice. Significant developments within the field of international arbitration have also transformed some of its core concepts and regulatory framework, and expanded its daily use in cross-border disputes. Lastly, foreign investment-related litigation has also evolved exponentially in ways unimaginable in the first half of the twentieth century.

However, there has not been adequate cross-fertilization between these disciplines. The absence of a proper interdisciplinary dialogue explains an important aspect of why several inconsistencies are still found within case law, regulation and scholarly writing on international investment arbitration. There are countless examples of the lack of productive dialogue between these three fields, which will be discussed in further detail later in this work (see esp. Chaps. XIII, XIV, XV and XVI).

Historically, public international law has largely dominated investment arbitration, which perhaps explains why its advocates routinely and unduly stretch the orthodox notions of their discipline. Yet, private international law and its new underpinnings are better suited to address several complex issues currently facing investment claims, at least in relation to the applicable substantive law of these disputes. Foreign ventures raise contractual and other issues that public international law is largely ill-suited to solve.

However, mainstream public international law experts have historically proven unreceptive to developments from the private law domain. This was observed by Sir Hersch Lauterpacht almost one hundred years ago when he wrote:

---

2. W. Jenks, *Common Law of Mankind*, New York, Frederick A. Praeger, 1958, p. 85.

> "The warning 'beware of private law' has become a catchword uncritically accepted, eagerly copied, and widely disseminated; and its prestige is undimmed by the fact that the banished phantom reappears with unfailing regularity under the garb of 'general jurisprudence'." [3]

Another problem stems from unawareness in other disciplines that private international law has evolved to be better suited to resolve applicable law problems in a dynamic cosmopolitan setting. For example, old rigid nineteenth-century conflict of laws formulas have significantly transformed in recent decades: today, flexible conflict of laws mechanisms and uniform substantive law rules have increased in popularity and influence.

A shift must occur to rebalance the equilibrium of approaches within international investment arbitration. Of course, public international law will always dominate to a certain extent within a field that typically addresses international customary law and the violation of treaties. However, private international law and its recent developments deserve much closer attention, particularly in relation to certain specific matters, such as determining the applicable substantive law.

Lord Arnold McNair noted that public international law gave birth to the legal system that was considered applicable to international investments. Nonetheless he also recognized private law principles "from which tribunals can enrich and develop Public International Law" [4]. It is true that, as Michael Bogdan cautions, borrowed legal concepts must be applied thoughtfully to international law since they follow a domestic perspective and may thus become obsolete [5]. However, this is not always the case and the chapters that follow will devote particular attention to advances in related disciplines that potentially or factually impact international investment arbitration outcomes.

This book addresses a wide array of legal topics, some of which are granted a more in-depth study. Particular attention will be paid

3. H. Lauterpacht, *Private Law Sources and Analogies of International Law*, London, Longmans, Green and Co., 1927, p. 23.

4. Lord McNair, "The General Principles of Law Recognized by Civilized Nations", *British Yearbook of International Law*, Vol. 33 (1957), p. 6.

5. M. Bogdan, "General Principles of Law and the Problem of Lacunae in the Law of Nations", *Nordic Journal of International Law / Nordisk Tidsskrift for International Ret*, Vol. 46 (1977), p. 51. See also ILC (M. Vázquez-Bermúdez, Special Rapporteur), Second Report on General Principles of Law, A/CN.4/741, https://documents-dds-ny.un.org/doc/UNDOC/GEN/N20/093/44/PDF/N2009344.pdf?OpenElement, accessed 3 March 2022, at p. 55.

to applicable substantive law matters related to the investment arbitration mechanism of the International Centre for Settlement of Investment Disputes (ICSID) [6]. Why? ICSID's substantial body of jurisprudence shows that it is the leading institution offering dispute resolution services within the investment arbitration field [7]. Moreover, even though the ICSID arbitral mechanism has received scholarly attention, a considerable imbalance still exists within the literature on international commercial arbitration, in general, relating, for instance, to the International Chamber of Commerce (ICC) [8] or the United Nations Commission on International Trade Law (UNCITRAL) arbitral mechanisms [9] – the rules of which also may apply in investment claims.

Aspects of these and other dispute resolution services nonetheless merit consideration, mainly in relation to the intricacies that distinguish the applicable substantive law in investment arbitration from commercial arbitration. This book will also devote particular attention to the Permanent Court of Arbitration (PCA), which has a pioneering role within contemporary international arbitration, particularly in investment-related matters – a development that promises to expand in the coming years [10].

Due to concerns of overbreadth, this book will not address the many aspects of the arbitral process that have or might benefit from further interaction with recent developments within private international law, such as parallel litigation and *lis pendens*, or enforcement issues [11]. While it is not possible to make precise analogies (especially regarding the ICSID mechanism), several studies about these topics have been

6. Convention on the Settlement of Investment Disputes Between States and Nationals of Other States, 18 March 1965, Washington, 17 UST 1270, TIAS 6090, 575 UNTS 159.

7. Among others, Muchlinski refers to ICSID as "[t]he most important arbitral institution in the field of investment disputes". P. Muchlinski, "Policy Issues", in P. Muchlinski, F. Ortino and C. Schreuer (eds.), *The Oxford Handbook of International Investment Law*, New York, Oxford University Press, 2008, p. 41.

8. See https://iccwbo.org/dispute-resolution-services/arbitration/rules-of-arbitration, accessed 3 March 2022.

9. See https://uncitral.un.org/en/texts/arbitration, accessed 3 March 2022.

10. See https://pca-cpa.org/en/home, accessed 3 March 2022.

11. In this regard, see e.g. G. A. Bermann, "International Arbitration and Private International Law (General Course on Private International Law)", *Recueil des cours*, Vol. 381 (2016), pp. 177-216. Another telling topic that is catching attention is *iura novit curia*. For an excellent recent contribution regarding this issue in investment arbitration, see S. Loizou, "Establishing the Content of the Applicable Law in International Arbitration", in F. Ferrari and S. Kröll (eds.), *Conflict of Laws in International Commercial Arbitration*, New York, NYU Center for Transnational Litigation and Commercial Law / Juris, 2019, p. 443.

extensively undertaken in commercial arbitration scholarship [12], and their discussion will remain outside the scope of this work.

The focus throughout this book on the applicable substantive law is relevant because it is "[o]ne of the most difficult, under-theorized, and contentious questions in investment arbitration" [13]. This relative lack of scholarly attention is surprising, considering its importance. Indeed, it can determine the outcome of a dispute, and applying the wrong law can lead to the annulment of an award [14].

The substantive law applicable to an investment dispute constitutes a sufficiently broad and controversial topic to justify consideration on its own. Several questions related to this issue have often been ignored, neglected or improperly handled thus far. For instance, while ICSID has operated for over fifty years and has issued a large number of awards, it has recently been noted that "little progress has been made in better understanding [its] conflict-of-law system" and that "arbitral tribunals address conflict-of-law problems often only superficially" [15], or fail to provide any reasoning at all [16].

---

12. For instance, see G. Cordero-Moss and D. P. Fernández Arroyo, "Private International Law and International Commercial Arbitration: A Dialogue about the Usefulness and Awareness of the Former for the Latter", in V. Ruíz Abou-Nigm and M. B. Noodt Taquela (eds.), *Diversity and Integration in Private International Law*, Edinburgh, Edinburgh University Press, 2019, pp. 310-324.

13. A. Bjorklund and L. Vanhonnaeker, "Article 42", in J. Fouret, R. Gerbay and G. M. Alvarez (eds.), *The ICSID Convention, Regulation and Rules: A Practical Commentary*, Cheltenham, Edward Elgar, 2019, pp. 347-348. "[T]he method of establishing the content of the applicable law is one of the most important, albeit seldom examined, topics in the theory and practice of international arbitration"; also Loizou, *supra* note 11, p. 443.

14. In ICSID, the latter situation can occur on the ground of "excess of authority" (Art. 52 of the ICSID Convention). In arbitrations governed by UNCITRAL Model Law-inspired solutions, awards can be set aside on similar grounds (Art. 34 (2) (iii)). Under the New York Convention on Recognition and Enforcement of Foreign Awards, an arbitral tribunal's disregard for the applicable law chosen by the parties is arguably a ground for refusing recognition and enforcement contemplated in Article V (1) *(d)*. However, there is uncertainty as to how courts might decide in such a circumstance, and there is no uniform answer found in case law. See G. A. Bermann (ed.), *Recognition and Enforcement of Foreign Arbitral Awards: The Interpretation and Application of the New York Convention by National Courts*, Cham, Springer, 2017, pp. 51-52.

15. J. A. Bischoff, "Conflict of Laws and International Investment Arbitration", in F. Ferrari and S. Kröll (eds.), *Conflict of Laws in International Commercial Arbitration*, New York, NYU Center for Transnational Litigation and Commercial Law / Juris, 2019, p. 745. He cites cases such as *Eiser Infrastructure Limited and Energía Solar Luxembourg SARL* v. *Spain*, ICSID Case No. ARB/13/36, Award (4 May 2017), paras. 324-325; *Charanne BV and Construction Investments SARL* v. *Spain*, SCC Case No. 062/2012, Award (21 January 2016), paras. 15, 21.

16. In *Libananco Holding Co. Limited* v. *Republic of Turkey*, ICSID Case No. ARB/06/8, Final Award (2 September 2011), para. 113 and *Saba Fakes* v. *Republic of Turkey*, ICSID Case No. ARB/07/20, Award (14 July 2010), paras. 125 *et seq.*, tribunals assessed the validity of shares by applying Turkish law but provided no

In recent decades, international investment arbitration has experienced a rapid growth, often described as an "explosion" or "revolution" [17]. Foreign investment disputes do not fall under a subgenre of an existing discipline and are "dramatically different from anything previously known in the international sphere" [18]. Perhaps "neither of the two paradigms which gave birth to investment treaty law – International Commercial Arbitration and Public International Law – themselves contain the necessary concepts for constructively developing this new field" [19].

Even though multidisciplinary approaches are needed for international investment arbitration, the field falls mainly under the domain of public international law. This is problematic for, in the words of Pierre Lalive,

> "too many distinguished public international lawyers seem to have little experience or understanding in problems on choice of law (and conversely, practitioners in domestic, private or commercial law, are too often blind to the practical importance or effectiveness of the Law of Nations)" [20].

Lucy Reed, in turn, stresses that the paradox of "[p]rivate lawyers . . . playing on a traditionally public international stage, and public lawyers . . . in urgent need of traditionally private sector skills" [21] needs to be addressed if the investment arbitration system wants to move forward.

C. *Structure of this book*

This book is divided into three parts (public international law, private international law and arbitration) and consists of twenty-two chapters.

---

reasoning. In *Total SA* v. *Argentine Republic*, ICSID Case No. ARB/04/1, Decision on Liability (27 December 2010), para. 39, the Tribunal applied Argentinean law without discussion. In *Caratube International Oil Company LLP and Devincci Salah Hourani* v. *Kaz*, ICSID Case No. ARB/13/13, Award (27 September 2017), the Tribunal applied contract law, domestic investment protection law and customary law without comprehensive reasoning.

17. S. P. Subedi, *International Investment Law: Reconciling Policy and Principle*, Oxford, Hart Publishing, 2008, pp. 1-2.

18. J. Paulsson, "Arbitration Without Privity", *ICSID Review: Foreign Investment Law Journal*, Vol. 10 (1995), pp. 232, 256.

19. D. Kalderimis, "Investment Treaty Arbitration as Global Administrative Law: What This Might Mean in Practice", in C. Brown and K. Miles (eds.), *Evolution in Investment Treaty Law and Arbitration*, Cambridge, Cambridge University Press, 2011, p. 149.

20. "Concluding Remarks", in E. Gaillard and Y. Banifatemi (eds.), *Annulment of ICSID Awards: The Extend of Review of the Applicable Law in Investment Treaty Arbitration*, New York, Juris, 2004, pp. 297, 313.

21. L. Reed, "Mixed Private and Public International Law Solutions to International Crises", *Recueil des cours*, Vol. 306 (2003), p. 193.

The first chapters mainly address public international law matters. After these preliminary remarks of Chapter I, Chapter II addresses fundamental notions on foreign investments protection. Chapters III through IX deal with the evolution of public international law, particularly customary international law, treaties, general principles of law and other sources in relation to foreign investments.

Chapters X through XIV relate to private international law issues first, and then to their relationship with public international law. Specifically, Chapter X refers to the evolution and recent changes within private international law, whereas Chapter XI describes the path toward "uniform law" and Chapter XII addresses the International Institute for the Unification of Private Law (UNIDROIT) Principles and investment arbitration. Chapter XIII expands on the public and private international law relationship in foreign investments, and Chapter XIV concentrates on the particularities of foreign investment contracts and the public-private relationship.

Chapters XV through XXI concentrate specifically on arbitration and applicable substantive law issues related to this dispute resolution system. Chapter XV refers to investment arbitration tribunals, and Chapter XVI to the applicable law rules in their respective arbitral mechanisms. Chapter XVII focuses on choice of law, Chapter XVIII follows with a discussion on the absence of choice and Chapter XIX deals with the applicable substantive law in arbitration *ex aequo et bono*. Chapter XX addresses the corrective and supplemental role of international law and Chapter XXI tackles the issue of public policy [22].

Finally, Chapter XXII connects all the book's topics in the concluding remarks.

---

22. The law is stated as it was in March 2022.

CHAPTER II

FUNDAMENTAL NOTIONS ON INTERNATIONAL INVESTMENT PROTECTION

A. An area in dramatic flux

Foreign investment is one of the oldest fields within public international law; however, it has remained remarkably underdeveloped for most of its history. In the famous *Sabbatino* case heard in 1964, the US Supreme Court stated that "[t]here are few if any issues in international law today on which opinion seems to be so divided as the limitations on a State's power to expropriate the property of aliens" [23].

A few years later, in 1970, the famous *Barcelona Traction* case was heard by the International Court of Justice (ICJ), which wrote that

> "considering the way in which the economic interests of States have proliferated, it may at first sight appear surprising that the evolution of law has not gone further and that no generally accepted rules in the matter have crystallized on the international plane" [24].

Statements like these may be no longer true [25]. Five decades after *Barcelona Traction*, rapid changes began to occur within the body of

23. *Banco Nacional de Cuba* v. *Sabbatino*, 276 US 398, Judgment (23 March 1964), para. 45.

24. *Barcelona Traction, Light and Power Co. (Belgium* v. *Spain)*, Judgment (5 February 1970), *ICJ Reports 1970*, p. 47, https://www.icj-cij.org/public/files/case related/50/050-19700205-JUD-01-00-EN.pdf, accessed 3 March 2022. Even in 2009, Dolzer wrote:

"A decade ago, investment treaty law was firmly in place, but both the corresponding procedural setting and the understanding of the main principles were still in their infancy. . . . A few decisions had addressed individual significant issues but had not really developed a full roadmap or opened up all the major pathways into the interior of the unknown regions of the new terrain."

See R. Dolzer, "Contemporary Law of Foreign Investment: Revisiting the Status of International Law", in C. Binder, U. Kriebaum, A. Reinisch and S. Wittich (eds.), *International Investment Law for the 21st Century: Essays in Honour of Christoph Schreuer*, Oxford, Oxford University Press, 2009, p. 819.

25. Regarding the *Sabbatino* case, Lowenfeld writes that the above-transcribed statement could not be made at the beginning of the third millennium. A. F. Lowenfeld, *International Economic Law*, 2nd ed., Oxford, Oxford University Press, 2008, p. 591.

law, arbitral case law and scholarly commentary related to the field [26]. In fact, foreign investment was recently described as "one of the most vibrant areas of research, interest and concern" [27] in public international law. Its consolidation has been a "technical and sociological process" regarding not only its substantive and procedural aspects but also in relation to a required specialist knowledge and expertise, backed by an epistemic community with its own networks, conferences, journals, newsletters and mailing lists [28].

These developments have proven beneficial, considering that investment-related matters raise complex issues beyond the language of the treaties and awards interpreting them. Such issues include, for example, "the movement of power balances among States, the dominance and retreat of particular economic theories at given periods and the prevailing viewpoints within the arbitral community" [29].

In fact, international investment law suffers a prolongation of the battle of ideologies between liberal and communitarian ideas in relation to the individual and society in general. That battle exposes different views on State sovereignty and societal self-determination versus the protection of foreign property, and critics of the regime point out the "unwarranted advantages for foreign investors and capital-exporting States" in detriment to countries in emerging economies [30].

---

26. J. E. Alvarez, "The Public International Law Regime Governing International Investment", *Recueil des cours*, Vol. 344 (2011), p. 205.

27. E. De Brabandere, *Investment Treaty Arbitration as Public International Law: Procedural Aspects and Implications* (Cambridge Studies in International and Comparative Law), Cambridge, Cambridge University Press, 2014, p. 1.

28. The following is stated in A. Mills, "The Public–Private Dualities of International Investment Law and Arbitration", in C. Brown and K. Miles (eds.), *Evolution in Investment Treaty Law and Arbitration*, Cambridge, Cambridge University Press, 2011, p. 102:

"Nevertheless, participants in the practice (or study) of international investment law are likely to come from more generalist training as part of either the world of public international law or international commercial arbitration, bringing with them certain perspectives and technical skills shaped by that experience."

See also E. Gaillard, "Sociology of International Arbitration", in D. D. Caron, S. Schill, A. Cohen Smutny, E. E. Triantafilou, and C. Nelson Brower (eds.), *Practising Virtue: Inside International Arbitration*, Oxford, Oxford University Press, 2015.

29. M. Sornarajah, *The International Law on Foreign Investment*, 3rd ed., Cambridge, Cambridge University Press, 2010, p. xvi.

30. S. Schill, *The Multilateralization of International Investment Law*, Cambridge, Cambridge University Press, 2009, p. 7. "International investment law constitutes the stage of the pitted confrontation between liberal and communitarian approaches to the world economy", J. d'Aspremont, "International Customary Investment Law: Story of a Paradox", in T. Gazzini and E. De Brabandere (eds.), *International Investment Law: The Sources of Rights and Obligations*, Leiden/Boston, Martinus Nijhoff, 2012, pp. 6-7. See an interesting perspective regarding criticisms of the current international

International investment "remains the largest external source of finance for developing economies" [31]. The law related to the field qualifies as a hot topic in the legal profession not only because of the large sums of money typically involved but also due to its convergence with contemporary political themes related to sovereignty, globalization, finance, trade, environment, development, human rights and health [32].

Remarkably little attention has been paid to the "theoretical impropriety of applying public international law *stricto sensu*" in several matters related to foreign investments, particularly regarding the applicable substantive law. This is problematic as public international law lacks suitable rules on many of these issues [33]. As will be argued throughout this book, private law and private international law often offer more appropriate tools to address several of these problems [34].

The disciplinary confusion extends to the terminology: for instance, some may refer to this field as "international investment law" [35], others call it "international development law" or analogous terms [36]; in the specific context of foreign investment contractual arrangements, it is also possible to find the expression "international contract law" [37].

---

investment regime in A. Mazzoni and M. C. Malaguiti, *Derecho del Comercio Internacional*, Valencia, G. Giappichelli Editore / Tirant Lo Blanch, 2021, pp. 228-235.

31. UNCTAD 2018 World Investment Report, Key Messages, p. xii.

32. P. d'Argent, "Introduction", in T. Gazzini and E. De Brabandere (eds.), *International Investment Law: The Sources of Rights and Obligations*, Leiden/Boston, Martinus Nijhoff, 2012, p. 1.

33. P. Guggenheim, "I Traité de Droit International Public" (1953) *apud* P. Kahn, "The Law Applicable to Foreign Investments: The Contribution of the World Bank Convention on the Settlement of Investment Disputes", *Indiana Law Journal*, Vol. 44 (1968), pp. 16-17.

34. For an in-depth discussion, see Chap. XIII.A *infra*, "Public and private law notions".

35. Schill, *supra* note 30, p. 1.

36. Bradlow characterizes international development law as "a branch of public international law that deals with rights and duties of states and other actors in the development process, and it includes economic, environmental and human law concerns", in D. D. Bradlow, "Differing Conceptions of Development and the Content of International Development Law", in *International Sustainable Development Law*, Vol. 1, United Kingdom, Eolss Publishers, 2010, p. 24 (originally published in *South African Journal on Human Rights*, Vol. 47 (2005)). The word "development" for this purpose refers to a national, not international context. See also S. Sucharitkul, "The Nature and Sources of International Development Law" (p. 48) and A. Carty, "The Concept of International Development Law" (pp. 59-60), both also in *International Sustainable Development Law*, Vol. 1, United Kingdom, Eolss Publishers, 2010.

37. "According to proponents, its first postulate is the sanctity and immutability of the terms of the contract", M. Sornarajah, "The Myth of International Contract Law", *Journal of World Trade Law*, Vol. 15, No. 3 (1981), p. 188.

B. The protection of international investments

Domestic legislation in the field typically includes specific regulations in areas such as property ownership, taxation, currency control, transfer of technology, environmental obligations and corporate governance [38].

By contrast, international treaties usually impose open-textured standards, regulating State conduct to guarantee foreign investment protection [39]. Indeed, investment treaties mitigate the risk of investment overprotection over time, the risk associated with suing a State and, finally, the risk of non-payment [40].

In addition, investment guarantees and obligations are often negotiated within contracts signed between the investor and the State [41]. Customary international law and other sources referred to in the following chapters may also have their say on investment protection [42].

International investments create employment and bring about a transfer of knowledge, capital and technology [43]. However, their typically large scale can become problematic insofar as investors may

---

38. Decades ago, Lord Shawcross noted that

> "a number of investment-receiving countries have made arrangements and introduced municipal legislation designed to create a better feeling of security and to encourage foreign investment. These measures . . . may reflect the proper view of international law".

However,

> "[f]rom unhappy experience in the past, foreign investors have retained their fear that measures thus unilaterally enacted and not part of the country's fundamental laws can equally easily be unilaterally revoked".

Rt. Hon. Lord Shawcross, Q. C., "The Problems of Foreign Investment in International Law", *Recueil des cours*, Vol. 102 (1961), pp. 359-360. This phenomenon explains the proliferation of treaties on the matter.

39. Z. Douglas, *The International Law of Investment Claims*, Cambridge, Cambridge University Press, 2009, pp. xxii-xxiii; J. Arato, "The Private Law Critique of International Investment Law", *American Journal of International Law*, Vol. 113, No. 1 (2019), p. 7.

40. J. Arato, "The Logic of Contract in the World of Investment Treaties", *William & Mary Law Review*, Vol. 58, No. 351 (2016), p. 366.

41. Situations may arise in which claims based on different sources are dealt with in the same arbitral proceedings. In *Pac Rim Cayman LLC* v. *The Republic of El Salvador*, ICSID Case No. ARB/09/12, Decision on the Respondent's Jurisdictional Objections (1 June 2012), para. 5.45, the Tribunal stated that it

> "finds no juridical difficulty in having an ICSID arbitration based on different claims arising from separate investment protections and separate but identical arbitration provisions, here CAFTA and the Investment Law".

42. See Chapter IX.A, *infra*, "Plurality of legal sources in foreign investments".

43. S. E. Blythe, "The Advantages of Investor-State Arbitration as a Dispute Resolution Mechanism in Bilateral Investment Treaties", *The International Lawyer*, Vol. 47, No. 2 (2013), pp. 273-290.

influence the economic and political actions of governments. Other potential issues stem from the flow of profits overseas and the negative impact of exploiting the host State's natural resources [44].

As such, the regulation of international investments must be balanced and suited to the specific needs of the field. While today there exists an impressive web of treaties, national laws and other sources to regulate foreign investment, several flaw within the current system persist. Many of its problems emerge from the fact that treaties on the matter, and international customary law in general, provide for substantive standards that are elusive or abstract, which creates uncertainties regarding the law substantively applicable to a contract or dispute [45]. This book will deal with this matter extensively.

Further, critics point out that the balance often turns against States [46]. For instance, they highlight the significant lobbying power of multinational corporations and their influence in shaping transnational rules [47]. Complications and complexities also arise from the growing professionalization of non-State actors operating at the international level, such as third-party *amicus curiae* intervening as stakeholders in investment claims, or legal advocacy groups at the national and

44. See J. Bonnitcha, "Assessing the Impacts of Investment Treaties: Overview of the Evidence", International Institute for Sustainable Development Report, Geneva, 2017, https://www.iisd.org/system/files/publications/assessing-impacts-investment-treaties.pdf, accessed 3 March 2022; J. Pohl, "Societal Benefits and Costs of International Investment Agreements: A Critical Review of Aspects and Available Empirical Evidence", OECD Working Papers on International Investment, 2018, http://www.oecd-ilibrary.org/finance-and-investment/societal-benefits-and-costs-of-international-investment-agreements_e5f85c3d-en, accessed 3 March 2022.

45. For example, the "fair and equitable treatment" standard. For the most common substantive standards included in BITs, see Chap. V.E, *infra*, "Bilateral investment treaties".

46. Subedi criticizes the legal loopholes and lacunae found in investment treaties that have often been negotiated by countries under pressure from international organizations. He also notes that many problems within the investment system derive from messy privatization programs managed by political leaders and government officials who are often incompetent and corrupt, as well as unsound and faulty commercial contracts often concluded by governments under the influence of corrupt officials. Subedi further alludes to the assistance provided by sophisticated lawyers to foreign investors, whereas many governments do not have appropriate advice in this area. See Subedi, *supra* note 17, p. 33. According to Jean Ho, "Today, scholars disagree on multiple concerns ranging from investor obligations to excessive damages awards. Contradiction flourishes when every narrative on international investment law tempts the resourceful scholar to craft a distinctive and memorable counter narrative". See J. Ho, "The Art of Contradiction in International Investment Law", *British Yearbook of International Law*, Oxford, Oxford University Press, 2022, p. 1.

47. M. Sornarajah, *The Settlement of Foreign Investment Disputes*, The Hague, Kluwer Law International, 2000, p. 9.

international level [48]. Besides, foreign investment matters intersect with several areas of law in relation, for instance, to the administrative law police powers of States, environmental matters and human rights issues, among others still lacking appropriate regulation [49].

Human rights provide a clear example. Such matters are not addressed in most investment treaties and, when they are, regulation is often not comprehensive [50]. Unsurprisingly, divergent interpretations arise in case law in this regard. This situation notably occurred in the *Suez*, *Saur* and *Urbaser* cases [51], arising from actions adopted by Argentina in its 2001-2002 financial crisis that impacted companies investing in its water and sewage services. Argentina argued that the measures emerged from a necessity to safeguard its obligations under human rights treaties, in particular the right to water. Only the *Urbaser* judgment from 2016 showed a human rights-friendly approach for interpretive purposes [52]. This focus was furthered in the

48. B. Hess, "The Private-Public Divide in International Dispute Resolution", *Recueil des cours*, Vol. 388 (2018), pp. 106 ff.

49. As noted by Priscilla Pereira de Andrade and Nitish Monebhurrun, when investment agreements "do provide for environmental protection, this is normally done in a non-mandatory way, thereby becoming grist to the mill of the common belief that the social and environmental externalities generated by investment activities cannot be effectively regulated or that regulation, in such cases, only acts as a friendly pressure", P. Pereira de Andrade and N. Monebhurrun, "Mapping Investors' Environmental Commitments and Obligations", in J. Ho and M. Sattorova (eds.), *Investors' International Law*, Oxford, Hart Publishing / Bloomsbury, 2021, p. 288.

50. Resolution A/HRC/RES/26/9, adopted by the UN Human Rights Council on 14 July 2014, emphasized that states have an obligation and the primary responsibility for promoting and protecting human rights and fundamental freedoms and protecting against any abuses committed within their jurisdiction, including by third parties such as corporations. On 14 July 2014, the UN Human Rights Council adopted Resolution A/HRC/RES/26/9 on the elaboration of a legally binding instrument on transnational corporations and other business enterprises with respect to human rights. To this end, it created an open-ended intergovernmental working group on this issue to elaborate a legally binding agreement on human rights applicable to transnational corporations and other business enterprises. At the OAS, the Americas have also addressed the issue of "conscious and effective regulation of business in the area of human rights". See CJI/RES. 232 (XCI-O/17); CJI/doc.522/17 rev.2; CJI/RES. 205 (LXXXIV-O/14); AG/RES. 2887 (XLVI-O/16). See also General Assembly Resolutions AG/RES. 1786 (XXXI-O/2001); AG/RES. 2887 (XLVI-O/16); A/HRC/RES/26/9, https://www.oas.org/en/sla/iajc/annual_reports.asp, accessed 18 June 2022, p. 141 ff.

51. *Suez, Sociedad General de Aguas de Barcelona SA, and InterAguas Servicios Integrales del Agua SA* v. *The Argentine Republic*, ICSID Case No. ARB/03/17, Decision on Liability (30 July 2010), para. 240. *SAUR International SA* v. *Republic of Argentina*, ICSID Case No. ARB/04/4, Decision on Jurisdiction and Liability (6 June 2012), paras. 330-331. *Urbaser SA and Consorcio de Aguas Bilbao Bizkaia, Bilbao Biskaia Ur Partzuergoa* v. *The Argentine Republic*, ICSID Case No. ARB/07/26, Award (8 December 2016), para. 1200.

52. "The BIT has to be construed in harmony with other rules of international law of which it forms part, including those relating to human rights." *Urbaser* v. *Argentina*,

case *Phoenix* v. *Czech Republic*. In a clash between human rights and investment obligations, the Tribunal held that "an interpretation attempting to 'harmonize' the investment treaty in place with human rights commitments remains the best-case scenario for the protection of human rights" [53].

Moreover, treaties, investment contracts and even national laws usually provide for dispute resolution through arbitration. However, by their very nature, arbitrators typically concentrate more on resolving the dispute than on "the shape and direction" of investment law, which often creates inconsistent awards [54]. This disparity is further aggravated by the lack of a corpus addressing substantial matters within international investment law [55].

Relying on arbitration to settle investment disputes also brings into question by some critics the legitimacy of this mechanism in general, as decisions do not come from international courts staffed by public servants but from private arbitrators. Other controversies relate to questions of transparency in arbitrator appointment, possible conflicts of interest and the high costs involved in arbitral proceedings, among others [56].

---

ibid., p. 318, para. 1200. See also C. McLachlan, "The Principle of Systemic Integration and Article 31 (3) *(c)* of the Vienna Convention", *International and Comparative Law Quarterly*, Vol. 54, No. 2 (2005), pp. 279-320.

53. "To take an extreme example, nobody would suggest that ICSID protection should be granted to investments made in violation of the most fundamental rules of protection of human rights, like investments made in pursuance of torture, of genocide, or in support of slavery or trafficking of human organs" (*Phoenix Action, Ltd.* v. *The Czech Republic*, ICSID Case No. ARB/06/5, Award (15 April 2009), para. 78). See further in S. Steininger, "The Role of Human Rights in Investment Law and Arbitration: State Obligations, Corporate Responsibility, and Community Empowerment", MPIL Research Paper Series No. 2020-16, https://ssrn.com/abstract=3595457, accessed 3 March 2022, p. 8.

54. Examples of absurd situations emerge from the *Lauder* and *CME* awards, issued within ten days of each other. *Ronald S. Lauder* v. *The Czech Republic*, UNCITRAL, Final Award (3 September 2001); *CME Czech Republic BV* v. *The Czech Republic*, UNCITRAL, Partial Award (13 September 2001). One case failed and the other succeeded in the amount of FFF353 million USD, equal to the Czech Republic's entire healthcare budget.

55. "Nonetheless, arbitral tribunals have generally shown concern for the future shape and direction of the law, since publication of their decisions and awards has exposed the differences in how tribunals qualify facts and understand the law", A. Rigo Sureda, *Investment Treaty Arbitration Judging Under Uncertainty*, Cambridge, Cambridge University Press, 2012, p. 139.

56. J. D. Fryand and J. I. Stampalija, "Forged Independence and Impartiality: Conflicts of Interest of International Arbitrators in Investment Disputes", *Arbitration international*, Vol. 30, No. 2 (2014), pp. 189-264.

This and other uncertainties described above have often created a regulatory chill in countries that are hesitant to adopt local law reforms for fear that they may invite claims as a consequence [57].

Many of these issues have received international attention, most notably in three forums: UNCITRAL, the United Nations Conference on Trade and Development (UNCTAD) and ICSID [58]. At UNCITRAL, for instance, discussions even include a proposal to create a Multilateral Investment Court [59], or an appellate mechanism [60], among other matters [61].

---

57. C. Brown and K. Miles (eds.), *Evolution in Investment Treaty Law and Arbitration*, Cambridge, Cambridge University Press, 2011, pp. 3-4.

58. Alvarez envisages that

> "[. . .] in 15 years the most likely description of the investment regime will remain what it is today: a confusing spaghetti bowl of international investment agreements with diverse substantive standards and procedures for adjudicating them. He foresees that the investment regime's spaghetti bowl is likely to become more, not less, complex. Over the next few years, States will be exercising more, not fewer, options. In the end, there will be more noodles in the regime's bowl, more substantive and procedural choices, not fewer".

See J. E. Alvarez, "ISDS Reform: The Long View", IILJ Working Paper 2021/6, p. 37.

59. See the latest survey released by the School of International Arbitration, Centre for Commercial Law Studies, Queen Mary University of London, prepared with the support of the Corporate Counsel International Arbitration Group. It found (among other things) the following:

> "While respondents would welcome regulation in this area, they think third-party funding in ISDS should be permitted and be available to investors as a commercial decision. Respondents expressed mixed views on the introduction of an appeals mechanism in ISDS and nine in ten respondents would be opposed to a re-hearing of the tribunal's factual and legal findings. On balance, respondents do not favor the creation of a multilateral investment court."

"2020 QMUL-CCIAG Survey: Investors' Perceptions of ISDS", May 2020, http://www.arbitration.qmul.ac.uk/media/arbitration/docs/QM-CCIAG-Survey-ISDS-2020.pdf, accessed 3 March 2022, p. 5. Cf. I. Hallak, "Multilateral Investment Court: Overview of the Reform Proposals and Prospects", European Parliament Briefing 2020, https://www.europarl.europa.eu/RegData/etudes/BRIE/2020/646147/EPRS_BRI(2020)646147_EN.pdf, accessed 3 March 2022.

60. See, for instance, in this regard: M. L. Jaime, "Reshaping Investor-State Dispute Settlement Through an Appellate Review Mechanism", *The Investor-State Dispute Settlement System: Reform, Replace or Status Quo?*, The Hague, Kluwer Law International, 2021, pp. 138 *et seq*. See also M. L. Jaime, "A New Legal Framework for Improving Investor-State Dispute Settlement (ISDS)", in L. Cadiet, B. Hess and M. Requejo Isidro (eds.), *Privatizing Dispute Resolution: Trends and Limits* (Studies of the Max Planck Institute Luxembourg for International, European and Regulatory Procedural Law, No. 18), Baden-Baden, Nomos, 2019, pp. 485 ff.

61. Such as third-party funding, dispute prevention methods, exhaustion of local remedies, shareholder claims and reflective loss, treaty parties' interpretations, security for costs, frivolous claims, third-party participation, multiple proceedings and counterclaims, code of conduct, selection and appointment of arbitrators, and the creation of an advisory center. See "Possible Reform of Investor-State Dispute Settlement", Note by the Secretariat, UN Doc. A/CN.9/WG.III/WP.166 (30 July 2019).

UNCTAD advances the less ambitious agenda of modernizing old-generation treaties to contemplate human rights, environmental, health and other concerns [62]. In turn, ICSID approved, in 2022, an amendment to its arbitration rules, seeking greater transparency and providing the option to fast-track proceedings [63].

The International Institute of Sustainable Development (IISD) has also had a remarkable voice in the debate on balancing investment protection with environmental protection. It even advanced a Model International Agreement on Investment for Sustainable Development in this regard [64].

However, there is currently no global initiative to launch a comprehensive corpus addressing the substantive applicable law concerns. In its absence, one of the central messages of this book is the need for more timely and appropriate handling of – *inter alia* – issues related to private international law and private law.

C. *Definition of international investments*

The legal protection afforded to foreign investments must be distinguished from the regime governing international transactions in goods or services. This particular safeguarding is warranted by the fact that international investments intend to establish a long-term relationship in a given country, usually with the State itself or a public entity. At least in principle, these investments, often called "foreign direct investments" [65], also differ from activities in which the investor's stakes are small. These minor-scale investments may not garner this special international protection since businesses are not exposed to the same level of risk [66].

There are varying definitions of the term "investment" within national laws. Indeed, some domestic laws do not even define the term [67]. For

---

62. See "Phase 2 of IIA Reform: Modernizing the Existing Stock of Old-Generation Treaties", IIA Issues Note (June 2017). See also UNCTAD, "Investment Policy Framework for Sustainable Development", Doc. No. UNCTAD/DIAE/PCB/2015/5.

63. Available at https://icsid.worldbank.org/resources/rules-amendments, accessed 17 June 2022.

64. IISD, "Model International Agreement on Investment for Sustainable Development", April 2005, www.iisd.org/investment, accessed 3 March 2022.

65. Sometimes also called direct foreign investment (DFI). See J. W. Salacuse, *The Law of Investment Treaties*, 3rd ed., Oxford, Oxford University Press, 2021, p. 45.

66. D. Collins, *An Introduction to International Investment Law*, Cambridge, Cambridge University Press, 2016, p. 3.

67. The well-known civil law distinction between absolute ownership of things *(in rem)* and rights or claims stemming from contractual or non-contractual obligations

this reason, investment treaties usually describe investments in broad terms, referring to "every kind of asset" and then listing the forms of investment non-exhaustively, such as property, rights and interests of every nature [68].

The Convention on the Settlement of Investment Disputes Between States and Nationals of Other States ("ICSID Convention") was designed as a tool to resolve investment disputes. However, the term "investment" was deliberately not defined [69]. Several definitions were considered and ultimately rejected in light of "the essential requirement of consent of the parties" [70]. While no specific definition of the term exists within the Convention, some cases have nonetheless referred to its Article 25 (1) for the purpose of establishing jurisdiction, where the term can also be found [71].

One approach to defining the term "investment" within ICSID case law consists of analyzing the wording of the particular investment treaty. This approach was adopted by the *ad hoc* Annulment Committee in *MHS* v. *Malaysia* [72].

A second method examines the traits common to many large-scale investments, such as a significant contribution of money or other assets

---

(in personam) is relevant, although constitutional protections against deprivation of ownership also cover to some extent the second category. G. Sacerdoti, "Bilateral Treaties and Multilateral Instruments on Investment Protection", *Recueil des cours*, Vol. 269 (1997), p. 306.

68. See UNCTAD, Scope and Definitions: A Sequel (Series on Issues in International Investment Agreements (hereafter IIA), Series Two), 6 April 2011, https://unctad.org/system/files/official-document/diaeia20102_en.pdf, accessed 3 March 2022.

69. Lowenfeld, *supra* note 25, p. 539.

70. J. Fouret, R. Gerbay and G. M. Alvarez (eds.), *The ICSID Convention, Regulation and Rules: A Practical Commentary*, Cheltenham, Edward Elgar, 2019, p. 114. The authors also refer to ICSID, *History of the ICSID Convention*, Vol. I-1, p. 116; Vol. II-1, pp. 285-286, 492-493; Vol. II-2, pp. 843-844, 972. This consent of the parties, however, is given weight, but is not conclusive, as stated by the Tribunal in *Československa Obchodni Banka, AS* v. *The Slovak Republic*, ICSID Case No. ARB/97/4, Decision of the Tribunal on Objections to Jurisdiction (24 May 1999), para. 68.

71. The objective definition of investment was also applied outside the ICSID context, in the UNCITRAL case: *Romak SA (Switzerland)* v. *Republic of Uzbekistan*, PCA Case No. AA280, Award (26 November 2009). The decision was criticized in *Guaracachi America Inc. and Rurelec PLC* v. *Plurinational State of Bolivia*, PCA Case No. 2011-17, Award (31 January 2014), para. 364. The Tribunal stated:

> "[I]t is not appropriate to import 'objective' definitions of investment . . . when in the context of a non-ICSID arbitration such as the present case. On the contrary, the definition of protected investment, at least in non-ICSID arbitrations, is to be obtained only from the (very broad) definition contained in the BIT."

72. *Malaysian Historical Salvors, SDN, BHD* v. *Government of Malaysia*, ICSID Case No. ARB/05/10, Decision on Annulment (16 April 2009), paras. 58-61.

of economic value [73], a certain duration of time for the investment, an element of risk and a contribution to the host country's development [74]. This approach is known as the *Salini* test [75].

While the *Salini* test has been described as "debatable" by some scholars [76], it has nonetheless been influential in deciding several arbitral cases, among them *Saipem SpA* v. *Bangladesh* [77] and *MHS* v. *Malaysia* [78]. Other cases have held that the *Salini* test traits "must be considered as mere examples and not necessarily as elements that are required for the existence of an investment" [79]. As stated by Zachary Douglas, there is a premium for precision in defining a protected investment, and the subjectivity encountered in the *Salini* test makes it unfit for that purpose [80].

While investments may be defined in a multitude of ways, it is equally important to distinguish between types of investments. Foreign direct

---

73. According to Douglas, "the stated objective of investment treaties is to stimulate flows of private capital into the economies of the contracting States", Douglas, *supra* note 39, p. 162.

74. *Salini Costruttori SpA and Italstrade SpA* v. *Kingdom of Morocco*, ICSID Case No. ARB/00/4, Decision on Jurisdiction (23 July 2001), para. 52. It is worth noting that while the *Salini* test has received some level of resistance, "[t]he first three criteria – contribution, risk, and duration – have since been systematically adopted by ICSID tribunals", Fouret, Gerbay and Alvarez, *supra* note 70, p. 117.

75. Even though its origins can be traced to the prior case *Fedax NV* v. *The Republic of Venezuela*, ICSID Case No. ARB/96/3, Decision on Objections to Jurisdiction (11 July 1997), para. 43.

76. C. L. Lim, J. Ho and M. Paparinskis, *International Investment Law and Arbitration: Commentary, Awards and other Materials*, Cambridge, Cambridge University Press, 2018, p. 284. The economic development that results from investment in a State (as noted in the first paragraph of the Preamble to the ICSID Convention) was considered irrelevant in *LESI SpA and ASTALDI SpA* v. *People's Democratic Republic of Algeria*, ICSID Case No. ARB/05/3, Award (12 November 2008). See also *Saba Fakes* v. *Turkey*, *supra* note 16, para. 110. In contrast, the *ad hoc* Committee in *Patrick Mitchell* v. *Democratic Republic of the Congo*, ICSID Case No. ARB/99/7, held that "the existence of a contribution to the economic development of the host State as an essential – although not sufficient – characteristic or unquestionable criterion of the investment, does not mean that this contribution must always be sizable or successful" (Decision on the Application for Annulment of the Award (1 November 2006), para. 33).

77. *Saipem SpA* v. *The People's Republic of Bangladesh*, ICSID Case No. ARB/05/7, Decision on Jurisdiction (21 March 2007).

78. *Malaysian Historical Salvors* v. *Malaysia*, *supra* note 72, Award on Jurisdiction (17 May 2007).

79. P. Bernardini, "ICSID Versus Non-ICSID Investment Treaty Arbitration", in M. A. Fernandez-Ballester and D. Arias Lozano (eds.), *Liber Amicorum Bernardo Cremades*, Madrid, La Ley / Wolters Kluwer España, 2010, p. 170. The Annulment Committee in *Malaysian Historical Salvors* v. *Malaysia*, *supra* note 72, Award on Jurisdiction (17 May 2007) did not consider the *Salini* criteria before applying a broad definition of the term "investment" in the applicable investment treaty.

80. Douglas, *supra* note 39, p. 191.

investment in a manufacturing plant, for instance, can be distinguished from "portfolio investments" by virtue of the investor's lasting interest in the venture, in which they hold a significant stake. By contrast, portfolio investments involve holding the securities of companies.

These transactions present a particular problem [81]. Portfolio investments involve the acquisition of shares or the raising of capital through security instruments for ventures in another country without controlling the company in question [82]. The problem is that several treaties include shares in their definition of foreign investment [83], which raises the following question: what happens when the foreign venture does not have the "control" [84]? Moreover, granting portfolio investments the same protection that foreign direct investments are afforded under treaties negates the alleged underlying benefits of international investment legal regimes. This situation happens insofar as, for example, the transfer of knowledge and increasing employment that typically result from foreign direct investment are not as easy to identify in the case of portfolio investments [85]. Scholars have argued

---

81. *The Encyclopedia of Public International Law* defines "foreign investment" as "a transfer of funds or materials from one country (called the capital-exporting country) to another country (called the host country) in return for a direct or indirect participation in the earnings of that enterprise", in Vol. 8, p. 246. This definition was criticized as "being broad enough to include portfolio investment". The IMF Balance of Payments Manual (1980), para. 408, used a narrower definition which excluded portfolio investment. See Sornarajah, *supra* note 29, p. 8.

82. The definition of a "controlling" share varies according to the circumstances:

> "For companies with widely-dispersed, publicly-held shares, effective control can occur with very small percentage holdings. Most countries, including the United States, consider – for the purposes of data collection under their national law – a stake of 10 percent in the ordinary shares of an enterprise sufficient to constitute the minimum threshold for foreign 'control'. However, foreign direct investment typically also involves the existence of a long-term relationship between a direct investor and its foreign affiliate, which usually means a significant degree of influence on the management of that affiliate."

Citing Alvarez, *supra* note 26, pp. 205-206.

83. For example, the Energy Charter Treaty contains an open-ended definition of "investment" (Art. 1 (6)). Other treaties with closed definitions of "investment", such as Article 1 *(r) (ii)* of the 2009 Canada-Jordan BIT, expressly include shares.

84. In the ICSID case *AMT* v. *Zaire*, the Tribunal held that investments via the share capital of a local entity were eligible for protection under the United States-Zaire BIT. *American Manufacturing and Trading Inc.* v. *Republic of Zaire*, ICSID Case No. ARB/93/1, Award (21 February 1997), paras. 5.08-5.15. In the ICSID case *CMS* v. *Argentina*, the Tribunal held that the American claimant's minority shares in an Argentine company qualified as a protected investment. *CMS Gas Transmission Co.* v. *The Republic of Argentina*, ICSID Case No. ARB/01/8, Decision on Objections to Jurisdiction (17 July 2003), paras. 36-65. A similar decision was reached in *Suez* v. *Argentina*, *supra* note 51, Decision on Jurisdiction (16 May 2006), para. 51.

85. Collins, *supra* note 66, p. 76.

that the latter should not be granted protection under international investment treaties "unless specifically included in the definition of foreign investment in the relevant treaty" [86].

Problems also arise from certain indirect investments, such as holding shares in a local entity via one or several intermediary companies. An ICSID tribunal considered this situation an "investment" even though it was not expressly included in the treaty [87]. Another tribunal drew the same conclusion for unconventional financial investments that did not necessarily involve an inflow of funds into the host State or the active management of a given venture [88].

Loans [89], government bonds and related security entitlements [90] have also been considered "investments" for the purposes of legal protection under the broad headings of the treaties' definition of the term, such as "assets", "claims to money" or "obligations". Tribunals usually do not look at these transactions in isolation but consider the operation as a whole. Several financial instruments were qualified as investments in recent cases [91]. Decisions in this regard considered straightforward loans, negotiable instruments, sovereign bonds, oil price hedges [92] and

86. See Sornarajah, *supra* note 29, pp. 9-10.

87. See, for instance, *Señor Tza Yap Shum* v. *Republic of Peru*, ICSID Case No. ARB/07/6, Decision on Jurisdiction and Competence (19 June 2009).

88. In *Fedax* v. *Venezuela*, *supra* note 75, Decision on Objections to Jurisdiction (11 July 1997), paras. 39-40, the Arbitral Tribunal determined that the Venezuelan promissory notes that had been acquired by the claimant from the original holder in the secondary market by way of endorsement constituted an investment under the Netherlands-Venezuela BIT.

89. *Československa* v. *Slovak Republic*, *supra* note 70, Decision (24 May 1999), para. 77.

90. *Abaclat et al.* v. *The Argentine Republic*, ICSID Case No. ARB/07/5, Decision on Jurisdiction and Admissibility (4 August 2011), para. 713 *(ix)*; also *Ambiente Ufficio SpA et al.* v. *The Argentine Republic*, ICSID Case No. ARB/08/9, Decision on Jurisdiction and Admissibility (8 February 2013), paras. 547-548.

91. Although this outcome depends on the applicable treaty and the facts of the case. See ICC Commission Report, Financial Institutions and International Arbitration, International Chamber of Commerce (ICC) 2016, https://iccwbo.org/content/uploads/sites/3/2016/11/icc-financial-institutions-and-international-arbitration-icc-arbitration-adr-commission-report.pdf, accessed 3 March 2022, p. 7. See, for instance, *Oko Pankki Oyj, VTB Bank (Deutschland) AG and Sampo Bank PLC* v. *The Republic of Estonia*, ICSID Case No. ARB/04/6, Award (19 November 2007); *Fedax* v. *Venezuela*, *supra* note 75, Award (9 March 1998); *Abaclat* v. *Argentina*, *supra* note 90, Decision on Jurisdiction and Admissibility (4 August 2011).

92. They were considered as a qualifying investment in three of the following ICSID cases but not in a fourth case: *Abaclat* v. *Argentina*, *supra* note 90, Decision on Jurisdiction and Admissibility (4 August 2011); *Ambiente* v. *Argentina*, *supra* note 90, Decision on Jurisdiction and Admissibility (8 February 2013); *Giovanni Alemanni* v. *The Argentine Republic*, ICSID Case No. ARB/07/8, Decision on Jurisdiction and Admissibility (17 November 2014); *Poštová banka, as and ISTROKAPITAL SE* v. *Hellenic Republic*, ICSID Case No. ARB/13/8, Award (9 April 2015).

even a bank guarantee to constitute investments[93]. Further, process financing and hedge funds are increasingly involved in cross-border investment disputes[94].

A 2016 ICC report detected that around fifty cases both within and outside the ICSID system dealt with financial institutions or financial product-related matters[95]. Several cases decided on jurisdictional issues related to the investment subject matter *(ratione materiae)*[96]. Other cases dealt with the standing of the investor *(ratione personae)*[97], and others with the place of the investment *(ratione loci)*[98].

---

93. Considered to be a qualifying investment in a PCA case under the UNCITRAL Arbitration Rules but denied that benefit in an ICSID case. *Joy Mining Machinery Ltd.* v. *Arab Republic of Egypt*, ICSID Case No. ARB/03/11, Award on Jurisdiction (6 August 2004). Cases also relate to the ability to require bank regulators to adhere to the right to fair and equitable treatment, such as *Deutsche Bank AG* v. *Democratic Socialist Republic of Sri Lanka*, ICSID Case No. ARB/09/2, Award (31 October 2012); *Antoine Goetz* v. *République du Burundi*, ICSID Case No. ARB/95/3, Award (10 February 1999), involving a balancing of legitimate regulatory interests and interests that are perceived as not being legitimate (*Renée Rose Levy de Levi* v. *Republic of Peru*, ICSID Case No. ARB/10/17, Award (26 February 2014), paras. 157 ff.), or discriminatory (*Goetz* v. *Burundi*, *ibid.*, Award; *Valeri Belokon* v. *Kyrgyz Republic*, UNCITRAL, Award (24 October 2014).

94. See, for instance, *Oko Pankki Oyj* v. *Estonia*, *supra* note 91, Award (19 November 2007); *Fedax* v. *Venezuela*, *supra* note 75, Award (9 March 1998); *Abaclat* v. *Argentina*, *supra* note 90, Decision on Jurisdiction and Admissibility (4 August 2011).

95. ICC Commission Report, *supra* note 91, pp. 7 ff.

96. For instance, *Alex Genin, Eastern Credit Limited, Inc. and AS Baltoil* v. *The Republic of Estonia*, ICSID Case No. ARB/99/2, Award (25 June 2001); *British Caribbean Bank Ltd.* v. *Government of Belize*, PCA Case No. 2010-18, Award (19 December 2014); *Československa* v. *Slovak Republic*, *supra* note 70, Award (29 December 2004); *Hesham Talaat M. Al-Warraq* v. *Republic of Indonesia*, UNCITRAL, Final Award (15 December 2014); *Invesmart BV* v. *Czech Republic*, UNCITRAL, Award (26 June 2009); *KT Asia Investment Group BV* v. *Republic of Kazakhstan*, ICSID Case No. ARB/09/8, Award (17 October 2013); *Metalpar SA and Buen Aire SA* v. *The Argentine Republic*, ICSID Case No. ARB/03/5, Decision on Jurisdiction (27 April 2006), Award on the Merits (6 June 2008); *Oko Pankki Oyj* v. *Estonia*, *supra* note 91, Award (19 November 2007); *Poštová banka* v. *Hellenic Republic*, *supra* note 92, Award; *Rafat Ali Rizvi* v. *Republic of Indonesia*, ICSID Case No. ARB/11/13, Award on Jurisdiction (16 July 2013).

97. See *ABCI Investments NV* v. *Republic of Tunisia*, ICSID Case No. ARB/04/12, Decision on Jurisdiction (18 February 2011); *Blue Bank International & Trust (Barbados) Ltd.* v. *Bolivarian Republic of Venezuela*, ICSID Case No. ARB/12/20, Award (26 April 2017); *Continental Casualty Company* v. *The Argentine Republic*, ICSID Case No. ARB/03/9, Award (5 September 2008); *Daimler Financial Services AG* v. *Argentine Republic*, ICSID Case No. ARB/05/1, Award (22 August 2012); *Renée Rose Levy* v. *Peru*, *supra* note 93; and *Valle Verde Sociedad Financiera Sl* v. *Bolivarian Republic of Venezuela*, ICSID Case No. ARB/12/18, Decision on Provisional Measures (25 January 2016).

98. For instance, *Fedax* v. *Venezuela*, *supra* note 75, Award (9 March 1998); *British Caribbean Bank* v. *Belize*, *supra* note 96; *Giovanni Alemanni* v. *Argentina*, *supra* note 92.

Having learned the lessons of the past, modern investment treaties now address many of the matters that had previously remained unsettled [99]. Thus, many of the issues addressed above have now been clarified [100]. Still, portfolio investments, loans, bonds and related security entitlements raise particularly challenging private international law questions considering the multiple jurisdictions that can be involved.

The definition of an "investment" is an important one for determining the jurisdiction of an investment tribunal. For instance, Article 25 of the ICSID Convention extends the power of ICSID tribunals to "investment" disputes but, as has been previously mentioned, does not define the term. Party autonomy alone is not sufficient to transform any business relationship into an investment for the purposes of the ICSID Convention: defining an investment under the Convention requires an objective test [101].

Whether an investment can be considered "foreign" depends on the nationality of the investor [102]. Existing domestic law and investment

---

99. For instance, Article 1 of the US Model BIT's 2004 and 2012 versions describe an "investment" as

> "every asset that an investor owns or controls, directly or indirectly, that has the characteristics of an investment, including such characteristics as the commitment of capital or other resources, the expectation of gain or profit, or the assumption of risk. Forms that an investment may take include: *(a)* an enterprise; *(b)* shares, stock, and other forms of equity participation in an enterprise; *(c)* bonds, debentures, other debt instruments, and loans; *(d)* futures, options, and other derivatives; *(e)* turnkey, construction, management, production, concession, revenue-sharing, and other similar contracts; *(f)* intellectual property rights; *(g)* licenses, authorizations, permits, and similar rights conferred pursuant to domestic law; and *(h)* other tangible or intangible, movable or immovable property, and related property rights, such as leases, mortgages, liens, and pledges".

100. Recent treaties have narrowed the scope of protection by expressly excluding portfolio investments, including the EFTA, the Mexico FTA (signed 27 November 2000, entered into force on 1 July 2001, Art. 45) and commercial contracts (for example, Canada Model BIT (2004), Art. 1), or by requiring that investments have certain inherent characteristics by reference to criteria associated with the *Salini* test (US Model BIT (2012)). Other States have limited the scope of their treaties by excluding certain classes of disputes arising out of investments in certain sectors. For instance, in 1974, Jamaica excluded legal disputes arising directly out of an investment relating to minerals or other natural resources. Prior to its withdrawal from ICSID in 2009, Ecuador provided a similar notice under Article 25 (4) of the ICSID Convention in 2007 in respect of disputes arising out of investments in the natural resources sector.

101. Bjorklund and Vanhonnaeker, *supra* note 13, p. 350.

102. Double nationality can be an issue affecting jurisdictional purposes. ICSID decisions have favored formal nationality, rather than the test of effective nationality, in determining whether an individual qualifies as a "national of another [ICSID] Contracting State" under the Convention. See, for instance, *Ioan Micula, Viorel Micula, SC European Food SA, SC Starmill SRL and SC Multipack SRL* v. *Romania*, ICSID Case No. ARB/05/20, Decision on Jurisdiction and Admissibility (24 September 2008), para. 101; *Waguih Elie George Siag and Clorinda Vecchi* v. *The Arab Republic of Egypt*,

treaty provisions will be relevant in this regard [103], which usually refer to the law of the State where nationality is claimed [104]. This approach is consistent with State sovereignty in determining the criteria for nationality [105]. The issue of dual nationals submitting investment claims between a host State and a contracting State has been controversial [106].

The nationality of legal entities or juridical persons is determined by the criteria of incorporation or the seat of the company, subject to relevant agreements, treaties and legislation. This was the case in *AES* v. *Argentina* [107]. The nationality requirement must be met at the time of the alleged breach of the obligation, as acquiring a particular nationality in order to prosecute a claim under a corresponding treaty is not permissible. Treaty shopping is acceptable; *forum* shopping is not [108].

ICSID Case No. ARB/05/15, Decision on Jurisdiction (11 April 2007), para. 201. See the issue of nationality in C. Schreuer *et al.*, *The ICSID Convention: A Commentary on the Convention on the Settlement of Investment Disputes Between States and Nationals of Other States*, 2nd ed., Cambridge, Cambridge University Press, 2009, pp. 552-553.

103. According to Article 1 of the Hague Convention on Certain Questions Relating to the Conflict of Nationality Laws (1930), "it is for each State to determine under its own law who are its nationals", but "this law shall be recognized by other States in so far as it is consistent with international conventions, international custom and the principles of law generally recognized with regard to nationality", Douglas, *supra* note 39, p. 77. There is a general consensus between national laws and international laws on this topic, but the problem lies in the precise interaction between investment treaties and municipal law.

104. See, for instance, deciding in this sense: *Hussein Nuaman Soufraki* v. *The United Arab Emirates*, ICSID Case No. ARB/02/7, Award (7 July 2004), para. 55. Other cases follow similar lines, for instance, *Siag and Vecchi* v. *Egypt*, *supra* note 102, Decision on Jurisdiction (2007), paras. 195-201; *Ioan Micula* et al. v. *Romania*, *supra* note 102, Decision on Jurisdiction and Admissibility (24 September 2008), paras. 86, 101.

105. Some treaties also include additional requirements such as residence (see, for example, Article 1 (3) *(b)* of the Treaty between the Federal Republic of Germany and the State of Israel concerning the Encouragement and Reciprocal Protection of Investments, signed on 24 June 1976, entered into force on 14 April 1980), or domicile (see, for example, Art. 1 of the Agreement between the Government of Denmark and the Government of the Republic of Indonesia Concerning the Encouragement and the Reciprocal Protection of Investments, signed on 30 January 1968, entered into force on 10 March 1970).

106. To read more about the position of ICSID tribunals on the matter, see Fouret, Gerbay and Alvarez, *supra* note 70, pp. 165-169. The ILC also addressed the issue in its fifty-eighth session in Geneva, 1 May-9 June and 3 July-11 August 2006, published in Fragmentation of International Law: Difficulties Arising From the Diversification and Expansion of International Law, Report of the Study Group of the International Law Commission, finalized by Martti Koskenniemi, 13 April 2006, A/CN.4/L.682 (hereafter "ILC Fragmentation Report"), https://legal.un.org/ilc/documentation/english/a_cn4_l682.pdf, accessed 3 March 2022, pp. 218 ff.

107. *AES Corporation* v. *The Argentine Republic*, ICSID Case No. ARB/02/17, Decision on Jurisdiction (26 April 2005), para. 78.

108. Douglas, *supra* note 39, pp. 290-291.

Some treaties provide additional requirements for protection under the treaty, such as the effective conducting of business in the home State [109]. Even where these additional requirements are not present, tribunals generally conduct a formal review of the definition of an investor in the treaty [110]. As a result, investors frequently formally make use of particular corporate structures to ensure investment treaty protection [111]. Tribunals have declared this type of corporate strategizing valid unless undertaken with a lack of good faith, or as an "abusive manipulation of the system" in the case of claims arising before the corporate restructuring [112]. Some treaties also provide protection for investments made by legal entities incorporated in the host State that are controlled by entities incorporated under a contracting State [113].

D. International investment contracts and other foreign investments generating State responsibility

1. International investment contracts

These contracts regulate the usually long-term relationship between the host State and the foreign investor [114]. The substantive rules of

---

109. See, for instance, the Agreement on Encouragement and Reciprocal Protection of Investments between the Kingdom of the Netherlands and the Argentine Republic, signed on 20 October 1992, entered into force on 1 October 1994, Article 1 *(b)*.

110. *Yukos Universal Ltd. (Isle of Man)* v. *The Russian Federation*, PCA Case No. AA 228, Interim Award on Jurisdiction and Admissibility (30 November 2009). Also in *Venezuela Holdings, BV*, et al. (case formerly known as *Mobil Corporation, Venezuela Holdings, BV,* et al.) v. *Bolivarian Republic of Venezuela* (hereafter *Venezuela Holdings* v. *Venezuela* refers to the whole history of the case, ICSID Case No. ARB/07/27, Decision on Jurisdiction (10 June 2010), para. 165. But see *TSA Spectrum de Argentina SA* v. *The Argentine Republic*, ICSID Case No. ARB/05/5, Award (19 December 2008), paras. 160-162.

111. This procedure was recognized as valid, for instance, in *Aguas del Tunari SA* v. *Republic of Bolivia*, ICSID Case No. ARB/02/3, Decision on Respondent's Objections to Jurisdiction (21 October 2005), para. 330.

112. *Venezuela Holdings* v. *Venezuela*, *supra* note 110, Decision on Jurisdiction (10 June 2010), para. 176, which cites *Phoenix* v. *Czech Republic*, *supra* note 53, Award (15 April 2009), para. 113. See also *Tidewater Inc. et al.* v. *The Bolivarian Republic of Venezuela*, ICSID Case No. ARB/10/5, Decision on Jurisdiction (8 February 2013), para. 146.

113. For instance, Article 1 (2) *(c)* of the Argentina-France BIT extends protection to "legal persons effectively controlled directly or indirectly by nationals of one of the Contracting Parties or by legal persons having their registered office in the territory of one of the Contracting Parties and constituted in accordance with legislation of the latter" (Agreement between the Government of the French Republic and the Government of the Republic of Argentina on the Encouragement and the Reciprocal Protection of Investments, signed on 3 July 1991, entered into force on 3 March 1993, Article 1 (2) *(c)*. Free translation from the French original).

114. J. Sicard-Mirabal and Y. Derains, *Introduction to Investor-State Arbitration*, The Hague, Kluwer Law International, 2018, p. 12.

these agreements are frequently complemented by a provision specifying the law applicable to the relationship and, generally, an arbitral clause [115].

International investment contracts are usually drafted in sectors in which the State exercises a monopoly under local legislation [116]. These contracts may govern projects such as public service concessions, public-private partnerships or build-operate-transfer work within the construction industry. Foreign investment contracts may also relate to tourism sites, housing projects and licensing of telecommunications services. See further discussion on this point in Chapter XIV.

International investment contracts also often regulate the exploitation of natural resources. These contracts are referred to as "concession agreements", but this is not a strict term of art [117]. This terminology conceals the bilateral character of the transaction, "and moreover it is often used, popularly, to denote the area in respect of which the agreement is made" [118]. This is why some prefer to call them "economic development agreements" [119] or *convention d'établissement* [120].

These international investment contracts or "economic development agreements" usually require substantial capital and input of high-level skills, in addition to management and organizational capacities and collateral responsibilities for infrastructure. The States are incentivized

---

115. Kahn, *supra* note 33, p. 7.

116. UNCTAD, State Contracts (IIA, Series One), 2004, https://unctad.org/en/Docs/iteiit200411_en.pdf, accessed 3 March 2022, p. 3.

117. *Ibid.*

118. McNair, *supra* note 4, p. 1. Igbokwe considers this a terminological sophistry suggesting that foreign investment contracts, rather than being mutually beneficial to both the foreign investor and the host State, are essentially geared toward the economic development of the host State and thus deserving the protection by international law. V. C. Igbokwe, "Determination, Interpretation and Application of Substantive Law in Foreign Investment Treaty Arbitrations", *Journal of International Arbitration*, Vol. 23, No. 4 (2006), p. 271.

119. McNair, *supra* note 4, p. 1. See also, for instance, in C. T. Curtis, "Legal Security of Economic Development Agreements", *Harvard International Law Journal*, Vol. 29, No. 2 (1988), p. 332; G. R. Delaume, "State Contracts and Transnational Arbitration", *American Journal of International Law*, Vol. 75, No. 4 (1981), p. 786. Sole Arbitrator R.-J. Dupuy refers to this terminology in *Texaco Overseas Petroleum Co./California Asiatic Oil Co.* v. *Government of Libya*, Award of the Merits (19 January 1977), 17 ILM, p. 1, paras. 36, 40-45, at 45 *(c)*. The arbitrator cites: M. Bourquin, "Arbitration and Economic Development Agreements", *The Business Lawyer*, Vol. 15 (1960); A. A. Fatouros, "Government Guarantees to Foreign Investors", *Columbia Law Review*, Vol. 63, No. 3 (2007); J. N. Hyde, "Economic Development Agreements", *Recueil des cours*, Vol. 105 (1962); A. Verdross, "The Status of Foreign Private Interests Stemming from Economic Development Agreements with Arbitration Clauses", *Selected Readings on Protection by Law of Private Foreign Investments*, Vol. 117 (1964).

120. Kahn, *supra* note 33, p. 7.

to allow such foreign involvement as they do not have (or barely have) the means to accomplish the task themselves [121].

These agreements, usually of long duration, involve a variety of obligations mostly performed in the territory of the host State and within the framework of its administrative system [122]. Even though these contracts are usually governed by the law of the host country, they also give rise to international legal obligations related to the treatment of the investor [123].

Unlike ordinary commercial arrangements, international investment contracts raise significant public policy considerations. Elements of public law are relevant during their negotiation, conclusion, operation and termination. Since terminating foreign investment contracts may have implications for public goods or necessities, the rules regarding damages may differ from those typically found within ordinary commercial agreements. Termination rights may also be different: while commercial contracts and foreign investment contracts may be terminated due to contractual breaches, international investment contracts may also be terminated where the performance of the contractual obligations is made wholly or partially impossible due to State action [124].

The elements of public policy-based control and discretion that are common to international investment contracts may favor the State over the investor and may subject the other party to the risk of interference in its commercial expectations for entering into the agreement. It is at this juncture that public international law may become important [125]. Further nuances of international investment contracts and the applicable substantive law will be dealt with in Chapters XVII-XIX.

2. *Other international investments generating State responsibility*

Foreign direct investments are protected by local statutes and are subject to certain advantages such as fiscal incentives. This is often

121. A.V. M. Struycken, "Arbitration and State Contracts", *Recueil des cours*, Vol. 374 (2015), p. 29.

122. J. Crawford and A. Sinclair, "The UNIDROIT Principles and their Application to State Contracts", in "UNIDROIT Principles of International Commercial Contracts: Reflections on their Use in International Arbitration", *ICC International Court of Arbitration Bulletin* (hereafter *ICC Ct. Bull.*), special supplement published in book form, Paris, ICC Publishing, 2002 (hereafter *ICC Ct. Bull.* Special 2002), p. 58.

123. Muchlinski, *supra* note 7, p. 7.

124. UNCTAD, State Contracts, *supra* note 116, p. 5.

125. See Chap. XIV, *infra*, "Particularities of foreign investments contracts and the public-private relationship".

the case with investments made in developing countries. These types of investments usually also benefit from the protection of treaties, for instance, which may open the door for public international law remedies when appropriate to respond to undue measures taken by the host States.

Domestic investment incentives typically correspond to purely administrative law matters. The domestic regimes establishing the fiscal incentives, for instance, usually do not contain a provision determining the applicable law, nor do most basic investment laws or codes. Treaties, in turn, typically establish broad standards of protection but do not include comprehensive treatment of the applicable law and its intricacies. Determining the law applicable to the investment contract, therefore, generates several collateral issues, which will be dealt with later in this book [126].

As previously mentioned, both domestic legislation and investment treaties typically set arbitration as the default dispute resolution mechanism. If an investment claim arises, however, only the State is bound to accept this recourse to arbitration. The investors are not obliged to do so unless they consider recourse to the arbitral mechanism appropriate.

This matter raises the question of whether, in the absence of privity, one could recur to arbitration [127]. The issue was resolved in the affirmative in the famous *SPP* v. *Egypt* case [128]. As later stated by Jan Paulsson, the attorney in the case,

---

126. For a detailed analysis, see Chaps. XVII and XIX, *infra*, on choice of law in investment claims.

127. Arbitration is built on consent; however, "arbitration without consent exists". See G. Kaufmann-Kohler and H. Peter, "Formula 1 Racing and Arbitration: The FIA Tailor-Made System for Fast Track Dispute Resolution", *Arbitration International*, Vol. 17 (2001), p. 186.

128. See *Southern Pacific Properties (Middle East) Limited* v. *Arab Republic of Egypt*, ICSID Case No. ARB/84/3, Decision on Jurisdiction (14 April 1988), para. 118:

> "It is true, as Egypt has emphasized in these proceedings, that consent by a State to the jurisdiction of an international tribunal involves a waiver of sovereign immunity. The Tribunal would note, however, that the waiver which results from Article 8 is illusory in several respects. In the first place, because of the hierarchic nature of the first paragraph of Article 8, the Government of Egypt may avoid the Centre's jurisdiction by agreeing with the investor on some other form of dispute settlement. Second, in those cases where a bilateral treaty is applicable, that treaty will take precedence over ICSID arbitration unless it provides for such arbitration, in which case Egypt has already waived its jurisdictional immunity and consented to the Centre's jurisdiction. Finally, Article 8 only becomes operative after the investment has been approved by Egyptian authorities. Thus, even if all of the jurisdictional prerequisites of Article 25 of the Washington Convention are satisfied, Article 8 does not effect a waiver of sovereign immunity unless and until

"arbitration without privity is a delicate mechanism . . . But if the mechanism is applied judiciously, it will help fill a void that now exists in the absence of compulsory jurisdiction, and thus contribute to enhancing the legal security of international economic life" [129].

Several ICSID decisions invoking the unilateral offer to arbitrate followed the *SPP* v. *Egypt* ruling [130]. In the words of Aron Broches, agreements to ICSID jurisdiction may be expressed by States in contracts, or alternatively in treaties or in their laws [131].

Egypt approves the investment in question without reaching agreement with the investor on some other form of dispute settlement."

129. Paulsson, *supra* note 18, p. 232.

130. J. Paulsson, "The Pyramids Case", *Collected Courses of the International Academy for Arbitration Law*, Vol. 1 (2014), pp. 11, 20-21.

131. A. Broches, "The Convention on the Settlement of Investment Disputes: Some Observations on Jurisdiction", *Columbia Journal of Transnational Law*, Vol. 5 (1966), p. 263.

CHAPTER III

EVOLUTION OF FOREIGN INVESTMENTS UNDER PUBLIC INTERNATIONAL LAW UNTIL THE NINETEENTH CENTURY

A. Introduction

While the legal regime regulating foreign investments has long been rooted in public international law, it remained underdeveloped until the later part of the twentieth century [132]. The origins of the foreign investment legal protection may be traced to ancient times; however, developments leading to the current state of affairs began to unfold in the Middle Ages.

Justice Oliver Wendell Holmes Jr. once wrote in a decision, "a page of history is worth a volume of logic" [133]. A brief reference to its historical evolution is helpful to understand both the current state of affairs within foreign investment law and the challenges lying ahead regarding applicable law, upon which much of this book is focused.

B. Medieval lex mercatoria *and arbitration*

The expression *lex mercatoria*, attributed to an anonymous late thirteenth-century author [134], refers to common understandings and usages established within the merchant communities of medieval Western Europe, which was markedly cosmopolitan [135]. This *lex* did not consist of an organized corpus of written rules but of consuetudinary

132. Collins, *supra* note 66, p. 1.

133. *New York Trust Co.* v. *Eisner*, 256 US 345, Judgment (16 May 1921), para. 6.

134. Contributing to the Colfore collection included in the "Little Red Book of Bristol", R. Zimmermann, *Estudios de Derecho Privado Europeo*, Madrid, Civitas Ediciones, 2000, p. 198. An interesting perspective on the origins of *lex mercatoria* can be found in Albrecht Cordes, "Conflicts in 13th Century Maritime Law: A Comparison between Five European Ports", *Oxford University Comparative Law Forum*, Vol. 2 (2020), https://ouclf.law.ox.ac.uk/conflicts-in-13th-century-maritime-law-a-comparison-between-five-european-ports/, accessed 3 March 2022.

135. H. J. Berman and F. J. Dasser, "The 'New' Law Merchant and the 'Old': Sources, Content, and Legitimacy", in T. E. Carbonneau (ed.), Lex Mercatoria *and Arbitration: A Discussion of the New Lew Merchant*, 2nd ed., The Hague, Juris / Kluwer International, 1998, p. 53.

norms based on good faith [136] and party autonomy [137]. The usages of the *lex mercatoria*, constantly changing, were complemented by standardized notarial documents [138].

Every once in a while, compilations [139] of the *lex mercatoria* were presented, among them: the Little Red Book, written in 1280 and published in medieval Bristol; the *Rôles d'Oléron* published at the end of the twelfth century in France, comprising usages from the Atlantic coast; and the *Consulado del Mar*, compiled in fourteenth-century Barcelona, containing usages from the Mediterranean and the Bay of Biscay. The Rules of Wisby and the Laws of the Hanse Towns did the same with the usages from the Baltic Sea, and, in Italy, the Amalfi Laws compiled decisions from the Maritime Tribunal [140].

One of the special features of the *lex mercatoria* was the resolution of conflicts either by merchants themselves or by mercantile tribunals [141]. This mechanism was both agile and informal, entrusting the decision-making to peer merchants or to other individuals who typically had no legal training. Decision-makers usually avoided legal technicisms and abstract scholastic reasoning, tending instead to decide *ex aequo et bono* [142].

The flourishing cities of medieval Western Europe attempted to attract foreign merchants by concluding commercial treaties guaranteeing freedom of trade and by rendering the circulation of goods exempt from taxation. An agreement between Venice and Pavia dating back to 840 is the oldest on record, and others extended throughout the centuries in Europe and even outside the Latin Christian world [143]. Rulers also

---

136. See H. J. Berman, *Law and Revolution, The Formation of the Western Legal Tradition*, Cambridge, MA / London, Harvard University Press, 1983, pp. 348-350.

137. See C. M. Schmitthoff, "International Business Law: A New Law Merchant, II Current Law and Social Problems", in C. Cheng (ed.), *Clive M. Schmitthoff's Selected Essays on International Trade Law*, Dordrecht, Martinus Nijhoff, 1961, p. 24.

138. Berman, *supra* note 136, p. 341.

139. R. Goode, "Usage and Its Reception in Transnational Commercial Law", *International and Comparative Law Quarterly*, Vol. 46 (1997), p. 5.

140. J. C. Fernández Rozas, *Ius Mercatorum, Autorregulación y unificación del Derecho de los negocios transnacionales*, Madrid, Editorial Colegios Notariales de España, 2003, pp. 31-32.

141. Berman, *supra* note 136, p. 346.

142. Schmitthoff, *supra* note 137, p. 24.

143. For example, Venice concluded a far-reaching commercial treaty with the Byzantine Empire in 992 CE, and another in 1082 CE: S. C. Neff, *Justice Among Nations: A History of International Law*, Cambridge, MA, Harvard University Press, 2014, p. 87.

offered help to merchants who had been mistreated by advancing claims on their behalf against foreign governments [144].

In international relations, arbitration clauses first appeared within treaties as early as the twelfth century but only became commonplace toward the end of the thirteenth century. To use modern terminology, international arbitration claims corresponded mostly to mediation or amiable composition proceedings.

The language used in such affairs was imprecise [145]. Moreover, in the Middle Ages, it became difficult to distinguish between private and public arbitration proceedings since both mechanisms overlapped. For example, conflicts between two princes often passed from the private to the public sphere [146]. Procrustean attempts to place medieval arbitration proceedings into a modern categorical framework prove difficult and offer a useful warning that such modern analogies may be unhelpful [147].

C. Medieval arbitration in matters among sovereigns

In the Middle Ages, arbitrators in the above matters derived their powers, in hierarchical order, from the Pope or Emperor, then from the monarch via delegation [148], and then from the monarch's representatives.

These adjudicators usually lacked the necessary competence for effective decision-making and often failed to remain completely impartial. Concerned with the interests of their own jurisdiction, they also typically avoided formulating general principles that could later be used against them. Similarly, decision-makers preferred not to provide reasons in their decisions to avoid being bound to particular precedents

---

144. In this regard, they made use of "reprisals", a sort of combination of claims made by rulers on behalf of nationals and in furtherance of just wars. The use of force was exercised in the form of capturing property, rather than the use of physical violence to attack individuals. Usually, force was used by the injured party himself and not by the armed forces of his country, and often was not used against the actual wrongdoer but against surrogate parties who had not personally committed the original wrong. See *ibid.*, p. 88.

145. A. Keller, "Inter-State Arbitration in Historical Perspective on International Arbitration", in T. Schultz and F. Ortino (eds.), *The Oxford Handbook of International Arbitration*, Oxford, Oxford University Press, 2020, pp. 848-849.

146. *Ibid.*, p. 848.

147. C. G. Roelofsen, "International Arbitration and Courts", *The Oxford Encyclopedia of the History of International Law*, Oxford, Oxford University Press, 2012, pp. 152-153.

148. For instance, King William I, or King Louis IX, acted in several conflicts. Keller, *supra* note 145, p. 847.

in the future and to escape the eventual criticism of jurists, which could produce a result incompatible with royal sovereignty [149].

For these reasons, litigants were often distrustful of arbitration for causes between sovereigns, which was a major threat to the system as a whole.

D. The emergence of the theoretical foundations for the protection of aliens

Public international law emerged from the late medieval *ius gentium* tradition. Influential writers such as Francisco de Vitoria, Alberico Gentili, Hugo Grotius, Samuel von Pufendorf, Christian Wolff and Emer de Vattel "sculpted international law into substantially its modern form" [150]. Collectively, the work of these writers loosened the close link that had been forged in the Middle Ages between natural law and *ius gentium* and transformed international law into a branch of law in itself [151]. In doing so, these early theorists borrowed heavily from private law [152]. At the time, Roman law, the *ius commune* within Western Europe [153], was universally regarded as the standard against which to measure justice [154].

---

149. C. Rousseau, *Derecho Internacional Público*, 3rd ed., Barcelona, Editorial Ariel, 1966, p. 489.

150. J. Crawford, *Brownlie's Principles of Public International Law*, 8th ed., Oxford, Oxford University Press, 2012, pp. 3-4.

151. Neff, *supra* note 143, p. 141. Also, Crawford, *ibid.*, at p. 7:

> "The process of separating international law from natural law was spurred on by the Reformation and the religious wars, notably the Thirty Years War which ended with the Peace of Westphalia (1648). Natural law emerged from Roman law and the traditions of the Roman Church, which created a universal *ius naturale*, of which *ius gentium* or the "law of peoples" was a subset. Natural law was thus universal and laid the foundation for many of the early theorists' work. Willingly or not, these thinkers contributed to the separation of *ius gentium* from *ius naturale* and its formation into a law of nations, which applied specifically to the rulers of States."

152. Lauterpacht, *supra* note 3, pp. 10 ff.

153. H. Coing, *Derecho Privado Europeo*, Madrid, TI, Editorial Fundación Cultural del Notariado, 1996, p. 38. It had suppletive value regarding local laws and was recurrently used for interpretive purposes. F. Wieacker, *Historia del Derecho Privado de la Edad Moderna*, Granada, Editorial Comares SL, 2000, pp. 52-53.

154. H. C. Gutteridge, "Comparative Law and the Law of Nations", *British Yearbook of International Law*, Vol. 21 (1944), p. 4. A recent report of the ILC on *ius cogens*, to cite one of several examples, also finds antecedents of the idea in classical Roman law. ILC, First Report on *Jus Cogens*, Chap. IX, by Dire Tladi, Special Rapporteur, A/CN.4/693, Sixty-Eighth Session, Geneva, 2 May-10 June and 4 July-12 August 2016, https://legal.un.org/ilc/reports/2016/english/chp9.pdf, accessed 9 June 2022, p. 9.

Sovereigns and governments received advice from experts trained as civil lawyers, who turned their attention to the legal affairs of States. When addressing international problems, these experts inevitably resorted to the legal notions that they had absorbed in their civil law studies, most of which derived from Roman law, in particular its private law [155]. Modern international law was developed beginning with the Peace of Westphalia in 1648 until the middle of the nineteenth century, during which time the vast majority of experts were lawyers trained in the Roman system. As such, it is unsurprising that the historical source of international law is Roman law [156], in particular, its *ius gentium*.

As to the origins of this notion of *ius gentium*, ancient Roman civil law *(ius civile)* did not apply between foreigners and Roman citizens, and decisions were rendered *ex aequo et bono*. As the Roman Empire expanded in power and influence, the application of foreign legal notions became commonplace, and it became increasingly clear that certain basic ideas of law applied to all people. These accepted notions led to the creation of the *ius gentium*, which merged with the civil law into a single system in the latter days of the Roman Empire [157].

Centuries later, the Lutheran and Calvinist Reformations of the sixteenth century ruptured the legal and political unity of Europe, following which the same *ius gentium* inspired Grotius and others in their writings to address the legal relationships between sovereigns. In this context, *ius gentium* grew to be understood as a body of norms containing fundamental and universally shared legal concepts drawn from Roman private law [158].

During this time, the protection of foreign investments beyond Europe became central to the creation and development of public international law [159]. The arguments at the time in favor of such international investment protection ran as follows. When European traders traveled to Asia, Africa or Latin America, local law did not apply since the foreign merchants were already subject to their own

155. R. Zimmermann, "Roman Law and the Harmonisation of Private Law in Europe", in A. Hartkamp *et al.* (eds.), *Towards a European Civil Code*, 4th ed., The Hague, Kluwer Law International, 2011, pp. 27-53.

156. Sir. H. Waldock, "General Course on Public International Law", *Recueil des cours*, Vol. 106 (1962), p. 54.

157. C. T. Kotuby, Jr. and L. A. Sobota, *General Principles of Law and International Due Process: Principles and Norms Applicable in Transnational Disputes*, Oxford, Oxford University Press, 2017, p. 7.

158. For Grotius these concepts included, among other things, *pacta sunt servanda*, *ibid.*, p. 8.

159. Sornarajah, *supra* note 29, p. 18.

national laws, which applied to their international transactions. As such, the property purchased by merchants could not be nationalized or seized via local enactments. In short, national laws could not violate international obligations – and this protection gave rise to the notion of an "international minimum standard" [160].

Moreover, the functions of the State and the investor intersected during this period of European expansionism. One clear example is found in the relationship between the European States and their respective national corporations, notably the Dutch East India Company (Verenigde Oostindishe Compagnie, or the "VOC"), the British East India Company and the French East India Company [161]. These corporations not only conducted commercial affairs but also advanced their home State's political positions, entered treaties, founded and administered settlements, engaged in military conquest and built fortifications [162].

Vitoria sustained the view that alien traders must receive treatment equal to the nationals of the State. In turn, Grotius advanced an alternative position, according to which foreigners must observe some external standard, usually higher than national standards. In his view, nationals in underdeveloped legal systems were only granted minimal legal protection, which would have been unacceptable to traders from abroad. Both Vitoria and Grotius shared the belief that the law should further the free movement of trade and investments across State boundaries. Both thinkers wished to advance the expansion of European trade. In fact, historians consider Grotius's book *Freedom of the Seas* (1608) to have enabled the entry of European powers into Asia and Africa [163].

---

160. Subedi, *supra* note 17, pp. 7-8. See also M. Paparinskis, *The International Minimum Standard and Fair and Equitable Treatment*, Oxford, Oxford University Press, 2013.

161. K. Miles, *The Origins of International Investment Law: Empire, Environment and the Safeguarding of Capital*, Cambridge, Cambridge University Press, 2013, p. 33.

162. *Ibid.*, pp. 33-34. At pp. 41-42:

> "The merging of State interests with those of private investors as international rules protecting foreign investments were being developed resulted in close relationships being established between States and investors throughout the nineteenth century, embedded within the very nature of the law. Inevitably, such conditions contributed to creating a sense of 'otherness' of international investment law. The separateness of international investment law was most visible in excluding the host State from legal protection within the relevant laws."

163. See Sornarajah, *supra* note 29, pp. 19-23. Miles, *supra* note 161, p. 19:

> "Emerging from an international legal system established amongst European nations, the rules on foreign investment protection evolved throughout the

E. Friendship, Commerce and Navigation Treaties

In the aftermath of hostilities ended by the Treaty of Utrecht in 1713, States began to conclude treaties that incorporated provisions protecting property and economic interests [164]. A network of similar instruments dominated the European legal landscape in the middle of the seventeenth century. These texts were the antecedents to modern bilateral investment treaties. They covered a wide range of issues beyond investment and trade, also incorporating provisions on immigration, taxation and matters that are today understood as human rights [165].

Grotius's view that local law should not apply to Europeans, who were already subject to their "more civilized law", was enshrined in Friendship, Commerce and Navigation treaties. This exclusion was essential to ensure that investors received better treatment than natives in local communities. Local law often provided extreme punishments such as execution for petty crimes, emphasizing the need to maintain order in an environment lacking a permanent military presence. Over time, the preferential treatment given to foreigners was phased out by the notion of an international minimum standard of protection. This standard has survived as of today as a principle of customary international law, offering a check on the arbitrariness of the exercise of State power over individuals [166].

Friendship, Commerce and Navigation treaties, "a sort of latter-day successor to the law merchant of the Middle Ages", were important international trade tools, forming "a framework for international protection of foreign capital" [167]. They were also sources of transnational norms, as the contents of many treaties contained significant overlap and included a series of basic rights granted to individuals in their

---

'colonial encounter' as a tool to protect the interests of capital-exporting States and their nationals. International investment principles were drafted and claimed to be both universal and impartial, while essentially offering protection for investors and establishing obligations for capital-importing States in order to facilitate trade and investment."

164. Treaty of Peace and Friendship between Great Britain and Spain, signed 13 July 1713, 28 Consol. TS 295, Articles VII, VIII, IX, XV. See C. Brown, "Resolving International Investment Disputes", in N. Klein (ed.), *Litigating International Law Disputes: Weighing the Balance*, Cambridge, Cambridge University Press, 2014, p. 403.

165. See, for example, the Treaty of Friendship, Commerce and Navigation, US-Federal Republic of Germany, 29 October 1954, cited in J. F. Coyle, "The Treaty of Friendship, Commerce and Navigation in the Modern Era", *Columbia Journal of Transnational Law*, Vol. 302 (2013), p. 304.

166. Collins, *supra* note 66, p. 9.

167. Miles, *supra* note 161, pp. 24-25.

commercial activities. Merchants also benefited from such provisions, even though they were not parties to these treaties. The equal treatment of foreigners and nationals regarding to taxation and access to justice was also typically included and later became commonplace, as well as what later became known as the most-favored-nation clause (MFN): each party was entitled to equal treatment under the local State law, and the extension to them of the same favorable treatment provided to parties of other nationalities [168].

As the name of these treaties suggests, and contrary to modern bilateral investment agreements, Friendship, Commerce and Navigation agreements were not exclusively (or even primarily) vehicles to protect investments abroad [169]. The treaties included some protections for investors, but their primary objective was to promote international trade and improve international relations, allowing access to ports and granting navigation rights through territorial waters [170].

These agreements concluded for centuries by major colonial powers even became a common part of foreign investment policy in the United States until after World War II. However, their popularity had largely faded by the 1960s. Countries that gained their independence after World War II were often unwilling to accept the obligations contained in such agreements, leading to the birth of a new type of investment protection enshrined in bilateral investment treaties (BITs) [171].

Also, several treaties signed by Congo in 1885, Morocco in 1906, China in 1922 and Turkey in 1923 were modeled after the Congo General Act of 1885 and provided for "equality of opportunity" concerning commerce in their territories. Further, a regime of the so-

---

168. "The first most-favored-nation clause that clearly included this element of futurity appeared in a bilateral treaty between England and Spain in 1667. These provisions later appeared in several treaties thereafter", Neff, *supra* note 143, pp. 200-204. As highlighted by Mazzoni and Malaguti, the most-favored-nation clause had great relevance since it liberalized access to internal markets. Mazzoni and Malaguti, *supra* note 30, p. 31.

169. In these times, commerce referred to the trading of goods by merchants, and not "investment" from abroad. Direct investment by multinational corporations, or instances where consortia set up permanent operations in host countries, were not contemplated at that time. See Collins, *supra* note 66, p. 34.

170. "While these treaties contained provisions protecting against expropriation, requiring full protection and security, and fair and equitable treatment, their primary purpose was to establish closer commercial and political relations between the contracting parties. This reflected their original design as instruments for the United States, as a then newly independent State, to participate in international trade relations", Schill, *supra* note 30, p. 29.

171. J. Basedow, "The Law of Open Societies: Private Ordering and Public Regulation of International Relations General Course on Private International Law", *Recueil des cours*, Vol. 360 (2013), p. 90.

called A- and B-mandates was established by the League of Nations after World War I with comparable provisions on equal opportunity. These initiatives aimed to ensure non-discriminatory treatment from the European powers in relation to trade and investment. However, the advent of World War II and other events put an end to international cooperation based on multilateral principles concerning substantive investment rights [172].

F. International mixed claims commissions

Even though arbitration is one of the oldest international dispute resolution mechanisms, its popularity declined steadily after the Middle Ages until it was revived with the mixed claims commissions, established by the Jay Treaty of 1794 [173]. As noted by John Merrills, this instrument is considered the predecessor to the prevailing modern methods for resolving international investment claims [174].

The mechanism instituted by the Jay Treaty blended juridical and diplomatic considerations targeted at reaching negotiated settlements [175]. Even though this treaty granted an arbitral mechanism that is very different from those used today [176], it proved innovative in many respects [177] and ushered in the modern era of international arbitration [178].

The Jay Treaty established mixed claims tribunals (or commissions) with sitting arbitrators. This allowed States, for the first time, to bypass direct diplomatic channels in their negotiations [179]. Unlike modern commissions, these mixed claims tribunals followed a strictly juridical procedure and delivered reasoned awards [180]. The first two commissions created by the Jay Treaty did not have a significant impact

172. Schill, *supra* note 30, p. 30.

173. For more on Jay arbitrations and their legacy, see Roelofsen, *supra* note 147, pp. 160 ff.

174. Keller, *supra* note 145, p. 851. The Jay Treaty followed the precedent that had been set by the 1648 Treaty of Münster between the Netherlands and Spain as part of the Peace of Westphalia. V.V. Veeder, "Inter-State Arbitration", in T. Schultz and F. Ortino (eds.), *The Oxford Handbook of International Arbitration*, Oxford, Oxford University Press, 2020, p. 217.

175. J. Merrills, "The Place of International Litigation in International Law", in N. Klein (ed.), *Litigating International Law Disputes: Weighing the Options*, Cambridge, Cambridge University Press, 2014, p. 3.

176. Veeder, *supra* note 174, p. 217.

177. Keller, *supra* note 145, p. 852.

178. B. Cheng, *General Principles of Law as Applied by International Courts and Tribunals*, Cambridge, Cambridge University Press, 2006, p. 387.

179. Keller, *supra* note 145, pp. 855-856.

180. Merrills, *supra* note 175, p. 3.

on the development of public international law. The third commission, however, importantly influenced this discipline when affirming that an arbitral ruling should necessarily conform to the essential principles of the law of peoples *(ius gentium)* [181]. It frequently invoked general principles of law, albeit not always under that name [182]. For instance, in the 1798 *Jamaica* case, the Tribunal used the terminology "principles of justice" and decided that "where there is no fault, no omission of duty, there can be nothing whereon to support a charge of responsibility or justify a complaint" [183].

These tribunals heard many cases, and a significant body of case law emerged [184]. Over the course of five years, the mixed claims commissions that had been established under the Jay Treaty issued 536 awards [185]. Between 1798 and 1804, three mixed claims commissions were responsible for resolving a significant portion of the pending litigation between the United States and Great Britain related to, among other matters, the determination of the frontier with Canada and the payment of credits claimed by a British subject [186].

The main issues dealt with by these commissions was related to the measure of damages and the tribunal's right to determine its own jurisdiction. Several of these judgments, such as *Croft*, *Williams* and *Fabiani*, borrowed solutions from private law in matters related to damages, prescription and admission [187]. The decisions that emerged therefrom became recognized as established rules within public international law.

These mixed commissions also provided a model for many of the standing tribunals that the United States formed with Latin American States in the nineteenth century. These tribunals were composed of nationals from the United States, of the affected countries, and nationals of a third State [188].

---

181. Keller, *supra* note 145, p. 857.
182. Cheng, *supra* note 178, p. 387.
183. *Ibid.*, p. 218.
184. Neff, *supra* note 143, pp. 328-329.
185. D. J. Bederman, "The Glorious Past and Uncertain Future of International Claims Tribunals", in M. W. Janis (ed.), *International Courts for the Twenty-First Century*, Dordrecht, Martinus Nijhoff, p. 167.
186. Rousseau, *supra* note 149, p. 90.
187. These cases are mentioned in Lauterpacht, *supra* note 3, p. 39.
188. At the beginning, one expert was assigned to each litigant, and a third to adopt the decision in case of disagreement after; mixed arbitral commissions were later composed of three to five commissaries (one or two for each interparty and a third to break ties). Rousseau, *supra* note 149, p. 90.

Also, the 1871 Treaty of Washington between the United States and Britain led to a mixed commission award in the famous *Alabama* case, the first arbitration to occur between two world powers [189]. The decision was rendered in 1872 by a five-member commission.

Withdrawal of British support for the mixed claims commissions' system led to its eventual collapse. Nonetheless, States increasingly showed their willingness to accept arbitration [190]. By the end of the nineteenth century and the beginning of the twentieth, approximately 300 bilateral arbitration treaties had been concluded [191].

G. Gunboat diplomacy

The early slow development of the international foreign investment legal regime can be explained by reference to the colonial expansion of the eighteenth and nineteenth centuries. At the time, the protection enjoyed by imperial powers was largely sufficient for them to safely invest in their colonies without further legal safeguards. As such, there was no pressing need for the development of public international law for the purpose of protecting investments. For this reason, evolution occurred mainly on the American continent, where the United States did not have the colonial dominance to secure the investments of its nationals. Herein, power became the final arbiter. The use of overt or covert force in foreign investment-related matters continued well after World War II [192].

In this context, the United States and, on occasion, also European States used force to guarantee the extraterritorial application of their national law in order to protect investor rights. Known as gunboat diplomacy, this strategy was in many ways an antecedent of modern diplomatic protection. Through gunboat diplomacy, States exercised their discretion to intervene on behalf of their citizens abroad,

189. *Ibid.*, p. 490.

190. The Alabama Commissions' disputing parties consented, for the first time in history, to arbitration before a panel of jurists appointed mostly by neutral governments, charged with a mandate to apply specific rules. "From then on, the trajectory of arbitration shifted decisively towards a judicial model." See Keller, *supra* note 145, pp. 861-862.

191. "Only the United States signed twenty-two in the two-year period of 1908-9. However, the treaties had important caveats and usually the key decision whether the matter was arbitrable corresponded to each State. Unsurprisingly, arbitration did not flourish as would be expected. However, in the period 1794-1900, around 177 arbitrations took place, half of them in the period between 1880 and 1900." Neff, *supra* note 143, pp. 328-330.

192. Sornarajah, *supra* note 29, pp. 20-21.

demanding protection and compensation from the host State directly. This discretion was ultimately legitimized by both the Permanent Court of International Justice (PCIJ) and the ICJ [193].

In the nineteenth century, Latin American countries defended the application of their own laws and constitutions, while the United States insisted on applying international standards. The discussion had little to do with the taking of alien property in the context of economic reforms. This situation was generally related to the taking of property by mobs due to political vendettas. Early writers did not appear to see this distinction. The seizing of property for political reasons or by elite groups is one thing, but the seizing of property for the sake of economic reform is another entirely [194].

In many parts of the world under colonial rule or in protectorates such as those in the Middle East, foreign investments were protected through military power and thus gunboat diplomacy was sufficient [195].

As such, the development of an international system for assigning responsibility for injuries to the property of aliens occurred primarily in regions with no colonial regime in place, particularly in Latin America, which received significant investment from the United States. The international minimum standards for the treatment of aliens were, to a large extent, based upon American standards [196] rooted in turn in the French Declaration of the Rights of Man and of the Citizen of 1789 [197]. Article 17 of the Declaration states:

> "Property being a sacred and inviolable right, no one can be deprived of it, unless a legally established public necessity demands it, under the condition of a just and prior indemnity." [198]

---

193. Collins, *supra* note 66, p. 11.

194. Sornarajah, *supra* note 29, p. 21.

195. *Ibid.*, p. 36.

196. It may be useful to compare the international minimum standard with actual State practice. Here, one may refer to State practice as indicated in their own constitutional laws. The terms of the Fifth Amendment of the Constitution of the United States are familiar in this regard: "No person shall . . . be deprived of life, liberty or property without due process of law nor shall private property be taken for public use without just compensation." This principle of manifest justice and honesty has even, in its actual language, affected the development of other municipal systems. Lord Shawcross, *supra* note 38, p. 348.

197. Lowenfeld, *supra* note 25, p. 47.

198. Declaration of the Rights of Man and of the Citizen, France's National Constituent Assembly, 1789, Article 17.

H. Diplomatic protection in the nineteenth century

1. Scenario

Traditionally within public international law, individuals have lacked both legal subjectivity and standing, as their home States represented and provided them with legal protection. In this way, *diplomatic* protection was the main procedural mechanism used to remedy the situation [199].

Investor home States had interest not only in protecting their nationals abroad but also in advancing their own economic and political objectives. In his writing, Swiss jurist Emerich de Vattel (1714-1767) declared that whoever injures a citizen injures their State, which must protect that citizen – hence the origin of the notion of diplomatic protection [200].

Customary international law throughout the nineteenth century was generally understood to accept a minimum standard of treatment for the protection of investment property. Lack of compliance with this standard generated State responsibility and entitled a foreign State to intervene. Injury to an investor became, by extension, an injury to their State, which could respond to such an injury on behalf of its own nationals. State responses varied from military intervention to diplomatic appeals [201].

2. The Latin American response

Host States in Latin America saw the doctrine of diplomatic protection as another tool used by the United States and European powers to undermine Latin American sovereignty [202], and began to argue that their citizens should not be placed in a worse legal position than that accorded to foreigners. From the 1860s onward, many Latin American States advocated in favor of applying national treaty rules to investment contracts and disputes, which expressly contradicted the privileged standing granted to foreigners within customary international law [203]. These States also relied on the doctrine of sovereignty and sovereign equality to assert their right to expropriate or nationalize

199. Hess, *supra* note 48, p. 106.
200. Salacuse, *supra* note 65, pp. 67-68.
201. Miles, *supra* note 161, p. 47.
202. Salacuse, *supra* note 65, p. 69.
203. Miles, *supra* note 161, pp. 49-50.

foreign investments, so long as fair compensation was provided. The underlying logic emphasized that the very notion of sovereignty subjected foreigners residing within a national territory to the law of the land [204].

Latin American countries striving for greater sovereign control over their domestic economy mainly invoked the Calvo and the Drago Doctrines, detailed in the following section [205]. The situation was different in other developing areas of the world, such as Asia, the Middle East and parts of Africa. A system of extraterritorial jurisdiction prevailed in these areas since their institutions and laws were considered inferior to (or radically different from) those of Western States. As such, investors desired to remain under the jurisdiction and laws of their home States for their own protection.

According to Donald Shea, the principle of extraterritoriality was never fully established in Latin America, partly because of State sensitivity to the prerogatives of sovereignty, the European origins of their institutions and because they enjoyed a better bargaining position as a result of the Monroe Doctrine advanced by the United States against European colonialism in the Americas. In this scenario, aliens frequently resorted to diplomatic protection in order to guarantee their investments in the region. Fearful of economic or political imperialism, Latin American countries designed ingenious devices to blunt the effects of diplomatic protection, the most successful of which was the Calvo Doctrine [206].

Although superficially following the liberal-democratic ideal, these countries were inexperienced when it came to the democratic process. The resulting instability and disorder manifested itself in a series of injuries to the persons and property of resident aliens. Legal deficiencies led the investors' home governments to demand stronger protection

---

204. "For instance, Article 9 of the Convention on the Rights and Duties of States, one of the first international instruments to support the idea of national treatment, provided that States exercise jurisdiction upon all inhabitants within their national territorial limits. Nationals and foreigners enjoy the same legal protection, and national authorities and the foreigners may not claim rights beyond those that are also granted to nationals", Subedi, *supra* note 17, p. 8.

205. B. M. Cremades, "Disputes Arising out of Foreign Direct Investment in Latin America: A New Look at the Calvo Doctrine and Other Jurisdictional Issues", *Dispute Resolution Journal*, Vol. 59, No. 2 (2004), p. 80. See also B. Olmos Giupponi, "The Protection of Foreign Direct Investment in Latin America: Where Do We Stand on International Arbitration?", *Journal of International Arbitration*, Vol. 32, No. 2 (2015), p. 119.

206. D. R. Shea, *The Calvo Clause: A Problem of Inter-American and International Law and Diplomacy*, Minneapolis, University of Minnesota Press, 1955, pp. 3-5.

from Latin American States by threatening intervention. Originally, the intervention of foreign governments on behalf of their citizens was based on the principle of comity. As this type of State intervention became more frequent, they became a matter of legal right, forming the basis of diplomatic protection [207].

3. Calvo Doctrine

The Calvo Doctrine responded to the European and North American colonialist practice of diplomatic intervention through the use of claims commissions. These tribunals systematically decided against Latin American countries, which resulted in the payment of considerable damages and the loss of territory [208]. The Argentine jurist Carlos Calvo (1822 [209]-1906) condemned these interventions, and his views were widely accepted in the region [210].

The Calvo Doctrine was based on the generally accepted rules of national sovereignty, equality of States and territorial jurisdiction [211]. Its core ideas can be summarized in three parts. First, since sovereign States are free and independent, they cannot suffer interference of any sort by other States, either by force or diplomatically. Second, foreign investors should receive no better treatment than that accorded to the host States' own nationals. Each State could establish its own standard of treatment, which had to be accepted by foreigners conducting business there. Third, settlement should be achieved by the domestic courts of the host State alone [212]. As argued by Shea, accepting these concepts would eliminate the negative or "enemy" effects of diplomatic protection [213].

---

207. *Ibid.*, p. 10.

208. Mexico, in particular, suffered the consequences, including even foreign military interventions: J. L. Siqueiros, "Arbitral Autonomy and National Sovereign Authority in Latin America", in T. E. Carbonneau (ed.), Lex Mercatoria *and Arbitration: A Discussion of the New Lew Merchant*, 2nd ed., The Hague, Juris / Kluwer International, 1998, pp. 219-220.

209. See F. Perez Aznar, "Revisiting Carlos Calvo on the 200th Anniversary of his Birth", *EJIL Talk*, https://www.ejiltalk.org/revisiting-carlos-calvo-on-the-200th-anniversary-of-his-birth/, accessed 3 June 2022.

210. H. Accioly, *Tratado de Derecho Internacional Público*, Madrid, Instituto de Estudios Políticos, 1958, pp. 285-286.

211. Shea, *supra* note 206, p. 19.

212. J. Ho, *State Responsibility for Breaches of Investment Contracts*, Cambridge, Cambridge University Press, 2018, p. 11. See an interesting perspective in H. A. Grigera Naón, "Arbitration and Latin America: Progress and Setbacks", Fresh fields Lecture, *Arbitration International*, Vol. 21, No. 2 (2004), pp. 127-175.

213. Shea, *supra* note 206, pp. 19-20.

The Calvo Doctrine was received with much enthusiasm by Latin American States [214], which led to "Calvo Clauses" being included in national constitutions [215], treaties [216] and in the contractual agreements of many Latin American nations. "Calvo Clauses" guaranteed that foreign investors would have at most the same rights as nationals, and that the conflicts would be decided by local courts [217]. As such, investors would have little need of diplomatic protection from their own governments.

The Calvo Doctrine extended to regions beyond Latin America [218]. Later resolutions, even within the framework of the United Nations in the 1960s and 1970s, have also echoed this doctrine [219].

---

214. In the First International Conference of American States in 1889, the *ad hoc* Commission on International Law (without the support of the United States) concluded: "Foreigners are entitled to enjoy all the civil rights enjoyed by natives and they shall be accorded all the benefits of said rights in all that is essential as well as in the form or procedure, and the legal remedies incident thereto, absolutely in like manner as said natives. A nation has not, nor recognizes in favour to foreigners, any other obligations or responsibilities than those which in favour of the natives are established in like cases by the constitution and the laws", see J. B. Scott, *The International Conferences of American States (1889-1928)*, Oxford, Oxford University Press, 1931, p. 45.

215. See A. S. Hershey, "The Calvo and Drago Doctrines", *American Journal of International Law*, Vol. 1, No. 1 (1907), pp. 26-45; Olmos Giupponi, *supra* note 205, p. 115.

216. For instance, Article 21 of the "treaty of friendship, commerce and navigation" between Italy and Colombia of 1894 stated the following:

> "The Contracting Parties express their desire to avoid all types of dispute which might affect their cordial relations and agree that, in connection with disputes which involve individuals arising out of criminal, civil or administrative matters, their diplomatic agents will abstain from intervening except in cases of denial of justice or extraordinary or unlawful delay in the administration of justice."

217. J. Wong, "Umbrella Clauses in Bilateral Investment Treaties: Of Breaches of Contract, Treaty Violations, and the Divide Between Developing and Developed Countries in Foreign Investment Disputes", *George Mason Law Review*, Vol. 14 (2006), p. 145:

> "Under general international law, it is unclear whether a state breaching a contract with an investor qualifies per se as a violation of an international obligation. Such a breach may simply be treated as a domestic commercial matter. As such, investors were often forced to resolve any disputes over their contracts with the host state in that state's municipal courts and under its domestic laws, which were vulnerable to unilateral variation by the state."

218. W. Shan, "Is Calvo Dead?", *American Journal of Comparative Law*, Vol. 55, No. 1 (2007), p. 129.

219. General Assembly (GA) Resolution 3281 (XXIX) (Charter of Economic Rights and Duties of States), UN GAOR, Twenty-Ninth Session, Supp. No. 31 (1974) 50, Articles 2 (2) *(a)*, 4 *(g)*; UNGA Res. 626 (VII) of 21 December 1952 (on the Right to exploit freely Natural Wealth and Resources); UNGA Res. 1803 (XVII), 14 December 1962 (Permanent Sovereignty over Natural Resources); UNGA Declaration on the Establishment of a New International Economic Order, Resolution 3201 (S-VI) (1 May 1974). Human Rights Council, Protect, Respect and Remedy: A Framework for Business and Human Rights, Report of J. Ruggie, Special Representative of the Secretary-General on the issue of human rights and transnational corporations and

Nonetheless, the Calvo Clauses generated many controversies as well. Whether or not Calvo Clauses were valid became one of the most disputed questions within international diplomacy and jurisprudence [220]. Those who advocated for their invalidity argued that States had inherent rights to bring claims on behalf of their nationals due to violations of their rights as alien investors. Any waiver in this regard could not be enforced against a foreign State [221].

In fact, few decisions have admitted the total validity of the Calvo Clauses. They have been declared valid when the relationship in question is between the foreign investor and the defendant State. However, the same is not true for matters between the injured individual and the claimant State. Calvo Clauses have not been taken into account in case of any denial of justice and have even been declared categorically null in such situations [222].

A leading decision in this regard was rendered by the United States-Mexican Claims Commission in the *North American Dredging Company* case [223]. In it, the Tribunal declared the invalidity of the clause. The Tribunal wrote:

> "Under Article 18 of the contract [the Calvo clause] . . . the present claimant is precluded from presenting to its government any claim relative to the interpretation or fulfillment of this contract. . . . As the claimant voluntarily entered into a legal contract binding itself not to call as to this contract upon its Government to intervene on its behalf, and as all of its claim relates to this contract, and as therefore it cannot present its claim to its Government for interposition or espousal before this Commission, the second ground to the motion to dismiss is sustained." [224]

In the 2002 Third Report on Diplomatic Protection by the United Nations International Law Commission (ILC) to the UN General

---

other business enterprises), A/HRC/8/5, 7 April 2008, para. 14. These UN resolutions will be further addressed in Chap. IV.

220. "Perhaps no other problem in international law has been so indecisively arbitrated before international tribunals or as vehemently disputed among nations", Shea, *supra* note 206, p. 5.

221. As "an interesting comment on the state of development of international law", Neff points out that this dispute has not been definitively resolved even as of the present day, Neff, *supra* note 143, pp. 276-277.

222. Rousseau, *supra* note 149, p. 369.

223. *North American Dredging Co. of Texas (United States* v. *United Mexican States)* (31 March 1926), reproduced in *American Journal of International Law*, Vol. 20 (1926), p. 800.

224. See Shea, *supra* note 206, p. 263. See also Salacuse, *supra* note 65, p. 86.

Assembly, the Special Rapporteur noted that the Calvo Clause was of limited effect in that it did not constitute a complete bar to diplomatic intervention. Moreover, an alien could not by means of a Calvo Clause waive rights that under international law belonged to his government [225].

Most Latin American countries abandoned the Calvo Doctrine when they adopted BITs *en masse* [226], as will be seen in the next chapters [227].

Notably, the recent United States-Mexico-Canada Trade Agreement (USMCA) eliminates resort to international dispute settlement mechanisms between the United States and Canada [228]. Further, a return to the Calvo Doctrine can *de facto* occur if States follow UNCTAD's lead in replacing treaties with others so constrained with respect to resort to international dispute settlement mechanisms that few claimants will in fact use them [229].

225. See these and other arguments in UNGA, "Diplomatic Protection", Report of the International Law Commission, Fifty-Fourth Session (29 April to 7 June and 22 July to 16 August 2002), GAOR Fifty-Seventh Session, Supp. No. 10 (A/57/10), chap. V, p. 162.

226. See Schill, *supra* note 30, p. 42.

227. See, in particular, Chapter V.E, *infra*, "Bilateral investment treaties".

228. As do some other treaties, such as the US-Australia BIT, the EU-Investment China Agreement and the EU-UK Trade and Cooperation Agreement. See Alvarez, *supra* note 58, p. 18.

229. *Ibid.*, pp. 18-19.

CHAPTER IV

CUSTOMARY INTERNATIONAL LAW AND FOREIGN INVESTMENTS AFTER THE NINETEENTH CENTURY

A. Scenario

Diplomatic records from the nineteenth century until the creation of the League of Nations reflect that although statesmen believed themselves to be living and acting under a rule of law system, no common organs existed to maintain order, enforce the observance of the law, settle disputes or develop the law institutionally [230].

In 1896, William Edward Hall referred to a "rough jurisprudence of nations" [231], alluding to the largely customary state of affairs in public international law at the time. Soon after, however, this state of affairs began to change dramatically.

B. Creation of the first world arbitration court

The institution of the Permanent Court of Arbitration was an important step forward. The PCA emerged through the Convention on the Pacific Settlement of Disputes [232] and entered into force in 1900, ushering in what historians describe as "the age of internationalism in law" [233]. The PCA was created at the Hague Peace Conference of 1899 and was a remarkable innovation for its time. At that time, the smaller European countries, some Asian States and Mexico also participated alongside the larger Western powers [234].

The Convention's main achievement was the establishment of what is sometimes referred to as the world's first international court [235], dealing

230. Waldock, *supra* note 156, pp. 7-9.

231. W. E. Hall, *A Treatise on International Law*, Oxford, Oxford University Press, 1895, p. xxvii.

232. Its constitutive instruments are the Convention for the Pacific Settlement of International Disputes of 1899 (29 July 1899, 32 Stat 1779, TS 392) and its 1907 revision (Convention for the Pacific Settlement of International Disputes), 18 October 1907, 36 Stat 2199, 1 Bevans 557.

233. Keller, *supra* note 145, p. 866.

234. For more information on the history of the Hague Peace Conferences and the PCA, see https://www.icj-cij.org/en/history, accessed 3 March 2022.

235. Friedrich Martens played a "pivotal role", first by supporting the concept of a permanent court of arbitration, and second by convincing Andrew Carnegie to donate funds for the creation of a courthouse to serve the PCA, which today still stands out

not only with arbitration but also with other methods of peaceful dispute resolution, such as good offices and mediation. The instrument adopted the expression "obligatory arbitration" in reference to an agreement by States to arbitrate in advance of any dispute, prior to determining the specific forum for arbitration. In comparison, the 1871 Washington Treaty, for instance, was restricted to addressing existing disputes alone, leaving a gap for an agreement to arbitrate future claims [236].

Dispute resolution between States through arbitration had become widespread after 1815 as a result of its frequent use among the young Latin American republics. Important developments that paved the way for the Hague Conference of 1899 include the Panama Conference of 1826 and the 1880 General, Permanent and Absolute Arbitration Treaty between Colombia and Chile [237]. By the end of the nineteenth century, it became necessary to introduce arbitration mechanisms not only for existing disputes but also to address the possibility of future claims between States [238]. The idea crystallized in the creation of the Permanent Court of Arbitration.

The label "permanent" seems appropriate, as the institution continues to exist to the present day. The word "court" was perhaps less happily chosen since the term usually relates to judicial settlement. In addition, the PCA does not have a fixed standing or continuous existence [239]. Arbitrators on the PCA roster "soon became a kind of global Who's Who of prominent international law academics". However, after arbitrators appointed to a specific panel discharge their task, they disband, or "melt back . . . to await a future summons that might, or might not, come" [240]. The list of arbitrators became the only "permanent" feature

---

as one of the icons of international arbitration. See A. Eyffinger, "Friedrich Martens: A Founding Father of the Hague Tradition; The Fourth Friedrich Martens Memorial Lecture", *ENDC Proceedings*, Vol. 15 (2012), p. 14.

236. Veeder, *supra* note 174, p. 216.

237. Keller, *supra* note 145, p. 858.

238. Veeder, *supra* note 174, p. 217.

239. "The Permanent Court of Arbitration is no more than a list of potential arbitrators and an administrative structure facilitating the establishment of arbitral tribunals", A. Pellet and D. Müller, "Part Three, Statute of the International Court of Justice, Ch. II, Competence of the Court, Article 38", in A. Zimmermann, C. J. Tams, K. Oellers-Frahm and C. Tomuschat (eds.), *The Statute of the International Court of Justice: A Commentary* (Oxford Commentaries on International Law), 3rd ed., Oxford, Oxford University Press, 2019, p. 824.

240. Neff, *supra* note 143, p. 331:

> "A point of contention in the negotiations that led to the establishment of the PCA related to the reasoning given in awards. In judicial dispute resolution, it was generally accepted that reasons must be provided in the judgments. However, the same was not so widely accepted regarding arbitration. Friedrich Martens,

of the Court. As once written by Friedrich Martens, the PCA constitutes "an idea which occasionally assumes shape and then disappears" [241]. Evidently, the PCA's name and its objectives were a compromise to achieve unanimity [242].

The Convention also established a permanent bureau in The Hague with similar functions to those of a court registry or secretariat. Moreover, the Convention laid down rules of procedure to govern the conduct of arbitrations.

The PCA began operating in 1902; its first two cases involved Latin America. The second case concerned foreign investment in Venezuela [243] and involved a blockade of Venezuelan ports by Germany, Great Britain and Italy due to non-payment of obligations owed to alien investors. This conflict did not serve as the basis for the development of "gunboat diplomacy" by States but legitimated this strategy by prioritizing the debts of the countries participating in the blockade [244].

Despite its success, all were not satisfied with the 1899 Convention. Some found the idea of creating the PCA unacceptable; others felt that it did not go far enough. Still others resisted arbitration because it was slow, costly and complex [245]. Nonetheless, in the words of V. V. Veeder, the birth of the Permanent Court of Arbitration marks the development of modern inter-State arbitration [246].

C. The Drago Doctrine, the Porter Convention and the equality of States

At the Second Hague Peace Conference of 1907, negotiators made serious efforts to establish an international court of justice, which

---

for example, was strongly opposed to a general rule requiring arbitrators to give reasons. He considered that achieving unanimity among arbitrators was more important than the giving of reasons. Doing so could have the undesirable effect of eliciting dissenting opinions from arbitrators who might otherwise have quietly acquiesced. This position did not prevail in the drafting of the PCA Convention at the First Hague Conference, but is indicative of the discussions of the time regarding the distinction between arbitration and judicial settlement."

241. Keller, *supra* note 145, p. 869.

242. Veeder, *supra* note 174, p. 222.

243. *Arbitraje sobre el Tratamiento Preferente de las Reclamaciones de las Potencias Bloqueadoras contra Venezuela* (1903).

244. M. Doe Rodríguez and J. L. Aragón Cardiel, "Causas y azares: el renacimiento de la Corte Permanente de Arbitraje en América Latina en el campo de las inversiones extranjeras", in A. Tanzi, A. Asteriti, R. Polanco Lazo and P. Turrini (eds.), *International Investment Law in Latin America: Problems and Prospects*, Leiden, Brill Nijhoff, 2016, pp. 576-577.

245. Keller, *supra* note 145, p. 870.

246. Veeder, *supra* note 174, p. 224.

only materialized years later as the Permanent Court of International Justice [247].

The Second Hague Peace Conference was also the first international conference to hold a discussion regarding the standing of individuals to bring cases against States before international courts beyond questions of diplomatic protection [248]. Member States later authorized the PCA to use the ample mandate given by this and the prior Hague conventions to administer, in 1934, the first arbitration involving a non-State party (*Radio Corporation of America* v. *China*) [249]. Until then, the PCA had administered exclusively inter-State disputes [250].

The Second Hague Peace Conference of 1907 adopted the Convention of the Peaceful Resolution of International Disputes [251], also known as the Porter Convention in honor of its chief proponent, American diplomat Horace Porter. This instrument concretized the idea of the sovereign equality of States, a cornerstone of contemporary international law [252].

The Porter Convention has only ever occupied a "modest place" in the history of international law due to the limitations it set upon the use of armed force. This was the first such restraint ever included within a multilateral instrument [253]. The Convention also set arbitration as an alternative to the use of force, becoming the first instrument to guarantee protection for State investments [254]. As such, it provided the framework for the conclusion of bilateral arbitration treaties that granted investors a direct cause of action [255].

According to the Calvo Doctrine, the standards established by each State should apply within its territory. In 1902, when the United

---

247. Waldock, *supra* note 156, pp. 7-9. See also W. Goldschmidt, "Transactions Between States and Public Firms and Foreign Private Firms (A Methodological Study)", *Recueil des cours*, Vol. 136 (1972), p. 237.

248. Doe Rodríguez and Aragón Cardiel, *supra* note 244, pp. 579-580.

249. *Radio Corporation of America* v. *National Government of the Republic of China*, 1934-01, Award (13 April 1935), (1935) 3 RIAA, p. 1621. See Doe Rodríguez and Aragón Cardiel, *supra* note 244, p. 579.

250. Three PCA tribunals heard investment cases: *(i) The Orinoco Steamship Company Case (United States of America/Venezuela)*, (1909) 11 RIAA, p. 227; *(ii) Canevaro claim (Italy/Peru)*, 1910-01, (1910) 11 RIAA, p. 227; and *(iii) Arbitraje sobre las Reclamaciones Francesas contra Perú (Francia/Perú)*, (1914) 1 RIAA, p. 215. See Doe Rodríguez and Aragón Cardiel, *supra* note 244, p. 578.

251. Signed in 1907, in force in 1910, 36 Stat 2241, 1 Bevans, 607.

252. Doe Rodríguez and Aragón Cardiel, *supra* note 244, p. 577.

253. Neff, *supra* note 143, p. 338.

254. Doe Rodríguez and Aragón Cardiel, *supra* note 244, p. 578.

255. N. Blackaby, C. Partasides, A. Redfern, and M. Hunter, *Redfern and Hunter on International Arbitration*, 6th ed., Oxford, Kluwer International Law / Oxford University Press, 2015, p. 442.

Kingdom, Germany and Italy subjected Venezuela to a naval blockade, this position was supplemented and narrowed by the "Drago Doctrine", advanced by Luis María Drago, the Argentinean Minister of Foreign Affairs. Drago sustained that States should not resort to the use of force in order to collect debts on behalf of their nationals: State sovereignty in accordance with international law should lead to immunity from execution measures, but not immunity from adjudication [256].

The Porter Convention did not, however, completely prohibit the use of armed force in service of the collection of debt for private parties [257]. Because the instrument left the question of armed intervention up to the investor powers and considering that Latin American States did not ratify the convention (with the exception of Mexico), this "acceptance" of the Drago Doctrine did not allay the fears and suspicions of the nations in this region [258].

D. The creation and consolidation of the world's court of justice

In 1920, the League of Nations approved the creation of the Permanent Court of International Justice, tasked not only with hearing international disputes but also with rendering advisory opinions about any claim or question referred to it by the League of Nations. The PCIJ maintained its permanent seat at the Peace Palace in The Hague alongside the Permanent Court of Arbitration. Unlike the PCA, however, the PCIJ became a permanently constituted body, accessible to States for the judicial settlement of international disputes.

The enabling statute of the PCIJ specifically listed the sources of law that could apply to contentious cases and advisory opinions, including treaties and customary international law. Between 1922 and 1940, the PCIJ decided twenty-nine contentious cases. At the same time, several hundred treaties and other international instruments granted the PCIJ jurisdiction over disputes [259].

The outbreak of World War II was the death knell of the PCIJ. In 1945, the newly established United Nations created the International Court of Justice (ICJ) as one of its organs alongside the General Assembly, the

256. Neff, *supra* note 143, p. 338.

257. "The convention left a loophole wide enough for an armada to sail through by providing that the renunciation of the use of force was not applicable "when the debtor state refuses or neglects to reply to an offer of arbitration, or, after accepting the offer, prevents any *pinionsc* from being agreed on, or, after the arbitration, fails to submit to the award", Shea, *supra* note 206, p. 15.

258. *Ibid.*, p. 15.

259. Available at https://www.icj-cij.org/en/history, accessed 3 March 2022.

Security Council, the Economic and Social Council, and others. For the sake of continuity, however, the ICJ based its statute on the enabling statute of the PCIJ, which was formally dissolved in 1946 [260].

The ICJ also has its seat in The Hague. The Court is tasked with settling international disputes and rendering advisory opinions on legal questions referred to it by authorized UN organs and other specialized agencies. It is composed of fifteen judges who are elected for nine-year terms by the UN General Assembly and the Security Council. The Registry is the permanent administrative secretariat of the Court [261].

The first case submitted to the ICJ was *Corfu Channel* (*United Kingdom* v. *Albania*) in 1947 [262]. Between 22 May 1947 and 11 November 2019, the ICJ accepted 178 cases [263].

One of the characteristics of our time is the multiplication of international courts. Still, the ICJ undoubtedly remains the solar center for international claim disputes, due to its general *(ratione materiae)* and universal *(ratione personae)* scopes, its role as the main auxiliary organ of the United Nations (Art. 92, UN Charter), and for concentrating many of the most publicly transcendent cases in a milieu that has permitted the consistent application of authoritative case law for almost a century [264].

Despite its international importance, the ICJ has only played a modest role in developing international investment legal matters. Because its jurisdiction is limited to State-to-State disputes, whether an investment dispute will be heard before the ICJ is contingent on the willingness of States to submit such disputes to the Court. Many States have generally proven to be unwilling to exercise this right. Further, the ICJ has construed the consent of States quite narrowly. Moreover, the Court has been reluctant to move beyond positive law – that is, to establish norms of behavior where there is no corresponding treaty or comparable evidence of universal consensus to determine the issue [265].

---

260. *Ibid.*

261. Available at https://www.icj-cij.org/en/court, accessed 3 March 2022.

262. *Corfu Channel (United Kingdom of Great Britain and Northern Ireland* v. *Albania)*, ICJ, proceedings began 22 May 1947.

263. Available at https://www.icj-cij.org/en/cases, accessed 3 March 2022.

264. A. Remiro Brotóns, *Derecho Internacional*, Valencia, Tirant Lo Blanch, 2010, p. 631.

265. Lowenfeld, *supra* note 25, p. 511. The ICJ has jurisdiction *rationae personae* when it comes to States that have accepted its jurisdiction (34.1 of the Statute). Its jurisdiction *rationae materiae* applies to questions of international law, to the interpretation of treaties, breaches of international obligations and reparations for breaches of international obligations (36.2).

Three foreign investment-related cases were submitted to the Court after World War II, and all were dismissed. In all cases, the ICJ avoided dealing with the underlying question of host State responsibility *vis-à-vis* foreign investors [266]. For instance, in the *Anglo-Iranian* case [267], the ICJ determined that it lacked jurisdiction. Similarly, the *ELSI* case [268] added little to the existing international investment legal landscape [269]. In *Barcelona Traction*, the best-known of the ICJ investment cases [270], the Court ruled that special agreements could provide substantive protections or avenues for dispute settlement. However, customary law would not be built from these agreements, or at least had not been consolidated at the time. As stated by Andres F. Lowenfeld, the Court saw "an intense conflict of systems and interests" and decided to get out of the way [271].

In matters related to foreign investments, the ICJ (as well as other tribunals and national courts) faced a lack of consensus in the field ambiguous precedents and even ideological conflicts. Many decisions avoided dealing with relevant legal issues or relied on the conflict of laws doctrine to avoid having to make general declarations on the substantive law applicable to the international dispute. Moreover, arbitral tribunals generally ordered compensation for foreign investors that had been deprived of their property by the host State, but they differed when it came to calculating reparation amounts [272].

E. Sources of law in the Court's statute

Historically, the most important attempt to specify sources of international law comes from Article 38 of the Statute of the PCIJ [273], copied almost verbatim by Article 38 of the Statute of the ICJ.

---

266. Unlike what happened in the *Chorzów Factory* (*infra* note 325) case decided by the PCIJ, discussed in further sections of this chapter. *Ibid.*, pp. 511-512.

267. *Anglo-Iranian Oil Co. (United Kingdom* v. *Iran)*, Preliminary Objection (22 July 1952), *ICJ Reports 1952*, p. 93, https://www.icj-cij.org/public/files/case-related/16/016-19520722-JUD-01-00-EN.pdf, accessed 22 June 2022.

268. *Elettronica Sicula SpA (ELSI) (United States of America* v. *Italy)* (1987).

269. Lowenfeld, *supra* note 25, p. 518.

270. *Barcelona Traction*, *supra* note 24; A. Reinisch and L. Malintoppi, "Methods of Dispute Resolution", in P. Muchlinski, F. Ortino and C. Schreuer (eds.), *The Oxford Handbook of International Investment Law*, Oxford/New York, Oxford University Press, 2008, p. 716.

271. Lowenfeld, *supra* note 25, p. 515.

272. *Ibid.*, pp. 533-534.

273. 16 December 1920, 112 BFSP 317.

The provision does not mention the term "source" and deals strictly with "court law" [274]. However, Article 38 is applied by the ICJ as its governing provision and is frequently cited by other tribunals. As such, Article 38, considered an authoritative statement of sources of public international law, is now generally accepted in practice [275]. For instance, a UNCITRAL Tribunal in *Merrill & Ring Forestry LP* v. *Canada* (2010) stated that

> "[t]he meaning of international law can only be understood today with reference to Article 38 (1) of the Statute of the International Court of Justice" [276].

The doctrine of sources is central to the adjudicatory exercise of public authority and the formation of a perception of the immanent intelligibility and neutrality of a legal regime. Paradoxically, as noted by Jean d'Aspremont, it received limited attention and theoretical reflection in international investment legal writing, which has mechanically and uncritically transposed general public international law developments into the discipline [277]. Nuances in this regard will be addressed in later passages of this work.

F. Customary international law in the ICJ Statute

"International custom", or "customary international law", referred to as the oldest and the original source of public international law as well as of law in general [278], "is unwritten law deriving from practice accepted as law" [279].

On the one hand, customary international law refers to the *process* by which certain rules of international law are formed. On the other hand, it consists of the *rules themselves* that were created through this

274. R. Y. Jennings, "General Course on Principles of International Law", *Recueil des cours*, Vol. 121 (1967), p. 331.

275. *Ibid.*, pp. 331-332. See also M. Fitzmaurice, "History of Article 38 of the Statute of the International Court of Justice: The Journey from the Past to the Present", in S. Besson and J. d'Aspremont (eds.), *The Oxford Handbook of the Sources of International Law*, Oxford, Oxford University Press, 2017.

276. *Merrill & Ring Forestry LP* v. *Canada*, UNCT/07/1, NAFTA Award (31 March 2010, F. O. Vicuña, K. W. Dam and J. W. Rowley, arbs.), para. 184.

277. d'Aspremont, *supra* note 30, p. 8.

278. R. Jennings and A. Watts (eds.), *Oppenheim's International Law*, 9th ed., London/New York, Longman, 1996, p. 25.

279. ILC, Report on the Work of the Seventieth Session (2018), chap. V: Identification of Customary International Law, A/73/10, https://legal.un.org/ilc/reports/2018/english/chp5.pdf, accessed 3 March 2022, p. 122.

process. These rules may not necessarily be universal in scope, but all existing general rules of international law are customary [280].

Article 38 (1) of the ICJ Statute states that "the Court shall apply: . . . b. international custom, as evidence of a general practice accepted as law". The wording of this provision is *prima facie* defective. It alludes to "international custom, as evidence of a general practice accepted as law". However, the existence of a custom does not mean that it has been generally accepted. As stated by Ian Brownlie, legal advisors, courts, governments and commentators must ask themselves two separate but related questions: is there a general practice, and is it accepted as international law [281]?

The standard conception of customary international law has created significant uncertainty and generated endless debates [282]. Many argue that the traditional customary international law doctrine lacks legitimacy, is inefficient, has little value in the world and might even be harmful [283]. According to one critic, the dominant customary international law doctrine "is not only incorrect but insidious" [284]. By the same token, Robert Y. Jennings also points out that custom in international law ended up becoming "a catch-all for anything that is not either conventional law or general principles" [285]. This is particularly striking in international investment matters, toward which a very permissive and loose concept of customary law developed in the pre-1945 era [286].

James Crawford [287] also writes that the notion of custom is "like a repeated mantra which dissolves on examination" [288]. In emphasizing consent to each individual rule, the notion of custom challenges the very idea of international law as a system. In practice, customary

280. T. Treves, "The Expansion of International Law", *Recueil des cours*, Vol. 398 (2019), pp. 142-143.

281. Crawford, *supra* note 150, p. 23.

282. These debates relate to the definition of custom and customary international law, the relative significance of practice and *pinion juris*, and other conceptual matters within the traditional conception of customary international law. See E. A. Posner and J. L. Goldsmith, "A Theory of Customary International Law", *Chicago Unbound Journal* (University of Chicago Law School, Faculty Scholarship), 1999, p. 118.

283. M. Hakimi, "Making Sense of Customary Law", *Michigan Law Review*, Vol. 118 (2020), p. 1489.

284. *Ibid.*, p. 1536.

285. Jennings, *supra* note 274, p. 336.

286. d'Aspremont, *supra* note 30, p. 12.

287. J. Richard Crawford *(in memoriam)*, international law scholar, advocate, arbitrator and judge, significantly contributed to reshaping the paradigms of the discipline in the last decades.

288. J. Crawford, "Chance, Order, Change: The Course of International Law (General Course on Public International Law)", *Recueil des cours*, Vol. 365 (2013), p. 85.

international law is a consciousness, but it is not a false consciousness. Customary international law is constantly in motion and has evolved over time as States and other actors engage in dialogue and contribute incrementally to its development through collective judgments [289].

In any case, custom is generally assumed to have two principal requirements: practice and *opinio juris*. The latter is understood not as a subjective inquiry into the motives for following the practice but as the general sentiment among States that there is a requirement of law [290]. Hence, when there is a practice but no *opinio juris*, no "custom" can be born – the practice is a mere "usage" with no corresponding sense of obligation [291].

"Custom" and "usage", therefore, are terms of art that have different meanings in public international law. Unlike custom, a usage is a general practice that does not correspond to any obligation [292]; for example, ceremonial salutes at sea or the granting of parking privileges to diplomatic vehicles [293].

In sum and to follow the wording of the ICJ, both the existence of a general practice and the acceptance of that practice as law *(opinio juris)* "must be fulfilled" in order for that practice to become custom [294].

---

289. *Ibid.*, p. 58:

> "[Article 38 (1) (b) of the Statute] just invites confusion: 'international custom, as evidence of a general practice accepted as law' [emphasis added] . . . The three elements 'international custom', 'general practice' and 'accepted as law' – seem to be in the wrong order. It might better have said 'a general practice accepted as law, as evidence of international custom'. And why is the one element, 'international custom', merely described as 'evidence'? The implications are doubly puzzling. What other evidence would you want of a general practice accepted as law than that it was international custom – or vice versa? If you showed that there was such a general practice accepted as law [emphasis added], what could disqualify it from being customary?"

290. An ILC report in this regard states that "one must look at what States actually do and seek to determine whether they recognize an obligation or a right to act in that way. This methodology, the 'two-element approach', underlies the draft conclusions and is widely supported by States, in case law, and in scholarly writings". ILC, Seventieth Session Report, *supra* note 279, chap. V, p. 125.

291. The requirement both of consistent practice, and of the general opinion, is implicit in the well-known passage from the judgment of the ICJ in the *Asylum* case – *Colombia* v. *Peru*, Judgment (20 November 1950), *ICJ Reports 1950*, pp. 276-277; Jennings, *supra* note 274, p. 335.

292. Conclusion 9 of an ILC report in this regard states that the requirement "that the general practice be accepted as law (*opinio juris*) means that the practice in question must be undertaken with a sense of legal right or obligation". The text of the draft Conclusions on Identification of Customary International Law is available at https://legal.un.org/ilc/reports/2018/english/chp5.pdf, accessed 3 March 2022.

293. Crawford, *supra* note 150, p. 23.

294. *North Sea Continental Shelf (Federal Republic of Germany/Netherlands)*, Judgment (20 February 1969), *ICJ Reports 1969*, p. 3, at p. 44, para. 77; *Jurisdictional*

The practice must have gained such widespread acceptance among States that it may be considered to be the expression of a legal right or obligation (namely, that it is required, permitted or prohibited as a matter of law) [295]. The test must answer the question of whether there has been a general practice accepted as law [296].

The material sources of custom that have been officially recognized include diplomatic correspondence, policy statements, press releases, opinions of government legal advisors, official manuals on legal questions, executive decisions, practice orders to military forces, legislation, international and national juridical decisions, recitals in treaties and other instruments, the practice of international organs, and UN resolutions relating to legal questions (notably the General Assembly), the value of which depends on the circumstances [297].

Reports of the ILC, some recognizing the existence of a rule of customary international law and others not [298], have been received in cases heard before the ICJ as well as before other courts and tribunals [299].

Immunities of the State (Germany v. *Italy: Greece intervening)*, Judgment (2 February 2012), *ICJ Reports 2012*, p. 99, at pp. 122-123, para. 55; *Continental Shelf (Libyan Arab Jamahiriya/Malta)*, Judgment (21 March 1984), *ICJ Reports 1985*, p. 13, pp. 29-30, para. 27.

295. For example, in the *Jurisdictional Immunities of the State* case, an examination into State practice through an extensive survey of national legislation, judicial decisions, claims and other official statements (which were found to be accompanied by *pinion juris*) served to identify the scope of State immunity under customary international law, *Germany* v. *Italy: Greece intervening*, *ibid.*, Judgment (2 February 2012), at pp. 122-123, para. 55 and pp. 122-139, paras. 55-91. Regional and particular customary international law was not fully developed in the ILC Conclusions on Identification of Customary International Law, and the matter raises several issues, addressed in G. R. Bandeira Galindo, "Particular Customary International Law and the International Law Commission: Mapping Presences and Absences", *Questions of International Law*, Vol. 86 (2021), pp. 3 ff.

296. ILC, Seventieth Session Report, *supra* note 279, chap. V, p. 125. The ALIC Guide states that "customary international law refers to obligations arising from general and consistent practices of States that they follow out of a shared sense of legal obligation *(pinion juris)*". UNIDROIT/IFAD Legal Guide on Agricultural Land Investment Contracts, September 2021, https://www.unidroit.org/wp-content/uploads/2021/10/ALICGuidehy.pdf, accessed 23 May 2022, p. 22.

297. Crawford, *supra* note 150, p. 24. See also Conclusions 6 and 10 of the ILC Draft Conclusions on Identification of Customary International Law, *supra* note 292, p. 120.

298. ILC, Seventieth Session Report, *supra* note 279, chap. V, p. 142.

299. See, for example, *Gabčíkovo-Nagymaros Project (Hungary/Slovakia)*, Judgment (25 September 1997), *ICJ Reports 1997*, p. 7, at p. 40, para. 51; *Responsibilities and obligations of States with respect to activities in the Area*, Advisory Opinion (1 February 2011), *ITLOS Reports 2011*, p. 10, at p. 56, para. 169; *Prosecutor* v. *Elizaphan Ntakirutimana and Gérard Ntakirutimana*, Case Nos. ICTR-96-10-A and ICTR-96-17-A, Judgment (Appeals Chamber, 13 December 2004), International Criminal Tribunal for Rwanda, para. 518; *Dubai-Sharjah Border Arbitration*, Award

In 2012, the ILC included the question of customary international law in its program of work [300], and the debates summarized in the resulting report underscore that "customary law remained highly relevant despite the proliferation of treaties and the codification of several areas of international law" [301].

The report also notes that while treaties are only binding upon the parties thereto, they "may have an important role to play in recording and defining rules deriving from custom, or indeed in developing them" [302]. Moreover, Article 38 of the 1969 Vienna Convention refers to the possibility of "a rule set forth in a treaty . . . becoming binding upon a third State as a customary rule of international law, recognized as such" [303].

The 2018 UN General Assembly resolved to "take note in a resolution of the draft conclusions [of the ILC report] on identification of customary international law" and to "ensure their widest dissemination" [304]. This report can be considered the most authoritative recent statement to offer guidance on customary international law [305].

G. Customary international law of foreign investments at the dawn of the twentieth century

At the beginning of the twentieth century, the "law of aliens" of "customary international law" focused on the protection of foreign

---

(19 October 1981), 91 ILR, pp. 543-701, at p. 575; 2 BvR 1506/03, German Federal Constitutional Court, Order of the Second Senate (5 November 2003), para. 47.

300. In 2012, this commission included in its program of work the topic "Formation and evidence of customary international law". The Commission decided to appoint Mr Michael Wood as Special Rapporteur for the topic. In 2013, the Commission received the first report, and decided to change the title of the topic to "Identification of customary international law", https://legal.un.org/ilc/summaries/1_13.shtml, accessed 3 March 2022.

301. Treves, *supra* note 280, pp. 138-139.

302. *Continental Shelf (Libyan Arab Jamahiriya/Malta)*, Judgment (21 March 1984), pp. 29-30, para. 27:

> "It is of course axiomatic that the material of customary international law is to be looked for primarily in the actual practice and *pinion juris* of States, even though multilateral conventions may have an important role to play in recording and defining rules deriving from custom, or indeed in developing them."

303. ILC, Seventieth Session Report, *supra* note 279, chap. V, p. 143.

304. The work of the Commission on the topic as described above has been proceeding in accordance with the successive resolutions adopted by the General Assembly. UNGA Res. 67/92 (14 December 2012); UNGA Res. 68/112 (16 December 2013); UNGA Res. 69/118 (10 December 2014); UNGA Res. 70/236 (23 December 2015); UNGA Res. 71/140 (13 December 2016).

305. ILC, Seventieth Session Report, *supra* note 279, chap. V, p. 123. For criticisms to the ILC Conclusions, see Hakimi, *supra* note 283, pp. 1504 ff.

nationals and their property, and not on whether an "investment" was made. In addition, only the State could initiate investment claims on behalf of its nationals through the exercise of diplomatic protection.

Customary international law distilled several standards applicable to international investments [306]; gaining particular relevance were those related to the minimum protection granted to aliens, and to compensation for expropriation.

1. Minimum standard of protection

Customary international law asserted that a minimum standard of public international law could not be evaded by national law. This safeguard drew on the doctrine of State responsibility for the protection of foreign investors and alien property against injury. States were not required to accept investors in their territory, but once an investment had been made, a certain minimum standard of treatment had to be observed [307]. In 1910, the US Secretary of State Elihu Root wrote:

> "The condition upon which any country is entitled to measure the justice due from it to an alien by the justice which it accords to its own citizens is that its system of law and administration shall conform to this general standard. If any country's system of law and administration does not conform to that standard, although the people of the country may be content or compelled to live under it, no other country can be compelled to accept it as furnishing a satisfactory measure of treatment to its citizens." [308]

Therefore, in principle, foreign investors should be subject to the standard of "national treatment". However, this treatment was insufficient for aliens if it was not in accordance with a minimum standard generally

306. W. M. Reisman, "Canute Confronts the Tide: States versus Tribunals and the Evolution of the Minimum Standard in Customary International Law", *ICSID Review: Foreign Investment Law Journal*, Vol. 30 (2015), p. 622:

> "Where there is a convergence of practice and pinion juris among a significant number of such tribunals, it may serve as evidence of customary international law. Hence, in the context of customary international law in investment law, BITs and decisions of tribunals adjudicating the disputes arising from these investment treaties have come to play a significant role in the ongoing formation of law in this field. These two sources are particularly important . . . because much of international investment law is developed through them – they represent State practice and pinion juris in this area of law."

307. Subedi, *supra* note 17, p. 9.

308. E. Root, "The Basis of Protection to Citizens Residing Abroad", *American Journal of International Law*, Vol. 4 (1910), p. 521.

accepted by nations. Even though customary international law did not grant aliens the right to acquire property, exercise a profession or work in foreign territory, its international minimum standard granted them protection against expropriation [309].

The scope of application of this international minimum standard was restricted to curtail clearly excessive State measures. In the *Neer* case decided in 1926, the Mexico-United States General Claims Commission ruled that isolation of this minimum standard of treatment "should amount to an outrage, to bad faith, to wilful neglect of duty, or to an insufficiency of governmental action so far short of international standards that every reasonable and impartial man would readily recognize its insufficiency" [310].

Contrarily, the principle of equality, enshrined in the Calvo Doctrine [311], advocated that host States need not treat aliens any better than their own nationals. As equals in the international system, States are not subject to any legislative authority other than their own. Any alien doing business in a host country must accept its laws and understand the risks involved. In a famous correspondence to US Secretary of State Cordell Hull, the Mexican Foreign Minister Eduardo Hay argued strongly in favor of the principle of equality, stating that:

> "[T]he foreigner who voluntarily moves to a country which is not his own, in search of a personal benefit, accepts in advance, together with the advantages he is going to enjoy, the risks to which he may find himself exposed. It would be unjust that he should aspire to a privileged position." [312]

---

309. Schill, *supra* note 30, p. 26.

310. *L. Fay H. Neer And Pauline Neer (USA)* v. *United Mexican States*, Decision (15 October 1926). See a recent citation in *BG Group PLC* v. *The Republic of Argentina*, UNCITRAL, Final Award (24 December 2007), IIC 321 (2007), paras. 275-310. Other claim cases reached similar conclusions, finding that the test, broadly speaking, is whether aliens are treated in accordance with "the ordinary standards of civilization", *Roberts (US)* v. *Mexico* (2 November 1926) I Opinions of Commissioners, General Claims Commission (US and Mexico, 1923) 100, 105 (1927). Also whether the "international minimum standard has been extended to cover the instances of discrimination against aliens, denial of justice and injuries to aliens' economic interests (e.g. expropriation)". *France* v. *Great Britain* (1931), (1933) 27 AJIL 153, 160. See Salacuse, *supra* note 65, p. 71. 57 American Law Institute, Restatement of the Law 2nd citing "*France* v. *Great Britain* (1931)" (1933) 27 AJIL 153, 160. See also A. Freeman, *The International Responsibility of States for Denial of Justice*, London, Longmans, Green and Co., 1938, p. 502 ff.

311. Latin America's response to the international minimum standard was the doctrine of national treatment. Salacuse, *supra* note 65, p. 67.

312. "Official Documents" (1938), 32 AJIL Supp. 181, 188. Salacuse, *supra* note 65, p. 70:

The decrees of nationalization adopted after the Russian Revolution bolstered this position in another region since they drew no distinction between Russian nationals' and foreign-owned property [313].

In contrast, the United States and European countries maintained that host States have an obligation under public international law to observe an international minimum standard in the treatment of aliens and their property. According to this position, if the standards prevailing in a given State are too low, even if nationals and aliens are treated alike, the norms of international law may be violated [314].

This minimum standard of protection ultimately prevailed in the twentieth century, as did the right of home countries to extend diplomatic protection to their nationals injured abroad, reflected in the decision of the PCIJ in the famous *Chorzów Factory* case referred to below, as well as several arbitral awards [315].

The scope and content of the international minimum standard remains the object of incommensurable controversy, thereby putting

---

> "The Mexican Minister cited Article 9 of the Convention on the Rights and Duties of States, which was signed at Montevideo in 1933. According to this instrument, 'nationals and foreigners are under the same protection of the law and the national authorities, and foreigners may not claim rights other than or more extensive than those of nationals'. In response, US Secretary of State Cordell Hull stated that 'when aliens are admitted into a country the country is obligated to accord them that degree of protection of life and property consistent with the standards of justice recognized by the law of nations'. He denied that this was a claim of special privilege in contravention of the Montevideo Treaty and maintained that confiscation could not be excused by the 'inapplicable doctrine of equality'."

313. d'Aspremont, *supra* note 30, p. 11.

314. "This view became prevalent in customary international law during the nineteenth and the first half of the twentieth centuries; with the expansion of Western economic powers, the spread of European colonialism, and American influence in Latin America and Asia, the principle of a minimum international standard became dominant, at least among Western States" (Salacuse, *supra* note 65, p. 65).

315. In the *Hopkins* case before the United States-Mexico General Claims Commission of 1923, the Tribunal concluded that

> "it not infrequently happens that under the rules of international law applied to controversies of an international aspect a nation is required to accord aliens broader and more liberal treatment than it accords to its own citizens under municipal laws. The reports of decisions made by arbitral tribunals long prior to the Treaty of 1923 contain many such instances. There is no ground to object that this amounts to a discrimination by a nation. It is not a question of discrimination but a difference in their respective rights and remedies. The citizens of a nation may enjoy many rights which are withheld from aliens, and, conversely, under international law aliens may enjoy rights and remedies which the nation does not accord to its own citizens".

Hopkins (US) v. *Mexico* (21 March 1926) I Opinions of Commissioners, General Claims Commission (US and Mexico, 1923) 42, 50-1 (1927). See Salacuse, *supra* note 65, p. 70.

into question the customary status commonly attributed to that rule [316]. The standard originated from Western conceptions. However, the emerging specific needs and prerogatives of developing nations, and a greater emphasis on human rights have moved the needle forward and helped create new perspectives related to the minimum acceptable standard of treatment for investors [317]. This and other controversies regarding the standard continue unsettled as of today.

2. *Prompt, effective and adequate compensation*

(a) *Compensation for expropriation*

According to the Calvo Doctrine, State sovereignty results in all land and other natural resources belonging to the State. Thus, no foreign investor can own the resources of another State.

Both Mexico and the Soviet Union have followed this rule in the past, launching expropriation and nationalization campaigns without offering investors proper compensation, claiming justification in the doctrine of State sovereignty. The Western States responded by recognizing the right to expropriate or nationalize according to international law rules, that is, "coupled with prompt, adequate and effective compensation" [318].

For Mexico after the drafting of its constitution in 1917 as well as for other Latin American countries the social function of property recognized in their laws did not grant those States a right to expropriate without compensation. However, compensation did not need to be prior or prompt, and the State's ability to pay was an important factor in determining its appropriate amount. This is the case where major construction projects are owned by States, such as electric power generation, petroleum exploration or railroads, as well as for the redistribution of land pursuant to agrarian reform programs. According to the Calvo Doctrine, aliens have no greater right to protection than

316. d'Aspremont, *supra* note 30, pp. 10-11.

317. A. F. M. Maniruzzaman, "International Development Law as Applicable Law to Economic Development Agreements: A Prognostic View", *Wisconsin International Law Journal*, Vol. 20, No. 1 (2001), p. 50. The Calvo Doctrine, the Russian Revolution and the Mexican objection have not been deemed sufficient to prevent the emergence of a customary minimum standard; international investment tribunals have, in the great majority, considered that the international minimum standard, as expressed by the *Neer* formula, constitutes customary international law, although its evolutive character has occasionally been recognized in *Pope and Talbot Inc.* v. *Canada*, *infra* note 501, 31 May 2002, paras. 59 ff., *ADF Group* v. *United States*, ICSID No. ARB(AF)/00/1, Award, 9 January 2003, para. 173. See also d'Aspremont, *supra* note 30, p. 24.

318. Subedi, *supra* note 17, p. 15.

nationals. Furthermore, some States required land and commercial property owners to incorporate in the host country and renounce all forms of protection in their home country [319].

Therefore, unlike the Soviet Union, Mexico did not deny compensation to foreigners but maintained that it did not necessarily need to be prompt, adequate or effective. How compensation for expropriation was to be arranged depended on the ability of the State.

Years of negotiation ended in a claims commission formed in 1927 to consider the claims of United States investors affected by expropriation and nationalization measures in Mexico. By 1938, however, compensation had still not been paid, resulting in an intensification of diplomatic efforts by the United States. Cordell Hull, the American Secretary of State at the time, engaged in diplomatic exchanges and advanced views on the appropriate compensation to be paid. He noted that the national constitutions of many American republics include the principle of just compensation. In an international investment context, Hull advocated in favor of prompt, adequate and effective payment for expropriation and nationalization. His views are referred to as the "Hull Formula", which is generally followed by developed countries and by the United States in particular and has become a "stable fixture within international law" [320].

According to the Hull Formula, the fair market value of an expropriated resource should be determined according to the price that willing buyers and sellers would agree to pay in an arm's-length transaction [321]. This formula did not, however, apply literally in practice. As stated by Lowenfeld:

> "'Prompt' did not exclude payments over time; 'adequate' was often not the equivalent of full value; 'effective' meant that the taking state could not subject the compensation to taxation or exchange controls, but did not exclude more or less voluntary agreement by the former owner to reinvest some or all of the

319. Lowenfeld, *supra* note 25, p. 473.
320. *Ibid.*, pp. 15-18.
321. In recent times, the Tribunal in *Starrett Housing Corporation* v. *Iran*, referred to the fair market value as "the price [at which] a willing buyer would buy . . . and the price at which a willing seller would sell . . . on condition that none of the two parties [is] under any kind of duress and that both parties have good information about all relevant circumstances involved in the purchase", *Starrett Housing Corporation, Starrett Systems, Inc. and others* v. *The Government of the Islamic Republic of Iran, Bank Markazi Iran and others*, Iran-United States Claims Tribunal (hereafter IUSCT), Award No. 314-24-1 (14 August 1987), paras. 18, 27, 274.

compensation in the taking state in sectors not designated for nationalization." [322]

Later formulas advocated for a "just" or "appropriate" compensation, taking into account, in some circumstances, the State's capacity to pay the amount [323].

Notably, Rapporteurs of the Revised Restatement (Third) of the Foreign Relations Law of the United States refused in the early stages of its drafting to insert the "prompt, adequate, and effective" formula as black letter, asserting that they did "not think that that can be said as an honest statement of customary international law" [324].

(b) *Compensation for other types of breaches*

Regarding other types of breaches beyond expropriation, the classic and often-cited precedent for determining compensation emerged from the *Chorzów Factory* case [325]. The decision in this case established the principle that reparations must, as far as possible, negate all the consequences of the illegal act and return the injured party to the position they would have been in had the wrongful act not been committed [326].

---

322. Lowenfeld, *supra* note 25, p. 494.

323. *Ibid.*, p. 494. The question of whether the abovementioned Hull Formula constitutes customary international law has attracted much attention in international legal scholarship. See d'Aspremont, *supra* note 30, p. 25. The exact standard of compensation remaining subject to variations was recognized by the Arbitral Tribunal in *CME* v. *Czech Republic*, *supra* note 54, Final Award (14 March 2003), para. 497.

324. Revised Restatement (Third) of the Foreign Relations Law. Professor Louis Henkin, the chief reporter for this Restatement, affirmed this in the Fifty-Ninth Annual Meeting, ALI PROC. (1982), pp. 238-239:

> "The Restatement's view would seem to represent the current position of most Western States on the standard of compensation due to investors for the illegal acts of host States under international law. More recently, that view is reflected in Article 31 (2) of the Articles on Responsibility of States for Internationally Wrongful Acts, which provides that a State responsible for an internationally wrongful act is 'under an obligation to make full reparation for the injury caused by [its] internationally wrongful act'." (cited in Salacuse, *supra* note 65, p. 79)

325. *Factory at Chorzów (Germany* v. *Poland)*, Judgment (13 September 1928), PCIJ, Ser. A, No. 17 (1928), p. 28.

326. Jennings, *supra* note 274, p. 475:

> "This famous case elaborated on the distinction between the measure of damages due in reparation to the claimant State and the damage actually suffered by the individual concerned. The rights or interests of an individual and the corresponding damages caused by their violation are inherently distinct from the rights belonging to a State, the rights of which may also be infringed by the same wrongful act. In short, the damage suffered by an individual can never be identical to that which will be suffered by a State; such a comparison can only be useful as a scale for the calculation of the reparations due to the State."

Some writers and tribunals argue that the *Chorzów Factory* case established the basic principle of compensation. Others interpret it as advancing the proposition that unlawful expropriation entitles the injured party to greater compensation, or even the lawful expropriation of private property (where the only violation is failure to pay compensation). Unlawful expropriation occurs where a treaty or concession provision has been violated, or in instances of discriminatory treatment. Yet another interpretation maintains that the *Chorzów Factory* case does not reflect customary law at all. Nonetheless, it remains one of the most cited cases in the history of investment claims, and it is still relevant today, particularly regarding reparations to compensate an injured party for the commission of an unlawful act [327].

H. Diplomatic protection from the twentieth century onward

For centuries, customary international law recognized diplomatic protection in the event of injury to an investor. In providing diplomatic protection, the State acts as the subject and the wronged individual as the object in the claim against an opposing State for an internationally wrongful act [328].

States exercising diplomatic protection proceed as if the grievance to their own national constitutes, by extension, an injury to the State itself. As seen in Chapter III, this approach is rooted in Vattel's writings, dating back to 1758 [329]. Many years later, in the 1924 *Mavrommatis Palestine Concession* case, the PCIJ recognized diplomatic protection as "an elementary principle of international law" [330]. Other PCIJ and

327. Lowenfeld, *supra* note 25, p. 475. Examples of modern cases applying the *Chorzów* formula are: *MTD Equity Sdn Bhd & MTD Chile SA* v. *Republic of Chile*, ICSID Case No. ARB/01/7, Award (25 May 2004), paras. 570, 633; *Petrobart Limited* v. *The Kyrgyz Republic*, SCC Arbitration No. 126/2003, Award (29 March 2005), IIC 184 (2005); *Azurix Corporation* v. *Argentine Republic*, ICSID Case No. ARB/01/12, Award (14 July 2006), paras. 409, 423; *SD Myers Inc.* v. *Government of Canada*, UNCITRAL, Partial Award (13 November 2000), IIC 249, paras. 311, 313; *Metalclad Corporation* v. *The United Mexican States*, ICSID Case No. ARB(AF)/97/1, Award (30 August 2000). Exceptionally, restitution has also been granted. *Mr Franck Charles Arif* v. *Republic of Moldova*, ICSID Case No. ARB/11/23, Award (8 April 2013), para. 559.

328. See definition in draft Articles on Diplomatic Protection with commentaries, https://legal.un.org/ilc/texts/instruments/english/commentaries/9_8_2006.pdf, accessed 3 March 2022, p. 26

329. See also *ibid.*, p. 27.

330. *Mavrommatis Palestine Concession (Greece* v. *United Kingdom)*, Judgment (Objection to Jurisdiction of the Court, 30 August 1924), PCIJ, Ser. A, No. 2, p. 20; *Reparation for Injuries Suffered in the Service of the United Nations*, Advisory Opinion (11 April 1949), *ICJ Reports*, p. 181; *Barcelona Traction*, *supra* note 24.

ICJ cases have since followed this ruling [331]. Renowned decisions such as the *Chorzów Factory* case [332], the *Barcelona Traction* case [333] and the *ELSI* case [334] all involved investment claims brought by way of diplomatic protection [335].

After World War II, most peace treaties followed the traditional pattern of diplomatic protection for individuals' economic losses, where they were not directly caused by military operations that had already been settled by conciliation commissions (in which State agents presented claims on behalf of their nationals). Arbitral tribunals competent to address individual claims of this type were not established [336].

Important changes began to occur at this time as injured individuals were increasingly granted standing and empowered by investment tribunals and human rights courts [337].

In this scenario, diplomatic protection is no longer optimal for foreign investors. Once their home government has espoused the claim, it effectively "owns" it. Therefore, the investors' home State controls how the claim will be made, the conditions, if any, of a settlement, or even the abandonment of a claim if it considers this justified in light of other factors in the relationship with the host country, such as security considerations or broader economic concerns [338]. Therefore, this decision of the State to pursue the cause or not on behalf of its nationals

331. Therefore, the continued validity of the "Mavrommatis formula" is beyond doubt, Douglas, *supra* note 39, p. 13. For instance, in the *Panevezys-Saldutiskis Railway* case, the Court stated that "it is the bond of nationality between the State and the individual which alone confers upon the State the right of diplomatic protection, and it is as a part of the function of diplomatic protection that the right to take up a claim and to ensure respect for the rules of international law must be envisaged" (*Panevezys-Saldutiskis Railway (Estonia* v. *Lithuania)*, Judgment (28 February 1939), PCIJ, Sers. A/B, No. 76, p. 16).

332. *Certain German Interests in Polish Upper Silesia (Germany* v. *Poland)*, Judgment (25 August 1926), PCIJ, Ser. A, No. 7; *Chorzów*, *supra* note 325, Judgment (13 September 1928).

333. *Barcelona Traction*, *supra* note 24.

334. *Elettronica Sicula SpA (ELSI)*, Judgment (20 July 1989), *ICJ Reports 1989*, p. 15, para. 128. Recently, *Ahmadou Sadio Diallo (Republic of Guinea* v. *Democratic Republic of the Congo)*, Preliminary Objections (24 May 2007), *ICJ Reports 2007*, p. 582; Judgment (30 November 2010), *ICJ Reports 2010*, p. 639.

335. Brown, *supra* note 164, p. 401. The surge in claims by private parties against States in the era of investment treaties should not be surprising. Lauterpacht observed that the origin of most international claims lies in injuries suffered by private parties. See H. Lauterpacht, *The Development of International Law by the International Court*, London, Stevens, 1958, pp. 31-32; Rigo Sureda, *supra* note 55, p. 3.

336. Hess, *supra* note 48, p. 116.

337. *Ibid.*, pp. 107-117.

338. "In such a situation, the injured investor is left with no redress either against the offending host country or its unsympathetic home country. A further complication involved a home country's ability to extend diplomatic protection to nationals who are

usually derives from political considerations, in a process that many investors and capital-exporting States have perceived as inadequate [339].

Moreover, since the end of the gunboat diplomacy era, diplomatic protection in many cases did not necessarily result in a meaningful remedy. It often ended in an exchange of written or oral statements between governments since the matter could only be brought to an international tribunal with the consent of the States concerned. Therefore, as noted by Jeswald Salacuse, diplomatic protection proved to be a very uncertain and often ephemeral remedy for injured international investors [340].

However, despite these pitfalls, diplomatic protection still plays a considerable role in the safeguarding of the injured individual at the international level generally, and within international trade law more specifically. The continued importance of diplomatic protection is reflected in the 2006 adoption of the ILC Draft Articles on Diplomatic Protection with commentaries [341].

I. Mixed claims commissions in the twentieth century

In the Latin America of the early twentieth century, investment disputes were often resolved by mixed claims commissions through an inter-State arbitral process. These tribunals lasted well into the late 1930s, as was the case for the commission established by the United States and Mexico before World War II to settle Mexican agrarian expropriations [342].

This commission was established in 1923 and dealt both with "special" claims of alleged injuries to American nationals caused by the revolutionary disturbances in Mexico and "general" claims of alleged injuries of all sorts by Mexico to Americans and vice versa. Special claims of this type led to the filing of more than 3,000 documents.

---

shareholders in foreign corporations, such as occurred in the criticized decision in the *Barcelona Traction* case", Salacuse, *supra* note 65, p. 71.

339. S. E. Foster, "International Investment Arbitration and Transparency", in V. Ruíz Abou-Nigm, K. McCall Smith, and D. French (eds.), *Linkages and Boundaries in Private and Public International Law*, Oxford, Hart Publishing, 2018, p. 201.

340. *Ibid.*, p. 72.

341. Draft Articles on Diplomatic Protection, *supra* note 328.

342. "Mexico further concluded general claims conventions with six European countries in the period between 1924-27 (Britain, France, Germany, Italy, Spain, and Belgium). A general mixed claims commission was also established by Panama and the United States in 1926. These claims commissions, in the aggregate, produced an avalanche of case law that was far greater and more varied than that of the Permanent Court of International Justice", Neff, *supra* note 143, pp. 357-358.

However, the only two final decisions rendered turned out to be highly controversial. Eventually, in 1934, the remaining special claims were settled by a lump sum payment made by Mexico to the United States government, which then distributed the sum internally. A larger number of general claims were filed, but they also ended in a global lump sum settlement made in 1941 [343].

Interestingly, this United States-Mexican Claims Commission [344] argued for the potential application of public international law, private international law and municipal law depending on the nature of the claim [345].

Claims commissions were also widely used to achieve settlement of war-related claims in peace treaties after the world wars [346]. The agreements negotiated after World War I established large-scale dispute settlement systems to deal with the consequences of economic warfare. Thirty-six so-called "mixed arbitral tribunals" were granted jurisdiction over commercial contracts, private debts and damage to property, among others. However, these tribunals did not contribute to the advancement of the law in this field due to contradictory case law, treaty norms deviating from established practices and massive renunciations and settlements [347].

The mixed arbitral tribunals put in place at the end of World War I created a unique situation. Individuals were given direct access to these courts in order to pursue their claims against former enemy

343. *Ibid.*, p. 357.

344. *Illinois Central Railroad Company (USA)* v. *United Mexican States*, American-Mexican Claims Commission, Decision (31 March 1926), paras. 23-24.

345. Hess, *supra* note 48, p. 36:

> "The United States-Mexico Claims Commission distinguished between four types of international claims. First are the claims between nationals of two different countries. These cases are considered to be international even when Public International Law declares one of the municipal laws involved to be exclusively applicable. The second type of international claims are claims between two national governments in their own right. In these types of cases, Public International Law applies. The third type are claims between citizens of one country and the Government of another country in its public capacity. Here, in order to determine the applicability of national or international law, the question arises whether and to what extent the legal relationships are of a private or public law nature. And finally, claims between a citizen of one country and the Government of another country acting in a civil capacity. International law applies in this case, even if it merely makes use of national law in order to find a solution. Today, one must add to the list of types of international claims the exercise of authority and transactions made by international organizations, and the growing use of (commercial) arbitration in international matters."

346. *Ibid.*, p. 108.

347. See *ibid.*, pp. 112-116.

States. These cases were not considered international, nor between States, and therefore did not generally trigger the application of "true" international law (except for treaty interpretation). In some situations, tribunals resorted to private international law and referred to national laws, but they also frequently made use of general principles of law and equity. For instance, a German-Portuguese Tribunal stated that

> "in the absence of rules of international law applicable to the facts in litigation, the arbitrators ought to fill the gap by deciding according to the principles of equity while remaining with the spirit (*sens*) of international law applied by analogy, and in taking account of its evolution" [348].

A different situation has arisen due to the creation of the United Nations Compensation Commission (UNCC), a subsidiary organ of the UN Security Council established by its Resolution 692. The UNCC was active primarily between 1991 and 2005 in claims for compensation losses resulting from Iraq's unlawful invasion and occupation of Kuwait in 1990-1991.

The UNCC Is not technically an international tribunal but rather an administrative mass claims processing program [349]. Nonetheless, its panels applied international law principles as well as internal UNCC rules to claims brought before it [350]. Interestingly, its decisions have reflected principles recognized both in public and private law [351]. In particular, the UNCC acknowledged that certain provisions of the UNIDROIT Principles of International Commercial Contracts ("UNIDROIT Principles"), referred to in Chapter XII of this book, are an expression of general principles, particularly regarding

---

348. P. C. Jessup, *Transnational Law*, New Haven, CT, Yale University Press, 1956, p. 96.

349. *Ibid.*, pp. 123-124.

350. Ho, *supra* note 212, p. 9.

351. See Reed, *supra* note 21, p. 225. Other recent mixed commissions dealt with claims regarding *Bosnia and Herzegovina*, *Kosovo*, and *Eritrea and Ethiopia* conflicts. See also Hess, *supra* note 48, pp. 127-128. At pp. 130-131, Hess states:

> "Contemporary proceedings regulating the bringing of claims are highly standardized: individual claims are categorized, grouped and bundled. Small claims are usually represented by States or international agencies. Large claims are brought by affected individuals and businesses themselves. The old *leitmotif* of diplomatic protection – that the claim of the individual must be fully espoused by its home State – is replaced by the modern idea of 'representation'. In addition, the victim can choose between different © for the enforcement of claims."

force majeure [352] and the duty to mitigate the losses of the opposing party [353].

J. Multilateral efforts for a global instrument on State responsibility

Unlike the trade in goods, in foreign investment there is no single definitive multilateral treaty text equivalent to, for instance, the General Agreement on Tariffs and Trade (GATT), or a sole overarching institution comparable to the World Trade Organization (WTO). As noted by José Alvarez, the state of affairs remains stalled, but not for lack of trying [354]. Six codification projects for foreign investment matters were advanced between the 1920s and the 1990s. Four of these initiatives derived from States and two from private actors [355]. All turned out to be unsuccessful. Although these projects originated from different initiatives, the notion of property as defined by these drafts resembles the definitions of "investment" within many contemporary bilateral and multilateral treaties.

1. Early efforts

Until the end of World War II, the requirements for diplomatic protection had begun to mirror those of customary international law, such as State international responsibility for the denial of justice to aliens and a minimum standard in the treatment of foreign investors. An important body of case law and writings emerged in this regard.

The "high-water mark of this analysis" is reflected in the 1929 Harvard Draft on "The Law of Responsibility of States for Damage Done in their Territory to the Person or Property of Foreigners" [356]. Nonetheless, at the 1930 Hague Codification Conference, the disparity of views regarding its content, reflecting a lack of customary international law consensus on the matter, led to the abandonment of the project [357].

The Havana Charter of 1948 [358] was another effort to negotiate rules regarding foreign investment, under the auspices of the United Nations'

352. UNCC, Report and Recommendations Made by the Panel of Commissioners concerning Part One of the First Instalment of Claims by Governments and International Organizations (Category "F" Claims), UN Doc. S/AC.26/1997/6 (18 December 1997), pp. 23, 27, 32.

353. *Ibid.*, para. 79.

354. Alvarez, *supra* note 26, p. 213.

355. The Abs-Shawcross Draft Convention and the Harvard Convention were initiatives by private actors. Ho, *supra* note 212, pp. 45-46.

356. C. McLachlan, "Investment Treaties and General International Law", *The International and Comparative Law Quarterly*, Vol. 57, No. 2 (2008), pp. 365-366.

357. Ho, *supra* note 212, p. 48.

358. Havana Charter for an International Trade Organization (Havana Charter, ITO Charter 1948) (United Nations [UN]) UN Doc. E/CONF.2/78.

attempt to form an international trade organization. Though the Havana Charter never came into force, it did pave the way for the negotiation and finalization of the GATT [359].

The first draft of the Havana Charter was submitted to the UN Social and Economic Committee in 1946 by the United States. The initial draft contained no provisions regarding foreign investment. A charter on economic development was later added to the American proposal [360]. The charter, signed in March 1948 on behalf of fifty-three countries, dealt with some investment matters in Articles 11 and 12, but ultimately eliminated one of the draft provisions requiring States to give compensation to individuals for property taken into public ownership, with certain exceptions. The charter was ultimately officially dropped in 1950, for reasons other than those related to the existing investment provisions [361].

2. Abs-Shawcross Draft Convention

After the failure of the Havana Charter, a wave of expropriations occurred in the 1950s in communist countries and numerous recently independent States. Several proposals were made in reaction. In 1959, Herman Abs and Hartley Shawcross advanced the most influential document [362]. Their Draft Convention on Investments Abroad [363] was inspired by an earlier proposal from Shawcross.

This Draft Convention, formally endorsed by the ICC [364] – which also administers international arbitrations – was never tabled for ratification

359. General Agreement on Tariffs and Trade ("GATT"), adopted 30 October 1947, entered into force 1 January 1948, 55 UNTS 187; General Agreement on Tariffs and Trade [1947 and 1994]. It laid the foundation for the multilateral trading system. See Havana Charter (1948), in *Max Planck Encyclopedia of International Law*, 2014.

360. "The Havana Charter for an International Trade Organization was envisaged to constitute, together with the International Monetary Fund and the International Bank for Reconstruction and Development (now the World Bank), the third pillar of the Bretton-Woods system and was originally conceived as an international organization that encompassed competences regarding both trade and investment", Schill, *supra* note 30, p. 32.

361. Lowenfeld, *supra* note 25, p. 483. Schill notes that "the project stopped being a priority to the United States due to matters such as internal politics and divergence of the business sector in this country with the limited provisions on investment protection of the document, among other reasons. Since the participation of the United States was considered crucial for establishing the ITO, this first effort to order international investment relations under the aegis of an international organization also failed to receive sufficient support from other States", Schill, *supra* note 30, p. 34.

362. *Ibid.*, p. 35.

363. H. Abs and H. Shawcross, "The Proposed Convention to Protect Private Foreign Investment: A Round Table", *Journal of Public Law*, Vol. 9 (1960), p. 115.

364. Sornarajah, *supra* note 29, p. 68.

by States. Nonetheless, it represents an extraordinary attempt to introduce an international Magna Carta for foreign investors.

In the postwar period, customary international law experienced no new important developments in the field of foreign investments. Against this background, the Abs-Shawcross Draft Convention provided a template for bilateral investment treaties, which had a huge impact on subsequent treaty practice. Its substantive standards represented an acceptable articulation of the consensus that had been reached regarding foreign investment within customary international law. Further, as stated by Campbell McLachlan, the Draft Convention was "clothed in language which avoided reigniting some of the pre-War controversies by offering new scope for flexibility" [365]. Besides, the explanatory notes accompanying this instrument were described as reflecting rules of customary international law [366].

The Abs-Shawcross Draft Convention did not contain provisions comprehensively dealing with the substantial applicable law. However, it did include safeguards for investors, for instance in Article II relating to contractual protection [367], which imposed the observance of undertakings given in relation to investments made by nationals of other countries. Further, Article III provided that no State should take any measures against nationals of another party that may directly or indirectly deprive them of their property, except under due process of law. Moreover, these measures also must not discriminate or run contrary to the party's undertakings and should be followed by payment of just and effective compensation. In turn, Article VI provided for the mandatory application of any present or future treaty or municipal law that conferred more favorable treatment to any of the parties' nationals [368].

According to Article VII of the Draft Convention, disputes were to be submitted, with the parties' consent, to arbitration. Where the parties did not consent to arbitration and had not agreed to settle the dispute through other specific means, the controversy could be submitted to the ICJ. No reference to the applicable law in these proceedings emerges from the Draft Convention.

---

365. McLachlan, *supra* note 356, p. 367.

366. A. R. Parra, "Applicable Substantive Law in ICSID Arbitrations Initiated Under Investment Treaties", *ICSID Review: Foreign Investment Law Journal*, Vol. 16, No. 1 (2001), p. 22.

367. See Ho, *supra* note 212, p. 54.

368. See Abs and Shawcross, "Draft Convention on Investments Abroad", in *ibid.*, *supra* note 363.

Importantly, the draft instrument pioneered the idea of the injured party's right to also have access to arbitration claims against the State responsible for the injury caused. The drafters did not present this idea as greatly innovative, as individuals at the time could gain access to international tribunals directly through, for instance, the Central American Court of Justice, certain mixed arbitral tribunals, as well as bodies such as the Court of the European Community, the European Commission of Human Rights and the administrative tribunals of international organizations [369].

The Abs-Shawcross Draft Convention was submitted to the Organisation for Economic Co-operation and Development (OECD), which never adopted the instrument. Nonetheless, it did serve as the basis for the OECD Draft Convention on the Protection of Foreign Property, published in 1962 [370].

3. Harvard Draft Convention

Prior to this first OECD draft, in 1961 the Harvard Draft Convention on the Responsibility of States for Injuries to the Economic Investment of Aliens included a moderate principle of qualified protection for foreign investments. The Harvard Draft Convention was not ratified by any State, nor is it cited by modern-day international tribunals [371].

4. OECD Draft Convention

In the 1960s, capital-exporting governments discussed three options for multilateral investment protection: a substantive code, an investment insurance organization and a convention on investor-State arbitration. These proposals were debated at the OECD and the World Bank. Unlike the three failed attempts to achieve a substantive code mentioned previously, however, the World Bank succeeded in creating instruments related to investor-State arbitration (the ICSID Convention, discussed in Chapter XIV) and in generating a multilateral investment

369. In this sense, Parra states that no real departure from legal tradition exists here to suggest that similar rights are to be conferred on individuals in connection with investment matters. Parra, *supra* note 366, p. 15.

370. OECD, Draft Convention on the Protection of Foreign Property, 2 ILM, p. 241 (1962), https://www.oecd.org/investment/internationalinvestmentagreements/39286571.pdf, accessed 3 March 2022.

371. Ho, *supra* note 212, p. 57.

insurance mechanism (referred to in the next chapter). Both of these initiatives obtained widespread support [372].

On the contrary, the 1962 OECD Draft Convention on the Protection of Private Foreign Investment, essentially a modified version of the Abs-Shawcross Draft Convention, did not enjoy the same fate [373].

This OECD Draft Convention included in its Article 2 the principle of *pacta sunt servanda*, according to which all contractual obligations must respect international law. Article 3 of the Draft concerned expropriation and provided that no State should take any measures that deprive – either directly or indirectly – a national of another State of their property unless taken in the public interest and under due process of law, in a non-discriminatory manner, and unless the seizure of property is accompanied by provision for the payment of just compensation [374]. Article 5 stated that upon any breach of the convention, the party responsible must make full reparation.

The OECD Draft Convention contained no express reference as to which substantive law should be applied to foreign investments. The preamble of the Convention only made reference to the desire to strengthen international economic cooperation based on "international law" and mutual "confidence".

During negotiations, British officials declared that the OECD Draft Convention was "a dead duck" [375]. The Draft Convention did not gain traction due to partisan overtones and the implicit rejection of the vast majority of States [376], which in fact did not participate in its drafting [377]. In the ten years during which it was discussed (1956-1966), at no point did the Convention garner widespread support. Since it was planned, as a multilateral convention, to also be open for signature to non-OECD members, it failed: the timing could not have been more unfavorable for an instrument to gain the support of developed and developing countries [378].

The slow death of the Draft Convention accelerated in earnest when European governments realized that they could obtain more robust

372. See T. St John, "The Creation of Investor-State Arbitration, on International Arbitration", in T. Schultz and F. Ortino (eds.), *The Oxford Handbook of International Arbitration*, Oxford, Oxford University Press, 2020, pp. 797-799.

373. *Ibid.*, p. 797.

374. OECD, Draft Convention on the Protection of Foreign Property, *supra* note 370.

375. St John, *supra* note 372, p. 797.

376. Ho, *supra* note 212, p. 49.

377. Lim, Ho and Paparinskis, *supra* note 76, p. 64.

378. Schill, *supra* note 30, pp. 36-37.

investment law standards through the negotiation of bilateral treaties [379]. Despite its failure, together with its direct predecessors, the Draft Convention in fact significantly influenced the drafting of the bilateral instruments negotiated in the 1960s and 1970s [380].

K. UN initiatives on international investments

Once the European States relinquished their colonies, they found it convenient to adopt the existing American system of international investment protection. By contrast, developing States in Africa and Asia generally defended the Calvo Doctrine [381]. This conflict of ideologies and interests led to a period of insecurity concerning which customary international rules should apply to foreign investments [382].

Between 1945 and 1970, a wave of expropriations took place in many regions of the world [383]. All States of Eastern Europe nationalized land and private industrial property, including that of aliens, with the exception of Greece, China and later Cuba. Utilities, mines and other companies in Bolivia, Brazil, Argentina, Peru and Guatemala, among others, were also seized. Well-known cases include the expropriations of Dutch properties in Indonesia (1958-1959), the nationalization of the Anglo-Iranian Oil Company's properties in Iran (1951) and Egypt's nationalization of the Suez Canal Company (1956). In the early 1970s, most Arab nations, from Algeria to Saudi Arabia and Iraq, either nationalized or ended the concessions of major oil companies. Negotiations generally followed after such campaigns, but the agreed-upon compensations rarely ever came close to fitting within the Hull Formula [384].

Neither the Hull nor the Calvo proposals were a reliable guide concerning the potential international legal sources of State obligations to investors, but they were not irrelevant either. Agreements on lump sum money compensations were driven by political and economic considerations, generally without an attempt to fit them into international legal doctrine [385].

379. St John, *supra* note 372, p. 798. In addition, the OECD abandoned efforts to arrive at a Code of Good Behavior in 1967.
380. Schill, *supra* note 30, p. 39.
381. Sornarajah, *supra* note 29, p. 37.
382. R. Dolzer and C. Schreuer, *Principles of International Investment Law*, 1st ed., Oxford, Oxford University Press, 2008, pp. 4-5.
383. It should be noted that this phenomenon also extended to the UK and France.
384. Lowenfeld, *supra* note 25, pp. 484-485.
385. *Ibid.*, p. 485.

Several efforts were made to address the conventional regulation of international customary law, first under the umbrella of the League of Nations in 1929, and later at the United Nations after the 1950s, which adopted the resolutions referred to in the following pages.

1. UN Resolution 1803 (XVII) of 14 December 1962

Since one of the fundamental principles of the UN Charter is the sovereign equality of States [386], countries gaining independence relied on the doctrine of permanent sovereignty over their natural resources to renegotiate agreements that had been made in colonial times. To regain control over such agreements, the *pacta sunt servanda* or the sanctity of existing agreements entered into conflict with – in the words of Surya Subedi – "one of the most powerful doctrines of international law: the sovereignty of States" [387].

Latin American countries such as Uruguay and Chile pushed to introduce the sovereignty of States doctrine into the UN Agenda. General Assembly Resolution 626 (VII) of 1952 supported the idea of economic self-determination. Subsequently, the Third Committee of the General Assembly adopted in 1955 a draft article on the right of self-determination [388].

The Commission on Permanent Sovereignty over Natural Resources was established in 1958. Alongside the Economic and Social Council, the Commission conducted efforts that led to General Assembly Resolution 1803 (XVII) of 1962 on the Permanent Sovereignty of States over their Natural Resources [389].

This resolution was the first document regarding expropriation under certain conditions (including appropriate compensation) to gain near-universal support [390]. It included the aspirations of developing nations, as well as parts of the Hull Formula. The resolution attempted to record (and perhaps shape) customary international law on matters that the world was deeply divided upon, which explains why its language was

386. The Charter of the United Nations, signed on 26 June 1945, Article 2.

387. Subedi, *supra* note 17, p. 21.

388. It stated the following: "The peoples may, for their own ends, freely dispose of their natural wealth and resources without prejudice to any obligations arising out of international economic co-operation, based upon the principle of mutual benefit, and international law. In no case may a people be deprived of its own means of subsistence."

389. *Ibid.*, p. 22.

390. Curtis, *supra* note 119, p. 328. Paragraph 8 of the resolution stated: "Foreign investment agreements freely entered into *by, or between,* sovereign states shall be observed in good faith", UN GAOR Supp. (No. 17) at 15, UN Doc. A/5217 (1962).

evasive[391]. Overall, General Assembly Resolution 1803 (XVII) was considered "the most widely accepted international instrument on foreign investment law" that articulated existing agreed-upon principles within customary international law[392].

The document symbolized a sort of consensus between developed and developing countries regarding expropriation with compensation, in accordance with the law of the expropriating State and with public international law. The resolution also declared investment agreements between States and private parties to be binding[393]. Controversies were to be referred to the jurisdiction of the State that had committed the alleged wrongful act, but parties could agree to settle their dispute by arbitration or international adjudication (the choice of which was binding)[394].

The famous *Texaco* v. *Libya* award of 1977[395], which, as stated by Robert von Mehren and Nicholas Kourides, "should be of immense value and importance to the international legal community", constituted a forceful and influential attempt to treat this Resolution 1803 (XVII) as a reflection of customary international law[396]. Chapter VIII of this book will further elaborate on this award.

2. *Subsequent United Nations New Order resolutions and the "New International Economic Order"*

In 1966, the UN General Assembly rendered Resolution 2158 on the Permanent Sovereignty over Natural Resources. Some 104 countries voted in favor of this resolution, while six abstained, including the

391. *Ibid.*, p. 486.

392. Subedi, *supra* note 17, p. 23. See also Schill, *supra* note 30, p. 38.

393. Paragraph 8 of Resolution 1803, stating the requirement that investment agreements "by, or between, states" be observed in good faith, was introduced by the US and Great Britain for the specific purpose of protecting investment agreements. Resolution 1803 therefore specifically recognizes the status in international law of investment agreements between States and private investors". See 17 UN GAOR C.2 (850th mtg.) at p. 325, 325-26, UN Doc. A/C.2/SR.850 (1962). Also Curtis, *supra* note 119, p. 328.

394. In addition, the resolution states that in cases where authorization is granted, the capital imported and the earnings on that capital shall be governed by the terms of the authorization, by the national legislation in force, and by international law. Lowenfeld, *supra* note 25, p. 489; Declaration 4 of Resolution 1803, https://www.un.org/ga/search/view_doc.asp?symbol=A/RES/1803%28XVII%29, accessed 3 March 2022.

395. *Texaco* v. *Libya*, *supra* note 119, *Ad hoc* Award on the Merits (19 January 1977).

396. R. B. von Mehren and P. N. Kourides, "International Arbitrations between States and Foreign Private Parties: The Libyan Nationalization Cases", *American Journal of International Law*, Vol. 75, No. 3 (1981), p. 551.

United States. This resolution received substantial criticism for its lack of clarity [397]; however, it became highly relevant for the discussions that followed at the United Nations.

Some years after, General Assembly Resolution 3171 of 1973 went so far as to claim that expropriations do not create an obligation for "appropriate compensation" according to domestic standards [398]. It received 108 votes in favor, one against and sixteen abstentions, including ten Western European countries and the United States, indicating their lack of support for the resolution [399].

After obtaining a majority of votes, the developing nations attempted to introduce an agenda more favorable to their interests. This attempt to establish a New International Economic Order was recognized by the General Assembly through Resolution 3201 (S-VI) of 1974 and the Programme of Action on the Implementation of the Declaration through Resolution 3202 (S-VI) [400], adopted by the Charter of Economic Rights and Duties of States via General Assembly Resolution 3281 of 1974.

Article 4 of the Declaration recognizes the "full permanent sovereignty of every State over its natural resources and all economic activities", and that:

> "In order to safeguard these resources, each State is entitled to exercise effective control over them and their exploitation with means suitable to its own situation, including the right to nationalization or transfer of ownership to its nationals, this right being an expression of the full permanent sovereignty of the State. No State may be subjected to economic, political or any other type of coercion to prevent the free and full exercise of this inalienable right."

In the words of Lowenfeld, most of what had come before was gone [401]. Not only were States not compelled to grant preferential treatment to foreign investment – something not incorporated as such into public international law – but it appeared that there now existed no right for equal treatment. Simply put, there was now no prohibition of arbitrary or discriminatory treatment of foreign investment or investors.

---

397. Lowenfeld, *supra* note 25, p. 490.
398. UNGA Res. 3171, 28 UN GAOR Supp. No. 30, at 52 (17 December 1973), UN Doc. A/9030, reprinted in *American Journal of International Law*, Vol. 68 (1974), p. 381.
399. *Ibid.*, p. 491.
400. Subedi, *supra* note 17, p. 24.
401. Lowenfeld, *supra* note 25, p. 492.

The right to nationalize or expropriate foreign-owned property was restated, with no requirement of public purpose or public utility. This Charter of Economic Rights and Duties of States attempted to repudiate a system that the developing States had little or no participation in creating. Francisco V. García-Amador, Rapporteur of the ILC Articles on State Responsibility, wrote that

> "at least insofar as measures affecting foreign-owned property are covered, [the effect] is to place State responsibility outside the realm of international law" [402].

The Charter of Economic Rights and Duties of States adopted the "appropriate compensation" standard but rejected some of the key aspects of the Hull Formula. Instead, the document emphasized the application of national rather than public international law on matters related to expropriation and nationalization. For this reason, many developed countries did not support the Charter [403], which has been described as "the most far-reaching and controversial" resolution of the United Nations on international economic law. The reasoning of sole Arbitrator Dupuy in *Texaco* v. *Libya* even dismissed the idea that the Charter reflected customary international law, considering this circumstance as one of the reasons for its lack of acceptance [404].

The dissonance between capital-exporting and capital-importing States in this regard occurred at a time in which BITs began to proliferate under the auspices of countries looking to attract investment [405]. Moreover, the UN resolutions at the time did not necessarily reflect the

402. *Ibid.*, p. 492.

403. Subedi, *supra* note 17, p. 26.

404. *Texaco* v. *Libya*, *supra* note 119, *Ad hoc* Award on the Merits (19 January 1977), 52 ILR, p. 389 (1977), para. 88. Jean d'Aspremont notes that "arbitral tribunals gave very little weight to the UN GA resolutions defiant of the Western capital-protective vision. Only the International Court of Justice in the Barcelona Traction case and the arbitrator in the *Texaco* v. *Libya* award remained lucid and clear-sighted about the state of the law of investment protection in the post-1945 period", d'Aspremont, *supra* note 30, pp. 14-15.

405. Lord Shawcross, *supra* note 38, p. 341:

> "This type of movement of money, techniques, and skills became more important than ever. Political and social changes naturally led to much more clamorous and urgent demands by the populations of developing regions for more rapid progress and a fairer share in the economic prosperity that occurred as a result of globalization. During this time, large-scale bilateral and multilateral assistance plans also began to emerge by the governments of the more prosperous countries, as well as through intergovernmental institutions like the International Bank for Reconstruction and Development."

rules of international law in the sense, for instance, of Article 42 (1) of the ICSID Convention relating to the applicable substantive law [406].

However, the aforementioned UN resolutions may be applied by incorporation into an agreement, through a reference to a treaty or by extension due to their reflection of customary international law in matters such as nationalization [407]. The award in the ICSID case *Amco* v. *Indonesia* [408] is an example of this argumentation [409].

L. *Efforts for a multilateral instrument in the 1990s*

In the 1960s, there was no real consensus on the law related to foreign investments nor was there any inclination to craft legal rules. Related international instruments used very open language, such as "Members undertake . . . to give due regard" [410]. In the famous 1964 *Sabbatino* case, the Supreme Court of the United States wrote that customary international law had fallen into a state of considerable legal uncertainty in the field [411].

By the mid-1970s, "numerous ingredients and influences" [412] had shaped the customary international law of protecting foreign investments. States often preached one thing before the United Nations but in practice behaved differently when it came to the negotiation of bilateral and multilateral agreements. Scholarly commentary on this issue exists along a broad spectrum, with many authors completely denying that public international law applied to the protection of international investment and others advocating for the continuing relevance of the Hull Formula and its antecedents [413].

Christopher Curtis observes that the radical resolutions of the early 1970s have not been reiterated in the General Assembly. This silence

406. See Chap. XVI.I, *infra*, "Applicable substantive law in the ICSID Convention".
407. Schreuer *et al.*, *supra* note 102, p. 612.
408. *Amco Asia Corporation and others* v. *Republic of Indonesia*, ICSID Case No. ARB/81/1, Award (20 November 1984).
409. For cases, see Schreuer *et al.*, *supra* note 102, p. 611.
410. Lowenfeld, *supra* note 25, p. 483.
411. Lim, Ho and Paparinskis, *supra* note 76, p. 12.
412. Lowenfeld, *supra* note 25, p. 416.
413. *Ibid.*, pp. 495-496. "Moreover, investors' home countries had good reason to emphasize the importance of adequate compensation. From 1960 to mid-1974, some sixty-two different developing countries engaged in 875 nationalizations or takeovers of foreign enterprises. The majority of the cases (591) took place in ten States. As a result, disputes about the existence and nature of obligations to pay compensation for the expropriation of alien property under international law increased dramatically", Salacuse, *supra* note 65, pp. 87-88.

should be interpreted as a refusal of a critical proportion of nations to adhere to the views expressed therein [414].

By the beginning of the 1980s, little progress had been achieved without the support of developed countries, which maintained their opposition to this new economic order. As a result, other international actors came under pressure to act or respond, such as the World Bank, the OECD and the WTO [415].

The World Bank had already established the ICSID dispute resolution mechanism, but in 1992 it adopted a set guidelines or non-binding principles on foreign investments [416]. In turn, the Uruguay Round, the same that led to the creation of the WTO, also led to the adoption of the Agreement on Trade-Related Investment Measures (TRIMs), which applies to investment measures affecting trade in goods [417].

For its part, the OECD began to draft an ambitious Multilateral Agreement on Investment (MAI) in 1995. This agreement aimed to create a comprehensive general framework to guide international investment, also available to non-OECD countries, incorporating high standards of liberalization, investment protection and effective dispute settlement procedures [418].

The Draft MAI Negotiating Text, further referred to as the MAI, was the resulting international attempt to draft a global instrument on State responsibility that also incorporated general rules related to the substantial applicable law [419]. Its provisions resembled those contained in Article 42 of the ICSID Convention. Parties could select the applicable rules of law, and in the absence of their choice, the MAI determined

---

414. "Those resolutions are best understood as political assertions of the moment. They represented the crest in the tide of decolonization and followed hard upon the first major OPEC price increase, which seemed to herald a new era of wealth and power for the developing world. But now the developing States recognize their continuing need for investment capital from developed countries as well as among themselves, and a different pattern of international instruments has emerged", Curtis, *supra* note 119, p. 359.

415. Subedi, *supra* note 17, p. 28.

416. World Bank Group, Legal Framework for the Treatment of Foreign Investment, Vols. 1 and 2, 1992. The text of the guidelines is reproduced in 31 ILM, p. 1363 (1992).

417. See https://www.wto.org/english/tratop_e/invest_e/invest_info_e.htm#:~:text=The%20Agreement%20on%20Trade%2DRelated,which%20violate%20basic%20WTO%20principles, accessed 23 July 2022.

418. OECD, "OECD Begins Negotiations on A Multilateral Agreement on Invest ment", Paris, 1995, https://www.oecd.org/investment/internationalinvestmentagreements/43389907.pdf, accessed 3 March 2022.

419. This text is the consolidated version of the agreement considered in the MAI negotiations course up to the point where they were discontinued in April 1998. OECD, The Multilateral Agreement on Investment: Draft Consolidated Text, http://www.oecd.org/daf/mai/pdf/ng/ng987r1e.pdf, accessed 3 March 2022.

the law of the contracting party (including its rules on the conflict of laws), the law governing the authorization or agreement and the rules of international law as may be applicable to the dispute, depending on the particular case (Art. V (D) (14), para. 1.*b)*) [420].

Among the investor-State procedures included in the MAI, Article V (D) (2) stated that the parties could agree to arbitration using a different set of rules, such as ICSID or others [421].

The MAI also established a "fair and equitable treatment and full and constant protection and security" for investments, to be no less favorable than that required by international law (Art. IV, 1.1.1) [422]. The MAI further included rules related to the expropriation and protection of foreign investors: expropriation must be in the public interest, conducted on a non-discriminatory basis and in accordance with due process of law. Additionally, payment of prompt, adequate and effective compensation should be afforded (Art. IV.2 of the MAI).

The text of these provisions was generally in accordance with the standards of mainstream investment treaties in place at the time. Unfortunately, negotiations for the formal adoption of the MAI were discontinued in 1998 [423] due to a failure to reach a consensus on several issues, and also due to the lack of participation of developing nations in the formal discussions, which generated strong resistance from countries such as India. Influential non-governmental organizations also expressed strong concerns regarding issues such as labor and environmental standards [424].

M. Draft Articles on State Responsibility

State responsibility may derive – *lato sensu* – from any of its breaches of public international law, ranging from an error made by a petty

420. The MAI draft established different rules depending on the kind of dispute: investor-State disputes or disputes among States. *State-to-State procedures* were to be decided following the MAI's rules, "interpreted and applied in accordance with the applicable rules of international law" (Art© (C) (6) (a)). In turn, *investor-State procedures* concerning an alleged breach of an obligation that caused loss or damage to the investor or its investment were to be decided in accordance with the *MAI rules* and interpreted and applied under the *applicable rules of international law* (Art. V (D) (14), para. 1.a)).

421. If available, the ICSID Convention; the ICSID Additional Facility; the Arbitration Rules of UNCITRAL; or the Rules of Arbitration of the ICC. See OECD MAI, *supra* note 419.

422. The reference to international law in this article was considered critical and worded in the most straightforward manner, as noted in the Commentary to the Draft Consolidated MAI. *Ibid.*, p. 29.

423. Ho, *supra* note 212, p. 51.

424. See these and other reasons in Schill, *supra* note 30, pp. 53-58.

official to an act of aggression, such as when British destroyers struck Albanian mines laid in the Corfu Channel [425]. Originally, the doctrine of State responsibility dealt with the State's public responsibility due to the breach of an international obligation owed to another State [426].

After the nineteenth century, in particular, difficulties began to arise regarding the outrageous behavior of States toward aliens. In order to deal with this conduct, an appreciation of the law of State responsibility was required in the context of the growing customary law on foreign investments. In these situations, States were only indirectly injured when their nationals were affected, in comparison with the direct harm generally referred to in discussions of direct State responsibility [427].

The law of "State responsibility" developed in this stricter sense, regarding the indirect injury of a State affecting the national of another country [428]. Originally, State responsibility was created to protect individuals and, subsequently, foreign companies and their business concerns [429]. Within this logic, a State could incur legal liability for its interference and be obligated to compensate the injured party. It is therefore clear that the obligations contained in international investment treaties create a situation where a wide range of domestic regulations and acts may become unlawful under public international law [430].

In the mid-twentieth century, Robert Jennings stated that "possibly no part of the law is more in need of reassessment than that concerning the responsibility of States" [431].

---

425. *Corfu Channel* case, Merits, Judgment (9 April 1949), *ICJ Reports 1949*, p. 4.

426. Jennings, *supra* note 274, p. 474. The concept of responsibility "in its true meaning is substantially similar to responsibility in municipal private law". See Cheng, *supra* note 178, p. 389.

427. Jennings, *supra* note 274, p. 474.

428. *Ibid.*, p. 474.

429. In the *Barcelona Traction* case, the ICJ stated the following: "When a State admits into its territory foreign investments of foreign nationals, whether natural or juristic persons, it is bound to extend to them the protection of the law and assumes obligations concerning the treatment to be afforded them" (*Barcelona Traction*, *supra* note 24, para. 33). In the *Roberts* claim, the General Claims Commission held that "Facts with respect to equality of treatment of aliens and nationals may be important in determining the merits of a complaint of mistreatment of an alien. But such equality is not the ultimate test of the propriety of the acts of authorities in the light of international law. That test is, broadly speaking, whether aliens are treated in accordance with ordinary standards of civilization" (The *Roberts*, *Hopkins*, and *British Claims in the Spanish Zone of Morocco* cases of 1926: *Harry Roberts (USA)* v. *United Mexican States*, General Claims Commission, Decision (2 November 1926), (1926) 4 RIAA, pp. 77-81, para. 8; *George W. Hopkins (USA)* v. *United Mexican States*, Decision (31 March 1926), (1926) 4 RIAA, p. 411; and *British Claims in the Spanish Zone of Morocco*, Decision (1925), (1925) 2 RIAA, p. 617, respectively).

430. Collins, *supra* note 66, p. 66.

431. Jennings, *supra* note 274, p. 474.

Nowadays, the law of State responsibility is to a large extent reflected in the work of the ILC. At the 1930 League of Nations Conference, an attempt to codify this matter was launched [432]. The United Nations later took up the initiative, and after almost forty-five years and thirty reports, a draft was finally approved [433].

Special Rapporteur and Cuban jurist Francisco V. García-Amador wrote an initial report in 1956 that attempted a comprehensive codification on the responsibility stemming from injury to aliens [434]. García-Amador was succeeded in 1961 by Italian jurist Roberto Ago, who established the basic structure and orientation of the project to codify the law of State responsibility. Ago contributed more abstract general rules relating to State responsibility, offering a distinction between primary and secondary rules. This approach avoided some of the contentious issues that had previously posed problems. Ago stated that

> "it is one thing to define a rule and the content of the obligation it imposes, and another to determine whether that obligation has been violated and what should be the consequences of the violation" [435].

As such, Ago's proposal does not deal with the content of international obligations, which is the focus on the primary rules of State responsibility "whose codification would involve restating most of substantive customary and conventional international law" [436]. Instead, emphasis is placed upon the secondary rules, or "the general conditions under international law for the State to be considered responsible for wrongful actions or omissions, and the legal consequences which

---

432. See Report to the General Assembly, *Yearbook of the International Law Commission* (1949), p. 281.

433. Text adopted by the Commission at its fifty-third session, in 2001, and submitted to the General Assembly as a part of the Commission's report covering the work of that session. ILC, Draft Articles on Responsibility of States for Internationally Wrongful Acts, with commentaries, November 2001, https://legal.un.org/ilc/texts/instruments/english/draft_articles/9_6_2001.pdf, accessed 3 March 2022, Supplement No. 10 (A/56/10), chap. IV.E.1.

434. F. V. García-Amador, First Report on International Responsibility, UN Doc. A/CN.4/SER.A/1956/Add.1, *Yearbook of the International Law Commission* (1956), p. 175, para. 6.

435. *Yearbook of the International Law Commission*, Vol. 2 (1970), p. 306, para. 66 *I*, https://legal.un.org/ilc/publications/yearbooks/english/ilc_1970_v2.pdf, 11 March 2022.

436. ILC Draft Articles on State Responsibility, *supra* note 433, p. 31, para. 1 (https://legal.un.org/ilc/texts/instruments/english/commentaries/9_6_2001.pdf, 11 March 2022).

flow therefrom" [437]. Ago's proposal determines which acts qualify as internationally wrongful, the circumstances under which wrongful action may be attributed to the State, the general defenses to liability and the consequences of liability.

The final version of the ILC Draft Articles on Responsibility of States for Internationally Wrongful Acts was adopted by Resolution 56/83 of 2001 [438]. This initiative was brought "to the attention of Governments without prejudice to the question of their future adoption or other appropriate action" [439].

There appears to be a general consensus that the Articles on Responsibility of States for Internationally Wrongful Acts is currently the most authoritative document on the law of State responsibility, although it does not cover all of its aspects under public international law [440]. The draft articles were even cited by the ICJ in the *Gabčíkovo-Nagymaros Project* case [441].

N. Evaluation and recent developments in customary international law

Customary international law developed particularly to ascertain and fill gaps in Friendship, Commerce and Navigation treaties, which did not address several issues related to investors and evolved around the practice and the home laws of the aliens. General principles of law, case law and doctrinal writings relied on these developments. Subedi states that, therefore, international investment matters followed the law imposed by investor countries. As a result, tensions often arose between the application of the law of the host State and the application of international law, which was generally aligned with the practice of investor countries [442].

---

437. *Supra* note 435.

438. See https://www.un.org/en/ga/sixth/68/StateRes.shtml, accessed 18 May 2022.

439. UNGA Res. 56/83 (12 December 2001), https://documents-dds-ny.un.org/doc/UNDOC/GEN/N01/477/97/PDF/N0147797.pdf?OpenElement, accessed 11 March 2022, para. 3.

440. K. Hobér, "State Responsibility and Attribution", P. Muchlinski, F. Ortino and C. Schreuer (eds.), *The Oxford Handbook of International Investment Law*, New York, Oxford University Press, 2008, p. 550. See also Remiro Brotóns, *supra* note 264, p. 405.

441. *Gabčíkovo-Nagymaros*, *supra* note 299, Judgment (25 September 1997), paras. 47, 50, 79, 83.

442. Subedi, *supra* note 17, p. 10.

Customary international law was highly unsatisfactory. Many issues that emerged (particularly in recent times) such as the right of foreign investors to make foreign transfers or to bring their own managers to the host country, were not addressed [443].

Salacuse notes other problems. One of them arises from the often-vague international customary rules, subject therefore to varying interpretations. This situation was reflected, for instance, in the manner of how compensation was to be calculated. Disagreements between nations of the Global North and South aggravated the divergences. As seen, developing countries considered mainstream customary international law as an imposition of the developed world. Moreover, no effective enforcement dispute resolution was available to investors. In sum, international customary law was incomplete, vague, contested and without an effective enforcement mechanism [444]. This situation led to the negotiation of investment treaties, as described in the next chapter.

Today, the role of customary international law in foreign investments has changed. This is particularly true with the proliferation of treaties since the 1990s due to the demise of the Soviet Union and the growing number of bilateral instruments that have been concluded in the interim. Since then, States have begun to focus on new ways of attracting foreign investment [445]. The dominant strategy in this new era has been "not to oppose classical customary law, but instead to attract additional foreign investment by granting more protection to foreign investment, now on the basis of treaties" [446].

Customary law still has an important position in international law, particularly in the absence of an applicable treaty [447]. In this situation, customary international law provides answers to matters such as the minimum standard for the treatment of aliens, the prohibition of the denial of justice and State responsibility for injury to aliens [448].

443. Salacuse, *supra* note 65, p. 94.

444. *Ibid.*, p. 96.

445. Parra, *supra* note 366, p. 22.

446. Dolzer and Schreuer, *supra* note 382, p. 5.

447. Collins, *supra* note 66, p. 28. Besides this "lacuna-filling effect", international customary law has an "interpretation-harmonizing effect" when treaties are interpreted in light of general public international law. Jean d'Aspremont also talks about a "multilateralizing effect": "Customary international law, in this sense, is the only tool that allows the multilateralization of a regime which otherwise would be of a solely contractual nature. It constitutes the only realistic route to ensuring the true multilateralization of the investment protection regime", d'Aspremont, *supra* note 30, pp. 27-28.

448. A problem arises with the extension to international investment of developments from customary international law in general, such as in relation to the doctrine of

There are numerous precedents in which ICSID tribunals have applied the rules of customary international law, such as the principles of State responsibility [449], the principle of respect for acquired rights [450], the consequences of a state of necessity [451], the denial of justice [452], the standard of protection in case of an insurrection [453], nationalization in breach of a stabilization clause [454] or compensation for expropriation [455], including the already mentioned *Chorzów Factory* standard for

---

necessity in situations of *force majeure*, that will normally apply to acts of war and, under certain conditions, to harm caused by insurrection and civil war. It has been doubted whether necessity exists as an omnibus category, and in any event its availability as a defense is circumscribed by rigorous conditions. While necessity has been argued before investment tribunals, its recognition is usually denied, as occurred in *Neptune* and *Russian Indemnity*, and before courts, in *Gabčíkovo-Nagymaros* (*supra* note 299), and *M/V SAIGA (No. 20)*. In *LG&E Energy Corp.* v. *Argentina*, the Tribunal affirmed the necessity "should be only strictly exceptional and should be applied exclusively when faced with extraordinary circumstances" (*LG&E Energy Corp., LG&E Capital Corp., and LG&E International, Inc.* v. *Argentine Republic*, ICSID Case No. ARB/02/1, Decision on Liability (3 October 2006), para. 228. A similar decision was rendered in *CMS* v. *Argentina*, *supra* note 84, Award (12 May 2005), paras. 379 ff.

449. *Southern Pacific* v. *Egypt*, *supra* note 128, Award (20 May 1992), para. 85; *CMS* v. *Argentina*, *supra* note 84, Decision of the Tribunal on Objections to Jurisdiction (17 July 2003), para. 108; *Tokios Tokelés* v. *Ukraine*, ICSID Case No. ARB/02/18, Decision on Jurisdiction (29 April 2004), para. 102; *Jan de Nul NV and Dredging International NV* v. *Arab Republic of Egypt*, ICSID Case No. ARB/04/13, Decision on Jurisdiction (16 June 2006), para. 89; *Azurix* v. *Argentina*, *supra* note 327, Award (2006), para. 50; *Saipem* v. *Bangladesh*, *supra* note 77, Decision on Jurisdiction and Recommendation on Provisional Measures (21 March 2007), para. 148; *Ioannis Kardassopoulos* v. *The Republic of Georgia*, ICSID Case No. ARB/05/18, Decision on Jurisdiction (6 July 2007), para. 190.

450. *Amco Asia* v. *Indonesia*, *supra* note 408, Award (20 November 1984), para. 248 *(v)*.

451. *CMS* v. *Argentina*, *supra* note 84, Award (12 May 2005), paras. 304-331; *LG&E* v. *Argentina*, *supra* note 448, Decision on Liability (3 October 2006), paras. 245-266; *Enron Corporation and Ponderosa Assets, LP* v. *Argentine Republic*, ICSID Case No. ARB/01/3, Award (22 May 2007), paras. 294-313; *CMS* v. *Argentina*, *supra* note 84, Decision of the *ad hoc* Committee on the Application for Annulment of the Argentine Republic (25 September 2007), paras. 101-150; *Sempra Energy International* v. *Argentine Republic*, ICSID Case No. ARB/02/16, Award (28 September 2007), paras. 333-354, 392-397.

452. *Amco Asia* v. *Indonesia*, *supra* note 408, Award in Resubmitted Proceeding (5 June 1990), paras. 122-138.

453. *Asian Agricultural Products Ltd. (AAPL)* v. *Democratic Socialist Republic of Sri Lanka*, ICSID Case No. ARB/87/3, Award (27 June 1990), 4 *ICSID Reports*, p. 246, para. 72.

454. *AGIP SpA* v. *People's Republic of Congo*, ICSID Case No. ARB/77/1, Award (30 November 1979), paras. 84-88.

455. *SARL Benvenuti & Bonfant* v. *People's Republic of the Congo*, ICSID Case No. ARB/77/2, Award (15 August 1980), para. 4.64; *Amco Asia* v. *Indonesia*, *supra* note 408, Award (20 November 1984), para. 188; *Compañía del Desarrollo de Santa Elena SA (CDSE)* v. *Republic of Costa Rica*, ICSID Case No. ARB/96/1, Award (17 February 2000), 39 ILM, p. 1317, paras. 68-95.

determining the appropriate amount of compensation for wrongful expropriation [456].

Foreign investments have also generated a wide array of soft law or non-binding instruments (see further in Chap. XI), particularly in topics that lack the international consensus required for the establishment of a treaty. Such matters include, for instance, corporate responsibility, upon which the UN Global Compact has been working since 1999, a list of ten principles in the areas of human rights, labor rights, environmental protection and anti-corruption [457]. Other soft law initiatives include the UN Norms on the Responsibilities of Transnational Corporations and Other Business Enterprises with regard to Human Rights (2003) [458], the UN Guiding Principles on Business and Human Rights (2011) [459] and the influential OECD Guidelines for Multinational Enterprises (first issued in 1976, most recently updated in 2011) [460]. Another relevant recent development is the Legal Guide on Agricultural Land

---

456. *Compañía de Aguas del Aconquija SA and Vivendi Universal SA* v. *Argentine Republic*, ICSID Case No. ARB/97/3, Award (20 August 2007), paras. 8.2.2-8.2.7; *Liberian Eastern Timber Corporation (LETCO)* v. *Republic of Liberia*, ICSID Case No. ARB/83/2, Award (31 March 1986), 2 *ICSID Reports*, p. 366; *Southern Pacific* v. *Egypt*, *supra* note 128, Award on the Merits (20 May 1992), paras. 160-168; *Goetz* v. *Burundi*, *supra* note 93, Award, para. 72; *Československa* v. *Slovak Republic*, *supra* note 70, Decision (24 May 1999), para. 32; *Bayindir Insaat Turizm Ticaret Ve Sanayi AS* v. *Islamic Republic of Pakistan*, ICSID Case No. ARB/03/29, Decision on Jurisdiction (14 November 2005), para. 178; *El Paso Energy International Co.* v. *Argentine Republic*, ICSID Case No. ARB/03/15, Decision on Jurisdiction (27 April 2006), paras. 117-136; *Enron* v. *Argentina*, *supra* note 451, Award (22 May 2007), para. 396. *M Emilio Agustin Maffezini* v. *Kingdom of Spain*, ICSID Case No. ARB/97/7, Decision of the Tribunal on Objections to Jurisdiction (25 January 2000), paras. 25 ff.; *Generation Ukraine Inc.* v. *Ukraine*, ICSID Case No. ARB/00/9, Award (16 September 2003), paras. 13.1-13.6; *Saipem* v. *Bangladesh*, *supra* note 77, Decision on Jurisdiction and Recommendation on Provisional Measures (21 March 2007), paras. 150-153; *Tokios Tokelés* v. *Ukraine*, *supra* note 449, Decision on Jurisdiction (29 April 2004), paras. 53-56; *CMS* v. *Argentina*, *supra* note 84, Decision of the Tribunal on Objections to Jurisdiction (17 July 2003), para. 48; *Camuzzi International SA* v. *The Argentine Republic*, ICSID Case No. ARB/03/2, Decision on Objections to Jurisdiction (11 May 2005), paras. 144, 145; *Sempra* v. *Argentina*, *supra* note 451, Decision on Objections to Jurisdiction (11 May 2005), paras. 156-157.

457. F. Dasser, "Soft Law in International Commercial Arbitration", *Recueil des cours*, Vol. 402 (2019), p. 417.

458. Norms on the Responsibilities of Transnational Corporations and Other Business Enterprises with regard to Human Rights, 2003, https://digitallibrary.un.org/record/501576#record-files-collapse-header, 11 March 2022.

459. UN Guiding Principles on Business and Human Rights, 2011, https://www.ohchr.org/documents/publications/guidingprinciplesbusinesshr_en.pdf, 11 March 2022.

460. OECD Guidelines for Multinational Enterprises, https://www.oecd.org/daf/inv/mne/48004323.pdf, 11 March 2022. The OECD, in turn, has a Code of Liberalization of Capital Movements, 2010, http://www.oecd.org/dataoecd/10/62/39664826.pdf, accessed 3 March 2022.

Investment Contracts (ALIC) by UNIDROIT and the International Fund for Agricultural Development (IFAD)[461].

461. UNIDROIT/IFAD ALIC Legal Guide, *supra* note 296.

CHAPTER V

TREATIES AND FOREIGN INVESTMENTS

A. Developments in the twentieth century

As seen in the two previous chapters, from the wording of Friendship, Commerce and Navigation agreements signed from the seventeenth century onward emerged certain substantive obligations that evolved under international customary law. Attempts at a multilateral level to codify these substantive obligations faced significant setbacks after World War II. Among them are the failed OECD projects aimed at the creation of a universal instrument with substantive obligations addressing the matter.

Under the aegis of the United Nations, the ILC ultimately abandoned the "enormously ambitious" [462] draft code of Cuban jurist Francisco V. García-Amador on the protection of aliens. Instead, the ILC focused on the creation of a non-binding instrument (the Draft Articles on Responsibility of States for Internationally Wrongful Acts). As described in Chapter IV, the Draft Articles on State Responsibility only dealt with matters such as the consequences for breaches of international obligations (secondary rules) but did not address issues related to the substantive obligations themselves (primary rules). Similarly, the ILC's work on diplomatic protection from 2006 [463] expressly limits itself to secondary rules [464].

Since these initiatives, no other significant codification project within the field of State responsibility has been undertaken. Instead, States have opted *en masse* to conclude bilateral, regional and multilateral investment treaties, including free trade agreements (FTAs) that incorporate specific chapters regulating foreign investment.

---

462. J. Crawford, *The International Law Commission's Articles on State Responsibility*, Cambridge, Cambridge University Press, 2002, p. 15.

463. Draft Articles on Diplomatic Protection, *supra* note 328. Text adopted by the ILC at its fifty-eighth session in 2006 and submitted to the General Assembly as a part of the Commission's report covering the work of that session (A/61/10). The report, which also contains commentaries on the draft articles, appears in the *Yearbook of the International Law Commission*, Vol. 2 (2006), Part 2.

464. McLachlan, *supra* note 356, pp. 366-367.

B. Treaties

Article 38 of the Statute of the ICJ, generally considered the most authoritative statement on the sources of public international law, mentions international conventions and custom at the outset (Art. 38 (1)) [465]. Per Ian Brownlie, treaties and custom comprise the most important sources of public international law [466].

In recent times, the balance is shifting toward treaties. There are, as of today, more than 70,000 treaties dominating the international law landscape [467]. Of particular importance is the Charter of the United Nations, which is the basic legal instrument of the international community [468].

Long ago, Hugo Grotius suggested that treaties share many traits with private law contracts. Centuries later, the US Supreme Court considered treaties not as acts of legislation but rather as contracts between sovereign nations (for instance, in *Olympic Airways* v. *Husain* [469]).

Of course, there are certain characteristics that are unique to treaties alone, reflected in the widely ratified Vienna Convention on the Laws of Treaties (VCLT) [470], which is an instrument generally accepted as reflecting customary international law [471]. Article 2 (1) *(a)* of the VCLT defines a treaty as

> "an international agreement concluded between States in written form and governed by international law, whether embodied in a single instrument or in two or more related instruments and whatever its particular designation" [472].

---

465. See Article 38 (1) of the Statute of the International Court of Justice, https://www.icj-cij.org/en/statute, accessed 3 March 2022.

466. Crawford, *supra* note 150, p. 22.

467. See D. B. Hollis (ed.), *The Oxford Guide to Treaties*, Oxford, Oxford University Press, 2020, p. viii.

468. Jennings and Watts, *supra* note 278, p. 31.

469. *Olympic Airways* v. *Husain*, 316 F.3d 829 (9th Cir. 2002).

470. Vienna Convention on the Law of Treaties ("VCLT"), opened for signature 23 May 1969, entered into force 27 January 1980, 1155 UNTS 331, reprinted in 8 ILM, p. 679 (1969), https://www.oas.org/legal/english/docs/Vienna%20Convention%20Treaties.htm, accessed 3 March 2022, see Article 2 (1) *(a)*.

471. R. K. Gardiner, "The Vienna Convention Rules on Treaty Interpretation", in D. B. Hollis (ed.), *The Oxford Guide to Treaties*, Oxford, Oxford University Press, 2020, p. 460. This is the case even with those rules of the convention which would otherwise be excluded for reasons such as their pre-dating the Vienna Convention, or because a State concerned with the issue under interpretation is not a party to the Vienna Convention. See also R. K. Gardiner, *International Law*, London, Pearson Longman, 2003, p. 79.

472. See Article 2 (1) *(a)*, VCLT, *supra* note 470.

The ICJ has interpreted this definition as reflective of customary international law [473], and most States and writers endorse this statement as well [474]. However, this definition has also been widely recognized as incomplete. For instance, agreements by other non-State subjects of international law would not qualify, which is an omission [475].

An instrument need not bear the title of "treaty" to qualify as one. In practice, many different titles are also used, including "act", "agreed minute", "charter", "convention", "covenant", "declaration", "memorandum", "note verbale", "protocol" and "statute" [476].

The primary international legal effect of a treaty is to trigger the foundational international legal principle of *pacta sunt servanda*, according to which its provisions become binding upon the parties and must be performed by them in good faith (Art. 26 of the VCLT). Moreover, a treaty also carries with it secondary international legal effects, including those emerging from the law of treaties, State responsibility and any other specific regimes tied to the treaty's subject matter. The VCLT, and customary international law more generally, will regulate the validity, interpretation, application, breach and termination of a State's treaties [477].

In addition, treaties exercise a constant influence in the formation of customary rules, declaring, crystallizing or even generating them [478], and may provide indicators of what is considered good practice in international law. As such, treaties are important international tools that can exert influence on national-level policy and legal decision-making,

---

473. *Maritime Delimitation in the Indian Ocean (Somalia* v. *Kenya)*, Preliminary Objections, Judgment (2 February 2017), *ICJ Reports 2017*, p. 3, at p. 21, para. 42; *Land and Maritime Boundary between Cameroon and Nigeria (Cameroon* v. *Nigeria: Equatorial Guinea intervening)*, Judgment (10 October 2002), *ICJ Reports 2002*, p. 249, para. 263.

474. On this topic, see the recent document approved by the Inter-American Juridical Committee of the OAS and presented by United States jurist Duncan Hollis, acting as Rapporteur: Guidelines of the Inter-American Juridical Committee for Binding and Non-Binding Agreements, http://www.oas.org/en/sla/iajc/docs/themes_recently_concluded_Binding_and_Non-Binding_Agreements_GUIDELINES.pdf, accessed 3 March 2022.

475. This is the case in the Vienna Convention on the Law of Treaties between States and International Organizations or between International Organizations, adopted on 21 March 1986, not yet in force, 25 ILM, p. 543 (1986).

476. *Pulp Mills on the River Uruguay (Argentina* v. *Uruguay)*, *ICJ Reports 2010*, Judgment (20 April 2010), pp. 132-150 (treating an unsigned joint press statement as an "agreement"), in OAS CJI Guidelines, *supra* note 474.

477. Part V, VCLT, *supra* note 470.

478. Remiro Brotóns, *supra* note 264, p. 216.

as well as on businesses, for instance regarding free, prior and informed consent for investments affecting indigenous people [479].

Malcolm Shaw notes that three main techniques deal with the interpretation of treaties. An objective approach puts an emphasis on the text and the words used. Another school seeks the intention of the parties from a subjective perspective. A third technique employs a teleological approach to center the object and purpose of the treaty as the backdrop for the interpretation of particular treaty provisions [480].

The rules of interpretation of the VCLT reflect customary international law, as decided by the ICJ and other international tribunals on several occasions [481], and the provisions of the VCLT mirror the three approaches prevailing in public international law [482]. As noted by Remiro Brotóns:

> "Article 31 conceives interpretation as a combined operation which, under the umbrella of the good faith principle, come under equal conditions the three criteria of interpretation: grammatical, logical-systematical or contextual and teleological. Text, context, object and purpose of the treaty are intrinsic elements of interpretation since they, in one way or another, reflect the agreement of the parties." [483]

Article 31 (1) of the VCLT states that treaty language is presumed to have its natural and ordinary contextual meaning. A corollary of this provision is the principle of *effet utile*: the words of a substantive treaty provision should be given some rather than no effect. A further corollary is that each treaty must be interpreted in its own terms and in its own right [484].

---

479. UNIDROIT/IFAD ALIC Legal Guide, *supra* note 296, p. 22.

480. "This teleological school of thought has the effect of underlining the role of the judge or arbitrator, since he will be called upon to define the object and purpose of the treaty, and it has been criticized for encouraging judicial law-making", M. N. Shaw Q.C., *International Law*, 6th ed., Cambridge, Cambridge University Press, 2008, pp. 932-933.

481. For example, *The Genocide Convention (Bosnia* v. *Serbia)* case, *ICJ Reports 2007*, paras. 160 ff.; *Indonesia/Malaysia* case, *ICJ Reports 2002*, p. 625, 645-646; *Botswana/Namibia* case, *ICJ Reports 1999*, p. 1045; *Libya/Chad* case, *ICJ Reports 1994*, p. 6, 21-22, 100 ILR, p. 1, 20-21; *Qatar* v. *Bahrain* case, *ICJ Reports 1995*, p. 6, 18, 102 ILR, p. 47, 59. Other courts and tribunals have done likewise: see e.g. the GATT Dispute Settlement Panel Report on United States Restrictions on Imports of Tuna in 1994, 33 ILM, p. 839, 892; the case *Concerning the Auditing of Accounts between the Netherlands and France*, Arbitral Award (12 March 2004), para. 59, and the *Iron Rhine (Belgium/Netherlands)*, Arbitral Award (24 May 2005), para. 45.

482. Shaw, *supra* note 480, p. 933.

483. Remiro Brotóns, *supra* note 264, p. 375.

484. J. Crawford, "Treaty and Contract in Investment Arbitration", *Arbitration International*, Vol. 24, No. 3 (2008), pp. 354-355.

In addition, the interpretation of a treaty must take into account its context (Art. 31 (2) of the VCLT), including the preamble, annexes, any other instrument made by the parties in connection and all aspects of the agreement, from the words employed to the intention of the parties and the aims of the particular document. It is not possible to exclude completely any one of these components [485]. Further, Article 31 (3) *(c)*) includes the principle of "systemic integration", whereby international obligations are interpreted by reference to their normative environment [486]. Since treaties form part of public international law, their provisions exist alongside rights and obligations established by other treaty and customary international law rules, forming a coherent and meaningful whole. In this regard, as the Arbitral Tribunal in the *Georges Pinson* case stated, a treaty must be deemed "to refer to such principles for all questions which it does not itself resolve expressly and in a different way" [487].

Moreover, if the interpretation according to Article 31 needs confirmation, or leads to a manifestly ambiguous, obscure, absurd or unreasonable result, Article 32 authorizes signatories to recur in a supplementary way to the preparatory works *(travaux préparatoires)* of the treaty and the circumstances of its conclusion [488].

Therefore, for example, as decided in the *Amoco* v. *Iran* case, "customary international law may be useful in order to fill in possible lacunae of the law of the Treaty, to ascertain the meaning of undefined terms in its text or, more generally, to aid interpretation and

485. Shaw, *supra* note 480, p. 933. See the *US Nationals in Morocco* case, *ICJ Reports 1952*, p. 176, 196; 19 ILR, p. 255, 272; the *Beagle Channel* case, HMSO, 1977, p. 12; 52 ILR, p. 93; the *Young Loan* arbitration, 59 ILR, p. 495, 530.

486. Article 31 (3) *(c)* of the VCLT provides: "There shall be taken into together account with the context: . . . *(c)* any relevant rules of international law applicable in the relations between the parties".

487. ILC Fragmentation Report, *supra* note 106, pp. 207-209. Many issues arise in relation to this matter in investment arbitration. For instance, in *Esphahanian* v. *Bank Tejarat* the question arose whether a claimant who had dual Iran/US nationality might bring a claim before the Tribunal. The Tribunal expressly employed Article 31 (3) *(c)* of the VCLT in order to justify reference to a wide range of materials on the law of diplomatic protection in international law. These materials supported the Tribunal's conclusion that the applicable rule of international law was that of dominant and effective nationality. *Esphahanian* v. *Bank Tejarat*, 2 *Iran-United States Claims Tribunal Reports* (hereafter IUSCTR), p. 157 (1983-I), 161. See also, to like effect, IUSCT Case No. A/18, 5 IUSCTR, p. 260 (1984-I); ILC Fragmentation Report, pp. 218-219. The matter of dual nationals is, however, highly controversial in investment arbitration.

488. Shaw, *supra* note 480, p. 935.

implementation of its provisions" [489]. Conversely, the preparatory work and circumstances of its conclusion must not be taken into account when they do not confirm the clear meaning given to a treaty provision by applying the general rule of Article 31, which includes "systemic integration". Article 32, therefore, only applies in a supplementary way [490].

C. *Treaties and international investments*

While customary international law traditionally prevailed in the past in disputes involving foreign investments, treaties are now the primary means through which aliens seek protection of their rights [491]. Crude substantive standards set out in customary law or in articulations of general principles shift the needle toward the existence of a "treatified" law on investment protection. Contemporary treaties sometimes incorporate the classic customary rules, and other times move beyond them [492].

In the modern era, a web of bilateral, regional and multilateral investment treaties [493] make up the landscape for the protection of foreign investors that fall under their provisions. These treaties provide for standards of protection that, when breached, result in liability under international law [494].

Some treaties also confer safeguards on contractual rights, the extent of which is highly controversial [495]. Modern investment treaties

489. *Amoco International Finance Corporation* v. *Iran*, IUSCT Case No. 56, 15 IUSCTR, p. 189 (1987-II), at 222, para. 112. See also ILC Fragmentation Report, *supra* note 106, p. 95.

490. R. Gardiner, *Treaty Interpretation*, 2nd ed., Oxford, Oxford University Press, 2017, p. 410.

491. Collins, *supra* note 66, p. 33.

492. "Modern treaties sometimes clarify the classic ambiguities or replace the unsatisfactory solutions. Other times, they sometimes permit different approaches to exist simultaneously, and other times maintain a constructive ambiguity regarding the precise relationship between the different rules", M. Paparinskis, "Investment Treaty Interpretation and Customary Investment Law: Preliminary Remarks", in C. Brown and K. Miles (eds.), *Evolution in Investment Treaty Law and Arbitration*, Cambridge, Cambridge University Press, 2011, p. 65.

493. UNCTAD maintains a complete and user-friendly International Investment Agreements Navigator, see https://investmentpolicy.unctad.org/international-investment-agreements, accessed 3 March 2022.

494. Hollis, *supra* note 467, pp. 6-7. "Treaties do not provide international tribunals with a *carte blanche*; the rules for prosecuting claims in investment treaty arbitration must be fair and just and the system for the resolution of investment disputes must be internally coherent and sustainable for the duration of the treaty", *ibid.*, p. xxiii.

495. Ho, *supra* note 212, pp. 50-51. "The root of the problem is that investment treaties tend to say nothing, or only very little, about how they relate to contracts.

have left a significant degree of uncertainty when it comes to the way international law rules interact with contracts [496]. Rapporteur García-Amador's ILC project on State responsibility, discussed previously, advanced the position that non-performance of State contracts could give rise to international responsibility. The idea generated much opposition until finally expunged by his successor, Rapporteur Roberto Ago, as will be further addressed in Chapter XIV. Until today, there is still no comprehensive corpus offering clear guidance on the matter.

Another controversy relates to the interaction between treaties and customary international law [497]. The ILC Articles on State Responsibility recognize the existence of distinct regimes of State responsibility by incorporating an important *lex specialis* reservation in Article 55 [498]. If a treaty exists, it prevails over customary international law.

For instance, in *CMS* v. *Argentina* [499], Argentina successfully raised the defense of necessity according to customary international law (as codified in Article 25 of the ILC Articles on State Responsibility), precluding assignment of liability to Argentina for breach of its obligations under Article 11 of the US-Argentina Bilateral Investment Treaty. The *ad hoc* Annulment Committee confirmed the interpretation that Article 11 of the treaty *(lex specialis)* takes precedence over Article 25 as *lex generalis* (international customary law).

In relation to this matter, an ILC report explains that systemic interpretation must be performed under

> "presumptions, one positive, the other negative: *(a)* According to the positive presumption, parties are taken 'to refer to general

---

Investment treaties largely do not spell out the consequences of their application to contracts for questions related to breached obligations, defenses, forum selection, calculating damages, or the whole host of terms articulating the life of any contractual agreement", Arato, *supra* note 40, p. 355.

496. Arato, *supra* note 39, p. 19.

497. In *Ghella* v. *Venezuela*, the Tribunal determined that the invoking the ILC as a source of consent leading to jurisdiction is not possible. *Ghella SpA* v. *República Bolivariana de Venezuela and CA Metro de Valencia*, ICC Case No. 24776/JPA, Final Award (16 March 2022), para. 163.

498. These articles do not apply where and to the extent that the conditions for the existence of an internationally wrongful act or the content or implementation of the international responsibility of a State are governed by special rules of international law. The ILC's Articles clarify secondary obligations from a reservation in Article 33.2, "This Part is without prejudice to any right, arising from the international responsibility of a State, which may accrue directly to any person or entity other than a State", Hollis, *supra* note 467, pp. 95-96.

499. *CMS* v. *Argentina*, *supra* note 84, Decision of the *ad hoc* Committee on the Application for Annulment of the Argentine Republic (25 September 2007) (Gillaume, Elaraby, Crawford).

principles of international law for all questions which [the treaty] does not itself resolve in express terms or in a different way'[648]; *(b)* According to the negative presumption, in entering into treaty obligations, the parties intend not to act inconsistently with generally recognized principles of international law or with previous treaty obligations towards third States"[500].

Typically, investment cases refer to customary international law "where the treaty rule is unclear or open-textured and its meaning is determined by reference to a developed body of international law, or the terms used in the treaty have a recognized meaning in customary international law, to which the parties can therefore be taken to have intended to refer". Examples flow from the construction of the terms "fair and equitable treatment" and "full protection and security", interpreted by the North American Free Trade Agreement (NAFTA) Free Trade Commission in *Pope & Talbot* v. *Canada*[501].

D. *Investment treaty regime*

In the mid-1970s, the customary international law related to the protection of international investments was the subject of much development and modification. While several developing States often preached one thing in the United Nations, as described in the previous chapter, they practiced another in the negotiation and drafting of their bilateral and multilateral agreements[502]. Today, foreign investments not subject to any investment treaty protection whatsoever are the exception to the general norm[503].

Many instruments incorporate a certain degree of investment protection, ranging from those referring specifically to foreign investments, such as bilateral or multilateral investment treaties[504], to others containing some rules on the topic. For instance, many WTO Agreements contain certain rules on investment that are rather marginal in comparison with the other matters dealt with in the bilateral investment treaties, as will be further addressed below[505].

500. See ILC Fragmentation Report, *supra* note 106, p. 234.
501. *Pope & Talbot Inc.* v. *Canada* (31 May 2002), NAFTA Arbitral Tribunal, 41 ILM, p. 1347, citing the Interpretation of the NAFTA Free Trade Commission. See ILC Fragmentation Report, *supra* note 106, p. 235.
502. Lowenfeld, *supra* note 25, p. 495.
503. Lim, Ho and Paparinskis, *supra* note 76, p. 57.
504. The UNCTAD website provides a database of international investment agreements at http://investmentpolicyhub.unctad.org/IIA, accessed 3 March 2022.
505. See Sec. F in this chapter, *infra*, "Multilateral and regional investment treaties".

As noted by Jeswald Salacuse, one can characterize the existing body of investment treaties as a *regime*, with significant differences from other international regimes. The international investment regime has three features. One, it has largely been constructed bilaterally, rather than multilaterally. Two, it gives rise to private and decentralized decision-making. And three, in contrast to the WTO, no multilateral international organization supports the foreign investment regime [506].

E. Bilateral investment treaties

1. The first BITs

In the 1950s, the United States signed seventeen Friendship, Commerce and Navigation treaties [507]. Since these instruments dealt with investment-related issues, some texts referred to them as bilateral investment treaties (BITs). However, the 1959 agreement between Germany and Pakistan (which entered into force in 1962) is generally considered the first modern bilateral investment treaty [508]. Much of the inspiration for this and the later treaties came from the 1959 Abs-Shawcross Draft Convention on Investments Abroad and the 1967 OECD Draft Convention on the Protection of Foreign Property [509].

These bilateral treaties essentially guaranteed foreign investments non-discriminatory treatment, protection and security, just compensation in the event of expropriation and freedom from restrictions on the transfer of capital and returns [510]. While they did not contain a dispute resolution clause that could be invoked by injured investors, these first modern investment treaties did open the door to other, similar instruments for investment protection. The 1968 BIT between Indonesia and the Netherlands was the first to introduce a provision to settle claims with foreign investors via an arbitration offer [511].

---

506. Salacuse, *supra* note 65, pp. 9-20.
507. Collins, *supra* note 66, p. 35.
508. Treaty between the Federal Republic of Germany and Pakistan for the Promotion and Protection of Investment, signed on 25 November 1959, http://investmentpolicyhub.unctad.org/Download/TreatyFile/1387, accessed 3 March 2022.
509. Parra, *supra* note 366, p. 22.
510. A. R. Parra, *The History of ICSID*, Oxford, Oxford University Press, 2012, p. 21.
511. See https://investmentpolicy.unctad.org/international-investment-agreements/treaties/bit/1987/indonesia---netherlands-bit-1968, accessed 18 May 2022.

2. *Later evolution*

By 1989, there were 385 BITs in force. UNCTAD reported the existence of approximately 900 BITs at the beginning of the 1990s, which jumped to over 2,900 by the end of the decade [512]. According to UNCTAD, by the end of December 2020 there were 2,659 international investment agreements in force, among them BITs and other economic agreements that include investment-related provisions, referred to as Treaties with Investment Provisions or "TIPs" [513].

Interestingly, more than 770 BITs were negotiated between developing States in the 2000s, which outnumbered the number of treaties negotiated between developing and developed States [514].

3. *Common features in most BITs*

There is a "surprising degree of uniformity" between most BITs, as they are often based upon model treaties that had been drafted by "the main capital-exporting nations" [515]. BITs converge in structure, scope and content, which is particularly striking considering the failures to achieve a global multilateral investment treaty and the flexibility that a bilateral instrument brings about in tailoring specific rights and obligations [516].

Most bilateral investment treaties are divided into three parts: scope, substantive protection and dispute settlement [517]. They are generally preceded by a preamble, followed by definitions of "investment" and "investors", and then conditions on the admission of a foreign investor. They also contain standards and guarantees to be observed by host States, followed by miscellaneous protections regarding currency transfer and the hiring of personnel. Finally, BITs incorporate dispute settlement mechanisms geared toward resolving issues between States and, more significantly, between investors and States (usually setting arbitration as the default mechanism).

---

512. Sornarajah, *supra* note 29, p. 2.
513. UNCTAD Investment Policy Monitor, No. 24, February 2021, pp. 7-8.
514. Dolzer and Schreuer, *supra* note 382, p. 21.
515. Blackaby *et al.*, *supra* note 255, p. 470. Although differences exist, for instance, between the United States' most investor-protective 1987 model, adopted in many treaties, and later models. Moreover, Alvarez notes that seemingly identical BIT guarantees – such as FET – exist within treaties whose object and purpose may be as different as is suggested by the respective preambles of the proposed Norway BIT of 2007 and that of the US Model BIT of 1987. See Alvarez, *supra* note 26, pp. 316-317.
516. Schill, *supra* note 30, p. 11.
517. Collins, *supra* note 66, pp. 38-39.

Thus, investors can avail themselves of the treaty protections both in terms of the standards of treatment and the choice of forum. In addition, BITs typically grant investors standing to bring forward claims on their own.

4. Substantive standards included in BITs

BITs generally include clauses such as the guarantee of non-expropriation or equivalent measures without compensation; fair and equitable treatment; the right to national treatment; the rights to most-favored-nation status and to non-discriminatory treatment; full protection and security; no arbitrary or discriminatory measures impairing the investment; free transfer of funds related to investments; and, last but not least, umbrella clauses. These substantive standards are explained below.

(a) *Guarantee of non-expropriation or equivalent measures without compensation*

One of the most frequently invoked guarantees within investment claims is the obligation to compensate for expropriation [518]. This guarantee is also articulated in a similar fashion within investment treaties [519], which usually require that expropriation be for a public

518. For instance, an ICC report notes that

> "in cases regarding State interference to financial institutions, prohibition of expropriation is one of the standards mostly invoked. Expropriation claims by investors in financial institutions have been invoked at a secondary level, mainly because FET claims seem to be more successful for investments in financial institutions and products. A characteristic obstacle for claimants is that, in order to claim expropriation, the investors must show that they were substantially deprived of the economic value of their investments as a result of State interference; at the same time, it is extremely difficult to distinguish the reduction in investment value caused by such interference from the decrease in value caused by financial crises generally".

ICC Commission Report, *supra* note 91, p. 14.

519. For example, Article 3 (1) of the United States-Argentina BIT states:

> "Investments shall not be expropriated or nationalized either directly or indirectly through measures tantamount to expropriation or nationalization ('expropriation') except for a public purpose; in a non-discriminatory manner; upon payment of prompt, adequate and effective compensation; and in accordance with due process of law and the general principles of treatment provided for in Article II (2). Compensation shall be equivalent to the fair market value of the expropriated investment immediately before the expropriatory action was taken or became known, whichever is earlier; be paid without delay; include interest at a commercially reasonable rate from the date of expropriation; be fully realizable; and be freely transferable at the prevailing market rate of exchange on the date of expropriation."

purpose, performed in accordance with due process and accompanied by payment of prompt, adequate and effective compensation [520].

> "To qualify for compensation, expropriation can be either direct or indirect. Direct expropriation refers to the outright physical seizure of property or its title [521]. By contrast, indirect expropriation originates from measures that amount to a substantial deprivation of the use and value of the investment, regardless of the fact that actual title to the asset may still remain with the investor." [522]

In *Total* v. *Argentina*, an ICSID Arbitral Tribunal wrote that:

> "Under international law a measure which does not have all the features of a formal expropriation could be equivalent to an expropriation if an effective deprivation of the investment is thereby caused. An effective deprivation requires, however, a total loss of value of the property such as when the property affected is rendered worthless by the measure, as in case of direct expropriation, even if formal title continues to be held." [523]

In determining whether an indirect expropriation has occurred, tribunals usually consider the economic impact and duration of the

---

520. Lim, Ho and Paparinskis, *supra* note 76, p. 323.

521. UNCTAD, Expropriation: A Sequel (IIA, Series Two), 2012, http://unctad.org/en/Docs/unctaddiaeia2011d7_en.pdf, accessed 3 March 2022, p. 7; *Crystallex International Corporation* v. *Bolivarian Republic of Venezuela*, ICSID Case No. ARB(AF)11/2, Award (4 April 2016), para. 667, cited in Lim, Ho and Paparinskis, *supra* note 76, p. 323; or, "formal or official withdrawal of property rights", Collins, *supra* note 66, p. 158, referring to decisions in the cases: *Sempra* v. *Argentina*, *supra* note 451, Award (2007), para. 280; *Enron* v. *Argentina*, *supra* note 451, Award (2007), para. 243.

522. OECD, "*'Indirect Expropriation'* and the *'Right to Regulate'* in International Investment Law", Working Paper on International Investment No. 2004/4 (September 2004), http://www.oecd.org/daf/inv/investment-policy/WP-2004_4.pdf, accessed 3 March 2022.

523. *Total* v. *Argentina*, *supra* note 16, paras. 195–196. The taking of control or interference in management by the State may also amount to an indirect expropriation. In *Sempra Energy International* v. *Argentine Republic*, it was stated that "depriving the investor of control over the investment, managing the day-to-day operations of the company, arresting and detaining company officials or employees, supervising the work of officials, interfering in administration, impeding the distribution of dividends, interfering in the appointment of official or managers, or depriving the company of its property or control in whole or in part" amounted to an indirect expropriation. *Sempra* v. *Argentina*, *supra* note 451, Award (September 28, 2007), para. 284. See also *Pope & Talbot* v. *Canada*, *supra* note 501, Award on Damages (31 May 2002); *PSEG Global, Inc., The North American Coal Corporation, and Konya Ingin Electrik Üretim ve Ticaret Ltd.* v. *Republic of Turkey*, ICSID Case No. ARB/02/5, Award (19 January 2007), para. 278.

governmental measures affecting the investment and the degree to which they have interfered with the investor's reasonable expectations [524].

In exceptional circumstances, the burdensome imposition of taxes can qualify as indirect expropriation as well [525].

Actions that run contrary to governmental assurances or undertakings can also fall within the category of indirect expropriation. In *CME* v. *Czech Republic*, the Tribunal determined that measures taken by the Czech regulatory authority interfered with the "economic and legal basis of CME's investment" and "destroy[ed] the legal basis ["the safety net"] of the Claimant's investment", which ruined the "commercial value of the investment" and thus amounted to expropriation [526].

In the absence of assurances or undertakings made by the government, however, a State exercising its bona fide capacity to regulate through the use of its police powers, for instance, should not be considered indirect expropriation, as was decided in the *Methanex* v. *USA* case [527]. In *Philip Morris* v. *Uruguay*, the Tribunal considered whether Uruguay's cigarette packaging measures constituted an indirect expropriation. The claimants argued that the host State's cigarette packaging regulations indirectly expropriated their intellectual property and destroyed their brand equity, with a substantial effect on profits. The Tribunal concluded that the measures in question were a valid exercise by Uruguay of its police powers aimed at protecting public health, and subsequently rejected the expropriation claim [528].

However, despite the wealth of case law that exists on this subject, the meaning of expropriation and the scope of the right to compensation in the context of environmental or public health regulation [529].

---

524. *LG&E remains* v. *Argentina unsettled*, *supra* note 448, Decision on Liability (3 October 2006), para. 190.

525. "A tax measure may be tantamount to expropriation if *(i)* it produces the effects required for any indirect expropriation and *(ii)* in addition, it is discriminatory, arbitrary, involves a denial of due process or an abuse of rights" (*Burlington Resources Inc.* v. *Republic of Ecuador*, ICSID Case No. ARB/08/5, Decision on Liability (14 December 2012), para. 375).

526. *CME* v. *Czech Republic*, *supra* note 54, Final Award (14 March 2003), paras. 551, 554, 555, and 591.

527. *Methanex Corporation* v. *United States of America*, UNCITRAL, Final Award on Jurisdiction and Merits (19 August 2005), para. 7.

528. *Philip Morris Brand Sàrl (Switzerland), Philip Morris Products SA (Switzerland) and Abal Hermanos SA (Uruguay)* v. *Oriental Republic of Uruguay*, ICSID Case No. ARB/10/7, Award (8 July 2016). See also *Philip Morris Asia Limited* v. *The Commonwealth of Australia*, UNCITRAL, PCA Case No. 2012-12.

529. B. Cremades and D. J. A. Cairns, "Contract and Treaty Claims and Choice of Forum in Foreign Investment Disputes", in N. Horn and S. Kröll (eds.), *Arbitrating Foreign Investment Disputes: Procedural and Substantive Legal Aspects* (Studies in

Now, simple contractual breaches made by the State outside of its sovereign regulatory capacity do not constitute an indirect expropriation [530]. This is not the case, however, when the State acts in its regulatory capacity and expropriates contractual rights by terminating the agreement by decree [531] or by performing a series of "sovereign acts designed illegitimately to end the concession or to force its renegotiation" [532]. Indeed, such acts will fall within the category of indirect expropriation.

Additionally, cases such as *CMS* v. *Argentina* [533] and *LG&E* v. *Argentina* [534] determined that a diminution in the value of an investment due to a violation of the standard of fair and equitable treatment does not constitute expropriation of either type, as the claimants in both cases remained in full control of their investment [535]. Other tribunals have determined that indirect expropriation can result from cumulative measures that together substantially reduce the value of the investment (known as creeping expropriation) [536]. In *Siemens* v. *Argentina*, the ICSID Tribunal wrote that:

> "By definition, creeping expropriation refers to a process, to steps that eventually have the effect of an expropriation. Obviously, each step must have an adverse effect but by itself may not be significant or considered an illegal act. The last step in a creeping expropriation that tilts the balance is similar to the straw that breaks the camel's back. The preceding straws may not

---

Transnational Economic Law, No. 19), The Hague, Kluwer Law International, 2004, p. 341.

530. *Waste Management Inc.* v. *United Mexican States*, ICSID Case No. ARB(AF)/00/3, Award (30 April 2004), para. 175. See also *Biwater Gauff (Tanzania) Ltd.* v. *United Republic of Tanzania*, ICSID Case No. ARB/05/22, Award (24 July 2008), para. 458. *Parkerings-Compagniet AS* v. *Republic of Lithuania*, ICSID Case No. ARB/05/8, Award (11 September 2007), paras. 443-445; *Azurix* v. *Argentina*, *supra* note 327, Award (2006), para. 315; *Suez* v. *Argentina*, *supra* note 51, Decision on Liability, paras. 140-145.

531. *Siemens AG* v. *The Argentine Republic*, ICSID Case No. ARB/02/8, Award (17 January 2007), para. 271.

532. *Vivendi* v. *Argentina*, *supra* note 456, Award (20 August 2007), para. 7.5.22.

533. *CMS* v. *Argentina*, *supra* note 84, Award (2005), para. 252-265.

534. *LG&E* v. *Argentina*, *supra* note 448, Decision on Liability (2006), paras. 198-200.

535. Lowenfeld, *supra* note 25, p. 562.

536. See UNCTAD, Taking of Property (IIA, Series One), 24 March 2000, http://unctad.org/en/docs/psiteiitd15.en.pdf, accessed 3 March 2022, p. 11. See also the Restatement (Third) of Foreign Relations Law of the United States, para. 712.

have a perceptible effect but are part of the process that led to the break." [537]

Many investment treaties refer to both direct and indirect expropriation, precisely in order to include creeping expropriations [538].

Indirect expropriations always involve prior assurances given to an investor followed by government action that wholly or significantly deprives them of their reasonable expectations regarding the investment [539]. As such, courts have ruled that it is the effects, rather than the intention, of the expropriation that are determinative [540].

Moreover, since the typical expropriation provision usually includes concepts such as discrimination and due process in its terms, it is not surprising that potential exists for blurring the lines between expropriation and other standards of treatment [541]. In general, tribunals have shown a tendency to construe indirect expropriation narrowly, considering the potential for the concept of direct expropriation to encompass a broad range of measures if not restricted [542].

---

537. *Siemens* v. *Argentina*, *supra* note 531, Award (17 January 2007), para. 263. See also *Biwater Gauff* v. *Tanzania*, *supra* note 530, Award (2008), para. 455; *Walter Bau AG* v. *The Kingdom of Thailand*, UNCITRAL, Award (1 July 2009), para. 10.10; Similarly, a tribunal determined that the refusal of a local agency to renew a permit for a landfill constituted expropriation, even though legal ownership of the assets was not affected. *Técnicas Medioambientales Tecmed SA* v. *United Mexican States*, ICSID Case No. ARB(AF)/00/2, Award (29 May 2003), para. 116, cited in Lowenfeld, *supra* note 25, p. 563. According to another tribunal that referred to *Tecmed* v. *Mexico*, the standard for determining creeping expropriation depends on the extent to which the measure in question constitutes a deprivation of the economic use and enjoyment of the land, as if the rights taken therefrom, such as income or benefits, ceased to exist: *Spyridonn Roussalis* v. *Romania*, ICSID Case No. ARB/06/01, Award (2011), para. 328, cited in Lim, Ho and Paparinskis, *supra* note 76, p. 336.

538. Lowenfeld, *supra* note 25, p. 559.

539. *Eureko BV* v. *Republic of Poland*, UNCITRAL, Partial Award of the *ad hoc* Committee (19 August 2005), 12 *ICSID Reports*, p. 331, para. 242; *Fireman's Fund Insurance Co.* v. *The United Mexican States*, ICSID Case No. ARB(AF)/02/01, Award (2006), para. 176; *ADC Affiliate Ltd. and ADC & ADMC Management Ltd.* v. *Republic of Hungary*, ICSID Case No. ARB/03/16, Award (2006), para. 424; *LG&E* v. *Argentina*, *supra* note 448, Decision on Liability (3 October 2006), para. 190.

540. *Vivendi* v. *Argentina*, *supra* note 456, Award (21 November 2000), para. 7.5.20; *CDSE* v. *Costa Rica*, *supra* note 455, Final Award (17 February 2000), paras. 71-72; *Phillips Petroleum Co. Iran* v. *Islamic Republic of Iran*, 21 IUSCTR, p. 79 (1989), paras. 115–116.

541. T. J. Grierson-Weiler and I. A. Laird, "Standards of Treatment", in P. Muchlinski, F. Ortino and C. Schreuer (eds.), *The Oxford Handbook of International Investment Law*, Oxford, Oxford University Press, 2008, p. 267.

542. Collins, *supra* note 66, p. 168.

(b) *Fair and Equitable Treatment*

Fair and equitable treatment is "perhaps the most important principle of foreign investment" legal matters [543], contained in almost all relevant investment treaties [544] and usually addressed therein at the beginning of the general treatment clauses [545]. At a minimum this standard means there can be no discrimination by nationality or origin in respect of such matters as access to local courts and administrative bodies, applicable taxes or governmental regulations. Fair and equitable treatment generally stands independent in investment treaties from other standards to make it clear that it applies even if no discrimination can be shown [546].

The Arbitral Tribunal in the *Waste Management* v. *Mexico* case described it in the following manner:

> "[T]he minimum standard of treatment of fair and equitable treatment is infringed by conduct attributable to the State and harmful to the claimant if the conduct is arbitrary, grossly unfair, unjust or idiosyncratic, is discriminatory and exposes the claimant to sectional or racial prejudice, or involves a lack of due process leading to an outcome which offends judicial propriety – as might be the case with a manifest failure of natural justice in judicial proceedings or a complete lack of transparency and candour in an administrative process. In applying this standard, it is relevant that the treatment is in breach of representations made by the host State which were reasonably relied on by the claimant." [547]

---

543. Subedi, *supra* note 17, p. 63

544. UNCTAD, Fair and Equitable Treatment: A Sequel (IIA, Series Two), 2012, http://unctad.org/en/Docs/unctaddiaeia2011d5_en.pdf, accessed 3 March 2022, pp. 17–35.

545. For instance, Article II (2) *(a)* of the United States-Argentina BIT states: "Investment shall at all times be accorded fair and equitable treatment, shall enjoy full protection and security and shall in no case be accorded treatment less than that required by international law."

546. Lowenfeld, *supra* note 25, p. 557.

547. *Waste Management* v. *Mexico*, *supra* note 530, Award (30 April 2004), para. 98. The Arbitral Tribunal in *Joseph Charles Lemire* v. *Ukraine* characterizes the fair and equitable treatment standard as requiring

> "an action or omission by the State which violates a certain threshold of propriety, causing harm to the investor, and with a causal link between action or omission and harm. The tribunal must determine if the State failed to offer a stable and predictable legal framework to the investor. The tribunal must also consider if the State had made specific representations to the investor, if due process was denied, and if the State acted with a lack of transparency. The tribunal must also take into consideration any harassment, coercion, abuse of power, or other bad faith

More recently, in *Mesa Power* v. *Canada* [548], the Tribunal referred to the award issued in the *Waste Management* v. *Mexico* case, confirming the elements mentioned in this decision [549].

One of the most important functions of the fair and equitable treatment standard is that it fills in the gaps left by the more specific standards. It is therefore seen as "a way to actually achieve the desired degree of security for investors that international treaties are designed to protect" [550].

A "sizeable number of contract-based fair and equitable claims" have been made on this standard, proving its relevance within international law [551]. There is a notable success rate for claims that invoke it, which fuels the perception that it is the most investment-friendly standard of protection [552]. Its popularity and success are related to the fact that a violation of this standard may be easier to establish than expropriation [553].

In addition, most treaties state the standard laconically, which has contributed to its controversiality [554]: in recent years, there have been a series of overly broad readings of the fair and equitable treatment standard, which has resulted in a backlash against investment arbitration [555]. As stated by Christian Sommer, the indeterminacy of this standard and the ample criteria of the arbitrators for its determination leads to uncertainties in the States receiving investments. More objective parameters are needed to guide the implementation of appropriate policies by host States [556].

One source of ambiguity is that the principle of fair and equitable treatment is included in treaties without any reference to an applicable

---

conduct on behalf of the State, and determine whether any of the State's actions should be considered arbitrary, discriminatory, or inconsistent".

(*Joseph Charles Lemire* v. *Ukraine*, ICSID Case No. ARB/06/18, Decision on Jurisdiction and Liability (14 January 2010), para. 284). See Blackaby *et al.*, *supra* note 255, p. 479.

548. *Mesa Power Group LLC* v. *Government of Canada*, PCA Case No. 2012-17, Award (24 March 2016).

549. *Ibid.*, para. 501.

550. Collins, *supra* note 66, p. 127.

551. Ho, *supra* note 212, pp. 90-91.

552. *Ibid.*, p. 101.

553. Lim, Ho and Paparinskis, *supra* note 76, p. 259.

554. Arato, *supra* note 39, p. 19.

555. Lim, Ho and Paparinskis, *supra* note 76, p. 260. In similar terms, Collins mentions that the breadth of the fair and equitable treatment clause is often a point of contention within the criticisms levied against investor-State dispute settlement, in particular relating to the excessive discretion of the arbitrators applying it. See Collins, *supra* note 66, p. 127.

556. C. Sommer, *Laudos Arbitrales del CIADI*, Buenos Aires, Astrea, 2016, pp. 30-31.

international standard against which to measure it. In the words of Giorgio Sacerdoti, this ambiguous language is "possibly [used] as a way of avoiding the divergence surrounding the latter and in order to give to it a direct content" [557]. The issue is raised recurrently when treaties use – as they do often – the expression "fair and equitable treatment in accordance with international law". Does this wording imply the traditional customary international law protection related to the minimum standard of treatment?

As seen in Chapter III, the "international minimum standard of treatment" (MST) within customary international law, enshrined in the *Neer* standard, referred to "an outrage", "bad faith", "wilful neglect of duty" or "an insufficiency of governmental actions". This formula was considered to be of quite limited application, and for this reason it was later expanded through treaties and through the notion of "fair and equitable treatment" and "full protection and security" of foreign investments. Much case law has since further discussed the intricacies of the fair and equitable treatment standard. However, the debate regarding its content is ongoing [558].

In fact, whether the fair and equitable treatment principle and the minimum international treatment standard are synonymous is the subject of much disagreement. Some consider both to be one and the same. Yet another view asserts that both standards are distinct. In particular, State respondents to treaty claims argue that "fair and equitable treatment" is a discrete and objective treaty standard, a particular form of *lex specialis* that can be found in many, but not all, such agreements, and does not necessarily correspond to the treatment required under customary international law [559].

The debate is, however, not yet settled [560]. In this regard, the ICSID Tribunal in the *Vivendi* v. *Argentina* case stated the following:

---

557. Sacerdoti refers to international instruments, and notes that Article 2 (2) *(c)* of the 1974 United Nations Charter of Economic Rights and Duties of States articulated only the national standard for the treatment of foreign investment, reflecting the critical view by the developing world of the minimum international standard as being vague and possibly biased, in Sacerdoti, *supra* note 67, p. 343.

558. UNCTAD, Fair and Equitable Treatment (IIA, Series One), 17 September 1999, http://unctad.org/en/Docs/psiteiitd11v3.en.pdf, accessed 3 March 2022, pp. 39-40.

559. See Grierson-Weiler and Laird, *supra* note 541, p. 262.

560. NAFTA Free Trade Commission, Notes of Interpretation of Certain Chapter 11 Provisions, issued on 31 July 2001, in Cremades and Cairns, *supra* note 529, p. 341. Mills, *supra* note 28, p. 104:

> "Those who view international investment law as a regime of emerging universal international standards are more likely to view an FET obligation as invoking the general standards of customary international law – characterising the object and

"The Tribunal sees no basis for equating principles of international law with the minimum standard of treatment . . . one should also look to contemporary principles of international law, not only to principles from almost a century ago." [561]

In contrast, the NAFTA Tribunal in *Mondev* v. *USA* considered the *Neer* standard to have evolved. According to the Tribunal, "[t]o the modern eye, what is unfair or inequitable need not equate with the outrageous or the egregious. In particular, a State may treat foreign investment unfairly and inequitably without necessarily acting in bad faith" [562]. Indeed, this is what would have occurred if the minimum standard within customary international law was applied.

Recently, arbitral tribunals have appeared less interested in the theoretical discussion regarding the distinction between the customary law minimum standard and the principle of fair and equitable treatment and focused their attention on determining the content of the latter [563].

In *Tecmed* v. *Mexico*, the Arbitral Tribunal wrote that fair and equitable treatment requires that "the basic expectations that were taken into account by the foreign investor to make the investment" be respected [564]. Subsequent decisions (that cited the *Tecmed* v. *Mexico* and

---

purpose of the BIT as part of a public multilateral *'standard setting'* process. By contrast, those who view international investment law as a series of negotiated bilateral agreements through which States define their mutual obligations in order to seek a competitive advantage are more likely to view an FET obligation as particular to the specific treaty under consideration – characterising the object and purpose of the BIT as defining the terms of a private *'contractual'* bargain."

561. *Vivendi* v. *Argentina*, *supra* note 456, Award 21 November 2000), para. 7.4.5. See also *Enron* v. *Argentina*, *supra* note 451, Award (22 May 2007), para. 258.

562. *Mondev International Ltd.* v. *United States of America*, ICSID Case No. ARB (AF)/99/2, Final Award (11 October 2002), para. 116.

563. Blackaby *et al.*, *supra* note 255, pp. 481-482. See *Saluka Investments BV* v. *Czech Republic*, UNCITRAL, Partial Award (17 March 2006), paras. 292-295. See also *CMS* v. *Argentina*, *supra* note 84, Award (12 May 2005), para. 284. Jean d'Aspremont notes that "Never has the question of the state of customary international law been more controversial than in connection with fair and equitable treatment. Despite its extremely low normative density – recognized in *Saluka Investments BV* v. *The Czech Republic* – it has been argued that fair and equitable treatment constitutes customary international law", d'Aspremont, *supra* note 30, p. 24. The decision in *Saluka* v. *Czech Republic* states: "such general standards represent principles that cannot be reduced to precise statements of rules [. . . . They] are susceptible of specification through judicial practice and do in fact have sufficient legal content to allow the case to be decided on the basis of law" (*Saluka* Award, *ibid.*, paras. 282–284).

564. The foreign investor expects the host State to act in a consistent manner, free from ambiguity and totally transparently in its relations with the foreign investor, so that it may know beforehand any and all rules and regulations that will govern its investments, as well as the goals of the relevant policies and administrative practices or directives, to be able to plan its investment and comply with such regulations. "The

Waste Management v. *Mexico* cases) stressed the need for a transparent and stable legal framework to identify the investors' "legitimate expectations" that require protection [565]. This "public law principle" of legitimate expectations is present in many domestic legal systems. As part of their general duty of fairness, States should act in a manner consistent with their prior statements of policy or intention, meeting the investor's expectations [566].

In this regard, the legitimate expectations of investors are relevant considerations for tribunals. Analysis of these expectations involves examining how the measure impacts "on the reasonable investment-backed expectations of the investor; and whether the state is attempting to avoid investment-backed expectations that the state created or reinforced through its own acts" [567]. However, as decided in the *LG&E* v. *Argentina* case, "the investor's fair expectations cannot fail to consider parameters such as business risk or industry's regular patterns" [568].

Case law considers breaches of the fair and equitable standard to imply the failure of public authorities to ensure due process, consistency and transparency [569], and indicate the lack of a predictable and stable environment, contrary to the legitimate expectations of the investor [570].

A fine balance must be drawn between State action and the fair treatment of investors in concordance with their legitimate expectations. While States should not have their regulatory autonomy frozen, they cannot treat investors unfairly or inequitably. In *CMS* v. *Argentina*, the Tribunal wrote that:

> "Save for the existence of an agreement, in the form of a stabilisation clause or otherwise, there is nothing objectionable

---

foreign investor also expects the host State to act consistently, i.e., without arbitrarily revoking any pre-existing decisions or permits issued by the state that were relied upon by the investor to assume its commitments as well as to plan and launch its commercial and business activities" (*Tecmed* v. *Mexico*, *supra* note 537, Award (29 May 2003), para. 154, in Alvarez, *supra* note 26, pp. 346-347).

565. *Ibid.*, pp. 346-347.

566. Crawford, *supra* note 484, p. 371.

567. *Saluka* v. *Czech Republic*, *supra* note 563, Partial Award (17 March 2006), para. 302. See also *CME* v. *Czech Republic*, *supra* note 54, Partial Award (13 September 2001), para. 611; *Tecmed* v. *Mexico*, *supra* note 537, Award (2003), para. 157.

568. *LG&E* v. *Argentina*, *supra* note 448, Decision on Liability (3 October 2006), para. 164.

569. *Ibid.*, para. 304. See also *Parkerings* v. *Lithuania*, *supra* note 530, Award (11 September 2007), paras. 335-336; *MTD* v. *Chile*, *supra* note 327, Award (25 May 2004), paras. 176-178.

570. *Maffezini* v. *Spain*, *supra* note 456, Award (2000), para. 83; *Encana Corporation* v. *Republic of Ecuador*, LCIA Case No. UN3481, Award (2006), 12 *ICSID Reports*, p. 427, para. 158.

> about the amendment brought to the regulatory framework existing at the time an investor made its investment. . . . What is prohibited however is for a State to act unfairly, unreasonably or inequitably in the exercise of its legislative power." [571]

It is highly contested whether the "unfair, unreasonable or inequitable" standard for State action truly protects an investor's "legitimate expectations" regarding regulatory changes. To use contract law terminology, does the fair and equitable treatment standard include an implied "stabilization" clause? A growing number of cases use concepts such as non-discrimination, fair and equitable treatment and legitimate expectation to the same end, but in so many different ways [572]. In any case, as explained by Julian Arato, "most tribunals accept that fair and equitable treatment requires protecting investor expectations to some degree" [573].

Investors expect State actions to be consistent, free from ambiguity and totally transparent. If these expectations of State behavior are met, aliens will be aware of the rules governing the investment well in advance and can plan their actions accordingly [574]. According to Alex Mills, in its perhaps strongest form, the standard entails "an obligation not to alter the legal and business environment in which the investment has been made" [575]. Put simply, States should be able to freely enact regulations in their territory, and investors must face a natural degree of regulatory risk, provided that State regulation is undertaken in good faith. The supervision, control, prevention and punitive powers of the State must be used for the purpose of assuring compliance with environmental and human health protection underlying such laws. Thus, substantive obligations in treaties should be interpreted narrowly,

---

571. *CMS* v. *Argentina*, *supra* note 84, Award (2005), para. 276; see also *Occidental Petroleum Corporation et al.* v. *Republic of Ecuador*, LCIA Case No. UN3467, Final Award (1 July 2004), para. 183.

572. Grierson-Weiler and Laird, *supra* note 541, p. 302.

573. Arato, *supra* note 39, p. 19; *Sempra* v. *Argentina*, *supra* note 451, Award (28 September 2007); *Enron* v. *Argentina*, *supra* note 451, Award (22 May 2007); *CMS* v. *Argentina*, *supra* note 84, Award (12 May 2005).

574. *Tecmed* v. *Mexico*, *supra* note 537, Award (29 May 2003), para. 154. See also the reference to the "stability and predictability of the business environment, founded on solemn legal and contractual commitments" in *CMS* v. *Argentina*, *supra* note 84, Award (12 May 2005), para. 284, and to "the obligation to grant and maintain a stable and predictable legal framework necessary to fulfill the justified expectations of the foreign investor", in *LG&E* v. *Argentina*, *supra* note 448, Decision on Liability (3 October 2006), para. 131. *Occidental* v. *Ecuador*, *supra* note 571, Final Award (1 July 2004), para. 191.

575. Mills, *supra* note 28, p. 109.

with a general deference to States where difficult questions of fact or policy arise [576].

Another important requirement for State behavior is that the regulations affecting foreign investments cannot be discriminatory in favor of domestic entities [577]. At a minimum, "fair and equitable treatment" means no discrimination by nationality or origin in matters such as access to local courts and administrative bodies, applicable taxes and administration of governmental regulations [578]. States must also ensure basic protection of their judicial systems, the violation of which can amount to a "denial of justice" [579]. In *Azinian* v. *Mexico*, the NAFTA Tribunal stated the following:

> "[A] denial of justice could be pleaded if the relevant courts refuse to entertain a suit, if they subject it to undue delay, or if they administer justice in a seriously inadequate way. . . . There is a fourth type of denial if justice, namely the clear and malicious misapplication of the law." [580]

(c) *The right to national treatment*

As previously mentioned, customary international law and investment treaties in general impose an obligation on the host State to treat the foreign investor in a manner that is at least as favorable as that granted to its own nationals in like circumstances. Foreign individuals should not be subject to additional requirements that put them at a

---

576. This approach is influenced by public law doctrines looking to balance private rights against public interests, as is the case within administrative law or human rights jurisprudence, whereas another, more traditional approach suggests a greater influence taken from private law doctrines such as contract, property law or estoppel. *Ibid.*, p. 110. McLachlan considers it "regrettable that, to date, no notable effort has been made in the investment arbitration jurisprudence to link the concept of 'fair and equitable treatment' with the specific standards of international human rights law. Reference to these sources would facilitate the application of standards which may be seen as genuinely common to civilized nations", McLachlan, *supra* note 356, p. 396.

577. *Parkerings* v. *Lithuania*, *supra* note 530, Award (11 September 2007), para. 332; *CMS* v. *Argentina*, *supra* note 84, Award (12 May 2005), para. 277.

578. Lowenfeld, *supra* note 25, pp. 556-557.

579. NAFTA tribunals held that a denial of justice constitutes a breach of the standard: see *The Loewen Group Inc. and Raymond L Loewen* v. *United States of America*, ICSID Case No. ARB(AF)/98/3, Award (26 June 2003), para. 132; *Waste Management* v. *Mexico*, *supra* note 530, Award (30 April 2004), para. 98; *International Thunderbird Gaming Corporation* v. *The United Mexican States*, UNCITRAL, Award (26 January 2006), para. 194, rejecting the investors' denial of justice claims.

580. *Azinian* et al. v. *Mexico*, ICSID Case No. ARB(AF)/97/2, Award on Jurisdiction and Merits (1999), 5 *ICSID Reports*, p. 272, para. 102.

competitive disadvantage in comparison to national investors [581]. The notion of "national treatment" has been described in a 1999 UNCTAD document as the "single most important standard of treatment enshrined in international investment agreements" [582].

Tribunals tend to approach claims of national treatment by asking three questions: are circumstances alike? Has the treatment been different? Is there a reasonable justification for such differential treatment [583]? This three-pronged test was established in *Saluka* v. *Czech Republic* [584] and was later replicated by several other tribunals [585].

(d) *The rights to most-favored-nation status and to non-discriminatory treatment*

The most-favored-nation (MFN) and non-discriminatory treatment standards "are not autonomous but comparative protection standards, as such varying case by case. They are usually contemplated in treaties [586], and recognized in case law" [587]. As a consequence, gains obtained in the benefits offered to one State automatically extend to others [588]. In addition to leveling the field among investors from different States, the MFN clause has the ancillary objective of promoting harmony on a global scale "by preventing favoritism on the grounds of nationality" [589].

---

581. On the national treatment right, see R. Dolzer and M. Stevens, *Bilateral Investment Treaties*, The Hague, Kluwer Law International, 1995, pp. 65-66; see also Cremades and Cairns, *supra* note 529, p. 340.

582. UNCTAD, National Treatment (IIA, Series One), 26 November 1999, p. 1.

583. Lim, Ho and Paparinskis, *supra* note 76, p. 299.

584. *Saluka* v. *Czech Republic*, *supra* note 563, Partial Award (2006). This award has been heavily criticized for extending treaty protection to self-induced investor expectations. Ho, *supra* note 46, p. 9.

585. *Quiborax SA, Non Metallic Minerals SA* v. *Plurinational State of Bolivia*, ICSID Case No. ARB/06/2, Award (16 September 2015), para. 247; *Lemire* v. *Ukraine*, *supra* note 547, para. 261; *Champion Trading Company and Ameritrade International, Inc.* v. *Arab Republic of Egypt*, ICSID Case No. ARB/02/9, Award (2006), para. 130; *Total SA* v. *Argentina*, *supra* note 16, Decision on Liability (2010), para. 344. The third element must be assessed under the specific circumstances of each case, as stated by the Tribunal in *Parkerings* v. *Lithuania*, *supra* note 530, Award (2007), para. 368.

586. Article 3 (1) of the United Kingdom-Egypt BIT, for instance, states: "Neither Contracting Party shall in its territory subject investments or returns of investors of the other Contracting Party to treatment less favourable than that which it accords to investment or returns of its own nationals or companies or to investments or returns of nationals or companies of any third State."

587. *Goetz* v. *Burundi*, *supra* note 93, Award, para. 121; *Nykomb Synergetics Technology Holding AB* v. *Republic of Latvia*, SCC, Award (16 December 2003), para. 64; *Saluka* v. *Czech Republic*, *supra* note 563, Partial Award (2006), para. 313.

588. Blackaby *et al.*, *supra* note 255, p. 486.

589. Collins, *supra* note 66, pp. 109-110.

Pia Acconci notes that typically the MFN treatment clause is concerned with how a State deals with foreign goods and persons when they enter its territory and thereafter. The standard essentially evaluates how the State treats investors during the post-establishment phase [590].

Non-discriminatory treatment prohibits measures that discriminate against the foreign investor [591]. The MFN standard, on the other hand, maintains that the nationals of one foreign country must not be treated less favorably than those of another. Of course, States are not obligated to treat all foreign nationals equally. However, a detrimental discriminatory differential treatment could be considered a violation of this standard [592]. A decision in this regard was rendered, for instance, in *Maffezini* v. *Spain* [593].

The MFN standard only applies "in like circumstances" between the foreign and domestic investor [594]. It applies to substantive rights such as taxation benefits, but cases have also extended it to apply to procedural matters as well, such as the determination of the dispute resolution mechanism [595]. As a result, recent investment treaties have tended to be explicit in excluding procedural rights from MFN clauses.

(e) *Full protection and security*

The full protection and security standard (FPS) is also difficult to define. Contrasting "with most of the other investor protections, which impose restrictions or prohibitions on certain types of host state activity,

590. P. Acconci, "Most-Favoured-Nation Treatment", in P. Muchlinski, F. Ortino and C. Schreuer (eds.), *The Oxford Handbook of International Investment Law*, Oxford, Oxford University Press, 2008, p. 381.

591. Cremades and Cairns, *supra* note 529, p. 341.

592. Sacerdoti, *supra* note 67, p. 344.

593. Decision of the Tribunal on Objections to Jurisdiction (25 January 2000), *ICSID Review: Foreign Investment Law Journal*, Vol. 15 (2001), p. 212, paras. 38-64. See Cremades and Cairns, *supra* note 529, p. 341. See also the discussions regarding the backlash to arbitration clauses in F. Pérez-Aznar, "The Use of Most-Favoured-Nation Clauses to Import Substantive Treaty Provisions in International Investment Agreements", *Journal of International Economic Law*, Vol. 20, No. 4 (2017), pp. 777, 801.

594. *Parkerings* v. *Lithuania*, *supra* note 530, Award (2007), para. 368; *United Parcel Service of America Inc.* v. *Government of Canada*, ICSID Case No. UNCT/02/1, Award (24 May 2007), paras. 173-184.

595. *Gami Investments Inc.* v. *The Government of the United Mexican States*, Award, UNCITRAL (15 November 2004), para. 114; *Parkerings* v. *Lithuania*, *supra* note 530, Award (2007), para. 371. *EDF International* et al. v. *Argentine Republic*, ICSID Case No. ARB/03/23, Award (2012), para. 929; Lim, Ho and Paparinskis, *supra* note 76, p. 320.

the 'full protection and security' clause seeks to impose certain positive obligations on the host state to protect investments"[596].

The FPS standard relates to the prevention of physical damages in the State's exercise of its governmental functions through policing and through the maintenance of law and order[597]. As decided in *AAPL* v. *Sri Lanka*[598], the standard is one of the most significant initiatives requiring the host State to exercise, within its means, due care (or the *obligation de moyens*), to protect investments. This standard does not impose "strict liability"[599]. While the Tribunal in *AAPL* v. *Sri Lanka* did not conclude that the government officials were themselves responsible for the harm done to the investment in question, they did conclude that the governmental authorities failed to take the appropriate precautionary measures to prevent such harm[600].

The Tribunal in *Wena* v. *Egypt*[601] assigned responsibility for the harm done to Egypt even if the State itself had not instigated the actions or participated in them[602]. In turn, the Tribunal in *The Eurotunnel Arbitration*[603] considered that the obligation to guarantee full protection and security was not simply a "best endeavors" obligation or an "obligation of means" but rather the imposition of an "obligation of conduct" on the host State[604]. Thus, the FPS standard is distinct from the protection provided by the State to its own nationals or to nationals of other countries[605].

The scope of the FPS standard has been extended to other circumstances beyond requiring the State to offer physical protection for investments[606]. For instance, other violations of the FPS standard include withdrawing an authorization or approval that is vital to

596. Blackaby *et al.*, *supra* note 255, p. 482.

597. Fair and Equitable Treatment (UNCTAD Series), *supra* note 544, p. 59. *AAPL* v. *Sri Lanka*, *supra* note 453, Final Award (27 June 1990); *AMT* v. *Zaire*, *supra* note 84, Award (21 February 1997); *Rumeli Telekom AS and Telsim Mobil Telekomunikasyon Hizmetleri AS* v. *Republic of Kazakhstan*, ICSID Case No. ARB/05/16, Award (29 July 2008).

598. *AAPL* v. *Sri Lanka*, *supra* note 453, Final Award (1990).

599. UNIDROIT Principles of International Commercial Contracts 2016, Article 5.1.4.

600. Lowenfeld, *supra* note 25, p. 558.

601. *Wena Hotels Ltd.* v. *Egypt*, ICSID Case No. ARB/98/4, Award (8 December 2000).

602. Lim, Ho and Paparinskis, *supra* note 76, p. 278.

603. *Channel Tunnel Group and Another* v. *UL Secretary for Transport and Another*, PCA, Partial Award (2007).

604. Lim, Ho and Paparinskis, *supra* note 76, pp. 278-279.

605. *Pantechniki SA Contractors & Engineers* v. *Republic of Albania*, ICSID Case No. ARB/07/21, Award (30 July 2009), paras. 81-84.

606. *AMT* v. *Zaire*, *supra* note 84, Award (21 February 1997).

the operation of the investment [607] or initiating a change in the legal framework governing an investment that makes it impossible for it to continue or maintain its contractual basis [608]. In short, the guarantee of full protection and security for investments has been extended to ensuring an investor's legal security [609].

(f) *No arbitrary or discriminatory measures impairing the investment*

Not all investment treaties use the term "arbitrary"; some instead refer to "unreasonable or discriminatory" measures. In the *National Grid* case, the Tribunal explained that both terms are synonymous: "[i]t is the view of the Tribunal that the plain meaning of the terms "unreasonable" and "arbitrary" is substantially the same in the sense of something done capriciously, without reason" [610].

Treaties typically do not define the concepts of "arbitrary" or "discriminatory" measures. For instance, Article II (3) *(b)* of the United States-Ecuador BIT provides that "[n]either Party shall in any way impair by arbitrary or discriminatory measures the management, operation, maintenance, use, enjoyment, acquisition, expansion, or disposal of investments" [611].

In the *ELSI* case, the ICJ stated that "[a]rbitrariness is not so much something opposed to a rule of law. . . . It is a wilful disregard of due process of law, an act which shocks, or at least surprises, a sense of juridical propriety" [612].

607. *Siag and Vecchi* v. *Egypt*, *supra* note 102, Award (2009), paras. 445-448; *AES Summit Generation Ltd. and AES-Tisza Erömü Kft* v. *Republic of Hungary*, ICSID Case No. ARB/07/22, Award (23 September 2010), para. 13.3.2; *Marion Unglaube and Reinhard Unglaube* v. *Republic of Costa Rica*, ICSID Case Nos. ARB/08/1 and ARB/09/20, Award (16 May 2012), para. 281. Other tribunals have rejected this extension of the standard: see e.g. *Rumeli* v. *Kazakhstan*, *supra* note 597, Award (2008), paras. 668-669; *AWG Group Ltd.* v. *Argentine Republic*, UNCITRAL, Decision on Liability (30 July 2010), paras. 174-177.

608. *Goetz* v. *Burundi*, *supra* note 93, Award, paras. 125-131.

609. Collins, *supra* note 66, p. 143.

610. *National Grid PLC* v. *The Argentine Republic*, UNCITRAL, Award (3 November 2008), para. 197.

611. Treaty between the United States of America and the Republic of Ecuador Concerning the Encouragement and Reciprocal Protection of Investment, signed on 27 August 1993, entered into force on 11 May 1997.

612. *Elettronica*, *supra* note 334, Judgment (20 July 1989), *ICJ Reports*, at p. 76 (1999), *Oxford Reports on International Courts of General Jurisdiction*, at p. 95 (1989), para. 128. See also *LG&E* v. *Argentina*, *supra* note 448, Decision on Liability (3 October 2006), para. 158.

While the intent of a discriminatory measure is relevant, its effect is the most important consideration [613]. In order for arbitrary or discriminatory measures to be found, therefore, bad faith is not required [614]. Instead, whether the measure discriminates without a reasonable basis regarding other investors in a similar or comparable situation will be indicative of arbitrary or discriminatory treatment [615].

As an example, the *Azurix* v. *Argentina* case involved an investment in a water concession subjected to government measures that incited consumers not to pay their bills, required the concessionaire not to apply the new tariffs resulting from a review and denied the concessionaire access to documentation on the basis of which it had been sanctioned. These governmental measures were considered by the Tribunal to be arbitrary [616].

(g) *Free transfer of funds related to investments*

This standard protects investors against restrictive foreign exchange controls or other related actions by the host State. Investments that qualify under this standard are, of course, the invested funds themselves, in addition to any amount related to the investment, including profit, dividend, interest, capital gain, royalty payment, management, technical assistance or other fee, or returns in kind. The relaxation of foreign exchange controls is therefore key to attract foreign investments, as these controls would have no strategic commercial purpose if the capital generated could not be effectively transferred across borders [617].

For instance, Article IV of the United States-Ecuador BIT provides:

> "Each Party shall permit all transfers related to an investment to be made freely and without delay into and out of its territory. Such transfers include: *(a)* returns; *(b)* compensation 'pur-

---

613. *Ibid.*, para. 262.

614. *Unglaube* v. *Costa Rica*, ICSID Case No. ARB/09/20, Award (2012), para. 263.

615. *Loewen* v. *USA*, *supra* note 579, Award (26 June 2003), para. 127. In this case, the Tribunal was considering the judgment of a US trial court. The Tribunal observed that bad faith or malicious intention is not an essential element of unfair and inequitable treatment; a lack of due process that offends a sense of judicial propriety is sufficient. Although the Tribunal found the trial court proceedings to be improper and discreditable, it nonetheless rejected the claimant's claim as a result of its failure to exhaust all remedies available under the US legal system.

616. *Azurix* v. *Argentina*, *supra* note 327, Award (2006), para. 393. In another case the Tribunal did not find arbitrariness in the measures taken by Argentina. See *El Paso* v. *Argentina*, *supra* note 456, Award (2011), paras. 319-325.

617. Collins, *supra* note 66, pp. 148-149.

suant to provisions of the treaty'; *(c)* payments arising out of an investment dispute; *(d)* payments made under a contract, including amortization of principal and accrued interest payments made pursuant to a loan agreement; *(e)* proceeds from the sale or liquidation of all or any part of an investment; and *(f)* additional contributions to capital for the maintenance or development of an investment." [618]

Often, treaties include exceptions that allow certain currency transfers to be restricted during unusual periods of low foreign exchange or balance of payment problems within the host State [619].

Few awards have considered this protection for the free transfer of funds. After Argentina moved in 2001 to restrict the transfers of currency abroad, the Arbitral Tribunal in *Metalpar* v. *Argentina* understood that the investor did not comply with the domestic procedure for the transfer of funds and therefore could not allege a breach [620]. Also, in *Continental Casualty* v. *Argentine Republic*, the Tribunal held that not every cross-border movement of funds will be "related to the investment" protected by the investment treaty [621]. In turn, in *White Industries* v. *India* the Tribunal dismissed a claim due to the fact that it related to the assertion of contractual rights, rather than to the movement of capital and the exchange of currency [622].

(h) *Umbrella clauses*

Umbrella clauses require host States to comply with specific obligations they have entered into with the investor, allowing the possibility of elevating contractual disputes to the international forum. For instance, the final sentence of Article 2 (2) of the Argentina-United States BIT states that "[e]ach Party shall observe any obligation it may have entered into with regard to investments" [623]. Since not all contractual breaches entail treaty breaches, umbrella clauses raise several issues, which will be addressed in Chapter XIV.

---

618. *Supra* note 611.
619. Blackaby *et al.*, *supra* note 255, p. 498.
620. *Metalpar* v. *Argentina*, *supra* note 96, Award (2008), para. 179.
621. *Continental Casualty* v. *Argentina*, *supra* note 97, Award (5 September 2008), para. 242.
622. *White Industries Australia Limited* v. *The Republic of India*, Final Award (30 November 2011), para. 13.2.3.
623. See Argentina-US BIT, https://investmentpolicy.unctad.org/international-investment-agreements/treaties/bit/162/argentina---united-states-of-america-bit-1991-, accessed 3 March 2022.

5. Evolution of the content of BITs

Prior to the 1970s, foreign investment was largely subject to "a thin regime of customary international law" [624]. Duties that emerged within this regime related to non-discrimination and arguably to rules concerning expropriation and the due process or denial of justice, which later became an integral part of the international minimum standard of treatment. Since the 1980s and particularly from the 1990s onward, a network of thousands of BITs has supplanted this regime.

The 1987 United States Model BIT established a model that was later followed by many subsequent BITs, particularly in the 1990s [625]. The 2004 US Model BIT, as well as most US investment protection instruments that have been drafted since, now include important changes that have remedied prior challenges arising out of the negotiation of BITs and subsequent dispute resolution [626]. If the 1987 United States BIT represented the triumph of the so-called Washington Consensus of the late 1980s, which promoted market-oriented reforms [627], the 2004 Model "reflects a new-found appreciation for the views of Carlos Calvo" [628]. From 2004 onward, therefore, the United States does not grant foreign investors more favorable rights than those enjoyed by its nationals [629].

---

624. Arato, *supra* note 39, p. 2.
625. Alvarez, *supra* note 26, pp. 276-277.
626. *Ibid.*, pp. 302-306:

> "Among the important changes are the following: (1) Narrow the definition of covered investments. (2) Narrow the scope of NT and MFN. Recent US investment treaties permit greater exceptions to both NT and MFN and indicate that MFN rights do not extend to grant treaty parties the benefits of prior, more expansive US BITs. (3) Eliminate the umbrella clause. (4) Eliminate the guarantee barring '*arbitrary and discriminatory*' treatment. (5) Narrow the scope of FET and full protection and security. (6) Reduce investors' rights to due process. The 2004 Model eliminates the clause from the 1987 Model that guaranteed investors' rights to local remedies. It also eliminates from the scope of investor-State arbitration claims for violation of investors' rights to participate in domestic administrative proceedings; indeed, the United States-Morocco FTA appears to omit any right to transparent local regulations or to a remedy in local courts. (7) Reduce the scope of indirect expropriation. (8) Limit claims based on violations of intellectual property rights. (9) Limit expropriation claims based on tax measures. (10) Include explicit recognition of States' rights to regulate to protect health, safety, and the environment. (11) Impose new restrictions on investor-State dispute settlement. (12) Make the "essential security" portion of the non-precluded clauses self-judging. (13) Authorize States' parties to issue interpretations of the treaty."

627. *Ibid.*, p. 309.
628. *Ibid.*, p. 166.
629. *Ibid.*, p. 312.

When early international investment treaties were being negotiated in and after the 1950s [630], the main concern was to protect investors against direct expropriation. However, in the modern international business environment direct expropriation is generally rare. Most modern investment claims involve more subtle forms of harmful government action, for instance, related to the renewal of licenses or to environmental or health concerns [631]. As such, it has become difficult to determine where to draw the line between reasonable actions taken by the State and indirect expropriation, as discussed in the *Philip Morris* awards [632].

To avoid these types of issues, contemporary treaties specifically tend to address matters related to health, the environment and human rights. Particularly, human rights issues have become relevant in several contexts within investment arbitration [633]. Within more than 3,000 investment treaties accounted for by UNCTAD, the term "human rights" has been included in 363, of which 260 are currently in force [634].

Several soft law instruments relate to foreign investments, such as the OECD Guidelines for Multinational Enterprises, the International Labour Organization's Tripartite Declaration of Principles concerning Multinational Enterprises and Social Policy and the United Nations Guiding Principles.

In addition, many contemporary treaties highlight that investors "should" adhere to international human rights standards or "encourage"

630. See Sec. E.1 of this chapter, *supra*.

631. See, for example, *Lao Holdings* v. *Lao People's Democratic Republic*, ICSID Case No. ARB(AF)/12/6 *(I)* and *Sanum Investments* v. *Laos People's Democratic Republic*, UNCITRAL, PCA Case No. 2013-13 in which both tribunals rejected the assertion that the State's refusal to renew a license to operate a gaming club, which had been renewed several times in the past, amounted to expropriation; *Tethyan Copper* v. *Pakistan*, ICSID Case No. ARB/12/1, in which the Tribunal decided that the State's refusal to grant a mining lease amounted to an indirect expropriation, reported in UNCTAD, IIA Issues Note (January 2021), pp. 21-22; also *Perenco Ecuador Ltd.* v. *Republic of Ecuador and Empresa Estatal Petróleos del Ecuador (Petroecuador)*, ICSID Case No. ARB/08/6, and *Burlington* v. *Ecuador*, *supra* note 525, in which the tribunals decided in favor of counterclaims by the State alleging that the Claimants violated a domestic law on environmental protection by causing environmental damage.

632. See *supra* note 528. See also, broadly related, WTO, Appellate Body, *Australia – Certain Measures Concerning Trademarks, Geographical Indications and Other Plain Packaging Requirements Applicable to Tobacco Products and Packaging*, WT/DS435/AB/R, WT/DS441/AB/R, WT/DS458/AB/R and WT/DS467/AB/R.

633. U. Kriebaum, "Human Rights and International Investment Arbitration", in T. Schultz and F. Ortino (eds.), *The Oxford Handbook of International Arbitration*, Oxford, Oxford University Press, 2020, p. 153.

634. UNCTAD, International Investment Agreements Navigator, https://investmentpolicy.unctad.org/international-investment-agreements/by-economy, accessed 3 May 2022.

international corporations to be mindful of corporate social responsibility standards [635]. Moreover, some treaties contain "legality clauses" that require foreign investors to comply with the domestic laws of the host State, including its human rights provisions [636]. Violation of these human rights standards can turn an infringement of domestic law into a treaty violation as well [637].

Although it is rare, treaties can also specify the direct human rights obligations of investors, as is the case with the very detailed Morocco-Nigeria BIT [638] signed in December 2016, which contains thirty-four articles [639].

F. Multilateral and regional investment treaties

Substantive and procedural standards set out in BITs also inspired the content of sectorial and regional agreements, such as NAFTA, later succeeded by USMCA, discussed below [640].

The incorporation of certain common terms within BITs into other international agreements contributed to the standardization of these types of clauses. However, attempts to achieve investment protection as a regime of general application have failed at the multilateral

635. For instance, Article 14 (2) *(b)* of the 2015 Brazilian Model Cooperation and Facilitation Investment Agreement states that "[t]he investors and their investment shall endeavour to comply with the following voluntary principles and standards for a responsible business conduct and consistent with the laws adopted by the Host State receiving the investment . . . *(b)* Respect the internationally recognized human rights of those involved in the companies' activities".

636. The 2016 Indian Model BIT, for example, states in Article 12.1 that "[i]nvestors and their Investments shall be subject to and comply with the Law of the Host States. This includes, but is not limited to, . . . *(v)* Law relating to human rights".

637. Steininger, *supra* note 53, p. 10.

638. O. Ejims, "The 2016 Morocco–Nigeria Bilateral Investment Treaty: More Practical Reality in Providing a Balanced Investment Treaty", *ICSID Review: Foreign Investment Law Journal*, Vol. 34, No. 1 (2019), pp. 62-84.

639. It states in Article 18, paragraph 2 that "[i]nvestors and investments shall uphold human rights in the host state". Those obligations become binding after the investment is made, and also extend to core labor standards (para. 3). Moreover, " '[i]nvestors and investments shall not manage or operate the investments in a manner that circumvents international environmental, labour and human rights obligations to which the host state and/or home state are Parties' (para. 4). A similarly binding formulation ('shall') conferring investor obligations can also be found in two regional investment agreements, namely Article 14 (2) of the Supplementary Act on Investment of the Economic Community of West African States (ECOWAS) from 2009 and Article 19 of the African Union's Draft Pan-African Investment Code (PAIC) from 2019. However, States remain reluctant to introduce binding obligations for foreign investors. Not even Morocco or Nigeria have included a similarly firm approach in their subsequently negotiated treaties", Steininger, *supra* note 53, p. 11.

640. See *infra* note 673.

level[641]. The majority of investment protection, therefore, is still contained in BITs. No relevant global treaties have been successful in establishing provisions for investment protection that are as robust or efficacious as those included in BITs[642].

1. Global initiatives

There exist, however, global instruments dealing with particular aspects related to foreign investments, among them the following:

(a) *MIGA and OPIC Risk Insurance*

The 1985 Convention establishing the Multilateral Investment Guarantee Agency (MIGA) was designed as an additional mechanism to protect foreign investment and to alleviate concerns related to non-commercial risks, promoting the flow of resources to developing countries[643]. MIGA provides guarantees to investors against risks such as war, civil disturbance or expropriation. Together with the World Bank and the International Finance Corporation (IFC), MIGA also offers advice to its members on attracting foreign investment[644].

Stephan Schill notes that as occurs with the ICSID Convention, the MIGA Convention does not impose direct obligations upon the member States relating to the treatment of foreign investment, which is one of the reasons for its acceptance, including many countries that were critical of bilateral investment treaties. States viewed this insurance framework as involving fewer restrictions on their sovereignty[645].

In 1992, the World Bank and the International Monetary Fund (IMF) asked MIGA to prepare a "legal framework" to promote foreign direct investment. The result was the Guidelines on the Treatment of Foreign Direct Investment[646]. Though these guidelines were advanced under the

641. G. Sacerdoti, "Investment Arbitration Under ICSID and UNCITRAL Rules: Prerequisites, Applicable Law, Review of Awards", *ICSID Review: Foreign Investment Law Journal*, Vol. 19 (2004), p. 4.

642. Sornarajah, *supra* note 29, p. 79.

643. Convention Establishing the Multilateral Investment Guarantee Agency, 1508 UNTS 100, signed on 10 November 1985, entered into force on 12 April 1988 ("MIGA Convention"). See also https://www.miga.org/about-us, accessed 3 March 2022.

644. Parra, *supra* note 510, p. 6.

645. "Notwithstanding, the accession to the MIGA Convention suggests a positive attitude of States vis-à-vis foreign investment and the desirability of its protection by international law, in particular when compared with the rhetoric of the New International Economic Order", Schill, *supra* note 30, p. 49.

646. World Bank Group, *supra* note 416, Vol. 2, http://documents1.worldbank.org/curated/en/955221468766167766/pdf/multi-page.pdf, accessed 3 March 2022.

auspices of the World Bank and the IMF and are therefore authoritative, they are not a treaty-like binding instrument [647].

The United States' Overseas Private Investment Corporation (OPIC), now known as the United States International Development Finance Corporation (DFC), also provides political risk insurance against losses incurred due to currency inconvertibility, government interference and political violence (including terrorism). The DFC also offers reinsurance to increase underwriting capacity [648].

(b) *World Trade Organization*

The establishment of the WTO in 1995 was the biggest advance in international trade reform since World War II. Building on the emerging number of bilateral trade agreements negotiated during and after reconstruction, it became evident that the system established by the GATT was insufficient in terms of appropriate rules for international trade. Following several rounds of multilateral trade negotiations conducted within the framework of the GATT, the nature of the multilateral trading system was transformed during the Uruguay Round, and the GATT was replaced with the WTO. The new system of trade rules that was established under the WTO, however, did not affect nor was intended to replace the existing framework of bilateral treaties [649].

The most notable feature distinguishing the WTO from the GATT is the creation of a wider scope of trade rules. The agreement establishing the WTO comprehends a single institutional framework encompassing the GATT, as modified by the Uruguay Round as well as other agreements and arrangements concluded under the auspices of the Uruguay Round [650]. The introduction of these "new issues" became the principal reason for the establishment of the WTO as a new international body: institutional reform was necessary to ensure cohesion not only within this new organization but also under the established dispute settlement rules [651].

647. Subedi, *supra* note 17, p. 34. See also World Bank Group, *supra* note 416, Vol. 2, p. 5.
648. See OPIC's legislative charter, 22 USCA, paras. 2191-2200b (2010).
649. C. Van Grasstek, *The History and Future of the World Trade Organization*, Cambridge, WTO / Cambridge University Press, 2013, p. 45.
650. The Marrakesh Agreement establishing the WTO includes, besides the main WTO Agreements (GATT, GATS and TRIPS), a number of other trade-related legal texts. See https://www.wto.org/english/docs_e/legal_e/legal_e.htm, accessed 23 March 2022.
651. Van Grasstek, *supra* note 649, p. 47.

Besides adopting the GATT in 1994 as a component of the WTO Agreements, the Uruguay Round of multilateral negotiations also resulted in the incorporation of other trade-related issues including trade in services, intellectual property rights and trade-related investment measures. "Investment issues" were added to the WTO Agreements, which was a significant change as it allowed for the rules to expand to include the trade in services and intellectual property. In practice, however, the Agreement on Trade-Related Investment Measures (TRIMs Agreement) proved to be less ambitious and consequential than the General Agreement on Trade in Services (GATS) and the Agreement on Trade-Related Aspects of Intellectual Property Law (TRIPS).

More specifically, the TRIMs Agreement is rather limited in scope and only applies to investment measures that affect the trade in goods; that is, measures prohibited by GATT Article III on national treatment or Article XI on quantitative restrictions. The TRIMs do not deal with investor-State issues [652]. Nonetheless, it leaves open for consideration whether, at a later date, it should be complemented with further provisions regarding investment and competition policy more broadly [653].

Regarding the other new issues dealt with in the Uruguay Round, both the TRIPS and the GATS have general effects on investment. The relation between enforceable intellectual property rights, trade and investment is rather complex. However, the minimum standard of protection provided in the WTO Agreements serves as the basis for more detailed provisions in BITs and FTAs involving jurisdictions with weak intellectual property right enforcement. The GATS deals with the provision of services through four different modes of supply including commercial presence in another country, broadly categorized as foreign investment within the services sector [654]. As such, services trade policies, as regulated by the GATS, are an important determinant of foreign direct investment.

Across the different WTO Agreements, the fundamental principle of trade without discrimination runs throughout, namely, in the form of MFN and national treatment principles. Notwithstanding, each agreement articulates these principles slightly differently, and some even allow certain exceptions under strict conditions.

---

652. Foster, *supra* note 339, p. 202.
653. WTO, Legal Texts: The WTO Agreements, https://www.wto.org/english/docs_e/legal_e/ursum_e.htm#eAgreement, accessed 3 March 2022.
654. Sornarajah, *supra* note 29, p. 1.

Only a few dispute cases referred to the WTO's Dispute Settlement Body (DSB), the specialized body in charge of hearing and resolving disputes between WTO members, have dealt with foreign investment matters. Since the DSB is limited to interpreting provisions of the different WTO Agreements, unlike ICSID cases, the DSB does not deal with traditional issues relating to foreign investment [655].

In principle, WTO panels and its appellate body issue "Reports" on disputes brought by the organization's members, which are later adopted by the DSB, unless all members decide not to do so. Overall, the DSB has a limited role in settling investment-related disputes related to, for instance, trade-related investment measures or other relevant WTO Agreements [656].

The WTO does impose certain investment requirements on member host States, such as rules prohibiting regulations that require particular levels of local procurement (local content requirements) [657] or rules that restrict the volume or value of imports as part of a trade-balancing requirements regime. Overall, however, WTO texts such as the TRIMs Agreement only provide a general regime for the regulation of foreign investment that is not quite as detailed as provisions usually found in BITs or other FTAs.

(c) *Energy Charter Treaty*

The Energy Charter Treaty (ECT), adopted in Lisbon in 1994, entered into legal force in April 1998. More than fifty States, plus the European Union and the European Atomic Energy Community, signed on to the treaty [658]. The ECT responded to the contemporary desire of European States to cooperate with Russia and the new Eastern European and

---

655. For instance, the case concerning *Certain Measures Affecting the Automobile Industry* (WT/DS44/R, Panel Report adopted by the DSB on 23 July 1998) was referred to the DSB and involved the compatibility of Indonesian local automobile industry requirements with Indonesia's TRIMS obligations. The Tribunal highlighted that the TRIMS Agreement concerns freedom for foreign investors who invest in a WTO member country. When the EC and the US challenged the Indonesian measures, the WTO Panel held that these measures were not consistent with Indonesia's obligations under the TRIMS Agreement. See Subedi, *supra* note 17, p. 38.

656. For instance, in the *Australia Tobacco Plain Packaging* case, the Panel (and subsequently the Appellate Body) analyzed whether the adopted plain packaging measures were inconsistent with Australia's obligations under the TRIPS Agreement, among others. WTO-AB, *Australia – Certain Measures Australia, supra* note 632.

657. See, for instance, Article IV of the WTO Agreement on Government Procurement.

658. Energy Charter Treaty, 2080 UNTS 95, signed on 17 December 1994, entered into force on 16 April 1998.

Central Asian States regarding the establishment of rules on foreign investments in the energy sector [659].

The ECT applies only to one, albeit very important, sector of the economy – the one related to energy. However, it has an important global reach, including countries such as Japan and Russia. Therefore, it is by no means a regional treaty [660]. Further, it does not limit itself to international investment matters but also covers trade, transit and the environment [661]. The ECT chapter on investment has given rise to significant investor-State litigation in recent years [662].

Obligations related to investment protection are enshrined in Part III of the ECT, which also includes provisions on investment promotion. Article 10 (1) contains a number of principles for the protection of foreign investments, though these do not go beyond the basic principles recognized in the majority of BITs, namely, fair and equitable treatment, most constant protection and security, and non-discriminatory measures. The last sentence of Article 10 (1) is an umbrella clause that emphasizes the principle of *pacta sunt servanda*, which imposes the obligation on contracting parties to comply with any obligation entered into in the investment contract. Article 13 (1) confirms the principle of full compensation following expropriation [663]. All the above provisions of Part III only protect investments once made. Therefore, its provisions relating to the making of investments are – in the words of Thomas Roe and Mathew Happold – largely hortatory [664].

Article 26 of the ECT concerns options for dispute resolution, according to which investors may choose to submit their disputes either to the national courts of the contracting party, a previously agreed-upon dispute settlement procedure or to arbitration under the ICSID, UNCITRAL or Stockholm Chamber of Commerce rules. Submitting

---

659. Sacerdoti, *supra* note 67, p. 265.

660. "It is consequently inaccurate to see the ECT as a European treaty; a perception exacerbated by a widespread, if erroneous, tendency to refer to it by the name of its precursor, the European Energy Charter. This is not, however, to say that the ECT did not have its origins in Europe nor that it was not meant to serve, inter alia, European States' interests", T. Roe and M. Happold, *Settlement of Investment Disputes Under the Energy Charter Treaty*, Cambridge, Cambridge University Press, 2011, p. 8.

661. "However, it is an extremely complex instrument and one that is, moreover, perhaps not always as well-drafted or coherent as it might be", Roe and Happold, *ibid.*; also d'Aspremont, *supra* note 30, p. 69.

662. Salacuse, *supra* note 65, p. 4.

663. K. Hobér, "Investment Arbitration and the Energy Charter Treaty", *Journal of International Dispute Settlement*, Vol. 1, No. 1 (2010), pp. 153-190.

664. "This was a major bone of contention during the negotiation of the ECT and efforts to agree a supplementary treaty covering the issue have so far been unsuccessful", Roe and Happold, *supra* note 660, p. 8.

a potential dispute to arbitration in any of these three forums may be done even in the absence of an arbitration agreement [665].

The ruling of the Court of Justice of the European Union (CJEU) in the *Achmea* case has caught the attention of the international investment arbitration community with regard to the question of whether its scope applies to the ECT's dispute resolution provision for intra-EU BITs. The CJEU declared that the Dutch-Slovak arbitration clause had an adverse effect on the autonomy of the EU law and, as such, rendered it unenforceable and incompatible with the EU legal framework. Particularly, the CJEU reasoned that the effectiveness of EU law may be undermined if EU-related disputes are referred to bodies that are outside of the jurisdiction of the EU [666].

The Agreement for the Termination of Bilateral Investment Treaties between the Member States of the European Union recently entered into force and implements the CJEU's reasoning within the *Achmea* case [667]. However, the agreement does not apply to intra-EU proceedings under the ECT. Instead, it expressly provides that "the EU and its Member States will deal with this matter at a later stage" [668].

2. *Regional investment initiatives*

(a) *North America*

The North American Free Trade Agreement (NAFTA) between Mexico, Canada and the US entered into force in 1994 [669]. Regarding investment protection, Chapter 11 appealed to the establishment of a "secure investment environment through the elaboration of clear rules

665. Alvarez, *supra* note 26, p. 427.

666. This matter has generated numerous cases at ICSID, mostly deriving from the ECT. The first case to dismiss an intra-EU objection at an ICSID level was the *Electrabel* v. *Hungary* case. *Electrabel SA v The Republic of Hungary*, ICSID Case No. ARB/07/19, Decision on Jurisdiction, Applicable Law and Liability (30 November 2012). The repercussions of the *Achmea* decision will have an impact worth monitoring in the years to come.

667. Agreement for the Termination of Bilateral Investment Treaties between the Member States of the European Union, preliminary considerations, https://eur-lex.europa.eu/legal-content/EN/TXT/?uri=CELEX%3A22020A0529%2801%29, accessed 3 March 2022.

668. The Preamble states in full that "CONSIDERING that this Agreement addresses intra-EU bilateral investment treaties; it does not cover intra-EU proceedings on the basis of Article 26 of the Energy Charter Treaty. The European Union and its Member States will deal with this matter at a later stage". See *ibid.*

669. North American Free Trade Agreement (NAFTA), 32 ILM, p. 612, signed on 17 December 1992, entered into force on 1 January 1994, Chap. 11.

of fair treatment of foreign investment" and aimed to "remove barriers to investment" and "provide effective means for the resolution of disputes" [670].

As such, NAFTA contained elaborate dispute settlement mechanisms. Under several preconditions, Chapter 11 also included provisions contemplating international arbitration against a host Government under either the ICSID Convention or its Additional Facility, or in accordance with the UNCITRAL Arbitration Rules [671]. NAFTA generated considerable case law and literature, indicating the extent to which it provided restraints on the exercise of regulatory powers by the signatory States [672].

The United States-Mexico-Canada Trade Agreement (USMCA), signed in November 2018, is the successor to NAFTA [673]. In December 2019, all three parties signed a protocol amending the original text of USMCA and on 1 July 2020, it entered into force [674]. The USMCA covers a range of trade-related issues between the three States, and includes chapters on rules of origin, technical barriers to trade, intellectual property, competition policy, labor, procurement, the environment and investment.

In comparison with NAFTA's Chapter 11, the availability of investor-State dispute settlement (ISDS) is narrowed under Chapter 14 of the USMCA. Though Chapter 14 still protects investment and investors through substantive obligations related to national treatment, MFN and direct expropriation, it departs in many ways from the previous Chapter 11. Mainly, the USMCA severely limits investors' abilities to enforce the substantive rights afforded to them under the Agreement, specifically in Canada, which was excluded from the ISDS mechanism provided in Chapter 14. As such, Mexican and American investors may only submit claims on the basis of national treatment, MFN treatment or direct expropriation, excluding, to some extent, common grounds for investment claims such as fair and equitable treatment and indirect expropriation.

---

670. See further in Dolzer and Schreuer, *supra* note 382, p. 28.

671. Alvarez, *supra* note 26, pp. 424-425.

672. Sornarajah, *supra* note 29, p. 80.

673. The treaty also carries two other names: Canada has adopted it as the Canada – United States – Mexico Agreement (CUSMA), while Mexico has settled on the title El Tratado entre México, Estados Unidos y Canadá (T-MEC).

674. Certain enumerated provisions will nonetheless remain in force for a limited time period.

As Canada is not a party to the dispute settlement mechanism included Chapter 14, this mechanism exists solely for the benefit of American and Mexican investors. In addition to that limitation, Chapter 14 now includes a local litigation requirement as a prerequisite for ISDS claims, except when "recourse to domestic remedies was obviously futile or manifestly ineffective" [675].

(b) *Asia*

In 2009, the Association of Southeast Asian Nations (ASEAN), comprised of ten Southeast Asian States, signed the ASEAN Comprehensive Investment Agreement (ACIA), which entered into force in 2012 [676]. The objective of the ACIA is "to create a free and open investment regime in ASEAN" through the progressive liberalization of the investment regimes of member States, the provision of enhanced protection to investors and investments, the improvement of transparency and predictability of the investment regime, the joint promotion of the region as an integrated investment area, and through the cooperation among ASEAN member States to create favorable conditions for their investors [677].

Moreover, ACIA Section B contains investment dispute settlement provisions and provides for investor-State arbitration under the ICSID Convention and ICSID Rules of Procedure for Arbitration Proceedings or ICSID Additional Facility Rules; under the UNCITRAL Arbitration Rules; before the Regional Centre for Arbitration at Kuala Lumpur; before other regional arbitration centers located within ASEAN countries; or before any other arbitration institution if agreed upon by the parties [678].

---

675. USMCA, Article 14.D.5 *(b)*, footnote 25.

676. The ten ASEAN member States have also begun to negotiate investment treaties as a group with individual non-ASEAN States, such as Korea, China and India. Unlike the EU treaties, in which the European Union is a separate treaty party, the ASEAN treaties do not provide that ASEAN is a separate contracting party in addition to the Association's ten member States. Since the EU and ASEAN treaties each have many more than two parties, one may have difficulty viewing them as BITs. On the other hand, considering that the ordinary dictionary definition of "bilateral" is "having two sides" (not two States), an analysis of the contents of these treaties and their negotiating histories reveals that substantively each of them is a two-sided agreement and therefore qualifies as a "bilateral investment treaty", Salacuse, *supra* note 65, pp. 5-6.

677. ASEAN Comprehensive Investment Agreement, Section A, Article 1, Objective, http://investasean.asean.org/files/upload/Doc%2005%20-%20ACIA.pdf, accessed 3 March 2022.

678. Article 33, *ibid.*, Section B.

Signed in 2020, the Regional Comprehensive Economic Partnership (RCEP) is the world's largest FTA in terms of the population covered and the cumulative GDP of signatory countries. Concluded by fifteen Asia-Pacific economies, it seeks to create an integrated market, rendering the trade of products and services between each country more easily available.

Article 10 of the RCEP sets out a number of provisions with regard to the promotion and protection of foreign investments, including the following standards of investment protection: national treatment (Art. 10.3); MFN treatment (Art. 10.4); fair and equitable treatment; full protection and security (Art. 10.5); and expropriation (Art. 10.13).

Though many of the RCEP provisions are similar to obligations found in other BITs, the RCEP does somewhat vary the formulation of its investment protection obligations. For example, the amended form of the fair and equitable treatment standard employed in the RCEP limits the scope of such protection to "the customary international law minimum standard of treatment of aliens" [679].

(c) *Central America*

The 2006 Dominican Republic-Central America Free Trade Agreement (CAFTA-DR) was concluded between the Dominican Republic, El Salvador, Costa Rica, Guatemala, Honduras, Nicaragua and the US and is the first FTA between the United States and Central American nations [680]. Chapter 10 of the CAFTA-DR specifically relates to investment and contemplates certain generic treaty rights that are frequently included within BITs, such as national treatment, the MFN treatment, the minimum standard of treatment, full protection and security, as well protection from expropriation without prompt, adequate and effective compensation [681].

(d) *Africa*

In Africa, "a multi-layered system of initiatives is bourgeoning on the continent to revamp the architecture of the international invest-

---

679. Regional Comprehensive Economic Partnership (RCEP) agreement to enter into force on 1 January 2022, see https://rcepsec.org/, accessed 3 March 2022.

680. CAFTA-DR Agreement, https://ustr.gov/trade-agreements/free-trade-agreements/cafta-dr-dominican-republic-central-america-fta, accessed 3 March 2022.

681. See *ibid.*, Chapter 10, Articles 10.3, 10.4, 10.5 and 10.7, https://ustr.gov/sites/default/files/uploads/agreements/cafta/asset_upload_file328_4718.pdf, accessed 3 March 2022.

ment law field according to African States' policy and development priorities" [682].

Since the mid-1990s and the early 2000s, African countries have signed numerous BITs. By July 2019, 897 out of the 2,971 BITs signed worldwide involved African States [683]. Presently, Africa comprises a complex web of various regional economic communities (RECs) [684]. Each African REC has at least one instrument relating directly or indirectly to investment.

Among these efforts, the Common Market for Eastern and Southern Africa (COMESA) was established in 2007, but it is not yet in force since the required threshold of ratification of at least six member States has not been met. It contains many innovative features, for instance, an investor obligation [685]. In 2016, COMESA finalized a Common Investment Agreement which revises the 2007 agreement [686].

---

682. M. Moïse Mbengue, "Africa's Voice in the Formation, Shaping and Redesign of International Investment Law", *ICSID Review: Foreign Investment Law Journal*, Vol. 34, No. 2 (2019), p. 455.

683. UNCTAD, "International Investment Agreement Database", http://investmentpolicyhub.unctad.org/IIA, accessed 3 March 2022. African countries also played a central role in the speedy entry into force of the ICSID Convention. Of the first twenty ratifications needed for the Convention to enter into force, fifteen came from African States, https://icsid.worldbank.org/about/member-states/database-of-member-states, accessed 3 March 2022.

684. Moïse Mbengue, *supra* note 682, fn. 79:

> "In West Africa, there are three RECs: the West African Economic and Monetary Union (UEMOA), the Mano River Union (MRU), and the Economic Community of West African States (ECOWAS). Central Africa has two groupings: the Economic Community of Central African States (ECCAS) and the Economic Community of Great Lakes Countries (ECGLC). In Eastern and Southern Africa, six groupings coexist: the Common Market for Eastern and Southern Africa (COMESA), the East African Community (EAC), the Inter-Governmental Authority on Development (IGAD), the Indian Ocean Commission (IOC), the Southern Africa Development Community (SADC), and the Southern African Customs Union (SACU). North Africa shares two RECs: the Arab Maghreb Union (AMU) and the Community of Sahel-Saharan States (CEN-SAD). As a consequence, today, of the 55 African countries, 28 retain dual membership, 20 are members of three RECs, the Democratic Republic of Congo belongs to four RECs, and six countries maintain singular membership."

685. Article 13 in this agreement provides that "COMESA investors and their investments shall comply with all applicable domestic measures of the Member State in which their investment is made". See Investment Agreement for the COMESA Common Investment Area, signed 23 May 2007, https://investmentpolicy.unctad.org/international-investment-agreements/treaty-files/3092/download, accessed 3 March 2022.

686. The instrument seeks to strengthen further the sustainable development dimension of foreign investment regulation and to safeguard the right of host States to regulate. The finalized text of 2016 was submitted to the COMESA Committee on Legal Affairs in September 2017. However, at the time of writing this article, the text has not been officially published and is not yet open for signature.

Also noteworthy are different instruments regulating investment within the Economic Community of West African States (ECOWAS) [687], among them the 2008 ECOWAS Supplementary Act on Investments [688] and the 2018 ECOWAS Common Investment Code (ECOWIC) [689], all modernizing the investment framework in the region.

In turn, the 2006 Southern Africa Development Community (SADC) advanced a Protocol on Finance and Investment (SADC Investment Protocol), currently in force [690]. In 2016, the SADC Investment Protocol was amended but is yet to be ratified. It is forward-looking and in line with African regional efforts of sustainable development promotion. The SADC region also adopted a Model Treaty, aiming to enhance the harmonization of investment regimes in the region and to provide an effective tool for the future conclusion of international investment agreements (IIAs) by SADC member States. It has an overarching objective of achieving sustainable development for the region. A first edition of the Model BIT was published in 2012 and has recently been updated via a second edition [691].

At the continental level, the Pan-African Investment Code, concluded in 2015, constitutes the first African-continent-wide investment code. It serves as the basis for the negotiations on the Investment Protocol to the Agreement establishing an African Continental Free Trade Area (AfCFTA), and also has the long-term goal of securing sustainable development.

It remains to be seen if the AfCFTA Investment Protocol will incorporate dispute resolution through a regional investment court. Relevant regional tribunals include the COMESA Court, established in 1988 as COMESA's judicial organ, the main purpose of which is to

---

UNCTAD, World Investment Report 2018: Investment and New Industrial Policies, 2018, https://unctad.org/en/PublicationsLibrary/wir2018_en.pdf, accessed 3 March 2022, p. 90.

687. ECOWAS Treaty (revised in 1993); the ECOWAS Protocol on Movement of Persons and Establishment; the ECOWAS Energy Protocol; as well as the ECOWAS Supplementary Act on Investments; https://investmentpolicy.unctad.org/international-investment-agreements/groupings/26/ecowas-economic-community-of-west-african-states-, accessed 3 March 2022.

688. ECOWAS Supplementary Act A/SA.3/12/08 Adopting Community Rules on Investment and the Modalities for their Implementation with ECOWAS, 2008.

689. Moïse Mbengue, *supra* note 682, fn. 97.

690. See SADC Protocol on Finance and Investment, signed 18 August 2006, http://investmentpolicyhub.unctad.org/Download/TreatyFile/273, accessed 3 March 2022.

691. SADC Model Bilateral Investment Treaty Template with Commentary, 2nd ed., June 2017 – also known as the Revised SADC Model BIT. The instrument is not publicly available but is on file with the author. Moïse Mbengue, *supra* note 682, fn. 108.

"[ensure] the adherence to law in the interpretation and application of [the] Treaty [establishing the Common Market for Eastern and Southern Africa]". The Community Court of Justice of ECOWAS was established in 1991 by the Protocol on the Community Court of Justice [692], and has the power to act as the arbitral tribunal of the community [693].

(e) *Middle East*

The Middle East relies upon a Unified Agreement for the Investment of Arab Capital in the Arab States, signed in 1980 and in force since 7 September 1981. The statutes of the Arab Investment Court came into force in 1988. Most members of the League of Arab States ratified the investment agreement, except Algeria and the Comoros [694].

(f) *South America*

The Common Market of the Southern Cone (MERCOSUR) prepared protocols related to the reciprocal promotion and protection of investments in 1994. To date, the only instrument in force related to the matter is the Protocol on Cooperation and Facilitation of Intra-MERCOSUR Investments, approved by MERCOSUR via Decision 3/17 [695] and ratified by Uruguay, Brazil and Argentina.

---

692. Protocol A/P.l/7/91 on the Community Court of Justice, signed 6 July 1991, entered into force provisionally 6 July 1991, definitively 5 November 1996; now amended by the Supplementary Protocol A/SP.1/01/05.

693. ECOWAS, Revised Treaty of the Economic Community of West African States, revised 24 July 1993, Article 16.

694. Members of the league are Algeria, Bahrain, Comoros, Djibouti, Egypt, Iraq, Jordan, Kuwait, Lebanon, Libyan Arab Jamahiriya, Mauritania, Oman, Palestine, Qatar, Saudi Arabia, Syrian Arab Republic, Somalia, Sudan, Tunisia, the United Arab Emirates and Yemen. See "Unified Agreement for the Investment of Arab Capital in the Arab States" in Economic Documents (League of Arab States) No. 3, UNCTAD website, http://investmentpolicyhub.unctad.org/Download/TreatyFile/2394, accessed 3 March 2022.

695. The protocol can be accessed at https://www.mre.gov.py/tratados/public_web/DetallesTratado.aspx?id=+uUEOsWR9wE3v91PDlXvnQ==, accessed 25 July 2022. This 2017 protocol substituted the 1994 "Protocolo de Colonia", which never entered into force as it failed to gather the four required ratifications as established in the Protocol. Available at https://www.mre.gov.py/tratados/public_web/DetallesTratado.aspx?id=QbqmyvQl7CGPrIugK4Iltg%3d%3d, accessed 25 July 2022. Further, a Protocol on the Promotion of Investments from non-MERCOSUR member States was approved via Decision 11/94. However, this protocol has yet to enter into force since it established a requirement of four ratifications and, to date, has only been ratified by three member states, https://www.mre.gov.py/tratados/public_web/DetallesTratado.aspx?id=MzFrhVNTCm7X+Ji9lTDZ0Q%3d%3d, accessed 25 July 2022. Regarding the content of these 1994 protocols, see, for instance, G. Argerich, "Protocolos de

One noteworthy feature of this protocol is the inclusion of a list of what the term "investment" does not cover, including bonds, debentures, loans and portfolio investments. Moreover, the fair and equitable treatment and full protection and security standards are expressly not covered by the protocol, nor are indirect expropriations. Among the protections the protocol *does* offer to investments are non-discrimination and protection against direct expropriations.

As to investment claims, the protocol first establishes a dispute prevention procedure that any member State may initiate. Only after exhausting this procedure may a member State activate any dispute resolution mechanism in force in MERCOSUR. Initiating the dispute prevention or the dispute resolution procedure of the protocol excludes the possibility of activating any arbitration right established under other BITs or agreements that might otherwise have been applicable.

On June 2019, the European Union and the MERCOSUR trade bloc reached a political agreement for the creation of a trade agreement that will aim at increasing bilateral trade and investment between the regions. A final version is still pending [696].

A recent study indicates that in Latin America, trends within the drafting of investment treaties and dispute settlement mainly follow comparable worldwide trends [697].

(g) *Other regional/bloc initiatives*

In Europe, the Treaty on the Functioning of the European Union includes provisions regarding international investment among the States of the Union, particularly in its Title IV, regarding the Free Movement of Persons, Services and Capital [698]. Further, the Lisbon Treaty, made

---

inversiones extranjeras del MERCOSUR, ¿instrumentos útiles para. el siglo XXI?", *DeCITA: direito do comércio internacional / derecho del comercio internacional*, eds. D. P. Fernández Arroyo, A. Dreyzin de Klor and L. Otávio Pimentel (eds.), No. 3 (2005), pp. 208-218.

696. See https://trade.ec.europa.eu/doclib/press/index.cfm?id=2039, accessed 3 March 2022 and https://www.mercosur.int/mercosur-cierra-un-historico-acuerdo-de-asociacion-estrategica-con-la-union-europea/, accessed 3 March 2022 for the EU and the MERCOSUR's press releases, respectively. The agreement in principle is available at https://trade.ec.europa.eu/doclib/docs/2019/june/tradoc_157964.pdf, accessed 3 March 2022.

697. R. P. Lazo and A. Wang, "Intra-Latin America Investor-State Dispute Settlement", in J. Chaisse, L. Choukroune and S. Jusoh (eds.), *Handbook of International Investment Law and Policy*, Singapore, Springer, 2019.

698. European Union: Consolidated Version of the Treaty on the Functioning of the European Union [2012] OJ C 329/49, https://eur-lex.europa.eu/legal-content/EN/TXT/?uri=celex%3A12012E%2FTXT, accessed 3 March 2022.

effective in 2009, grants EU institutions exclusive competence over direct foreign investment, an area previously within the exclusive competence of Member States [699]. After assuming competence over international investment for its members, the European Union negotiated several treaties on the matter, among them the 2016 EU-Canada Comprehensive Economic and Trade Agreement [700] and the 2019 EU-Vietnam Investment Protection Agreement [701].

The Comprehensive and Progressive Agreement for Trans-Pacific Partnership (CPTPP) is an FTA signed in 2018 by eleven countries in the Asia-Pacific [702]. It contains strong investment protections and guarantees [703]. The chapter related to investment covers the full life cycle of an investment and includes the core obligations of national treatment, MFN treatment, expropriation and compensation, performance requirements, and transfers. Although it does include investor-State dispute settlement provisions, the CPTPP has actually narrowed the scope for investors to make claims and excludes, for example, claims relating to investment contracts entered into with the government.

Finally, the Transatlantic Trade and Investment Partnership (TTIP) between the European Union and the United States had the potential

699. In what is the resulting "Consolidated Texts of the EU Treaties as Amended by the Treaty of Lisbon", at Article 207, the Treaty of Lisbon added just three words, i.e., "foreign direct investment", to the Union's competences, under the new title of External Action By The Union: "The common commercial policy shall be based on uniform principles, particularly with regard to . . . the commercial aspects of foreign direct investment . . .". With these three words the Union opened the door to a radical revision of the Union system with respect to foreign (including intra-EU) investments and the resolution of disputes arising out of them. Charles N. Brower, "Foreword", in J. Rafael Mata Dona and N. Lavranos (eds.), *International Arbitration and EU Law*, Cheltenham, Edward Elgar, 2021, pp. xix-xx.

700. Comprehensive Economic and Trade Agreement between Canada, of the One Part, and the European Union and its Member States, of the Other Part, signed in Brussels, 30 October 2016, https://ec.europa.eu/trade/policy/in-focus/ceta/ceta-chapter-by- chapter/, accessed 3 March 2022.

701. Investment Protection Agreement between the European Union and its Member States, of the One Part, and the Socialist Republic of Vietnam, of the Other Part, signed 30 June 2019, https://investmentpolicy.unctad.org/international-investment-agreements/treaty-files/5868/download, accessed 3 March 2022.

702. The CTPP entered into force on 30 December 2018 for Australia, Canada, Japan, Mexico, New Zealand and Singapore, on 14 January 2019 for Vietnam, and on 19 September 2021 for Peru. The ratification process in Brunei Darussalam, Chile and Malaysia is still to be completed. See https://www.dfat.gov.au/trade/agreements/in-force/cptpp/comprehensive-and-progressive-agreement-for-trans-pacific-partnership, accessed 3 March 2022.

703. The Comprehensive and Progressive Agreement for Trans-Pacific Partnership (CPTPP), https://www.mti.gov.sg/-/media/MTI/improving-trade/multilateral-and-regional-forums/CPTPP/cptpp_legal_text_21022018.pdf, accessed 3 March 2022.

to create a large and plurilateral regime that would have included rules on almost all aspects of trade and investment between the parties. However, negotiations were halted during the Trump Administration and, in 2019, the Council of the European Union declared that the negotiating directives for the TTIP had become obsolete [704].

G. Recent developments in relation to investment treaties

The Washington Consensus emerged from a shared belief in the value of open economies by several countries from the end of the 1980s and throughout the 1990s. The consensus propelled the spread of investment treaties worldwide. In spite of the backlash, countries continue to negotiate bilateral investment treaties, and the twenty-first century has seen initiatives to create "mega-regional economic groupings", or broad agreements such as the Trans-Pacific Partnership, TTIP and the Comprehensive Economic and Trade Agreement (CETA), among others [705].

However, again, none of these instruments (bilateral or multilateral) contain a comprehensive corpus of the applicable substantive law to international investments. Instead, they are generally limited to enunciating a few broad standards such as those described in this chapter.

704. Council Decision (EU) 2019, https://www.consilium.europa.eu/media/39180/st06052-en19.pdf, accessed 3 March 2022.
705. Salacuse, *supra* note 65, pp. 26-28.

CHAPTER VI

GENERAL PRINCIPLES AND PUBLIC INTERNATIONAL LAW

A. Legal theory considerations

Aristotle, "The Master of Those Who Know" [706], referred to "principles" *(archai)* as – literally – beginnings [707]. According to his teachings, principles are not only broader than rules but their relationship is teleological: rules are clarified by the purposes they serve, like a body's organs or the parts of a machine. Above all, Aristotle argues that principles describe what the society ultimately wishes to achieve [708].

These ideas were transposed into law through medieval scholars, particularly Saint Thomas Aquinas [709]. Within the Aristotelean tradition, systematic thinking required the exercise of prudence, understood as an ability to select actions for living a plain life. Prudence leads to judging actions as correct, even if the result cannot be explained. Rules fulfill objectives, but circumstances arrive in which the purpose of such rules is not met and, as a result, deviating from them becomes necessary. Using systematic thinking, one can determine which rule is appropriate in each situation, as well as any deviation that may be necessary according to higher principles [710].

Under the influence of René Descartes, Enlightenment philosophers approached systematic thinking differently, advocating for the extraction of rules from principles through deductive reasoning [711]. One of these deductive techniques considered certain Roman rules "maxims", that

---

706. D. Alighieri, *The Divine Comedy*, Inf. 4.131.

707. In *Metaphysics* A.1, Aristotle says that "everyone takes what is called 'wisdom' (*sophia*) to be concerned with the primary causes *(aitia)* and the starting points (or principles, *archai*)" (981b28). See *Stanford Encyclopedia of Philosophy*, https://plato.stanford.edu/entries/aristotle-metaphysics, accessed 3 March 2022.

708. J. Gordley, *Foundations of Private Law*, Oxford, Oxford University Press, 2006, p. 32.

709. Berman, *supra* note 136, pp. 132 ff.

710. Gordley, *supra* note 708, pp. 32-33. When a rule cannot be designed, or it is uncertain in a given case, it can be explained by reference to principles. Even though the rule cannot be defined, the principle can be observed in practice. It is frequently easier to observe general principles (*pacta sunt servanda*, unjust enrichment, etc.) than to determine their specific consequence. This difficulty is primarily due to the fact that principles can almost always be contrasted with others, as happens for example with *pacta sunt servanda* and *rebus sic stantibus* (hardship). *Ibid.*, pp. 37-38.

711. *Ibid.*, p. 32.

is, independent norms of universal validity [712]. Francisco Suárez and others referred to these maxims as general "principles" of universal validity that exist in conformity with reason, from which rules can be deduced. Contrary to the Aristotelean tradition, such thinkers advocated for the creation of an arsenal of principles or maxims of purely rational origin [713]. Within this view, formal deductive reasoning aimed to provide legal certainty. Formal reasoning in the law should be no different than the method applied in mathematics [714].

The method of formal reasoning in law goes in hand with the Cartesian method of seeking principles from which one can deduce particular rules. The result is to advance a system of principles, rather than engage in a teleological pursuit to arrive at an appropriate principle in a given case [715]. Formal reasoning also promoted the determination of general principles from particular situations that share common traits, particularly in response to the works of David Hume [716]. Deduction and induction thus occupy a central place in the formalistic approach to the determination of principles to achieve legal certainty.

Reasoning based on principles now takes teleological considerations into account and has progressively gained momentum [717]. Ronald Dworkin, "arguably the pivotal jurist of the last 40 years" [718], contributed to increasing the popularity of the teleological approach within the Anglo-American legal world after publishing an article in 1967 arguing against the positivist legal philosophy of his Oxford colleague Herbert Hart [719].

---

712. Paradoxically, the term *maxim* is of Aristotelean origin, referring to a "maximum proposition"; that is, a "universal". See Berman, *supra* note 136, p. 139.

713. M. Villey, *La formación del pensamiento jurídico moderno*, Portuguese trans. ed., São Paulo, Editorial Martins Fontes, 2005, pp. 413-414.

714. C. Perelman, *Lógica Jurídica*, Portuguese trans. of 1979 ed., São Paulo, Editorial Martins Fontes, 2000, p. 185.

715. Coing, *supra* note 153, p. 105.

716. The original source of what has become known as the "problem of induction" is in Book One, Part III, Section 6 of *A Treatise of Human Nature* by David Hume, published in 1739. In 1748, Hume gave a shorter version of the argument in Section IV of *An Enquiry Concerning Human Understanding*. See *Stanford Encyclopedia of Philosophy*, https://plato.stanford.edu/entries/induction-problem, accessed 3 March 2022.

717. Perelman, *supra* note 714, p. 185.

718. M. D. A. Freeman, *Lloyd's Introduction to Jurisprudence*· 9th ed., London, Sweet & Maxwell / Thomson Reuters, 2014, p. 593.

719. R. Alexy, *Tres escritos sobre los derechos fundamentales y la teoría de los principios*, Bogotá, Universidad Externado de Colombia, 2003, pp. 93-94. Dworkin states that "judges do and should rest their judgments on controversial cases on arguments of political principle, but not in arguments of political policy", R. Dworkin, *A Matter of Principle*, Cambridge, MA, Harvard University Press, 1985, p. 280. This

According to Dworkin, principles have a "dimension of weight", which distinguishes them from legal rules, that have an "either or" character [720]. Principles such as "no man should profit from his own wrong", differ from rules "in the character of the discretion they give" [721]. While rules are applicable in an all-or-nothing fashion, principles state

> "a reason that argues in one direction but (do) not necessitate a particular decision. . . . All that is meant, when we say that a particular principle is a principle of our law, is that the principle is one which officials must take into account, it is relevant, as a consideration inclining in one direction or another" [722].

Furthermore, principles have a weight or degree of importance that rules lack. Principles can conflict, and they often do. On the contrary, if rules clash, the introduction of a further rule will be necessary to resolve the conflict (for example, if law and equity conflict, equity prevails) [723]. An additional difference between principles and rules is that the force of a principle may become attenuated over a period of time. This does not occur with rules [724].

Robert Alexy and other renowned legal theorists have – also recently – advanced teleological approaches in the civil law world [725], in which debates regarding constitutionally recognized principles became commonplace [726]. According to this teleological approach, generality is

---

position has not been exempted from criticism. See for instance D. Moreno Rodríguez Alcalá, *Control judicial de la ley y derechos fundamentals. Una perspectiva crítica*, Madrid, Centro de Estudios Políticos y Constitucionales, 2011, pp. 281-285.

720. In contrast, values express our conceptions of the Good and are useful tools for lawmakers. Values can be individual or political, such as Liberty, Equality and Solidarity. Just as principles relate to law, values relate to lawmakers. Principles apply in legal interpretation (interpreting the legal system from within) and values apply in an evaluative perspective (evaluating the legal system from the outside). M. W. Hesselink, "'If You Don't Like Our Principles We Have Others'; On Core Values and Underlying Principles in European Private Law: A Critical Discussion of the New 'Principles' Section in the Draft CFR", in R. Brownsword, H. Micklitz, L. Niglia and S. Weatherill (eds.), *The Foundations of European Private Law*, Oxford, Hart Publishing, 2011, pp. 59-72, reproduced at http://ssrn.com/abstract=1514449, accessed 3 March 2022, see p. 60 (p. 2 in SSRN reproduction).

721. R. Dworkin, *Taking Rights Seriously*, Cambridge, MA, Harvard University Press, 1977, p. 24.

722. *Ibid.*, p. 26.

723. *Ibid.*, p. 26

724. *Ibid.*, p. 40.

725. A. Somek, "German Legal Philosophy and Theory in the Nineteenth and Twentieth Centuries", in Dennis Patterson (ed.), *A Companion to Law and Legal Theory*, Cambridge, MA, Blackwell, 1996, pp. 351-352.

726. R. Zimmermann and S. Whittaker (eds.), *Good Faith in European Contract Law*, Cambridge, Cambridge University Press, 2000, pp. 22-23. See also

not a necessary feature within principles. The outcome of a particular situation can be predicted through consideration of the different possibilities [727]. Therefore, principles can be identified if they justify the motive for a decision in one way or another [728].

In public international law, the 1903 *Gentini* case was decided using the teleological approach. The case held the following:

> "A rule . . . is essentially practical and, moreover, binding; there are rules of art as there are rules of government, while a principle expresses a general truth, which guides our action, serves as a theoretical basis for the various acts of our life, and the application of which to reality produces a given consequence." [729]

More recently, the ICJ tackled the teleological issue of weighing competing principles. Since there exists no overriding principle that can subsume and coordinate an apparent conflict, a weighing of competing principles must be made. In the *Gabčíkovo-Nagymaros* case, the ICJ subsumed economic development and environmental protection under the umbrella of sustainable development [730].

B. Some preliminary remarks on the term "principles" and the law

In current legal practice and commonplace scholarly writing [731], the term "principles", sometimes together with the words "general",

---

J. H. Merryman, *La Tradición Jurídica Romano-Canónica*, trans. E. L. Suárez, [Mexico City], Editorial México, Fondo de Cultura Económica, 2007, p. 276.

727. K. Larenz, *Derecho Justo, Fundamentos de Etica Jurídica*, Madrid, Editorial Civitas, 2001, pp. 32-33.

728. *Ibid.*, p. 36. Alexy advances three features within the teleological approach. The first is optimization: principles can be complied with to different degrees and should be realized to the greatest extent possible. Rules, in turn, are norms to be complied with; one should do exactly what they demand, not more nor less. Alexy, *supra* note 719, pp. 95-96. A second feature of principles is the collision law: between principles, there is no rule that takes precedence over the others. Principles must be assessed in each specific case, taking into account other complementary or contradictory principles. *Ibid.*, pp. 100-101. The third feature of principles is proportionality: since principles require the maximum possible realization, all factual and legal possibilities should be taken into account. Assessing which principle should prevail in a given situation is an important consideration. *Ibid.*, pp. 101-103.

729. Ital.-Ven. MCC (1903): *Gentini* Case, Ven. Arb. 1903, p. 720, at p. 725. See Cheng, *supra* note 178, p. 24.

730. *Gabčíkovo-Nagymaros*, *supra* note 299, Judgment (1997), p. 78, para. 140. Rigo Sureda, *supra* note 55, pp. 105-106.

731. Several usages of the word "principles" emerge from theoretical writings, as well as from legal opinions, pleadings and decisions. See, for instance, in J. A. Barberis, "Los Principios Generales de Derecho como Fuente del Derecho Internacional", *Revista IIDH*, Vol. 14 (1991), p. 23.

"universal" and "recognized", usually refers to rules of a more abstract and general character (such as *pacta sunt servanda* or good faith) [732]. On occasion, these general legal rules are qualified by the term "fundamental", which suggests ties to abstract basic values, such as those enshrined in the national constitutions of various States. At other times, the term "principles" is used as a synonym for "rules without the force of law", as in the UNIDROIT Principles [733] or the Hague Principles [734]. These and other uses of the word "principles" will be further addressed below.

The term "principles" remains "notoriously ill-defined" in theory [735] and has even sometimes been mocked for its lack of precision [736].

In private law, the expression "general principles of law" appeared in the Austrian Civil Code of 1811 and other nineteenth-century legal texts that codified private law both in Europe and in Latin America [737]. In these countries, writers and courts were faced with the following questions: in ascertaining the contents of general principles of law, should they look beyond their national frontiers? Are general principles of law conceived as having local roots, or do they transcend national boundaries [738]?

Numerous contemporary judgments by the Court of Justice of the European Communities and now the Court of Justice of the European Union also refer to "general principles of civil law" [739].

---

732. In this sense, in the *Gulf of Maine* case, the ICJ stated that "[t]he association of the terms 'rules' and 'principles' is no more than the use of a dual expression to convey one and the same idea, since in this context 'principles' clearly means principles of law, that is, it also includes rules of international law in whose case the use of the term 'principles' may be justified because of their more general and more fundamental character". *Delimitation of the Maritime Boundary in the Gulf of Maine Area (Canada* v. *USA)*, Merits (1984), *ICJ Reports 1984*, p. 246, para. 78.

733. See Chap. XII, *infra*.

734. See Chap. X.E.3, *infra*, "The Hague Principles".

735. Bermann, *supra* note 11, p. 353.

736. American comedian Groucho Marx said: "These are my principles. If you do not like them, well, I have others." The phrase was used in the title of a legal article by Hesselink, *supra* note 720, p. 68, fn. 41 (on p. 10 in SSRN reproduction).

737. L. D. Picaso, *Experiencias jurídicas y teoría del derecho*, 3rd ed., Barcelona, Editorial Ariel SA, 1993, pp. 216-218.

738. R. B. Schlesinger, "Research on the General Principles of Law Recognized by Civilized Nations", *American Journal of International Law*, Vol. 51, No. 4 (1957), p. 742.

739. See, for instance, in *Audiolux SA ea* v. *Groupe Bruxelles Lambert SA*, CJEU Case C-101/08, 15 October 2009; *Federal Republic of Germany* v. *Council of the European Union*, CJEU Case C-280/93, 5 October 1994. See also: *Société Thermale d'Eugénie-Les Bains*, ECJ Case C-277/95, 18 July 2007; *Annelore Hamilton* v. *Volksbank Filder eG*, ECJ Case C-412/06, 10 April 2008, para. 42; *Pia Messner* v.

In public international law [740], the term "principle" has been an object of intense doctrinal debate, and "is used rather loosely" [741]. Sometimes "principles" are equated to "rules", and other times "rules" include "principles" [742]. Every so often, the term "principle" refers to a general norm that explains and justifies more specific rules [743]. At times, treaties that are not even in force are considered reflective of the "principles of international law" [744]. On occasion, courts and tribunals merely state the existence of a principle without explaining where it has been derived from, for instance in the *Corfu Channel* case [745].

In the *ELSI* case, the ICJ used the terms "rule" and "principle" indiscriminately [746]. The French version of the ICSID Convention uses the expression "principes de droit international", the Spanish "normas de derecho internacional" and the English "rules of international law" (Art. 42 (1)). The preparatory work of the ICSID Convention indicates that the French term "principes" "should not be accorded any particular significance and should not be used to exclude the application of specific rules" [747]. In a highly criticized decision written in French, the *ad hoc* Committee in *Klöckner* v. *Cameroon* seemed to be unaware of

---

Firma Stefan Krüger, ECJ Case C-489/07, 3 September 2009, para. 26. Text of cases available at https://eur-lex.europa.eu/, accessed 3 March 2022.

740. Its decentralization makes it not only "silent on many matters, but also scattered into a mass of detailed rules and precedents which no common link would unite", A. Verdross, "Les principes généraux du droit applicable aux rapports internationaux", *Revue générale de droit international public*, Vol. 45 (1938), p. 52, as quoted in R. Kolb, *Theory of International Law*, Oxford, Hart Publishing, 2016, p. 137.

741. Much confusion derives from the use of the expression "fundamental principles of international law", which are at the top of the legal system and originate in treaty or custom (e.g. the principle of sovereign equality of States or the principle of the prohibition of the threat or the use of force), https://www.oxfordbibliographies.com/view/document/obo-9780199796953/obo-9780199796953-0063.xml, accessed 3 March 2022.

742. As seen, the confusion also originates in the ICSID Convention itself. The French version uses the term "principles" in Article 42 (1) when referring to applicable law, while the English and Spanish versions of the same provision respectively use the terms "norms" and "rules", https://icsid.worldbank.org/resources/rules-and-regulations/convention/overview, accessed 19 May 2022.

743. Rigo Sureda, *supra* note 55, p. 99.

744. In *Phillips* v. *Iran* (1989), the Tribunal ruled that the 1955 Treaty of Amity between the United States and Iran, whether or not in force, was a relevant source of law. *Phillips* v. *Iran*, *supra* note 540, para. 103.

745. *Corfu Channel*, *supra* note 425, p. 22. See also in the PCIJ *Chorzów* case, *supra* note 325, Claim for Indemnity (Jurisdiction), No. 9, p. 21; *Mavrommatis*, *supra* note 330, p. 12. Cf. Pellet (n. 4) 839, para. 266.

746. *Elettronica*, *supra* note 334, Judgment (20 July 1989), p. 42, para. 50. See also Rigo Sureda, *supra* note 55, p. 99.

747. See Schreuer *et al.*, *supra* note 102, p. 603.

other versions of the term and distinguished between "rules of law" and "principles of law" [748].

The PCIJ and later the ICJ have occasionally applied general principles as an integral part of public international law [749] in separate opinions issued by their individual judges [750]. However, the ICJ as a judicial body has generally remained rather cautious in its application of general principles. As a commentator, ICJ Judge Giorgio Gaja attributes this cautiousness to the "difficulty of engaging . . . in a comparative analysis" as well as the "risk of transgressing into the application of equity, which pursuant to Article 38 (2) ICJ Statute requires the parties' particular consent" [751]. Even though neither the ICJ nor its predecessor ever based a decision entirely on general principles, as noted by Mads Andenas and Ludovica Chiussi, this holds true also for treaties and custom, considering that these courts rarely base their decisions on only one source [752]. Moreover, no international court has ever indicated that it does not view general principles as a binding source of international law [753].

Beyond contradictions that exist within case law, there is a surprising dearth of literature on the use of general principles within public international law, especially as compared to doctrinal writings on treaties and custom as sources of law. The literature relating to principles is "quite time-bound"; waves of work were published immediately after the creation of the PCIJ, the ICJ and later during the 1960s [754]. During other times, commentary on the topic has been scarce.

---

748. *Ibid.*, p. 603. See also *Klöckner Industrie-Anlagen GmbH and others* v. *United Republic of Cameroon and Société Camerounaise des Engrais*, ICSID Case No. ARB/81/2, Decision on Annulment (3 May 1985), para. 68.

749. "Arguably, the Court has only referred to general principles of law a few times, once negating them, twice affirming them, and on other occasions relying on them in their decision-making. Its references mainly concern issues of procedure or evidence (not as a direct source of rights and obligations)", "The Use of Domestic Law Principles in the Development of International Law", *International Law Association Reports of Conferences*, Vol. 78 (2018), p. 1173.

750. Cheng, *supra* note 178, p. 388.

751. "Domestic Law Principles", *supra* note 749, p. 1173. See also: G. Gaja, "General Principles in the Jurisprudence of the ICJ", in M. Andenas, M. Fitzmaurice, A. Tanzi and J. Wouters (eds.), *General Principles and the Coherence of International Law*, Leiden, Brill, 2019, pp. 35 *et seq.*

752. M. Andenas and L. Chiussi, "Cohesion, Convergence and Coherence of International Law", in M. Andenas, M. Fitzmaurice, A. Tanzi and J. Wouters (eds.), *General Principles and the Coherence of International Law*, Leiden, Brill, 2019, p. 18.

753. See *Military and Paramilitary Activities in and against Nicaragua (Nicaragua* v. *United States of America)*, Merits, *ICJ Reports 1986*, p. 14, at 98-99.

754. More recent works have also been written on the topic, yet without diminishing the intellectual aura those earlier works still possess. See https://www.oxfordbiblio

General principles of law have been more important in areas of public international law that involve non-State actors, particularly in regard to foreign investments and arbitration [755]. This has been the case particularly in the early oil-related investment cases from the 1960s and 1970s, further analyzed in Chapter VIII.

C. Principles and customary international law

State practice, national legislation and domestic court decisions only become relevant as customary international law when accompanied by *opinio juris*, or the belief that the State is acting pursuant to a right or obligation within international law. A 2020 ILC report notes that the same is not necessarily true for general principles of law [756].

Both general principles and customary rules must find some form of acceptance by the international community. Unlike customary international law, principles are not recognized from the existence of a general practice [757]. However, principles can be extracted from existing norms of customary international law. In this regard, Paolo Palchetti notes that it is not entirely correct to say that principles precede customs since they are identified through a process of abstraction from pre-existing customary rules [758]. In the *Frontier Dispute (Burkina Faso/Mali)* case [759], a Chamber of the ICJ stated that at the time of the decision, the notion of *uti possidetis* (may you continue to possess such as you possess) was not yet considered a customary international law rule but could be recognized as a "general principle" [760] as it had gained recognition by the community of nations.

---

graphies.com/display/document/obo-9780199796953/obo-9780199796953-0063.xml, accessed 3 March 2022.

755. Schreuer *et al.*, *supra* note 102, p. 608.

756. ILC Second Report, *supra* note 5, p. 35. Cf. ILC (Special Rapporteur, Mr M. Vázquez-Bermúdez), Third Report of the ILC, 2022, A/CN.4/753, http://legal.un.org/docs/?symbol=A/CN.4/753, accessed 15 July 2022.

757. P. Palchetti, "The Role of General Principles in Promoting the Development of Customary International Rules", in M. Andenas, M. Fitzmaurice, A. Tanzi and Jan Wouters (eds.), *General Principles and the Coherence of International Law*, Leiden, Brill, 2019, p. 47.

758. "Then, these principles may become the basis of a deductive reasoning leading eventually to the identification of a new rule. Finally, through the accumulation of practice, this rule may acquire the status of a customary rule. So we have here, first, a movement from customary rules to general principles and, subsequently, from principles to customs", Palchetti, *supra* notc 757, p. 50.

759. *Frontier Dispute (Burkina Faso/Mali)*, Judgment (22 December 1986), *ICJ Reports 1986*, p. 554.

760. See *supra* note 756.

General principles therefore become relevant to address the emerging needs of the system in fast-evolving branches of public international law in which practice is lagging behind. They may very well evolve into customary rules or even be incorporated into treaties [761]. Sir Humphrey Waldock sagaciously noted that

> "there will always be a tendency for a general principle of national law recognized in international law to crystallize into customary law" [762].

The role of the general principles may be particularly relevant when a customary rule is undergoing a process of change and its content is still controversial because there are a variety of approaches by States. If considered a general principle it can be applied as a source [763].

D. Principles and policies

The distinction between principles and policies is a controversial topic that Dworkin wrote about extensively. According to Dworkin, policies are "a goal to be reached, generally an improvement in some economic, political or social feature of the community" [764].

This issue has been particularly addressed in the context of investment arbitration. Preambles to investment treaties refer to policies as goals to be reached, such as the economic or social improvement of a community. Some writers argue that principles do not necessarily advance policies but apply due to requirements of justice and fairness. In that case, it is not the role of tribunals to decide a dispute on the basis of such policies, but on a matter of principle [765].

---

761. Andenas and Chiussi, *supra* note 752, p. 18. An example is the principle of elementary considerations of humanity, which was mentioned in the *Corfu Channel* case in 1949, and later on incorporated into the 1984 Montreal Protocol to the Chicago Convention on International Civil Aviation, via Article 3.

762. Waldock, *supra* note 156, p. 62. See also Committee on Formation of Customary (General) International Law, "Final Report of the Committee: Statement of Principles Applicable to the Formation of General Customary International Law", in International Law Association Report of the Sixty Ninth Conference, London, 2000, p. 10-11. "With the evolution of international law, the distinction between general principles of law and international customary law has become increasingly blurred", A. Tanzi, "Conclusions: Testing General Principles of Law in International Investment Law: Between Principles and Rules of International Law", M. Andenas, M. Fitzmaurice, A. Tanzi and J. Wouters (eds.), *General Principles and the Coherence of International Law*, Leiden, Brill, 2019, p. 298.

763. Palchetti, *supra* note 757, p. 53.

764. Dworkin, *supra* note 721, p. 46.

765. For instance, "a tribunal would be on safer ground by making reference to the principle of estoppel or legitimate expectations to give content to the fair and equitable

At a high level of abstraction, however, the distinction between principles and policies may not be so clear: when an issue arises concerning the desirability of a given policy goal, this question will ultimately be one of principle. As such, principles and policies are related terms and do not exclude the relevance of the other [766].

E. Categories of general principles in public international law

Broadly, in public international law there are two categories of general principles of law: substantive and procedural. Substantive general principles apply to the conduct of both private parties and States. Both private parties and States are *inter alia* bound to abide by their contracts, act in good faith and refrain from wrongdoing [767].

Procedural general principles in public international law relate to the exercise of sovereign or adjudicative powers, and as such are applicable only to States and international tribunals. This category generally prescribes the treatment that all individuals are entitled to under the law, whether before a national court or an arbitral tribunal. Procedural general principles are the general principles of due process [768].

F. Functions of principles in public international law

Principles may be applied in different ways in this area of law. For instance, they can serve as interpretive guides, act as subsidiary sources of international law or may also have a corrective function. In this sense, principles "fill gaps left by customary or treaty rules and provide a tool for their interpretation". In interpretive matters they help avoiding or reducing fragmentation in the different subfields of public international law [769]. Moreover, parties and tribunals may recur to general principles to support their arguments and rules. In this persuasive function, invoking general principles may demonstrate that the conclusions are just or equitable, or that they are broadly accepted [770]. These different

---

standard of treatment, rather than appealing to the policy of achieving 'greater economic cooperation' between the contracting states to the treaty", Douglas, *supra* note 39, p. 83. See also Rigo Sureda, *supra* note 55, p. 101.

766. Rigo Sureda, *supra* note 55, pp. 101-102.

767. Kotuby and Sobota, *supra* note 157, p. 2.

768. *Ibid.*, p. 2.

769. Andenas and Chiussi, *supra* note 752, p. 10.

770. A. Carlevaris, "General Principles of Commercial law and International Investment Law", in M. Andenas, M. Fitzmaurice, A. Tanzi and J. Wouters (eds.), *General Principles and the Coherence of International Law*, Leiden, Brill, 2019, p. 224.

functions of the principles in public international law may be grouped as follows:

1. Principles as interpretive guides

At a basic level, general principles have a limited role [771], serving as interpretive guides to be applied alongside the law governing the relationship, which can be either an international treaty or customary law [772]. In accordance with the general rules for interpretation of public international law, general principles may clarify the obscure or uncertain – for instance, in interpreting terms "not susceptible to an ordinary or common meaning interpretation, or as a means for ascertaining the intent of the parties" [773].

2. Principles as subsidiary source of public international law

Some writers consider principles as no more than subsidiary sources of international law. According to this view, principles are only applicable when disputes arise that cannot be resolved using treaty or customary law alone, and the dispute requires an outcome beyond the status quo behavior of the parties [774]. Jeroen van den Boogaard notes that this was the function the drafters of the PCIJ Statute had in mind regarding general principles as a source of law [775].

On this topic, a British-United States Claims Arbitral Tribunal held that:

> "International law . . . may not contain, and generally does not contain, express rules decisive of particular cases; but the function of jurisprudence is to resolve the conflict of opposing rights and interests by applying, in default of any specific provisions of law, the corollaries of general principles, and so to find . . . the solution of the problem." [776]

---

771. General principles have a limited role in interpretive matters, for instance in international economic law. See Remiro Brotóns, *supra* note 264, p. 206.

772. Cheng, *supra* note 178, p. 390.

773. J. van den Boogaard, *Proportionality in International Humanitarian Law: Principle, Rule and Practice*, Amsterdam, Universiteit van Amsterdam, 2019, pp. 40-41.

774. Bogdan, *supra* note 5, p. 44. See also McNair, *supra* note 4, pp. 3-19.

775. "The principles of international law reinforce weak points of the law in this role or bridge gaps in general international law and in between specific branches of international law", Van den Boogaard, *supra* note 773, p. 41.

776. *Eastern Extension, Australasia and China Telegraph Co. Ltd. Case (British-United States Claims Arbitral Tribunal)*, (1923) 6 RIAA, p. 112, 114.

3. Principles offering precision to broad legal issues

General principles may also be applied to offer precision and give context to broad or amorphous legal provisions. For instance, the "fair and equitable treatment" standard for foreign investors is, on its own, an incomplete norm which grants adjudicators a considerable level of discretion in its application. An ICSID Tribunal expressly made use of general principles in determining the "precise content" of the fair and equitable treatment standard because

> "[t]reaties and international conventions . . . are not of great help to this end, as for the most part, they also contain rather general references to fair and equitable treatment and full protection and security without further elaboration" [777].

This use of general principles also refers to interpretive purposes but goes a step further by providing specific elements or attributes not expressly enunciated in the broad standards contained in the applicable law itself [778].

4. General principles as a legal system

Some commentators argue that general principles represent a legal system intermediate between municipal legal systems and public international law. They sometimes refer to the concept as "transnational law", *lex mercatoria* or the like [779]. The matter will be further addressed in Chapter XI [780].

---

777. *Merrill & Ring* v. *Canada*, *supra* note 276, paras. 186-187.

778. "For example, the FET standard was deemed violated where a host State seized and auctioned an investor's property after providing notice that, although compliant with local law, was considered inadequate when measured against universal norms. In this way, specific precepts common to all legal systems are useful to interpret broad investment protections", Kotuby and Sobota, *supra* note 157, pp. 32-33. See also A. Carlevaris, "The Use of the UNIDROIT Principles and Other Transnational Principles of Commercial Law in Treaty Arbitration: Hazards and Opportunities", *ICSID Review: Foreign Investment Law Journal*, Vol. 36, No. 3 (2021), p. 615.

779. "Some critics object that an economic development agreement cannot be governed by the general principles of law, because the general principles are not a legal system. It is true that the general principles, unlike municipal systems of law normally applied by domestic courts, do not constitute a unified system of law deriving binding effect from a sovereign government. As a practical matter, however, the general principles of law do form a coherent body of legal principles which are applied by arbitrators through the same process of judicial elaboration that characterizes other legal systems", Curtis, *supra* note 119, pp. 332-333.

780. See esp. Chap. XI.E., *infra*, "Non-State law and uniform law".

5. Principles as corrective tools

When the applicable national laws are insufficient to resolve a dispute, do not meet international standards or would yield an unacceptable result when applied in a particular case, courts and tribunals may apply principles to correct or supplement the gaps in national laws [781]. This corrective function is important within public international law because the domestic legislation must not be used as a mere blank sheet of paper with which any dictator or dominant group can do as they please [782].

The use of general principles as corrective tools is less common when the countries involved in the international dispute have developed legal systems, such as England or Italy. Using general principles for corrective purposes is more appropriate when the legal systems involved exhibit a marked contrast on certain important points of law, both in terms of their content and the stage of their development [783].

On occasion, domestic laws may be underdeveloped, unsuited to resolve a transnational dispute or, in some extreme cases, may be entirely unable to meet minimum standards of propriety and fairness [784]. In this situation, the use of general principles allows adjudicators greater flexibility in their interpretive task, harmonizing – in the words of Chaïm Perelman – equity and the law [785]. Following similar reasoning, a 2002 ICC decision interpreted local law in light of general principles internationally recognized such as *venire contra factum proprium* [786].

Comparative law may provide valuable corrective assistance to adjudicators faced with concepts or rules that exist exclusively within one (or a small number of) legal systems [787].

Resolving a transnational dispute through the application of general principles is perhaps less intrusive and less arbitrary than refusing to apply a particular foreign law on the grounds of public policy. In those

781. Kotuby and Sobota, *supra* note 157, p. 37. "[I]nternational standards . . . apply uniformly and are not dependent on the peculiarities of any particular national law. They take due account of the needs of international intercourse and permit cross-fertilization between systems that may be unduly wedded to conceptual distinctions [rather than] a pragmatic and fair resolution in the individual case", ICC Case No. 8385, in J. J. Arnaldez, Y. Derains and D. Hascher (eds.), *Collection of ICC Arbitral Awards 1996-2000*, The Hague, Kluwer Law International / ICC Publishing, 2003, p. 474, comments of Y. Derains.

782. Kotuby and Sobota, *supra* note 157, pp. 33-34.

783. McNair, *supra* note 4, p. 1.

784. Kotuby and Sobota, *supra* note 157, p. 32.

785. Perelman, *supra* note 714, p. 185.

786. ICC Arb. No. 10947/ESR/MS (June 2002), reprinted in *ASA Bulletin*, Vol. 22 (2/2004), p. 308, para. 30.

787. Gutteridge, *supra* note 154, p. 10.

cases, while the local law may have been completely displaced, it is not rejected due to its lack of compliance with the parochial "good morals" of the forum. Instead, local law must be understood as existing in harmony with the international standards enshrined in the applied principle [788]. Public policy issues will be addressed in greater detail in Chapter XXI.

6. *Principles as the ultimate source of rules of law*

Principles can also be understood as expressions of the sources of the different rules of law [789]. In 1984, the ICJ stated that the terms "rules" and "principles" can be considered as "a dual expression to convey one and the same idea" [790]. As stated in an International Law Association (ILA) report, if an argument can be advanced that a specific legal rule is generally accepted, then there is likely a common principle behind it that can be extracted. In this case, the rule therefore becomes an expression of the common principle [791].

7. *Principles as a "superconstitution" of public international law*

Some consider general principles to be the embodiment of the most important norms – the "superconstitution" – of international law [792]. According to this view, the existence of general principles is a testament to the fundamental unity of the law [793]. In this sense, general principles operate as "a centripetal force" for the interaction between diverse areas of law, such as international environmental law, international investment law and international human rights law. In this regard, Andenas and Chiussi ask

> "[w]hat would be left of the legal system if specialized courts and tribunals were allowed to ignore the common substantive and procedural rules of international law" [794]?

---

788. "This is also what differentiates the general principles from the *lex mercatoria*, which traditionally has little formal basis in a consensus of domestic laws", Kotuby and Sobota, *supra* note 157, pp. 34-35.

789. Cheng, *supra* note 178, p. 390.

790. *Delimitation of the Maritime Boundary*, *supra* note 732, Judgment (12 October 1984), pp. 288-290, para. 79.

791. "Domestic Law Principles", *supra* note 749, pp. 1236-1237.

792. Cheng, *supra* note 178, p. 5.

793. An unmistakable feature of international arbitral and judicial decisions is an assumption by international courts and tribunals that the universal concept of law exists, independently of any particular system. *Ibid.*, pp. 390-391.

794. *Ibid.*, pp. 33-34. General principles also show considerable potential to reduce the separation between international law and municipal legal systems.

The UNCITRAL tribunal in *Methanex* v. *USA* (2005) advanced this view in the following statement:

> "[T]he Tribunal agrees with the implication of Methanex's submission with respect to the obligations of an international tribunal – that as a matter of international constitutional law a tribunal has an independent duty to apply imperative principles of law or *jus cogens* and not to give effect to parties' choices of law that are inconsistent with such principles." [795]

G. Terminology

General principles are referred to using a variety of terms. For example, the 1979 Athens Resolution released by the Institute of International Law on "The Proper Law of the Contract in Agreements Between a State and a Foreign Private Person" alludes to "the principles common to . . . (domestic) systems, or the general principles of law, or the principles applied in international economic relations" [796]. The word "principles" also appears in other legal instruments, such as the 1954 Consortium Agreement with Iran [797], and is included in certain international contracts as well, such as those governing oil and gas investments in the Middle East (some of which have been the subject of landmark arbitrations in the past century). In those and other cases settled through arbitration, similar expressions have also been used by the tribunals [798]. Many of these cases will be referred to in Chapter VIII.

795. *Methanex* v. *USA*, *supra* note 527, Final Award of the Tribunal on Jurisdiction and Merits (3 August 2005), Part IV, Chapter C, Article 1105, NAFTA, para. 24.

796. The Athens resolution is cited in J. F. Lalive, "Contrats entre Etats ou entreprises étatiques et personnes privées: Développements récents", *Recueil des cours*, Vol. 181 (1983), pp. 51-52. Weil believes that, from the deliberations of the Institute, its members tried to ensure that the notion of general principles of law was considered autonomously with regard to international and domestic legal systems. See B. Oppetit, *Teoría del Arbitraje*, trans. E. Silva Romero, F. Mantilla Espinoza and J. Joaquín Caicedo Demoulin, Bogotá, Legis Editores, 2006, pp. 202-203.

797. The 1954 Agreement is governed by "principles of law common to Iran and the several nationals in which the other parties were incorporated and, in the absence of such common principles, then by and in accordance with principles of law recognized by civilized nations in general, including such of those principles as may have been applied by international tribunals".

798. "General principles of private international law" (*Aramco*); "general principles of law" (*Libya* v. *Texaco* and *Liamco*, 1977; *Aminoil* v. *Kuwait*, 1982; *Framatome* v. *Iran*, 1982); "generally admitted principles" (ICC Case No. 2152/1972); "general principles of law and justice" (ICC Case No. 3380/1980); "general principles of law that govern international transactions" (ICC Case No. 2291/1975); "general principles adopted by international arbitral jurisprudence" (ICC Case No. 3344/1981); "amply admitted general principles that govern international commercial law" (ICC Case

In the context of international State investment contracts, sometimes the terminology "transnational law" or *lex mercatoria* can also be found in reference to general principles [799].

For many years within public international law, the expression "recognized by civilized nations" has been used, alongside the terms, "principles" and "general principles". This terminology was used by Lewis Henry Morgan, an American anthropologist and lawyer who in 1877 published a treatise on ancient society. He classified human societies based on their level of cultural development, rather than on race or religious grounds. Further, Morgan divided peoples into three categories: civilized, barbarian and savage [800]. European Christian countries and some other former Western-hemisphere colonies fell into the category of "civilized nations". Western jurists considered themselves the legitimate interpreters of the "civilized law" [801].

For more than a century, customary international law employed similar terminology regarding the protection of foreign investors. For instance, in 1910 the American Secretary of State Elihu Root stated that countries must conform to "an established standard of civilization" in their treatment of aliens. This standard of justice was "of such general acceptance by all civilized countries as to form a part of the international law of the world" [802].

Article 38 of the Statute of the International Court of Justice refers to general principles as a source of public international law, describing them as "the general principles of law recognized by civilized nations". In the deliberations that occurred during the drafting of this provision, differences in opinion emerged regarding the purpose of including the

---

No. 3267/1979); "general principles of law applicable to international economic relationships" (ICSID Case, *Asia* v. *Republic of Indonesia*, 1983); "general principles of law comprised within" (ICC Case No. 3327/1981); "rules of law" (ICC Case No. 1641/1969).

799. See *supra* note 780.

800. "Non-Christian States with centralized governments (such as the Ottoman Empire, Persia, China, Japan, and Siam at the time) were considered part of the category of 'barbarian' States. In the category of 'savage' States were the myriad of tribal and national groups in Africa and the Pacific Islands", Neff, *supra* note 143, p. 311.

801. Y. Dezalay and B. G. Garth, *Dealing in Virtue: International Commercial Arbitration and the Construction of a Transnational Legal Order*, Chicago, University of Chicago Press, 1996, pp. 86-87. In 1900, at the Paris Exposition Fair and the First Congress of Comparative Law the French jurist Saleilles spoke of a *fonde commune* among legal systems. Lambert, also French, made reference only of countries in the same degree of civilization (*droit commun de l'humanité civilisée*), D. S. Clark, "Centennial World Congress on Comparative Law: Nothing New in 2000? Comparative Law in 1900 and Today", *Tulane Law Review*, Vol. 75 (2001), p. 885.

802. Neff, *supra* note 143, pp. 273-274.

expression, notably between the French Baron Descamps, the British Lord Phillimore and the US representative Elihu Root. Root ultimately abandoned his position and submitted to the positions of Descamps and Phillimore [803].

Baron Descamps was the chairman of the Advisory Committee of Jurists that had drafted the exact wording of Article 38. He proposed to refer to general principles as "the rules of international law as recognized by the legal conscience of civilized nations" [804]. Descamps explained that the expression referred to

> "the law of objective justice, at any rate in so far as it has twofold confirmation of the concurrent teachings of jurisconsults of authority and of the public conscience of civilized nations" [805].

Root considered that this definition was too wide and would lead to the application of "principles, differently understood in different countries" [806]. His amended proposal referred to "the general principles of law recognized by civilized nations", as included in Article 38 today [807]. No additional explanation for this choice of language was provided by the Committee's report, nor was the matter thoroughly discussed in the process of the Statute's formal adoption by the League of Nations [808].

Recently, the Drafting Committee working on the arbitral rules of the Permanent Court of Arbitration considered replacing the archaic expression "the law of civilized nations" with more modern language. However, the Committee ultimately decided against amending the expression for fear that such a change would lead to different interpretations of the traditional meaning of the provision [809]. Therefore, no amendments were made in this regard to the PCA Rules approved in 2012.

---

803. Cheng, *supra* note 178, pp. 14-15.

804. PCIJ, Advisory Committee of Jurists, Procès-verbaux of the Proceedings of the Committee, 16 June-24 July 1920, with Annexes, p. 306.

805. *Ibid.*, p. 324.

806. *Ibid.*, p. 308.

807. *Ibid.*, pp. 344-336.

808. Documents concerning the Action Taken by the Council of the League of Nations under Article 14 of the Covenant and the Adoption by the Assembly of the Statute of the Permanent Court. G. Gaja, "General Principles of Law", *Max Planck Encyclopedia of Public International Law*, 2013.

809. B. W. Daly, E. Goriatcheva and H. A. Meighen, *A Guide to the PCA Arbitration Rules*, Oxford, Oxford University Press, 2014, p. 137.

Bin Cheng adds to the debate that the expression "civilized nations" was originally used to refer to civilized "peoples" rather than civilized "States". The epithet "civilized" was used to exclude systems of law existing within "primitive" communities that had not yet been civilized. When applied to States on an international scale, however, the term must be understood differently [810].

Nowadays, in fact, it is widely accepted that the term "civilized" includes all members of the United Nations [811]. No State member of the United Nations can be considered "uncivilized" [812]. Recently, the Special Rapporteur of the ILC for the topic related to general principles suggested that the term "civilized nations" should be replaced in international instruments with the more appropriate term "community of nations" that was included in the International Covenant on Civil and Political Rights [813].

H. General principles and Article 38 of the ICJ Statute

The reference in ICJ Statute Article 38, paragraph 1 *(c)*, to general principles of law led to the further development of the concept within public international law. The records of the debate on this provision, discussed above, show a compromise between a series of differing opinions – according to Judge Giorgio Gaja – "especially on the question whether a general principle was to be regarded as part of international law only because it was already present in municipal systems" [814]. These differing views, according to Robert Jennings, have perhaps contributed to the disagreements regarding what is meant by

810. Cheng, *supra* note 178, p. 25.

811. *Reparation for Injuries Suffered*, *supra* note 330, at p. 219. See R. Monaco, *Sources of International Law,* in *Encyclopedia of Public International Law*, p. 471, interpreting as principles of some States that have a common legal evolution.

812. Bogdan states that "the term 'civilized nation' must at present be interpreted to mean any country which has a legal system consisting of rules for human behavior imposed and enforced by the state", in Bogdan, *supra* note 5, p. 45.

813. Article 15, paragraph 2, of the International Covenant on Civil and Political Rights. The treaty has more than 170 State parties and can therefore be considered widely accepted. As Article 15, paragraph 2, clearly refers to the source of international law listed in Article 38, paragraph 1 *I* of the ICJ Statute (*supra* note 465), it can be considered to reflect today's interpretation of the term "civilized nations". ILC Second Report, *supra* note 5, p. 4. See also *supra* note 756.

814. The Committee's report did not provide any additional explanation, nor was there any substantial discussion on the principles of law in the debates that led to the formal adoption of the PCIJ Statute by the League of Nations (Documents concerning the Action Taken by the Council of the League of Nations under Article 14 of the Covenant and the Adoption by the Assembly of the Statute of the Permanent Court). See Gaja, *supra* note 808.

the general principles referred to in Article 38 of the ICJ Statute. The only certainty in the definition of "general principles" is that they must refer to something different from international custom [815].

One understanding of the term "general principles" holds that they have been distilled from essential concepts found within domestic laws. In this regard, Hersch Lauterpacht explains that universal conceptions of law are extracted from generally recognized private law principles, although many public international lawyers are not aware of this [816]. Examples that illustrate the parallels between universal conceptions of law and private law principles are the principle of reparation for caused damage, the principles of interpretation of rules or the principles used for resolving conflicts of laws rules, many of which are referred to using Latin maxims [817]. Things have, however, evolved, and other examples have emerged in the realm of public international law, for instance, regarding the principle of humanity within international humanitarian law [818]. The matter will be further addressed in the following chapter.

Another perspective sees general principles as "nothing more or less than the principles of natural law", such as the natural law principle *nemo judex in re sua* (no one is the judge in his own case) [819]. According to Jennings, this approach can be regarded as complementary to the other distilling universal conceptions from private law, and both approaches have become interwoven in the entire fabric of the historical development of international law [820].

Another viewpoint sees the general principles of law as a sort of modern *ius gentium* for the regulation of international investment contracts [821]. In the end, this is simply a different approach to the same idea [822], applied in the specific context of foreign investments.

---

815. Jennings, *supra* note 274, p. 339.

816. Lauterpacht, *supra* note 3, pp. 36-37.

817. The judiciary has also developed a number of general principles of law, such as *audiatur et altera pars, actori incumbit onus probandi*, or the fact that the judge of merits is also judge of the incidental jurisdiction, https://www.oxfordbibliographies.com/view/document/obo-9780199796953/obo-9780199796953-0063.xml, accessed 3 March 2020.

818. *Ibid.*

819. However, its authority does not reach beyond this point. Lauterpacht, *supra* note 3, p. 178.

820. Jennings, *supra* note 274, p. 340.

821. From this perspective, international investment contracts evoke the Roman *ius gentium*, Rousseau, *supra* note 149.

822. Jennings, *supra* note 274, pp. 340-341:

"Whichever of these definitions of 'general principles of law' is adopted, it is clear that general principles are an entirely different kind of 'source' from either convention or custom. For instance, whether the principle *nemo judex in re sua* is regarded as a

I. Article 38 of the ICJ Statute and non liquet

The inclusion of "general principles" as a source of public international law in Article 38 of the ICJ Statute had a clear objective: to avoid *non liquet* [823]. The court can always apply general principles, notwithstanding a direct authorization of the parties. In contrast, Article 38 (2) of the ICJ Statute requires consent for equity adjudication [824].

Divergences in these discussions derive from differing civil law and Anglo-Saxon approaches as to the power of the adjudicator. In common law jurisdictions, a decision creates law, whereas the prevailing civil law view is that the adjudicator does not make law, but merely applies it. This is why to prevent a denial of justice, civil law systems make use of general principles of law [825]. Article 38 (3) of the ICJ Statute was designed specifically to avoid any issues that may arise regarding *non liquet* [826].

Article 38 of the ICJ Statute assumes the essential unity of all law and presents opportunities for progressive solutions to develop, filling apparent gaps and weaknesses [827]. Contrary to judges in domestic legal systems who have the duty to adjudicate even in cases of obscurity or insufficiency of the law, prior to Article 38 international judges had no such power, unless expressly authorized to resolve the dispute by the litigating parties [828].

Lauterpacht argues that Article 38 of the ICJ Statute represents the final and authoritative abandonment of the misleading doctrine that public international law constitutes a self-sufficing body of rules. The Committee of Jurists that drafted the ICJ Statute unanimously opined that public international law is incomplete and leaves many problems unanswered. Whereas a minority group advocated that the Court in these situations should pronounce a *non liquet* and declare itself unable

---

part of natural law, as a generalization derived from the municipal laws of civilized countries, or as belonging to a kind of modern *ius gentium*, the striking fact about this concept is that it is in conflict with the principle of traditional customary international law that no tribunal has jurisdiction over a sovereign State without that State's consent."

823. "The term *'non liquet'* literally means 'it is not clear'. In Roman law, it referred simply to the deferment of a case for insufficient information. But today, a finding of non liquet means that the court cannot decide a case due to a gap (or lacuna) in the law", D. Bodansky, "Non liquet", *Max Planck Encyclopedias of International Law*, 2006, https://opil.ouplaw.com/view/10.1093/law:epil/9780199231690/law-9780199231690-e1669#, accessed 31 March 2022.

824. Cheng, *supra* note 178, p. 20.

825. *Ibid.*, p. 16.

826. Bogdan, *supra* note 5, p. 37.

827. Rigo Sureda, *supra* note 55, p. 101.

828. Rousseau, *supra* note 149, p. 76.

to resolve the dispute, the majority of the Committee of Jurists believed that a decision must always be rendered, or else particular cases may amount to a denial of justice [829].

J. List of general principles of law

In 1957, Francis Mann conducted an extensive survey investigating the application of general private law principles in transactions between States, in particular with respect to civil and commercial law [830]. One of the objectives of his study was to question whether a common repository of general principles of law underpinning any and all legal systems truly exists, including within public and private international law. Mann notes that at least two of the principles that are commonly invoked – good faith in the performance of contractual obligations and *pacta sunt servanda* – are indisputably part of public international law [831].

According to a 2018 ILA report, tribunals typically make use of general principles when dealing with questions related to procedural law principles, contractual/private law principles (both of a general and more technical nature) and principles expanding upon the content of primary international law obligations, particularly within investment law. In some cases, municipal law principles were explicitly or implicitly excluded, the latter being most common in the foreign investment context [832]. For instance, in *SeaCo Inc.* v. *Iran* [833], the Tribunal rejected the principle of promissory estoppel because it "has not emerged as a rule of international law or as a general principle of law" [834].

It is an impossible task to exhaustively enumerate the principles of private law that can be regarded as "general" principles recognized by the international community. However, undoubtedly, some principles of private law were particularly useful in developing the law of nations, such as the impossibility of contractual performance, the doctrine of the abuse of rights and the doctrine of estoppel [835].

---

829. Lauterpacht, *supra* note 3, p. 67-68.
830. F. A. Mann, "Reflections on a Commercial Law of Nations", *British Yearbook of International Law*, Vol. 33 (1957); Reed, *supra* note 21, p. 20.
831. *Ibid.*, pp. 223-224.
832. "Domestic Law Principles", *supra* note 749 , p. 1198.
833. *SeaCo Inc.* v. *The Islamic Republic of Iran, The Iranian Meat Organization and others*, IUSCT Case No. 260, Award No. 531-260-2 (1992).
834. G. H. Aldrich, *The Jurisprudence of the Iran-United States Claims Tribunal: An Analysis of the Decisions of the Tribunal*, Oxford, Clarendon Press, 1996, pp. 169-170.
835. Gutteridge, *supra* note 154, pp. 5-6.

Several scholarly works [836] have summarized those principles generally applicable to international contractual disputes resolved through arbitration, which has a long tradition of invoking them [837]. In his 1988 work *New Lex Mercatoria: The First Twenty-five Years*, Lord Mustill identified twenty principles that are generally applied to international arbitration disputes [838], among them *pacta sunt servanda* (the binding character of contract), *rebus sic stantibus* (hardship) and good faith. Other authors have compiled similar collections of applicable general principles [839]. German Professor Klaus Peter Berger has even piloted the project of creating a database that aims at the "creeping" (i.e., the non-static and progressive) attempt to codify principles [840].

Principles are also an important legal source within international investment law. For instance, much of the legal support for ordering full compensation as a remedy for expropriation is based upon notions of unjust enrichment and acquired rights, which are considered general principles of law [841]. Compensation itself is considered a general principle of law [842].

Good faith and its corollaries are probably the most frequently cited example of a principle of international law also invoked in investment claims and broadly accepted in municipal legal systems [843]. For instance, in *Phoenix* v. *Czech Republic* the Tribunal stated that the

836. See E. Gaillard and J. Savage (eds.), *Fouchard Gaillard Goldman on International Commercial Arbitration*, The Hague, Kluwer Law International, 1999, pp. 830 ff. A further discussion relates to the issue of whether general principles of law are based on the normative activity of States, as stated by Gaillard, in E. Gaillard, *Teoría jurídica del arbitraje internacional*, trans. María Esmeralda Moreno, Asunción, La Ley Paraguaya / CEDEP / Thomson Reuters, 2010, p. 56, or based on comparative law, C. Brunner, *Force Majeure and Hardship under General Contract Principles: Exemption for Non-Performance in International Arbitration*, The Hague, Kluwer Law International, 2008, p. 5, not including only what the majority of States or legal systems regulate.

837. L. Craig, W. Park and J. Paulsson, *International Chamber of Commerce Arbitration*, 3rd ed., New York, Oceana Publications, 2000, p. 333.

838. He refers to them as principles or rules of *lex mercatoria*. L. Mustill, "New *Lex Mercatoria*: The First Twenty-Five Years", *Arbitration International*, Vol. 4, No. 2 (1988), pp. 86, 112-113.

839. For instance, in arbitration, Fouchard, Gaillard and Goldman find in arbitral awards principles relative to the validity, interpretation and performance of contracts. Gaillard and Savage, *supra* note 836, pp. 830 ff.

840. See http://www.trans-lex.org/, accessed 3 March 2022.

841. On unjust enrichment, see B. Juratowitch and J. Shaerf, "Unjust Enrichment as a Primary Rule of International Law", in M. Andenas, M. Fitzmaurice, A. Tanzi and J. Wouters (eds.), *General Principles and the Coherence of International Law*, Leiden, Brill, 2019, pp. 228 ff.

842. Sornarajah, *supra* note 29, p. 85.

843. Carlevaris, *supra* note 770, p. 219.

ICSID Convention and the BIT had to be construed with due regard to the international principle of good faith "also recognized in most, if not all, domestic legal systems. It appears therefore as a kind of 'Janus concept', with one face looking at the national legal order and one at the international legal order". And in most cases, but not in all, a violation of the international principle of good faith and a violation of the national principle of good faith go hand in hand. Therefore, ICSID tribunals that have relied on this principle in order to determine whether or not a protected investment exists have often relied on both dimensions of the principle [844].

K. Proof of general principles

General principles of law do not merely reflect the arbitrators' own personal sense of justice but constitute an important part of public international law and, as such, must be proven and not presumed [845]. There is a burden of proof for appealing to general principles of law, which has led them to be invoked less frequently in investment arbitration due to the relative difficulty of proving their existence within many of the world's major legal systems [846].

In practice, the express use of comprehensive comparisons to resolve international legal disputes is extremely rare [847]. Meg Kinnear has pointed out that arbitrators invoking such principles usually only explain them in vague terms. Only infrequently does extensive proof of the practice of general principles exist across different systems [848].

International tribunals "rarely reveal the methods they employ to determine general principles of law, and hardly ever refer to comparative law research" [849]. Waldock explains that

844. *Phoenix* v. *Czech Republic*, *supra* note 53, Award (15 April 2009), para. 109.

845. Schreuer *et al.*, *supra* note 102, p. 610.

846. M. Kinnear, "Treaties as Agreements to Arbitrate: International Law as the Governing Law", in A. Jan Van den Berg (ed.), *International Arbitration 2006: Back to Basics?* (ICCA Congress Series, No. 13), The Hague, Kluwer Law International, 2007, p. 428. Waldock points that "it has never been the practice of the Court or of arbitral tribunals to insist upon proof of the widespread manifestations of a principle or to indulge in elaborate comparative studies of the legal systems of the world", Waldock, *supra* note 156, p. 67.

847. Cheng, *supra* note 178, p. 392.

848. Kinnear, *supra* note 846, pp. 428-429.

849. Kotuby and Sobota, *supra* note 157, p. 24. "When international courts and arbitral tribunals have resorted to domestic principles in their legal reasoning, they seem to have done so cautiously, indirectly, and without clarifying how those principles were identified and how are they to be correctly applied", "Domestic Law Principles", *supra* note 749, p. 1171.

> "(t)ruth to tell, arbitral tribunals, which usually consist of one, three or five judges, have probably done no more in most cases than take into account their own knowledge of the principles of the systems in which the arbitrators were themselves trained".

Arbitrators tend to assume that the general principles that exist within their own legal system are also accepted elsewhere, but this is not always the case [850]. After extensive research on the topic, Rudolf Schlesinger points out that the adjudicators frequently justify their reasoning based on "a hunch, a hunch probably based upon the legal system or systems with which he happened to be familiar" [851].

In the famous ICSID case *Klöckner* v. *Cameroon*, the Annulment Committee pointed out that there had been a lack of authority to support the use of general principles in the annulled decision. The Committee ultimately concluded that the reasoning of the annulled award seemed more like a simple reference to equity rather than to general principles [852].

Therefore, the matter must be addressed with care. The next chapter will elaborate on general principles and the appropriate handling of comparative law in their regard.

---

850. Waldock, *supra* note 156, pp. 67-68.
851. Schlesinger, *supra* note 738, p. 734.
852. Schreuer *et al.*, *supra* note 102, p. 610.

CHAPTER VII

GENERAL PRINCIPLES OF PUBLIC INTERNATIONAL LAW AND COMPARATIVE LAW

A. General principles of private law, public law or public international law?

Historically, there has been a debate about whether general principles of public international law should be extracted from private law, public law or from public international law itself[853]. As will be seen in the following pages, the matter raises complexities associated with unsettled issues in relation to the comparative law method used to detect the existence of general principles.

1. Domestic law principles?

There is a widespread understanding that – despite some uncertainties in both doctrine and jurisprudence – general principles of law are essentially "those principles that are applied in domestic legal systems around the world, such as the principle of *pacta sunt servanda*" [854].

The origins of the use of domestic law principles can be traced to the emphasis in Roman law that international lawyers placed in their writings throughout the centuries. Roman legal maxims have undoubtedly played a significant role in the shaping of both general principles of law and public international law in its formative period.

Roman law developed on a case-by-case basis, usually with the underlying reasoning implicit in the discussion of the facts. Occasionally, "working rules of thumb" or maxims were provided to guide reasoning. Even though such general rules were intended to be applied in specific cases, they were formulated in general terms. These maxims were compiled into many collections and appear in Justinian's

853. Cheng, *supra* note 178, pp. 2-3. A 2020 report by the ILC in relation to this field states that "general principles of law comprise those: *(a)* derived from national legal systems; *(b)* formed within the international legal system", ILC Second Report, *supra* note 5, Draft Conclusion 3, p. 58.

854. See, for instance, in the recent UNIDROIT/IFAD ALIC Legal Guide, *supra* note 296, p. 22.

Corpus Iuris Civilis published in the sixth century. Medieval canonists reviewed these rules and added others, referring to them as *brocards* [855].

These maxims became particularly relevant in the development of public international law [856]. As described by Harold Gutteridge, the law of nations took concepts from Roman civil law which have been disguised in the garb of custom, reason or the law of nature [857]. Hersch Lauterpacht notes several examples of international arbitrations invoking Roman law as the *ratio scripta*. He argued that this use is justified: Roman law has become a part of the positive law of nations and has been used as a convenient expression of general principles of law in the absence of an international legal language [858].

Since law developed in the municipal sphere, it is natural to make reference to domestic law when looking for universal principles. When adjudicating an international dispute, international courts and tribunals have historically applied those principles underlying domestic laws that previously proved useful in providing substantial justice between individuals in similar circumstances [859]. According to Humphrey Waldock, almost every international lawyer must make use of the principles and notions of one or more national law systems. Likewise, international adjudicators are still encouraged in their training to draw upon legal ideas derived from national law. Since law is a reflection of the interests and needs of human society, many commonalities are to be found in the legal ideas of different national systems [860].

Statements were even made that the "law of nations is but private law 'writ large'" [861]. However, Gutteridge argues that a high degree of caution must be exercised before any private law principle or analogy can be accepted as conforming to the universal or general recognition

---

855. Kotuby and Sobota, *supra* note 157, pp. 8-9.
856. Waldock, *supra* note 156, p. 55.
857. Gutteridge, *supra* note 154, p. 2.
858. But beyond this its authority does not go. Lauterpacht, *supra* note 3, p. 178.
859. Cheng, *supra* note 178, p. 391.
860. Waldock, *supra* note 156, pp. 55-56. According to Lucy Reed, if the distilled wisdom of municipal law, in the form of general principles of law, has any relevance within public international law, it must be because there are common international needs that must be addressed and common methodological and practical problems that must be solved. Reed, *supra* note 21, p. 224. See also S. Vogenauer, "Sources of Law and Legal Method in Comparative Law", in M. Reimann and R. Zimmermann (eds.), *The Oxford Handbook of Comparative Law*, Oxford, Oxford University Press, 2006.
861. T. E. Holland, *Studies in International Law*, Oxford, Clarendon Press, 1898, p. 152. Gutteridge, *supra* note 154, p. 1.

standard for use on an international scale[862]. The matter will be addressed below.

2. Public law principles?

In one of his early works, Lauterpacht proposed that general principles emerged from private law. He later admitted that general principles should also include principles of public law or jurisprudence[863].

Judge Tanaka wrote in the ICJ *South West Africa Case (Second Phase)* of 1966 that so long as the "general principles of law" are not qualified, the "law" must be understood to embrace all branches of law, including municipal law, public law, constitutional law, administrative law, private law, commercial law, substantive and procedural law, and others[864].

Some principles such as those regarding State responsibility derive from private law. Others relating to adjudicatory proceedings are generally considered to originate in public and not private law[865]. In addition to these divergences, however, public and private law also overlap in many ways[866].

The *Chorzów Factory* and *Corfu Channel* cases decided by the PCIJ and the ICJ, respectively, contained statements that general principles of law can be found in both municipal law and international jurisprudence. Later, in 1984, Sir Robert Jennings referred to a "big change in content" in international law emerging from the "actual necessities arising from the juxtaposition of a larger number of States, all of them pushed by modern economic and technological developments into ever-increasing interdependence in even more matters; matters which therefore imperatively required regulation by international law"[867].

The trend accelerated in the twenty-first century with the emergence of more States and with technological advances that are creating new areas requiring regulation, among other developments[868]. Recently,

---

862. *Ibid.*, p. 1. According to Jenks, there is likely to be an increasing number of cases in which conflicts of law must be governed by international rather than national rules. Jenks, *supra* note 2, p. 51.

863. Lauterpacht did so in his book *The Function of Law in the International Community*, Oxford, Clarendon Press, 1933. See Cheng, *supra* note 178, p. 3.

864. *ICJ Reports 1966*, p. 294.

865. Cheng, *supra* note 178, p. 392.

866. Bogdan, *supra* note 5, p. 42.

867. R. Jennings, "Teachings and Teaching in International Law", in J. Makarczyk (ed.), *Essays in International Law in Honour of Judge Manfred Lachs*, The Hague, Martinus Nijhoff, 1984, pp. 121, 124.

868. R. Kolb, "General Principles of Law, Jus Cogens and the Unity of the International Legal Order", *Queen Mary Studies in International Law*, Vol. 27 (2019), p. 127.

for example, several ICSID cases have turned to public international law and even human rights law, in addition to domestic law, to resolve disputes [869].

An ILC report notes that practice and recent scholarship have revealed that all branches of national legal systems, including their private and public law, become potentially relevant when identifying a general principle of law. This appears to be the general understanding among scholars as well [870].

Within international investment arbitration, some awards have addressed primary rules of public international law, such as the fair and equitable treatment standard of investment treaties and its relationship with the good faith principle [871]. Other decisions rely on general principles to expand upon primary obligations. The ICSID Tribunal in *Total SA* v. *Argentina* performed "a comparative analysis of the protection of expectations in domestic jurisdictions", concluding that "[w]hile the scope and legal basis of the principle varies, it has been recognized lately both in civil law and common law jurisdictions within well-defined limits" [872].

Other cases deal with the law of treaties and secondary rules of State responsibility, both of which are bodies of law that are most often expressed at the level of general international law [873].

---

869. Grounding general principles in municipal law nonetheless remains the norm in part because there is "no consensus on the correct methodology for identifying and applying general principles on the international plane", Kotuby and Sobota, *supra* note 157, p. 15.

870. ILC Second Report, *supra* note 5, p. 22. It cites, for instance, *El Paso* v. *Argentina*, *supra* note 456, Award (31 October 2011), para. 622 ("rules largely applied *in foro domestico*, in private or public, substantive or procedural matters").

871. "Another series of cases relates to different aspects of the law of expropriation, mostly rendered by the Iran-United States Claims Tribunal. These cases directly engage with international law, rather than domestic principles", "Domestic Law Principles", *supra* note 749, p. 1188.

872. *Ibid.*; *Total* v. *Argentina*, *supra* note 16, paras. 128-130. Other decisions relate to proportionality. In *Occidental Petroleum Corporation and Occidental Exploration and Production Company* v. *The Republic of Ecuador (ii)*, ICSID Case No. ARB/06/11, Award (5 October 2012), paras. 402-403, and the Decision on Annulment (2 November 2015), para. 350, the Tribunal rejected the challenge, stating that "the Tribunal has convincingly explained that the principle of proportionality between intensity and scope of the illicit activity, and severity of the sanction is a general principle of punitive and tort law, both under Ecuadorian and under international law". Other decisions are more cautious, e.g. *Adel A Hamadi Al Tamimi* v. *Oman*, ICSID Case No. ARB/11/33, Award (3 November 2015), para. 261.

873. *Petrobart* v. *Kyrgyz Republic*, *supra* note 327, Award (29 March 2005), para. 23; *Eureko* v. *Poland*, *supra* note 539, Partial Award (19 August 2005), para. 177.

Further, other awards invoke private law principles that are solidly anchored in public international law, such as estoppel [874].

Andrea Carlevaris notes that, in practice, investment arbitral tribunals tend to commingle the nature and application of several general principles in domestic and international law. Consequently, it is rare for the tribunals to decide the outcome by identifying which national legal systems these principles belong to [875].

3. *Principles of public international law and not national law?*

Particularly in the era prior to the fall of the Iron Curtain, writers in socialist States asserted that the expression "general principles of civilized nations" only referred to principles of public international law. Some Western writers also adopted the same stance. According to Michael Bogdan, this position would empty Article 38 of the ICJ Statute of its meaning since it is clear that principles of public international law could already be invoked within the framework of conventional or customary international law. In fact, some examples of general principles of law are already part of international customary law, such as *pacta sunt servanda*, the right to self-defense and the duty to provide compensation for caused damage [876].

An ILC report on general principles of law formally acknowledges these concerns regarding principles in public international law. The report suggests that there is insufficient or inconclusive practice relating to them within public international law. Therefore, it remains extremely difficult to distinguish principles of public international law from customary international law. Finally, there is a risk that the criteria for identifying general principles of law may not be sufficiently stringent, which may open the door to rules of international law becoming invoked too easily [877].

---

874. Other examples include consent as a basis of international arbitration, *pacta sunt servanda*, and the principle according to which like cases should be decided alike. *Daimler* v. *Argentina*, *supra* note 97, Award (22 August 2012), paras. 52, 146, and 174.

875. "However, the practice of investment tribunals also shows the importance of an accurate choice-of-law analysis and the risk of annulment of the relevant decisions for excess power, violation of the arbitral mission or analogous standards, in the absence of a rigorous approach to the application of these principles", Carlevaris, *supra* note 770, p. 226.

876. Bogdan, *supra* note 5, p. 42.

877. ILC Second Report, *supra* note 5, p. 36.

According to the same report, three forms of general principles within international law can be identified, which are not mutually exclusive [878]. First, general principles of international law may be widely accepted in treaties and other international instruments, such as UN General Assembly resolutions [879]. Second, a principle of international law may underlie general rules of customary international law, in which case the methodology will be, essentially, deductive [880]. Third, a principle may be inherent or fundamental within the international legal system [881]. An example of an inherent general principle within public international law is the principle of consent to jurisdiction. This principle is a necessary consequence of the equality of sovereign States, in accordance to which its disputes may only be solved in an agreed-upon jurisdiction [882].

B. Unanimity or principles recognized by the majority of judicial systems?

1. The discussion

As a legal concept, principles of law raise many questions. Is it necessary for such principles to be identical in every system in order to be considered "general", or is it sufficient for them to exist in most systems worldwide?

To insist that these principles must be exactly similar throughout all systems of law would be impossible and would destroy (or seriously diminish) the value of making use of private law sources and analogies. In short, to insist that all principles of law must be the same would amount to granting veto powers to legal systems that still use outdated or idiosyncratic legal rules [883]. Furthermore, the wording of Article 38 of the ICJ Statute itself does not require recognition by all systems [884]. Any such quest for unanimity is both "utopian and impractical" [885].

878. *Ibid.*, Draft Conclusion 7, p. 53.
879. *Ibid.*, p. 39.
880. *Ibid.*, p. 45.
881. *Ibid.*, p. 38.
882. *Ibid.*, p. 47.
883. E. Gaillard, "Comparative Law in International Arbitration", *Ius Comparatum* (International Academy of Comparative Law), Vol. 1 (2020), p. 17.
884. Gutteridge, *supra* note 154, p. 5. See also R. David, *Traité élémentaire de droit civile compré : Introduction à l'étude des droits étrangers et à la méthode comparative*, Paris, Librairie Générale de Droit, 1950, p. 10.
885. J. Ellis, "General Principles and Comparative Law", *European Journal of International Law*, Vol. 22 (2011), p. 956.

Hersch Lauterpacht explains that when a public international lawyer determines which private law is to be applied to a dispute at hand, the exercise is not one of analogy but rather involves choosing the rules of a particular system of private law over another or selecting a universal private law (a kind of a modern *ius gentium* based on comparative jurisprudence) [886]. The choice between applicable private laws will be guided by considerations of legal justice. However, the choice of which private law will apply will ultimately turn on whether the rule or principle in question has been universally adopted in all – or at least the main – systems of private law jurisprudence [887].

As seen, not only private but also public law is relevant in the comparative analysis. The matter has recently received further refinements, as reflected below.

2. *A two-step analysis*

To identify general principles derived from national legal systems, an ILC report of 2020 established the following criteria:

> "*(a)* the existence of a principle common to the principal legal systems of the world; and *(b)* its transposition to the international legal system." [888]

This two-step analysis of general principles of law also appears in a 2020 report released by the ILA [889].

(a) *Commonality or representativeness*

As a first step, the comparative analysis must be wide and representative, reflecting the "principal legal systems of the world" [890]. This type of analysis is not an easy task, considering the uncertainties regarding comparative law and its method – or methods – as explained below.

---

886. Lauterpacht, *supra* note 3, p. 5. See in similar terms Rousseau, *supra* note 149, p. 77.

887. Lauterpacht, *supra* note 3, pp. 176-177. A different approach is sometimes advocated in private law. Berman and Dasser, for example, see a universal law with general principles not in comparative law but in the interaction and practices of merchants. Berman and Dasser, *supra* note 135, pp. 54-55.

888. ILC Second Report, *supra* note 5, Draft Conclusion 4, p. 35.

889. *Ibid.*, pp. 5-6. Cf. ILC Third Report, *supra* note 756.

890. ILC Second Report, *supra* note 5, Draft Conclusion 5, pp. 35-36.

(i) *Commonality and comparative law*

Comparative law methodology is a useful tool for regulatory reforms, for interpretive purposes [891] and for better understanding domestic systems [892]. In its report on general principles, the ILA referred to "functionalism" as "one of the primary comparative law methods" [893].

Functionalism prevails in modern comparative law [894]. The point of departure within the functional comparative law method is an analysis of the socioeconomic problem presented, and how it may be solved using the tools inherent within different legal systems. This strategy is known as *tertium comparationis* [895]. The use of comparative examples from different national systems worldwide can "illuminate the functional role that principles play with reference to how similar ideas have played out in domestic contexts" [896].

---

891. R. B. Ginsburg, "A Decent Respect to the Opinions of Humankind: The Value of a Comparative Perspective in Constitutional Adjudication", speech delivered to International Academy of Comparative Law, American University, 30 July 2010, transcript available at https://www.supremecourt.gov/publicinfo/speeches/viewspeech/sp_08-02-10, accessed 3 March 2022:

> "The law of nations, Chief Justice Marshall famously said in 1815, is part of the law of our land. Decisions of the courts of other countries, Marshall explained, show how the law of nations is understood elsewhere, and will be considered in determining the rule which is to prevail here. Those decisions, he clarified, while not binding authority for U. S. courts, merit respectful attention for their potential persuasive value.

Decades later, in 1900, the U. S. Supreme Court reaffirmed that

> '[i]nternational law is part of our law and must be ascertained and administered by [our] courts of justice . . . . [W]here there is no treaty, no controlling executive or legislative act or judicial decision, resort must be had to the customs and usages of civilized nations, and, as evidence of these, to the works of jurists and commentators, who by years of labor, research and experience, have made themselves peculiarly well acquainted with the subject of which they treat.'"

Within domestic systems the issue remains contentious, as occurred in the US with the famous position against comparative law of late Justice Scalia, to cite an example.

892. See, for example, in J. Gordley, "Is Comparative Law a Distinct Discipline?", *American Journal of Comparative Law*, Vol. 46, No. 4 (1998), p. 607. Lawson refers to the use of comparative law by jurists as escaping from prison to liberty. F. H. Lawson, *Selected Essays, Volume II: The Comparison*, Amsterdam, North-Holland, 1977, p. 73.

893. "In such a case, the reasoning process of the adjudicator to arrive at a decision should be summarized, including supporting evidence, in order to facilitate an eventual review if applicable", "Domestic Law Principles", *supra* note 749, p. 1235.

894. E. Jayme, "Identité Culturelle et Intégration : Le Droit International Privé Postmoderne, Cours général de droit international privé", *Recueil des cours*, Vol. 251 (1995), p. 105.

895. M. Siems, *Comparative Law*, Cambridge, Cambridge University Press, 2014, p. 26.

896. A. S. King, "General Principles and the Search for Legitimacy in International Arbitration: A Comparative Perspective", *Ius Comparatum* (International Academy of Comparative Law), Vol. 1 (2020), pp. 288-318.

Its modern origins can be traced to Ernst Rabel, one of the most influential comparative law jurists in the twentieth century [897]. In the 1930s, Rabel introduced this functional comparative law method, which involved a comparison not only of the language of different legal systems but also of the social realities behind them [898]. Rudolf Schlessinger, who received Rabel's teachings in the United States, published the first comparative law casebook [899] that utilized the functional method, and founded the famous Cornell Common Core Project at Cornell University [900]. From that point forward, functionalism began to expand throughout the world, and the "common core" approach reflects the mainstream of the twentieth century [901]. Functionalism even made its way into arbitration [902].

Arthur von Mehren was another early advocate of functionalism in the United States. He explained that, when approaching legal problems, the general frames of reference and legal reasoning techniques used in different legal systems around the world must be taken into account [903].

---

897. I. Schwenzer, "Development of Comparative Law in Germany, Switzerland, and Austria", in M. Reimann and R. Zimmermann (eds.), *The Oxford Handbook of Comparative Law*, Oxford, Oxford University Press, 2006, p. 76.

898. D. Gerber, "Sculpting the Agenda of Comparative Law: Ernst Rabel and the I of Language", in A. Riles (ed.), *Rethinking the Masters of Comparative Law*, Oxford, Hart Publishing, 2001, pp. 190-191.

899. R. B. Schlesinger, *Comparative Law: Cases and Materials*, Brooklyn, NY, Foundation Press, 1950.

900. U. Mattei, "The Comparative Jurisprudence of Schlesinger and Sacco: A Study in Legal Influence", in A. Riles (ed.), *Rethinking the Masters of Comparative Law*, Oxford, Hart Publishing, 2001, pp. 243-244. One cannot only trust what the jurists have to say, since there are important differences between the operative rules and the ones commonly mentioned. See M. Bussani, "Current Trends in European Comparative Law: The Common Core Approach", *Hastings International and Comparative Law Review*, Vol. 21 (1998), p. 5.

901. Siems, *supra* note 895, p. 31. Functionalism expanded its influence to Italy through Cappelletti, Pugliese and Gorla, who were also involved in Schlessinger's common core project. Gorla was later considered the father of the modern discipline of comparative law in Italy. E. Grande, "Development of Comparative Law in Italy", in M. Reimann and R. Zimmermann (eds.), *The Oxford Handbook of Comparative Law*, Oxford, Oxford University Press, 2006, p. 104. Functionalism and the search for the "common core" received impetus in Germany after an influential lecture by Zweigert in 1949, and his – in the words of Schwenzer – unparalleled comparative law book with Kötz. K. Zweigert and H. Kötz, *An Introduction to Comparative Law*, 3rd ed., New York, Oxford University Press, 1998. See Schwenzer, *supra* note 897, p. 93.

902. With regard to commercial arbitration in particular, Gaillard explains that State systems are a *fond commune* of arbitration. This position does not oppose State law but is based on the normative activities of States. Gaillard, *supra* note 836, p. 56.

903. A. T. von Mehren, "Civil Law Analogues to Consideration: An Exercise in Comparative Analysis", *Harvard Law Review*, Vol. 72 (1959), p. 1010. Von Mehren and Gordley's casebook on comparative law achieved remarkable success. A.T. von Mehren and J. Gordley, *The Civil Law System: An Introduction to the Comparative Study of Law*, Boston/Toronto, Little, Brown and Company, 1977.

When applied negatively, functionalism seeks to eradicate parochial preconceptions. When applied positively, it indicates which area of the foreign legal system must be investigated in order to arrive at an analogous solution [904].

In his approach to functionalism as a comparative law method, René David popularized reference to legal families in the 1964 edition of his book on comparative law [905], one of the leading texts on the subject in France and abroad [906]. The underlying assumption within the functional method is that similar solutions to legal problems emerge from other comparable international systems. Of course, this method is not absolute, and the particular outcome will depend on the specific case. Indeed, each legal system is a sociological phenomenon of its own and belongs to its own legal family. In this regard, David referred to four legal families: common law, civil law, socialist systems and a fourth residual classification [907]. Other scholars expressly mention other systems, such as Far Eastern, Hindu, Islamic and Nordic (Scandinavian). The division of legal systems into legal families is one of the landmark breakthroughs in twentieth-century comparative law [908], making it easy to classify and organize the vast volume of extant legal materials.

The creation of the *International Encyclopedia of Comparative Law* in the 1970s marked an important attempt to simplify access to and comparison of legal materials, and several volumes have since been published [909]. Emmanuel Gaillard notes that international arbitrators have been known to make use of this encyclopedia for this purpose [910]. Ultimately, however, this encyclopedia summarizes the law in many places, the perils of which are reflected in Lord Mustill's phrase that "a

904. Zweigert and Kötz, *supra* note 901, pp. 34-35.

905. The book draws upon an older text written by René David. *Grand Systemes* has been revised and edited many times. See B. Fauvarque-Cosson, "Development of Comparative Law in France", in M. Reimann and R. Zimmermann (eds.), *The Oxford Handbook of Comparative Law*, Oxford, Oxford University Press, 2006, pp. 45-46.

906. David, *supra* note 884.

907. In the end, the other classifications ended up confirming David's simpler division. U. Mattei, "Three Patterns of Law: Taxonomy and Change in the World's Legal System", *American Journal of Comparative Law*, Vol. 45 (1997), p. 9.

908. See J. L. Esquirol, "R. David: At the Head of the Legal Family", in A. Riles (ed.), *Rethinking the Masters of Comparative Law*, Oxford, Hart Publishing, 2001, p. 212. See also Wieacker, *supra* note 153, pp. 464-470.

909. See a thorough description of the endeavor in U. Drobnig, "The *International Encyclopedia of Comparative Law*: Efforts toward a Worldwide Comparison of Law", *Cornell International Law Journal*, Vol. 5, No. 2 (1972), http://scholarship.law.cornell.edu/cilj/vol5/iss2/, accessed 3 March 2022.

910. O. Lando, "The *Lex Mercatoria* in International Commercial Arbitration", *The International and Comparative Law Quarterly*, Vol. 34, No. 4 (1985), p. 750.

little learning is indeed a dangerous thing" [911]. Therefore, it and other comparative law materials must be used with great care.

Certain areas such as contracts and torts are more easily subject to the functional comparative law method that, in fact, is primarily used in private law. However, it has also been known to oversimplify issues and depart significantly from reality [912]. Moreover, there are matters in which no *tertium comparationis* exists, or where the different legal systems compared are not equally evolved [913].

Many other issues arise with the functional comparative law method. To what extent should the context of the rules be taken into account? The same questions arise with regard to procedural rules, the structure of courts, differences in legal history and the cultural and socioeconomic context in which the law developed [914]. Confusion also emerges with regard to the very term "functionalism", which is a misnomer: there is not one but several functional methods, not all methods are functional, and many times the functional methodology is difficult to identify [915].

The uncertainties of functionalism gave rise to other perspectives. For instance, a comparative law technique used to identify general principles employs the legal borrowing or transplantation method [916]. This technique analyzes historical transplants of rules, principles and legal structures [917]. For reasons of coercion (e.g., imposition of laws on

911. Mustill, *supra* note 838, p. 157.

912. R. Hyland, "Comparative Law", D. Patterson (ed.), *A Companion to Philosophy of Law and Legal Theory*, Oxford, Wiley-Blackwell, 1999 (repr. 2000), pp. 191-192.

913. Siems, *supra* note 895, pp. 26-28.

914. M. Van Hoecke, "Deep Level Comparative Law", in *id.* (ed.), *Epistemology and Methodology of Comparative Law*, Oxford / Portland, OR, Hart Publishing, 2004, p. 166.

915. R. Michaels, "The Functional Method of Comparative Law", in M. Reimann and R. Zimmermann (eds.), *The Oxford Handbook of Comparative Law*, Oxford, Oxford University Press, 2006, p. 342. Twinning refers to a "macro-comparison" corresponding to the *Grands Systèmes* of David, and a micro-comparison style preponderant after World War II in the works of Gutteridge, Lawson and Mason. In the end, all these scholarly works compare the systems of capitalist Western societies. The comparison is generally restricted to the realm of private law, notably comparisons between *common and civil law*, and descriptive, rather than prescriptive comparisons. For criticisms in this regard and critiques of functionalism in general, see W. Twinning, *Globalisation & Legal Theory*, London, Butterworths, pp. 89, 180. According to Constantinesco, the comparative law method leads to micro-comparisons, whereas comparative law as a science leads to macro-comparisons. Such comparisons do not exclude each other but are rather two complementary sides of the same coin. L.-J. Constantinesco, *Tratado de Derecho Comparado*, Vol. 1, Madrid, Editorial Tecnos, 1981, pp. 310-316.

916. Ellis, *supra* note 885, pp. 959 ff.

917. A. Watson, "Legal Transplants and European Private Law", *Electronic Journal of Comparative Law*, Vol. 4.4 (2000), available at www.ejcl.org, accessed 8 March 2022, p. 8.

colonies or conquered lands), prestige or guaranteeing better economic performance, among others, some borrowings end up prevailing in different legal systems [918]. Where legal borrowings prevail, they later become part of the general principles of the country's legal system.

The legal borrowing method became popular after its use in the 1970 Congress of the International Academy of Comparative Law, and later in the 1974 work of Alan Watson on legal transplants [919], followed in turn by Rodolfo Sacco [920].

The legal borrowing method has been the subject of several criticisms. Gunther Teubner stated, for example, that alien notions are unfit to a new environment and become "legal irritants", such as the transplant of the civil law concept of good faith to the common law [921]. Jaye Ellis offers further criticism related to current comparative law methodologies for identifying principles within private law. According to Ellis, the search for commonality or representativeness among legal principles has been justified on three unconvincing assumptions. One assumption is that the presence of a rule in many legal systems is evidence of its universal conception. The second assumption holds that the presence of the rule in many systems is evidence of State consent to the inclusion of that rule in its legal system. A third assumption concerns the democratic validity of international law, surmising that the adoption of domestic rule in a country warrants its production through legislative or democratic processes that ensure its legitimacy [922].

918. M. Graziadei, "Comparative Law as the Study of Transplants and Receptions", in M. Reimann and R. Zimmermann (eds.), *The Oxford Handbook of Comparative Law*, Oxford, Oxford University Press, 2006, pp. 456 ff.

919. *Ibid.*, pp. 442-443. See, in general, R. Sacco, *Trattato di diritto comparato*, 5th ed., Torino, Utet Giuridica, 1992. Sacco used the terminology of legal formants to allude to all the elements that contribute to the consolidation of a legal system, such as case law, doctrine, social structures, etc. See U. Mattei, *Comparative Law and Economics*, Michigan, University of Michigan Press, 1997, p. 104. See also J. C. Reitz, "How to Do Comparative Law", *American Journal of Comparative Law*, Vol. 46, No. 4 (1998), pp. 617 *et seq*. Örücü prefers the expression *legal transposition*. In its linguistic sense, "transplant" means moving to a new territory, which in juridical terms would be without a comparable civilization. Transposition can be used in reference to any expansion of law. Vid. E. Örücü, "Law as Transposition", *International and Comparative Law Quarterly*, Vol. 51, No. 2 (2002), p. 205; *id.*, in M. Van Hoecke Trees for (ed.), Legal Epistemology and Methodology of Comparative LawSystems, Oxford / Portland, OR, Hart Publishing, 2004, pp. 359-375.

920. Graziadei, *supra* note 918, pp. 456 ff.

921. J. M. Smits, "Comparative Law and its Influence on National Legal Systems", in M. Reimann and R. Zimmermann (eds.), *The Oxford Handbook of Comparative Law*, Oxford, Oxford University Press, 2006, p. 144.

922. Ellis, *supra* note 885, pp. 949, 970-971.

Regarding the distillation and transformation of municipal legal rules into principles suited to international society, such rules can only serve as sources of inspiration. "Borrowed" legal rules must be treated more like arguments rather than applied "in ways that their authors may never have anticipated, intended, or desired" [923]. A reckless engineer blindly borrows a part from an existing machine as he builds his own; a wise engineer uses the part from the existing machine as a source of inspiration, and designs an analogous part suited to the nuances of his machine's particular purpose and construction. Likewise, the distillation and transformation of municipal law into principles suited to international society must not result in the application of municipal rules and procedure "in ways that their authors may never have anticipated, intended, or desired" [924].

Gutteridge argues that there is no such thing as "comparative" law. The stages of analysis and synthesis of the rules of diverse systems that occur as part of the comparative legal analysis do not result in the formulation of any independent body of law. It would be preferable to use the term "comparative method" to "comparative law" [925]. However, several methods and purposes exist within the "comparative method", and therefore this term still remains fairly broad [926].

Three main approaches now exist in comparative law: one focuses on rules, another on their function to resolve similar problems in different legal systems (the functionalist approach), and a third on the culture in which diverse rules are embedded (the culturalist approach) [927]. The first approach has long been criticized by functionalists, who paradoxically also focus on legal rules and their functions in societies. Culturalists also begin their analysis with rules when placing them in their cultural contexts. The focus of all three of these approaches on rules, prominent in the Western legal tradition – in the words of Lena Salaymeh and

923. *Ibid.*, p. 971.

924. *Ibid.*, p. 971.

925. Gutteridge, *supra* note 154, p. 1. In similar terms regarding arbitration, recently Gaillard, for instance in E. Gaillard, "Transnational Law: A Legal System or a Method of Decision Making?", *Arbitration International*, Vol. 17, No. 1 (2001), pp. 59-72.

926. J. W. Cairns, "Development of Comparative Law in Great Britain", in M. Reimann and R. Zimmermann (eds.), *The Oxford Handbook of Comparative Law*, Oxford, Oxford University Press, 2006, p. 172.

927. "In spite of widely diverging methodological approaches, we can identify – albeit in a generalized and non-comprehensive fashion – shared assumptions in the discipline of comparative law that often contribute to the coloniality of the discipline", L. Salaymeh and R. Michaels, "Decolonial Comparative Law: A Conceptual Beginning", *Rabels Zeitschrift für ausländisches und internationales Privatrecht / Rabel Journal of Comparative and International Private Law*, Vol. 86 (2022), p. 170).

Ralf Michaels – "makes comparison with normative traditions or with systems that are not based on such legal rules difficult, if not impossible" [928].

Another important consideration is the difference between comparative law as used by academics and comparative law as referred to by tribunals or parliamentary advisors. Moreover, comparative law varies immensely within countries large and small [929]. According to John Reitz, most of the academics and legal practitioners that teach or write about comparative law have not been trained to do so but instead make use of multiple differing legal methods based on their own experience and convictions [930]. This lack of cohesion explains the poor theoretical ground upon which comparative law – which remains highly undertheorized [931] – is based [932]. As stated by the US Supreme Court, "[the] comparison of systems is slippery business" [933].

The preceding paragraphs explain why so many uncertainties surround the identification of general principles, and also the importance of the work of international organizations like UNIDROIT that devote significant resources to developing comparative law within several legal fields. The related work of this and other international organizations will be dealt with in greater detail in Chapter XI.

(ii) *Geographical representation*

Similar to the existence of a regional customary law, regional principles may emerge from the domestic laws that exist within a specific geographical zone. For example, the CJEU often refers to principles found in the domestic legal systems of its member States [934],

928. *Ibid.*, p. 171.

929. C. von Bar, "Comparative Law of Obligations: Methodology and Epistemology", in M. Van Hoecke (ed.), *Epistemology and Methodology of Comparative Law*, Oxford / Portland, OR, Hart Publishing, 2004, p. 124.

930. Reitz, *supra* note 919, p. 618.

931. The word "undertheorized" is used by Annelise Riles in the introduction to *Rethinking the Masters of Comparative Law* (2001), p. 1. See also D. E. López Medina, *Teoría impura del derecho, La transformación de la cultura jurídica latinoamericana*, Colombia, Editorial Legis, 2004, p. 74.

932. G. Samuel, "Epistemology and Comparative Law: Contributions from the Sciences and Social Sciences", in M. Van Hoecke (ed.), *Epistemology and Methodology of Comparative Law*, Oxford / Portland, OR, Hart Publishing, 2004, pp. 35-36.

933. *Intel Corp.* v. *Advanced Micro Devices, Inc.*, 542 US 241, 263, n. 15 (2004).

934. The Court, or the Advocate General, not only checks the commonality of the domestic principle but also if the principle fits the objectives of the EU. See e.g. Opinion of AG Lagrange in *Koninklijke Nederlandsche Hoogovens en Staalfabrieken* v. *ECSC High Authority*, Case C-14/61, [1962] ECR 485 ECLI:EU:C: 1962:19, pp. 282-283.

and EU legislation refers to general principles common to the domestic laws of its member States [935].

Regarding Article 9 of the ICJ Statute, Judge Christopher Weeramantry wrote that

> "the integrated values of any civilization are the source from which its legal concepts derive . . . international law would require a worldwide recognition of those values" [936].

Finding a principle that exists within all the main legal systems is not sufficient, therefore, if it does not enjoy significant geographical representation worldwide. For instance, a general principle of European civil law systems should also be identified in civil law countries belonging to other cultural lineages [937].

An ILC report on general principles states that different regions of the world should be represented in comparative legal analysis [938].

(iii) *Commonality in practice*

One of the most frequent examples of the identification of general principles in practice is the *Barcelona Traction* case, in which the ICJ referred to "rules generally accepted by municipal legal systems" [939], but there are numerous other examples. In *Highlands Insurance* v. *Iran* [940], for illustration, the Tribunal cited a comparative study of various national laws in support of its holding regarding offer and acceptance [941].

More recently, *Akzo Nobel Chemicals Ltd. and Akcros Chemicals Ltd.* v. *European Commission*, Case C-550/07, [2010] ECLI:EU:C:2010:512, paras. 69-76.

935. For example, Article 340 (2) of the TFEU states that "[i]n the case of non-contractual liability, the Union shall, in accordance with the general principles common to the laws of the Member States, make good any damage caused by its institutions or by its servants in the performance of their duties". See "Domestic Law Principles", *supra* note 749, p. 1237.

936. *Gabčíkovo-Nagymaros*, *supra* note 299, Order (5 February 1997), Separate Opinion of Judge Weeramantry, p. 245.

937. See "Domestic Law Principles", *supra* note 749, p. 1236.

938. ILC Second Report, *supra* note 5, p. 16.

939. *Barcelona Traction*, *supra* note 24, p. 38, para. 50. See also *Diallo*, *supra* note 334, Preliminary Objections, Judgment, *ICJ Reports 2007*, at p. 605, paras. 60-62; Merits, Judgment, *ICJ Reports 2010*, at p. 675, para. 104. ILC Second Report, *supra* note 5, p. 8.

940. Award No. 491-435-3 (1990).

941. Aldrich, *supra* note 834, p. 169. In *Combustion Engineering* v. *Iran*, the Tribunal made use of "principles of commercial and international law". It is widely accepted by municipal systems of law that enforceable contracts can be proven through evidence of performance. Award No. 506-308-2 (1991).

International tribunals have stated that a principle must emerge from national legal systems generally [942], from "all" legal systems [943], from the "main" or "major" legal systems [944], or from "many" [945] or a "majority" of legal systems [946].

For instance, in the *Alabama Claims* arbitration the United States referred to Roman law and the laws of England, "America" and the "Continent of Europe" to determine the meaning of the term "due diligence" employed in the Treaty of Washington of 1871 [947].

Other examples flow from ICSID cases. In *Amco* v. *Indonesia*, the Tribunal considered *pacta sunt servanda* a general principle of law recognized in civil law (France), common law (United States) and Islamic law (Libya and Saudi Arabia) systems. In its calculation of damages, the Tribunal referred to civil law systems (France and Indonesia) and common law systems (United Kingdom and United States) [948].

In turn, in *Total* v. *Argentina*, the Arbitral Tribunal referred to the protection of legitimate expectations as a general principle of law,

---

942. For example, *El Paso* v. *Argentina*, *supra* note 456, Award (31 October 2011), para. 622; *Questech, Inc.* v. *Ministry of National Defense of the Islamic Republic of Iran*, IUSCT Case No. 59, Award No. 191-59-1 (20 September 1985), 9 IUSCTR, p. 122; *Rockwell International Systems, Inc.* v. *Iran*, IUSCT Case No. 430, Award No. 438-430-1 (5 September 1989), 23 IUSCTR, p. 171, para. 92; ILC Second Report, *supra* note 5, p. 8.

943. For example, the *Queen case between Brazil, Norway and Sweden* (1871); *Corfu Channel*, *supra* note 425, Judgment (1949), p. 18; ILC Second Report, *supra* note 5, p. 9.

944. For example, *Certain Property (Liechtenstein* v. *Germany)*, Preliminary Objections, Judgment, *ICJ Reports 2005*, p . 6; Switzerland, Federal Council, "Rapport additionnel du Conseil fédéral au rapport du 5 mars 2010 sur la relation entre droit international et droit interne", *Federal Gazette*, 30 March 2011, pp. 3401-311. ILC Second Report, *supra* note 5, p. 9. The Restatement (Third) of Foreign Relations Law of the United States alludes to "general principles common to the major legal systems of the world". Kotuby and Sobota, *supra* note 157, p. 22.

945. For example, *LaGrand (Germany* v. *United States of America)*, Judgment, *ICJ Reports 2001*, p. 466; ILC Second Report, *supra* note 5, p. 9.

946. For example, *Libyan American Oil Company (Liamco)* v. *Libyan Arab Republic Relating to Petroleum Concessions*, Award (12 April 1977), 20 ILM, pp. 1-87 (1981), at 37; *Sea-Land Service, Inc.* v. *Iran*, Award No. 135-33-1 (20 June 1984), 6 IUSCTR, p. 168; *El Paso* v. *Argentina*, *supra* note 456, Award (31 October 2011), para. 623; ILC Second Report, *supra* note 5, p. 9.

947. *Alabama Claims of the United States of America against Great Britain*, Award (14 September 1872), (1872) 29 RIAA, pleading of the United States (at *Case of the United States, to Be Laid before the Tribunal of Arbitration, to Be Convened at Geneva under the Provisions of the Treaty between the United States of America and Her Majesty the Queen of Great Britain*, Concluded at Washington, 8 May 1871 (US Department of State, 1871), pp. 150-158); ILC Second Report, *supra* note 5, p. 10.

948. *Amco Asia* v. *Indonesia*, *supra* note 408, Award (20 November 1984), paras. 248, 266-267; ILC Second Report, *supra* note 5, p. 13.

"recognized lately both in civil law and in common law jurisdictions within well-defined limits". In support, the Tribunal referred to the legal systems of Argentina, England and Germany [949]. Similarly, in *Gold Reserve* v. *Venezuela*, the Tribunal held that "the concept of legitimate expectations is found in different legal traditions", in reference to Argentinean, English, French, German and Venezuelan law [950].

(iv) *Discretion and pragmatism*

A comprehensive survey of how different principles are interpreted within the world's varying domestic legal systems is beyond the capabilities of international courts and tribunals. After the fall of the Iron Curtain, two legal orders became particularly relevant: the civil and common law [951]. "For good or ill", the laws of Germany, France, England and the United States are the most frequently referenced because "these legal orders are easily accessible and, above all, have influenced the public law systems of many other countries" [952]. As an example, in an ICJ decision, Judge Bruno Simma addressed the matter of multiple tortfeasors by citing authorities from the United States, Canada, France, Switzerland and Germany, remarking that "the question has been taken up and solved by these legal systems with a consistency that is striking" [953].

Waldock highlights that, similar to the application of customary law, international tribunals that identify "general principles of law" must necessarily "exercise a considerable measure of discretion and appreciation" [954]. In the end, resolving an international dispute with reference to general principles is a pragmatic attempt to find the greatest agreement between the world's major legal systems on the issues relevant to the case at hand [955].

---

949. *Total* v. *Argentina*, *supra* note 16, para. 128. See also *Toto Costruzioni Generali SpA* v. *Republic of Lebanon*, ICSID Case No. ARB/07/12, Award (7 June 2012), para. 166; *Crystallex*, *supra* note 521, Award (4 April 2016), para. 546; ILC Second Report, *supra* note 5, p. 13.

950. *Gold Reserve Inc.* v. *Bolivarian Republic of Venezuela*, ICSID Case No. ARB(AF)/09/1, Award (22 September 2014), para. 576; ILC Second Report, *supra* note 5, p. 14.

951. Ellis, *supra* note 885, pp. 956-957.

952. Kotuby and Sobota, *supra* note 157, p. 26.

953. *Oil Platforms (Iran* v. *US)*, Judgment, *ICJ Reports 2003*, p. 161, at 324, paras. 66-74 (Separate Opinion of Judge Bruno Simma).

954. Waldock, *supra* note 156, p. 65.

955. W. Friedmann, "The Uses of 'General Principles' in the Development of International Law", *American Journal of International Law*, Vol. 57, No. 2 (1963), p. 284.

Soundness and persuasiveness could, therefore, be the criteria according to which general principles of law are identified. According to this strategy, adjudicators could present the actual line of reasoning that led them to identify a particular principle as useful or relevant to their legal analysis. This is precisely what Judge Stephen did in the *Erdemović* case. He presented the lessons he absorbed regarding the common law approach to duress in order to convince his audience that this defense was, in fact, available in the case at hand [956].

It is, of course, impracticable in a comparative legal analysis conducted in the course of resolving an international dispute to review every legal system in the world. Thus, a pragmatic approach is suggested. The comparative law answer is not expected to emerge as a matter of mathematical calculation of which domestic laws endorse the solution the most [957]. Rather, tribunals are expected to carry out wide and representative comparative analyses, covering different legal families and regions of the world [958]. As noted in an ILC report on general principles, establishing the "commonality" between principles is an empirical assessment of comparison of national systems to find shared principles [959].

(v) *Consequences of neglecting comparative law*

The ICSID *Klöckner* case [960] illustrates the dangers of neglecting an appropriate comparative analysis [961]. Rather than focusing on the Cameroonian governing law, the award based its decision on French law, upon which much of Cameroonian law is based. The Arbitral Tribunal adopted this approach based on the "basic principle" of "frankness and loyalty" emerging from French civil law. Moreover, the Tribunal stated – without providing any citation – that this basic principle was also a "universal requirement" inherent in "other national codes which we

---

956. Ellis, *supra* note 885, p. 971.

957. Statement of the ICJ Commission Member Mr Wood (A/CN.4/SR.3490, p. 8). Similarly, Judge Tanaka was of the view that "the recognition of a principle by civilized nations . . . does not mean recognition by all civilized nations" (*South West Africa (Second Phase)*, Judgment, *ICJ Reports 1996*, p. 6, Dissenting Opinion of Judge Tanaka, p. 299). ILC Second Report, *supra* note 5, p. 9.

958. ILC Second Report, *supra* note 5, pp. 9-10.

959. *Ibid.*, p. 17.

960. *Klöckner* v. *Cameroon*, *supra* note 748, Decision on Annulment (3 May 1985).

961. G. R. Delaume, "The Myth of the *Lex Mercatoria* and State Contracts", in T. E. Carbonneau (ed.), Lex Mercatoria *and Arbitration: A Discussion of the New Lew Merchant*, 2nd ed., The Hague, Juris / Kluwer International, 1998, p. 124.

know of" and both "English law and international law". The ICSID Annulment Committee found that this reasoning amounted to a failure to apply the proper law. The award was annulled on the basis that the Tribunal had not based their reasoning on "the law of the Contracting State," but instead "more on a sort of general equity than on positive law . . . or precise contractual provisions" [962].

Well-known subsequent ICSID awards dispense with comparative law analogies and positively formulate a substantive rule of law. Thus, in *LETCO* v. *Liberia* and *Amco* v. *Indonesia*, the Tribunal ruled that in the event of non-performance by the State, compensation is the only appropriate remedy [963].

(b) *Transposition to public international law*

General principles must not only be recognized by the community of nations but must also be capable of being transposed within the broader framework of public international law [964]. Early arbitral cases already alluded to this requirement of transposition. For instance, in the *North Atlantic Coast Fisheries* case, the Tribunal rejected the principle of "international servitude", noting that it would be incompatible with the principle of sovereignty [965].

Therefore, general principles must be compatible with the fundamental principles of public international law in this context [966]. In his widely cited *South West Africa* advisory opinion, Judge McNair wrote the following:

> "International law has recruited and continues to recruit many of its rules and institutions from private systems of law. . . . The way in which international law borrows from this source is not by means of importing private law institutions 'lock, stock and barrel', ready-made and fully equipped with a set of rules. It

962. "The Committee's decision has been criticized by academics and practitioners for annulling the final arbitration award too readily. However, this decision still serves as a cautionary tale: general principles of law must be supported by reference to positive rules of municipal or other relevant law". Kotuby and Sobota, *supra* note 157, p. 27. See also "Domestic Law Principles", *supra* note 749, p. 1235.

963. Delaume, *supra* note 961, p. 128.

964. ILC Second Report, *supra* note 5, p. 23. See also, for instance, in Jennings, *supra* note 274, p. 341; Reinisch and Malintoppi, *supra* note 270, p. 617; G. Cordero-Moss and D. Behn, "The Relevance of the UNIDROIT Principles in Investment Arbitration", *Uniform Law Review*, Vol. 19 (2014), pp. 585-586.

965. *North Atlantic Coast Fisheries Case (Great Britain, United States)*, Award (7 September 1910), (1910) 11 RIAA, pp. 167-226, 182.

966. ILC Second Report, *supra* note 5, p. 26.

> would be difficult to reconcile such a process with the application of 'the general principles of law' . . . the true view of the duty of international tribunals in this matter is to regard any features or terminology which are reminiscent of the rules and institutions of private law as an indication of policy and principles rather than as directly importing these rules and institutions." [967]

The structure of the national legal systems must be considered (with particular attention paid to the procedural frameworks) to determine whether, at the international level, the principle can be applied appropriately [968].

In a separate opinion concerning the private law principle *exceptio non adimpleti contractus* (that a party does not have to perform if the other fails to do so), Judge Simma stated that the transferability of general principles to the international legal arena requires amendment "in order for such a general principle to be able to play a constructive role also at the international level". In developed national systems, the functional *synallagma* [969] (equivalence) operates within the control of the courts when a party affected by its application

> "does not accept the presence of the conditions required to have recourse to our principle. What we encounter at the level of international law, however, will all too often be instances of non-performance of treaty obligations accompanied by invocation of

967. *International status of South-West Africa*, Advisory Opinion, *ICJ Reports 1950*, p. 128, Separate Opinion of Judge McNair, p. 146, at p. 148. Based on this, he found certain "general principles" common to "[n]early every legal system" (*ibid.*, p. 149). ILC Second Report, *supra* note 5, p. 19. See also "Domestic Law Principles", *supra* note 749, p. 1237; Waldock, *supra* note 156, p. 65.

968. *Ibid.*, p. 27. In a separate opinion in the *Barcelona Traction* case, Judge Fitzmaurice made the following statement:

"[W]hen private law concepts are utilized, or private law institutions are dealt with in the international legal field, they should not there be distorted or handled in a manner not in conformity with their true character, as it exists under the system or systems of their creation. But, although this is so, it is scarcely less important to bear in mind that conditions in the international field are sometimes very different from what they are in the domestic, and that rules which these latter conditions fully justify may be less capable of vindication if strictly applied when transposed onto the international level. Neglect of this precaution may result in an opposite distortion, – namely that qualifications or mitigations of the rule, provided for on the internal plane, may fail to be adequately reflected on the international, – leading to a resulting situation of paradox, anomaly and injustice."

Barcelona Traction, *supra* note 24, Separate Opinion of Judge Fitzmaurice, p. 65 and p. 67, para. 5.

969. "If one party to a reciprocal contract does not perform, the other party may refuse to counterperform", Zimmermann and Whittaker, *supra* note 726, p. 87, fn. 152.

our principle, but without availability of recourse to impartial adjudication of the legality of these measures. Absent the leash of judicial control, our principle will thus become prone to abuse; the issue of legality will often remain contested" [970].

Lord Hartley Shawcross offers a poignant example of the potential dangers of transposing a general principle within one domestic legal system into others internationally. The private law principle of *rebus sic stantibus* or unforeseen circumstances provides remedies for obligations that have become so onerous that, had the parties known how burdensome it would have become to complete the contract, the agreement would not have come into being. This is the case in, for example, contracts for the development of natural resources where circumstances may change dramatically, such as changes in the government that concluded the contract, political complexities, discovering a greater quantity of the resource than expected, or a different royalty rate established later in a neighboring country. If *rebus sic stantibus* remedies could be liberally invoked in this type of situation, the requirements of reciprocity would entitle the other party to avail themselves of the remedy where, for instance, heavy competition restricted its ability to export an agreed minimum of the mineral in question [971].

In certain circumstances, treaties or other international instruments can serve as evidence that a principle that exists in certain domestic settings may be transposed to the international legal system [972]. The UNIDROIT Principles provide a clear example in this regard. They will be further addressed in Chapters XI and XII.

---

970. Application of the Interim Accord of 13 September 1995 *(the former Yugoslav Republic of Macedonia* v. *Greece*, Judgment of 5 December 2011, *ICJ Reports 2011*, p. 695, Separate Opinion of Judge Simma, para. 13. ILC Second Report, *supra* note 5, p. 31.

971. Lord Shawcross, *supra* note 38, p. 356.

972. ILC Second Report, *supra* note 5, p. 32.

CHAPTER VIII

GENERAL PRINCIPLES AND INTERNATIONAL INVESTMENT CLAIMS

A. Principles in old international investment claims

Claims commissions and foreign offices throughout the eighteenth and nineteenth centuries referred to general principles to work out rough minimum standards of international investment protection, which they applied frequently in disputes arising from relationships between States. For example, the Anglo-American Board of Commissioners for the 1794 Jay Treaty alluded in this regard to "shared legal principles" [973].

Case law shows that general principles of law were used extensively even beyond the nineteenth century [974]. In 1910, the British-United States Claims Arbitral Tribunal stated the following:

> "International law, as well as domestic law, may not contain, and generally does not contain, express rules decisive of particular cases; but the function of jurisprudence is to resolve the conflict of opposing rights and interests by applying, in default of any specific provisions of law, the corollaries of general principles, and so to find . . . the solution to the problem." [975]

Many of these general principles recognized by international tribunals remain relevant today. This is the case, for instance, with the principle that contractual breaches do not violate international law *per se*, held in the *Martini* award and *International Fisheries Company* claim [976], and recently applied in the ICSID case *SGS Société Générale de Surveillance SA* v. *Islamic Republic of Pakistan* [977].

---

973. Kotuby and Sobota, *supra* note 157, p. 10.

974. Barberis, *supra* note 731, p. 18.

975. *Eastern Extension* (1923), *supra* note 776, *Nielsen's Reports*, p. 40, at pp. 75-76. Cheng, *supra* note 178, p. xiii.

976. *Martini Case (Italy* v. *Venezuela)*, (1903) 10 RIAA, p. 644; *International Fisheries Company Claim (USA* v. *United Mexican States)*, (1931) 4 RIAA, p. 691. See Ho, *supra* note 212, p. 42.

977. *SGS Société Générale de Surveillance SA* v. *Islamic Republic of Pakistan*, ICSID Case No. ARB/01/13, Decision of the Tribunal on Objections to Jurisdiction (6 August 2003), para. 166. However, the source of this principle was not specified therein. *Ibid.*, p. 41. Only contractual breaches *iure imperii* are considered potential violations of international law (*Shufeldt Claim*). This principle was held in Judge Hersch

B. Internationalization in the early natural resources' cases through the use of general principles

In the *Serbian Loans* case, the PCIJ stated that "[a]ny contract which is not a contract between States in their capacity as subjects of international law is based on the municipal law of some country" [978].

However, subjecting the entirety of a foreign investment contract to the national legal system of the State party would place the investor in an inferior position, subordinate to the free will of its co-contractor. States could escape liability by changing their domestic law for the matter. To avoid this imbalance of powers, "internationalization" emerged as a response [979].

This so-called "internationalization" refers to the equation of contractual obligations to international obligations [980]. If a breach of an internationalized investment contract by a State constitutes a violation of public international law [981], public authorities should be prevented from further acting outside of the conditions of the said agreement.

Foreign investment contracts throughout the mid-twentieth century were "internationalized" under the logic that foreign investors' lack of international standing could be overcome where States were willing to treat them as their equals. In these situations, principles of

---

Lauterpacht's separate opinion in *Certain Norwegian Loans (France* v. *Norway)*, Judgment (6 July 1957), *ICJ Reports 1957*, p. 9 at 61. In *Bankswith Ghana Ltd.* v. *The Republic of Ghana Acting as the Government of Ghana*, UNCITRAL, Award Save as to Costs (11 April 2014), the Tribunal credited the *Shufeldt Claim*, *infra* note 2048, as sole authority for this principle (paras. 11-68-11-69). The principle is, however, contested. See Ho, *supra* note 212, pp. 42-45. See also Chap. XIV, *infra*.

978. "The question as to which this law is forms the subject of that branch of law which is at the present day usually described as private international law or the 'doctrine of the conflict of laws'. The rules thereof may be common to several States and may even be established by international conventions or customs, and in the latter case may possess the character of true international law governing the relations between States. But apart from this, it has to be considered that these rules form part of municipal law", *Payment of Various Serbian Loans Issued in France (France* v. *Yugoslavia)*, Judgment (12 July 1929), PCIJ, Ser. A, No. 20, p. 42, cited in *Publications of the Permanent Court of International Justice*, Series A – No. 20/21, *Collection of Judgments*, A. W. Sijthoff, 1929, p. 41.

979. O. Spiermann, "Applicable Law", in P. Muchlinski, F. Ortino and C. Schreuer (eds.), *The Oxford Handbook of International Investment Law*, Oxford, Oxford University Press, 2008, p. 94.

980. The writings of F. A. Mann and W. Friedmann have given growth to the theory of internationalization since the 1960s. F. A. Mann, "State Contracts and State Responsibility", *American Journal of International Law*, Vol. 54 (1960), p. 572; W. Friedmann, "Half a Century of International Law", *Virginia Law Review*, Vol. 58, No. 8 (1964), p. 1333. See Lim, Ho and Paparinskis, *supra* note 76, p. 38.

981. *Ibid.*, p. 37.

international law could be applied to the agreement [982]. Creative law firms, particularly throughout the 1950s and 1960s, included carefully crafted clauses in their investor clients' international State contracts – such as legal stabilization clauses, choice of law clauses and arbitration clauses – to ensure that the "rules of the game" would not be changed unilaterally via State legislation [983].

The inclusion of stabilization clauses aimed to freeze the law and make the conditions of the investment immune to changes, insulating the contract from local courts and domestic law. This was a way of avoiding what the French scholars called *l'aléa de la souveraineté*, that is, the risk of legal changes made by the State to improve its contractual position or extricate itself from liability and thereby manipulate the contract balance to its advantage [984].

In the choice of law clause, the parties chose an undefined and quite general language (general principles of law and the like), which they felt was – and was recognized by arbitral tribunals as – a lesser evil than subjecting their relationship to local rules that might have been unpredictable or anachronistic.

Further, resolving foreign investment disputes through international arbitration was considered a way to ensure that rules of a transnational nature could apply, so that a sufficient degree of fairness would exist in the adjudication process [985].

The following hallmark arbitration cases helped consolidate internationalization via recurrence to general principles.

1. The Lena Goldfields Arbitration in 1930

The idea of internationalization surfaced in the 1930 *Lena Goldfields* award [986], rendered in the first international arbitration to apply a "general principle of law recognised by civilized nations" by reference to

---

982. Sornarajah, *supra* note 47, p. 226.

983. See the analysis in this regard of Sole Arbitrator R.-J. Dupuy in *Texaco* v. *Libya*, *supra* note 119, Award of the Merits (19 January 1977), 17 ILM, p. 1, paras. 36, 40-45. See also A. A. Fatouros, "International Law and the Internationalized Contract", *American Journal of International Law*, Vol. 74, No. 1 (1980), p. 135.

984. P. Bernardini, "International Arbitration and A-National Rules of Law", *ICC International Court of Arbitration Bulletin*, Vol. 15, No. 2 (2004), p. 59.

985. *Ibid.*

986. *Lena Goldfields* v. *USSR*, reported in *The Times*, 3 September 1930. See Lim, Ho and Paparinskis, *supra* note 76, p. 38.

Article 38 (1) *(c)* of the PCIJ, namely compensation for unjust enrichment [987].

In its decision, the Tribunal recognized that laws of the Soviet Union governed domestic matters of the concession agreement in the USSR, but that for other purposes, Article 38 of the ICJ Statute and its reference to general principles should be regarded as the proper law governing the contract.

The Tribunal took into account provisions in the concession agreement referencing "good faith", "good will" or "good conscience" as evidence of the parties' intention to "internationalize" their relationship. Georges Delaume questions this reasoning. He considers that failing an explicit reference to international law or to the general principles of law in an agreement, a "good faith" contractual provision is merely an elementary rule of contract law [988].

In a widely cited article, V. V. Veeder performs a thorough analysis of the *Lena Goldfields* award. He notes that the decision was an English award made with London as the seat of arbitration. The parties' concession agreement was not a treaty, and the dispute was not a State-State arbitration subject to public international law. Despite these facts, the *Lena Goldfields Case* arbitration was never treated by the parties or its arbitrators as a purely English arbitration. Be that as it may, the decision paved the way for developments in favor of the notion of internationalization. Further, over the years, legal commentators have treated the case as having a broader significance in both private and public international law [989]. Its reference to general principles of

987. See McNair, *supra* note 4, pp. 10-11. In 1977, this award was relied upon by Arbitrator Dupuy to support his reasoning in the *Texaco* v. *Libya* decision, which is referred to below.

988. Delaume further states that "[i]n this respect, to place excessive emphasis on isolated arbitral decisions rendered several decades ago in particular circumstances would be most unwise", Delaume, *supra* note 119, pp. 779-800.

989. V. V. Veeder, "The Lena Goldfields Arbitration: The Historical Roots of Three Ideas", *International and Comparative Law Quarterly*, Vol. 47 (1998), pp. 749-750. "However, the concession agreement contained no reference to the applicable law, and none was advanced in Lena Goldfields." Notice of Arbitration or Statement of Claim. The Soviet Union's correspondence during the arbitration proceedings did not contain any reference to the applicable law either. Only in the main hearing did Lena Goldfields' counsel argue that the Tribunal should apply general principles of law to its claim for unjust enrichment as the "proper law" governing the concession agreement. At this point, the Tribunal adopted the argument on general principles acting as the applicable law advanced by Lena Goldfields' counsel in relation to restitution for unjust enrichment. *Ibid.*, pp. 765-766. As explained by Veeder, it would have been dangerous for Lena Goldfields' counsel to subject the concession agreement to Soviet law as its only applicable law, while the substance of Lena Goldfields' case related, directly or indirectly, to the imposition of the Soviet policies, laws, and administrative regulations

law was described as a gigantic first step for international commercial arbitration, equivalent to the caveman's discovery of fire [990].

The *Lena* arbitration influenced the drafting of Articles 21 and 22 of the 1933 concession convention between the Persian Government and the Anglo-Persian Oil Company, which has inspired the drafting of concession agreements in the following years [991]. Article 22 of this concession agreement stated that

> "F. The award shall be based on the juridical principles contained in Article 38 of the Statutes *(sic)* of the Permanent Court of International Justice. There shall be no appeal against the award" [992].

Evidently, the parties to these concession contracts were not satisfied with the national law governing the agreement and felt it necessary to rely instead upon the general principles within which the agreements were intended to operate [993].

2. *Petroleum Development Ltd.* v. *The Sheikh of Abu Dhabi* [994]

This landmark case was critical to consolidate internationalization recurring to general principles. It involved a concession that had

---

at the highest level. It would also have been hopeless to argue for the application of English law to govern the contract, as English law did not fully recognize the principle of unjust enrichment at the time. The Tribunal accepted Lena Goldfields' argument with laconic language. *Ibid.*, pp. 766-767.

990. Spiermann, *supra* note 979, p. 93, who cites Veeder, *ibid.*

991. Sole Arbitrator Dupuy noted in the *Texaco* v. *Libya* decision: "There are many international contracts comparable to the contracts in dispute which refer to the general principles of law." It will suffice to cite here: the contract between Iran and Agip Mineraria of 24 August 1954 (Art. 40), the contract between Iran and the Consortium of 19 September 1954 (Art. 46), the contract between Kuwait and Kuwait Shell Petroleum Company of 15 January 1961 (Art. 35) and the contract between the United Arab Republic and Pan American UAR Oil Company, of 23 October 1963 (Art. 42). *Texaco* v. *Libya*, *supra* note 119, Award on the Merits (1977), 17 ILM, p. 1 (1978), 53 ILR, p. 389 (1977), at 41.

992. Veeder, *supra* note 989, pp. 750-751. McNair offers other examples. For instance. a concession granted by a Government in the Middle East stated that "[t]he award of arbitration shall be consistent with legal principles familiar to civilized nations". Article 4.6 of the 1954 Consortium Agreement between Iran, the National Iranian Oil Company and certain other international corporations (American, British, Dutch and French) refers to the "principles of law recognized by civilized nations in general, including such of those principles as may have been applied by international tribunals". See McNair, *supra* note 4, p. 8.

993. *Ibid.*, p. 9.

994. *Petroleum Development Ltd.* v. *The Sheikh of Abu Dhabi* (1951) 18 ILR, p. 144, reprinted in 1 ICLQ 247 (1952).

been granted by the Sheikh of Abu Dhabi to Petroleum Development (Trucial Coast) Limited in 1939. Article 17 of the agreement contained the provision that

> "[t]he Ruler and the Company both declare that they base their work in this Agreement on goodwill and sincerity of belief and on the interpretation of this Agreement in a fashion consistent with reason" [995].

In his 1951 decision, the arbitrator Lord Herbert Asquith considered that even though the contract was

> "made in Abu Dhabi and wholly to be performed in that country, no reasonable municipal system of law could be said to exist. . . . The Sheikh administers a purely discretionary justice with the assistance of the Koran; and it would be fanciful to suggest that in this very primitive region there is any settled body of legal principles applicable to the construction of modern commercial instruments" [996].

Lord Asquith also determined that English law was not applicable either, as Article 17 displaced domestic laws. He stated the following:

> "But, albeit English municipal law is inapplicable as such, some of its rules are in my view so firmly grounded in reason, as to form part of this broad body of jurisprudence – this 'modern law of nature.'" [997]

Lord Asquith excluded English law on the assumption that "it had recognized and absorbed the usages of international trade and the very principles of international law" [998]. He concluded that

> "the terms of that clause invite, indeed prescribe, the application of principles rooted in the good sense and common practice of the generality of civilised nations – a sort of 'modern law of nature'".

The first step in the award's reasoning was to free the interpretation of the concession agreement from any domestic system of law. Public international law did not apply since it was a contract between a State and a private entity. Applying domestic law would have gone against

995. McNair, *supra* note 4, pp. 8-9.
996. Cited in Lim, Ho and Paparinskis, *supra* note 76, p. 40.
997. McNair, *supra* note 4, p. 13.
998. David, *supra* note 884, p. 349.

the spirit of the transaction and risked creating an imbalance of power between the parties. As a second step, since no answer could be found within existing public international law, principles extracted from recognized national systems of law were used. This process reveals that some systems, even if they are developed, offer contradictory solutions to international legal problems. However, it is common for different systems to apply substantially the same principles, though in different forms. The expression "modern law of nature" was used by Lord Asquith in this sense [999].

From a critical stance, while English law was not applied in this case, Lord Michael Mustill notes that the principles used in the award resemble the reasoning taken within specific English cases [1000]. Moreover, in a discretionary manner, Lord Asquith accepted certain principles of English law that represented a "modern law of nature" but rejected others. For instance, he considered that the English rules of evidence and the feudally inspired principle that sovereign grants are to be construed against the grantee were peculiarities of English legal history [1001].

3. *The Ruler of Qatar, Aramco and Sapphire Cases*

The 1953 award *Ruler of Qatar* v. *International Marine Oil Co.* [1002] involved a concession agreement that contained no provision identifying the applicable law in the event of a dispute. Nothing in the concession agreement threw light on the applicable law to the relationship, and the sole arbitrator Sir Alfred Bucknill was confronted with the question of whether the proper law would be Islamic law or "the principles of natural justice and equity". Sir Bucknill ruled that Islamic law "does not contain a body of legal principles applicable to a modern commercial contract of this kind", and applied general principles of law within the case, accompanied by the qualification that such principles reflected "natural justice and equity and good conscience" [1003].

---

999. Friedmann, *supra* note 955, p. 284.

1000. L. Mustill, "The New *Lex Mercatoria*: The First Twenty-Five Years", in M. Bos and I. Brownlie (eds.), *Liber Amicorum for Lord Wilberforce*, Oxford, Clarendon Press, 1987, chap. 9, p. 168.

1001. *Petroleum* v. *Sheik*, *supra* note 994; Friedmann, *supra* note 955, p. 284. As Jessup states, the Tribunal might have invoked the rule *lex non conveniens*, if such a rule existed, as perhaps it should. Jessup, *supra* note 348, p. 82.

1002. *Ruler of Qatar* v. *International Marine Oil Co. Ltd.* (1953) 20 ILR, p. 534.

1003. *Ibid.*, 20 ILR, pp. 544-545.

In the 1958 *Saudi Arabia* v. *Arabian American Oil Co. (Aramco)* decision [1004], considering the lack of an express choice of law in the concession agreement, the Arbitral Tribunal took into account the *Serbian Loans* decision's reference to the applicability of a national law in accordance with private international law rules. Consequently, the Tribunal went on to declare the application, in principle, of the law of Saudi Arabia, given that it was one of the parties to the agreement and its performance was to occur in that jurisdiction as well [1005].

However, the Tribunal held that the regime of mining and oil concessions had remained embryonic in Islamic law [1006]. Since this law did not contain a definite rule relating to the exploitation of oil deposits, the Tribunal based its decision on the contractual nature of the relationship [1007], considering the concession agreement "the fundamental law of the Parties, and the Arbitration Tribunal is bound to recognize its particular importance". After doing so, the Tribunal stated that

> "[i]n so far doubts may remain on the content or on the meaning of the agreement of the Parties it is necessary to resort to the general principles of law and to apply them in order to interpret, and even to supplement, the respective rights and obligations of the parties".

For this conclusion the Arbitration Tribunal relied, by analogy, on the precedent of the *Lena Goldfields* case [1008].

1004. *Saudi Arabia* v. *Arabian American Oil Co. (Aramco)*, Award (23 August 1958), 27 ILR, p. 117, Award (23 August 1958), p. 168.

1005. In this regard, the award referred the PCIJ in its judgment in the *Serbian Loans* case (*supra* note 978) and the *Brazilian Loans* (*Payment in Gold of Brazilian Federal Loans Contracted in France (France* v. *Brazil*), Judgment (12 July 1929), PCIJ, Ser. A, No. 21, p. 232) case. The arbitrators reasoned that the Saudi Arabian law chosen by the parties must, where necessary, be interpreted and supplemented by general principles of law. See Bernardini, *supra* note 984, p. 3.

1006. See criticisms to the inadequate and unreasonable avoidance of Islamic law, and the arbitrators' lack of essential knowledge of Islamic jurisprudence and its approach to international contracts, in S. Alshahrani, "Ousting Choice of Law in International Contracts: Lessons from ARAMCO Case", *Asian International Arbitration Journal* (2019), pp. 125-128.

1007. "The concession was found to be contractual, and the Tribunal noted there was a requirement for the agreement to be ratified not only by the King of Saudi Arabia, but also by the competent organs of the company at its seat in the United States. The Tribunal ruled that the fact that the concession was ratified by a royal decree did not alter its status", R. Higgins, "The Taking of Property by the State: Recent Developments in International Law", *Recueil des cours*, Vol. 176 (1982), p. 299.

1008. See excerpts in Lim, Ho and Paparinskis, *supra* note 76, pp. 42-43.

This technique is referred to by Ole Spiermann as the horizontal approach since the contract and the national law are put on equal footing when it comes to determining the applicable law. After declaring the contractual nature of the relationship, the arbitrators opted for the application of general principles of law due to the risk of sounding too eccentric if they directly declared the applicability of public international law [1009].

In the 1963 *Sapphire Case* award [1010], the Tribunal also applied general principles of law, based upon reason and upon the common practice of civilized nations [1011]. In the absence of choice, sole arbitrator Pierre Cavin found no positive implication from the arbitral clause regarding the applicable law but stated that "it is possible to find there a negative intention, namely to reject the exclusive application of Iranian law" [1012], which was the national law of the State company.

The arbitrator wrote:

> "It is a fundamental principle of law, which is constantly being proclaimed by international courts, that contractual undertakings must be respected. The rule of *pacta sunt servanda* is the basis of every contractual relationship." [1013]

The arbitrator took into account that Article 28 of the concession agreement, "which confirms an intention already expressed in the preamble, [and] provides that the parties undertake to carry out its provisions according to the principles of good faith and good will, and to respect the spirit as well as the letter of the agreement". Drawing upon previous decisions in the *Lena Goldfields* arbitration and other early Middle East oil cases, the arbitrator expressed that "such a clause is scarcely compatible with the strict application of the internal law of a particular country. It much more often calls for the application of general principles of law" as enshrined in Article 38 of the ICJ Statute [1014].

1009. Spiermann, *supra* note 979, p. 96.

1010. Award, 15 March 1963, 35 ILR, p. 136, 172-176 (Cavin).

1011. Cited in Lim, Ho and Paparinskis, *supra* note 76, p. 44.

1012. *Ibid.*

1013. *Sapphire International Petroleum Ltd. (Sapphire)* v. *National Iranian Oil Co.* (1963) 35 ILR, p. 135.

1014. See experts in Lim, Ho and Paparinskis, *supra* note 76, p. 44. Delaume, *supra* note 119, p. 800:

> "Unlike similar agreements which provided for the application of the 'principles of law' or 'principles of law recognized by civilized nations', the Sapphire agreement made specific reference to the law of Iran, which was 'stabilized' in

This award has since received significant criticism due to the fact that the arbitrator erroneously justified his decision by construing the *force majeure* provision of the contract as a choice of law clause [1015]. Questionably, the arbitrator considered it perfectly legitimate to find in the *force majeure* provision "evidence of the intention of the parties not to apply the strict rules of a particular system but, rather, to rely upon the rules of law, based upon reason, which are common to civilized nations" [1016].

4. Three Libyan arbitration cases related to nationalization

In 1971, Libyan Colonel Muammar Khadafi nationalized several petroleum concessions. This had a tremendous impact upon the concession agreements that had been drafted previously. Specifically, the nationalization effort provoked numerous cases that – as will be seen below – yielded diverging decisions, even though the choice of law provisions within the concessions were identical [1017].

Clause 28, paragraph 7, of all the Libyan concession agreements stated the following:

> "The concession shall be governed by and interpreted in accordance with the principles of law of Libya common to the principles of international law and in the absence of such common principles, then by and in accordance with the general principles of law, including such of those principles as may have been applied by international tribunals."

---

several respects. It further contained a *force majeure* clause relieving the parties of their obligations in the event of impossibility to perform, *force majeure* being defined for the purpose as 'occurrences which are recognized as such by the principles of international law' (Art. 37 (2)). These provisions paint a composite picture of a transaction which nevertheless had its own characteristics. To construe the particular features of the transaction, including its choice-of-law elements, by reference to other agreements whose stipulations differed from those in the *Sapphire* case was, to say the least, a perilous exercise. Yet, this is exactly what the arbitrator did."

1015. Delaume, *supra* note 961, p. 117.

1016. The arbitrator further stated (Delaume, *supra* note 119, p. 801):

> "Their application is particularly justified in the present contract, which was concluded between a State organ and a foreign company, and depends upon public law in certain of its aspects. This contract has therefore a quasi-international character which releases it from the sovereignty of a particular legal system, and it differs fundamentally from an ordinary commercial contract."

1017. Bernardini, *supra* note 984, p. 60.

In turn, Clause 16 guaranteed the concession holders that their contractual rights would be protected, which could not be altered except by the mutual consent of the parties. Clauses 16 and 28 thus introduced a stabilization of rights provision, the arbitration and choice of law provisions [1018]. Three well-known awards decided controversies in this regard with different arguments, as shown below.

(a) *BP* v. *Libya award* [1019]

In this 1973 decision, sole arbitrator Judge Lagergren favored the application of "the principles common to Libyan law and to public international law". Only in the absence of such common principles would "the general principles of law" apply, regarded as reflecting the general principles of domestic laws as well [1020].

Judge Lagergren ruled that the concession established a direct contractual relationship between the respondent and the claimant [1021]. He then considered both the common law and the civil law approach to remedies. He concluded that within the common law, "the norm is damages and the exception is specific performance", while in civil law "specific enforcement is the normal remedy as regards all obligations and damages are awarded only when specific performance is not possible or the claim is for damages rather than specific relief" [1022]. As a consequence, BP's sole remedy was damages, and not *restitutio in integrum* [1023].

Criticizing this decision, René-Jean Dupuy noted that the PCIJ recognized and accepted that *restitutio in integrum* is an established principle of international law, and that since 1928 virtually all legal scholars have viewed the *Chorzów* statement on *restitutio in integrum* as a "declaration of principle" [1024]. Moreover, Delaume criticized the *BP* v. *Libya* award for lacking a rigorous comparative law analysis between the civil law and the common law and with regard to remedies for non-performance [1025]. In turn, Muthucumaraswamy Sornarajah

---

1018. von Mehren and Kourides, *supra* note 396, pp. 479-481.
1019. *BP Exploration Co. (Libya) Ltd.* v. *The Government of the Libyan Arab Republic*, Award (10 October 1973), 53 ILR, p. 297 (1979).
1020. Bernardini, *supra* note 984, p. 60.
1021. Higgins, *supra* note 1007, p. 301.
1022. von Mehren and Kourides, *supra* note 396, p. 499.
1023. *Ibid.*
1024. *Ibid.*, p. 535.
1025. Delaume, *supra* note 961, p. 126.

argued that the general principle of sanctity of contracts, on which the internationalization within this decision is based, has little application to State contracts even in regard to private contracts [1026].

(b) *The Texaco* v. *Libya case* [1027]

In his 1977 decision on this case, sole arbitrator René-Jean Dupuy analyzed the French doctrine of administrative contracts *(contrats administratifs)*, which allows the State to unilaterally amend or abrogate its provisions if public interest requires, to determine whether it constituted a general principle of law affecting the principle of sanctity of contracts. He concluded that the doctrine was a peculiarity of French law and was therefore not a general principle [1028].

Libyan law recognized the validity of the French *contrats administratifs* doctrine. Arbitrator Dupuy found, however, that the Texaco concession was not an administrative law contract as the agreement was not made in the public service, was not entered into by a public official and did not confer upon the administrative authority the power to alter or abrogate the agreement. Rather, the Texaco Concession Agreement included a stabilization clause [1029].

The foundations of any workable international society – in the benefit of the best interests of both the developed and the developing world – cannot be built on breached agreements and broken commitments. This is one of the central conclusions of the *Texaco* v. *Libya* case, particularly in reference to upholding the stabilization clause of the concession contract [1030].

Texaco v. *Libya* lists three possible ways that internationalization can occur: the contract may refer to "general principles of law" as the

---

1026. Sornarajah, *supra* note 47, p. 91.

1027. *Texaco* v. *Libya*, *supra* note 119, Award on the Merits (19 January 1977).

1028. Sornarajah, *supra* note 47, pp. 88-89:

"It would appear to be the case that English law (as adopted and developed in the Commonwealth countries) differentiates between private and public contracts. In any event, the proposition that a State uses its legislative and administrative powers to evade contractual undertakings which, due to changes in circumstances, become contrary to the public interest. American law generally recognizes the federal government is immune from liability due to contractual breaches whenever its sovereign actions violate the contracts it has entered into with private persons. This doctrine is known as the sovereign acts doctrine, which is justified on the basis that the State 'must be able to respond to changed circumstances that call for a policy response without undue inhibition'."

1029. Higgins, *supra* note 1007, pp. 299-300.

1030. von Mehren and Kourides, *supra* note 396, p. 552.

applicable law [1031], it may contain an arbitration clause [1032] or it may be an "economic development agreement" [1033].

Regarding the first two ways in which internationalization can take place (general principles and an arbitration clause), the award stated:

> "Even if one considers that the choice of international arbitration proceedings cannot by itself lead to the exclusive application of international law, it is one of the elements which makes it possible to detect a certain internationalization of the contract. . . . It is therefore unquestionable that the reference to international arbitration is sufficient to internationalize a contract, in other words, to situate it within a specific legal order – the order of the international law of contracts." [1034]

However, Arbitrator Dupuy did not offer a clear explanation of what was meant by the term "the international law of contracts" as governing law, and in what respect it differs from public international law or whether it is a manifestation of a distinct third category, the *lex mercatoria* [1035].

Moreover, Delaume questioned whether recourse to arbitration may necessarily have a *per se* determinative impact on the issue of applicable law; the primary purpose of arbitration is to avoid litigation before domestic courts [1036].

Dupuy decided that the contract should be ruled by public international law since the governing law clause referred primarily to "principles of international law" and to "general principles of law" on a

---

1031. "International arbitration case law confirms that the reference to the general principles of law is always regarded to be a sufficient criterion for the internationalization of a contract", para. 42, as cited in Lim, Ho and Paparinskis, *supra* note 76, p. 47.

1032. Dupuy has argued that the inclusion of international arbitration is *per se* sufficient to internationalize the contract. *Texaco* v. *Libya*, *supra* note 119, at 455. In contrast, Delaume notes: "It cannot be said that submission to arbitration should necessarily have a determinative impact upon the issue of applicable law", Delaume, *supra* note 119, pp. 784-819.

1033. According to Fatouros, the third method of internationalization "gives away the game". In the context of an economic development agreement, where the State party is a developing country, there is a presumption against limiting the sovereign authority of States. This principle is fundamental within international law and is widely accepted. However, this presumption has now been reversed, and inferences can be made favor limiting the sovereign authority of States to the benefit of private parties. Fatouros, *supra* note 983, p. 136.

1034. *Texaco* v. *Libya*, *supra* note 119, Award of the Merits (19 January 1977), 17 ILM, p. 1, paras. 36, 40-45 (Dupuy), p. 44.

1035. Maniruzzaman, *supra* note 317, p. 32.

1036. Delaume, *supra* note 961, p. 118.

subsidiary basis. Dupuy interpreted the latter in accordance with Article 38 of the ICJ Statute [1037].

The arbitrator further wrote:

> "International arbitration case law confirms that the reference to the general principles of law is always regarded to be a sufficient criterion for the internationalization of a contract. One should remember, in this respect, the awards delivered in *Lena Goldfields* v. *USSR* in 1930, *Petroleum Development Ltd.* v. *Sovereign of Abu Dhabi* in 1951, and *International Marine Oil Company* v. *Sovereign of Qatar* in 1953, and in *Sapphire International Petroleum Ltd.* v. *N10C*, all cases in which the arbitrators noted a reference to the general principles of law in order to reach their conclusions as to the internationalization of the contract." [1038]

Dupuy additionally determined that principles of Libyan law could govern only where they conformed with principles of international law "as applied between all nations belonging to the community of states". According to the arbitrator, clauses like these invoking general principles "tend to remove all or part of the agreement from the internal law and to provide for its correlative submission to . . . a system which is properly an international law system". This reasoning was intentional:

> "The recourse to general principles . . . is justified by the need for the private contracting party to be protected against unilateral and abrupt modifications of the legislation in the contracting State: it plays, therefore, an important role in the contractual equilibrium intended by the parties." [1039]

The award also held that "[a] third element of the internationalization of the contracts in dispute results from the fact that it takes on a dimension of a new category of agreements between States and private persons: economic development agreements" [1040].

1037. The applicable substantive law Clause 28 of the Deeds of Concession read as follows:

> "This concession shall be governed by and interpreted in accordance with the principles of the law of Libya common to the principles of international law and, in the absence of such common principles, then by and in accordance with the general principles of law, including such of those principles as may have been applied by international tribunals."

1038. *Texaco* v. *Libya*, *supra* note 119, Award of the Merits (19 January 1977), 17 ILM, p. 1, para. 42.

1039. Kotuby and Sobota, *supra* note 157, p. 46.

1040. *Texaco* v. *Libya*, *supra* note 119, Award of the Merits (19 January 1977), 17 ILM, p. 1, para. 44 *(c)*.

The award further notes that several elements characterize these agreements. First, their subject matter is particularly broad: they are not concerned only with an isolated purchase or performance but tend to bring to developing countries investments and technical assistance, particularly in the field of research and exploitation of mineral resources or in the construction of factories on a turnkey basis. Thus, they assume a real importance in the development of the country where they are performed. It will suffice to mention here the importance of the obligations assumed in the case under consideration by the concession holders in the matters of road and port infrastructures and the training on location of qualified personnel. The party contracting with the State was thus associated with the realization of the economic and social progress of the host country. Second, the long duration of these contracts implies close cooperation between the State and the contracting party and requires permanent installations as well as the acceptance of extensive responsibilities by the investor. Finally, because of the purpose of the cooperation between the contracting party and the State and the magnitude of the investments involved, the contractual nature of this type of agreement is reinforced: the emphasis on the contractual nature of the legal relation between the host State and the investor is intended to bring about an equilibrium between the goal of the general interest sought by such a relation and the profitability that is necessary for the pursuit of the task entrusted to the private enterprise. The effect is also to assure the private contracting party of a certain stability justified by the considerable investments that it makes in the country concerned. The investor must in particular be protected against legislative uncertainties, that is to say the risk of the municipal law of the host country being modified, and against any government measures which would lead to an abrogation or rescission of the contract. Hence the insertion, as in the case in question, of so-called stabilization clauses: these clauses tend to remove all or part of the agreement from the municipal law and likewise provide for either its submission to *sui generis* rules as stated in the *Aramco* award or to a proper international law system [1041].

1041. The *Texaco* award further states:

> "From this latter point of view, the following considerations should be noted, which were mentioned in the *Sapphire* award, and which stress the interest of the internationalization of the contract: 'Such a solution seems particularly suitable for giving the guarantees of protection which are indispensable for foreign companies, since these companies undergo very considerable risks in bringing financial and technical aid to countries in the process of development. It is in the interest of both parties to such agreements that any disputes between them should

Clause 28 (7) of the deeds of concession analyzed in the *Texaco* v. *Libya* decision was interpreted to determine that the principle of *restitutio in integrum* was the preferred remedy both in Libyan law and in international law. Dupuy reached the finding that specific performance (in the form of *restitutio in integrum*) is the "normal sanction for non-performance of contractual obligations and that it is inapplicable only to the extent that restoration of the status quo ante is impossible". He based his conclusions on arguments raised in international pleadings, the opinions of international scholars and *dicta* found in international decisions [1042]. The arbitrator therefore determined that the Libyan Government was legally bound to perform these deeds of concession as originally negotiated [1043].

The reasoning used in the *Texaco* v. *Libya* case is significant, due primarily to Dupuy's elaborate decision citing extensive scholarly authority. Moreover, the *Texaco* v. *Libya* case was the first major international arbitration to address the effect of the UN General Assembly's resolutions on the legal doctrine of permanent sovereignty over natural resources, discussed in Chapter VIII. Even though his reasoning tended to favor developing nations, Dupuy could not find any positive law source to support the binding legal effect of the Charter of Economic Rights and Duties of States. He determined that the very nature of the Charter, the circumstances surrounding it, the relevant statements made by States regarding the Charter, the States that voted on it and the text of its provisions all indicated that the Charter itself did not create customary international law. On the contrary, it was a clear challenge to the traditional Western view of international law. By contrast, State practice alone could lead to the development of customary international

> be settled according to the general principles universally recognized and should not be subject to the particular rules of national laws . . .' (*35 Int'l LR 136* (1963), pp. 175-176)."

Texaco v. *Libya*, *supra* note 119, para. 45 *(c)*; see text in Lim, Ho and Paparinskis, *supra* note 76, pp. 46-50. As mentioned in Lim, Ho and Paparinskis, p. 50:

> "It is apparent that none of the key awards contemplate the possibility that internationalization may not be defensible on legal grounds. As a result, no attempt is made to counter objections to investment contract internationalization. Sceptics soon latched onto this omission, and their reasoned objections to investment contract internationalization gave rise to a backlash against internationalization."

1042. *Texaco* v. *Libya*, *supra* note 119, Award (19 January 1977), paras. 101-109. Also Delaume, *supra* note 119, pp. 784-819, p. 806.

1043. von Mehren and Kourides, *supra* note 396, p. 499.

law [1044]. Dupuy concluded that only Resolution 1803 (XVII) of 1962 reflected the state of existing customary international law [1045].

(c) *The Liamco award*

In the *Liamco* award, sole arbitrator Sobhi Mahmassani went in a different direction and interpreted the choice of law clause as implying that "the law governing the Liamco concession agreement . . . is firstly Libyan law when the latter is consistent with international law, and secondly general principles of law" [1046].

Regarding the nature of the concessions, Mahmassani ruled that they were contractual in nature but were not administrative contracts. The arbitrator noted that the stabilization clause included in the agreements emphasized the contractual basis of the concession [1047].

Mahmassani considered the remedy of *restitutio in integrum* only in a peripheral fashion, as Liamco implicitly admitted the difficulty of ordering the remedy of restitution in kind. As such, the choice of law provision was not a vital element of the decision [1048]. In his award, Mahmassani pointed out that *restitutio in integrum* was a general principle of law accepted in both Libyan and international law. Nonetheless, this remedy was discarded due to "prevalent international practice" and because it was "practically incapable of compulsory execution" [1049].

5. *Critical perspective of the Libyan nationalization cases*

All three Libyan nationalization cases (*BP*, *Texaco*, and *Liamco*) were decided by arbitrators from different parts of the world: Sweden, France and Iran. While the three awards diverged significantly with regard to certain legal questions, these decisions have in common the notion that mining and petroleum concessions are contracts *simpliciter* and not unilateral acts nor administrative contracts [1050].

1044. *Ibid.*, pp. 528-529.

1045. *Texaco* v. *Libya*, *supra* note 119, Award on the Merits, (1977) 17 ILM, p. 1 (1978), 53 ILR, p. 389 (1977). See Salacuse, *supra* note 65, pp. 26-28, pp. 93-94.

1046. *Liamco*, *supra* note 946, Award (12 April 1977, S. Mahmassani, sole arb.), 20 ILM, p. 1 (1981). See Bernardini, *supra* note 984, p. 60.

1047. Higgins, *supra* note 1007, p. 300.

1048. von Mehren and Kourides, *supra* note 396, p. 500.

1049. This conclusion has been criticized by both von Mehren and Kourides as unconvincing. *Ibid.*, p. 544.

1050. Higgins, *supra* note 1007, p. 301.

Since in these cases Islamic law has typically been considered inadequate with respect to foreign investment contracts, the tribunals opted instead for the application of equitable or general principles of the law. In this regard, European writers suggested that public international law should apply, given that general principles are one of its sources [1051]. Sornarajah notes that many of the arguments in this regard can be traced to Lord Arnold McNair's seminal work. However, McNair carefully limited his view to refer only to situations where the host State's law was not sufficiently developed to apply to the contract [1052].

As seen, the different positions taken in the various Libyan awards mentioned have led to diverging conclusions regarding compensation for contractual breaches. The *BP* v. *Libya* and *Liamco* awards excluded full compensation since they did not identify any related principles that were common within Libyan and international law. By contrast, the *Texaco* v. *Libya* award found that the principles of both Libyan law and international law included *restitutio in integrum* as the typical sanction ordered for non-performance of contractual obligations [1053].

In both the *Liamco* and the *BP* awards, the arbitrators engaged in a comparative approach in the understanding that general principles of law applied. However, in the *Texaco* award, the arbitrator held that international law or the "international law of contracts" rather than the general principles applied as the governing law [1054].

1051. Sornarajah, *supra* note 47, p. 252.

1052. *Ibid.*, p. 254.

1053. Bernardini, *supra* note 984, p. 61. At p. 511:

> "The BP, Texaco, and Liamco arbitrations represent both approaches to determining the applicable law: first, the detachment from the municipal law of a State and second, the application of the municipal law of a State. In the BP arbitration, Judge Lagergren applied a detached system of general principles of law, and in the *Texaco* v. *Libya* and Liamco arbitrations, Sole Arbitrators Dupuy and Mahmassani applied municipal law, i.e., principles of Libyan law on the basis that they shared much in common with principles of international law. R. B. von Mehren and P. N. Kourides, p. 510. The BP award demonstrates the fact that a choice of law that is unattached to any sovereign may be completely practical and effective. In that case, sole Arbitrator Lagergren found in general principles of law the necessary elements to construe the contract, to determine whether it had been breached, and to decide upon a remedy. In his application of general principles of law, Lagergren had no more difficulty in construing the contract and determining that it had been breached than Dupuy and Mahmassani had in applying Libyan municipal law (common to international law) to decide the same issues. Likewise, with respect to the question of determining an appropriate remedy, although the choice-of-law approach required different conclusions, none of the sole arbitrators found that the law he was applying was inadequate for his purpose."

1054. *Liamco*, *supra* note 946, Award, 20 ILM, p. 35 (p. 67 of the award); *BP* v. *Libya*, *supra* note 1019, Award, 53 ILR, p. 329; *Texaco* v. *Libya*, *supra* note 119, Award, para. 41. See Delaume, *supra* note 119, p. 797.

These three conclusions are problematic. On the one hand, it is not clear what the content of this international law of contracts is [1055]. This explains why contrary to *Texaco* v. *Libya*, the *Aminoil* award rejected the application of transnational law or of a third legal order between national and international law [1056]. As was well observed by Delaume, the *Aminoil* decision further referred to below repudiates the *lex mercatoria*. By incorporating international law into the law of Kuwait and blending them into a single legal framework, the award obscured the role of international law as the ultimate controlling standard. In this way, the Tribunal found it necessary to test domestic rules against some external international norms that were capable of supplying a troubling "international public policy" that might justify the non-application of domestic law [1057].

On the other hand, a comparative analysis has its own perils. *Liamco* follows the *BP* v. *Libya* approach in this regard, and the latter has been criticized for lack of rigor in its civil and common law comparison [1058].

6. *The Aminoil case*

The 1982 *Aminoil* decision [1059], among others, adopted a different position than *Texaco* v. *Libya* regarding the doctrine of *contrats administratifs* [1060]. In that case, the State of Kuwait nationalized the petroleum concession granted to Aminoil, which had previously included a guarantee that the terms of the contract would remain stable.

According to Aminoil, the concession agreement had been wrongfully terminated by Kuwait in violation of international law and of a stabilization clause in the contract. Kuwait responded that it had agreed to this clause when it was still a "colonial" country, and that it therefore had no effect. The Tribunal did not agree with this argument since Kuwait had affirmed the validity of the stabilization clause after

---

1055. Therefore, Delaume considers that the *BP* and *Liamco* decisions are the road to follow. Even though it may not always be conducted in the same fashion or lead to identical conclusions, it is the proper way to give substantive meaning to those principles of law which are part and parcel of the law governing the contract. See *ibid.*, p. 809.

1056. Bernardini, *supra* note 984, pp. 61-62.

1057. Delaume, *supra* note 961, p. 120.

1058. *Ibid.*, p. 126.

1059. *The American Independent Oil Company (Aminoil)* v. *The Govt. of the State of Kuwait*, Award (24 May 1982), by a tribunal composed of Paul Reuter (chairman), Hamed Sultan and Sir Gerald Fitzmaurice, 66 ILR, p. 601-602, ILM, p. 976 (1982), 9 *ICCA Yearbook Commercial Arbitration* (hereafter YB Comm. Arb.) (1984), p. 71.

1060. Sornarajah, *supra* note 47, p. 90.

attaining full independence. A majority of the arbitrators on the panel held that the stabilization clause did not cover nationalization. The language of the clause was not specific enough, and the majority ruled that a limitation on the sovereign rights of a State could not be presumed. The arbitrators decided that the stabilization clause was intended to protect Aminoil against confiscatory measures. They further observed that after the nationalization Kuwait had made an offer for compensation. The arbitrators held that, therefore, the nationalization fell outside the scope of the clause, as it was not intended to be confiscatory [1061].

Delaume notes that unlike the earlier concession cases, wherein the States either engaged in bitter and protracted litigation or refused outright to participate in the proceedings, the *Aminoil* arbitration took place in a business-like atmosphere between parties seeking a solution to their dispute. Moreover, no attempt has been made to duplicate the *Texaco* ruling that submission to international arbitration might constitute an implicit choice of international law applicable to the substance of the dispute. This was even more the case since there was an express applicable law clause governing the substance of the dispute in *Aminoil* [1062].

The applicable law clause stated that

> "[t]he law governing the substantive issue between the Parties shall be determined by the Tribunal having regard to the quality of the Parties, the transnational character of their relations and the principles of law and practice prevailing in the modern world" [1063].

The Tribunal applied Kuwaiti law to many of the contractual issues, as it was "the law most directly involved". It also applied international

1061. "The majority also considered that, as a result of the many readjustments of the arrangements between the parties, including those of a financial nature, the original concession had in effect been transformed into a kind of association, with the result that the original stabilization clause had lost its former absolute character", G. R. Delaume, "The Proper Law of State Contracts Revisited", *ICSID Review: Foreign Investment Law Journal*, Vol. 12 (1997), p. 24.

1062. "The Texaco award assumption was an extreme example of the internationalization philosophy that inspired certain arbitrators in years past. Contrary to the arbitrator's opinion, the primary purpose of providing for the arbitral settlement of investment disputes is not to settle applicable law issues, but simply to remove these disputes from the jurisdiction of domestic courts, including not only those in the host State or the investor's country but also courts in other countries in which action might be brought as a result of forum shopping" (*ibid.*, p. 6).

1063. "It may be assumed from this vague formulation, redolent of a rule of conflict, that the parties failed to agree on a direct choice of applicable law", Bernardini, *supra* note 984, p. 61.

law alongside Kuwaiti law, stating that the two were not in conflict with one another. One of the central passages of the award stated that

> "if, as recalled above, international law constitutes an integral part of the law of Kuwait, the general principles of law correspondingly recognize the rights of the State in its capacity of supreme protector of the general interest" [1064].

The Tribunal thus recognized the possibility of applying both the law of the host State and international law as part of national law. However, the award fell short of directly addressing an important issue, namely the hierarchy between domestic and international law. Delaume notes that the fact that in addition to Kuwaiti law the Tribunal felt it necessary to refer also to the general principles may be an acknowledgment of the need to test domestic rules against external international norms [1065].

7. *Critical scholarly comments on the Middle East petroleum cases in this chapter*

Within the field of international investment arbitration, no concrete corpus or public international law doctrine exists to explain the legal sources that should be applied to foreign investments. Furthermore, the writings of publicists and the uncontested awards on which they are based have been referred to as "weak, manipulable, and mercenary" sources, many of which have been contradicted in the work of other publicists [1066]. These writings have been referred to as a "rarity", and when applied, the tribunal "chooses one over the other to suit the different circumstances, depending largely on the philosophical and other preferences the tribunal itself has for the solution" [1067].

The seminal work regarding general principles and international law was published by Bin Cheng in 1953. At the time, he only explored decisions of the ICJ (and its predecessor, the PCIJ) in addition to the rulings of certain *ad hoc* claims tribunals. The principles included in his work applied to disputes between States, describing good faith in terms of forbidding a State from abusing its rights, taking advantage of its

1064. "By reconciling Kuwaiti law and the general principles of law as legal sources that may be applied simultaneously, the Tribunal satisfied both the State, which had argued for the application of its own laws to all the issues in dispute, and Aminoil, which wanted general principles of law alone to be applied" (*ibid.*, p. 61).

1065. Delaume, *supra* note 1061, pp. 3-4.

1066. Sornarajah, *supra* note 47, p. 254. See also at p. 298 and citation of Dezalay and Garth, *supra* note 801.

1067. *Ibid.*, p. 16.

own wrongs, or taking inconsistent positions that disadvantage another State. For instance, Cheng explained that the principle of *pacta sunt servanda* developed in the context of international treaties and not State contracts. At the time, parties did not have a direct recourse against States, and diplomatic protection often trumped the grievances of the investors due to the weight and complexity of other facets of foreign relations. Today, this situation is totally different [1068].

The vagueness inherent in general principles of law and in the methods of their determination have led to their application in a manner considered by some writers to be detrimental to States. Sornarajah illustrates this situation by reference to the principle of the sanctity of contracts, rooted in nineteenth-century systems of freedom of contract and bargain. Modern developments have eroded the principle, yet the sanctity of contracts is still considered a general principle of law [1069]. As such, it is often relied upon in investment contracts that use stabilization clauses. In these situations, considering that State law can manipulate the "rules of the game" by making modifications to domestic laws in their favor [1070], party autonomy is expected to function optimally in favor of the investor. Sornarajah suggests, however, that party autonomy is expected to work well in export transactions but not in long-term investment contracts. Moreover, it applies well in international contracts with connecting factors normally in different places. Contrarily, investment contracts are largely affected by domestic regulation, for instance regarding environmental protection, customs controls and similar areas of public law. Sornarajah therefore concludes that reliance, in a nebulous system, of general principles of law incorporated via party autonomy is unwise [1071].

1068. Kotuby and Sobota, *supra* note 157, pp. 38-40. As stated by Wolfgang Friedmann, the principles of international law are constantly evolving due to changes in its social and moral foundations. Friedmann, *supra* note 955, p. 286.

1069. Sornarajah, *supra* note 47, p. 86.

1070. *Ibid.*, p. 282.

1071. *Ibid.*, pp. 284-286. Sornarajah, *supra* note 47, p. 289:

> "Some old cases refer to the application of external standards, but not exclusively. In the *Delgoa Bay Railway Case* (1900), the arbitrator found that Portuguese law applied, but also ruled that Portuguese law 'did not contain any particular provision on the decisive points that would depart from general principles of the common law of modern nations'. In the Schufeldt Claim (1930), there was a reference to the same laws in other legal systems, but the law of Guatemala was applied. In the Lena Goldfields arbitration (1936), the Tribunal decided that the dispute should be settled according to general principles. However, it did not do so attempting to create a universal system of law applicable to State contracts, but merely to demonstrate that the same solution will be achieved applying the legal systems of the other parties or other legal systems."

Another controversy related to general principles arises with regard to the remedy provided when parties argue that the tribunal has the power to order specific performance of the agreement. Even in cases involving breaches of international treaties, the remedy ordered is typically damages, except in situations involving territorial disputes. In foreign investment disputes, however, "the exorbitant claim" [1072] is made that the arbitral tribunal may order specific performance. According to Sornarajah:

> "The only reason for this is that it could facilitate the pursuit of the fruits of the concession that has been taken over through the domestic courts into whose jurisdiction such property is later taken. Here, again, theory is twisted to suit the convenience of foreign investment protection." [1073]

C. Recent evolution of general principles within investment arbitration

Since the 1970s, numerous changes have occurred within the field of international investment arbitration. Rather than States themselves, State-owned entities have increasingly been entering into investment contracts with private parties.

Further, in the last decades of the twentieth century, investors – who had previously occupied a dominant position in international trade – had to adapt to new patterns of conducting business. Concomitantly, a new generation of negotiators in Third World countries became steadily more familiar with the complexities of international investment contracts, and as a consequence, negotiation and implementation of State contracts have increasingly been conducted in a business-like manner. Moreover, Third World countries modernized their legal framework for attracting international investments. These developments led to the "metamorphosis" of investment agreements which was alluded to in the *Aminoil* award [1074].

Traditional concession agreements subject to general principles of international law have been replaced by new types of arrangements mostly subject to private domestic laws, such as service contracts, technical assistance contracts and build-operate-transfer agreements.

1072. This expression is used by Sornarajah, *supra* note 47, p. 289.
1073. *Ibid.*, p. 298.
1074. "New stipulations have appeared, which clearly illustrate a trend to 'relocalize' the relationship between investors and States under the State's own law", Delaume, *supra* note 1061, p. 2.

However, international arbitrators have shown a tendency to attenuate the application of domestic law by concurrently referring to other principles with a varying nomenclature, even where domestic law has been chosen by the parties. Arbitration laws and rules such as the ICC Rules of Arbitration (Art. 28 (4)) require arbitrators to take trade usages into account in all cases. The question nonetheless remains whether general principles fall within these categories [1075]. This matter will be addressed in Chapter XX.

In investment arbitration, the general principle of *pacta sunt servanda* invited tribunals to bring contractual arguments into play during the statutory interpretation of questions such as the legitimate expectations of foreign investors or the acquiescence of local authorities [1076].

Further, Andrea Carlevaris notes that although infrequent, application of the general principles of commercial law to the substance of an investment dispute may be relevant in situations in which, for example, the arbitral tribunal is faced with contractual claims and the broad language used in the relevant treaty covers disputes or investments. He also notes that situations may occur in which ascertaining a breach of the treaty requires analysis of a contractual relationship and of the parties' conduct in the context thereof. Even though here the relevant standards are those of public international law, ascertaining their breach may require an assessment of the conduct of the parties within the contractual relationship, for which purpose the general principles of commercial law could become relevant [1077].

Regarding the ICSID Convention, Aron Broches wrote that

> "the reference to international law in Article 42 . . . in reality, comprised (apart from treaty law) only such principles as that of good faith and the principle that one ought to abide by agreements voluntarily made and ought to carry them out in good faith" [1078].

1075. For instance, the award of 30 April 1982 in ICC Case No. 3896, 110 *Journal du Droit International* (hereafter JDI), p. 914 (1983), 10 YB Comm. Arb. (1985), p. 47, and in Sigvard Jarvin and Yves Derains (eds.), *Collection of ICC Arbitral Awards 1974-1985*, Paris/New York, ICC Publishing; Deventer/Boston, Kluwer Law and Taxation Publishers, 1990, p. 161; commented by B. Oppetit, "Arbitrage et contrats d'Etats: L'arbitrage Framatome et autres c. Atomic Energy Organization of Iran", 111 JDI, p. 37 (1984).

1076. Spiermann, *supra* note 979, p. 95.

1077. Carlevaris, *supra* note 770, p. 209.

1078. *History of the ICSID Convention: Documents Concerning the Origin and the Formulation of the Convention*, Vol. II-1, p. 985. The *History* is published by the ICSID in Washington in five volumes to date: Vol. I (1970), II-1 (1968), II-2 (1968), III (1968) and IV (1969). All were reprinted throughout the 2000s. See https://icsid.worldbank.org/resources/publications/the-history-of-the-icsid-convention.

Several ICSID arbitration cases made use of general principles. In the ICSID case *Inceysa* v. *El Salvador*, the Tribunal cited Article 38 of the ICJ Statute and proposed to describe general principles of law in the following terms:

> "[T]he general principles of law are an autonomous or direct source of International Law, along with international conventions and custom. Without attempting to define what the general principles of law are, the Tribunal notes that, in general, they have been understood as general rules on which there is international consensus to consider them as universal standards and rules of conduct that must always be applied and which, in the opinion of important commentators, are rules of law on which the legal systems of the States are based." [1079]

ICSID tribunals have invoked general principles such as good faith [1080], prohibition of corruption [1081], the principle that nobody can benefit from his or her own fraud *(nemo auditur propiam turpitudinem allegans)* [1082], *pacta sunt servanda* [1083], *exceptio non adimpleti contractus* [1084], estoppel [1085], unjust enrichment [1086], full compensation for

---

1079. *Inceysa Vallisoletana, SL* v. *Republic of El Salvador*, ICSID Case No. ARB/03/26, Award (2 August 2006), paras. 226-227.

1080. *Amco* v. *Indonesia*, Decision on Jurisdiction (25 September 1983), para. 47; *Inceysa, ibid.*, paras. 230 ff.

1081. *Wena Hotels* v. *Egypt*, *supra* note 601, Award (2000), para. 111; *World Duty Free Company* v. *Republic of Kenya*, ICSID Case No. ARB/00/7, Award (4 October 2006), paras. 138-157.

1082. *Inceysa*, *supra* note 1079, paras. 240 ff.

1083. *Adriano Gardella* v. *Cote d'Ivoire*, Award (29 August 1977), para. 4.3; *Amco* v. *Indonesia*, Award (20 November 1984), paras. 248 ff.

1084. *Klöckner* v. *Cameroon*, *supra* note 748, Award (21 October 1983), 2 *ICSID Reports*, p. 61 ff.; *Autopista* v. *Bolivia*, *supra* note 2716, Award (23 September 2003), para. 316.

1085. *Amco* v. *Indonesia*, *supra* note 1080, Decision on Jurisdiction (1983), para. 47; *Amco* v. *Indonesia*, Resubmitted Case: Award, 5 June 1990, paras. 144-145; *Klöckner* v. *Cameroon*, *supra* note 748, Decision on Annulment (1985), para. 123; *SPP (Middle East) Ltd.* v. *Arab Rep. of Egypt*, Decision on Jurisdiction I (27 November 1985), para. 63; *CSOB* v. *Slovakia*, Decision on Jurisdiction (24 May 1999), para. 47; *Gruslin* v. *Malaysia*, Award (27 November 2000), paras. 20.1-20.5; *Zhinvali* v. *Georgia*, Award (24 January 2003), paras. 244-248; *SGS* v. *Pakistan*, *supra* note 977, Decision on Jurisdiction (6 August 2003), paras. 122, 175-177; *SGS Société Générale de Surveillance SA* v. *Republic of the Philippines*, ICSID Case No. ARB/02/6, Decision on Jurisdiction (29 January 2004), para. 109; *Pan America/BP* v. *Argentina Pan American Energy LLC and BP Argentina Exploration Company* v. *The Argentine Republic*, ICSID Case No. ARB/03/13, Decision on Jurisdiction (27 July 2006), paras. 140-161; *ADC* v. *Hungary*, Award (2 October 2006), paras. 474, 475; *Fraport* v. *Philippines*, Award (16 August 2007), paras. 346, 347.

1086. *Amco* v. *Indonesia*, Resubmitted Case: Award (5 June 1990), paras. 154-156; *SPP* v. *Egypt*, *supra* note 1085, Award (20 May 1992), paras. 245-249; *Inceysa*, *supra* note 1079, Award (2 August 2006), paras. 253 *et seq*.

prejudice resulting from a failure to fulfill contractual obligations [1087], the principle of compensation in case of nationalization [1088], general principles of due process [1089], the principle that the claimant bears the burden of proof [1090], *res judicata* [1091], the prohibition of the abuse of right [1092], the duty to mitigate damages [1093], the principle that no one can transfer a better title than he or she has *(nemo plus iuris transferre potest quam ipse habet)* [1094], and the valuation of damages [1095].

The United States-Iran tribunals have also applied general principles, in accordance with the open-ended provision of Article V of the Claims Settlement Declaration of 1981. As stated in the *Amoco* v. *Iran* case [1096], this provision "contributed, to a greater extent than any other international compact, to the consolidation of the rule of international law that a State has the duty to respect contracts freely entered into with a foreign party" [1097].

1087. *Amco* v. *Indonesia, supra* note 1080, Award (1984), paras. 265-268.

1088. *Benvenuti* v. *Congo, supra* note 455, Award (15 August 1980), para. 4.64.

1089. *Amco* v. *Indonesia, supra* note 1080, Award (1984), paras. 199-201, Decision on Annulment (16 May 1984), paras. 75-79.

1090. *AAPL* v. *Sri Lanka, supra* note 453, Final Award (27 June 1990), para. 56; *Tradex Hellas* v. *Albania*, Award (29 April 1999), para. 74; *Middle East Cement* v. *Egypt*, Award (12 April 2002), para. 89; *Generation Ukraine* v. *Ukraine, supra* note 456, Award (16 September 2003), paras. 19.1-19.4; *Noble Ventures, Inc.* v. *Romania*, ICSID Case No. ARB/01/11, Award (12 October 2005), para. 100; *Salini* v. *Jordan*, Award (31 January 2006), paras. 70-75; *Saipem* v. *Bangladesh, supra* note 77, Decision on Jurisdiction (21 March 2007), para. 83; *Tokios Tokeles* v. *Ukraine, supra* note 449, Decision on Jurisdiction (29 April 2004), para. 121.

1091. *Amco* v. *Indonesia*, Resubmitted Case: Decision on Jurisdiction (10 May 1988), 1 *ICSID Reports*, p. 548 ff.

1092. *Saipem* v. *Bangladesh, supra* note 77, Decision (2007), paras. 154-158; *Siag* v. *Egypt, supra* note 102, Decision on Jurisdiction (11 April 2007), paras. 119, 125, 213.

1093. *Middle East Cement* v. *Egypt*, Award (12 April 2002), para. 166.

1094. *Mihaly International Corporation* v. *Sri Lanka*, ICSID Case No. ARB/00/2, Award (15 March 2002), para. 24.

1095. *Amco* v. *Indonesia*, Award (20 November 1984), para. 267; *Fedax* v. *Venezuela, supra* note 75, Award (9 March 1998), para. 30; *Enron* v. *Argentina, supra* note 451, Award (22 May 2007), para. 360.

1096. *Amoco* v. *Iran, supra* note 489, Award (14 July 1987), para. 177.

1097. See Spiermann, *supra* note 979, p. 99.

CHAPTER IX

OTHER SOURCES OF PUBLIC INTERNATIONAL LAW AND INVESTMENT LAW

A. Plurality of legal sources in foreign investments

Several instruments may govern the substantive and procedural rights and obligations of the foreign investments regime in a given country.

Many investment transactions are set out in contracts negotiated between the investor and the State or governmental agency. Violations of the investment contract may trigger contractual remedies or, when appropriate, State responsibility under public international law. These issues will be dealt with in Chapter XIV [1098].

Investments are often also granted protection by the domestic law of the host State. Typically, this local legislation applies in general to legal claims brought in the territory, as well as a residual source of law for contract claims in particular for gap-filling or interpretive purposes. Foreign investment protection safeguards of the host State's municipal law may also be invoked in international claims when their jurisdiction is available.

Violations of multilateral or bilateral international treaties are usually the source of foreign investment claims, and may also apply to international investment contracts, imposing a set of substantive standards such as fair and equitable treatment. Other sources of public international law may also apply, which adds additional safeguards. Such is the case for the customary international law in the instance of the doctrine of the state of necessity (which is only applied in exceptional circumstances) [1099]. Overlaps between all these sources of law applicable to international investments often occur as well.

Previous chapters have discussed treaties, international customary law and principles of law as applied to the international investment

1098. See esp. Chap. XIV.G, *infra*, "Breaches of contract violating public international law".

1099. Y. Shany, "Contract Claims vs. Treaty Claims: Mapping Conflicts Between ICSID Decisions on Multisourced Investment Claims", *American Journal of International Law*, Vol. 99, No. 4 (2005), p. 837.

regime. This chapter will address other potential applicable sources of law such as national legislation, scholarly works and legal precedents.

B. National legislation

After World War II, the legislation of several host States started providing protection for foreign investments. These national laws established numerous guarantees for these investments, such as free profit repatriation and safeguards against discrimination, among others that are typically contemplated within investment treaties.

National legislation also becomes relevant to international investments in the following way. In the past, in order for States to offer diplomatic protection for injuries to the investments made by their nationals, the prior exhaustion of local remedies was required. As such, domestic courts had to intervene first in dealing with issues related to national law. Where domestic courts were unable to provide an appropriate remedy, injured nationals would recur to an international tribunal for protection, which would apply international law to the dispute. In this scenario, national law became a pure question of fact.

By contrast, international investment arbitration was developed in line with a different set of rules. First, there is no requirement to exhaust local remedies prior to commencing an investment claim unless expressly agreed in the contract or provided in the investment treaty. Nonetheless, the law applicable to the investment contract is usually that of the host State alongside public international law [1100].

When an investment dispute arises, the law of the host State does not necessarily apply by default. While international tribunals will inform themselves of the content of local laws through expert submissions and other sources, determining the law applicable to an international investment dispute is a conflict of laws matter. In the case of inconsistency between national and international law, international law will prevail. In the majority of cases, however, there is no inconsistency, and both apply in parallel [1101].

Unlike treaties, international investment contracts are in principle governed by national law [1102], or – if chosen or applicable in absence of

1100. Crawford, *supra* note 484, p. 352.

1101. *Ibid.*, p. 353.

1102. According to the ILC, States may choose to use laws other than international law to govern their agreements. See *British Yearbook of International Law*, Vol. 2 (1996), p. 189, para. 6.

selection – uniform law such as the UNIDROIT Principles. Depending on the circumstances, however, States will incur international legal responsibility upon a breach of their obligations under the investment contract. Some key aspects of the investment agreement will also be subject to public international law, either because they have been designed to this effect or because its general safeguards will always be available. Some writings question whether this means that State contracts are, in fact, treaties, at least from the point of view of their legal effects [1103]. However, it is one thing to strengthen State contractual compliance with investment contracts by building upon the role of international law, and quite another to transmute State contracts into treaties [1104].

C. Teachings of the most highly qualified publicists

The doctrinal writings of leading publicists have historically contributed to the development of public international law. At its inception, writers such as Gentili, Grotius, Pufendorf, Bynkershoek and Vattel "were the supreme authorities of the sixteenth to eighteenth centuries and determined the scope, form and content of international law" [1105].

In the modern era, doctrinal writings also constitute a source of authority in the discipline. In this regard, Article 38 (1) *(d)* of the ICJ Statute refers to "the teachings of the most highly qualified publicists of the various nations, as subsidiary means for the determination of rules of law". The PCA Arbitration Rules likewise include a provision along similar lines [1106]. Further, an ILC report came to a similar conclusion [1107], stating that there are certain scholarly works or "teachings" that demonstrate that a principle is common in different legal systems [1108].

With the exception of the 1992 chambers judgment in the *Land, Island and Maritime Frontier Dispute* that mentioned "the successive editors

1103. F. Orrego Vicuña, "Of Contracts and Treaties in the Global Market", *Max Planck Yearbook of United Nations Law* (hereafter UNYB) (2004), p. 346.
1104. *Ibid.*, p. 347.
1105. Shaw, *supra* note 480, p. 112.
1106. The PCA Arbitration Rules provide in Article 35 1 *(a) iv* that the tribunal may apply "*iv.* Judicial and arbitral decisions and the teachings of the most highly qualified publicists of the various nations, as subsidiary means for the determination of rules of law".
1107. ILC Second Report, *supra* note 5, Conclusion 9, p. 56.
1108. *Ibid.*, p. 55.

of *Oppenheim's International Law* [1109]", the ICJ does not cite specific writers but refers in general to scholarly writings in certain matters that have reached general consensus as, for instance, an "almost universal opinion" or a view emanating from "all or nearly all writers" [1110].

Other tribunals, and investment arbitration tribunals in particular, regularly cite doctrinal writings in their awards. The use of secondary sources in this way stems from the historic unavailability of primary sources and difficulties in their interpretation, especially during times when the state of public international law was alarmingly uncertain. When no positive rules could be established, tribunals made use of natural law and Roman law as sources to support the reasoning in their awards, particularly as referenced in the works of the publicists [1111].

That practice still holds today. In ICSID arbitrations, for instance, the tribunals frequently cite scholarly writers [1112], and in particular, Christoph H. Schreuer's commentary on the ICSID Convention [1113]. Many well-established legal theories applicable to international investments can be sourced to the writings of publicists.

From a critical stance, Muthucumaraswamy Sornarajah argues that the internationalization of investment contracts – to cite an

---

1109. In the *Lotus* case, the Permanent Court referred to the "teachings of publicists", leaving expressly apart "the question as to what their value may be from the point of view of establishing the existence of a rule of customary law". *Lotus*, Judgment (7 September 1927), PCIJ, Ser. A, No. 10, pp. 4, 26. "This does not reflect the influence that these teachings have; there are a number of references in the opinions of the individual judges, which suggests that these views have probably been discussed during the deliberation", Pellet and Müller, *supra* note 239, pp. 962-963.

1110. For a list, see I. Brownlie, *Principles of International Law*, 7th ed., Oxford, Oxford University Press, 2008, p. 24, fn. 154.

1111. M. Virally, "The Sources of International Law", M. Sørensen (ed.), *Manual of Public International Law*, London, Macmillan, 1968, p. 153. See Rigo Sureda, *supra* note 55, p. 132. At p. 138:

> "Contrary to the system that existed in Rome, today tribunals and legal scholars cannot count on a Law of Citations to provide primary authorities such as Papinian, Paul, Ulpian, Modestinus and Gaius. If their opinions differed, the majority view was to be followed. If the numbers were equal, Papinian's view prevailed. If the numbers were equal and Papinian was silent, the judge could make up his own mind on the matter. Today, since we do not have emperors with such powers, counsel and arbitral tribunals have recognized the quality of scholarship and cogency of reasoning of those few who become 'highly respected publicists'. Thus, references to the work of the publicists within their judgments guaranteed that a more consensus-based procedure was followed, in comparison to that provided by imperial authority in the Roman system. However, relying on the work of publicists to support legal judgments in this way also resulted in a more prolonged process with less certainty of outcome."

1112. *Ibid.*, pp. 133-134.

1113. *Ibid.*, p. 134.

example – was created through reference to the writings of "highly qualified" publicists [1114]. By making use of such "low-order sources of international law" it is possible to refer to a wide array of private law resources to ensure that the law is developed in a way that is favorable to multinational corporations [1115].

Moreover, many scholarly writers and publicists not only record the state of the law as it is *(lex lata)* but also advocate for its development *(lex ferenda)*. On the other hand, many writings merely reflect the national or individual viewpoints of their authors. Further, the quality of scholarly writing varies immensely. As such, the impact of each work should be assessed independently on its own merits [1116]. Therefore, it is advisable to make use of the works of highly qualified publicists as public international law sources with prudence and caution.

D. The role of precedents

1. In general

Article 38 of the ICJ Statute treats both writings and judicial decisions as parallel "subsidiary means" [1117]. In practice, however, judicial decisions can be "of immense importance" [1118], perhaps more than scholarly writings and the work of publicists [1119].

The reasons for favoring the authority of precedents over scholarly writings has been explained in the following manner by Judge Sir Gerald Fitzmaurice in the 1958 *Symbolae Verziji* case:

1114. Sornarajah, *supra* note 47, p. 223.

1115. *Ibid.*, p. 5.

1116. The US Supreme Court in the *Paquete Habana* case referred to the works of jurists and commentators who, by years of labor, research and experience, have made themselves peculiarly well acquainted with the subjects of which they write. These scholarly works are intended to be used by the courts and tribunals as trustworthy evidence of the state of the law, rather than as speculations of what the law ought to be. *The Paquete Habana and The Lola*, US Supreme Court 175 US 677, Decision (8 January 1900), para. 65, https://www.law.cornell.edu/supremecourt/text/175/677, accessed 20 May 2022.

1117. Article 38 alludes to Article 59 of the ICJ Statute, *supra* note 465, according to which "[t]he decision of the Court has no binding force except between the parties and in respect of that particular case".

1118. Shaw, *supra* note 480, p. 109.

1119. Jennings, *supra* note 274, p. 342. Sir Humphrey Appleby once stated: "Avoiding precedents does not mean nothing should ever be done. It only means that nothing should ever be done for the first time" in "Doing the Honours", *Yes Minister*, Season 2, Episode 2 (BBC, first broadcast 2 March 1981), Crawford, *supra* note 288, p. 49.

> "When an advocate before an international tribunal cites juridical opinion, he does so because it supports his argument, or for its illustrative value, or because it contains a particularly felicitous or apposite statement of the point involved, and so on. When he cites an arbitral or judicial decision, he does so for these reasons also, but there is a difference – for, additionally, he cites it as something *which the tribunal cannot ignore*, which it is bound to take into consideration and (by implication) which it ought to follow unless the decision can be shown to have been clearly wrong, or distinguishable from the extant case, or in some way legally or factually inapplicable. Equally the tribunal, while it may well treat juridical opinion as something which is of interest but of no direct authority, and which the tribunal is free to disregard, will not usually feel free to ignore a relevant decision, and will normally feel obliged to treat it as something that must be accepted, or else – for good reason – rejected, but which must in any event be taken fully into account." [1120]

The ILC concluded in a report that "[d]ecisions of international courts and tribunals, in particular of the International Court of Justice, concerning the existence and content of general principles of law are a subsidiary means for the determination of such principles". The report also mentions that decisions of national courts can likewise be used as aids to determine the existence of general principles of law [1121]. Moreover, precedents of municipal courts may provide evidence of the existence of a customary rule or may serve as examples of how States actually behave, which can lead to establishing a new rule of international customary law [1122].

There is an important distinction between the *de facto* use of precedents and the "obligation" to follow them. Since precedents are considered a mere subsidiary source, previous decisions can merely –

1120. Jennings, *supra* note 274, p. 342.

1121. ILC Second Report, *supra* note 5, Draft Conclusion 8, p. 56.

1122. For instance, the following cases: *Thirty Hogsheads of Sugar, Bentzon* v. *Boyle*, 9 Cranch 191 (1815); the *Paquete Habana* 175 US 677 (1900); *The Scotia*, 81 US (14 Wall.) 170 (1871). Shaw, *supra* note 480, p. 112. J. d'Aspremont notes that "International Customary Law may perform a function of legitimizing and formalizing the *de facto stare decisis* and Jurisprudence Constante. Probably, the paramount advantage of customary international law is the adjudicative neutrality and immanent intelligibility which it provides to decisions of arbitral tribunals which commonly refer to other arbitral decisions", d'Aspremont, *supra* note 30, p. 28.

but rightly – serve as a source of inspiration or to add authority to a certain reasoning developed by a tribunal [1123].

The role of judicial precedents within arbitration proceedings is slightly distinct from that in litigation. Arbitrators must treat judicial decisions with great care and are not bound by such judgments in principle [1124].

Although Article 38 (1) of the ICJ Statute does not mention arbitral awards, it is generally accepted that they have the same authority as judicial decisions in the hierarchy of legal sources [1125]. Many diverse international tribunals also make use of precedents in their issuance of awards, as it can be seen in the decisions of the PCIJ, the ICJ, the European Court of Human Rights, and the Iran-United States Claims Tribunal, for example [1126]. In addition, rulings on foreign direct investments released by the WTO are or may also be relied upon [1127].

Arbitral tribunals in general regularly cite precedents in their awards. In this regard, in the landmark 1982 *Dow Chemical* case, the Tribunal stated that arbitral decisions progressively form a collection of jurisprudence that must be considered since they reflect the economic reality of the time and adjust to requirements within international commerce (to which international arbitration rules must be responsive) [1128].

2. *Precedents in international investment claims*

The practice of citing precedents in investment-related decisions comes from the early mixed claims commissions [1129]. This is "the most

1123. E. De Brabandere, "Arbitral Decisions as a Source of International Investment Law", in T. Gazzini and E. De Brabandere (eds.), *International Investment Law: The Sources of Rights and Obligations*, Leiden/Boston, Martinus Nijhoff, 2012, p. 286.

1124. "For instance, arbitrators that deal with contracts governed by German law are not necessarily bound to follow German case law, as German jurisprudence has only a *de facto*, not a *de jure*, precedential effect. Like German courts, arbitrators may even deviate even from long-standing case law emanating from the highest German court if they are convinced that the decision was wrong, or that the result reached by the higher court does not conform to the needs of international business", K. P. Berger, "To What Extent Should Arbitrators Respect Domestic Case Law? The German Experience Regarding the Law on Standard Terms", in F. Bortolotti and F. Mayer (eds.), *The Application of Substantive Law by International Arbitrators* (Dossiers ICC Institute of World Business Law), Paris, ICC Publishing, 2014, pp. 80-84.

1125. Ho, *supra* note 212, p. 68.

1126. Schreuer *et al.*, *supra* note 102, p. 610.

1127. Collins, *supra* note 66, p. 30.

1128. ICC Case No. 4131, Interim Award (23 September 1982), p. 899; P. Sanders, President, B. Goldman and M. Vasseur, JDI, p. 899 (1983), note Y. Derains.

1129. Ho, *supra* note 212, p. 11.

important example" illustrating that public international law grows not only out of the practice of States but has also been developed from a more sophisticated matrix than mere diplomatic exchanges. The significant role played by precedents within investment disputes originates, to a large extent, in the practice of mixed claims commissions and, later, in international arbitral practice [1130].

The "unusually prominent role of arbitral awards" in investment claims [1131] can be understood if one considers the few alternative places for guidance with respect to what the law is in this field [1132]. In a highly unregulated area such as investment contracts, arbitral awards were not only the first to offer guidance but also generated important legal content "if only because there is not much else at which to look" [1133].

In the resolution of investment-related disputes through arbitration, recourse to well-reasoned awards that have been issued on similar grounds is an invaluable analytical tool that can provide guidance to both States and investors, offering some clarity in a field marred by uncertainty. In contrast to the precedential value of arbitral awards, traditional customary international law has often proven unsuitable or has lost importance due to the growth of other kinds of precedents and legal sources.

Any discussion of precedents within international investment arbitration must be accompanied by the caveat that they be used with care. In addition to the variations that can be observed in how different tribunals use the precedents of other adjudicatory bodies, under certain rules they may not always have precedential effect. This was the case, for instance, under Article 1136 (1) of NAFTA, whereby a decision from one panel has no precedent effect on any other panel; Article 14.D.13 (7) of USMCA states likewise [1134].

3. The use of precedents in ICSID arbitration

According to the first part of Article 53 (1) of the ICSID Convention, "the award shall be binding on the parties". This may be read as

---

1130. Crawford, *supra* note 150, p. 93.
1131. Ho, *supra* note 212, p. 4.
1132. Alvarez, *supra* note 26, p. 358.
1133. Ho, *supra* note 212, p. 68 and authors cited. She makes the statement in the investment State contract's context, but it can be extended to foreign investments in general.
1134. "An award made by a tribunal has no binding force except between the disputing parties and in respect of the particular case", see https://ustr.gov/trade-agreements/free-trade-agreements/united-states-mexico-canada-agreement, accessed 28 September 2022.

excluding the applicability of the binding precedent principle to successive ICSID cases. Nothing in the *travaux préparatoires* of the ICSID Convention suggests that the doctrine of *stare decisis* should be applied under this mechanism [1135]. However, reference to ICSID's prior jurisprudence "has become a standard feature" in most rulings [1136].

A decision that relies primarily or exclusively on previous rulings may be subject to doubt, but no *ad hoc* committee has ever annulled an award for this reason. Nonetheless, from the perspective of tribunals, it appears wise to not expose their awards to challenges due to excess of powers or the failure to state reasons [1137].

Jurisprudence constante is a legal term of art that has extended into investment arbitration [1138]. It refers to an accumulation of judicial decisions that have decided similarly on a point of law. According to Frédéric Bachand and Fabien Gélinas, the main difference between the English notion of legal precedents and *jurisprudence constante* is the following: that precedents, as binding rules, derive from single decisions of hierarchically superior authority, while *jurisprudence constante* derives from a series of consistent decisions made by adjudicatory authorities of equal importance [1139]. Recurring to this broader concept of *jurisprudence constante*, tribunals tend to deviate from earlier "case law" only where there are cogent reasons. Tribunals thus adhere to a "softer *de facto* system of precedent" that nonetheless helps build a coherent and predictable body of international investment law [1140].

The notion of a "common legal opinion" or *jurisprudence constante* was first used by the Tribunal in *SGS* v. *Philippines* [1141]. The decision stated that:

> "Although different tribunals constituted under the ICSID system should in general seek to act consistently with each other,

1135. C. Schreuer and M. Weiniger, "A Doctrine of Precedent?", in P. Muchlinski, F. Ortino and C. Schreuer (eds.), *The Oxford Handbook of International Investment Law*, Oxford, Oxford University Press, New York, p. 1190.

1136. Schreuer *et al.*, *supra* note 102, p. 610.

1137. *Ibid.*, p. 1195.

1138. Ho, *supra* note 212, p. 75.

1139. F. Bachand and F. Gélinas, "Legal Certainty and Arbitration", T. Schultz and F. Ortino (eds.), *The Oxford Handbook of International Arbitration*, Oxford, Oxford University Press, 2020, p. 393.

1140. P. Janig and A. Reinisch, "General Principles and the Coherence of International Investment Law: of *Res Judicata*, *Lis Pendens* and the Value of Precedents", in M. Andenas, M. Fitzmaurice, A. Tanzi and J. Wouters (eds.), *General Principles and the Coherence of International Law*, Leiden, Brill, 2019, p. 296.

1141. Schreuer *et al.*, *supra* note 102, p. 611. See other cases cited in the same source.

in the end it must be for each tribunal to exercise its competence in accordance with the applicable law, which will by definition be different for each [investment treaty] and each Respondent State. Moreover, there is no doctrine of precedent in international law, if by precedent is meant a rule of binding effect of a single decision. There is no hierarchy of international tribunals, and even if there were, there is no good reason for allowing the first tribunal in time to resolve issues for all later tribunals." [1142]

Further, in *Duke Energy* v. *Ecuador* (2008), the ICSID Tribunal stated that it had a "duty to seek to contribute to the harmonious development of investment law, and thereby to meet the legitimate expectations of the community of States and investors towards establishing certainty in the rule of law" [1143].

The Tribunal in *AES* v. *Argentina* [1144] dealt in depth with the application of precedents to foreign investment disputes, in what is often considered "the most detailed examination of the role of precedent in investment arbitration to date" [1145]. The arbitrators analyzed whether tribunals

---

1142. *SGS* v. *Philippines*, *supra* note 1085, Decision on Jurisdiction (29 January 2004), para. 97.

1143. *Duke Energy Electroquil Partners & Electroquil SA* v. *Republic of Ecuador*, ICSID Case No. ARB/04/19, Award (18 August 2008). Another award held the following (*Bayindir* v. *Pakistan*, *supra* note 456, Award (27 August 2009), para. 145):

> "The Tribunal is not bound by previous decisions of ICSID tribunals. At the same time, it is of the opinion that it should pay due regard to earlier decisions of such tribunals. The Tribunal is further of the view that, unless there are compelling reasons to the contrary, it ought to follow solutions established in a series of consistent cases, comparable to the case at hand, but subject of course to the specifics of a given treaty and of the circumstances of the actual case. By doing so, it will meet its duty to seek to contribute to the harmonious development of investment law and thereby to meet the legitimate expectations of the community of states and investors towards certainty of the rule of law."

In another case, the Tribunal stated:

> "Where there is a convergence of practice and *opinio juris* among a significant number of such tribunals, it may serve as evidence of customary international law. Hence, in the context of customary international law in investment law, BITs and decisions of tribunals adjudicating the disputes arising from these investment treaties have come to play a significant role in the ongoing formation of law in this field. These two sources are particularly important . . . because much of international investment law is developed through them – they represent State practice and *opinion juris* in this area of law."

Eco Oro Minerals Corp. v. *Republic of Colombia*, ICSID Case No. ARB/16/41, Decision On Jurisdiction, Liability and Directions On Quantum (9 September 2021), para. 704, citing CL-0306. See also Reisman, *supra* note 306.

1144. *AES* v. *Argentina*, *supra* note 107, Decision on Jurisdiction (2005), p. 6 *et seq.*

1145. Schreuer and Weiniger, *supra* note 1135, pp. 1193-1194.

were permitted to use earlier decisions dealing with similar issues as a source of "comparison and . . . of inspiration". They observed that a tribunal may find with an issue of law "which, in essence, is or will be met in other cases whatever the specificities of each dispute may be. Such precedents may also be rightly considered, at least as a matter of comparison and, if so considered by the Tribunal, of inspiration". The same may be said for the interpretation given by a precedent decision or award to some relevant facts that are basically at the origin of two or several different disputes, keeping carefully in mind the actual specificities still featuring in each case [1146].

When dealing with international investment disputes, it is unsurprising that ICSID tribunals, among others, routinely refer to prior decisions and awards. These tribunals also make use of decisions and awards issued by other adjudicatory bodies on investment-related matters, such as the jurisprudence of the Iran-United States Claims Tribunal [1147].

In the context of an ICSID annulment proceeding, the *Continental Casualty* v. *Argentina* Committee remarked that "although there is no doctrine of binding precedent in the ICSID arbitration system . . . in the longer term the emergence of a *jurisprudence constante* in relation to annulment proceedings may be a desirable goal" [1148]. However, another *ad hoc* Committee concluded that "the mere fact that a Tribunal does not follow the prevailing jurisprudence on a given issue is not an error of law per se" [1149]. In *MCI* v. *Ecuador*, the *ad hoc* Committee decided that

---

1146. *AES* v. *Argentina*, *supra* note 107, Decision on Jurisdiction (26 April 2005), paras. 31-32.

1147. L. Ferguson Reed and J. Paulsson *et al.*, "ICSID Investment Treaty Arbitration", in L. Reed, J. Paulsson, N. Blackaby (eds.), *Guide to ICSID Arbitration*, 2nd ed., The Hague, Kluwer Law International, 2010, pp. 73-74. A. Rajput, "Problems with the Jurisprudence of the Iran–US Claims Tribunal on Indirect Expropriation", *ICSID Review: Foreign Investment Law Journal*, Vol. 30, No. 3 (2015), p. 590:

> "An empirical study surveying investment arbitration awards up to 2006 revealed that investment tribunals frequently rely on the decisions from the Iran-United States Claims Tribunal to serve as precedent. Among the 38 tribunals created under the ICSID Convention that deliver awards on merits, 17 of them (i.e. 44.7 percent) relied on the decisions of the Iran-United States Claims Tribunal in their reasoning. Over time, this reliance has only increased, including among ad hoc investment tribunals and those constituted under Chapter 11 of NAFTA."

1148. *Continental Casualty* v. *Argentina*, *supra* note 97, Decision on the Application for Partial Annulment, and the Application for Partial Annulment (16 September 2011), para. 84.

1149. *Summit Generation* v. *Hungary*, *supra* note 607, Decision of the *ad hoc* Committee on the Application for Annulment (29 June 2012), para. 99.

"the annulment mechanism is not designed to bring about consistency in the interpretation and application of international investment law" [1150].

As noted by Philipp Janig and August Reinisch, in the absence of an appeal mechanism in ICSID, the purpose of a *jurisprudence constante* is largely one of self-restraint of arbitrators based on a common understanding on legal issues and respect for other tribunals. However, nothing impedes newfound approaches from being more appropriate for a given case [1151].

Despite these safeguards, the embryonic institutionalization of investor-State dispute settlement, the lack of a rule of *stare decisis* and the absence of an appeals mechanism sometimes lead to notably inconsistent decisions. For instance, in *SGS* v. *Pakistan* and *SGS* v. *Philippines*, the tribunals interpreted similar umbrella clauses in two different investment treaties in a dissimilar manner [1152]. Stephen Schill notes that notwithstanding these divergences, by and large investment tribunals actively recognize consistency as a value in investment treaty arbitration [1153].

4. *Precedents in the Iran-United States Claims Tribunal*

While the Iran-United States Claims Tribunal has issued more decisions than any other international claims tribunal [1154], the precedential value of its awards should be assessed with caution. Its awards have been criticized due to their inconsistency [1155] and "considering that most of its decisions are rendered on direct and indirect expropriations" [1156].

1150. *MCI Power Group L.C. and New Turbine, Inc.* v. *Republic of Ecuador*, ICSID Case No. ARB/03/6, Decision on Annulment (19 October 2009), para. 24.

1151. Janig and Reinisch, *supra* note 1140, p. 287.

1152. The tribunals in *CME* v. *Czech Republic* and *Lauder* v. *Czech Republic* also reached contrary results in two proceedings that related to the same fact pattern but were brought by different claimants under two different BITs. Schill, *supra* note 30, p. 284.

1153. *Ibid.*, pp. 339-340.

1154. Rajput, *supra* note 1147, p. 590.

1155. Crook states that "inevitably, after many years and several hundred decisions, the Tribunal's handling of choice of law has not been wholly uniform. Arbitrators have come and gone; individual members have taken quite different approaches. Moreover, the Tribunal has four distinctive institutional configurations. All nine members sit en banc to hear some intergovernmental matters and important common issues. More frequently, the Tribunal sits in Chambers composed of three arbitrators. Each configuration has had its own approaches", in "Applicable Law in International Arbitration: The Iran–United States Claims Tribunal Experience", *American Journal of International Law*, Vol. 83 (1989), p. 286.

1156. "The Iran-United States Claims Tribunal rendered various awards on the nationality of the claimants, attributing the actions or omissions of public corporations and other entities to the State, and ultimately finding the States responsible", Rajput, *supra* note 1147, p. 590.

By contrast, other investment tribunals usually also deal with several other investment-related matters [1157].

5. *Precedents in the PCA Arbitration Rules*

These rules include an express provision dealing with the use of precedents. Article 35 (1) *(a) (iv)* was intended to increase the consistency and predictability of awards issued pursuant to them [1158].

An example of how precedents are employed in the PCA context can be seen in the *Yukos* v. *Russia* case. The Arbitral Tribunal discarded the "clean hands" doctrine invoked by Russia since it did not refer to any "majority decision where an international court or arbitral tribunal has applied the principle of 'unclean hands' in an inter-State or investor-State dispute" [1159].

E. *Other sources? A terminological conundrum*

As noted by Lassa Francis Lawrence Oppenheim, Article 38 of the Statute of the ICJ cannot be regarded as a necessarily exhaustive statement of the sources of international law for all time [1160]. A terminological conundrum emerges in this regard, as will be seen in the following pages.

1. *Rules of law*

Ben Wortley explains that the term "law" is generic, used in reference to rules designed to produce order and avoid anarchy. The term "rule

1157. "The law applied by investment tribunals is very different from that applied by the Iran-United States Claims Tribunal. Specifically, the influence of legal principles originating outside of public international law upon the Iran-United States Claims Tribunal renders it difficult to distinguish between the cases where international law was applied and where it was not. Even in cases involving indirect expropriation where international law was supposedly applied, it is rarely applied rigorously. As such, the importance of the choice of law on the outcome of a case cannot be understated. Where international law is not rigorously applied, the application of different laws in similar situations would lead to different outcomes, unless the contents of the applied laws are identical" (*ibid.*, p. 607).

1158. Daly, Goriatcheva and Meighen, *supra* note 809, p. 137.

1159. *Yukos* v. *Russia*, *supra* note 110, Final Award (18 July 2014), para. 1362. In *Obligation to Negotiate Access to the Pacific Ocean*, the ICJ noted that, in spite of the references to legitimate expectations that may be found in arbitral awards concerning investor-State disputes, "[i]t does not follow from such references that there exists in general international law a principle that would give rise to an obligation on the basis of what could be considered a legitimate expectation". See *Obligation to Negotiate Access to the Pacific Ocean (Bolivia* v. *Chile)*, Judgment of Merits (1 October 2018), *ICJ Reports 2018*, p. 559, para. 162. ILC Second Report, *supra* note 5, p. 55.

1160. Jennings and Watts, *supra* note 278, p. 45.

of law" is recognized in national legal systems, even though detailed "rules of law" may be formulated differently in different jurisdictions. The "rule of law" hence represents an attempt to order human relations, rather than leaving them to chance (as anarchists would do). In this way, the "rule of law" is "a conception that transcends State boundaries: it represents a common element of our civilization, even though legislation in different countries varies very widely in the language and manner of enunciation" [1161].

Therefore, the plural expression "rules of law" is understood to be wider than the term "law", encompassing both hard and soft law norms that have emerged on the international plane [1162]. According to Piero Bernardini, contractual practice and arbitral awards show references to a wide inventory of rules of law, such as public international law, general principles of law derived from comparisons between different national legal systems, drafts of international treaties not yet in force, the UNIDROIT Principles and the Principles of European Contract Law. Per Bernardini:

> "The following international legal sources are also impactful: rules of public or private organizations designed to harmonize trade practices in certain fields, such as the ICC Incoterms or the International Federation of Consulting Engineers (FIDIC) rules for construction contracts; general principles of international commercial law as applied by national and international tribunals; general standards and rules of international contracts; and international trade usages that are generally followed as contractual practices in a specific trade sector but do not amount to a consuetude." [1163]

As will be seen in Chapter XVI, however, not all the sources on this list strictly qualify as "applicable law" [1164], although many of these rules may serve for interpretive or gap-filling purposes or be incorporated by reference by the parties.

Early uses of the expression "rules of law" in reference to non-State law can be found in the 1960s in the drafting of the ICSID Convention,

---

1161. B. A. Wortley, "The Interaction of Public and Private International Law Today", *Recueil des cours*, Vol. 85 (1954).

1162. See *Aucoven* v. *Venezuela*, *supra* note 1084, Award (2003), G. Kaufmann-Kohler, K.-H. Böckstiegel and B. M. Cremades (eds.), para. 96.

1163. Bernardini, *supra* note 984, p. 67.

1164. *Ibid.*, pp. 67-68.

in addition to the arbitral laws of France and Djibouti [1165]. Subsequently, the language of "rules of law" was extended to arbitration laws and rules worldwide, appearing in numerous international and domestic instruments, as mentioned previously [1166].

Article 3 of the Hague Principles [1167] also adopts the expression "rules of law". The Working Group's [1168] decision to include this particular expression deliberately intended to open the door for the potential application of new scholarly, jurisprudential and legal sources that are created as the international arbitration field develop [1169].

2. *Soft law*

The emergence of the term "soft law" is credited to Lord Arnold McNair, one of the most renowned jurists of his time, President of the ICJ (1952-1955) and first President of the European Court of Human Rights (1959-1965) [1170]. The expression, however, was popularized in arbitration much later.

In a recent Hague Academy lecture, Felix Dasser mentions that, since 1985, he has spent considerable time conducting research on non-national legal standards such as *lex mercatoria* and does not recall having encountered the term "soft law" in international commercial arbitration until the late 2000s (and even then, only very occasionally) [1171].

1165. See United Nations, Settlement of Commercial Disputes: Revision of the UNCITRAL Arbitration Rules, A/CN.9/WG.II/WP.143/Add.1, https://daccess-ods.un.org/tmp/2802372.57480621.html, accessed 5 April 2022, p. 10.

1166. For instance, during the drafting of Article 35 of the PCA Arbitration Rules, the Drafting Committee discussed the possibility of the parties designating other legal sources as applicable rules of law, notably the ILC Draft Articles on State Responsibility, *supra* note 433. Daly, Goriatcheva and Meighen, *supra* note 809, p. 136.

1167. See Chap. XI.E.6, *infra*, "The Hague Principles and non-State Law".

1168. See *infra* note 1654.

1169. HCCH, Preliminary Document No. 1, Consolidated Draft, https://assets.hcch.net/docs/9436c200-bc46-40b7-817e-ae8f9232d306.pdf, accessed 20 May 2022.

1170. Dasser, *supra* note 457, p. 418:

> "According to Dupuy, Lord McNair coined the term to describe programmatory law that has not yet fully developed into (hard) law. Dupuy does not cite any source to support this claim, however. Later research has failed to identify a quote from Lord McNair with regard to the term 'soft law'. He may have used the term in his lectures on public international law at Cambridge University, though, but may have done so merely to distinguish between public international law *de lege lata* and *de lege ferenda*. The origin of the phrase therefore remains shrouded in mystery – which may explain its vagueness and malleability, and, by extension, its enduring popularity."

1171. Learning now that he studied soft law for years without knowing, reminds Dasser of Molière's *bourgeois gentilhomme* who was surprised to learn that he had unwittingly spoken prose all his life. *Ibid.*, p. 432.

According to Dasser, soft law is a "broad church". Many different instruments, texts and practices are regarded or labeled as "soft law". What these sources all share in common is that they are not State law. Aside from this commonality, there is little consensus on the exact definition of the term [1172].

Joachim Bonell nonetheless proposes a working definition of the term "soft law", describing it as a set of legal "instruments of a normative nature with no legally binding force, and which are applied only through voluntary acceptance" [1173].

3. A legal "subsystem" of the law of international institutions

Multiple actors are active within the field of foreign investments, all contributing in different ways to the development of international investment law. Notable actors include States, investors, multinational enterprises, non-governmental organizations and intergovernmental organizations. Their proliferation constitutes perhaps one of the most significant changes in public international law in recent decades, and their impact upon the available sources of law has been considerable [1174].

As noted by Peter Muchlinski, the intergovernmental organizations have formed a legal subsystem based on their constituent instruments, which, in turn, will also be governed by a subsystem of public international law (the law of international institutions). An intergovernmental organization, such as the OECD or the World Bank, may have a quasi-legislative power to develop substantive international rules and procedures governing its substantive field of activity. Intergovernmental organizations have, therefore, the power to develop rules applicable to international investments. For example, MIGA, a member of the World Bank Group, contributed to the creation of investment opportunities in developing countries by offering a specific, development-oriented investment insurance system that complements existing national investment insurance schemes [1175].

1172. *Ibid.*, p. 491.

1173. M. J. Bonell, "Soft Law and Party Autonomy: The Case of the UNIDROIT Principles", *Loyola Law Review*, Vol. 51 (2005), p. 229.

1174. Jennings and Watts, *supra* note 278, p. 45.

1175. Muchlinski, *supra* note 7, pp. 8-9.

Of noteworthy relevance are the works of the ILA [1176] and, in particular, of the ILC [1177]. The Articles on State Responsibility adopted by the ILC constitute "without doubt the most often-quoted document in investment treaty arbitral decisions" and have assisted in the development of consistent case law [1178].

The ICJ observed that resolutions emanating from bodies like the ILA and the ILC "even if they are not binding . . . can, in certain circumstances, provide evidence important for establishing the existence of a rule or the emergence of an *opinio juris*" [1179]. This statement holds particularly true when a resolution purports to declare the existence of a determined customary international law rule, in which case the resolution serves as evidence of its acceptance [1180]. According to the 2018 ILC report, "[c]onversely, negative votes, abstentions or disassociations from a consensus, along with general statements and explanations of positions, may be evidence that there is no acceptance as law" [1181].

In addition to ILA and ILC resolutions, UNCTAD and the OECD regularly generate reports describing and analyzing different developments within international law. While not emanating from

---

1176. The International Law Association was founded in Brussels in 1873. Its objectives, under its Constitution, are "the study, clarification and development of international law, both public and private, and the furtherance of international understanding and respect for international law". The ILA has consultative status, as an international non-governmental international organizations, with a number of the UN specialized agencies. See https://www.ila-hq.org, accessed 5 April 2022.

1177. Shaw, *supra* note 480, p. 120:

> "The International Law Commission was established by the United Nations General Assembly in 1947 with the purpose of promoting the progressive development of international law and its codification. It consists of thirty-four members from Africa, Asia, America and Europe, who remain in office for five years each and who are appointed from lists submitted by national governments. The Commission is aided in its deliberations by consultations with various outside bodies including the Asian–African Legal Consultative Committee, the European Commission on Legal Cooperation and the Inter-American Council of Jurists. See Articles 2, 3, and 8 of the Statute of the ILC. Many of the most important international conventions have grown out of the Commission's work. Apart from preparing such drafts, the International Law Commission also issues reports and studies, and has formulated such documents."

1178. "Although arbitrators' need for guidance has led them to apply the Articles to issues to which they do not apply or 'to apply them beyond the terms of the ILC's text'", Rigo Sureda, *supra* note 55, p. 138.

1179. *Legality of the Threat or Use of Nuclear Weapons*, Advisory Opinion, *ICJ Reports 1996*, pp. 254-255, para. 70 (referring to General Assembly resolutions).

1180. For instance, in *Aminoil*, *supra* note 1059, Final Award (1982), ILR, para. 143.

1181. ILC, Seventieth Session Report, *supra* note 279, chap. V, p. 148.

publicists *per se*, these reports may be regarded as equally authoritative as the teachings of the most highly qualified publicist [1182].

While resolutions originating from international organizations and intergovernmental conferences cannot create customary international law rules in themselves, an ILC report concludes that they can provide evidence of the existence of certain customary international law rules or contribute to their development [1183]. International reports and resolutions may also establish that a determined rule of customary international law is accepted as such by *opinio juris* [1184]. Resolutions like these reflect a general consensus – either unanimously or by some majority of the international community – on a particular matter, providing evidence of and contributing to the development of custom. By reducing customary law to written form, these resolutions share some of the characteristics of a codifying treaty. However, even though they contribute to developing customary law, clearly the process is not one of treaty making [1185].

4. Supranational systems for foreign investments?

According to Sornarajah, the supranational systems emerging out of case law and scholarly writings can be grouped into general principles of

---

1182. Collins, *supra* note 66, pp. 30-31.

1183. Reisman, *supra* note 306, p. 622:

> "Where there is a convergence of practice and *opinio juris* among a significant number of such tribunals, it may serve as evidence of customary international law. Hence, in the context of customary international law in investment law, BITs and decisions of tribunals adjudicating the disputes arising from these investment treaties have come to play a significant role in the ongoing formation of law in this field. These two sources are particularly important . . . because much of international investment law is developed through them – they represent State practice and *opinio juris* in this area of law."

1184. ILC draft Conclusions on Identification of Customary International Law, *supra* note 292, Conclusion 12 states literally the following (A/CN.4/L.908, p. 3):

> "1. A resolution adopted by an international organization or at an intergovernmental conference cannot, of itself, create a rule of customary international law. 2. A resolution adopted by an international organization or at an intergovernmental conference may provide evidence for determining the existence and content of a rule of customary international law or contribute to its development. 3. A provision in a resolution adopted by an international organization or at an intergovernmental conference may reflect a rule of customary international law if it is established that the provision corresponds to a general practice that is accepted as law *(opinio juris)*."

1185. "These and other solutions vary considerably in their legal significance. They may be given particular titles in certain cases, such as 'decisions' or 'recommendations', but such nomenclature, while it may be indicative of the legal effect of the resolution, is not conclusive", Jennings and Watts, *supra* note 278, pp. 48-49.

law, transnational law and *lex mercatoria* [1186]. Under his nomenclature, general principles emerge through a process of comparing different legal sources. *Seriatim*, transnational law exists as an intermediate system standing between public international law and national law to govern State contracts. In turn, *lex mercatoria* applies to State contracts involving foreign parties as well and was developed to apply to private international commercial transactions.

The expressions "general principles of law" and *lex mercatoria* have been used for centuries. However, it is usually recognized that Judge Philip Jessup only coined the expression "transnational law" in 1956 to reflect the general interpenetration of legal rules and systems across the world, in contrast to the dualistic picture put forward by legal positivism, which created a sharp separation between international and domestic law [1187].

Arghyrios Fatouros later contributed to the further development of the term. Under this conception, the law of international State contracts is nothing but a species falling under the genus of "transnational law", together with other species such as traditional public international law, private international law and international administrative law [1188]. Yet, Fatouros recognized that the authority proving the existence of a body of transnational law was largely confined to the opinion of individual scholars [1189].

The notion of transnational law developed largely from public international law, whereas *lex mercatoria* emerged from private law. To a large extent, both transnational law and *lex mercatoria* came about independently, but with numerous common features. Both developed thanks to the policy goal of promoting international commerce and investment through the creation of norms that provide security of businesses and commitments. Both were also invoked by arbitral tribunals and scholars using general principles of law as the primary

---

1186. Sornarajah also references the application of national law while also leaving room for principles of international law to apply. As such, the law of the State party remains the primary legal source, but the principles of international law may nonetheless apply through the "backdoor", Sornarajah, *supra* note 47, p. 257.

1187. Neff, *supra* note 143, p. 428.

1188. Jessup, *supra* note 348, p. 136. A. Fatouros, *Government Guarantees to Foreign Investors*, New York, Columbia University Press, 1962, p. 287.

1189. Sornarajah, *supra* note 47, p. 258. See recently in C. Menkel-Meadow, "Why and How to Study 'Transnational' Law", Legal Studies Research Paper Series No. 2011-19. She refers to "transnational" law as the "law that transcends or crosses borders but may not be formally enacted by States" (p. 103).

source from which the principles of the two systems are selected [1190]. However, the early Middle Eastern arbitral awards that mentioned transnational law failed to distinguish between transnational law and general principles of law, generally using them as synonyms. These awards were mentioned in Chapter VIII [1191].

According to Emmanuel Gaillard, comparative law has led to the development of general principles or transnational rules that, "from a terminological and conceptual standpoint, should be preferred to that of *lex mercatoria*" [1192]. However, general principles should not be understood as so general that they trump the application of the law chosen to apply to the contract. Rather, general principles privilege generally admitted rules over rules with local peculiarities. Perhaps it is preferable to refer to them as "transnational rules" to dispel any confusion [1193].

General principles within private international law will be discussed in the following chapter, and *lex mercatoria* will be further addressed in Chapter XI.

1190. *Ibid.*, p. 103.
1191. *Ibid.* See also Chap. X, *infra*.
1192. Gaillard, *supra* note 925, pp. 59-72.
1193. Gaillard, *supra* note 836, p. 135.

CHAPTER X

EVOLUTION AND RECENT CHANGES WITHIN PRIVATE INTERNATIONAL LAW

A. Introduction

Marginal or not, private international law has its role to play in investment arbitration. Over the past few decades, this discipline has evolved significantly, but its development has not generally received sufficient attention from other legal fields. Study of these developments can bring clarity to several issues related to the applicable substantive law in investment arbitration.

Throughout the nineteenth century, nation-States were consolidated and private international law emerged as an independent discipline in itself [1194]. These developments intensified the proliferation of "international" issues within private law matters such as what the applicable law should be for a contract that was executed in one State and performed in another. Similar conflict of laws problems also arise in federal systems such as the United States [1195]. Further complicating the issue of applicable law, several organizations also have standing within international law and can generate legal norms [1196].

According to Joseph Story (1779-1845), private international law is "a rather odd phrase". Story served as Justice of the US Supreme Court for more than thirty years and was "the first American legal scholar to be taken seriously outside the United States". He considered private international law "a most interesting and important branch of *public* law", or a part of the law of nations [1197].

1194. G. Kegel, "Introduction" (1986), in K. Lipstein (ed.), *Private International Law*, Vol. 3 of *International Encyclopedia of Comparative Law*, Tübingen, Mohr Siebeck; Leiden, Martinus Nijhoff, 2011, p. 5.

1195. S. C. Symeonides, W. Collins Perdue and A. T. von Mehren, *Conflict of Laws: American, Comparative, International, Cases and Materials* (American Casebook Series), St. Paul, MN, West Group, 1998, p. 1.

1196. J. Basedow, "The Effects of Globalization on Private International Law", in J. Basedow and Toshiyuki Kono (eds.), *Legal Aspects of Globalization, Conflict of Laws, Internet, Capital Markets and Insolvency in a Global Economy*, The Hague, Kluwer Law International, 2000, p. 4.

1197. A. Lowenfeld, "International Litigation and the Quest for Reasonableness", *Recueil des cours*, Vol. 245 (1994), pp. 27-28.

Today, in the common law, private international law has been consolidated, mainly under the term "conflict of laws" [1198]. Within civil law systems, the term "private international law" was first employed by French jurist Jean-Jacques Foelix in 1843, and its use has become commonplace. Private international law now exists as an independent discipline in the civil law world.

In many systems, conflict of laws principles do not emerge from legal enactments alone. In France, decisions of the Cour de cassation have shaped the development of private international law in many ways [1199]. In common law jurisdictions [1200], conflict of laws issues have generally been dealt with in scholarly writings. For this reason, Herma Hill Key states that conflict of laws is not a field of law but rather an arena of men (alluding to the importance of writers in shaping the discipline) [1201]. Historically, the subject matter was full of intellectual speculations that aimed at constructing coherent conflict of laws doctrinal systems, which explains the unique role played by scholars in its development [1202].

Not all private law matters fall within the scope of private international law. In most systems, it deals primarily with substantial and procedural matters within private international affairs [1203]. One

---

1198. This expression was adopted in the United Kingdom by Dicey and Morris, who noted that "conflict of laws" is also sometimes referred to as private international law. A. V. Dicey and J. H. Carlile Morris, *The Conflict of Laws*, Vol. 1, ed. L. Collins, 11th ed., London, Steven and Sons, 1987, p. 4. See also P. Dane, "Conflict of Laws", in D. Patterson (ed.), *A Companion to Philosophy of Law and Legal Theory*, Oxford, Wiley-Blackwell, 1999 (repr. 2000), p. 209. A. Briggs, *The Conflict of Laws* (Clarendon Law Series), Oxford, Oxford University Press, 2002, p. 2. Reimann considers both private international law and conflict of laws equally infelicitous. M. Reimann, "Comparative Law and Private International Law", in M. Reimann and R. Zimmermann (eds.), *The Oxford Handbook of Comparative Law*, Oxford, Oxford University Press, 2006, p. 1364.

1199. See *infra* note 1579.

1200. Dicey and Morris, *supra* note 1198, p. 8; F. Visher, "General Course on Private International Law", *Recueil des cours*, Vol. 232 (1992), p. 33, alludes to the strong influence of writers in the United States.

1201. F. K. Juenger, "General Course on Private International Law", *Recueil des cours*, Vol. 193 (1983), p. 319. Erik Jayme also notes the important influence of doctrine in this discipline, both in Europe and the United States. See Jayme, *supra* note 894, p. 80.

1202. B. Audit, *Droit International Privé*, 5th ed., Paris, Economica, 2008, pp. 22-23.

1203. D. P. Fernández Arroyo, *Derecho Internacional Privado (Una mirada actual sobre sus elementos esenciales)*, Córdoba, Advocatus, 1998, pp. 30-31, 36-37. Two matters are always present: jurisdiction and the applicable law. The matter of enforcement of judgments and arbitral awards may also eventually arise. Dicey and Morris, *supra* note 1198, p. 4. Y. P. Loussouarn, P. Bourel and P. de Vareilles-Sommières also include nationality and condition of aliens, in *Droit international privé*, 8th ed., Paris, Dalloz, 2004. See also, F. Rigaux, *Derecho Internacional Privado,*

of the issues addressed by this discipline is "conflict of jurisdictions" or "international procedural law", both at the litigation and at the enforcement stage. Another central issue is determining the law applicable to an international contract [1204].

Most of the theoretical debates that have occurred historically within private international law relate to the question of determining the applicable law. This issue is dealt with in more detail below.

Traditional conflict of laws and choice of law rules do not apply directly to substantive issues within a case. Instead, choice of law rules indicate which system of law is to apply to the contract, either domestic or from abroad. The "point of connection" or "connecting factor" is the technical means by which the applicable law will be determined, which will later be used to resolve the dispute. *Lex causae* is the expression that is generally used in this regard.

Connecting factors such as territoriality *(lex fori)*, nationality *(lex patriae)* and domicile *(lex domicilii)* relate to the capacity of the parties to contract. Connecting factors may also refer to elements of the parties' substantive relationship, such as the place of performance *(lex loci executionis)*, place of execution *(lex loci contractus)* or the law selected by the parties *(lex voluntatis)* to govern their international contract. Other examples of connecting factors include the place of the wrongdoing *(lex loci delicti)* within tort law and the location of the property *(lex rei sitae)* within property law.

Bilateral or multilateral investment treaties typically do not include choice of law rules. As such, arbitral tribunals apply the choice of law rules that are provided within the claims mechanism chosen, such as Article 42 of the ICSID Convention, further referred to in Chapter XVI. Detailed choice of law rules are, however, relatively rare within international dispute resolution instruments, and tribunals therefore typically make use of private international law and its principles to fill any gaps. Some choice of law rules, such as the *lex rei sitae* regarding immovables, have attained such universal recognition that

Parte General, Madrid, Editorial Civitas, 1985, pp. 99 *et seq.* For a full picture of the different positions, see Kegel, *supra* note 1194, pp. 3-4.

1204. In Germany, private international law only deals with the applicable law. See the different modern conceptions in G. Rühl, "Private International Law, Foundations", in J. Basedow *et al.* (eds.), *Encyclopedia of Private International Law*, Vol. 2: *Entries I-Z*, Cheltenham, Edward Elgar, 2017, p. 1380. De Ly warns about exaggerations in contractual matters, considering that the applicable law often only plays a residual role when the parties have clearly chosen a law to govern their contract, F. De Ly, *International Business Law and Lex Mercatoria*, Amsterdam, Elsevier Science / T.M.C. Asser Instituut, 1992, p. 60.

their application in foreign investment regimes as a "general principle of private international law" cannot generate controversy [1205].

Private international law also deals with the problem of "characterization", which is particularly relevant in investment-related matters. Some legal systems consider the transfer of tangible property a "property" issue, applying the *lex rei sitae* rule. On the other hand, other systems consider it a "contracts" issue, in which the choice of law rule will likely be different (related to the place of performance, closest connection, etc.). Matters connected to expropriation, for instance, will often require an inquiry into whether the property has been transferred and therefore acquired by the investor [1206]. In these circumstances, legal rules of universal application should govern, rather than parochial rules that come from particular domestic legal systems [1207]. These universal principles and rules are often enshrined in international instruments, such as the Rome I Regulation on Contractual Obligations [1208], referred to below [1209].

B. *Brief historical note*

The current state of affairs within private international law can be explained by looking back through history. As Kurt Nadelmann once expressed, in private international law, "everything worthy of trying has been tried before, under the same or other labels" [1210].

At times, substantive rules of purported universal application prevailed within private international law. At other times, conflict of laws rules triumphed. This chapter will deal mostly with conflict of laws rules, and the next two chapters with uniform law issues in international investment law.

1. *Roman law*

Roman law did not develop a conflict of laws system. The *ius gentium* applied among foreigners or between them and Roman citizens, and the

---

1205. Douglas, *supra* note 39, pp. 44-45.
1206. *Ibid.*, p. 45.
1207. *Macmillan Inc.* v. *Bishopsgate Investment Trust PLC* (No. 3) (1996) 1 WLR 387.
1208. See Douglas, *supra* note 39, pp. 45-46.
1209. See Chap. X.E., *infra*, "Modern international instruments".
1210. See, for instance, L. Brilmayer, *Conflict of Laws*, 4th ed., Boston, Aspen Law and Business, 1995.

ius civile governed the relationships between Roman citizens. In this personality-based system, citizenship therefore determined which law would be applied to a particular dispute between individuals [1211].

The *ius gentium*, which was also Roman substantive law [1212], contained several international elements – many of them rules derived from Greek law – that were to be applied to "transnational" relationships at the time. Medieval scholars such as Aldricus proposed the application of this transnational or universal substantive law (the *ius gentium*) in the Middle Ages [1213]. Had this system maintained its relevance, what we now understand as private international law would have been identified with the *ius gentium* [1214]. However, private international law ultimately developed mostly into a conflict of laws endeavor, as explained in the following pages.

2. *Statutists*

The true origins of the conflict of laws mechanism can be traced to continental Europe during the Middle Ages [1215]. Feudalism and the theory of territoriality prevailed north of the Alps [1216]. As such, conflict of laws problems did not exist in this part of Europe at the time [1217]. In the south, with the consolidation of Italian cities such as Florence, Bologna, Milan, Pisa and Padova, the linkages between people no longer arose as a result of their allegiances to the same feudal lords but developed due to their residence in the same city. As a result, conflict of laws issues arose due to the diversity of applicable municipal laws and the increasing commerce that occurred between cities [1218]. Formulas

---

1211. *Ius civile* could not be *ius gentium*, but the latter was necessarily *ius civile* and contributed to its evolution. V. Arangio-Ruíz, *Historia del Derecho Romano*, Madrid, Editorial Reus, 1994, p. 182.

1212. K. Siehr, "Private International Law, History of", in J. Basedow *et al.* (eds.), *Encyclopedia of Private International Law*, Vol. 2: *Entries I-Z*, Cheltenham, Edward Elgar, 2017, p. 1390. See also R. Sohm, *Historia e Instituciones del Derecho Privado Romano*, trans. P. Dorado, 7th ed., Madrid, España Moderna, 1898, pp. 103-105.

1213. M. Wolff, *Derecho Internacional Privado*, trans. A. Marín López of 2nd English ed., Barcelona, Editorial Bosch, 1958, p. 22.

1214. Juenger, *supra* note 1201, p. 141.

1215. Audit, *supra* note 1202, p. 61.

1216. F. H. Lawson, *A Common Lawyer Looks at the Civil Law*, Westport, VT, Greenwood Press, 1977 (originally delivered as a series of lectures in 1953), p. 15.

1217. Loussouarn, Bourel and Vareilles-Sommières, *supra* note 1203, p. 85. See also B. Audit and L. D'Avout, *Droit International Privé*, 7th ed., Paris, Economica, 2013, p. 210; M. E. Ancel, P. Deumier and M. Laazouzi, *Droit des contrats internationaux*, Paris, Sirey, 2017, pp. 152-153.

1218. J. Fawcett and P. North, *Cheshire and North's Private International Law*, 12th ed., London, Butterworth, 1992, p. 17.

developed to deal with these conflict of laws issues, many of which still exist today. For instance, the *lex rei sitae*, *lex domicilii* and the *lex loci contractus* all trace their roots to the Middle Ages.

These developments coincided with the reception of Roman law in the first universities, which were founded at that time [1219]. This occurred particularly after the *Glossa Ordinaria* of Accursius (1182-1260), which gave rise to statutory law in Europe. These academics made use of Roman texts to address legal problems, such as the phrase *cunctos populus* [1220]. The invocation of Roman texts was deceptive, however. Statutory law is a medieval (and not a Roman) creation [1221]. Medieval statutory law comprised a compilation of all usages of the time, and also incorporated some new elements when relevant [1222].

However, the *ius commune* has always operated as the general legal framework for resolving legal disputes. Therefore, the central question that emerged at the time was to what extent this "common law" could be excluded by statute [1223]. The answers to this question that emerged at the time attempted to conciliate the scientific pretense of the *ius commune* with the legislative autonomy of the Italian cities [1224].

Bartolus of Sassoferrato (1314-1357) is considered the father of private international law [1225]. His work introduced notable doctrinal refinements to the state of law at the time. Before his scholarly writings,

---

1219. Two major schools emerged in succession: first the "glossators", then the "commentators". The glossators only noted the difference between statutes, whereas the commentators advanced proposals to solve the different practical issues that arose at the time. See C. Donahue, "Comparative Law before the Code Napoléon", in M. Reimann and R. Zimmermann (eds.), *The Oxford Handbook of Comparative Law*, Oxford, Oxford University Press, 2006, pp. 12-13.

1220. It was the beginning of the *Codex Iustiniani* (Codex I, 1 on "*Cunctos populos*" of 529 AD), repeating the Edict of Thessalonica of 380 AD, which introduced Christianity into the entire Roman Empire. Siehr, *supra* note 1212, p. 1392.

1221. U. Drobnig and A. N. Makarov, "Sources" (1972), in K. Lipstein (ed.), *Private International Law*, Vol. 3 of *International Encyclopedia of Comparative Law*, Tübingen, Mohr Siebeck; Leiden, Martinus Nijhoff, 2011, p. 3.

1222. Wolff, *supra* note 1213, p. 21.

1223. Coing, *supra* note 153, pp. 186-187. Berman complains that "positivists" ignored these developments, centering their focus instead on the positive rules that existed within the different cities at the time. In practice, however, the law developed strongly with the *ius commune* acting as a backdrop. See H. J. Berman, "Is Conflict of Laws Becoming Passé?, An Historical Response", Emory University School of Law, Public Law & Legal Theory Research Paper Series, Research Paper No. 05-42, pp. 46-47.

1224. Wieacker, *supra* note 153, p. 102.

1225. Juenger considers that, until modern times, few developments occurred within the field of private international law. His eclecticism was several centuries ahead of its time, reflecting in many ways the legal pluralism that is now commonplace. See Juenger, *supra* note 1201, pp. 143-144.

a unilateral legal perspective prevailed, concentrating on the solutions offered within national law to conflict of laws problems.

One of Bartolus's primary contributions to the development of private international law was the introduction of a multilateral perspective within contractual matters. According to this approach, instead of determining the reach of the law of the forum, one must first consider the particularities of the legal relationship that exists between the parties, and from there determine the applicable law [1226]. For this reason, Bartolus proposed that the validity of the contract must be determined according to the place of its execution, irrespective of where the resolution of the dispute occurs, whereas the consequences of the agreement (for instance, non-performance, notice of default, prescription) must be analyzed according to the law of the place of performance of the contract. Only if the place of performance is not specified within the contract or cannot be easily determined should the contract be governed by the law of the forum [1227]. Within torts law (the law of delicts), the statutes of the city where the foreigner was being sued were to apply [1228].

Ben Wortley notes that Bartolus and Lucas de Penna, among other medieval scholars, broached many matters related to the discipline we now refer to as public international law [1229]. Conversely, in the seventeenth century, Hugo Grotius (considered the father of public international law) dealt with many issues that now form part of contemporary private international law [1230].

1226. P. J. Borchers, "The Triumph of Substance over Rules of Choice in International Commercial Transactions: From the *Lex Mercatoria* to Modern Standards", in M. J. Raisch and R. I. Shaffer (eds.), *Introduction to Transnational Legal Transactions*, New York, Oceana Publications, 1995, p. 144.

1227. H. Batiffol, *Les conflits de lois en matière de contrats. Étude de droit international privé comparé*, Paris, Sirey, 1938, pp. 21-22. See also M. Gutzwiller, "Le développement historique du droit international privé", *Recueil des cours*, Vol. 29 (1929), pp. 317-318.

1228. "The law of this jurisdiction was only to be applied if it could be established that the person who was being sued had lived in the city for so long that he actually ought to know the content of the relevant statue, or if his conduct falls under a prohibition common to all cities", B. P. Franzina, "Jurisdiction, Contracts and Torts", in J. Basedow *et al.* (eds.), *Encyclopedia of Private International Law*, Vol. 2: *Entries I-Z*, Cheltenham, Edward Elgar, 2017, p. 159.

1229. Wortley, *supra* note 1161, p. 248.

1230. In Book II, for example, Grotius deals with ownership (Chaps. II-IV), with family law, marriage and the right of association (Chap. V), with the diversity of laws about succession (Chap. VII, para. XI), with promises (he sets out the rule *locus regit actum*, for example) (Chap. XI, para. V), with contracts (he deals with double sales of the same object (Chap. XII, para. XV), with oaths (he deals with the acceptance of oaths for contractual purposes by persons who habitually swear by "false gods"

3. Territorialism

From the sixteenth to the eighteenth century in France, the law of the concerned territory was applied to legal disputes. Territorialism therefore has a feudal legacy [1231] that also developed at the time of the emergence of modern nation-States, which also coincided with the launching of Jean Bodin's "bestseller" text on territorial sovereignty in 1576 [1232]. The writings of Charles Dumoulin (1501-1566), Bertrand D'Argentré (1519-1590) and Guy Coquille (1523-1603) likewise emerged at that time, also dealing with relevant issues of territorialism. Dumoulin's territorialism was tempered by his theory of party autonomy. In turn, D'Argentré's closed territorialism [1233] strictly diverged from Guy Coquille's more policy-oriented position [1234].

As a corollary to the political independence initiatives that existed at the time, the Netherlands adopted the theory of territorialism as a result of their independence struggle with the Spanish Crown [1235]. However, the necessities of commerce in the region and the cosmopolitan spirit at the time tempered territorialism [1236], making use of the notion of *comitas* that had been introduced by Paul Voet (1619-1677) and further elaborated upon by his son Johanes Voet (1647-1714), who based comity on custom and self-interest.

Ulrik Huber (1636-1694) was the most influential jurist within the Dutch School. He elaborated upon the prior writings of Christian Rodenburg (1618-1668), who is frequently considered the first to use the expression "conflict of laws". Huber popularized this expression in an essay later included in his famous work *The Usus Modernus of Roman Law*, released in 1689 [1237]. In the section titled *De Conflicto Legum*, Huber dealt with problems relating to the conflict of laws [1238].

(Chap. XIII, para. XII), as well as with the general rules of interpretation (Chap. XVI). See Wortley, *supra* note 1161, p. 248.

1231. W. Goldschmidt, *Derecho Internacional Privado*, 8th ed., Buenos Aires, Ediciones Depalma, 1997, p. 71.

1232. On semantical refinements regarding territorialism, see Dane, *supra* note 1998, p. 211.

1233. Loussouarn, Bourel and Vareilles-Sommières, *supra* note 1203, pp. 92-93.

1234. Juenger, *supra* note 1201, pp. 146-147.

1235. Audit, *supra* note 1202, p. 68.

1236. H. Batiffol and P. Lagarde, *Traité de Droit International Privé*, Vol. 1, 8th ed., Paris, Librairie générale de droit et de jurisprudence, 1993, pp. 29-30.

1237. See Symeonides, Collins Perdue and von Mehren, *supra* note 1195, p. 10.

1238. Huber's writings concerning the territoriality of laws and the duty of temporary allegiance based on residence were strongly inspired by Roman law. Indeed, the European tradition of the *ius gentium* was strongly Roman in character, comprising both public and private branches of international law. See Wortley, *supra* note 1161, p. 249.

Huber advanced the ideas of sovereignty and *comitas* [1239] as a midway point between mere courtesy and a juridical obligation to apply a foreign law, derived from the tacit consent of nations and based on mutual tolerance and, ultimately, self-interest [1240]. For Huber, nothing could be more destructive to international commerce than neutralizing rights that had been validly acquired in another jurisdiction. Even though each State is sovereign, he advocated that it should not act in an arbitrary manner. Rather, States must take *comitas* into account and respect the requirements of international commerce [1241].

The work of Huber greatly influenced Lord Mansfield (1705-1793) and Sir William Blackstone (1723-1780) in England, long before 1834, when Story wrote his famous treatise on that subject. Huber also had a particularly strong influence on Albert Venn Dicey (1835-1922) and his theory of "vested rights" or acquired rights, who came to similar conclusions [1242].

However, *comitas* or the theory known as "vested rights" have also led to many doctrinal and practical uncertainties and have been described by Friedrich Juenger as "sheer sophistry" [1243].

4. *Nineteenth-century doctrinal developments*

The emergence and consolidation of private international law as an independent discipline can be traced back to the work of three individuals: an American judge (Joseph Story), a German professor (Friedrich Karl von Savigny) and an Italian politician and professor (Pasquale Stanislao Mancini).

Story (1779-1845) is considered the father of the modern conflict of laws system. His contributions to international law were influenced by the ideas generated by Bartolus and his followers, as well as by Huber and his theory of *comitas*. In his three-volume 1834 *Commentaries on the Constitution of the United States* [1244], Story adopted a multilateral stance, holding that any nation that refused to recognize common principles in private international law would soon find itself in a

1239. Juenger, *supra* note 1201, p. 148.
1240. See Symeonides, Collins Perdue and von Mehren, *supra* note 1195, p. 10.
1241. Fawcett and North, *supra* note 1218, p. 21.
1242. *Ibid.*, p. 21.
1243. Juenger, *supra* note 1201, p. 149.
1244. See D. S. Clark, "Development of Comparative Law in the United States", in M. Reimann and R. Zimmermann (eds.), *The Oxford Handbook of Comparative Law*, Oxford, Oxford University Press, 2006, p. 183.

"barbarous" state. For instance, Story argued that contracts should be interpreted in accordance with the rules recognized by all nations [1245].

Within Story's view of private international law, connecting factors were almost always territorial: the place of the tort, the place of the contract, and so on [1246]. To resolve contractual disputes, Story argued that decision-makers should not only consider the application of the local law *(lex fori)* but also the law of the place of execution of the contract (the *lex loci celebrationis*, within Dutch doctrinal writings) [1247]. This approach, however, was not intended to exclude alternative methods. In his *Swift* v. *Tyson* decision, Story cited Cicero and imagined an American federal system, analogous to the Roman *ius gentium*, "which would control interstate and international cases" [1248] and that contracts would be "governed by a general commercial law rather than conflicting State laws" [1249].

Savigny, the German professor (1779-1861), was also a multilateralist and took inspiration from Story's writings, which he considered "brilliant" [1250]. By focusing on the "seat" of the legal relationship [1251], Savigny made the applicable law independent from its result – that is, it could lead to the application of either national or foreign law [1252].

Having created a neutral mechanism for the determination of the applicable law, Savigny moved away from the theories of territorialism and *comitas*, which centered on the national law and the limitations of its application [1253].

Savigny's works marked the beginning of a "Copernican shift" [1254] that had also influenced medieval jurists. Rather than classifying

1245. Borchers, *supra* note 1226, p. 147.

1246. R. Michaels, "Story, Joseph", in J. Basedow *et al.* (eds.), *Encyclopedia of Private International Law*, Vol. 2: *Entries I-Z*, Cheltenham, Edward Elgar, 2017, p. 1663.

1247. He invoked an English case in this regard. *Scrimshire* v. *Scrimshire* (1753). Juenger, *supra* note 1201, pp. 152-153.

1248. *Ibid.*, p. 157.

1249. *Ibid.*, p. 136.

1250. M. F. C. de Savigny, *Sistema de Derecho Romano Actual*, Vol. 6, 2nd ed., Madrid, Centro Editorial de Góngora, 1924, pp. 121-122.

1251. *Ibid.*, p. 136.

1252. The Savignean multilateral tradition never considered State interest a primordial consideration. State interests are central to the unilateral traditions, which emphasize political rather than private considerations. See H. Muir Watt, "New Challenges in Public and Private International Legal Theory: Can Comparative Scholarship Help?", in M. Van Hoecke (ed.), *Epistemology and Methodology of Comparative Law*, Oxford / Portland, OR, Hart Publishing, 2004, p. 277.

1253. Visher, *supra* note 1200, p. 32.

1254. Even though according to Yanguas Messía, in two centuries Suárez anticipated Savigny's international community of States doctrine. See J. De Yanguas Messía,

laws according to their subject matter, Savigny's neutral mechanism focused on determining the seat within every legal relationship [1255]. To determine the seat within a particular legal relationship, the following concepts were fundamental: the theory of domicile regarding personal capacity, *lex rei situs* in relation to property, and the place of execution and performance in respect to contracts [1256]. Due to the proximity between torts law and criminal law, Savigny argued that the *lex fori* should apply, rather than the law of the place of the tort [1257].

Savigny supported the unification of private international law through treaties [1258], thus advocating in favor of universal conflict of laws solutions via public international law instruments (i.e., treaties).

Until recently, many scholars gave or presaged a "farewell to Savigny" [1259]. However, while the Savignean method has diluted in utility within private international law, it still serves as an important departure point for private international law and as a basis for modern thinking [1260]. His work illustrated what can be done by following a general formula within international law [1261].

Savigny's writings have been translated into several languages and have been cited as authoritative in common law and civil law countries alike. His formula focusing on the seat inspired Otto von Gierke's "center of gravity test" in the civil law world. Savigny's theories have shaped the development of the common law as well, notably the Westlake "proper law" theory in England, which led to the development of the "closest or most significative connection" test [1262]. The Restatement (Second) of "Conflict of Laws" of 1971 (Secs. 145, 188) refers to the closest connection or the "most significant relationship" [1263].

Derecho Internacional Privado, Parte General, 3rd ed., Madrid, Editorial Reus, 1971, p. 93.

1255. Savigny, *supra* note 1250, p. 136.

1256. Prior to the development of the Savignean tradition, determining the seat turned on which type of rule was to apply: territorial or personal. Now, determining the seat centers around the relevant connecting factor, and not to which type of rule applies. See O. Kahn-Freund (ed.), *General Problems of Private International Law*, Leiden, A. W. Sijthoff, 1974, pp. 97-98.

1257. M. Sonnentag, "Savigny, Friedrich Carl von", in in J. Basedow *et al.* (eds.), *Encyclopedia of Private International Law*, Vol. 2: *Entries I-Z*, Cheltenham, Edward Elgar, 2017, pp. 1610-1611.

1258. Savigny, *supra* note 1250, p. 137.

1259. Jayme, *supra* note 894, p. 81.

1260. Khan-Freund, *supra* note 1256, p. 142.

1261. Wolff, *supra* note 1213, pp. 35-36.

1262. On the evolution of the proper law in England, see *ibid.*, pp. 409-410.

1263. After Savigny and Gierke, in *Auten* v. *Auten*, the New York Court of Appeals referred to "grouping of contracts" and "most significant contacts". Both notions

The Italian professor, Mancini (1817-1888)[1264], presented an inaugural lecture at the University of Torino in 1851 where he advocated against the territorialism theory and favored nationalism as a basis for private international law[1265]. Mancini's doctrine is considered internationalist, rather than territorialist, since his theory holds that the application of a foreign law should be an international obligation, rather than a matter of courtesy[1266].

Mancini was one of the founders of the Hague Conference on Private International Law[1267], and perhaps the most vehement and notorious proponent at his time of the unification of the discipline through treaties[1268]. Mancini's unification theories as a universal aspiration were put into practice by Dutch professor Tobías Asser (1838-1913), due to whose influence the Dutch Government invited several European countries to codify private international law in 1892[1269]. The Hague Conference on Private International Law came into being the following year and has constituted an intergovernmental organization since 1955[1270].

C. *The first private international law treaties*

1. *Montevideo Treaties*

Under the influence of contemporary European thinkers, the Americas took the lead in the codification of private international law as early as 1867[1271].

---

were later merged into the "most significative relationship" concept, adopted in the Restatement (Second). See Juenger, *supra* note 1201, p. 179.

1264. Mancini was followed by influential jurists Weiss of France and Laurent of Belgium, G. Kegel, "Fundamental Approaches" (1986), in K. Lipstein (ed.), *Private International Law*, Vol. 3 of *International Encyclopedia of Comparative Law*, Tübingen, Mohr Siebeck; Leiden, Martinus Nijhoff, 2011, p. 7.

1265. P. S. Mancini, *Direito Internacional (Diritto Internazionale Prelezioni)*, trans. Ciro Mioranza, Rio Grande do Sul, Editora Unijuí, 2003.

1266. Audit, *supra* note 1202, p. 72.

1267. Kegel, *supra* note 1264, p. 9.

1268. Q. Alfonsín, *Curso de Derecho Privado Internacional*, Montevideo, Ediciones Idea, 1955, pp. 275-276.

1269. See Wolff, *supra* note 1213, p. 44.

1270. See *infra* note 1320.

1271. The creation of norms to govern private international law can be traced back to 1867 and the conversations that occurred between diplomatic representatives of Bolivia, Chile, Ecuador and Peru. D. P. Fernández Arroyo, *La Codificación del Derecho Internacional Privado en América Latina*, Madrid, Eurolex, 1994, p. 87. For more information regarding the applicable law to international contracts in Latin America, see also M. M. Albornoz, *La loi applicable aux contrats internationaux dans les pays du Mercosur*, Tese datilografada, Université Paris II, 2006;

In 1889, nine private international law treaties were signed in Montevideo, each of them dealing with specific civil, commercial, procedural and other matters [1272]. Ratification was perhaps eased because those particular topics were addressed in different instruments [1273]. These early Montevideo Treaties remain binding today in Argentina, Bolivia, Colombia, Paraguay, Peru and Uruguay.

The Treaty on International Civil Law that specifically addresses the issue of choice of law within international contracts has generated controversial solutions regarding the absence of choice and remains silent concerning party autonomy [1274].

Regardless, the Montevideo Treaties should be applauded as the first international codification initiative within private international law that also maintains its relevance today. In relation to international contracts, these treaties were a century ahead of their time in anticipating the European conventional framework and more than 120 years ahead of the universal instrument on the topic adopted in 2015 by the Hague Conference on Private International Law. These developments will be addressed further later in this chapter.

In 1940, new treaties were signed in Montevideo (ratified only by Argentina, Paraguay and Uruguay) that reaffirmed the earlier solutions regarding the absence of choice of law provisions and also codified the general rule that when the applicable law comes into question, the law of the place of performance should apply (with some exceptions) with regard to contracts.

F. V. d. C. Cerqueira, "Proposition d'un système dualiste de détermination de la loi applicable aux contrats internationaux dans l'espace juridique du Mercosur", PhD thesis, Université de Strasbourg, 2010; T. B. De Maekelt, "General Rules of Private International Law in the Americas: New Approach", *Recueil des cours*, Vol. 177 (1982).

1272. (1) Treaty on International Civil Law of 12 February 1889; (2) Treaty on International Commercial Law of 12 February 1889; (3) Treaty on International Penal Law of 23 January 1889; (4) Treaty on International Procedural Law of 11 January 1889; (5) Convention on the Exercise of Liberal Professions of 4 February 1889; (6) Treaty for the Protection of Literary and Artistic Property of 11 January 1889; (7) Convention on Commercial and Industrial Trademarks of 16 January 1889; (8) Convention on Letters Patent of 16 January 1889; (9) Additional Protocol to Treaties on Private International Law of 13 February 1889. Information at http://opil.ouplaw.com/page/Treaties-Montevideo, accessed 20 May 2022.

1273. T. B. De Maekelt, *Teoría General del Derecho Internacional Privado*, Academia de Ciencias Políticas y Sociales, Caracas, 2005, p. 29.

1274. Regarding critics, see D. Hargaín and G. Mihali, *Régimen Jurídico de la Contratación Mercantil Internacional en el MERCOSUR*, Buenos Aires, Julio César Faira, 1993, p. 39. On the issue of party autonomy in the Treaties of 1889, see R. Santos Belandro, *El Derecho Aplicable a los Contratos Internacionales*, 2nd ed., Montevideo, Editorial Fundación de Cultura Universitaria, 1998, pp. 55-56.

Furthermore, these later treaties provided that each State should choose for itself whether it accepts the principle of party autonomy. In the absence of clear provisions to that effect in domestic legislation, the principle of party autonomy becomes very controversial, as seen in relevant cases arising in Brazil [1275], Paraguay [1276] and Uruguay [1277].

Article 37 of the 1940 Montevideo Treaty uses the place of performance of the contract as a connecting factor to govern issues related to formation, characterization, validity, effects, consequences and performance of the contract. Article 33 of the 1889 Montevideo Treaty was the original source of this provision.

This approach raises concerns when the place of performance of the contract occurs in more than one State. Moreover, the place of performance may not be known at the time the contract is concluded or it could change later on. The presumptions established in Article 38 of the 1940 Montevideo Treaty attempted to resolve these problems. These presumptions applied to contracts "on specific and individually identified things", contracts "on specific types of things", "referring to fungible things" and contracts "for the provision of services". At the same time, Article 40 of the 1940 Montevideo Treaty provides that the law of the "place of execution" of the contract will be applicable to those contracts for which the place of performance cannot be determined at the time the contract is concluded [1278].

Nonetheless, these solutions have proven problematic and have led to additional challenges. For instance, international contracts and the obligations arising therefrom often have more than one place of performance. As such, it becomes impossible to determine which law

---

1275. See N. de Araújo (ed.), *Contratos Internacionais*, 2nd ed., Rio de Janeiro, Renovar, 2000, pp. 320-324.

1276. See J. A. Moreno Rodríguez, "Autonomía de la Voluntad en el Derecho Internacional Privado Paraguayo", in Tatiana B. De Maekelt, *Homenaje a Tatiana Maekelt*, Asunción, CEDEP, 2010, pp. 409 *et seq*.

1277. See, in general, C. Fresnedo de Aguirre, *La Autonomía de la Voluntad en la Contratación Internacional*, Montevideo, Editorial Fundación de Cultura Universitaria, 1991. Currently, there is an important shift on this topic, analyzing in a broader perspective in the following excellent work, D. Opertti Badán, "El Derecho Internacional Privado en tiempos de globalización", *Revista Uruguaya de Derecho Internacional Privado*, Vol. 6, No. 6 (2005).

1278. Goldschmidt, *supra* note 1231, p. 396. A factor in its success was also the political ingredient of the Bolivarian dream of the continental "unión", toward which these treaties were considered an important step, L. Pereznieto Castro, *Los Principios de UNIDROIT y la Convención Interamericana sobre el Derecho Aplicable a los Contratos*, Instituto de Investigaciones Jurídicas, Ser. H, Estudios de Derecho Internacional Público, No. 27, Universidad Nacional Autónoma de México, México, DF, 1998, p. 244.

applies unless the contract refers to a specific service or "characteristic" obligation and the respective place of performance of such an obligation is clearly determined.

However, referring to "characteristic" obligations in the contract also creates discrepancies in practice as well. For instance, the following questions must be posed: does the contract refer to the physical place of performance, or to the domicile, habitual residence or establishment of the obligor of the characteristic performance? Furthermore, determining the characteristic performance can become unclear within swap agreements, distribution agreements and in complex contractual relationships generally, given that international contracts tend to be complex transactions. Worse yet, this solution tends to favor the application of the law of the domicile of the parties that are in a dominant position when it comes to the sale of goods or provision of services in international transactions [1279].

As such, while the approach established in the Montevideo Treaties in the absence of choice of law is still defended by some scholars in the field, it has also created many controversies [1280]. Critics of this approach argue that the adjudicator is not granted the flexibility to determine whether there are closer connections than those provided in advance by the legislator, nor are the solutions offered by these treaties clearly presented [1281].

2. *Bustamante Code*

Many States in the Americas, such as Brazil, Chile and Venezuela, did not incorporate the Montevideo Treaties into their national legislation. Instead, they ratified the Bustamante Code of 1928, which had been

1279. Hargaín and Mihali, *supra* note 1274, pp. 31, 39.

1280. See D. P. Fernández Arroyo and C. Fresnedo de Aguirre, "Obligaciones contractuales: aspectos generales", in D. P. Fernández Arroyo *et al.* (ed.), *Derecho Internacional Privado de los Estados del MERCOSUR: Argentina, Brasil, Paraguay, Uruguay*, Buenos Aires, Zavalía, 2003, p. 949. See also several contributions in C. Fresnedo de Aguirre and G. Lorenzo Idiarte, *Jornadas 130 Aniversario Tratados de Montevideo 1889*, Montevideo, Fundación de Cultura Universitaria, 2019.

1281. This criticism is considered controversial by other scholars who maintain that significant flexibility can be derived from the Additional Protocols to the Treaties of 1889 and 1940, and subsequently, by the Inter-American Convention on General Rules of Private International Law. Article 9 of the Inter-American Convention on General Rules of Private International Law, is an example of a provision providing this flexibility, adopted in Montevideo at CIDIP-II, signed on 8 May 1979 and entered into force on 10 June 1981.

adopted as a result of the sixth Pan-American Conference that took place in Havana, Cuba.

It remains unclear whether the Bustamante Code endorses the principle of party autonomy. Further, where an international contract does not specify a choice of law, the solutions provided in the Bustamante Code – which differ from those in the Montevideo Treaties – are unsatisfactory [1282]. The Code provides that, where appropriate, contracts shall be governed by the law that is common to the parties and that determines capacity. If no such law exists, the law of the place of conclusion of the contract should apply, according to Article 186. However, it is unlikely for there to be a law common to the parties to determine capacity given that in international commercial contracts a party's domicile – a criterion that at times prevails over nationality in Latin American civil law – is almost always different for each party. Therefore, since the criterion of a "law common to the parties to determine capacity" (or "personal common law") will rarely be met, the criterion of "place of conclusion" is widely used instead, with its corresponding challenges (as noted above) [1283]. When it comes to formal requirements, the law of the place of conclusion and performance of the contract (Art. 180) apply cumulatively. This solution has also been criticized [1284].

In general, scholars have observed that the Bustamante Code is very confusing when it comes to contractual matters. The Code has scarcely been used by national courts, and when used it is often in a merely suppletive way within the lacunae of national legislation [1285]. The question of the application of the Code when States have made generic reservations (which has been done by Bolivia, Chile, Costa Rica, Ecuador and El Salvador) is also controversial [1286].

1282. Bustamante Code, Articles 175-186. See also A. Sánchez, *Derecho Internacional Privado*, Vol. 2, 3rd ed., Habana, Cultural, 1943.

1283. Araújo, *supra* note 1275, p. 163.

1284. Article 180. Cf. OAS, Guide on the Law Applicable to International Commercial Contracts in the Americas, 2019, https://www.oas.org/en/sla/dil/publications_Guide_Law_Applicable_International_Commercial_Contracts_Americas_2019.asp, pp. 77-78.

1285. J. Samtleben, in Araújo, *supra* note 1275, p. 161. See also J. Dolinger, "The Bustamante Code and the Inter-American Conventions in the Brazilian System of Private International Law", in J. Kleinheisterkamp and G. A. Lorenzo Idiarte (eds.), *Avances del Derecho Internacional Privado en América Latina, Liber Amicorum Jürgen Samtleben*, Montevideo, Editorial Fundación de Cultura Universitaria, 2002, pp. 133 *et seq.*

1286. See OAS Guide, *supra* note 1284, p. 20.

D. Legislation

National legislation around the globe regulating private international law matters remained scarce or anachronistic throughout the nineteenth century. This is the case, for instance, with the French Civil Code of 1804, the Austrian Civil Code of 1811, the Code of the Canton of Zurich of 1854, the Italian Civil Code of 1865, the Chilean Civil Code of 1855 and the Argentinean Civil Code of 1869 [1287].

Modern legislation arrived well after the nineteenth century. As noted by Symon Symeonides, the codification movement throughout the 1960s began slowly, gained momentum around the turn of the twentieth century and continued into the twenty-first century. Beginning in continental Europe, the codification movement has since spread to other continents and to countries from all legal families and traditions [1288]. The first completed codification occurred in Madagascar in 1962, followed by the codification initiative within the former Czechoslovakian State, which was adopted in 1963 and went into effect in 1964. From that point onward, many other countries followed suit. Altogether, without considering the European Union Regulations, the last decades have produced at least ninety-four national (or, in some cases, subnational) codifications or re-codifications [1289].

In contractual matters, contemporary laws are now generally aligned with the solutions provided for in modern international instruments, referred to below, which tribunals and writers frequently consider an expression of general private international law principles.

1287. S. C. Symeonides, *Codifying Choice of Law Around the World: An International Comparative Analysis*, Oxford, Oxford University Press, 2014, p. 2.

1288. *Ibid.*, p. 3.

1289. *Ibid.*, p. 12. For instance, in Africa, the following countries codified private international law: Gabon (1972), Senegal (1972), Guinea-Bissau (1973), Mozambique (1975), Algeria (1975), Angola (1977), and Tunisia (1998); in Asia: Afghanistan (1977), Jordan (1977), United Arab Emirates (1985), North Korea (1995), Vietnam (1995), South Korea (2001), Mongolia (2002), Japan (2007), Turkey (1982 and 2007), Taiwan (2010), and China (1985, 1987, 1999 and 2010); in Europe: Albania (1964 and 2011), Poland (1965 and 2011), Portugal (1967), Spain (1974), Hungary (1979), Austria (1979), Germany (1986 and 1999), Switzerland (1987), Russia (1991, URSS and 2002), United Kingdom (1995), Italy (1995), Belgium (2004), The Netherlands (2001 and 2011), and Czech Republic (2012); and in the Americas: Ecuador (1970), Peru (1984), Mexico (1988), Quebec (1991), Panama (1992) and Venezuela (1998). Paraguay enacted Law 5393 "on the law applicable to international contracts" in 2015, and Uruguay enacted its "General Law of Private International Law" (Law No. 19.920), in November 2020. See commentaries on the Uruguayan reform in *Comentarios a la nueva Ley General de Derecho Internacional Privado* (No. 19.920 del 17 de noviembre de 2020), Montevideo, Ediciones Idea, 2022.

E. *Modern international instruments*

1. *Rome Convention and the Rome I Regulation*

Almost a century after the Montevideo Treaties of 1899, a treaty was signed in 1980 to regulate conflict of laws problems in international contracts in Europe. The "Rome Convention" entered into force in 1991 and was accompanied by an official report designed by Professors Mario Giuliano and Paul Lagarde to assist with its interpretation [1290]. In 2008, following the transfer of certain legislative powers to the European Union, the Rome Convention was substituted, with some modifications and additions, for the European Union's Regulation on the Law Applicable to Contractual Obligations, also known as "Rome I" [1291].

Both instruments cover matters related to the law applicable to international contracts, outline the principle of party autonomy and the limits thereof and also provide criteria to determine the applicable law in the absence of choice of law provisions in the agreements themselves.

When it comes to the uncertainty that had previously existed with respect to party autonomy in certain international instruments, the Rome I Regulation settled the issue in its favor. Where the contract does not include a choice of law provision, the Rome I Regulation suggests choosing the place of characteristic performance [1292]. The direct application of non-State law is also discarded in Rome I; non-State law only becomes applicable if it has been explicitly incorporated in the contract [1293].

The Rome Convention of 1980 adopted the "closest connection" formula in the absence of choice of law provisions. However, a set of guidelines was designed to arrive at an understanding of "characteristic performance" compatible with the closest connection formula.

1290. M. Giuliano and G. Lagarde, Report on the Convention on the Law Applicable to Contractual Obligations, OJ C 282/1, 1980, https://eur-lex.europa.eu/LexUriServ/LexUriServ.do?uri=CELEX:31980Y1031(01):EN:HTML, accessed 20 June 2022.

1291. Regulation of the European Parliament and of the Council on the law applicable to contractual obligations (17 June 2008), 593/2008/EC, [2008] OJ L177/6. Rome I is binding on all EU Member States other than Denmark, where the Rome Convention remains applicable.

1292. See Article 4 of the Rome I Regulation on the applicable law in the absence of choice.

1293. See criticisms to this circumstance in M. J. Bonell, "El reglamento CE 593/2008 sobre la ley aplicable a las obligaciones contractuales ('Roma I')", in J. Basedow, D. P. Fernández Arroyo and J. A. Moreno Rodríguez (eds.), *Cómo se Codifica hoy el Derecho Comercial Internacional*, Asunción, CEDEP / La Ley Paraguaya, 2010.

These guidelines generated considerable criticism and disparities [1294]. Moreover, Juenger considered the very concept of characteristic performance to be a "Gordian Knot" [1295] of dubious efficacy in swaps, distribution contracts and complex international relationships in general. Making matters worse, the concept of characteristic performance confers a capricious privilege in favor of the application of the law of the party that controls the provision of goods and services in international transactions [1296].

The reforms that generated Rome I clarified some of the previous issues [1297] but resulted in rather rigid rules that determine which law applies in different scenarios in order to determine characteristic performance (Art. 4) [1298]. This choice was made to increase predictability in the matter. However, as noted by George Bermann, several interpretive perambulatory clauses exist within Rome I, which suggests less certainty than was originally sought in the drafting of the instrument [1299].

The proposed solutions for absence of choice in Rome I were characterized as a "labyrinth" or a "jungle" [1300], and even an "inferno" in some

1294. See A. Bonomi, "The Principles of Party Autonomy and Closest Connection in the Future EC Regulation 'Rome I' on the Law Applicable to Contractual Obligations", *DeCITA: direito do comércio internacional / derecho del comercio internacional*, eds. D. P. Fernández Arroyo, A. Dreyzin de Klor and L. Otávio Pimentel (eds.), No. 3 (2005), pp. 332-342, 338. Bonomi, for instance, advocated instead for the closest connection rule of the 1994 Mexico Convention (*ibid.*, pp. 340-341). See also criticisms in E. Hernández-Bretón, "La Convención de México (CIDIP V, 1994) como modelo para. la actualización de los sistemas nacionales de contratación internacional en América Latina", in *DeCITA*, Vol. 9, Asunción, CEDEP, 2008, p. 178.

1295. This allusion refers to the Greek legend of a knot declared "impossible to untangle"; an oracle prophesied that whoever could untangle the knot would conquer the East. Alexander Magnus cut it with his sword.

1296. F. K. Juenger, "The UNIDROIT Principles of Commercial Contracts and Inter-American Contract Choice of Law", in *Contratación Internacional, Comentarios a los Principios sobre los Contratos Comerciales Internacionales del UNIDROIT*, México, Universidad Nacional Autónoma de México, Universidad Panamericana, 1998, pp. 206-207.

1297. See G. A. Bermann, "Rome I: A Comparative View", in F. Ferrari and S. Leible (eds.), *Rome I Regulation: The Law Applicable to Contractual Obligations in Europe*, Munich, Sellier, 2009, p. 350.

1298. The instrument does not contemplate the closest connection rule found, for instance, in the Mexico Convention. However, its rigid conflict rules lead to the place of characteristic performance. U. Magnus, "Article 4 Rome I Regulation: The Applicable Law in the Absence of Choice", in F. Ferrari and S. Leible (eds.), *Rome I Regulation: The Law Applicable to Contractual Obligations in Europe*, Munich, Sellier, 2009, p. 29.

1299. The recitals to the regulation seem disturbingly similar to the "comments" and "reporters' notes" within the North American Restatements which, in contrast to Rome I, only attempt to have a persuasive value. Bermann, *supra* note 1297, p. 357.

1300. *Ibid.*, p. 358.

cases [1301]. It is necessary to refer to the perambulatory clauses within Rome I in order to resolve interpretation issues, but such detailed rules diminish the value of broad or flexible formulas [1302]. Given the rich variety of commercial relations, it becomes unlikely that a mechanical rule appropriate for one type of contract will be appropriate for another as well.

This kind of flexibility existed in British law until 1991 (when the Rome Convention came into effect in the United Kingdom) thanks to the proper law of the contract formula [1303], which is analogous to the closest connection test in its search for characteristic performance [1304]. Similarly, in the United States, while it is necessary to take a State-by-State approach to the conflict of laws analysis, the domestic States that follow the Second Restatement have adopted the flexible closest connection or "most significant relationship" formula for contracts that do not involve the sale of goods [1305].

Finally, according to Article 19 of the Consolidated version of the Treaty on European Union and Articles 251 *et seq* of the Consolidated version of the Treaty on the Functioning of the European Union (TFEU), the CJEU shall assure the uniform interpretation of community law throughout the EU. The CJEU frequently – although not as a matter of course – uses the comparative method for inspiration when interpreting EU law [1306].

1301. U. P. Gruber, "Insurance Contracts", in F. Ferrari and S. Leible (eds.), *Rome I Regulation: The Law Applicable to Contractual Obligations in Europe*, Munich, Sellier, 2009, pp. 110-111.

1302. J. H. C. Morris, *The Conflict of Laws*, 7th ed., eds. David McClean and Kisch Beevers, London, Sweet and Maxwell / Thomson Reuters, 2009, p. 369.

1303. In English law, the "proper law of the contract" rule existed until 1991 (when the Rome Convention entered into force). Morris, *supra* note 1302, p. 352. See analysis of the case *Dynamit AG* v. *Rio Tinto Co.* (1918), in G. Dannemann, "Comparative Law: Study of Similarities or Differences?", in M. Reimann and R. Zimmermann (eds.), *The Oxford Handbook of Comparative Law*, Oxford, Oxford University Press, 2006, pp. 394-395. Such a concept approximates to the closest connection instead of to the search for a characteristic performance. C. G. J. Morse, "England", in C. G. J. Morse and M. Rubino-Sammartano (eds.), *Public Policy in Transnational Relationships*, Deventer/Boston, Kluwer Law and Taxation Publishers, 1991, p. 71.

1304. On the regime in England after withdrawal from the European Union, see M. Ahmed, *Brexit and the Future of Private International Law in English Courts*, Oxford, Oxford University Press, 2022.

1305. Restatement (Second) of Conflict of Laws of 1971 (Secs. 145, 188). This solution prevails in the majority of States. Symeonides, Collins Perdue and von Mehren, *supra* note 1195, p. 139. For the sale of goods that are not governed by the CISG, Section 1-301 *(b)* of the UCC provides that when the parties have not made an effective choice, the UCC (as codified in that State) "applies to transactions bearing an appropriate relation to this state". On the evolution of the proper law in England, see Wolff, *supra* note 1213, pp. 409-410.

1306. See T. Kadner Graziano, F. Garcimartín Alférez and G. Van Calster, "European Union Perspectives on the Hague Principles", in D. Girsberger, T. Kadner Graziano

It remains to be seen what interpretative developments of Rome I will occur in the absence of choice. Perhaps the Mexico Convention can be better relied upon as an expression of general principles on the law applicable to international contracts, as explained in the OAS Guide that will be addressed below.

2. Mexico Convention

By the mid-twentieth century, a general feeling existed in the Americas that the instruments mentioned above were highly unsatisfactory. First, they contained questionable solutions, and second, significant divergences existed among them. In addition, several States on the continent had not ratified any of these instruments, in particular those based upon common law traditions, which further contributed to complexity in the matter.

The establishment of the Organization of American States (OAS) in 1948 brought with it new hope that complexities within the region's conflict of laws system would finally be resolved. After careful evaluation, the OAS decided against developing a general code such as the Bustamante Code. Instead, it concentrated its efforts on working toward the gradual codification of particular topics within the field of private international law [1307].

The OAS tabled new private international law instruments at the Inter-American Specialized Conferences on Private International Law (CIDIPs). The CIDIPs are diplomatic conferences organized pursuant to Article 122 of the Charter of the OAS. To date, seven CIDIPs have been held, which have resulted in the adoption of twenty-six international instruments (including conventions, protocols, uniform law documents and one model law) on various topics.

However, it was only at the Fifth Inter-American Specialized Conference on Private International Law (CIDIP-V, which took place in Mexico City in 1994) that the issue of choice of law in international contracts was addressed. The Inter-American Convention on the Law Applicable to International Contracts, commonly known as the "Mexico Convention", resulted from CIDIP-V. The Mexico Convention

---

and J. L. Neels (eds.), *Choice of Law in International Commercial Contracts: Global Perspectives on the Hague Principles*, Oxford, Oxford University Press, 2021, p. 751.

1307. See J. M. Arrighi, "El proceso actual de elaboración de normas Interamericanas" *Jornadas de Derecho Internacional* (2001); E. Villalta, "El Derecho Internacional Privado en el Continente Americano", in J. A. Moreno Rodríguez and C. Lima Marques (eds.), *Los servicios en el Derecho Internacional Privado*, Asunción, ASADIP, 2014, p. 23 ff.

recognizes party autonomy, and in the absence of choice, adopts the closest connection formula [1308].

Article 9, paragraph 1, of the Mexico Convention provides that "[i] f the parties have not selected the applicable law, or if their selection proves ineffective, the contract shall be governed by the law of the State with which it has the closest ties [connections]". This is known as "the proximity principle".

In deciding the applicable law, "[t]he Court will take into account all objective and subjective elements of the contract to determine the law of the State with which it has the closest ties [connections]" (Art. 9, para. 2, first sentence). This provision is consistent with Article 11 when it refers to a "State with which the contract has close [connections]". Another interpretation has been advanced that when determining the "closest connection" one must evaluate all the possible circumstances, as well as the territorial circumstances related to the conclusion, performance, domicile or establishment, dispute resolution clause, currency, prior negotiations, and others. These "objective" connections are to be considered together with the "subjective" connections that arise from different clauses and circumstances before, during and after the conclusion of the contract and which indicate the legitimate expectations of the parties [1309].

In making its determination, a court shall also take into account "the general principles of international commercial law recognized by international organizations" (Art. 9, para. 2, second sentence).

During the process of drafting the Mexico Convention, the US delegation proposed the "closest connection" formula, the intention that led to a transnational, non-State law, rather than to a domestic law [1310]. Around the same time, the UNIDROIT Principles were coming into the limelight, approximately two decades after their inception as a project and later drafting. Juenger, a member of the US delegation, argued that the reference to "general principles" should clearly include the UNIDROIT Principles [1311].

1308. Articles 7 (party autonomy) and 9 (closest connection).

1309. OAS Guide, *supra* note 1284, para. 351.

1310. "If the parties have not selected the applicable law, or if this election proves ineffective, the contracts shall be governed by the general principles of international commercial law accepted by international organizations", F. K. Juenger, "The Inter-American Convention on the Law Applicable to International Contracts: Some Highlights and Comparisons", *American Journal of Comparative Law*, Vol. 42, No. 2 (1994), p. 391.

1311. See also F.K. Juenger, "Conflict of Laws, Comparative Law and Civil Law: The *Lex Mercatoria* and Private International Law", *Louisiana Law Review*,

After considerable discussions during CIDIP-V, a compromise was reached [1312]. Regarding the rule that was ultimately adopted, one interpretation is that the role of *lex mercatoria* or non-State law has been reduced to that of an auxiliary element that, together with the objective and subjective elements of the contract, helps the adjudicator identify the law of the State with the closest connection to the agreement. Another interpretation mirrors Juenger's argument and favors the application of non-State law where a choice of law has not been made [1313]. In Juenger's own words:

> "[E]ven in countries that fail to ratify the Convention, its provisions can be considered an expression of inter-American policy that judges ought to consult in rendering their decisions. Once courts as well as arbitrators begin to rely on them, the Principles can furnish the necessary legal infrastructure for this Continent's ever-increasing economic and legal integration." [1314]

The Mexico Convention also contains a flexible formula that can be applied in the determination of the applicable law [1315]. Article 10 provides that:

> "In addition to the provisions in the foregoing articles, the guidelines, customs, and principles of international commercial law as well as commercial usage and practices generally accepted

---

Vol. 60 (2000), p. 1133, at 1148. The relevance of this opinion is highlighted by José Siqueiros, the original drafter of the Mexico Convention, since the former was the one who had proposed the compromise solution. J. L. Siqueiros, "Los Principios de UNIDROIT y la Convención Interamericana sobre el Derecho Aplicable a los Contratos Internacionales", in *Contratación Internacional, Comentarios a los Principios sobre los Contratos Comerciales Internacionales del UNIDROIT*, México, Universidad Nacional Autónoma de México, Universidad Panamericana, 1998, p. 223.

1312. Juenger, *supra* note 1310, p. 391.

1313. The preparatory works of the CIDIP-V reveal that there had also been discussion as evidenced in the preparatory works that discussions did occur regarding whether the term "international organizations" incorporates all of the elements of *lex mercatoria*. Report of the Rapporteur of the Commission I on the Law Applicable to International Contractual Arrangements, OEA/Ser.K/XXI.5, CIDIP-V/doc.32/94 rev.1. This understanding existed prior to the further development of this idea in more recent times.

1314. Juenger, *supra* note 1310, p. 236.

1315. Although the analogous wording of Article 9 had been suggested by common law jurists, Article 10 of the Mexico Convention was proposed by Gonzalo Parra Aranguren, President of the Venezuelan delegation, who hailed from the civil law tradition. Inter-American Convention on the Law Applicable to International Contracts, OAS Doc. OEA/Ser.K/XXI.5 (17 March 1994). See also "La Quinta conferencia Especializada Interamericana sobre Derecho Internacional Privado (CIDIP V), México, 1994", *Revista de la Fundación Procuraduría General de la República*, pp. 219-220.

shall apply in order to discharge the requirements of justice and equity in the particular case."

In the Americas, a similar flexible formula provided in Article 9 of the 1979 OAS Inter-American Convention on General Rules of Private International Law has been accepted for many years and has been ratified by several countries in the region [1316].

Even though the Mexico Convention was generally welcomed by the international community [1317], it has, unlike other continental instruments that have been widely received, so far only been ratified by Mexico and Venezuela. There is much speculation as to why the Convention was not ratified by more countries. Perhaps the legal establishments in the various States were not sufficiently prepared to integrate the solutions proposed by the Mexico Convention into their domestic laws [1318], or perhaps States did not know how to bring the Mexico Convention into effect without ratifying it. Aside from ratification, States could have simply transferred its provisions into a national law on the matter, as was done, for instance, in 1998 by Venezuela [1319].

3. The Hague Principles

The Hague Conference on Private International Law (hereinafter, the Hague Conference or HCCH) is undoubtedly the most prestigious

---

1316. Argentina, Brazil, Colombia, Guatemala, Paraguay, Ecuador, Mexico, Peru, Uruguay and Venezuela. See http://www.oas.org/juridico/spanish/firmas/b-45.html, accessed 21 April 2020. On this topic, see further in Chap. XX, *infra*.

1317. In fact, the modern solutions offered by the Mexico Convention have been applauded by international scholars. See R. Herbert, "La Convención Interamericana sobre Derecho Aplicable a los Contratos Internacionales", *Revista uruguaya de derecho internacional privado*, No. 1 (1994), p. 45; J. Tálice, "La autonomía de la voluntad como principio de rango superior en el Derecho Internacional Privado Uruguayo", in *Liber Amicorum in Homenaje al Profesor Didier Opertti Badán*, Montevideo, Editorial Fundación de Cultura Universitaria, 2005, pp. 560-561, stating that it deserves to be ratified or incorporated into the internal laws of the countries through other means.

1318. See J. A. Moreno Rodríguez and M.M. Albornoz, "Reflexiones emergentes de la Convención de México para la elaboración del futuro instrumento de La Haya en materia de contratación internacional", published in Spanish at http://alumnosmdag.blogspot.com/2011/04/reflexiones-emergentes-de-la-convencion.html. In English: "Reflections on the Mexico Convention in the Context of the Preparation of the Future Hague Instrument on International Contracts", *Journal of Private International Law*, Vol. 7, No. 3 (2011), p. 493.

1319. Hernández-Bretón, *supra* note 1294, p. 170. On the Venezuelan Law, see T. B. de Maekelt, C. Resende and I. Esis Villaroel, *Ley de Derecho Internacional Privado Comentada*, Vol. I-II, Caracas, Universidad Central de Venezuela, 2005. In particular, in Vol. II, the work of J. Ochoa Muñoz and F. Romero on the applicable law to international contracting and the *lex mercatoria*, pp. 739-832.

organization in the world codifying conflict or choice of law rules [1320]. The organization advanced the initiative of drafting the Hague Principles on Choice of Law in International Contracts, now commonly referred to as "the Hague Principles", which are likely to become very influential in years to come [1321].

The success of the Rome Convention led the Hague Conference to undertake studies throughout the early 1980s regarding the possibility of adopting a similar instrument. Given the difficulties in obtaining mass ratification of the proposed convention, this initiative was ultimately discarded, as insufficient ratification would have led to its failure. In recent years, however, the matter had been taken up again, and the feasibility studies that took place between 2005 and 2009 indicate that perhaps a different type of instrument could prove successful and productive [1322].

Accordingly, a working group was convened in 2010 [1323] that advocated for the development of a "soft law" document rather than a "hard law" instrument, inspired by the drafting technique of the highly praised UNIDROIT Principles. After more than four years of work, the Hague Principles were finally adopted in 2015 [1324].

1320. Further, the Hague Conference is the oldest of The Hague's international legal institutions, H. van Loon, "The Hague Conference on Private International Law", *The Hague Justice Journal*, Vol. 2 (2007), p. 4; in this article the former Secretary-General of the organization describes its important work.

1321. See, for instance, L. Radicati Di Brozolo, "Non-National Rules and Conflicts of Laws: Reflections in Light of the UNIDROIT and Hague Principles", *Rivista di diritto internazionale privato e processuale*, Vol. 48, No. 4 (2012), pp. 841–864.

1322. The preparatory works are available at https://www.hcch.net/en/publications-and-studies/details4/?pid=6297&dtid=61, accessed 6 May 2022.

1323. N.B. Cohen (United States); The Hon. Justice Clyde Croft (Australia); S.E. Darankoum (Canada); A. Dickinson (United Kingdom); A.S. El-Kosheri (Egypt); B. Fauvarque-Cosson (France); L. G. E. Souza Jr. (Brasil); F. J. Garcimartín Alférez (Spain); D. Girsberger (Switzerland); Y. Guo (China); M. E. Koppenol-Laforce (Netherlands); D. Martiny (Germany); C. McLachlan (New Zealand); J. A. Moreno Rodríguez (Paraguay); J. L. Neels (South Africa); Y. Nishitani (Germany); R.F. Oppong (United Kingdom); G. Saumier (Canada); I. Zykin (Russia). The following observers also joined the Working Group: M. J. Bonell (UNIDROIT); F. Bortolotti (International Chamber of Commerce); T. Lemay (UNCITRAL); F. Mazza (Arbitration Court of the International Chamber of Commerce); K. Reichert (International Bar Association); P. Werner (International Swaps and Derivatives Association). Later on, T. Kadner Graziano (Switzerland) and S. Symeonides (Cyprus) joined the Working Group.

1324. For more details on the work of the Working Group and the context surrounding the drafting of The Hague Principles, see M. Pertegás, "The Provenance of the Hague Principles", in D. Girsberger, T. Kadner Graziano and J. L. Neels (eds.), *Choice of Law in International Commercial Contracts: Global Perspectives on the Hague Principles*, Oxford, Oxford University Press, 2021, pp. 141-150. For information about the future promotion and possible work of The Hague Principles, see J. Ribeiro-Bidaoui, "HCCH:

While the UNIDROIT Principles address substantive law issues, the Hague Principles are limited to choice of law issues, specifically in relation to party autonomy [1325]. The absence of choice is not addressed by the Hague Principles, perhaps because this would have made the project too ambitious, and perhaps also because it makes little sense to regulate these issues in a soft law instrument [1326].

The Hague Principles are not a formally binding instrument, such as a convention that States are obliged to apply or incorporate into their domestic law directly. Instead, they are a non-binding set of principles intended to guide the reform of domestic laws related to choice of law. As its Commentary emphasizes, the Hague Principles may thus be considered "an international code of current best practice with respect to the recognition of party autonomy in choice of law in international commercial contracts, with certain innovative provisions as appropriate" [1327].

Of course, there are multiple additional uses of the Hague Principles, such as serving as a model for legislators and as an interpretive tool for parties, judges and arbitrators [1328].

Paraguay reproduced the Hague Principles almost verbatim in its law on international contracts, which has been in operation since January 2015 [1329]. Similarly, the Hague Principles have also played a role in existing or future legislation in jurisdictions such as the Republic of

---

Roadmap for the Promotion of the HCCH Principles, with a Focus on the Role of International Organizations", in *ibid.*, pp. 151-177.

1325. Regarding the relation between The Hague Principles and the UNIDROIT Principles (as well as the CISG), see the joint work of the HCCH, UNCITRAL and UNIDROIT on the future Tripartite Legal Guide to Uniform Legal Instruments in the Area of International Commercial Contracts (with a focus on sales). This Guide aims to create a roadmap to navigate the existing uniform law texts in the area of international sales law, primarily though not exclusively, the CISG, the UNIDROIT Principles of International Commercial Contracts and the HCCH Principles. It is an effort to clarify the interaction among these instruments, promoting uniformity, certainty and clarity in this area of the law. The publication of the Legal Guide has been authorized by all three organizations in 2020. For more information, see https://www.unidroit.org/instruments/commercial-contracts/tripartite-legal-guide, accessed 15 September 2022.

1326. This matter was widely discussed in the deliberations of the Working Group in The Hague, in which the author of this work participated.

1327. Commentary I.15, available at https://www.hcch.net/en/instruments/conventions/full-text/?cid=135, accessed 15 September 2022.

1328. See Ribeiro-Bidaoui, *supra* note 1324, pp. 151-177.

1329. Law 5393 on the law applicable to international contracts, available at https://www.hcch.net/en/publications-and-studies/details4/?pid=6300&dtid=41, accessed 6 May 2022. See J. A. Moreno Rodríguez, "The New Paraguayan Law on International Contracts: Back to the Past?", in *Eppur si muove: The Age of Uniform Law – Essays in Honour of Michael Joachim Bonell to Celebrate His 70th Birthday*, Vol. 2, Rome, UNIDROIT, 2016, https://ssrn.com/abstract=2958771, accessed 13 May 2022

the Congo, Indonesia, Australia, the European Union, Russia and Mexico [1330].

While it has only been in existence for a short time, in many other jurisdictions the Hague Principles have also been used as persuasive authority by courts in the interpretation, supplementation and development of applicable private international law rules and principles, such as in the European Union, Hong Kong, India, Japan, Singapore, Argentina, Brazil, Mexico, Canada, the United States, and many others [1331].

The Hague Principles have been described as "ground-breaking" for being the first legal instrument to address choice of law issues in international contracts at a global level. The Hague Principles have also benefited from being advanced by an international organization that has been working with diverse stakeholders for many years [1332]. Additionally, their principles are balanced and straightforward, contemplating both commercial interests in expanding party autonomy and States' interest in restricting the parties' choice of law in exceptional circumstances when it is manifestly incompatible with public policy.

The Hague Principles may have much more influence in jurisdictions that have no codified regime of choice of law in international contracts and in which the courts have no – or have only very limited – experience dealing with transborder commercial transactions. For example, this is the case in many developing countries in parts of Asia, Africa and Latin America. This does not imply that the Hague Principles will not have an influence in jurisdictions that have already adopted modern choice of law rules. In these jurisdictions, discussions have begun as to whether (and if so, to what extent) the Hague Principles are superior to, or more sophisticated than, those in their national laws [1333], and may prove useful – at the least – for interpretive purposes.

1330. See D. Girsberger, T. Kadner Graziano and J. L. Neels, "General Comparative Report", in *id.*, *Choice of Law in International Commercial Contracts: Global Perspectives on the Hague Principles*, Oxford, Oxford University Press, 2021, p. 15; See also Ribeiro-Bidaoui, *supra* note 1324, p. 153 ff.

1331. An Argentine Appeals Court also used the Hague Principles as an interpretive tool even before their final adoption. *DG Belgrano SA* v. *Procter and Gamble Argentina SRL*, Courtroom A of the Cámara Nacional de Apelaciones en lo Comercial, 2003. Other jurisdictions are more skeptical, in particular about the prospects of any eventual influence of the Hague Principles on their legislation or application by the courts (e.g. China, South Korea, Iran, Lebanon, Norway, Western Balkans and Uruguay). See Girsberger, Kadner Graziano and Neels, "General Comparative Report", *ibid.*, pp. 15-16.

1332. For example, they were endorsed by UNCITRAL, APEC and the ICC. See J Ribeiro-Bidaoui, *supra* note 1324, pp. 157-158.

1333. See "General Comparative Report", *supra* note 1330, p. 17; See also Ribeiro-Bidaoui, *supra* note 1324, p. 158 ff.

4. OAS Guide

In 2015, after the approval of the Hague Principles and the enactment of the Paraguayan law on international contracts [1334], the Inter-American Juridical Committee of the OAS (CJI) sent a questionnaire on the subject of international contracts to all the national governments in the Americas [1335]. Based on the responses received [1336], the CJI finally decided to move ahead with drafting a guide on the law applicable to international contracts [1337].

Over twenty years have passed since the adoption of the Mexico Convention. Given that the Hague Principles incorporated subsequent developments that created greater clarity for conflict of laws problems and introduced innovative solutions, the CJI reviewed several options for drafting the guide. It ultimately decided against embarking on a process to revise the Mexico Convention, as negotiating and adopting a convention is a highly complicated and costly process that requires political will and considerable resources. The drafting of other instruments, such as model laws and legislative guidelines, have proven to be simpler processes and just as effective a means of advancing harmonization in private international law.

The CJI concluded that, at this stage in the development of applicable law issues, it would be much more effective for American States to

1334. Law No. 5393 of 2015, "Law Applicable to International Contracts", has nineteen articles. Articles 1 to 10 and Articles 13 and 14 on choice of law basically reproduce the Hague Principles with small modifications. Articles 11, 12, 15 and 16 primarily address those situations where no choice of law had been made and reproduce almost verbatim the corresponding provisions in the Mexico Convention. Lastly, Article 17 on public policy is aligned with the solution provided by the Hague Principles and Article 18 addresses the legislation that must be revoked as a result of this law.

1335. OAS, Questionnaire on the Implementation of the Inter-American Conventions on Private International Law, CJI/doc.481/15.

1336. The CJI and the Department of International Law of the OAS (DIL) were headed by legal expert Dante Negro and had the benefit of the involvement of Jeannette Tramhel, Senior Legal Officer, who also devoted a great deal of time to the project with assistance from various interns prepared a status report of the matter. The Inter-American Convention on the Law Applicable to International Contracts and the Furtherance of its Principles in the Americas, OEA/SG, DDI /doc.3/16; see also The Law Applicable to International Contracts, OEA/Ser.Q, CJI/doc.487/15 rev. 1.

1337. The DIL prepared a highly comprehensive synopsis that covered a range of topics to be addressed, including information highlighted by several jurists in the region who pledged their assistance where their domestic law was concerned. Promoting International Contracts Law in the Americas: A Guide to Legal Principles, OEA/Ser.Q, CJI/doc.XX/16. In addition, CJI Member Dr Elizabeth Villalta prepared a comparative analysis of the Mexico Convention (1994) and the Hague Principles, both concerning international contracts, which was also most useful as preparatory material (The Law Applicable to International Contracts, CJI/doc.464/14 rev.1).

adopt or revise domestic laws in order to establish a certain consistency with the guidelines endorsed by the OAS based on international rules and best practices recognized by the Hague Conference and other relevant international bodies.

A draft guide was prepared in Spanish by CJI member José A. Moreno Rodríguez (who was also the drafter of the Paraguayan law on international contracts) acting as Rapporteur, with the support of the Department of International Law of the OAS (DIL). The draft guide was the culmination of intensive research, consultations and drafting activities, in line with input received from the CJI at subsequent meetings [1338].

Finally, in 2019, the CJI adopted the Guide on the Law Applicable to International Commercial Contracts in the Americas (the OAS Guide) [1339]. The OAS Guide consistently relies on the main instruments in force on the subject, including Rome I (the EU regulation), the Hague Principles and, in particular, the Mexico Convention. Provisions from those instruments (and even some comments on the Hague Principles) have been directly copied in the draft OAS Guide so as to maintain their fidelity to the original text. It must be considered that, among other uses, the Hague Principles are intended to serve as a model for

1338. The question of a prospective guide to international contracts has been discussed at previous meetings of the CJI, at Washington, DC, in March 2016, and in Rio de Janeiro in October 2016 and March 2017. At those meetings, the CJI had the opportunity to consider the different preparatory materials contained in the appendixes to the within draft Guide, including the enriched synopsis prepared by the DIL. The Rapporteur worked in close collaboration with the DIL and the Guide benefited from significant input from several jurists and organizations. The draft Guide was considered by UNCITRAL, UNIDROIT, HCCH and by prominent regional and international legal experts, such as Hans van Loon, Daniel Girsberger, Jürgen Samtleben, Diego Fernández Arroyo, Joachim Bonell, Geneviève Saumier, Alejandro Garro, Marta Pertegás, Luca Castellani, Anna Veneziano, Paula All, Neale Bergman, Brooke Marshall, Maria Blanca Noodt Taquela, Nádia de Araújo, Cristian Giménez Corte, Lauro Gama, Frederico Glitz, Valerie Simard, Jaime Gallegos, Ignacio Garcia, Francisco Grob D., Antonio Agustin Aljure Salame, Lenin Navarro Moreno, Elizabeth Villalta, Pedro Mendoza, Nuria González, Mercedes Albornoz, Jan L. Neels, David Stewart, Antonio F. Perez, Soterios Loizou, Cecilia Fresnedo, Claudia Madrid Martes, Eugenio Hernández-Bretón, Gustavo Moser, Anayansy Rojas, José Manuel Canelas, Felipe Ossa, Francisco González de Cossío, Alfredo Bullard, Fernando Cantuarias Salaverry, Roger Rubio and Dyalá Jiménez Figueres. The American Bar Association Section on International Law provided valuable comments, as did the Department of Justice Canada. Many of the legal experts involved are also officers and members of ASADIP, which brings together the region's top experts in the field. In a statement dated 10 January 2019, ASADIP expressed its support for the draft Guide. Afterwards, on 4 March 2019, ASADIP supported the final draft. These backings were expressed pursuant to a mandate from the ASADIP General Assembly granted on 9 November 2018, available at www.asadip.org, accessed 6 May 2022.

1339. See OAS Guide, *supra* note 1284.

legislators. There are fourteen OAS member States of the HCCH [1340], and the working group that drafted the Hague Principles included representatives from this region. As such, the Hague Principles reflect the positions of many States in the Americas that are part of the HCCH.

When dealing with applicable law in arbitration, the OAS Guide focuses in particular on the 1958 New York Convention, ratified or acceded to by nearly all States in the Americas [1341], and on the UNCITRAL Model Law, which has promoted harmonization by inspiring legal reforms throughout the American continent [1342]. These reforms contributed significantly to increasing acceptance throughout the region of the principle of party autonomy and recognition of the utility of uniform law instruments within the realm of international commercial contracts.

The OAS Guide has several objectives, among them to support efforts by OAS member States to modernize their domestic laws on international commercial contracts in accordance with international standards. The OAS Guide provides assistance to contracting parties and their counsel in the Americas in the drafting and interpretation of international commercial contracts. The OAS Guide also provides guidance to judges and arbitrators in the interpretation and supplementation of domestic laws, particularly on international commercial contract matters that are not dealt with under domestic law [1343].

The OAS Guide begins with a "summary of specific recommendations" to legislators, judges, the parties and their advisors on international contracts. It then contains a table of contents, a list of abbreviations and another list of terms in Latin and other languages used in the document. After these lists, the text of the Guide itself is presented (with eighteen

---

1340. At the diplomatic session, many of the OAS Member States recommended that the document should be approved. The meeting of the Special Commission on the Choice of Law in International Contracts took place on 16 November 2012; The report is available at https://assets.hcch.net/docs/735cb368-c681-4338-ae8c-8c911ba7ad0c.pdf, accessed 6 May 2022.

1341. The exceptions are Belize, Grenada, Saint Kitts and Nevis, Saint Lucia and Suriname.

1342. UNCITRAL Model Arbitration Law, current status at http://www.uncitral.org/uncitral/en/uncitral_texts/arbitration/1985Model_arbitration_status.html. According to the website, legislation based on the Model has been adopted in the following OAS Member States: Canada (federally and all provinces and territories), Chile, Costa Rica, Dominican Republic, Guatemala, Honduras, Jamaica, Mexico, Nicaragua, Peru, United States (certain states only) and Venezuela. Argentina has also advanced new legislation (Arbitration Law, enacted 26 July 2018). Uruguay has also approved legislation to adopt the Model law, available at http://ciarglobal.com/uruguay-aprobado-por-el-senado-el-proyecto-de-ley-de-arbitraje-comercial-internacional/, accessed 6 May 2022.

1343. See OAS Guide, *supra* note 1284, p. 18.

parts), addressing issues of party autonomy, absence of choice and public policy, among others. Finally, the document includes annexes that incorporate a table comparing the Mexico Convention and the Hague Principles, a table of laws, a table of cases and a list of databases and other electronic sources used in preparing various parts of the draft OAS Guide. References to the OAS Guide will be made throughout this book.

5. Other regional efforts

Currently, there is no regional instrument that has been approved for use in regulating international contracts within the African region. Two efforts are worth mentioning: the OHADA initiative, and a project originated by the University of Johannesburg.

The Organization for the Harmonization of Business Law in Africa (OHADA), created in 1993, aims at creating simple, modern and harmonized business law rules within its seventeen member States [1344]. OHADA did not propose any comprehensive codification of private international law. Rather, specific private international law provisions appear in different drafts [1345], such as the proposal to regulate obligations [1346]. In preparing this draft, only the Rome I Regulation was taken into account, even though the draft was completed in December 2015 after the approval of the Hague Principles [1347].

1344. OHADA Member States includes Benin, Burkina Faso, Cameroon, Central African Republic, Côte d'Ivoire, Congo, Comoros, Gabon, Guinea, Guinea-Bissau, Equatorial Guinea, Mali, Niger, Democratic Republic of Congo, Senegal, Chad and Togo.

1345. See J. Monsenepwo, "The Organization for the Harmonization of Business Law in Africa and the Hague Principles", in D. Girsberger, T. Kadner Graziano and J. L. Neels (eds.), *Choice of Law in International Commercial Contracts: Global Perspectives on the Hague Principles*, Oxford, Oxford University Press, 2021, p. 250.

1346. With the support of UNIDROIT, in 2002 the OHADA Council of Ministers began drafting a Uniform Act on the law of contracts. After preparatory work and consultations with experts from nine OHADA Member States, a Preliminary Draft Uniform Act on Contract Law and its Explanatory Notes was completed. Based on the UNIDROIT Principles, this first Preliminary Draft contained only substantive law rules related to contractual matters. On 12 December 2007, the OHADA Council of Ministers decided to relaunch the preparation of a Uniform Act on Contract Law with the Foundation for Continental Law. OHADA and the Foundation for Continental Law created a Working Group which submitted a Preliminary Draft Uniform Act on the Law of Obligations in the OHADA Region to the OHADA Council of Ministers in 2015. Unlike the first preliminary Draft, which focused solely on contract law, the new Draft contains conflict of laws rules regarding the law applicable to contractual obligations and other contractual matters. *Ibid.*, p. 251. See also M. Fontaine, "The Draft OHADA Uniform Act on Contracts and the UNIDROIT Principles of International Commercial Contracts", *Uniform Law Review*, Vol. 9, No. 3 (2004), pp. 573-584.

1347. *Ibid.*, p. 252. It is argued that, in that context, the Hague Principles could inform a revision of the conflict of laws title of the Projet de texte uniforme portant

The African Principles of Commercial Private International Law are intended to form a set of model laws for use by the African Union or its member States on matters ranging from the applicable law to international contracts, international obligations, sales, and others [1348]. Their drafting was heavily influenced by modern instruments such as the Hague Principles [1349]. The project is conducted by the Research Centre for Private International Law in Emerging Countries at the University of Johannesburg [1350].

There is no regional instrument governing international contract law in Asia either. The Asian Principles of Private International Law (APPIL) have recently been proposed and constitute a comprehensive set of private international law principles that are generally recognized within the different Asian jurisdictions. It is a non-binding (soft law) instrument that aims at providing guidance for the possible future harmonization of international contract law across Asia, for use within Asian legislation, as well as by national courts, practitioners and academics. APPIL was strongly inspired by the Hague Principles and other global and regional instruments, such as the Rome I Regulation, the Mexico Convention and the UNIDROIT Principles [1351].

---

droit general des obligations dans l'espace OHADA (2015), see J. L. Neels, "The Role of the Hague Principles on Choice of Law in International Commercial Contracts in the Revision of the Preliminary Draft Uniform Act on the Law of Obligations in the OHADA Region", *Tydskrif vir Hedendaagse Romeins, Hollandse Reg / Journal of Contemporary Roman – Dutch Law*, Vol. 81, No. 3 (2018), p. 464.

1348. "The various model laws are provisionally called the African Principles on the Law Applicable to International Contracts of Sale, the African Principles on the Law Applicable to International Commercial Contracts, the African Principles on the Law Applicable to Non-contractual Obligations, and the African Principles on Jurisdiction in International Civil and Commercial Cases. The first two model laws may perhaps be combined under the title of the second (the African Principles on the Law Applicable to International Commercial Contracts)." Quote from J. L. Neels and E. A. Fredericks, "The African Principles of Commercial Private International Law and the Hague Principles", in D. Girsberger, T. Kadner Graziano and J. L. Neels (eds.), *Choice of Law in International Commercial Contracts: Global Perspectives on the Hague Principles*, Oxford, Oxford University Press, 2021, p. 239.

1349. *Ibid.*, p. 239. See also J. L. Neels and E. A. Fredericks, "An Introduction to the African Principles of Commercial Private International Law", *Stellenbosch Law Review*, Vol. 29 (2018), pp. 347-356.

1350. See Neels and Fredericks, *supra* note 1348, p. 239.

1351. N. Takasugi and B. Elbalti, "Asian Principles of Private International Law", in D. Girsberger, T. Kadner Graziano and J. L. Neels (eds.), *Choice of Law in International Commercial Contracts: Global Perspectives on the Hague Principles*, Oxford, Oxford University Press, 2021, pp. 399-401:

> "The origins of the APPIL date back to 1997 and the initiative launched by Professor Hiroshi Matsuoka, who launched a research project with Korean academics on the harmonization of Private International Law between Korea and Japan. This bilateral scholarly cooperation continued until 2011 and resulted

The scope of the APPIL project was originally very ambitious, as it aimed to cover the major areas of private international law. However, after the first meeting, it became clear that the project had to be narrowed. The result was the preparation of a set of principles covering topics such as international jurisdiction in civil and commercial matters, general rules of choice of law, choice of law for contracts, choice of law for torts, recognition and enforcement of foreign judgments in civil and commercial matters, and judicial support for international commercial arbitration. The document is expected to be published in the near future [1352].

F. Private international law in investment claims related to contracts

Yuliya Chernykh notes that only on some occasions are the parties to a contract and the parties to a treaty-based dispute absolutely identical. In many other instances, the parties to a treaty-based dispute have merely a certain proximity to the parties to a contract. Sometimes, the foreign investor acting as a claimant concludes agreements with a broad range of State-related entities, such as a ministry or a State-owned enterprise, that are not formally respondents in investment treaty arbitration. At other times, discussions in an investment claim relate to contracts concluded between a claimant and a third party. Every so often, issues arise in relation to contracts concluded between the State and companies connected with the foreign investor [1353]. All these agreements may raise private international law issues.

---

in a number of scholarly publications. One year later, a new scholarly initiative supported by a Japanese government fund was launched, igniting the APPIL project. The project was undertaken under the supervision of the 'APPIL Steering Committee'. It started with the creation of an APPIL research study group involving scholars representing ten Asian jurisdictions. In 2013, the Commission on the Asian Principles of Private International Law (CAPPIL) was created. Members of the CAPPIL held their first meeting in December 2015. Two other meetings were held in 2016 and 2017, during which the drafting of the APPIL was completed. Their publication is expected to be delivered soon."

On the APPIL, see also W. Chen and G. Goldstein, "The Asian Principles of Private International Law: Objectives, Contents, Structure and Selected Topics on Choice of Law", *Journal of Private International Law*, Vol. 13 (2017).

1352. Takasugi and Elbalti, *supra* note 1351, pp. 401-402.

1353. "Even contracts concluded between the parties, none of which are formally a party to treaty-based disputes, may also appear as objects to be ascertained in investment treaty arbitration", Y. Chernykh, *Contract Interpretation in Investment Treaty Arbitration: A Theory of the Incidental Issue* (International Litigation in Practice, No. 12), Leiden/Boston, Brill Nijhoff, 2022, p. 19.

Some investment contracts, such as concession and license agreements, have a strong public law element and, consequently, lessened levels of party autonomy [1354]. Arbitral decisions have dealt with a variety of these contracts, such as concession agreements for the operation of the national vehicle registry [1355], the provision of services [1356], water and sewage/water distribution services [1357], the exploration of natural resources [1358], concession agreement for the operation of pipelines [1359], mine operation contracts [1360] and license agreements [1361].

Also, typical commercial agreements have been recognized as investment contracts, such as the financial risk management (hedging) agreement discussed in *Deutsche Bank* v. *Sri Lanka* [1362]. Other cases have dealt with discussions related to leases [1363], loans [1364] and

---

1354. Discussions in this regard were addressed in *Enron* v. *Argentina*, *supra* note 451, Award (22 May 2007), para. 220.

See also *Azurix* v. *Argentina*, *supra* note 327, Award (2006), paras. 54, 62, 290; Decision on the Application for Annulment of the Argentine Republic (1 September 2009), para. 134 *(f)*.

1355. *Talsud SA* v. *The United Mexican States*, ICSID Case No. ARB(AF)/04/4, Award (16 June 2010), paras. 4-44.

1356. *IBM World Trade Corporation* v. *República del Ecuador*, ICSID Case No. ARB/02/10, Decision on Jurisdiction and Competence (22 December 2003), paras. 54-63; *Millicom International Operations BV and Sentel GSM SA* v. *The Republic of Senegal*, ICSID Case No. ARB/08/20, Decision on Jurisdiction of the Arbitral Tribunal (16 July 2010), paras. 8, 97; *SGS* v. *Pakistan*, *supra* note 977, Decision (2003), paras. 135, 160-161.

1357. *Azurix* v. *Argentina*, *supra* note 327, Award (2006), paras. 41, 114-119; *Impregilo SpA* v. *Argentine Republic*, ICSID Case No. ARB/07/17, Award (21 June 2011), paras. 14-15, 322-323.

1358. *Chevron Corporation (USA) and Texaco Petroleum Company (USA)* v. *The Republic of Ecuador*, UNCITRAL, PCA Case No. 34877, Partial Award on the Merits (30 March 2010), paras. 33, 448-451; *Chevron Corporation and Texaco Petroleum Company* v. *The Republic of Ecuador (II)*, PCA Case No. 2009-23, Third Interim Award on Jurisdiction and Admissibility (27 February 2012), paras. 3.7-3.12.

1359. *Ron Fuchs* v. *The Republic of Georgia*, ICSID Case No. ARB/07/15, Award (3 March 2010), paras. 94-103, 318-322, 331-341; *Kardassopoulos* v. *Georgia*, *supra* note 449, Award (3 March 2010), paras. 94-103, 318-322, 331-341).

1360. *Crystallex*, *supra* note 521, Award (4 April 2016), paras. 18-20, 205, 481-483, 698-700.

1361. *Enron* v. *Argentina*, *supra* note 451, Decision on Jurisdiction (Ancillary Claim) (2 August 2004), paras. 23, 47-52, Award (22 May 2007), paras. 43, 151-155; *Ulysseas, Inc.* v. *The Republic of Ecuador*, UNCITRAL, Interim Award (28 September 2010), paras. 67-72, 149-163.

1362. *Deutsche Bank* v. *Sri Lanka*, *supra* note 93, Award, paras. 12-14.

1363. *Mamidoil Jetoil Greek Petroleum Products Societe SA* v. *Republic of Albania*, ICSID Case No. ARB/11/24, Award (30 March 2015), paras. 81, 648; *Generation Ukraine* v. *Ukraine*, *supra* note 456, Award (16 September 2003), paras. 18.23-18.42; *Lee John Beck and Central Asian Development Corporation* v. *Kyrgyz Republic*, Award (13 November 2013), paras. 2-3, 26, 37; *Flemingo DutyFree Shop Private Limited* v. *the Republic of Poland*, Award (12 August 2016), paras. 60-82, 546-560.

1364. *Československa* v. *Slovak Republic*, *supra* note 70, Award (29 December 2004), paras. 30-31, 239-257, 272-278, 303-313; (loan and security agreement) *British Caribbean Bank* v. *Belize*, *supra* note 96, paras. 168-175.

other credit agreements [1365], pledge agreements [1366], construction agreements [1367], electricity purchase agreements [1368], farmout agreements [1369], privatization agreements [1370], sale contracts [1371], service agreements [1372], settlement agreements [1373], joint venture agreements and partnerships [1374], share purchase agreements [1375], trust contracts [1376], and many others [1377].

1365. *Waste Management* v. *Mexico*, *supra* note 530, Award (30 April 2004), paras. 50-51, 102-103, 118-129.

1366. *Hassan Awdi, Enterprise Business Consultants, Inc. and Alfa El Corporation* v. *Romania*, ICSID Case No. ARB/10/13, Award (2 March 2015), paras. 58-60, 220-221, 368-383.

1367. *Bayindir* v. *Pakistan*, *supra* note 456, Award (27 August 2009), paras. 13-22, 252-356; *Garanti Koza LLP* v. *Turkmenistan*, ICSID Case No. ARB/11/20, Award (19 December 2016), paras. 4-5, 331-337, 346-354.

1368. *Mercer International Inc.* v. *Government of Canada*, ICSID Case No. ARB(AF)/12/3, Award (6 March 2018), paras. 3.82-3.85.

1369. *Occidental* v. *Ecuador (ii)*, *supra* note 872, Award (5 October 2012), paras. 92, 127-134, 331, 386.

1370. *Plama Consortium Limited* v. *Republic of Bulgaria*, ICSID Case No. ARB/03/24, Award (27 August 2008), paras. 84, 113-114; *Vincent J. Ryan, Schooner Capital LLC, and Atlantic Investment Partners LLC* v. *Republic of Poland*, ICSID Case No. ARB(AF)/11/3, Award (24 November 2015), paras. 53-55, 75-83, 254-258; *Hassan Awdi* v. *Romania*, *supra* note 1366, Award (2015), paras. 368-383; *Telefónica SA* v. *The Argentine Republic*, ICSID Case No. ARB/03/20, Decision of the Tribunal on Objections to Jurisdiction (25 May 2006), para. 87.

1371. *Siag and Vecchi* v. *Egypt*, *supra* note 102, Award (1 June 2009), paras. 507-510, 528-529, 577-584.

1372. *Luigiterzo Bosca* v. *Lithuania*, Award (17 May 2013), paras. 166-178; *Karkey Karadeniz Elektrik Uretim AS* v. *Islamic Republic of Pakistan*, ICSID Case No. ARB/13/1, Award (22 August 2017), paras. 690-698.

1373. *Lemire* v. *Ukraine*, *supra* note 547, Decision on Jurisdiction and Liability (14 January 2010), paras. 114-115; *William Nagel* v. *The Czech Republic*, SCC Case No. 049/2002, Final Award (9 September 2003), paras. 225-244; *Noble Ventures* v. *Romania*, *supra* note 1090, Award (12 October 2005), paras. 198-202.

1374. *Fuchs* v. *Georgia*, *supra* note 1359, Award (3 March 2010), paras. 318-330; *Kardassopoulos* v. *Georgia*, *supra* note 449, Award (3 March 2010), paras. 318-330; *Gustav F W Hamester GmbH & Co. KG* v. *Republic of Ghana*, ICSID Case No. ARB/07/24, Award (18 June 2010), paras. 22-27, 263-266; *EDF (Services) Limited* v. *Republic of Romania*, ICSID Case No. ARB/05/13, Award (8 October 2009), paras. 47-64, 245-246; *Société Générale in respect of DR Energy Holdings Limited and Empresa Distribuidora de Electricidad del Este, SA* v. *The Dominican Republic*, LCIA Case No. UN7927, Award on Preliminary Objections to Jurisdiction (19 September 2008), paras. 46-47.

1375. *Swisslion DOO Skopje* v. *The former Yugoslav Republic of Macedonia*, ICSID Case No. ARB/09/16, Award (6 July 2012), paras. 180-181.

1376. *Empresa Electrica del Ecuador, Inc. (EMELEC)* v. *Republic of Ecuador*, ICSID Case No. ARB/05/9, Award (2 June 2009), paras. 53, 86 ff.

1377. Such as an offtake agreement (*Koch Minerals Sàrl and Koch Nitrogen International Sàrl* v. *Bolivarian Republic of Venezuela*, ICSID Case No. ARB/11/19, Award (30 October 2017), paras. 2.15, 4.11-4.17, 6.58-6.71, 7.41-7.51), a pooling agreement among corporate shareholders (*Fraport AG Frankfurt Airport Services Worldwide* v. *Republic of the Philippines (ii)*, ICSID Case No. ARB/11/12, Award (10 December 2014), paras. 113-114, 442-468), usufruct contract (*Railroad Development Corporation (RDC)* v. *Republic of Guatemala*, ICSID Case No. ARB/07/23, Award (29 June 2012), paras. 82–84), a so-called "road map agreement" as a specific agreement evidencing undertakings on the part of the State to enable an investment

Moreover, standard contract forms, such as those provided by FIDIC in relation to international construction contracts [1378], have been addressed in international investment disputes [1379]. Further, investment claims may raise discussions in relation to agreements that are not investment contracts *per se* [1380].

Contractual matters addressed in investment claims typically relate to choice of law and dispute resolution clauses, provisions on currency adjustment, exclusivity, *force majeure*, limitation of liability or waiver of liability clauses, linguistic discrepancy, notification, penalty, price, renegotiations, stabilization clauses and economic equilibrium, termination clauses and other interpretive matters [1381].

The private international law instruments discussed some pages above, such as Rome I and the Mexico Convention, can be of great assistance in addressing these and other contractual issues raised in foreign investment claims. The same holds true with uniform law, which will be referred to in the next chapter.

Interesting problems also arise regarding the "incidental or preliminary question" issue. In private international law the "incidental or preliminary question" discussion arises when a rule of law attaches specific effects to an existing legal status or relationship. When the adjudicators must make a decision on a legal matter, they may first

project (*Unglaube* v. *Costa Rica*, ICSID Case No. ARB/08/1, Award (2012), paras. 75-76, 170; 185-191, 250 and *Unglaube* v. *Costa Rica*, ICSID Case No. ARB/09/20, Award (2012), paras. 75-76, 170; 185-191, 250), a contract on salvage (*Malaysian Historical Salvors* v. *Malaysia*, *supra* note 72, Award on Jurisdiction (17 May 2007), paras. 107-146; Decision on the Application for Annulment (16 April 2009), para. 60 ff.), bareboat charters (*Inmaris Perestroika Sailing Maritime Services GmbH* et al. v. *Ukraine*, ICSID Case No. ARB/08/8, Decision on Jurisdiction (8 March 2010), paras. 66–88), contract on immigration control, personal identification and electoral information (*Siemens* v. *Argentina*, *supra* note 531, Decision on Jurisdiction (3 August 2004), paras. 23-25, 174–180, Award (6 February 2007, paras. 128-150), donation of land plots agreement (*Unglaube* v. *Costa Rica*, ICSID Case No. ARB/08/1, Award (2012), paras. 49-59, 170-197; *Unglaube* v. *Costa Rica*, ICSID Case No. ARB/09/20, Award (2012), paras. 49-59, 170-197), funding agreement (third-party funding) (*Teinver SA, Transportes de Cercanías SA and Autobuses Urbanos del Sur SA* v. *The Argentine Republic*, ICSID Case No. ARB/09/1; Decision on Jurisdiction (21 December 2012), paras. 239-259; Award (21 July 2017), paras. 224-233). See Chernykh, *supra* note 1353, pp. 22-25.

1378. These forms are provided by the International Federation of Consulting Engineers. See https://fidic.org/node/7089, accessed 20 May 2022.

1379. See *Bayindir* v. *Pakistan*, *supra* note 456, Decision on Jurisdiction (14 November 2005), paras. 14-15.

1380. As happened in *Daimler* v. *Argentina*, *supra* note 97, Award (22 August 2012), paras. 146-153; *MNSS BV and Recupero Credito Acciaio NV* v. *Montenegro*, ICSID Case No. ARB(AF)/12/8, Award (4 May 2016), paras. 158-159, 164. See Chernykh, *supra* note 1353, pp. 15-21.

1381. *Ibid.*, pp. 26-28.

be required to decide on the presupposed status or relationship if its existence or validity is disputed [1382]. For example, a claim on the registration of shares (principal issue) may require a prior decision on the validity of the contract on their transfer (preliminary or incidental issue).

The matter, first raised in the 1930s [1383], is controversial in national courts regarding the application of the *lex fori* or *lex causae*, and no clear preference can be formulated *in abstracto* [1384]. It is clear, however, that as stated in Article 8 of the Inter-American Convention on General Rules of Private International Law, "[p]revious, preliminary or incidental issues that may arise from a principal issue need not necessarily be resolved in accordance with the law that governs the principal issue".

In investment treaty claims, controversies can arise regarding the jurisdiction over a claim for a breach of an international investment contract. The tribunal must then interpret the agreement, which may involve also, for instance, assessing an environmental regulation that modifies the contractual rights. The investor may consider the regulation incompatible with a protection of the investment treaty. In this case, public international law may apply to an incidental question raised in the context of a contractual claim [1385]. If not considered a violation of public international law, the law governing the contract in accordance with private international law will apply [1386].

1382. A. Bonomi, "Incidental (Preliminary) Question", in J. Basedow *et al.* (eds.), *Encyclopedia of Private International Law*, Vol. 1: *Entries A-H*, Cheltenham, Edward Elgar, 2017, 2017, p. 912.

1383. Wilhelm Wengler's work in 1934 was very influential in this regard. George Melchior and Hans Lewald also contributed to the treatment of the issue at the time. See W. Wengler, "The Law Applicable to Preliminary (Incidental) Questions" (1988), in K. Lipstein (ed.), *Private International Law*, Vol. 3 of *International Encyclopedia of Comparative Law*, Tübingen, Mohr Siebeck; Leiden, Martinus Nijhoff, 2011.

1384. A. Bonomi, "Incidental (Preliminary) question", in J. Basedow, G. Rühl, F. Ferrari and P. de Miguel Asensio (eds.), *Encyclopedia of Private International Law*, Vol. 2, Cheltenham, Edward Elgar, 2017, p. 922. Juenger is highly critical on the matter, and states that this self-inflicted embarrassment of private international law cannot be adequately resolved. See Juenger, *supra* note 1201, pp. 196-197.

1385. "If the regulation is adjudged to be contrary to an investment treaty standard, then the only consequence is that the regulation is a nullity; there can be no remedy from international law on that account (i.e., an award of damages for a breach of an international obligation) because the secondary rules of State responsibility do not apply to a claim for breach of contract. The breach is then examined in accordance with the law governing the contract", Douglas, *supra* note 39, p. 50.

1386. The matter was addressed in *AGIP SpA* v. *Government of the People's Republic of the Congo*, 1 ICSID Rep 306.

In this regard, Yuliya Chernykh rightly suggests that the private international law notion of incidental or preliminary question can provide "an essential theoretical framework capable of safeguarding its distinguishable legal nature and ensuring application of the proper law to it" [1387]. Moreover, the conceptualization of the matter as an incidental issue may enable justice to be done without blocking a procedure in investment treaty arbitration. The arbitral tribunal can decide on its jurisdiction without waiting for the issue to be resolved by another adjudicatory body [1388].

G. Capacity

Capacity within international contracts is not regulated in the Hague Principles, and no universal principle exists in this regard. Divergent perspectives emerge from private international law rules. Many jurisdictions consider capacity a matter of personal status, whereas the Restatement (Second) of Conflict of Laws considers it a question of *lex contractus*.

Moreover, different approaches exist in national laws for determining the law applicable to an individual and legal entities (the *lex societatis*, in particular [1389]). Some international instruments also address the matter.

In Latin America, the 1940 Montevideo Treaty adopted criteria of the law of the country within which the company was recognized as a legal person. The 1989 Montevideo Treaty changed this approach and adopted a new criterion in favor of the law of the country in which the company is domiciled. Under the Bustamante Code, the applicable law is that of the place in which the company was constituted [1390].

In turn, in 1979 the OAS advanced the Inter-American Convention on Conflicts of Laws Concerning Commercial Companies, which sets

---

1387. Chernykh, *supra* note 1353, p. 375.

1388. "For investment treaty arbitration, an approach to contract interpretation as the incidental issue means that the jurisdiction of treaty-based tribunals is not blocked until the issue is resolved as the *principal issue* in the relevant contract-based procedures. The tribunals' decisions on the content of contractual provisions thus rendered would not have the same final effect as the decisions of courts or tribunals that exercise contract interpretation in the framework of contractual claims as the *principal* issue" (*ibid.*, pp. 376-377).

1389. Bischoff, *supra* note 15, p. 762.

1390. See C. Lima Marques and C. Fresnedo de Aguirre, "Personas jurídicas", in D. P. Fernández Arroyo *et al.* (ed.), *Derecho Internacional Privado de los Estados del MERCOSUR: Argentina, Brasil, Paraguay, Uruguay*, Buenos Aires, Zavalía, 2003, pp. 557-561.

the place of incorporation as the connecting factor (Art. 2). An identical rule emerges from the 1984 Inter-American Convention on Personality and Capacity of Juridical Persons in Private International Law, which refers to the "law of the place of its organization" (Art. 2).

At a global level, the Hague Convention on the Recognition of the Legal Personality of Foreign Companies, Associations and Institutions includes identical criteria in its Article I, although it did not receive sufficient ratification to enter into force [1391].

Similarly, the Institut de Droit International issued the recommendation that:

> "A company which is recognized in accordance with the preceding provisions enjoys all rights which are conferred upon it by the law by which it is governed, except rights which the State by which it is recognized refuses to grant either to foreign nationals in general or to companies of a corresponding type governed by its own law." [1392]

The matter was addressed by the ICJ in the *Barcelona Traction* case of 1970. The Court stated:

> "[I]nternational law has had to recognize the corporate entity as an institution created by States in a domain essentially within their domestic jurisdiction. This in turn requires that, whenever legal issues arise concerning the rights of States with regard to the treatment of companies and shareholders, as to which rights international law has not established its own rules, it has to refer to the relevant rules of municipal law." [1393]

Issues of capacity may technically arise in investment arbitration, although they rarely do in practice. In the first of the *Amco* v. *Indonesia* cases, the Tribunal held that "one should apply the law of the state of incorporation to determine whether such a company, though dissolved, is still an existing legal entity for any specified legal purpose" [1394]. In this case, the Tribunal chose the place of incorporation as a connecting factor.

1391. Convention of 1 June 1956 concerning the Recognition of the Legal Personality of Foreign Companies, Associations and Institutions, https://www.hcch.net/en/instruments/conventions/full-text/?cid=36, accessed 9 May 2022.

1392. Douglas, *supra* note 39, p. 78.

1393. *Barcelona Traction*, *supra* note 24, para. 38.

1394. 202 (Preliminary Objections) 1 *ICSID Reports*, p. 543, 562.

According to Zachary Douglas, "the law applicable to the issue of whether a legal entity has the capacity to prosecute a claim before an investment treaty tribunal is the *lex societatis*" [1395]. As has been noted, however, the connecting factor can vary in domestic laws between the place of incorporation and the seat of the legal entity [1396].

Despite the differences that exist in different national laws and international instruments, they all share a common goal: to determine the law that has the closest connection to the case, without having to resort to the *lex fori* [1397]. This matter must be distinguished from the discussion in Chapter II regarding whether a claimant company fulfills nationality requirements under the applicable international investment agreement for jurisdictional purposes [1398].

1395. Rule 8 of Douglas, *supra* note 39, p. 78. He invokes the following cases: *Impregilo SpA* v. *Islamic Republic of Pakistan,* ICSID Case No. ARB/03/3 (Preliminary Objections) 12 *ICSID Reports*, p. 245, 269-70/115-24; *(Semble): Amco Asia* v. *Indonesia*, *supra* note 408, No. 2 (Preliminary Objections) 1 *ICSID Reports*, p. 543, 562; *Consortium Groupement LESI-DIPENTA* v. *People's Democratic Republic of Algeria*, ICSID Case No. ARB/03/8 (Preliminary Objections), paras. 38 *(ii)*, 39. *(Semble): Biwater Gauff* v. *Tanzania*, *supra* note 530, Merits, para. 323.

1396. For instance, in the Netherlands, the law of incorporation determines the power of the legal entity "to perform acts and to act at law", and in Switzerland, it governs the "capacity to have and exercise rights and obligations". In Germany, the "real seat" doctrine determines the company's legal status and standing to sue. The ECJ held that this choice of law rule is incompatible with the freedom of establishment guaranteed in the EC Treaty. In that case, the German courts failed to recognize the standing a company that had been incorporated in the Netherlands but had its seat determined to be in Germany. See Überseering BV and Nordic Construction Company Baumanagement GmbH (NCC) (2002) ECR I-09919, 200 Warsaw Session, 1965.

1397. "Although this principle is vague, it is a principle that can and should be applied by tribunals", Bischoff, *supra* note 15, 762.

1398. Article 42.1 of the ICSID Convention deals with the question of whether capacity is included. The consequences may be inappropriate where the parties' choice of a "neutral law" leads that law to be applied where questions arise as to whether the host State's representatives were entitled to agree on a choice of law clause. For instance, the choice of law agreement in *Kaiser* v. *Jamaica* specifically excluded the application of Jamaican rules on capacity "which could throw doubt upon the authority or ability of the Government to enter into the . . . Agreement" (*Kaiser Bauxite Company* v. *Jamaica*, ICSID Case No. ARB/74/3, Jurisdiction and Competence (6 July 1975), para. 12). Considering the clear wording of 42.1, it is not possible to exclude certain questions from the scope of this article. Further support for this conclusion is found in article 42.2, which prohibits *non liquet*. Article 42.1 is the only source for determining the applicable law. In the absence of choice, the *renvoi* provided for in Article 42.1.s.2 of the ICSID Convention will most likely direct the tribunal to the application of the proper law of the company. Thus, the problem emerges when interpreting badly drafted choice of law agreements, rather than in interpreting Art. 42.1 of the ICSID Convention in general. See Bischoff, *supra* note 15, pp. 753-754.

H. Torts and other international conflict of laws instruments

1. Torts

In the Americas, the Montevideo Treaties follow the traditional *lex loci delicti* rule (Art. 38 of the 1889 Treaty, and Art. 43 of the 1940 Treaty)[1399]. Article 167 of the Bustamante Code, in turn, rules that obligations generated by torts follow the law of the jurisdiction where they were committed[1400]. In the United States, the classic *lex loci delicti* rule, included in Section 377 of Beale's first 1934 Restatement of Conflict of Laws was discarded in case law and legal practice. Instead, one should determine the proper law of the tort considering its center of gravity or more significant contacts[1401].

At a global level, the Hague Conference addressed the issue of the law applicable to torts in two conventions: the Hague Convention of 4 May 1971 on the Law Applicable to Traffic Accidents[1402], and the Hague Convention of 2 October 1973 on the Law Applicable to Products Liability[1403].

The Rome II Regulation followed, establishing for the first time in modern history non-contractual rules applicable to all EU Member States except Denmark. Article 28 of the Rome II Regulation establishes that the two Hague Conventions prevail over the norms in their respective contracting States.

The general *lex loci delicti* rule has remained constant throughout these developments, with certain exceptions to party autonomy, both

1399. *Lex loci delictus*, also known as *lex loci delicti*, is the Latin term for "law of the place where the delict [tort] was committed". It holds that the substantive law of the place where the tort occurs applies. For more on the topic, see P. Terblanche, "*Lex Fori* or *Lex Loci Delicti*? The Problem of Choice of Law in International Delicts", *Comparative and International Law Journal of Southern Africa*, Vol. 30, No. 3 (1997), pp. 243–63.

1400. J. Basedow, "Bustamante, Antonio Sánchez de", in J. Basedow *et al.* (eds.), *Encyclopedia of Private International Law*, Vol. 1: *Entries A-H*, Cheltenham, Edward Elgar, 2017, p. 248.

1401. C. Fresnedo de Aguirre, "Obligaciones Extracontractuales", in D. P. Fernández Arroyo *et al.* (ed.), *Derecho Internacional Privado de los Estados del MERCOSUR: Argentina, Brasil, Paraguay, Uruguay*, Buenos Aires, Zavalía, 2003, pp. 1171-1182.

1402. In force since 1975. On its adoption status, see https://www.hcch.net/en/instruments/conventions/status-table/?cid=81, accessed 9 June 2022. See also T. Kadner Graziano, "Products Liability", in J. Basedow *et al.* (eds.), *Encyclopedia of Private International Law*, Vol. 2: *Entries I-Z*, Cheltenham, Edward Elgar, 2017, pp. 1709-1716.

1403. In force since 1977. On its adoption status, see https://www.hcch.net/en/instruments/conventions/status-table/?cid=84, accessed 20 May 2022.

by an *ex post* and an *ex ante* (under certain circumstances) choice of applicable law [1404]. In torts-related disputes, investment tribunals have applied the law of the tort, in accordance with generally accepted principles of private international law [1405].

2. *Property*

Regarding property, both of the Montevideo Treaties on International Commercial Law (Art. 26 of the 1889 Treaty, and Art. 32 of the 1940 Treaty) and the Bustamante Code (Art. 105) apply the *lex loci rei sitae* [1406].

The relevant international instruments, such as the Mexico Convention and the Hague Convention, do not address property-related matters within contracts. Commentary 1.31 of the Hague Principles provides that the Hague Principles "only determine the law governing the mutual rights and obligations of the parties, but not the law governing rights *in rem*"; that is, they do not address matters such as whether the transfer actually conveys property rights without the need for further formalities, or whether the purchaser acquires ownership free of the rights and claims of third parties. Such questions are typically governed by domestic laws specific to conveyances [1407].

According to Douglas,

> "[t]he law applicable to an issue relating to the existence or scope of property rights comprising the investment is the municipal law of the host state, including its rules of private international law" [1408].

1404. Kadner Graziano, *supra* note 1402, pp. 1709-1716. The authoritative text in this regard may be considered: A. A. Dickinson, *The Rome II Regulation: The Law Applicable to Non-Contractual Obligations*, Oxford, Oxford University Press, 2010.

1405. *Lex loci rei sitae* (Latin for "law of the place where the property is situated"), also known as *lex situs*, is the doctrine that the law governing the transfer of title to property is dependent upon and varies with the location of the property. See *Isiah* v. *Bank Mellatt*, IUSCT Case No. 35-219-2 (30 March 1983), 2 IUSCTR, p. 232; *Sea-Land Service*, *supra* note 946.

1406. See B. Pallarés, "Bienes Materiales", in D. P. Fernández Arroyo *et al.* (ed.), *Derecho Internacional Privado de los Estados del MERCOSUR: Argentina, Brasil, Paraguay, Uruguay*, Buenos Aires, Zavalía, 2003, pp. 885-889.

1407. See also the OAS Guide, *supra* note 1284, p. 89.

1408. Douglas, *supra* note 39, p. 52.

This private international law-originated solution was applied in several cases [1409], since public international law does not provide substantive property law rules [1410].

The *lex situs* principle applies for matters related to tangible property. For instance, the domestic law of the land would govern to define the scope of a mortgagee's right over tangible property which comprises the investment. Intangible property is treated differently across the various private international law systems. In some, the law of the domicile of the debtor applies, and the domicile of the creditor applies in others. Where the law of debtor applies and the debtor is domiciled in the host State, investment protection regimes may become available [1411].

If the investment is done in shares, investment protection may also arise when these have been acquired in accordance with the law of the jurisdiction where the company was incorporated. In the United Kingdom, legal ownership commences once the investment is entered onto the share register. For registry to occur, however, it is not sufficient to accept delivery of share certificates, as would be the case in other jurisdictions such as New York [1412].

3. Bonds and loans

International regulation is scarce on issues related to bonds and loans. The League of Nations promoted the Convention Providing a

---

1409. *AIG Capital Partners, Inc. and CJSC Tema Real Estate Company* v. *Republic of Kazakhstan*, ICSID Case No. ARB/01/6, Merits, 11 *ICSID Reports*, p. 7, 48/10.1.4; *Zhinvali* v. *Georgia*, Preliminary Objections, 10 *ICSID Reports*, p. 3, 69/301; *Encana* v. *Ecuador*, *supra* note 570, Merits, p. 476-477/184-188; *Nagel* v. *Czech Republic*, Merits, *supra* note 1373; *SwemBalt* v. *Latvia*, Merits, para. 35; *Saluka* v. *Czech Republic*, *supra* note 563, Merits, para. 204; *Bayview* v. *Mexico*, Preliminary Objections, paras. 98, 102, 118; *Fraport* v. *Philippines*, Preliminary Objections, para. 394; *Azinian* v. *Mexico*, *supra* note 580, Merits, pp. 289/296; *BG* v. *Argentina,* Merits, paras. 102, 117; *Victor Pey Casado and President Allende Foundation* v. *Republic of Chile*, ICSID Case No. ARB/98/2, Award (8 May 2008), paras. 179–230.

1410. Treaties do not either. An exception of an international treaty that does create and regulate rights in rem is the UNIDROIT Convention on International Interests in Mobile Equipment (2001), https://www.unidroit.org/instruments/security-interests/cape-town-convention/, accessed 20 May 2022.

1411. Douglas, *supra* note 39, p. 55. The clearest endorsement of the principle in Rule 4 is the award in *Encana* v. *Ecuador*, *supra* note 570. The Tribunal ruled that "for there to have been an expropriation of an investment or return (in a situation involving legal rights or claims as distinct from the seizure of physical assets) the rights affected must exist under the law which creates them, in this case, the law of Ecuador". A similar statement of principle can be found in *Thunderbird* v. *Mexico*, *supra* note 579, Merits: "compensation is not owed for regulatory takings where it can be established that the investor or investment never enjoyed a vested right in the business activity that was subsequently prohibited" (para. 208). See Douglas, *supra* note 39, p. 56.

1412. *Ibid.*, pp. 52-53.

Uniform Law for Bills of Exchange and Promissory Notes (Geneva 1930) after the Hague Conference failed to regulate the matter in 1910 and 1912. However, the instrument was ratified by twenty-seven countries, mostly from Europe – none from Africa or Oceania and only a few from Asia [1413]. Brazil was the only country in the Americas that adopted the convention, which was approved twenty-two years after the instrument was brought before the Secretary-General of the League of Nations [1414].

In turn, the UN Convention on International Bills of Exchange and International Promissory Notes (New York, 1988) did not receive the necessary ratifications to enter into force [1415].

Regionally, the Montevideo Treaties contained provisions on bills of exchanges and promissory notes (Arts. 26 and 34 of 1889 Treaty and Arts. 32 and 33 of 1940 Treaty). The Bustamante Code also addresses bills of exchange in Articles 263-273.

The Inter-American Convention on Conflict of Laws concerning Bills of Exchange, Promissory Notes, and Invoices, adopted at CIDIP-I in 1975, substituted with its regulation the above Montevideo and Bustamante rules for the countries ratifying the OAS instrument [1416].

Article 5, paragraphs *(c)* and *(d)*, of the Mexico Convention exclude obligations deriving from securities and from secured transactions. The Hague Principles do not contain a similar provision. Rome I deals with securities and pledges or other security rights over claims in Article 14.

A 2016 ICC Commission report notes that localizing an investment in an infrastructure project for the purpose of determining whether an investment treaty applies is different from localizing financial instruments, such as bonds and loans. In the latter case, specific connecting factors need to be considered [1417]. Transnational finance instruments can be designed to avoid conflicts of laws problems by containing choice of law and choice of forum clauses. Loans that do not

---

1413. See https://legacarta.intracen.org/instrument/184980-convention-providing-uniform-law-bills-exchange-promissory-notes/#:~:text=The%20League%20of%20Nations%20Geneva,laws%20related%20to%20these%20documents, accessed 9 May 2022.

1414. Legislative approval was granted in 1964, through the Legislative Decree No. 54 of 1964, and finally entered into force through the Decree No. 57.663 of 24 January 1966, see M. B. Noodt Taquela, "Títulos Valores", in D. P. Fernández Arroyo *et al.* (ed.), *Derecho Internacional Privado de los Estados del MERCOSUR: Argentina, Brasil, Paraguay, Uruguay*, Buenos Aires, Zavalía, 2003, p. 1202.

1415. See https://uncitral.un.org/en/texts/payments/conventions/bills_of_exchange/status, accessed 9 May 2022.

1416. Noodt Taquela, *supra* note 1414, p. 1209, 1212.

1417. ICC Commission Report, *supra* note 91, p. 6.

include a choice of law clause would be subject to the *lex contractus*. Bonds that do not contain a choice of law clause can be reasonably presumed to be subject to the law of the market where the bond was issued, as it has the closest connection to the bond [1418].

4. Secured transactions

The Montevideo Treaties and the Bustamante Code are generally considered to be the first private international law regulations dealing with security rights over movable assets [1419].

At a global level [1420], there were several early attempts to develop a system of international recognition of security rights, including the International Convention of 10 April 1926 for the Unification of Certain Rules relating to Maritime Liens and Mortgages [1421], the International Convention of 6 May 1993 on Maritime Liens and Mortgages [1422] and the Geneva Aircraft Convention in 1948 [1423].

More recently, UNIDROIT, the Hague Conference and UNCITRAL have actively promoted a series of instruments addressing secured transactions [1424].

1418. M. Lehmann, "Guarantees", in J. Basedow *et al.* (eds.), *Encyclopedia of Private International Law*, Vol. 1: *Entries A-H*, Cheltenham, Edward Elgar, 2017, pp. 1709-1716; D. P. Fernández Arroyo, "Modalidades Contractuales Específicas", in D. P. Fernández Arroyo *et al.* (ed.), *Derecho Internacional Privado de los Estados del MERCOSUR: Argentina, Brasil, Paraguay, Uruguay*, Buenos Aires, Zavalía, 2003, p. 1158.

1419. Fernández Arroyo, *ibid.*, p. 1102.

1420. See, in this regard, E. M. Kieninger, "Security Interests in Mobile Equipment (Uniform Law)", in J. Basedow *et al.* (eds.), *Encyclopedia of Private International Law*, Vol. 2: *Entries I-Z*, Cheltenham, Edward Elgar, 2017, pp. 1621-1623.

1421. International Convention for the Unification of certain Rules relating to Maritime Liens and Mortgages, 1926.

1422. International Convention on Maritime Liens and Mortgages, 1993, https://treaties.un.org/pages/ViewDetails.aspx?src=TREATY&mtdsg_no=XI-D-4&chapter=11&clang=_en, accessed 9 May 2022

1423. Convention on the International Recognition of Rights in Aircraft, 1948. For more information https://treaties.un.org/pages/showDetails.aspx?objid=0800000280 14032c, accessed 9 May 2022.

1424. Such as the UNIDROIT Convention on International Factoring (Ottawa, 1988), the UNIDROIT Convention on International Financial Leasing (Ottawa, 1988), the United Nations Convention on the Assignment of Receivables in International Trade (New York, 2001, the UNCITRAL Legislative Guide on Secured Transactions (2007) and Supplement on Security Rights in Intellectual Property (2010), the UNIDROIT Model Law on Leasing (2008), the Convention on the Law Applicable to Certain Rights in Respect of Securities Held with an Intermediary (The Hague, 2006), prepared by the Hague Conference UNIDROIT Convention on Substantive Rules for Intermediated Securities (Geneva, 2009), the "Cape Town" Convention and its Protocols, referred to in the following footnote. for more information on how these instruments complement each other, see UNCITRAL, Hague Conference and UNIDROIT texts on security

Both conflict of laws and "uniform law" solutions emerge from these instruments. As will be seen in the next chapter, uniform law instruments propose substantive rights solutions directly. For instance, the Cape Town Convention (Convention of 16 November 2001 on International Interests in Mobile Equipment) sought to create internationally registered uniform security rights. The Cape Town Convention was a major success and has been ratified by eighty-three countries [1425].

I. The problems with "orthodox" private international law

Private international law has been criticized for being unduly technical, process-driven and, above all, a matter of domestic law [1426]. The discipline has seen the growth of conflict of laws "technocrats" [1427], many of whom preach unintelligibly, with pernicious consequences in the real world [1428]. Private international law experts have often been referred to as "conflictualists" rather than "internationalists", obsessed with the domestication of international relationships [1429].

The difficulties of conflictualism are patent. Conflict of law national rules diverge alarmingly, and the idea of a universal treaty on the matter has been a chimera. Therefore, notorious uncertainty exists regarding the applicable law.

---

interests, comparison and analysis of major features of international instruments relating to secured transactions. See https://uncitral.un.org/sites/uncitral.un.org/files/media-documents/uncitral/en/uncitral-hcch-unidroit-e.pdf, accessed 9 May 2022.

1425. Additional Protocols that are not yet in effect deal with other matters such as space, railway, agricultural, mining and construction equipment. Protocol of 16 November 2001 to the Convention on International Interests in Mobile Equipment on matters specific to aircraft equipment; Luxembourg Protocol of 23 February 2007 to the Convention on International Interests in Mobile Equipment on matters specific to railway rolling stock; Protocol of 9 March 2012 to the Convention on International Interests in Mobile Equipment on matters specific to space assets; and Protocol for Matters Specific to Mining, Agriculture and Construction Equipment (MAC Protocol, https://www.unidroit.org/secured-transactions, accessed 17 June 2022). For the official commentary of the Cape Town Convention, see R. Goode, *Convention on International Interests in Mobile Equipment and Protocol thereto on Matters Specific to Aircraft Objects: Official Commentary*, 5th ed., 2022, https://www.unidroit.org/instruments/security-interests/cape-town-convention/official-commentary/.

1426. V. Ruíz Abou-Nigm, K. McCall Smith and D. French, "Introduction: Systemic Dialogue: Identifying Commonalities and Exploring Linkages in Private and Public International Law", in *id.*, *Linkages and Boundaries in Private and Public International Law*, Oxford, Hart Publishing, 2018, p. 1.

1427. It is thus conceived as domestic private international law. See Audit, *supra* note 1202, p. 3.

1428. Juenger, *supra* note 1201, pp. 134, 262, 320.

1429. R. David, *Los Grandes Sistemas del Derecho Contemporáneo*, Portuguese translation by H. A. Carvalho, 4th ed., São Paulo, Editorial Martins Fontes, 2002, p. 25.

Moreover, in many parts of the world, such as in Russia, Indonesia, China or Latin America, it is often impossible to render an opinion on the domestic law or predict a court decision. Some codes or laws may be so old or heavily amended that it is impossible to know if the text at hand is the appropriate one [1430].

Local peculiarities, legislation, case law and doctrinal developments can often only be handled appropriately by adjudicators and parties practicing in that national jurisdiction, and the situation is even more complicated when one of the parties does not come from the same legal tradition [1431]. A well-known study conducted by Max Rheinstein found that adjudicators erred in the application of the law in thirty-six of the forty cases included in a leading casebook on private international law. In the other four cases, the result was correct, but with flaws in the reasoning [1432]. Evidently, an adjudicator not familiarized with a given national legal system is prone to err when applying a law that they simply do not understand.

In several settings, the application of national law is highly inappropriate, such as when a transaction has so many international components that a domestic legal system cannot govern it [1433].

1430. In some parts of the world, corruption, which makes case law unpredictable, is also a problem "and the price of a judgment can be learned for the asking, of members of local Bars, in American dollars", H. P. Glenn, "An International Private Law of Contract", in P. Borchers and J. Zekoll (eds.), *International Conflict of Laws for the Third Millennium*: *Essays in Honor of Friedrich K. Juenger*, New York, Transnational Publishers, 2001, pp. 58-59.

1431. Regarding, for instance, the terms "consideration", "implied terms", "misrepresentation" or "frustration". Y. Derains, "The ICC Arbitral Process. Part. VIII. Choice of the Law Applicable to the Contract and International Arbitration", *ICC International Court of Arbitration Bulletin*, Vol. 6, No. 1 (1995), foreword.

1432. See O. Lando, "Principles of European Contract Law and UNIDROIT Principles: Moving From Harmonisation to Unification", *Uniform Law Review*, Vol. 8 (2003), p. 126; Kaufmann-Kohler, remembering the cases in which she acted as arbitrator, governed by the laws of Germany, France, England, Poland, Hungary, Portugal, Greece, Turkey, Lebanon, Egypt, Tunisia, Morocco, Sudan, Liberia, Korea, Thailand, Argentina, Colombia, Venezuela, Switzerland, Illinois and New York, asked herself whether she actually knew these legal systems. She answered that, except for the law of New York, which she learned years ago and does not pretend to know today, and the law of Switzerland, which she actively practices, the answer is clearly "no". See Committee on International Commercial Arbitration, "International Commercial Arbitration Committee's Report and Recommendations on Ascertaining the Contents of the Applicable Law in International Commercial Arbitration", *Arbitration International*, Vol. 26, No. 2 (2010), p. 198. Therefore, the possibilities of erring in the application of a foreign law and its interstices are clearly high.

1433. See V. Ruíz Abou-Nigm, "The *'Lex Mercatoria'* and its Current Relevance in International Commercial Arbitration", *DeCITA: direito do comércio internacional / derecho del comercio internacional*, No. 2 (2004), pp. 109-110.

Cyberspace also leaves the territorial conceptions fundamental to the application of most domestic laws without a foundation [1434]. A scholar commenting on the challenges posed by the Internet concluded that "conflicts law is not dead yet but is on its deathbed" [1435].

Moreover, conflict of laws rules reward "forum shoppers" that when feasible pursue litigation in places with rules benefiting their claims, which frustrates the search for certainty and predictability in transactions [1436]. Besides, not infrequently, faced with a dilemma between "conflictual justice" and "material justice" [1437], adjudicators seek to dodge the matter entirely by escaping into concepts such as characterization, international public policy and *fraude à la loi*. Even human rights have been invoked to "limit" what States can do in private international law matters. A landmark decision in this sense was rendered by the German Constitutional Court in 1971 [1438], followed by others such as the Italian Corte di Cassazione in 1987 [1439], and the CJEU [1440].

It is no wonder that Frank Visher characterized private international law as the most debated branch in law, with divergences in its principles, methods and objectives [1441]. David Cavers talks of "six centuries of frustration" [1442], Jean-Paulin Niboyet referred to it as a mental game with infinite complications, and Barbara Bucholz as a labyrinth construed by professors drunk on their own theories. In the words of William Prosser:

1434. L. Lessig, *Code and Other Laws of Cyberspace*, New York, Basic Books, 1999, p. 192.

1435. S. Symeonides, "Private International Law: Idealism, Pragmatism, Eclecticism", *Recueil des cours*, Vol. 384 (2017), p. 352.

1436. Juenger, *supra* note 1311, p. 1138.

1437. Following the terminology of Kegel, see S. C. Symeonides, "Material Justice and Conflicts Justice in Choice of Law", in P. Borchers and J. Zekoll (eds.), *International Conflict of Laws for the Third Millennium: Essays in Honor of Friedrich K. Juenger*, New York, Transnational Publishers, 2001, pp. 125-128.

1438. Decision of 4 May 1971, BverfGE 31, 58 (Spanierenentscheidung).

1439. Decision of 26 February 1897, Corte Constituzionale, No. 71/1987.

1440. For instance, it referred to the four liberties (of movement, persons, services and capital) and the principle of non-discrimination to guarantee recognition of a corporation in member States (*Centros* v. *Erhvervs-og Selskabsstyrelsen*, Case C-212/97, 1999, ECR-I, 1459). See Reimann, *supra* note 1198, pp. 1392-1393. Moreover, as stated by Paulsson, national laws themselves contain corrective norms which are formidable. They can be derived from principles contained, for instance, in the national constitutions, or from ratified treaties; national courts have both the duty and the authority to apply them. J. Paulsson, *The Idea of Arbitration*, Oxford, Oxford University Press, 2013, p. 232.

1441. Visher, *supra* note 1200, p. 21.

1442. Symeonides, *supra* note 1435, p. 352.

> "The realm of the conflict of laws is a dismal swamp, filled with quaking quagmires, and inhabited by learned but eccentric professors who theorize about mysterious matters in a strange and incomprehensible jargon. The ordinary court, or lawyer, is quite lost when engulfed and entangled in it." [1443]

René David refers to orthodox private international lawyers as "champions of the past", fossilized in the four walls of academia [1444] and thus running the risk that new law will be established notwithstanding their teaching of outmoded systems not effective in practice [1445].

Failures such as those described in the paragraphs above lead defenders of orthodox private international law to a methodological pluralism that "because it explains everything . . . explains nothing" [1446], thus adding to the confusion.

J. Recent developments

In his Hague Academy General Course, Symeon Symeonides expressed that today's world is less homogeneous, more mobile and far more complex and multipolar than the world in which Savigny wrote [1447]. In this context, while private international law may be less idealistic and less "pure" than the classical model, "it is richer and more pragmatic, vibrant, sophisticated, flexible, and pluralistic than ever before" [1448].

Domestic nationalization movements and the consolidation of modern States throughout the nineteenth century led to a boom within the field of private international law, understood as a discipline intended to solve "conflicts of national laws". As seen, on a theoretical level, the basis of orthodox "conflictualism" has suffered numerous attacks, and the system has proven ineffective when it comes to responding to the necessities of transnational commercial activity. In today's world, though, things are changing. Private international law is capable of responding to the needs of a multijurisdictional world, characterized by the permeability

1443. W. Prosser, "Interstate Publication", *Michigan Law Review*, Vol. 51 (1952-1953), p. 971.
1444. See David, *supra* note 1429, p. 26.
1445. See *ibid.*, p. 26.
1446. Juenger, *supra* note 1201, p. 254.
1447. Symeonides, *supra* note 1435, pp. 351-352.
1448. *Ibid.*, p. 352.

of national frontiers, the progressive interconnectedness of societies and economies, and the internationalization of individual lives [1449].

Contemporary changes within private international law are significant and have far-reaching impacts. Party autonomy has become consolidated as a principle within international contracts. As such, parties can effectively avoid the unpredictable "conflictualism" that can occur in international transactions by including clear choice of law provisions within their agreements.

In addition, the field of arbitration has developed into a widespread means for solving commercial disputes, providing arbitrators with powerful tools to arrive at appropriate decisions beyond the automatic application of national laws in accordance with conflict of laws mechanisms [1450]. As stated by David, "[a] complete renewal of private international law, as it was conceived in the 19th century, is therefore in view and such a development may be aided to a large extent by commercial arbitration" [1451].

International organizations have responded to the need to harmonize norms governing transborder commercial activities and thus to leave behind the outdated "conflictualism" that exists in this field [1452]. Remarkable efforts to propose norms governing international commercial transactions include those of UNIDROIT, created in 1926 under the auspices of the then League of Nations [1453]; UNCITRAL, established in 1966 [1454]; and private organizations such as the ICC [1455].

1449. "Private International Law is no longer exclusively anchored inside a single legal order reaching towards its fringes, but increasingly departs from a comparative and extra-legal, i.e., economic or social, point of view. This point of view serves as the starting point for private actors – individuals and incorporate bodies alike – for orientating themselves and achieving legal certainty in a multi-jurisdictional environment governing their transnational activities", Basedow, *supra* note 171, p. 36.

1450. D. Fernández Arroyo and M. Moïse Mbengue, "Public and Private International Law in International Courts and Tribunals: Evidence of an Inescapable Interaction", *Columbia Journal of Transnational Law*, Vol. 56, No. 4 (2018), p. 802. See also D. P. Fernández Arroyo, "Denationalising Private International Law: A Law with Multiple Adjudicators and Enforcers", in A. Bonomi and G. P. Romano (eds.), *Yearbook of Private International Law Vol. XX – 2018/2019*, Cologne, Otto Schmidt, 2020, pp. 31-46.

1451. R. David, *Arbitration in International Trade*, Deventer/Boston, Kluwer Law and Taxation Publishers, 1985, p. 351.

1452. Bonell highlights the multiple initiatives toward unification or at least harmonization of national laws as characteristic of our time. See M. J. Bonell, "International Uniform Law in Practice, Or Where the Real Trouble Begins", *American Journal of Comparative Law*, Vol. 38 (1990), pp. 865 *et seq*.

1453. See www.unidroit.org, accessed 9 May 2022.

1454. See www.uncitral.org, accessed 9 May 2022.

1455. See http://www.iccwbo.org, accessed 9 May 2022.

A growing "differentiation" between private international law rules has been occurring within a great variety of legal institutions and for a wide array of conflict of laws issues [1456]. This development goes in hand with the increasing "flexibilization" of conflict of laws rules in order to better cater the legal analysis to the particular needs of the case [1457].

For instance, Article 15.1 of Switzerland's 1987 Code on Private International Law states the following: "The law designated by this Code shall not be applied in those exceptional situations where, in light of all circumstances, it is manifest that the case has only a very limited connection with that law and has a much closer connection with another law". Paul Lagarde notes that escape clauses such as these allow for the applicable rule to be substituted when appropriate [1458].

In addition to increasing "differentiation" and "flexibilization" within public international law, recent years have seen an increasing "materialization" in the field, reflected in the use of public policy *(ordre public)* or alternative connecting factors to achieve substantive results. Uniform law rules adopted in international instruments have progressively gained momentum, many of them formally incorporated by States [1459].

Uniform law and comparative law have become increasingly relevant in this new era of private international law, marked by a strong eclecticism in the search for predictability within private transborder transactions.

1456. Private international law serves many functions. When the objective is to coordinate between multiple legal systems, classical conflict of laws rules may be appropriate. When social, economic or political "integration" is considered, conflict of laws rules designed to incorporate policy considerations may be more appropriate, as occurs with international contract rules. H. Kronke, "Most Significant Relationship, Governmental Interests, Cultural Identity, Integration: 'Rules' at Will and the Case for Principles of Conflict of Laws", *Uniform Law Review*, Vol. 9, No. 3 (2004), p. 476. See also P. Hay, "Flexibility Versus Predictability and Uniformity in Choice of Law: Reflections on Current European and United States Conflicts Law", *Recueil des cours*, Vol. 226 (1991), pp. 396-397.

1457. Basedow, *supra* note 171, pp. 39-40. In Europe, flexibilization has been a tendency since the second half of the twentieth century, M. Reimann, "Domestic and International Conflicts Law in the United States and Western Europe", in P. Borchers and J. Zekoll (eds.), *International Conflict of Laws for the Third Millennium*: *Essays in Honor of Friedrich K. Juenger*, New York, Transnational Publishers, 2001, p. 114. Kegel notes the existence of "pragmatists" in modern European private international law, seeking for workable practical results, Kegel, *supra* note 1264, p. 12.

1458. P. Lagarde, "Public Policy" (1994), in K. Lipstein (ed.), *Private International Law*, Vol. 3 of *International Encyclopedia of Comparative Law*, Tübingen, Mohr Siebeck; Leiden, Martinus Nijhoff, 2011, p. 3.

1459. Basedow, *supra* note 171, p. 40.

Private international law has also experienced a gradual "proceduralization" that has shifted attention away from the choice of the applicable law to a greater focus on procedural issues, such as jurisdiction and the recognition and enforcement of foreign decisions, as well as judicial cooperation across national borders [1460]. An emphasis is thus placed on many other aspects of private international law beyond questions of the applicable law.

Numerous States have also recently updated their domestic legislation in line with these international developments in an attempt to harmonize domestic laws that are relevant to private international law and uniform law [1461].

States no longer have a monopoly on enacting conflict of law rules. In many jurisdictions, private international law is decentralized from within. For instance, in the European Union the States have largely relinquished their legislative power with respect to private international law in favor of developing uniform solutions applicable to all European States. Much of what we describe as domestic private international law now originates outside the domestic sphere of States. Indeed, private international law, like public international law, may now play a regulatory function [1462].

Furthermore, the European Court of Human Rights has repeatedly dealt with the compatibility of private international law with human rights. In various contexts, individual private international law provisions have been held to infringe human rights [1463].

1460. *Ibid.*, p. 40.

1461. "Ever since World War II, there has been a notable growth in the practical significance and utility of Private International Law. Private International Law also clearly emerges from the need felt by legislators in numerous countries to codify existing rules of Private International Law. Andreas Bucher has listed approximately 30 comprehensive statutes that have been enacted worldwide in the 30 years since the Austrian Act of 1978, and the codification movement has kept its pace in the more recent past" (*ibid.*, p. 39). See also Symeonides, *supra* note 1287.

1462. Fernández Arroyo and Moïse Mbengue, *supra* note 1450, p. 802.

1463. "The declaration that a certain rule infringes a human right often relates to a specific factual situation and the result produced by the rule in that context. It is generally the result that offends justice and human rights, not the abstract rule as such. This makes it difficult to infer new and better conflict rules from that case law. The Court's judgments should rather be taken as impulses directed toward the defendant State to reconsider the regulation of a specific area of the law. That may occur at the national level, but an international regulation is often more suited for the cross-border situations at issue", J. Basedow, "The Hague Conference and the Future of Private International Law: A Jubilee Speech", *Rabels Zeitschrift für ausländisches und internationales Privatrecht / Rabel Journal of Comparative and International Private Law*, Vol. 82, No. 4 (2018), pp. 922-943.

Modern private international law can thus be characterized as working toward the goals of coordination, unification and harmonization. Different modalities are employed in this regard, such as formally binding conventions and protocols, non-binding (soft law) instruments and rules, hortatory principles, legislative guidance and best practices [1464].

The conflict of laws methodology did not and will not disappear, however. In matters related to foreign investments specifically, tribunals will continue to make use of conflict of laws rules when necessary or pertinent [1465]. Since private international law has evolved significantly, stakeholders in investment claims must be aware of its developments.

1464. D. Stewart, "How Private International Law Contributes to Economic Development and the Rule of Law", in D. P. Fernández Arroyo and C. Lima Marques (eds.), *Derecho internacional privado y derecho internacional público: un encuentro necesario*, Asunción, CEDEP, 2011, p. 106.

1465. Delaume, *supra* note 961, p. 130.

CHAPTER XI

TOWARD A UNIFORM PRIVATE INTERNATIONAL LAW

A. Uniform law for international contracts

With regard to international contracts in particular, the "conflicts method" exists alongside the "uniform" or "uniform law method" [1466], which is also referred to as the "material" [1467], "privatist" [1468] or "universalist" technique. Thomas Carbonneau writes that the universalist school sees private international law as an evolving body of substantive transnational law [1469]. The conflicts method seeks localization of the relationship in a national law, whereas the uniform method advocates in favor of substantive transnational solutions in international matters [1470].

In transborder transactions, parties should be aware of the law governing their relationship. Surprising foreign legal rules may conflict with this goal. Even when parties choose a third country's law to govern their contract, they often do so mainly for the sake of neutrality. However, parties using a third country's law rarely have an in-depth

---

1466. C. Schmitthoff, *Commercial Law in a Changing Economic Climate*, 2nd ed., London, Sweet & Maxwell, 1981 (orig. 1977), p. 21; C. Schmitthoff, "International Business Law: A New Law Merchant", *Current Law and Social Problems*, Vol. 2 (1961), p. 129; G. Kegel, "The Crisis of Conflict of *Laws*", *Recueil des cours*, Vol. 112 (1964), p. 91; Pereznieto Castro, *supra* note 1278, p. 210.

1467. Or of "progressive materialization". See D. P. Fernández Arroyo, "El derecho internacional privado en el diván – Tribulaciones de un ser complejo", in *Derecho internacional privado y Derecho de la integración, Libro homenaje a Roberto Ruíz Díaz Labrano*, Asunción, CEDEP, 2013, pp. 32-34.

1468. G. A. Lorenzo Idiarte, "¿Cuándo un Contrato es Internacional? Análisis Desde una Perspectiva Regional", in J. Kleinheisterkamp and G. A. Lorenzo Idiarte (eds.), *Avances del Derecho Internacional Privado en América Latina, Liber Amicorum Jürgen Samtleben*, Montevideo, Editorial Fundación de Cultura Universitaria, 2002, p. 107. See also Q. Alfonsín, *Teoría del Derecho Internacional Privado*, Montevideo, Ediciones Idea, 1982, p. 350.

1469. Within this conception, private international law is transformed from a choice of law system to a set of material rules that regulate transnational dealings and activities. T. Carbonneau, "The Remaking of Arbitration: Design and Destiny", in *id.* (ed.), Lex Mercatoria *and Arbitration: A Discussion of the New Lew Merchant*, 2nd ed., The Hague, Juris / Kluwer International, 1998, p. 30.

1470. For an analysis of the "dilemma" and the relationship between the uniform and the conflicts method, see Jayme, *supra* note 894; D. Opertti Badán, "Conflit de lois et droit uniforme dans le droit international privé contemporain dilemme ou convergence?", *Recueil des cours*, Vol. 359 (2012); C. P. Pamboukis, "Droit international privé holistique: droit uniforme et droit international privé", *Recueil des cours*, Vol. 330 (2008), pp. 41 *et seq.*

knowledge of its content, and (for instance) the subtleties of its rules as developed and applied within the case law may be unexpected [1471].

Furthermore, parties often expressly or implicitly wish that their transaction be governed by a neutral law. This situation may occur, for instance, if a contracting party is a State or a State entity. In this case, by selecting a transnational or uniform law, the other party avoids exposure to potential changes in the legal system of the State party and the State does not submit to the law of a foreign country [1472].

In other instances, national laws do not provide answers to questions that may arise in a particular case [1473]. In fact, many national systems are ill-equipped to handle international transactions. For example, a buyer rejecting goods presents more significant issues in an international sale, in which certain obligations not contemplated in municipal laws such as reselling or conservation should be imposed [1474]. The language used within foreign laws and the absence of uniform legal terminology worldwide may also be a problem. On occasion, selecting domestic laws to govern an international contract is unsatisfactory, due to pride or other political reasons. The problem is even more significant when the foreign law is completely unknown to the parties or for whatever reason not wanted at all. Obtaining information on the foreign law

---

1471. F. Bortolotti and F. Mayer (eds.), *The Application of Substantive Law by International Arbitrators* (Dossiers ICC Institute of World Business Law), Paris, ICC Publishing, 2014, p. 8. Berger asks the following question: when the parties choose German law as a neutral body of rules without any knowledge of its subtleties, the arbitral tribunal should apply an awkward long-standing case law in Germany that requires certain standard term clauses to be "bargained for in detail". While this strict formula makes sense in consumer transactions, German law also applies this formula to business transactions, where the presumption of the parties' professional competence would not require the same degree of legal protection. The matter was addressed in an interim award issued in January 2001, rendered by the Arbitral Tribunal in ICC Arbitration No. 10279. The Tribunal decided not to apply the local interpretation, considering that they were dealing with experienced international businesspeople and companies and arguing that it "would be inconsistent with commercial reality". Berger, *supra* note 1124, pp. 80-84.

1472. See J. Lew, L. Mistelis and S. Kröll, *Comparative International Commercial Arbitration*, The Hague, Kluwer Law International, 2003, paras. 18-41, fn. 11.

1473. Such as interests not contemplated in Islamic law; matter decided in the case *SPP* v. *Egypt* (1992), *supra* note 1085. See also Glenn, *supra* note 1430, pp. 58-59.

1474. Moreover, several factors are unique to international transactions, such as the distance between importers and exporters and other requirements such as import and export licenses that depend upon the local authorities or upon other matters. R. David, "The International Unification of Private Law" (1971), in *id.* (ed.), *The Legal Systems of the World/Their Comparison and Unification*, Vol. 2 of *International Encyclopedia of Comparative Law*, Tübingen, Mohr Siebeck; Leiden, Martinus Nijhoff, 2011, pp. 11-12.

may also be extremely time-consuming and costly, posing further complications for the parties.

It must also be considered that contemporary multipartite arrangements for large economic development projects involving a State usually encompass the implementation of industrial, engineering or mining ventures and normally require the combined contributions of suppliers of machinery, equipment and technology, contractors and consulting engineers. In these situations, avoiding potential conflicts between the parties can be a great challenge. The complexity of these contractual frameworks may not find appropriate response in traditional domestic notions of contract law and conflict of law mechanisms [1475].

Therefore, a uniform law should ideally govern international transactions [1476], unless the application of a particular national law is desirable to achieve a specific purpose, for instance, where the parties chose Californian law due to its advanced state of development with regard to high-tech regulation [1477]. Of course, there are matters for which national law is most suited, for instance regarding overriding mandatory rules. This issue is dealt with in Chapter XXI.

B. Tools to achieve a uniform law

The terms "unification" and "harmonization" are often used interchangeably. Strictly speaking, unification implies the adoption of common legal rules by more than one State or region [1478]. By contrast,

---

1475. Delaume, *supra* note 961, p. 115.

1476. Uniform laws are also suitable substantive rules for multi-State problems. A. T. von Mehren and D. T. Trautman, "Jurisdiction to Adjudicate: A Suggested Analysis", *Harvard Law Review*, Vol. 79 (1966), p. 1121; see also A. von Mehren and D. Trautman, *The Law of Multistate Problems*, Boston/Toronto, Little, Brown, and Company, 1965. It is regrettable that the courts have not paid more attention to von Mehren's famous article in the *Harvard Law Review* for special substantive rules on multistate problems. J. A. R. Nafziger, "Memoriam: A. T. von Mehren", *Harvard Law Review*, Vol. 119, No. 7 (2006).

1477. If a party chose a national law because it desired a rigid solution for a specific case, it can state so and thus exclude the possibility of considering other laws or transnational law. See Brunner, *supra* note 836, pp. 30-32.

1478. For the differences between unification and harmonization, see K. Boele-Woelki, "Unifying and Harmonizing Substantive Law and the Role of Conflict of Laws", *Recueil des cours*, Vol. 340 (2010), pp. 299 *et seq*. For Boele-Woelki, "on the one hand, the unification of law is conceived as the process for providing identical rules to different countries, so that the same solution applies universally (or in a given geographical area in which unification is sought). Harmonization of law, on the other hand, indicates the process by which similar or analogous rules are adopted". See also Pamboukis, *supra* note 1470, pp. 42-43.

harmonization provides greater flexibility; it does not necessarily refer to uniform texts but rather to the alignment of legal criteria based on common foundations, model laws or uniform principles. Both conflict of laws rules and substantive laws can be subject to unification and harmonization.

An "international treaty" or "convention" is the instrument traditionally used by States to adopt common rules as part of a unification effort, by building upon existing solutions or creating new ones [1479]. Indeed, many successful treaty instruments have been drafted. However, a drawback of the treaty format is that it can often be difficult to secure ratification. Negotiations between States with different legal traditions or with divergent policy objectives may be challenging, and often require that compromises and concessions be made that result in a final contractual text that is inadequate or even inoperable, which unsatisfied parties ultimately refuse to ratify. In an effort to obtain ratifications, mechanisms such as "reservations" are often used, which create the illusion of unity while ultimately subverting unification. Further complicating the issue, drafters usually exclude the issues on which no consensus has been reached. As such, although treaties continue to abound, they also have their limitations.

International treaties may pose limitations as they are relatively inflexible and may be incapable of responding to changes in rapidly evolving commercial practices. Treaties are often not drafted to account for such commercial changes, which poses additional interpretive challenges.

Conventions on commercial law subjects frequently seek to codify certain commercial usages, customs or practices as "law". However, when treaties are drafted by State governments rather than by the merchants whom the treaties will supposedly serve, such instruments may fail to gain widespread acceptance precisely because they do *not* reflect community practices or perceptions. One must keep in mind, however, that the role of the State is also to safeguard the interests and rights of those who are not part of the dominant voice within the mercantile community.

Other uniform law texts that operate within the context of international treaties include the Convention Providing a Uniform Law for Bills of

1479. An example of the adoption of common rules is the term "party autonomy", which can be found in the 1955 Hague Sales Convention. The term "party autonomy" has subsequently become so widespread that it has become a common term to express the principle in many subsequent instruments.

Exchange and Promissory Notes (Geneva, 1930) and the Convention Providing a Uniform Law for Cheques (Geneva, 1931) [1480]. These two conventions set out uniform laws that contracting States agreed to introduce into their legislations. Today, these mechanisms have largely been discarded; Since uniform laws are designed to be incorporated in their entirety into domestic law, they are often seen as infringing on States' sovereign authority to create legislation within their jurisdiction.

To remedy these challenges posed by uniform law mechanisms, the concept of the "model law" was devised. A model law is an instrument drafted by an eminent organization that subsequently recommends its adoption by States. The UNCITRAL Model Law on International Commercial Arbitration (UNCITRAL Model Law) is an example of this kind of instrument [1481]. However, true unification is often not achieved through the drafting and adoption of model laws either since national legislators may revise, adapt or even disregard model law provisions. The more general the subject matter of the model law, the greater the likelihood that national legislators will ignore its provisions.

Additional "soft law" methods exist that aim at legal harmonization. Contrary to "hard law" texts, States are not expected to formally adopt a wide variety of instruments through treaty ratification or legislation. Nonetheless, these instruments can still have a significant influence upon the practice and development of the law. Soft law legal methods may generate a type of "statement of the law", also called "principles". Soft law also includes legislative guides that offer examples of draft texts in the form of rules and regulations and other types of guides and like instruments [1482].

Examples of soft law instruments include the UN Convention on the Assignment of Receivables in International Trade (New York, 2001), which promotes the availability of capital and credit at more affordable rates across national borders and facilitates the movement of goods and services across borders. The UN Legislative Guide on Secured Transactions (2007) builds on the UN Convention on the Assignment

---

1480. Convention Providing a Uniform Law for Bills of Exchange and Promissory Notes, 7 June 1930, Geneva, 143 UNTS 257; Convention Providing a Uniform Law for Cheques, 1 January 1934, Geneva, 143 UNTS 355.

1481. UNCITRAL Model Law on International Commercial Arbitration, adopted 21 June 1985, with amendments adopted in 2006, https://uncitral.un.org/sites/uncitral.un.org/files/media-documents/uncitral/en/19-09955_e_ebook.pdf, accessed 9 May 2022.

1482. On soft law and hard law, see further in Mazzoni and Malaguiti, *supra* note 30, pp. 135 *et seq*. See also Chap. XI, *infra*.

of Receivables in International Trade and applies to transactions that create a security right in a movable asset, with a view to promoting the availability of secured credit [1483]. In 2016, a legislative guide was proposed on the matter [1484].

C. Relevant uniform law instruments

Several uniform law instruments exist, but two are particularly germane as they address choice of law issues related to international contracts and investment arbitration: the UN Convention on Contracts for the International Sale of Goods (CISG) [1485], and the UNIDROIT Principles of International Commercial Contracts. Additionally, there are also some important ongoing regional efforts to develop uniform laws on contracts as well as private sector initiatives that have been influenced by other arbitral instruments.

1. UN Convention on Contracts for the International Sale of Goods

Known widely by its English acronym, UNCITRAL was established in 1966 under the aegis of the United Nations with the objective of "the promotion of the progressive harmonization and unification of the law of international trade". Its general mandate is to reduce and eliminate barriers created by differences between domestic laws that govern international trade and commerce.

1483. The UNCITRAL Legislative Guide on Secured Transactions: Supplement on Security Rights in Intellectual Property (2010) supplements the Legislative Guide in developing laws that make credit more available and at a lower cost to intellectual property owners and other intellectual property rights holders. The UNCITRAL Guide on the Implementation of a Security Rights Registry (2013) builds on the Legislative Guide and its Supplement to assist States in the establishment of a publicly accessible registry in which information about the potential existence of a security right in a movable asset may be registered. In 2011, UNCITRAL approved the UNCITRAL, Hague Conference and UNIDROIT Texts on Security Interests to assist policymakers and legislators in comparing and analyzing the major features of international instruments relating to secured transactions. See https://uncitral.un.org/en/texts/securityinterests, accessed 9 May 2022.

1484. In 2017, UNCITRAL proposed a Guide to Enactment (2017) to explain the thrust of the Model Law and its relationship with other UNCITRAL texts on secured transactions. In 2019, UNCITRAL adopted the Practice Guide to the UNCITRAL Model Law on Secured Transactions, which illustrates the types of secured transactions that can be undertaken under the Model Law and provides step-by-step explanations of how to engage in the most common and commercially important secured transactions. See https://uncitral.un.org/en/texts/securityinterests, accessed 9 May 2022.

1485. United Nations Convention on Contracts for the International Sale of Goods, concluded 11 April 1980, entered into force on 1 January 1988, 1489 UNTS 3.

One of the well-known products of UNCITRAL is the CISG, which was adopted in 1980 and entered into force in 1988 [1486]. Peter Huber has referred to the CISG as one of the success stories in the international unification of the law [1487], as it amalgamates the substantive law on the international sale of goods among its contracting States, addresses aspects of contract formation for the international sale of goods, provides substantive rights for the buyer and the seller and deals with matters related to the fulfillment and non-fulfillment of each of these obligations.

Many of these issues dealt with by the CISG are common to contracts in general. In fact, several State contract laws are drawn from the provisions of the CISG, which has become the prototype for almost all subsequent contract legislation [1488], and more reform occurred within the field in the first twenty years after the CISG entered into force than in the fifty years prior to its drafting [1489]. In addition, in some States the CISG has been used by judges to interpret or supplement domestic law [1490].

The CISG has been referred to as a common law "Trojan Horse" within the civil law [1491] since it has brought many common law solutions into the civil law. The massively positive reception of the CISG within national legislation in many regions and its widespread use in domestic case law both demonstrate its unifying power.

Testifying to its widespread influence, the CISG has been ratified by more than ninety States worldwide [1492]. It is estimated that at least

---

1486. Studies leading to the drafting of the CISG were initially published by the remarkable comparatist Ernst Rabel in 1936. Gerber, *supra* note 898, p. 196.

1487. P. Huber, "Some Introductory Remarks on the CISG", *Internationales Handelsrecht*, Vol. 6 (2006). Similar remarks are made in Zimmermann, *supra* note 134, p. 119.

1488. R. Goode, "International Restatements of Contract and English Contract Law", *Uniform Law Review*, Vol. 231, No. 1 (1997), p. 236.

1489. J. Basedow, "Towards a Universal Doctrine of Breach of Contract: The Impact of the CISG", *International Review of Law and Economics*, Vol. 25 (2005), p. 487.

1490. For instance, in Brazil, see *Diário de Justiça do Estado do Rio Grande do Sul* (DJE), Appellate Court of the State of Rio Grande do Sul, Case No. 70072362940, Twelfth Chamber, 16 February 2017. See also in El Salvador, Second Civil and Commercial Court of San Salvador, 28 February 2013, Ruling No. PC-29-12, to cite some examples.

1491. P. Schlechtriem, "The German Act to Modernize the Law of Obligations in the Context of Common Principles and Structures of the Law of Obligations in Europe", *Oxford University Comparative Law Forum* (2002), https://ouclf.law.ox.ac.uk/the-german-act-to-modernize-the-law-of-obligations-in-the-context-of-common-principles-and-structures-of-the-law-of-obligations-in-europe/, accessed 9 May 2022.

1492. Status of CISG Membership, http://www.uncitral.org/uncitral/en/uncitral_texts/sale_goods/1980CISG_status.html, accessed 9 May 2022.

two-thirds of world commerce is or could be governed by the CISG, if not excluded expressly by the contracting parties [1493]. Despite its wide acceptance, contracting parties may decide to exclude its application or, subject to certain limitations, abrogate or vary the effect of its provisions (Art. 6, CISG) [1494]. As the CISG recognizes the principle of party autonomy, the exclusion or variation of any of the provisions of the CISG may be achieved by choosing the law of a non-contracting State or the internal domestic substantive law of a contracting State to govern the parties' contract (for example, a national civil commercial code). This possibility of allowing a national law to be chosen by opting out of the CISG may have significant consequences in jurisdictions where national law does not fully recognize party autonomy [1495].

Conversely, even if it has not been ratified by the State of the contracting parties involved in a dispute, the CISG may be implemented as an expression of non-State law when adjudicators are authorized to apply uniform law as the governing law [1496]. However, this issue continues to be the subject of much debate.

1493. P. Huber, "Comparative Sales Law", in M. Reimann and R. Zimmermann (eds.), *The Oxford Handbook of Comparative Law*, Oxford, Oxford University Press, 2006, p. 954.

1494. Some commentators have stated that contracting parties often choose to exclude application of the CISG. However, the actual percentage of parties that choose to opt out of the CISG has been the object of several studies that have yielded different results, in light of the different methodologies used. Recent comprehensive studies have been carried out by Gustavo Moser. See L. G. M. Moser, *Rethinking Choice of Law in Cross-Border Sales*, The Hague, Eleven International, 2018, pp. 25-32. Moser states: "Whilst the rate of CISG opt-out cannot be overlooked and should be further discussed and investigated, a commonality to note among all these studies is that such rate appears to be linked to 'lack of familiarity' with the CISG and perhaps a 'fear of the unknown'. However, the claim that the CISG is 'widely excluded' is not supported by empirical evidence" (p. 31). Anecdotal evidence indicates that opting out is often related to dependency patterns, without full consideration of the underlying reasons. The current general trend appears to be toward further acceptance of the CISG, rather than less.

1495. See L. Castellani and C. Emery, "UNCITRAL Perspectives on the Hague Principles", in D. Girsberger, T. Kadner Graziano and J. L. Neels (eds.), *Choice of Law in International Commercial Contracts: Global Perspectives on the Hague Principles*, Oxford, Oxford University Press, 2021, p. 179.

1496. The CISG can be applied as an expression of "general principles of international trade" (see, for example, *Steel Bars Case*, ICC Arbitration Case No. 6653, March 1993). It can also be applied as an expression of "general standards and rules of international contracts" (see, for example, *Printed Banknotes Case*, ICC Arbitration Case No. 9474, February 1999). Moreover, the CISG can be applied as an expression of "trade usages" (see, for example, *Cowhides Case*, ICC Arbitration Case No. 7331, 1994; *Hotel Materials Case*, ICC Arbitration Case No. 7153, 1992). Originally cited in C. R. Emery and J. Salasky, "Arbitration and UNCITRAL's Sales Conventions", *Slovenska arbitražna praksa*, Vol. 2, No. 1 (2013), https://ssrn.com/abstract=2394516, accessed 9 May 2022, pp. 28-34.

Judicial and arbitral interpretations of the CISG have also expanded its influence. Hundreds of cases dealing with the CISG, including judicial decisions and arbitral awards, have been made available on the UNCITRAL website [1497].

2. *UNIDROIT Principles of International Commercial Contracts*

Also known as the "Rome Institute", UNIDROIT was created in 1926 under the auspices of the League of Nations. Its purpose is to modernize and harmonize private international law, with a primary focus on commercial law. UNIDROIT currently counts more than sixty member States [1498].

UNIDROIT's efforts are directed toward the development of material solutions to international commercial problems. In other words, the organization has embarked on a quest for the development of a "uniform substantive law" and only exceptionally toward the drafting of "conflict of laws" rules. UNIDROIT has been in existence for over ninety years, during which time it has generated over sixty texts (including conventions) and conducted numerous studies that have led to the creation of model laws and guides on a wide range of subjects [1499].

From among these efforts, the drafting of the UNIDROIT Principles is one of the most significant accomplishments. The UNIDROIT Principles was first published in 1994, although work on the subject began in the 1970s. The 1994 edition of the UNIDROIT Principles contains a preamble and rules (or articles) relating to general contract provisions, contract formation, validity, interpretation, content, performance and non-performance. These rules are accompanied by detailed commentary, including illustrations, all of which form an integral part of the UNIDROIT Principles. Given that the same thirteen OAS member States were members of UNIDROIT at the time of the adoption of the

1497. See https://uncitral.un.org/en/texts/salegoods; also UNILEX database on CISG, http://www.unilex.info/instrument/cisg, accessed 9 May 2022.

1498. Current UNIDROIT Membership available at https://www.unidroit.org/about-unidroit/membership, accessed 9 May 2022.

1499. In this way, UNIDROIT has an ample mandate: in principle, no private international law topic is excluded from its application, L. Ferrari Bravo, "La contribución de UNIDROIT al proceso de unificación del derecho privado", in F. Mestre-Lafay and P. Nissing de Seume (eds.), *Los Principios de UNIDROIT: ¿Un derecho común de los contratos para. las Américas? : actas : hacia un nuevo régimen para la contratación mercantil internacional : los principios de UNIDROIT sobre los contratos comerciales internacionales : Valencia, Venezuela-6-9 noviembre 1996*, Rome, UNIDROIT, 1998, p. 14.

UNIDROIT Principles in 1994, that work can be assumed to reflect the consensus reached with the direct or indirect involvement of these States [1500].

A revised and enlarged version of the UNIDROIT Principles was released in 2004, with the addition of five chapters on agents, third-party rights, damages, assignment of rights, transfer of obligations, assignment of contracts and limitation periods. The 2010 edition, in turn, addressed new topics on joint and several obligations and the invalidity of contracts covering unlawful or immoral subject matter. The most recent version is the 2016 edition, which better takes into account matters related to long-term contracts, which may be relevant in both international commercial contracts and foreign investment contracts.

To support the use of the UNIDROIT Principles, in 2013 UNIDROIT approved the Model Clauses for the Use of the UNIDROIT Principles. The Model Clauses are

> "primarily based on the use of the UNIDROIT Principles in transnational contract and dispute resolution practice, *i.e.*, they reflect the different ways in which the UNIDROIT Principles are actually being referred to by parties or applied by judges and arbitrators" [1501].

The Model Clauses are offered for parties wishing to make reference to the UNIDROIT Principles in different contexts: as the rules of law governing the contract, as terms incorporated into the contract, as a tool to interpret and supplement the CISG when the latter is chosen by the parties and as a tool to interpret and supplement the applicable domestic law, including any international uniform law instrument incorporated into that law [1502].

Judicial and arbitral interpretations of the UNIDROIT Principles have also expanded their influence. Many of these court deci-

1500. See OAS Guide, *supra* note 1309.

1501. Model Clauses for the Use of the UNIDROIT Principles of International Commercial Contracts, https://www.unidroit.org/instruments/commercial-contracts/upicc-model-clauses, accessed 9 May 2022. See also M. J. Bonell, "Model Clauses for the use of the UNIDROIT Principles of International Commercial Contracts", *Uniform Law Review*, Vol. 18, Nos. 3-4 (2013), pp. 473-475.

1502. UPICC Model Clauses, *ibid.* For the use of the UNIDROIT Principles, in general, see J. A. Estrella Faria, "The Influence of the UNIDROIT Principles of International Commercial Contracts on National Laws", *Uniform Law Review*, Vol. 21 (2016).

sions and arbitral awards have been compiled in the UNILEX database [1503].

The drafting of the UNIDROIT Principles was influenced by the "Restatements" prepared by the American Law Institute, an organization of eminent jurists in the United States that organizes, summarizes and "restates" predominant trends in jurisprudence within various fields of domestic law. Although similar in appearance to the rules contained in codes of civil law jurisdictions, these Restatements do not share that same legal status in the United States [1504].

Therefore, rather than the word "restatement", the term "principles" was selected to capture the non-State character of the UNIDROIT Principles. Evidently, the drafters wished to ensure that the UNIDROIT Principles would be free from possible semantic connotations suggestive of the world's predominant civil and common law systems. As such, the drafters intentionally did not refer to the UNIDROIT Principles as a code, which implies legislative sanctioning, nor as a restatement. Instead taking advantage of the vagueness of the term, the drafters decided to refer to them as "principles". Technically, however, most of the legal norms within the UNIDROIT Principles are expressed as precise rules, not principles in a broader and more general sense.

The objective of the UNIDROIT Principles is to serve as a central and fundamental instrument within international commercial law in various contexts. For legislators, the UNIDROIT Principles may serve as a source of inspiration for contract law reforms. In fact, the UNIDROIT Principles, among other international influences, were considered during the revision process of the Argentine Civil and Commercial Code, the law of obligations in Germany, contract law in the Republic of China and in various African countries [1505].

For contracting parties that are subject to different legal systems or that speak different languages, the UNIDROIT Principles can serve as a guideline for drafting their contracts and can offer a neutral body of law (akin to a *lingua franca*) [1506]. This may be accomplished in different

1503. For more information, see http://www.unilex.info/instrument/principles, accessed 9 May 2022.

1504. However, although the aim is to describe rules adopted by courts, at times, they also offer suggestions that would amount to changes in the law.

1505. See Estrella Faria, *supra* note 1502, p. 238.

1506. K. P. Berger, "International Arbitral Practice and the UNIDROIT Principles of International Commercial Contracts", *American Journal of Comparative Law*, Vol. 46, No. 1 (1998), p. 129. As stated by Mayer, if the contract without law is not theoretically inconceivable, the submission of an international contract to non-State rules such as the UPICC is lesser so. The arbitrator can apply these rules exactly in the same way that

ways. For instance, the UNIDROIT Principles may serve as a source of legal terminology. In civil law systems, the terms "debtor" and "creditor" are used, whereas in common law, the terms "obligor" and "obligee" are preferred, with the terms "debtor" and "creditor" only being used when monetary payments are involved. To bridge this gap, the UNIDROIT Principles use the terms "obligor" and "obligee" "to better identify the party performing and the party receiving performance of obligations . . . irrespective of whether the obligation is nonmonetary or monetary" [1507]. In addition, the UNIDROIT Principles may serve as a checklist for parties to ensure that they have included all potentially relevant provisions in their international contracts.

Moreover, parties to international contracts may directly choose the UNIDROIT Principles as the applicable law. The selection of the UNIDROIT Principles may be combined with the choice of domestic law to cover supplementary issues, considering that the Principles alone may not be sufficient in all circumstances and may need to be complemented by a more comprehensive regime as is usually provided by national law. However, the reverse is also possible: the UNIDROIT Principles can serve as a "means of interpreting and supplementing domestic law". If entitled to do so, adjudicators may also apply the UNIDROIT Principles in situations in which the parties have not chosen an applicable law, rather than having to resort to conflict of laws mechanisms [1508].

The UNIDROIT Principles [1509] is "perhaps the strongest candidate for treatment as non-State law in the international commercial arbitration context". They have given a new impetus to non-State law or *lex mercatoria* [1510], providing it a concrete existence [1511]. Dieter Martiny considers the *lex mercatoria* to not even qualify as non-State law because it does not meet the requirement of being a set of rules [1512]. By contrast, the UNIDROIT Principles can be "grasped by the hand"

---

they apply State rules. See P. Mayer and V. Heuzé, *Droit International Privé*, 7th ed., Paris, Montchrestien, 2001, p. 477.

1507. UNIDROIT Principles, Article 1.11, Comment 4.

1508. See A. Garro M. and J. A. Moreno Rodríguez (eds.), *Use of the UNIDROIT Principles to Interpret and Supplement Domestic Contract Law* (*Ius Comparatum*: Global Studies in Comparative Law, Vol. 51), Cham, Springer, 2021.

1509. Bermann, *supra* note 11, p. 358.

1510. Berger, *supra* note 1506, p. 519.

1511. J. D. M. Lew, "The UNIDROIT Principles as Lex Contractus Chosen by the Parties and Without an Explicit Choice-of-Law Clause. The Perspective of Counsel", in *ICC Ct. Bull.* Special 2002.

1512. D. Martiny, "Die Haager Principles on Choice of Law in International Commercial Contracts", *Rabels Zeitschrift für ausländisches und internationales*

and after an analysis of arbitral cases, Allan Farnsworth concludes that arbitrators consider them an expression of general principles of international commercial law or *lex mercatoria* [1513]. In fact, the UNIDROIT Principles have been used in arbitration when arbitrators are called upon to adjudicate according to international usages or custom or general principles of international commerce [1514]. Moreover, they have been used for interpretive or supplementary purposes and are regularly consulted by arbitral tribunals [1515]. Indeed, all seven chapters of the 1994 version of the UNIDROIT Principles have been referred to by arbitrators in their decisions [1516].

For courts and arbitral tribunals, the UNIDROIT Principles may provide the necessary criteria to interpret and supplement existing international instruments such as the CISG as well as national laws [1517].

A recent report issued by the International Academy of Comparative Law finds that, in most national jurisdictions surveyed, the UNIDROIT Principles are interpreted alongside other national or international legal

---

Privatrecht / Rabel Journal of Comparative and International Private Law, Vol. 79, No. 3 (2015), p. 638.

1513. E. A. Farnsworth, "The Role of the UNIDROIT Principles in International Commercial Arbitration (2): A US Perspective on their Aims and Application", in *ICC Ct. Bull.* Special 2002, p. 22. See also L.G. Radicati di Brozolo, "Arbitrage commercial international et lois de police : considérations sur les conflits de juridictions dans le commerce international", *Recueil des cours*, Vol. 315 (2005), p. 842 *in fine.* Brozolo mentions the 2010 ICSID case *Lemire* v. *Ukraine*, *supra* note 547, in which it was determined that the UNIDROIT Principles should not be considered a traditional source of law: they are a manifestation of transnational law (*ibid.*, p. 844).

1514. Several decisions illustrating this principle appear in the UNILEX database. Only recently, the China Justice Observer website referred to a CIETAC arbitration case in which the UNIDROIT Principles were applied for the first time under the CIETAC rules. In this case, the parties chose Singapore law as the applicable law. Given that Singapore law was unclear, the Arbitral Tribunal presumed – with the agreement of the parties – that the UNIDROIT Principles were consistent with Singapore law and were therefore applicable, unless one party could prove otherwise. See https://www.chinajusticeobserver.com/a/chinas-first-public-arbitration-case-under-the-unidroit-principles, accessed 9 May 2022.

1515. H. Kronke, "The UNIDROIT Principles of International Commercial Contracts", in *ICC Ct. Bull.* Special 2002.

1516. Mayer and Heuzé, *supra* note 1506, pp. 106-107.

1517. Regarding the use of the UNIDROIT Principles to interpret and complement the CISG, see Castellani and Emery, *supra* note 495, pp. 182 ff. For the authors, "It may be appropriate to use the UNIDROIT Principles to interpret and complement the CISG in those cases when the two texts share common principles. However, this may not be possible when the CISG and the UNIDROIT Principles adopt different approaches. Moreover, the States that adopted the CISG did not consent to having those general principles elaborated upon or supplanted by a different body at a different time" (p. 182). The authors also noted that, "In recognition of this issue, the UNCITRAL Secretariat made written submissions, proposing, for example, an alternative draft that made reference first to the principles underlying the CISG and then recourse to the UNIDROIT Principles" (pp. 182-182).

sources [1518]. Several examples also appear in a recent study released by the International Bar Association [1519].

The next chapter will extensively discuss the use of the UNIDROIT Principles within investment arbitration beyond its originally envisaged application to commercial law matters.

3. Regional unification efforts

Over roughly the same period, a group of academics known as the Commission on European Contract Law – many of whom were also involved in the drafting of the UNIDROIT Principles – began efforts to develop a uniform law instrument. Although non-governmental, the group was created by the European Parliament [1520], and included representatives from all member States of the EU. Its efforts have resulted in a body of work known generally as the Principles of European Contract Law (PECL) [1521].

The PECL were published in 1995 (Part I), 1999 (Parts I and II jointly) and 2003 (Part III). Several provisions of the PECL are identical or very similar to those of the UNIDROIT Principles. In addition to rules, commentary and illustrations, the PECL contain valuable notes on European comparative law as well.

1518. Garro and Moreno Rodríguez, *supra* note 1508, pp. 68-69:

> "In fact, the UNIDROIT Principles are rarely applied on their own in the absence of the parties' choice and the parties rarely choose the Principles as the applicable law. And when the Principles are chosen, more often than not they are not applied as a whole to the exclusion of any other law . . . Yet, looking back at the number of arbitral awards and judicial decisions that have acknowledged the role played by the UNIDROIT Principles over time, one is left with the impression that the Principles continue to offer a comprehensive and well-balanced legal regime that will continue to gain in influence internationally. In fact, even in those jurisdictions where the courts are unlikely to cite the UNIDROIT Principles, their leading commentaries on domestic contract law rarely fail to make some comparative reference to some individual UPICC provisions while discussing domestic contract law issues."

1519. "In most cases, the UNIDROIT Principles are used as a means of interpreting and supplementing the applicable domestic law" (Perspectives in Practice of the UNIDROIT Principles 2016: Views of the IBA Working Group on the Practice of the UNIDROIT Principles 2016, Foreword, p. 5).

1520. Resolution A2-157/89, and then again in 1994 (Resolution A3-0329/94). Most of the members of the committee were academics from the fifteen Member States but did not receive instructions from their governments. See O. Lando, "Principles of European Contract Law", paper presented at the EU-Japan Legal Dialogue (Contracts) Symposium, Kyoto, Japan, 21-22 November 1996, p. 10.

1521. See https://www.trans-lex.org/400200/_/pecl/, accessed 9 May 2022; Cf. O. Lando and H. Beale (eds.), *Principles of European Contract Law Parts I and II*, The Hague, Kluwer Law International, 2000.

The PECL have not received any formal recognition by the EU [1522]. However, arbitral precedents have invoked them, such as ICC Case No. 10022 of 2000 involving a common commercial usage [1523]. The House of Lords had already cited them by 2001 in *Director General of Fair Trading* v. *First National Bank* [1524].

Another academic initiative has resulted in the soft law instrument known as the Draft Common Frame of Reference (DCFR), which was drafted in a similar way to the PECL [1525]. The European Parliament welcomed the presentation of the DCFR in 2008 and, while recognizing it as "merely an academic document" with the next steps being "a highly political exercise", it pointed out that in the future, the document may range "from a non-binding legislative tool to the foundation for an optional instrument in European contract law" [1526].

Both the PECL and the DCFR may lead to the development of additional instruments in the future that might include the possibility of choosing the PECL as the applicable law, which Rome I does not currently allow. In its preamble, Rome I specifies that it may be incorporated into contracts by direct reference and, should the EU adopt substantive law rules, the parties may choose those rules as well [1527].

1522. See discussion in Commission of the European Communities, Communication from the Commission to the Council and the European Parliament on European Contract Law, Brussels, 11.07.201. COM (2001) 398 Final, https://eur-lex.europa.eu/legal-content/EN/TXT/?uri=CELEX:52001DC0398, accessed 9 May 2022.

1523. See www.unilex.info, accessed 9 May 2022.

1524. Von Bar, *supra* note 929, p. 126. Another academic initiative has resulted in the *soft law* instrument known as the Draft Common Frame of Reference (DCFR), the drafting technique of which was very similar to that used for the PECL. C. von Bar, E. Clive and H. Schulte-Nölke (eds.), *Principles, Definitions and Model Rules of European Private Law: Draft Common Frame of Reference (DCFR)*, Berlin, De Gruyter, 2008. The European Parliament welcomed the presentation of the DCFR in 2008 and, while recognizing it as "merely an academic document" with the next steps as "a highly political exercise", pointed out that in the future, the document may range "from a non-binding legislative tool to the foundation for an optional instrument in European contract law" (European Parliament resolution of 3 September 2008 on the common frame of reference for European contract law, OJ C 295 E/91. 4 December 2009). See, on the relationship of this instrument with the UNIDROIT Principles, M. J. Bonell and R. Peleggi, "UNIDROIT Principles of International Commercial Contracts and Draft Common Frame of Reference: A Synoptical Table", *Uniform Law Review*, Vol. 14 (2009), pp. 437-554.

1525. *Principles, Definitions and Model Rules of European Private Law, Draft Common Frame of Reference (DCFR)*, C. von Bar, H. Schulte-Nölke *et al.* (eds.), 2008.

1526. EP resolution (2008), OJ C 295 E/91, *supra* note 1524.

1527. Perambulatory paragraphs 13 and 14, respectively. Proposal for a Regulation of the European Parliament and of the Council on a Common European Sales Law, COM/2011/0635 final – 2011/0284 (COD), https://eur-lex.europa.eu/legal-content/en/TXT/?uri=CELEX:52011PC0635, accessed 9 May 2022. See also Kadner Graziano, Garcimartín Alférez and Van Calster, *supra* note 1306, pp. 749-778.

In the Americas, by comparison, efforts toward a process of regional integration have not led to the advancement of any official uniform law initiatives [1528]. Article 1 of the Treaty of Asunción (establishing the Southern Common Market, also known as MERCOSUR) is noteworthy as it refers to the commitment by State Parties "to harmonize their legislation in relevant areas in order to strengthen the integration process". However, this initiative has not been realized in respect of uniform law [1529].

In Africa in 2002, the OHADA Council of Ministers began drafting a uniform act on the law of contracts with the support of UNIDROIT. After completing the preparatory work and consultations with experts from OHADA member States, a preliminary draft of the Uniform Act on Contract Law was finalized. Based on the UNIDROIT Principles, this first preliminary draft encompassed only substantive contract law rules. In December 2007, the OHADA Council of Ministers decided to relaunch the preparation of the Uniform Act on Contract Law with the Foundation for Continental Law. OHADA and the Foundation for Continental Law created a working group that submitted a preliminary draft of the Uniform Act on the Law of Obligations for the OHADA Region to the OHADA Council of Ministers in 2015 [1530]. The document is still pending approval as of 2022.

4. *Private sector harmonization initiatives*

Harmonization is promoted not only by public organizations, but by private sector initiatives as well.

One type of instrument that has been designed to promote harmonization is referred to as "standardized terms". Notably, the ICC advances several normative instruments that can be incorporated

---

1528. A group of scholars of the region prepared Principles of Latin American Contract Law, see http://pldc.uexternado.edu.co/, accessed 9 May 2022. Its impact in practice remains to be seen. A recent newcomer to the field of codification is the Organization for the Harmonization of Business Law in the Caribbean (OHADAC), whose work to prepare OHADAC Principles on International Commercial Contracts could contribute toward garnering support from Caribbean States, see http://www.ohadac.com/, accessed 9 May 2022.

1529. Treaty establishing a Common Market between the Argentine Republic, the Federal Republic of Brazil, the Republic of Paraguay and the Eastern Republic of Uruguay (Common Market of the South [MERCOSUR]) 2140 UNTS 257.

1530. Unlike the first Draft, which focused solely on contract law, the new Draft also contained conflict of laws rules regarding the law applicable to contractual obligations. See Monsenepwo, *supra* note 1345, pp. 250 ff.

into agreements by reference [1531]. Examples include the International Commercial Terms (Incoterms) [1532] and the Uniform Customs and Practice for Documentary Credits (UCP) [1533]. Although instruments such as these are usually satisfactory and sufficiently neutral in form and substance, they provide only a partial solution due to their limited scope. Moreover, they presume the existence of an overarching legal framework that governs the contract. Nonetheless, both the Incoterms and the UCP are considered by many to be highly successful, in part because they are specialized and narrowly focused, and in part because the organization that promulgates the instruments has the ability to modify them in response to changed commercial circumstances.

Another tool frequently used is the "standard contract" that is accepted within a specific economic sector. One example of a standard contract is the Conditions of Contract for Works of Civil Engineering Construction (1987), prepared under the auspices of FIDIC and commonly referred to as the "FIDIC Contract". Another example is the standard international forms of contract of the Grain and Feed Trade Association, which are widely used in international trade for agricultural products. In the financial field, the use of the Global Master Repurchase Agreement published by the International Capital Market Association stands out internationally, as does the ISDA Master Agreement for Derivative Contracts published by the International Swaps and Derivatives Association [1534].

Model contracts are also developed by intergovernmental and non-governmental organizations. One example is the Model Contract for the International Commercial Sale of Goods, prepared by the International Trade Centre [1535].

While they are useful international tools, these standard contracts may present problems within the general framework of contract law. As they are usually prepared by or for business entities operating in the world's largest commercial centers, they may be of limited use in other

---

1531. For information on the ICC, see https://iccwbo.org/about-us/, accessed 9 May 2022.

1532. For information on Incoterms, see https://iccwbo.org/resources-for-business/incoterms-rules/incoterms-rules-2010/, accessed 9 May 2022.

1533. For information on the UCP, see http://store.iccwbo.org/icc-uniform-customs-and-practice-for-documentary-credits, accessed 9 May 2022.

1534. See http://fidic.org/; https://www.gafta.com; https://www.icmagroup.org; https://www.isda.org.

1535. International Trade Centre, Model Contracts for Small Firms: Legal Guidance to Doing International Business, 2010, Chapter 3. International Commercial Sale of Goods, http://www.intracen.org/itc/exporters/model-contracts/, accessed 20 May 2022.

applications. Moreover, in most cases the content of standard contracts is formulated unilaterally, for unilateral benefit and the drafting is inevitably influenced by legal concepts from the respective countries of origin.

So-called "codes of conduct" are also available and can be prepared either by private entities or intergovernmental organizations. They generally take the form of compilations of rules in specific subjects or industries. Codes of conduct are characterized by flexibility, voluntary compliance and self-governance, rather than by State regulation. An example is the International Code of Advertising and Marketing Communication Practice, which has also been developed by the ICC [1536]. An example from Factors Chain International is the Code of International Factoring Customs [1537].

Bar associations, such as the International Bar Association (IBA), the American Bar Association and the Union Internationale des Avocats, also formulate "private soft law rules". An example thereof is the IBA's Rules on the Taking of Evidence in International Arbitration, which are used worldwide [1538].

Other non-governmental organizations such as the American Law Institute, the European Law Institute, the European Group of Private International Law, and the American Association of Private International Law (ASADIP) have also collaborated, along with the international community, to launch various codification efforts over the years in partnership with UNCITRAL, UNIDROIT, HCCH and the OAS. Some non-governmental organizations have even advanced their own soft law proposals, such as the ASADIP Principles on Transnational Access to Justice (Transjus) [1539].

D. Uniform interpretation

Considerable efforts are required to develop harmonized conflict of laws rules and uniform law texts. However, to achieve a harmonized

1536. Advertising and Marketing Communication Practice (Consolidated ICC Code), 2011, https://iccwbo.org/publication/advertising-and-marketing-communication-practice-consolidated-icc-code, accessed 9 May 2022.

1537. H. J. Sommer, "Factoring, International Factoring Networks and the FCI Code of International Factoring", *Uniform Law Review*, Vol. 3 (1998), pp. 685-691. See also https://fci.nl/en/solutions/factoring/model-law-for-factoring, accessed 9 May 2022.

1538. International Bar Association, IBA Rules on the Taking of Evidence in International Arbitration, 2010 edition, https://www.ibanet.org/MediaHandler?id=def0807b-9fec-43ef-b624-f2cb2af7cf7b, accessed 9 May 2022.

1539. Text approved by the ASADIP Assembly in Buenos Aires on 12 November 2016, http://www.asadip.org/v2/?page_id=231, accessed 9 May 2022.

interpretation of international rules it is not enough for international and domestic provisions to be similar. The intended goal of harmonization by means of international instruments may be defeated if provisions are interpreted solely from a domestic and not from a comparative perspective.

To address this challenge, in recent years there has been an increase in the practice of including instructions in uniform law instruments whereby courts are encouraged to take into account their international nature and the need to promote their uniform enforcement [1540]. One example of this is Article 7.1 of the CISG, which states that "[i]n the interpretation of this Convention, regard is to be had to its international character and to the need to promote uniformity in its application and the observance of good faith in international trade". CISG Article 7.1 inspired the drafting of Article 1.6 of the UNIDROIT Principles, which contains similar language [1541].

Various conflict of laws instruments also refer to the need to take into account their international nature and the importance of ensuring uniform interpretations of their provisions worldwide. Article 18 of the Rome Convention is an example of this. Although no equivalent provision exists within Rome I, it is a regulation and therefore, it must be interpreted uniformly based on Article 288 of the TFEU. This European provision marks an important distinction from the system of uniform interpretation existing in other regions of the world. In this regard, the CJEU contributes toward the uniform interpretation of Rome I through its so-called "preliminary rulings" made at the request of a court of an EU Member State.

The preamble of the Mexico Convention conveys the desire to "continue the progressive development and codification of private international law" and the "advisability of harmonizing solutions to international trade issues", and that, in light of the need to foster economic interdependence and regional integration, "it is necessary to

1540. In this regard, under the initiative of UNICITRAL, the three Secretariats of UNCITRAL, HCCH and UNIDROIT have been working together on a Tripartite Legal Guide to Uniform Legal Instruments in the Area of International Commercial Contracts (with a focus on sales). This future Legal Guide aims at providing a roadmap to the existing texts in the area of commercial contracts prepared by each organization, primarily the CISG, the UNIDROIT Principles and The Hague Principles. The objective is to provide an assessment of interactions between the texts, their actual and potential use, application and impact, with the goal to facilitate promotion of their appropriate use, uniform interpretation and adoption. The publication of the Legal Guide has been authorized by all three organizations in 2020. See https://www.unidroit.org/instruments/commercial-contracts/tripartite-legal-guide, accessed 9 May 2022.

1541. For the discussions regarding the use of the UNIDROIT Principles to interpret and complement the CISG, see Castellani and Emery, *supra* note 495, pp. 182 ff.

facilitate international contracts by removing differences in the legal framework for them".

The objectives expressed in the preamble can be achieved in those States that decide to ratify the instrument or, alternatively, decide to incorporate the solutions presented in the Mexico Convention into their domestic laws. However, such formal acts alone are not enough: formally adopted provisions must be interpreted uniformly. Article 4 of the Mexico Convention provides some guidance in this regard:

> "For purposes of interpretation and application of this Convention, its international nature and the need to promote uniformity in its application shall be taken into account."

Although the Hague Principles do not contain a provision similar to that of the Mexico Convention regarding uniform interpretation, the Hague Principles are a soft law instrument and clearly include the objective of harmonization throughout. The Hague Principles contain provisions that can be adopted by parties around the world in the exercise of party autonomy. For instance, paragraphs 2, 3 and 4 of the preamble state that "they may be used as a model for national, regional, supranational or international instruments" and "may be used to interpret, supplement and develop rules of private international law" and "may be applied by courts and by arbitral tribunals".

It is anticipated that widespread use of the Hague Principles will lead to uniformity of interpretation in accordance with its rules. The word "develop" is used by the Hague Principles but not found in other texts such as the CISG (Art. 7 (1)), the UNCITRAL Model Law (Art. 2 (A) (1)) or the Mexico Convention (Art. 4). The fact that the word "develop" is included within the Hague Principles suggests that this instrument may have a possible impact on archaic and unpredictable domestic private international law rules, a statement which may be considered "revolutionary" [1542].

The uniform interpretation of international texts is also facilitated through the collection and dissemination of judicial decisions and arbitral rulings [1543].

1542. For discussions regarding the use of the Hague Principles to interpret and complement the CISG and the "battle of forms" issue, see Castellani and Emery, *supra* note 495, pp. 183 ff. See also P. Winship, "The Hague Principles, the CISG, and the 'Battle of the Forms'", *Penn State Journal of Law & International Affairs*, Vol. 4 (2015), p. 151.

1543. See e.g. http://www.unilex.info/dynasite.cfm?dssid=2377&dsmid=14311, accessed 9 May 2022.

The OAS Guide likewise advocates in favor of uniform interpretation, encouraging judges, arbitrators, contracting parties and lawyers to consider the ultimate goal of unification and harmonization of law and to remain informed of developments on the interpretation of instruments that may influence the specific transaction at hand [1544].

E. Non-State law and uniform law

The term "State law" is used synonymously with "national", "municipal", "domestic", "internal" or "local" law. Within comparative law and international practice more generally, terminology differs in reference to non-State law (or non-State rules of law). This expression covers a broad range of topics, from universal principles, customs, usages and practices to standard trade terms. These topics have little if anything in common, except that they do not emanate from any State source that works to create "binding" law. Arbitration has been a fertile ground for the development and refinement of these notions, using the term "rules of law", which is less broad. Various types and articulations of non-State law are described in the following pages.

1. Custom and usages

"Custom", like tradition, refers to the practice of repeating a particular action or pattern of behavior [1545]. Today, the term "custom" is employed interchangeably with "usages" and is generally used only within public international law [1546].

Commercial understandings that arise from contractual practices that had traditionally been called "customs" are now referred to as "usages" [1547] and are accepted within the legal, business and arbitration communities [1548]. Instruments such as the UNCITRAL Model Law

1544. OAS Guide, *supra* note 1309, Recommendations 4.1 to 4.4.

1545. H. P. Glenn, *Legal Traditions of the World*, 2nd ed., Oxford, Oxford University Press, 2004. On difficulties regarding the term custom, see M. Akehurst, "Custom as a Source of International Law", *British Yearbook of International Law*, Vol. 47 (1975), p. 53. I. Bentekas, "The Private Dimension of the International Customary Nature of Commercial Arbitration", *Journal of International Arbitration*, Vol. 25, No. 4 (2008), pp. 455-456.

1546. Goode, *supra* note 139, p. 7n.

1547. Berman and Dasser, *supra* note 135.

1548. G. Aksen, "The Law Applicable in International Arbitration: Relevance of Reference to Trade Usages", in A. J. van den Berg (ed.), *Planning Efficient Arbitration Proceedings: The Law Applicable in International Arbitration* (ICCA Congress Series, No. 7), The Hague, Kluwer Law International, 1996.

(Art. 28 (4)), the CISG (Arts 8 (3) and Art. 9) [1549] and the UNIDROIT Principles (Art. 1.9) [1550] accept this terminology.

In this sense, the term "usages" is broader than "customs" as it covers not only practices that are generally accepted in a particular trade or sector but also those considered by the parties to be implied expectations [1551]. Given that "usages" do not require the same element of obligation required in customary public international law (known as *opinio juris*), the parties' implied expectations are enough for "usages" to emerge [1552].

Although usages can be proven, their institutionalization by an organization (governmental or otherwise) helps establish a common understanding of expressions that are frequently used in international commercial contracts. One example is the CISG, which may not always apply to the transaction as a matter of law but as a reflection of trade usages. Other well-known examples emanate from the ICC, a global association that has institutionalized usages in several of its regulatory instruments, such as the Incoterms, a set of rules that cover standard terms used in international trade. These instruments have become "part of the daily language of commercial trade" and are regularly incorporated into international contracts and various domestic laws [1553].

1549. As Schlechtriem explains, CISG Article 8 (3) has a different function than Article 9 (2). Article 8 (3) does not work to fill a gap but to interpret the parties' declaration. P. Schlechtriem, *Uniform Sales Law: The UN-Convention on Contracts for the International Sale of Goods*, Vienna, Manz, 1986. The term custom of public international law was considered but discarded. J. O. Honnold, *Uniform Law for International Sales under the 1980 United Nations Convention*, 3rd ed., The Hague, Kluwer Law International, 1999 (1st ed. 1982).

1550. However, the UNIDROIT Principles do not define the term "usages", even though the matter was discussed in the early drafting process of the instrument. See S. Vogenauer (ed.), *Commentary on the UNIDROIT Principles of International Commercial Contracts (PICC)*, 2nd ed., Oxford, Oxford University Press, 2015 (1st ed. 2008), p. 233.

1551. Berman and Dasser, *supra* note 135, p. 65. Regarding usages that have become uniform within a commercial community, Judge Learned Hand stated: "I cannot see why judges should not hold men to understandings which are the tacit presupposition on which they deal." *Künglig Jarnvägsstyrelsen* v. *Dexter & Carpenteer, Inc.*, 299 F 991, SDNY, 1924; Berman and Dasser, *ibid.*, p. 57.

1552. See Derains, *supra* note 1431, p. 2. However, in many domestic legal systems such as France, Italy and Spain, "customs" have normative force and offer a source of rights to fill in gaps where the law is silent. By contrast, "usages" serve to interpret or clarify the will of the parties, and will only have normative force in a limited number of cases. The key difference between customs and usages here is that it is not necessary for the normative force of customs to be proven, however it must be proven for usages. In the Mexico Convention of 1994 on the applicable law to international contracts, the term "customs" was included in a row along with and alternate to "usage" (Art. 10).

1553. See https://iccwbo.org/, accessed 20 May 2022. See, for instance, Article 51 of the Venezuelan law of PIL of 1998; Article 2651 of the Argentine Civil and

Usages can be incorporated by specific intent or by implication when arbitrators determine that they must have been within the parties' contemplation [1554]. Usages can fill gaps in the contract, can serve as guides to interpret the ordinary meaning of those terms and can help resolve their ambiguities [1555].

Usages and fair dealing rules are generally adaptable and often give adjudicators a better guide than rigid local rules [1556]. Since international commercial usages generally develop more rapidly than the law, they are also used in arbitration to fill gaps in the applicable law [1557]. When usages are repeatedly referred to within international cases, they begin to develop into a form of case law [1558]. According to Orsolya Toth, even though arbitrators make an effort to "take into account" trade usages, they hesitate when determining the relevant usage and applying it to the dispute. "Often, the focus shifts from the examination of market *practice* to the analysis of the terms of the *contract.* Consequently, what should properly be a matter of assessing evidence about market practice transforms into an exercise in contract interpretation." [1559] Arbitrators often refer to trade usages in the "applicable law" section of the award [1560]. On occasion, "usage is applied as though it were the

---

Commercial Code; Article 51 of the Draft Law of DIPr of Uruguay; Article 852 *et seq.* of the Commercial Code of Bolivia (which refer to Incoterms) and Article 1408 (which refers to Documentary Credits); Article 3 of Resolution 112/2007 of the Directorate of National Taxes and Customs of Colombia (Cf. OAS Guide, *supra* note 1309, p. 48).

1554. See Craig, Park and Paulsson, *supra* note 837, pp. 331-332; Y. Derains and E. A. Schwartz, *El Nuevo Reglamento de Arbitraje de la Cámara de Comercio Internacional: Guía de Arbitraje Comercial Internacional*, Oxford, Oxford University Press, 2001, p. 225. The implication comes from the applicable law. For example, Article 9 (2) of the CISG provides for the incorporation of international trade usages if the parties knew or ought to have known about the usage and, in international trade, it is widely known to, and regularly observed by, parties to contracts of the type involved in the particular trade concerned. The same is provided in Article 1.9 of the UPICC.

1555. Berman and Dasser, *supra* note 135, p. 57.

1556. Carbonneau, *supra* note 1469, p. 37.

1557. Examples are ICC Cases 1472/1968 and 8873/1997. See Craig, Park and Paulsson, *supra* note 837, p. 331.

1558. See D. P. Fernández Arroyo, "Cuestiones Claves del Arbitraje Internacional", in E. Gaillard and D. P. Fernández Arroyo (eds.), *Cuestiones Claves del Arbitraje Internacional*, Asunción, CEDEP; Bogotá, Universidad del Rosario, 2013, p. 225. In ICC Case No. 4131/1982, presided by Pieter Sanders, it was stated: "The decisions of tribunals progressively create case law which should be taken into account, because it draws conclusions from economic reality and conforms to the needs of international commerce, to which rules specific to international arbitration, themselves successively elaborated, should respond". ICC Awards 146, 465. See Craig, Park and Paulsson, *supra* note 837, pp. 638-639.

1559. O. Toth, *The Lex Mercatoria in Theory and Practice*, Oxford, Oxford University Press, 2017, p. 259.

1560. Final Award in Case No. 6527/1991, *Austrian Buyer* v. *Turkish Seller*, 18 YB Comm. Arb. (1993), p. 44, and in J.-J. Arnaldez, Y. Derains, D. Hascher (eds.),

governing law, albeit this is not expressly admitted" [1561]. In several circumstances, usages have been decisive to the outcome of the dispute, "at times overshadowing the applicable law" [1562]. Gerald Aksen states that in almost any controversy, custom and usage play a prominent part in deciding the substance of the dispute [1563].

In many jurisdictions, while the term "usages" refers to conduct established by third and other parties within international commerce, the term "practices" is limited to the past conduct of the contracting parties themselves. In some jurisdictions, these terms are defined within legislation [1564]. Research has indicated that arbitrators usually rely on usages and, to a lesser extent, the prior negotiations of the parties [1565].

The term "practices" is employed in uniform law instruments. Thus, for example, Article 1.9 of the UNIDROIT Principles states that "the parties are bound by any usage to which they have agreed and by any practices which they have established between themselves". This language is identical to CISG Article 9 (1) and is also in line with the subjective approach proposed in CISG Article 8 (3) [1566].

Collection of ICC Arbitral Awards 1991-1995, The Hague, Kluwer Law International / ICC Publishing, 1997, pp. 185, 187-188; Final Award in Case No. 5485/1987, *Bermudian company* v. *Spanish company*, in S. Jarvin, Y. Derains, J.-J. Arnaldez (eds.), *Collection of ICC Arbitral Awards 1986-1990*, The Hague, Kluwer Law International / ICC Publishing, 1994, pp. 199, 209; Final Award in Case No. 5713/1989, *Seller* v. *Swiss Buyer*, 15 YB Comm. Arb. (1999), p. 70, and in *Collection of ICC Arbitral Awards 1986-1990* (1994), pp. 223, 225; Interim Award in Case No. 7645/1995, *Slovakian Supplier* v. *Korean Buyer*, 26 YB Comm. Arb. (2001), p. 130, and in J.-J. Arnaldez, Y. Derains, D. Hascher (eds.), *Collection of ICC Arbitral Awards 2001-2007*, The Hague, Kluwer Law International / ICC Publishing, 2009, p. 18. See Toth, *supra* note 1559, p. 259.

1561. See the *Turkish Seller* and *Spanish Joint Venture* cases, *ibid.*, in Toth, *supra* note 1559, p. 259.

1562. *Swiss Buyer* (1989). As a matter of practice, it seems that trade usages are part of the applicable law used to determine international contract disputes. Aksen, *supra* note 1548, p. 478. The difficulty is that this is done overtly in most cases. An exception is ICC Interim Award in Case No. 5314/1988, *Manufacturer* v. *Licensor*, 20 YB Comm. Arb. (1995), p. 35; Toth, *supra* note 1559, p. 260.

1563. Aksen, *supra* note 1548, 1996, p. 471.

1564. For example, the US UCC, Sec. 1-303, distinguishes between *course of performance* (a term that is not easy to translate into Spanish but which is closely linked to the contract and prevails over the following two terms), *course of dealing* or prior practices between the parties and *usage of trade* or uses.

1565. C. R. Drahozal, "Of Rabbits and Rhinoceri: A Survey of Empirical Research on International Commercial Arbitration", *Journal of International Arbitration*, Vol. 20, No. 1 (2003), p. 30.

1566. The notion of implied usages is of significance since it leads that rules not advanced by States can be imposed to the parties. B. Audit, "The Vienna Sales Convention and the *Lex Mercatoria*", in T. E. Carbonneau (ed.), Lex Mercatoria *and Arbitration: A Discussion of the New Lew Merchant*, 2nd ed., The Hague, Juris / Kluwer International, 1998, pp. 176-177.

2. General principles

General principles of commerce emerge from their widespread acceptance in different legal systems: this is why they generally have a broader reach than usages [1567]. For this reason, Roy Goode argues that a usage is restricted to a specific activity. Once that activity gains general acceptance, it will become a general principle [1568]. This was the view put forward by the Tribunal in ICC Case No. 3380/1980 [1569]. As a result, the burden of proof for usages is generally higher than for general principles [1570].

General principles of law appear in some national civil and commercial codes or in other national and conflicts of law rules across various jurisdictions. The term "general principles" is also used in this sense in specific uniform law instruments, such as the CISG. CISG Article 7 (2) established that matters are to be settled "in conformity with the general principles on which it is based". Similarly, the UNIDROIT Principles has expressly specified that general principles will apply when the parties have agreed that their contract be governed by "general principles of law, the *lex mercatoria* or the like" [1571].

"3. New" lex mercatoria

Sometimes, one must look back to see forward. In *The Tempest*, Shakespeare wrote: "what is past is prologue". When it comes to the *lex mercatoria*, what is past is also what is to come [1572].

The *lex mercatoria* or "new *lex mercatoria*" doctrine emulated the law of merchants of the Middle Ages and surged in popularity in the second half of the twentieth century, particularly after Berthold Goldman's renowned contribution [1573]. The *lex mercatoria* has been

---

1567. Oppetit, *supra* note 796, pp. 205-207.

1568. Goode, *supra* note 139, pp. 16-17.

1569. Presided over by Pierre Lalive. ICC Case No. 3380/1980 *apud* Craig, Park and Paulsson, *supra* note 837, p. 102.

1570. Some usages are broad, and others are specific, but widely followed – such as the granting of a reasonable period of time to examine letters of credit or the apparent good order of documents. The degree of specificity of usages may be relevant when it comes to seeking recognition by an arbitral tribunal, since the more general the usage, the greater its assimilation to general principles of law will be and the lesser will be the burden of proving that it is generally known. See Goode, *supra* note 139, p. 12.

1571. Preamble to the UNIDROIT Principles.

1572. Y. Fortier, "The New, New *Lex Mercatoria*, or, Back to the Future", *Arbitration International*, Vol. 17, No. 2 (2001), p. 128.

1573. B. Goldman, "Frontières du droit et lex mercatoria", *Archives de philosophie du droit*, Vol. 9 (1964), p. 184; Zumbansen highlights Jessup's contribution in 1956

relied upon in several arbitral decisions [1574], with the Middle Eastern cases dealing with concession agreements leading the way [1575]. The legal rationales articulated in these awards has echoed beyond the context of investment contracts to other areas of international contracts as well [1576]. These cases were discussed in Chapter VIII.

An arbitral award characterized the *lex mercatoria* as a "set of norms of international commerce developed in practice and reaffirmed by national tribunals" [1577]. In 1981, the French Cour de cassation held that a *lex mercatoria* decision is not made in equity, and as such an award resolving the dispute in accordance with general principles of commercial law – or *lex mercatoria* – should not be annulled (*Fougerolle* v. *Banque de Proche Orient*) [1578]. This was followed by other decisions made by the Cour de cassation and the appeals courts in France [1579]. In 1982, the Austrian Supreme Court refused to annul an ICC award (*Pabalk Ticaret* v. *Ugilor/Norsolor*) in which the arbitrator had applied the *lex mercatoria* [1580] rather than national law, even though no prior reference to the *lex mercatoria* had been made by the parties [1581].

(Jessup, *supra* note 348), P. Zumbansen, "Transnational Law", in J. M. Smits (ed.), *Elgar Encyclopedia of Comparative Law*, Cheltenham, Edward Elgar, 2006, p. 738. Schlessinger and Schmitthoff also made important contributions in the field.

1574. In 1969, one of the first cases applying *lex mercatoria* understood the absence of a choice of national law implicitly gave the arbitrator the duty to apply the corresponding rules of law or commercial usages. ICC Case No. 1641/1969. Craig, Park and Paulsson, *supra* note 837, p. 333. For a detailed account of the "new" *lex mercatoria*, see further the critical remarks of Felix Dasser in Dasser, *supra* note 457, p. 474.

1575. Spiermann, *supra* note 979, p. 90.

1576. Sornarajah, *supra* note 47, p. 249.

1577. Award of the Arbitration and Mediation Centre of Paris, Case No. 9246, 22 YB Comm. Arb. (1997), p. 31.

1578. The award can be considered a first step in favor of finding *lex mercatoria* as *lex fori* in international arbitration. See De Ly, *supra* note 1204, pp. 255-256.

1579. In *Compañía Valenciana de Cementos Portland* v. *Société Primary Coal Inc.* (1989), the Appellate Court of Paris attributed legal standing to principles and usages known as *lex mercatoria*. Jayme, *supra* note 894, p. 87. In 1993 the Court alluded to a substantive rule of the international law of arbitration (*Dalico Contractors* v. *Comité de la Municipalité de Khoms El Mergeb* (J. M. García Represa, F. Mantilla-Serrano and C. Núñez-Lagos, "Panorama de Jurisprudencia Francesa (por el Capítulo Francés del Club Español del Arbitraje)", *Revista del Club Español del Arbitraje*, Vol. 3 (2008), p. 101. The same line was followed in *Uni-Kod* (2004) and *Némesis* (1ª Sala Civil, 2005). In 2007, in *PT Putrabali Adyamulia* v. *Rena Holding*, the Court of cassation confirmed the existence of an arbitral legal order different of national legal systems. The case is of great relevant due to the theoretical framework it provides for this matter in France, see P. Pinsolle, "The Status of Vacated Awards in France: the Cour de cassation Decision in Putrabali", *Arbitration International*, Vol. 24, No. 2 (2008), pp. 277-278.

1580. De Ly, *supra* note 1204, p. 257.

1581. See Lando, *supra* note 910, p. 757.

In England, a favorable attitude toward the *lex mercatoria* can be traced back to the 1978 *Eagle Star* v. *Yuval* case [1582] and subsequently to the landmark 1987 *Deutsche Schachtbau-und Tiefbohr-Gessellschaft mbH* v. *Ras Al Khaimah National Oil Co. and Shell International Petroleum Co. Ltd.* case [1583]. The Italian Court of Cassation also decided in favor of applying the *lex mercatoria* in the 1982 *Damiano* case, as did the Swedish Supreme Court in *Götaverken Arendal AB* v. *Libyan General Maritime Transport Co.* [1584]. Recent relevant decisions from the Americas include a 2017 ruling by the Court of Appeal of the State of Rio Grande do Sul in Brazil, which referred to non-State law such as *lex mercatoria* [1585] and another 2014 ruling by the Supreme Court of Justice in Venezuela [1586].

At the theoretical level, there is no consensus regarding the notion of *lex mercatoria* [1587]. Some scholars ambitiously [1588] consider the *lex mercatoria* an autonomous order for international transactions that exists independent of national systems [1589]. Others understand the *lex mercatoria* as rules emerging from arbitral awards and international conventions [1590] that can serve as an alternative to national laws [1591]. Still others, such as Goldman [1592], consider the *lex mercatoria* a

1582. J. H. Dalhuisen, *Dalhuisen on International Commercial, Financial and Trade Law*, Oxford, Hart Publishing, 2000, p. 118.

1583. International Law Association, London Conference, 2000, Committee on International Commercial Arbitration, Interim Report on Public Policy as a Bar to Enforcement of International Arbitral Awards, pp. 27-28, available at https://www.ila-hq.org/, accessed 9 May 2022.

1584. Visher, *supra* note 1200, p. 143.

1585. Proceedings No. 70072362940, *supra* note 1490, Judgment of February 2017. As to the law governing the contract, the Court of Appeal noted that according to Article 9 (2) of the Introductory Law to Brazilian Civil Code, Danish law should apply as it was the law of the place of the conclusion of the contract. However, the Court held that whenever the contract was pluriconnected (as in the case at hand), the traditional *lex loci celebrationis* rule should be disregarded in favor of a more flexible approach leading to the application of the CISG and the UNIDROIT Principles as an expression of the so-called "new *lex mercatoria*".

1586. Venezuelan Supreme Court of Justice on *lex mercatoria*, see http://catedradipr.org/diprwp/wp-content/uploads/2015/11/VENEZUELA-2014-12-2-TSJ-SCC-BANQUE-ARTESIA-NEDERLAND.pdf, accessed 9 May 2022.

1587. The following positions are perhaps an oversimplification, for didactic purposes, of the several views advanced regarding the standing of *lex mercatoria*.

1588. G. Born, *International Commercial Arbitration: Commentary and Materials*, 2nd ed., New York, Transnational Publishers, 2001.

1589. This position was advocated by Schmitthoff. See Schmitthoff, *supra* note 137, pp. 32-36. See also Berman and Dasser, *supra* note 135, p. 53.

1590. Born, *supra* note 1588, p. 556.

1591. Berman and Dasser, *supra* note 135, p. 53.

1592. See Goldman, *supra* note 1573, p. 21. These different notions have been advanced in the arbitral context. Craig, Park and Paulsson, *supra* note 837, p. 623. See also T. Carbonneau, "A Definition and Perspective Upon the *Lex Mercatoria* Debate",

simple complement to national law emerging from trade usages and expectations [1593]. Lawrence Craig, William Park and Jan Paulsson argue that the conception of the *lex mercatoria* as a complement to national law is "the most practical significant notion" and that the *lex mercatoria* may therefore be seen as an "expansion of the notion of usages" [1594]. Under this conception, arbitrators may apply the *lex mercatoria* alongside a national law. However, arbitrators must be cautious of declaring the *lex mercatoria* the sole applicable law without an express indication of consent from the parties as this may invite litigation in the specific case and would generate controversy about the role of the *lex mercatoria* more generally [1595].

According to Emmanuel Gaillard, any discussion surrounding the appropriate role for the *lex mercatoria* depends on how arbitration is conceptualized [1596]. Some scholars consider arbitration the result of a recognition by a given legal system in which the tribunal is seated. Other scholars understand the arbitral process as resulting from all the legal systems potentially involved, including the seat of arbitration and the various places of enforcement. Others still consider arbitration the result of an autonomous arbitral legal order founded on the normative activity of States (known as the *ordre juridique arbitral*) [1597]. This last conception is more open to the application of non-State rules [1598]. Paulsson advances another perspective, which is equally open to extra-State normativity [1599]. In a pluralist world comprised of States and other forms of non-State arrangements, he underlines the importance of understanding the capacity of a variety of social institutions for authoritative decision-making [1600].

---

in *id.* (ed.), Lex Mercatoria *and Arbitration: A Discussion of the New Lew Merchant*, 2nd ed., The Hague, Juris / Kluwer International, 1998, p. 12. For a theoretical analysis of the discussions: Oppetit, *supra* note 796, pp. 208-213. For a discussion of the sources, see J. Bell, "Public Law in Europe: Caught Between the National, the Sub-National and the European?", in M. Van Hoecke (ed.), *Epistemology and Methodology of Comparative Law*, Oxford / Portland, OR, Hart Publishing, 2004, p. 260.

1593. Craig, Park and Paulsson, *supra* note 837, p. 633. Lew's position that *lex mercatoria* should be equated to *ex aequo et bono* amiable composition has not received much support, see Born, *supra* note 1588, p. 556.

1594. Craig, Park and Paulsson, *supra* note 837, pp. 633-634.

1595. *Ibid.*, pp. 336-337.

1596. See full in Gaillard, *supra* note 836, fn. 115. The book translates E. Gaillard, *Aspects philosophiques du droit de l'arbitrage international*, Leiden, Martinus Nijhoff, 2008.

1597. Gaillard, *supra* note 836, pp. 46-47.

1598. *Ibid.*, pp. 127-148. Paulsson considers it a ferment of two generations of scholarly fervor in France. Paulsson, *supra* note 1440, p. 39.

1599. *Ibid.*

1600. *Ibid.*, p. 50.

Some scholars argue that the *lex mercatoria* does not exist [1601]; that it is "a phantom created by professors of the Sorbonne" [1602], a non-subject [1603], a Loch Ness monster that appears in a precedent invoking it [1604], a wicked misnomer, or a contradiction in terms [1605]. Other commentators criticize the advancement of the *lex mercatoria* by a group of scholars who sat on arbitration panels and expressed their views in various arbitral awards, choosing rules that they found appropriate based on their own subjective preferences [1606].

Internationally renowned arbitrators understand the *lex mercatoria* as an alternative to applying national law, consistent with the necessities of international commerce [1607]. Between these polarizing opinions, many "cautious well-wishers" can be found, who see a progressive development of the *lex mercatoria* and aim for its consolidation [1608].

More than any other factor, the difficulty of determining the content of a universal or transnational law has typically stood in the way of any serious discussion concerning the usefulness of the *lex mercatoria* [1609]. Disparities between the terminology used to refer to the *lex mercatoria* further complicate the issue. It is possible that the expression has become overburdened with meaning [1610]. The Institute of International Law undertook several studies on this topic during the early 1990s but failed to pay attention to the theoretical basis of the *lex mercatoria* or whether it represents an independent legal order or not. Instead, these studies focused more practically upon the validity and enforceability of *lex mercatoria* rules. The most salient debate regarding the *lex mercatoria* may therefore concern its practical significance [1611] and how adjudicators deal with this legal concept in practice. The debate

1601. See B. Goldman and F. A. Mann, "Introduction", in T. E. Carbonneau (ed.), Lex Mercatoria *and Arbitration: A Discussion of the New Lew Merchant*, 2nd ed., The Hague, Juris / Kluwer International, 1998, p. xix.

1602. See G. Teubner, "Breaking Frames: The Global Interplay of Legal and Social Systems", *American Journal of Comparative Law*, Vol. 45 (1997), p. 151.

1603. Mustill, *supra* note 1000, p. 149.

1604. Ruíz Abou-Nigm, *supra* note 1433, p. 105.

1605. A. F. Lowenfeld, "Lex Mercatoria: An Arbitrator's View", in *ICC Ct. Bull.* Special 2002.

1606. Sornarajah, *supra* note 47, pp. 242-243.

1607. *Ibid.*, p. 85. Park, however, states that the *lex mercatoria* has only a "marginal impact on the practice of international arbitration", in W. Park, *Arbitration of International Business Disputes: Studies in Law and Practice*, 2nd ed., Oxford, Oxford University Press, 2014, p. 593.

1608. Berman and Dasser, *supra* note 135, p. 55.

1609. Fortier, *supra* note 1572, pp. 121-128.

1610. Craig, Park and Paulsson, *supra* note 837, p. 625.

1611. Borchers, *supra* note 1226, pp. 150-151. Juenger considers similarly, see Juenger, *supra* note 1311, p. 265.

surrounding the *lex mercatoria* consequently shifts from the formal sources to the adjudication methods [1612].

Nevertheless, deliberations over the proper way to define the *lex mercatoria* continue, with intense debates over its terminology, sources and whether it constitutes an autonomous legal regime that exists independently from domestic legal systems.

In investment arbitration, the *lex mercatoria* is linked to the efforts to create a transnational legal system applied to foreign investment contracts that cannot be changed by the State when previously agreed upon to be the applicable law. Thus, the *lex mercatoria* becomes a tool for the achievement of this objective through the principle of the sanctity of contracts [1613].

4. *Other terms*

In reference to non-State law, the terms customs, usages, principles and the *lex mercatoria* are used most frequently. However, the following terms are also frequently employed to refer to non-State law: transnational law, non-State rules of law, *droit a-national* (a-national law) [1614], world law, global law, uniform law or even expressions such as *lex constructionis*, *lex electrónica*, *lex marítima*, *lex petrolea* [1615], *lex arbitralis* [1616], *lex informatica* [1617], *lex mediatica* [1618], *lex sportiva* [1619], and so on.

1612. De Ly, *supra* note 1204, p. 315. This is more so today when gaining acceptance that application and interpretation of law is in certain way a creative process generating new law. See also Vogenauer, *supra* note 860, pp. 885-886.

1613. According to Sornarajah, "the *lex mercatoria* does have some credibility when it is applied to private transactions in ordinary international commerce. The idea is to build upon this credibility and introduce the concept into the area of foreign investment agreements, which involves State participation and State policies", Sornarajah, *supra* note 47, pp. 244-245.

1614. This term is believed to have been coined by the late Professor P. Fouchard in his work *L'arbitrage commercial international*, Paris, Dalloz, 1965.

1615. A. De Jesús O., "The Prodigious Story of the Lex Petrolea and the Rhinoceros. Philosophical Aspects of the Transnational Legal Order of the Petroleum Society", *TPLI Series on Transnational Petroleum Law*, Vol. 1, No. 1 (2012), available at www.lexpetrolea.org, accessed 9 May 2022.

1616. See H. Smit, "Proper Choice of Law and the *Lex Mercatoria* Arbitralis", in T. E. Carbonneau (ed.), Lex Mercatoria *and Arbitration: A Discussion of the New Lew Merchant*, 2nd ed., The Hague, Juris / Kluwer International, 1998, p. 96.

1617. R. Lorenzetti, *Comercio Electrónico*, Buenos Aires, Abeledo-Perrot, 2001, p. 39.

1618. Related to intellectual property. A López-Tarruella Martínez, *Contratos Internacionales de Software*, Valencia, Tirant Lo Blanc, 2006, p. 322.

1619. For instance, Arbitral Award 2002/A/593, Court of Arbitration for Sport (CAS), which in the case *Football Association of Wales (FAW)* v. *Union des Associations Européenes de Football (UEFA)* refers to the *contra proferentem* rule as a general principle of the *lex sportiva*.

5. *Developments of* lex mercatoria *in practice*

Yves Dezalay and Bryan Garth point out that international commercial arbitration began to grow at an overwhelming rate worldwide, particularly after the oil-related disputes of the 1970s [1620] that were decided by well-known law professors or former judges with a profound theoretical knowledge of international law, as well as non-State law issues (usages, principles, etc.) [1621].

This situation subsequently evolved, and this informal justice system that had been dominated by European academics transformed into an "offshore" arbitral justice system mostly monopolized by large American and English law firms. Arbitral "technocrats" emerged from this new system, substituting for the previous "grand old men" of arbitration. These technocrats invoked the specialization and technical knowledge that many had acquired working in the secretariat of arbitral institutions that hire young lawyers to administer arbitral cases. These practitioners emphasized the value of precedents and the detailed analysis of the facts of the case. By contrast, scholars had an important advantage over their practitioner counterparts when it came to the theoretical aspects of arbitral cases and could also comfortably deal with non-State law (or *lex mercatoria*), a topic that has now been amply discussed and researched within the academic world. Nonetheless, since the pendulum swung toward a stronger emphasis on the work of the great Anglo-American law firms within the international arbitration field, the role of non-State law or *lex mercatoria* gradually diminished [1622].

Now, when discussing the technocratic and academic approaches, much of the data is contradictory. The defenders of the technocratic approach refer to data that proves the widespread application of State law as opposed to the incidence of non-State law. For instance, the ICC has reported that in 95 percent of disputes referred to ICC arbitration in 2020, the parties included a choice of law clause in their contracts, and in 98 percent of the cases, they chose national laws. The ICC notes that these choices do not necessarily coincide with the law applied to the merits of the dispute [1623].

1620. Dezalay and Garth, *supra* note 801, p. 63.
1621. *Ibid.*, chap. 2.
1622. *Ibid.*, chap. 3.
1623. English law and the law of the United States were more frequently chosen, accounting for a quarter of all contracts. Other common choices were the laws of Switzerland, France and Brazil. See *ICC Dispute Resolution 2020 Statistics*, 2021, p. 17. See also G. Cuniberti, "The International Market for Contracts: The Most

However, some years ago, a study of 2,733 lawyers conducted by Klaus Peter Berger found that approximately one-third of those surveyed knew of at least one case in their practice in which parties had referred to "transnational" law in their contracts, and more than 40 percent had knowledge of at least one arbitral proceeding in which the term had been used [1624]. More recent research conducted using 136 extensive questionnaires and qualitative data based on sixty-seven in-depth interviews found that the use of transnational law was fairly common in the arbitral setting: approximately 50 percent of those interviewed used the term "transnational law" at least "sometimes" [1625].

Even more recently, in 2014 the Kluwer Arbitration Blog invited responses to its survey on the use of soft law instruments in international arbitration. Users were asked to report on their real-life encounters with the UNIDROIT Principles, the *lex mercatoria* and other similar instruments. The results of the survey for the UNIDROIT Principles and the *lex mercatoria* were strikingly similar, which may suggest that they can be used interchangeably. Around 50 percent of the blog's users reported that they had used both instruments occasionally, whereas about 20 percent reported that they always or regularly use them [1626].

Attractive Contract Laws", *Northwestern Journal of International Law & Business*, Vol. 34 (2013), pp. 475-476. Cuniberti conducted an empirical study of more than 4,400 international contracts concluded by 12,000 parties based on an analysis of data published with respect to the contractual practices of parties participating in ICC arbitrations. His study was conducted from 2007-2012 and revealed that, when international commercial parties agreed to choose a law other than their own to apply to their contract, they generally choose the law of one of five jurisdictions: England, Switzerland, United States, France and Germany. However, as it has been pointed out, the selection of non-State law was not included in this research, K. Boele-Woelki, "¿Traen consigo algún cambio los Principios de La Haya sobre la elección de la ley ivan s ra a los contratos comerciales internacionales?", in D. P. Fernández Arroyo and J. A. Moreno Rodríguez (eds.), *Contratos Internacionales*, Washington, DC, ASADIP / OAS, 2016, p. 97.

1624. See Drahozal, *supra* note 1565, p. 30.

1625. *2010 International Arbitration Survey: Choices in International Arbitration*, Queen Mary, University of London, School of International Arbitration and White & Case, p. 11. See also C. R. Drahozal, "Empirical Findings: On International Arbitration", in T. Schultz and F. Ortino (eds.), *The Oxford Handbook of International Arbitration*, Oxford, Oxford University Press, 2020, p. 659.

1626. The survey was conducted within the Fondecyt (National Foundation for Scientific and Technological Development, Chile) Project No. 1110437. E. Mereminskaya, B. Mir and A. Jana Abogados, *Results of the Survey on the Use of Soft Law Instruments in International Arbitration*, June 2014, http://arbitrationblog.kluwerarbitration.com/2014/06/06/results-of-the-survey-on-the-use-of-soft-law-instruments-in-international-arbitration/?doing_wp_cron=1589810344.7918469905853271484375, accessed 9 May 2022.

6. The Hague Principles and non-State law

In the discussions of the working group that prepared the draft Hague Principles, three options for the choice of non-State rules were considered: (1) reserving non-State rules for arbitration, (2) allowing the choice of non-State law regardless of the dispute settlement mechanism, or (3) omitting all references to non-State law, thereby leaving it open to interpretation by judges and arbitrators.

The first option would have been equivalent to maintaining the *status quo*. Indeed, while most modern arbitration rules offer the option to choose non-State law as the legal framework for an international contract, most courts of law do not. The third option (omitting all references to non-State law) would have allowed the arbitral tribunal or court to determine the applicable law on their own, which could give rise to uncertainties. Ultimately, the Hague Conference opted for the second option, that is, to allow non-State law to be chosen regardless of the dispute resolution method [1627]. This view was credited with "levelling the playing field" [1628], or "bridging the gap" [1629], between arbitration and litigation, at least in countries that have adopted the UNCITRAL Model Law. Today, where legislators or courts have accepted rules such as Article 3 of the Hague Principles, it is no longer necessary to include an arbitral clause to assure that the choice of non-State law will be respected.

Writers have expressed doubts about the extent to which choosing non-State law in arbitration or litigation meets an existing commercial need. Others have raised the issue of a democratic deficit [1630] in sources of law beyond the State [1631].

1627. L. Gama Jr. and G. Saumier, "Non-State Law in the (Proposed) Hague Principles on Choice of Law in International Contracts", in *El Derecho internacional Privado en los procesos de integración regional, Jornadas de la ASADIP 2011*, San José, Costa Rica, 24-26 November, ASADIP / Editorial Jurídica Continental, 2011, pp. 62-63.

1628. M. Pertegás and B. A. Marshall, "Harmonization Through the Draft Hague Principles on Choice of Law", *Brooklyn Journal of International Law*, Vol. 39 (2014), p. 979.

1629. G. Saumier, "Designating the Unidroit Principles in International Dispute Resolution", *Uniform Law Review*, Vol. 17 (2011), p. 533.

1630. See H. Muir Watt, "Party Autonomy in International Contracts: From the Makings of a Myth to the Requirements of Global Governance", *European Review of Contract Law*, Vol. 6, No. 3 (2010), pp. 250-283.

1631. B. A. Marshall, "The Hague Choice of Law Principles, CISG, and PICC: A Hard Look at a Choice of Soft Law", *American Journal of Comparative Law*, Vol. 66 (2018), pp. 175-217.

In response, Symeon Symeonides wrote that that the admission of non-State norms in the Hague Principles met the parochial resentments of a coalition of yesterday's men, and he recognized that the drafting of this issue in the Hague Principles was not ideal [1632]. According to Daniel Girsberger and Neil Cohen, "apologists of a more classical, state-focused legal system may neglect the fact that globalization has already diminished the role of State law". Moreover, "empirical research has proved that major players in international trade increasingly refer to non-State law". They also express their doubts

> "that the new rule will either strengthen or weaken the role of State courts vis-à-vis arbitration; other factors will undoubtedly be more important (such as the quality of the judges). It is not intended to create competition between arbitration and court proceedings in international litigation but, rather, to make a supplementary offer in favor of the parties' needs" [1633].

The application of non-State law under the Hague Principles is not unlimited. According to Article 11 (1) of the instrument, even where the choice of non-State law is accepted, mandatory rules of the forum may still apply irrespective of the law chosen by the parties. Article 11 (2) and (4) of the Hague Principles extend this possibility under certain circumstances to mandatory provisions and to public policy rules that emanate from another law. Likewise, according to Article 11 (3) of the Hague Principles:

> "[A] court may exclude the application of a provision of the law [or of 'non-State law'] chosen by the parties only if and to the extent that the result of such application would be manifestly incompatible with fundamental notions of public policy *(ordre public)* of the forum." [1634]

1632. Symeonides, *supra* note 1287, p. 143. Mankowski is also a severe critic of the non-State law provisions of the Principles, in "Article 3 of the Hague Principles: The Final Breakthrough for the Choice of Non-State Law?", *Uniform Law Review*, Vol. 22 (2017), p. 369.

1633. D. Girsberger and N. B. Cohen, "Key Features of the Hague Principles on Choice of Law in International Commercial Contracts", *Uniform Law Review*, Vol. 22 (2017), pp. 328-329.

1634. "On the other hand, the approach adopted by the Hague Principles requires further analysis into whether rules that are mandatory in domestic scenarios should also be mandatory when the contract is international. This may depend on their specific aim, the given factual situation and the proximity between the case and the forum", "General Comparative Report", *supra* note 1330, pp. 49 *et seq.*

(a) *Types of non-State law to be chosen according to the Hague Principles*

Once the arbitral tribunal has decided to apply non-State law, it has to establish the content of "this kind of stuff" [1635]. This is not an easy exercise, but arbitrators must "cope" with it, as expressed in a noteworthy ICC arbitral award [1636].

The Hague Principles give content to "this kind of stuff". Its Article 3 indicates the joint criteria that are required to determine the legitimacy of non-State law. The requirement of "neutrality" calls for a body of rules capable of resolving the problems that are commonly encountered in transnational contracts, whereas the prerequisite of "balance" was established to address the problem of unequal bargaining power leading to the application of unfair or inequitable rules of law. In turn, the "set of rules" chosen must "allow for the resolution of common contract problems in the international context" and must not merely constitute a small number of provisions [1637].

Article 3 of the Hague Principles provides that parties may submit their international contract to non-State rules which are "generally accepted on an international, supranational, or regional level as a neutral and balanced set of rules". This latter requirement is intended to dissuade the parties from choosing vague or unclear categories as the applicable rules of law [1638]. Examples of generally accepted sets of rules include the UNIDROIT Principles, the PECL and the DCFR.

In addition, the Hague Principles allow the CISG and the UNIDROIT Principles to be chosen as "rules of law" when they are not applicable to the case at hand under its own terms [1639]. The Hague Principles offer

---

1635. A. Briggs, *The Conflict of Laws*, 3rd ed., Oxford, Oxford University Press, 2013, p. 237. See citation in Toth, *supra* note 1559, p. 207.

1636. *Ministry of Defence and Support for Armed Forces of the Islamic Republic of Iran* v. *Westinghouse Electric Corp.*, ICC Arbitral Award No. 7375/1996 (5 June 1996), 11 (12) Mealey's Int'l Arb. Rep. A-1, http://www.unilex.info/principles/case/625, accessed 20 May 2022.

1637. Unilaterally drafted contractual clauses or conditions clearly do not qualify as non-State law that can be chosen as applicable law, since they fail to meet the requirement of constituting a sufficiently complete and appropriate body of rules chosen through the exercise of party autonomy (Commentary [3.10], https://www.hcch.net/en/instruments/conventions/full-text/?cid=135, accessed 15 September 2022).

1638. See Pertegás and Marshall, *supra* note 1628, pp. 997-998.

1639. "Both the UNIDROIT Principles and the CISG are expressly mentioned as examples that may be chosen as the applicable law within the official commentary to the Hague Principles. Choosing to apply unwritten statements of non-State law presents a more serious challenge as they tend to be incomplete and unstructured, and their content is less well-defined. It is also uncertain whether, and to what extent, unwritten

a valuable contribution in this regard as no other private international law rules have allowed the parties to deviate from an instrument's normal scope of application and choose it as the law applicable to their contract [1640]. Choosing the CISG through the Hague Principles may respond to a clear commercial need. In fact, a 2015 UNCITRAL commentary wrote, in relation to its instruments, ". . . the use of the Hague Principles, as appropriate" in arbitration [1641]. This is a significant advancement as the CISG has been qualified by Reinhard Zimmermann as "the most significant instrument for unification of private law" [1642]. Further highlighting the impact of the ability to choose the CISG and the UNIDROIT Principles as the applicable law under the Hague Principles, a study conducted by Giles Cuniberti detected that the CISG is the non-State law most frequently chosen [1643].

As stated by Yves Fortier, the UNIDROIT Principles, the CISG and the PECL are all "workable tools" for arbitration, marked by informality and pragmatism – it is the "new, new *lex mercatoria*" [1644].

Ralph Michaels, a strong critic of the Hague Principles when it comes to the regulation of non-State law, argues that principles such as the UNIDROIT Principles cannot serve as the applicable law because they do not cover as many contract law issues as State systems

statements of non-State law contribute to legal certainty and predictability" (Bermann, *supra* note 11, p. 361). For more information regarding the use of the UNIDROIT Principles as the rules of law governing the contract and their relation with the Hague Principles, see A. Veneziano, "The Model Clauses for the Choice of the UNIDROIT Principles of International Commercial Contracts and Article 3 of the Hague Principles", in D. Girsberger, T. Kadner Graziano and J. L. Neels (eds.), *Choice of Law in International Commercial Contracts: Global Perspectives on the Hague Principles*, Oxford, Oxford University Press, 2021, pp. 189-199. See also UNCITRAL, HCCH and UNIDROIT Legal Guide to Uniform Instruments in the Area of International Commercial Contracts, with a Focus on Sales, https://uncitral.un.org/sites/uncitral.un.org/files/media-documents/uncitral/en/tripartiteguide.pdf, accessed 9 May 2022.

1640. This has given rise to problems across various sectors. For example, multimodal transport that is governed by a single contract of carriage but involves transportation by sea and land as well results in the contract being subject to different regulatory regimes. See generally S. M. Carbone, "Multimodal Carriage Contracts", in J. Basedow *et al.* (eds.), *Encyclopedia of Private International Law*, Vol. 2: *Entries I-Z*, Cheltenham, Edward Elgar, 2017, p. 1262.

1641. United Nations, Report of the United Nations Commission on International Trade Law on the Work of its Forty-Eighth Session, UN Doc. A/70/17 (2015), https://undocs.org/A/70/17, accessed 9 May 2022, para. 240.

1642. Zimmermann, *supra* note 134, p. 119.

1643. G. Cuniberti, "Three Theories of Lex Mercatoria", *Columbian Journal of Transnational Law*, Vol. 52 (2014), pp. 396-403.

1644. Fortier, *supra* note 1572, pp. 121-128 (after note 123). "A powerful advantage of written soft law principles, such as the UNIDROIT Principles, is precisely their written form, and, more particularly, their presentation in a structured and authoritative text around which all discussions will revolve", Bermann, *supra* note 11, p. 360.

do [1645]. However, as stated by Pierre Lalive, while it is true that the *lex mercatoria* is incomplete, no domestic system can be considered complete either [1646]. Moreover, the incompleteness of rules of law "does not have to be a practical disadvantage". This is also the case because instruments such as the UNIDROIT Principles provide a balanced set of rules that are "neutral" and designed to be used throughout the world, irrespective of the legal traditions and the economic and political conditions of the countries in which they are to be applied [1647].

The Hague Principles allow the parties to choose different laws for different parts of the contract (Art. 2 (2)). Therefore, State law and non-State law may coexist in accordance with the needs of the parties [1648]. Moreover, as highlighted by prominent comparatist René David, domestic laws are not typically appropriate for the regulation of international transactions [1649].

(b) *Potential conflicts between Article 3 of the Hague Principles and other models for choosing non-State law*

As stated earlier, Article 3 of the Hague Principles drafted by the Working Group plainly provided: "In these Principles a reference to law includes rules of law", whereas the compromise text now includes the requirements of "generally accepted", "set of rules" and "neutral and balanced".

Michaels offered a harsh critique of this provision, stating that the original provision would "at least have made analytical sense", and that the additions introduced by the Special Commission in 2012 "made a problematic rule far worse". Michaels considers the formula for

1645. R. Michaels, "The UNIDROIT Principles as Global Background Law", *Uniform Law Review*, Vol. 19 (2014), pp. 643-668.

1646. P. Lalive, "Transnational (or Truly International) Public Order and International Arbitration", in P. Sanders, *Comparative Arbitration Practice and Public Policy in Arbitration* (ICCA Congress Series, No. 3), The Hague, Kluwer Law International, 1986, fn. 186.

1647. See UPICC Model Clauses, *supra* note 1501, Clause 1, General Remarks.

1648. This is also the solution provided by the Model Clauses for the Use of the UNIDROIT Principles of International Commercial Contracts. Model Clauses No. 1 states that "parties wishing to choose the UNIDROIT Principles as the rules of law governing their contract may *(i)* choose the UNIDROIT Principles without any reference to other legal sources; *(ii)* choose the UNIDROIT Principles supplemented by a particular domestic law; or *(iii)* choose the UNIDROIT Principles supplemented by "generally accepted principles of international commercial law", UPICC Model Clauses, *supra* note 1501.

1649. David, *supra* note 1474, pp. 11-12.

choosing arbitration too narrow, given that the requirements introduced by the Special Commission do not exist in arbitral laws [1650].

Indeed, Article 28 of the UNCITRAL Model Law does not include the requirements of Article 3 of the Hague Principles. Jürgen Basedow questions whether

> "the arbitrators [could] declare a set of rules forming part of the contract as too fragmentary or too one-sided in order to be treated as the applicable law under Article 3 if the same set of rules can be expected to be regarded as the applicable law in court proceedings under the national provision implementing Article 28 of the UNCITRAL Model Law"?

Basedow considers the role of Article 3 of the Hague Principles to be "a bit opaque". If the drafters wanted to reinforce the general tendency toward non-State law emerging from Article 28 of the Model Law, they should have copied it verbatim, he believes. If the purpose of Article 3 was "to clarify the concept of 'rules of law' used in Article 28 . . . it should have been made clear at least in the Commentary and would raise some doubts as to its legitimacy" [1651].

In response, it could be argued that Article 28 of the Model Law refers to two situations regarding non-State law. The first situation arises in the context of Article 28 (1), dealing with the issue of "applicable law", but with no guidance as to what qualifies as such. In this sense, the Hague Principles can prove useful, as both arbitrators and judges may implement the national provision of Article 28 (1) to assist them in identifying what qualifies as applicable non-State law in arbitration (this matter is still open and very controversial in this discipline). The second situation emerges from Article 28 (4) of the Model Law. This provision deals with non-State law in a different context, referring mostly to non-State law as trade usages in interpretation of contractual terms. The Hague Principles do not have a say on this matter.

A prominent member involved in the drafting of the Hague Principles recognizes that "as is often the case, the phrasing of a compromise text leaves much to be desired" [1652], considering that "drafting by committee

1650. R. Michaels, "Non-State Law in the Hague Principles on Choice of Law in International Contracts", in K. Purnhagen and P. Rott (eds.), *Varieties of European Economic Law and Regulation: Liber Amicorum for Hans Micklitz*, Cham, Springer, 2014.

1651. J. Basedow, "The Hague Principles on Choice of Law: Their Addressees and Impact", *Uniform Law Review*, Vol. 22 (2017), pp. 314-315.

1652. Symeonides, *supra* note 1287, p. 145.

to reach compromise often yields results that are less than optimal" [1653]. José Antonio Moreno Rodríguez presided over an *ad hoc* committee set up in The Hague at the Special Commission meeting of 2012 due to the obstinate refusal of the European Union delegation to accept non-State law in the Hague Principles. Ultimately, the only text that proved acceptable to that delegation was the one finally approved in this *ad hoc* Committee following a proposal by Francesca Mazza [1654]. It was felt at the time by a majority of delegates that a compromise text was a lesser evil than refusing to admit non-State law altogether [1655].

The final drafting of the Hague Principles on this issue is not ideal. However, it opened the door for the acceptance of non-State law within the Hague Principles, which otherwise would not have been possible. As argued by Patrick Glenn, the development of non-State law is ultimately the work of legal practitioners, academics and judges whose primary contribution results from an openness and possible acceptance of non-State legal normativity [1656]. Finally, as stated by Geneviève Saumier, while the criteria in the Hague Principles "can serve to identify 'rules of law' that successfully meet the requirements, the provision remains operational" [1657].

In the context of international investment claims, the final text of Article 3 of the Hague Principles clearly paves the way for the use, for instance, of the UNIDROIT Principles as applicable chosen law or even in absence of choice situations, as will be explained in the next chapter.

1653. G. Saumier, "The Hague Principles and the Choice of Non-State 'Rules of Law' to Govern an International Commercial Contract", *Brooklyn Journal of International Law*, Vol. 40, No. 1 (2014), pp. 24-28.

1654. Mazza was one of the Working Group observers and acted at that time on behalf of the ICC Court of Arbitration.

1655. Dickinson, one of the members of the Working Group on the Hague Principles, also formulated a strong objection to the reforms introduced by the Special Commission. He argued that anyone interpreting the Hague Principles should simply ignore the additions, in "A Principled Approach to Choice of Law in Contract", *Journal of International Banking and Financial Law*, Vol. 2 (2013), p. 152.

1656. H. P. Glenn, "Harmony of Laws in the Americas", Office of the Assistant Secretary for Legal Affairs, Legal Harmonization in the Americas: Business Transactions, Bijuralism and the OAS General Secretariat, 2002, p. 43. This considers the broad recognition of party autonomy and the importance of commercial custom and practice to govern the law on international contracts.

1657. "Only time will tell whether Art 3 is a bold step forward or a step in the wrong direction . . . With such minimal downside risk it is a step worth taking, if only to see where it leads", Saumier, *supra* note 1653, p. 28.

7. The applicability of non-State law in other private international law instruments

As discussed in the previous chapter, the Rome I Regulation only admits the incorporation of non-State law by reference [1658], whereas the Mexico Convention shows greater openness in this regard (even if several of the concepts used in the Convention may cause some interpretation problems). For instance, Article 9, paragraph 2, of the Mexico Convention refers to "the general principles of international commercial law recognized by international organizations"; while Article 10 refers to "the guidelines, customs, and principles of international commercial law as well as commercial usage and practices generally accepted" [1659].

Part Six of the OAS Guide deals with the complex problem of non-State law and various related terminologies, such as uses, customs and practices, principles and the *lex mercatoria.* In line with the Hague Principles, the Guide uses the term "rules of law" and advocates that domestic legal regimes on the law applicable to international commercial contracts "should recognize and clarify choice of non-State law" (Recommendation 6.1). Moreover, the Guide encourages moving beyond the status quo, as do the Hague Principles [1660], admitting non-State law not only in the arbitral setting but also in the judicial context as a choice of law and as an interpretive tool (see Recommendation 6.2).

Under the OHADA draft law, although parties may choose to designate the applicable law to their contract, Article 234 of the Uniform Act on General Commercial Law does not determine whether parties can choose rules of law to govern their contract. Hence, under Article 10 of the OHADA Treaty, this question is governed by the national law of each member State. No OHADA member State allows parties litigating in national courts to designate non-State law to govern their contract. Conversely, the first sentence of Article 15 (1) of the Uniform Act on Arbitration Law allows the parties to choose not only State law but also rules of law *(règles de droit)* to govern their arbitral proceedings [1661].

1658. See paragraph 13 of the preamble to the Rome I Regulation, which states that the regulation "does not preclude parties from incorporating by reference into their contract a non-State body of law or an international convention" (consider also perambulatory para. 14).

1659. See OAS Guide, *supra* note 1309, p. 51.

1660. Gama and Saumier, *supra* note 1627, pp. 62-63.

1661. See Monsenepwo, *supra* note 1345, p. 255.

Similarly, the Preliminary Draft of 2015 does not recognize the option to choose non-State law when a dispute is brought before the court of an OHADA member State [1662].

In a considerable number of jurisdictions worldwide, with respect to proceedings in State courts, parties are not allowed to choose non-State law as the law governing their contract. In these jurisdictions, the law governing the contract must be a State law. If the parties choose non-State law to govern their contract, a domestic court will not recognize this choice and will determine the applicable State law on its own using international conflict rules. This is the case, for instance, in the European Union, in OHADA (and its member States), in Hong Kong, Singapore, South Korea, New Zealand, Mexico, Bolivia, and many other jurisdictions [1663]. In a considerable number of other countries, the question has not yet been decided and therefore remains open, such as in common law Africa, India, Russia, Indonesia, and others. In all these jurisdictions, the parties will only be able to incorporate non-State law into their contract by way of reference (i.e., by the rule of law being integrated within the terms of the contract) [1664].

In a small minority of jurisdictions, the parties are explicitly allowed to choose non-State law to govern their international commercial contracts. This possibility is expressly recognized in Article 3.4 of the draft APPIL [1665]. In the Americas, Paraguayan legislation accepts this possibility, as do the laws in Panama, Venezuela and, very recently, Uruguay [1666].

1662. See Neels, *supra* note 1347.

1663. See "General Comparative Report", *supra* note 1330, pp. 44-45.

1664. *Ibid.*

1665. See Takasugi and Elbalti, *supra* note 1351, pp. 399-413.

1666. See OAS Guide, *supra* note 1309, p. 53. Regarding Uruguay, the new "General Law of Private International Law" (Law No. 19.920), adopted in November 2020, expressly establishes in its Article 45 (2): "In accordance with the provisions of Articles 13 and 51 of this law, the parties may choose rules of law generally accepted at the international level as a set of neutral and balanced rules, provided that these emanate from international organizations to which the Oriental Republic of Uruguay is a party" (translation from Spanish by the author).

CHAPTER XII

THE UNIDROIT PRINCIPLES AND INVESTMENT ARBITRATION

A. Limited role of the UPICC in investment arbitration?

The UNIDROIT Principles (referred to by their acronym "UPICC" in this chapter for the sake of brevity) were initially designed as a tool for international commercial transactions. It is, therefore, understandable that they performed a limited role in international investment arbitration.

However, their importance in this field has been growing in recent years [1667], as reflected in the scholarly writings and cases cited in this chapter.

Further, the UPICC's most recent 2016 edition, which better takes into account matters related to long-term contracts, is envisaged by its drafters to be relevant in both international commercial agreements and foreign investment contracts [1668].

UNIDROIT has also developed, along with the IFAD, an ALIC to be used in this context in particular. The Guide contains references to both public and private international principles and standards, as well as good contractual practices applicable to agricultural land investment contracts. This guidance within the ALIC is consistent with, and reaffirms, the applicability of the UPICC in this scenario [1669].

This chapter will address the relevance of the UPICC as a reflection of general principles of public international law. After, it will refer to its use in private international law or uniform law in several contexts of international investments, including their applicability to issues

---

1667. A. Reinisch, "The Relevance of the UNIDROIT Principles of International Commercial Contracts in International Investment Arbitration", *Uniform Law Review*, Vol. 19 (2014), p. 622. See also P. Bernardini "UNIDROIT Principles and International Investment Arbitration", *Uniform Law Review*, Vol. 19 (2014), p. 563. Others, like Maniruzzaman, for instance, discard their applicability to foreign investment contracts, in Maniruzzaman, *supra* note 317, p. 30.

1668. See, for instance, Article 1.11 states that, "Depending on the context, examples of long-term contracts may include . . . investment or concession agreements".

1669. The Guide ALIC Guide was approved by the UNIDROIT Governing Council at its ninety-ninth session in September 2020. The Draft is available at https://www.unidroit.org/english/documents/2020/study80b/s-80b-alic-draft-e.pdf, accessed 9 May 2022.

related to the COVID-19 pandemic. The chapter will conclude with an evaluation of and remarks on the future prospects of the UPICC in the investment arbitration context.

B. UPICC and public international law

Not all the provisions included in the UPICC reflect a norm recognized in most legal systems [1670]. According to its drafters, however, many of the answers presented in the UPICC are "better solutions" than those found in other systems worldwide [1671].

Only the UPICC provisions that do reflect principles generally accepted worldwide qualify as "general principles of law", so long as they may be applied on a public level [1672] in accordance with Article 38 of the ICJ Statute. The United Nations Compensation Commission (UNCC), for example, referred to the UPICC provisions as an expression of general principles, particularly those concerning *force majeure* [1673].

Most investment arbitration cases deal with treaty claims rather than contract claims. However, even in treaty-related claims, investment tribunals rely on concepts codified by the UPICC as an expression of general principles. Some commercial contract principles contained therein are general enough that they may be relied upon both in contractual and treaty-related relationships between investors and host States [1674].

1670. "When considering domestic principles during the drafting of hard and soft law instruments, it has not always been clear whether all of the principal legal systems of the world were considered." See "Domestic Law Principles", *supra* note 749, p. 1171.

1671. "The question of the influence of soft law instruments that are not well recognized but nevertheless forward-looking remains a difficult one to answer. These laws do not merely reflect the state of law existing at a particular time – they attempt to inculcate new legal rules that offer fair and balanced policies", H. Gabriel, "The Use of Soft Law in the Creation of Legal Norms in International Commercial Law: How Successful Has It Been?", *Michigan Journal of International Law*, Vol. 40, No. 3 (2019), p. 432.

1672. "In this situation, and to the extent that the UPICC are considered to be an expression of generally recognized principles, they may be considered to constitute sufficient proof of the existence of a particular principle and, thus, avoid the criticism that was made in the Klöckner annulment decision. However, a reference to the UPICC will not always be a substitute for proving content of the principle itself. For example, there does not seem to be a uniform understanding of the principle of good faith in international trade. Therefore, the UPICC may not provide sufficient evidence to prove the specific content of a general principle of good faith in international law", Cordero-Moss and Behn, *supra* note 964, p. 587.

1673. UNCC, S/AC.26/1997/6, *supra* note 352, p. 23, 27, 32.

1674. Reinisch, *supra* note 1667, pp. 609-610. Professor Pedro Mendoza kindly read this chapter and commented the following:

In *El Paso* v. *Argentina*, the Tribunal was faced with the issue of the preclusion of wrongfulness in certain situations. In its reasoning, the Tribunal inquired whether the UPICC existed as a "general principle of law recognized by civilized nations" in the sense of Article 38 (1) *(c)* of the ICJ Statute. The Tribunal concluded that the UPICC indeed were a sort of international restatement of the law of contracts, reflecting rules and principles applied by the majority of national legal systems [1675].

The *Gemplus* v. *Mexico* case offers another example, wherein the Tribunal applied the UPICC to corroborate a general principle clearly forming part of public international law, such as the harm reparation principle [1676]. Likewise, in *Ministry of Defense and Support for the Armed Forces of the Islamic Republic of Iran* v. *Cubic Defense Systems, Inc.*, the Arbitral Tribunal and the American Court that decided in favor of the recognition of the arbitral award (the US District Court for the Southern District of California) applied the UPICC as an expression of "general principles of international law" [1677]. Many other decisions also relied on the UPICC as "general principles of law", recognized as applicable within international trade law [1678].

C. UPICC and private international law

1. UPICC as a "general part" of investment contracts

As has been mentioned, there exists no comprehensive corpus of substantive law matters related to international investments. Few

---

"Some authors have expressed some reservation as to the relevance of the UPICC when it comes to the international law of treaties, especially on issues of treaty formation and validity, given the greater need to ensure the stability of treaties. See, for example, Dörr/Schmalenbach (eds.), Vienna Convention on the Law of Treaties: Commentary, Springer 2018, Article 48, paragraph 3, Article 49 paragraph 5, on error and fraud respectively. There, the area of overlap may be relatively small. In other areas, like State responsibility, the overlap might be greater, which explains findings like the ones in El Paso Energy, where the UPICC were used to confirm a rule already codified in Article 23 of the Articles on State Responsibility."

1675. *El Paso* v. *Argentina*, *supra* note 456, Award (31 October 2011). While the ILC Draft Articles are used as the primary source of such a general principle, the UPICC are helpful in corroborating the existence of similar principles in other national legal systems. See Cordero-Moss and Behn, *supra* note 964, p. 595.

1676. *Ibid.*, p. 593.

1677. ICC International Court of Arbitration, Paris 7365/FMS (5 May 1997), in L. Gama, "Les principes d'UNIDROIT et la loi régissant les contrats de commerce", *Recueil des cours*, Vol. 406 (2019), p. 146.

1678. *Ibid.*, p. 144 ff.

(and broad) provisions are found within investment treaties, whereas investment contracts usually focus on matters related to the particular venture and do not deal with general contract law questions.

The UPICC may therefore be of further use [1679] when treated as general principles of law applicable to international contracts [1680]. This is particularly true with respect to the UPICC chapters on formation, validity, performance and non-performance, which contain several provisions particularly suited to the special needs of long-term contracts in general and investment contracts in particular [1681].

2. UPICC as a neutral law chosen by the parties or the tribunal

A fear of the so-called *alea de la souveraineté* (risk of sovereignty) may lead investors to wish to apply the UPICC instead of the law of the home State. In doing so, investors may avoid potential future amendments to local laws that may place them at a disadvantage [1682].

The parties may choose the UPICC either directly or indirectly. When chosen directly, the UPICC must be considered the applicable law, regardless of whether they have been selected before or after a dispute arises – they must apply directly in accordance with the parties' choice [1683].

In the second case, tribunals may apply the UPICC in a neutral fashion when the parties generically refer to "principles of the [host country's domestic law] common to the principles of international law", "generally accepted principles of international commercial law", "usages and customs of international trade", or the like [1684]. The same occurs when the UPICC are considered by tribunals as a manifestation of the *lex mercatoria*, as was recognized in the second of the *Lemire* v. *Ukraine* cases [1685].

Even when domestic laws show a reluctance to accept the choice of non-State rules as the law governing the contract, the situation is very different in the arbitral field. For instance, Article 28 of the UNCITRAL

1679. M. J. Bonell, "International Investment Contracts and General Contract Law: A Place for the UNIDROIT Principles of International Commercial Contracts?", *Uniform Law Review*, Vol. 17 (2012), Nos. 1-2, p. 141.

1680. See Gama, *supra* note 1677, p. 143.

1681. Bonell, *supra* note 1679, p. 146.

1682. Bernardini, *supra* note 1667, p. 563.

1683. This choice might be express or implied. Gama, *supra* note 1677, pp. 127 ff.

1684. Bonell, *supra* note 1679, p. 143.

1685. *Lemire* v. *Ukraine, supra* note 547, Decision on Jurisdiction and Liability (14 January 2010), para. 110.

Model Law expressly accepts the choice of rules of law. Thus, in disputes that fall under model law rules, the UPICC might be applicable as the law governing the contract, even excluding any domestic law [1686]. The same occurs in arbitrations that are conducted under Article 42 (1) of the 1965 ICSID Convention.

3. UPICC in the absence of choice

It is rare for the parties to have clearly chosen the UPICC as the law applicable to their contract in investment-related matters.

In the second of the two *Lemire* cases [1687], the Tribunal applied the UPICC due to the fact that the parties could not agree on a specific national law to govern their contract or apply to their dispute [1688]. The reasoning of the Tribunal in this case is, however, unclear [1689], and does not shed much light on the matter.

Now, then, where the parties have not chosen an applicable law, the tribunal should not necessarily automatically opt for the application of non-State law. In ICC Case No. 7319 of 1991 [1690], the tribunal applied the Irish substantive law following the Rome Convention provision on absence of choice, determining that this instrument governed the relationship for both parties. In situations like this, according to Horacio Grigera, it is safer to apply an instrument that is common to both parties (the Rome Convention in this case) in order to avoid the risk of the award being challenged [1691].

In any event, in situations of absence of choice, the arbitrators must first hear the parties on the law that they consider most appropriate to govern the substance of the dispute [1692] if they did not discuss this issue in their submissions [1693].

1686. For the binding force of the parties' choice in arbitration and State courts, see Gama, *supra* note 1677, pp. 128 *et seq.*

1687. *Lemire* v. *Ukraine*, *supra* note 547, para. 109.

1688. See Reinisch, *supra* note 1667, pp. 610-611. Bonell refers to the *voie directe* powers of the tribunal. Bonell, *supra* note 1679, p. 144.

1689. Cordero-Moss and Behn, *supra* note 964, p. 582.

1690. *Collection of ICC Arbitral Awards 1996-2000* (2003), p. 300 ff.

1691. H. Grigera Naón, "UNIDROIT Principles as Proper Law", in C. Benicke and S. Huber (eds.), *National, International, Transnational: Harmonischer Dreiklang im Recht, zum 70, Festschrift für Herbert Kronke, Geburtstag*, Bielefeld, Verlag Ernst / Werner Gieseking, 2020, p. 127.

1692. Gama, *supra* note 1677, pp. 169-170.

1693. In the context of an *iura novit arbiter* (the UPICC was not considered in the case), a similar statement (with citations) regarding discussion by the parties was made in *Carlos Rios y Francisco Javier Rios c. República de Chile*, ICSID Case No. ARB/17/16.

D. UPICC as an interpretive aid

In addition to their primary application as the law governing the contract, the UPICC may also be used on a subsidiary basis to interpret or supplement the international conventions and national laws that might be applicable to the investment relationship [1694]. In this regard, Ralf Michaels notes that, "like *ius commune* and common law", the UPICC "serve as a global background law" that is increasingly used by judges and legislators to justify their decisions through reference to a global consensus (whether imagined or real). In short, Michaels points out that the UPICC "are becoming, more and more, a sort of general benchmark against which legal arguments take place" [1695].

International tribunals have relied upon the UPICC in this way to resolve investment disputes. For instance, in the *Al-Kharafi* v. *Libya* case, the Tribunal referred to the UPICC to support its reasoning for the amount of damages awarded [1696], which were among the highest granted in the history of investment arbitration [1697]. The *Petrobart* v. *Kyrgyzstan* case conducted under the Stockholm Chamber of Commerce arbitration rules offers another example where the Tribunal referred to the UPICC to justify its award on interests [1698]. Further, in the ICSID case *AIG* v. *Kazakhstan*, the arbitrators referred to Article 7.4.8 of the UPICC in relation to the broad acceptance of the "duty to mitigate damages" [1699]. Finally, the defense of non-performance *(exceptio non adimpleti contractus)* was addressed in 2005 by the *ad hoc* Tribunal in *Eureko* v. *Poland* [1700]. In its decision, the Tribunal referred to the exception as contemplated in Article 7.1.3 of the UPICC [1701].

1694. No. 1 of The Model Clauses for the Use of the UNIDROIT Principles of International Commercial Contracts states that parties wishing to choose the UNIDROIT Principles as the rules of law governing their contract may *(i)* choose the UNIDROIT Principles without any reference to other legal sources; *(ii)* choose the UNIDROIT Principles supplemented by a particular domestic law; or *(iii)* choose the UNIDROIT Principles supplemented by "generally accepted principles of international commercial law", UPICC Model Clauses, *supra* note 1501.

1695. Michaels, *supra* note 1645, pp. 643-668.

1696. *Mohamed Abdulmohsen Al-Kharafi & Sons Co.* v. *Libya and others*, *Ad Hoc* Arbitration, Final Arbitral Award (22 March 2013).

1697. Reinisch, *supra* note 1667, p. 614.

1698. *Petrobart* v. *Kyrgyz Republic*, *supra* note 327, Award (29 March 2005).

1699. *AIG* v. *Kazakhstan*, *supra* note 1409, Award (7 October 2003).

1700. *Eureko* v. *Poland*, *supra* note 539, Partial Award (19 August 2005), para. 167.

1701. "but it stressed that it only applied to cases of conditional or simultaneous performance 'if the other party is not willing and able to perform'. Since the parties had simultaneously performed their waiver agreement by ending and not merely suspending all claims, the Tribunal could not identify any non-performance justifying the resubmission of the waived claims", Reinisch, *supra* note 1667, p. 616. See

E. UPICC as corroboration of national law

The UPICC may serve to legitimize the conclusions reached by tribunals in their interpretation of national laws [1702].

For instance, in *African Holding* v. *Congo*, the Tribunal stated that under Congolese law and in accordance with the UPICC, it was not necessary for the contract to be in writing. Moreover, the conduct of the parties proved the existence of a construction contract [1703]. Other examples may be found in *AIG* v. *Kazakhstan*, *Sax* v. *City of Saint Petersburg*, *Al-Kharafi* v. *Libya* [1704] and *Suez* v. *Argentina* [1705].

F. The supplementary or corrective function of the UPICC

An Arbitral Tribunal found that a former Soviet country had not yet fully developed its legal framework regarding the market economy, which contained several gaps and ambiguities pertinent to a dispute. The Tribunal supplemented the country's national law by applying the UPICC in its place [1706].

This is another important function of the UPICC: it may supplement anachronistic or unsophisticated legal systems that cannot appropriately deal with certain issues regarding, for instance, the formation, validity, performance and non-performance of an investment contract [1707].

A more contentious issue regards the potential *corrective* function of the UPICC in the arbitration context [1708]. As will be seen further in

---

criticisms in light of the absence of a more rigorous examination of the applicability of the UNIDROIT Principles in Cordero-Moss and Behn, *supra* note 964, p. 590.

1702. Cordero-Moss and Behn, *supra* note 964, p. 596. This is the use more extended regarding the UNIDROIT Principles reported cases in practice. See Garro and Moreno Rodríguez, *supra* note 1508, pp. 68-69.

1703. *African Holding Company of America, Inc. and Société Africaine de Construction au Congo SARL* v. *Democratic Republic of the Congo*, ICSID Case No. ARB/05/21, Award (29 July 2008).

1704. *Al-Kharafi* v. *Libya*, *supra* note 1696, Award (2013).

1705. In corroboration of its conclusions in favor of the obligation to negotiate in cases of hardship, the Tribunal cited the UNIDROIT Principles and the Principles of European Contract Law. *Suez* v. *Argentina*, *supra* note 51, Dissenting Opinion of Arbitrator Pedro Nikken, para. 48.

1706. The energy supply system in the State in question was fundamentally changed by law, making it possible for the power station constructed by the US company to supply energy at profitable prices. Given this, the Tribunal found that the application of the national law of that State should be supplemented by taking the UPICC into consideration, particularly Articles 1.4, 6.2.2/6.2.3 and 7.1.7. See Dolzer, *supra* note 24, p. 825.

1707. See Garro and Moreno Rodríguez, *supra* note 1508. See also Gama, *supra* note 1677, pp. 187 *et seq.*

1708. Cordero-Moss and Behn, *supra* note 964, p. 595.

Chapter XX, international and uniform law may play a corrective role when in relation to national law. Moreover, the UPICC have been used in treaty arbitration cases as a confirmation of a rule that is already part of customary international law [1709].

G. UPICC as invoked by the parties

In several investment arbitration cases, the parties invoked the UPICC in their submissions. This was the case, for instance, in *PSEG* v. *Turkey* [1710], *Limited Liability Company AMTO* v. *Ukraine* [1711], *Meerapfel* v. *Central African Republic* [1712], *Azurix* v. *Argentina*, *Kardassopoulos & Fuchs* v. *Georgia* [1713], *SGS* v. *Paraguay* [1714], *Chevron* v. *Ecuador* [1715] and *Micula* v. *Romania* [1716].

Even though the tribunals in these cases did not cite the UPICC in their decisions, they may very well have relied upon the substance of its provisions in their reasoning when evaluating the parties' arguments. As such, determining the specific influence of the UPICC in these cases remains difficult.

As an example, in *PSEG* v. *Turkey*, the Arbitral Tribunal addressed the issue of good or bad faith in negotiations. It used words such as "reasonable" (para. 127), "lack of diligence" or "silence" (para. 157), and also addressed the question of "Were the Parties Engaged in Subsequent Negotiations in Bad Faith?" (paras. 159 to 178). Many of the arguments therein included could well have also cited, in their support, the UPICC and its rules and comments on good and bad faith.

H. Aspects of investment contracts in which the UPICC may be useful

The following examples illustrate circumstances where the UPICC may be used to interpret investment contracts. Many of these

---

1709. Bernardini, *supra* note 1667, p. 569.

1710. *PSEG* v. *Turkey*, *supra* note 523, Decision on Jurisdiction (4 June 2004).

1711. SCC Award No. 80/2005 (26 March 2008), para. 34. The claimant invoked Article 7.4.9 of the PICC to support its claim for interest.

1712. *M. Meerapfel Söhne AG* v. *Central African Republic*, ICSID Case No. ARB/07/10, Award (12 May 2011).

1713. *Ioannis Kardassopoulos & Ron Fuchs* v. *Georgia*, ICSID Case No. ARB/05/18 and ICSID Case No. ARB/07/15, Award (3 March 2010).

1714. *SGS Société Générale de Surveillance* v. *Republic of Paraguay*, ICSID Case No. ARB/07/29, Award (10 February 2012).

1715. *Chevron* v. *Ecuador (II)*, *supra* note 1358, Partial Award (20 March 2010), para. 382.

1716. *Ioan Micula* et al. v. *Romania*, *supra* note 102, Award (11 December 2013).

provisions – such as those related to long-term contracts and changes of circumstances – may be particularly relevant considering the situation created by the COVID-19 pandemic.

1. Determining when a binding agreement has been reached

Many long-term contracts and investment contracts involve lengthy negotiations. The UPICC contain provisions determining when a binding agreement has been reached (Art. 2.1.1) [1717], and determining the precise time of the conclusion of the contract (Official Comments to Art. 5.3.1) [1718].

2. Extended negotiations

Investment contracts are usually arrived at after extensive negotiations. Article 2.1.15 of the UPICC deals with negotiations that have been made in bad faith and can be useful to determine the offending party's liability. In addition, when parties put their agreement in writing and declare that their document constitutes the final agreement, Article 2.1.17 related to merger clauses may be helpful [1719]. In these situations, even though prior statements cannot be used to contradict or supplement the final contract, they may still serve an interpretive purpose [1720].

3. Interest rates

On this issue, the Iran-United States Claims Tribunal invoked UPICC Article 7.4.9 (2), which provides "[that] the rate of interest shall be the average bank short-term lending rate to prime borrowers prevailing for the currency of payment at the place for payment, or where no such rate exists at that place, then the same rate in the State of the currency of payment" [1721].

1717. See the ICSID awards of 23 July 2008 and 4 June 2004. A delicate issue can also arise regarding the identification of the public party to a contract (for example, is it the State or the signatory State entity or the controlling government ministry). The UPICC can be of assistance when there are misrepresentations in this regard. See Crawford and Sinclair, *supra* note 122, pp. 61-67.

1718. Bonell, *supra* note 1679, pp. 146-147.

1719. Referred to in the ICSID Award of 14 January 2010.

1720. Bonell, *supra* note 1679, p. 148.

1721. *The Islamic Republic of Iran* v. *The United States of America*, IUSCT Case No. 602-A15(IV)/A24-FT, Decision (2 July 2014), http://www.unilex.info/principles/case/1856, accessed 10 May 2022.

4. Gross disparity

Often, developing countries do not have equal bargaining power *vis-à-vis* major corporations. Article 3.2.7 of the UPICC concerning gross disparity may be invoked in these situations. Moreover, Article 7.4.13 concerning payment for non-performance may be referenced to prevent abuses regarding "penalty" or "liquidated damages".

5. Remedies for illegality

Article 3.3.1 of the UPICC on "contracts infringing mandatory rules" and Article 3.3.2 on "restitution" deal with situations of illegality and may be very useful in determining remedies where corruption has occurred [1722].

6. Supervening events

Articles 6.2.2 and 6.2.3 of the UPICC address hardship or supervening circumstances that lead to a fundamental alteration of the equilibrium of the contract, as well as the appropriate remedies for each.

By contrast, Article 7.1.7 relates to *force majeure*. Termination, adaptation or renegotiation are all remedies contemplated for hardship. In situations of *force majeure*, the only remedy provided by the UPICC is an excuse for non-performance: there is no possibility of the adjudicator adapting the contract, nor a duty of the parties to renegotiate (as provided by the UPICC in the case of hardship) [1723].

In reference to hardship, Stefan Kröll praises the solutions offered by the UPICC. He states that although they were initially intended for international commercial contracts, they offer a flexible balancing of the conflicting interests involved in investment contracts [1724].

Furthermore, the dissenting opinion of arbitrator Pedro Nikken in the *Suez* v. *Argentina* investment case stresses the potential of the UPICC to evaluate whether a contractual renegotiation due to hardship constitutes a breach of the fair and equitable treatment standard [1725].

1722. See Bonell, *supra* note 1679, p. 150.

1723. Bonell, *supra* note 1679, p. 155. See a detailed treatment of the matter in Crawford and Sinclair, *supra* note 122, pp. 67-75.

1724. S. Kröll, "The Renegotiation and Adaptation of Investment Contracts", in N. Horn and S. Kröll (eds.), *Arbitrating Foreign Investment Disputes: Procedural and Substantive Legal Aspects* (Studies in Transnational Economic Law, No. 19), The Hague, Kluwer Law International, 2004, p. 466.

1725. *Suez* v. *Argentina*, *supra* note 51, Dissenting Opinion of Arbitrator Pedro Nikken, para. 48.

7. Duty of cooperation

Article 5.1.3 of the UPICC aims to guarantee cooperation between the parties. This provision can be important in long-term agreements, particularly in investment contracts.

8. Stabilization clauses

Clauses that insulate the contract against legislative changes within the host country that may affect the investment raise interesting issues. In particular, the question remains open whether such safeguards within investment contracts (which are often also supported by investment treaties as well) can override regulatory measures enacted to advance legitimate public objectives such as public health, safety, environment, and food and water shortages. In these cases, the application of the UPICC would mandate the parties to negotiate a solution in good faith at the outset rather than just imposing upon the host State the duty to compensate the injured parties for the emergency measures taken [1726].

9. Termination

UPICC provisions related to the termination of contracts may be particularly useful in investment contracts as well. Articles 7.3.1 to 7.37 relate to termination for non-performance, and Article 5.1.8 refers to contracts concluded for an indefinite period [1727].

10. Estoppel and duty of best efforts

The Tribunal in the second of the *Lemire* cases relied on the estoppel/ *venire contra factum proprium* principle enshrined in Article 1.8 of the 2004 version of the UPICC when it determined that a party cannot invoke a specific contractual breach that it had previously condoned. The same Tribunal also invoked the duty of best efforts located in Article 5.1.4 of the 2004 version of the UPICC to find that a mere delay in procuring licenses did not violate this obligation [1728].

1726. Boncll, *supra* note 1679, p. 156
1727. *Ibid.*, p. 158.
1728. *Lemire* v. *Ukraine*, *supra* note 547, Decision on Jurisdiction and Liability (14 January 2010), paras. 134, 154, 199.

11. Damages

The UPICC provisions related to damages have also been applied in investment arbitrations. In *Gemplus* v. *Mexico*, the Tribunal referred to Article 7.4.2 in relation to lost profits [1729]. In *El Paso* v. *Argentina*, the arbitrators mentioned Articles 7.1.6 and 7.1.7 of the 2004 version of the UPICC to find exemptions from liability for non-performance. The Tribunal interpreted the investment according to these provisions and decided that the exemption did not apply to Argentina [1730].

12. Interest rate

In *Sax* v. *City of Saint Petersburg* [1731], the Arbitral Tribunal quoted Article 7.4.9 in its determination of the interest rate. However, the Tribunal did not rely solely on the UPICC but reasoned that the "average bank short-term lending rate to prime borrowers of the currency in question at the place for payment" was a "frequently used formula in international arbitration" [1732].

13. Mitigation of damages

There is convincing evidence that the duty to mitigate the other party's loss has been generally accepted within international practice. This principle is reflected in Article 7.4.8 of the UPICC relating to the mitigation of harm [1733].

A UNCC panel decided that Article 7.4.8 reflects a general principle of law [1734], recognized both in public and private law [1735].

1729. *Gemplus and Talsud* v. *Mexico*, ICSID Case No. ARB(AF)/04/3, Award (16 June 2010).

1730. *El Paso* v. *Argentina*, *supra* note 456, Award (31 October 2011). See Reinisch, *supra* note 1667, pp. 617-618.

1731. *Sax* v. *City of Saint Petersburg (Sax)*, *Ad hoc* UNCITRAL Arbitration, Award (30 March, 2012).

1732. Reinisch, *supra* note 1667, p. 618.

1733. "(1) The non-performing party is not liable for harm suffered by the aggrieved party to the extent that the harm could have been reduced by the latter party's taking reasonable steps. (2) The aggrieved party is entitled to recover any expenses reasonably incurred in attempting to reduce the harm." Full text available at https://www.unidroit.org/instruments/commercial-contracts/unidroit-principles-2010/chapter-7-section-4/, accessed 28 September 2022. This duty is also contemplated in Article 77 of the CISG and in other instruments.

1734. UNCC, S/AC.26/1997/6, *supra* note 352, para. 79.

1735. Reed, *supra* note 21, p. 225.

I. The UPICC and ex aequo et bono arbitrations

In these proceedings [1736], even though the arbitrators are not tied to a specific legal system, they must become familiar with the stipulations of the contract, look at the intention of the parties and interpret and supplement ambiguous texts. In completing this mission, even in their internal forum, the arbitrators will likely find the UPICC a useful tool [1737]. As summarized by Russel Weintraub, in these situations the UPICC may provide the adjudicators with a reliable guide on how to act [1738].

J. UPICC and the COVID-19 crisis

The COVID-19 pandemic caused a global economic slowdown and significantly affected the business operations of many sectors [1739]. Arguably, the world of contracts has not suffered such an unforeseeable, global and intense interference since at least the outbreak of World War I. The effects on contractual relations of such an event are clear: the volume of orders collapsed, deadlines were not met and liquidity was depleted while operating costs accumulated. Investors may find it impossible to continue on agreed terms, and States may also not be in a position to keep their word. Matters of public policy and new legislation issuing mandatory norms might have a considerable impact. What is the way forward?

The UPICC may offer guidance for many issues relating to foreign investments, particularly concerning State contracts [1740]. The open nature of the UPICC furnishes the parties and interpreters with a much-needed flexibility in such an extreme context, constituting an efficient tool to offer a nuanced solution that can help preserve valuable contracts.

1736. See Chap. XIX, *infra*.

1737. Siqueiros, *supra* note 1311, p. 227.

1738. R. J. Weintraub, "Lex Mercatoria and The UNIDROIT Principles of International Commercial Contracts", in P. Borchers and J. Zekoll (eds.), *International Conflict of Laws for the Third Millennium: Essays in Honor of Friedrich K. Juenger*, New York, Transnational Publishers, 2001, p. 142.

1739. See note of the UNIDROIT Secretariat on the UNIDROIT Principles of International Commercial Contracts and the Covid-19 health crisis, https://www.unidroit.org/unidroit-releases-secretariat-note-on-the-unidroit-principles-of-international-commercial-contracts-and-covid-19, accessed 10 May 2022.

1740. For a detailed analysis of the relevance of the UPICC to interpret the equitable and fair treatment standard and other open-ended clauses in State contracts, see Reinisch, *supra* note 1667, pp. 609-622.

Especially in mid-to-long-term contracts, and in view of the temporary nature of the impediment, mechanisms that allow for an adequate renegotiation and proportionate allocation of losses ultimately help preserve contracts and maximize value for the jurisdiction involved.

In this regard, the UNIDROIT Secretariat prepared a document purporting to help parties use the UPICC "*(i)* . . . when implementing and interpreting their existing contracts or when drafting new ones in the times of the pandemic and its aftermath"; as well as to "*(ii)* assist courts and arbitral tribunals or other adjudicating bodies in deciding disputes arising out of such contracts; and *(iii)* provide legislators with a tool to modernise their contract law regulations, wherever necessary, or possibly even to adopt special rules for the present emergency situation" [1741].

The first known court decision relying on the UPICC on matters related to the pandemic was rendered on 30 April 2020, by the Rechtbank of Amsterdam [1742].

K. Evaluation and future prospects of the UPICC

The UPICC have enormous potential in the legal field of foreign investments. They may apply not only to international investment State contracts but also to public international law issues when tribunals consider the UPICC reflect general principles in this area.

It is true that the available information reflects that the UPICC have only been used in few cases. However, and even though much writing focuses on ICSID arbitrations, a significant number of investment cases are heard before other forums such as the ICC [1743], or other arbitral mechanisms including *ad hoc* arbitrations. The resulting awards are

---

1741. *Supra* note 1739, p. 2. See also M. M. Albornoz, "Contratos internacionales con COVID-19", in N. González Martín (ed.), *COVID-19 y su circunstancia. Una visión jurídica plural de la pandemia*, Vol. 1: *Marcos normativos*, México, Universidad Nacional Autónoma de México / Instituto de Investigaciones Jurídicas e Instituto de Estudios Constitucionales del Estado de Querétaro, 2021, https://archivos.juridicas.unam.mx/www/bjv/libros/14/6566/5.pdf, accessed 13 June 2022, pp. 1-23.

1742. See note prepared by Professor Michael Joachim Bonell and Ms Eleonora Finazzi Agrò, see https://www.unidroit.org/unidroit-covid-19/#1456405893720-a55ec26a-b30a, accessed 10 May 2022. In the same link, the UNIDROIT Secretariat notes that other instruments may also be useful, such as the UNIDROIT/FAO/IFAD Guide on Contract Farming, the Convention on International Interests in Mobile Equipment and the UNIDROIT/IFAD ALIC.

1743. Indeed, an ICC decision, in ICC Case No. 7110, has been regarded "as the official *entrée* of the Principles into international arbitration". See Crawford and Sinclair, *supra* note 122, p. 59.

rarely published and even when they are, the parties' pleadings are rarely made publicly available [1744].

Moreover, recent developments, such as the 2016 version of the UPICC and the ALIC Guide approved in 2020, strongly signal that UNIDROIT considers that their applicability must not be limited to commercial contracts and can be extended to the investment context.

A reason for the lack of reliance on the UPICC within investment claims may be due to the arbitrators' backgrounds. Arbitrators trained in commercial arbitration are more prone to accept the UPICC than panels composed of public international law specialists [1745]. For example, Professor Rajski, a member of the working group that drafted the UPICC, was also a member of the tribunal in *Eureko* v. *Poland* that decided to apply them. Similarly, Piero Bernardini was also a member of the same working group and formed part of the tribunals in *AIG* v. *Kazakhstan* and *El Paso* v. *Argentina*, which invoked the UPICC as well. In the same vein, several Iran-United States Claims Tribunal decisions relied on these principles, likely due to the influence of Herbert Kronke, a member of the Tribunal and former Secretary-General of UNIDROIT.

The UPICC represent one of the most impressive achievements in uniform law history. Since they were initially designed as a tool for international commercial transactions, it is understandable that in their inception they performed a limited role in foreign investment claims. However, their importance in this field has been growing in recent years and should enhance exponentially if well understood their content and potential.

1744. J. Hepburn, "The UNIDROIT Principles of International Commercial Contracts and Investment Treaty Arbitration: A Limited Relationship", https://www.academia.edu/28252754/The_UNIDROIT_Principles_of_International_Commercial_Contracts_and_Investment_Treaty_Arbitration_A_Limited_Relationship, accessed 9 May 2022, pp. 33-34. A revised version of this paper appears in *International and Comparative Law Quarterly*, Vol. 64 (2015), p. 905. See Dolzer, *supra* note 24, p. 825.

1745. Bernardini, *supra* note 1667, p. 563. See also Reinisch, *supra* note 1667, p. 622. Remarkably, prominent commentators with special expertise in international commercial arbitration (and not public international law specialists) have observed this movement away from domestic law within commercial arbitration.

CHAPTER XIII

PUBLIC AND PRIVATE INTERNATIONAL LAW RELATIONSHIPS IN INVESTMENT LAW

The former Hague Academy Secretary-General Yves Daudet once posed the following question: in a globalized society such as ours, where public and private actors intermingle in commercial and political activities, how can public and private international law disregard their mutual developments [1746]? Publicists may take inspiration from private international law to address their problems, and privatists may draw upon public international lawyers in their endeavors.

Today, there is an "unconvincing separation between public and private international law" [1747]. The cracking *(resquebrajamiento)* within their traditional concepts [1748] has led the two disciplines to intertwine "to a degree that they become difficult to distinguish" [1749].

However, there is a remarkable gap in scholarly writings discussing the relationship between them [1750]. This is particularly troubling. Although it may not always be apparent to those on the battlefield, bridging the methodological and teleological gap between private and public law is a necessity for both disciplines. Thus, the new generation of international lawyers is faced with the challenge of perceiving the existing opportunities to merge both disciplines, especially during moments of crisis [1751].

1746. Y. Daudet, prologue to D. P. Fernández Arroyo and C. Lima Marques (eds.), *Derecho internacional privado y derecho internacional público*: *un encuentro necesario*, Asunción, CEDEP, 2011, pp. 22-23.

1747. Lowenfeld, *supra* note 1197, p. 26.

1748. T. B. Maekelt, "Relaciones entre el derecho internacional privado y el derecho internacional público", in D. P. Fernández Arroyo and C. Lima Marques (eds.), *Derecho internacional privado y derecho internacional público*: *un encuentro necesario*, Asunción, CEDEP, 2011, p. 57.

1749. Orrego Vicuña, *supra* note 1103, p. 342.

1750. D. Opertti Badán, "Derecho internacional público y derecho internacional privado. Hacia un diálogo renovado", in D. P. Fernández Arroyo and C. Lima Marques (eds.), *Derecho internacional privado y derecho internacional público*: *un encuentro necesario*, Asunción, CEDEP, 2011, p. 76.

1751. Reed, *supra* note 21, p. 193.

A. Private and public law notions

In ancient Rome, Ulpianus connected public law to the State and private law to the individual [1752]. Centuries later, Francis Bacon referred to public law as the sinews of government, and to private law as the sinews of property [1753].

Thus, the classical understanding of public law addresses interactions between individuals and the State, comprising topics such as constitutional, administrative, criminal or tax law, while private law governs relationships between private individuals such as property, contract, torts and unjust enrichment [1754].

The public-private law divide applies primarily to substantive law matters. Within the realm of dispute resolution, this distinction establishes the jurisdiction of different courts (civil and administrative) that apply different procedures [1755]. The public-private law divide is primarily found in continental law systems, but it also exists in certain parts of the common law world [1756].

As stated by Francis Mann, it is dangerous to treat public-private law distinctions as exhaustive or invariably correct and precise, "while in truth they merely constitute a primitive and initial guide" [1757]. The fundamental weakness of the divide is the absence of a consensus on

---

1752. The formula of Ulpianus according to whom *publicum jus est quod ad statum rei Romanae spectat, privatum quod ad singulorum utilitatem*.

1753. E. Works of 1803, VII, 440.

1754. See Arato, *supra* note 39, p. 8.

1755. Hess, *supra* note 48, p. 21.

1756. *Ibid.*, p. 21. J. A. Maupin, "Public and Private in International Investment Law: An Integrated Systems Approach", *Virginia Journal of International Law*, Vol. 54, No. 2 (2014), p. 410:

> "Both common law and civil law systems historically recognized a distinction between these two types of law, though on the basis of different legal philosophies. Public law had, from this point of view, two major components: constitutional law in the classic sense – the law by which the governmental structure is constituted – and administrative law – the law governing the public administration and its relations with private individuals. In private legal relations the parties were equals and the State the referee. In public legal relations the State was a party, and as a representative of the public interest (and successor to the prince) it was a party superior to the private individual. In the English common law tradition, by contrast, private law rights included not only rights in property and contract but also rights of personal security and personal liberty. These private common law rights were held to pre-exist statutory (or codified) law – a view subsequently transferred to American law as well. Regulatory claims by individuals against the government did not originally fall under the domain of public law."

1757. F. A. Mann, "Conflict of Laws and Public Law", *Recueil des cours*, Vol. 132 (1971), pp. 117-118.

the dividing line between the two disciplines at both the domestic and international levels [1758].

The twenty-first century has seen an expansion of the gray area that exists between public and private law, where mercantile activities involve States' regulatory interests as well as their commercial conduct and domestic agencies [1759]. Entire fields of law exist within this gray area – administrative contracts, the regulation of corporations and patent law, to name a few. The State also acts as a commercial party in a variety of legal arrangements ranging from buying and selling property, to contracting with citizens and foreigners, to investing in private businesses, joint ventures and State-owned enterprises. International investment arbitration exists at the border of these State-sponsored commercial activities, and as such it can be understood both from public and private law perspectives [1760].

Moreover, even though the public-private law distinction dominates the teaching curricula of modern legal education, there is hardly any private law field that can nowadays be adequately understood without a strong and often decisive admixture of public law. For instance, numerous statutory public law regulations – regarding standard terms, for instance – increasingly affect private contract law [1761].

Legal doctrine concerning the public-private law divide developed in several directions: some scholars advocate for a merging of the two disciplines, while others argue for the preservation of the divide by reinforcing it from a public law perspective in light of recent regulatory developments.

B. The distinction between public and private international law

Public and private international law emerged from a single international law of nations [1762]. In the Anglo-American usage, the term "international law" was popularized by Jeremy Bentham, who intended it to refer to *public* international law when used without qualification. On

1758. Hess, *supra* note 48, p. 275.
1759. *Ibid.*, p. 276.
1760. "That is, both in terms of how far it accomplishes its goals of investment protection and promotion, and in terms of how it affects domestic legal institutions", Arato, *supra* note 39, p. 8.
1761. "Moreover, a new category of government contracts developed that, although technically considered private contracts, produced distinctly public law principles (such as the French *contrat administratif*)", Friedmann, *supra* note 955, p. 281.
1762. Fernández Arroyo and Moïse Mbengue, *supra* note 1450, p. 800.

the other hand, *private* international law is a separate subject – usually referred to as "conflict of laws" in the common law world [1763]. The close relationship between public and private international law began to fade in the nineteenth century, and by the early years of the twentieth century the understanding of both as entirely separate disciplines prevailed [1764].

Historically, public international law has consisted of sources emanating from the international community of States, within which governments preside over defined territories. It applies to States [1765], to international organizations created by States [1766] and to individuals when pertinent under international treaties or customary international law [1767].

Public international law exists outside any municipal law, although national laws can influence its development if they are applied regularly around the world. National law can become relevant in matters such as international investment claims, in which it has been challenged by investors for unduly interfering with their commercial activities in another State. In turn, public international law is used to determine whether the application of national laws is acceptable or not in particular transborder relationships [1768].

While public international law deals with the relationships between sovereign States and international organizations, private international law encompasses transactions between individuals and private entities [1769]. The fundamental premise of the public-private law distinction is that certain areas of the law are inherently "public" and others inherently "private". The distinction is more meaningful to civil law lawyers, since public and private law have historically developed separately and on entirely different premises within civil law systems.

1763. Wortley, *supra* note 1161, pp. 247-248.

1764. A. Mills, "Public International Law and Private International Law", in J. Basedow *et al.* (eds.), *Encyclopedia of Private International Law*, Vol. 2: *Entries I-Z*, Cheltenham, Edward Elgar, 2017, p. 1450.

1765. In the case of the SS *Lotus*, the PCIJ stated: "International law governs relations between independent States. The rules of law binding upon States therefore emanate from their own free will as expressed in conventions or by usages generally accepted as expressing principles of law and established to regulate the relations between these co-existing independent communities or with a view to the achievement of common aims", *Fr.* v. *Turk*, *Lotus* judgment (1927), *supra* note 1109, para. 444.

1766. This extension was made in the ICJ advisory opinion in *Reparation for Injuries Suffered*, *supra* note 330, at p. 174.

1767. Maupin, *supra* note 1756, p. 406.

1768. Collins, *supra* note 66, pp. 27-29.

1769. Stewart, *supra* note 1464, p. 81.

Differences in theories of individual autonomy and the rule of law for the State within the civil law world illustrate this divide [1770].

For many of its experts, public international law is the only truly "international" law since private international law is largely made up of domestic laws, rules and principles governing questions of jurisdiction, conflict of laws and the enforcement of judgments [1771].

However, this understanding of both disciplines is no longer accurate. Public international law deals with the rights and obligations of individuals and other non-State entities, such as international corporations [1772]. Private international law is not limited to domestic regulation – it also includes international rules and procedures that are applicable to private law relationships [1773].

Hersch Lauterpacht emphasizes three points of contact between public and private international law. The first refers to situations in which legal relationships generally regulated by public international law are shaped "in accordance with or after the analogy of private law. This occurs, for instance, when a matter of sovereignty over a territory is decided applying the rules of prescription" [1774].

The second public-private point of contact occurs when the State or its entities conduct business between themselves, outside the scope of the "rights and duties of imperium". This takes place, for example, when States grant a loan or a purely economic lease to one another [1775].

The third point of contact occurs where public international law determines or influences private rights such as those applying to aliens [1776].

1770. Reed, *supra* note 21, pp. 202-203.

1771. "Both public and private international law have been considered misnomers. Private international law is not technically 'international' because it does not transcend State boundaries but merely deals with situations potentially falling within the scope of municipal law. Private international law is a sort of co-ordinating law, but that is organized *by means of and at the level of municipal law.* On the other hand, it is argued that public international law operates and is created truly *international*, but is not really law. This is because, by definition, law cannot extend to contractual creations under no superior authority and, more importantly, with no safeguarding sanctions" (*ibid.*, p. 203).

1772. "[I]t can no longer be admitted that companies operating internationally are immune from becoming subjects of international law" (*Urbaser* v. *Argentina*, *supra* note 51, paras. 1195-1196).

1773. Stewart, *supra* note 1464, pp. 81-82.

1774. Lauterpacht, *supra* note 3, p. 3.

1775. *Ibid.*, p. 4.

1776. Those cases in which parties to a treaty make use of private law principles to assert private law rights are of particular importance. Lauterpacht, *supra* note 3, p. 4.

Furthermore, functional connections exist between public and private international law as well. For example, significant public-private connections happen within public policy norms [1777], which will be addressed in Chapter XXI.

C. The influence of private law in the development of public international law

Many publicists avoid the use of private law in their work. In their view, recourse to private law was perhaps justified in the formative period of public international law but "has subsequently impeded its growth, and ought to be discouraged" [1778]. However, a critical examination shows that private law in fact had a positive influence on the development of public international law. This discipline in many cases ultimately adopted private law solutions without regard for the so-called "special character" of international relations [1779].

As pointed out in Chapter IV, domestic law is generally more complex than public international law and has developed a more advanced set of legal principles frequently used in the latter [1780]. At its core, the legal notion of responsibility, for example, is substantially similar in both public international law and municipal law [1781]. In fact, many international legal doctrines such as estoppel and the strict performance of contractual obligations [1782] derive from domestic legal norms which, according to Jaye Ellis, "may escape our notice because they have become such a familiar part of the international landscape" [1783].

1777. Mills, *supra* note 1764, p. 1451. He also mentions the example of the rule of comity (pp. 1448-1449).

1778. "Making use of private law principles is considered an unfortunate imitation strategy that ignores the special structure of international relations and, by introducing the intricacies of municipal law, threatens to thwart all attempts to develop international law into a fruitful and creative scientific discipline. Even in those rare cases in which an author is forced to adopt a private law solution due to the types of legal relationships he is presented with, making use of private law through analogy is usually accompanied by caveats or by apologetic explanations", Lauterpacht, *supra* note 3, p. vi.

1779. Lauterpacht, *supra* note 3, p. vii. As stated by Justice Brett Kavanaugh, "Private law, being in general more developed than international law, has always constituted a sort of reserve store of principles upon which the latter has been in the habit of drawing [because] a principle which is found to be generally accepted by civilized legal systems may fairly be assumed to be so reasonable as to be necessary to the maintenance of justice under any system" (*Doe VIII* v. *Exxon Mobil Corp.*, 654 F.3d 11, 54 (D.C. Cir. 2011), Kavanaugh, J., dissenting).

1780. Bogdan, *supra* note 5, p. 43.

1781. *Ibid.*, p. 389.

1782. Gutteridge, *supra* note 154, p. 4.

1783. Ellis, *supra* note 885, p. 950.

Moreover, the relations between sovereign States strongly resemble the dealings between private citizens, in that both are equal before the law [1784].

In addition, the writings of civil law lawyers such as Portalis, Geny, Bonnecase and others have contributed to the development of public international law [1785].

In international arbitration, moreover, both governments and tribunals frequently made use of private law [1786]. This is precisely because general principles of law that are adopted by customary and conventional public international law emanate from private law [1787]. For instance, in the famous *Alabama* arbitration of 1871, the Tribunal seated in Geneva dealt with private law matters such as the different forms of *culpa* within Roman law, the measure of damages and whether the awarding of interest should be admitted. The *Behring Sea* arbitration of 1893 between the United States and Great Britain addressed private law issues as well, including the legal doctrines of property, possession, damages and prescription [1788].

According to Lauterpacht, arbitral tribunals make use of private law rules because recourse to analogy is necessary within international relations and because international law is not always sufficiently developed to provide a solution itself [1789]. In his words, it is in "rules of private law that we see embodied the principles of legal justice and of international progress" [1790]. In practice, international arbitral tribunals either expressly state that a particular private law rule is applicable to the case in question or render a decision which they describe as being

---

1784. Bogdan, *supra* note 5, pp. 42-43.
1785. Cheng, *supra* note 178, p. 3.
1786. See Chap. III, *supra*.
1787. Lauterpacht, *supra* note 3, p. vii.
1788. *Ibid.*, p. 39. At p. 41:

> "In the famous North Atlantic Fisheries arbitration between Great Britain and the United States before the Hague Court, the matter of servitudes was discussed by the parties and analyzed by the Tribunal. The *Russian Indemnity* case between Russia and Turkey, decided in 1912 by the Hague Court as well, is another classic example of the application of private law rules by both the parties and the Tribunal itself, especially those principles governing the question of moratory interest. Ultimately, the case was decided by the application of a private law rule akin to estoppel."

1789. *Ibid.*, p. ix.
1790. He laments, however, that "the recourse to private law has been so frequently abused by writers lacking in originality and falling back upon ready-made constructions, by unscrupulous lawyers and diplomats championing doubtful causes, and by skillful counsel at international arbitrations, that some prefer to dispense with it altogether" (*ibid.*, p. xi).

based on a general principle of law or a rule of universal jurisprudence (although the principle may be identical to provisions that exist within private law). Private law is used even more frequently in cases where States appear as parties before international tribunals [1791].

Neither the ICJ nor its predecessor cite many judicial precedents outside their own jurisprudence. However, when in accordance with Article 38 of the ICJ Statute they recur to private international law principles, they thereby incorporate into the corpus of their own decisions what has thitherto been considered *private international law* norms [1792].

In the landmark *Serbian Loans* case dealing with the "gold clauses" [1793], the private international law doctrine of the "proper law" was clearly stated and accepted by the PCIJ [1794]. As expressed by Ben Wortley, private international law rules may indeed become inevitable when States choose municipal law to apply to their dealings with each other [1795].

In this regard, the PCIJ stated the following:

> "Any contract which is not a contract between States in their capacity as subjects of international law is based on the municipal law of some country. The question as to which this law is forms the subject of that branch of law which is at the present day usually described as private international law or the doctrine of the conflict of laws. The rules thereof may be common to several States and may even be established by international conventions or customs, and in the latter case may possess the character of true international law governing the relations between States. But apart from this, it has to be considered that these rules form part of municipal law." [1796]

Following this reasoning, an international tribunal may apply national or municipal systems of law in the resolution of international disputes, including national private international law rules or non-State law where pertinent [1797], such as the UNIDROIT Principles.

1791. *Ibid.*, pp. 302-303.
1792. Wortley, *supra* note 1161, p. 302.
1793. *Serbian Loans*, *supra* note 978, Judgment (12 July 1929), p. 41.
1794. Wortley, *supra* note 1161, p. 302.
1795. *Ibid.*, p. 303.
1796. *Serbian Loans*, *supra* note 978, Judgment (1929), p. 41.
1797. In the *Serbian Loans* (*supra* note 978) and *Brazilian Loans* (*supra* note 1005) cases, the PCIJ recognized a distinction between the mode of payment

D. The evolving notion of public international law itself

The evolution of private international law has been addressed in Chapters X and XI. In turn, public international law has also been expanding throughout history, both in the extension of its scope of application and in the increased complexity of the techniques for its implementation [1798]. It now applies to new areas of the law, such as environmental matters, international trade and outer space exploration [1799], and incorporates new values into its corpus, such as the protection of human rights [1800].

Public international law is also becoming increasingly fragmented [1801], with a growing number of instruments developing on their own at different times, across distinct regions and with several uses. Despite the growing number of public international law instruments that exist independently from one another, mutual relationships exist among them, which can generate conflicts [1802].

Public international law has not just expanded horizontally to embrace the new States established since the end of the Second World War. Instead, further complicating the field, it grants rights and obligations to a wide array of distinct legal entities [1803]. International organizations are capable of concluding treaties, incurring international responsibility, receiving and embarking upon diplomatic missions and generating public international law rules.

The United Nations, for instance, can even use force or sanctions in the same way that States can [1804]. Public international law cannot in

---

and the substance or value of the debt. This distinction has previously been accepted by private international law courts, and has become even more common since the resolution of the Gold Clause Cases. Wortley, *supra* note 1161, pp. 303-304.

1798. Treves, *supra* note 280, p. 43.

1799. Shaw, *supra* note 480, p. 45.

1800. "The values of democracy and good economic governance have been more controversial, but have nonetheless been met with support by Public International Law scholars. New values make their way into international legal practice through the use of expressions such as 'the common heritage of mankind', 'equal but differentiated responsibilities', and the very notion of the 'international community'. Although these notions are vague, they are often incorporated in rules and challenge interpreters to determine their scope within each particular case", Treves, *supra* note 280, p. 45.

1801. ILC Fragmentation Report, *supra* note 106.

1802. "Law-making treaties are beginning to develop in a number of historical, functional, and regional groups that are separate from one other and whose mutual relationships are, in some respects, analogous to those of separate municipal legal systems", C. Wilfried Jenks, "The Conflict of Law-Making Treaties", *British Yearbook of International Law*, Vol. 30 (1953), p. 403.

1803. Shaw, *supra* note 480, p. 45.

1804. Treves, *supra* note 280, p. 44.

the contemporary era be understood without reference to the growth in the number and influence of intergovernmental institutions, foremost among them the United Nations in terms of its core importance in the process of diplomatic relations, international cooperation and norm creation. Furthermore, the existence of the Security Council as an executive organ with powers to adopt resolutions that are binding in certain circumstances upon all member States is unique in the history of international relations [1805].

Moreover, new mechanisms emerge from traditional customary law and treaties, such as "soft law" codifications. At the same time, international courts and tribunals have been expanding their presence and work in recent years [1806].

The international legal field and profession have also been growing due to the presence of legal advisors employed by States, offices representing governments in conferences and meetings and international organizations that employ international lawyers. There are also a growing number of courts and international tribunals that have shaped the role of international adjudicators into, "if not a profession, at least a not so rare occupation for specialists in international law" [1807].

It is clear, therefore, that public international law has been developing and moving into new domains with increasingly complex evolving relationships. However, it also often lacks its own rules and must borrow them from municipal systems, as occurs, for instance, with sovereign insolvency rules [1808] and others described in Chapter XIII.

E. Public international law influences in private international law

Public international law can be understood as the father (or at least older brother) of private international law, affecting the fields of human rights, investments, international banking law, environmental law, the law of international organizations and the law of treaties [1809], among others. Andreas Lowenfeld states that "public law is no longer

1805. Shaw, *supra* note 480, p. 47.
1806. Treves, *supra* note 280, p. 45.
1807. *Ibid.*, p. 46.
1808. "Domestic Law Principles", *supra* note 749, p. 1170.
1809. Fernández Arroyo, *supra* note 1467, p. 19. "Given the interdependence of domestic and international law in areas such as human rights, environment, criminal liability, and commerce, international law can learn much from municipal legal systems. The source general principles of international law is one important point of contact between international and municipal law", Ellis, *supra* note 885, p. 949.

out of bounds for international lawyers, that private international law embraces public law, and indeed that this is where the action is" [1810].

Many scholars have pointed out the futility of contraposing monism and dualism in public international law [1811]. Monism considers public international law and domestic law to be parts of the same legal system [1812]. In both, the individual person ultimately remains the subject of legal regulation, and thus public international law shares the same creators and aspirations as municipal law [1813]. Dualism views public international law as separate from domestic law and operating on a different level. International law rules regulate relations in the international society, whereas municipal law is concerned with individual citizens in their relations with one another and the State [1814]. For this reason, proponents of dualism argue that public international law must be incorporated into domestic law to be enforced by national laws [1815].

Bridges built between public international law and domestic law have rendered the traditional interplay between monism and dualism merely theoretical. Public international law has become increasingly aware of the existence of domestic legal systems and their importance for the implementation of its rules. For instance, certain international judges apply a mixture of international and domestic law in their judgments, while others engage in a detailed examination of domestic law in order to draw conclusions for the application of international law rules. States often accept that violations of certain domestic law obligations equate to violations of obligations under international law [1816].

1810. Lowenfeld, *supra* note 1197, p. 308.

1811. G. Galindo, "Revisiting Monism's Ethical Dimension", in J. Crawford and S. Nouwen (eds.), *Select Proceedings of the European Society of International Law*, Vol. 3, Oxford, Hart Publishing, 2010, p. 141.

1812. From a monist perspective, Kelsen states that the majority of public international law rules are incomplete and must be supplemented by national law. The international legal order only has meaning as part of a universal legal order, that also includes national legal orders. Monist. H. Kelsen, *Principios de Derecho Internacional Público*, Buenos Aires, El Ateneo, 1965 (translation of *Principles of International Law*, New York, Rinehart & Company, Inc., 1952), p. 345.

1813. C. C. Joyner, *International Law in the 21st Century*, Lanham, MD, Rowman and Littlefield, 2005, p. 39.

1814. *Ibid.*, p. 38.

1815. International law cannot ever function as the law of the land for a State except through municipal custom or statutory enactment. *Ibid.*, pp. 38-39.

1816. Treves, *supra* note 280, p. 45.

F. A blurring distinction

If the term "private international law" is indeed a misnomer, the term "public international law" is even more inappropriate [1817]. According to Francis Mann, there is very little to be gained by searching for the distinction between the two branches of law [1818].

International lawyers have a somewhat expansionist tendency to view issues – such as anything included in a treaty – as automatically "a matter" of international law [1819]. This propensity exists within private international law as well. However, the public-private law divide has blurred [1820]. The relationship between public and private international law has proven to be far more nuanced than traditional distinctions would suggest [1821].

Legal scholars historically distinguished between the public and private spheres along three classical axes. The first is the division between public and private actors; the second, between public law and private law; and the third, between public international law and private international law [1822]. Distinctions along these axes no longer contemplate (and perhaps never reflected) reality. Changes in the relations among States, individuals and multinational corporations have led scholars and practitioners to reconsider the traditional boundaries of each discipline. For example, non-State actors now exert considerable influence in the development of public international law. Further, international economic and investment legal matters have become central features of public international law. Moreover, the growing corpus of international human rights law indicates that individuals have been (re)discovered as subjects of public international law [1823].

1817. Mann, *supra* note 1757, p. 120.

1818. *Ibid.*, p. 121.

1819. A. Mills, "Connecting Public and Private International Law", in V. Ruíz Abou-Nigm, K. McCall Smith and D. French (eds.), *Linkages and Boundaries in Private and Public International* Law, Oxford, Hart Publishing, 2018, p. 16.

1820. Hess, *supra* note 48, pp. 24 ff.

1821. "Asserting a strict divide between public and private international law masks the necessary confluence between the two disciplines and has left both public and private international law scholars and practitioners blind to the numerous ways in which they interact. The artificial divide has restricted our ability to draw on legal theories, arguments, and techniques developed in one area of the law to resolve analogous issues in the other", Fernández Arroyo and Moïse Mbengue, *supra* note 1450, p. 799.

1822. Maupin, *supra* note 1756, p. 33.

1823. Fernández Arroyo and Moïse Mbengue, *supra* note 1450, p. 801.

No sensible criterion exists to distinguish public from private international law such as purpose, subject matter, origin or rules [1824]. For too long, the theoretical separation between the two disciplines masked the functional connections that exist between them. However, this relationship has long been evident to practitioners whose work cuts through artificial academic boundaries [1825], and actual cases reveal that the public-private law distinction is now fading. For instance, in *PSEG* v. *Turkey*, one of the central issues involved a concession contract and its ultimate private law status [1826].

Consequently, in the words of Zachary Douglas, there is nothing revolutionary about abandoning the dichotomy [1827]. There is hope that the binary public-private law distinctions in international law will be left in the past and considered a divide that served, at best, a descriptive purpose [1828].

Furthermore, as mentioned previously, public international law expanded into numerous areas including environmental law and human rights law. One of the most pressing problems posed by this development concerns the interaction between these areas. A range of legal reasoning techniques are available to public international law lawyers, but it is unclear whether they are appropriate to address several issues in the new context. In such cases, private international law may be a potential source of further methods useful to address these questions. These techniques would still strive to accommodate multiple legal orders that are normatively equal [1829]. Public international law instruments (State immunity) and private international law instruments (jurisdiction, conflict of laws, acts of State, non-justiciability) are often applied together [1830].

1824. Remarks by L. Brilmayer and A. Bucher in "The Increasing Focus of Public International Law on Private Law Issues", *Proceedings of the ASIL Annual Meeting*, Vol. 86 (1992), p. 456, at pp. 473-474; remarks by M. Janis in "Academic Workshop: Should We Continue to Distinguish between Public and Private International Law?", *Proceedings of the ASIL Annual Meeting*, Vol. 79 (1987), pp. 352-353; R. G. Steinhardt, "The Privatization of Public International Law", *George Washington Journal of International Law and Economics*, Vol. 25 (1991), p. 523. Reed, *supra* note 21, p. 202.

1825. Mills, *supra* note 1764, p. 1450.

1826. See *PSEG* v. *Turkey*, *supra* note 523, Award (19 January 2007), especially in para. 194.

1827. Douglas, *supra* note 39, p. 7.

1828. Ruíz Abou-Nigm, McCall Smith and French, *supra* note 1426, p. 9.

1829. Mills, *supra* note 1819, p. 29.

1830. Hess, *supra* note 48, p. 276.

While the distinction between public international law and private international law may increasingly become less meaningful [1831], it still ought to be considered given the current state of affairs. However, in a globalized world featuring a modern multilevel legal structure, private and public international law must be thought of as complementary to one another [1832].

G. Public and private law concepts in foreign investments

1. The discussion

Aspects of both public and private law can be found in the law applicable to foreign investments. José Alvarez notes that his Hague Academy courses on investment arbitration were placed under the umbrella of "public international law". There was some resistance to this idea within the Academy. According to Alvarez, some scholars maintain that foreign investment regimes should continue to be framed in private international law terms [1833]. However, many public international law scholars take the opposite view, and consider international investment law as a sub-branch of their discipline.

Investment tribunals may make use of both public and private international law in questions related to jurisdiction. For example, in *Amco* v. *Indonesia*, consent to arbitration was interpreted both on the basis of Indonesia's private international law and the ICSID Convention [1834]. In *SPP* v. *Egypt*, the Tribunal recurred both to the VCLT according to public international law and to the Egyptian rules of statutory interpretation according to private international law [1835].

The interaction between public and private international law typically occurs within "compound choice of law clauses" that are commonly found in foreign investment relationships. While treaties or investment contracts sometimes only refer to public international law or the domestic law of the home State, in most cases the choice of law rules in the contract refer to both. These provisions are known as compound

1831. Orrego Vicuña, *supra* note 1103, p. 357.
1832. Hess, *supra* note 48, p. 278.
1833. Alvarez, *supra* note 26, pp. 260-261.
1834. *Amco Asia* v. *Indonesia*, *supra* note 408.
1835. *Southern Pacific* v. *Egypt*, *supra* note 128, 3 *ICSID Reports* 142 (1988). "These awards suggest that jurisdictional questions are governed by their own system combining public and private international law", Fernández Arroyo and Moïse Mbengue, *supra* note 1450, p. 826.

choice of law clauses [1836], addressed in several cases, including *Fedax* v. *Venezuela* [1837], *Maffezini* v. *Spain* [1838], *Goetz* v. *Burundi* [1839] and the renowned *Wena* v. *Egypt* case [1840].

There are three basic types of claims that can be pursued by investors against States: treaty-based, contract-based and statute-based. Treaty-based claims originate in public international law. Contract-based claims generally call for the application of private international law. Statute-based claims may involve either public or private international law, a mixture of both, or neither of the two disciplines, depending on the domestic statute. According to Julie Maupin, these three types of claims do not involve purely private dispute settlement nor public governance alone. Rather, all of them encompass the reconciliation of the States' obligations toward investors with their obligations toward non-investors. This reconciliation transcends the public-private divide [1841].

2. A workable distinction?

Maupin considers the persistence of the public-private debate within international investment law "baffling" and the distinction between the two disciplines to be "artificial, unworkable, or even downright pernicious" [1842].

The term "public" is often reserved exclusively for States and subnational levels of government, whereas the label "private" applies to all non-State actors. For example, in *Abaclat* v. *Argentina* [1843], the State (representing the "public") is put in peril by the financial claims of non-State (private) actors [1844].

At other times, the public-private differentiation is made between the individual and the collective. In the *Phillip Morris* v. *Uruguay* case [1845], it was feared that privately held intellectual property rights

1836. *Ibid.*, p. 827.
1837. *Fedax* v. *Venezuela*, *supra* note 75, para. 30 (1998).
1838. *Maffezini* v. *Spain*, *supra* note 456, 5 *ICSID Reports*, p. 419, paras. 50-57, 77 (2000).
1839. *Goetz* v. *Burundi*, *supra* note 93, 6 *ICSID Reports*, p. 3 (1999).
1840. *Wena Hotels* v. *Egypt*, *supra* note 601. See also Fernández Arroyo and Moïse Mbengue, *supra* note 1450, pp. 832-833.
1841. Maupin, *supra* note 1756, pp. 406-407.
1842. *Ibid.*, p. 373.
1843. *Abaclat* v. *Argentina*, *supra* note 90, Decision on Jurisdiction and Admissibility (August 04, 2011).
1844. Maupin, *supra* note 1756, p. 401.
1845. *Philip Morris* v. *Uruguay*, *supra* note 528, Award (8 July 2016).

might render public health regulation too expensive for the State (public)[1846]. However, the differentiations that occur within this sphere do not constitute a meaningful public-private divide within foreign investment law[1847].

Further, a commercial and investment arbitration divide cannot be used to consider the former system as "private" and the latter as "public". Of greater importance is the application of procedural minimum standards and the respect of public policy in both types of proceedings. Considering these issues through the lens of private or public international law does not capture the complexities of the legal relationships involved[1848].

3. *Clash of two professions: Arbitration experts versus public international law professors*

The public-private law divide has produced important legal debates, issues and inconsistencies within international investment[1849].

Investor-State arbitration actors often approach the public-private law distinction from different perspectives, such as public international law or commercial arbitration. Since different fundamental assumptions underly each of these perspectives, diverse interpretations of the public-private distinction emerge as well[1850].

For these reasons, some scholars advocate the need for specialists specifically in the field of investment claims since many arbitrators have no grounding in international law and approach it from a commercial perspective without regard for the public law elements present in the disputes. The "treatification" of investment disputes has put the public interest at the core of investment arbitration and has triggered the publicization of arbitration proceedings[1851], which demands expertise in public international law. Generalist knowledge of public international law will not suffice in this case, though, since the legal regime of

1846. Maupin, *supra* note 1756, p. 401.
1847. *Ibid.*, p. 406.
1848. Hess, *supra* note 48, p. 277.
1849. Mills, *supra* note 28, p. 116.
1850. The same occurs within the civil and common law paradigm. See J. Sicard-Mirabal and Y. Derains. "Introduction to Investor-State Arbitration", in *id.*, *supra* note 114, p. 2. See also Fernández Arroyo and Moïse Mbengue, *supra* note 1450, p. 824.
1851. Y. Radi, "Balancing the Public and the Private in International Investment Law", in H. Muir Watt and D. P. Fernández Arroyo (eds.), *Private International Law and Global Governance*, Oxford, Oxford University Press, 2014, pp. 164-165.

investment claims has been expanding so rapidly [1852]. In essence, the contemporary discourse in international investment law can be divided into two camps: private dispute settlement and public regulation [1853].

4. Epistemic communities

The concept of epistemic communities has become commonplace in the field of international arbitration. It refers to the potential lens through which we look at different social groups competing for authority within a legal field. In the future, academic debates over epistemic communities promise to intensify [1854].

Maupin believes that the public-private divide that exists within international investment arbitration is rooted in "the sociologically fractured epistemic community of international investment lawyers". Arbitrators that come from private law or commercial arbitration backgrounds approach the field from a private law perspective. By contrast, investment law scholars usually come from public international law backgrounds and see the debate in public law terms. "To a person with a hammer, everything looks like a nail." [1855] This divide is clearly visible when participating in conferences organized by public law scholars and representatives of the arbitration community.

From a private law perspective, investment arbitration emerges from disparate and isolated international agreements, entered into by States looking for competitive advantages in the field. In the absence of a coherent international regime for resolving investment disputes, private law advocates would have arbitral tribunals look to techniques applied in interpreting and enforcing private contractual arrangements. Tribunals would likewise focus on the intentions of the State parties and on the context of contractual arrangements involved in the dispute. From this perspective, "international investment law appears as a specialized subject of international commercial dispute resolution" [1856].

This purely private law perspective regards investment arbitration as having little or no public impact. Obligations to investors are considered akin to private contractual commitments, and investment arbitration

---

1852. Sornarajah, *supra* note 29, p. 7fn.
1853. Maupin, *supra* note 1756, p. 393.
1854. A. Bianchi, "Epistemic Communities in International Arbitration", in T. Schultz and F. Ortino (eds.), *The Oxford Handbook of International Arbitration*, Oxford, Oxford University Press, 2020, p. 590.
1855. Maupin, *supra* note 1756, p. 413.
1856. Mills, *supra* note 28, pp. 99-100.

is understood as an extension of ordinary commercial arbitration. The process by which investor-State disputes are decided is modeled on international commercial arbitration. In addition, the majority of investment arbitrators hail from a commercial arbitration background and most recent investor-State disputes involved claims for breach of contract, which brings them within the realm of ordinary commercial disputes [1857].

Arbitrators do not operate as judges. Their decisions are not subject to appeals for the sake of consistency. For instance, the requirement that arbitrators give reasons (according to the ICSID Convention) [1858] "is a process requirement", in the sense that it aims to ensure that the tribunal does not proceed arbitrarily. This requirement is not designed to allow for a substantive review of the tribunal's reasoning [1859].

Arbitrators' skills lie "in procedural fairness, forensic and witness skills, effective case management and, above all else, producing a timely and enforceable decision". Arbitrators are tasked with interpreting the words of the treaty "in light of the submissions of the parties". Previous decisions, usually derived from instruments that are worded differently than the case at hand, are often dismissed for lacking binding force [1860].

Within this perspective, consistency cannot be aspired to as one of the goals of international arbitration [1861]. In fact, according to an influential

---

1857. "Since the private dispute settlement model functions quite well in these circumstances, so it is no surprise that arbitrators with commercial law backgrounds became the go-to appointees for resolving these disputes", Maupin, *supra* note 1756, pp. 394-395.

1858. Articles 48 (3) and 52 (1) *I* of the ICSID Convention.

1859. Crawford, *supra* note 484, p. 353. He finds the current level of dissensus on core questions disturbing. Crawford argues that the carpet looks very much as if different people have started from different ends without many common threads. International arbitration has become a crazy quilt rather than a Persian rug.

1860. "In their decisions, tribunals will often embark on an extensive recounting of the procedural history of the arbitration, contrasted with concise legal reasoning unburdened by exegesis, express reliance on extrinsic material, or controversial conceptual baggage", Kalderimis, *supra* note 19, p. 149.

1861. Mills, *supra* note 28, p. 104:

> "Such an arbitrator may prefer to take a looser approach to characterising the obligations that are applicable to States, making questions of fact more decisive, presenting the applicable standard as one which is 'subjective and depends heavily on a factual context', or identifying it as 'a flexible one which must be adapted to the circumstances of each case', perhaps focusing on the expectations of the particular investor, or on considerations of 'equity'. Arbitrators may be wary of defining the law between States in a forum in which only one is represented. They may be conscious of their own lack of law-making legitimacy, or simply cautious of reducing their own value in the market in which arbitrators themselves compete for work by appearing to commit themselves to particular principles or approaches."

view of the international arbitration function, it is unwise to search for a *jurisprudence constante* in the system. Instead, a greater focus should be placed on "the patterns of decisions" and "an acceptable spectrum of views" [1862].

Further complications stem from the differences between two types of arbitral cases: contract-based arbitrations and treaty-based arbitrations. In contract-based arbitrations, the tribunal should ensure that the parties fulfill their reciprocal contractual commitments by applying the principle of party autonomy. As a corollary matter, the tribunal must also decide the issues based on the contract and the award may not impact the rights of third parties not before the tribunal.

In treaty-based arbitrations, however, only the respondent State intervenes. The home State of the investor (the other party to the treaty) does not participate in the proceeding, and therefore cannot express its views on the proper interpretation of the treaty. Further, treaties often contain open-textured provisions (like "fair and equitable treatment") that contrast with the usual specificity of contractual obligations. Thus, tribunals must use their discretion more widely within treaty-based arbitrations. This circumstance can "inadvertently impact" the rights of third parties not litigating before the investment arbitral tribunal. Moreover, investment treaties bestow obligations only upon States, not upon investors, which generates accountability problems due to the asymmetry of the parties [1863]. Practitioners who view arbitration from a private law perspective generally do not take sufficient account of the differences between contract-based and treaty-based disputes [1864].

If the arbitrator sees his role as more "quasi-judicial", he or she is more likely to identify the content of the legal rules applicable to the parties to provide guidance for future cases (even if not strictly necessary to resolve the dispute). A quasi-judicial role in this sense relates to the extension of the arbitrators' reasons, their focus on factual or legal analysis and the place played by precedents in their reasoning. Consistency with other international investment decisions will also be a concern for arbitrators taking on this role [1865].

A sociological argument has been advanced according to which the arbitration and public international law communities are incomplete if

1862. Crawford, *supra* note 484, p. 353.
1863. See, in general, Goldschmidt, *supra* note 247. Regarding the asymmetrical nature of the transactions, see, in particular, pp. 326-327.
1864. Maupin, *supra* note 1756, pp. 395-396.
1865. Mills, *supra* note 28, pp. 102-103.

they do not take into account other stakeholders such as State lawmakers and treaty negotiators, civil society activists, the in-house counsel of large multinational companies and the institutional personnel who staff the major arbitration institutions [1866]. This argument adds further complexities to the public-private law divide within international investment arbitration. The epistemic community has become increasingly diverse and has been fragmented into subcommunities, or parallel communities. As a result, there are more diverse discourses in arbitration today than thirty years ago [1867].

There are also ongoing discussions concerning the very idea of arbitration itself [1868]. In the words of Ralf Michaels, arbitration is not a purely private mechanism but involves a mixture of private and public laws. The exact configuration of this blend in arbitration remains unclear [1869], and the public-private mixture is even more nebulous within investment arbitration.

Andrea Bianchi also views the public-private debate within arbitration from a professional "mindset". The fact that some arbitrators hail from a public international law background makes them particularly sensitive to State interests. As such, States may appoint public international lawyers more often than others in investment arbitrations. The reverse may be true for commercial or corporate lawyers. Treaty interpretation illustrates this divide. Commercial lawyers tend to identify the object and purpose of treaties as the promotion and protection of investments, while public international law lawyers are more prone to weigh the different interests involved, particularly the legitimate interest of the host State [1870]. These differences in strategy are not due to any particular ideological bias but rather to the professional "mindset" that each category of lawyers inevitably carries with them [1871].

1866. Maupin, *supra* note 1756, pp. 413-414.

1867. T. Schultz and N. Ridi, "Arbitration Literature", in T. Schultz and F. Ortino (eds.), *The Oxford Handbook of International Arbitration*, Oxford, Oxford University Press, 2020, p. 21.

1868. Renowned recent works in this regard are: Paulsson, *supra* note 1440; Gaillard, *supra* note 836.

1869. R. Michaels, "Arbitration as Private and Public Good", in T. Schultz and F. Ortino (eds.), *The Oxford Handbook of International Arbitration*, Oxford, Oxford University Press, 2020, p. 401.

1870. As in *SGS* v. *Philippines* and *El Paso* v. *Argentina*. *SGS* v. *Philippines*, *supra* note 1142, Decision (2004); *El Paso* v. *Argentina*, *supra* note 456, Decision on Jurisdiction (2006).

1871. Bianchi, *supra* note 1584, p. 586.

5. *Investment arbitration as public international law or global administrative law?*

Attila Tanzi recalls the age-old debate on the alleged hybridity of the body of international investment law, in which the ostensibly significant commercial component of international investment arbitration, linked to the private law interest of foreign investors, has been countered by the consideration of the public law relevance of the constraints that it provides on the exercise of the sovereign powers of host States. In this debate one can find those propounding the import of domestic public law principles into the body of international investment law [1872].

In contrast to commercial arbitration, Daniel Kalderimis notes that public international law teaches one to look at the evolution and crystallization of States' practices and principles over time [1873]. The public international lawyer tends to systematize, look for coherence and universality, and to identify and advance the progressive development of both international law and international investment law as a global "public" legal order [1874].

Eric De Brabandere explains that investment arbitration has shifted from a primarily private law dispute resolution mechanism to one focused more on public international law [1875]. The private law dimension of international investment arbitration has thus become subsidiary; investment treaty arbitration cannot be equated to a private or commercial dispute settlement method [1876].

In fact, scholars that advocate for reforms of the mechanism for resolving foreign investment claims usually argue that the regime must be designed as a public law system "to better capture its pressure on national regulatory policy" [1877].

1872. Tanzi, *supra* note 762, p. 302.

1873. Kalderimis, *supra* note 19, p. 159.

1874. Mills, *supra* note 28, pp. 101-102.

1875. This moves away from theories that either characterize investment treaty arbitration as "hybrid" legal system or equate it to public/administrative law. See De Brabandere, *supra* note 27, pp. 1-2.

1876. *Ibid.*, p. 9. Friedmann states that analogies to private law are no longer accurate. "With the growing importance of international legal relations between public authorities and private legal subjects, public law will be an increasingly fertile source of international law", Friedmann, *supra* note 955, p. 295.

1877. "Scholars that advocate for such reforms view the 'public law frame' as key to securing national sovereignty and democratic values, supposing that public law language, doctrines, and institutions will be more responsive to public values. However, this emphasis upon public law has caused various controversies, and important voices remain unconvinced. Nonetheless, the reliance upon public law has clearly reshaped

In his 2007 book *Investment Treaty Arbitration and Public Law*, Gus van Harten notes that investment treaty arbitration is often considered a form of reciprocally consensual adjudication between an investor and a State. He argues that investment treaty arbitration should be viewed as a public law dispute resolution mechanism for two reasons: first, because the system is established by a sovereign act of the State, and second, because investment treaty arbitration is primarily used to resolve disputes arising from the exercise of sovereign authority. The system engages the regulatory relationship between the State and individuals, rather than a reciprocal relationship between individuals that are equal before the law [1878].

Van Harten contends that international investment arbitration is best viewed as a transnationalized form of "public law", in that it essentially reviews the validity of State regulatory actions in a manner that is reminiscent of domestic constitutional or administrative law systems. Different expressions are used in this regard, such as "constitutionalizing economic globalization", "a form of spontaneously emerging global administrative law", "comparative public law" or "international public law" (not to be confused with public international law) [1879].

According to this view, bilateral investment treaties are not international investment agreements; they are global administrative law instruments. As such, arbitrators working with bilateral investment treaties must demonstrate that they understand and can contribute to the development of sound and legitimate international regulatory principles [1880].

Investment arbitration enforces norms that are analogous to those found within the public law of States [1881]. It performs functions that can be likened to those performed by high courts when interpreting constitutional texts.

International investment law can, therefore, be understood as serving a constitutional function for the emerging global economy. Like constitutions, its rules restrict State action and, moreover, they

---

the debate, with States adopting the rhetoric of public law in advocating for reforms in the fields of international investment law and arbitration", Arato, *supra* note 39, p. 8.

1878. G. van Harten, *Investment Treaty Arbitration and Public Law*, Oxford, Oxford University Press, 2007, p. 45. See Kalderimis, *supra* note 19, pp. 145-146.

1879. Maupin, *supra* note 1756, pp. 397-398.

1880. Kalderimis, *supra* note 19, p. 159.

1881. S. Schill, *International Investment Law and Comparative Public Law*, Oxford, Oxford University Press, 2010, p. 15.

create and safeguard the interests of the international community in the functioning of the global economic system [1882].

The strict nineteenth-century distinction between public and private law assumes that governmental action is limited to certain public functions such as defense, the administration of justice and the police force, while the bulk of social and economic activities is carried out between private subjects. As has been discussed in this chapter, this public-private distinction is no longer accurate. States have progressively assumed greater responsibilities in areas of economic and social welfare, and this process has been repeated in the international sphere. Traditionally, public international law applied to diplomatic relations, the establishment of formal jurisdictional limitations and to military actions. Contemporary public international law has been extended and now applies to several "welfare" functions, which has created an entirely new field of international economic aid. These new interests within public international law were ushered in by a myriad of public international organizations, which has led to the development of a growing body of international administrative law [1883].

The theory of a global administrative law assumes that there is a widespread consensus regarding certain international investment legal standards. Within this view, any such consensus leads to the creation of an international investment law "regime", and treaty interpretation must unfold in the "broader context of international investment agreements and arbitral awards" [1884]. Within global administrative law, treaty interpretation is based upon analogous rules emanating from domestic public law (like administrative law) or from international investment law. As such, both domestic public law rules and international investment legal rules are understood as new developments within global administrative law. In global administrative law, international investment law thus emerges as "a specialized subject of public international law" dealing with interconnected treaties, customary international law standards and general principles of purported universality [1885].

1882. "Investment treaties comprise constitutional traits by establishing legal principles that serve as a yardstick for the conduct of States vis-à-vis foreign investors. Furthermore, investment treaties establish standards that can be effectively implemented by means of investor-State arbitration" (*ibid.*, p. 373).

1883. Friedmann, *supra* note 955, p. 282.

1884. Mills, *supra* note 28, p. 99.

1885. *Ibid.*, p. 99.

6. Investment arbitration as a hybrid legal system or a new development

Some consider the international investment legal framework a hybrid or *sui generis* system [1886]. It is public international law in the sense that it consists of legal commitments made by sovereign States at the international level [1887]. Foreign investment legal matters also comprise private law elements, and in this sense, this area can be viewed as a field of transnational contract law governed both by domestic legal systems and international law rules [1888].

However, the legal characterization of foreign investment as a "hybrid" system is an excessively simple way of disentangling a complex web of legal relations and tends to blur the underlying legal relations between foreign investors and host States [1889].

On the other hand, scholars have rightly stated that international investment treaty law is a new development that requires new thinking. Therefore, public international law principles that have been developed for a different paradigm will only be of limited practical use when applied within international investment treaty law [1890].

1886. Z. Douglas, "The Hybrid Foundations of Investment Treaty Arbitration", *British Yearbook of International Law*, Vol. 74, No. 1 (2003), pp. 152-153.

1887. "Its points of intersection with other regimes of Public International law relate to 'treatification', fragmentation, impact of non-States parties, globalization and its discontents, etc.", Alvarez, *supra* note 26, p. 481.

1888. Collins, *supra* note 66, p. 1.

1889. De Brabandere, *supra* note 27, p. 4.

1890. Kalderimis, *supra* note 19, p. 154.

CHAPTER XIV

PARTICULARITIES OF FOREIGN INVESTMENT CONTRACTS AND THE PUBLIC-PRIVATE RELATIONSHIP

A. A particular legal regime for State contracts

State contracts is an area in which private and public law notoriously intersect. State contracts cannot be approached from a purely contractual point of view without taking public law factors into consideration, and vice versa. There are specific rules that apply to State contracts, such as those regulating their formation, execution and termination. These rules transcend the public-private divide.

B. Differences between international investment contracts and domestic or commercial contracts

Unlike domestic contracts, international investment contracts may be governed by public international law rules [1891] or other rules that exist outside the law of the host State [1892]. The law of the host State usually applies to international investment contracts. However, these contracts may also give rise to public international law obligations regarding the treatment of the investor [1893].

In the 1922 *Electricity Company of Warsaw* case [1894], the sole arbitrator held that international investment contracts such as concessions "are not pure institutions of private law, but present a mixture of private and public legal characters" [1895]. In the *Lighthouse* case between France and Greece, the PCIJ stated that "a contract granting a public utility concession does not fall within the category of ordinary instruments of private law" [1896].

1891. Orrego Vicuña, *supra* note 1103, p. 349. In the words of Lord McNair, "it is Public International Law that has given birth to the legal system that has gradually become recognized as applicable to foreign investment contracts. For instance, for Article 38 of the ICJ Statute merely places on record one of the main sources of the rules of Public International Law", McNair, *supra* note 4, p. 7.

1892. Sornarajah, *supra* note 29, p. 85.

1893. Muchlinski, *supra* note 7, p. 7. UNCTAD, State Contracts, *supra* note 116.

1894. 3 RIAA, p. 1687.

1895. McNair, *supra* note 4, p. 2.

1896. 51 PCIJ, Ser. A/B, No. 62, p. 20 (17 March 1934).

Unlike ordinary commercial contracts concluded with a State party [1897], public law elements pervade the negotiation, conclusion, operation and termination of international investment agreements.

In domestic systems such as in France, Belgium and Italy, international investment contracts are considered "administrative contracts" *(contrats administratifs)*. These undertakings are subject to special rules, for instance regarding State capacity to enter into them, the areas that can be regulated by these agreements, and other intricacies involving their review and scrutiny. Usually, international investment contracts affect State interests and may potentially involve a State's financial and other resources [1898].

Administrative contracts can be distinguished from ordinary contracts in that they recognize the administration's unilateral powers of control in the public interest. The administration may suspend, vary or rescind the contract, transfer it to another party, or take it over itself. The contract is always subject to the changing needs of the public service. Even though no exact equivalent exists in common law systems, similar developments unfolded through the standard forms and terms of government contracts, granting authorities certain powers of termination or modification balanced by an obligation to indemnify the private party [1899].

Special rules applicable to international investment contracts exist beyond private law, for instance in cases in which external circumstances require State contracts to be terminated due to public considerations. For example, the French Conseil d'Etat (the country's administrative law tribunal) decided that compensation will be limited to the *damnum emergens*, that is, to actual losses suffered by expenses and commitments incurred in the execution of the contract, as distinct from the expectation of profits that can be awarded in private law agreements. A similar approach is followed within the common law [1900].

The blend of public and private law in State contracts is clearly reflected in the arbitral award issued by the President of the Swiss

---

1897. The US Supreme Court stated in *Lynch* v. *The United States* (1934) 292 US 571 at p. 579 that "when the United States enters into a commercial relation, its rights and duties are governed by the law applicable to contracts between private parties".

1898. UNCTAD, State Contracts, *supra* note 116, pp. 3-4.

1899. Friedmann, *supra* note 955, pp. 291-292.

1900. "Generally, United States and British standard government contracts restrict the compensation payable in the event of an exercise of a special power of determination by the governmental contractor in accordance with these principles", Friedmann, *supra* note 955, p. 293.

Federal Tribunal in the *Alsing* case [1901]. In its decision, the adjudicator analyzed both public and private law elements in a supply agreement. He decided to interpret aspects of this administrative contract "according to the norms of private law and by the application of the principles of good faith". A growing number of international economic transactions also apply a blend of public and private concepts, especially where both parties are public authorities or where one is a public authority and the other a private subject [1902].

International investment contracts provide mutual benefits and obligations for the State on the one hand and the private party on the other. These undertakings are usually made in accordance with relevant laws and regulations (such as those respecting mining or petroleum) and a concession or license is issued thereunder. The more State agreements become assimilated into the concept of "administrative contracts" or its analogues, the more governments may claim a power to rectify and amend the arrangements they enter into [1903].

Termination of international investment contracts may be tied to public requirements. In these cases, the rules regarding damages may differ from those that apply to ordinary commercial contracts. Moreover, the means of contract termination may be different. Both State and ordinary contracts may be terminated due to breaches, but State contracts are typically ended in cases where performance has been made wholly or partially impossible due to State action. The

---

1901. The award, dated 22 December 1954, is fully reported by Schwebel, "The Alsing Case", *International and Comparative Law Quarterly*, Vol. 8 (1959), p. 320 ff. See *infra* note 2559.

1902. Friedmann, *supra* note 955, pp. 294-295.

1903. Higgins, *supra* note 1007, p. 298. At 298-299:

> "Legal systems diverge. However, basic features of a concession are twofold 'a State act and the vesting of property rights in the concessionaire'. A public service concession is one by which the concessionaire undertakes a public service and obtains his profit from the charges incurred by the users of the service. The extent to which such a concession is purely contractual or at least partly regulatory will depend upon the particular concession concerned. A variation is the public works concession, whereby the concessionaire undertakes to build and maintain a public work, such as a hydro-electric factory. It is apparent that mining concessions – whether for oil or minerals – are different in character from the public service concession in that they do not contain any provisions in favor of third-party users. Although a proportion of the revenues from the venture may be used by the State for public purposes, the mine itself is not destined to public use. The status of a mining concession is viewed variously in different jurisdictions. In French law, for example, it is regarded as *sui generis*, having some of the characteristics of a unilateral act of State and some of a contract. Tribunals have in recent years dealt in very diverse ways with this question of the status of the particular concession with which they are concerned."

public policy-based control and discretion may tip the balance in favor of the State and may subject the other party to the risk of interference in its commercial expectations for entering into the contract. As such, public international law has developed rules to protect investors in these situations due to concerns about the "in-built superiority of host country institutions" and partiality of local courts [1904].

If, after a time, a State receiving an investment wishes to be free of the contract, alter its terms, or cancel it, these circumstances may be contemplated in the contract. Where an investor-State contract provides for its own modification and termination, the question arises as to whether the State is entitled to alter or terminate the contract for reasons not contemplated therein. Even though the contract is subject to local law, according to the public international law doctrine of acquired rights, once a right has come into existence under the local law, it cannot be deprived of its international significance by any State action that runs contrary to the law of nations [1905].

Therefore, following these international developments, the obligations arising from foreign investment contracts may be rooted in an external system other than domestic law, at least for matters related to termination and dispute resolution [1906]. Proposals have been advanced in this regard under customary international law [1907] and, although several

1904. UNCTAD, State Contracts, *supra* note 116, p. 5.

1905. Lord Shawcross, *supra* note 38, p. 352.

1906. UNCTAD, State Contracts, *supra* note 116, p. 6. From a comparative review, Christopher Curtis (*supra* note 119, pp. 337-338) concludes that

> "there is no general principle of law recognizing an inherent power in the government to terminate or modify the legal rights of those with whom it contracts. In the case of international State contracts for a long period of time, the government may reserve a power to modify or terminate the agreement. One means is the renegotiation clause, but it may not be enough to attract long term investments. This is where stabilization clauses come into play, negating conclusively that the agreement is intended to be an administrative contract or otherwise subject to governmental power to affect the rights of the foreign investor. Notwithstanding, even though no general principle of law recognizing an inherent power in governments to terminate their contracts exist, this circumstance does not impede a government from expropriating property comprising the foreign investor's contract rights".

1907. Claim by the British Government before the ICJ in 1951: *Anglo-Iranian Oil*, 1952 *ICJ Pleadings* 124 and *Oral Arguments and Documents* 84 (2 July). Also, claim by the Greek Government in the *Ambatielos* case (*Greece* v. *UK*), 1953 *ICJ Pleadings* 71 (May 1953). Similarly, the argument advanced by Switzerland in *Certain Norwegian Loans*, *supra* note 977, p. 61. None of the cases in which these arguments were made ended up in judgment on the issue. ILC Fourth Report on International Responsibility, UN Doc. A/CN.4/119, *Yearbook of the International Law Commission*, Vol. 2 [1959], p. 30 ff.. See also Add. to the Sixth Report (A/CN.4/134/Add.1 of 11 December 1961), Article 10 (3) and Commentary 23. 5.

matters have been left unsolved, investment treaties also address these issues.

In reference to the field of foreign investment contracts, some scholarly writings refer to a "public international law contract" [1908] and others to "quasi-international agreements" [1909] or "partly international agreements", and so on. [1910]. Some writers have argued that as soon as international law applies to contracts, an "international law of contracts" is created [1911] "even if only partial, thin, and rudimentary" [1912].

C. Absence of a public international law corpus applicable to international contracts

Public international law lacks an appropriate corpus of rules applicable to the regulation of usually complex foreign investment contractual relationships [1913]. In 1950, Martin Wolff stated that public international law "has no answer to the questions" raised in contract law regarding formation, invalidity and breach. The law of nations did not develop legal techniques "sufficiently well-equipped to answer the numerous questions of private law, which arise in a litigation between the State and a private person" [1914].

1908. Maniruzzaman, *supra* note 317, p. 8.

1909. Because – at least considering the balance of forces existing at the time the theory was set forth – they are agreements between equals. See Kahn, *supra* note 33, p. 14. See also R. B. Lillich, "The Law Governing Disputes under Economic Development Agreements: Re-Examining the Concept of Internationalisation", in R. B. Lillich and C. N. Brower (eds.), *International Arbitration in the Twenty-First Century: Towards Judicialization and Uniformity*, New York, Transnational Publishers, 1993, p. 92. Alshahrani notes also the characterization of oil concessions as a "quasi-international treaty", *supra* note 1006, p. 129.

1910. Maniruzzaman, *supra* note 317, p. 9.

1911. See the seminal article: Fatouros, *supra* note 983, pp. 134-141. In an also influential article, Sornarajah states: "International lawyers have built up 'an international contract law' which has as its first postulate the sanctity and immutability of the terms of the contract. State Contracts governed by public international law", Sornarajah, *supra* note 37, pp. 187-188.

1912. "What remains to be determined is what kind of rules emerge from the international law of contracts: whether this regime should be understood as thin or thick, rudimentary or sophisticated; and what values such choices might serve", Arato, *supra* note 40, p. 369.

1913. S. J. Toope, *Mixed International Arbitration: Studies in Arbitration between States and Private Persons*, Cambridge, Cambridge University Press, 1990, p. 78. Toope cites Battifol, Lipstein and Verhoven in support of the view that there is no public international law on the subject of foreign investment contracts. See Sornarajah, *supra* note 47, p. 253.

1914. M. Wolff, "Some Observations on the Autonomy of Contracting Parties in Conflict of Laws", *Transactions of Grotius Society*, Vol. 35 (1950), p. 152.

This statement remains true today. In 1970, the ILC expunged the topic of contractual breaches from its codification project on State responsibility. In the words of the Special Rapporteur Roberto Ago,

> "[t]he violation by a State of a contractual obligation does not constitute, in and of itself, the objective element of an internationally wrongful act and is not at all capable of giving rise to State responsibility; the violation is subject to a different legal order, be it national or some other law" [1915].

According to Jean Ho, since the ILC's codification project on State responsibility, no detailed study on the law of State responsibility on contractual breaches has emerged [1916]. While there have been substantial efforts to codify rules regarding international transactions such as the sale of goods, documentary credits, bills of exchange, and others, little attention has been paid to the development of public international law rules addressing the diverse aspects of foreign investment contracts [1917].

While no formal codification effort has emerged related to State responsibility for contractual breaches, various international organizations have nonetheless embarked on partial soft law codification efforts. For example, the United Nations released the Draft Code of Conduct on Transnational Corporations, and the World Bank released the Guidelines on the Treatment of Direct Foreign Investment [1918]. However, these guidelines leave many issues unaddressed [1919], and it remains to be seen what their impact will be in practice.

The ICJ has done little to advance the law in this area, missing the opportunity to contribute to the field of foreign investment in two important cases: the 1952 *Anglo-Iranian Oil Company* case [1920] and the 1970 *Barcelona Traction* case [1921]. Further, ICSID and other investment

---

1915. R. Ago, Fifth Report on State Responsibility to the ILC, 22 March 1976, UN Doc. A/CN.4/291, pp. 12-13.

1916. Ho, *supra* note 212, p. 2.

1917. Maniruzzaman, *supra* note 317, p. 41.

1918. See The Draft UN Code of Conduct on Transnational Corporations, UN Doc. E/1990/94 (1990); The World Bank Guidelines on the Treatment of Foreign Direct Investment, 31 ILM, p. 1363-1384 (1992).

1919. Maniruzzaman, *supra* note 317, pp. 53-54.

1920. *Anglo-Iranian Oil*, *supra* note 267, Judgment (22 July 1952).

1921. *Barcelona Traction*, *supra* note 24. In this case, the Court found that it had no jurisdiction. However, in the *ELSI* case (*Elettronica*, *supra* note 334, Judgment (20 July 1989)), the ICJ dealt with certain important issues, such as: the requisition of a US company in Italy in violation of the bilateral Friendship, Commerce and Navigation treaty between the USA and Italy, the interpretation and status of the treaty, the exhaustion of local remedies and compensation for damages.

arbitration decisions dealing with State responsibility for contract breaches have been contradictory. A famous article written by Brigitte Stern discusses three important ones (*Texaco* v. *Libya*, *BP* v. *Libya* and *Liamco* v. *Libya*) that originated in similar factual scenarios but were resolved differently [1922].

In the context described in the above paragraphs, the conundrum of State accountability regarding foreign investment contracts is important due to the lack of an appropriate corpus to regulate the matter comprehensively [1923]. Indeed, any search for appropriate wide-ranging contractual rules applicable to State contracts within public international law will be in vain [1924]. To worsen matters, the law of nations offers different visions of most of its core issues [1925].

The overemphasis on the public law frame within foreign investment law allowed a wide range of private law problems to continue unaddressed and has arguably even contributed to their continuity [1926]. On the other hand, private law and private international law may serve as useful tools to resolve issues related to investment legal matters in general, and issues related to investment contracts in particular [1927].

1922. B. Stern, "Trois arbitrages, un même problème, trois solutions", *Revue de l'Arbitrage*. She makes reference to the following cases: *Texaco* v. *Libya*, *supra* note 119, 53 ILR, p. 389 (1979); *BP* v. *Libya*, *supra* note 1019, 53 ILR, p. 297 (1997); *Liamco*, *supra* note 946, 20 ILM, p. 1 (1981).

1923. Toope, *supra* note 1913, p. 78.

1924. Maniruzzaman, *supra* note 317, p. 29 (emphasis added). As noted by Douglas, public international law does not contain a single body of secondary rules regarding State responsibility for wrongful acts committed by a State. This is particularly evident in the case of international treaties that confer rights directly upon non-State actors such as the European Convention of Human Rights, the Iran-US Agreement, NAFTA, the Energy Charter and the ICSID Convention. These treaties create mechanisms for non-State actors to hold contracting States responsible internationally in a manner that transcends the traditional dichotomy between public and private international law. The secondary obligations generated by State responsibility in these cases have a different legal character from the secondary obligations that arise between States. See Douglas, *supra* note 39, p. 94.

1925. International law is the result of a difficult process of conciliating different visions in fundamental matters. G. S. Tawil, "Los conflictos en materia de inversión, la jurisdicción del CIADI y el derecho aplicable: a propósito de las recientes decisiones en los casos 'Vivendi', 'Wena' y 'Maffezini'", *TR LALEY* AR/DOC/18093/2001, V.

1926. Arato, *supra* note 39, p. 6.

1927. See Sornarajah, *supra* note 47, pp. 6-7. In view of this lack of a comprehensive corpus on the matter, Stephan Schill advocates for "at least scholarly efforts on interdisciplinary approaches, such as economic analysis or comparative constitutional principles that structure the State–market relationship, such as property rights, contract enforcement, and others, as well as comparisons with other international law regimes of the global economy, including the WTO regime and human rights treaties", in Schill, *supra* note 1881, pp. 376-377.

As such, faced with the lack of an appropriate corpus to address these problems, decades ago tribunals started to make use of general principles of law in accordance with Article 38 of the ICJ Statute. In doing so, tribunals have embarked on the process of "internationalizing" foreign investment contracts.

D. The "internationalization" of contractual obligations?

As seen in Chapter VIII, "internationalization" refers to the equating of contractual obligations to international obligations. According to this theory, the breach of an investment contract by a State amounts to a breach of its international obligations under public international law [1928]. The fundamental objective of the internationalization theory is to neutralize the power of the home State to change the rules of its foreign investment contracts by subjecting them to a law other than the municipal law. Public international law constrains abuses to foreign investors by host countries. The domestic legal system may be an instrument for such abuse, which gives rise to the necessity to internationalize the dispute [1929]. Views diverge in this regard. Some refer to the applicability of a "transnational law" to foreign investment contracts, others to "general principles of law", or to the contract itself as independent and sovereign. Others directly point to public international law [1930].

Internationalization remains an unresolved legal issue within international investments. Typically, arbitral awards that decide in favor of internationalization have not produced detailed substantive law rules suitable for governing international investment contracts. Moreover, as will be seen in the following sections, municipal law will not necessarily be displaced in many situations [1931]. As such, internationalization

1928. Orrego Vicuña, *supra* note 1103, p. 345.
1929. G. Cordero-Moss, "Foreword", in Chernykh, *supra* note 1353.
1930. Igbokwe, *supra* note 118, p. 270. Sornarajah, for instance, notes that State contracts are governed by public international law, Sornarajah, *supra* note 37, p. 187.
1931. The internationalization of investment relationships – whether they be contractual or otherwise – has certainly not led to a radical "denationalization" of the legal relations springing from international investment to the point that the domestic law of the host State would be deprived of all relevance or application in the interests of an exclusive role for international law. It merely signifies that these relations relate at once – in parallel, one might say – to the sovereign supremacy of the host State in domestic law and to the international undertakings to which it has subscribed. See *Goetz* v. *Burundi*, *supra* note 93, Award, para. 98.

resolves nothing in itself[1932]. For this reason, numerous theories have been proposed to justify the internationalization of foreign investments contracts, as addressed below.

1. *Internationalization via general principles*

As mentioned previously in Chapter IV, the early twentieth-century petroleum cases revealed that general principles of law are more appropriate than domestic laws in the resolution of disputes between foreign investors and host States that are developing nations. As such, internationalization has emerged to fill the gaps in the laws of developing States regarding foreign investment disputes [1933].

However, this theory regarding the role of internationalization has been put into question by scholarly writings that demonstrated that laws of developing countries often provided adequate protection for investors within investment contracts. Further, it was observed that the "international law principles" that were applied within foreign investment disputes were, in fact, solutions that had been adopted by developed jurisdictions (such as Britain) in their private laws. Some scholars have put into question whether this result necessarily reflected general principles of internationally recognized law [1934].

2. *Equating contracts to treaties*

Other scholarly writings have equated State contracts to inter-State treaties governed by public international law, which is yet another aspect of internationalization [1935]. The basis for this view is the international law principle of *pacta sunt servanda* (applicable to both treaties and contracts) which limits the ability of States to dictate measures interfering with contractual performance [1936]. Applied to the theory of internationalization, the principle of *pacta sunt servanda* sanctions

1932. According to Fatouros, "internationalization of State contracts led, paradoxically, to their privatization. In much of the doctrine and in the limited practice extant, the trend points to a pervasive limitation of the host State's sovereign authority within its own territory" (Fatouros, *supra* note 983, p. 141).

1933. This was a conscient technique for a tribunal adopting a point of view external to the national legal system, yet the imperialist underpinnings were unattractive even at the time. See Spiermann, *supra* note 979, p. 96. See also Ho, *supra* note 212, p. 185.

1934. *Ibid.*, p. 188.

1935. Maniruzzaman refers to it as a "Strict Internationalist School", *supra* note 317 , p. 9.

1936. *Ibid.*, p. 5.

the performance of State obligations toward individuals in the same way that it sanctions the performance of State obligations toward one another [1937].

In principle, however, State contracts are governed by their applicable private law, which is typically domestic law. Moreover, the *pacta sunt servanda* principle also loses value considering that under public international law, the sanctity of contracts is not absolute [1938]. The *rebus sic stantibus* principle applies to unforeseen circumstances justifying departures from the contractual agreement.

3. *The inviolability of contractual rights*

Another view of the utility of internationalization focuses on this aspect. In *Aramco* [1939], it was decided that contractual rights are acquired rights and, as such, are inviolable under international law [1940]. As remarked by Jean Ho, it is puzzling how commentators have uncritically credited this award for the proposition that a State cannot interfere with contractual rights without violating public international law. Treating acquired rights as absolute rights is a fundamental departure from the international law on acquired rights as laid down in the case of *German Interests in Polish Upper Silesia* (*Germany* v. *Poland*) [1941].

By purporting to insulate contractual rights from future changes, stabilization clauses may be used to attempt to engineer inviolable contractual rights. This is reflected in the argument that any interference with contractual rights by the host State is a breach of the stabilization clause, which, in turn, constitutes a violation of international law [1942].

The attempt to insulate contracts from changes through stabilization clauses generated several controversies. This principle refers to material restitution that fully restores the affected contractual rights. Except for *Texaco* v. *Libya*, all other tribunals that have dealt with this issue refused to apply the remedy of *restitutio in integrum*. If monetary compensation can act as a remedy for interference with contractual

1937. Ho, *supra* note 212, p. 183.
1938. *Ibid.*, p. 187.
1939. See Chap. VIII.B.3, *supra*, "The *Ruler of Qatar*, *Aramco* and *Sapphire* cases".
1940. *Aramco*, *supra* note 1004, Award, ILR, p. 1963, p. 205.
1941. (Merits) (1926), PCIJ, Ser. A, No. 7, p. 22. See Ho, *supra* note 212, p. 189. Ho also refers to other cases before the European Courts of Human Rights, arbitral tribunals and arbitral courts that did not treat acquired rights as absolute rights. *Ibid.*, pp. 190-191.
1942. *Ibid.*, p. 192.

rights, the prerogatives emanating from the stabilization clause are no different from regular contractual rights [1943].

Factoring stabilization clauses into the quantification of damages for a breach of contract seems a better way to integrate the foreign investor's risk minimization strategy without attempting to engineer inviolable contractual rights. In the past, stabilization clauses have typically been included in the older investment contracts concluded between wealthy Anglo-American or European investors and impoverished, less-developed host States. However, those days are likely over. A 2009 study failed to find any stabilization clauses within investment contracts that insulate all contractual rights from interference by the host State [1944].

4. *Internationalization through umbrella clauses*

In principle, a State breaching a contract with an investor may simply be treated as a domestic law matter. Investors were often forced to resolve disputes over their contracts in the State's municipal courts and under its domestic laws, vulnerable to unilateral variation. It was in this context that the umbrella clause first arose [1945]. Umbrella clauses are provisions in investment treaties by which States agree to comply with all their contractual obligations to investors. A breach of contract thus becomes a breach of the umbrella clause [1946]. As such, the legal

1943. *Ibid.*, pp. 192-194.

1944. *Ibid.*, pp. 194-195.

1945. "Specifically, scholars have traced its origins to a 1954 draft settlement agreement involving the Anglo-Iranian Oil Company's (AIOC) claims regarding Iran's oil nationalization program. In 1951, AIOC's interests under a long-standing oil concessionary contract with Iran were effectively expropriated when a change in government led to the enactment of the Iranian Oil Nationalization Law, which placed all oil operations in Iran in the government's hands. Thereafter, AIOC pursued a range of ultimately unsuccessful legal options for redress, including a failed attempt to arbitrate the claims", Wong, *supra* note 217, p. 145. For an extensive treatment of the history of the umbrella clause, see A. C. Sinclair, "The Origins of the Umbrella Clause in the International Law of Investment Protection", *Arbitration International*, Vol. 20 (2004), pp. 413-418.

1946. A. Siwy, "Contract Claims and Treaty Claims", in C. Baltag (ed.), *ICSID Convention after 50 Years: Unsettled Issues*, The Hague, Kluwer Law International, 2016, p. 215. "The very purpose and the effect of an umbrella clause in an investment treaty is to transform breaches of obligations the State has undertaken with respect to the foreign investor and its investment, including contractual obligations, into treaty breaches", S. Alexandrov, "Breaches of Contract and Breaches of Treaty: The Jurisdiction of Treaty-based Arbitration Tribunals to Decide Breach of Contract Claims in *SGS* v. *Pakistan* and *SGS* v. *Philippines*", *Transnational Dispute Management*, Vol. 5 (2006), p. 556.

effect [1947] of umbrella clauses is to transform contractual claims into treaty claims [1948].

The typical umbrella clause provides that the host State "shall observe any obligation it may have entered into with regard to investments". If umbrella clauses are meant to stabilize contractual rights in the same way as stabilization clauses, then they can be understood to continue the work of engineering inviolable contractual rights [1949], thus reintroducing internationalization into investment protection.

Umbrella clause claims are unusual because they sometimes evince an overlap between contract claims and treaty claims, which have traditionally been considered distinct. If the host State breaches an umbrella clause within an investment treaty, its international responsibility will be engaged due to its violation of a treaty obligation. What is less clear is whether a host State's breach of a separate contractual obligation is sufficient to violate the umbrella clause [1950].

This confusion arose in the aftermath of the *SGS* v. *Pakistan* cases [1951]. Article 11 of the Switzerland-Pakistan investment treaty provided the following: "Either Contracting Party shall constantly guarantee the observance of commitments it has entered into with respect to the investments of the investors of the other Contracting Party." According to the decision in the *SGS* v. *Pakistan* case, the umbrella clause cannot have the effect of automatically elevating breaches of contract under municipal law to breaches of the treaty [1952]. In rejecting SGS's interpretation of Article 11 without proposing an alternative, the award has been criticized for appearing to strip Article 11 of any legal effect. Anyways, with or without umbrella clauses, host States must adhere to their obligations under international law.

James Crawford identifies four theories regarding umbrella clauses. One renders an "extremely narrow interpretation" of umbrella clauses [1953], according to which they are operative only where it is

1947. Orrego Vicuña, *supra* note 1103, p. 353.
1948. Hobér, *supra* note 440, p. 575.
1949. Ho, *supra* note 212, p. 196.
1950. *Ibid.*, p. 196.
1951. *SGS* v. *Pakistan*, *supra* note 977, Decision (2003).
1952. *Ibid.*, para. 172.
1953. Position promoted by States fighting in United Nations Permanent Sovereignty Over Natural Resources, UNGA Res. 1803 (XVIII) (14 December 1962), GAOR Supp. UNGA 17, 15; UN General Assembly Resolution on a Charter of Economic Rights and Duties of States, UNGA Res. A/Res/3281(XXIX) (12 December 1974).

possible to discern the shared intent of the parties that any breach of contract also constitutes a breach of the treaty [1954].

A second position limits umbrella clauses to breaches of contract committed by the host State in the exercise of their sovereign authority, but not in their commercial capacity [1955]. As such, the umbrella clause will not protect the "commercial aspects" of the contract and will only shield the investor from "significant interference by governments or public agencies" [1956].

A third view evokes the other extreme and maintains that the effect of umbrella clauses is to internationalize investment contracts, thereby transforming contractual claims into treaty claims that are directly subject to treaty rules [1957].

Finally, the fourth view holds that umbrella clauses are operative and may form the basis for a substantive treaty claim, but do not convert contractual claims into treaty claims. Umbrella clauses may nonetheless provide a basis for the treaty claim, even if they do not include a generic claims clause. However, the umbrella clause will not change the proper law of the contract nor its provisions for dispute settlement [1958].

Crawford points out difficulties in the first three positions. The first theory of the utility of umbrella clauses effectively deprives the umbrella clause of any content, contrary to the principle of *effet utile* and to the apparent intent of the drafters [1959]. The second and third theories create uncertainties that may lead to arbitrary results [1960]. They raise the issue

---

1954. This approach was taken first by the Tribunal in *SGS* v. *Philippines* (*supra* note 1142, Decision on Jurisdiction (29 January 2004), paras. 125, 128) and has since also been adopted by several other tribunals. See e.g. *Noble Ventures* v. *Romania*, *supra* note 1090, Award (12 October 2005), paras. 61, 62; *SGS* v. *Paraguay*, *supra* note 1714, Award (2012), para. 91; *Plama* v. *Bulgaria*, *supra* note 1370, Award (2008), paras. 185-187.

1955. The tribunals in *El Paso* v. *Argentina*, *supra* note 456, Decision on Jurisdiction (27 April 2006), para. 70 and *Pan American* v. *Argentina*, *supra* note 1085, Decision on Preliminary Objections (27 July 2006), para. 101.

1956. *CMS* v. *Argentina*, *supra* note 84, Award (12 May 2005), para. 299. *Sempra* v. *Argentina*, *supra* note 451, Award (September 28, 2007), para. 305. See other decisions in Ho, *supra* note 212, pp. 209-211.

1957. *Fedax* v. *Venezuela*, *supra* note 75, Decision on Jurisdiction (11 June 1997), 5 *ICSID Reports* 186, Award (9 March 1998), 5 *ICSID Reports* 200, para. 29; *Eureko* v. *Poland*, *supra* note 539, Partial Award (19 August 2005), paras. 244-260, cf. Dissenting Opinion of Rajski, para. 11; *Noble Ventures* v. *Romania*, *supra* note 1090, Award (12 October 2005), paras. 46-62; *SGS* v. *Philippines*, *supra* note 1142; *CMS* v. *Argentina*, *supra* note 84, Decision of the *Ad hoc* Committee on the Application for Annulment of the Argentine Republic (25 September 2007).

1958. Crawford, *supra* note 484, p. 368.

1959. *Ibid.*, p. 368.

1960. "The second theory imposes a characterisation test at the level of breach that is not warranted by the text of the contract and which is capable of producing

of what quality of breach is required for a violation of the contract to constitute a breach of an umbrella clause [1961].

According to Crawford, the position that should be favored is the one he refers to as "integrationist", in line with the decision of the *ad hoc* committee in *CMS* v. *Argentina* (annulment). As applied to standard umbrella clauses, the integrationist view maintains the distinction between treaty claims and contract claims. As such, contractual claims are governed by their own applicable law. These claims allow enforcement to occur without internationalization and without transforming the character and content of the underlying obligation. In the integrationist view, the umbrella clause is an additional mechanism for the enforcement of claims, but the basis of the transaction remains the same [1962].

The divergences that exist between the different theories of umbrella clauses are still manifest today, as reflected in contemporary cases. In two claims launched against Paraguay (one by BIVAC, the other by SGS), the arbitral tribunals arrived at the exact opposite conclusions regarding the jurisdiction of national courts and tribunals, as provided for in the umbrella clause in the investment treaty contracts [1963].

arbitrary results" (*ibid.*, pp. 368-369). "No doubt there are genuine concerns driving the restrictive view, which is to a significant extent a reaction against the equal and opposite defects of the third view. However, State laws or regulations should not be equated to obligations entered into by the State. Similarly, umbrella clauses should not be regarded as implicitly freezing the laws of the State at the date of admission of In investment. In the absence of express stabilization, investors take the risk that the host State's obligations under its own law may change, and the umbrella clause will not reduce this risk. According to this view, an umbrella clause might even enable an investor to evade agreed-upon exclusive jurisdiction arrangements in the investment contract, whether they provide for dispute resolution through domestic courts or through international arbitration" (*ibid.*, p. 370).

1961. Siwy, *supra* note 1946, p. 217:

> "In addition to the quality of the breach required to trigger an umbrella clause, an additional question is raised regarding the privity of contracts and its relationship to umbrella clauses. Investment agreements are often not concluded by a State or one of its organs, but by separate legal entities that are controlled or wholly owned by the State. It is doubtful that a breach of a contract entered into by legal entities that are separate from the State can also amount to a breach of the umbrella clause. In any case, at the most, under an umbrella clause a host State may be liable for breaches of a contract even in the absence of the use of *puissance publique*. In this case, however, the contractual obligation must bind the State itself."

1962. Crawford, *supra* note 484, p. 370.

1963. Both tribunals held that the umbrella clause brings contractual obligations into the investment treaty. However, their final conclusions were different. The *BIVAC* Tribunal declared the claim inadmissible since the parties had agreed to the exclusive jurisdiction of national courts, *Bureau Veritas, Inspection, Valuation, Assessment and Control, BIVAC BV* v. *Republic of Paraguay*, ICSID Case No. ARB/07/9, Decision on Jurisdiction, fn. 156, paras. 141-142 and 159. On the contrary, the *SGS* Tribunal

Controversies and the lack of conclusive answers to issues raised by umbrella clauses make them less attractive to States. Even though reliance on them has a relatively low rate of success, the trend to exclude umbrella clauses is gaining momentum [1964].

E. The difference between contract and treaty claims

According to Francisco Orrego Vicuña, "[n]ot long ago teachers of international law used to explain that treaties are like contracts, only between States. Today it is necessary to explain that contracts are like treaties, only between individuals and the State" [1965].

However, an investment agreement is not a treaty, nor is it even analogous to a treaty. Hence, the analogous application of treaty rules to investment agreements should not be accepted [1966]. In this regard, the Iran-United States Claims Tribunal held in the *Amoco* v. *Iran* case [1967] that while "a State has the duty to respect contracts freely entered into with a foreign party," this rule must not be equated with the *pacta sunt servanda* principle. States are not bound by their contracts with private parties in the same way that they are committed by treaties entered into with other sovereign States. Any conclusion to the contrary has no basis in law or equity [1968].

In the landmark *Vivendi* v. *Argentina* decision, the ICSID Arbitral Tribunal held that

> "[w]hether there has been a breach of the BIT and whether there has been a breach of the contract are different questions. Each of these claims will be determined by reference to its own proper or applicable law – in the case of the BIT, by international law, in the case of the Concession Contract, by the proper law of the contract" [1969].

---

decided that the forum selection clause did not bar its jurisdiction, *SGS* v. *Paraguay*, *supra* note 1714, Decision on Jurisdiction, fn. 156, paras. 162-171.

1964. Chernykh notes that according to the UNCTAD Investment Policy Hub, as of January 2019, the provision has been relied upon in 125 cases and its breach was found only in seventeen cases, i.e. 13.6 percent. She also notes that her calculations show that the umbrella clause was increasingly used in the first five decades from its appearance, reaching 52.11 percent of the concluded agreements, whereas the last sixteen years (calculated up to 2017) witnessed an abrupt decline from 52.11 percent to 22.98 percent, i.e. by 29.13 percent, in Chernykh, *supra* note 1353, p. 48.

1965. Orrego Vicuña, *supra* note 1103, p. 341.

1966. Maniruzzaman, *supra* note 317, pp. 5-6.

1967. *Amoco* v. *Iran*, *supra* note 489, Award (14 July 1987), p. 21, paras. 242-243.

1968. Maniruzzaman, *supra* note 317, p. 6.

1969. *Vivendi* v. *Argentina*, *supra* note 456, Decision on Annulment (3 July 2002), para. 96.

Vivendi v. *Argentina* is considered the leading case shining light on the contract-treaty distinction. According to its award, the breach of an investment contract must be assessed under the proper contract law, while the breach of an investment treaty is a question for international law [1970]. This ruling was endorsed in many subsequent ICSID decisions. For instance, in *Impregilo* v. *Pakistan* [1971], the Tribunal held that "[e]ven if the two perfectly coincide, they remain analytically distinct, and necessarily require different enquiries" [1972].

However, overlapping may occur. When a State commits, through the signing of a treaty, to comply with a contract, any breach of the contract will also constitute a breach of an international obligation – except when a State commits the breach to avoid committing another wrongful act. Even though they are conceptually different, according to Crawford, the breach of a contract may, in certain contexts, also entail or imply the breach of a treaty [1973].

F. Law applicable to contract claims

In the *Ambatielos* case, the ICJ [1974] stated that it

> "cannot accept the view that the contract signed between the Iranian Government and the Anglo-Persian Oil Company has a double character [of a contract and an international agreement]. It is nothing more than a concessionary contract between a government and a foreign corporation".

In fact, not every breach of contract generates State responsibility under public international law [1975]. State responsibility is relevant, for instance, when it comes to determining remedies. However, contractual

---

1970. Crawford, *supra* note 484, p. 358.

1971. In this case, the ICSID Tribunal held that the taking of contractual rights could, potentially, constitute expropriation (or a measure having an equivalent effect). The Tribunal noted that the case at hand did not involve nationalization or expropriation in the traditional sense of those terms but behavior that could, at least in theory, constitute an indirect expropriation (or a measure having an effect equivalent to expropriation). In *Aguas del Tunari* v. *Bolivia*, an ICSID Tribunal made it clear that it did not have. *Aguas* v. *Bolivia*, *supra* note 111, Decision on Respondent's Objections to Jurisdiction (21 October 2005), para. 119. Subedi, *supra* note 17, p. 147.

1972. *Impregilo* v. *Pakistan*, *supra* note 1395, Decision on Jurisdiction (22 April 2005), para. 258. Brown, *supra* note 164, pp. 427-428.

1973. Crawford, *supra* note 484, pp. 357-358.

1974. *Ambatielos*, *supra* note 1907; 11 (*Anglo-Iranian Oil*), 1952 *ICJ Pleadings* 111 *et seq.* (July 1952); 12 *id.* at 112. See also ICC Award in Case No. 3327/1981, 109 JDI (Clunet), p. 971 and in *Collection of ICC Arbitral Awards 1974-1985* (1990), p. 433.

1975. De Brabandere, *supra* note 27, p. 29.

remedies in domestic laws, such as punitive damages, liquidated damages or contractual penalties, are not available and cannot be awarded under public international law [1976].

State responsibility cannot be invoked under public international law for several reasons. First, foreign investors are not considered full subjects within international law, and State contracts do not in principle create public international law obligations for either of the contracting parties. Moreover, it would be unfair if a private alien could invoke State responsibility for breach of contract under public international law because the investor has different concerns to those of the State, such as the welfare of the country or equivalent obligations to the public. As such, foreign investors should not be entitled to take advantage of the State party's superior position as a subject within public international law by acting as an international subject without the corresponding duties or obligations [1977].

In contract-based disputes subject to arbitration, parties can subject their contract to the law of the host State, or some other law [1978]. If the contract is silent, tribunals recur to private international law techniques [1979]. In the 1929 case of *Payment of Various Serbian Loans Issued in France*, the PCIJ decided that agreements that are not concluded between international law subjects will be governed by national law [1980]. As a result, an agreement that is not a treaty will be subject to municipal law or non-State law when applicable [1981].

When it comes to ICSID arbitration, in the *travaux préparatoires* of the ICSID Convention, the Austrian delegate expressed that "in cases where an investor complained of action which affected the performance of the contract", the tribunals were "merely a substitute for the domestic courts and would apply municipal law" [1982].

1976. Siwy, *supra* note 1946, p. 218.

1977. "In addition, since a national's right to diplomatic protection is tied to his State, it cannot be transferred to the former without disrupting the latter's foreign policy and international relations with other States at least on the question of international claims", Maniruzzaman, *supra* note 317, pp. 25-26.

1978. According to Cremades and Cairns, a contract claim is likely to be determined according to the Host State's law relating to administrative contracts. Cremades and Cairns, *supra* note 529, p. 330.

1979. Thus, Rule 11 of Douglas states: "The law applicable to an issue relating to a claim founded upon a contractual obligation, tort or restitutionary obligation, or an incidental question relating thereto, is the law governing the contract, tort or restitutionary obligation in accordance with generally accepted principles of private international law", Douglas, *supra* note 39, p. 90.

1980. *Serbian Loans*, *supra* note 978, Judgment, at 41.4.

1981. See *supra* note 978.

1982. *History of the ICSID Convention*, *supra* note 1078, II-1, p. 400, fn. 73.

Several cases illustrate this conclusion. In *(SOABI)* v. *Senegal* (1988), an ICSID tribunal ruled that "the national law applicable to the relations of two Senegalese parties in respect of a project that was to take place in Senegal, can only be Senegalese law". The Tribunal referred to the agreements under discussion as "government contracts", subject primarily to the Senegalese Code of Governmental Obligations [1983]. In turn, the Tribunal in *Aucoven* v. *Venezuela* (2003) applied national law to the merits of the contractual claims [1984]. Similarly, in *Noble Ventures* v. *Romania* (2005), the Tribunal recalled the

> "well-established rule of general international law that in normal circumstances per se a breach of a contract by the State does not give rise to direct international responsibility on the part of the State" [1985].

Similarly, the Iran-United States Claims Tribunal applied national law to questions relating to the relationship within the investment contract, as was the case in *Sea-Land Service, Inc.* v. *Government of the Islamic Republic of Iran, Ports and Shipping Organizations (PSO)* (1984) [1986] and in *Dic of Delaware et al.* v. *Tehran Redevelopment Corp. (TRC) et al.* (1985), which dealt with the enforceability of an alleged verbal agreement for the third phase of a project [1987].

Following the same logic, the NAFTA case *Waste Management* v. *Mexico* (2004) did not apply public international law to a mere breach of contract [1988].

G. Breaches of contract violating public international law

For a State to incur responsibility under public international law for breach of contract, the State's actions must have been arbitrary, violating an agreement in a "clear and discriminatory departure" from

---

1983. *Société Ouest Africaine des Bétons Industriels (SOABI)* v. *Senegal*, ICSID Case No. ARB/82/1, Award (25 February 1988), para. 5.02.

1984. *Aucoven* v. *Venezuela, supra* note 1084, Award (2003), paras. 222-227.

1985. *Noble Ventures* v. *Romania, supra* note 1090, Award (12 October 2005), para. 53; *SGS* v. *Pakistan, supra* note 977, Decision (2003), para. 167: "[A] violation of a contract entered into by a State with an investor of another State, is not, by itself, a violation of international law."

1986. *Sea-Land Service, supra* note 946, at Section II (A) *(i)*.

1987. *Dic of Delaware* et al. v. *Tehran Redevelopment Corp.* et al., Award No 176-255-3 (26 April 1985), 8 IUSCTR, p. 144 (1985), at sec. B (1). Regarding enforceability, the Tribunal applied Iranian law to hold that the agreement was unenforceable due to insufficient evidence of the definiteness of the agreement.

1988. *Waste Management* v. *Mexico, supra* note 530, Award (30 April 2004).

the governing law or incurring "unreasonable departure from the principles recognized by the principal legal systems of the world" [1989]. State arbitrariness can also result from a denial of justice such as limiting access to its courts, refusing to arbitrate after clearly committing to do so, or failing to comply with a judicial or arbitral award [1990]. In this sense, denial of justice is an international delict that gives rise to causes of action under public international law [1991].

The Commentary to Article 4 of the ILC's Articles of the Responsibility of States for Internationally Wrongful Acts (Draft Articles on State Responsibility) rules on the matter, stating that a contractual breach by a State does not automatically entail a breach of international law. Instead, it suggests that "something further is required before international law becomes relevant, such as a denial of justice by the courts of the State in proceedings brought by the other contracting party" [1992].

Following the same logic, Section 712 of the Restatement of the Foreign Relations Law of the United States (revised in 1986) rejects the principle that governmental acts to alter or abrogate the terms of a State contract constitute violations of public international law. Actions of a more egregious nature are required, such as a discriminatory breach

---

1989. Alexandrov, *supra* note 1946, p. 564.

1990. The Separate Opinion of Judge Tanaka, in *Barcelona Traction*, *supra* note 24, at p. 144, states that "denial of justice occurs in the case of such acts as – 'corruption, threats, unwarrantable delay, flagrant abuse of judicial procedure, a judgment dictated by the executive, or so manifestly unjust that no court which was both competent and honest could have given it. . . . But no merely erroneous or even unjust judgment of a court will constitute a denial of justice". C. T. Curtis explains that "[t]he traditional rule of international law has been that a State's breach of a contract with a foreign national is not of itself an international wrong. Some additional element is required, something pronounced and manifestly unfair. But it has never been completely clear what that additional element is. One factor that will raise a breach of contract to the level of an international wrong is a 'denial of justice'. The investor may assert a claim of denial of justice if the contracting State provides no forum in which the investor's claim may be heard or if the investor does not receive a fair hearing in the available forum", Curtis, *supra* note 119, p. 326.

1991. Maniruzzaman, *supra* note 317, p. 26.

1992. ILC Draft Articles on State Responsibility, *supra* note 433, p. 87, Art. 4, Comment 6. States are responsible under international law for contractual breaches when they have frustrated the contractual dispute settlement mechanism, leaving the foreign investor with no recourse to contractual remedies to redress a contractual wrong. Both the *SGS* v. *Pakistan* Tribunal and the *SGS* v. *Philippines* Tribunal agreed that there would be a viable treaty breach claim if the investor were prevented from submitting disputes to the contractual dispute settlement mechanism. The very recent decision in the *Waste Management* case also recognized that the availability and the viability of a contractual dispute settlement mechanism was critical to determining whether certain acts violated substantive provisions of the treaty. Alexandrov, *supra* note 1946, pp. 564-565.

or a breach of contract for governmental (rather than commercial) reasons [1993].

It is widely accepted in arbitral precedents that a contract cannot, in itself, create legitimate expectations under public international law. For instance, in *Parkerings* v. *Lithuania*, *Duke* v. *Ecuador* [1994] and *Hamester* v. *Ghana* [1995], the existence of legitimate expectations and of contractual rights were considered to be two entirely separate issues [1996]. As decided in the latter case, "it is not sufficient for a claimant to invoke contractual rights that have allegedly been infringed" to advance a claim for a violation of the fair and equitable treatment standard" [1997]. The Tribunal in *Impregilo* v. *Argentina* came to a similar conclusion [1998].

Long before then, in the *Neer* claim decided in 1926, the Tribunal had already held on the issue of denial of justice that the "minimum standard of treatment" for aliens under customary international law entails "an outrage, to bad faith, to willful neglect of duty, or to an insufficiency of governmental action so far short of international standards that every reasonable and impartial man would recognize its insufficiency" [1999].

The *Neer* claim case did not deal with contractual protection, as did the 1927 decision in the *Chattin* claim [2000] regarding contractual non-performance. The Tribunal did not consider mistreatment a

1993. The commentary on Section 712 of the Restatement of the Foreign Relations Law of the United States provides that "[u]nder Subsection (2) a State is responsible under international law for such a repudiation or breach only if it is discriminatory . . . or if it is akin to an expropriation in that the contract is repudiated or breached for governmental rather than commercial reasons and the State is not prepared to pay damages". See more in F. Beveridge, *Globalization and International Investment*, London, Routledge, 2017.

1994. The Tribunal established that in its dealings with Electroquil, INECEL did not behave in a manner different from that of a "normal" contracting party. The establishment of the Payment Trust did not imply the exercise of sovereign power. According to the Tribunal, any private contractor may undertake to establish a payment trust. As such, Electroquil's expectations under the PPA 95 must be regarded as "mere" contractual expectations that are not protected under the BIT. See *Duke Energy* v. *Ecuador*, *supra* note 1143, Award (2008), para. 358.

1995. *Parkerings* v. *Lithuania*, *supra* note 530, Award (11 September 2007), para. 344, emphasis original. Siwy, *supra* note 1946, p. 211.

1996. *Gustav* v. *Ghana*, *supra* note 1374, Award (18 June 2008), para. 335.

1997. Thus, even if the impugned actions were "sovereign" in nature and attributed to Ghana, the alleged contract violations could not have amounted to a violation of the FET standard based on the theory of "legitimate expectations". *Ibid.*, para. 337.

1998. The Tribunal considered the existence of legitimate expectations and the existence of contractual rights as two separate issues. Contractual acts "cannot amount to a violation of the fair and equitable treatment standard based on a theory of legitimate expectations" (*Impregilo* v. *Argentina*, *supra* note 1357, Final Award (2011), paras. 292, 294).

1999. *USA* v. *United Mexican States*, (1926) 4 RIAA, p. 60, 61.

2000. *Ibid.*, in Ho, *supra* note 212, p. 94.

breach of contract that was sufficient, in and of itself, to engage State responsibility [2001]. As such, the Tribunal preserved denial of justice as the minimum standard of treatment recognized within the *Neer* claim.

Case law emerging after the *Neer* claim dealing with customary international law determined that aggravating circumstances turn a breach of contract into a breach of public international law, such as arbitrariness [2002] and State exercise of its sovereign power [2003] to unduly interfere with contract performance [2004].

The legal basis for finding breaches of contract changed when States gradually stopped practicing diplomatic intervention to protect the interests of their nationals that had entered into international investment treaties. Today, injured investors can directly pursue claims against the host State.

Previously, within international investments it was thought that any denial of justice violated the international minimum standard within customary international law. Now, the "fair and equitable treatment protection" standard is included in virtually all investment treaties, allowing investors to pursue States internationally for breaches of contract that amount to its violation [2005]. In this regard, the approach for interpreting fair and equitable treatment in the context of contractual breaches approximates it to the denial of justice under the minimum standard within customary international law [2006].

The doctrines of non-arbitrariness and respect for due process have emerged from arbitral precedents as the key components within the fair and equitable treatment protection standard [2007]. For instance, while bad faith conduct undoubtedly violates the standard, it is often not identified as its component in international jurisprudence. Other components of the fair and equitable treatment standard identified by tribunals include

---

2001. *Ibid.*, pp. 94-95.

2002. *USA* v. *El Salvador*, (1902) 15 RIAA, p. 467; *USA* v. *Mexico* (1931), *supra* note 976; *Great Britain* v. *United Mexican States*, (1930) 5 RIAA, p. 115.

2003. *Delagoa Bay Railway Arbitration (USA* v. *Portugal)*, in US Department of State, *Papers Relating to the Foreign Relations of the United States*, Washington, DC, Government Printing Office, 1900. *Cheek Claim (USA* v. *Siam)*, Award (21 March 1898); *Robert R. Brown (USA* v. *Great Britain)*, (1923) 6 RIAA, p. 120.

2004. See Ho, *supra* note 212, p. 96.

2005. *Ibid.*, p. 101.

2006. Alexandrov, *supra* note 1946, p. 560. The core standard of treatment for investment contracts is further preserved by the growing trend in investment treaty practice pegging FET to MST. This obliges arbitral tribunals that are tasked with adjudicating contract-based FET claims to first ascertain what the MST for investment contracts is, and to then assimilate FET to that core standard. Ho, *supra* note 212, p. 101.

2007. Orrego Vicuña, *supra* note 1103, p. 346.

the safeguarding of investor expectations, freedom from State coercion for renegotiations and cancellations, and harassment [2008].

The following question arises: what additional factor is required for a breach of contract by a State to become a breach of public international law [2009]?

H. Additional factor for considering breach of contract a breach of international law

Arbitral precedents have failed to determine in a consistent manner when breaches of contract by a State constitute breaches of public international law [2010]. As discussed below, various responses to this question have been advanced.

1. Exercise of power (iure imperii)

The *iure imperii* exercise of power has been classified by Alfred Siwy as the dominant approach to determining breaches of public international law by States [2011].

In this regard, a distinction must be made between State actions performed *iure gestionis* (for commercial or private matters) and State actions performed *iure imperii* (in the exercise of sovereign authority or *puissance publique*) [2012].

2008. Ho, *supra* note 212, p. 138.

2009. Siwy, *supra* note 1946, p. 210.

2010. "Cases involving breaches of contract have invariably also given rise to complex disputes about the jurisdiction of the treaty-based tribunal tasked with adjudicating their dispute. The main questions dealt with in these cases have focused on whether these tribunals can hear claims based on the breach of a contract as a preliminary question to determining a breach of a treaty, the jurisdiction of treaty-based tribunals to hear claims for breaches of contracts that do not amount to breaches of international law, and the relevance of contractually agreed upon dispute resolution provisions. There are currently no uniform answers to these questions" (*ibid.*, p. 209).

2011. *Ibid.*, p. 213.

2012. In *Saudi Arabia* v. *Nelson*, US Supreme Court Justice Souter, stated:

> "Under the restrictive, as opposed to the absolute, theory of foreign sovereign immunity, a state is immune from the jurisdiction of foreign courts as to its sovereign or public acts *(jure imperii)*, but not as to those that are private or commercial in character *(jure gestionis)* . . . a state engages in commercial activity under the restrictive theory where it exercises only those powers that can also be exercised by private citizens, as distinct from those powers peculiar to sovereigns. Put differently, a foreign state engages in commercial activity for purposes of the restrictive theory only where it acts in the manner of a private player within the market."

Saudi Arabia v. *Nelson*, 507 US 349, 359-360 (1993). See also Sicard-Mirabal and Derains, *supra* note 1850, p. 12.

State breaches that could also have been committed by a private party are not considered acts *iure imperii*, and do not violate public international law. This was the case in the *Bayindir* v. *Pakistan* [2013] and *Impregilo* v. *Pakistan* decisions [2014]. In the latter award, the Tribunal held that "[o]nly the State in the exercise of its sovereign authority *('puissance publique')*, and not as a contracting party, may breach the obligations assumed under the BIT" [2015].

In *Bureau Veritas* v. *Paraguay*, the Tribunal stated that Paraguay did not exercise its sovereign powers via the adoption of legislation or regulatory acts, did not exercise police powers, nor did it ignore any court judgment. Further, it noted that "[a]ttempts to mislead, distort, conceal or otherwise confuse a contractual partner are strategies open to and used by both public and private persons" [2016]. Something more is required [2017].

Crawford criticizes this approach of distinguishing between acts *iure imperii* and *iure gestionis*. He notes that nowhere in Articles 4 and 12 of the ILC Draft on State Responsibility is there a requirement to prove any particular motive, whether financial or "governmental" in this regard [2018].

2. *Other elements beyond acts* iure imperii

In *Waste Management* v. *Mexico* [2019], the Tribunal decided that if a violation of a contract amounted to "an outright and unjustified

2013. Which held generally that "a breach of FET requires conduct in the exercise of sovereign powers". *Bayindir* v. *Pakistan*, *supra* note 456, Award (27 August 2009), para. 377. Siwy, *supra* note 1946, p. 212.

2014. In this case, the Tribunal was tasked with decide on various claims deriving from a construction contract under which a dam of the Indus was to be built, *Impregilo* v. *Pakistan*, *supra* note 1395, Decision on Jurisdiction (22 April 2005). The investor argued that Pakistan had committed various breaches of the BIT due to their alleged interference with the establishment of the dispute resolution board under the construction contract and due to the fact that the investor lacks the capacity to raise claims for additional costs under the contract.

2015. *Ibid.*, para. 260. In *CMS* v. *Argentina*, *supra* note 84, Award (12 May 2005), para. 299, the Arbitral Tribunal stated: "Purely commercial aspects of a contract might not be protected by the treaty in some situations, but the protection is likely to be available when there is a significant interference by governments or public agencies with the rights of the investor."

2016. *BIVAC* v. *Paraguay*, *supra* note 1963, Further Decision on Objections to Jurisdiction (9 October 2012), para. 241.

2017. *Ibid.*, para. 227.

2018. Crawford, *supra* note 484, p. 356. All those members of the Sixth Committee who responded to the specific question on this issue confirmed that classifying the acts of State organs as *iure imperii* or *iure gestionis* was an irrelevant consideration. See Report of the ILC, 1998, A/53/10, para. 35; Crawford, *supra* note 484, p. 35.

2019. *Waste Management* v. *Mexico*, *supra* note 530, Award (30 April 2004), para. 115.

repudiation of the transaction", a breach of public international law may be found in cases where the aggrieved party was left with no remedy to "address the problem" [2020]. As stated by Siwy, the Tribunal in this case alluded to both the repudiation of the transaction and the lack of capacity to address courts or an arbitral tribunal [2021].

According to Christopher Curtis, action taken by States pursuant to "general and unobjectionable legislation" not specifically directed against the contracting party would probably not be considered arbitrary [2022].

The following actions may violate the fair and equitable treatment standard: cumulative acts and omissions, coerced renegotiations, bad faith, and arbitrariness. In this regard, the 2017 Comprehensive Economic and Trade Agreement between Canada and the European Union (CETA) provides in its Article 8.10 (2) that breaches of fair and equitable treatment may occur

> "if a measure or a series of measures constitutes: *(a)* denial of justice, in criminal, civil or administrative proceedings; *(b)* fundamental breach of due process, including a fundamental breach of transparency, in judicial and administrative proceedings; *(c)* manifest arbitrariness; *(d)* targeted discrimination on manifestly wrongful grounds such as gender, race or religious belief; *(e)* abusive treatment of investors, such as coercion, duress and harassment".

Confiscatory breach, in which the investor's rights are taken away without adequate compensation, is internationally wrongful [2023].

Some decisions are erroneously cited as establishing that a breach of contract amounts to a treaty violation. For instance, in *Mondev* v. *USA* [2024] the Tribunal rejected the claim that the local court's decision amounted to denial of justice. This ruling is "a far cry from stating that a breach of contract amounts to a breach of treaty" [2025]. The *SGS* v. *Paraguay* decision has also been erroneously cited as establishing that a violation of contract leads to a breach of public international law.

2020. See Subedi, *supra* note 17, p. 148.
2021. Siwy, *supra* note 1946, p. 214.
2022. Curtis, *supra* note 119, p. 327.
2023. *Ibid.*, p. 327.
2024. *Mondev* v. *USA*, *supra* note 562, Award (11 October 2002). The decision has been misinterpreted to have concluded that a breach of contract is also constitutes a breach of international law. A closer reading of the award reveals that this is an erroneous interpretation. See *Ibid.*, para. 134.
2025. See Siwy, *supra* note 1946, pp. 214-215.

This interpretation is wrong [2026]. At most, the *SGS* v. *Paraguay* decision recognizes that non-payment violates the fair and equitable treatment if proof of bad faith or arbitrariness can be found [2027].

I. Non-contractual investment claims

Non-contractual claims within foreign investments are usually rooted in public international law. However, non-contractual claims can also be brought under national law alone, or together with public international law. Combined claims launched under national and public international law may arise when required under the relevant investment treaty, or in cases where it is necessary to refer to national law to verify the existence and content of the investor's rights *vis-à-vis* the host State [2028].

In *Iurii Bogdanov, Agurdino-Invest Ltd., Agurdino-Chimia JSC* v. *Government of the Republic of Moldova* (2005), the foreign investor alleged that the host State violated the principle of non-retroactivity of legislation. Sole Arbitrator Moss dismissed the claim, applying the Moldovan Foreign Investment Act [2029].

As to the relevance of national law within international investment claims, the PCIJ considered matters related to national law as merely factual [2030]. However, as pointed out by Douglas, the principle that municipal laws are to be treated as facts before an international court or

---

2026. *Ibid.*, p. 215. The decision turned on issues of jurisdiction. The Tribunal stated the following:

> "A State's non-payment under a contract is, in the view of the Tribunal, capable of giving rise to a breach of a fair and equitable treatment requirement, perhaps, where the non-payment amounts to a repudiation of the contract, frustration of its economic purpose, or substantial deprivation of its value. Whether anything more than a wrongful refusal to pay, and, if so, what more, is required to prevail on a claim of breach of a fair and equitable treatment standard are questions for the merits."

SGS v. *Paraguay*, *supra* note 1714, Decision on Jurisdiction (12 February 2010), para. 146.

2027. Ho, *supra* note 212, p. 121.

2028. Ho, *supra* note 212, p. 146. "For a private person to have a claim under international law arising from the deprivation of its property, it must hold that property in accordance with applicable rules of domestic law" (*Vestey Group Ltd.* v. *Venezuela*, ICSID Case No. ARB/06/4, Award (15 April 2016), para. 257).

2029. Governmental Regulation No. 482 of 1988. *Iurii Bogdanov, Agurdino-Invest Ltd., Agurdino-Chimia JSC* v. *Government of the Republic of Moldova*, SCC Institute, Award (22 September 2005), Sections 1.3, 4.1.

2030. *Polish Upper Silesia*, *supra* note 332, at p. 19 (25 May 1926). *Fouad Alghanim & Sons Co. for General Trading & Contracting, WLL* et al. v. *Jordan*, ICSID Case No. ARB/13/38, Award (14 December 2017), para. 345.

tribunal is debatable. Some situations do not generate controversy, such as when the international court decides a maritime boundary dispute and takes into account municipal laws asserting legal rights over the disputed area to determine whether the doctrine of acquiescence in international law can be invoked by one of the State litigants. It is able to do so in this context because the matter is governed exclusively by international law [2031].

Moreover, the violation of domestic law may not necessarily entail a breach of international law, as decided by the ICJ in the *ELSI* case [2032]. However, when violating its domestic law, the State may also have breached public international law. In such a situation, interpretation of domestic law becomes a preliminary step: when evaluating the lawfulness or unlawfulness of the State's conduct, domestic law must be considered as a fact from the point of view of public international law [2033]. National law is, of course, also relevant to questions such as whether an investment is valid, whether a representative was empowered to act on behalf of the State, or in determining the nature of a private entity. Further examples include environmental impact assessments, zoning changes, taxation, immigration and identifying the appropriate currency to be used in calculating and adjusting tariffs [2034].

J. Public international law governs the violation of international obligations

When States breach their international obligations, the characterization and consequences of the violation are governed by public international law [2035].

2031. Douglas, *supra* note 39, pp. 69-70. In *Total SA* v. *Argentina*, when considering the role of Argentina's domestic law in determining the content and the extent of the investor's economic rights as they existed in Argentina's legal system, the Tribunal rejected the view that Argentinean law was only relevant as "factual evidence". The Tribunal stated that it believes that Argentine law has a broader role than that of just determining factual matters. The content and the scope of Total's economic rights must be determined by the Tribunal in light of Argentina's legal principles and provisions. Moreover, the extensive reliance by the Claimant on Argentina's acts of a legislative and administrative nature governing the gas, electricity and hydrocarbons sectors, as well as the extensive discussion between the parties regarding the content and extent of Total's rights in respect of the operation of its investments, is a recognition that Argentina's domestic law plays a prominent role. See *Total SA* v. *Argentina*, *supra* note 16, Decision on Liability (2010), para. 39.

2032. *Elettronica*, *supra* note 268, Judgment (20 July 1989), para. 124.

2033. Sacerdoti, *supra* note 641, p. 22.

2034. Spiermann, *supra* note 979, pp. 111-112. See also pp. 113-115.

2035. In this regard, Douglas promotes his Rule 12 as follows: "The law applicable to an issue relating to the consequences of the host state's breach of an investment treaty

According to Article 2 of the ILC's Draft Articles on State Responsibility, an internationally wrongful act will be found when two conditions are met. First, the conduct (either an action or an omission) must be attributable to the State under public international law. Second, it must constitute a breach of one of the State's international obligations.

In turn, Article 3 of the Draft Articles provides that whether an action is considered internationally wrongful will be governed by public international law. This determination is independent from, and prevails over, applicable domestic legal rules. However, as explained in the official commentary to Article 3:

> "[I]nternal law will often be relevant to the question of international responsibility. In every case it will be seen on analysis that either the provisions of internal law are relevant as facts in applying the applicable international standard, or else that they are actually incorporated in some form, conditionally or unconditionally, into that standard." [2036]

In line with these provisions, the *ad hoc* Committee in the *MTD* case "characterized international law as the *lex causae* in a case based on a breach of an investment treaty" [2037]. In *Wena* v. *Egypt*, the

obligation is to be found in a *sui generis* regime of state responsibility for investment treaties", Douglas, *supra* note 39, p. 94.

2036. ILC, Commentary to Art. 3, para. 7, reprinted in Crawford, p. 89. Crawford, *supra* note 484, pp. 354, 357. There is no *a priori* definition of what is or is not international. This is even true regarding acts that *a priori* may relate to internal affairs. Furthermore, there is no "presumption of the restrictive interpretation of treaties", as was decided in the first PCIJ case, *The Wimbledon*, in 1923, PCIJ Ser. A, No. 1. In the *Loewen* case, the Tribunal stated the following: "There is no warrant for transferring rules derived from private law into a field of international law where claimants are permitted for convenience to enforce what are in origin the rights of party States. *Loewen* v. *USA*, *supra* note 579, Award (26 June 2003), 7 *ICSID Reports* 442. See Crawford, *supra* note 484, pp. 354-355.

2037. *MTD* v. *Chile*, *supra* note 327, Decision on the Application for Annulment (21 March 2007), paras. 72, 61. Spiermann, *supra* note 979, p. 108, 109; *AAPL* v. *Sri Lanka*, *supra* note 453; *Wena Hotels* v. *Egypt*, *supra* note 601; *CMS* v. *Argentina*, *supra* note 84; *Enron* v. *Argentina*, *supra* note 451; *Sempra* v. *Argentina*, *supra* note 451. Douglas's Rule 12 states that "The law applicable to an issue relating to the consequences of the host state's breach of an investment treaty obligation is to be found in a sui generis regime of state responsibility for investment treaties". *Wintershall Aktiengesellschaft* v. *Argentine Republic*, ICSID Case No. ARB/04/14, Award (8 December 2008), para. 113. The ILC Draft Articles on State Responsibility, *supra* note 433, contains no rules and regulations of State responsibility *vis-à-vis* non-State actors: tribunals are left to determine "the ways in which State responsibility may be invoked by non-State entities" from the provisions of the text of the particular treaty under consideration, Douglas, *supra* note 39, p. 94.

Tribunal held that "international law can be applied by itself, if the appropriate rule is found in this ambit" [2038]. In deciding that compound interest should be awarded in the case, the Tribunal relied on public international law, as interest is an integral part of the calculation of damages under the formula well-known therein of prompt, adequate and effective compensation. In this case, it would have been unwise to rely on principles of national law that are clearly less generous in the granting of interest.

K. A private law approach to investment contracts?

1. The problem

Investment treaties contain provisions that, if violated, constitute breaches of State duties. There is no need to refer to national law or public international law to find a breach of the State's obligations within international investments, as both national law and public international law apply when specifically included in the agreement or treaty [2039]. These provisions constitute the core of generic treaty rights that are usually drafted in similar terms, which has contributed to the development of a growing arbitral jurisprudence in relation to treaty rights [2040].

Treaty interpretation presents several challenges, as treaty rights are notoriously vague and drafted in broad standards rather than as precise obligations [2041]. Treaty rights have generated significant debate in commentary and case law, and has left the following questions unanswered: what is included in the "international minimum standard" of treatment? What constitutes "fair and equitable treatment"? Who is entitled to "fair and equitable treatment"? The controversies related to treaty rights are not limited to these questions, however, and many other issues have arisen that have yielded contradictory responses within case law and scholarly writing [2042]. As stated by Julie Maupin,

2038. Cremades and Cairns, *supra* note 529, p. 330.

2039. R. Kreindler, "The Law Applicable to International Investment Disputes", in N. Horn and S. Kröll (eds.), *Arbitrating Foreign Investment Disputes: Procedural and Substantive Legal Aspects* (Studies in Transnational Economic Law, No. 19), The Hague, Kluwer Law International, 2004, pp. 405-406.

2040. Cremades and Cairns, *supra* note 529, p. 340.

2041. Maupin, *supra* note 1756, p. 382.

2042. Subedi, *supra* note 17, p. 57.

"the absence of clear guidelines leads arbitrators, hailing from different backgrounds, to advance contradicting interpretations" [2043].

Further, investment treaties generally fail to address the extent to which treaties displace private law institutions and values in practice. In the realm of foreign investment, treaties include provisions related to property rights (real, personal and intellectual), contracts, enterprises and equity interests in business organizations such as stocks and shares. What treaties generally omit to mention, however, is how these private law matters interact with them. This issue has also been largely neglected in modern scholarly writing in which, according to Julian Arato, "major problems of fairness, efficiency and equitable distribution have been missed" [2044].

2. Contracts as investments

Investment treaties do not properly assimilate contracts to property, but they have successfully assimilated contracts to investments. When treaties list contractual rights as protected within the agreement, such rights will become subject to expropriation [2045]. Several investment

2043. Maupin, *supra* note 1756, pp. 382-384:

"Moreover, the textual ambiguities pose quandaries concerning the very nature of the international investment law field. Since investors can launch claims against host States for violating their treaty obligations, are investors considered rights-holders within international investment treaties? If they are not rights-holders, should they merely be considered third-party beneficiaries who hold a derivative interest in the States' observance of their reciprocal legal obligations (since the investors themselves are not parties to the treaty)? In short, treaty standards are often so vague that it becomes difficult to distinguish between rights and interests. Perhaps this explains why arbitral tribunals have tended to merge the two. The fair and equitable treatment standard, for example, has been interpreted as requiring States to protect the legitimate expectations of investors concerning their investments. Do investors then have a right to the protection of their legitimate expectations, or merely an *interest* in protecting their expectations? Since vague treaty standards will be interpreted, in practice, by arbitrators rather than by the treaty drafters themselves, it seems strange to label components of the treaty 'rights'. On the other hand, if investors can obtain compensation when State behavior violates their legitimate expectations, then the academic distinction between rights and interests becomes moot in any event. The ambiguity of the legal obligations here has created an environment wherein investors' perceptions appear to matter more than legal doctrine in the articulation of their rights within international investment law. Once again, this emphasis upon investors' expectations fuels the concern that international investment law favors private investor rights over competing public interest concerns."

2044. Arato, *supra* note 39, pp. 2-8.

2045. Ho, *supra* note 212, pp. 157-158. It is well established under international law that the taking of a foreign investor's contractual rights constitutes expropriation or a measure having an equivalent effect. Alexandrov, *supra* note 1946, p. 559.

treaties[2046] have included contracts in the definition of "investment", which has led arbitral precedents to develop inconsistently on this issue. A problem arises here because tribunals often confuse the logics of contract and property[2047].

The argument in favor of assimilating contract law and foreign investment legal protection holds that intrusion in contractual rights is a form of deprivation of property rights, and public international law prohibits such interference unless done for a public purpose, on a non-discriminatory basis, and appropriate or fair compensation is offered[2048]. Thus, the breach of contractual rights is considered as an act of expropriation or deprivation of property rights[2049].

However, property claims are different from contract disputes. Contracts involve the parties' individual choices. As such, the underlying logic of contract law is one of customization, which can be contrasted with the underlying logic of property law that focuses on standardization. Arbitral investment tribunals implicitly, but routinely, interpret investment instruments as generating a wide set of rigid implied terms that are applicable to investment contracts[2050].

The drafting of rigid and stable protections within treaties make sense when property is involved. For instance, clear property law provisions allow investors to properly plan and execute a land development project. In these cases, mandatory property law rules offer little room for agreeing parties to choose how the law will apply to their holdings. For example, *numerus clausus* is one of the fundamental principles of property law and refers to the idea that both the number and content of property rights is limited[2051]. By contrast, party autonomy is the

---

2046. Also para. 712 of the United States Restatement on Foreign Relations Law (1987) makes applicable the rules on expropriation of property to contractual interference.

2047. Arato, *supra* note 39, p. 29.

2048. Contract as property was recognized in the PCA case *Norwegian Shipowners' Claim (Norway* v. *United States)*, PCA Case No. 1921-01, Award (13 October 1922), (1922) 1 RIAA, p. 307. See also *Shufeldt Claim (Guatemala* v. *United States)*, Award (24 July 1930), (1930) 2 RIAA, p. 1079. The PCIJ assimilated contractual to property rights in *Polish Upper Silesia*, *supra* note 332, Merits, at p. 12. Following similar logic, the Tribunal in *SPP* v. *Egypt* (1992), *supra* note 1085, held that "it has long been recognized that contractual rights may be indirectly expropriated". This decision was cited in *Wena Hotels* v. *Egypt*, *supra* note 601. Furthermore, in *Bayindir* v. *Pakistan* the Tribunal decided that contractual rights could be subject to expropriation, *Bayindir* v. *Pakistan*, *supra* note 456, Decision on Jurisdiction (14 November 2005), para. 255.

2049. Maniruzzaman, *supra* note 317, p. 53.

2050. Arato, *supra* note 39, p. 3. See also Arato, *supra* note 40, p. 368.

2051. B. Akkermans, "The Numerus Clausus or Property Rights", in M. Graziadei and L. Smith (eds.), *Comparative Property Law: Global Perspectives*, Cheltenham,

dominant principle within contract law [2052]. As such, contract law can be understood to follow the logic of choice.

While this one-size-fits-all model works well for contracts related to property, it makes little sense if applied to non-property assets. The property law model creates unfair *ex post* constraints and surprise costs for States seeking to regulate in the public interest and makes investment more difficult, costly and unappealing for all parties *ex ante*. Some arbitral decisions in this field have shown a greater appreciation for the logic of contract law, but the uncertainty of an unpredictable international investment regime on the matter and its ambiguities in the prospective effects of contractual choices renders bargaining *ex ante* extremely inefficient [2053].

As expressed by Louis Kaplow and Steven Shavell, "parties make contracts when they have a need to make plans". The drafting of robust and specific contracts prevents opportunistic behavior that might otherwise occur over the course of the relationship and hinder the fulfillment of the contractual obligations [2054]. Moreover, assurances given by one party encourages the other party's reliance, thus increasing the value of the transaction. For instance, a factory owner may be

Edward Elgar, 2017, p. 100. There is more freedom in this regard in the common law than in the civil law systems, Gordley, *supra* note 708, p. 49.

2052. Akkermans, *ibid.*, p. 100.

2053. "Arbitral tribunals have tended to blur the logic of contract and property law, thus limiting the capacity of States and investors to bargain for terms they prefer. Blending contract and property law in this way requires the inclusion of contractual terms that are extremely favorable to the investor, which are unlikely to be efficient in every circumstance. At the same time, tribunals have prevented States from regulating choice where they deem it appropriate in the interest of extrinsic values such as policing public corruption", Arato, *supra* note 39, p. 50.

2054. L. Kaplow and S. Shavell, "Economic Analysis of Law", Harvard Law School, John M. Olin Center for Law, Economics and Business, Discussion Paper No. 251, February 1999, p. 29. Moreover, investment treaties diminish the State's capacity to regulate the limits of contractual freedom, which, in turn, limit party autonomy by policing the agreement in the bargaining process, pushing parties to share certain information and by preventing abuses through the doctrine of good faith, among others. *Bankswitch* v. *Ghana* demonstrates the regulatory functions of contract law may be distorted in the context of anti-corruption norms. Specifically, in the interests of boosting transparency and public accountability, Ghana's constitution limited the executive's ability to unilaterally enter into contracts with foreigners by requiring parliamentary approval for State contracts entered into. This was necessary to reduce corruption and its effects on the public. Even though the constitutional requirement was not satisfied, the Tribunal considered the contract valid "under a lenient promissory estoppel rule, which was supposedly grounded in customary international law" (*Bankswitch* v. *Ghana*, UNCITRAL Award (except for costs), 11 April 2014, paras. 11.73-11.75). This decision displaces national constraints on contract formation and distorts the State's capacity to regulate government corruption. See Arato, *supra* note 39, pp. 27-28.

unwilling to spend money to customize machinery for a particular transaction unless he has full assurance that the other party will not breach the contract[2055].

3. The logic of private law and the interaction between treaty and contract law

Treaties typically do not specify how they relate to contracts. They do not detail how exactly they apply, for instance, with respect to contractual breach, defenses, forum selection, damages, and the rights and obligations that generally emerge from the contractual relationship. Rather, treaties generally apply to agreements either explicitly or implicitly, and sometimes even equate the breach of the State contract with the violation of the treaty due to the presence of the umbrella clause[2056]. Therefore, where treaties do not include specific provisions relating to their interaction with contract law, contract rules must be applied[2057].

In sum, investment treaties do not clarify the scope and content of their rules applicable to contracts. Moreover, investment treaties do not deal with the ways in which their rules interact with contracts and mandatory rules. Arbitral precedents on this topic have generated contradictory decisions: most tribunals assume that treaty rules are mandatory and that they can only rarely be discarded through the parties' agreement[2058].

This confusion stems from equating treaty rights to property-style rules, which prevents parties from including specific contractual provisions relating to substantive duties, forum selection and damages. Tribunals tend to apply the treaty over the agreed-upon contractual terms, in an approach that "turns the logic of contract on its head". The contractual bargain may be rewritten *ex post*, which hampers the parties' capacity to negotiate on risk and price *ex ante*. In that case, parties are less incentivized to contract in the first place, which benefit neither States nor investors *ex ante*[2059].

2055. R. Craswell and A. Schwartz, *Foundations of Contract Law*, New York, Foundation Press, 1994, p. 14. See also C. J. Goetz and R. E. Scott, "Enforcing Promises: An Examination of the Basis of Contract", *Yale Law Journal*, Vol. 89 (1980).

2056. Arato, *supra* note 40, p. 355.

2057. Bogdan, *supra* note 5, pp. 39-40.

2058. Arato, *supra* note 39, pp. 19-25. See also Arato, *supra* note 40, p. 357

2059. Arato, *supra* note 39, p. 4. See also Arato, *supra* note 40, p. 414. As put by Kaplow and Shavell, contracts will stimulate all manner of investments, Kaplow and Shavell, *supra* note 2054, p. 30.

Arato distinguishes between "default rules", "sticky default rules" and "mandatory rules" [2060]. Default rules have a supplementary and gap-filling function, and the parties can contract around them. On the other hand, mandatory rules prevail over the parties' agreement [2061]. Sticky default rules stand somewhere in between. Parties can agree otherwise, but they typically require the adoption of certain formalities to opt out [2062].

Some tribunals assume that investment treaty provisions are mandatory, as was the case in the *Argentine Gas* cases [2063] and in *SGS* v. *Paraguay* [2064].

Other decisions consider investment treaties as default rules with "varying degrees of stickiness" [2065]. In the *Kardassopoulos* and *Crystallex* cases, for instance, treaty provisions were viewed as "highly sticky defaults" to be applied unless the parties use language that clearly and specifically precludes their application [2066].

Certain tribunals consider treaty provisions simple default rules that can be left aside by the parties [2067]. This was the case, for instance, in *SGS* v. *Philippines* and *Oxus Gold* v. *Uzbekistan.* Further, when considering the relationship between contract arrangements and the standard of fair and equitable treatment, the *ad hoc* Committee in *MTD* v. *Chile* reasoned that:

> "The obligations of the host State towards foreign investors derive from the terms of the applicable investment treaty and not

2060. Arato, *supra* note 40, p. 363.

2061. In the United States, these implied terms that are read into the contract are referred to as default rules. In Germany, they are referred to as *dispositives Recht*, and in France as *lois supplétives*. E. A. Farnsworth, "Comparative Contract Law", in M. Reimann and R. Zimmermann (eds.), *The Oxford Handbook of Comparative Law*, Oxford, Oxford University Press, 2006, p. 919. The UNIDROIT Principles refer to mandatory and non-mandatory rules. See Commentary to Article 1.5 of the UNIDROIT Principles.

2062. Arato, *supra* note 40, p. 363.

2063. *Sempra* v. *Argentina*, *supra* note 451, Award (28 September 2007); *Enron* v. *Argentina*, *supra* note 451, Award (22 May 2007); *CMS* v. *Argentina*, *supra* note 84, Award (12 May 2005).

2064. *SGS* v. *Paraguay*, *supra* note 1714, Decision on Jurisdiction (12 February 2010). Also *Venezuela Holdings* v. *Venezuela*, *supra* note 110, Award (9 October 2014), paras. 11, 61, 373.

2065. Arato, *supra* note 40, p. 395.

2066. *Crystallex*, *supra* note 521, Award (4 April 2016), para. 482; *Kardassopoulos* v. *Georgia*, *supra* note 449; *Fuchs* v. *Georgia*, *supra* note 1359.

2067. See *SGS* v. *Philippines*, *supra* note 1142, Decision (2004), para. 134; *Oxus Gold* v. *Republic of Uzbekistan*, UNCITRAL, Final Award (17 December 2015), para. 958; see also *BIVAC* v. *Paraguay*, *supra* note 1963, Decision on Jurisdiction (29 May 2009), para. 148.

from any set of expectations investors may have or claim to have. A tribunal which sought to generate from such expectations a set of rights different from those contained in or enforceable under the BIT might well exceed its powers, and if the difference were material might do so manifestly." [2068]

Indeed, the general and vague formula of legitimate expectations cannot substitute for what was agreed upon in the contract. In the words of Crawford, a legitimate expectation "is not a licence to arbitral tribunals to rewrite the freely negotiated terms of investment contracts" [2069].

In extreme cases, it is possible that the contract completely prevails over the treaty. In these cases, domestic law provides background rules. This hypothesis, however, runs contrary to the text of most treaties when considering contracts as covered investments. Another position holds that treaties do not prevail over the parties' express agreement but provide rules that supplant any conflicting domestic law rule. This is the approach of the Vienna International Sales Convention (CISG) [2070].

The *Parkerings* v. *Lithuania* decision follows this logic, implicitly considering the fair and equitable treatment principle as a default rule. The decision also held that parties are free to "ratchet up" the level of protection that fair and equitable treatment would entail by negotiating for a stabilization clause in the contract [2071]. In other words, treaty and contract law cannot be neatly separated from one another, but the parties can control the scope of fair and equitable treatment. The *Parkerings* case and subsequent similar decisions differ markedly from the *Argentine Gas* cases in treating the fair and equitable treatment principle as a default rule, the scope of which can be altered by contract [2072].

As seen, another position holds that treaties contain "sticky default rules". Within this view, parties may opt out by observing certain formalities or by making a clear statement [2073]. The *MNSS* v. *Montenegro*

2068. *MTD* v. *Chile*, *supra* note 327, Award (25 May 2004), Decision on the Application for Annulment (21 March 2007), para. 67.

2069. Crawford, *supra* note 484, p. 373.

2070. Arato, *supra* note 40, pp. 369-370.

2071. *Parkerings* v. *Lithuania*, *supra* note 530, Award (11 September 2007), para. 332. In similar lines, see also *EDF* v. *Romania*, *supra* note 1374, Award (2009), para. 217; *Philip Morris* v. *Uruguay*, *supra* note 528.

2072. *Sempra* v. *Argentina*, *supra* note 451, Award (28 September 2007); *Enron* v. *Argentina*, *supra* note 451, Award (22 May 2007); *CMS* v. *Argentina*, *supra* note 84, Award (12 May 2005).

2073. Arato, *supra* note 40, pp. 370-371.

decision provides a meaningful example in this regard, holding that exceptionally clear language must be used to contract around treaty standards. The Tribunal stated that "investors may waive the rights conferred to them by treaty provided [the] waivers are explicit and freely entered into" [2074]. In the *Crystallex* case, the Tribunal ruled that "any such waiver would have to be formulated in clear and specific terms" [2075], and that waiver "is never to be lightly admitted as it requires knowledge and intent of forgoing a right, a conduct rather unusual in economic transactions" [2076].

On the extreme opposite end of the spectrum, a fourth position holds that treaty terms that impose mandatory rules cannot be waived. The *Argentine Gas* cases provide the archetypal example of this [2077]. Once triggered, the fair and equitable treatment principle applies equally to property and to contracts and remains unaffected by anything the contract says about the scope of stabilization, or even the waiver of treaty rights. In this sense, the treaty effectively displaces any contractually agreed-upon rule. As such, the fair and equitable treatment principle leaves States and investors stuck with an implied stabilization clause, notwithstanding any agreement on the contrary [2078].

Crawford notes that the investment contract allocates risks and opportunities, which is relevant in determining whether there has been fair and equitable treatment in the contractual relationship. This standard "should not be used as a substitute for the actual arrangements agreed between the parties, or as a supervening and overriding source of the applicable law" [2079]. In any case, ascertainment of the contractual content becomes an indispensable part of the decision on the legitimate

2074. *MNSS* v. *Montenegro*, *supra* note 1380, Award (4 May 2016). The Tribunal in *Aguas del Tunari* refused to "read an ambiguous clause as an implicit waiver of [International Centre for Settlement of Investment Disputes (ICSID)] jurisdiction," adding that "silence as to the question is not sufficient". *Aguas* v. *Bolivia*, *supra* note 111, Decision on Jurisdiction (21 October 2005), paras. 119, 122.

2075. *Crystallex*, *supra* note 521, Award (4 April 2016) para. 48.

2076. *Ibid.*, para. 481. According to Arato, "reading between the lines, the justification for this approach may have been information-forcing – to protect investors who might not be aware of their rights (and leverage) under an investment treaty ex ante", Arato, *supra* note 39, p. 22.

2077. *Sempra* v. *Argentina*, *supra* note 451, Award (28 September 2007); *Enron* v. *Argentina*, *supra* note 451, Award (22 May 2007); *CMS* v. *Argentina*, *supra* note 84, Award (12 May 2005); Arato, *supra* note 39, p. 19.

2078. In *Venezuela Holdings* v. *Venezuela*, the Tribunal held that it could not give effect to potentially limiting compensation provisions in the underlying concession contract, *Venezuela Holdings* v. *Venezuela*, *supra* note 110, Award (9 October 2014), para. 225.

2079. Crawford, *supra* note 484.

expectations of a foreign investor, and contract interpretation appears on the scene at this juncture. As well noted by Yuliya Chernykh, to decide if there has been a violation of the fair and equitable standard, a tribunal should look to and interpret the contractual arrangement:

> "Interpretation thus exercised is driven by a necessity to ascertain the expectations of a foreign investor that are protected by international investment law." [2080]

Mandatory rules are justified when values should be protected, such as the intrinsic logic of contract, the equality of information, the protection of unsophisticated parties and extrinsic public goods such as anti-corruption initiatives. Sticky default rules offer less protection and will not be undercut if opted out of by sophisticated parties. As such, mandatory and sticky default rules should be the exception.

Arato argues that the optimal approach is to, at least in principle, privilege contractual arrangements over background treaty rules. If background treaty rules are given precedence, there must be a justification in terms of values, incentives and risks, and this justification may not be based on broad formalisms regarding the relationships between treaty and contract, or international law and domestic law. In this way, States secure their future regulatory autonomy by including risk-control mechanisms in their contracts such as limitations on damages and *force majeure* clauses. If treaties call for the respect of investment contracts, treaty-contract matters should be drawn from the private law logic of the contract [2081].

This debate does not pit "investor-friendly" and "state-friendly" approaches against one another. *Ex ante*, neither rigidity nor flexibility clearly favors one party or the other. Rigidity affects the State's future regulatory autonomy. If foreign investors may flexibly negotiate secure contractual obligations in their contracts with States, in the end, the investment is protected when the terms of the bargain are followed, rather than when a treaty is invoked to rewrite the agreement [2082].

2080. Chernykh, *supra* note 1353, p. 40.
2081. Arato, *supra* note 39, pp. 26-27; Arato, *supra* note 40, p. 399.
2082. Arato, *supra* note 40, pp. 402-403. At 415-416:

> "Privileging the treaty over terms in the contract may make sense under certain limited circumstances – as, for example, a sticky default in cases when informational asymmetries seem likely to create a market failure or otherwise undermine the goals of the investment treaty. Given their centrality in the investment treaty system, forum selection provisions might be a plausible candidate. Constraints on choice might also be justified based on values completely extrinsic to contract-as

Treaties may be drafted with these intricacies in mind. The CISG provides a good example of this. Parties may exclude the application of the CISG, derogate from it, or vary the effect of any of its provisions (Art. 6). Treaties may expressly declare some norms as mandatory, or even as sticky default rules with specific opt-out provisions. Treaties that are drafted in this way will ensure predictability and efficiency for both States and investors [2083].

However, these types of reforms to the contract-treaty interaction are ultimately unrealistic since any such changes would require thousands of treaties to be amended [2084]. A more immediate solution may come from guidelines produced by soft law instruments [2085]. Where no such soft law rules are available, however, treaty interpretation must overcome the public/private dichotomy in the interest of identifying appropriate answers that balance the parties' agreement with a regime that protect investments whose *ex ante* and *ex post* actions benefit both States and investors.

---

might be the case with general exceptions clauses in certain BITs modelled on GATT Article QX. But in any case, adjudicators ought to view such situations as exceptional, and carefully justify deviation from the norm of privileging party choice."

2083. Arato, *supra* note 39, p. 52.

2084. *Ibid.*, p. 371.

2085. The OAS Inter-American Juridical Committee, for instance, entrusted José Antonio Moreno Rodríguez as Rapporteur for a future guide on the law applicable to international investments in the Americas. See https://www.oas.org/en/sla/iajc/current_agenda.asp, accessed 16 August 2022.

CHAPTER XV

INVESTMENT ARBITRATION TRIBUNALS

A. Foreign investment disputes

The expression "Investor-State Dispute Settlement" (ISDS) is nowadays widely used [2086] to refer to the international dispute resolution mechanisms available to the investor when "the rules of the game have changed". Domestic court systems complement the ISDS system; the existence of international law mechanisms does not eliminate the need to encourage the development of domestic court remedies where rights are adjudicated in an impartial, fair and predictable manner [2087]. However, municipal court systems do not always offer an appropriate environment for the adjudication of claims. As a result, other dispute resolution mechanisms have been developed.

Historically, foreign investors that had been wronged in an international transaction invoked the diplomatic protection of their States to espouse their claims. As has been discussed throughout this work, International Claims Commissions and the ICJ rendered important decisions in this regard. In the modern era, arbitration has become an extended mechanism for the resolution of investment-related conflicts. In fact, arbitration is now considered the primary method of resolving international investment disputes between States and individuals or corporations [2088].

Two separate international investment claims mechanisms are available through arbitration. The first deals with disputes between States, which generally concern the interpretation or application of a

2086. For instance, UNCITRAL established a Working Group on "Investor-State Dispute Settlement Reform", https://uncitral.un.org/en/working_groups/3/investor-state, accessed 11 May 2022. Article 33 of the UN Charter and Chapter IV of the ICJ Statute list the following methods for the pacific settlement of disputes between States: negotiation, inquiry, mediation, conciliation, arbitration, judicial settlement and resort to regional agencies or arrangements (to which good offices should be added), see https://www.icj-cij.org/en/history, accessed 11 May 2022.

2087. S. Franck, "Foreign Direct Investment, Investment Treaty Arbitration and the Rule of Law", *McGeorge Global Business and Development Law Journal* (2006), p. 367. At p. 368: "Fostering the development of the rule of law in national courts not only develops local judicial institutions, but it also promotes confidence in the overall process of resolving investment disputes."

2088. Blackaby *et al.*, *supra* note 255, p. 1.

treaty. The *Lucchetti* v. *Peru* case is a rare example of this device in action [2089]. The second arbitral mechanism resolves disputes between foreign investors and States and is used much more frequently. The advantage of this type of investment arbitration is that it does not potentially generate an international conflict between States and external factors do not influence the claim [2090].

The *Mavrommatis Palestine Concessions* case is an example of political considerations impacting the dispute [2091]. In 1914 and 1916, the Ottoman Empire granted Mr Mavrommatis (a Greek citizen) certain concessions, which were not affirmed in full by the British Government after its seizure of the Ottoman territory containing the concession following World War I. The Greek Government later brought a claim regarding this concession against the British Government on behalf of Mavrommatis on the basis of diplomatic protection. The claim was ultimately heard before the PCIJ. Referring to the political ramifications of resolving international investment disputes, Thomas Franck described the case in the following manner:

> "[W]hat had been a quarrel between businessmen and an administrator became a dispute pitting Britain against Greece, kingdom against kingdom, national pride against national pride." [2092]

In the early 1920s, few (if any) options existed for aliens such as Mavrommatis to pursue their claims against States. Today, investors in several jurisdictions can count on international arbitration in this regard. Consequently, rather than pursuing the claim before the ICJ, foreign investors recurring to arbitration no longer require the cooperation of the other party. Further, this dispute could result in an award that is enforceable and recognizable around much of the world [2093]. As such, arbitration provides a valuable alternative to pursuing interna-

---

2089. *Empresas Lucchetti, SA and Lucchetti Peru, SA* v. *The Republic of Peru* (2007), ICSID Case No. ARB/03/4, Preliminary Objections, 12 *ICSID Reports*, p. 219, 221/227. Peru apparently sought a favorable interpretation of the BIT in the State/State arbitration to assist its case in the investor/State arbitration. See Douglas, *supra* note 39, p. 3.

2090. Doe Rodríguez and Aragón Cardiel, *supra* note 244, p. 598.

2091. *Mavrommatis* Judgment, *supra* note 330.

2092. T. Franck, *The Structure of Impartiality: Toward the Organisation of World Law*, New York, Macmillan Company, 1968, p. 214.

2093. D. D. Caron, "The Nature of the Iran-United States Claims Tribunal and the Evolving Structure of International Dispute Resolution", *American Journal of International Law*, Vol. 84 (1990), https://lawcat.berkeley.edu/record/1113853, accessed 9 June 2022, p. 151.

tional investment claims through diplomatic protection. The latter has proven to be both politically contentious and less efficient in practice [2094].

B. Arbitration

1. Origins

The official website of the ICJ refers to numerous examples of arbitration in ancient Greece, in China, among the Arabian tribes, in maritime customary law, in medieval Europe, and in Papal practice [2095]. In fact, supporters of the arbitral mechanism often trumpet the wisdom of the ages in tracing its origins [2096]. However, as warned by Jan Paulsson, much of the support for the international arbitral mechanism is found in the opening pages of books about arbitration, consisting of selective quotations and anecdotes, and is "unlikely to pass muster with serious historians nor are they likely to give us solid ground for modern construction" [2097].

2. Evolution of arbitration in private law

In Roman private law, the public authority (the Praetor-Consul) delegated its adjudicating functions to citizens known as *arbiters* or *iudex* [2098]. These adjudicators were typically laymen exercising common sense and did not require a thorough knowledge of the law since they acted in close contact with jurists and often requested their opinions [2099].

Similarly, rather than relying on public adjudicators, in the Middle Ages merchants frequently referred their disputes to peers, trustworthy third parties and honorable citizens who acted as arbitrators. The merchants organized themselves into fairs and corporations and

2094. *Ibid.*, p. 152.

2095. See https://www.icj-cij.org/en/history, accessed 11 May 2022.

2096. For a contemporary reference to the ancient roots of arbitration, see W. W. Park, "Arbitration and Law", in T. Schultz and F. Ortino (eds.), *The Oxford Handbook of International Arbitration*, Oxford, Oxford University Press, 2020, pp. 40-41.

2097. Paulsson, *supra* note 1440, p. 10.

2098. Arangio-Ruíz, *supra* note 1211, pp. 87-88.

2099. This system was even institutionalized in imperial Rome, after the Emperor granted a determined group of experts the *ius respondendi ex auctoritate principis*. Among these jurists, historic names such as Papinian, Ulpianus, Modestinus and others can be found. See F. Schulz, *Derecho Romano Clásico*, Barcelona, Editorial Bosch, 1960, p. 13. Regarding arbitration in Roman law, see D. Roebuck and B. de Loynes de Fumichon, *Roman Arbitration*, Oxford, Holo Books, 2004.

developed their own statutes. Kings, feudal lords and other authorities allowed the merchants to organize their own system of justice. As a result, numerous tribunals were successively created. These forums have frequently been considered arbitral tribunals due to the freedom granted to the parties to choose their adjudicators and due to the application of rules beyond those provided for in local customs [2100].

The subsequent consolidation of nation-States and the proliferation of the doctrine of State sovereignty throughout the past centuries, among other factors, contributed to the retreat of arbitration. In 1790, the French Constituent Assembly had considered arbitration as "the more reasonable method for terminating disputes among citizens" [2101]. However, some decades later, in 1843 a landmark case rendered in France ruled arbitration clauses invalid, except in exceptional circumstances. The French Court deciding this case went on to state that if these clauses were considered valid, arbitration may be chosen over other dispute resolution methods too often and individuals would be deprived of the basic guarantees recognized by State tribunals. This position remained unchanged until 1925, when France reformed their Code of Commerce and the possibility of referring court cases to arbitration arose once more [2102].

The same fear that arbitration would become the dominant dispute resolution mechanism also existed in the common law. English judges' financial compensation used to depend almost exclusively on fees they charged the litigants for the cases in which they intervened. Fixed salaries were non-existent. Such a situation clearly contributed to the hostility toward arbitration in England [2103].

2100. According to David, these tribunals must be considered to form part of a distinct justice system separate from the public authorities, rather than forming an entirely new arbitration system. Arbitration in Roman law has followed a similar path. In Rome, arbitration could be convened via the *stipulatio*, establishing a sanction (penalty clause) in case the other party failed to comply with the sanctions ordered by the tribunal. Arbitration could also be convened in a "consensual" contract, but the arbitrator's ruling could be revised by the judge if manifestly unjust or if contrary to good faith. See David, *supra* note 1451, p. 13.

2101. French Law of 16-24 August 1790, Art. 1°: "As arbitration is the most reasonable means of terminating disputes between citizens, the legislators shall not make any provision that would diminish either the favor of the efficiency of an agreement."

2102. T. Várady, J. J. Barceló III and A. T. von Mehren, *International Commercial Arbitration: A Transnational Perspective*, 4th ed., London, Thomson Reuters, 2009, pp. 58-60.

2103. *Ibid.*, p. 65.

In the United States, the popularity of arbitration began with the Arbitration Act of 1925 [2104]. The arbitral mechanism started consolidating in 1932, when the Supreme Court decided that in light of the clear intention of Congress, the traditional judicial hostility toward arbitration must be reversed [2105]. France also modified its legislation in the 1960s, adding provisions that helped to consolidate arbitration as a viable domestic dispute resolution mechanism. Today the French Code of Civil Procedure – as adopted in decrees promulgated on 14 May 1980, 12 May 1981 and 13 January 2011 – applies to international arbitration as codified in Articles 1504 to 1527. The Arbitration Act of 1996 modernized the matter in a similar fashion in England [2106].

Following the same logic, States that are active in international commerce have become signatories to the essential international conventions and reformed their local laws to favor arbitration. As a result, it has now been consolidated as an influential dispute resolution mechanism in many regions of the world. Arbitration is widely used in significant international commercial transactions, being the preferred post-Covid-19 method of resolving transborder disputes for 90 percent of respondents to a recent comprehensive survey, either on a standalone basis (31 percent) or in conjunction with other alternative dispute resolution mechanisms (59 percent) [2107].

The enactment of pivotal international instruments strongly contributed to the flourishing of commercial arbitration in recent times. The New York Convention was concluded within the United Nations framework and now has more than 160 State parties from across all continents [2108]. Primarily, the New York Convention has been referred

---

2104. This law established a basic statutory regime for arbitration. The law currently in vigor has separate chapters for both domestic arbitration (Chapter 1) and international arbitrations (Chaps. 2 and 3). US FAA, 9 USC, paras. 1-16 (domestic and non-New York or Inter-American Convention international arbitrations), paras. 201-208 (New York Convention), paras. 301-307 (Inter-American Convention).

2105. See *Marine Transit Corporation* v. *Dreyfus* (1932), in R. M. Mosk, "Comments on Enforceability of Awards", A. J. Van Den Berg (ed.), *New Horizons in International Commercial Arbitration and Beyond* (ICCA Congress Series, No. 12), The Hague, Kluwer Law International, 2005, p. 328.

2106. See Born, *supra* note 1588, pp. 152-154.

2107. In 2021, White and Case and the Queen Mary University of London conducted a survey on adapting arbitration to a changing world, see https://arbitration.qmul.ac.uk/media/arbitration/docs/LON0320037-QMUL-International-Arbitration-Survey-2021_19_WEB.pdf, accessed 28 June 2022.

2108. Convention on the Recognition and Enforcement of Foreign Arbitral Awards, signed 10 June 1958, entered into force 7 June 1959, 330 UNTS 3, current status at http://www.uncitral.org/uncitral/en/uncitral_texts/arbitration/NYConvention_status.html (accessed 11 May 2022). The first convention to deal with the matter was the Treaty on International Procedural Law of 11 January 1889, Title III. The Bustamante

to as "the most effective instance of international legislation in the entire history of commercial law" [2109] and as "one of the cornerstones of international arbitration" [2110] leading to the availability of an effective mechanism for the enforcement of international commercial arbitral awards. According to George Bermann, the New York Convention is highly valued by the international arbitration community due to its paramount importance worldwide [2111].

Several relevant regional arbitration instruments exist as well, such as the 1964 European Convention on International Commercial Arbitration (comprising thirty-one State parties) [2112] and the Inter-American Convention on International Commercial Arbitration, also known as the "Panama Convention", ratified by sixteen States [2113].

The 1985 Model Law of the UNCITRAL, modified in 2006 [2114], has also been a major success in creating a framework for international arbitration worldwide [2115]. More than 110 jurisdictions [2116] have passed legislation based on the UNCITRAL Model Law and other arbitration-friendly regulations such as the UNCITRAL Arbitration Rules of 1976,

---

Code of 1928 in the Americas also contains a provision regarding enforcement in its Article 432. At a global level, the topic was first addressed in the 1922 Geneva Protocol on Arbitration Clauses in Commercial Matters (27 LNTS 158, 1924) which was ratified by the United Kingdom, Germany, France, Japan, India, Brazil and about two dozen other nations. The Geneva Convention for the Execution of Foreign Arbitral Awards of 1927 expanded the enforceability of awards rendered pursuant to arbitration agreements subject to the Geneva Protocol. Geneva Convention on the Execution of Foreign Arbitral Awards ("Geneva Convention"), 92 LNTS 302 (1929).

2109. This much cited quote can be found in M. Mustill, "Arbitration: History and Background", *Journal of International Arbitration*, Vol. 6, No. 2 (1989), p. 43

2110. Blackaby *et al.*, *supra* note 255, p. 61.

2111. Bermann, *supra* note 14, p. xiii.

2112. European Convention on International Commercial Arbitration, Geneva, signed 21 April 1961, entered into force 7 January 1964, https://treaties.un.org/pages/ViewDetails.aspx?src=TREATY&mtdsg_no=XXII-2&chapter=22&clang=_en#:~:text=The%20Convention%20was%20prepared%20and,the%20Economic%20Commission%20for%20Europe%2C, accessed 28 June 2022.

2113. Mexico, Brazil, Argentina, Venezuela, Colombia, Chile, Ecuador, Peru, Costa Rica, El Salvador, Guatemala, Honduras, Panama, Paraguay, Uruguay and the United States. Inter-American Convention on International Commercial Arbitration, 1975, www.oas.org/juridico/english/Sigs/b-35.html, accessed 11 May 2022.

2114. UNCITRAL Model Arbitration Law, *supra* note 1342.

2115. Blackaby *et al.*, *supra* note 255, p. 63.

2116. Including Australia, Bahrain, Bermuda, British Virgin Islands, Brunei, Bulgaria, Canada, Costa Rica, Cyprus, Denmark, Dominican Republic, Fiji, Germany, Georgia, Hong Kong, India, Ireland, Japan, Malaysia, Mauritius, Mexico, Montenegro, New Zealand, Nigeria, Norway, Peru, the Russian Federation, Scotland, Singapore, Spain, Sweden, Tunisia, Turkey and various US, Australian and Canadian subnational jurisdictions. See Born, *supra* note 1588, p. 143.

modified in 2010 and 2013 [2117]. Within the scope of private commercial disputes, the UNCITRAL instruments recognize the possibility of referring controversies to non-State adjudicators whose decisions have the authority to put an end to conflicts. These instruments provide very limited possibilities to appeal awards before State courts – intervention by domestic adjudicators is only available if due process or public policy was clearly affected.

3. Evolution of arbitration in public international law

Three types of arbitration existed in the public international law field during the Middle Ages [2118]: arbitration provided by a head of State, by a mixed commission or by a tribunal.

Arbitration by a head of State was rooted in the old European tradition that justice as political power comes from above – that is, justice is dispensed by the Pope or Emperor, and then by the prince or his delegate. This system led parties to litigation to distrust State-appointed adjudicators, who they felt were preoccupied with and influenced by the interests of their own State over the dispensation of impartial justice. Further, to avoid being bound by precedent in their adjudication of future disputes and out of concern that juridical criticism might undermine royal sovereignty, decisions rendered by heads of State rarely gave reasons [2119].

Arbitration before mixed commissions, described in Chapter III, was handicapped, in principle, by the fact that such judgments were sometimes considered less authoritative than those before an adjudicator wielding State authority. Problems also arose when the adjudicator was a national of one of the State parties involved in the dispute. Notwithstanding, arbitrations before mixed commissions did present some advantages, as the experts in their panels typically gave detailed (often prolix) reasons [2120].

2117. See https://uncitral.un.org/en/texts/arbitration/contractualtexts/arbitration, accessed 11 May 2021.

2118. Gary Born refers to several examples of inter-State "arbitration" in antiquity. One of the striking features was the large number of arbitrators within tribunals (variously, 600 Milesians, 334 Larissaeans, and 204 Cnidians) which arguably reflect a quasi-legislative, rather than adjudicatory, function. Other "arbitrations" appear to have been more in the nature of non-binding mediation, or political consultation, than true arbitration. See Born, *supra* note 1588, pp. 8-10.

2119. Rousseau, *supra* note 149, p. 489.

2120. *Ibid.*, p. 490.

According to Ian Brownlie, even though arbitration is an old practice, it was revived through international law in the late eighteenth and nineteenth centuries. Mixed commissions and individual arbitrators often acted partly as conciliators as well. In such cases, they applied the concepts of "law and equity" within awards that were not necessarily well-reasoned [2121].

In contrast, nineteenth-century arbitration became progressively oriented toward the judicial model. Adjudicators tended to be independent and impartial experts with recognized technical competence whose decisions were increasingly well-reasoned and in accordance with the law. The famous 1872 Alabama arbitration case between the United States and England illustrates this evolution [2122]. The decision was rendered by five tribunal members in accordance with the Treaty of Washington of 1871 [2123].

Despite this advancement, arbitration made insufficient progress throughout the nineteenth century. This was partially due to the fact that arbitral tribunals were only established on occasion and required the prior negotiation of the parties. In addition, these tribunals were frequently inclined to encourage settlements, which gave the awards a diplomatic character. Many awards were only supported by weak legal reasoning, which made the development of international case law difficult. This situation changed in 1899 after the First Hague Conference which, in an agreement revised in 1907, created the Permanent Court of Arbitration (as discussed in Chapter IV).

In the twentieth century, all three types of arbitration (head of State, mixed commission and tribunal) can still be found. Arbitration before a head of State was reserved for certain matters such as the establishment of borders after both world wars (which were typically decided by sole arbitrators) [2124]. Mixed commission arbitrations have also continued, typically seated in the jurisdiction where the dispute first occurred in order to facilitate the investigations of the issues discussed (usually

2121. I. Brownlie, "International Law at the Fiftieth Anniversary of the United Nations", *Recueil des cours*, Vol. 255 (1995), p. 118.

2122. Rousseau, *supra* note 149, p. 490.

2123. See Chap. III, *supra*.

2124. An example arises of the territorial transfers which took place after World War I upon the division of the former Austro-Hungarian Monarchy. The disputes were submitted to arbitrators designated by the Council of the League of Nations. Two well-known cases arose in this way – the *Sopron-Koszeg Local Railway Company* v. *Austria and Hungary* and the *Barks-Pakrac Railway* cases. See Lord Shawcross, *supra* note 38, pp. 357-358.

related to damages). Finally, arbitration cases before arbitral tribunals flourished significantly throughout the past century [2125].

According to Brownlie, arbitration in public international law does not differ significantly from dispute resolution by international courts, although the term "arbitration" is reserved for tribunals with a limited calendar of business that are typically devoted to a single claim [2126]. Today, dispute resolutions before both arbitral tribunals and courts have judicial-like qualities in the sense that they must resolve the claims in accordance with established rules. Notwithstanding the fact that permanent international courts have existed since 1920, the practice of arbitration continued. The standards applicable to them have become consistent and reasoned awards have been the rule [2127].

Hersch Lauterpacht regrets that in advocating for the creation of a court of international justice, some writers misleadingly asserted that arbitration before the PCIJ was non-judicial and largely consisted in resolving disputes through compromises. In fact, only in exceptional cases and when expressly instructed by the parties did arbitrators act under the PCA mechanism as "amicable referees" [2128]. The overwhelming majority of PCA arbitral awards observe strict legal considerations in both form and substance. The distinction between arbitration and judicial settlement is made for an entirely separate reason. In contrast to arbitration, the PCIJ (currently the ICJ) comprises a permanent body of judges who follow a fixed and well-ordered procedure and resolve disputes in accordance with universally recognized rules of law [2129].

John Merrills explains that, traditionally, one of the primary appeals of arbitration was the resolution of legal disputes while improving relations between the parties through a binding resolution handed down by a third party. With this purpose in mind, territorial and boundary disputes were frequently referred to the arbitral forum. As an advantage of arbitration, the parties can define the matters to be addressed by the tribunal; that is, they can establish the scope of the tribunal's jurisdiction through agreement. The parties can also provide directives as to the criteria to be applied in the decision such as the applicable law, and they can even instruct the arbitrators to resolve the dispute on the basis of

---

2125. Rousseau, *supra* note 149, pp. 501-503.
2126. Brownlie, *supra* note 2121, p. 118.
2127. *Ibid.*, p. 119.
2128. For instance, the award in the *Alsop Claim* of 5 July 1911 between the United States and Chile, where King George V acted as an "amiable compositeur" in virtue of the arbitration agreement. See A. J., v., 1911, p. 1079.
2129. Lauterpacht, *supra* note 3, pp. 64-65, fn. 4.

equity or any other grounds. Further, parties can choose the arbitrators who will hear their dispute, which increases trust among the parties and is "a factor of fundamental importance in international litigation". The parties may also make procedural arrangements on the conduct and payment of the proceedings [2130].

4. International investor-State arbitration

This mechanism emerged as a common ground between submitting international disputes to domestic courts and States' intervention to protect their nationals' investments and other rights under diplomatic protection [2131].

The rules against the use of force enhanced the role of arbitration in the twentieth century with the support of capital-exporting States. In the early twentieth century, a number of disputes were settled by inter-State arbitration as a result of States bringing investment claims on behalf of their nationals. The 1922 *Norwegian Shipowners' Claims* case is a well-known example of a dispute resolved by an inter-State arbitral tribunal [2132]. The *Chorzów Factory* case is another notable claim that arose as a result of the change in frontiers between Germany and the newly re-established Poland at the end of World War I. The controversy arose after the Polish Government seized control of a nitrogen factory built when the territory was German. As seen in Chapter IV, this case is well-known for its formula for determining just compensation, particularly the phrase "reparation must, as far as possible, wipe out all the consequences of the illegal act and re-establish the situation which would have existed if that act had not been committed" [2133].

Investment arbitration has become one of the most important dispute resolution mechanisms in international law [2134]. This is so because, as stated in the *Wintershall* v. *Argentina* case, investor-State arbitration "combines a public law system of State liability with

2130. Merrills, *supra* note 175, pp. 3-5. International arbitration has traditionally been defined as arbitration between States. As the First Hague Peace Conference in 1899 stated, "international arbitration has as its object the settlement of disputes between states". Article 15 of the Convention for the Pacific Settlement of International Disputes (1889). Sornarajah, *supra* note 47, p. 151.

2131. Orrego Vicuña, *supra* note 1103, p. 348.

2132. *Norwegian Shipowners' Claims*, *supra* note 2048, referred to in Lowenfeld, *supra* note 25, p. 474. Another well-known case is the *Martini* case of 1930, *Italy* v. *Venezuela*, 3 May 1930. See more in Reinisch and Malintoppi, *supra* note 270, p. 718.

2133. Lowenfeld, *supra* note 25, p. 475.

2134. De Brabandere, *supra* note 27, p. 1.

private arbitration" [2135]. In the words of Christoph Schreuer, investment arbitration lies at the borderline of international and domestic law [2136].

C. The ICSID revolution

1. The ICSID idea

The creation of the International Centre for Settlement of Investment Disputes (ICSID), "the world's largest and most experienced international organization dedicated to dispute resolution" [2137] in the field, brought about significant new developments which, in light of subsequent advances in international law, now appear almost commonplace. According to ICSID Secretary-General Meg Kinnear:

> "Although its drafters certainly understood the extraordinary potential of the ICSID mechanism, it is probably fair to say that many observers did not grasp the transformative nature of this system until two or three decades after it came into force." [2138]

In turn, August Reinisch and Loretta Malintoppi highlight the "tremendous success" of the mechanism [2139].

Before ICSID was created, most investor-State disputes arose over individually negotiated contracts. Investor-State claims proceeded as ordinary breach-of-contract claims, resolved through international commercial arbitration [2140]. Where no investor-State contracts had been

---

2135. *Wintershall* v. *Argentina*, *supra* note 2037, Final Award (8 December 2008), para. 160 (2).

2136. C. Schreuer, "The Relevance of Public International Law in International Commercial Arbitration: Investment Disputes", publication details unknown, available at http://roboalbanconuevomundo.com/pdf/bnm-memorial-de-meritos/anexo%20vii.%20doctrina/anexo%2028.pdf, p. 3.

2137. G. Flores, "The Forefront of International Investment Law: Modernizing the Rules and Regulations of ICSID", *Manchester Journal of International Economic Law*, Vol. 16 (2019), p. 94.

2138. M. Kinnear, "Foreword", in J. Fouret, R. Gerbay and G. M. Alvarez (eds.), *The ICSID Convention, Regulation and Rules: A Practical Commentary*, Cheltenham, Edward Elgar, 2019, pp. iv.

2139. Reinisch and Malintoppi, *supra* note 270, p. 692.

2140. Maupin, *supra* note 1756, p. 376:

> "Twenty-six cases of this kind were brought under ICSID between 1965 and 1990, none of which produced any notable public outcry. However, the fall of the Berlin Wall brought about a sea change for the regime. With the simultaneous opening up of so many markets in Eastern Europe, a sort of gold rush ensued. Multinational companies from developed countries raced to seize upon new investment opportunities in previously closed economies. In these circumstances, taking the time to negotiate an investment contract with each host State's government – assuming that a company had sufficient market power to do so – could mean losing out to more flexible competitors. Bilateral investment treaties (BITs) granting generalized protections to broad classes of foreign investors stepped in to fill this gap."

negotiated, investment disputes were resolved mostly in national courts applying their domestic laws. Individuals had very little chance of success if they intended to bring claims against States or State entities. States could bring international claims on behalf of their nationals, but otherwise there was no direct recourse.

Within this legal landscape, the ICSID Convention "broke new ground" [2141]. This instrument allowed investors to escape diplomatic protection schemes, avoid national jurisdictions and act directly against a State [2142], making use of public international law where applicable. State immunity also became much restricted under the ICSID Convention due to the exclusion of local remedies and the possibility of enforcing awards directly within territories of the State's parties [2143]. Thus, according to Schreuer, "the dispute settlement process is depoliticized and subjected to objective legal criteria" [2144].

The previous Friendship, Commerce and Navigation treaties were replaced by bilateral investment treaties, which, after the creation of ICSID, prompted treaty drafters to attempt to escape diplomatic protection by incorporating a clause establishing the consent of the State to arbitrate with covered investors [2145]. In 1969, the ICSID Secretariat released a document listing a series of model clauses tailored to bilateral investment treaties and disseminated it widely. Before, no bilateral investment treaty included investor-State arbitration clauses. In the words of St. John, the Secretariat's model clauses "are the centralized origin of investment treaty arbitration" [2146].

By including an arbitration option within treaties, investment legislation and contractual arrangements, host States seek to improve their international investment climate. However, important questions have been raised regarding whether the possibility of recurring to arbitration defectively attracts foreign capital [2147], as also seen in Chapters II and III. In addition, by consenting to ICSID arbitration, host States

2141. Blackaby *et al.*, *supra* note 255, p. 54.

2142. Reinisch and Malintoppi, *supra* note 270, p. 692. Standing of the individual in international law was recently recognized by the ICJ in the *LaGrand* and *Avena* cases. *LaGrand Germany* v. *USA*, *supra* note 945, Judgment (2001), pp. 493-494, paras. 76-77. *Avena and Other Mexican Nationals Mexico* v. *United States of America*, Judgment (31 March 2004), *ICJ Reports 2004*, p. 12, 35-36.

2143. Lauterpacht, *supra* note 3; Schreuer *et al.*, *supra* note 102, p. ix.

2144. *Ibid.*, p. 416.

2145. Blackaby *et al.*, *supra* note 255, p. 444.

2146. St John, *supra* note 372, p. 808.

2147. Franck, *supra* note 2087, p. 357. Private dispute resolution provisions created by the parties to enforce specific negotiated commercial contracts may be a more direct, effective and reliable manner of controlling investment-related risk. Empirically

may protect themselves against other forms of international litigation. Consenting to ICSID arbitration also allows States to effectively shield themselves against diplomatic protection launched by opposing States to protect their nationals [2148].

One of the advantages of the ICSID Convention is that it places disputes under the framework of an international treaty operating as the only source of regulation of the different aspects of the dispute. ICSID provides a "self-contained system of arbitration" that is autonomous and independent of national legal systems [2149].

The Convention has been specifically designed to resolve investment-related disputes and to be immune to State interference. The competence of arbitral tribunals is determined under the Convention. This marks a distinct difference from international commercial arbitrations, where national courts play a significant role in jurisdictional disputes. In addition, ICSID decisions cannot be set aside in national courts [2150] – they are only subject to an ICSID annulment procedure as described below [2151]. This marks a significant difference from the New York Convention model, where awards can be reviewed by the domestic courts of the arbitral seat and by the jurisdiction where enforcement proceedings must occur.

The ICSID Convention only provides a procedural framework for resolving investment-related disputes and does not contain substantive rules governing the relationship between host States and foreign investors [2152]. There have been several proposals to provide further guidance in this issue, but they were discarded during the negotiation of the Convention [2153]. Strong conflicting positions in this regard would have jeopardized the whole project [2154].

The only applicable conflicts of laws provision is Article 42 of the Convention, which merely indicates which substantive rules may apply

---

speaking, it is unclear whether investment treaty arbitration adversely affects the rule of law and/or discourages investment. See *ibid.*, p. 365.

2148. Schreuer *et al.*, *supra* note 102, p. xi.

2149. Regarding this context and ICSID pros, cons and challenges, see Bernardini, *supra* note 79, pp. 187-188.

2150. Even though the enforcement of such awards remains subject to local rules granting States immunity from execution.

2151. See *infra* note 2184.

2152. Its neutrality and apolitical approach to investor-State relations were – in the words of Stephan Schill – arguably the decisive factors for the success of the Convention at a time when substantive investment protection standards were highly controversial. See Schill, *supra* note 1881, p. 47.

2153. See *History of the ICSID Convention*, *supra* note 1078, II, pp. 418 *et seq.*

2154. Schreuer *et al.*, *supra* note 102, p. 550.

in light of party autonomy or where the parties have not chosen an applicable law. This will be discussed in Chapters XVI and XVIII.

Contrary to the underlying logic of the Calvo Doctrine and the New Economic International Order, the ICSID Convention appeared at a moment during which developing States were insisting upon the application of their laws and local remedies before the United Nations. ICSID ushered in a new era of dispute resolution, serving as a catalyst for the widespread conclusion of bilateral investment treaties concluded pursuant to its rules [2155].

2. *Origins of the ICSID Convention*

The foundations for the ICSID Convention were laid more than a century prior, with the 1899 and 1907 Conventions for the Pacific Settlement of International Disputes [2156], which established the Permanent Court of Arbitration. These Conventions created "mixed arbitrations" that would later prove useful, particularly in influencing the 1962 PCA arbitration rules that were instrumental in the preparation of the ICSID Convention [2157].

Economist John Maynard Keynes envisioned three global institutions born in the 1944 United Nations Monetary and Financial Conference of Bretton Woods: The International Bank for Reconstruction and Development (IBRD), the International Monetary Fund (IMF), and the International Trade Organization, which later became the World Trade Organization (WTO). The IBRD was the largest of these organizations and the precursors to the others [2158], established to assist

2155. Subedi, *supra* note 17, pp. 30-32. As stated by the ICSID Tribunal in *SDG* v. *Argentina,* the creation of ICSID and the adoption of bilateral investment treaties offered foreign investors assurances that investment disputes that might arise would not be subject to the delays and political pressures that result from adjudication in national courts. Indeed, the possibility of resolving disputes through international arbitration was designed to offer host States a way to avoid political pressures of the investor's national State. The ICSID Tribunal went on to highlight the significance of international arbitration in the following words: "We remain persuaded that assurance of independent international arbitration is an important – perhaps the most important – element in investor protection" (*Gas Natural SDG* v. *the Argentine Republic*, ICSID Case No. ARB/03/10, Decision of the Tribunal on Preliminary Questions on Jurisdiction (17 June 2005), para. 29).

2156. Reprinted in Permanent Court of Arbitration, Basic Documents 1 and 17 (2005). See Parra, *supra* note 510, p. 11.

2157. Doe Rodríguez and Aragón Cardiel, *supra* note 244, p. 580. "In the late 1950s, the Permanent Court of Arbitration highlighted the possibility of moving forward in this direction, but it was the World Bank that had the political acumen and the institutional resources to make this a reality", St John, *supra* note 372, p. 801.

2158. Parra, *supra* note 510, p. 2.

in the reconstruction of Europe after World War II. As such, the IBRD became the "world's premier institution" for developing countries.

The World Bank was also formed to be a specialized agency of the United Nations. Created in 1945, it began operating the following year [2159]. The World Bank comprises many institutions (collectively called the "World Bank Group"), with the IBRD as its main organ. Membership in the World Bank is conditioned upon membership in the IMF [2160]. As a development institution, the World Bank is concerned with capital flowing from developed to developing countries [2161].

The World Bank created a plan for the settlement of disputes between private parties and host States under the auspices of a neutral institution "to which almost every state outside the Soviet bloc belonged" [2162]. As a result, it advanced the ICSID Convention. ICSID is the only non-financial institution within the World Bank Group, departing in several respects from the organizational pattern of the others [2163].

Before the creation of the ICSID Convention, the IBRD intervened in the settlement of various disputes by good office, mediation and conciliation. This experience facilitated the negotiations that led to the creation of ICSID. Aron Broches, then General Counsel of the World Bank, played a key role in its creation.

The ICSID Convention was first discussed in 1962 and approved by Executive Directors on 18 March 1965, before entering into force on 14 October 1966 with twenty ratifications [2164]. The ICSID Convention

2159. At this moment in time, it was informally being referred to as the "World Bank", which was later officially adopted. *Ibid.*, p. 2.

2160. C. Baltag, "The ICSID Convention: A Successful Story – The Origins and History of the ICSID", in *id.* (ed.), *ICSID Convention after 50 Years: Unsettled Issues*, The Hague, Kluwer Law International, 2016, pp. 2-3. It should be noted, however, that the term "World Bank" is now officially used to refer both to the IBRD and its affiliate, the International Development Association (IDA). See Parra, *supra* note 510, p. 2.

2161. A. Broches, "The Convention on the Settlement of Investment Disputes between States and Nationals of Other States", *Recueil des cours*, Vol. 136 (1972), p. 343.

2162. Lowenfeld, *supra* note 25, p. 537.

2163. Parra, *supra* note 510, p. 10. There are currently five organizations within the World Bank Group: ICSID, IBRD, IDA, IFC and MIGA. Each of the five World Bank Group organizations contribute to the overall goal of reducing poverty worldwide. See https://icsid.worldbank.org/about, accessed 11 May 2022.

2164. See *History of the ICSID Convention*, *supra* note 1078, II 2, p. 1041. The contracting States to the ICSID Convention must be member States of the IBRD or parties to the ICJ Statute, and which the Administrative Council of the ICSID invited to sign the Washington Convention. See also Baltag, *supra* note 2160, pp. 2-3.

now has 164 signatories and 157 deposited ratifications [2165]. Notable exceptions include Russia (signed but not deposited) and Brazil [2166].

The Rules and Regulations of the ICSID Convention [2167] entered into force on 1 January 1968. Small amendments were made in 1984 and new Rules and Regulations came into effect on 1 January 2003. On 21 March 2022, ICSID member States again approved a comprehensive set of amendments, entering into effect on 1 July 2022. The new rules for arbitration and conciliation aim to reduce the time and cost of cases. Novel expedited arbitration rules are also now available. The new rules also aim to create greater transparency by enhancing public access to ICSID orders and awards. Further, they address, for the first time, third-party funding [2168].

3. *ICSID functioning*

The ICSID Convention establishes a Centre with a separate international legal personality (Arts. 1 and 18), just like the ICJ. Unlike the ICJ, however, ICSID attempted to create a depoliticized forum for the parties to resolve their disputes, with the help of arbitrators chosen in accordance with the mechanism.

In fact, ICSID does not conduct arbitrations itself (Art. 1). Rather, ICSID provides facilities and services, for example keeping lists of possible arbitrators (Art. 12), screening and registering arbitration requests (Art. 36, para. 3), assisting in the constitution of tribunals and in the conduct of proceedings (Art. 38), adopting rules and regulations (Art. 6), and drafting model clauses for investment agreements [2169].

2165. Available at https://icsid.worldbank.org/about/member-states/database-of-member-states, accessed 9 June 2022. On 21 June 2021, Ecuador signed again the ICSID Convention, becoming the 164th State to do so. See https://icsid.worldbank.org/news-and-events/news-releases/ecuador-signs-icsid-convention, accessed 9 June 2022.

2166. Available at https://icsid.worldbank.org/about/member-states/database-of-member-states, accessed 9 June 2022.

2167. The Rules and Regulations of the ICSID Convention included the Administrative and Financial Regulations, the Rules of Procedure for the Institution of Conciliation and Arbitration Proceedings ("Institutional Rules"), the Rules of Procedure for Conciliation Proceedings ("Conciliation Rules") and the Rules of Procedure for Arbitration Proceedings ("Arbitration Rules"). See https://icsid.worldbank.org/services/overview, accessed 11 May 2022.

2168. Also, the amended rules provide that broader access to ICSID's dispute resolution rules and services, providing States and investors access to Additional Facility arbitration and conciliation where one or both disputing parties is not an ICSID contracting State. Regional Economic Integration Organizations (REICs) – such as the European Union – may also be a party to proceedings under the amended Additional Facility Rules. See https://icsid.worldbank.org/resources/rules-amendments, accessed 13 June 2022

2169. Reinisch and Malintoppi, *supra* note 270, pp. 698-699.

The Centre provides facilities for arbitration, conciliation, mediation and fact-finding [2170]. The official languages of ICSID are English, French and Spanish.

The Administrative Council is the governing body of ICSID, which adopts the rules and regulations of the Centre and approves its annual reports and budget. The Administrative Council has no role in the administration of cases [2171].

The Secretariat is headed by a Secretary-General and comprises two Deputy Secretaries-General and approximately seventy staff of diverse backgrounds and nationalities [2172]. The Secretary-General is the legal representative and the principal officer of the Centre and is responsible for its internal administration [2173].

ICSID maintains a Panel of Conciliators and a Panel of Arbitrators. Each contracting State may appoint four persons to each panel who may (but need not) be its nationals [2174]. The Chairman of the Administrative Council may appoint ten persons to each Panel, each with a different nationality. Under certain circumstances, such as an absence of agreement between parties [2175], the Chairman of the Administrative Council may appoint the arbitrators and conciliators.

ICSID enjoys the same privileges and immunities as other international organizations [2176].

4. Some basic features of the ICSID arbitration mechanism

It is commonly said that the ICSID arbitration mechanism draws upon the thinking, procedure and structure of commercial arbitration [2177]. Against this common assertion, Antonio Parra argues that the

---

2170. The Secretary-General may also act as an appointing authority or as the authority deciding a proposal to disqualify an arbitrator in non-ICSID disputes. See https://icsid.worldbank.org/services, accessed 11 May 2022.

2171. The Administrative Council is formed by the representatives of the member States or, in their absence, by the governors of the World Bank of each member State. The President of the Bank is the Chairman of the Administrative Council and has no vote in the Council.

2172. See https://icsid.worldbank.org/about/secretariat, accessed 11 May 2022.

2173. C. Schreuer, "Article 11 Functions of Secretary-General", in Schreuer *et al.*, *supra* note 102, pp. 37-38.

2174. Article 13 of the ICSID Convention.

2175. The circumstances of Articles 30, 38 and 52 of the ICSID Convention.

2176. C. Kettlewell, "International Centre for Settlement of Investment Disputes", in J. Fouret, R. Gerbay and G. M. Alvarez (eds.), *The ICSID Convention, Regulation and Rules: A Practical Commentary*, Cheltenham, Edward Elgar, 2019, p. 26. Thus, ICSID representatives and employees cannot be prosecuted because they have jurisdiction immunity in respect to acts done in their official character.

2177. See Caron, *supra* note 2093, p. 154.

provisions of the Convention and its implementing regulations and rules are not based on private arbitration models but rather on the provisions of other public international law instruments [2178]. Divergences like this are reflected in the inconsistencies found in practice when ICSID-related matters are approached exclusively from commercial arbitration or public international law standpoints.

According to Broches, "the most striking feature of the Convention" from a legal perspective is that it provides a private individual or a corporation a forum to pursue States directly, "thus contributing to the growing recognition of the individual as a subject of international law" [2179].

Similarly to the ICJ Statute, within the ICSID Convention contracting States have no obligation to submit disputes to the Centre where the parties have not consented to its jurisdiction [2180]. Therefore, the ICSID jurisdiction is not compulsory *per se*. It requires written consent of the parties either in an investment agreement or otherwise. According to the ICSID preamble, "no Contracting State shall by the mere fact of its ratification, acceptance or approval of this Convention and without its consent be deemed to be under any obligation to submit any particular dispute to conciliation or arbitration" [2181].

To avoid the risks of obstruction, consent to ICSID cannot be unilaterally withdrawn (Art. 25, para. 1), the tribunal enjoys exclusive jurisdiction (Art. 41), and the awards are binding and enforceable (Arts. 53 and 54). Further, the Centre may appoint an arbitrator where the parties have failed to do so (Art. 38), and the parties' lack of cooperation will not prevent the proceedings from continuing (Art. 45).

Consent alone is not enough to establish ICSID jurisdiction, however. The Centre has limited jurisdiction in relation to the character of the

---

2178. "For example, the Conventions for the Pacific Settlement of Disputes, the Statute and Rules of the ICJ, the Model Rules on Arbitral Procedure of the ILC, the Articles of Agreement, By-Laws and Loan Regulations of the IBRD, etc. Moreover, from the start ICSID's development was connected to the development of investment treaties. The Abs-Shawcross Draft Convention on Investments Abroad and the OECD Draft Conventions on the Protection of Foreign Property combined substantive standards of treatment of investment with arbitration procedures for the settlement of investor-State disputes as well as State-State disputes", Parra, *supra* note 510, p. 321.

2179. Broches, *supra* note 2161, p. 350.

2180. This is noted in the Preamble, which also makes clear that it is not the purpose of the Convention, or the expectation of the contracting States, that all matters affecting foreign investment should be removed from national jurisdiction. See Broches, *supra* note 2161, pp. 349-350.

2181. See the full text at https://icsid.worldbank.org/rules-regulations/convention/icsid-convention/preamble, accessed 20 July 2022.

parties and the nature of the dispute [2182]. In this regard, Article 25 of the ICSID Convention establishes jurisdictional requirements relating to the nature of dispute *(ratione materiae)* and the parties to the dispute *(ratione personae)*. More specifically, the nature of the dispute must arise directly out of the investment and the parties involved must be contracting States or constituent subdivisions (when so agreed) and nationals of other contracting States, including "any juridical person, which, because of foreign control, the parties have agreed should be treated as a national of another Contracting State for the purposes of the Convention" [2183].

These limitations *ratione materiae* and *ratione personae* led to the creation of the ICSID Additional Facility Rules, to enable arbitrations that do not fall under these jurisdictional requirements. The Additional Facility Rules are discussed in the pages below.

In ICSID proceedings, arbitral tribunals normally comprise three arbitrators: one selected by each party and the third chosen jointly by them if they can agree, or else by the ICSID Chairman. According to Article 39, the majority of the arbitrators must be nationals of States other than the host State or the State of the investor. This requirement distinguishes ICSID proceedings from arbitrations conducted under other institutional rules.

5. *Arbitration review mechanism*

ICSID has created a review mechanism within the system for the annulment of the awards under exceptional circumstances in order to safeguard against the violation of fundamental principles relating to the process (Art. 52 of the ICSID Convention, Arts. 50 and 52-55 of the Arbitration Rules) [2184].

Grounds for annulment are the following: the tribunal was not properly constituted or had manifestly exceeded its powers; there was

---

2182. Broches, *supra* note 2161, pp. 352-353.

2183. Article 25 (2) *(b)* of the ICSID Convention.

2184. The Updated Background Paper on Annulment for the Administrative Council of ICSID May 2016 is a very useful guide in this regard. See https://icsid.worldbank.org/resources/publications/background-papers-annulment, accessed 11 May 2022. The grounds for annulment in the ICSID Convention derive from the 1953 ILC Draft Convention on Arbitral Procedure, which was an effort to codify existing international law on arbitral procedure in State-to-State arbitrations. See Documents of the Fifth Session Including the Report of the Commission to the General Assembly, *Yearbook of the International Law Commission*, Vol. 2 [1953], p. 211, UN Doc. A/CN.4/SER.A/1953/Add.1 (Art. 30 of the Draft Convention on Arbitral Procedure).

corruption on the part of one of the members of the tribunal; there was a serious departure from one of the fundamental procedural rules; or the award failed to state the reasons on which it is based.

Annulment applications must be filed within 120 days of the award being rendered [2185]. The Chairman of the Administrative Council then appoints three persons from the Panel of Arbitrators to form an *ad hoc* Committee that will decide the application, and finally reject or uphold the award in whole or in part. If the *ad hoc* Committee annuls the award, a party is entitled to request resubmission to a newly constituted tribunal to obtain a new award on the matter [2186].

The first two *ad hoc* Annulment Committees constituted under the ICSID mechanism in the *Klöckner* v. *Cameroon* and *Amco* v. *Indonesia* cases exercised broad powers of review, which has been criticized [2187]. In *Klöckner*, the Committee determined that while the tribunal had properly identified the applicable law to the dispute, it did not apply this law and instead based its decision on a "broad equitable principle without establishing its existence in positive law" [2188]. A similar analysis was performed by the Committee in the *Amco* v. *Indonesia* case: the issue discussed was not the incorrect determination of the law governing the dispute but rather the tribunal's failure to apply an essential provision of that law [2189].

Later annulment committees created a higher threshold for annulling awards based on other reasons instead of based on an incorrect application of the applicable law [2190]. However, applying the wrong law

---

2185. If there is an allegation of corruption, the application must be made within 120 days after the corruption was discovered and no later than three years after the award was rendered. See https://icsid.worldbank.org/services/arbitration/convention/process/post-award-remedies, accessed 11 May 2022.

2186. *Ibid.*

2187. Reinisch and Malintoppi, *supra* note 270, p. 700.

2188. *Klöckner* v. *Cameroon, supra* note 748, Decision on Annulment (1985), para. 79.

2189. *Amco Asia* v. *Indonesia, supra* note 408, Decision on Annulment (16 May 1986), para. 23.

2190. See e.g. *Maritime International Nominees Establishment (MINE)* v. *Republic of Guinea*, ICSID Case No. ARB/84/4, Decision on Annulment (22 December 1989), para. 5.04; *Amco (resubmitted)*, Decision on Annulment (17 December 1992), paras. 7.18-7.29; *Wena Hotels* v. *Egypt, supra* note 601, Decision on Annulment (5 February 2002), paras. 21-55; *CDC Group PLC* v. *Republic of Seychelles*, ICSID Case No. ARB/02/14, Decision on Annulment (29 June 2005), paras. 44-47; *Repsol* v. *Ecuador*, ICSID Case No. ARB/01/10, Decision on Annulment (January 208, 007), para. 38; *MTD* v. *Chile, supra* note 327, Decision on Annulment (March 21, 2007), paras. 44-48, 59-77; *Soufraki* v. *UAE, supra* note 104, Decision on Annulment (5 June 2007), paras. 35-37, 79-114; *Lucchetti* v. *Peru, supra* note 2089, Decision on Annulment (5 September 2007), para. 98.

could still lead to the annulment of the award on the grounds of the manifest excess of powers of the tribunal [2191].

6. *First ICSID cases and evolution*

From the creation of ICSID in 1966 until 1987, all the cases submitted to ICSID tribunals were brought under concession contracts containing an ICSID arbitration clause [2192]. Indeed, the ICSID mechanism was primarily intended to apply to cases involving these contracts, even though the *travaux préparatoires* of the Convention also made clear that State consent to arbitration could be established through the provisions of an investment law [2193].

The Centre "began life quietly" [2194]. The ICSID Convention entered into force two years before the first bilateral investment agreement in 1968 included investor-State arbitration under its mechanism [2195]. Then came a proliferation of bilateral or multilateral treaties accepting the ICSID Convention or its Additional Facility Rules for the resolution of investment disputes. BITs multiplied quickly, beginning with around forty treaties negotiated in 1979 to around 3,000 at present. This propagation has led to an impressive number of cases involving arbitration, Additional Facility arbitration and conciliation.

The first case submitted to ICSID was the 1972 *Holiday Inns* v. *Morocco* arbitration [2196], resulting from an investment concession contract. The first investment treaty case, registered in 1987, was *Asian Agricultural Products Ltd. (AAPL)* v. *Sri Lanka*. Prior to the *AAPL* case, twenty-three non-investment treaty cases had been registered at ICSID. The flow of cases afterwards has been impressive [2197]. By the

---

2191. Updated Background Paper on Annulment for the Administrative Council of ICSID, https://icsid.worldbank.org/sites/default/files/publications/Background%20Paper%20on%20Annulment%20April%202016%20ENG.pdf, accessed 11 May 2022, p. 57

2192. Brown, *supra* note 164, p. 427.

2193. Blackaby *et al.*, *supra* note 255, p. 443.

2194. *Ibid.*, p. 55.

2195. Agreement on Cooperation Between Netherlands and Indonesia (with Protocol and Exchanges of Letters Dated on 17 June 1968). See Bjorklund and Vanhonnaeker, *supra* note 13, p. 349.

2196. *Holiday Inns SA and others* v. *Morocco*, ICSID Case No. ARB/72/1, Decision on Jurisdiction (12 May 1974).

2197. Caseload statistics can be consulted at https://icsid.worldbank.org/resources/publications/icsid-caseload-statistics, accessed 11 May 2022.

end of 2019, a total of 745 ICSID arbitrations had been registered since its founding [2198].

7. *ICSID Additional Facility Rules*

The ICSID Additional Facility was created on 27 September 1978, and its rules were published that year with non-binding explanatory comments. The Additional Facility Rules have subsequently been amended in 2002, 2006 and 2022 [2199].

The proceedings under its rules could only be convened for the conciliation or arbitration of investment disputes under certain circumstances [2200] since the Facility is not available for the settlement of ordinary commercial disputes [2201].

These Additional Facility Rules apply to legal disputes that do not directly arise out of an investment, provided that at least one side is a party of the ICSID Convention or national of a State party to this treaty. The Additional Facility Rules also govern fact-finding proceedings between a State and a national of another State [2202].

Additional Facility proceedings may be administered by the ICSID Secretariat and benefit from the Centre's institutional support and expertise. However, the ICSID Convention and its rules of enforcement do not apply to Additional Facility awards [2203]. Questions of enforcement are typically governed by the New York Convention on the Recognition and Enforcement of Foreign Arbitral Awards, when duly ratified.

2198. While only four ICSID awards were made between 1971 and 1980, nine were made between 1981 and 1990, eighteen were made between 1991 and 2000, ninety-six were made between 2001 and 2010 and 197 were made between 2011 and 2019. ICSID, *The ICSID Caseload: Statistics* 7 (2020).

2199. See https://icsid.worldbank.org/resources/rules-and-regulations/additional-facility-rules/overview. On the last amendment, see https://icsid.worldbank.org/resources/rules-amendments, accessed 24 June 2022.

2200. The Additional Facility is responsible for the administration of the following proceedings: *(i)* conciliation or arbitration proceedings for the settlement of investment disputes arising between parties one of which is not a contracting State or a national of a contracting State; *(ii)* conciliation or arbitration proceedings between parties at least one of which is a contracting State or a national of a contracting State for the settlement of disputes that do not directly arise out of an investment; and *(iii)* fact-finding proceedings. See Baltag, *supra* note 2160, p. 19.

2201. Article 2, para. *b* of the Additional Facility Rules must be read in conjunction with Article 4, paragraph 3. A condition thus emerges that the underlying transaction must have features which distinguish it from an ordinary commercial transaction. Certain investments nexus emerges as a precondition. In practice, only the first group of cases has been relevant. Reinisch and Malintoppi, *supra* note 270, p. 704.

2202. Additional Facility Rules, Article 2.

2203. Additional Facility Rules, Article 3.

The ICSID Additional Facility Rules became particularly relevant in the context of NAFTA, since the United States was a party to ICSID, but Canada and Mexico were not at the time [2204]. Articles 1120 and 1122 of NAFTA gave parties the option to resort to Additional Facility arbitration or UNCITRAL arbitration. Since Mexico and Canada were not parties to ICSID, only UNCITRAL arbitration was available to them under NAFTA [2205]. In fact, the first ICSID Additional Facility Rules case of 1997, *Metalclad* v. *Mexico*, derived from NAFTA [2206].

Under Annex 14.D.3 of the recent United States-Mexico-Canada Agreement (USMCA), for investment disputes between Mexico and the US, claimants may submit a claim under the following rules: the ICSID Additional Facility Rules, the UNCITRAL Arbitration Rules or any other arbitration rules provided that both the claimant and respondent agree [2207].

The USMCA represents a significant change from the system created under NAFTA since it eliminates Canada from the investor-State arbitration system altogether. Moreover, the USMCA significantly curtails investor-State arbitration for US and Mexican investors. In contrast to NAFTA, when a dispute arises the USMCA requires the investor to exhaust local remedies for a minimum of thirty months, unless recourse to local courts is "obviously futile". In addition, only

---

2204. *Ibid.*, p. 705.

2205. Another example is the 1994 Free Trade Agreement between Mexico, Colombia and Venezuela, https://investmentpolicy.unctad.org/international-investment-agreements/treaties/treaties-with-investment-provisions/3122/colombia-mexico-venezuela-fta, accessed 24 June 2022. Articles 17 and 18 of the Agreement grant the investor option to institute ICSID arbitration, Additional Facility Arbitration or UNCITRAL arbitration, depending on the state of ratification of the ICSID Convention by the State in question.

2206. Baltag, *supra* note 2160, pp. 20-21:

> "Except for disputes where counterclaims were raised, at least one case brought by a State against an investor was registered under ICSID: *Gabon* v. *Société Serete SA* Of the total number of cases, around 60% were submitted based on the offer expressed by the contracting States pursuant to their BITs; around 16% based on consent to the arbitration clauses contained in contracts between investors and the contracting State(s); about 9 percent were based on the investment law of the host State; and around 9 percent on the provisions of the Energy Charter Treaty ('ECT'). As to the nature of disputes, 26 percent came from the oil, gas, and mining industries; 17 percent from electric power and other energy; 9 percent from transportation; a 7 percent tie from construction and finance, respectively; 6 percent from information and communication; 5 percent related to water, sanitation, and flood protection; 4 percent from agriculture, fishing, and forestry; and 3 percent from service and trade; while the remaining of 12 percent of claims were based upon other activities."

2207. Available at https://ustr.gov/sites/default/files/files/agreements/FTA/USMCA/Text/14-Investment.pdf, accessed 11 May 2022.

specific matters may be claimed under the USMCA mechanism, such as discrimination and direct expropriation [2208].

D. The UNCITRAL Rules and international investment claims

Other investment tribunals operate pursuant to the UNCITRAL Arbitration Rules or rules drawn upon them. The UNCITRAL Rules, considered "one of the most successful instruments of a contractual nature in the field of international trade law" [2209], and which inspired commercial arbitration rules worldwide [2210], appeared in 1976 and were not designed specifically to apply within international investment claims. However, they have been used in the investment arbitration context for many years.

The UNCITRAL Rules (or their adoption with minor modifications by many arbitral institutions) have been included in several investment treaties [2211] after they were first adopted in the treaty between France and Panama in 1982 [2212]. Panama did the same with several other treaties. Other countries such as Cuba, Haiti, Panama, Poland, Russia, Bulgaria and China followed suit [2213].

2208. The USMCA precludes claims for indirect or creeping expropriation, violation of the minimum standard of treatment and violation of an investor's legitimate expectations. See Born, *supra* note 1588, pp. 127-128.

2209. R. Sorieul, "Foreword", in C. Croft, C. Kee and J. Waincymer, *A Guide to the UNCITRAL Arbitration Rules*, Cambridge, Cambridge University Press, 2013, p. xxi.

2210. For several decades, these rules have been the mainstay of international commercial arbitration by their adoption as the applicable arbitration rules under various arbitration regimes, and by serving as benchmark, or guide, to institutions in the development of their own arbitration rules. See Croft, Kee and Waincymer, *ibid.*, p. 1.

2211. J. Levine, "Navigating the Parallel Universe of Investor-State Arbitrations under the UNCITRAL Rules", in C. Brown and K. Miles (eds.), *Evolution in Investment Treaty Law and Arbitration*, Cambridge: Cambridge University Press, 2012, p. 372.

2212. St John, *supra* note 372, p. 822.

2213. For example Russia-Poland BIT (1992); Bulgaria-Russia BIT (1993); Russia-Cuba BIT (1993): Congo-Italy BIT (1994); Hong Kong SAR-Switzerland BIT (1994); Dominican Republic-Spain BIT (1995); Russian Federation-Sweden BIT (1995); Kyrgyzstan-Pakistan BIT (1995); Oman-United Kingdom BIT (1995): Hong Kong SAR-Italy BIT (1995); France-Hong Kong SAR BIT (1995); Argentina-Cuba BIT (1995); Bulgaria-United Kingdom BIT (1995); Cuba-Lebanon BIT (1995): Armenia-Egypt BIT (1996); Eritrea-Italy BIT (1996); Italy-Russian Federation BIT (1996); Argentina-Vietnam BIT (1996); Cuba-Romania BIT (1996); Bulgaria-Vietnam BIT (1996); BLEU (Belgium-Luxembourg Economic Union)-Hong Kong SAR BIT (1996); Cuba-France BIT (1997); Hong Kong SAR-Japan BIT (1997); Hong Kong SAR-Korea, Republic of BIT (1997); Egypt-Russian Federation BIT (1997); Iran-Switzerland BIT (1998); Argentina-Russian Federation BIT (1998); Hong Kong SAR-United Kingdom BIT (1998). See also J. Dahlquist, *The Use of Commercial Arbitration Rules in Investment Treaty Disputes: Domestic Courts, Commercial Arbitration Institutions and Tribunal Jurisdiction*, Leiden, Brill, 2021, pp. 35-36.

Besides the UNCITRAL Arbitration Rules themselves, the most frequently used UNCITRAL-inspired rules are the ICC Rules of Arbitration, the SCC Arbitration Rules and the ICSID Additional Facility Rules [2214].

Investment treaties often offer investors the choice between different dispute resolution options. For instance, Article 10 (5) of the Netherlands-Argentina BIT provides that "the investor concerned may submit the dispute either to" ICSID or an *ad hoc* arbitration tribunal established under the UNCITRAL Rules [2215]. Most multilateral investment treaties also offer a choice between the ICSID and UNCITRAL Rules, among other options [2216].

The ICSID and UNCITRAL Rules are similar in most aspects. As such, Judith Levine has noted that the substantive outcome should be the same regardless of whether the ICSID or UNCITRAL Rules are invoked [2217]. There is also a common pool of arbitrators currently employed in both ICSID and non-ICSID arbitrations [2218].

There is less information regarding UNCITRAL than ICSID arbitrations, as more institutions are involved, *ad hoc* arbitrations are commonly selected and significant differences exist when it comes to publication of the awards [2219].

2214. Dahlquist, *ibid.*, p. 4.

2215. Agreement on Encouragement and Reciprocal Protection of Investments Between the Kingdom of the Netherlands and the Argentine Republic, signed 20 October 1992, entered into force 1 October 1994.

2216. For instance, the Agreement Establishing the ASEAN-Australia-New Zealand Free Trade Area (AANZFTA), signed 27 February 2009, entered into force 1 January 2010, [2010] ATS 1, Article 21 (1); United States-Dominican Republic-Central America Free Trade Agreement, signed 28 May 2004 (entered into force for the United States on 28 February 2006, El Salvador 1 March 2006, Honduras and Nicaragua 1 April 2006, Guatemala 1 July 2006, Dominican Republic 1 March 2007, Costa Rica 1 January 2009), Article 10.16 (3) (offering ICSID, ICSID Additional Facility UNCITRAL Arbitration Rules); Energy Charter Treaty, signed 17 December 1994, entered into force 16 April 1998, 2080 UNTS 95, Article 26 (4). See Levine, *supra* note 2211, p. 373.

2217. Levine, *supra* note 2211, p. 377. This has not, however, been the case in matters such as double nationality.

2218. C. L. Lim, J. Ho and M. Paparinskis, *International Investment Law and Arbitration: Commentary, Awards and other Materials*, 2nd ed., Cambridge, Cambridge University Press, 2021, p. 198.

2219. "Various public sources make clear that a significant number (over 120) of investor-State cases have been brought under the UNCITRAL Rules. One might assume that even more investor-State disputes have been taking place away from the public eye. One source suggests that in recent years, there were more investor-State arbitrations commenced under the UNCITRAL Rules than the ICSID Convention", Levine, *supra* note 2211, p. 370.

Even though almost half of all known investment treaty disputes are arbitrated under "non-ICSID" rules, Joel Dahlquist points out that there is limited research on this phenomenon, perhaps because investment arbitrations under commercial rules tend to be less publicized, making them less likely targets for research [2220].

The few studies that exist diverge in this regard. A 2013 UNCTAD survey of known investment arbitrations revealed that 61 percent were ICSID cases and roughly 25 percent of known cases were arbitrated under the UNCITRAL Rules, while the SCC Rules represented 5 percent of the known cases and "other rules" 8 percent [2221].

The study contemplated known arbitration, which in the words of Dahlquist favors ICSID arbitration and does not correspond with the real figures [2222].

A more illustrative study was undertaken in 2012 by the OECD Investment Division. From a random sample of 1,660 bilateral investment treaties, 96 percent allow for investors to initiate arbitration, and from the surveyed clauses, 56 percent of the treaties offer the investor the opportunity to choose from more than one type of arbitration.

This possibility of a broad spectrum of choices is also called the "cafeteria approach", preferred primarily by the United Kingdom, Belgium and Luxembourg [2223].

As stated, many institutions follow or are inspired by UNCITRAL Arbitration Rules. Among them, the Permanent Court of Arbitration and other institutions of relevance that do so will be referred to below.

2220. Dahlquist, *supra* note 2213, p. 6.

2221. UNCTAD, Recent Developments in Investor-State Dispute Settlement, UNCTAD/WEB/DIAE/PCB/2013/3, p. 4.

2222. For example, the "other rules" category in the UNCTAD study includes eight known ICC cases, whereas the material studied for Chapter IV of this book shows that the number of actual ICC cases at the time was significantly higher. See Dahlquist, *supra* note 2213, pp. 21-22.

2223. For instance, the Saint Lucia-United Kingdom BIT (1983); BLEU-Turkey BIT (1986); Malta-United Kingdom BIT (1986); Dominican Republic-United Kingdom BIT (1987); BLEU-Malta BIT (1987); BLEU-Poland BIT (1987); Antigua and Barbuda-United Kingdom BIT (1987); Grenada-United Kingdom BIT (1988); Bolivia-United Kingdom BIT (1988). France-Panama BIT (1982), Article 8. 81 Panama-United States of America BIT (1982), Article VI. 82; Panama-United Kingdom BIT (1983); Panama-Switzerland BIT (1983), which appears to be the first time an UNCITRAL clause is accompanied by an appointing authority (the PCA); Germany-Panama BIT (1983).

E. Permanent Court of Arbitration

Currently, the PCA has 122 member States [2224]. It offers several services such as arbitration, conciliation, fact-finding commissions, good offices and mediation. Moreover, the PCA has been appointed as the nominating authority (among other functions) under the UNCITRAL Rules [2225].

The PCA administers cases under its own procedural rules as well as under the UNCITRAL Rules. It also administers *ad hoc* proceedings according to the provisions of negotiated treaties. Additionally, as an appointing authority, the PCA is responsible for deciding arbitrator challenges.

The PCA has a three-part organizational structure. The Administrative Council oversees its policies and budgets. The Members of the Court are potential arbitrators, and the Secretariat is the appointing authority [2226]. The arbitrators, however, need not necessarily be selected from among the list of the Members of the Court.

The Secretariat, known as the International Bureau, is headed by the Secretary-General. The International Bureau has its seat in The Hague [2227] and provides administrative support to tribunals and commissions, serving as the official channel of communication for the PCA and ensuring the safe custody of documents [2228]. The PCA has offices in Port Louis (Mauritius), Singapore and Buenos Aires [2229].

The 2012 PCA Arbitration Rules, currently in effect, draw upon prior rules of the 1990s and the UNCITRAL Rules [2230], with certain

2224. Contracting Parties which have acceded to one or both of the PCA's founding conventions. Status at https://pca-cpa.org/en/about/introduction/contracting-parties/, accessed 20 July 2022.

2225. Doe Rodríguez and Aragón Cardiel, *supra* note 244, p. 582. See also J. Bordaçahar and J. I. Massun, "La Corte Permanente de Arbitraje y su nueva sede en Buenos Aires: Una oportunidad para. acercar el arbitraje moderno a la región", *Revista del Colegio de Abogados de la Ciudad de Buenos Aires*, Vol. 80, No. 1 (2020), p. 81. In 2021, the PCA handled 49 requests related to its appointing authority services. See https://pca-cpa.org/en/about/annual-reports, accessed 11 May 2022.

2226. Article 6, 8-10, PCA Arbitration Rules 2012.

2227. See https://pca-cpa.org/en/about, accessed 11 May 2022.

2228. "The International Bureau provides services such as financial administration, logistical and technical support for meetings and hearings, travel arrangements, and general secretarial and linguistic support. It also provides administrative support to tribunals or commissions conducting PCA dispute settlement proceedings outside The Netherlands", vid. https://pca-cpa.org/en/about/structure/international-bureau, accessed 11 May 2022.

2229. *Ibid.*

2230. "These rules effectively consolidate and replace the PCA's existing four sets of rules (although the older rules were not withdrawn and technically remain in

changes made in order to address the public international law issues that may arise in disputes [2231]. For example, according to Article 1.2, by submitting disputes to the PCA, States waive their immunity. In addition, the applicable law provision of the PCA Rules makes reference to the ICJ Statute, as will be discussed in the next chapter [2232].

Created more than a century ago, the PCA originally focused on States. Now, the PCA rules apply to States, State-controlled entities, intergovernmental organizations and private parties. Even though inter-State disputes continue to be one of the PCA's most important activities, mixed arbitrations involving these other parties have expanded substantially and represent a majority of the active PCA cases in 2022 [2233].

Until 1932, only twenty cases had been filed at the PCA. Decisions over the course of its history dealt with matters concerning territorial sovereignty, State responsibility, the interpretation of treaties or contracts, fishing rights and financial matters. One of the most famous cases to be heard throughout this time is the *Island of Palmas* case [2234].

The workload of the PCA has grown significantly since the 1990s. In 2012, Levine wrote that the PCA has administered over fifty cases in the last ten years, compared to none in the previous decade [2235]. The numbers keep growing. During 2021, the PCA administered 204 cases, comprising: seven inter-State arbitrations; 115 investor-State arbitrations arising under bilateral/multilateral investment treaties or national investment laws; eighty arbitrations arising under contracts involving a State, intergovernmental organization, or other public entity; and two other proceedings [2236].

The PCA has a network of agreements in four continents. According to those agreements, cases administered by the PCA have certain privileges and immunities analogous to those granted to the United

---

existence). By combining the PCA's existing sets of rules into a single new instrument, the drafting committee sought to streamline the process of PCA arbitrations and to ensure that multi-party disputes can be submitted more easily to PCA Arbitration. The 2012 PCA Rules are similar to the 2010 and 2013 UNCITRAL Rules, providing greater flexibility to the parties than the PCA's earlier rules, but are also specifically tailored to cases involving States, State-controlled entities and intergovernmental organizations", Born, *supra* note 1588, p. 210.

2231. Daly, Goriatcheva and Meighen, *supra* note 809, p. 11.

2232. See Chap. XVI, *infra*.

2233. Bordaçahar and Massun, *supra* note 2225, pp. 79-80.

2234. H. Jonkman, "The Role of the Permanent Court of Arbitration in International Dispute Resolution (Addresses)", *Recueil des cours*, Vol. 279 (1999), p. 39.

2235. Levine, *supra* note 2211, p. 371.

2236. See https://pca-cpa.org/en/about/annual-reports, accessed 11 May 2022.

Nations, as well as inviolability for acts performed in the exercise of its functions. Likewise, non-party participants in proceedings such as witnesses and experts have the corresponding privileges and immunities that come with the exercise of their functions [2237].

The PCA also received a significant boost thanks to its involvement in the establishment of the Iran-United States Claims Tribunal in The Hague. This Tribunal was originally seated at the premises of the PCA in the Peace Palace until it moved to its own offices in 1982 [2238].

F. Iran-United States Claims Tribunal

1. Origins and evolution

In the past, mixed claims commissions were "quasi-institutionalized and semi-permanent arbitration" [2239]. The most innovative and recent example is the Iran-United States Claims Tribunal, established by the so-called Algiers Accord of 1981 [2240].

After the Organization of the Petroleum Exporting Countries (OPEC) embargo caused oil prices to nearly double between 1973 and 1974, the Shah of Iran conducted a massive industrialization and modernization program, negotiating many private investments and long-term contracts with American companies. The 1979 Iranian Revolution led to the reverse of these policies under Iran's new revolutionary government, which also nationalized a substantial number of American assets without compensation. A hostage crisis at the US Embassy in Tehran led to an American blockade of Iran and the freezing of Iranian assets in the US [2241].

Private American bankers played a pivotal role in the negotiations that led to the Algiers Accord appeasing diplomatic tensions and the release of the fifty-two American hostages [2242]. The agreement provided

2237. Bordaçahar and Massun, *supra* note 2225, p. 85.
2238. Jonkman, *supra* note 2234, p. 30.
2239. Reinisch and Malintoppi, *supra* note 270, p. 717.
2240. Claims Settlement Declaration of Algiers, 19 January 1981, 20 ILM, p. 223 (1981). The text of the Algiers Accords (1981), including the Declaration of the Government of the Democratic and Popular Republic of Algeria (General Declaration) and the Declaration of the Government of the Democratic and Popular Republic of Algeria Concerning the Settlement of Claims by the Government of the United States of America and the Government of the Islamic Republic of Iran (Claims Settlement Declaration), can be accessed at 1 IUSCTR, p. 3 (1981-1982).
2241. Lowenfeld, *supra* note 25, p. 542.
2242. "The bankers and their lawyers broke an impasse that had withstood all the tools in the Public International Law arsenal: diplomatic talks, a unanimous decision of the International Court of Justice, a Security Council resolution, and a personal

for the liberation of the hostages and the establishment of a mixed claims commission to settle disputes between both countries, including private claims. All parties involved had something at stake: a significant number of US investors sought compensation for the nationalization of their assets in Iran, breaches of contract and similar harms. Iran had billions of US dollars deposited (and after frozen) in US banks, which in turn faced exposure to a potential default on billions of dollars of loans by Iran's government.

In 1999, Hans Jonkman described the Iran-United States Claims Tribunal as potentially conducting "the most important arbitration in the history of international law to date". Its most valuable contribution was ending a very serious international dispute through an effective peaceful settlement mechanism [2243].

2. *Mandate of the Tribunal*

The mandate of the Iran-United States Claims Tribunal is the adjudication of disputes arising out of alleged violations of property rights in the aftermath of the Iranian Revolution. An impressive series of cases resulted [2244]. Their decisions run to more than thirty volumes and have made a momentous contribution to international law in addition to the Tribunal breaking ground on issues such as expropriation and State responsibility [2245]. The rulings in these and other matters caught the attention of scholars and other international tribunals with widespread citations.

The Tribunal has jurisdiction in two categories of claims: between private parties and the United States and in inter-State claims between the United States and Iran. Thousands of cases have been heard related to several matters involving, for instance, investment rights, expropriation, compensation and valuation issues. The decisions of the Iran-United States Claims Tribunal are made public and are frequently considered persuasive sources of authority on relevant investment arbitration issues raised before other tribunals [2246].

---

démarche by the UN Secretary-General, and even a failed US military rescue attempt. To do so, these private actors did not make use of Public International Law theories and principles. These largely 'unsung heroes' used the everyday tools of bankers and banking lawyers including legal opinions, audits and accounting calculations, delicate consultations structured so as not to violate US antitrust laws, and wire transfer instructions". Reed, *supra* note 21, pp. 195-196.

2243. Jonkman, *supra* note 2234, p. 40.

2244. Neff, *supra* note 143, pp. 445-446.

2245. Merrills, *supra* note 175, pp. 3-5.

2246. Reinisch and Malintoppi, *supra* note 270, p. 718.

From a private-public law perspective, it is challenging to characterize the Iran-United States Claims Tribunal as either a public or private claims resolution body. While the substance of disputes heard by the Tribunal often arose from private law contracts (regarding sales and services), such contracts were often concluded with or between State entities. All these relationships were affected by the political consequences of revolution [2247].

The Iran-United States Claims Tribunal is a creature of public international law and can hear both public and private matters. As such, it is neither an entirely private nor public body – it is of a hybrid nature [2248]. This question of determining the nature of the Tribunal has generated great academic interest that is perhaps disproportionate to its practical importance [2249].

The considerable number of cases heard, the monetary sums involved, the continuity of the Tribunal, the high-profile status of its members and the many controversial issues raised have together made the Iran-United States Claims Tribunal a "milestone in the evolution of the international law of investment, as well as of dispute settlement" [2250].

3. *A peculiar procedure*

The Iran-United States Claims Tribunal is comprised of nine members, also referred to as arbitrators or judges [2251]. The Tribunal

---

2247. Tribunal clearly held that it was a new forum substituting traditional forum protection. Case No. A/18, *Jurisdiction Over Claims of Persons with Dual Nationality*, 5 IUSCTR, p. 251 (1984), at 261-262. See Hess, *supra* note 48, p. 122.

2248. In *Dual Nationality, ibid.*, p. 219, 261, the Tribunal characterized itself in the following way:

> "While the Tribunal is clearly an international tribunal established by treaty and while some of its cases involve disputes between the two Governments and involve the interpretation and application of public international law, most disputes (including all those bought by dual nationals) involve a private party on one side and a Government or Government-controlled entity on the other, and may involve primarily issues of municipal law and general principles of law. In such cases it is the rights of the claimant, not of his national that are to be determined by the Tribunal. . . . Although this Tribunal is not an organ of a third State, it is also not, as noted above, a tribunal where claims are espoused by a State at its discretion and decided solely by reference to public international law."

This characterization clearly demonstrates that the Tribunal sees itself as a hybrid form of dispute resolution, often required to apply both public and private international law to resolve matters that come before it. See Fernández Arroyo and Moïse Mbengue, *supra* note 1450, pp. 849-850.

2249. Reed, *supra* note 21.

2250. Lowenfeld, *supra* note 25, p. 553.

2251. Claims Settlement Declaration (1981), Article III (three of the members are appointed by the US; three by Iran; and three by party-appointed members acting jointly or, in absence of agreement, by an appointing authority.

applies rules or procedures based on a variation of UNCITRAL Rules that have been modified and adapted to address the complexities and the sheer size of the cases that are typically handled by the Tribunal [2252].

According to David Caron, "one of the most innovative and intellectually satisfying aspects" of the Tribunal is that it operates under a rather complete internal world. As a result, there is little need for the parties to request assistance from powers outside of the Tribunal. The Tribunal has also established a fund that supports and guarantees its functioning, which is sourced from a portion of the Iranian assets that the United States had frozen [2253].

The Claims Settlement Declaration of 1981 compels Iran and the United States to give effect to the Tribunal's awards within their national legal orders. Article IV (3) and Article IV (1) of the Claims Settlement Declaration states that "[a]ll decisions and awards of the Tribunal shall be final and binding" [2254]. Therefore, awards issued by the Tribunal cannot be revised or reversed by domestic courts, either under the New York Convention or through any other means [2255].

While recognizing that it can err, the Tribunal decided that it alone is capable of revising the awards that it issues [2256]. Throughout its

---

2252. "The Iran-United States Claims Tribunal applied, and indeed still applies to the few outstanding cases, the 1976 UNCITRAL Rules, albeit in a slightly modified version. Even though the State parties initially attempted to modify the UNCITRAL Rules, they ultimately failed to reach an agreement and it instead fell upon the Tribunal itself to alter the Rules in order to make them more suitable for the very specific task at hand. Most alterations done by the Tribunal in the document known as the Final Tribunal Rules of Procedure (FTRP)", Dahlquist, *supra* note 2213, p. 67.

2253. "With the Algerian Government acting as escrow agent for the Security Account pursuant to the Tribunal's instructions, the Security Account assures the availability of funds to satisfy most of awards issued by the Tribunal", Caron, *supra* note 2093, p. 129.

2254. In *Islamic Republic of Iran* v. *United States of America* (1998), IUSCT Case No. A/18, 5 IUSCTR, p. 261, it was decided that the United States has violated its obligation under the Algiers Declarations to ensure that a valid award of the Tribunal be treated as final and binding, valid and enforceable in the jurisdiction of the United States (fn. 231, para. 83). In *Anaconda-Iran, Inc.* v. *Government of the Islamic Republic of Iran and the National Iranian Copper Industries Company* it was stated: "[D]ue to the provisions establishing the Security Account, a settlement by this Tribunal gives successful United States' claimants the additional benefit of a guaranteed execution of the awards" (Interlocutory Award, 10 December 1986), 13 IUSCTR, p. 223, para. 104).

2255. *Iran* v. *United States*, *ibid.*, paras. 64, 70. See also *Islamic Republic of Iran* v. *United States of America*, Case A/21, Decision No. Dec. 62-A21-FT (4 May 1987), 14 IUSCTR, p. 324, 330, para. 14.

2256. See *Iran* v. *United States*, Case A/27, fn. 231, para. 64, fn. 6. Cf. *Ram International Industries, Inc.* et al. *and Air Force of the Islamic Republic of Iran*, Decision No. DEC 118-148-1 (28 December 1993), paras. 20, 29 IUSCTR, p. 383, 390; *Seifi*, p. 43, fn. 220. But see *Iran* v. *United States*, Case A/27, fn. 218, para. 64 ("[T]he Tribunal is not prepared to hold that it has an inherent power to revise a final and binding award").

existence, the Tribunal never subjected itself to the laws of its seat in the Netherlands [2257] and it stated that is clearly "subject to international law" [2258]. In fact, the Tribunal avoided the application of Dutch law to procedural and substantive issues [2259]. Further, even when the parties made a clear choice of applicable law, the Tribunal has demonstrated an inclination to apply general principles of law instead [2260].

4. Assessment

The Iran-United States Claims Tribunal has been referred to as "the most significant arbitral body in history" and its awards have been described as "a gold mine of information for perceptive lawyers". However, some find its decisions unpersuasive "since they involve a special type of arbitration, and their rulings are not applicable elsewhere" [2261]. The Tribunal has also been perceived as a commercial arbitration tribunal deciding on private rights rather than a claims settlement commission applying public international law [2262].

Lucy Reed notes that the Tribunal has contributed significantly to the progress and codification of international law generally, providing important jurisprudence in matters regarding expropriation, compensation, various issues of State responsibility and the determination of interest on monetary awards [2263]. The UNCITRAL Rules also found widespread authoritative application in this context, generating commentaries that have contributed to their enhanced and increasingly popular position in international arbitration practice [2264].

Reed also points out many of the Tribunal's weaknesses. She notes that the majority of awards emerged from the lowest common legal and political denominator between the judges, "hence with a reasoning

2257. *Iran* v. *United States*, *supra* note 2254, Decision No. Dec 32-A18-FT (6 April 1984).

2258. *Anaconda* v. *Iran*, *supra* note 2254, Interlocutory Award (1986), para. 97.

2259. Reed, *supra* note 21, p. 275.

2260. "Though usually in conjunction with at least a perfunctory reference to the relevant rules of applicable municipal law" (*ibid.*, p. 275).

2261. "The Iran-United States Claims Tribunal may be viewed as a gigantic experiment in international dispute resolution, rather than merely a claims settlement device created to resolve this particular group of disputes. As such, the precedential value of the Tribunal's decisions remains unclear to some. Millions of dollars have been spent on its operation and hundreds of awards have been rendered, yet it is apparently common to view the Tribunal's work as unique, but inapplicable in other dispute resolution contexts", Caron, *supra* note 2093, p. 104.

2262. Rajput, *supra* note 1147, pp. 589-615.

2263. Reed, *supra* note 21, p. 284.

2264. *Ibid.*, p. 284.

that could usefully have been more elaborate". However, this weakness is also found in decisions from the ICJ, as well as other international tribunals [2265].

G. Investment arbitration under other institutional rules

Investment treaties or contracts also sometimes refer to other rules emanating from international institutions such as the International Chamber of Commerce (ICC) [2266], the London Court of International Arbitration (LCIA) [2267], the Arbitration Institute of the Stockholm Chamber of Commerce (SCC) [2268], the Swiss Chambers' Arbitration Institution [2269], the Vienna International Arbitral Centre (VIAC) [2270] and the Kuala Lumpur Regional Centre for Arbitration [2271], among

2265. *Ibid.*, p. 285.

2266. See in this regard: Arbitration Involving States and State Entities under the ICC Rules of Arbitration: Report of the ICC Commission on Arbitration and Alternative Dispute Resolution Task Force on Arbitration Involving States or State Entities, 2012, https://iccwbo.org/content/uploads/sites/3/2016/10/ICC-Arbitration-Commission-Report-on-Arbitration-Involving-States-and-State-Entities.pdf, accessed 11 May 2022). "There have been relatively few publicly known investment treaty arbitrations under the ICC Rules. Still, the rules are frequently referred to in bilateral investment treaties: after the ICSID Rules, the UNCITRAL Rules and ICSID's Additional Facility Rules, they are in a safe fourth spot with a total of 127 references in the twentieth-century treaties studied", Dahlquist, *supra* note 2213, p. 46.

2267. The LCIA has administered a handful of investment disputes under the UNCITRAL Rules. See Dahlquist, *supra* note 2213, p. 38.

2268. "The SCC benefits from a historical reputation as a forum for disputes arising out of the East-West trade. The starting point for this development was the 'Optional Arbitration Clause for Use in Contracts in USA-USSR Trade – 1977'. The SCC also cultivated early ties with Chinese entities. Many of the largest and most complex Chinese foreign trade and investment disputes have been SCC disputes, and a significant portion of SCC cases still involves Chinese parties. The first Chinese BIT to be concluded, in 1982, was with Sweden", Dahlquist, *supra* note 2213, pp. 40-41. "Furthermore, it is unusual that treaties refer exclusively to the SCC Rules. Almost every reference is coupled with alternative options: ICSID, UNCITRAL, ICC, or – most commonly – a combination of several rules" (*ibid.*, p. 45).

2269. As of 1 June 2021, the Swiss Chambers' Arbitration Institution (SCAI) became a Swiss limited company and was renamed the Swiss Arbitration Centre. Its majority shareholder is the Swiss Arbitration Association. This change was accompanied by the entry into force, also on 1 June 2021, of the revised Swiss Rules of International Arbitration. See https://www.swissarbitration.org/resources/swiss-rules-2021, accessed 11 May 2022.

2270. In 2021 the Vienna International Arbitral Centre adopted the VIAC Rules of Investment Arbitration, offering a set of specialized arbitral rules to accommodate the unique features of investment arbitration, including the involvement of sovereign parties and the implication of issues of public interest and public policy. See https://www.viac.eu/en/investment-arbitration/content/vienna-rules-investment-2021-online, accessed 11 May 2022).

2271. The Asian International Arbitration Centre (Malaysia) (AIAC) Arbitration Rules 2021 takes effect from 1 August 2021. Any reference to the Kuala Lumpur

others [2272]. These rules tend to follow similar patterns, inspired by the UNCITRAL Rules [2273].

High-profile cases have been submitted to the ICC Rules, such as the *Deutsche Shachtbau* case [2274], or to the LCIA Rules, such as the *Occidental* case [2275]. The SCC Rules have been expressly mentioned in the Energy Charter Treaty and in many other bilateral investment treaties signed by successor States of the former Soviet Union [2276].

Recent developments include the signing of the 2016 Comprehensive Economic and Trade Agreement (CETA) between Canada and the EU and of the EU-Vietnam Free Trade Agreement (EVFTA). Both the CETA and the EVFTA are innovating in the field, as they provide the establishment of a permanent court and an appellate body, instead of the *ad hoc* arbitral tribunals historically used in trade and investment agreements [2277].

The 1993 Treaty creating the Organization for the Harmonization of Business Law in Africa (OHADA) is another example of a unique development in the field of international investment arbitration. According to its preamble, the signatory heads of State and governments declared themselves "willing to promote arbitration as an instrument for resolving contractual disputes [after confirming their commitment]

Regional Centre for Arbitration (KLRCA) in any written law or in any instrument, deed, title, document, bond, agreement or working arrangement shall be construed as a reference to the AIAC. See https://admin.aiac.world/uploads/ckupload/ckupload_20210801103608_18.pdf, accessed 11 May 2022.

2272. "There are also references in treaties to the Istanbul Center for Commercial Arbitration; the Arbitration Court of Chamber of Economy of Bosnia and Herzegovina in Sarajevo; the Regional Cairo Center for International Commercial Arbitration. As of 2012, the center in Cairo has been involved in three unpublished treaty cases. There are no investment treaty cases reported at any of the other institutions", Dahlquist, *supra* note 2213, p. 38.

2273. G. Born, *International Commercial Arbitration*, 3rd ed., The Hague, Kluwer Law International, 2021, pp. 2365-2366. See also K. H. Böckstiegel, "Commercial and Investment Arbitration: How Different are they Today? The Lalive Lecture 2012", *Arbitration International (The Journal of the London Court of International Arbitration)*, Vol. 28, No. 4 (2012), pp. 577-590, https://cdn.arbitration-icca.org/s3fs-public/document/media_document/media113644853030910bckstiegel_lalive_lecture_offprint.pdf, accessed 28 June 2022.

2274. *Deutsche Schachtbau-und Tiefbohr-Gesellschaft mbH* v. *Ras Al Khaimah Nat'l Oil Co.*, English Ct. App., 2 All ER (1987). ILA Interim Report on Public Policy, *supra* note 1583, pp. 27-28. ICC rules progressively gained relevance, see ICC Commission Report on Arbitration Involving States, *supra* note 2266.

2275. *Occidental Exploration and Production Company* v. *The Republic of Ecuador*, England and Wales Court of Appeal (9 September 2005).

2276. Reinisch and Malintoppi, *supra* note 270, p. 709.

2277. Born, *supra* note 2273, p. 128.

to build a stream of confidence in their countries' economies to create a new development hub in Africa" [2278].

The treaty, later revised, is currently in force in seventeen African countries and is open to all African States, whether or not they are members of the African Union. The OHADA Treaty institutes a dual legal system, where national laws coexist with the business legislation instituted by OHADA. This legislation supersedes national laws covered by the same subject matter, thereby modernizing business legislation [2279].

The OHADA organization is comprised of the Conference of Heads of States, the Council of Ministers, the Common Court of Justice and Arbitration (CCJA), the Permanent Secretary and the High Regional School of Magistracy. The CCJA is a supranational court working toward the uniform application of the OHADA acts [2280].

Among other roles, the OHADA organization operates both as an arbitral institution and as a court of final appeal for arbitral awards. As stated by Jimmy Kodo, many multinational companies that deal in minerals sign agreements with investment arbitration clauses with OHADA State parties, available both for commercial and investor-State arbitration [2281].

H. International investment ad hoc *arbitrations*

Some foreign investment arbitration cases have been conducted as *ad hoc* proceedings [2282]. For instance, the famous *Aminoil* case [2283]

2278. Official Journal of OHADA, No. 4 (1 November 1997), p. 1.

2279. See M. J. Vital Kodo, *Arbitration in Africa under OHADA Rules*, The Hague, Kluwer Law International, 2020, pp. 1-2.

2280. *Ibid.*, p. 3.

2281. *Ibid.*, p. 4.

2282. "There are several ad hoc arbitration clauses with procedural specificities included in the treaty, without necessarily referring to any set of arbitration rules. Some versions of such ad hoc clauses are modelled on the State-State arbitration clause included in the same treaty, such as example Netherlands-Oman BIT (1987); China-Poland BIT (1988); Switzerland-Uruguay BIT (1988) and others . . . A tendency can be detected towards the end of the 1980s to provide that the *ad hoc* tribunal shall either apply the UNCITRAL Rules or decide its own rules of procedure 'in compliance' with these rules. For example, BLEU (Belgium-Luxembourg Economic Union)-Czech Republic BIT (1989); Poland-Sweden BIT (1989); Bulgaria-China BIT (1989): Norway-Poland BIT (1990); France-Slovakia BIT (1990); Netherlands-Slovakia BIT (1991); . . . China-Qatar BIT (1999) . . . Some ad hoc clauses also refer to the ICSID Arbitration Rules as the guiding procedural rules for such and ad hoc tribunal (for instance, the Chinese treaties before the Chinese ratification of the ICSID Convention) or to the ICSID and SCC Rules (China-Italy BIT (1985) and China-Ghana BIT (1989)", Dahlquist, *supra* note 2213, pp. 37-38.

2283. *Aminoil*, *supra* note 1059, Final Award (24 March 1982).

was subject to procedural rules "on the basis of natural justice and of such principles of trans-national arbitration procedure as it may find applicable" [2284].

When bilateral investment treaties provide for *ad hoc* arbitration, the mechanism is usually the following: the arbitral tribunal is composed of three arbitrators, two of which are chosen by the parties that independently appoint one arbitrator each. These party-appointed arbitrators then appoint the third arbitrator, who acts as chairman. The third arbitrator must be a national of a third State not involved in the proceedings. A few BITs also specify that the third country shall be a State "which maintains diplomatic relations with both Contracting Parties" [2285]. If there is no agreement on the third arbitrator, the task is entrusted to an impartial appointing authority. The same applies when one of the parties does not appoint an arbitrator. Recent BITs have been consistent in relying upon authorities to select the third arbitrator, such as the President of the ICJ, the Chairman of the ICC, the Secretary-General of the PCA or the Secretary-General of the United Nations, who may be approached to this end by either party [2286].

Problems may arise when the *ad hoc* clauses do not expressly indicate a set of rules but directs that tribunal to decide its own procedural regulations. Difficulties may be overcome when the parties agree to the application of certain rules, such as in the case in *ECE Projektmanagement* et al. v. *Czech Republic*, based on the 1990 German-Czech Republic BIT [2287]. With the parties' consent, the Tribunal applied the 1976 UNCITRAL Rules. The same approach was adopted by the *Saar Papier* tribunal, thereby effectively turning these awards into

2284. Other cases. See more in Reinisch and Malintoppi, *supra* note 270, pp. 711-712.

2285. See, for example, the BIT between the United Arab Emirates and the Hellenic Republic https://investmentpolicy.unctad.org/international-investment-agreements/treaty-files/5357/download, accessed 20 July 2022.

2286. Sacerdoti, *supra* note 67, pp. 430-431. "On the other hand, a number of important agreements include complex arbitration clauses that provide for completely autonomous arbitration, independent from the *lex loci arbitratus*, modelled on the practice between States. On occasion, the choice of arbitrators has also been referred to the President of the ICJ. This model has been defined as 'quasi-international' arbitration: its binding nature derives from the international principles that recognize the legality of entering into such an agreement by a State as an exercise of its sovereignty" (*ibid.*, pp. 416-417).

2287. *ECE Projektmanagement & Kommanditgesellschaft Panta Achtundsechzigste Grundstücksgesellschaft mbH & Co.* v. *The Czech Republic*, UNCITRAL, PCA Case No 2010-5, Award (19 September 2013).

UNCITRAL awards, despite the States providing for "pure" *ad hoc* arbitration in the treaty [2288].

Ad hoc arbitrations have the advantage of procedural flexibility, but difficulties usually arise when the parties or their lawyers [2289] do not cooperate, or when they are not supported by an adequate legal system in the place of arbitration [2290]. Perhaps this explains why there appears to be hesitation to organize *ad hoc* arbitrations [2291]. Companies and States increasingly include in their contracts a reference to institutional rules [2292], which are often more predictable than an *ad hoc* procedure [2293], but still allow the tribunal and the parties to "work out the details of arbitral procedures in particular cases as they see fit – much as they are in ad hoc arbitrations" [2294].

An *ad hoc* arbitration may be more procedurally complicated than under ICSID rules. However, Giorgio Sacerdoti points out that *ad hoc* arbitrations are not always more complex when managed professionally and with cooperation of the parties. Moreover, *ad hoc* arbitrations can bring other advantages as well, such as increased confidentiality.

Unlike ICSID arbitrations, *ad hoc* proceedings open up the possibility of challenges before national courts in the jurisdictions where the award is decided or enforced, and this may cause uncertainty for the parties (in order to assess beforehand if the country of the seat has a competent and efficient judicial system, correctness and speed are guaranteed). This was the case in Sweden in *CME* v. *Czech Republic*, conducted as an *ad hoc* arbitration pursuant to the provisions of the parties' BIT [2295].

2288. Dahlquist, *supra* note 2213, p. 38.

2289. Blackaby *et al.*, *supra* note 255, p. 43.

2290. *Ibid.*

2291. A 2008 study detected a preference for institutional arbitration over *ad hoc* arbitration. Interviewees expressed "that the main reason for using institutional arbitration was the reputation of the institutions and the convenience of having the case administered by a third party", see PWC and Queen Mary University, International Arbitration: Corporate Attitudes and Practices 2008, https://www.pwc.co.uk/assets/pdf/pwc-international-arbitration-2008.pdf, accessed 12 May 2022. This survey was not exclusively concerned with foreign investment disputes but international arbitration in general.

2292. Reinisch and Malintoppi, *supra* note 270, p. 712.

2293. Born, *supra* note 2273, p. 2365.

2294. *Ibid.*, p. 2365.

2295. "Further, the CME/Lauder arbitrations demonstrate that commercial arbitration can be quite expeditious, leading to the awarding and payment of a substantial monetary award", Sacerdoti, *supra* note 641, pp. 46-47.

I. Internationalized and territorialized tribunals distinction

A distinction is sometimes made between "internationalized" and "territorialized" tribunals [2296]. Territorialized tribunals operate under the legal framework of the State of the seat under rules similar to the ones of international commercial arbitration. In this regard, investment claims heard before territorialized tribunals are filed pursuant to rules such as the UNCITRAL Arbitration Rules for *ad hoc* cases, the PCA Rules or the ICC Rules, among others.

Internationalized tribunals, such as ICSID tribunals and the Iran-United States Claims Tribunal, are governed by their constituent documents and the rules of public international law. When it comes to ICSID tribunals, in the 2002 case *Mihaly* v. *Sri Lanka* the Tribunal wrote that it "maintains that the jurisdiction of the Centre . . . is based on the ICSID Convention and the rules of general international law. It does not operate under any national law in particular" [2297]. By contrast, in Case A/27 the Iran-United States Claims Tribunal stated that "it was established by an international agreement [that…t]he Tribunal is 'clearly an international tribunal' . . . 'and it is subject to international law'" [2298].

Several criteria have been advanced to characterize a tribunal as "international". For instance, some scholars suggest that internationalized tribunals apply international law. However, that is also the case for national courts. In a plausible response, Elisabeth Kjos proposes three interrelated criteria for determining whether a tribunal is truly "internationalized": their mandate must be determined within a treaty; they must be insulated from applying the law of the seat (which has been relinquished by the State in question); and the State must be treaty-bound to comply with the tribunal's decisions without launching enforcement proceedings under instruments such as the New York Convention. In combination, these three factors ensure that these tribunals operate in the international legal order. Their *lex arbitri* is public international law [2299].

2296. H. E. Kjos, *Applicable Law in Investor-State Arbitration: The Interplay Between National and International Law* (Oxford Monographs in International Law), Oxford, Oxford University Press, 2013, pp. 19 *et seq.*

2297. *Mihaly* v. *Sri Lanka*, *supra* note 1094, Award (15 March 2002), para. 19. In the same line the following case: *Abaclat* v. *Argentina*, *supra* note 90, Dissenting Opinion of Professor Georges Abi-Saab (28 October 2011), para. 6.

2298. *Iran and United States*, Case No. A/27, Award No. 586-A27-FT (5 June 1998), para. 58 (citing *Dual Nationality*, *supra* note 2247, p. 261, fn. 228); *Anaconda* v. *Iran*, *supra* note 2254, Interlocutory Award, fn. 230, para. 97).

2299. Kjos, *supra* note 2296, p. 45.

Territorialized tribunals, in contrast, remain linked to a specified domestic jurisdiction. Norms such as the national *lex loci arbitri* provide the normative framework when the arbitration is pending, and in the post-award review [2300].

J. Jurisdictional overlaps

There is a substantial jurisdictional overlap between competing jurisdictions, which has generated much confusion in practice [2301]. For instance, the 2012 US Model BIT [2302] allows claimants to submit their claim to arbitration under the ICSID Convention or under the UNCITRAL Arbitration Rules or under any other rules, provided that both parties agree (Art. 24 of the 2012 US Model BIT) [2303]. Even in the absence of a specific agreement, parties are not *per se* prevented from accessing national courts (Art. 26, first sentence, ICSID Convention).

Investment-related matters can often be decided by international arbitration tribunals, the ICJ or the WTO in some cases. They may also be resolved by regional tribunals such as the European Court of Human Rights [2304].

Since investors may typically choose between different dispute resolution mechanisms (international, regional and even national), "investment institution shopping" has become a widespread but controversial practice in investment arbitration [2305].

In contrast to internationalized tribunals, awards resulting from territorialized arbitrations conducted under institutional rules or in *ad hoc* cases may be subject to judicial scrutiny. For example, in Switzerland the Supreme Court has recently – for the first time – partially annulled an

---

2300. Dahlquist, *supra* note 2213, p. 283. At 284-285, Dahlquist notes that

> "court decisions in set-aside proceedings constitute a growing body of case law in investment treaty arbitration, especially on frequent jurisdictional questions. . . . However, speaking generally, domestic courts are unfamiliar with both international sources, and with those from comparative domestic jurisdictions. Even the most frequently used courts seem to approach these issues with limited reference to the practice of other courts in similar positions. No dialogue or co-ordination between courts can be expected. . . . In the individual cases, therefore, the responsibility rests primarily with the disputing parties, who may bring relevant case law from other seats to the attention of the court seized".

2301. Reinisch and Malintoppi, *supra* note 270, p. 692.

2302. 2012 US Model Bilateral Investment Treaty, https://ustr.gov/sites/default/files/BIT%20text%20for%20ACIEP%20Meeting.pdf, accessed 12 May 2022.

2303. Reinisch and Malintoppi, *supra* note 270, p. 693.

2304. See Chap. V.F.2, *supra*, "Regional investment initiatives".

2305. Hess, *supra* note 48, p. 137.

arbitral award issued in an investment arbitration. The Supreme Court decided that the tribunal, constituted under the UNCITRAL Arbitration Rules, had wrongly declined jurisdiction to decide an investment treaty claim brought by Clorox España SL against Venezuela [2306]. The Swiss Supreme Court had been dealing with an increasing number of investment arbitration cases in recent years, but it had never before annulled an investment arbitration award [2307].

2306. Supreme Court, 4A_306/2019, 25 March 2020 (in French).

2307. F. Spoorenberg and D. Franchini, "First Annulment of investment Arbitration Award by the Supreme Court", 2 July 2020, *International Law Office Newsletter*.

CHAPTER XVI

ARBITRATION AND THE APPLICABLE LAW

A. Arbitration as a sui generis *alternative to State or international courts*

By recurring to arbitration, the parties entrust one or more arbitrators to decide disputes that arise from their agreement [2308]. Arbitration always tackles juridical controversies, which discards purely factual proceedings on non-legal matters [2309].

Resolving disputes through arbitration is an alternative to recurring to domestic courts composed of public servant adjudicators. In contrast to the appellate review mechanisms usually available under national court systems, finality is one of the most salient features of arbitration. Arbitral awards can generally only be scrutinized under the narrow lenses of procedural fairness, jurisdiction and public policy [2310]. As a result, arbitrators have significant latitude to apply substantive law. Undoubtedly, parties who choose arbitration over judicial proceedings can expect some differences in the handling of legal sources of law as well as in the process itself [2311].

International commercial arbitration flourished between merchants in days of old and in recent decades has once again regained momentum [2312]. Commercial arbitration has several specificities that distinguish it from labor and consumer arbitration [2313], which have also seen a recent expansion. This matter will not be dealt with in this book, which will primarily focus on developments related to the applicable substantive

2308. See David, *supra* note 1451, p. 5.

2309. Oppetit, *supra* note 796, pp. 26-27, 278-279.

2310. Born, *supra* note 2273, p. 80.

2311. A. F. Lowenfeld, "Lex Mercatoria: An Arbitrator's View", in T. E. Carbonneau (ed.), Lex Mercatoria *and Arbitration: A Discussion of the New Lew Merchant*, 2nd ed., The Hague, Juris / Kluwer International, 1998, p. 90.

2312. The Explanatory Note to Article 1 of the UNCITRAL Model Law gives the term "commercial" an ample connotation of business transactions that are exemplified therein. Commentaries to the Preamble of the UNIDROIT Principles also include similar definitions. See https://uncitral.un.org/sites/uncitral.un.org/files/media-documents/uncitral/en/19-09955_e_ebook.pdf, p. 1, fn. 2, and https://assets.hcch.net/docs/5da3ed47-f54d-4c43-aaef-5eafc7c1f2a1.pdf, p. 29, accessed 20 July 2022.

2313. Lalive, *supra* note 1646, fn. 37 ff. A particular problem is also presented in arbitration regarding distribution agreements. See also Mosk, *supra* note 2105, p. 329.

law brought about by the explosive expansion of international investment arbitration in recent years.

Before World War II, international arbitration was generally considered a simple means of dispute resolution, tolerated by States as an alternative to local tribunals. The *jurisdictional* theory of arbitration reflected this tendency, according to which both judges and arbitrators are vested with decision-making power derived from their sovereign. As a result, the jurisdictional theory of arbitration held that national laws and conflict of laws systems should prevail [2314]. The *contractual* theory of arbitration took a different stance, by focusing on the parties' agreement. The contractual theory was advanced in times of inappropriate national regulation during which, for instance, the enforcement of arbitral awards was justified as distinct from the restrictive regime for the enforcement of judicial decisions [2315].

After the development of numerous regulatory instruments [2316], the autonomous, *sui generis* or mixed character of arbitration has gained strength [2317]. As explained by René David, arbitration is subject to complex rules. It is governed by norms related to contracts, procedural regulations connected with the administration of justice and rules specifically developed for arbitration. Long-sterile discussions regarding the appropriate rules for regulating arbitration ought to be abandoned [2318].

2314. A. T. von Mehren, "International Commercial Arbitration and Conflict of Laws", in "Essays in Honor of Hans Smit", eds. Thomas Carbonneau and Vratislav Pechota, *American Review of Arbitration*, Vol. 3 (1992), p. 59. According to Silva Romero, two conceptions of justice are found on the theoretical plane: the first is universalist and the other is nominalist, which places significant importance upon the seat of the arbitration and the impact of local rules, in "Introducción", in F. Mantilla-Serrano (ed.), *Arbitraje Internacional, Tensiones actuales*, Bogotá, Legis, Comité Colombiano de Arbitraje, 2007, pp. xiv-xiv.

2315. Gaillard, *supra* note 836, p. 19.

2316. Such as the arbitral conventions and modern legal enactments discussed in this chapter.

2317. Some commentators have even argued that arbitration should be considered "autonomous", existing outside the contractual, jurisdictional, or hybrid systems. According to this view, the arbitrator will even be granted the status of an "international judge" (Gaillard, *supra* note 836, pp. 69 ff.). It is unclear what doctrinal or practical consequences result from this argument. The theory was developed by French scholars based on the thesis that "the juridicity of arbitration is rooted in a distinct, transnational legal order, that could be labeled as the arbitral legal order, and not in a national legal system", Born, *supra* note 2273, p. 241.

2318. David, *supra* note 1451, p. 78.

B. Arbitrators' broad discretion

Arbitrators enjoy greater decision-making freedom than public servant adjudicators [2319]. Gabrielle Kaufmann-Kohler characterizes this broad discretion as "truly striking" due to its far-reaching impact on the case [2320]. This latitude derives from the broad powers granted to arbitrators in mainstream legislation, combined with the fact that most jurisdictions allow no review on the merits of their award.

It would be a misconception to consider this broad discretion as *carte blanche* permission for the arbitrator to casually choose whichever rule seems the best fit for the dispute. According to Marc Blessing, such a view would be completely misguided. In fact, the exact opposite occurs in arbitration: the arbitrator must consider all the possibilities that exist for the case at hand, opt for a reasoned solution that conforms to international standards and emphasize in the decision the effort expended on that analysis [2321]. To perform this task, Lord Goff of Chieveley writes that "it is better to have a feast of contrasting sources, festering with ideas, than a single hygienic package, wrapped in polythene" [2322].

Arbitral discretion is a key feature of international commercial arbitration, as is made clear by the prevailing methodologies for resolving arbitral conflicts of laws that will be discussed in this and in the following chapters. As the substantive law governing the contract shapes the parties' rights and obligations, the arbitrator's discretion has the capacity to significantly affect the outcomes of each case [2323]. Hence, the freedom that arbitral tribunals enjoy to determine the applicable law is both a challenge and a responsibility, in particular when the contract includes no choice of law clause [2324].

2319. Stressed in a recent article: L. Radicati di Brozzolo, "Competition between Cross-Border Dispute Settlement Mechanisms", in C. Benicke and S. Huber (eds.), *National, International, Transnational: Harmonischer Dreiklang im Recht, zum 70, Festschrift für Herbert Kronke, Geburtstag*, Bielefeld, Verlag Ernst / Werner Gieseking, 2020, p. 451.

2320. G. Kaufmann-Kohler, "Arbitral Precedent: Dream, Necessity or Excuse?", *Arbitration International*, Vol. 23, No. 3 (2007), p. 364.

2321. M. Blessing, "Choice of Substantive Law in International Arbitration", *Journal of International Arbitration*, Vol. 14, No. 2 (1997), p. 48.

2322. Cited by J. M. Smits, "The Europeanisation of National Legal Systems", in M. Van Hoecke (ed.), *Epistemology and Methodology of Comparative Law*, Oxford / Portland, OR, Hart Publishing, 2004, p. 239.

2323. This discretion can be qualified either as a blessing or a curse, depending on one's perspective. See B. Hayward, *Conflict of Laws and Arbitral Discretion: The Closest Connection Test* (Oxford Private International Law Series), Oxford, Oxford University Press, 2017, p. 2.

2324. Bermann, *supra* note 11, p. 267, para. 369.

Lucy Reed observes that "a particularly startling example" of an overreach of an arbitrator's discretion is found in the (in)famous *Norsolor* award [2325].

In that decision, the Tribunal, seated in Austria, awarded compensation to the Turkish agent of the French company that terminated the agency agreement.

It did so even though neither French nor Turkish law provided for compensation [2326]. The award withstood scrutiny in both Austria [2327] and France [2328], demonstrating the respect of these States' courts for arbitral discretion.

Perhaps the Arbitral Tribunal overstepped its discretion in that case, however, because it based its decision in a rule of law that neither of the parties could have contemplated at the time that they concluded the contract [2329]. Hard cases make bad law [2330], and the *Norsolor* award demonstrates that arbitral discretion must be exercised cautiously.

Recently, an ICSID Annulment Tribunal stated very clearly that:

> "The acknowledgement that a tribunal has discretion is merely a general affirmation of one of the powers of a tribunal, but such general affirmation, in the context of the award, cannot be the sole reason to award a nominal value of damages. The acknowledgement by the Tribunal of its discretion is a stand-alone affirmation that has no clear connection with the preceding paragraphs so that the reasoning of the Tribunal from the premises to the conclusion can be followed." [2331]

2325. Reed, *supra* note 21, p. 228.

2326. ICC Case No. 3171/1979, [1983] Rev. Arb., p. 525, 9 YB. Comm. Arb. (1984), p. 109.

2327. See Oberster Gerichtshof, *Pabalk Ticaret Ltd. Sirketi* v. *Norsolor SA*, RIW, Vol. 29 (18 November 1982) (1983), p. 868, note Seidl-Hohenveldern, PIPV, Vol. 4 (1984), p. 97, KTS, Vol. 44 (1983), p. 666, note Schlosser, 110 JDI, p. 645 (1983) note Seidl-Hohenveldern.

2328. See Cass. Cív. 1re, 9 October 1984, *Société Pabalk Ticaret Sirketi v. Société Norsolor*, 112 JDI (1985) note Kahn; [1985] RD, p. 101 note Robert; 24 ILM, p. 360 (1985); 11 YB. Comm. Arb. (1986), p. 484; *Journal of International Arbitration*, Vol. 2, No. 2 (1985), p. 67, note Thompson.

2329. Reed, *supra* note 21, p. 228.

2330. The phrase "hard cases make bad law" was used by Justice Oliver Wender Holmes in *Northern Securities Co.* v. *United States*, 193 US 197, 400 (1904) (J. Holmes, dissenting).

2331. *Perenco Ecuador Ltd.*, *supra* note 631, Decision on Annulment (28 May 2021), para. 467.

C. *A neutral forum for international matters*

1. *A neutral forum for private parties*

In transborder litigation, the parties commonly have the option of submitting their disputes to either a national court or to international arbitration. Subjecting their dispute to domestic courts carries the risk that the parties may have to litigate in another country before adjudicators trained to decide according to "domestic" criteria and who ignore the problems and necessities of transborder commerce. In short, there is a risk that local judges will be influenced by their own legal system, which poses a significant risk to the foreign party. As Humphrey O'Sullivan famously quipped in 1831, "there is little use in going to law with the devil while the court is held in hell" [2332].

Moreover, the foreign party will have to seek lawyers from that jurisdiction whom they may be unfamiliar with or in whom they do not have sufficient confidence. Furthermore, the adjudication process may be conducted in a language other than that specified in the contract, requiring the documents to be translated, which once again leads to additional costs, delays and potential misunderstandings [2333].

In contrast to these challenges, arbitration provides an effective means to resolve international disputes in a neutral forum and before arbitrators normally acquainted with international commercial matters. Furthermore, arbitrators are often capable of approaching the conflict with a cosmopolitan view – and even in different languages depending on the needs of the parties [2334].

An adjudicator that has been trained in comparative law will, consciously or unconsciously, look at the problem with *an international eye*. Arbitrators are human beings and, as such, cannot dissociate themselves from the frames of reference, social influences and networks that surround them. As stated by Burkhard Hess, there is a common understanding within the arbitration community

2332. "Diary of Humphrey O'Sullivan, 6 January 1831", in Park, *supra* note 1607, p. 423.

2333. Blackaby *et al.*, *supra* note 255, pp. 28-29.

2334. The tendency to apply transnational law in arbitration is particularly strong in areas where national laws are developing at different paces in particular areas such as frustration, invalidity and interest. See H. Smit, "Proper Choice of Law and the *Lex Mercatoria Arbitralis*", in T. E. Carbonneau (ed.), Lex Mercatoria *and Arbitration: A Discussion of the New Lew Merchant*, 2nd ed., The Hague, Juris / Kluwer International, 1998, p. 109.

regarding the methods of determining and interpreting the applicable law and the procedural due process standards that should be applied [2335]. Even when recurring to national laws, arbitrators are likely to do so "in a way that better fits the transnational environment of arbitration" [2336].

A 1989 resolution of the Institute of International Law rejects juridical and philosophical objections to the "non-national" character of arbitration, highlighting the inherent differences between arbitrators and national judges [2337]. It is undeniable that international arbitration has features that distinguish it from litigation before domestic adjudicators. In general, parties that choose arbitration often do so in an effort to avoid "legalist" solutions to their commercial conflicts. On the one hand, businesspeople frequently feel that the State courts do not understand the realities of commercial exchange. On the other hand, the arbitrators (whose power derives from the parties' agreement) are expected to prioritize the rules that the parties had chosen to govern their relationship – that is, the terms of their contract and the corresponding arbitral norms.

Arbitrators are not considered delegates of the State that must abide by local rules in their application of the law. Instead, arbitrators are appointed by the parties directly, or according to the mechanism chosen by them. Moreover, the mobile character of arbitration allows parties to avoid adjudication in hostile national environments and instead conduct their dispute in jurisdictions where they can control important procedural and substantive aspects of the conflict regarding the applicable law. When it comes to substantive law, the parties can establish their own applicable rules and require – or expect from the Tribunal – that non-State norms and principles be applied when appropriate [2338], thus liberating themselves from inadequate domestic

---

2335. Hess, *supra* note 48, p. 193.

2336. T. Schultz, "The Ethos of Arbitration", in T. Schultz and F. Ortino (eds.), *The Oxford Handbook of International Arbitration*, Oxford, Oxford University Press, 2020, p, 243.

2337. Institute of International Law, Resolution on Arbitration Between States, State Enterprises or State Entities, and Foreign Enterprises, Institute of International Law, Articles on Arbitration between States, State Enterprises, or State Entities and Foreign Enterprises, *Annuaire d'Institut de droit international*, Vol. 63-I (1989), pp. 31-201; Explanatory Note by A. T. von Mehren, "Arbitration Between States and Foreign Enterprises: The Significance of the Institute of International Law's Santiago de Compostela Resolution", *ICSID Review: Foreign Investment Law Journal*, Vol. 5, No. 1 (1990), p. 54.

2338. von Mehren, *supra* note 2314, p. 62.

rules regulating international commerce and instead making use of a dispute resolution mechanism with transnational criteria [2339].

As stated by William Park, the arbitral mechanism carries significant advantages when applied to international transactions not only due to its speed and reduced cost (which are also important factors) but also due to an increased degree of fairness inherent in the arbitral process [2340]. For instance, arbitrators are empowered to apply general principles and may refuse to apply "unlawful laws" that run afoul of the minimum standards of international law [2341]. Thus, in *SPP* v. *Egypt*, it was decided that "Egyptian law must be construed so as to include [general] principles [. . . and the] national laws of Egypt can be relied upon only in as much as they do not contravene said principles" [2342].

Rather than lamenting a *lex dura, sed lex* emerging from domestic law, the arbitrators' discretion may lead them to apply general principles better suited to the case at hand [2343]. In this regard, Marc Blessing notes that companies that are active in the international market can select a national law to govern their international contracts. In the event of a dispute, however, they can expect that the arbitral tribunals will render a decision based on the fundamental notions and general principles in accordance with the expectations of the parties. In short, the arbitrator cannot act as a slave or machine who blindly applies the local tools to find a solution to the conflict [2344].

Emmanuel Gaillard explains that the rejection by arbitrators of outcomes without sufficient comparative law support accelerates the evolution of national laws. For example, the arbitral practice of rejecting the leniency of national law in favor of certain questionable practices to obtain contracts eventually led even to the adoption of the OECD Anti-Bribery Convention [2345].

2. *A neutral forum for State contracts*

The neutrality of arbitration is also of particular relevance regarding contractual relationships with State or State enterprises. In order

2339. F. K. Juenger, "Contract Choice of Law in the Americas", *American Journal of Comparative Law*, Vol. 45 (1997), p. 202.
2340. Park, *supra* note 2096, p. 69.
2341. Kotuby and Sobota, *supra* note 157, p. 46.
2342. *Southern Pacific* v. *Egypt*, *supra* note 128, Award (20 May 1984), para. 84.
2343. *Westinghouse*, *supra* note 1636.
2344. Blessing, *supra* note 2321, p. 42.
2345. Gaillard, *supra* note 836, p. 150.

to remain attractive to international investment, States offer, via arbitration, a neutral forum to solve future disputes, as the other party often wishes to resolve them outside of national courts and without necessarily applying the local laws [2346].

When it comes to determining the law applicable to a dispute, domestic courts are guided by their own mandatory private international law rules. Depending on how the host State incorporates international law into its municipal legal order, domestic courts may give preference to the application of national over international law, even if the former clearly contradicts the latter. National judges often lack the expertise to apply international law, which adds to an (actual or perceived) perception of partiality already fed by national judges' sensitivity to domestic public opinion [2347].

Moreover, choosing the laws of another country may be impractical because States frequently act not only commercially *(iure gestionis)* but in the exercise of their sovereignty *(iure imperii)*. Finally, there is a risk that the third country's law will be dismissed, particularly in expropriation cases [2348]. For these reasons, foreign parties often consider national courts to be unattractive dispute resolution forums [2349].

Regarding State contracts, it is commonly held that arbitral tribunals do not have a *lex fori* on the basis of which to choose applicable law. An early example is the 1958 award in *Aramco*, in which the Tribunal founded this approach on principles of equality between the parties as well as State immunity. The ruling was upheld in subsequent awards, albeit on different grounds, and it is now commonplace in international arbitration at large [2350].

2346. Already in 1958, in *Saudi Arabia* v. *Arabian American Oil Company (Aramco)* (1958) the Tribunal stated that the jurisdictional immunity of States "excludes the possibility, for the judicial authorities of the country of the seat, of exercising their right of supervision and interference in the arbitral proceedings which they have in certain cases", *Aramco*, *supra* note 1004, Award (23 August 1958), p. 136, 154-155 (1963).

2347. As noted by Reinisch and Malintoppi, *supra* note 270, p. 696.

2348. *Ibid.*, p. 696.

2349. *Ibid.*

2350. Spiermann, *supra* note 979, p. 93. The Tribunal in *Aramco* concluded that "the arbitration, as such, can only be governed by international law", rather than the law of the seat, Geneva, Switzerland. *Aramco*, *supra* note 1004, Award, pp. 154-156, fn. 52. In *Texaco* v. *Libya* (1977), sole Arbitrator Dupuy ruled that "[o]ne cannot accept that the institution of arbitration should escape the reach of all legal systems and be somehow suspended in vacuo" and that, therefore, the arbitration was "directly governed by international law", *Texaco* v. *Libya*, *supra* note 119, Award (9 January 1977), fn. 32, Dupuy (sole arb.), para. 16. In *Liamco* v. *Libya*, sole Arbitrator Mahmassani, sitting in Geneva, stated that "in his procedure [he] shall be guided as much as possible by the general principles contained in the [Model Rules] on Arbitral

D. *Private international law and arbitration*

Arbitration has been referred to as "the quintessential private international law endeavor" [2351]. No other field of law better reflects the functions of private international law, and arbitration provides an eminently suitable window through which to examine its challenges [2352]. In fact, as stated by George Bermann,

> "[i]t is not much of an exaggeration to view international arbitration as something of a private international law 'playground'" [2353].

It is not surprising, therefore, that reputable international arbitrators also tend to be outstanding private international law scholars [2354].

The concepts and vocabulary that private international law bring to bear are largely the same in the litigation and arbitration contexts [2355]. However, the specific form that private international law notions take may differ in these settings. For example, the concept of public policy has its refinements in the arbitration context [2356], which will be further discussed in Chapter XXI. These subtle nuances present challenges in the application of traditional private international law notions in arbitration.

Conflicts questions that arise in arbitration can be "at least as complex as those in litigation", if not more so [2357]. As stated by Filip De Ly, the difficulties and complexities in international arbitration stem from the fact that arbitrators in commercial cases not only face the conflict of laws question regarding "which law" applies but also the question of

---

Procedure of the International Law Commission" (*Liamco*, *supra* note 946, Award (12 April 1977, S. Mahmassani, sole arb.), 20 ILM, p. 1 (1981)).

2351. Bermann, *supra* note 11, p. 17.

2352. *Ibid.*, p. 20.

2353. G. A. Bermann, "Private International Law in International Arbitration", in F. Ferrari and D. P. Fernández Arroyo (eds.), *Private International Law: Contemporary Challenges and Continuing Relevance*, Cheltenham, Edward Elgar, 2019, p. 482.

2354. F. Ferrari and D. P. Fernández Arroyo, "Introduction", in *id.* (eds.), *Private International Law: Contemporary Challenges and Continuing Relevance*, Cheltenham, Edward Elgar, 2019, p. 4.

2355. For instance, regarding questions such as characterization, the application by an arbitral tribunal on its own motion of a conflict rule, the methods for ascertaining the contents of the applicable law (*iura novit curia*), and public policy. See F. De Ly, "Conflicts of Law in International Arbitration: An Overview", in F. Ferrari and S. Kröll (eds.), *Conflict of Laws in International Commercial Arbitration*, New York, NYU Center for Transnational Litigation and Commercial Law / Juris, 2019, p. 3.

2356. Bermann, *supra* note 11, p. 23.

2357. Hayward, *supra* note 2323, p. 2.

"which system of Private International Law" applies [2358]. Numerous answers to these questions are possible depending on the case, including national laws, conventions such as Rome I or the Mexico Convention, or principles of private international law, among others. This matter will be addressed in further detail in the following paragraphs.

The Report on the Fragmentation of International Law to the ILC defined conflict as "a situation where two rules or principles suggest different ways of dealing with a problem" [2359]. There are several situations in which conflicts questions may significantly impact the outcome of the dispute, for instance regarding the formation, performance, termination, interpretation and calculation of damages in international contracts [2360].

Lacunae, ambiguities or interpretive divergences on the applicable law not only complicate the resolution of disputes but can also contribute to their emergence. If the parties do not know which rules apply to their relationship, they may contribute to the conflict unnecessarily by failing to comply with unclear obligations. Moreover, a party acting in bad faith can take advantage of any uncertainty related to the applicable law and attempt to use it to serve its own self-interest [2361].

2358. F. De Ly, "Conflicts of Law in International Arbitration: An Overview", *International Arbitration, in Conflict of Laws in International Commercial Arbitration*, in F. Ferrari and S. Kröll (eds.), *Conflict of Laws in International Commercial Arbitration*, New York, NYU Center for Transnational Litigation and Commercial Law / Juris, 2019, p. 1.

2359. ILC Fragmentation Report, *supra* note 106, Conclusions, para. 25. See also Conclusions, para. 14 (2).

2360. Hayward, *supra* note 2323, pp. 33-34:

> "This situation can occur for instance, in the following situations: contract formation disputes, disputes involving an alleged oral contract, disputes where reference is sought to extrinsic materials to interpret a written contract; disputes involving the enforcement of good faith obligations, disputes involving a complaint over non-disclosure disputes involving an alleged premature contract termination, disputes involving the termination of a contract for breach, disputes over the foreseeability of damages, disputes involving a claim for punitive damages, disputes involving the enforcement of an agreed sum payable upon breach; disputes over the interest rate applicable, disputes involving an excuse claim based on frustration or impossibility, disputes over the legal consequences of bribery or corruption connected to a contract, disputes over the applicable limitation period, disputes over the availability of set-off, and many others."

2361. Derains, *supra* note 1431, p. 10. In the experience of Detlev Vagts, a high percentage of arbitral controversies relate not to the validity of the international contract itself but to its interpretation and scope. See D. F. Vagts, "Arbitration and the UNIDROIT Principles", in *Contratación Internacional, Comentarios a los Principios sobre los Contratos Comerciales Internacionales del UNIDROIT*, México, Universidad Nacional Autónoma de México, Universidad Panamericana, 1998, p. 272.

Determining the applicable law continues to be considered an "esoteric" exercise exacerbated by legal academia [2362]. Some experts such as Thomas Clay consider private international law to be the law of conflict and argue that arbitration negates these conflicts by providing material rules to resolve them – a transnational law *par excellence* [2363]. Expressions like the latter perhaps explain why conflict of laws issues are often ignored in arbitration. Fortunately, recent initiatives such as Bermann's General Course at The Hague Academy of International Law have illustrated the importance of handling conflict of laws issues appropriately [2364].

Private international law, both uniform law and conflict of laws rules, may become relevant in resolving international disputes, and grasping them suitably can be crucial for the outcome of the case and to preserve the legitimacy of the arbitration and the predictability of the award [2365]. Hence, international arbitral practice must keep up to date on the recent developments in private international law.

E. "Orthodox" conflict of laws rules in the nascent stages of the international arbitral system

In the period immediately following World War II, arbitration emerged under the orthodox private international law conflicts of law system, described in Chapter X. Numerous instruments were drafted to regulate this emerging international field, among them the 1958 New York Convention, the 1961 Geneva Convention and even the 1987 Swiss Private International Law Act, which has a chapter on arbitration [2366].

2362. L. Silberman and F. Ferrari, "Getting to the Law Applicable to the Merits in International Arbitration and the Consequences of Getting It Wrong", Law and Economics Research Paper Series, New York University School of Law, 2010, p. 25.

2363. T. Clay, "La importancia de la sede del arbitraje en el arbitraje internacional: ¿es todavía relevante?", in F. Mantilla-Serrano (ed.), *Arbitraje Internacional, Tensiones actuales*, Bogotá, Legis, Comité Colombiano de Arbitraje, 2007, pp. 193-194.

2364. Bermann, *supra* note 11, pp. 130-135.

2365. "Far from being the retrograde and arbitration-hostile mechanism that it has long been suspected of being, Private International Law in effect gives instruments to ensure that arbitration maintains its effectiveness", G. Cordero-Moss, "Private International Law in Arbitration", in M. Pfeiffer, J. Brodec, P. Bríza and M. Zavadilová (eds.), *Liber Amicorum – Monika Pauknerova*, Prague, Wolters Kluwer, 2021, pp. 94-95.

2366. At the time, perhaps international arbitration was not so important in Switzerland. See Cordero-Moss and Fernández Arroyo, *supra* note 12, p. 312.

However, these texts have been interpreted with a cosmopolitan eye. For instance, the rules regarding the application of non-State law [2367] in the New York Convention [2368] have been interpreted progressively, as recognized by the Cairo Declaration of the International Law Association in April 1992. More specifically, according to this declaration, if arbitrators apply transnational rules of law in lieu of a national law, the validity of the award may not be questioned for this reason alone when the parties selected them or when they remained silent regarding the applicable law [2369].

Today, arbitration is typically transnational in nature. The international arbitration field incorporates common terms, common practices, the same leading arbitrators and the most significant institutions competing to develop the most attractive dispute resolution services for transnational business. In contemporary international practice, classical private international law, based on the selection of a national law according to the location of some connecting factors, does not meet the challenges handled by arbitration. A new private international law, providing for the flexible application of domestic laws and the application of uniform law and other techniques where appropriate, is now consolidated [2370]. The evolution of private international law in this regard was discussed in Chapters X and XI.

F. Current trends of conflict of laws in arbitration

Modern trends are reflected in the 1976 UNCITRAL Arbitration Rules, modified in 2010, and the 1985 UNCITRAL Model Law, modified in 2006 [2371]. From the provisions contained therein, particularly Articles

2367. An example is: *Ministry of Defense and Support of the Armed Forces of the Islamic Republic of Iran* v. *Cubic Defense Systems, Inc.* In this case, enforcement of an award applying the UNIDROIT Principles as an expression of non-State law or general principles was accepted as not violating the arbitration mandate in accordance with Article V (1) *I* of the New York Convention. Sixty-Fifth ILA Conference in El Cairo, 26 April 1992, in E. Gaillard (ed.), *Transnational Rules in International Commercial Arbitration*, Paris, ICC Publishing, 2003, p. 247.

2368. Bermann, *supra* note 14.

2369. Gaillard, *supra* note 2367, p. 247.

2370. Cordero-Moss and Fernández Arroyo, *supra* note 12, p. 312. "Moreover, in arbitral proceedings, the use of classical Private International Law is exceptional. Private International Law may only have a role at the limits of the arbitral proceedings, or outside of them. Thus, the parties may in certain circumstances request judicial support for the arbitration, but not for the proceedings *per se* conducted by the arbitral tribunals themselves. Courts, in providing assistance for arbitration, may also make use of Private International Law tools" (*ibid.*, p. 312).

2371. UNCITRAL Model Arbitration Law, *supra* note 1342.

33 (currently Art. 35) of the UNCITRAL Arbitration Rules and Article 28 of the Model Law, it has been rightly stated that "[a]rbitrators are no longer the 'slaves' of conflict rules; rather, they appear to be the masters". In resolving an international dispute, arbitrators can choose a conflict of laws "system", a "rule", or can "directly" determine the appropriate "law" or "rules of law" to govern the contract [2372].

It is true that where the parties have not selected an applicable law, the Model Law prevents the arbitrators from choosing it directly; Article 28 (2) states in this regard that the Tribunal "shall apply the law determined by the conflict of laws rules which it considers applicable". However, the provisions regarding the applicable substantive law should not be considered mandatory [2373]. Further, as explained by Pierre Mayer, since the Model Law does not include a mechanism to review awards, arbitrators that ignore this provision do not put the validity of the decision into question. Certain exceptions to this rule exist in jurisdictions such as England where, unless agreed otherwise, parties can appeal an award on the merits [2374].

Moreover, Model Law Article 28 (4) states that in all cases the tribunal must take the contract and usages into account [2375]. This rule prevails over conflict rules and does not depend on the will of the parties, thereby granting significant flexibility to the arbitrators in their determination of the applicable law [2376]. This will be further discussed in Chapter XIX.

Modern instruments discussed in Chapters X and XI, such as the Hague Principles, and for the Americas, the OAS Guide, can be of particular assistance to arbitrators in determining the applicable substantive law, since they provide guidance on acceptable general principles of private international law that arbitrators may apply [2377].

2372. Toth, *supra* note 1559, p. 206.

2373. As noted – for instance – by Blessing, in *Introduction to Arbitration: Swiss and International Perspectives* (Swiss Commercial Law Series, ed. N. P. Vogt, No. 10), Basel / Frankfurt am Main, Helbing und Lichtenhahn, 1999, para. 627.

2374. In England, Article 69 of the Arbitration Act of 1996. See Mayer and Heuzé, *supra* note 1506, pp. 69-70.

2375. Institutional rules (such as the ICC, Art. 21 (2)) and international arbitration rules (such as UNCITRAL, Art. 35 (3)) require that arbitral tribunals consider relevant trade usages in their decision-making. A similar requirement is also found in some national legislation, such as the Netherlands Arbitration Act 1986 (Art. 1054 (4)). See Blackaby *et al.*, *supra* note 255, p. 213.

2376. This applies even to the eventual application of *lex mercatoria* or international law, at least with regards to the application of fundamental principles to the case at hand. See Dalhuisen, *supra* note 1582, p. 119.

2377. L. Gama, D. Girsberger and J. A. Moreno Rodríguez, "Perspectives on the Hague Principles in International Commercial Arbitration", in D. Girsberger, T. Kadner

Several awards refer to arbitrators' ample or discretionary power to determine the applicable substantive law [2378]. However, arbitrators should be careful in exercising their discretion in this regard. Lucy Reed points to a 1989 ICC Case No. 5713 [2379] in which the tribunal applied a similar provision regarding trade usages in the ICC Rules [2380] and the Vienna Sales Convention, which caught the parties by surprise since it was not the law of the contract and neither party referred to it in their briefs [2381].

G. *Peculiarities of international investment arbitration*

Arbitrators dealing with foreign investment claims must typically interpret whether the State has actually implemented the guarantees that the investor alleges it enjoys under the applicable investment law,

---

Graziano and J. L. Neels (eds.), *Choice of Law in International Commercial Contracts: Global Perspectives on the Hague Principles*, Oxford, Oxford University Press, 2021, p. 200. The Hague Conference on Private International Law publishes a table which presents a non-exhaustive list of arbitral institutions that either have incorporated the HCCH Principles into their own institutional rules or are advertising or facilitating their use in other ways. The table is based on information provided by the institutions and is updated on a yearly basis. The third survey on the HCCH Principles reveals increasing awareness and wider use of the HCCH Principles among international arbitral institutions and tribunals. See https://www.hcch.net/en/publications-and-studies/details4/?pid=6800, accessed 12 May 2022.

2378. Silberman and Ferrari mention the following awards: ICC Award No. 2930/1982, 9 YB Comm. Arb. (1984), p. 105, 106; Cairo Regional Center for International Commercial Arbitration (CRCICA), No. 120/1998, Partial Award (23 June 2000), in A. Eldin (ed.), 2 *Arbitral Awards of the Cairo Regional Centre for International Commercial Arbitration* (hereafter AACRCICA), p. 25 (2000), 28; ICC Award No. 3540/1980, 7 YB Comm. Arb. (1982), p. 124, 128; ICC Award No. 2730/1982, in *Collection of ICC Arbitral Awards 1974-1985* (1990), p. 490, 491; ICC Award No. 1422/1966, in *Collection of ICC Arbitral Awards 1974-1985* (1990), p. 185, 186. Silberman and Ferrari note that the discretionary power cannot go to the extreme of the court ignoring any conflict of laws approach, as stated, for example, in ICC Award No. 8113/1995, 25 YB Comm. Arb. (2000), p. 324, 325, cited in Silberman and Ferrari, *supra* note 2362, p. 13.

2379. *Swiss Buyer* (1989), *supra* note 1560.

2380. ICC Rules of Arbitration, in force 1 January 1998, ICC Publication No. 581, 1997, reprinted in 36 ILM, p. 1604 (1997), 22 YB Comm. Arb. (1997), p. 347, Article 13 (5).

2381. "The parties were presumably taken by surprise. Not only were their respective States not parties to the Vienna Sales Convention, but the contract was concluded in 1979, a year before the text of the convention was even finalized. Furthermore, the Tribunal did not appear to have reviewed the factual matter of whether the Convention codified pre-existing and widely accepted practice in the area of trade concerned. In fact, the Convention established a two-year time limit for the buyer's notice of non-conformity, which is substantially longer than most municipal sales laws require. In these circumstances, the Tribunal's finding that 'equities' warranted the application of the Vienna Sales Convention is open to criticism for arbitrariness", Reed, *supra* note 21, pp. 226-227.

treaty or contract. In principle, these types of disputes go beyond what is traditionally dealt with in international commercial arbitration [2382].

However, arbitrators have great flexibility in investment claims when it comes, for instance, to interpreting open-textured treaty standards. As in commercial arbitration, they are not bound by rigid prescriptions nor by the provisions of a single domestic system. Giorgio Sacerdoti thus concludes that, in the end, investment arbitration

> "does not appear so far apart from international commercial arbitration, notwithstanding its public international law features and the national public interest often involved in international investment disputes" [2383].

ICSID tribunals exercise this discretion, for instance, when determining whether the compensation due for a lawful expropriation attracts simple or compound interest. In the *CDSE* v. *Costa Rica* case [2384], the Tribunal stated:

> "Even though there is a tendency in international jurisprudence to award only simple interest, this is manifested principally in relation to cases of injury or simple breach of contract. The same considerations do not apply to cases relating to the valuation of property or property rights. In cases such as the present, compound interest is not excluded when it is warranted by the circumstances." [2385]

The Tribunal found the available authorities indecisive and ambiguous [2386], and drew support from the Special Rapporteur of the ILC on the Proposed Draft Convention on State Responsibility, where it

---

2382. Sicard-Mirabal and Derains, *supra* note 114, pp. 9-10.

2383. Sacerdoti, *supra* note 641, p. 47. As noted by Cheng, the existence of a universal concept of law outside of any particular legal system is an unmistakable feature of international arbitral tribunals and courts. International law is precisely the application of this universal concept, which has long been applied in the relations between individuals and is now applied to the relations between States, Cheng, *supra* note 178, pp. 390-391. From a critical perspective, Sornarajah states that the flexibility and cosmopolitanism of arbitration helped "internationalize" foreign investment contracts. It is "unlikely that the International Court would have assisted in the creation of such a theory as ideological cleavages within it would have led to the manifestation of the different views on the settlement of foreign investment disputes", Sornarajah, *supra* note 29, p. 156. The history of the *Anglo-Iranian Oil*, *supra* note 267, (in which the ICJ refused jurisdiction) indicated quite early that the judges would not take a uniform position on foreign investment issues.

2384. *CDSE* v. *Costa Rica*, *supra* note 455.

2385. *Ibid.*, para. 97.

2386. *Ibid.*, paras. 98-102.

found that "compound interest certainly is not unknown or excluded in international law" [2387]. The arbitrators concluded that "the determination of interest is a product of the exercise of judgment, taking into account all of the circumstances of the case at hand and especially considerations of fairness which must form part of the law to be applied by this Tribunal" [2388]. In its reasoning, the Tribunal explained that the interest owed to the owner who lost property and did not receive compensation should reflect the additional earnings he would have received had the amount been reinvested.

According to Reed, the ICSID Tribunal's reasoning in the *CDSE* v. *Costa Rica* case is not so different from other decisions, including the one rendered in the ICC Case No. 5713 mentioned above [2389]. Due to the wider margin of discretion available to tribunals under public international law, ICSID tribunals may appear more justified in setting the compensation amount as "what is appropriate in the circumstances". Nonetheless, the aim of these tribunals remains the same: to adapt the choice of law rule to select the rule that, in the circumstances, will yield the most appropriate and equitable result [2390].

H. Choice of law in investment arbitration

Investment arbitration is a stimulating "field trip" for anyone interested in the interplay between the national and international legal orders [2391]. The law applicable in investment claims may involve a multitude of layers. Public international law has a particular bearing in

---

2387. According to whom "compound interest should be awarded whenever it is proved that it is indispensable in order to ensure full compensation for the damage suffered by the injured State", G. Arangio-Ruíz, Report, UN Doc. A/CN.4/425 and Corr.1 and Add.1 and Add.1/Corr.1, *Yearbook of the International Law Commission*, Vol. 2-I (1989), p. 30, as quoted in the award, *ibid.*, para. 102. The text of the Draft Articles on the International Responsibility of States, Article 44 (2), UN Doc. A/51/10 (1996), reprinted in 37 ILM, p. 440 (1998), states what follows: "For the purposes of the present article, compensation covers any economically assessable damage sustained by the injured State, and may include interest and, where appropriate, loss of profits".

2388. "It is not the purpose of compound interest to attribute blame to, or to punish, anybody for the delay in the payment . . .; it is a mechanism to ensure that the compensation awarded the Claimant is appropriate in the circumstances" (*CDSE* v. *Costa Rica*, *supra* note 455, Award, paras. 103-104).

2389. See *supra* note 2379.

2390. Reed notes "that the ICSID Tribunal purported to safeguard the legitimate expectations of the parties in its choice of applicable law. This element of the arbitral dispute resolution process that typically is not spelled out in commercial arbitration jurisprudence", Reed, *supra* note 21, p. 230.

2391. Kjos, *supra* note 2296, p. 297.

the field. However, the point of reference can also be the commercial contract or contractual relationships underlying the investment.

In investment treaties, laws or investor-State contracts, choice of law clauses often refer to the law of the host State, sometimes provide for stabilization clauses or mention the law of a third State (such as in the case of bonds). Moreover, choice of law clauses in investor-State contracts generally refer to international law, general principles of law [2392] or the standards of protection provided for in the bilateral investment treaty [2393].

Some treaties list principles or rules of international law but omit national laws. Other treaties combine both domestic and international laws, and others mention the national law of the host States and contracts between the disputing parties, while omitting any reference to international law [2394]. A common formula in the treaties lists the following sources, in no particular hierarchical order: *(a)* the host State's law; *(b)* the BIT itself and other treaties; *(c)* any contract relating to the investment; and *(d)* general international law [2395].

How does the tribunal determine the applicable law in the investment arbitration context? Arbitral tribunals generally do not have any choice of law rules of the forum to apply. Therefore, they are in need of their own "transnational" choice of law rules [2396].

Decades ago, Lord McNair advocated persuasively in favor of getting rid of the notion that the only choices of law available in foreign investment-related matters are public international law and the national system of law associated with either of the parties [2397]. The issue then becomes determining which rules, principles or "system" applies.

2392. In referring to general principles of law, choice of law clauses agree on the formulations of the principles to be applied in the determination of responsibilities. This was the case, for instance, in *Alabama Claims*, *supra* note 947. Brownlie writes that "interesting choice of law clause occurred in the *compromis* between *Greenpeace Stichting International* v. *The French State* (1987). This arbitration was based on a *compromis* or Special Agreement in which France accepted responsibility for the destruction of the Rainbow Warrior in Auckland harbour. The issue in this arbitration was exclusively about the quantum of damage, the compensation for the destruction of the vessel. The choice of law clause stipulated that the applicable law was *either* the law of England, *or* the law of New Zealand, or the law of France. No further criteria were indicated. The Decision of the Tribunal is not in the public domain", Brownlie, *supra* note 2121, p. 95.

2393. Hess, *supra* note 48, p. 140.

2394. Such as Article 26 (6) of the Energy Charter Treaty.

2395. Dolzer and Schreuer, *supra* note 382, p. 290.

2396. Arguably, the need for transnational choice of law rules in the public international law context was already recognized by the PCIJ in the *Serbian Loans* cases in the 1920s. *Serbian Loans*, *supra* note 978. Mills, *supra* note 1819, p. 31.

2397. McNair, *supra* note 4, p. 3.

As stated, most investment treaties provide for arbitration, and many specify the applicable law, which is usually a blend of the national law of the host State concerned and the general principles of international law. Many treaties, however, do not address this issue, or refer to broad and generic principles by using formulas such as "generally recognized rules and principles of international law". Moreover, the law to be applied by the tribunal varies from one dispute settlement mechanism to another. Some give ample discretion to the tribunal, while others refer to conflict of laws rules or rules of international law [2398].

It is also common for several sources of law to apply at once. For instance, in the ICSID Additional Facility Rules arbitration case *Tecmed* v. *Mexico* (2003) [2399], the applicable law clause included in the BIT listed the treaty itself as well as international law provisions as pertinent in the event of a dispute. This clause was interpreted by the Tribunal in accordance with Article 38 of the ICJ Statute. In its discussion of expropriation, the Tribunal referred to the case law of the European Court of Human Rights, the Inter-American Court of Human Rights and the Iran-United States Claims Tribunal [2400].

I. Applicable substantive law in the ICSID Convention

1. The content of Article 42

Determining the applicable substantive law has been a major topic since the very beginning of the drafting of the ICSID Convention [2401]. This instrument provides a procedural framework for the conduct of international investment arbitrations. The ICSID Convention also contains a choice of law provision (Art. 42) attempting to remove any uncertainty and unpredictability in this regard [2402].

Article 42 of the ICSID Convention provides the following:

2398. For instance, Article 21 of the 2021 ICC Arbitration Rules provide that in the absence of choice, the *voie directe* applies, which gives ample discretion to the arbitrators. By contrast, Article 28 of the UNCITRAL Model Law refers to traditional conflict of laws rules that the tribunal considers appropriate, as discussed in Chap. XVIII, *infra*. Article 42 of the ICSID Convention contemplates the application of "the law of the Contracting State party to the dispute (including its rules on the conflict of laws) and such rules of international law as may be applicable".

2399. *Tecmed* v. *Mexico*, *supra* note 537, Award (29 May 2003).

2400. *Ibid.*, para. 116.

2401. Lowenfeld, *supra* note 25, p. 539.

2402. Bjorklund and Vanhonnaeker, *supra* note 13, p. 349. On similar lines, Schreuer, *supra* note 2173, p. 550. The following issues are not governed by Article 42: jurisdiction, nationality and *ius standi* in particular of minority shareholders (see cases in *ibid.*, pp. 551-553).

> "(1) The Tribunal shall decide a dispute in accordance with such rules of law as may be agreed by the parties. In the absence of such agreement, the Tribunal shall apply the law of the Contracting State party to the dispute (including its rules on the conflict of laws) and such rules of international law as may be applicable.
>
> (2) The Tribunal may not bring in a finding of *non liquet* on the ground of silence or obscurity of the law.
>
> (3) The provisions of paragraphs (1) and (2) shall not prejudice the power of the Tribunal to decide a dispute *ex aequo et bono* if the parties so agree."

In contrast to the procedural provisions scattered throughout the ICSID Convention, Article 42 deals with the applicable substantive law [2403]. Neither the New York Convention nor the Inter-American Convention contains comparable choice of law provisions [2404]. Article 28 of the UNCITRAL Model Law and Article 35 of the UNCITRAL Arbitration Rules are analogue provisions to Article 42 of the ICSID Convention.

Article 42 (1) of the ICSID Convention proceeds from the principle of the freedom of the parties to choose the law they consider most appropriate for their relationship [2405]. Where the parties have not chosen an applicable law, the tribunal may refer to both domestic and international law rules. Aron Broches, considered "the founding father of the Convention", explained Article 42 in the following terms:

> "The tribunal will first look at the law of the host State and that law will in the first instance be applied to the merits of the dispute. Then the result will be tested against international law. That process will not involve the confirmation or denial of the host State's law, but may result in not applying it where that law, or action taken under that law, violates international law. In that sense . . . international law is hierarchically superior to national law under Article 42 (1)." [2406]

2403. Broches, *supra* note 2161, p. 388.

2404. Born, *supra* note 2273, p. 125.

2405. On the freedom of choice of law more generally, see K. Lipstein, "International Arbitration Between Individuals and Governments and the Conflict of Laws", in Bin Cheng and E. D. Brown (eds.), *Contemporary Problems of International Law: Essays in Honour of Georg Schwarzenberger on his Eightieth Birthday*, London, Stevens & Sons, 1988, p. 177. Schreuer *et al.*, *supra* note 102, pp. 21, 557.

2406. Broches, *supra* note 2161, p. 388.

Schreuer notes that Article 42 combines flexibility with certainty. Flexibility is provided by granting the parties maximum autonomy to determine the applicable rules. Certainty is provided by ensuring that the tribunal will find appropriate rules where the parties have made no such choice. Flexibility emerges from the first sentence of paragraph 1 regarding the agreement of the parties and from paragraph 3 that extends party autonomy to equitable principles. Certainty emerges from the second sentence of paragraph 1, setting the host State's law as applicable, in conjunction with international law in the absence of agreement. Paragraph 2 prohibits a finding of *non liquet* by the tribunal [2407].

However, a closer look at Article 42 shows that the twofold process (party autonomy and the absence of choice) is more complicated than it seems [2408]. These complexities will be addressed below and in further chapters.

2. *Interplay of national and international law in the ICSID Convention*

Article 42 of the ICSID Convention was designed for the purpose of applying to contract claims [2409]. And in the first twenty years of the ICSID Convention, the claims raised generally regarded breaches of investment contracts [2410]. Subsequently, in a remarkable way the bulk of

---

2407. Schreuer *et al.*, *supra* note 102, p. 550 ff. "In drafting this provision, here the drafters followed the example set by the Model Draft on Arbitral Procedure adopted by the United Nations International Law Commission. The provision, which is not found in either the old or the new ICJ Statutes reflects the view that existing international law provides the international judge or arbitrator with sufficient elements to render a decision on the dispute, contrary to earlier positivist views that the international legal order was incomplete", Broches, *supra* note 2161, pp. 388-389.

2408. Bjorklund and Vanhonnaeker, *supra* note 13, p. 352.

2409. Applying Article 42 of ICSID to "directly and unreservedly to treaty claims involves a strong element of absurdity", Spiermann, *supra* note 979, p. 107. "In the course of drafting the ICSID Convention, a number of suggestions were made concerning possible international law rules that might be applied by tribunals. These rules include the protection against discriminatory treatment, the obligation to act in good faith, the prohibition of measures contrary to international public policy, *pacta sunt servanda*, the exhaustion of local remedies, and rules on State succession" (*History of the ICSID Convention*, *supra* note 1078, II, pp. 419, 570, 801, 985). "Mr. Broches pointed out that, apart from treaty law, the reference to international law in Article 42 was only composed of principles such as good faith and the principle that one ought to abide by agreements voluntarily made" (*ibid.*, p. 985).

2410. Half of those cases involved the applicable law selected by the parties, which is usually the law of the home State. In the case *Mobil* v. *New Zealand*, the ICSID arbitration clause stipulated that "[a]n Arbitral Tribunal shall apply the law of New Zealand". (See *Attorney General of New Zealand* v. *Mobil Oil New Zealand*, High Court of New Zealand, Judgment (1 July 1987), in *ICSID Review: Foreign Investment Law Journal*, Vol. 2 (1987), p. 497, 502. However, stabilization or "freezing" clauses are

the ICSID cases expanded to primarily deal with treaty claims. Only a minority of bilateral investment treaties specify the applicable law, and those that contain such provisions always list the substantive provisions of the bilateral investment treaty itself [2411].

The drafting of Article 42 was designed to be acceptable to developing countries that were suspicious of the law applicable to the merits of the dispute. Article 42 did not provide a definitive solution to the question of the applicable law and which norm should prevail in case of conflict [2412].

Since the very beginning, attitudes toward the interplay between national law and international law have been polarized [2413]. In principle, the law of the contracting State should be applied to resolve the dispute [2414], but in numerous ICSID awards, international law has a "complementary" and "subsidiary" role when the law of the contracting State is lacking [2415]. These roles will be dealt with in Chapter XX.

3. The applicability of public international law under Article 42 of the ICSID Convention

As noted by Meg Kinnear, resort to public international law has become so common that in ICSID arbitration the tribunals rarely question the analytical basis for applying it, beyond the mere fact that the breach is based on an international treaty. Even though, in theory, other laws should be applied, in practice public international law has

---

typically included (such as in *MINE* v. *Guinea*, *supra* note 2190 (22 December 1989), para. 94). Other cases referred to national and international law, "so that application of the former might if necessary be complemented or tempered by the latter" (*AGIP* v. *Congo*, *supra* note 454, Award (30 November 1979), para. 323, cited in Parra, *supra* note 510, pp. 178-179).

2411. Spiermann, *supra* note 979, p. 107.

2412. V. C. Igbokwe, "Developing Countries and the Law Applicable to International Arbitration of Oil Investment Disputes", *Journal of International Arbitration*, Vol. 14 (1997), pp. 114-115.

2413. See *ibid.*, p. 102.

2414. E. Gaillard and Y. Banifatemi, "The Meaning of 'and' in Article 42(1), Second Sentence of the Washington Convention: The Role of International Law in the ICSID Choice of Law Process", *ICSID Review: Foreign Investment Law Journal*, Vol. 18, No. 2 (2003), p. 391. "In several ICSID cases, the applicable substantive law in investment arbitration combines international law and the law of the host State . . . where the parties have chosen the applicable law and also where the parties have made no such choice. . . . In non-ICSID arbitrations between investors and host States, tribunals have also applied a combination of international law and host State law. Furthermore, where there is a contradiction between international law and host State law, international law typically prevails", Dolzer and Schreuer, *supra* note 382, pp. 292-293.

2415. Gaillard and Banifatemi, *ibid.*, p. 381.

played an important role as the law governing relationships that emerge from a treaty [2416].

In the negotiation process of the ICSID Convention, there was repeated concern that the simple reference to international law rules was too unspecific [2417]. The drafting history document states that "[t]he term 'international law' as used in this context should be understood in the sense given to it by Article 38 (1) of the Statute of the International Court of Justice, allowance being made for the fact that Article 38 was designed to apply to inter-State disputes" [2418]. It is debatable if this provides a complete picture of contemporary international law. Nonetheless, the drafting history makes clear that ICSID tribunals are directed to look at the full range of sources of international law in resolving disputes, in a similar way as the ICJ [2419].

The reference of Article 42 of the ICSID Convention to "rules of international law" must "be understood as compromising the general international law, including customary law", and not just the applicable treaty [2420]. This was the case in the *LG&E* v. *Argentina* and *ADC* v. *Hungary* decisions [2421].

It must be considered that Article 38 of the ICJ Statute was also designed to apply to inter-State disputes. Article 42 of the ICSID Convention does not transpose the rules that apply to relationships between States to links between States and investors. Hence, if tribunals refer to customary international law rules, they must first establish their applicability to individuals as well [2422].

Article 42 also comprises the following general principles of public international law: good faith and the principle that one ought to abide by agreements voluntarily made and ought to carry them out in good faith.

2416. Kinnear, *supra* note 846, p. 443.

2417. *History of the ICSID Convention*, *supra* note 1078, II-1, pp. 330, 418, 570, 801.

2418. *Ibid.*, Vol. II-2, p. 962.

2419. Schreuer *et al.*, *supra* note 102, pp. 604-606. See also NAFTA, Energy Charter and Vienna Convention, especially for interpreting BITs.

2420. Of course, this does not exclude the possibility of applying national law, and host-State law in particular, to other issues in the case. Article 42 provides for the application of national law, which also follows in any event from the hybrid character of investment arbitration. See McLachlan, *supra* note 356, p. 399.

2421. *LG&E* v. *Argentina*, Decision on Liability (3 October 2006), para. 89. *ADC* v. *Hungary*, Award (2 October 2006), para. 290.

2422. Bischoff, *supra* note 15, p. 758. See also International Bank for Reconstruction and Development, Report of the Executive Directors on the Convention on the Settlement of Investment Disputes between States and Nationals of Other States (18 March 1965).

4. Autonomous interpretation of Article 42

Arbitral tribunals often only address conflict of laws problems superficially and are satisfied with referring to Article 42 of the ICSID Convention or to the corresponding choice of law provision within the investment treaty [2423]. However, a closer look may lead to a different outcome in certain situations, which justifies several discussions in this book related to the applicable substantive law.

Article 42 is the *lex fori* designed to give guidance to ICSID tribunals in determining the appropriate applicable substantive law [2424]. The provision must be interpreted autonomously, taking general principles of law into account when relevant.

For private law-related matters, the arbitrators may apply – as an expression of general principles – uniform law instruments like the CISG [2425] and the UNIDROIT Principles. Where a tribunal does not consider it appropriate or cannot establish general principles of uniform law in a particular case, it can resort to general conflict of laws principles instead [2426]. The Hague Principles that reflect them can be of great help in this regard, as well as other instruments such as Rome I and the Mexico Convention.

Where general principles cannot be established, there will be no *non liquet*. The ICSID Convention provides guidance in these situations (specifically, Art. 42, para. 1, Sec. 2), opening the door for the application of the law of the host State and its conflict of laws rules in particular [2427].

5. Conflict of laws rules under the ICSID Additional Facility Rules

Rule 68 of the ICSID Additional Facility Rules states:

> "Applicable Law
>
> (1) The Tribunal shall apply the rules of law designated by the parties as applicable to the substance of the dispute. Failing such designation by the parties, the Tribunal shall apply: *(a)* the

2423. Bischoff, *supra* note 15, p. 745.
2424. Schreuer *et al.*, *supra* note 102, pp. 554-557.
2425. Bischoff, *supra* note 15, p. 761.
2426. "If the tribunal is faced with a choice between several national laws, it will choose the 'proper law' by the application of generally accepted principles of Conflict of Laws or Private International Law" (*History of the ICSID Convention*, *supra* note 1078, Vol. II-1, p. 570).
2427. Bischoff, *supra* note 15, p. 762.

law which it determines to be applicable; and *(b)* the rules of international law it considers applicable.

(2) The Tribunal may decide *ex aequo et bono* if the parties have expressly authorized it to do so and if the law applicable to the arbitration so permits."

Despite the difference in wording with Article 42 of the ICSID Convention, the result of the application of both provisions should be the same in most situations [2428].

J. Conflict of laws before the Iran-United States Claims Tribunal

1. The applicable law provision of the Claims Settlement Declaration

Article V of the Claims Settlement Declaration [2429] refers both to "choice of law rules" and "principles of commercial and international law". It also states that the tribunal must take into account "relevant usages of the trade, contract provisions and changed circumstances" [2430].

In an oft-cited case, the Iran-United States Claims Tribunal wrote:

> "It is difficult to conceive of a choice of law provision that would give the Tribunal greater freedom in determining case by case the law relevant to the issues before it. Such freedom is consistent with, and perhaps almost essential to, the scope of the tasks confronting the Tribunal, which include not only claims of a commercial nature, such as the one involved in the present case, but also claims involving alleged expropriations or other public acts, claims between the two Governments, certain claims between two banking institutions, and issues of interpretation and implementation of the Algiers Declarations. Thus, the Tribunal

2428. The same comment was made in reference to the prior rules by Cordero-Moss and Behn, *supra* note 964, p. 577.

2429. The provision states "[t]he Tribunal shall decide all cases on the basis of respect for law, applying such choice of law rules and principles of commercial and international law as the Tribunal determines to be applicable, taking into account relevant usages of the trade, contract provisions and changed circumstances".

2430. "Article V differs with the UNCITRAL Model Law and Rules, inter alia, because instead of preserving the primacy of the parties' contract, the terms of the contract are placed on a par with trade usages and 'changed circumstances'. Arbitrators are granted a broad authority to choose not only the appropriate choice of law rules, but also to apply whatever principles of substantive commercial and international law they find appropriate, whether or not the parties have made their own choice", S. A. Baker and M. D. Davis, *The UNCITRAL Arbitration Rules in Practice: The Experience of the Iran-United States Claims Tribunal*, Deventer/Boston, Kluwer Law International, 1992, p. 178.

may often find it necessary to interpret and apply treaties, customary international law, general principles of law and national laws, 'taking into account relevant usages of the trade, contract provisions and changed circumstances' as Article V directs." [2431]

2. Eclecticism

Article V of the Claims Settlement Declaration contains a particularly complicated choice of law provision. As such, the Iran-United States Claims Tribunal has proceeded cautiously when applying it [2432], looking primarily at the clauses of the contract under consideration. Instead of recurring to Iranian or US conflict of laws rules, the Iran-United States Claims Tribunal usually applies general principles of law and non-State law or the *lex mercatoria* (but does not necessarily mention these sources by name). This hesitation mirrors the general reluctance of international tribunals to apply domestic conflict of laws provisions to public international law disputes. In matters related to expropriations or administrative decisions rendered against foreigners, the Iran-United States Claims Tribunal generally applies public international law [2433].

For political reasons, Article V offers little guidance regarding the interplay between public and private international law. In the 1980 negotiations there was no agreement on the system of law or conflict of laws rules that would govern the claims. Therefore, the negotiators thought it best to leave the adoption of choice of law rules to the discretion of the Tribunal [2434].

Conscious of this flexibility, the Tribunal has applied Article V liberally [2435]. It referred to Article V as a "novel system for determining applicable law . . . according to this system the Tribunal is not required to apply any particular national or international system" [2436]. However, the Iran-United States Claims Tribunal adjudicators also expressed that they do not enjoy "a discretionary freedom . . . as the Tribunal is given a rather precise indication as to the factors which should

2431. *CMI International Inc.* v. *Ministry of Roads and Transport*, Award No 99-245-2 (27 December 1983), 4 USCTR, p. 263 (1983), 267-268.

2432. Abercrombie and Davies highlight as "the most striking thing about the Tribunal's choice of law jurisprudence" its "paucity", Baker and Davis, *supra* note 2430, p. 178.

2433. Hess, *supra* note 48, p. 120.

2434. Fernández Arroyo and Moïse Mbengue, *supra* note 1450, p. 850.

2435. *Benjamin R Isaiah* v. *Bank Mellat*, Award No 35-219-2 (30 March 1983), 2 IUSCTR, p. 232 (1983), 237.

2436. *Anaconda* v. *Iran, supra* note 2254, p. 199, 232.

guide its decision" [2437]. In the *Mobile Oil Iran* v. *Iran case* (1987), the Tribunal ruled that "in determining the choice of law in a given case, the Tribunal should examine relevant legal principles and rules as well as the specific factual and legal circumstances of the case" [2438].

In its application of the law to a particular dispute, the Iran-United States Claims Tribunal is influenced to a large extent by the nature of the dispute. In particular, the Tribunal has applied relevant public international law norms in several cases. For instance, in *Amoco* v. *Iran* [2439], the Tribunal held that customary international law determined whether just compensation was required for property taken. Likewise, the Tribunal applied customary international law to other public international law issues such as the determination of interest [2440], attribution [2441], succession of rights and obligations [2442] and the nationality of dual nationals [2443].

In addition, determining the applicable law in private claims can be extremely complex. To avoid political sensitivities, the Tribunal bases its decisions on neutral factors such as the contract between the parties or the general principles of law that are common to them [2444]. In *Mobil Oil Iran, Inc.* v. *Iran*, the Tribunal determined that the Agreement should not be governed by the domestic laws of one party, showing its reluctance to place one party's domestic law above the other's [2445].

Judge Lagergren, the first President of the Iran-United States Claims Tribunal, explains the Tribunal's attitude in the following terms: "The Tribunal has avoided applying any national conflict of laws rules, but instead applied general principles of conflict of laws". In the same vein, in *FMC Corporation* v. *Iran* (1987), Judge Bahrami Ahmadi stated that the Tribunal "cannot, as an international forum, apply the choice of law rules of that state in which it has been convened, even in commercial

2437. *Ibid.*

2438. *Mobil Oil Iran, Inc.* v. *Government of the Islamic Republic of Iran*, IUSCT Award No. 311-74/76/81/150-3 (14 July 1987), 16 IUSCTR, p. 3 (1987), para. 72.

2439. *Amoco* v. *Iran*, *supra* note 489, paras. 223, 246-248; similar determinations of applicable law were made in *Shahin Shaine Ebrahimi* v. *Iran*, IUSCT Case No. 560-44/46/47-3 (12 October 1994), 30 IUSCTR, p. 174 (1994); *Nat'l Iranian Oil Co.*, 10 IUSCTR, p. 180 (1986), 184-187.

2440. *McCollough and Company, Inc.* v. *Ministry of Post, Telegraph and Telephone*, 11 IUSCTR, p. 3 (1986), 26-31; *Sylvania Technical Systems Inc.* v. *Iran*, 8 IUSCTR, p. 298 (1985), 320-322.

2441. *Sea-Land Service*, *supra* note 946; *Rankin* v. *Iran*, 17 IUSCTR, p. 135 (1986).

2442. *Oil Field of Texas, Inc.* v. *Iran, National Iranian Oil Company and Oil Service Company of Iran*, 1 IUSCTR, p. 347 (1982), 361.

2443. *Dual Nationality*, *supra* note 2247.

2444. Fernández Arroyo and Moïse Mbengue, *supra* note 1450, p. 851.

2445. *Mobil Oil* v. *Iran*, *supra* note 2438, p. 27.

claims, whereby the two Governments deemed it necessary to lay down rules for selecting the applicable law" [2446].

Further, in *Harnischfeger Corp.* v. *Ministry of Roads and Transportation* [2447], the Tribunal applied general principles of private international law (i.e., the "most significant connection" principle) to conclude that the United States Uniform Commercial Code was the applicable law [2448]. In *Economy Forms Corporation* v. *Iran* [2449], the Tribunal also applied general principles of private international law, considering the "closest connection" or "centre of gravity" a generally accepted principle [2450].

3. Criticisms

The freedom granted to the Iran-United States Claims Tribunal through Article V inspired the development of a creative and eclectic approach (or variety of approximations) to the choice of law, which has been the subject of various criticisms. George Aldrich expressed that it "is impossible to define any coherent set of choice of law rules followed by the Tribunal" [2451]. In a dissenting opinion, Judge Mosk expressed his frustration in the following terms:

> "The majority's opinion in this case . . . might be more comprehensible if it contained a discussion of the source of the law applied. . . . [T]here appears to be choice-of-law issues. Indeed, in the Partial Award, the Tribunal specifically discussed its choice of law with respect to transactions similar to those involved. . . . Yet, in the instant matter, the Tribunal gives little indication that

2446. *FMC Corporation* v. *[Iranian] Ministry of National Defence* et al., IUSCT Case No. 353, Award (12 February 1987), Dissenting Opinion, Judge Ahmadi, at sec. B (1). In *Sapphire* (1963), Arbitrator Cavin followed "the view of some eminent specialists in Private International law [that] since the arbitrator has been invested with his powers as a result of the common intention of the parties he is not bound by the rules of conflict in force at the forum of arbitration". *Sapphire*, *supra* note 1013, Award (15 March 1963, Cavin, sole arb.), p. 169.

2447. *Harnischfeger Corp.* v. *Ministry of Roads and Transportation*, IUSCT Case No. 144-180-3, 7 IUSCTR, p. 90 (1984).

2448. Similar application was made in *Queens Office Tower Assocs.* v. *Iran Nat'l Airline Corp.*, 2 IUSCTR, p. 247 (1983), 250.

2449. *Economy Forms Corporation* v. *Government of the Islamic Republic of Iran et al.*, IUSCT Award No. 55-165–1, 3 IUSCTR, p. 42 (1984).

2450. See Fernández Arroyo and Moïse Mbengue, *supra* note 1450, pp. 852-853.

2451. Aldrich, *supra* note 834, p. 156. "The flexibility of choice of law has impacted the decision-making process of the Tribunal generally. The options of applicable law have been so conflated that it becomes difficult to decide which cases are strictly applying international law", Rajput, *supra* note 1147, pp. 589-615.

it considered the possibility that different laws might apply to different transactions and to different issues involved in the case. One cannot discern from the majority's opinion how the majority derived whatever legal principles it invokes." [2452]

Aniruddha Rajput has further criticized the Tribunal; while claiming to apply general principles of law, it failed to rigorously determine which municipal law principles could be considered as such. Instead, the Tribunal has relied upon secondary material for a comparative study [2453]. In fact, the Tribunal has even acknowledged that it has not referred to laws from a sufficient number of jurisdictions [2454]. Moreover, in some cases, the parties were also unable to provide assistance to the Tribunal in determining whether the principles it was applying could be considered general principles [2455].

Taking these criticisms into account, international arbitrators must proceed with caution when referring to awards rendered by the Iran-United States Claims Tribunal dealing with choice of law issues. When it comes to determining the applicable law under Article V, an arbitrator's discretion is only as good as the arbitrator himself.

K. Applicable law in investment arbitrations under the UNCITRAL Arbitration Law and Rules

In "territorialized" arbitration tribunals operating under UNCITRAL-inspired legislation and rules, the methodology for determining the applicable substantive law is linked to the *lex arbitri* [2456]. When it comes to the enforcement of the awards emerging therefrom, the New

2452. *Harnischfeger* v. *Ministry*, *supra* note 2447, Final Award, Dissenting Opinion of Judge R. M. Mosk (1985), fn. 239, p. 141.

2453. Rajput, *supra* note 1147, p. 609. See also *Housing and Urban Serv Int'l, Inc.* v. *Gov't of the Islamic Republic of Iran*, IUSCT Award No. 201-174-1 (22 November 1985), 9 IUSCTR, p. 313 (1985), p. 332, fn. 22; *Dic* v. *Tehran*, *supra* note 1987; *Morrison-Knudsen Pacific Limited* v. *Ministry of Roads and Transportation (MORT) and Iran*, Award No 143-127-3 (13 July 1984), 7 IUSCTR, p. 54 (1984); *CMI* v. *Ministry of Roads*, *supra* note 2431, p. 270.

2454. *TCSB, Inc.* v. *Islamic Republic of Iran*, IUSCT Award No 114-140-2 (16 March 1984), 5 IUSCTR, p. 160 (1984), 172.

2455. *Harnischfeger* v. *Ministry*, *supra* note 2447, Award No 175-180-3, Dissenting Opinion of Richard M Mosk (26 April 1985), 8 IUSCTR, p. 119, 140-141.

2456. This connection was advanced by Arbitrator Lagergren in the *British Petroleum Exploration* case (although his discussion centered more on pragmatic than legal reasons). *BP* v. *Libya*, *supra* note 1019, Award (10 October 1973), pp. 308-309 (Lagergren, sole arb.). However, in his decision Arbitrator Lagergren made clear that the connection between the applicable law and the *lex arbitri* exists primarily for procedural matters, and not necessarily substantive issues.

York Convention may be applied in arbitrations arising out of public international law since the application of this method is not confined to commercial disputes alone [2457].

Most of the world's relevant jurisdictions are aligned with Article 28 of the UNCITRAL Model Law regarding the applicable substantive law, according to which:

> "(1) The arbitral tribunal shall decide the dispute in accordance with such rules of law as are chosen by the parties as applicable to the substance of the dispute . . . (2) Failing any designation by the parties, the arbitral tribunal shall apply the law determined by the conflict of laws rules which it considers applicable . . . (4) In all cases, the arbitral tribunal shall decide in accordance with the terms of the contract and shall take into account the usages of the trade applicable to the transaction."

This provision was inspired by Article 33 of the 1976 UNCITRAL Arbitration Rules.

These texts refer to "rules of law", precisely within the understanding that this term is broader than simple references to "law" alone, which is typically understood as referring to "domestic law". Where the parties have not specified an applicable law, Article 28 refers to "the law determined by the conflict of laws rules which it considers applicable". This norm replicates Article 33 of the UNCITRAL Arbitration Rules.

The revised provision, now Article 35 of the 2010 UNCITRAL Arbitration Rules (which is identical within the 2013 UNCITRAL Arbitration Rules) [2458], removed the reference to "determined by the conflict of laws rules". Thus, Article 35 of the UNCITRAL Arbitration Rules grants the tribunal greater flexibility in determining the law applicable to the dispute. As noted by Judith Levine, cases where public international law could be applicable also fall within the purview of Article 35 [2459]. The intricacies of Model Law Article 28 and the corresponding Article 35 of the 2010 UNCITRAL Arbitration Rules will be dealt with in further detail in the following chapters.

Several arbitral institutions base their rules on the UNCITRAL Arbitration Rules. The Permanent Court of Arbitration did so in its

---

2457. Hess, *supra* note 48, p. 187.
2458. UNCITRAL Arbitration Rules (with new Art. 1, para. 4, as adopted in 2013), https://uncitral.un.org/sites/uncitral.un.org/files/media-documents/uncitral/en/uncitral-arbitration-rules-2013-e.pdf, accessed 12 May 2022.
2459. Levine, *supra* note 2211, p. 406.

2012 rules, adding certain adjustments in order to reflect the public international law elements that may arise in disputes [2460]. For example, according to the 2012 rules, States that submit their disputes to the PCA waive their immunity from jurisdiction (Art. 1.2) [2461]. Moreover, Article 35 of the PCA Rules mirrors Article 28 of Model Law regarding the law applicable to the substance of the dispute. Article 35 of the PCA Rules first establishes the application of "the rules of law designated by the parties". Where no applicable law has been chosen and both parties are States, the arbitral tribunal shall apply international law [2462]. In disputes between intergovernmental organizations and private parties, the tribunal will

> "have regard both to the rules of the organization concerned and to the law applicable to the agreement or relationship out of or in relation to which the dispute arises, and, where appropriate, to the general principles governing the law of intergovernmental organizations and to the rules of general international law" [2463].

Bilateral investment agreements that do not refer to ICSID arbitration contemplate *ad hoc* arbitration under the UNCITRAL Arbitration Rules, with or without indicating an authority to appoint the arbitrators. In other cases, arbitration may be administered by institutions such as the International Chamber of Commerce or the Stockholm Chamber of Commerce. All these instances will ultimately be governed by the local arbitration law's choice of law provisions, the awards will be subject to scrutiny by domestic courts, and recognition and enforcement will likely be subject to the 1958 New York Convention on Recognition and Enforcement of Foreign Arbitral Awards [2464].

2460. Daly, Goriatcheva and Meighen, *supra* note 809, p. 11.

2461. *Ibid.*, p. 12.

2462. "*(a)* . . . by applying: *i.* International conventions, whether general or particular, establishing rules expressly recognized by the contesting States; *ii.* International custom, as evidence of a general practice accepted as law; *iii.* The general principles of law recognized by civilized nations; *iv.* Judicial and arbitral decisions and the teachings of the most highly qualified publicists of the various nations, as subsidiary means for the determination of rules of law. *(b)* In cases involving only States and intergovernmental organizations, apply the rules of the organization concerned and the law applicable to any agreement or relationship between the parties, and, where appropriate, the general principles governing the law of intergovernmental organizations and the rules of general international law."

2463. In such cases, the arbitral tribunal shall decide in accordance with the terms of the agreement and shall take into account relevant trade usages *(c)*.

2464. Awards rendered pursuant to the rules of the ICSID Additional Facility, which is also provided for in some BITs and in NAFTA Article 1130, are also subject to the New York Convention. See Sacerdoti, *supra* note 641, p. 9.

The choice of dispute resolution forum can influence the choice of law to be applied to the dispute. For instance, Article 26, paragraph 4 of the Energy Charter Treaty (ECT) allows the investor to choose between and among four different arbitral forums: ICSID, the ICSID Additional Facility, UNCITRAL *ad hoc* arbitrations or the Stockholm Chamber of Commerce. Since the arbitral rules of each of these forums has a slightly different provision regarding the choice of law in the absence of party agreement, the investor can directly influence the choice of law to be applied by selecting the forum that most favors his interests [2465].

Prior to the creation of ICSID, older investment agreements continuously made reference to *ad hoc* tribunals, which could be tailormade by the parties themselves [2466]. A discussion of the intricacies of these tribunals and their functioning can be found in the previous chapter.

L. Determining the applicable law under different treaties

Three types of scenarios arise in investment arbitration. In the first scenario, arbitration proceedings conducted under the ICSID rules arise from contracts between investors and the host State (or the entities under the host State), where Article 42 applies to deal with the applicable substantive law. This scenario is mostly historical, with exceptions such as the *Caratube* and *Perenco Ecuador Ltd.* cases [2467].

The second scenario – also mainly of historical importance – has recently arisen in the *Pac Rim* v. *El Salvador* case [2468]. In contrast to the first scenario, it refers to ICSID arbitrations that arise out of national protection legislation. States can express their consent to arbitration

2465. "Going even further, if the investor were not happy with the progress of the arbitral proceedings and the law applied under its rules, he could bring a local court action or contractual arbitration under the ECT, and later bring an application for arbitration pursuant to Article 26 of the ECT (this action would be brought notwithstanding the provisions of Art. II.3 United Nations Convention on the Recognition and Enforcement of Foreign Arbitral Awards of 10 June 1958)", Kreindler, *supra* note 2039, pp. 408-409. "It is indeed clear from Article 26 of the ECT that only disputes of an international character are subject to the ECT settlement mechanism provided for in the Treaty. When it comes to disputes that may arise between contracting parties concerning the application or interpretation of the Treaty, Article 27 provides that disputes that are not amicably settled may be submitted to an ad hoc tribunal constituted according to ECT Article 27 (3)", Alvarez, *supra* note 26, p. 427.

2466. Sornarajah, *supra* note 29, p. 286.

2467. *Caratube* v. *Kazakhstan*, *supra* note 16, para. 290; *Perenco Ecuador Ltd.*, *supra* note 631, Remaining Issues of Jurisdiction and on Liability (12 September 2014). See Bischoff, *supra* note 15, p. 748.

2468. *Pac Rim* v. *El Salvador*, *supra* note 41, Award (14 October 2016), para. 5.62.

in municipal laws under the ICSID Convention (Art. 25, para. 1). In contrast to contractual cases, the offer to arbitrate in the second scenario is potentially directed at an unlimited number of investors. In these types of disputes, the ICSID Convention will govern the applicable law, but the law of the host State will also maintain its relevance [2469].

The first two scenarios are rooted in the procedural approach to international arbitration; that is, dispute settlement provisions in the contract or in national laws that refer to the ICSID Arbitration Rules.

The third scenario refers to a class of cases that emerge from investment treaties. These cases may be decided under the ICSID Arbitration Rules or under other applicable commercial arbitration rules [2470]. Interesting questions often arise within these cases since the investment treaties themselves often contain their own applicable law provisions outside of the arbitration rules themselves.

Many of these treaties refer only to "international law" as the applicable law. This is the case, for instance, with Article 1131 of NAFTA (currently Annex 14.D.3 of the USMCA), and Article 26, paragraph 6 of the ECT [2471].

2469. Bischoff, *supra* note 15, p. 749.
2470. *Ibid.*, pp. 749-750.
2471. *Ibid.*, p. 750.

CHAPTER XVII

CHOICE OF LAW IN INVESTMENT CLAIMS

A. Party autonomy in private international law

In domestic law, party autonomy relates to individuals' ability to freely determine the content of their relationship within the limits of the local legal system. In private international law, party autonomy refers to the parties' power to choose the law applicable to their relationship. In this context, party autonomy gives the parties the option to select this law *ex ante*, instead of leaving this power to the adjudicator *ex post*. In this regard, party autonomy is comparable to the technique of establishing the eventual damages payable pursuant to a penalty clause beforehand [2472].

Party autonomy has become entrenched in modern private international law and promises further consolidation within the discipline in the coming years [2473]. For this reason, Erik Jayme argues that there has been an "irresistible extension" of party autonomy in the field [2474]. The principle of party autonomy is extremely attractive. There is no one better suited than the parties to determine the law that will govern their relationship; it is preferable for them to determine the parameters of their contract themselves, rather than granting the legislator this power beforehand or the adjudicator this authority after a dispute has arisen. Party autonomy grants the parties many benefits [2475], including legal certainty [2476].

While party autonomy is perhaps the most widely accepted principle in contemporary private international law, debates continue regarding

---

2472. A vindication of Weber's theory of the "calculability of risk" for contractual relationships, Kahn-Freund, *supra* note 1256, p. 196.

2473. Fernández Arroyo, *supra* note 1203, p. 92. Conflicts method is excluded, since the matter is now how to interpret the exact will of the contracting parties. V. Heuzé, *La réglementation française des contrats internationaux, Étude critique des méthodes*, Lille, GLN Editions, 1990, p. 14.

2474. See Jayme, *supra* note 894, p. 148.

2475. It protects legitimate expectations, generates efficiency by reducing costs of eventual dispute resolution and facilitates transborder transactions. See http://www.hcch.net/upload/wop/contracts_2012pd01e.pdf, accessed 13 May 2022, p. 13.

2476. Visher, *supra* note 1200, p. 126, pp. 132 and following. See also, more recently, A. L. Calvo Caravaca, "Fundamentos Teóricos de la Autonomía de la Voluntad en los Contratos Internacionales", *Revista Jurídica del Notariado*, No. 111 (July-December 2020), p. 169. See also Basedow, *supra* note 1196, p. 8.

its modalities, parameters and limitations. Already in the 1977 *Texaco* v. *Libya* case, the Tribunal wrote that this principle appears "as universally accepted, even though it may not always have the same meaning or the same scope" [2477].

Debates regarding party autonomy vary from the method of choice – which can be explicit or tacit – of the applicable law; whether a connection is required between the selected law and the domestic laws of the State of the parties to the contract; whether non-contractual issues can be included in the choice of law; which State, if any, can impose limitations on the parties' selection; and whether non-State rules can be chosen [2478]. These matters will be addressed in this chapter.

B. Evolution

Even though examples of party autonomy exist throughout the ages [2479], the work of sixteenth-century French jurist Charles Dumoulin contains the modern origins of the principle [2480]. When criticizing the law of the execution of the contract *(lex loci contractus)*, Dumoulin argued that determining the parties' choice of applicable law was the most important exercise in contract interpretation [2481].

Nineteenth-century European codifications do not include this principle, but party autonomy was present in the writing of the French Jean-Jacques Foelix, the German Friedrich Carl von Savigny and the Italian Pasquale Stanislao Mancini. The principle became integrated into French case law between 1840 to 1874, before it was finally formalized in the 1910 Cour de cassation decision in *American Trading Company* v. *Québec Steamship Company Limited* [2482]. In Germany, party autonomy is rooted in Article 2 (1) of the Constitution and is also included in Section 1051 of the German Code of Civil Procedure

2477. *Texaco* v. *Libya*, *supra* note 119, Award (9 January 1977), para. 16. See also *Liamco*, *supra* note 946, Award (12 April 1977).

2478. S. C. Symeonides, "Party Autonomy in Rome I and II From a Comparative Perspective", K. Boele-Woelki, T. Einhorn, D. Girsberger and S. Symeonides (eds.), *Convergence and Divergence in Private International Law: Liber Amicorum Kurt Siehr*, The Hague, Eleven International, 2010, pp. 514-515.

2479. P. Borchers traces the origins to Hellenic Egypt (120-118 CE), in Borchers, *supra* note 1226, p. 152. Juenger also notes important medieval precedents, in Juenger, *supra* note 1201, p. 84 and p. 189.

2480. Fawcett and North, *supra* note 1218, p. 20.

2481. Loussouarn, Bourel and Vareilles-Sommières, *supra* note 1203, p. 91. See also Audit, *supra* note 1202, p. 66.

2482. *American Trading Company* v. *Quebec Steamship Company*, Cour de cassation, 5 December 1910.

(ZPO). Article 25 of the Italian Civil Code recognizes the principle of party autonomy, as well as Article 1511 of the French Code of Civil Procedure, Article 1511 and Article 187 (1) of the Swiss Federal Act on Private International Law of 1987 [2483], and several other laws across continents [2484].

In England, adjudicators did not apply foreign law until the mid-nineteenth century. This changed in 1865 with the adoption of the "proper law" formula, which refers to the law that the parties intended to apply [2485]. As stated by Lord Wright before the English Privy Council in the 1939 *Vita Food Prods. Inc.* v. *Unus Shipping Co. Ltd.* case:

> "[W]here there is an express statement by the parties of their intention to select the law of the contract, it is difficult to see what qualifications are possible, provided the intention expressed is bona fide and legal, and provided there is no reason for avoiding the choice on the ground of public policy." [2486]

In the United States, party autonomy had been recognized since 1825 before ultimately being rejected in the first Restatement of Conflict of Laws of 1934 despite court decisions to the contrary. Finally, the second Restatement of Conflict of Laws of 1971 reintegrated the principle via Article 187 (2) [2487], as did the Uniform Commercial Code (UCC) [2488].

2483. See in this regard the Judgment of 13 May 2005, Geneva Cour de Justice, in *ASA Bulletin*, Vol. 24 (2006), p. 128, 132-33.

2484. See *infra* note 2519.

2485. L. Collins (ed.), *Dicey, Morris and Collins on The Conflict of Laws*, 15th ed., London, Sweet & Maxwell, 2012, para. 32-006 and Supp. 2019.

2486. *Vita Food Prods. Inc.* v. *Unus Shipping Co. Ltd.*, AC 277 (English Privy Council), 1939, p. 290. Morse, *supra* note 1303, p. 60. Other cases reaffirmed the principle of party autonomy, such as *R.* v. *International Trustee for the Protection of Bondholders, AG* (1937) and *Assunzione* (1954), referred to in R. H. Graverson, *Comparative Conflict of Laws: Selected Essays*, Vol. 1, Amsterdam, North-Holland, 1977, pp. 289-290. Lord Reid expressed the following in *Whitworth St. Estates (Manchester) Ltd.* v. *James Miller & Partners Ltd.*, AC 583, 603 (House of Lords), 1970: "Parties are entitled to agree what is to be the proper law of their contract. . . . There have been from time to time suggestions that parties ought not to be so entitled, but in my view there is no doubt that they are entitled to make such an agreement, and I see no good reason why, subject it may be to some limitations, they should not be so entitled."

2487. However, the status of the principle across the United States is not as simple as it might appear. The rules of the First Restatement continue to be applied in a number of states. Even when, in those domestic states in which the party autonomy rules of the Second Restatement have been adopted, their precise application requires an understanding of First Restatement methods. In addition, for sales of goods not governed by the CISG, Article 2 of the UCC, as supplemented by Article 1 thereof, will apply. Under the UCC, the parties are free to choose the domestic state or sovereign nation whose laws will govern their transaction, as long as the transaction bears a reasonable relation to the state or country selected (UCC para. 1-301 *(a)*).

2488. The original version of UCC para. 1-105 (1), in effect in most US states, provides that "when a transaction bears a reasonable relationship to this state and also

Around the same time, the US Supreme Court recognized the principle of party autonomy in the 1972 *Bremen* v. *Zapata* case [2489] and the 1974 *Scherk* v. *Alberto-Culver Co.* case [2490]. As argued by Georges Delaume, the US Supreme Court made a significant contribution to the harmonious regulation of international transactions in these cases, liberating international transactions from many of the domestic constraints in place at the time [2491]. The Court specifically reaffirmed party autonomy in the arbitral context in the 1985 *Mitsubishi Motors Corporation* v. *Soler Chrysler-Plymouth Inc.* case [2492].

As early as the nineteenth century, the party autonomy principle experienced significant resistance in other regions such as Latin America [2493], in countries like Brazil, Uruguay and Paraguay [2494]. Within some jurisdictions that did not recognize "foreign" dispute resolution mechanisms or laws, the reasoning of the Calvo and Drago Doctrines was relied upon until ultimately being abandoned in the 1980s [2495].

---

to another state or nation the parties may agree that the law of either this state or of such other state or nation shall govern their rights and duties". A recent revision of the UCC adopted a more "pro-enforcement" approach to choice of law clauses, largely deleting the so-called "reasonable relationship" requirement (contained in the original text). See US UCC para. 1-105 (1) (1995), superseded by US UCC para. 1-301 (2001).

2489. *The Bremen* v. *Zapata Offshore Co.*, 407 US 1, 92 S.Ct. 1907, 1972. That case, however, dealt specifically with selection of forum, not choice of law. As the case has had "negative treatment" by some, its authority has been questioned.

2490. The decision holds that party autonomy is "an almost indispensable precondition to achievement of the orderliness and predictability essential to any business transaction" (*Scherk* v. *Alberto-Culver Co.*, 417 US 506 (1974), 516).

2491. G. R. Delaume, "What is an International Contract, An American and a Gallic Dilemma", *International & Comparative Law Quarterly*, Vol. 28, No. 2 (1979), pp. 258-266. In effect, in *Zapata* (1972) and *Scherk* (1974), the Court emphasized that they were dealing with experimented and sophisticated parties, who were negotiating in equal positions.

2492. Other known cases of appeals courts are the following: *Karaha Bodas Co. LLC* v. *Perusahaan Pertambangan Minyak Dan Gas Bumi Negara*, 500 F.3d 111 (2d Cir. 2007); *Cohen* v. *Chase Bank NA*, 679 F.Supp.2d 582, 591 (DNJ 2010); *Nurettin Mayakan* v. *Carnival Corp.*, 721 F.Supp.2d 1201 (MD Fla. 2010); *Tierra Right of Way Servs. Ltd.* v. *Abengoa Solar Inc.*, 2011 WL 2292007 (D. Ariz.).

2493. See an account on the matter in Fresnedo de Aguirre, *supra* note 1277. More recently, see Grigera Naón, *supra* note 212, pp. 127-175.

2494. See the discussion in Moreno Rodríguez, *supra* note 1276. See also M. M. Albornoz, "Choice of Law in International Contracts in Latin American Legal Systems", *Journal of Private International Law*, Vol. 6, No. 1 (2010), p. 58. See also D. Hargaín and G. Mihali, *Régimen Jurídico de la Contratación Mercantil Internacional en el MERCOSUR*, B. de F., Buenos Aires, cited in C. Esplugues Mota and D. Hargaín (eds.), *Derecho del comercio internacional: Mercosur-Unión Europea*, Madrid, Editorial Reus; Montevideo, Editorial B de F, 2005, p. 304.

2495. Born, *supra* note 2273, p. 2883. For instance, in the Interim Award in ICC Case No. 10947, *supra* note 786, p. 318, it was stated: "The influence of the Calvo Doctrine which refers to the sovereignty of states and that they are not to abide by the jurisdiction of other sovereign states [was a] historical mistake." See also *Ebrahimi* v. *Iran*, *supra* note 2439, p. 170; *First Travel Corp.* v. *Iran*, IUSCT Case No. 206-34-1, Award (3 December 1985), 12 YB Comm. Arb. (1987), p. 257.

Resistance against party autonomy has been gradually reversing in Latin American jurisdictions, signaled by its wide acceptance in the arbitration laws of recent decades throughout the region. Other legal reforms followed this same path. In Paraguay, for instance, scholarly opinions were divided regarding the solution adopted by the Civil Code until 2013, when the Supreme Court decided to accept the principle of party autonomy [2496]. In 2015, Paraguay finally enacted its Law No. 5393 on the "Law Applicable to International Contracts" [2497], which draws upon the Hague Principles and the Mexico Convention and their ample acceptance of party autonomy [2498]. Uruguay has also recently modified Article 2399 of the Appendix to its Civil Code, and in November 2020 adopted the General Law on Private International Law (Law 19.920), which recognizes the principle of party autonomy [2499].

In Brazil, the Introductory Law to the Norms of Brazilian Law (LINDB) currently contains no express provision on this matter [2500]. Brazilian judicial decisions have been contradictory, with some accepting party autonomy and others rejecting it [2501]. There have been efforts over the past few years to introduce changes to the Brazilian system. The latest proposal to amend the LINDB (Bill 4.905) is, at the time of writing, at an impasse before Congress. This amendment would introduce a new Article 9, the first paragraph of which would acknowledge party autonomy [2502]. However, Brazilian law currently

---

2496. Acuerdo and Sentencia No. 82, 21 March 2013, in *Reconstitución del Expte. Hans Werner Bentz c. Cartones Yaguareté SA s/Incumplimiento de contrato*. The Court cited expressly the author of this contribution. See J. A. Moreno Rodríguez (ed.), *Derecho internacional privado y Derecho de la integración, Libro homenaje a Roberto Ruíz Díaz Labrano*, Asunción, CEDEP, 2013, p. 381.

2497. See https://www.bacn.gov.py/leyes-paraguayas/4553/ley-n-5393-sobre-el-derecho-aplicable-a-los-contratos-internacionales, accessed 13 May 2022.

2498. The law has nineteen articles. Articles 1 to 10 and Articles 13 and 14 on choice of law almost entirely reproduce the Hague Principles. See Moreno Rodríguez, *supra* note 1329.

2499. See its openness toward the party autonomy and non-State law in E. Florio de León, "The New Uruguayan Private International Law: An Open Door to Party Autonomy in International Contracts", *Uniform Law Review*, Vol. 26, No. 1 (2021), pp. 4-10.

2500. See, for instance, N. de Araújo (ed.), *Contratos Internacionais*, 4th ed., Rio de Janeiro, Renovar, 2009, pp. 89-90.

2501. It has been accepted, for example, in the following: TJsP, DJe 30 November 2011, Apel. Cív. 9066155-90.2004.8.26.0000; TJSP, j. 06 June 2008, Apel. Cív. 9202485-89.2007.8.26.0000; and rejected in others, for example: TJSP, j. 19 February 2016, Apel. Cív. 2111792-03.2015.8.26.0000; TJsP, DJe 09 January 2012, Apel. Cív. 0125708-85.2008.8.26.0000.

2502. Article 9: "The international contract between professionals, businessmen and traders is governed by the law chosen by the parties, and the agreement of the parties recognizes party autonomy in arbitration or whenever the CISG – which was ratified and is in force in Brazil – is applied.

C. Party autonomy in private international law instruments

Jayme notes that party autonomy underlies in several charters and instruments setting out fundamental international rights, such as Article 29, paragraph 1, of the Universal Declaration of Human Rights, which holds that "[e]veryone has duties to the community in which alone the free and full development of his personality is possible" [2503].

In its 1991 session in Basel, the International Law Institute formulated a resolution regarding party autonomy. In its Article 2, paragraph 1, the resolution specified that the parties are free to determine the law applicable to their contract. Meanwhile, Article 3, paragraph 1, establishes that the law applicable to the contract derives from the parties' consent [2504].

The principle of party autonomy has been incorporated within important private international law treaties such as the 1955 Hague Convention on the Law Applicable to International Sale of Goods, the Hague Convention of 1978 on the Law Applicable to Agency, the 1986 Hague Convention on the Law Applicable to Contracts for the International Sale of Goods, and various other universal, continental and regional instruments.

In Europe, Article 3 of the 1980 Rome Convention recognizes party autonomy. Article 3 of the European Union Regulation on the Law Applicable to Contractual Obligations, known as Rome I, also recognizes this principle. In the Americas, the 1994 Mexico Convention recognizes party autonomy in its Article 7, as does the recent OAS Guide on the Applicable Law to International Commercial Contracts [2505].

Party autonomy is considered the *leitmotif* of the Hague Principles [2506] and can be found in its Article 2. This coincides with the near-universal recognition of the principle as expressed in responses to questionnaires

---

on this choice must be express. 1. The choice must refer to the entire contract, but no connection between the law chosen and the parties or the transaction is required."

2503. See Jayme, *supra* note 894, p. 147.

2504. Text available at https://www.idi-iil.org/app/uploads/2017/06/1991_bal_02_en.pdf, accessed 13 May 2022.

2505. See OAS Guide, *supra* note 1284.

2506. Documentavailableathttp://www.hcch.net/upload/wop/contracts_2012pd01e.pdf, accessed 13 May 2022, p. 5.

submitted by the Hague Conference in 2007 [2507]. As will be seen further below, these principles can be very useful in clarifying several issues regarding party autonomy and its complexities.

D. Party autonomy in arbitration

A 1992 ICC award stated that the arbitrator's primary duty is to base his decision on the law chosen by the parties [2508]. Much earlier, in the 1958 *Saudi Arabia* v. *American Oil Company* case, the Arbitral Tribunal followed the 1929 PCIJ decision in a renowned case of loans to Brazil. The Tribunal reaffirmed the private international law principle that requires arbitrators to first apply the law that has been expressly selected by the parties [2509]. Other arbitral decisions relating to natural resources concessions also reached a similar conclusion [2510]. One tribunal, for instance, held that

> "the arbitrator has no power to substitute his own choice to that of the parties, as soon as there exists an expressed, clear and unambiguous choice, and no sufficient reason has been put forward to refuse effects to such a choice" [2511].

2507. Preliminary Document No. 5 of the Hague Conference Secretariat, https://assets.hcch.net/docs/cb1ca59e-5e69-4a86-b9f1-e929075fdef2.pdf, accessed 13 May 2022, p. 4.

2508. ICC Award No. 6474/1992, 25 YB Comm. Arb. (2000), p. 283. The Indian Supreme Court stated that "in international commercial arbitrations parties are at liberty to choose, expressly or by necessary implication, the law and the procedure to be made applicable" (*Bhatia Int'l* v. *Bulk Trading SA*, 4 SCC 105, para. 25 (Indian S.Ct.), 2002). In turn, a Singapore Court of Appeals expressed the following: "The need to respect party autonomy . . . in deciding . . . the substantive law to govern the contract, has been accepted as the cornerstone underlying judicial non-intervention in arbitration" (*Tjong Very Sumito* v. *Antig Invs. Pte Ltd.*, (2009) SGCA 41, para. 28 (Singapore Ct. App.)). See also Final Award in ICC Case No. 18203, 41 YB Comm. Arb. (2016), p. 276, 280; Interim Awards and Final Award in ICC Case No. 4145 (1984), 12 YB Comm. Arb. (1987), p. 97, 101.

2509. Giuliano and Lagarde, *supra* note 1290, pp. 138 ff.

2510. *Sapphire* (1963), *supra* note 1013; *Texaco* v. *Libya* (1977), *supra* note 119. See also Final Award in ICC Case No. 18203, 41 YB Comm. Arb. (2013), p. 276, 280; *Hoechst GmbH* v. *Genentech, Inc.*, Third Partial Award in ICC Case No. 15900/JHN/GFG (5 September 2012); Final Award in ICC Case No. 13450, in J.-J. Arnaldez, Y. Derains and D. Hascher (eds.), *Collection of ICC Arbitral Awards 2012-2015*, The Hague, Kluwer Law International / ICC Publishing, 2019, p. 725, 727; Final Award in ICC Case No. 8938, 24 YB Comm. Arb. (1999), p. 174; *Korean Buyer*, Interim Award, *supra* note 1560, p. 131; Final Award in ICC Case No. 6379, 17 YB Comm. Arb. (1992), p. 212; Award in ICC Case No. 1581, *ICC Ct. Bull.*, Vol. 6, No. 1 (1995), p. 14, 15; Award in ICC Case No. 1512/1971, 1 YB Comm. Arb. (1976), p. 128, 130; CRCICA Case No. 20/1990, Award (22 April 1992), 1 AACRCICA, p. 29 (2000); Final Award in *German Coffee Association* case of 28 September 1992, 19 YB Comm. Arb. (1994), p. 48; *HimpurnaCal. Energy Ltd.* v. *PT (Persero) Perusahaan Listruik Negara*, Final Award in *Ad Hoc* Case of 4 May 1999, 25 YB Comm. Arb. (2000), p. 13, 23-24.

2511. Award in ICC 1512, *supra* note 1510, p. 130.

Arbitration is a creature of party autonomy. Nowadays, in most jurisdictions, parties can have their disputes settled through arbitration and may select the applicable substantive law to govern their relationship [2512]. Recent statistics show that commercial arbitration agreements typically include a choice of substantive law provision as well [2513].

Determining the applicable law does not, in itself, resolve many of the issues that may arise in this regard [2514]. Private international law can be of great assistance in this regard, as will be discussed throughout this chapter.

E. Party autonomy in arbitral instruments

The principle of party autonomy underlies the 1958 New York Convention, the 1975 Inter-American Panama International Commercial Arbitration Convention and the 1979 Inter-American Convention on Extraterritorial Validity of Foreign Judgments and Arbitral Awards [2515]. Although none of these instruments directly address the question of the applicable law, party autonomy is recognized when it comes to the value of the arbitral clause, the arbitral process itself and the recognition of the award. It is further understood, or may be inferred, that clauses

2512. "In court litigation, party autonomy is not universally accepted, contrasting with its wide acceptance in arbitration. As noted by Bermann, herein lies a fundamental difference between Private International Law in the litigation and arbitration settings", G. A. Bermann, *International Arbitration and Private International Law*, Leiden, Nijhoff, 2017, p. 353.

2513. Born, *supra* note 2273, p. 2876. Choice of law clauses were included in substantive contractual provisions in 95 percent of all ICC cases registered in 2020. These covered the laws of 127 different nations, states, provinces and territories – the highest number to date. The most frequently selected *lex contractus* was English law with 122 cases (13 percent of all cases registered), the laws of a US state (104 cases), followed by Swiss law (66 cases), French law (56 cases) and the laws of Brazil (42 cases). Of the contracts, 2 percent included a reference to rules or instruments other than national laws, such as the CISG, the UNIDROIT Principles and the ICC Incoterms. ICC Dispute Resolution 2020 Statistics, International Chamber of Commerce, 2021, https://iccwbo.org/publication/icc-dispute-resolution-statistics-2020/, accessed 13 May 2022), p. 17.

2514. L. Silberman and F. Ferrari observe that even when the parties have chosen the applicable law in the contract, that choice may raise issues that arbitrators will have to address that cannot be dealt with by simply applying the law chosen, in "Getting to the Law Applicable to the Merits in International Arbitration and the Consequences of Getting it Wrong", in F. Ferrari and S. Kröll (eds.), *Conflict of Laws in International Commercial Arbitration*, New York, NYU Center for Transnational Litigation and Commercial Law / Juris, 2019, p. 374.

2515. Inter-American Convention on Extraterritorial Validity of Foreign Judgments and Arbitral Awards, adopted at Montevideo at CIDIP-II, signed 8 May 1979 and entered into force 14 June 1980.

relating to the choice of law applicable to the merits of the matter must also be respected [2516].

The 1961 European Convention on International Commercial Arbitration expressly recognizes party autonomy, providing in Article VII that "the parties shall be free to determine, by agreement, the law to be applied by the arbitrators to the substance of the dispute" [2517]. Similarly, MERCOSUR's Arbitral Agreement of 1998 states in Article 10 that "the parties may choose the law that is to apply in resolving the controversy" [2518].

F. Party autonomy in arbitration laws and rules

The UNCITRAL Model Law includes the principle of party autonomy in Article 28 (1). Domestic laws on arbitration in a number of States worldwide equally show an openness to party autonomy [2519]. This widespread acceptance can also be observed in several arbitration rules. For example, the principle is contemplated in Article 33 of the 1976 version (Art. 35 as revised in 2010 and 2013) of the UNCITRAL Arbitration Rules, which has served as inspiration for diverse arbitration rules worldwide [2520], among them Article 35 (1) of the PCA Rules [2521].

2516. M. B. Noodt Taquela, "El derecho aplicable por los árbitros al fondo del asunto", in J. C. Rivera and D. P. Fernández Arroyo (eds.), *Contratos y Arbitraje en la Era Global*, Asunción, CEDEP/ASADIP, 2012, p. 87.

2517. European Convention on International Commercial Arbitration, concluded 21 April 1961 and entered into force 7 January 1964, https://www.arbitrationindia.com/geneva_convention_1961.html, accessed 13 May 2022.

2518. *Acuerdo Sobre Arbitraje Comercial Internacional del MERCOSUR*, Decision by MERCOSUR Council No. 03/98 of 23 July 1998, http://www.sice.oas.org/Trade/MRCSRS/Decisions/dec0398.asp, accessed 13 May 2022.

2519. Such as Articles 1478 and 1511 of the Code de Procédure Civile Français; Sections 1051, 1 and 4 of the German Code of Civil Procedure (ZPO); Article 46 (1) *(a)* of the English Arbitration Act of 1996; Article 187 of the Swiss Private International Law Act of 1987; Article 1054 (2) of the Netherlands Code of Civil Procedure; para. 406 (1) of the Austrian ZPO, Article 36 (1) of the Japanese Arbitration Law; Schedule 1, Article 28 (1) of the Singapore International Arbitration Act; Article 1710 (1) of the Belgian Judicial Code; para. 48 (1) of the Swedish Arbitration Act; Article 28 (1) of Russian International Arbitration Law; Article 34 (2) Spanish Arbitration Act; Article 28 (1) of the Chilean Arbitration Law; Article 2 of the Brazilian Arbitration Law; and many others.

2520. Várady, Barceló III and von Mehren, *supra* note 2102, p. 70. Examples are Article 21 (1) of the 2017 ICC Rules; Article 31 (1) of the 2016 SIAC Rules; Article 31 (1) of the 2014 ICDR Rules; Article 22 (3) of the 2020 LCIA Rules; Article 33 (1) of the 2012 Swiss Rules; Article 36 (1) of the 2018 HKIAC Rules; Article 24 (1) of the 2018 DIS Rules; Article 27 (1) of the 2018 VIAC Rules; and Article. 61 *(a)* of the 2020 WIPO Rules.

2521. In the PCA Rules, party autonomy can lead to selection among various sources of international law, transnational principles such as those set out in the UNIDROIT Principles, and different combinations of rules. See Daly, Goriatcheva and Meighen, *supra* note 809, p. 136.

G. Party autonomy and the legitimate expectations of the parties

Several writings insist upon the necessity of protecting the parties' legitimate expectations [2522]. According to Yves Derains, the expression should not be confused with the will of the parties. First, the parties' legitimate expectations do not always manifest themselves expressly. Second, during precontractual negotiations the parties may have opposing viewpoints regarding the applicable law that they do not specify in the contract. In addition, the express or implied choice of law does not exclude the possibility that in certain cases, the arbitrator can fairly be expected to consider a rule that the parties did not specify or had expressly excluded. This scenario is most likely to occur in matters related to public policy [2523].

However, the principle of reasonable expectations demands that the parties not be met with obligations imposed by the law that are unreasonable, excessive or unforeseeable [2524].

The principle of *favor validitatis* is also closely linked to this principle since the parties should reasonably expect that an act freely entered into by them will give rise to legal consequences. In situations in which the choice of law cannot be implied with reasonable certainty, the *favor validitatis* principle should be the starting point [2525]. This matter will be again addressed at the end of this chapter.

H. Party autonomy in investment arbitration

In the 1982 *Aminoil* decision, it was stated that party autonomy looms large in investment arbitration. In that case, the Tribunal did not find it necessary to base the principle of party autonomy on a specific legal system. According to Ole Spiermann, this decision implies that party autonomy has reached a non-controversial, or universal, recognition within the international investment arbitration field [2526].

2522. Jayme, *supra* note 894, p. 204, who in turn cites Pierre Lagarde. In fact, the justification of private international law *(conflict of laws)*, as pointed out by Dicey and Morris, is to protect legitimate expectations of parties. Dicey and Morris, *supra* note 1198, p. 5.

2523. Derains, *supra* note 1431, p. 2.

2524. P. E. Nygh, "The Reasonable Expectations of the Parties as a Guide to the Choice of Law in Contract and in Tort", *Recueil des cours*, Vol. 251 (1995), pp. 295-296, p. 343.

2525. "It is argued that the Rule of Validation should be the basic principle where the parties have not made an express choice. Where they have made an express choice leading to invalidity, then there is no reasonable ground against invalidity. Where the choice is implied, the conclusion that an invalidating law was intended should be avoided" (*ibid.*, p. 343).

2526. Spiermann, *supra* note 979, pp. 101-102.

In foreign investment claims, when it comes to the motives for selecting a particular legal system, the parties may be driven by the desire to achieve certainty of the law governing their relationship or may wish to select a law familiar to them or one with appropriate protection of the rights of aliens [2527].

The law most closely connected will presumably be the most practical choice of applicable law [2528] as it helps achieve greater legal predictability and limits the opportunity for forum shopping [2529]. Moreover, a State party to an investment relationship may insist on applying its own domestic law as a matter of principle or national prestige [2530].

The choice of the applicable law may range from the law of the host State to the choice of international law, to the exclusion of domestic law [2531]. Between these two extremes, general principles of law, or even sometimes "rules of natural justice or equity", may be chosen by the parties [2532]. Some commentary even advocates for the application of the so-called "transnational law" or non-State law [2533]. This terminology, and its nuances, has already been dealt with in Chapter XI.

The principle of party autonomy is enshrined in the ICSID Convention. It states that the tribunal "shall decide a dispute in accordance with such rules of law as may be agreed by the parties" (Art. 42). Only in the absence of a choice of law may the tribunals resort to the second sentence of Article 42 (1) and apply the law of the host State (including its conflict of laws rules) and "such rules of international law as may be applicable" [2534].

Freedom of choice was a recurrent theme in the *travaux préparatoires* of the ICSID Convention [2535], as many discussions occurred relating to the possibility that this liberty might be exploited to the advantage of the foreign investor [2536]. Nonetheless, the Convention finally recognized the principle in its Article 42 (1) [2537]. By giving priority to the rules of

2527. Schreuer *et al.*, *supra* note 102, p. 557, para. 21.

2528. Bjorklund and Vanhonnaeker, *supra* note 13, p. 352. See also Schreuer *et al.*, *supra* note 102, p. 557, p. 557.

2529. Bischoff, *supra* note 15, p. 747.

2530. Schreuer *et al.*, *supra* note 102, p. 557, p. 557.

2531. Dolzer and Schreuer, *supra* note 382, pp. 81-82.

2532. *Ibid.*, pp. 81-82.

2533. See Igbokwe, *supra* note 2412, pp. 103 *et seq*.

2534. Bjorklund and Vanhonnaeker, *supra* note 13, p. 352.

2535. See *History of the ICSID Convention*, *supra* note 1078, I, pp. 190-192.

2536. Schreuer *et al.*, *supra* note 102, p. 557, p. 557.

2537. Thus, Aron Broches states that "[t]he first sentence is intended to settle one of the more difficult questions in international arbitration, namely that of the freedom of

law adopted by the parties, the drafters of the Convention were faithful to their general system of granting the will or consent of the parties a primary role in the functioning of the arbitration [2538].

Even though the Iran-United States Claims Settlement Declaration does not make explicit reference to party autonomy, Article V alludes to "choice of law rules" and "contract provisions" and leads to the interpretation that choice of law agreements must be respected, particularly since party autonomy is also a general principle of international law [2539]. As stated in the 1986 *Anaconda* v. *Iran* case, the tribunal is "required to take seriously into consideration the pertinent contractual choice of law rules" [2540].

Territorialized arbitral tribunals will, in turn, take into account provisions of their arbitral laws, a great number of which recognize party autonomy in line with the UNCITRAL Model Law.

I. Choice of law mechanisms in investment arbitration

1. Choice of law in the international investment contract

The parties can choose the applicable substantive law in their investment contracts, as it is many times the case.

In this regard, ICSID even provides a model clause [2541]. According to its Explanatory Comments, parties may refer to national law, international law, a combination of the two, or a law frozen in time or subject to certain modifications [2542]. Earlier versions specifically

---

the parties to choose the law applicable to the merits of the dispute", in Broches, *supra* note 2161, p. 389.

2538. These views coincide with those of the drafters of the European Convention on International Commercial Arbitration of 21 April 1961 and the Hague Convention on the Law Applicable to International Sales of Goods, which was signed in 1955 and went into effect in 1964. See Kahn, *supra* note 33, pp. 6-7.

2539. See A. F. M. Maniruzzaman, "State Contracts in Contemporary International Law: Monist versus Dualist Controversies", *European Journal International Law*, Vol. 12, No. 2 (2001), p. 322. Cited in Kjos, *supra* note 2296, p. 69.

2540. *Anaconda* v. *Iran*, *supra* note 2254, Interlocutory Award (10 December 1986), para. 131. See also *FMC* v. *Ministry of National Defence*, *supra* note 2446, fn. 9, Award, Dissenting Opinion of Judge Ahmadi, at sec. B.1.

2541. The 1993 ICSID Model Clauses state the following in regard to the "Specification of System of Law" (Clause 10): "Any Arbitral Tribunal constituted pursuant to this agreement shall apply *specification of system of law* [as in force on the date on which this agreement is signed] [subject to the following modifications . . .]". 4 *ICSID Reports*, p. 364. See more in http://icsidfiles.worldbank.org/icsid/icsid/staticfiles/model-clauses-en/13.htm#a, accessed 1 September 2022.

2542. 1981 Model Clauses, Clause XVII, 1 *ICSID Reports*, p. 206.

referred to international law and a formula according to which the parties could exclude the application of a particular legal system [2543].

Most of the ICSID cases that arose in its first twenty years of operation involved alleged breaches of investment contracts. In about half of them, the parties had determined the law to be applied to their disputes and referred, with a few exceptions, to the law of the State party to the claim. This was the case, for instance, in *Mobil* v. *New Zealand* [2544].

In situations like these, when the State party was a developing nation, the choice of law "rarely referred to its law in such unadorned terms" [2545]. The choice of law was usually accompanied by a stabilization or "freezing" clause so that the law would be applied as in force on the date of the contract [2546], such as the provision in the 1971 agreement of the parties in *MINE* v. *Guinea* [2547]. In other cases, reference was made to the law of the State party alongside international law, in order to complement or temper the application of the national law. This was the case, for example, in the arbitration clause of the 1974 agreement between the parties in *AGIP* v. *Congo* [2548].

2. *Choice of law in a national law or in an investment treaty*

When there is no investment contract, or no applicable law clause in the contract, the choice of law together with the offer to arbitrate can be made in the investment legislation of the country itself or in the investment treaty. In such a case, by referring the dispute to arbitration the investor is understood to consent to the applicable law [2549]. In this regard, for instance, in the 2007 *Siemens* v. *Argentina* case, the ICSID Tribunal stated that since the applicable BIT provided an offer to arbitrate, by accepting Argentina's offer, "Siemens agreed that this should be the law to be applied by the Tribunal. This constitutes an

2543. 1968 Model Clauses, Clauses XIX-XXI, 7 ILM, pp. 1175-1176 (1968).

2544. *Attorney General of New Zealand* v. *Mobil Oil New Zealand*, High Court of New Zealand, Judgment, 1 July 1987, in *ICSID Review: Foreign Investment Law Journal*, Vol. 2 (1987), p. 497, 502.

2545. Parra, *supra* note 510, pp. 178-179.

2546. *Ibid.*, pp. 178-179.

2547. *MINE* v. *Guinea*, *supra* note 2190, *Ad hoc* Committee Decision (22 December 1989), para. 94.

2548. *AGIP* v. *Congo*, *supra* note 454, Award (30 November 1979), para. 323.

2549. In the ICSID Convention cases initiated under BITs in the period 2000 to 2010, the arbitrators generally held international law, including the provisions of the BIT, to be applicable (with domestic law also found to be relevant in many instances). Parra, *supra* note 510, pp. 303-304.

agreement for purposes of the law to be applied under Article 42 (1) of the Convention" [2550].

Other BITs contain an express choice of law provision as well [2551]. Moreover, in plurilateral treaties, related provisions can be found in the Energy Charter Treaty, the older NAFTA, the current USMCA (though only for the benefit of American and Mexican investors), and in the Central America-Dominican Republic-United States Free Trade Agreement [2552].

3. Choice of law in home State legislation

Home State investment legislation can also express its consent to the arbitral process and to the applicable law. Naturally any investment venture pursued according to this legislation falls within the scope of its regulation [2553], as provided, for instance, in Venezuela's Investment Law [2554].

J. Choice of State or non-State law in investment arbitration

1. Choice of the law of the host State

According to Richard Kreindler, when an arbitration clause is included in an international investment contract, the parties rarely agree to the application of the host State's law [2555]. In turn, treaties usually

2550. *Siemens* v. *Argentina*, *supra* note 531, Award (6 February 2007), para. 76, cited in Parra, *supra* note 510, p. 304. See also *Goetz* v. *Burundi*, *supra* note 93, Award, para. 94. Cf. *History of the ICSID Convention*, *supra* note 1078, II, p. 267, fn. 54.

2551. For instance, the Australia-Argentina BIT includes an applicable law provision that permits the tribunal to apply the terms of the treaty, the law of the host State and relevant principles of international law. Another example can be found in the Portugal-Turkey BIT, which permits the tribunal to apply the terms of the treaty (which may be considered an implicit choice of international law) and national law of the contracting party in whose territory the investment was made, including the rules relative to conflicts of law.

2552. Cordero-Moss and Behn, *supra* note 964, p. 579.

2553. *Ibid.*, p. 509.

2554. Article 2 of Decree No. 356/1999, "Law on Promotion and Protection of Investments", provides: "This Law-Decree shall apply both to investment already existing in the country at the time it comes into force, and to investments made afterwards, as well as to investors in one or the other. The provisions hereof shall not, however, apply to any controversy, claim or difference arising from occurrences or actions that took place before the effective date hereof."

2555. Kreindler, *supra* note 2039, pp. 403. Contrastingly, years ago Delaume wrote that the overwhelming of State contracts, to the extent that they contain a stipulation of applicable law, provide for the applicability of the law of the host State. In certain cases, whose number appears to be decreasing, the parties seek to "internationalize" or "de-localize" some of the major features of the agreement in an obvious attempt to refer, in some manner, to public international law, which can either stand alone or act in conjunction with domestic rules [2556].

ICSID arbitration cases dealing with the selection of the law of the host State are "relatively rare" [2557]. An example flows from the 1988 *MINE* v. *Republic of Guinea* case, in which Guinean law was chosen by the parties and applied by the Tribunal without reference to the choice of law clause. Instead, the Tribunal alluded to the principle of good faith within the French Civil Code, deciding that Guinean law derives from French law [2558].

Territorialized tribunals have also applied domestic law when so agreed upon by the parties. In *Alsing Trading Co.* v. *Greece* (1954), involving an alleged breach of contract, the arbitrator wrote that "the plaintiffs accepted before the arbitration tribunal that the case be judged according to Greek law, as requested by the defendant" and the law of the host State was to be applicable to the dispute [2559]. In turn, in *National Oil Corporation (NOC)* v. *Libyan Sun Oil Company* (1985/1987), the ICC Tribunal applied the doctrine of *force majeure* as found within the Libyan Civil Code and within the case law of the countries' Supreme Court. When awarding damages, the Tribunal made references to reports by Libyan legal experts [2560]. Further, in *Zeevi Holdings Ltd.* v. *Republic of Bulgaria and The Privatization Agency of Bulgaria* (2006), the UNCITRAL Tribunal applied Bulgarian law, which had been expressly chosen in the privatization agreement [2561].

---

withdraw the relationship from the reach (and possible change) of the host State's law. See Delaume, *supra* note 119, p. 796.

2556. Kreindler, *supra* note 2039, pp. 403-404.

2557. *New Zealand* v. *Mobil*, *Tanzania Electric Supply Company Limited* v. *Independent Power Tanzania Limited*, ICSID Case No. ARB/98/8, Final Award (12 July 2001). Schreuer *et al.*, *supra* note 102, p. 557, p. 558-559. Stabilization clause, *Atlantic Triton Company Limited* v. *People's Revolutionary Republic of Guinea*, ICSID Case No. ARB/84/1, Award (21 April 1986), 3 *ICSID Reports*, p. 17; *MINE* v. *Guinea*, *supra* note 2190, p. 559.

2558. *MINE* v. *Guinea*, *supra* note 2190, Award (6 January 1988), D. E. Zubrod, J. Berg and D. K. Sharpe (eds.), sec. A, at sec. 8. Although not properly a choice of law issue, interestingly the IUSCT in *Questech.* v. *Iran* (1985), considering that the contract did not contain any provision designed to protect the investor against unilateral changes by the State party, did not entertain with public international law matters and decided to apply national law. *Questech* v. *Iran*, *supra* note 942, Award (20 September 1985). See also *FMC* v. *Ministry of National Defence*, *supra* note 2446, Award (12 February 1987), Dissenting Opinion of Bahrami Ahmadi, at sec. B.1.

2559. *Alsing Trading Company Ltd.* v. *Greece*, Award (22 December 1954), 23 ILR, p. 633, paras. 637-638.

2560. *National Oil Corporation* v. *Libyan Sun Oil Company*, ICC Case No. 4462, First Award (on *force majeure*) (31 May 1985), 29 ILM, p. 565 (1990), paras. 615, 608.

2561. *Zeevi Holdings Ltd.* v. *Republic of Bulgaria and The Privatization Agency of Bulgaria*, UNCITRAL Case No. UNC39/DK, Final Award (25 October 2006), paras. 104-105.

2. Choice of a third State's law

In commercial arbitration, parties frequently select the law of a third country law and a neutral seat to "delocalize" the transaction [2562]. This is not the case in foreign investment State contracts. Selecting a neutral third country law as applicable can potentially create greater difficulties if the investor's activities are closely linked to the host State or strongly connected its legislation in matters such as employment, taxation, and so forth.

Commercial transactions such as transportation or sales contracts are relatively straightforward and simple when it comes to the parties' obligations. In international investment contracts, however, the investor undertakes obligations under guarantees provided by the host State. The fulfillment of these obligations may require the investor to enter into a series of contracts on matters such as sales, purchases, construction and the hiring of personnel. Each of these obligations will have its own status and most of them will likely be performed in the country where the investment is made. In turn, the host State will assume those obligations that are within its control, such as tax arrangements and exemptions, customs tariffs, and so on. For these reasons, it is often difficult or impractical to choose any law other than the host State's to govern the contract [2563].

The situation is different for investment contracts that take the form of loans, for example, as laws other than the State's own law are often chosen. In fact, loan contracts frequently select the law of the lender's country as the applicable law. Less recurrently, the law of a third country that has an important financial center is also chosen [2564]. It is

2562. On delocalization, see J. A. Moreno Rodríguez, *Derecho Aplicable y Arbitraje*, Madrid, Thomson, 2014, pp. 346-350; R. Goode, "The Role of the *Lex Loci Arbitri* in International Commercial Arbitration", *Arbitration International*, Vol. 17, No. 1 (2001), pp. 21-22. Thereby described as "denationalized, anational, floating or drifting arbitrations". See also P. Read, "Delocalization of International Commercial Arbitration: Its Relevance in the New Millennium", *American Review of International Arbitration*, Vol. 10 (1999), p. 186.

2563. "After studying eighty such agreements, Delaume does not cite a single clause adopting the law of a third State. The author has never encountered any. On the other hand, the law of the host State is quite often chosen. Delaume enumerates about fifty instances. It should be added that a rather large number of investment codes and laws provide, at least tacitly, for the application of the law of the host State to agreements concluded under them", Kahn, *supra* note 33, pp. 12-13.

2564. Examples are *SPP* v. *Egypt*, *supra* note 1085, Award (20 May 1992), para. 225; *CDC* v. *Seychelles*, Award (17 December 2003), para. 43; and *Colt Industries* v. *Korea* (this case was settled and discontinued with no published record of the proceedings). See Schreuer *et al.*, *supra* note 102, p. 557, pp. 559-560.

also common for the parties to select the law of the State from where the loan is issued, rather than the law of the borrowing State or of the jurisdiction in which the borrower is a subordinate agency.

According to Philip Kahn, traditional conflict of laws issues still prevail here since these loan contracts closely resemble traditional international commercial contracts rather than complex direct investment agreements with strong public law elements [2565]. Therefore, choosing a neutral third country law may be desirable for certain investments, such as those involving loans or licensing agreements [2566].

Some ICSID cases have expressly dealt with the choice of a third State's laws [2567].

3. *Choice of the investor's home State law*

In the ICSID case *Colt Industries* v. *Korea*, the parties chose the law of the investor's home country because the investment encompassed technical and licensing agreements for the production of weapons and was, in the parties' view, most closely connected with the licensor's home country [2568]. In *World Duty Free* v. *Kenya*, due to substantial similarities in both systems involved, the Tribunal had no problem applying the awkward wording of choice of both laws [2569].

When it is both feasible and desirable to apply a law other than that of the host State, such as the domestic law of the investor, it is important for the parties to choose the governing law expressly. If they do not, the tribunal will apply the second sentence of Article 42 (1) and will likely make use of the law of the State party to the dispute (together with any applicable international law) even if it is not the law most closely connected to the transaction [2570].

2565. Kahn, *supra* note 33, p. 13.

2566. Kreindler, *supra* note 2039, p. 404.

2567. *Southern Pacific* v. *Egypt*, *supra* note 128, Award on the Merits (10 May 1992), para. 225; *CDC* v. *Seychelles*, *supra* note 2190, Award (17 December 2003), para. 43; *World Duty Free* v. *Kenya*, *supra* note 1081, Award (4 October 2006), paras. 158-159. See Bjorklund and Vanhonnaeker, *supra* note 13, p. 353.

2568. *Colt Industries Operating Corporation* v. *Republic of Korea*, ICSID Case No. ARB/84/2. See also Schreuer *et al.*, *supra* note 102, p. 557, p. 560.

2569. *World Duty Free* v. *Kenya*, *supra* note 1081, Award (4 October 2006), paras. 158-159.

2570. Schreuer *et al.*, *supra* note 102, p. 557, p. 560.

4. *Choice of non-State law*

(a) *In international arbitration in general*

The parties are free to select the non-State rules of law that they accept and agree to be treated as binding and enforceable, despite these norms originating outside of State organs.

There is no prohibition against enforcing awards that apply non-State law. In fact, non-State law was applied in the 2011 *Ministry of Defense and Support of the Armed Forces of the Islamic Republic of Iran* v. *Cubic Defense Systems, Inc.* case, under the New York Convention. In that case, the Tribunal applied the UNIDROIT Principles as general principles in the issuance of the arbitral award [2571]. As recognized by the 1992 Cairo Declaration of the International Law Association, if arbitrators apply transnational rules or principles in lieu of a national law, the validity of the award may not be questioned for this reason alone when the parties selected non-State law or when they remained silent regarding the governing law [2572].

The 1961 European Convention on International Commercial Arbitration recognizes party autonomy in Article VII to select "the law to be applied by the arbitrators to the substance of the dispute" [2573]. Dominique Hascher advocates in favor of a progressive interpretation of this instrument, admitting that the parties may select the *lex mercatoria* and general principles (i.e., non-State Law) [2574].

Also admitting party autonomy, Article 10 of MERCOSUR's Arbitral Agreement of 1998 relates to the applicability of "private international law and its principles" and of the "law of international trade". The latter expression in particular has been understood to imply the acceptance of non-State law [2575].

The UNCITRAL Model Law includes the principle of party autonomy in its Article 28 (1) for the selection of rules of law. According to the UNCITRAL commentary on this article, the term "rules of law" is

2571. Silberman and Ferrari, *supra* note 2514, pp. 427-428. In a recent judgment, the Paris Court of Appeal rejected a claim for annulment of an international arbitral award where the Arbitral Tribunal had decided to apply the UNIDROIT Principles to the merits of the case: Cour d'appel de Paris, 25 February 2020, *Prakash Steelage* v. *Uzuc* (Cour d'appel de Paris – Pôle 01 ch 01 – 25 février 2020 – No. 17/18001). The holding of the ruling may well extend to investment claims.

2572. See Gaillard, *supra* note 2367, p. 247.

2573. Broches, *supra* note 2161, p. 389.

2574. D. Hascher, "European Convention on International Commercial Arbitration (European Convention, 1961): Commentary", 20 YB Comm. Arb. (1995), pp. 1030-1031.

2575. See Moreno Rodríguez, *supra* note 2562, p. 332.

understood more broadly than "law" and includes rules "that have been elaborated by an international forum but have not yet been incorporated into any national legal system" [2576].

Domestic arbitration laws in a number of States worldwide equally show an openness toward non-State law, such as Articles 1478 and 1511 of the Code de Procédure Civile Français; Section 1051 of the German ZPO; Article 46 (1) *(a)* of the English Arbitration Act of 1996; Article 187 of the Swiss Private International Law Act of 1987; Article 1052 (2) of the Netherlands Code of Civil Procedure [2577]; among many others. The law of Panama deserves special mention here: not only is it open to non-State law, but it also provides that in international arbitration, the UNIDROIT Principles must be taken into account, thereby legitimizing that body of non-State provisions [2578].

Allowing the parties to select "rules of law" according to the principle of party autonomy can also be observed in several arbitration rules, for example in Article 33 of the 1976 version (Art. 35 as revised in 2010 and 2013) [2579] of the UNCITRAL Arbitration Rules (which has inspired

---

2576. Explanatory Note by the UNCITRAL secretariat on the 1985 Model Law on International Commercial Arbitration as amended in 2006, https://uncitral.un.org/en/texts/arbitration/modellaw/commercial_arbitration, accessed 27 June 2022, p. 33. In this regard, both the English official commentary and the Dutch explanatory text to the arbitration laws of these countries introduced the understanding that the *lex mercatoria* is included in the expression "rules of law". Explanatory notes to the project in 1985, drafted by a departmental advisory committee of arbitration, stated that this section applies to Article 28 of the Model Law (Department of Trade and Industry, Consultative Paper, Sections 1 and 2: Draft Clauses of an Arbitration Bill, p. 38). (Notes, Art. 1:101 PECL, commentary 3 *(a)*). The explanatory Dutch text (Document No 18464) is found in De Ly, *supra* note 1204, p. 250.

2577. The legislative history indicates that this provision leads not only to national law but also may be derived from *lex mercatoria*. See A. H. van den Berg, "National Report", 12 YB Comm. Arb. (1987), p. 25.

2578. Article 56, National and International Arbitration in Panama, Law 131 of 2013. The provision reproduces in this regard Article 27 of a prior Panamanian Arbitration Law. An Arbitral Tribunal seated in Panama invoked Articles 7.4.2 and 7.4.3 of the UNIDROIT Principles in a discussion related to damages in an *ex aequo et bono* arbitration, considering that Article 27 of the Panama Arbitration Law orders the tribunal to take them into account. Arbitral Award dated 24 February 2001, Arbitral Tribunal of the city of Panama, cited in www.unilex.info, accessed 13 May 2022.

2579. UNCITRAL Arbitration Rules (1976), adopted by the UN General Assembly on 15 December 1976. UN Doc. A/RES/31/98; UNCITRAL Arbitration Rules (as revised in 2010), adopted by the UN General Assembly on December 6, 2010, UN Doc. A/RES/31/98; texts available at https://uncitral.un.org/en/texts/arbitration/contractualtexts/arbitration, accessed 13 May 2022. Adjustments to the new rules are discussed in Revision of the UNCITRAL Arbitration Rules: A Report by Jan Paulsson and Georgios Petrochilos, commissioned by the UNCITRAL Secretariat, Draft for Comments, 31 March 2006. Discussions in this regard are reflected in the documents A/CN.9/614, paras. 122-124, A/CN.9/641, paras. 106-113 and A/CN.9/684, paras. 91-100.

numerous other arbitration rules worldwide) [2580] and in Article 35 (1) of the PCA Rules [2581].

The situation is different when it comes to litigation in court. Party autonomy is not universally accepted, and non-State law is only admitted in a minority of jurisdictions [2582]. Article 3 of the Hague Principles attempts to "level the field" in this regard, proposing to extend party autonomy to litigation as well, as seen in Chapter XI. The OAS Guide, also discussed in Chapter XI, has a similar objective [2583].

Non-State law seems, however, not to be usually selected by the parties in their international relationships – a commonplace statement made by scholars and practitioners. Perhaps there is a "prisoner's dilemma" here because the parties tend to assume that the choice of non-State law will be rejected by the courts. As argued by Fabio Bortolotti, even within arbitration, the parties often mitigate this uncertainty by selecting domestic laws to minimize the risks of invalidity based on what has been decided by domestic tribunals at the seat or at the eventual place of enforcement [2584].

Regarding the manner in which the parties must manifest their choice of application of international law, general principles or trade usages, an ICC Tribunal decided that:

> "[T]he failure of the parties to agree on the law governing the Agreement cannot, in the sole arbitrator's opinion, be interpreted as an implied reference to some vague international legal or trade principles. Such reference must be made expressly and, if not expressly, then in an implied manner which gives reasonable certainty to the arbitrators or the courts, respectively, that the parties indeed agreed to submit their dispute to a national law or international trade principles, particularly considering the fact

---

2580. Várady, Barceló III and von Mehren, *supra* note 2102, p. 70. Examples are Article 21 (1) of the 2017 ICC Rules; Article 31 (1) of the 2016 SIAC Rules; Article 31 (1) of the 2014 ICDR Rules; Article 22 (3) of the 2020 LCIA Rules; Article 33 (1) of the 2012 Swiss Rules; Article 36 (1) of the 2018 HKIAC Rules; Article 24 (1) of the 2018 DIS Rules; Article 27 (1) of the 2018 VIAC Rules; and Article 61 *(a)* of the 2020 WIPO Rules.

2581. The expression includes various sources of international law, transnational principles such as those set out in the UNIDROIT Principles, and different combinations of rules. See Daly, Goriatcheva and Meighen, *supra* note 809, p. 136.

2582. Such as in Paraguay and Uruguay. As noted by Bermann, herein lies a fundamental difference between private international law in the litigation and arbitration settings. Bermann, *supra* note 2512, p. 353.

2583. Part Six of the OAS Guide, *supra* note 1309.

2584. Bortolotti and Mayer, *supra* note 1471, p. 7.

that such a national laws and principles, if not properly defined, are difficult if not impossible to assess." [2585]

(b) *In investment arbitration*

In investment arbitration, as discussed, Article 42 (1) of the ICSID Convention directs the Tribunal to "decide a dispute in accordance with such rules of law as may be agreed by the parties". The expression "rules of law" is understood to comprise both State and non-State law [2586]. In the ICSID case *Joseph Charles Lemire* v. *Ukraine*, the Tribunal ruled that:

> "Given the parties' implied negative choice of any municipal legal system, the Tribunal finds that the most appropriate decision is to submit the Settlement Agreement to the rules of international law, and within these, to have particular regard to the UNIDROIT Principles." [2587]

In the United States-Iran context, in *Ministry of Defence and Support for Armed Forces of the Islamic Republic of Iran* v. *Westinghouse Electric Corp.* (ICC Award No. 7375, 5 June 1996) at Section III it was decided that if a contract

> "does not contain a choice of law provision, then this must be viewed as a 'shouting silence', at least an 'alarming silence', *'un silence inquiétant'*; thus, a silence which must ring a bell and requires the Tribunal to look 'behind' so as to understand why the Parties have failed to include 'the obvious'".

The Tribunal concluded that the absence of a choice of law clause "must be understood as a so-called 'implied negative choice' of the Parties . . . in the sense that none of the Parties' national laws should be imposed on any of the Parties". Having found that neither Iranian law nor the law of the United States or Maryland was applicable, the Tribunal chose to apply a "de-nationalized solution", according to which it would "decide legal issues by having regard to the terms of the Contract and, where necessary or appropriate, by applying truly international standards as reflected in, and forming part of, the so-called 'general principles of law'" [2588].

2585. ICC Case No. 7319/1992, 24 YB Comm. Arb. (1999), p. 145.
2586. Schreuer *et al.*, *supra* note 102, p. 557, p. 563.
2587. *Lemire* v. *Ukraine*, *supra* note 547, Decision on Jurisdiction and Liability (14 January 2010), para. 111.
2588. See also Kjos, *supra* note 2296, p. 73.

5. Choice of public international law

Public international law can also be selected by the parties to govern their relationship. The expression "rules of law" is broad enough to encompass the possibility. The 1979 Athens Resolution of the Institute of International Law states:

> "The parties may in particular choose as the proper law of the contract either one or more domestic legal systems or the principles common to such systems, or the general principles of law, or the principles applied in international economic relations, or international law, or a combination of these sources of law." [2589]

In the selection of public international law, the parties may even refer to a treaty that is not in force, as was the case in *CSOB* v. *Slovakia* [2590], or they may opt for a non-binding code of conduct such as the World Bank's 1992 Guidelines on the Treatment of Foreign Direct Investment [2591]. In this sense, the term "rule of law" can mean that not only existing norms can be chosen, but the parties can also adopt their own rules by reference to a non-binding document as the law governing their contract [2592].

Article 35 of the PCA Rules offers another example of the selection of public international law. The PCA Drafting Committee noted in discussions prior to the final text that parties could, for example, choose the ILC's Draft Articles on Responsibility of States for Internationally Wrongful Acts as the applicable rules of law for their contract [2593].

In the context of the ICSID Convention, Article 42 (1) provides for the application of the "relevant" rules of international law, and not "all" international law rules, as observed by the Tribunal in the *LG&E* v. *Argentina* case [2594]. The selection of "public international law" as the only governing law may be problematic, as will be described in the following paragraphs.

Investors see the selection of public international law as a way of avoiding the laws of the State where the investment was made, perceiving it as a neutral solution to these challenges. Public international law

---

2589. The Athens resolution is cited in Lalive, *supra* note 796, pp. 51-52. Bernardini, *supra* note 984, p. 59.

2590. *CSOB* v. *Slovakia*, Decision on Jurisdiction (24 May 1999), paras. 36-55.

2591. See Chapter V, *supra* note 646.

2592. Schreuer *et al.*, *supra* note 102, p. 557, p. 564.

2593. Daly, Goriatcheva and Meighen, *supra* note 809, p. 136.

2594. Bjorklund and Vanhonnaeker, *supra* note 13, p. 358, citing: *LG&E* v. *Argentina*, *supra* note 448, Decision on Liability (3 October 2006), para. 88.

copes satisfactorily with cases in which the government seeks to modify the contract in its favor, unilaterally divesting the private party of its contractual rights. Indeed, its application shields against such unilateral modifications by States acting under their own law. According to Christopher Curtis, if submission to public international law involves some difficulty and even uncertainty of result, that may well be a price that the parties find is worth paying [2595].

In a recent Hague Academy course, Anton Struycken stated that square negative answer emerges to the question of whether private law companies can be the subject of public international law [2596]. However, he also questions why public international law should not be a subject capable of evolution, like other fields of law, to give adequate answers to real new problems, such as regulation of space, transborder pollution, deep-sea mineral rights and terrorism [2597].

Struycken goes even further in favor of public international law as the *lex fori* of the arbitration of State contracts. For instance, where the constitution of the tribunal is not always readily agreed upon once a party asks for arbitration, a solution must be provided for. This was the case when Libya refused to appoint an arbitrator in the *Texaco* v. *Libya* arbitration. Professor Dupuy was appointed not by a State court but by the ICJ President. Struycken also argues that aspects of the rules are a matter of public international law, and that the arbitrators must limit themselves to the public policy values of public international law. Therefore, public international law applies regardless of what the parties to a State contract had in mind [2598].

These conclusions, and in general the applicability of public international law to State contracts is – as noted by Cristopher Curtis – a highly controversial topic [2599]. In the words of Peter Mankowski,

2595. Curtis, *supra* note 119, p. 344.

2596. Struycken, *supra* note 121, p. 36.

2597. "It is my and others' thesis that public international law has to render adequate services to the world community and to show inventiveness and willingness to do so. Our problem is that an arbitral award for a dispute affecting directly or indirectly both Home State and Host State needs a robust *lex fori* in order to be binding on them. There should be no room for the arbitral award being considered as rendered without *lex fori*, i.e., in the blue sky. A new chapter of public international law has had to be developed, not identical to that of treaty law" (*ibid.*, p. 38).

2598. "Given those far-reaching consequences of public international law being the home base, the *lex fori* of the arbitration, one cannot but agree with Professor Weil that public international law applies regardless of what parties to the State contract had in mind. Parties to the contract cannot set aside public international law where it applies, and parties are not in a position to decide that public international law applies where it does not" (*ibid.*, pp. 38-39).

2599. Curtis, *supra* note 119, p. 342.

public international law "is a dark horse" and is ill-suited for investment matters related to, for instance, breaches of contracts or default. This situation is understandable considering that public international law has traditionally acted primarily between States [2600].

Unsurprisingly, some experts consider that referring only to international law, general principles or usages to govern the transaction is "not advisable". There are usually several specific provisions of the host State's law that should be considered, making reference to international law alone quite impractical.

Only very few State contracts select public international law as the sole law governing their dispute. It is more common for contracting parties to an international investment to choose a combination of legal systems, including the host State's law and general principles of law or international rules and principles [2601].

There are a great variety of clauses in this regard. Many express that the agreement will be governed by general principles of law recognized by civilized nations [2602] or, in addition, by international law [2603]. Many provide for some combination of national and non-national laws arranged in a complex hierarchy [2604]. The common objective of these

2600. The "principles of international law", achieving five scores in ICC arbitration in 2014, fares little if any better. The intended choice fails for its inherent imprecision, not for the formal source of its intended object. Article 3 of the Hague Principles cannot help over this hurdle. See Mankowski, *supra* note 1632, p. 383.

2601. Maniruzzaman, *supra* note 317, p. 32. "Certain 'internationalizing' clauses are simply formulated and compare with ordinary choice-of-law clauses, such as the following: 'The arbitrators shall base their decision on equity and the principles of international law'. Other provisions are more complex in the sense that the choice of law consists of a combination of alternatives culminating in a reference to the general principles of law", Delaume, *supra* note 119, p. 797.

2602. For instance, the Agreement between the Government of Abu Dhabi and Amerada Hess Petroleum Abu Dhabi Ltd., 13 October 1980, Article 35 *(G)*, reprinted in Basic Oil Laws and Concession Contracts: Middle East (Supp. 75) at 5 (Barrows 1982).

2603. For instance, in *Elf Aquitaine Iran (France)* v. *National Iranian Oil Company (NIOC)* of 1982, 96 ILR, p. 254 (Art. 41.5 of the Agreement between NIOC and ERAP): "The Arbitration Board or the sole arbitrator in arriving at the award, shall in no way be restricted by any specific rule of law, but shall have the power to base his award on considerations of equity and generally recognized principles of law and in particular International Law."

2604. For instance, the Draft Agreement between American Indep. Oil Co. and the Gov't of Kuwait, 1973, annex 1, pr. 2, Article XII: "Taking account of the different nationalities of the parties, the agreements between them shall be given effect, and must be interpreted and applied, in conformity with principles common to the laws of Kuwait and of the State of New York, United States of America, and in the absence of such common principles, then in conformity with principles of law normally recognized by civilized States in general, including those which have been applied by international tribunals", reprinted in *Aminoil*, *supra* note 1059, Award (1982), ILR, p. 560. See also the Deeds of Concession executed by the Gov't of Libya on the one hand and Texaco Overseas Petroleum Co. and California Asiatic Oil Co. on the other,

clauses is to insulate the agreement wholly or partially from the political risk of changes in the host State's law to the investor's detriment [2605].

In several public international law conventions, arbitrators are expressly instructed to render their decision in accordance either with principles "of justice, equity, and the law of nations" or other similar formulas [2606]. These instruments show that conventional public international law rules alone are often insufficient for the resolution of international disputes. Hersch Lauterpacht adds that public international law rules further prove inadequate due to the fact that arbitral provisions in treaties to address them are often one of the most important items dealt with during negotiations [2607].

Noteworthily, both the USMCA and the Energy Charter Treaty contain clauses on the applicable law that refer only to the respective treaty and rules of international law [2608]. Under the heading "Governing Law", Article 14.D.9 of the USMCA, Annex 2 of Chapter 14 specifies that "when a claim is submitted under Article 14.D.3.1 (Submission of a Claim to Arbitration), the tribunal shall decide the issues in dispute in accordance with this Agreement and applicable rules of international law". In turn, Article 26 (6) of the ECT provides that "[a] tribunal established under paragraph (4) shall decide the issues in dispute in accordance with this Treaty and applicable rules and principles of international law".

---

cf. 28, reprinted in the *TOPCO* award, 53 ILR, p. 389 (1977), 442; Agreement for Petroleum Exploration and Production between the Ministry of Energy and Minerals of the People's Democratic Republic of Yemen (South Yemen) and Canadian Oxy Offshore Int'l Ltd., 15 September 1986, Article 27.3 *(d)*, reprinted in Basic Oil Laws and Concession Contracts: Middle East (Supp. 75) at 5 (Barrows 1982); Sale and Purchase Agreement between Iran and a Consortium of Oil Companies, 1973, art. 29, reprinted in *Mobil Oil* v. *Iran*, *supra* note 2438, Mealey's Lit. Rep. (Iranian Claims), p. 928, 941, para. 59.

2605. Curtis, *supra* note 119, pp. 320-321.

2606. For instance, Article 7 of the unratified Hague Convention XII relative to the Establishment of an International Prize Court, the 1910 Convention establishing the British-American Claims Arbitral Tribunal, the Hague Conventions for the Pacific Settlement of International Disputes and the PCIJ Statute. See Lauterpacht, *supra* note 3, p. 62.

2607. *Ibid.*, pp. 62-63. Waldock takes a critical perspective, considering that decisions of individual arbitral tribunals covering general principles of law should be approached with more caution than those of the World Court. Article 9 of the ICJ Statute ensures the selection of a Court representing different legal systems of the world, serving as "a certain guarantee as to the use made by the Court of its power to determine and apply general principles of national law", Waldock, *supra* note 156, p. 68.

2608. Article 26 (6) of the ECT provides: "A tribunal established under paragraph (4) shall decide the issues in dispute in accordance with this Treaty and applicable rules and principles of international law."

K. Formalities for the choice of law

Arbitration instruments usually do not address the issue of formalities for the choice of law. As such, private international law, and in particular the Hague Principles, can be of assistance. As stated in these, to facilitate transborder activity, the parties' choice of law should not be restricted by formal requirements. Particularly, per Commentary 5.3 of the Hague Principles:

> "[M]ost legal systems do not prescribe any specific form for the majority of international commercial contracts, including choice of law provisions (see Art. 11 CISG; Art. 1 (2) (first sentence) UNIDROIT Principles and Art. 3.1.2 UNIDROIT Principles) . . . [m]any private international law codifications employ comprehensive result-oriented alternative connecting factors in respect of the formal validity of a contract (including choice of law provisions), based on an underlying policy of favoring the validity of contracts *(favor negotii)* (see, *e.g.*, Art. 13 Mexico City Convention; Art. 11 (1) Rome I Regulation)." [2609]

In the ICSID context, the provision for choice of law and determination of the applicable law (Art. 42, para. 1, Sec. 1) is ambiguous. Considering that Article 25, paragraph 1, explicitly requires "consent in writing" regarding the dispute resolution clause, it can be argued that, absent this requirement in Article 42, the parties can agree on a choice of law in any form. This reasoning is endorsed by the *travaux préparatoires*, specifying that whether the term "agreement" includes implicit agreements was an issue discussed during the Convention's negotiation. The Drafting Committee decided that the term "agreement" should include implicit agreements, but a clarification sought by two delegations was, however, not included [2610].

The Hague Principles can aid in the interpretation of the ICSID Convention on this matter. Under these principles, choice of law is, in principle, not subject to any requirement of form, unless otherwise agreed by the parties (Art. 5). Agreements regarding the choice of law can be made orally or via electronic communication [2611]. This solution

2609. Commentary 5.3 of the Hague Principles.

2610. *History of the ICSID Convention*, *supra* note 1078, II, p. 570.

2611. This same logic regarding formal validity is reflected in Part Nine of the OAS Guide, *supra* note 1309. This Guide, together with the Hague Principles, constitute strong advocacy for change. This is particularly true in Latin America, where written form is a requirement in many domestic laws. According to the Guide, domestic

is consistent with protecting the parties' legitimate expectations which, as seen above, includes the *favor validitatis* principle.

Of course, this also applies to the choice of law clause. The remainder of the contract must comply with the formal requirements applicable to it. As such, if a particular law is chosen, the formal requirements of that law must be met within the contract [2612].

L. *Dépeçage*

1. *Concept*

In private international law, the French term *dépeçage* (or "splitting" of the law) refers to the division of the legal relationship so that different parts may be governed by different laws.

There are numerous reasons why the parties may wish for different laws to govern diverse parts of their relationship. For example, in an international sale, the majority of contractual obligations might be governed by the law of a single State, yet it would be preferable for the conditions under which the seller must obtain inspection certificates to be governed by the law of the State of the final destination of the goods, or that the deadline for the purchaser to report any defect in the goods conveyed be governed by the law of the place of delivery. Another example is that of a clause that provides for the payment of capital and interest, at the creditor's option, in one or more States and in the currency of a particular State. In that case, the parties will often agree that the law of the State in which payment is to be made will govern matters related to the sum to be paid and the form of payment [2613].

Dépeçage is a manifestation of the principle of party autonomy; it does not fall within the nineteenth-century orthodox localization or nationalization doctrines [2614].

---

regimes should not contain any requirements as to form unless otherwise agreed by the parties. Furthermore, adjudicators, in determining the formal validity of a choice of law, should not impose any requirements as to form, unless otherwise agreed by the parties or as may be required by applicable mandatory rules. However, contracting parties and counsel should take into account any mandatory rules as to form that may be applicable.

2612. Official Comment of the Hague Principles 5.5.

2613. Another example of this approach is the so-called Bermuda Form insurance policy, which contains a choice of law clause providing for the application of New York law, save for specific issues which are governed by English law. See Born, *supra* note 2273, p. 2962.

2614. In fact, Ronald Herbert, one of the Uruguayan negotiators of the Mexico Convention, said that the *dépeçage* provision within that instrument may be profoundly at odds with the Montevideo Treaties, in Herbert, *supra* note 1317, p. 91.

Scholars that oppose *dépeçage* argue that it only provides minimal advantages in comparison to the risks that it entails, due to technical problems that could arise from discrepancies in the knowledge and application of the different laws that have been chosen. *Dépeçage* is also considered to be a weapon in the hands of the stronger party to the detriment of the weaker one because aspects of the applicable law that may favor the former can be accorded more prominence than is appropriate. Nevertheless, critics of the concept of *dépeçage* must admit that certain issues, such as those related to the form of the contract and capacity, may be more appropriately governed by different laws and the mandatory rules of the forum [2615].

Legal writers who argue in favor of *dépeçage* point out that party autonomy is available to parties in order to better regulate their interests, where appropriate [2616]. Thus, this principle serves the intent of the parties, and mandatory rules or public policy rules are available to prevent *dépeçage* from being used by the stronger party against the weaker one. Overriding mandatory rules and public international law rules are available to guard against its abuse [2617].

Dépeçage also raises the possibility that part of the applicable law would be public international law [2618]. The same situation may happen with non-State law. For instance, substantive obligations can be submitted to the law of one State and the interpretive criteria may emerge from non-State law, such as the UNIDROIT Principles [2619].

Dépeçage may be used in two situations. First, it may be employed where legislation specifically provides that the parties may choose more than one law to govern the contract, as is provided in certain domestic codifications such as Article 3111 (3) of the Québec Civil Code and Article 1210 (4) of the Russian Civil Code. *Dépeçage* may also be used where the parties have partially chosen the applicable law and the rest

2615. J. G. Rodas, "Elementos de Conexão do Direito Internacional Privado Brasilero Relativamente às Obrigações Contratuais", in N. de Araújo (ed.), *Contratos Internacionais*, 3rd ed., São Paulo, Editora Revista dos Tribunais, 2002, p. 21.

2616. Santos Belandro, *supra* note 1274, pp. 100-102.

2617. Some advocate that through *dépeçage* could be avoided imperative rules of the law that would have been applied *(lex causae)*. This, even denied by some, would lead according to Visher to the *contrat sans loi*. The prevailing position is to grant ultimate control of *dépeçage* to the forum. See Visher, *supra* note 1200, pp. 140-141.

2618. D. Caron, L. M. Caplan and M. Pellonpää, *The UNCITRAL Arbitration Rules: A Commentary*, Oxford, Oxford University Press, 2006, p. 129.

2619. Thomas Webster notes that the use of principles of international law frequently occurs in investment-related disputes, in *Handbook of UNCITRAL Arbitration: Commentary, Precedents and Materials for UNCITRAL Based Arbitration Rules*, London, Sweet & Maxwell / Thomson Reuters, 2010, p. 513.

of the contractual obligations must be determined objectively. Rome I expressly permits this partial choice, specifying that the parties may choose the law applicable to part of the contract only (Art. 3.1). The Mexico Convention follows the same lines [2620].

A third situation may occur if the law chosen by the parties does not cover all the issues that may arise. For example, if a contract is governed by the CISG, there are matters that the CISG itself excludes under Article 4, such as the validity of the contract and the effects on property, for example the goods sold [2621].

Article 2.2 of the Hague Principles provides that: "The parties may choose *(a)* the law applicable to the whole contract or to only part of it; and *(b)* different laws for different parts of the contract". Because the Hague Principles include non-State law within the meaning of "law" such as is provided in Article 3, non-State sources can also be chosen.

The Hague Principles also discuss the reasons for which many choices of applicable law might be made (for instance, a clause about the exchange rate may be subject to another legal system) and the corresponding risks of such choices (contradiction and inconsistency in determining the rights and obligations of the parties) [2622]. If there is a partial choice of applicable law and no indication that the law will govern the rest of the contractual relationship, "the law that will apply to that remainder will be determined by the court or the arbitral tribunal according to the rules applicable in the absence of a choice" [2623]. The Hague Principles also state that "in practice, such partial or multiple choices [of law] may concern the contract's currency denomination, special clauses relating to performance of certain obligations, such

2620. It states in Article 7 that the choice of law "selection may relate to the entire contract or to a part of same". Hence, it enshrines voluntary *dépeçage*. Involuntary *dépeçage* is provided for in Article 9 of the Mexico Convention, paragraph 3 of which states: "Nevertheless, if a part of the contract were separable from the rest and if it had a closer tie with another State, the law of that State could, exceptionally, apply to that part of the contract." This can occur, for instance, when an adjudicator decides to apply either the rules of a third State connected to the contract or mandatory rules or policies.

2621. In accordance with Article 7 (2) of the CISG, "questions concerning matters governed by the CISG which are not expressly settled in it are to be settled in conformity with general principles", but issues not addressed by the CISG will have to be governed by the supplementary law that the parties have chosen and, in the absence of such a choice, it will be necessary to determine the applicable law, in which case, two different laws may govern the contract. The Bustamante Code uses *dépeçage* to regulate separately the different issues of the contractual relationship (for instance, Arts. 169-172, 176, 181 and 183).

2622. Hague Principles, Commentary 2.6.

2623. Hague Principles, Commentary 2.7.

as obtaining governmental authorizations, and indemnity/liability clauses" [2624].

2. Dépeçage *in arbitration*

The arbitral forum has its peculiarities and the issue of *dépeçage* is not addressed expressly in either the UNCITRAL Model Law or the UNCITRAL Arbitration Rules. According to scholarly doctrine, *dépeçage* is widely accepted pursuant to the principle of party autonomy, which as discussed previously clearly prevails in the arbitration context [2625].

In investment arbitration, *dépeçage* is particularly likely to occur where the overall relationship is governed by separate agreements concluded at different times and that regulate distinct issues [2626]. *Dépeçage* can also result in the application of "different legal regimes or laws to different aspects of the parties' relationship" [2627], as occurred in the ICSID case *Southern Pacific Properties (Middle East) Limited* v. *Arab Republic of Egypt* [2628].

In fact, the parties may decide upon the applicable law from among certain pieces of legislation within a particular legal system. The ICSID Tribunal in *Aucoven* v. *Venezuela* endorsed this method by stating that Article 42 (1) in its first sentence refers to "rules of law" and not systems of law, regarding which it is generally interpreted that the wording entitles the parties to agree on a partial choice of law and select specific rules from a system of law [2629]. Accordingly, Article 42 (1) does not mandate the choice of an entire system of law but opens the possibility of choosing rules of law selectively [2630].

2624. Hague Principles, Commentary 2.9.

2625. This interpretation is advocated, for instance, regarding Article 35 (1) of the UNCITRAL Arbitration Rules of 2010. Webster, *supra* note 2619, p. 513. "Split" choice of law clauses generally give rise to no serious questions as to validity. As a matter of fact, they are permitted under most legal systems. See Born, *supra* note 2273, p. 2962. He notes that some institutional rules provide for the possibility to split the applicable law, providing, for example, that the arbitral tribunal "shall apply the substantive law(s) or rules of law designated by the parties as applicable to the dispute" (2014 ICDR Rules, Art. 31 (1)). Other examples: 2020 LCIA Rules, Article 22 (3); 2017 SCC Rules, Article 27 (1).

2626. Schreuer *et al.*, *supra* note 102, p. 557, p. 564.

2627. Bjorklund and Vanhonnaeker, *supra* note 13, p. 355.

2628. *Southern Pacific* v. *Egypt*, *supra* note 128, Award on the Merits (10 May 1992), paras. 224-225.

2629. *Aucoven* v. *Venezuela*, *supra* note 1084, Award (2003), para. 96.

2630. Schreuer *et al.*, *supra* note 102, p. 557, p. 563.

Notwithstanding, where the parties have not clearly chosen an applicable law (or multiple laws), the agreement should not be interpreted lightly to contain a choice of different laws for different questions. In relationships where tribunals have concluded that the parties have only made a partial law choice (i.e., they agreed to apply the BIT), tribunals have not hesitated to find the applicable law to the remaining questions pursuant to ICSID, Article 42, paragraph 1, Section 2 [2631].

Dépeçage can be voluntary or involuntary. Where *dépeçage* is involuntary, the adjudicator decides upon the partial application of other laws or imperative norms [2632]. For example, the Tribunal in *Wena* v. *Egypt* found that the parties had chosen the BIT as "the primary source of applicable law for this arbitration". The Tribunal noted that the BIT was a short and limited document that did not specify all the applicable rules and decided instead to apply both equity and law. The Tribunal also decided to apply international law rules by virtue of the pleadings made by the parties [2633].

The situation is different where the parties have chosen an entire legal system to govern their contract, which would incorporate its own gap-filling system [2634].

M. Reasonable connection of the law chosen

1. In private international law

Historically, it was believed that the law chosen by the parties should have some connection either to them or to the transaction itself. This principle of "reasonable connection" might have originated under the influence of doctrines such as "localization" in the nineteenth century. Even today, in some domestic legal systems, the law chosen must be substantially related to the parties or to their transaction, or there must be another reasonable ground to justify the parties' choice of a particular law. This happens in the United States, which contemplates it in its Restatement (Second) of Conflict of Laws [2635].

2631. Although in theory the parties are free to agree on a BIT's exclusive application, excluding the complementary application of ICSID Convention's Article 42, paragraph 1, section 2, the parties' agreement should only be read in such way if it clearly states so, as it bears the risk of lacunae. See Bischoff, *supra* note 15, p. 765.

2632. Santos Belandro, *supra* note 1274, p. 104.

2633. *Wena Hotels* v. *Egypt*, *supra* note 601, Award (2000), para. 79. This decision was annulled considering its vague references to equity. *Wena Hotels* v. *Egypt*, Decision on Annulment (5 February 2002).

2634. Schreuer *et al.*, *supra* note 102, p. 594.

2635. Not in England: *Steel Authority of India Ltd.* v. *Hind Metals Inc.* (1984). See Morse, *supra* note 1303, p. 62.

The Mexico Convention does not expressly address the issue of the reasonable connection of the law chosen, although scholars have argued that, by virtue of the principle of party autonomy, a "neutral" law can be chosen freely [2636]. A similar interpretation has been advanced in relation to Rome I [2637].

This issue has been addressed expressly in the Hague Principles [2638]. Article 2.4 of the Principles states that "[n]o connection is required between the law chosen and the parties or their transaction". The Commentary to the Principles states that "this provision is in line with the increasing delocalization of commercial transactions". It states further that "[t]he parties may choose a particular law because it is neutral as between the parties or because it is particularly well-developed for the type of transaction contemplated (e.g., a State law renowned for maritime transport or international banking transactions)" [2639].

Also, Resolution 1979 of the Institut de Droit International expressly states that a connection between the contract and the chosen law is not required (Arts. 1 and 2). It is only where the parties have failed to choose an applicable law that the contract shall be subject to the rules of law with which the contract has the closest link (Art. 1) [2640].

2. *Reasonable connection in arbitration*

With respect to arbitration, the issue of the reasonable connection of the law chosen has not been clarified in either the UNCITRAL Arbitration Rules or in the Model Law. Arbitral decisions have been made that, under a broad interpretation of the principle of party autonomy, would allow the parties to choose any law to govern their contract, even if

2636. See J. A. Moreno Rodríguez, *La Convención de México sobre el Derecho Aplicable a la Contratación Internacional*, Washington, DC, OAS, 2006, III, D, 7.

2637. H. Heiss, "Party Autonomy", in F. Ferrari and S. Leible (eds.), *Rome I Regulation: The Law Applicable to Contractual Obligations in Europe*, Munich, Sellier, 2009, p. 2. Rome I is silent with respect to the connection requirement (Art. 3), except for two types of contracts: contracts for the carriage of passengers (Art. 5.2) and insurance contracts covering small risks (Art. 7.3). This silence is interpreted to mean that a connection is generally not necessary, except for the two types of contracts mentioned.

2638. A reasonable connection does not appear neither in the Hague Conventions of 1955 on the Law Applicable to International Sales of Movables, the 1986 Convention on International Sales of Goods, nor in the 1978 Convention on the Law Applicable to Contracts of Intermediaries and Representation.

2639. Commentary 2.14, Hague Principles. Part Twelve of the OAS Guide contains a similar discussion, see *supra* note 1309.

2640. See Sec. T of this chapter, *infra*, "Stabilization clause". See also *Annuaire d'Institut de droit international*, Vol. 58-II (1979), pp. 192-195.

it is not obviously related to the dispute [2641]. Nevertheless, arbitrators must act with considerable caution in this area, given that failure to acknowledge public policy issues connected to the case can be the basis for setting aside an award or preventing its enforcement pursuant to Article V (2) *(b)* of the New York Convention [2642]. This requirement flows from arbitrators' general duty to issue enforceable awards.

The reasonable connection requirement is less appropriate in investment arbitration as it is generally more rational and desirable to adjudicate disputes in an unrelated neutral legal system [2643]. Within such a mechanism, there is no reason to require a connection between the contract and the chosen law [2644]. Unsurprisingly, it is generally accepted that ICSID arbitration, for example, does not require a reasonable connection between the law and the transaction [2645].

N. Renvoi

1. In private international law

The doctrine of *renvoi* concerns the following question: does the application of a specific domestic law also include its private international law provisions? If so, those rules may refer the matter back to another law, which may pose certain challenges.

This issue has been fiercely debated in private international law circles [2646] and has been solved by Article 8 of the Hague Principles [2647]. This provision states that "[a] choice of law does not refer to rules of private international law of the law chosen by the parties unless the parties expressly provide otherwise". The Hague Principles Commentary on Article 8.2 explains that this choice of law "avoids the possibility of an unintentional *renvoi* and therefore conforms to the parties' likely intentions". The Commentary continues that,

2641. See, for example, ICC 4145, *supra* note 2508.
2642. Caron, Caplan and Pellonpää, *supra* note 2618, pp. 124-125.
2643. Schreuer *et al.*, *supra* note 102, p. 564.
2644. Spiermann cites in this regard the case *Elf Aquitaine* v. *NIOC*, *supra* note 2603, paras. 15 and 17), in Spiermann, *supra* note 979 , p. 102.
2645. Schreuer *et al.*, *supra* note 102, p. 564.
2646. Kahn-Freund, *supra* note 1256, p. 285. P. Kahn has shown a critical view toward *renvoi* by stating that, in the end, despite all those authors who favored *renvoi*, he considered it as an unnecessary complication in the contractual area, Kahn, *supra* note 33, pp. 26-27.
2647. Consistent with other Hague Conventions. Consolidated version of preparatory work leading to the draft Hague principles on the choice of law in international contracts – drawn up by the Permanent Bureau, available at http://www.hcch.net/upload/wop/contracts_2012pd01e.pdf, accessed 13 May 2022, p. 26.

nevertheless, in accordance with the principle of party autonomy, parties are allowed by way of exception "to include in their choice of law the private international law rules of the chosen law, provided they do so *expressly*".

The OAS Guide takes a similar approach to Article 20 of Rome I and Article 17 of the Mexico Convention. All these instruments reject *renvoi*, and as such, any reference to the law of a country refers to its substantive law rather than to its conflict of laws rules [2648].

2. Renvoi *in arbitration*

In the UNCITRAL Model Law, there is also a presumption against the *renvoi* principle. Article 28.1 provides that "[a]ny designation of the law or legal system of a given State shall be construed, unless otherwise expressed, as directly referring to the substantive law of that State and not to its conflict of laws rules".

Linda Silberman and Franco Ferrari note that, unsurprisingly, the arbitral rules that deal with the matter exclude *renvoi*, primarily because it undermines legal certainty. As such, generally, the choice of law or legal system of a given State is construed to refer directly to the substantive law of that State and not to its conflict of laws rules [2649].

Arbitral case law regarding the principle of *renvoi* has been contradictory. Some ICC awards exclude *renvoi* [2650], while others accept the principle [2651].

Article 42 (1) of the ICSID Convention states the following:

> "The Tribunal shall decide a dispute in accordance with such rules of law as may be agreed by the parties. In the absence of such agreement, the Tribunal shall apply the law of the Contracting

2648. Silberman and Ferrari, *supra* note 2514, p. 391.

2649. *Ibid.*, fn. 114. The following rules address the matter: Article 27 (1) of the VIAC Rules of Arbitration and Mediation (2018); for similar, if not identical, wording, see Article 33 (2) of the DIAC Rules (2007); Article 46 of the English Arbitration Act 1996; Article 36 (1) of the Japanese Arbitration Act of 25 July 2003; Article 28 (1) of the Danish Arbitration Act of 24 June 2005; Article 34 (2) of the Spanish Law 60/2003 on Arbitration of 23 December 2003; Article 23 (1) of the Arbitration Rules of the German Institution of Arbitration (1998); Article 27 (2) of the Arbitration Institute of the SCC (2017).

2650. ICC Case No. 5505/1987, Preliminary Award, 13 YB Comm. Arb. (1988), p. 110, 117-118.

2651. ICC Award No. 1704/1977, *Collection of ICC Arbitral Awards 1974-1985* (1990), p. 312, 313.

State party to the dispute (including its rules on the conflict of laws) and such rules of international law as may be applicable."

As seen, within the ICSID Convention, the concept of *renvoi* is contemplated in the second sentence of Article 42 (1). The decision of its drafters to include *renvoi* in the second sentence rather than the first may be taken as an indication that it should not be interpreted within the first sentence whatsoever. Moreover, this provision on *renvoi* refers to "rules of law" rather than to a "system of law", and only a legal system as a whole could be expected to also contain conflict of law rules [2652]. According to Andrea Bjorklund and Lukas Vanhonnaeker:

> "When referring to 'whole law' of the host State, the drafters of the ICSID Convention envisaged that the application of the second sentence of Article 42 (1) would not inevitably lead to the application of that law to the substance of the claim. Therefore, if a claim is more closely connected with another law that that of the host State, it is probable that the rules on conflict of laws of the host State would dictate its application. In any way, the arbitrators are granted great discretion with the Article 42 provision when deciding the applicable law." [2653]

If *renvoi* is to be applied according to principles that prioritize the parties' intentions, it must be assumed that, when choosing the applicable law, they did not intend to subject their relationship to the uncertainty of *renvoi* – to an undetermined system of law. However, in the drafting of their choice of law clause, the parties can avoid this outcome by making express reference to the substantive rules of law that they wish to be applied. The parties can also expressly include or exclude the application of national conflict of laws within the law chosen in order to avoid problems of interpretation [2654].

This situation can also occur once litigation arises. In this sense, the Tribunal in *Amco* v. *Indonesia* held that: "[A]s to Indonesian law, there is no need to enter into a discussion of its conflicts of laws' rules".

2652. Schreuer *et al.*, *supra* note 102, pp. 567-568.
2653. Bjorklund and Vanhonnaeker, *supra* note 13, p. 357.
2654. Schreuer *et al.*, *supra* note 102, p. 568. The Convention's drafting history explains the highly unusual phenomenon of a choice of law clause containing a reference to the conflict rules of the chosen laws. Schreuer cites Broches when assuring that: "The idea was to take some of the rigidity out of the automatic reference to the host State's law in case another system of law has stronger contacts to the transaction and a court of the host State would apply that other system of law" (*ibid.*, p. 601).

Indeed, claimants as well as respondents were constantly referring, in their discussion on the merits, to the substantive law of Indonesia [2655].

Where the parties have not chosen an applicable law, the residual rule within Article 42 directs the tribunal to examine the host State's law to determine whether or not another system of law is referred to. If no other legal system is applicable within this rule, the tribunal may then proceed to apply the host State's rules [2656]. This will most typically occur in commercial loan contracts or licensing agreements.

O. Supervening choice of law

Article 2.3 of the Hague Principles states that a choice of law may be made or modified at any time. However, a choice of law or modification made after the contract has been concluded may not prejudice its formal validity or the rights of third parties. This solution is in line with Rome I (Art. 3 (2)), the Mexico Convention (Art. 8.1), recent legislation [2657] and arbitral precedents [2658], which have resolved many of the controversies of the past [2659].

As stated in Commentary 2.10 to the Hague Principles, Article 2.3 is a consequence of the principle of party autonomy. Commentary 2.12 clarifies that third-party rights cannot be affected by this provision. In the example provided, if a third party provides a guarantee and the choice of law is later amended to impose greater liability on one of the contracting parties, although the modification is effective between the contracting parties, such a change will not affect the responsibility of the guarantor. This commentary provides significant clarity on the

2655. *Amco* v. *Indonesia*, Award (20 November 1984), para. 148. This reasoning was also endorsed by the Tribunal in *LG&E* v. *Argentina*, Decision on Liability (3 October 2006), para. 87.

2656. Schreuer *et al.*, *supra* note 102, p. 601.

2657. For instance, the Japanese Law of Private International Law of 2006 (Art. 9), the Russian Civil Code (Art. 1210 (3)) and the Argentinean Civil and Commercial Code (Art. 2651, para. *a*).

2658. *Foreign Trade Court of Arbitration attached to the Serbian Chamber of Commerce*, Award (23 January 2008), http://www.unilex.info, accessed 29 June 2022. Another precedent: *Ad hoc* Arbitral Tribunal, Award (17 December 1975), 4 YB Comm. Arb. (1979), p. 192, 193. The matter has not, however, been addressed by the UNCITRAL Model Law or the UNCITRAL Arbitration Rules.

2659. In Italy, for instance, prior to the Rome Convention the Supreme Court decided that this should not be admitted (1966, Decision No. 1.680, in *Assael Nissim contro Crespi*), which was strongly questioned by Italian doctrine (see Report by M. Giuliano and P. Lagarde, Report on the Convention on the Law Applicable to Contractual Obligations, 11 December 1992, in C. Esplugues Mota (ed.), *Contratación Internacional*, Valencia, Tirant lo Blanch, 1994; comment to Article 3.

appropriate timing and modulations of contract modification. However, for greater certainty, it would be preferable for these clarifications to be clearly expressed in the instrument itself, rather than interpretation by way of reference to domestic laws.

The Hague Principles commentary also makes it clear that as they

> "do not generally seek to resolve what are commonly considered to be procedural issues . . . if the choice or modification of the choice of law occurs during the dispute resolution proceedings, the effect . . . may depend on the *lex fori* or the rules governing the arbitration proceedings" [2660].

In investment arbitration, the initiation of arbitration proceedings or the first session of the tribunal may be good opportunities to agree on a choice of law. However, this can also be done at some later state of proceedings [2661].

In the ICSID context, a literal reading of the language of Article 42 may permit the parties to adopt rules of law up to the time the Centre assumes authority. The parties may even determine their rules of law during the course of the arbitration proceedings [2662] since the competence of the ICSID Centre is founded on the presence of a dispute and not upon the legal regime under which the investment was made. Nevertheless, it remains true that, usually, only the parties to an international investment contract will have chosen the rules of law applicable to a dispute [2663].

2660. Hague Principles, Commentary 2.13. The OAS Guide modeled itself on this solution offered by the Hague Principles. In its recommendations, the OAS Guide provides that domestic laws should specify that a choice of law can be modified at any time but that such a modification does not prejudice its formal validity or the rights of third parties. See OAS Guide, *supra* note 1309, Part Nine, pp. 111 ff.

2661. Schreuer *et al.*, *supra* note 102, p. 568. In *Gardella* v. *Cote de Ivoire*, it is unclear if the Tribunal decided under 42 (1) or (2). The Tribunal said: "Both parties admit that their agreement is governed by the law of the Ivory Coast. Gardella has pleaded, it is true, that the law of the Ivory Coast ought to apply, in this case, within the framework and in the context of public international law. However, Gardella has not drawn any other conclusion from that argument than that it is necessary to have regard to the rule 'pacta sunt servanda' and to the principle of good faith, principles which are equally recognized by the law of the Ivory Coast as well as by French law", *Gardella* v. *Côte d'Ivoire*, *supra* note 1083, Award (29 August 1977), para. 4.3.

2662. *SOABI* v. *Senegal*, *supra* note 1983, Award (25 February 1988), para. 5.02; *AAPL* v. *Sri Lanka*, *supra* note 453, Final Award (27 June 1990), para. 22. See Bjorklund and Vanhonnaeker, *supra* note 13, p. 356.

2663. Kahn, *supra* note 33, p. 8.

P. Severability

The term "severability" in the context of arbitration refers to the situation where the invalidity of an international contract will not necessarily affect or cause the invalidity of the choice of law agreement. For example, if a contract of sale is invalid, the choice of law clause contained within that agreement (or as separately agreed upon) will remain unaffected. Moreover, the effectiveness or invalidity (regardless of whether substantive or formal) of the contract must be evaluated according to the applicable law specified within the agreement in which it was selected. It should be noted that severability is not the same as *dépeçage*.

This severability principle, long accepted in arbitral cases regarding the separability of the arbitration clause from the contract, is aligned with recent instruments related to the choice of law (Rome I) [2664] and to forum selection (2005 Hague Convention on Choice of Court Agreements).

Severability flows from Article 12, paragraph 1, of the Mexico Convention [2665]. The Hague Principles refer explicitly to severability. Article 7 of the Hague Principles states that "a choice of law cannot be contested solely on the ground that the contract to which it applies is not valid". Thus, if the choice of law agreement is not affected, any allegation of the main contract's invalidity must be examined in accordance with the law chosen by the parties. Part Eleven of the OAS Guide deals with the concept of severability along the same lines.

The Hague Principles provide the example of a contract that has been rendered invalid on the grounds of mistake, which does not necessarily invalidate the choice of law agreement unless that agreement is also affected by the same defect. Another example is that of a corporation that enters into a contract which, according to the corporate law of its home

---

2664. Article 10, Regulation (EC) No. 593/2008 of the European Parliament and of the Council of 17 June 2008 on the law applicable to contractual obligations (Rome I).

2665. Which provides that: "The existence and the validity of the contract or of any of its provisions, and the substantive validity of the consent of the parties concerning the selection of the applicable law, shall be governed by the appropriate rules in accordance with Chapter 2 of this Convention." That provision clearly indicates that the validity of the choice of law should be assessed according to the rules contained in Chapter 2. Because party autonomy is enshrined therein, if a choice of law was made, that law will govern all matters related to the validity of the consent of the parties concerning that choice. However, according to paragraph 2 of Article 12, "to establish that one of the parties has not duly consented, the judge shall determine the applicable law, taking into account the habitual residence or principal place of business". This interpretation is advanced by the OAS Guide, *supra* note 1309, p. 146.

State, should have been subject to shareholder approval. Nevertheless, this would not automatically invalidate the choice of law agreement, which must be considered separately. For this provision to be applied properly, it does not matter whether the clause has been provided for in the main contract or in a separate agreement. If it is alleged that the parties did not enter into a contract, the principle of severability only takes effect if it is demonstrated that there was a valid choice of law agreement [2666].

The Hague Principles also indicate that the substantive or formal invalidity of the main contract does not automatically mean that the choice of law agreement is null and void; it can only be declared null and void for reasons that affect the choice of law agreement specifically. The nullity of the main contract may or may not affect the parties' choice of law – this depends on the specific circumstances of the case. For instance, arguments focused on invalidating the consent of the parties in the main contract do not presume to challenge their consent to the choice of law agreement, unless there are circumstances that demonstrate the absence of consent in both agreements [2667].

The Hague Principles give the example of a contract that contains an agreement that it is governed by a law under which the contract is considered invalid due to lack of consent. The lack of consent cannot be said to extend to the choice of law agreement. As a result, that law applies to determine the consequences of invalidity, notably the entitlement to restitution when the contract has been performed, either in whole or in part [2668].

When the defect affects both the main contract and the choice of law agreement, the situation is entirely different. The examples given in the Hague Principles are the invalidity of the contract due to bribery or because one of the parties lacked capacity. Violations such as these would invalidate both agreements [2669].

Q. Express and tacit choice of law in international contracts

Parties may choose the law applicable to their contracts either expressly or tacitly. Party autonomy applies as long as the parties have effectively exercised their desire to make that choice. An express

2666. Hague Principles, Commentary 7.2.
2667. Hague Principles, Commentary 7.8.
2668. Hague Principles, Commentary 7.9.
2669. Hague Principles, Commentary 7.10.

choice of the applicable law clearly arises from the agreement and may be either verbal or written. On occasion, express choice is made with reference to an external factor, such as the location of one of the parties' establishments. The Hague Principles provide the example of the parties entering into a contract that "shall be governed by the law of the State of the establishment of the seller" [2670].

At times, it may be difficult to be certain whether the parties have agreed upon a choice of law. In these cases, the arbitrators should not try to ascertain the hypothetical will of the parties.

A restrictive approach suggests that the adjudicator should be limited to verifying the choice of law as reflected in the contractual terms, excluding any inquiry into outside circumstances. This is how Article 2 (2) of the 1955 Hague Sales Convention is interpreted [2671].

A broad viewpoint reveals that the judge will not only examine the express terms of the contract but will also take into account the circumstances of the case or "the conduct of the parties". This is provided for in the 1978 Hague Agency Convention (Art. 5 (2)) and the 1986 Hague Sales Convention (Art. 7 (1)) [2672].

The Rome Convention followed almost verbatim the Hague Agency Convention by providing in Article 3 (1) that the choice "must be express or demonstrated with reasonable certainty by the terms of the contract or the circumstances of the case". In their official commentary to the Rome Convention, Mario Giuliano and Paul Lagarde stated that tacit intent is certain, for example, when the parties choose a contract type governed by a particular legal system, when there is a previous contract specifying the choice of law, when there is reference to the laws or provisions of a specific country or when a contract forms part of a series of transactions and a system of law was chosen for the agreement on which the other transactions rest [2673].

Andrea Bonomi states that had the drafters of the Rome Convention considered the choice of law, they would have wished to distinguish the tacit choice of law from purely hypothetical selections. However, the line between tacit and hypothetical choices of law is difficult to draw

2670. Hague Principles, Commentary to Article 4.
2671. OAS Guide, *supra* note 1309, p. 127.
2672. *Ibid.*, p. 128.
2673. Report on the Convention on the law applicable to contractual obligations (Rome Convention), by M. Giuliano and P. Lagarde, http://aei.pitt.edu/1891/1/Obligations_report__Guiliano_OJ_C_282.pdf, accessed 13 May 2022.

in practice, and English and German tribunals have been less strict than other European tribunals in finding tacit choice of law selections [2674].

Despite some proposals to eliminate it [2675], Rome I (in line with the Rome Convention) continues to allow tribunals to accept the parties' tacit choice of law, provided that their choice is "expressly or clearly demonstrated by the terms of the contract or the circumstances of the case" (Art. 3.1). There has been a change in terminology from that of the Rome Convention that has to do, above all, with strengthening the English version of the text (as well as the German version). Specifically, Rome I requires that a tacit choice must be "clearly demonstrated", and not just "demonstrated with reasonable certainty". This does not aim to change the spirit of the prior Rome Convention rule. Rather, this change simply aims to bring the English and German versions in line with the French text of the instrument [2676].

In the United States, the Restatement (Second) Conflict of Laws contains a "less demanding" solution [2677], which reads:

> "Even when the contract does not refer to any state, the forum may nevertheless be able to conclude from its provisions that the parties did wish to have the law of a particular state applied. So, the fact that the contract contains legal expressions, or makes references to legal doctrines, that are peculiar to the local law of a particular state may provide persuasive evidence that the parties wished to have this law applied." [2678]

Article 7, paragraph 1, of the Mexico Convention states that "the parties' agreement on this selection must be express or, in the event that there is no express agreement, must be evident from the parties' behaviour and from the clauses of the contract, considered as a whole". For this reason, all the contract's points of connection must be considered, such as the place of formation and performance, language, currency and the forum or place of arbitration.

The issue of the choice of applicable law was subject to intense debate in the discussions leading up to the drafting of the Mexico Convention. It is clear from the language of the article that the conduct

2674. See further on this issue and its alternatives in Bonomi, *supra* note 1294, pp. 335-336, that references the German decisions of the Bundersgerichtshoff of 1997 and 1999.

2675. *Ibid.*, p. 336.

2676. Heiss, *supra* note 2637, p. 1.

2677. Born, *supra* note 2273, p. 2941.

2678. Restatement (Second) Conflict of Laws, para. 187, comm. a (1971).

of the parties and the clauses of the contract are indices to be considered cumulatively by the court, and that they must enable the court to reach a conclusion that is "evident". Otherwise, Article 9 will be applied as if the parties had not chosen an applicable law at all. That is, the Mexico Convention does not accept a hypothetical choice of law; a clear and obvious intention to choose the applicable law is required. For example, if the parties to the contract refer to the specific rules of a particular State in the choice of law clause and their behavior is consistent with the content of that clause, the court may consider that the choice of the law of that State is "evident" [2679].

According to Article 4 of the Hague Principles, "a choice of law . . . must be made expressly or appear clearly from the provisions of the contract or the circumstances". This allows for the choice of law to be express or tacit, so long as it is clear. The OAS Guide points in the same direction [2680].

The issue was subject to intense scrutiny during discussions of the Hague Working Group as well [2681]. Given the lack of consensus in comparative law, it was thought that the parties should be encouraged to be explicit in their choice of law. For greater certainty, the decision was made to adopt the formula that the choice of law "should be made expressly, or follow clearly from the provisions of the contract or the circumstances". Most of the experts expressed concern that the standard of "manifestly clear intentions" would be very high, in particular for certain States that require lower standards for other substantive aspects of the contract.

According to the commentary of the Hague Principles, the relevant circumstances may consist of the parties' behavior and other factors related to the conclusion of the contract. This principle may also be applicable in the case of related contracts. Thus, if the parties have

---

2679. Fernández Arroyo and Fresnedo de Aguirre, *supra* note 1280, pp. 999-1000. According to Parra Aranguren's interpretation, the possibility to separate a national judge and a substantive law of international origin (international conventions or other principles) remains open. See also D. Operti Badán and C. Fresnedo de Aguirre, *Contratos Comerciales Internacionales*, Montevideo, Fundación de Cultura Universitaria, 1997, p. 33. See criticisms in D. Hargaín, "Contratos comerciales en el MERCOSUR: Ley aplicable y juez competente", *Revista de Derecho del MERCOSUR*, No. 1 (1997), p. 95.

2680. Part Eight of the OAS Guide refers to express or tacit choice of law, stressing that, one way or another, the choice should be evident or appear clearly from the provisions of the contract and its circumstances, see *supra* note 1309.

2681. For a review of the preparatory works of the Hague Principles, see https://www.hcch.net/en/publications-and-studies/details4/?pid=6297&dtid=61, accessed 30 June 2022.

made the express choice to use the law of a particular State to govern their contracts in prior dealings, and the circumstances do not indicate any intention to change this practice, the adjudicator may conclude that the parties had the clear intent for the contract under consideration to be governed by the law of that same State, even though an express choice does not appear therein [2682].

The choice must be clear from the existence of conclusive evidence [2683]. The Hague Principles further state that it is widely accepted that the adoption of a model form used generally in the context of a specific legal system may signal the parties' intent for the contract to be governed by that system, although there is no express statement to that effect. The example provided is a marine insurance contract in the form of a Lloyd's policy. Given that this contract model is based on English law, its use by the parties may indicate their intent to subject the contract to that legal system [2684]. The same occurs when the contract contains terminology that is characteristic of a specific legal system or contains references to domestic provisions evidencing that the parties had that legal system in mind and intended to subject the contract to it [2685].

R. Tacit choice in commercial arbitration

Article 28 (1) of the UNCITRAL Model Law provides that "[t]he arbitral tribunal shall decide the dispute in accordance with such rules of law as are chosen by the parties as applicable to the substance of the dispute". The UNCITRAL Arbitration Rules of 2010 refer to the rules of law "designated by the parties" as applicable to the substance of the dispute.

It follows from these texts that for a choice of law to be valid, it is not necessary that the parties communicate that choice expressly. However, because the new rules use the word "designate", there is nonetheless an expectation that the choice of law be unambiguous [2686].

The reference in the Arbitration Rules of 2010 to "the rules of law designated by the parties" is an invitation for the arbitral tribunals to determine whether there has been any indirect indication as to the governing rules. For instance, even if the parties have not expressly

2682. Hague Principles, Commentary 4.13.
2683. Hague Principles, Commentary 4.14.
2684. Hague Principles, Commentary 4.9.
2685. Hague Principles, Commentary 4.10.
2686. Caron, Caplan and Pellonpää, *supra* note 2618, p. 125.

agreed on the law applicable to their contract, they may have referred to various provisions within a particular legal system, which could indicate that they intended to choose the laws of that system as the applicable law.

With respect to arbitral awards, in a 1975 case it was declared that a tacit selection of the applicable law will be found where both the claimant and the respondent based their arguments on provisions of the same law [2687]. In another award, it was understood that the selection of the seat of the arbitration should not necessarily imply that the law of the seat should govern the contract [2688]. Ultimately, tacit selection must be clearly or obviously communicated. As was expressed in another arbitral award, tacit selection must result from a clear and non-ambiguous interpretation of the terms of the contract or the circumstances [2689].

The Hague Principles also address the issue of tacit choice in the context of arbitration. According to the second sentence of Article 4, the parties' selection of an arbitral tribunal is not sufficient to indicate, on its own, that the parties have made a tacit choice of the applicable law. The Hague Principles state that the parties may have chosen a tribunal because of its neutrality or specialization, and not necessarily because they desired a particular law to be applied to their contract. Nevertheless, an arbitration agreement that refers disputes to a clearly specified forum may be one of the primary factors to consider in the determination of a tacit choice of applicable law [2690].

S. Express and tacit choice in investment arbitration

1. Express choice

A choice of law may be made expressly in the investment contract, in the investment law of the host State, in the investment treaty or in a subsequent agreement between the parties.

2687. *Ad hoc* Arbitral Tribunal, *supra* note 2658, p. 193.

2688. Caron, Caplan and Pellonpää, *supra* note 2618, p. 126. There is however precedent decided in the contrary. In the case *China International Economic and Trade Arbitration Commission*, Arbitral Award No. 0291-1, it was understood that by opting for an arbitration administered by the CIETAC with seat in China, the parties were tacitly selecting Chinese law, http://www.unilex.info. In *Schiedsgericht der Handelskammer Hamburg*, 21 March 1996, it was stated that the selection of German law could be inferred from the parties' agreement to refer their disputes to the German arbitral tribunal.

2689. ICC Preliminary Award 5505/1987, *supra* note 2650, p. 118.

2690. Hague Principles, Commentary 4.11.

Explicit choice of law provisions in treaties are the exception and not the rule [2691]. Nonetheless, a number of BITs contain choice of law clauses that serve as the basis for an agreement on the choice of law between the host State and the investor. In this regard, the Tribunal in *Goetz* v. *Burundi* held that the applicable law is determined in the investment treaty. The Republic of Burundi has decided in favor of the applicable law in the Belgium-Burundi investment treaty and investors also made this choice by initiating an arbitration based on such an instrument [2692]. The tribunals in *Middle East Cement* v. *Egypt* and *Siemens* v. *Argentina* also decided in accordance with this criterion [2693].

Multilateral treaties in which the contracting States offer consent to arbitration to investors may also contain provisions stating the applicable law. In this regard, the USMCA, Article 14.D.9, Annex 2 of Chapter 14, states that "the tribunal shall decide the issues in dispute in accordance with this Agreement and applicable rules of international law". A similar provision is found in Article 26 of the Energy Charter, which was applied in the *Kardassopoulos* v. *Georgia* case, in which the Tribunal quoted the provisions of the treaty to determine that it could only decide the disputed issues considering the applicable rules and principles of international law [2694].

2. Vagueness of rules on tacit choice in investment arbitration

The ICSID Convention does not deal with the issue of express and tacit choice in arbitration. Instead, the Convention leaves the issue to be decided in accordance with conflict of laws rules. Within this context, the following question arises: should the ICSID Convention be interpreted on its own or should the conflict of laws rules of the host State be considered on a residual basis [2695]? The only thing which is certain is the vagueness of ICSID Article 42 as to the form which the adoption of the governing law by the parties should take [2696].

Case law provides little guidance in this regard. The first ICSID case to ever discuss this issue was *Holiday Inns* v. *Morocco*, wherein the Tribunal held that an implied agreement would only be acceptable

2691. Cordero-Moss and Behn, *supra* note 964, p. 579.
2692. *Goetz* v. *Burundi*, *supra* note 93.
2693. *Middle East Cement* v. *Egypt*, Award (12 April 2002), paras. 86, 87. *Siemens* v. *Argentina*, *supra* note 531, Award (6 February 2007), para. 76.
2694. *Kardassopoulos* v. *Georgia*, Decision on Jurisdiction (6 July 2007), para. 146.
2695. Bischoff, *supra* note 15, p. 760.
2696. Kahn, *supra* note 33, p. 10.

in the event that the specific circumstances would exclude any other interpretation of the parties' intention [2697]. In *CDSE* v. *Costa Rica*, the Tribunal stated that the choice of applicable law must be clear and unequivocal [2698]. Therefore, the situation must be limited to cases in which such an agreement can be ascertained with reasonable certainty [2699]. In *Benvenuti* v. *Congo*, the determination of the choice of law provision was done first by looking at the agreement of the parties (which was silent on the matter) and then by resorting to Article 42 (1) of the Convention, which led to the application of the law of the contracting State and the principles of international law on the matter [2700]. In this situation, Georges Delaume advocates for the tribunal to first determine whether a choice of law clause that has been agreed upon does, in fact, exist before proceeding to an analysis of the applicable law on the basis of the first or second sentence of Article 42 (1) [2701].

Article V of the 1981 Iran-United States Claims Settlement Declaration also does not deal with the issue of express and tacit choice in arbitration.

There does not appear to be any case decided before the Iran-United States Claims Tribunal in which the parties had explicitly agreed to the application of international law. Indeed, it was the practice in Iran

---

2697. "The Tribunal had to consider whether the consent to treat a locally incorporated company as a national of another country should be express or implied. The Tribunal confirme that the terms of Article 25 (2) *(b)* created an exception to the ICSID Convention and therefore one would expect that parties should express themselves clearly and explicitly with respect to such a derogation. Such an agreement should therefore normally be explicit", J. D. M. Lew, "ICSID Arbitration: Special Features and Recent Developments", in N. Horn and S. Kröll (eds.), *Arbitrating Foreign Investment Disputes: Procedural and Substantive Legal Aspects* (Studies in Transnational Economic Law, No. 19), The Hague, Kluwer Law International, 2004, pp. 267-282, esp. 270, and 633. This paragraph was quoted by the Tribunal in *Cable Television of Nevis Ltd. and Cable Television of Nevis Holdings Ltd.* v. *The Federation of St Kitts and Nevis*, ICSID Case No. ARB/95/2, in *ICSID Review: Foreign Investment Law Journal*, Vol. 13, No. 1 (1998), p. 328, p. 370. The Tribunal decided in that case that it did not have jurisdiction.

2698. "Article 42 (1) of the ICSID Convention does not require that the parties' agreement as to the applicable law be in writing or even that it be stated expressly. However, for the Tribunal to find that such an agreement was implied it must first find that the substance of the agreement, irrespective of its form, is clear" (*CDSE* v. *Costa Rica*, Award (17 February 2000), in *ICSID Review: Foreign Investment Law Journal*, Vol. 15 (2000), p. 190, para. 63.

2699. Kjos, *supra* note 2296, p. 80.

2700. *Benvenuti* v. *Congo*, *supra* note 455, Award (15 August 1980), para. 4.2. See Schreuer *et al.*, *supra* note 102, p. 593.

2701. G. R. Delaume, "The Pyramids Stand: The Pharaohs Can Rest in Peace", *ICSID Review: Foreign Investment Law Journal*, Vol. 8 (1993), p. 241. In the same sense, see Schreuer *et al.*, *supra* note 102, p. 572.

before the Revolution to subject contracts concluded with Iranian governmental entities to the laws of Iran[2702].

In certain cases, such as *Mobil Oil Iran* v. *Iran* (1987), the Tribunal has nevertheless found an implied choice of international law by examining the nature of the contract[2703]. In that case, the Tribunal reasoned as follows:

> "In view of the international character of the [Agreement], concluded between a State, a State agency and a number of major foreign companies, of the magnitude of the interests involved, of the complex set of rights and obligations which it established, and of the link created between this Agreement and the sharing of oil industry benefits throughout the Persian Gulf Countries, the Tribunal does not consider it appropriate that such an Agreement be governed by the law of one Party. This conclusion is in accord with the spirit of Article 29 and with the usages of trade, as expressed in agreements between States and foreign companies, notably in the oil industry, and confirmed in several recent arbitral awards."[2704]

Thus, the Tribunal concluded that the law applicable to the contract was Iranian law for interpretive issues, and the general principles of commercial and international law for all other issues. The law applicable to the party's liability was found to be international law[2705].

3. *Clear and unequivocal choice*

ICSID tribunals have recognized the possibility of an indirect choice of law, for instance in a clearly implicit agreement or in a reference by the parties to an instrument with a clause on applicable law[2706], "thus giving a broad meaning to the first sentence of Article 42 (1)"[2707].

2702. A. Avanessian, *The Iran-United States Claims Tribunal in Action*, London, Graham & Trotman / Martinus Nijhoff, 1993, p. 239, fn. 19 *apud* Kjos, *supra* note 2296, p. 220.

2703. *Mobil Oil* v. *Iran*, *supra* note 2438, Partial Award (14 July 1987).

2704. *Ibid.*, para. 80.

2705. *Ibid.*, para. 81.

2706. *Československa* v. *Slovak Republic*, *supra* note 70, Award (29 December 2004), para. 63; *ADC & ADMC* v. *Hungary*, *supra* note 539, Award of the Tribunal (2 October 2006) para. 290; *UAB E energija (Lithuania)* v. *Republic of Latvia*, ICSID Case No. ARB/12/33, Award (22 December 2017), para. 792.

2707. Bjorklund and Vanhonnaeker, *supra* note 13, p. 352.

In *CDSE* v. *Costa Rica*, it was held that an agreement on the choice of law would have to be clear and unequivocal [2708]. The Tribunal found that although Article 42 (1) of the ICSID Convention did not require that the parties' arrangement as to the applicable law be in writing or even that it be stated expressly, the agreement still had to be clear and unequivocal. To determine that such an agreement was implied, the tribunal must first conclude that the substance of the arrangement is clear. Such did not occur in that case [2709].

In turn, the *CME* v. *Czech Republic* case involved UNCITRAL Arbitration Rules that emerged from the Netherlands-Czech bilateral investment treaty [2710]. In that case, the Tribunal decided that the choice of the applicable law could not be implied and must be made "clearly and unequivocally" [2711]. This is a matter of interpretation of the parties' intention, as opposed to an interpretation of the ICSID Convention itself [2712].

4. Choice of law as implied from a law in the parties' contract

Another method of determining the choice of law involves searching for an indirect or implicit choice of law either in the original agreement or in the subsequent conduct of the parties.

In this regard, reference to a specific part of the host States' legislation in the agreements between the parties may amount to a general choice of its law. This argument was accepted in *LETCO* v. *Liberia* [2713]. In that case, the opening paragraph of the investment contract specified that the contract had been concluded under the General Business Law of Liberia. The Tribunal understood that such language seemed "to indicate an express choice by the parties of the Law of Liberia as

---

2708. *CDSE* v. *Costa Rica*, Award (17 February 2000), paras. 28, 35, 37, 40, 60-68.

2709. Schreuer *et al.*, *supra* note 102, p. 558 mentions paragraph 63 of the Award, in which the Tribunal explains the rationale behind its conclusion.

2710. *CME Czech Republic BV* v. *The Czech Republic*, Final Award (14 March 2003), 9 *ICSID Reports*, p. 264, 348 (2006), para. 91, in Y. Banifatemi, "The Law Applicable in Investment Treaty Arbitration", in K. Yannaca-Small (ed.), *Arbitration Under International Investment Agreements: A Guide to the Key Issues*, Oxford, Oxford University Press, 2010, p. 198.

2711. *CME Czech Republic BV* v. *The Czech Republic*, Final Award (14 March 2003), 9 *ICSID Reports*, p. 264, 348 (2006), para. 91. It is also interesting the reasoning of the Svea Court of Appeal following the Czech Republic's application for annulment of the Partial Award of 13 September 2001. Svea Court of Appeal, *The Czech Republic* v. *CME Czech Republic BV*, Judgment (15 May 2003), 42 ILM, p. 919, 965 (2003). See Banifatemi, *supra* note 2710, pp. 198-199.

2712. *Ibid.*, p. 199.

2713. *LETCO* v. *Liberia*, *supra* note 456, Award (31 March 1986), para. 35.

the law governing the Concession Agreement". However, the Arbitral Tribunal in that case also took international law into account [2714].

With that stipulation in mind, a mere reference by the parties to an item of the host State's law is not sufficient indication of the parties' intention to choose that entire legal system as the applicable law. Further, acceptance of an offer to consent to jurisdiction cannot be taken as a choice of the host State's law [2715]. This was decided by the Tribunal in *Aucoven* v. *Venezuela* [2716], in which the application of Venezuelan law was only partially accepted [2717]. The Preamble of the Concession Agreement in that case stated that the contract would be governed by certain specified Venezuelan decrees "and the provisions of any other laws, regulations, or other documents as may be applicable". The Arbitral Tribunal ruled that the parties could easily have adopted language showing their common intent to choose Venezuelan law as the general applicable law. Failing any indication to this effect, no agreement on Venezuelan law could be found [2718].

5. Choice of law if the parties argue on the basis of the same law

Another method to determine the parties' choice of applicable law involves looking at the parties' submissions in the course of the

2714. *Ibid.*, para. 36, in which the Tribunal wrote that: "The only question is whether Liberian law is applied on its own (as the law chosen by the parties) or in conjunction with applicable principles of public international law." The question was left open in *Southern Pacific* v. *Egypt*, *supra* note 128, Decision on Jurisdiction (14 April 1988). The preamble to the Heads of Agreement referred to Egyptian Laws No. 1 and No. 2 of 1973 and Law No. 43 of 1974. In this case, the parties disputed whether the parties had agreed or not to apply Egyptian law. The respondent contended that the parties had implicitly agreed to apply it, in view of the first sentence of Article 42 (1). The claimants rejected this position, sustaining that it is the second sentence of Article 42 (1) which becomes operative, so that the Tribunal shall apply the "law of the Contracting state party . . . and such rules of international law as may be applicable". The Tribunal saw this circumstance of "very little, if any, practical significance", since national and international law should be applied to the merits regardless of an implicit choice for Egyptian law. *SPP* v. *Egypt*, *supra* note 1085, Award (20 May 1992), para. 78. The dissenting opinion of El Mahdi, at section III (3) *(i)* stated the following: "[I]t is mandatory to decide upon the issue of whether or not the parties to the present dispute agreed upon the choice of the Applicable Law. . . . [T]he plain language of article (42/1) first sentence [ICSID Convention], does not give room but to the exclusive application of the law that the parties have chosen as the applicable law to govern their relationship."

2715. Schreuer *et al.*, *supra* note 102, pp. 570-571.

2716. *Autopista Concesionada de Venezuela, CA* v. *Bolivarian Republic of Venezuela*, ICSID Case No. ARB/00/5, Award (23 September 2003).

2717. Schreuer *et al.*, *supra* note 102, p. 593.

2718. *Autopista* v. *Venezuela*, *supra* note 2716, Award (2003), para. 94.

proceedings or at their reliance upon a treaty as an indirect choice of law. As a general proposition, any agreement on choice of law should be proven and not inferred by the tribunal without evidence [2719].

In *Asian Agricultural Products Limited (AAPL)* v. *Democratic Socialist Republic of Sri Lanka* (1990), for the first time an ICSID tribunal's jurisdiction was determined to derive from an investment treaty [2720]. The treaty contained no provision related to the applicable law, and the Tribunal understood that the parties' pleadings "demonstrated their mutual agreement to consider the BIT as being the primary source of the applicable legal rules" [2721]. The dissent noted that the respondent had no choice but to respond to the arguments of claimant and refer to the laws the opposing party had cited, but that this does not amount to an implied choice of law [2722]. The Arbitral Tribunal could also have directly applied the second sentence of Article 42 (1) of the ICSID Convention, deciding the applicability of both Sri Lankan and international law [2723].

In other cases, ICSID tribunals relied upon the parties' submissions merely to corroborate their findings on applicable law. For instance, the tribunals in the first award in *Amco* v. *Indonesia*, in *Wena* v. *Egypt* and in *Enron* v. *Argentina* decided that the parties' references and pleadings involving a specific law allowed for that law to be applied to their contract [2724].

In *Biloune and Marine Drive* v. *Ghana*, the UNCITRAL Tribunal considered the parties' pleadings and referred to customary international law despite the agreement in their contract to the application of the laws of Ghana. The Tribunal stated that "there is no indication that Ghanaian law diverges on the central issue of expropriation from customary

2719. Schreuer *et al.*, *supra* note 102, p. 570. "The assumption of a hypothetical agreement interpreted from the objective circumstances of a case is sometimes used in Private International Law but would not be in line with the meaning of Article 42 (1) and is likely to undermine the residual rule of its second sentence. In virtue of this, the French version of the ICSID Convention adopts the terminology 'agreed' in its drafting, implying that the parties must take a positive action to justify choice of law" (*ibid.*, p. 593).

2720. *AAPL* v. *Sri Lanka*, *supra* note 453, Award (27 June 1990), p. 246.

2721. *Ibid.*, paras. 246, 250, 256.

2722. *Ibid.*, Dissenting Opinion by Asante, para. 299.

2723. "Holding the BIT to be the principal source of applicable law was logical in the circumstances. As in most of the many other BIT cases that were to follow, the claim in AAPL was based on asserted breaches by the respondent of its obligations under the BIT – notably, in AAPL, the obligation to accord covered investments 'full protection and security'." Under the UK-Sri Lanka BIT Article 2 (2), it would have made little sense to judge such a claim mainly by reference to domestic host State law, Parra, *supra* note 510, p. 184.

2724. *Wena Hotels* v. *Egypt*, *supra* note 601, Award (2000), para. 79. *Enron* v. *Argentina*, *supra* note 451, Award (22 May 2007), para. 209.

principles of international law. On the contrary, both Parties explicitly treated those principles as governing the issue of expropriation" [2725].

6. *Reference to certain aspects of a law through the parties' implied choice*

Any assertion that the inclusion of a domestic law provision or an entire piece of legislation within an agreement amounts to a general choice of that law is unconvincing. This is particularly so in the context of an arrangement that grants the parties a significant latitude in combining, selecting and excluding parts of different legal systems. Moreover, certain aspects of the domestic law of the host State will almost inevitably be applicable. Therefore, the reference to certain domestic law provisions within an agreement cannot be seen as clarifying certain details regarding the application of the law and should not be interpreted as an implicit general choice of that law [2726].

7. *Tacit agreement and the selection of arbitration*

No conclusions in regard to the applicable law may be drawn from the fact that a dispute has been submitted to international arbitration, nor can a choice of law derive from the jurisdiction where the proceedings are to take place. On the contrary, in what has been qualified as a "clearly erroneous decision" [2727], the District Court in *MINE* v. *Guinea* based its finding of the applicability of US law on the fact that ICSID arbitration was expected to take place in that country [2728].

Some treaties that provide for ICSID arbitration contain their own rules to decide the applicable law. In these cases, acceptance by the investor of an offer to consent to jurisdiction also implies the acceptance of the clause on the applicable law specified within the treaty. This acceptance can be shown by initiating proceedings on the basis of the treaty's dispute resolution provision [2729].

2725. See *Biloune and Marine Drive Complex Ltd.* v. *Ghana Investments Centre and the Government of Ghana*, Award on Jurisdiction and Liability (27 October 1989), secs. I, VI and F.

2726. Schreuer *et al.*, *supra* note 102, p. 573.

2727. *Ibid.*, p. 570.

2728. *Maritime International Nominees Establishment* v. *Republic of Guinea*, US Court of Appeals District of Columbia Circuit Decision (12 November 1982).

2729. Schreuer *et al.*, *supra* note 102, p. 576.

8. Arbitration as an implicit choice of public international law

Early cases found that the inclusion of an arbitration clause in a contract leads to the implicit acceptance of public international law as the parties' choice of applicable law. In *Texaco* v. *Libya* (1977), the Arbitral Tribunal stated: "[One] process for the internationalization of a contract consists in inserting a clause providing that possible differences which may arise in respect of the interpretation and the performance of the contract shall be submitted to arbitration." [2730]

The same conclusion had been reached in the *Sapphire* case (1963); however, the decision was subject to different reasoning. The Tribunal held that "if no positive implication can be made from the arbitral clause, it is possible to find there a negative intention, namely, to reject the exclusive application of Iranian law" [2731]. On this basis, the Tribunal went on to apply international law.

A significant number of treaties referring to the ICSID mechanism do not provide for any express choice of law. Strictly speaking, the absence of a choice of law should lead to the application of the default Article 42 (1), Section 2, that reads "in absence of such agreement" [2732]. However, several ICSID tribunals considered these situations as involving an implicit choice of public international law. The tribunals in *Middle East Cement* v. *Egypt* [2733], *MTD* v. *Chile* [2734], *CSOB* v. *Slovakia* [2735] and *ADC* v. *Hungary* [2736] all adopted this view [2737].

2730. *Texaco* v. *Libya*, *supra* note 119, fn. 53, Award on the Merits (19 January 1977), para. 44.

2731. *Sapphire*, *supra* note 1013, Award (1963), p. 140, para. 173. Sole Arbitrator Cavin stated: "[A] reference to rules of good faith, together with the absence of any reference to a national system of law, leads the judge to determine, according to the spirit of the agreement . . . not to apply the strict rules of a particular system but, rather, to rely upon the rules of law, based upon reason, which are common to civilized nations. These rules are enshrined in Article 38 of the Statute of the International Court of Justice as a source of law, and numerous decisions of international tribunals have made use of them and clarified them."

2732. Schreuer *et al.*, *supra* note 102, p. 578.

2733. *Middle East Cement* v. *Egypt*, Award (12 April 2002), para. 86.

2734. *MTD* v. *Chile*, *supra* note 327, Award (25 May 2004).

2735. *CSOB* v. *Slovakia*, Award (29 December 2004), para. 61.

2736. *ADC & ADMC* v. *Hungary*, *supra* note 539, Award (2 October 2006), para. 290.

2737. In *LG&E* v. *Argentina* the Tribunal discussed but did not follow the concept of an implicit choice of international law through the invocation of the BIT. *LG&E* v. *Argentina*, Decision on Liability (3 October 2006), para. 85. However, although the Tribunal addressed the issue of applicable law under the second sentence of Article 42 (1), its solution came very close to an implicit choice of law. See Schreuer *et al.*, *supra* note 102, p. 580.

In *MCI* v. *Ecuador*, the claimant argued that "the Tribunal should consider that no such agreement exists, the force of the second part of Article 42 (1) of the Convention is such that international law must be applied". For its part, Ecuador argued that its own domestic law should be applied. In the end, the Tribunal decided that it

> "finds no evidence of any agreement on the law applicable to this dispute. Therefore, the Tribunal considers that it must respect the provisions of the second part of Article 42 (1) of the ICSID Convention, i.e., in the absence of an agreement, the Tribunal shall apply Ecuadorian law, including its rules of private international law and such rules of international law as may be applicable" [2738].

Similarly, this argument was rejected in *LG&E* v. *Argentina* (2006). In that case, the Tribunal stated that "these elements do not suffice to say that there is an implicit agreement by the parties as to the applicable law, a decision requiring more decisive actions". Consequently, no implied agreement was deemed to be present [2739].

In other cases, the tribunal resorted directly to the application of Article 42 of the ICSID Convention since the applicable investment agreement contained no choice of law clause [2740]. This rationale was subsequently followed by the tribunals in *Vestey Group* v. *Venezuela* and *Ioan Micula* et al. v. *Romania* [2741].

Furthermore, the Tribunal in *Goetz* v. *Burundi* (1999) held that

> "choice of law clauses in investment protection treaties frequently refer to the provisions of the treaty itself, and more broadly, to international law principles and rules. This leads to a remarkable comeback of international law, after a decline in practice and

---

2738. *MCI* v. *Ecuador*, *supra* note 1150, Award (31 July 2007), paras. 214-217.

2739. *LG&E* v. *Argentina*, *supra* note 448, Decision on Liability (3 October 2006), para. 85. See also *MCI* v. *Ecuador*, *supra* note 1150, Award, para. 217.

2740. Bischoff, *supra* note 15, p. 760.

2741. The decisions on this matter read as follows. In *Vestey* v. *Venezuela*, *supra* note 2028, para. 117, the Tribunal determined: "The Parties have not agreed on the rules of law that govern the merits of this dispute. Consequently, the Tribunal shall apply, in addition to the Treaty, Venezuelan law and international law when appropriate." In *Ioan Micula* et al. v. *Romania*, *supra* note 102, Award (11 December 2013), para. 287, the Tribunal followed this line by ruling that: "The Parties note that the BIT does not contain a choice of law clause (C-SoC, para. 170; R-CM, para. 72; R-Rejoinder, para. 230). Accordingly, Article 42 (1) of the ICSID Convention directs the Tribunal to apply the host State's law (here, Romanian law) and 'such rules of international law as may be applicable'".

jurisprudence, in the legal relations between host States and foreign investors"[2742].

In *Quirobax SA and Non-Metallic Minerals SA* v. *Bol.*, the Tribunal determined that "except for the undisputed application of the BIT, the Parties have not agreed on the rules of law that govern the merits of this dispute. Consequently, the Tribunal shall apply Bolivian law and international law when appropriate"[2743].

Since claimants regularly assert violations of the substantive treatment standards contained in the treaties, in the absence of express choice of law provisions, these public international law standards are considered the rules of law applicable to the dispute. Whether such an implicit choice of law encompasses other rules of public international law, such as customary international law or general principles, is less clear[2744].

T. Stabilization clause

When a national law is chosen, a question arises whether that law should be understood according to its own terms at the time the agreement was concluded or should be interpreted in the way in which it may have been amended by subsequent legislation. As pointed out by Aron Broches, a mere reference to the law of a country must be understood to be a reference to that law as it exists at the time when the dispute arises[2745].

Stabilization clauses work to counter this default effect and are intended to exclude legislation passed by States after the conclusion of a contract that would defeat, cancel or gravely affect its conditions. As expressed in the case *Liberian Eastern Timber Corporation* v. *Liberia*, "otherwise the contracting State may easily avoid its contractual obligations"[2746].

2742. *Goetz* v. *Burundi*, *supra* note 93, paras. 488-489.

2743. *Quirobax* v. *Bolivia*, *supra* note 585, Award (2015), para. 91. This decision is also aligned with *Venezuela Holdings* v. *Venezuela*, *supra* note 110, Award (9 October 2014), para. 221 and with *Electrabel* v. *Hungary*, *supra* note 666, Decision on Jurisdiction, Applicable Law and Liability (30 November 2012), paras. 4.18, 4.192. With another rationale, the Tribunal in *LG&E* v. *Argentina* questioned that claiming a breach could result in an implicit choice of law but did not question that choice of law agreements can be made implicitly. See *LG&E* v. *Argentina*, *supra* note 448, Decision on Liability (2006), para. 96.

2744. Schreuer *et al.*, *supra* note 102, p. 578.

2745. Broches, *supra* note 2161, p. 390.

2746. *LETCO* v. *Liberia*, *supra* note 456, Award (31 March 1986), para. 368.

Changes to legislation can be expected in light of altering social, economic and technological conditions. For instance, governments may decide to make adjustments to labor law, to make reasonable changes to tax law or to update technical safety standards and regulations. As such, the parties may specifically agree to exempt the investor from certain fiscal, foreign exchange or social security legislation [2747]. Since investing in developing countries involves many uncertainties not only of the expected economic but also political risk, to not discourage these endeavors the technique of express stabilization of particular terms of the agreements is valid under international law and should be recognized as such in any forum in which the issue arises [2748].

The situation is different when it comes to legislation that defeats undertakings freely made by the host State and that affect the root of the legal relationship, thus creating an environment in which the investor can no longer operate. Direct or indirect expropriations, or actions selectively directed toward particular investors or a group of investors, cannot be tolerated for this reason [2749]. In these situations, if the stabilization clause is governed by the law of the host State, the rules of the game will change significantly, and minimum standards of protection will only be maintained if the transaction is governed by international law [2750].

In *Elf Aquitaine Iran* v. *NIOC*, the Tribunal held that

> "a State which has itself entered into an international agreement or has permitted companies or institutions controlled by it to enter into such agreement regulated as lex contracts by recognized principles of international law is not free to change the *lex contractus* by subsequent legislation" [2751].

2747. Schreuer *et al.*, *supra* note 102, p. 564.
2748. Curtis, *supra* note 119, p. 365.
2749. Schreuer *et al.*, *supra* note 102, p. 592.
2750. Bischoff, *supra* note 15, p. 766.
2751. *Elf Aquitaine* v. *NIOC*, *supra* note 2603, para. 19. In an ICC case, the Tribunal found that the chosen law was Utopian law, "purely and simply", as opposed to utopian law "in its evolution". The Tribunal stated that "it cannot be accepted that the parties which do simply accept that the validity and effectiveness of a contractual clause as fundamental as an arbitration clause should be subject to a sort of condition entirely within the power of one party, the occurrence of which would depend solely on the will of the State of which the public organization party to the said contract and to the undertaking to arbitrate is an instrumentality" (*Company Z and others* v. *State Organization ABC*, Award (April 1982), YB Comm. Arb. (1983), p. 114). See Spiermann, *supra* note 979, p. 97.

The ICSID Convention does not address the problem of the stabilization clause. The drafting history of the Convention revealed that the drafters were generally aware of this issue, however no obvious solution was offered [2752]. In reference to the final text of Article 42, Broches suggested that the parties may decide to stabilize their contractual relationship by incorporating a particular law as of a certain date. In that case, if the host State subsequently amends its law in order to defeat the rights of the investor, the tribunal would be free to disregard such a change on the grounds that it violated international law [2753]. Stabilization clauses do not prevent the law from being changed but rather communicate a promise that legal variations will not apply to investors or will be accompanied by compensation for any adverse consequences caused by such changes.

Stabilization clauses are generally accepted within investment arbitral decisions [2754]. For instance, in the ICSID case *AGIP* v. *Congo*, the Tribunal demonstrated not only a general deference to stabilization clauses but also a willingness to accept them as part of international law, thereby shielding them against any unilateral abrogation through host State legislation [2755]. Stabilization clauses have not featured as centrally in other cases but were still referred to and favored by tribunals in *LETCO* v. *Liberia* [2756], *MINE* v. *Guinea* [2757], *CMS* v. *Argentina* [2758] and *Duke Energy* v. *Peru* [2759], among others.

2752. "It was suggested that subsequent legislation should not apply if it were to the detriment of the investor. However, Broches manifested that the issue is up to the parties to decide" (*History of the ICSID Convention*, *supra* note 1078, II, p. 502).

2753. "Phrased in a more abstract manner, the question is whether the Tribunal can apply international law where international law is not in terms included in the rules of law agreed by the parties pursuant to the first sentence of Article 42 (1). This is a difficult question on which I hesitate to express a firm opinion. However, I submit that in this situation the application by the Tribunal of international law rules is at least permissible to the extent that these rules are "the law of the land", which is to say that they would presumably be applied by the national courts of the host country", Broches, *supra* note 2161, p. 390.

2754. *Texaco* v. *Libya*, *supra* note 119, Award (19 January 1977), 17 ILM, p. 1, 24 (1978); *Aminoil*, *supra* note 1059, Award (1982), 66 ILR, pp. 586 *et seq.*; Schreuer *et al.*, *supra* note 102, p. 588. ICSID Model Clause 10 of 1993, 4 *ICSID Reports*, p. 364.

2755. Schreuer *et al.*, *supra* note 102, p. 589. *AGIP* v. *Congo*, *supra* note 454, Award (30 November 1979), paras. 68-70.

2756. *LETCO* v. *Liberia*, *supra* note 456, Award (31 March 1986).

2757. *MINE* v. *Guinea*, *supra* note 2190, Decision on Annulment (22 December 1989), paras. 6.33. 6.36.

2758. *CMS* v. *Argentina*, *supra* note 84, Award (12 May 2005), paras. 145 151.

2759. *Duke Energy International Peru Investments No. 1 Ltd.* v. *Republic of Peru*, ICSID Case No. ARB/03/28, Decision on Jurisdiction (1 February 2006), paras. 24-31, 85. See more in Schreuer *et al.*, *supra* note 102, pp. 590-591.

Stabilization clauses are also accepted by Article 3 of the 1979 Resolution of L'Institut de Droit International. Article 1 states that "[c] ontracts between a State and a foreign private person shall be subjected to the rules of law chosen by the parties or, failing such a choice, to the rules of law with which the contract has the closest link". Article 3 states that "[t]he parties may agree that domestic law provisions referred to in the contract shall be considered as being those in force at the time of conclusion of the contract" [2760].

There are diverse stabilization clauses. Commonly, these provisions express that the agreement may not be changed except by mutual consent [2761]. Also, the clauses may be more specific on the restriction to the governmental powers, like when they stabilize the level of taxes or royalties [2762], considering that these are the principal means of dividing the benefits of the enterprise and limiting the return to the investor [2763].

Moreover, stabilization clauses can be grouped into a number of categories. One of them, sometimes called an "intangibility" clause, establishes that the State may not unilaterally modify or terminate the contract [2764]. Another (the so-called "stabilization clause *stricto sensu*" group) provides that the governing law of the contract shall be that of the execution of the agreement, thereby excluding subsequent changes in the contracting State's law [2765]. A third group of clauses provides that the agreement shall be performed consistently with "good will" or in "good faith" and can also be regarded as a type of stabilization clause. The requirement of performance in good faith precludes unilateral modification or termination [2766].

2760. *Annuaire d'Institut de droit international*, Vol. 58-II (1979), pp. 192-195 and also 72, 74 and 84.

2761. See e.g. Guinea-Bissau, 1982 Offshore Model Contract for Agreements between PETROMINAS (a State company) and Foreign Private Companies, Article 31.1, reprinted in Basic Oil Laws and Concession Contracts: South and Central Africa (Supp. 71) at 48 (Barrows 1983).

2762. See e.g. Agreement between Revere Jamaica Alumina Ltd. and the Gov't of Jamaica, Mar. 10, 1967, Articles12, 13, discussed in *Revere Copper and Brass, Inc.* v. *Overseas Private Inv. Corp.*, 56 ILR, p. 258, 273 (1978).

2763. Curtis, *supra* note 119, p. 321.

2764. See e.g. Agreement between the Gov't of the Yemen Arab Republic (North Yemen) and Deutsche Shell AG; Agreement between the Gov't of Abu Dhabi and Amerada Hess Petroleum Abu Dhabi Ltd., Art. 34.

2765. See e.g. Agreement between the Republic of Liberia and Liberia Iron and Steel Corp.; Joint Venture Agreement between ONAREP (a State company) and Amoco Morocco Oil Co., 17 June 1982, Article 13.3, reprinted in Basic Oil Laws and Concession Contracts: North Africa (Supp. 62) at 29 (Barrows 1983).

2766. Curtis, *supra* note 119, pp. 346-347.

U. Pactum de lege utenda

An international contract sets out the parties' rights and obligations. The parties may or may not decide upon a choice of law to govern their contract and may do so either in the main contract or in a separate agreement. When a choice of law is made by the parties, the law governing the main contract is derived from that choice; however, the question arises as to which law will serve as the basis upon which to assess the validity and consequences of that choice of law agreement. This delicate question refers to the *pactum de lege utenda*, or the selection of the law *(electio juris)* [2767]. This may create a vicious circle since once the law has been chosen, the governing law will derive from the will of the parties. Even in this circumstance, however, the question still remains regarding which law the *pactum* is based upon [2768].

Various alternatives have been proposed to address this issue. One option is to apply the *lex fori* (the law of the place of litigation) to the choice of law clause, which may still, however, frustrate the parties' intent [2769]. Another option is to apply the law that would have governed the contract in the absence of the parties' choice. This is also an imperfect solution, however, as it suffers from the very uncertainties that the parties intended to avoid by including the choice of law clause in the contract. The same uncertainties emerge when applying international substantive rules, as was decided in a controversial 1988 arbitral decision [2770].

Another option to address this issue is to apply the law selected in the choice of law clause, which was the strategy followed in several

2767. De Ly, *supra* note 1204, pp. 65-66.

2768. Briggs, *supra* note 1198, p. 149.

2769. In several cases, arbitrators applied the law of the seat. For instance, Final Award in ICC Case No. 16168, in *Collection of ICC Arbitral Awards 2012-2015* (2019), p. 205; ICC Preliminary Award 5505/1987, *supra* note 2650; Award in ICC Case No. 3916, 111 JDI (Clunet), p. 930 (1984); Award in ICC Case No. 1598, in *Collection of ICC Arbitral Awards 1974-1985* (1990), p. 19; Partial Award in CRCICA 120/1998, *supra* note 2378. See arguments in favor and against in Born, *supra* note 2273, pp. 2892-2893. Other awards appear to uphold the validity of choice of law clauses, generally in circumstances where the law of the arbitral seat would also do so. Final Award in ICC 8938, *supra* note 2510; Partial Award in ICC Case No. 5073, 13 YB Comm. Arb. (1988), p. 53, 57 *et seq.*

2770. Final Award in Arbitration Chamber of Paris Case No. 9392/9462 of 16 January 1998, 26 YB Comm. Arb. (2001), p. 13. In this case, in the absence of a choice of law clause, the Tribunal seated in Paris applied "international rules" and "usages generally accepted in international commerce".

arbitral cases [2771]. This is also the solution proposed by Article 10 (1) of the Hague Sales Convention and by Article 116 (2) of the Swiss Private International Law Act [2772].

Gary Born points out that there is substantial evidence of an international consensus regarding the parties' autonomy to select the law governing their contract, and the validity of that choice as a general principle of international law. He suggests that the law chosen by the parties should be applied by international arbitral tribunals [2773]. This consensus is reflected in relevant private international law instruments, such as Rome I (Art. 3.5), the Mexico Convention (Art. 12) and the Hague Principles (Art. 6).

Nevertheless, this solution creates problems in those cases where the choice of law was not properly agreed upon. In this regard, Article 3.5 of Rome I provides that consent is determined by the law that would be applied if that agreement existed (the third option mentioned above). This is consistent with the aim of giving the greatest possible effect to the intent of the parties, presupposing that the agreement exists in line with respect for the principle of party autonomy. Similarly, pursuant to Article 12, paragraph 1, of the Mexico Convention, the substantive validity of the parties' consent to the selection of the applicable law will be governed by the law chosen by the parties.

A similar approach is taken in Article 6.1 of the Hague Principles, which provides that "whether the parties have agreed to a choice of law is determined by the law that was purportedly agreed to" [2774]. Nevertheless, Article 6.2 provides that:

> "[T]he law of the State in which a party has its establishment determines whether that party has consented to the choice of law if, under the circumstances, it would not be reasonable to make that determination under the law specified in [this Article]."

2771. Award in ICC Case No. 16655, *International Journal of Arab Arbitration*, Vol. 4, No. 2 (2012), p. 125; Partial Award in ICC Case No. 12363/ACS, *ASA Bulletin*, Vol. 24 (2006), p. 462; Award in the ICC Case No. 9651, UNILEX (UNIDROIT Principles); Final Award in ICC 6379, *supra* note 2510; ICC Preliminary Award 5505/1987, *supra* note 2650; *Cvoro* v. *Carnival Corp.*, Partial Award in ICDR Case No. 01-14-0001-0023 of 30 September 2015.

2772. See *supra* note 2809.

2773. Born, *supra* note 2273, pp. 2893-2894.

2774. The Hague Principles constitute the first international instrument to address the issue known as the "battle of forms" regarding choice of law, particularly in relation to this issue (Arts. 2.1.19 to 2.1.22 of the UNIDROIT Principles do so in relation to substantive law).

As noted in the Hague Principles, this is similar to Article 12, paragraph 2, of the Mexico Convention, which states that "to establish that one of the parties has not duly consented, the judge shall determine the applicable law, taking into account the habitual residence or principal place of business" [2775]. This provision also corresponds to Article 10.2 of Rome I.

The Hague Principles underscore the exceptional nature of Article 6.2. Duress, fraud, mistake or other defects of consent are some of the grounds that parties can invoke to demonstrate the absence of an "agreement" [2776]. In order to invoke these grounds, the parties must meet two concurrent conditions: first, "under the circumstances, it would not be reasonable to make that determination under the law specified in Article 6.1"; and second, "no valid agreement on the choice of law can be established under the law of the State in which a party invoking this provision has its establishment". This can occur in cases of duress or fraud, as well as in situations where one of the parties has remained silent in response to a contractual offer. To illustrate this situation, the Hague Principles provide the example of an offer stipulating that the law of a specific State will govern the contract. If silence equals acceptance according to the law of that State but not under the law of the place where the party receiving the offer has its establishment, it would not be reasonable for that party to be bound by the contract [2777].

In principle, the OAS Guide favors the applicability of the law chosen by the parties. However, it admits that the law of the State in which a party has its establishment may prevail under certain circumstances [2778].

In the context of investment arbitration, a difficult issue arises if the host State's domestic law contains provisions limiting its authority to enter into certain types of arrangements pertaining to the applicable law. For instance, some domestic legal systems attempt to curtail the capacity of the government to submit to international arbitration or to

2775. Hague Principles, Commentary, 6.4.
2776. Hague Principles, Commentary 6.7.
2777. Hague Principles, Commentary 6.28.
2778. The provision from Article 6.2 of the Hague Principles is in the middle between Rome I, which leads to the law applicable had the agreement existed (Art. 3.5) – with the aim of giving maximum effect to party autonomy – and the Mexico Convention, according to which the law of the place of establishment of the affected party is applicable (Art. 12). According to the OAS Guide, adjudicators, in determining whether parties have agreed to a choice of law, should take into account Article 6 of the Hague Principles and Article 12, paragraph 2 of the Mexico Convention.

consent to the application of systems of law other than their own. In *Kaiser* v. *Jamaica*, the choice of law provision in the 1969 agreement purported to exclude, *inter alia*, any rule of Jamaican law "which could throw doubt upon the authority or ability of the Government to enter into this . . . Agreement" [2779].

The question may be formulated as follows: can a State contract out of one of its own legal rules that limit its freedom to enter into agreements? The answer is complex. Much will depend on whether the domestic provision is seen to affect the State's capacity to contract, thereby resulting in the agreement's nullity or whether the provision is seen as a simple prohibition that does not affect the validity of the agreement. Where any doubt arises, it will be preferable to uphold the validity of the agreement, especially where the investor has relied in good faith on the host State's capacity to contract. Nevertheless, provisions of this kind in domestic law should be a cause for concern and should be investigated thoroughly before relying on a contractual clause purporting to exclude them [2780].

In validating the choice of law agreement [2781], some arbitral tribunals will consider the law of the State where the award is to be enforced and determine whether this law is consistent with the solution of domestic laws [2782]. This is a variation of the validation principle that attempts to avoid implausible and uncommercial results by selecting an applicable law that will give effect to the parties' agreement. This strategy has been adopted in what Born considers "well-reasoned international arbitral awards" [2783] and commentary. If the chosen law would invalidate an international contract or material provisions of it, the validation

2779. *Kaiser* v. *Jamaica*, *supra* note 1398, Decision on Jurisdiction (6 July 1975), para. 12.80. In this sense: Institute of International Law, Articles on Arbitration between States, State Enterprises, or State Entities and Foreign Enterprises, *Annuaire d'Institut de droit international*, Vol. 63-II (1989), p. 328, Article 4.

2780. Schreuer *et al.*, *supra* note 102, pp. 565-566.

2781. For instance, Partial Award in ICC Case No. 7920, 23 YB Comm. Arb. (1998), p. 80; ICC Preliminary Award 5505/1987, *supra* note 2650; Interim Award in ICC 4145, *supra* note 2508, p. 100 *et seq.*

2782. For instance, Restatement (Second) Conflict of Laws, para. 200 comment c (1971); *Kahler* v. *Midland Bank*, [1950] AC 24 (House of Lords); *NV Handel My J. Smits Imp.-Exp.* v. *English Exps. (London) Ltd.*, [1955] 2 Lloyd's Rep. 317 (English Ct. App.); *Etler* v. *Kertesz*, (1960) 26 DLR2d 209, 222 (Ontario Ct. App.).

2783. Final Award in ICC Case No. 13954, 35 YB Comm. Arb. (2010), p. 218, 236; ICC Partial Award 7920, *supra* note 2781, pp. 81-83; Y. Derains, "Observations Following Award in ICC Case No. 5953", 117 JDI (Clunet), p. 1056 (1990); Interim Award in ICC 4145, *supra* note 2508; Preliminary Award in ICC Case No. 2321, 1 YB Comm. Arb. (1976), p. 133.

principle should be understood as providing for an implied exception to the parties' selection of the chosen law, instead applying the law of the arbitral seat with regard to the relevant issues [2784].

2784. "The rationale is that the parties intended that their negotiations and contract have meaning and effect, rather than none, and that application of the law of the arbitral seat in order to accomplish this is consistent with that intention, even if not expressly stated. Nor should this analysis be regarded as doing violence to the parties' agreement; rather, it seeks to reconcile inconsistent parts of an agreement, just as rules of construction do in other contexts, by giving effect to the specific (substantive obligation) while implying an exception to the general (choice-of-law provision)", Born, *supra* note 2273, p. 2895.

CHAPTER XVIII

ABSENCE OF CHOICE OF LAW IN INVESTMENT LAW

A. Absence of choice of substantive law in international commercial transactions

The principle of party autonomy allows parties that opt for arbitration to also choose the substantive law applicable to their relationship. However, they often fail to do so [2785]. The parties may not choose an applicable choice of law due to simple oversight, they may not have considered it necessary or they may have found it difficult to come to an agreement. The parties may also have intentionally avoided discussing the matter of the applicable law due to difficulty reaching a consensus or out of fear that such discussions might prevent a final agreement [2786]. Further, the parties may have exercised their autonomy and made a choice of law but under certain circumstances that selection may be subsequently deemed invalid [2787].

In the absence of an effective choice of law, the question arises as to which law should be applied. Clarity in this respect can help to prevent disputes and, in the event of legal action, can also help orient the parties in asserting their positions and providing the adjudicator with guidance in issuing a decision.

The absence of a choice of applicable law in transborder commercial transactions is addressed in national legislation and several private international law instruments, such as the Rome I Regulation and the Mexico Convention, and the OAS Guide. The Hague Prin-

---

2785. According to a renowned survey undertaken some years ago by White & Case LLP and School of International Arbitration, Centre for Commercial Law Studies of Queen Mary based on a quantitative methodology (online questionnaires) and qualitative (personal telephone interviews), 51 percent of respondents believe that the applicable law is the first issue that should be decided, and 23 percent believe that it is an issue of fundamental importance (White & Case LLP/School of International Arbitration – University of Queen Mary, "2010 International Arbitration Survey: Choices in International Arbitration", p. 8. See https://arbitration.qmul.ac.uk/media/arbitration/docs/2010_InternationalArbitrationSurveyReport.pdf, accessed 16 May 2022.

2786. See Blessing, *supra* note 2321, p. 44. On reasons why the parties may opt to not select the rules of law to the dispute, see Award in ICC 7319/1992, *supra* note 2585, pp. 144-145.

2787. Magnus, *supra* note 1298, p. 27.

ciples, however, do not deal with this question, as explained in Chapter X.

This chapter will confirm that arbitrators are in a fundamentally different position than judges and are generally granted a broader discretion by arbitration laws. This discretion is further expanded when there is no choice of law provision at all [2788].

B. Absence of choice in international commercial arbitration conventions

The 1958 New York Convention contains no provision addressing the absence of a choice of applicable substantive law [2789]. A little later, the 1961 European Convention on International Commercial Arbitration dealt with this matter in its Article VII, which states the following: "Failing any indication by the parties as to the applicable law, the arbitrators shall apply the proper law under the rule of conflict that the arbitrators deem applicable." This provision does not refer to conflict rules of the seat, thereby granting arbitrators discretion to apply the rules that they deem applicable [2790].

In the Americas, the Panama Convention offers a similar solution for when the parties have failed to choose a law to be applied to their relationship. The Convention refers to Article 30 of the Inter-American Commercial Arbitration Commission (IACAC) Rules, which states that "[f]ailing any designation by the parties, the arbitral tribunal shall apply the law determined by the conflict of laws rules which it considers applicable". This rule is identical to that of the UNCITRAL Model Law, discussed below.

The MERCOSUR Arbitral Agreement of 1998 grants arbitrators and the parties the same authority when it comes to determining the applicable law. Article 10 states that:

> "The parties may choose the law to be applied to resolve the dispute based on private international law and its principles, as

2788. "This is due to the fact that arbitral tribunals operate in a universe lacking anything resembling fixed choice of law principles", Bermann, *supra* note 2512, pp. 271-272. The author also questions the following: "Why subject arbitral tribunals to choice of law rules (or rules of civil procedure) designed for the institutions – national courts – to which arbitral rules are precisely meant to be an alternative? Such rules were neither conceived nor intended to apply to any bodies other than the courts of the jurisdiction that adopted them" (*ibid.*, pp. 257-258).

2789. Silberman and Ferrari, *supra* note 2514, p. 380.

2790. Blackaby *et al.*, *supra* note 255, p. 223.

well as on international commercial law. If the parties failed to specify their choice of law, the arbitrators shall decide according to the same sources."

The instrument also allows for the possibility of selecting not only domestic but also uniform law, first, when it refers to "international commercial law", and second, where reference is made to private international law "and its principles", which includes both conflict of laws and uniform law rules [2791].

C. Absence of choice in the Arbitration Model Law

According to the UNCITRAL Model Law, "[f]ailing any designation by the parties, the arbitral tribunal shall apply the law determined by the conflict of laws rules which it considers applicable" (Art. 28 (2)).

The UNCITRAL commentary states that where the parties have not chosen an applicable law, the arbitral tribunal must adhere to traditional guidelines. Therefore (at least in principle), the arbitrators are required to apply private international law rules, which may bring about uncertainties due to the fact that arbitrators lack a national forum. For this reason, some States have not adopted this provision and have instead granted arbitrators the freedom to choose the law that they deem appropriate [2792].

Even though the UNCITRAL Model Law and the domestic legislation that follows it adhere to more traditional criteria regarding the applicable law in the absence of a choice, these instruments may be interpreted broadly in a way that does not yield "domestic" results. Model Law Article 28 (2) appears to constrain the arbitrator and does not grant him the freedom to choose the applicable law. Nevertheless, it has been argued that an arbitrator who disregards this provision does not put his or her award in jeopardy, as the Model Law does not grant State courts the power to review the reasoning that led to the determination of the applicable law [2793].

2791. Moreno Rodríguez, *supra* note 2562, p. 332.

2792. For example, see Article 57 (2) of the Peruvian arbitration legislation.

2793. However, while it is true that there is no judicial control in this matter in the annulment remedy or the New York Convention, it is necessary to consider this aspect within the provisions regarding public policy. Excess of arbitrators' mandate and due process concerns may arise in this regard. Moreover, some tribunals considered that the arbitral seat's conflicts rules are mandatory, as occurred with an English-seated tribunal, according to which, "[t]he place of this arbitration is London, and on any question of choice of law I must therefore apply the relevant rules of the private international law of England" (Final Award in ICC Case No. 5460, 13 YB Comm. Arb. (1988), p. 104). See also Chap. XXI and note 3381, *infra*.

Several writers [2794] and arbitral awards refer to arbitrators' ample and discretionary powers to select the applicable law in the absence its choice [2795]. Of course, that discretionary power cannot become so extreme as to ignore any conflict of laws approach, as noted in a 1995 ICC award [2796].

D. Approaches for absence of choice in UNCITRAL arbitration

There are major differences regarding the approach that should be taken by a tribunal to determine the applicable law in the absence of an effective choice by the parties. As stated by Pierre Mayer, no international consensus has been reached on this matter. Various legal approaches have developed in different jurisdictions, and older methods have not always been replaced by newer ones [2797]. The following sections will highlight some of the most noteworthy approaches taken by arbitral tribunals in determining the applicable law in the absence of a choice made by the parties.

1. Conflict of laws rules of the seat

Originally, the majority of arbitral awards tended to give priority to the conflict of laws rules of the place of arbitration when determining the applicable law in the absence of the parties' choice. In fact, an old 1957 resolution made by the Institute of International Law following the Sauser-Hall Report stated: "The rules of choice of law in the state of the seat of the arbitral tribunal must be followed to settle the law applicable to the substance of the dispute." [2798]

This approach received tacit support by tribunals worldwide for quite some time, especially in the common law world [2799]. Indeed, the

2794. P. Mayer, "El Derecho o las Normas Aplicables al Fondo de la Controversia", in J. C. Rivera and D. P. Fernández Arroyo (eds.), *Contratos y Arbitraje en la Era Global*, Asunción, CEDEP/ASADIP, 2012, pp. 69-70.
2795. See, for instance, ICC 2930/1982, *supra* note 2378, p. 106; CRCICA 120/1998, *supra* note 2378, p. 28; ICC 3540/1980, *supra* note 2378, p. 128; ICC 2730/1982, *supra* note 2378, p. 491; Award in ICC 1422/1966, *supra* note 2378, p. 186.
2796. ICC 8113/1995, *supra* note 2378, p. 325. See Silberman and Ferrari, *supra* note 2514, p. 397, fn. 149.
2797. Mayer, *supra* note 2794, p. 68.
2798. Article 11 of the Institute of International Law's Resolution on Arbitration in Private International Law, adopted during the Amsterdam session held on September 18-27, 1957, reprinted in Institut de Droit International (1992), Tableau des Résolutions Adoptées (1957-1991), p. 243.
2799. Mann is frequently cited in this regard, vid. P. Sanders (ed.), *International Arbitration: Liber Amicorum for Martin Domke*, The Hague, Martinus Nijhoff, 1967, pp. 158 ff.

Restatement (Second) of Conflict of Laws of the United States notes that the selection of the seat of the arbitration presumes a "demonstration of the intent for the local law of the country to govern the contract in its entirety" [2800].

However, determining the seat of arbitration is often an unpredictable process, especially when the decision is made by the arbitral tribunal or an arbitral institution rather than by the parties. In addition, the parties may choose the seat of arbitration for reasons other than its conflict of laws rules, such as the political neutrality of the country, its proximity or the logistical services it offers.

Several writings criticize or refer to this position as "anachronical" [2801]. As stated in the *Sapphire* case:

> "Contrary to a State judge, who is bound to conform to the conflict law rules of the State in whose name he metes out justice, the arbitrator is not bound by such rules. He must look for the common intention of the parties, and use the connecting factors generally used in doctrine and in case law and must disregard national peculiarities." [2802]

Recent awards tend to reflect the emerging trend that, upon determining the law applicable to the substance of the case, the arbitrator will set aside the conflict of laws rules of the forum [2803]. National courts have confirmed this interpretation [2804].

2800. Restatement (Second) Conflict of Laws, para. 218, comment *b*.

2801. Fouchard, *supra* note 1614, paras. 546 et seq. (1965); P. Lalive, "Le droit applicable au fond par l'arbitre international", *Droit International et Droit Communitaire*, Vol. 33 (1991), p. 41; G. J. Kaufmann-Kohler, "Aspects de la mise en œuvre du droit en arbitrage", *Revue de Droit Suisse* (1988), p. 414. Mayer, *supra* note 2794, pp. 68-69.

2802. *Sapphire*, *supra* note 1013, *Ad hoc* Award (15 March 1963), 35 ILR, p. 136, 170 (1967).

2803. *Westinghouse*, *supra* note 1636, Award (1996), A-37; *Ad hoc* Arbitral Tribunal, Award of 10 October 1973, 5 YB Comm. Arb. (1980), p. 143, 148; ICC Award 2637/1975, in *Collection of ICC Arbitral Awards 1974-1985* (1990), p. 13, 15; Award in ICC 1422/1966, *supra* note 2378, p. 186; CRCICA 120/1998, *supra* note 2378, p. 28; ICC Award No. 4434 of 1983, in *Collection of ICC Arbitral Awards 1974-1985* (1990), p. 458, 459; Award in ICC 2730/1982, *supra* note 2378, p. 491; Final Award in ICC Case No. 18643, 44 YB Comm. Arb. (2019), p. 145, 157; Partial Award in ICC 8113/1995, *supra* note 2378, p. 325; Final Award in *Turkish Seller* (1993), *supra* note 1560, p. 44; Award in ICC Case No. 6030, discussed in H. Grigera Naón, "Choice-of-Law Problems in International Commercial Arbitration", *Recueil des cours*, Vol. 289 (2001), p. 228, fn. 227; Award in ICC 3540/1980, *supra* note 2378, p. 127, 128; Final Award in ICC Case No. 2073, 33 YB Comm. Arb. (2003), p. 63, 73; Award in ICC 2930/1982, *supra* note 2378; Award in *Ad hoc* Arbitration of 10 October 1973, 5 YB Comm. Arb. (1980), p. 143, 148.

2804. *Scherk*, *supra* note 2490, p. 519, n. 13 (US S.Ct. 1974); *Konkar Indomitable Corp. v. Fritzen Schiffsagentur und Bereederungs GmbH*, 1981 US Dist. LEXIS 9637,

George Bermann argues that inferring the parties' selection of conflict of laws rules based on their selection of the place of arbitration would be "to misconceive the meaning of *lex arbitri*". In selecting the seat, the parties are unlikely to have taken into account local rules on court litigation within that particular jurisdiction. This result "would also be perverse" since, by resorting to arbitration, the parties intended to escape the application of the rules of that jurisdiction during litigation [2805].

Taking a different stance, Gary Born recently argued that the numerous pronouncements that the rule has been wholly abandoned in international arbitration are wrong. In many cases, arbitrators continue to apply the choice of law [2806], or even the substantive laws of the arbitral seat [2807]. This is even provided for in the mandatory national arbitration laws of Switzerland, Germany and Japan [2808]. However, this issue remains controversial. For instance, scholars have noted that Article 187 of the Swiss law is so flexible that, in practice, it does not restrict the arbitrators' freedom to apply the law that they favor [2809]. This

pp. 6-7 (SDNY); *Compagnie d'Armement Maritime SA* v. *Compagnie Tunisienne de Navigation SA* [1971] AC 572, 600 (House of Lords). See Born, *supra* note 2273, p. 2849.

2805. Bermann, *supra* note 11, pp. 271-272.

2806. Born, *supra* note 2273, p. 2855. See Award in ICC Case No. 10303, discussed in Grigera Naón, *supra* note 2803, p. 230; Award in ICC Case No. 8385, *supra* note 781; Award in ICC Case No. 7262, discussed in Grigera Naón, *ibid.*, p. 231; Interim Award in ICC Case No. 6149, 20 YB Comm. Arb. (1995), p. 41; Preliminary Award in ICC Case No. 6401, 7 (1) Mealey's Int'l Arb. Rep. B-1 (1992); ICC Final Award 5460, *supra* note 2783, p. 106; Award in ICC 3540/1980, *supra* note 2378; *Gil* v. *Watson*, Final Award in ICDR Case No. 50-20-1300-0952 of 18 September 2015; Award in *Budapest Chamber of Commerce and Industry*, Case No. VB96074 of 10 December 1996; Award in *Czechoslovak Chamber of Commerce*, 9 January 1975, 2 YB Comm. Arb. (1973), p. 143; Partial Award in *Hamburg Chamber of Commerce*, 21 March 1996, 22 YB Comm. Arb. (1997), p. 35; Award in *USSR Chamber of Commerce and Industry*, 6 October 1977, 5 YB Comm. Arb. (1980), p. 209 (applying Soviet conflicts rules).

2807. In the Interim Award in ICC Case No. 11061, discussed in Grigera Naón, *supra* note 2803, pp. 266-68, it was expressed: "it seems to us not unreasonable to attribute an intention of the parties who have chosen Singapore as the venue for the resolution of their disputes, to submit themselves also to the law of Singapore, be it procedural or substantial".

2808. Arbitral tribunals seated in these jurisdictions have applied the statutory conflict of laws rule in many cases, for instance: Award on Preliminary Issues of ICC Case No. 12171, *ASA Bulletin*, Vol. 23 (2005), p. 256, 259; Award in ICC Case No. 9415, discussed in Grigera Naón, *supra* note 2803, p. 227, fn. 226; Award in ICC 1598, *supra* note 2769, p. 19; Partial Award in *Hamburg Chamber*, *supra* note 2806, p. 36; Final Award in *Ad hoc* case of 29 December 1998, 24 YB Comm. Arb. (1999), p. 13, para. 6. See Born, *supra* note 2273, p. 2856.

2809. Official translation at https://www.fedlex.admin.ch/eli/cc/1988/1776_1776_1776/en, accessed 29 September 2022.

conclusion is reflected in a 1993 award made in Geneva in ICC Case No. 7154 [2810].

2. Substantive law of the seat

Sporadically, views in favor of applying the substantive law of the seat are promoted [2811], particularly in less-developed jurisdictions [2812]. This was also the view traditionally held in the United States, reflected in the Restatement (Second) Conflict of Laws, which held that:

> "Provision by the parties in a contract that arbitration shall take place in a certain state may provide some evidence of an intention on their part that the local law of this state should govern the contract as a whole. This is true not only because the provision shows that the parties had this particular state in mind; it is also true because the parties must presumably have recognized that arbitrators sitting in that state would have a natural tendency to apply its local law." [2813]

In the past, decisions of this kind were also rendered in English cases, such as the 1968 case *Tzortzis & Sykias* v. *Monark Line AB* heard before the Court of Appeals [2814]. In that case, the contract between Swedish sellers and Greek buyers had no connection with England

2810. It was held that the contract in dispute had closer connections with "the law which preserves its existence than with the law which denies it" (*Algerian shipowner* v. *French shipyard*, 121 JDI, p. 1059 (1994), and observations by Y. Derains).

2811. For instance, Award in ICC Case No. 2735, in *Collection of ICC Arbitral Awards 1974-1985* (1990), p. 301, 302.

2812. G. Born, *supra* note 2273, notes that

> "the view is emphatically rejected in all developed jurisdictions. The parties' choice of an arbitral seat is not an implied choice of substantive law: the choice of the arbitral seat is a choice of a national arbitration regime, which governs the arbitral procedures, and will often have nothing at all to do with the parties' underlying commercial transaction and relationship. The selection of the arbitral seat does not independently either constitute or connote an implied selection of the law of the arbitral seat to govern the parties' underlying contract or other commercial relationship".

2813. Restatement (Second) Conflict of Laws, para. 218 comment *b* (1971).

2814. 1 Lloyd's Rep. 337, 413 (English Ct. App.). See also these other cases, where the House of Lords considered that the selection of London as arbitral seat constitutes choice of English substantive law: *NV Vulcaan* v. *AS Ludwig Mowinckels Rederi*, [1938] 2 All ER 152 (House of Lords) (selection of London as arbitral seat constitutes choice of English substantive law); *Kwik Hoo Tong Handel Maatschappij* v. *James Finlay & Co.* [1927] AC 604 (House of Lords); *Spurrier* v. *La Cloche* [1902] AC 446 (House of Lords); Problems in International Arbitration 126 (1986).

whatsoever despite its arbitration clause designating London as the seat of arbitration.

This position has been criticized and slowly eroded both in doctrine [2815] and in case law. As stated in a renowned 1990 ICC award, "[i]t is appropriate to eliminate forthwith the law of the forum, whose connection with the case is purely fortuitous" [2816]. In another award, the Tribunal wrote:

> "[I]t is highly debatable whether a preferred choice of the *situs* of the arbitration is sufficient to indicate a choice of governing law. There has for several years been a distinct tendency in international arbitration to disregard this element, chiefly on the ground that the choice of the place of arbitration may be influenced by a number of practical considerations that have no bearing on the issue of applicable law." [2817]

3. *Conflict of laws rules of another jurisdiction*

When it comes to applying conflict of laws rules of another jurisdiction, international case law has articulated different positions. First, the law of the State of the arbitrator may be applied to the dispute on the basis that the arbitrator has better knowledge of his or her own law [2818]. This position is unconvincing as it suggests that arbitrators are unable to apply conflict of laws rules other than their own – a position that has long been rejected. In addition, the arbitrator's home State may have no connection to the dispute whatsoever, apart from it being his or her country of origin, which would create a connection to the dispute even more tenuous than that of the seat of the arbitration. This approach also raises the practical challenge of how to determine the arbitrator's country of origin – that is, whether the determining factor should be the arbitrator's nationality, citizenship, domicile or residence. Moreover, in practice an arbitral tribunal tends to be composed of arbitrators from different States [2819].

A different position gives effect to the law of the State whose courts would have had jurisdiction if there had been no arbitration agreement

2815. Born, *supra* note 2273, p. 2847.

2816. Award in ICC 1422/1966, *supra* note 2378, p. 186; Award in SCC Case No. 117/1999, 2002:1 *Stockholm Arbitration Reports*, p. 59, 64.

2817. . SCC 117/1999, *ibid.*

2818. As in ICC Award No. 3130 of 1980, in *Collection of ICC Arbitral Awards 1974-1985* (1990), pp. 417-418, fn. 16.

2819. Silberman and Ferrari, *supra* note 2514, p. 403.

to begin with [2820]. This approach has not prevailed either, because arbitration is not comparable to the dispute resolution mechanism of a State. Moreover, in some cases, conflicts of jurisdiction may arise due to differences in State rules in this regard.

Another method that has been suggested is to apply the law of the State where the award will be enforced [2821]. This approach is impractical, however, because it is unpredictable and also neglects the fact that the award may be enforced in more than one State. In any case, awards often reflect the solutions that arbitrators find based on the arguments put forward by the parties in order to avoid surprising the parties with an unexpected award or legal ruling.

4. Cumulative application of the rules of all States with a connection

Under this approach, arbitrators should perform a comparative exercise to determine whether there is any conflict between the legal systems connected to the case [2822]. This method, applied in many arbitral cases [2823], has the advantage of being consistent with the transnational nature of international commercial arbitration, in addition to being more in line with the parties' expectations [2824]. Performing a conflicts check also reduces the possibility of challenges alleging that the wrong

---

2820. See Born, *supra* note 2273, p. 2864.

2821. *Ibid.*, p. 2864.

2822. Some time ago this system was mentioned by Craig, Park and Paulsson as the most frequently used by arbitrators in ICC cases. Craig, Park and Paulsson, *supra* note 837, pp. 326-327.

2823. ICC Interim Award 6149, *supra* note 2806. See also: CRCICA 120/1998, *supra* note 2378, p. 29; ICC 7319/1992, *supra* note 2585, p. 142 ff.; ICC Award No. 7250/1992, *ICC Ct. Bull.*, Vol. 7 (1996), p. 92 ff.; ICC Award No. 7197/1992, 138 JDI (Clunet), p. 1029 ff. (1993); ICC Award No. 6281 of 1989, 15 YB Comm. Arb. (1990), p. 96, 97; *Manufacturer* v. *Licensor*, *supra* note 1562; Award in ICC Case No. 4996 of 1985, 113 JDI, p. 1131 ff. (1986); ICC Award No. 3043 of 1978, in *Collection of ICC Arbitral Awards 1974-1985* (1990), p. 358, 359; ICC 2930/1982, *supra* note 2378, pp. 105-106; Award in ICC 2730/1982, *supra* note 2378, p. 491; ICC Award No. 2438 of 1975, in *Collection of ICC Arbitral Awards 1974-1985* (1990), p. 253, 254; ICC 1704/1977, *supra* note 2651, pp. 312-314; ICC Award 1512/1971, *supra* note 1510; ICC Award No. 1434/1975, in *Collection of ICC Arbitral Awards 1974-1985* (1990), p. 262, 265; ICC Award No. 953 of 1956, 3 YB Comm. Arb. (1978), p. 214, 214-215; Final Award in ICC Case No. 12193, *International Journal of Arab Arbitration*, Vol. 1, No. 2 (2009), p. 449, 451; Award in ICC Case No. 2272, in *Collection of ICC Arbitral Awards 1974-1985* (1990), p. 11; *Carolina Brass, Inc.* v. *Arya Shipping Lines*, IUSCT Case No. 252-10035-2, Award (12 September 1986), 12 IUSCTR, p. 139 (1986). See Silberman and Ferrari, *supra* note 2514, pp. 403-404, fn. 190.

2824. Mayer, *supra* note 2794, p. 71, who cites the following awards applying this method: Award ICC 7319/1992, *supra* note 2585: Award ICC Case No. 8451/1998; ICC Case No. 12193, Award (2004), *ICC Ct. Bull.*, Vol. 19, No. 1, p. 125.

law was applied [2825]. Further, this approach grants the arbitrators broad discretion to decide which conflict of laws rules are connected to the dispute and must be taken into account.

Nevertheless, this mechanism carries certain challenges as well. Performing this type of conflicts check is often quite costly and is only useful when the rules are similar or convergent, or at least aim toward the same outcome unless it is sufficient to "adopt the law that appears most frequently as the applicable law". As such, the persuasive value of this approach is inversely proportional to the number of applicable laws that arise from the application of the various sets of conflict of laws rules.

5. *Application of general private international law principles*

An alternative to the conflict of laws approach is the application of "general principles" of private international law.

As an example in practice, in *SwemBalt AB* v. *Latvia*, the Tribunal relied on principles of general private international law, applying the law of the seat, Denmark, after considering that the link with Sweden was not sufficiently strong. The Tribunal also took into account that the parties had not provided the arbitrators with information on relevant Latvian law [2826]. This method also takes a comparative approach but focuses less upon the connection between these rules and the contractual relationship in dispute [2827].

In line with this approach, arbitrators have tended to turn to international conventions for guidance regarding these general principles. This is especially true when it comes to the Rome Convention and now

2825. Silberman and Ferrari, *supra* note 2514, p. 305; ICC 3540/1980, *supra* note 2378, p. 127.

2826. *SwemBalt AB* v. *Latvia*, Award (23 October 2000), para. 46. See also ICC Award 7197/1992, *supra* note 2823, p. 1028; Interim Award in ICC Case No. 5717, *ICC Ct. Bull.*, Vol. 1, No. 2 (1990), p. 22 (1990); Award in ICC Case No. 4650, in *Collection of ICC Arbitral Awards 1986-1990* (1994), p. 67, 68; Award in ICC Case No. 4237/1985, 10 YB Comm. Arb. (1985), p. 52, 55; Award in ICC Case No. 3316, in *Collection of ICC Arbitral Awards 1974-1985* (1990), p. 87, 88; Award in ICC 2930/1982, *supra* note 2378; Award in ICC Case No. 2680, in *Collection of ICC Arbitral Awards 1974-1985* (1990), p. 334; Award in ICC Case No. 1717, in *ibid.*, p. 191; Final Award in ICC Case No. 8672, *ICC Ct. Bull.*, Vol. 12, No. 1 (2001), p. 117, 118; Preliminary Award in ICC Case No. 4710, *ASA Bulletin*, Vol. 3 (1985), p. 65, 70; CIETAC Award of 2 September 2005, UNILEX (UNIDROIT Principles); ICC Interim Award 6149, *supra* note 2806; Partial Award in CRCICA 120/1998, *supra* note 2378, p. 28; *Harnischfeger* v. *Ministry*, *supra* note 2447, Partial Award (13 July 1984), 7 IUSCTR, p. 90 (1984), 99.

2827. Craig, Park and Paulsson, *supra* note 837, p. 327.

the Rome I Regulation, regardless of whether these instruments were applicable under their own terms [2828].

Identifying "general principles" of private international law may nonetheless be a difficult task, which explains why arbitrators typically recur to these international instruments instead [2829]. Even though, in principle, international instruments reflect only a consensus of the countries ratifying them [2830], arbitral tribunals have also applied them even if not in force [2831]. Tribunals have adopted formulas such as the closest connection rule, the characteristic performance rule [2832], the "proper law of the contract" rule [2833] and the "law of the seller" in sales contracts [2834].

Several of these "general principles" of private international law may be found in international instruments. For instance, the closest connection formula [2835] is included in the Rome I Regulation [2836] and the Mexico Convention [2837]. Some arbitral awards also relied upon the

---

2828. *Ibid.*, p. 328.

2829. *Turkish Seller* (1993), *supra* note 1560, p. 46; ICC Award No. 6360 of 1990, *ICC Ct. Bull.*, Vol. 1 (1990), p. 24.

2830. See Silberman and Ferrari, *supra* note 2514, pp. 408-409.

2831. For instance, *Turkish Seller* (1993), *supra* note 1560, p. 46.

2832. ICC Arbitral Award Case No. 8486 of 1996, 24 YB Comm. Arb. (1999), p. 162, 166; *Swiss Buyer* (1989), *supra* note 1560; ICC Arbitral Award Case No. 2879 of 1978, in *Collection of ICC Arbitral Awards 1974-1985* (1990); Award in ICC 2730/1982, *supra* note 2378; ICC Arbitral Award No. 2558 of 1976, in *ibid.*

2833. ICC Arbitral Award Case No. 2583 of 1976, in *Collection of ICC Arbitral Awards 1974-1985* (1990); ICC 1512, *supra* note 1510.

2834. ICC Arbitral Award Case No. 3894 of 1981, in *Collection of ICC Arbitral Awards 1974-1985* (1990).

2835. In ICC Award 4237/1985, *supra* note 2826, p. 55, the Tribunal stated: "The decided international awards published so far show a preference for the conflict rule according to which the contract is governed by the law of the country with which it has the closest connection." See Interim Award of 17 July 1992 and Final Award in SCC Case of 13 July 1993, 22 YB Comm. Arb. (1997), p. 197, para. 18. See also awards cited by Silberman and Ferrari, *supra* note 2514, pp. 408-409, fn. 214.

2836. Bermann criticizes some writers, like Born, who, in Bermann's view, mistakenly posits that the Regulation applies directly in arbitral proceedings taking place in the European Union, in Bermann, *supra* note 11, p. 278.

2837. See Award in ICC 7319/1992, *supra* note 2585, p. 146; Award in ICC Case No. 7205, 122 JDI 1031 (1994); Partial Award of 17 May 2005 and Final Award of 5 July 2005, Nederlands Arbitrage Instituut, 31 YB Comm. Arb. (2006), p. 172, 179; Nederlands Arbitrage Instituut, Interim Award of 10 February 2005, 32 YB Comm. Arb. (2007), p. 93, 99-100; ICC Arbitral Award Case No. 9771 of 2001, 30 YB Comm. Arb. (2004), p. 46, 54; ICC Arbitral Award Case No. 7205 of 1993, 122 J. Dr. Int., p. 1031 (1995); ICC 6360/1990, *supra* note 2829, p. 24; ICC 2730/1982, *supra* note 2378, p. 491. The following award applied both the 1955 Hague Sales Convention and the Rome Convention: Award in ICC Case No. 10274, 29 YB Comm. Arb. (2004), p. 89, 91.

1955 Hague Sales Convention [2838] and the Hague Convention of 14 March 1978 on the Law Applicable to Intermediary Agreements and Agency [2839]. The Rome II Regulation on non-contractual obligations can also be taken into account when pertinent [2840].

Applying general private international law principles carries certain advantages, which were reflected in the award issued in ICC Case No. 8385. In that case, the Tribunal stated that

> "the application of international standards offers many advantages. They apply uniformly and are not dependent on the peculiarities of any particular national law. They take due account of the needs of international intercourse and permit cross-fertilization between systems that may be unduly wedded to conceptual distinctions and those that look for a pragmatic and fair resolution in the individual case. [. . . T]he Tribunal therefore judges it preferable to apply the standards of international commerce dictated by the needs of the international marketplace" [2841].

Despite these advantages, use of this approach has been limited because it increases the uncertainty of the conflict of laws analysis by requiring a two-part analysis, without producing noticeable benefits. This approach requires the tribunal to first identify that the law of a certain State is applicable. Second, the tribunal must then identify the conflict of laws rules of that State. Ultimately, those conflict of laws rules must be applied in order to determine the substantive law, which in turn entails carrying out another potentially complex analysis [2842].

2838. Final Award in ICC Case No. 8117, *ICC Ct. Bull.*, Vol. 12, No. 1 (2001), p. 69; Award in ICC Case No. 6281, in *Collection of ICC Arbitral Awards 1991-1995* (1997), p. 409; Final Award in ICC Case No. 5885, 16 YB Comm. Arb. (1991), p. 91, 92; Award in ICC Case No. 5118, in *Collection of ICC Arbitral Awards 1986-1990* (1994), p. 318; ICC Preliminary Award 5505/1987, *supra* note 2650, p. 119.

2839. ICC Award 4996 (1985), *supra* note 2823; ICC Award No. 6523/1991, *Austrian company* v. *Turkish company*, *ICC Ct. Bull.*, Vol. 7, No. 1 (1996), p. 88; ICC Award No. 7329/1994, *French agent* v. *Italian manufacturer*, *ICC Ct. Bull.*, Vol. 7, No. 1 (1996), p. 93.

2840. Reg. (EC) No. 864/2007. See Webster, *supra* note 2619, pp. 524 ff.

2841. Award in ICC Case No. 8385, *supra* note 781; *Swiss Buyer* (1989), *supra* note 1560, p. 71; ICC Arbitral Award Case No. 3779/1981, 9 YB Comm. Arb. (1984), p. 124, 126; Award in ICC 2930/1982, *supra* note 2378, p. 106; ICC Arbitral Award 2637/1975, *supra* note 2803; ICC Arbitral Awards in Cases No. 2475 and No. 2762 of 1977, in *ibid.*; ICC Arbitral Award 2438/1975, *supra* note 2823. See also Silberman and Ferrari, *supra* note 2514, p. 407, fn. 205.

2842. *Ibid.*, p. 403, fn. 188.

6. Non-State law

Applying non-State law instead of domestic law may be desirable in different scenarios. For instance, it is possible that the applicable local law does not offer a viable answer to resolve the dispute. It could be that the local law may not address the interest payable on a loan (this is often the case in Islamic law) or may not contain a legal framework to regulate contracts concluded online. In addition, the laws of the parties may provide opposing solutions and conflict of laws rules alone may not determine the outcome.

In such cases, the application of non-State law offers a neutral method for resolving the dispute without treading on the sensitivities of the eventual "losing party". Likewise, if an identical answer would be found by applying either the law of the two parties, or the law of the State with the closest connection to the contract, or non-State law, the adjudicator may resort to non-State law directly without having to declare a "winner".

On occasion, an arbitral tribunal may consider an approach that leads to the choice of a domestic law unsatisfactory because it would require municipal law (designed for domestic commerce) to be applied to an international transaction. In any case, prior to resolving these issues, the arbitrators must hear the parties' positions prior to making a decision [2843].

Even though non-State law is not often applied in arbitration, this possibility is nonetheless "a distinctive quality of the law of international arbitration" [2844]. The UNCITRAL Model Law refers to "rules of law" in Article 28 (1) related to party autonomy. Therefore, the parties may clearly select non-State law since the expression "rules of law" encompasses it and domestic law. However, Article 28 (2), for situations of absence of choice, raises controversies since it only refers to "law" and not "rules of law".

Lord Mustill has argued that this must have been a disappointment to the *lex mercatorists* and an obstacle to the growth of non-State law [2845]. However, he made this argument in 1987 and subsequent developments have proven otherwise. Influential doctrine has advocated in favor of an extensive interpretation of this provision [2846]. According to this view, no

---

2843. Goode, *supra* note 139, p. 31.
2844. Bermann, *supra* note 11, p. 284.
2845. Mustill, *supra* note 1000, p. 181.
2846. Gaillard, *supra* note 836, p. 124. See also V. R. Collins and M. M. Albornoz, "On the Dwindling Divide between the Public and Private: The Role of Soft Law

public policy principle will be violated if this liberal interpretation of the Model Law is followed [2847].

Unfortunately, neither the 2010 nor the 2013 revisions to the UNCITRAL Rules referred directly to rules of law, as other arbitral mechanisms have. Article 21 (1) of the 2017 ICC Rules, for instance, refer to rules of law in all cases, stating that "[i]n the absence of any such agreement [on the applicable substantive law], the arbitral tribunal shall apply *the rules of law which it determines to be appropriate*" [2848].

The issue has been addressed in some domestic legislation. For example, in France the new Code of Civil Procedure provides that the arbitral tribunal may resolve disputes according to the rules of law that the parties have chosen or, failing that, according to those it deems appropriate, taking into account commercial practices [2849]. Arbitrators' autonomy to determine the rules of law to be applied in their resolution of disputes is also enshrined in the Belgian Code of Civil Procedure (Art. 1700), the Dutch Code of Civil Procedure (Art. 1054), the Swiss Law of Private International Law (Art. 87 (1)) and the Italian Code of Civil Procedure (Art. 834).

Writers have stressed that if arbitrators have doubts on whether to apply non-State law, they should take relevant domestic laws into consideration. If possible, the award should make clear that the application of the *lex mercatoria* does not lead to a result that is incompatible with national laws within a conflict of laws analysis [2850]. Following this logic, a 1992 ICC award (Case No. 7319) ruled that where national law has not been expressly selected, an implied selection of non-State law such as "general principles of law" or *lex mercatoria* should not be inferred [2851].

By contrast, ICC Case No. 3131 (1984) considered the difficulty of finding compelling reasons to apply a national law. In that case, the Tribunal took into account the international nature of the agreement

---

Instruments in Global Governance", in V. Ruíz Abou-Nigm, K. McCall Smith and D. French (eds.), *Linkages and Boundaries in Private and Public International* Law, Oxford, Hart Publishing, 2018, p. 117.

2847. For more information regarding public policy, see Chap. XXI, *infra*.

2848. See also 2016 SIAC Rules, Article 31 (1); 2014 ICDR Rules, Article 31 (1); 2020 LCIA Rules, Article 22 (3); 2018 HKIAC Rules, Article 36 (1); 2016 ACICA Rules, Article 39 (1); 2007 DIAC Rules, Article 33 (1); 2015 NAI Rules, Article 42; 2017 SCC Rules, Article 27 (1); 2018 VIAC Rules, Article 27 (2); 2020 WIPO Rules, Article 61 (a).

2849. As amended by Decree 2011-48 of 2011, Article 1511.

2850. Caron, Caplan and Pellonpää, *supra* note 2618, p. 129. In similar terms this warning is made by Craig, Park and Paulsson, *supra* note 837, p. 337.

2851. Partial Award in ICC 7319/1992, *supra* note 2585, p. 145.

and left aside Turkish or French legislation, applying the *lex mercatoria* instead [2852]. In turn, in the Final Award issued in ICC Case No. 16816 (2015), the sole arbitrator held that *lex mercatoria*, as reflected in UNIDROIT Principles, were the most appropriate "rules of law" in absence of parties' choice [2853].

Considering that French law allows arbitrators to decide the dispute in accordance with "rules of law", in French courts an award has been upheld designating the *lex mercatoria* in the absence of a choice by the parties [2854].

There are certain widespread concerns that the uniform or transnational rules method, which involves the application or taking into account of non-State law, will lead to greater uncertainty. These concerns are unjustified. In fact, applying non-State law leads to greater predictability of the outcome in comparison with the classic conflict of laws approach. Parties that have not made a choice of law for their contract may be more surprised by the application of an unknown domestic law than by the application of a non-State set of rules that is reflective of broad international consensus [2855].

Where the parties have not made an effective choice of law, Part Thirteen of the OAS Guide offers the "closest connection" solution contained in the Mexico Convention. As discussed, this instrument can also be considered to enshrine private international law principles. The Guide states that if adjudicators find that transnational rules are more appropriately suited to the dispute at hand and thus more closely connected to the case than national law, they must apply them directly. In this regard, the Guide clarifies one of the central interpretive problems related to the Mexico Convention [2856]. In fact, choosing the

---

2852. Award in ICC Case No. 3131, 9 YB Comm. Arb. (1984), p. 109, 110. In the Partial and Final Awards in ICC Case No. 9875, considering the difficulties to find decisive factors qualifying either Japanese or French law as applicable to the contract reveal the inadequacy of the choice of a domestic legal system to govern a case like this, the Tribunal decided that "[t]he most appropriate 'rules of law' to be applied to the merits of this case are those of the *'lex mercatoria'*, that is the rules of laws and usages of international trade which have been gradually elaborated by different sources". Partial and Final Awards in ICC Case No. 9875, discussed in Grigera Naón, *supra* note 2803, pp. 237-38.

2853. Final Award in ICC Case No. 16816, 40 YB Comm. Arb. (2015), p. 236, 264.

2854. *Valenciana* case, Judgment (13 July 1989) (Cour de cassation, Chambre civile 1, 22 October 1991).

2855. Gaillard, *supra* note 836, p. 126.

2856. Article 9 of the Mexico Convention stipulates in regard to determining the law of the closest connection that "the general principles of international commercial law accepted by international organizations" are to be taken into account. This was a compromise solution reached by the negotiators of the Mexico Convention after the

law with the closest connection to the dispute may not necessarily lead the adjudicators to apply a domestic law but may reveal that the *lex mercatoria* or other forms of non-State law are most appropriate. Indeed, in many cases applying uniform law instruments like the UNIDROIT Principles might be preferable to the conflict of laws approach.

E. Voie directe

As stated, while arbitrators have traditionally made use of the conflict of laws rules of the place of arbitration or the arbitrator's home State, more recently there has been a tendency to apply the ones of all States with a connection to the case at hand or, alternatively, the conflict of laws rules which the arbitrators themselves consider relevant in each case. Recently it has even become possible to allow the arbitrators to determine the applicable substantive law they consider to be "directly" appropriate *en voie directe*. This term is a well-known term in arbitration and has frequently been invoked in arbitral awards [2857].

Voie directe allows the arbitrators to choose the law most suited to the dispute without having to resort to any conflict of laws rule [2858]. By contrast, arbitrators using the *voie indirecte* method will identify the applicable law by first consulting a previously identified, and presumably neutral, choice of law rule and then applying it [2859].

In an important demonstration of support, the *voie directe* method was specifically put forward by the 1989 Declaration of Santiago de Compostela of the Institute of International Law. The 1989 Declaration

---

US delegation had proposed the direct application of the UNIDROIT Principles in the absence of choice. Friedrich Juenger, the US delegate, understood that the agreed-upon formula nonetheless led directly to the UNIDROIT Principles. See Juenger, *supra* note 1311, pp. 1133, 1148. The relevance of this opinion is highlighted by J. Siqueiros, the original drafter of the Mexico Convention, since he was the one who proposed the compromise solution. See also Siqueiros, *supra* note 1311, p. 223. Regarding a similar provision included in the Venezuelan private international law, the Supreme Court of Venezuela stated that the closest connection formula leads to the *lex mercatoria*, which is comprised of commercial customs and practices. Vid. *Banque Artesia Nederland, NV* v. *Corp. Banca, Banco Universal C.A.*, 2014, Exp. 2014-000257, www.unilex.info, accessed 16 May 2022.

2857. As an example, ICC 3540/1980, *supra* note 2378, p. 128.

2858. Gaillard and Savage, *supra* note 836, p. 876.

2859. Bermann, *supra* note 11, p. 274. "Significantly, a distinction between *la voie indirecte* and *la voie directe* is largely unknown in private international law generally. If national courts conduct any choice of law analysis at all, they are likely to identify a choice of law principle before identifying the chosen law, i.e., to proceed via *la voie indirecte*. They will draw the relevant choice of law principle from the principles set forth in the forum's private international law legislation or jurisprudence" (*ibid.*, p. 276).

departed from its formula put forward in 1957 that involved applying the law of the seat, and accepted the *voie directe* mechanism, as it reflected dominant thinking within the field at the time[2860].

The *voie directe* method has been incorporated into the modern arbitration laws of several States[2861]. The UNCITRAL Arbitration Rules of 2010 and 2013 also accept the *voie directe* method. Article 35 of these rules states: "1. The arbitral tribunal shall apply the rules of law designated by the parties as applicable to the substance of the dispute. Failing such designation by the parties, the arbitral tribunal shall apply the law which it determines to be appropriate."

Contrasting with the 1976 version of the rules, Article 35 (1) of the UNCITRAL Rules authorizes the arbitrators to avoid a private international law exercise and, instead, directly choose the applicable

---

2860. Taking into account von Mehren's report, Article 6 of the resolution states the following:

> "The parties have full autonomy to determine the procedural and substantive rules and principles that are to apply in the arbitration. In particular (1) a different source may be chosen for the rules and principles applicable to each issue that arises and (2) these rules and principles may be derived from different national legal systems as well as from non-national sources such as principles of international law, general principles of law, and the usages of international commerce. To the extent that the parties have left such issues open, the tribunal shall supply the necessary rules and principles drawing on the sources indicated in Article 4."

Article 4 states:

> "Where the validity of the agreement to arbitrate is challenged, the tribunal shall resolve the issue by applying one or more of the following: the law chosen by the parties, the law indicated by the system of private international law stipulated by the parties, general principles of public or private international law, general principles of international arbitration, or the law that would be applied by the courts of the territory in which the tribunal has its seat. In making this selection, the tribunal shall be guided in every case by the principle in *favorem validitatis*."

Institute de Droit Session of Santiago de Compostela – 1989 Arbitration Between States, State Enterprises, or State Entities, and Foreign Enterprises, Eighteenth Commission, Rapporteur: Messrs Eduardo Jiménez de Aréchaga and Arthur von Mehren, https://www.idi-iil.org/app/uploads/2017/06/1989_comp_01_en.pdf, accessed 16 May 2022.

2861. It is recognized, for instance, in the laws of France (Article 1511 of the Code of Civil Procedure, amended in 2011); the Netherlands (Art. 1054 (2) of the Code of Civil Procedure); Spain (Spanish Arbitration Act, Art. 34 (2)); and Austria (Art. 603 (2) of the Code of Civil Procedure, RGBI. Nr. 113/1895 as amended by the 2013 Amendment to the Arbitration Act, BGBI. Nr. 118/2013). In Latin America, *voie directe* is enshrined in the laws of Colombia (Art. 101 of the National and International Arbitration Statute of 2012); Mexico (Art. 1445 of the Commercial Code and 628 of the Code of Civil Procedure of Mexico City, Federal District, *ad contrario*) and Peru (Art. 57 of Legislative Decree 1071 of 2008). In Peru, not only does the legislation provide for *voie directe*, it also expressly authorizes the arbitrators to apply "legal rules" that they deem appropriate, without providing reasons or applying conflict of laws rules.

law [2862]. Thomas Webster praises this change with respect to the 1976 rules, expressing that the reference to the conflict of laws rules within the 1976 Rules was seen as unnecessarily complicating the arbitral proceedings [2863].

However, the new UNCITRAL Arbitration Rules maintain the distinction between "rules of law" that can be selected in the exercise of party autonomy and the "law" to be determined by the arbitrators (directly or in *voie directe*) in situations where the parties have not chosen an applicable law.

When amendments to the UNCITRAL Arbitration Rules were discussed, different points of view were expressed regarding whether or not an arbitral tribunal had the discretion to designate "rules of law" where the parties had not made an effective choice of law. It was decided that the rules should be consistent with Article 28 (2) of the UNCITRAL Model Law, which specifies that the arbitral tribunal may apply the "law" rather than the "rules of law" that it determines must be applicable [2864].

A different solution has been adopted (permitting tribunals to adopt "rules of law") in the recent reform to rules of relevant arbitration centers, such as those of the ICC and the American Arbitration Association, among others [2865].

In applying the *voie directe* method, the arbitrator will likely also consider private international law principles [2866] in his or her internal reasoning. However, the arbitrator has no obligation to provide an explanation or legal basis for the application of these principles [2867]. This remains true despite the fact that in the absence of a different agreement made by the parties, under most arbitration rules the award

2862. The Working Group that drafted the Rules expressed its support to the wording that confers the arbitral tribunal broad discretion when determining the applicable regulation (A/CN.9/641, *supra* note 2579, paras. 106-112). Article 35 *(d)* of the PCA Rules also refers to the law and not rules of law in situations of *voie directe*.

2863. Webster, *supra* note 2619, p. 512.

2864. See Explanatory Note by the UNCITRAL Secretariat, https://uncitral.un.org/sites/uncitral.un.org/files/media-documents/uncitral/en/19-09955_e_ebook.pdf, accessed 16 May 2022, p. 33.

2865. 2021 ICC Rules, Article 21 (1), 2016 SIAC Rules, Article 31 (1); 2014 ICDR Rules, Article 31 (1); 2020 LCIA Rules, Article 22 (3); 2018 HKIAC Rules, Article 36 (1); 2016 ACICA Rules, Article 39 (1); 2007 DIAC Rules, Article 33 (1); 2015 NAI Rules, Article 42; 2017 SCC Rules, Article 27 (1); 2018 VIAC Rules, Article 27 (2); 2020 WIPO Rules, Article 61 *(a)*.

2866. For instance, in the Partial Award in ICC 8113/1995, *supra* note 2378, p. 325, the arbitrator decided not to determine the proper law directly but through the application of an appropriate rule of conflict.

2867. Blessing, *supra* note 2321, p. 55.

should "contain the reasons on which it is based" [2868]. It must do so, but it is not necessary to invoke private international law principles.

Gary Born argues that without conducting a conflict of laws analysis, arbitrators who directly apply a commonly applicable substantive law do little to further the interests of predictability or fairness [2869]. In particular, when the outcome of the case differs depending on which law is applied, arbitrators would not choose the law applicable to the dispute according to the expected outcome. As such, the expected outcome will not always lead the arbitrators to choose the same method. Depending on the circumstances of each case, the method that appears to be the most solidly supported will vary. Conflict of laws rules will therefore always have their say in international arbitration, and may even be necessary to tackle certain matters, for instance, capacity [2870].

Indeed, the *voie directe* method should not be considered arbitrary. In any case, concepts that form part of the conflict of laws approach, such as the "closest connection" or "place of performance", can be used as a point of reference [2871]. Particularly when the result varies depending on what law is applied, it is essential that arbitrators are not suspected of having selected a particular law with the outcome already in mind. Depending on the circumstances of each case, the arbitrator must apply the method that has the greatest legal support [2872].

Another issue relates to the "direct" method and the applicability of non-State law. This situation may occur especially in cases where the parties have made a so-called "implied negative choice"; that is, when it can be inferred from the circumstances that the parties intended to exclude the application of any domestic law. This may happen, for instance, where one of the parties is a State or a government agency and both parties have made it clear through lengthy negotiations that neither of them would accept the application of the other's domestic law or that of a third State; where the parties have expressly chosen as the applicable law "general principles of international commercial law", "principles of natural justice", "the *lex mercatoria*", or the like without further defining these terms; where the parties referred to non-existent

---

2868. Article 26.1 of 1998 LCIA Rules; Article 27 (1) of 2006 VIAC Rules of Arbitration and Conciliation.

2869. Born, *supra* note 2273, p. 2854.

2870. Silberman and Ferrari, *supra* note 2514, p. 420, fn. 272.

2871. Webster, *supra* note 2619, p. 515.

2872. Mayer, *supra* note 2794, pp. 77-78, citing ICC 7319/1992, *supra* note 2585. He also refers to the Award rendered in 1999, ICC Case No. 10988, *ICC Ct. Bull.*, Vol. 19, No. 1, p. 118. See Mayer, *supra* note 2794, pp. 76-77.

"laws" such as "European law", "Latin American law" or "Principles and Rules of the ICC"; or, finally, where the parties chose the Incoterms or the UCPs, among others, as the applicable law.

However, the same result is also often achieved in so-called multi-connected cases; that is, when the contract is silent as to the applicable law but presents connecting factors with a multitude of States, none of which are enough to justify the application of the respective domestic law to the exclusion of all the others. As demonstrated by the numerous arbitral awards reported in the UNILEX database [2873], in these types of cases, arbitral tribunals worldwide are often no longer insistent upon the application of a particular domestic law nor upon the law applicable to the substance of the dispute. Instead, arbitral tribunals may prefer to resort to a balanced, comprehensive and internationally recognized set of rules of law such as the UNIDROIT Principles.

George Bermann highlights the alternative of applying non-State law by way of *voie directe*. In doing so, arbitrators may apply substantive uniform law that has an identifiable content and an international flavor, if only because it is not anchored in a particular legal system. Bermann also writes that perhaps the best example of such a body of law is the UNIDROIT Principles or the CISG, which tribunals have found most appropriate to address the problems of the transborder relationship [2874].

In any case, whether an arbitral tribunal follows the *voie directe* or *voie indirecte* solution, it enjoys very considerable freedom when it comes to the choice of law. In this regard, arbitral tribunals also have a measurably greater liberty than courts do [2875].

F. The absence of choice in international investment law

Investment contracts, national laws and treaties often neglect applicable law issues. This is particularly the case within investment treaties. Some provide for the application of a certain law, combinations of laws or rules of law. However, most do not contain an explicit reference [2876].

Arbitral regulations provide some guidance in this regard. For instance, the second sentence of Article 42 (1) of the ICSID Convention

---

2873. Scc http://unilex.info/principles/cases/article/102/issue/1224#issue_1224, accessed 16 May 2022.
2874. Bermann, *supra* note 11, p. 282.
2875. *Ibid.*, p. 275
2876. Ferguson Reed and Paulsson, *supra* note 1147, p. 73.

includes an applicable substantive law provision and imposes a two-step process: first, tribunals must determine whether a law was chosen, consistent with the fundamental principle of party autonomy. Second, in the absence of such a choice, the arbitrators "shall apply the law of the Contracting State party to the dispute (including its rules on the conflict of laws) and such rules of international law as may be applicable".

This twofold process is more complicated than it seems [2877]. According to Schreuer, where there is no clear indication of a choice of law [2878], "the tribunal should assume absence of such agreement and apply the residual rule" [2879]. The most difficult and controversial task for arbitrators to complete is likely managing the relevance of their application and the eventual interaction of the laws of the host State and international law [2880].

In ICSID practice, tribunals dealing with treaty claims generally apply the substantive provisions of the treaty itself (such as fair and equitable treatment) and other sources of public international law, such as international customary law or general principles. The laws of a host State usually have a role to play in these cases as well, such as determining whether the investment was made in accordance with their

---

2877. *Ibid.*, pp. 351-352.

2878. "To make this determination may be made simply by a search of any contractual document which governs their relationship for an explicit choice of law clause, failing which the tribunal may conclude that there is no agreement on choice of law. This was the method adopted in *Benvenuti & Bonfant* v. *Congo*", Schreuer *et al.*, *supra* note 102, p. 592.

2879. *Ibid.*, p. 593.

2880. Bjorklund and Vanhonnaeker, *supra* note 13, p. 360. Schreuer *et al.*, *supra* note 102, p. 583:

> "The question remains whether international law will be taken into account by an ICSID tribunal where it is not included in the formula on choice of law agreed to by the parties. At first appearance a negative reply is indicated by the juxtaposition of the first and second sentences of Article 42 (1): whereas the second sentence includes a reference to applicable rules of international law, the first sentence does not. A. Broches has explained this omission as a matter of drafting technique. The first sentence speaks of 'rules of law' rather than of a system of national law. Since such 'rules of law' may be national as well as international, a separate reference to international law would have been out of place: Broches, *Convention, Explanatory Notes and Survey*, p. 668. The principle of freedom of choice of law also indicates that a failure to mention international law in an agreement actually amounts to a negative choice of law effectively excluding its applicability. Several authors have, in fact, drawn this conclusion, arguing that the application of international law in this situation would violate the parties' declared will. Nevertheless, the practice of ICSID Tribunals, the overwhelming weight of writerly opinion, and important policy considerations all indicate that there is at least some place for International law even in the presence of an agreement on choice of law which does not incorporate it. *Letco* v. *Liberia*, Award, 31 March 1986, 2 ICSID Reports 358."

rules or ensuring that compensation for expropriation was accurately calculated [2881].

In the first twenty years of the ICSID Convention and up until the 1990s, most of the cases involved breaches of investment contracts. Half of them included a choice of law agreement related to the substance of the dispute, and almost all cases referred to the law of the State party of the dispute [2882]. In the remaining cases, no applicable law had been agreed upon [2883]. As such, the appropriate handling of choice of law issues became of utmost relevance [2884], and several disputes decided by ICSID dealt with this matter. This was the case, for instance, in *Benvenuti* v. *Congo* [2885], *SOABI* v. *Senegal* [2886], *LETCO* v. *Liberia* [2887], *CDSE* v. *Costa Rica* [2888] and *MCI* v. *Ecuador* [2889].

Most of the ICSID disputes heard after 2000 involved BITs, and in the absence of a choice the arbitrators generally applied international law due to the fact that the claims invariably asserted breaches of the BIT in question [2890].

For investment claims conducted in accordance with UNCITRAL-inspired mechanisms, as seen in this chapter, the Model Law states that in the absence of a choice of law, the arbitral tribunal shall apply "the law determined by the conflict of laws rules which it considers applicable" (Art. 28 (2)). This traditional approach has been reflected in many arbitration laws and rules governing investment arbitration cases. Others, such as the ICC Arbitration Rules, are more forward-looking, and allow for the *voie directe* approach. These and related matters have been approached earlier in this chapter.

The PCA Rules also draw upon the UNCITRAL Model Law and include provisions that apply directly to States and intergovernmental parties. In the absence of a choice of law, Article 35.1.*b* of the PCA Rules states that:

> "In cases involving only States and intergovernmental organizations, apply the rules of the organization concerned and the

2881. Ferguson Reed and Paulsson, *supra* note 1147, p. 73.
2882. Parra, *supra* note 510, p. 178.
2883. *Ibid.*, p. 179.
2884. Kreindler, *supra* note 2039, pp. 407-408.
2885. *Benvenuti* v. *Congo*, *supra* note 455, Award (15 August 1980), paras. 4.1-4.4.
2886. *SOABI* v. *Senegal*, *supra* note 1983, Award (25 February 1988), paras. 5.01-5.37.
2887. *LETCO* v. *Liberia*, *supra* note 456, Award (31 March 1986), paras. 34-37.
2888. *CDSE* v. *Costa Rica*, *supra* note 455, Award (17 February 2000), paras. 60-67.
2889. *MCI* v. *Ecuador*, *supra* note 1150, Award (31 July 2007), para. 217.
2890. Parra, *supra* note 510, p. 303.

law applicable to any agreement or relationship between the parties, and, where appropriate, the general principles governing the law of intergovernmental organizations and the rules of general international law."

Certain national arbitration laws and arbitration rules direct tribunals to apply national law to the exclusion of international law in the absence of an agreement by the parties [2891]. Notwithstanding, international law may apply in a supervening way as will be further elaborated in Chapter XX.

G. Conflict of laws mechanisms in investment arbitration

Investment tribunals have often sought to avoid clear statements regarding the applicable substantive law and evade a rigid application of the law of the host State [2892]. Numerous conflict of laws formulas have been advanced in the absence of a choice of law: the center of gravity, the place of characteristic performance, the law of the place where the contract was formed, the law of the place of performance, the law of the place where the tort took place, the law of the place where the legal act took place, the law of the place where the object is situated and the law of the place of domicile, among others [2893]. The application of the different formulas exemplified above depends on the relevant issue and the conflict of laws system governing the relationship.

Regarding the selection of the applicable conflict or uniform law rules, as in international commercial arbitration, several approaches exist within international investment law that will be discussed in the following sections.

1. The conflict of laws system of the host State

Negotiations during the drafting of the ICSID Convention show that early discussions and draft versions of the instrument did not refer to

2891. Kjos mentions as an arguable example, in this regard, the CRCICA Arbitration Rules (in force from 1 March 2011) which in its Article 35 (1) expressly states that: "The arbitral tribunal shall apply the rules of law designated by the parties as applicable to the substance of the dispute. Failing such designation by the parties, the arbitral tribunal shall apply the law which has the closest connection to the dispute", Kjos, *supra* note 2296, p. 77.

2892. Bischoff, *supra* note 15, p. 755.

2893. Kreindler, *supra* note 2039, pp. 407-408.

the law of the host State. The applicability of national and international law rules was referenced; however, no mention was made of the law of the host State [2894]. The drafters of the Convention opted for such an open-ended formula in Article 42 to aid arbitral tribunals in determining the proper applicable law by applying generally accepted conflict of laws rules or private international law [2895]. By following this approach, arbitrators could expect to determine the law with the most significant connection to the dispute. The law of the host State will be applicable in most cases, but other national laws may also be applicable in others [2896].

This solution was criticized during the drafting of the Convention for being too vague and broad [2897], particularly by delegates of developing countries [2898]. As a consequence, the final version of the ICSID Convention contemplates the application of the law of the State party to the dispute, including its conflict of laws rules [2899]. Therefore, tribunals should generally apply the law of the host State unless its choice of law rules lead to the application of a different law [2900]. Several ICSID cases applied the law of the host State [2901], such as *Benvenuti* v. *Congo* [2902], *Cable TV* v. *St. Kitts and Nevis* [2903], *Amco* v.

2894. *History of the ICSID Convention*, *supra* note 1078, I, pp. 190, 192.

2895. *Ibid.*, II, pp. 79, 110, 267, 330, 506, 570. Article 42, paragraph 1, second sentence, states: "In the absence of such agreement, the Tribunal shall apply the law of the Contracting State party to the dispute (including its rules on the conflict of laws) and such rules of international law as may be applicable."

2896. *Ibid.*, pp. 514, 571, 800.

2897. A. Broches, "The Convention on the Settlement of Investment Disputes between States and National of Other States: Applicable Law and Default Procedure", in P. Sanders (ed.), *International Arbitration: Liber Amicorum for Martin Domke*, The Hague, Martinus Nijhoff, 1967, pp. 12, 13 *et seq*.

2898. *History of the ICSID Convention*, *supra* note 1078, II, pp. 418, 419, 466, 513, 515-516, 653, 660, 663, 800-802. See also Douglas, *supra* note 39, p. 130.

2899. See Schreuer *et al.*, *supra* note 102, p. 594.

2900. Bjorklund and Vanhonnaeker, *supra* note 13, p. 368. This solution according to Schreuer is clearly in favor of host States' law. "The qualifying words at the end of the sentence ("as may be applicable") cannot be meant to interpret this decision contingent on the particular circumstances of the case, since these words do not refer to the law of the contracting State party to the dispute. Other systems of domestic law are excluded unless their application is mandated by the host State laws' conflict rules", Schreuer *et al.*, *supra* note 102, p. 595.

2901. *Ibid.*, p. 596.

2902. The Tribunal decided to apply Congolese as well as international law. Vid. *Benvenuti* v. *Congo*, *supra* note 455, Award (15 August 1980), para. 4.2.

2903. *Cable Television*, *supra* note 2697, Award (13 January 1997), paras. 6.02, 6.25.

Indonesia[2904], *SOABI* v. *Senegal*[2905], *Genin* v. *Estonia*[2906] and *MCI* v. *Ecuador*[2907].

Christoph Schreuer notes that the clear victory of the application of the law of the host State in ICSID arbitration is mitigated by four factors. First, the law of the host State is generally the one that is most closely connected to the dispute and, as such, the law would likely be applied anyways. Second, the second sentence of Article 42 (1) explicitly includes conflict of laws rules. Therefore, if there are stronger connections to another legal system, it is likely that *renvoi* will lead to the application of that law regardless. Third, the parties may exercise party autonomy in accordance with the first sentence of Article 42 (1) and select other rules if applying the host State's law would lead to unsatisfactory results. Finally, the host State's law is also subject to the corrective function of international law[2908], a matter that will be further dealt with in Chapter XX.

2. *Cumulative application of the rules of all States with a connection to the dispute*

As has been mentioned, cumulatively applying the rules of all States with a connection to the dispute is an approach consistent with the transnational nature of international arbitration. The cumulative application of these laws is also more in line with the parties' expectations and reduces the possibility of challenges arising that allege that the wrong law was applied. This approach was adopted by the ICSID tribunals in cases such as *SOABI* v. *Senegal*[2909] and *Klöckner* v. *Cameroon*[2910].

2904. "[T]he Tribunal has to apply Indonesian law, which is the law of the Contracting State Party to the dispute, and such rules of international law as the Tribunal deems to be applicable, considering the matters and issues in dispute" (*Amco Asia* v. *Indonesia*, *supra* note 408, Award (20 November 1984), para. 148).

2905. The Tribunal characterized the contracts as "government contracts", the effect and execution of which are governed primarily by the Code of Governmental Obligations. It appears from the position of the Government as stated in its Counter-Memorial (p. 11) and that of SOABI contained in its Reply (p. 7) that both parties agree that the applicable law is Senegalese administrative law. Vid. *SOABI* v. *Senegal*, *supra* note 1983, Award (25 February 1988), para. 5.02.

2906. *Genin* v. *Estonia*, *supra* note 96, para. 350.

2907. *MCI* v. *Ecuador*, *supra* note 1150, Award (31 July 2007), para. 217.

2908. Schreuer *et al.*, *supra* note 102, p. 595.

2909. *SOABI* v. *Senegal*, *supra* note 1983, Award (25 February 1988), paras. 5.01-5.37.

2910. *Klöckner* v. *Cameroon*, *supra* note 748, Award (1983), 2 *ICSID Reports*, p. 59. This decision was annulled, as explained in Chap. VII.B.2.*(v)*, *supra*, "Consequences of neglecting comparative law".

3. Conflict of laws rules of another State

Tribunals may also apply conflict of laws rules from another State. This possibility emerges, for example, from the second sentence of Article 42 (1) of the ICSID Convention. This rule states that "[i]n the absence of such agreement, the Tribunal shall apply the law of the Contracting State party to the dispute (including its rules on the conflict of laws) and such rules of international law as may be applicable".

According to this provision, the host State's law applies in the absence of choice, and its conflict of laws rules may lead to the application of another substantive law [2911].

4. The application of general principles of private international law

Some investment arbitration cases have referred to general principles of private international law [2912]. For instance, in the *SPP* case, an ICC tribunal expressed the following:

> "May we observe, *ad abundantiam*, that failing contractual designation of the governing law the same result (i.e., reference to the law of the host country) would also normally be achieved by applying the ordinary principles on conflict of laws." [2913]

Similarly, several ICSID tribunals have also applied "general principles of conflict of laws" by recurring to the closest connection test [2914]. This approach seeks to ensure greater predictability and limit opportunities for forum shopping [2915].

The closest connection test was also used in the *ad hoc* foreign investment case *Wintershall AG* et al. v. *Government of Qatar* [2916], and in various Iran-United States Claims Tribunal decisions, such as in *Economy Forms Corporation* v. *Government of the Islamic Republic of Iran* et al., and *Harnischfeger Corp.* v. *Ministry of Roads & Transportation* [2917].

2911. Bischoff, *supra* note 15, p. 757.

2912. *Liamco*, *supra* note 946, Award (1977), 20 ILM, p. 1, 32, fn. 53; *Aramco*, *supra* note 1004, Award (23 August 1958), 27 ILR, p. 117, 156-157 (1963). *Westinghouse*, *supra* note 1639, fn. 89, at sec. III.

2913. *SPP* v. *Egypt*, *supra* note 1085, ICC Award No. 3493, Award (16 February 1983), para. 49.

2914. Schreuer *et al.*, *supra* note 102, p. 560.

2915. Bischoff, *supra* note 15, p. 747.

2916. *Wintershall AG* v. *Government of Qatar*, Partial Award (5 February 1988) and Final Award (31 May 1988), at p. 800, 802, 821-823.

2917. *Economy Forms*, *supra* note 2449, at sec. III (1). Aldrich, *supra* note 834, p. 159. See also *Harnischfeger* v. *Ministry*, *supra* note 2447, Partial Award (13 July 1984).

5. Application of public international law

How public international law should be applied where the parties have not agreed upon an applicable law will depend on the context of the dispute and the nature of the relationship more broadly [2918]. In some cases, however, the application of public international law will be clear – for instance, with several issues related to treaty claims [2919].

In the context of ICSID arbitrations, public international law may always be applicable in a supervening way, according to Article 42, paragraph 1 (second sentence), of the ICSID Convention. This matter will be further elaborated in Chapter XX.

It is also clear that public international law will apply when appropriate in Iran-US Tribunal decisions due to the broad wording of Article V of the 1981 Iran-United States Claims Settlement Declaration, a provision addressed extensively in Chapter XVI.

In territorialized arbitrations, if the arbitral rules authorize the tribunal through *voie directe* to apply the appropriate "rules of law" (for example, as in ICC arbitrations), no questions will arise regarding the power of the arbitrators to decide the dispute applying public international law if pertinent. Difficulties may emerge regarding the more traditional solution, found in the UNCITRAL Rules, of deciding which "law" to apply (and not rules of law) in the absence of the parties' choice [2920]. Notwithstanding this provision, when appropriate,

---

2918. Justice Aikens stated in *Ecuador* v. *Occidental* (2001) that the "rights are granted under public international law . . . must be determined on principles of public international law". *Republic of Ecuador* v. *Occidental Exploration and Production Company*, High Court of Justice, Queen's Bench Division, Commercial Court (29 April 2005), [2005] EWHC 774 (Comm) (per Mr Justice Aikens), para. 61.

2919. Kjos, *supra* note 2296, p. 235. In international investment agreement cases, the treaty is *lex specialis* and its provisions "supersede principles of customary international law". Unless those principles are general principles of international law in the nature of *jus cogens*" (*Teinver SA* et al. v. *Arg.*, ICSID Case No. ARB/09/01, Award (21 July 2017), para. 475). But as decided by the Tribunal in *Emmis International* v. *Hungary*, a tribunal "has to apply international law as a whole to the claim, and not the provisions of the BIT in isolation". *Emmis International Holding, BV et al.* v. *Hung.*, ICSID Case No. ARB/12/2, Objection under ICSID Arbitration Rule 41 (5) (11 March 2013), para. 78; *MTD* v. *Chile*, *supra* note 327, Annulment (21 March 2007) para. 61. Interesting questions arise where, like in case of EU law and intra-EU IIAs, several treaties potentially conflict. See e.g. Case C-284/16 *Slowakische Republik* v. *Achmea BV*, http://eur-lex.europa.eu/legal-content/EN/TXT/?uri=CELEX:62016CJ0284, accessed 16 May 2022 (6 March 2018), where the court found that arbitration clauses in intra-EU IIAs are contrary to EU law; the underlying dispute was *Achmea BV (formerly Eureko BV)* v. *Slovak*, UNCITRAL, PCA Case No. 2008-13, Final Award (7 December 2012). See Bischoff, *supra* note 15, pp. 758-759.

2920. Kjos, *supra* note 2296, pp. 80-81.

arbitrators may apply public international law and in general rules of law, as advocated earlier in this chapter.

The ICSID Additional Facility Rules attempt to eliminate complications on this issue when referring to the combined application of "*(a)* the law determined by the conflict of laws rules . . . and *(b)* such rules of international law as the Tribunal considers applicable" [2921].

The applicability of public international law in investment claims raises several other issues that have been further addressed in Chapter XVII (J) (5).

6. Uniform law techniques or recurrence to non-State law

What has been discussed in this chapter regarding the applicability of non-State law to commercial arbitrations also bears on the investment arbitration context.

In the famous 1989 case *Deutsche Schachtbau-und Tiefbohr GmbH* v. *R'As Al Khaimah National Oil Co. (Rakoil)* [2922], in the absence of an express choice of law, the Tribunal considered the application of national law inappropriate. It referred to "what has become common practice in international arbitrations particularly in the field of oil drilling concessions", which "must have been known to the parties . . . and should be regarded as representing their implicit will". The Tribunal decided the case by referring to "internationally accepted principles of law governing contractual relations" [2923].

In *Ministry of Defence and Support for Armed Forces of the Islamic Republic of Iran* v. *Westinghouse Electric Corp.* (1996) [2924], the Tribunal took into account that *(i)* the parties did not operate within the same environment and legal culture; *(ii)* that they did not have a long history of cooperation, and then proceeded to address all the potential outcomes given that the contract did not contain extensive or detailed provisions. In this context, the absence of a choice of law provision was considered by the Tribunal to be a "shouting silence", or at the very least an "alarming silence" or *un silence inquiétant* that required the Tribunal to look "behind" to determine the parties' intentions. The Tribunal found that the parties had made an "implied negative choice" excluding the application of either of the parties' national law. Instead,

2921. ICSID Additional Facility Rules (2006), Article 54 (1).
2922. ICC Case No. 3572, Final Award (1987), 14 YB Comm. Arb., p. 111 (1989), 117.
2923. *Ibid.*
2924. *Westinghouse*, *supra* note 1636, Award (1996).

the Tribunal decided in favor of a "de-nationalized solution", according to which it would "decide legal issues by having regard to the terms of the Contract and, where necessary or appropriate, by applying truly international standards as reflected in, and forming part of, the so-called 'general principles of law'" [2925].

7. The law of the contract: contrat sans lois*?*

The theory that international contracts, and in particular international State contracts, are not subject to any rules other than those of the agreement itself is not only questionable on theoretical grounds but can also create practical problems regarding issues not contemplated therein [2926].

The decision in *MINE* v. *Guinea* [2927], according to Schreuer, "goes a long way towards reducing the impact of domestic law but stops short of making the agreement a *contrat sans loi*" [2928].

In any case, if the tribunal does not find guidance in the contract regarding a particular issue, the prohibition of *non liquet* in Article 42 (1) of the ICSID Convention can lead to the application of other sources such as general principles [2929].

8. Voie directe

The delicate balance between flexibility and predictability is a unique feature of the ICSID Convention [2930]. As noted by Antonio Parra, the tribunals in the *Wena* v. *Egypt* case [2931], the *CMS* case [2932] and others appear to have interpreted the second sentence of Article 42 (1) of the ICSID Convention as allowing a similar freedom: several modern commercial arbitration rules grant the tribunal the power to determine the applicable law through *voie directe* [2933].

2925. *Westinghouse*, *supra* note 1636, fn. 86, at sec. III. See Kjos, *supra* note 2296, p. 73.

2926. Schreuer *et al.*, *supra* note 102, p. 562.

2927. *MINE* v. *Guinea*, *supra* note 2190.

2928. Schreuer *et al.*, *supra* note 102, p. 562.

2929. *Ibid.*, p. 563.

2930. *Ibid.*, p. 595.

2931. *Wena Hotels* v. *Egypt*, *supra* note 601.

2932. *CMS* v. *Argentina*, *supra* note 84.

2933. Parra considers this interpretation difficult to reconcile with this drafting history and the text of the second sentence of Article 42 (1) requiring the application of the national law "and" applicable international law rules. Moreover, the interpretation, developed as a pragmatic solution in the context of modern BIT cases, seemed less

Zachary Douglas notes that Article 42 (1) provides no guidance as to the circumstances in which national law or international law should be applied by the tribunal. In his words:

> "[T]he default rule does not purport to set out the connecting factors that would enable the tribunal to decide the proper law of a particular issue. Article 42 is not therefore a choice of law rule in the true sense of the term. It simply recognizes the competence of the tribunal to apply both national and international law." [2934]

Similarly, Article V of the 1981 Claims Settlement Declaration for the Iran-United States Tribunal also grants the arbitrators the freedom to apply those rules and principles that they determine to be appropriate in the case at hand.

As seen previously in this chapter, this *voie directe* freedom also exists in several UNCITRAL-inspired arbitration laws and rules governing territorialized investment arbitrations.

---

self-evidently sensible for the setting of contract claims uppermost in the minds of the drafters in the mid-1960s. All this seemed to testify to the wisdom, in investment treaty cases, of situating applicable law where possible under the first sentence of Article 42 (1), as was done in the ADC case in particular, in Parra, *supra* note 510, p. 306.

2934. The Limitations of Article 42 (1) are implicit in the report of the Executive Director on the ICSID Convention. "(T)he Tribunal must apply the law of the State party to the dispute (unless that law calls for the application of some other law), *as well* as such rules of international law as may be applicable." There is no attempt to provide the tribunal's applicant of these sources of law. The original wording was even more unequivocal: "[i]n the absence of any agreement between the parties concerning the law to be applied . . . the Arbitral Tribunal shall decide the dispute submitted to it in accordance with such rules of law, whether national or international, as it shall determine to be applicable" (Working Paper in the form of a Draft Convention (5 June 1962), in *History of the ICSID Convention*, *supra* note 1078, II, p. 21 *apud* Douglas, *supra* note 39, p. 129).

CHAPTER XIX

THE APPLICABLE SUBSTANTIVE LAW IN INVESTMENT ARBITRATION *EX AEQUO* ET BONO

A. Equity in the law

In *Nicomachean Ethics* and *Rhetoric*, Aristotle referred to equity as "super justice", correcting the harsh application of rules [2935]. Roman law used the word *aequitas* in this same sense [2936]. Another perspective derives from Christian theology, which understands equity as correcting the application of the law not only to achieve justice but also for the sake of charity, grace or piety [2937]. Equity was used in this sense within medieval scholarship: it was understood as clemency when required by good conscience [2938].

In the modern era, legal rules operate in two ways: they either amply delegate equitable powers to adjudicators [2939] or recognize equitable principles, such as good faith, that the adjudicator must apply alongside other rules [2940].

In England, when referring to equity, common lawyers generally prefer to speak about justice, fairness and good conscience [2941] due to

---

2935. Aristotle, *Nicomachean Ethics*, trans. W. D. Ross, http://classics.mit.edu//Aristotle/nicomachaen.html, accessed 12 May 2022), Book V, 10, Book VI, 11, Book VIII, 10. *Aristotle, Rhetoric*, trans. W. Rhys Roberts, http://classics.mit.edu//Aristotle/rhetoric.html, accessed 12 May 2022, Book I, Parts 13, 15.

2936. Villey, *supra* note 713, p. 62. Erasmus distorts the phrase *summun ius summa injuria*, used by Cicero to criticize procedural formalism. Erasmus criticized the medieval Bartolists for their fixation on written texts. The texts must be applied with equity, the spirit of the texts and natural reason in mind. See *ibid.*, p. 541.

2937. *Ibid.*, p. 330.

2938. H. J. Berman, *Law and Revolution*, Vol. 2: *The Impact of the Protestant Reformations on the Western Legal Tradition*, Cambridge, MA / London, Harvard University Press, 2003, p. 196.

2939. From this perspective, equity may be understood in the contexts of adapting law to particular areas or choosing between several different interpretations of the law (equity *infra legem*), filling gaps in the law (equity *praetor legem*) and as a reason for not applying unjust laws (equity *contra legem*). See M. Akehurst, "Equity and General Principles of law", *International and Comparative Law Quarterly*, Vol. 25, No. 4 (1976), p. 801. See also Judge Weeramantry, the *Jan Mayen* case, *ICJ Reports 1993*, pp. 226-234, 99 ILR, pp. 594-602.

2940. Contemplated, for instance, in Article 1.7 of the UNIDROIT Principles. Zimmermann and Whittaker, *supra* note 726, p. 31.

2941. David, *supra* note 1451, p. 375.

certain historical developments. In the past, in contrast to common law courts, English equity courts avoided the strict application of precedents *(stare decisis)* to the controversies submitted to them, and their decisions in turn generated equitable principles [2942]. Eventually, equity courts and the principles they articulated were absorbed by the common law.

Harold Berman finds a theoretical basis for common law equity in Lutheran philosophy, in particular the writing of Johann Oldendorp (1480-1567). For Oldendorp, in all cases the adjudicator should go beyond the legal texts and their spirit, both from the point of view of justice in each particular case and also to guarantee ultimate consistency within the rules themselves. This thinking is reflected in the Anglo-American conception of judicial discretion [2943].

In the words of John Henry Merryman, common law judges do not need to encapsulate the dispute within the parameters created by the legislator. Even in cases in which it is appropriate to apply a particular law, the adjudicator still maintains certain powers to adjust the law to the facts. If the parameters are inadequate, the adjudicator can make minor changes to adjust. This power is even greater in precedents. By contrast, within the civil law the legislature always controls the parameters [2944]. Although this understanding has been tempered in recent years, the evolving role of the judge within the civil law does not mean that they are free to deviate from the path of the law proper.

According to Lucy Reed, the impact of equitable considerations on the applicable substantive law is "a troubling issue in both private

2942. Perelman, *supra* note 714, p. 13.

2943. Berman, *supra* note 2938, p. 96. "The common law concept of equity found fertile ground within the international law field. For instance, in many cases decided by the British-American Claims Tribunal under the Convention of 1910, the tribunals denied claims that had no support in rules "of international law and of equity". In addition, the term "justice" is used in arbitration treaties when defining "legal justice" and is generally interpreted in this way by arbitral tribunals as well. In the *Delagoa Railway* arbitration case [*supra* note 2003], for example, the arbitrator had to decide according to what he would deem 'most just'", Lauterpacht, *supra* note 3, pp. 65-66. Pellet and Müller have criticized Anglo-Saxon jurists that seem to have sometimes yielded to the temptation to transpose the common law principle "lock, stock, and barrel", in Pellet and Müller, *supra* note 239, p. 875. In turn, Oppenheim notes that the English "equity" bears a very specialized meaning, which is not normally imported into that term in international law. The meaning of "equity" in a national sense may, however, be relevant to the meaning of that term in a treaty. See Jennings and Watts, *supra* note 278, p. 43.

2944. Recognizing that the law can sometimes be harsh or inadequate, it is preferable to leave in hand of the adjudicator a discretion provided by these equitable principles, which is many times considered a menace in traditional civil law systems. See Merryman, *supra* note 726, pp. 102-103.

and public international law" [2945]. In a discrete number of instances, the applicable law incorporates equitable considerations directly and instructs the tribunal to take account of them [2946]. In these situations, equity can be considered an intrinsic attribute of the rules of law (equity *infra legem*) or can constitute the very content of said rules (equity *intra legem*) and fill gaps within the law (equity *praeter legem*) [2947]. In other cases, the tribunal is not required to base its decision upon strict rules of law [2948], and may come to a final adjudication by "correcting" the law (or despite the law entirely) via the mere application of the principles of fairness and justice (equity *contra legem*) [2949]. This chapter will make particular reference to equity in these latter cases, particularly in relation to arbitration.

B. *Equity in arbitration*

In arbitration, equitable powers are interpreted in several ways [2950]. First, equitable powers dictate that the tribunal must observe the applicable law but ignore purely formalistic rules, such as the observance of a particular form in a contract. Second, equitable powers may require that the tribunal follow the applicable law but may allow particular rules that operate unfairly in the case at hand to be ignored [2951].

2945. Reed, *supra* note 21, pp. 225-226.

2946. This was the case within the Continental Shelf Delimitation judgment. See e.g. *Continental Shelf (Tunisia/Libyan Arab Jamahiriya)*, Judgment, *ICJ Reports 1982*, p. 18; *Delimitation of the Maritime Boundary*, *supra* note 732, Judgment (1984).

2947. E. Milano, "General Principles Infra, Praeter, Contra Legem? The Role of Equity in Determining Reparation", in M. Andenas, M. Fitzmaurice, A. Tanzi and J. Wouters (eds.), *General Principles and the Coherence of International Law*, Leiden, Brill, 2019, p. 66. See also Pellet and Müller, *supra* note 239, p. 875.

2948. On *ex aequo et bono* awards, see e.g. UNCITRAL Arbitration Rules, approved by UNGA Res. 31/98, Article 33 (2), reproduced in *Yearbook of UNICTRAL*, Vol. 8 (1977), p. 7, 15 ILM, p. 701 (1976), 2 YB. Comm. Arb. (1977) p. 161: "[t]he arbitral tribunal shall decide as *amiable compositeur* or *ex aequo et bono* only if the parties have expressly authorized the arbitral tribunal to do so and if the law applicable to the arbitral procedure permits such arbitration".

2949. Milano, *supra* note 2947, p. 66. See also Pellet and Müller, *supra* note 239, p. 875.

2950. As noted in Blackaby *et al.*, *supra* note 255, p. 217.

2951. These two interpretations go in line with the award issued in ICC Case No. 3327, *supra* note 1974, which characterized arbitration in equity as putting less emphasis on the legal aspect of the claim and more emphasis upon its technical, psychological and commercial aspects. Equity provides the arbitrator with a means to limit the effects of the law in the dispute, and instead grants a greater emphasis upon other factors, according to the factual circumstances and the requirement to maintain a reasonable commercial policy. See Gaillard and Savage, *supra* note 836, p. 836.

Third, the tribunal may have to decide cases in accordance with general principles of law instead of per the contract or the ostensibly applicable legislation [2952]. Finally, equitable powers may – sporadically – permit the tribunal to completely ignore all rules of law and decide the case according to its own conscience [2953]. According to Alan Redfern and Martin Hunter, this last interpretation of equitable powers has been rejected in arbitration scholarly writings [2954].

Arbitration in equity is also referred to as "amiable composition" [2955]. Even though the issue generated debates [2956], the terms *ex aequo et bono* and *amiable compositeur* are used interchangeably [2957]. Due to terminological disparities, both expressions are found in the UNCITRAL Rules and Model Law [2958].

Equitable (or *ex aequo et bono*) arbitration was consolidated by the canon lawyers during the Middle Ages. In their view, the arbitrator must consider and define the rights and obligations of the parties at the outset of the arbitration. However, that examination will not be final since the

2952. In an ICC arbitration governed by the laws of Ecuador, the Tribunal arrived at a conclusion in accordance with "established principles of international arbitration" and the general principle of *venire contra factum proprium*. As seen in this example, an "interpretation" of domestic law may be perceived as an alteration or correction of it – especially to a State that takes a different view of its own law. See Kotuby and Sobota, *supra* note 157, p. 32.

2953. For instance, ICC Case No. 5103, Award, 115 JDI (Clunet), p. 1206 (1988). See also *Soubaigne* v. *Limmereds Skogar*, Paris Cour d'Appel, Judgment (15 March 1984), 1985 Rev. Arb., p. 285, according to which the arbitrators must seek the fairest solution.

2954. "To the extent that they do agree, commentators seem to suggest that even an arbitral tribunal that decides 'in equity' must act in accordance with some generally accepted legal principles. In many (or perhaps most) cases, this means that the arbitral tribunal will reach its decision based largely on a consideration of the facts and on the provisions of the contract, while trying to ensure that these provisions do not operate unfairly to the detriment of one of the parties", Blackaby *et al.*, *supra* note 255, p. 217.

2955. According to the Paris Court of Appeal, "arbitrators acting as *amiables compositeurs* have an obligation to ensure that their decision is equitable or else they would betray their duty and give rise to a cause for annulment" (Paris Cour d'Appel, 11 January 1996, p. 351).

2956. Definitions of both of these terms vary. Some authorities conclude that *amiables compositeurs* are first obliged to reach a "legal" result, and then adjust it (if necessary) in light of equitable considerations. Other authorities hold that arbitration *ex aequo et bono* involves considerations of equity and fairness, in addition to, or without having to refer to, legal rules. See the UNCITRAL, Report on the Work of its Ninth Session, UN Doc. A/31/17, Annex II, para. 172 (1976). In *Yesodei Hatorah College Inc.* v. *Trustees of the Elwood Talmud Torah Congregation* (2011), the Tribunal used indistinctively the expressions *ex aequo et bono* or *amiable compositeur*. VSC 622, paras. 69-70 (Victoria Sup. Ct.).

2957. Hayward, *supra* note 2323, p. 27. See, for instance, Gaillard and Savage, *supra* note 836, p. 835.

2958. Caron, Caplan and Pellonpää, *supra* note 2618, p. 134.

arbitrator must also apply the equitable consideration of reestablishing harmony between litigants [2959].

In the United States, arbitrators were not historically obligated to give reasons and their awards could not be reviewed due to errors of law. As a result, the arbitration system was compared to *ex aequo et bono* or *amiable compositeur* [2960]. By contrast, English law did not allow arbitration *ex aequo et bono* until the passing of the Arbitration Act of 1996, which permits it in Section 46 (1) *(b)*.

With some exceptions [2961], today numerous regulations around the world provide for arbitration *ex aequo et bono*, as reflected in Article 28 (3) of the Model Law [2962]. The explanatory note to the Model Law elaborates on this provision and its application because the principle of *ex aequo et bono* had not previously been commonly known or applied across the world's legal systems [2963].

Some national laws even went further than the Model Law, stating that the arbitrators must decide according to equitable principles unless expressly agreed otherwise. This recalls the origin of *ex aequo et bono* arbitration as – in the words of Redfern and Hunter – a "friendly" dispute resolution mechanism, which runs contrary to the law-based process it has become [2964].

In addition, Article VII (2) of the European Convention of 1961 includes a provision on *amiables compositeurs* [2965], as does the

2959. See David, *supra* note 1451, pp. 86-87.

2960. C. Patilla Robertson and V. Castro Hurtado, "La amigable composición", *Boletín Informativo del Capítulo Mexicano de la Cámara Internacional de Comercio*, No. 53 (2007), p. 2237.

2961. Russian International Arbitration Law, Article 28; Bulgarian Arbitration Law, Art. 38.

2962. French Code of Civil Procedure, Article 1512. German ZPO, para. 1051 (3); Hong Kong Arbitration Ordinance, para. 64 (3); Swiss Law on Private International Law, Article 187 (2); Belgian Judicial Code, Article 1710 (3); Netherlands Code of Civil Procedure, Article 1054 (3); Italian Code of Civil Procedure, Article 822; Japanese Arbitration Law, Article 36 (3); Québec Code of Civil Procedure, Article 944 (10); South Korean Arbitration Act, Article 29 (3), etc. In the United States, the Restatement of the US Law of International Commercial and Investor-State Arbitration, para. 1-1 Reporters' Note b (2019) states the following: "The definition of arbitral tribunal includes bodies empowered to act *ex aequo et bono* (or as *amiable compositeur*)."

2963. UNCITRAL Secretariat's Explanatory Note, https://uncitral.un.org/sites/uncitral.un.org/files/media-documents/uncitral/en/19-09955_e_ebook.pdf, accessed 13 May 2022, p. 34.

2964. For example, Ecuador's Law of Arbitration No. 145/1997 stated at Section 3: "The parties will decide whether the arbitrator shall decide in law or in equity. Unless otherwise agreed, the award shall be in equity." See Blackaby *et al.*, *supra* note 218.

2965. Hascher, *supra* note 2574, p. 1030. The European Convention states that "the arbitrators shall act as *amiables compositeurs* if the parties so decide and if they may do so under the law applicable to the arbitration" (Art. VII (2)).

MERCOSUR Arbitration Agreement of 1998 [2966]. Provisions on *amiables compositeurs* can also be found within the UNCITRAL Arbitration Rules and the PCA Arbitration Rules [2967], among others following these models [2968].

In practice, parties agree to arbitration *ex aequo et bono* in extremely rare cases. Gary Born notes that at most 2-3 percent of all commercial arbitration agreements include *ex aequo et bono* provisions [2969]. According to Nobumichi Teramura, "despite its many distinguished proponents over time, *ex aequo et bono* – the idea of deciding disputes on the basis of what an adjudicator regards as fair and equitable – has failed to take hold in international commercial arbitration" [2970]. The unpopularity of *ex aequo et bono* arbitration is due to its perceived unpredictability [2971], which has caused the arbitration community to

---

2966. Article 9; the convention recognizes the influence of the UNCITRAL Model Law both in its *considerando* and when remitting to its solutions in Article 25. See MERCOSUR/CMC/DEC. No. 3/98, https://www.mercosur.int/documentos-y-normativa/normativa/, accessed 9 June 2022.

2967. Other arbitral rules also include similar provisions. For instance, Art. 35.2 of the PCA Arbitration Rules states: "The arbitral tribunal shall decide as *amiable compositeur* or *ex aequo et bono* only if the parties have expressly authorized the arbitral tribunal to do so."

2968. For instance, Article 21.3 of the International Chamber of Commerce Arbitration Rules, Article 22.4 of the London Court of International Arbitration Rules and Article 34.3 of the American Arbitration Association – International Centre for Dispute Resolution (ICDR) Rules require authorization from the parties to allow the arbitral tribunal to act as *amiable compositeur* or *ex aequo et bono*. *Ex aequo et bono* arbitrations are also allowed in other rules, such as Article 35 (2) of the PCA Arbitration Rules, Article 27 (3) of the SCC Rules and Article 35 (2) of the Swiss Rules of International Arbitration, among others.

2969. Born, *supra* note 2273, pp. 2987-2988. Drahozal studied 500 arbitration agreements between 1987 and 1989, of which only 3 percent contained such provisions. See C. R. Drahozal, "Commercial Norms, Commercial Codes, and International Commercial Arbitration", *Vanderbilt Journal of Transnational Law*, Vol. 33 (2000), p. 129. More recently, in 2018, the ICC reported only one arbitration involving a contract authorizing arbitrators to decide *ex aequo et bono*, out of more than 800 ICC arbitrations filed in 2018. In 2016 and 2017, of the nearly 1,000 arbitrations filed in each year, there were no reported ICC case on the matter. See ICC, 2018 ICC Dispute Resolution Statistics, 2019:2 *ICC Dispute Resolution Bulletin* (hereafter *ICC Disp. Resol. Bull.*), p. 13, 22 (2019); ICC, 2017 Dispute Resolution Statistics, 2018:2 *ICC Disp. Resol. Bull.*, p. 51, 61; ICC, 2016 ICC Dispute Resolution Statistics, 2017:2 *ICC Disp. Resol. Bull.*, p. 106, 113.

2970. N. Teramura, *Ex Aequo et Bono as a Response to the 'Over-Judicialisation' of International Commercial Arbitration*, The Hague, Kluwer Law International, 2020.

2971. "States' unwillingness to authorise courts and tribunals to decide *ex aequo et bono* is easy to comprehend. To grant an *ex aequo et bono* mandate for unspecified future disputes, states need to come to terms with the greater uncertainty that inheres in this type of adjudication. After all, states may be 'more comfortable with the law as it is than as it should be'. This is rather to be expected, even if it is not 'a great aspiration to justice'" (C. Titi, *The Function of Equity in International Law*, Oxford University Press, 2021, p. 154).

overlook its potential usefulness in redressing the "overjudicialization" of the proceedings in a balanced manner. The overjudicialization of arbitration usually brings about the overregulation of the proceedings and the adoption of litigation techniques that reduce flexibility and lead to an escalation of costs for both parties [2972]; *ex aequo et bono* arbitration could provide a remedy for these problems.

C. *Express agreement for* ex aequo et bono *arbitration*

Article 28 (3) of the Model Law requires that *ex aequo et bono* arbitration be expressly agreed upon [2973], either at the beginning or in the course of the proceedings [2974]. Tacit agreement is not valid [2975]. For this reason, an Egyptian court annulled an award decided *ex aequo et bono* when the arbitrator was not properly authorized [2976], and the same has occurred in other jurisdictions [2977].

Something similar occurred in the ICSID *Klöckner* v. *Cameroon* case, where there was also no agreement to decide the case *ex aequo et bono*. The *ad hoc* Committee held that "an excess of powers might consist not only in failure to apply the governing law but also in a solution in equity where there was a requirement to decide in law" [2978]. Similarly, in the ICSID *MINE* v. *Guinea* case, the *ad hoc* Committee confirmed

2972. Teramura, *supra* note 2970, p. 9.

2973. In similar lines: French Code of Civil Procedure, Art. 1512; Swiss Law on Private International Law, Art. 187 (2); Belgian Judicial Code, Art. 1710 (3); Netherlands Code of Civil Procedure, Art. 1054 (3). Similar provision flows from arbitration rules (2013 UNCITRAL Rules, Art. 35 (2); 2017 ICC Rules, Art. 21 (3); 2016 SIAC Rules, Art. 31 (2); 2014 ICDR Rules, Art. 31 (3); 2020 LCIA Rules, Art. 22 (4); 2018 HKIAC Rules, Art. 36 (2); 2017 SCC Rules, Art. 27 (3).

2974. Schreuer *et al.*, *supra* note 102, p. 633.

2975. A Canadian court ruled that the contract included an express agreement to allow for *ex aequo et bono* arbitration when the parties agreed that the contract may be interpreted as an "honorable agreement". The Court also stated that the Tribunal was exempted of all formalities to reach a decision. *Liberty Reinsurance Canada* v. *QBE Insurance and Reinsurance (Europe) Ltd.*, Ontario Superior Court of Justice, Canada (20 September 2002).

2976. Case No. 72/117, Court of Appeals of Cairo, Egypt, Ruling (8 January 2002), UNCITRAL Digest of Case Law on the Model Law, pp. 153, 88, https://uncitral.un.org/sites/uncitral.un.org/files/media-documents/uncitral/en/mal-digest-2012-e.pdf, accessed 13 May 2022.

2977. See also *Gold Reserve* v. *Venezuela*, *supra* note 950, 146 F.Supp.3d 112, 134 (DDC 2015); Case No. 10-14.687 (French Cour de cassation Cív. 1), Judgment (12 October 2011); Judgment (22 June 2005), 34 Sch 10/05 (Oberlandesgericht München); Judgment (13 May 2009), Case No. 34525 (Colombia Consejo de Estado), in Born, *supra* note 2273, p. 3592.

2978. *Klöckner* v. *Cameroon*, *supra* note 748, Decision on Annulment (1985), para. 59.

the principle that a decision based on equity without authorization may constitute "an excess of powers", considering that "unless the parties had agreed on a decision *ex aequo et bono*, a decision not based on any law would constitute a derogation from the Tribunal's terms of reference" [2979].

D. Conflict of laws in ex aequo et bono *arbitrations*

Even within *ex aequo et bono* arbitrations, recourse to conflicts methodologies may still be necessary [2980]. Arbitrators are free to use national law as a point of departure and subsequently exclude its effects if necessary, or they may directly apply the solution they consider equitable in the circumstances [2981]. Also, if authorized to decide *ex aequo et bono*, arbitrators may apply non-State law to support their reasoning [2982], and may refer, for instance, to the UNIDROIT Principles [2983].

Furthermore, if the parties include a clause in their contract selecting a law with arbitration of equity, arbitrators should first determine the governing law and then evaluate whether or not its application is appropriate in the circumstances [2984]. Interestingly, in the *Atlantic Triton* v. *Guinea* case, the parties included a choice of law provision (referring to the law of the host State) as well as a clause authorizing the Tribunal to decide the arbitration *ex aequo et bono*. The Tribunal decided to apply the law of Guinea to certain aspects of the decision, and equitable principles to others [2985].

2979. *MINE* v. *Guinea*, *supra* note 2190, Decision on Annulment (22 December 1989), para. 5.03.

2980. Hayward, *supra* note 2323, p. 27.

2981. "Applicable Law Chosen by The Parties", in Gaillard and Savage, *supra* note 836, pp. 836-837. According to Born, where parties combine a choice of law clause with an amiable composition or *ex aequo et bono* provision, arbitrators will typically take the latter approach. Born, *supra* note 2273, p. 2991. See, for example, ICC Case No. 2216, Award (1975), 102 JDI (Clunet), p. 917; ICC Case No. 2139, Award (1975), 102 JDI (Clunet), p. 929; *Ad hoc* case in Paris, Award (21 April 1997), UNILEX (UNIDROIT Principles) (choice of Russian law supplemented by UNIDROIT Principles).

2982. Bermann, *supra* note 11, pp. 285-286.

2983. Case No. 1795, Final Award in Chamber of National and International Arbitration of Milan (1 December 1996), 24 YB Comm. Arb. (1999), p. 196. In the ICSID *Benvenuti* v. *Congo* case, the parties authorized the Tribunal to decide *ex aequo et bono*. For its decision, the Tribunal took into account rules of law. *Benvenuti* v. *Congo*, *supra* note 455, Award (15 August 1980), in Schreuer *et al.*, *supra* note 102, p. 636.

2984. Born, *supra* note 2273, pp. 2240-2241.

2985. *Atlantic Triton*, *supra* note 2557, p. 19, 23, in Schreuer *et al.*, *supra* note 102, p. 636.

Some domestic courts have interpreted the inclusion of a choice of law clause as inconsistent with granting the tribunal the power to decide *ex aequo et bono* [2986]. However, a preferable interpretation is that such an inclusion should cause arbitrators to *(i)* recur to the conflict of laws mechanism and *(ii)* mitigate any harsh or unfair results through the application of equitable principles [2987].

E. Mandatory rules and ex aequo et bono *arbitration*

The situation is different with mandatory rules since arbitrators exercising *ex aequo et bono* powers "are bound by mandatory rules of law" [2988].

Consequently, the parties cannot evade the application of mandatory rules of law by agreeing to arbitration *ex aequo et bono* [2989], as was held in ICC Case No. 2216. In the same vein, the Tribunal in ICC Case No. 1677 decided that it did not have the power to render a decision that would run contrary to morality and public policy [2990].

Therefore, when mandatory rules might be in play, arbitrators can feel the need to make clear in their decision that no such rules have been violated. Failure to do so may subject the award to annulment or may prevent its enforcement [2991].

2986. *Wilko* v. *Swan*, 201 F.2d 439, 444 (2d Cir. 1953); *Fudickar* v. *Guardian Mut. Life Ins. Co.*, 62 NY 392, 401 (NY 1875); ICC Award 4237/1985, *supra* note 2826. See Born, *supra* note 2273, p. 2990.

2987. In this regard, in ICC Case No. 3755 the Tribunal stated: "According to a more liberal interpretation which is more widely used in arbitration, the arbitrators invested with the authority of *amiable compositeurs* have the right to deviate from the applicable positive law according to the rules of international private law, given that they consider it is necessary and just, in conformity with the general objective of the contract, and more generally, when it is in view of a solution to this dispute. In this case, the arbitrators do not have to justify their divergence from the law which is normally applicable to the case" (Final Award, *ICC Ct. Bull.*, Vol. 1, No. 2 (1990), p. 25. See also ICC Award 3327/1982, *supra* note 1974, JDI, p. 975; ICC Case No. 13509, Award; ICC Award 5118, *supra* note 2838.

2988. Teramura, *supra* note 2970, p. 149. See also Born, *supra* note 2273, p. 2993. In the ICC Case No. 1677, the Tribunal decided that an arbitrator sitting as amiable compositeur is not "according to general principles . . . authorized to take a decision contrary to an absolutely constraining law, particularly the rule concerning public order or morals" (Award, in *Collection of ICC Arbitral Awards 1974-1985* (1990)).

2989. This contradicts the conventional concept of mandatory rules of law, Teramura, *supra* note 2970, p. 149.

2990. Patilla Robertson and Castro Hurtado, *supra* note 2960, pp. 4-5.

2991. Gaillard and Savage, *supra* note 836, pp. 840, 1508. 61. David, *supra* note 1451, pp. 411-412.

F. Observance of the terms of the contract in ex aequo et bono *arbitration?*

Can arbitrators disregard terms of the parties' contract? In the 1982 ICC Case No. 3938, the sole arbitrator acting as *amiable compositeur* determined that the principles that an arbitrator can apply to correct an overly strict application of legal rules are not valid with regard to the contract. This is because the contract must be understood as a particular body of rules that emerges from the parties' negotiation [2992].

Other scholarly writings have also reached a similar conclusion, arguing that when deciding *ex aequo et bono*, arbitrators may depart from the terms of the parties' contract by fashioning a fair and equitable result, provided that they do not rewrite the structure or material terms of the agreement [2993].

Articles 28 (4) of the UNCITRAL Model Law and 35 (3) of the UNCITRAL Arbitration Rules expressly state that in all cases, arbitrators must take into account the terms of the contract and contract usages when interpreting a particular contract [2994].

A majority of scholarly writings accept that without modifying the contract as a whole, the arbitrators acting as *amiables compositeurs* may still refuse to apply certain rights created by the contract, or at the very least reduce or extend their effects [2995]. Arbitrators could, for instance, recur to hardship rules [2996] or reduce the effects of contractual terms, as was decided by the Court of Appeals of Paris in 1988 in the *Société Unijet* case [2997]. However, arbitrators may not alter the structure of the agreement and may not substitute the contractual obligations for new terms that the parties have not agreed on [2998]. In short, arbitrators cannot create new rights or obligations, nor can they eliminate the obligations from the agreement altogether [2999], as this would disrupt the

2992. *Ibid.*, p. 838.

2993. See, for instance, Born, *supra* note 2273, p. 2988, citing the following authorities: *Parfums Stem France* v. *CFFD* (Paris Cour d'Appel), 1991 Rev. Arb., p. 669, Judgment (19 April 1991), 673; *Unijet SA* v. *Sarl Int'l Bus. Relations Ltd.*, Judgment (6 May 1988), 1989 Rev. Arb., p. 83, 86 (Paris Cour d'Appel); ICC Case No. 3344, Award, 109 JDI (Clunet), p. 978 (1982); ICC Award 3327/1982, *supra* note 1974; *Ad hoc* case, Final Award (10 December 1997), 3 Unif. L. Rev., p. 178 (1998).

2994. Webster, *supra* note 2619, p. 529.

2995. Gaillard and Savage, *supra* note 836, p. 839.

2996. *Ibid.*, p. 839.

2997. *Société Unijet SA* v. *SARL International Business Relations Ltd. (IBR)*, Paris Court of Appeals, Ruling (6 May 1988).

2998. Gaillard and Savage, *supra* note 836, pp. 839.

2999. *As decided in Coderre* v. *Coderre*, [2008] QCCA 888 (Québec Ct. App.); *Louis Dreyfus SAS* v. *Holding Tusculum BV*, [2008] QCCS 5903 (Québec Super. Ct.). See Born, *supra* note 2273, p. 2988.

bargain struck in the contract or would risk running beyond the parties' intentions [3000].

An issue arises when tribunals authorized to decide *ex aequo et bono* do so by strictly applying the relevant law. In this sense, it has been determined that applying the relevant law does not imply that the result is not "equitable" [3001]. Similarly, it has been decided that a tribunal that merely applies the law without taking equitable considerations into account violates its mandate [3002].

If an arbitral tribunal decides *ex aequo et bono* without the parties' authorization to do so, the award may risk annulment and non-recognition on the grounds that it exceeded its authority [3003]. However, Born notes that national courts are generally reluctant to rule that arbitrators have exceeded their authority by acting *ex aequo et bono* [3004].

G. Is there a duty to motivate or decide equitably in ex aequo et bono *arbitration?*

In *ex aequo et bono* arbitrations, the parties can free the arbitrators of their duty to provide reasons [3005]. If the parties do not exempt the arbitrators of this duty, they must give reasons.

3000. *Sté Parfums Stem France* v. *CFFD*, Judgment (19 April 1991), 1991 Rev. Arb., p. 669, 673 (Paris Cour d'Appel).

3001. *Unijet SA* v. *Sarl Int'l Bus. Relations Ltd.*, Judgment, Paris Cour d'Appel (6 May 1988), 1989 Rev. Arb., p. 83; *Soubaigne* v. *Limmereds Skogar*, Paris Cour d'Appel, Judgment (15 March 1985), 1985 Rev. Arb., p. 285, 287. See Born, *supra* note 2273, p. 2992.

3002. *Halbout* v. *Epoux Hanin*, French Cour de cassation Cív. 2 (15 February 2001), 2001 Rev. Arb., p. 135; *Centrale Fotovista* v. *Vanoverbeke* (15 January 2004), 2004 Rev. Arb., p. 908, 912. See Born, *supra* note 2273, p. 2992.

3003. *DBM Blending BV* v. *WRT Beheers BV (Amsterdam Rechtbank)*, Judgment (18 April 2007); *SA SDMS Int'l* v. *Cameroon Telecommunications – Camtel*, Judgment (17 January 2008), 33 YB Comm. Arb. (2008), p. 484, 486 (Paris Cour d'Appel); French Cour de cassation Cív. 1, Judgment (12 October 2011), 2012 Rev. Arb., p. 93.

3004. Born, *supra* note 2273, p. 2990. In this regard, he cites *Certain Underwriters at Lloyd's* v. *BCS Ins. Co.*, 239 F.Supp.2d 812 (N.D. Ill. 2003); Case No. 80-13.177, French Cour de cassation Cív. 2, Judgment (30 September 1981); Swiss Fed. Trib., Judgment (14 November 1990), DFT 116 II 634; Judgment (14 March 2011), 34 Sch 08/10 (Oberlandesgericht München); *Food Servs. of Am. Inc.* v. *Pan Pac. Specialties Ltd.*, [1997] CanLII 3604 (BC Sup. Ct.). In *SA Fleury Michon* v. *Pac. Dunlop Ltd.*, 2001 Rev. Arb., p. 731, Paris Cour d'Appel, Judgment (November 16, 2000), the Court refused to consider whether arbitrators vested with powers of *amiable composition* had exceeded their authority where they had "not shown any deliberate intention either to base their decision on other grounds than those provided under the law, or to modify or moderate the consequences of contractual provisions based on equity considerations", as doing so would constitute impermissible review on merits.

3005. Article 31 (2) of the ICC Rules of Arbitration and Alternative Dispute Resolution (2012 version). See also G. Blanke, "Antitrust Arbitration under the

In the *Fotovista* case, the Paris Court of Appeal annulled an award made in amiable composition because the arbitrator did not provide reasons for applying French law in his award [3006].

In reference to ICSID arbitration, Christoph Schreuer notes that the arbitrators must provide reasons in *ex aequo et bono* arbitrations as well, "although the burden of reasoning may be somewhat lighter than in the case of decisions based on law" [3007].

In short, arbitral tribunals have the power, but not the duty, to decide in accordance with equitable principles. For instance, in the *Brig Macedonian* case, "the arbitrator did not appear to expressly rely on equity, despite his *ex aequo et bono* mandate" [3008]. Something similar happened in the *James Pugh* case [3009]. Arbitrators may decide not to apply such principles, for instance if the award will be enforced in jurisdictions where arbitration in equity is not provided for by law [3010].

H. Equity in international law

Both the ICJ and the PCIJ have been granted by their statutes the power to decide *ex aequo et bono*, provided that the parties agree. However, even though *ex aequo et bono* clauses have been contemplated in a considerable number of treaties, no litigation before the PCIJ and ICJ emerged following these provisions.

In the *Cayuga Indians* case [3011] the tribunal distinguished *ex aequo et bono* jurisdiction from its possibility to apply equity as a general principle [3012]. In the *Diversion of Waters from the River Meuse* decision,

---

ICC Rules", in G. Blanke and P. Landolt (eds.), *EU and US Antitrust Arbitration: A Handbook for Practitioners*, The Hague, Kluwer Law International, 2011, p. 1849.

3006. *Société Centrale Fotovista* v. *Vanoverbeke* et al. (2004), CA Paris (15 January 2004), in Webster, *supra* note 2619, p. 528.

3007. Schreuer *et al.*, *supra* note 102, p. 637.

3008. *Case of the Brig Macedonian (United States* v. *Chile)*, Decision of the King of Belgium (15 May 1863), in C. Titi, *The Function of Equity in International Law*, Oxford, Oxford University Press, 2021, p. 146.

3009. In the matter of the death of James Pugh (Great Britain, Panama), (1944) 3 RIAA, p. 1439, in Titi, *ibid.*, p. 146.

3010. Caron, Caplan and Pellonpää, *supra* note 2618, p. 136.

3011. After the division of the Cayuga Nation between Great Britain and the United States as a consequence of the War of 1812, the Cayuga Indians remained on the Canadian side of the US-Canada border. As a matter of "international law and of equity", the Cayuga Indians were considered entitled to an appropriate share of the annuity payable by the United States under a treaty with Great Britain. Cayuga Indians; *Great Britain* v. *US*, *Nielsen's Reports*, p. 203 (1926), 307; 29 PCIJ, Ser. A/B, No. 70 (1937).

3012. It reasoned that, contrary to *ex aequo et bono* decision-making, in its case it was a matter of invoking general and universally admitted principles of justice and right dealing, as against the harsh operation of strict doctrines of legal personality in

the PCIJ emphasized its importance [3013], and applied an equitable principle originating in one of the early maxims of English equity, that "he who seeks equity must do equity" – analogue to the *venire contra factum proprium* principle derived from the Roman law and familiar to modern continental systems [3014].

Thus, also in public international law, the use of expressions such as "rules of justice", "equity" and "general principles of law" do not mean that a settlement outside the law – or *ex aequo et bono* – can be reached [3015] without express authorization [3016].

States only exceptionally confer *ex aequo et bono* powers upon international courts and tribunals. On the rare occasions when tribunals are instructed to act *ex aequo et bono*, they discharge their powers conservatively. For instance, in *Free Zones*, a "sharply divided" PCIJ refused to decide *ex aequo et bono* [3017]. It held that such powers are of "an absolutely exceptional character" and could only derive from "a clear and explicit provision to that effect" [3018].

---

an anomalous situation for which such doctrines were not devised. See Titi, *supra* note 3008, p. 36.

3013. *Diversion of Water from Meuse (Netherlands* v. *Belgium)*, 1937 PCIJ, Ser. A/B, No. 70, Judicial Year 1937 (28 June). In that case, a claim by the Netherlands against Belgium arising out of a Belgian diversion of the river waters for canal purposes, was rejected on the grounds that the Netherlands itself had previously done exactly the same.

3014. "The *venire contra factum proprium* principle holds that one who, by word or conduct, willfully causes another to believe in the existence of a certain state of things and induces him to act on the strength of that belief, is precluded from averring against that party a different state of things as existing at the same time", Friedmann, *supra* note 955, pp. 287-288.

3015. "Article 38 of the PCIJ makes this principle clear. After having adopted 'the general principles of law as recognised by civilized nations' as an acceptable source of decision-making, the PCIJ concluded: 'This provision shall not prejudice the power of the Court to decide a case *ex aequo et bono*, if the parties agree thereto'. Other arbitration conventions contain similar provisions. However, unless the arbitrator is expressly instructed to settle the dispute *ex aequo et bono*, he is under the obligation to decide the case based upon principles of legal justice", Lauterpacht, *supra* note 3, pp. 63-64.

3016. *Free Zones of Upper Savoy and the District of Gex (France* v. *Switzerland)*, PCIJ Ser. A, No. 24, 6 December 1930, Order 1930, n. 35 [3], in Titi, *supra* note 3008, p. 143.

3017. *Free Zones of Upper Savoy and the District of Gex (France* v. *Switzerland)*, Order (6 December 1930), PCIJ Ser. A, No. 24.

3018. See in Titi, *supra* note 3008, pp. 142-143. "In Haya de la Torre, the ICJ held that a choice among the various courses of action propounded by the parties could not be based on 'legal considerations, but only on considerations of practicability or of political expediency'. The ICJ remarked that the parties themselves were better placed to make the choice and directed them to settle their dispute with regard to 'considerations of courtesy and good neighbourliness'. According to Gerald Fitzmaurice, this amounted to a recommendation that the parties should turn to negotiations 'in a spirit of good faith and good will'" (*ibid.*, pp. 144-145).

Wolfgang Friedmann notes that there has been considerable discussion on the question of whether equity is part of the law to be applied, or whether it is an antithesis to law. This latter conception of equity can be understood in the sense in which the term *ex aequo et bono* is used in Article 38, paragraph 2, of the ICJ Statute [3019]. According to Aron Broches, in these cases, the tribunal "may not only take into account equitable considerations *infra legem*, that is in interpreting the law, or *praeter legem*, that is in supplementing the law, but may decide *contra legem*, in disregard of the law, when considerations of equity and justice so require" [3020]. This does not mean that the tribunal can act capriciously or arbitrarily. The tribunal must proceed in accordance with objective considerations of what is fair and just and must not reach a result that could not be explained on rational grounds [3021].

As seen, the "*ex aequo* proceedings" are one thing, but the "principle of equity" is quite another. In non *ex aequo* proceedings, equity may be applied not *contra legem* (Art. 38 (2), of the ICJ Statute), but as a general principle of law in accordance with Article 38 (1) *(c)* of the ICJ Statute.

In the *Barcelona Traction* case, the ICJ did not consider that the Belgium Government could intervene in the proceedings "by considerations of equity" [3022]. *A contrario*, these considerations could have had this result. The *Barcelona Traction* example is a confirmation of the large measure of appreciation that the Court must apply to the sources of law in each case. Article 38 of the ICJ Statute is, in this way, a toolbox from which to select the appropriate rules to be applied: treaties, customary law or general principles. But this is not altogether a disadvantage – it allows the Court to adapt its decisions to the particular circumstances of the case and, as has been aptly noted, "the absence of priorities among the sources of law in Article 38 (1) *(a)* *(b)*, and

3019. Friedmann, *supra* note 955, p. 287.
3020. Broches, *supra* note 2161, p. 395.
3021. *Ibid.*, p. 395. For instance, in the Chaco case between Bolivia and Paraguay, both disputing States decided that their boundary would be determined by the Presidents of United States, Uruguay, Peru, Chile, Brazil and Argentina in their capacity as "arbitrators in equity . . . acting *ex aequo et bono*". The arbitrators took into account several factors as geographic and economic needs, the parties' demands as to their mutual security, the opinions of the military assessors, among others, which convinced the arbitrators "of the equitableness of the fronter line that they suggested", *Chaco (Bolivia, Paraguay)*, 3 RIAA, p. 1817, 1938 in Titi, *supra* note 3008, p. 146.
3022. The Court literally stated that it was "not of the opinion that, in the particular circumstances of the present case, jus standi [was] conferred on the Belgian Government by considerations of equity". *Barcelona Traction, supra* note 24, p. 48, para. 101.

(c) has afforded a valuable degree of flexibility in the preparation of judgments" [3023].

I. Equity in investment arbitration

Some decades ago, Aron Broches noted that equity in arbitration can be important in major investments that typically unfold over long periods of time. Since it is difficult to predict future developments, it is often problematic to agree on fair or suitable terms to govern the entire course of an agreement. When new developments raise contentious issues, *ex aequo et bono* decisions can not only settle controversies but also encourage cooperation between investors and host States [3024]. If renegotiating the contractual terms turns out to be impossible, Schreuer argues that "*ex aequo et bono* decisions may be a second-best method to achieve a result which is fair and suitable to changed circumstances" [3025].

Contrary to generally accepted criteria, in the UNCITRAL investment case *Parienti* v. *Panama*, the Tribunal decided that in the absence of an express provision, it would conduct an arbitration in equity [3026]. Later, however, this award was set aside by the Supreme Court of Panama because the Tribunal acted *ex aequo et bono* without the express agreement of the parties [3027].

In ICSID arbitrations, the choice of law may extend beyond legal rules *stricto sensu* to principles of equitable justice (Art. 42 (3), ICSID Convention). Authorization must also be express in this investment claims context. As was noted in the *CME* v. *Czech Republic* case, a tribunal is not allowed to decide *ex aequo et bono* without the parties' authorization [3028]. Following the same logic, the Tribunal in the *Zhinvali* v. *Georgia* case held that "Article 42 (3) of the ICSID Convention provides that an ICSID tribunal only has the power to decide a dispute *ex aequo et bono* if the parties so agree" [3029].

3023. Pellet and Müller, *supra* note 239, pp. 935-936.

3024. Broches, *supra* note 2161, pp. 395-396.

3025. Schreuer *et al.*, *supra* note 102, p. 632.

3026. *Laurent Jean-Marc Parienti* v. *Autoridad de Transito y Transporte Terreste and Panama*, UNCITRAL, Award in Equity (27 January 2005), in Titi, *supra* note 3008, pp. 149-150.

3027. Supreme Court of Justice (Panama), Judgment (20 September 2006). Later, the arbitral award received exequatur in France. See Titi, *supra* note 3008, p. 150.

3028. Spiermann, *supra* note 979, p. 92.

3029. *Zhinvali* v. *Georgia*, Award (24 January 2003), para. 418 in Schreuer *et al.*, *supra* note 102, p. 635.

In the *Amco* v. *Indonesia* case, the Annulment Committee stated:

> "Neither does the ad hoc Committee consider that any mention of 'equitable consideration' in the Award necessarily amounts to a decision *ex aequo et bono* and a manifest excess of power on the part of the Tribunal. Equitable considerations may indeed form part of the law to be applied by the Tribunal, whether that be the law of Indonesia or international law. . . . The ad hoc Committee thus believes that invocation of equitable considerations is not properly regarded as automatically equivalent to a decision *ex aequo et bono*." [3030]

The Tribunal in *Tecmed* v. *Mexico* case [3031] and the Annulment Committee in *MTD* v. *Chile* reasoned in similar terms [3032, 3033].

Acting *ex aequo et bono* without authorization can be considered an annullable error for manifest excess of powers [3034]. This is so considering that:

3030. *Amco* v. *Indonesia*, Decision on Annulment (16 May 1986), paras. 26, 28. *Ibid.*, p. 637.

3031. The Tribunal in the *Tecmed* v. *Mexico* case, *supra* note 537, stated the following: "[T]he fact that a tribunal may take equitable considerations into account without deciding *ex aequo et bono* was also recognized in the ICSID Additional Facility case of *Tecmed* v. *Mexico*. The Tribunal found that an Arbitral Tribunal may consider general equitable principles when setting the compensation owed to the Claimant, without thereby assuming the role of an arbitrator *ex aequo et bono*", Award (29 May 2003), para. 190.

3032. The *ad hoc* Committee in the *MTD* v. *Chile* case explained that considerations of fairness and the balancing of interests do not necessarily make a decision *ex aequo et bono* (Decision on Annulment, 21 March 2007, para. 48).

3033. ICSID committees' analysis of the outer contours of the *ex aequo et bono* mandate tends to confirm the view that *ex aequo et bono* adjudication is something quite distinct from the discretion that tribunals have anyway. See Titi, *supra* note 3008, p. 154.

3034. *Amco Asia* v. *Indonesia*, *supra* note 408, Decision on Annulment (16 May 1986), para. 28 and Decision on the Applications for Annulment of the 1990 Award and the 1990 Supplemental Award (3 December 1992), para. 7.28; *MINE* v. *Guinea*, *supra* note 2190, Decision on Annulment (14 December 1989), para. 5.03; *MTD* v. *Chile*, *supra* note 327, Decision on Annulment (21 March 2007), para. 45 (citing *MINE* v. *Guinea*); *CMS* v. *Argentina*, *supra* note 84, Decision on Annulment (25 September 2007), para. 50 (citing *MINE* v. *Guinea*); *Azurix* v. *Argentina*, *supra* note 327, Decision on Annulment (1 September 2009), para. 136; *Enron* v. *Argentina*, *supra* note 451, Decision on Annulment (30 July 2010), para. 218 (citing *Azurix* v. *Argentina*); *Lemire* v. *Ukraine*, *supra* note 547, Decision on Annulment (8 July 2013), para. 237; *Adem Dogan* v. *Turkmenistan*, para. 98, n. 15; *Total SA* v. *Argentina*, *supra* note 16, Decision on Annulment (1 February 2016), para. 198; *Antoine Abou Lahoud and Leila Bounafeh-Abou Lahoud* v. *Democratic Republic of the Congo (DRC)*, ICSID Case No. ARB/10/4. See Titi, *supra* note 3008, p. 151. Decision on Annulment, 29 March 2016 [118]; *Mobil Exploration and Development Argentina and Mobil Argentina* v. *Argentina*, ICSID Case No. ARB/04/16, Decision on Annulment (8 May 2019), para. 67.

"Annulment may be granted on a number of limited grounds, including manifest excess of powers. According to the case law, a tribunal's failure to apply the applicable law may give rise to manifest excess of powers. Since under the ICSID Convention the possibility of jurisdiction *ex aequo et bono* is part of the provision on applicable law, then logically resort to *ex aequo et bono* powers where none have been given may constitute an annullable error for manifest excess of powers." [3035]

Still, authorization for deciding *ex aequo et bono* can be given after the dispute has arisen [3036].

According to Schreuer, the flexibility granted by Article 42 (3) to decide a case according to equitable principles comes at considerable cost to predictability [3037]. Perhaps this explains why the *Benvenuti* v. *Costa Rica* and *Atlantic Triton* cases are the only reported ICSID cases where an *ex aequo et bono* resolution was handed down [3038].

With respect to "territorialized arbitrations", some jurisdictions do not accept equitable principles. When seated in these countries, tribunals are not permitted to decide *ex aequo et bono*. This does not occur in ICSID arbitrations, as they are free from the interference of domestic rules. Choosing the place of an ICSID arbitration is thus purely a matter of convenience and will have no impact on matters such as the selection of *ex aequo et bono* arbitration [3039].

In relation to Iran-United States claims, the wording of Article V of the 1981 Claims Settlement Declaration for the Iran-United States Tribunal was subsequently incorporated into the first paragraph of Article 33 of the Tribunal Rules of Procedure, which adds the following second paragraph: "(2) The arbitral tribunal shall decide *ex aequo et bono* only if the arbitrating parties have expressly and in writing authorized it to do so". This is a modified version of Article 33 and is included in the current Article 35 of the UNCITRAL Rules. No case has yet been decided by the Tribunal on such a basis [3040].

3035. Titi, *supra* note 3008, p. 151.
3036. Broches, *supra* note 2161, p. 396.
3037. Schreuer *et al.*, *supra* note 102, p. 631
3038. Bjorklund and Vanhonnaeker, *supra* note 13, p. 359.
3039. Schreuer *et al.*, *supra* note 102, p. 638.
3040. C. N. Brower and J. D. Brueschke, *The Iran–United States Claims Tribunal*, The Hague, Martinus Nijhoff, 1998, p. 632.

CHAPTER XX

THE CORRECTIVE AND SUPPLEMENTAL ROLE OF INTERNATIONAL LAW

A. A "broader brush" in international transactions

Roy Goode coined the expression "broader brush" in reference to the interpretation of national laws in a transnational setting with "an eye on international usage" [3041]. Domestic legal systems have open formulas that grant broad powers to adjudicators, including the authority to interpret general principles such as good faith, *force majeure* and hardship. Here, taking a cosmopolitan perspective that also incorporates aspects of comparative law has proven to be a very effective interpretive tool [3042]. The impact of comparative law in domestic systems is undeniable [3043], which has led James Gordley, for instance, to persuasively argue for a switch from a positivistic and nationalist approach to a transnational and functional approach to contract interpretation [3044]. By the same token, Klaus Berger has referred to an "internationally useful construction of domestic laws" [3045].

This comparative construction within domestic law has even firmer roots when applied to international relationships. As stated by Yves Derains, it is impossible to separate the law from the language of its

---

3041. R. Goode, "The Adaptation of English Law to International Commercial Arbitration", *Arbitration International*, Vol. 8 (1992), p. 1. In the arbitration context, Bruno Oppetit uses the expression "legal acculturation", Oppetit, *supra* note 796, pp. 278-279.

3042. Brunner, *supra* note 836, pp. 30-32.

3043. The influence of comparative law in the interpretation of domestic laws is emphasized in Zweigert and Kötz, *supra* note 901, p. 19. As stated by Zimmermann, we are living in an age of post-positivism, "Roman Law and the Privatization of Private Law in Europe", in A. Hartkamp *et al.* (eds.), *Towards a European Civil Code*, 4th ed., The Hague, Kluwer Law International, 2011, p. 51; in regard to German law, see R. Zimmermann, "The German Civil Code and the Development of Private Law in Germany", *Oxford University Comparative Law Forum* (2006), https://ouclf.law.ox.ac.uk/the-german-civil-code-and-the-development-of-private-law-in-germany/, , accessed 16 May 2022, after note 144. In France, even the "internists", albeit refusing to be labeled as comparatists, resort to comparison, whether consciously or not. See Fauvarque-Cosson, *supra* note 905, p. 59. For developments in England, see Vogenauer, *supra* note 860, p. 876. In the United States, see Clark, *supra* note 1244, p. 179.

3044. Gordley, *supra* note 892, p. 607.

3045. See the full citation in the very interesting article by Ruíz Abou-Nigm, *supra* note 1433, p. 111.

expression. For instance, regarding the terms "consideration", "implied terms", "misrepresentation" and "frustration"[3046], it is necessary for adjudicators to embark upon an ample (or broad-brush) interpretation of the applicable law when one of the parties does not hail from a common law tradition[3047].

Moreover, as stated by Jan Paulsson, national laws themselves contain robust corrective norms. These norms can be derived from principles contained, for instance, in national constitutions, or in ratified treaties – regarding human rights, for instance – and national courts have both the duty and the authority to apply them[3048]. Further, whether or not the parties have referred to international principles, these concepts can act as important tools with which the application of national laws can be corrected. This is particularly relevant when domestic legislation departs from the international status quo[3049].

In addition, the laws governing contractual relationships are almost entirely dispositive. Many aspects of the applicable law can be excluded through an agreement of the parties or by the adjudicators in the course of exercising their corrective interpretation[3050].

The express or implicit selection of a governing law does not exclude the possibility that, in certain cases, adjudicators can fairly be expected to take into account the operation of a rule that the parties did not include in their contract or, at the very least, that they did not expressly exclude[3051].

3046. Derains, *supra* note 1431, p. 6.

3047. Even in domestic laws, as pointed out by Jürgen Basedow, usages should be considered incorporated, for instance in a contractual relationship, as an implied consent of the parties, when they are widely known in a given sector of economic activity, and in this sense, they should prevail over suppletive provisions of national law. J. Basedow, "El derecho privado estatal y la economía: el derecho comercial como una amalgama de legislación pública y privada", in J. Basedow, D. P. Fernández Arroyo and J. A. Moreno Rodríguez (eds.), *Cómo se Codifica hoy el Derecho Comercial Internacional*, Asunción, CEDEP / La Ley Paraguaya, 2010, pp. 9-10.

3048. Paulsson, *supra* note 1440, p. 232.

3049. Blessing, *supra* note 2321, p. 42.

3050. R. Goode, "Contract and Commercial Law: The Logic and Limits of Harmonisation", *Ius Commune Lecture* (2003), pp. 8-9.

3051. Derains, *supra* note 1431, Bulletin 10. As creatures of the parties' consent, arbitrators must show special fidelity to shared expectations expressed in the contract or treaty: W. W. Park, "Fidelity to Contract Commitments in Commercial Arbitration: Contract Language and Change Circumstances", in UNIDROIT (ed.), *Eppur si muove: The Age of Uniform Law. Essays in honour of Michael Joachim Bonell to celebrate his 70th birthday*, Vol. 1, p. 893. See also D. M. Vicente, "La autonomía privada y sus distintos significados a la luz del derecho comparado", in D. P. Fernández Arroyo and J. A. Moreno Rodríguez (eds.), *Contratos Internacionales*, Washington, DC, ASADIP / OAS, 2016, p. 74.

The following example is illustrative of this point. The Federal Supreme Court of Switzerland dismissed a claim to annul an arbitral award based on the fact that the arbitrator used both the CISG and the UNIDROIT Principles to determine what constituted "material breach" under Swiss law – even though the parties had selected Swiss law as the applicable law. Confirming the arbitral award, the Tribunal explained that the reference to these instruments did not imply the application of international law. On the contrary, reference both to the CISG and the UNIDROIT Principles was considered perfectly legitimate under Swiss law, especially in light of the fact that the parties in an international commercial contract could reasonably have been expected to have accepted international concepts within both instruments [3052].

When the parties choose a third country's law as applicable to the contract, they typically do so with the aim of finding a neutral solution, but rarely have an in-depth knowledge of its content. The subtleties of the third country's legal rules as articulated within its national case law may be surprising to a foreign party [3053]. As an example, Berger argues that when parties choose German law as the neutral third country law without any knowledge of its subtleties, the arbitral tribunal should not apply the awkward long-standing case law in Germany requiring certain standard term clauses to be "bargained for in detail". While this strict formula makes sense in consumer transactions, German law also applies this formula to business transactions, where the presumption of the professional competence of the parties would not require the same degree of legal protection. The matter was addressed in an Interim Award issued in January 2001, rendered by an arbitral tribunal in ICC Case No. 10279. The Tribunal decided not to follow the local interpretation of the issues in the case, as the parties to the dispute were experienced international businesspeople and companies, making any local application "inconsistent with commercial reality" [3054].

According to Berger, in cases involving sophisticated business entities, the law that will be applied will depend largely on the parties' expectations. It is fair to assume that, in choosing to resolve their dispute through arbitration instead of domestic courts, the parties expect the adjudicators "to refrain from a 'mechanical' application of the law". Instead, arbitrators should take into account the economic

3052. Schweizerisches Bundesgericht (Switzerland), No. 4A 240/2009, 16 December 2009, http://www.unilex.info/principles/case/1513, accessed 16 May 2022.
3053. Bortolotti and Mayer, *supra* note 1471, p. 8.
3054. Berger, *supra* note 1124, pp. 80-84.

circumstances of the case and the international context in which the parties operated. Most arbitration laws and rules give the arbitrators the mandate of considering trade usages that "underscores the objective of arbitration to provide resolutions of international disputes in a manner that accord with the commercial expectations of the parties and practices in the trade concerned" [3055].

Of course, this situation will be fundamentally different in situations in which the foreign parties, following the advice of their lawyers, for instance, have selected a law such as the German for the very reason that it provides a strict law on general contract terms [3056].

This whole matter calls for careful scrutiny. Christoph Brunner proposes a case-by-case analysis to consider the legitimate interests of the parties. If a party chooses a national law because it desires a rigid solution for a specific case, it may do so and thus exclude the possibility of considering other laws or transnational law [3057]. If the parties have no such desire, the adjudicator should have the discretion to reach an appropriate solution by taking into consideration the circumstances of the contract and the international environment in which the relationship developed.

The "broader brush" that enables usages, principles and equity to be taken into account by the tribunal coincides with Martin Wolff's visionary perspective, when he declared several decades ago that a private international law system lacking a supranational vision would be contrary to justice [3058].

B. *Corrective formulas in private international law instruments*

The matter of corrective or "flexible" formulas is controversial in comparative law when it comes to their terminology and scope [3059]. In the Americas, a flexible or corrective formula has been accepted for many years through Article 9 of the 1979 OAS Inter-American Convention on General Rules of Private International Law, which has been ratified by several countries in the region [3060]. This Convention

3055. *Ibid.*, pp. 89-90.
3056. *Ibid.*, pp. 80-90.
3057. Brunner, *supra* note 836, pp. 30-32.
3058. Wolff, *supra* note 1213, p. 15.
3059. As stated in the comment to Article 1:105 of the European Principles of Contract Law (PECL). An escape clause is strongly defended for instance by the Swiss Professor Visher, commenting on an escape clause of Article 15 of the Swiss Law of Private International Law. See Visher, *supra* note 1200, p. 106.
3060. Argentina, Brazil, Colombia, Guatemala, Paraguay, Ecuador, Mexico, Peru, Uruguay and Venezuela. See http://www.oas.org/juridico/spanish/firmas/b-45.html, accessed 16 May 2022.

admits equitable solutions to achieve justice in particular cases, notwithstanding the provisions of national laws that are potentially applicable to the transaction [3061].

The spirit of this formula is replicated in Article 10 of the Mexico Convention. The solution has also been received in the private international law rules of Mexico, Venezuela and Paraguay [3062].

C. Broader brush in international arbitration

René David explains that local legislation cannot always achieve the objectives of justice due to the fact that legislators have been conditioned by history and have typically taken other factors into account as well, including the inevitable abstraction and general character of the legal instruments they draft. In short, legislators can only aspire to an approximative form of justice. Therefore, arbitrators should not adhere to a legal rule when the circumstances of the case clearly indicate that it does not adjust to requirements of justice [3063].

In ICC Case No. 2375 of 1975 between a Spanish and a Bahamian company, the Tribunal rejected the application of Spanish law in the interpretation of a series of contracts within the dispute. The Tribunal recognized Spanish law as applicable to the formalities of

---

3061. Article 9 of this Convention states that "the different laws that may be applicable to various aspects of one and the same juridical relationship shall be applied harmoniously in order to attain the purposes pursued by each of such laws. Any difficulties that may be caused by their simultaneous application shall be resolved in the light of the requirements of justice in each specific case". Ronald Herbert and Cecilia Fresnedo de Aguirre have pointed out that said article draws upon American doctrines of Currie (of governmental interests) and Cavers (of equitable solutions), contrary to the abstract and automatic system in place before in Latin America. The adoption of these doctrines has the merit of having left open an ample interpretive field to relax the rigid criteria of the continent up until then. See C. Fresnedo de Aguirre and R. Herbert, "Flexibilización Teleológica del Derecho Internacional Privado Latinoamericano", in J. Kleinheisterkamp and G. A. Lorenzo Idiarte (eds.), *Avances del Derecho Internacional Privado en América Latina, Liber Amicorum Jürgen Samtleben*, Montevideo, Editorial Fundación de Cultura Universitaria, 2002, p. 57. See also Herbert, *supra* note 1317, pp. 89-90.

3062. Under the title "equitable harmonization of interests", Article 12 of the Paraguayan Law copies that provision. Accordingly, it states that: "In addition to the provisions in the foregoing articles, the guidelines, customs, and principles of international commercial law as well as commercial usages and practices generally accepted shall apply in order to discharge the requirements of justice and equity in the particular case." This equitable or corrective formula will, therefore, apply both when the law was chosen and in the absence of choice. See Moreno Rodríguez, *supra* note 1329, pp. 1171-1173.

3063. R. David, C. Jauffret-Spinosi and M. Goré, *Les grands systèmes de droit contemporains*, 12th ed., Paris, Dalloz, 2016, p. 412.

incorporation and the regulation of operations in Spain. However, the Tribunal ultimately considered that the interpretation of the contractual relationship and the prior negotiations between the parties ought to be examined under the lens of general principles and international usages [3064].

The "broader brush" powers are expressly acknowledged in many jurisdictions around the world [3065]. Article 28 (4) of the UNCITRAL Model Law states that in all cases, the terms and conditions of the contract and the commercial usages and practices applicable to the transaction must be taken into account [3066].

This flexible formula, originally included in the European Convention on Arbitration of 1961 (Art. VII), has been qualified by a leading arbitrator as one of the most significant accomplishments of the twentieth century, having contributed to liberating arbitration from the confines of local perceptions [3067].

This formula is also reflected in several arbitration rules, such as in Article 35 (3) of the UNCITRAL Rules, Article 35 (1) *(d)* of the PCA Rules and Article 21 (2) of the ICC Rules [3068].

The Model Law, and most other national arbitration statutes and institutional rules, require that trade usages be considered "in all cases". This expansive language resolves any doubts regarding the appropriateness of using trade usages both in situations when there is a choice of law agreement and when there is not [3069].

Relevant trade usages must be proven in particular cases, unless arbitrators are familiar with them and make this clear to the parties

---

3064. Craig, Park and Paulsson, *supra* note 837, p. 332.

3065. A notable exception is England. The drafters of the Arbitration Act, 1996 declined to provide for arbitrators to take "trade usages" into account, on the grounds that developed legal systems already took such considerations into account in fashioning and applying rules of commercial law. English Arbitration Act, 1996, para. 46; UK Departmental Advisory Committee on Arbitration Law, Report on the Arbitration Bill, 1996, para. 222. See Born, *supra* note 2273, p. 2984.

3066. Similar provisions are included in several arbitration laws, such as the French Code of Civil Procedure, Article 1496 (2); the German ZPO, para. 1051 (4); the Netherlands Code of Civil Procedure, Article 1054 (4); the Japanese Arbitration Act, Article 36 (4); the Chilean International Commercial Arbitration Law, Article 28 (4); the Paraguayan Law on Arbitration and Mediation, Article 32; the Peruvian Arbitration Law, Article 117 (3); and others.

3067. Blessing, *supra* note 2321, p. 54. Hascher speaks of a progressive interpretation of the convention, favoring the *lex mercatoria* and international principles, in Hascher, *supra* note 2574, pp. 1030-1031.

3068. 2018 DIS Rules, Article 24 (3); 2016 SIAC Rules, Article 31 (3); 2017 Lima Chamber of Commerce Rules, Article 21 (2); 2019 Milan Rules, Article 3 (4); 2010 Paraguay Arbitration Center Rules, Article 35; and others.

3069. Born, *supra* note 2273, p. 2985.

from the outset [3070], or provide a timely opportunity to discuss them. The institutionalization of trade usages, for instance by the ICC within the Incoterms, has helped tremendously in their identification. Standard-form contracts such as those that exist within the shipping trade, the commodity markets and the oil industry may also achieve international recognition when applied uniformly by different national courts [3071].

Now, the fact that trade must be taken into account in all cases should never enable arbitrators to ignore the applicable law [3072]. In the Final Award in ICC Case No. 13954, it was stated that "[t]rade usages do not constitute rules of law and cannot take precedence over the applicable law or dispense with the necessity of identifying it". Similar reasoning emerges from other awards as well [3073].

In particular reference to the UNIDROIT Principles, in the award in ICC Case No. 33/2014 the Tribunal refused to apply these principles as trade usages, concluding that

> "the arbitral tribunal does not find grounds to apply the [UNIDROIT] Principles since the Parties agreed to apply the Russian law, and, when the dispute was being considered, there were raised no issues which would require the reference to UNIDROIT [Principles] as trade usages" [3074].

A different situation arises when the parties agree that particular trade usages apply to their relationship. In these cases, the arbitrators must apply those trade usages [3075] and consider them no differently than they would understand a particular contractual term that had been included in the contract. In this way, trade usages that the parties have agreed upon must be considered and enforced by the tribunal in the same way as any other aspect of the parties' agreement [3076].

3070. Blackaby *et al.*, *supra* note 255, pp. 213-214.

3071. *Ibid.*, p. 214.

3072. Gaillard and Savage, *supra* note 836, para. 1514. According to Born, this is the prevailing position among commentators. Born, *supra* note 2273, pp. 2985-2986.

3073. See Partial Award in ICC Case No. 10022, *ICC Ct. Bull.*, Vol. 12, No. 2 (2001), p. 100. See also ICC Final Award 13954, *supra* note 2783, p. 234.

3074. See also Partial Award in ICC Case No. 10021 (2000).

3075. For instance, in *Tube City IMS LLC* v. *Anza Capital Partners LLC*, Final Award in ICC Case No. 18991; Final Award in ICC Case No. 18981, 43 YB Comm. Arb. (2018), p. 184; Final Award in ICC Case No. 14581, 37 YB Comm. Arb. (2012), p. 62; Final Award in ICC Case No. 11849, 31 YB Comm. Arb. (2006), p. 148; Final Award in ICC Case No. 8502, *ICC Ct. Bull.*, Vol. 10, No. 2 (1999), p. 72; *Bagadiya Bros. Pvt Ltd.* v. *Churchgate Nigeria Ltd.*, Final Award in LCIA Case No. 91309 (25 July 2014); *Pointer Inv. H.K. Ltd.* v. *Wisco Am. Co. Ltd.*, First Partial Award in HKIAC Case No. A14127 and A14179 (17 November 2015).

3076. Born, *supra* note 2273, p. 2986.

Under a different view, renowned commentators have argued that the flexible formula authorizes the application of usages or non-State rules such as the UNIDROIT Principles [3077], as was also decided in arbitral awards. For instance, in the Final Award in ICC Case No. 18728 [3078], the arbitrator cited Article 21.2 of the ICC Arbitration Rules and concluded that "[t]he UNIDROIT Principles is part of the international commercial usages, which the Sole Arbitrator is explicitly authorized to take into consideration". Likewise, in the Final Award in ICC Case No. 8502 [3079], the Tribunal held that the choice of Incoterms and the Uniform Customs and Practices for Documentary Credits (UCP 500) demonstrated the parties' intent for their contract to be governed by generally accepted international trade principles such as the UNIDROIT Principles [3080].

In a recent survey conducted between experienced arbitrators in the United States, more than a quarter of respondents indicated that at least some of the time they "feel free to follow [their] own sense of equity and fairness in rendering an award even if the result would be contrary to the applicable law" [3081]. This is exactly what happened in the 1983 Iran-United States Claims Tribunal case *CMI International, Inc.* v. *Iran*, wherein the arbitrators did not adhere to the parties' selection of the law of Idaho. The Tribunal ignored the law chosen by the parties after considering that their own task as arbitrators was to search for justice and equity [3082].

Two Latin American-seated arbitrations invoked Article 28 (4) of the Model Law in this regard, as did an arbitral tribunal seated in Costa

3077. Blackaby *et al.*, *supra* note 255, p. 212. Mayer even talks about the application of the UNIDROIT Principles in all situations, not as *lex contractus*, but specifically, when the content of a determined norm of the *lex contractus* is not clearly established or is manifestly inadequate. See P. Mayer, "The Role of the UNIDROIT Principles in ICC Arbitration Practice", in *ICC Bull.* Special 2002, pp. 75-76.

3078. ICC Case No. 18728, Final Award, 43 YB Comm. Arb. (2018), p. 108, 141.

3079. ICC Award 8502/1999, *supra* note 3075.

3080. Other ICC awards in this direction are the following: *Manufacturer* v. *Licensor*, Interim Award, *supra* note 1562; ICC Case No. 3896, 111 JDI (Clunet), p. 58, Award (1984); ICC Case No. 3493, Award, 9 YB Comm. Arb. (1984), p. 111.

3081. T. J. Stipanowich and Z. P. Ulrich, "Arbitration in Evolution: Current Practices and Perspectives of Experienced Commercial Arbitrators", *American Review of International Arbitration*, Vol. 25 (2014), pp. 479-480. There remain, however, two responses that indicate the need for further inquiry. First of all, although nearly three-quarters (74.2 percent) of respondents never "feel free to follow [their] own sense of equity and fairness in rendering an award even if the result would be contrary to applicable law", the other quarter (25.8 percent) do, at least some of the time. It is not entirely clear how these latter arbitrators interpret their mandate, but their response should encourage deeper discussion about the ethical as well as legal implications of such choices. *Ibid.*, pp. 455-456.

3082. Silberman and Ferrari, *supra* note 2362, p. 34.

Rica [3083] and another seated in Argentina. In the Argentinean case, notwithstanding the fact that both parties had chosen Argentinean law as the applicable law, the Arbitral Tribunal applied the UNIDROIT Principles instead as an expression of international commercial usages reflecting the solutions of different legal systems as well as a reflection of international contract practice. In ignoring the parties' choice of law, the Tribunal determined that Article 28 (4) of the UNCITRAL Model Law on International Commercial Arbitration should prevail over any domestic law [3084].

Are arbitrators operating *contra legem* in cases such as these? Rejecting the parties' choice of law is controversial, but it may be argued that when the parties select an applicable substantive law and a Model Law jurisdiction, the parties are also choosing Model Law Article 28 (4) and its corrective powers. The extent of this selection is, of course, a matter for another discussion. Evidently, however, some discretion has been granted to the adjudicator regarding whether national rules not of an overriding mandatory character should be applied [3085]. In any case, the parties should have a chance to discuss in the proceedings the rule to be purportedly applied by the arbitrator.

Moreover, as stated by Fernández Arroyo, Article 2A of the 2006 reform to the Model Law stresses the international origin of the Model Law and the necessity of promoting uniformity in its application. This provision acts as another argument in favor of cosmopolitism [3086]. In fact, the cosmopolitan character of arbitration makes it an ideal scenario for disputes to be resolved in the international field, even when national

---

3083. *Ad hoc* Arbitration in Costa Rica (30 April 2001), available at www.unilex.info, accessed 16 May 2022. In turn, the arbitral Tribunal references other ICC Awards in this regard – Awards 8908/1996 and 8873/1997, in *ICC Ct. Bull.*, Vol. 10, No. 2 (1999), pp. 78 ff.

3084. *Ad hoc* Arbitral Award (10 December 1997), available at www.unilex.info, accessed 16 May 2022.

3085. Ferrari states that the international arbitration cannot be more international than the national rules applicable to a given issue in a specific case allow the arbitration to be, in "How International Should International Arbitration Be? A Pea in Favour of a Realistic Answer", in *Eppur si muove: The Age of Uniform Law – Essays in Honour of Michael Joachim Bonell to Celebrate His 70th Birthday*, Vol. 2, Rome, UNIDROIT, 2016, p. 848. Many responses can be given to defend a different view, but one of them is that when the parties select an arbitral jurisdiction that in its laws contemplates a corrective formula, this authorizes the arbitrators to reach solutions of justice.

3086. D. P. Fernández Arroyo, "Los precedentes y la formación de una jurisprudencia arbitral", in E. Gaillard and D. P. Fernández Arroyo (eds.), *Cuestiones Claves del Arbitraje Internacional*, Asunción, CEDEP; Bogotá, Universidad del Rosario, 2013, pp. 233-234.

law has been selected by the parties [3087]. In the words of Lord McNair, arbitration itself affords some evidence, albeit inconclusive on its own, of the parties' belief in the inadequacy of the national law to resolve their dispute [3088].

Marc Blessing echoes many of the criticisms that scholars have made about Article 28 (4), in particular the observation that the dual reference found therein

> "would only complicate matters, would provide uncertainty and thus should rather be avoided, giving preference to one clear national legal system to prevail".

In response, Blessing argues that these critics

> "have either never had a single arbitration to adjudicate where these issues were at the heart of the dispute, or else they have not learned to realize that local or national perceptions and laws are often short-sighted, engineered under a purely local focus and do not deserve to be of an authoritative nature in a large international context" [3089].

D. The "brooding omnipresence" of public international law in investment arbitration

Richard Lillich wrote that international law is treated "much like a brooding omnipresence" hovering over international arbitrations: it is there and may be used by arbitrators when they believe that international law must be invoked in order to achieve a just resolution of an investment dispute [3090].

3087. International arbitration is frequently seen as a reason in itself for internationalizing the national applicable law. Members of an arbitral tribunal may find it less complicated than national judges to do so. See Spiermann, *supra* note 979, pp. 93-94.

3088. McNair, *supra* note 4, p. 10. When a pattern that repeats itself in arbitral case law, when the circumstances in which this occurs in international transactions involves different laws, foreign languages or different currencies, to cite examples, "a type of jurisprudence is generated, by repeated decisions dealing with similar transnational fact patterns, which by definition cannot be derived from a purely national context". Mann characterizes the jurisprudence of international tribunals as result-oriented rather than rules-oriented: "The idea and the ideals of international tribunals have in the past not been circumscribed by legalism. The practice of international tribunals has, on the whole, been characterized by careful analysis of the facts against the background of *broad* principles of law", Reed, *supra* note 21, p. 276.

3089. Blessing, *supra* note 2321, p. 42.

3090. Cited by Spiermann, *supra* note 979, p. 100.

After the famous *Serbian Loans* case [3091] decided by the PCIJ, and for a long time afterward, it was understood that international contracts were governed by the municipal law of a particular country to the potential exclusion of international law. Nowadays, in the context of foreign investment contracts and relationships in general, it is commonly accepted that international law operates as a framework that must be respected by domestic law [3092], even where international law has not been explicitly chosen by the parties [3093]. This was the case, for example, in *MCI* v. *Ecuador* (2007) [3094], *Sempra Energy International* v. *Argentine Republic* (2007) [3095] and *Duke Energy* v. *Peru* (2008) [3096].

International law may be applied in a supplementary fashion or corrective fashion. It can often be difficult to discern, however, the best way to proceed in this regard in a particular case. Rudolf Dolzer notes that the primary doctrinal issue is not the applicability of international law to a foreign investment dispute but the particular role it will play in this context. According to what criteria can the arbitrator make a choice between the applicability of international and domestic law rules? How can general principles of law relevant to investment law be identified? Within which circumstances can it be assumed that investors have waived their rights under international law [3097]? The remaining part of this chapter will deal with these issues.

E. Supplemental application of international law or national law

When there are gaps within the applicable law, arbitrators must deal with the issue of supplementation. *Non liquet* is not an alternative in situations where there is "silence or obscurity in the law" as provided, for instance, in Article 42 (2) of the ICSID Convention [3098]. This matter was also discussed in Chapter VI in relation to Article 38 of the ICJ Statute and the *non liquet* principle.

3091. *Serbian Loans, supra* note 978, Judgment (1929).
3092. Dolzer, *supra* note 24, p. 829.
3093. Schreuer *et al., supra* note 102, p. 585.
3094. *MCI* v. *Ecuador, supra* note 1150, Award (31 July 2007), para. 218.
3095. *Sempra* v. *Argentina, supra* note 451, Award (28 September 2007), para. 238.
3096. In *Duke Energy* v. *Peru* (2006), the Tribunal stated that "even if the law of Peru were held to apply to the interpretation of the [investment agreement], this Tribunal has the authority and duty to subject Peruvian law to the supervening control of international law" (*supra* note 2759, Decision on Jurisdiction (1 February 2006), para. 162).
3097. Dolzer, *supra* note 24, p. 830.
3098. See, in this regard, *History of the ICSID Convention, supra* note 1078, II-2, pp. 802-804, fn. 73.

The supplementary role of international law is expressly recognized in bilateral investment treaties and multilateral treaties such as the Energy Charter Treaty (Art. 26), NAFTA (Art. 1131) and the USMCA (Art. 14.D.9). When investors decide to pursue their claims in arbitration, they consent to this supplementary role provided for in the relevant treaty.

The *ad hoc* Annulment Committee in the *Klöckner* case (1985) stated that principles of international law may have "a complementary role (in the case of a 'lacuna' in the law of the State)" [3099]. Also, the *ad hoc* Annulment Committee in the *Amco* v. *Indonesia* case (1986) applied rules of international law to "fill up lacunae in the applicable domestic law" [3100]. This was similarly decided in the resubmitted case of *Amco* v. *Indonesia* (1990) [3101], in *Aucoven* v. *Venezuela* [3102] and in the *Micula* case [3103].

In *Enron Corporation Ponderosa Assets, LP* v. *Argentine Republic* (2007), the Tribunal stated the following:

> "While on occasions *[sic]* writers and decisions have tended to consider the application of domestic law or international law as a kind of dichotomy, this is far from being the case. In fact, both have a complementary role to perform, and this has begun to be recognized." [3104]

By contrast, in *AAPL* v. *Sri Lanka*, the Tribunal stated that

> "[t]he Bilateral Investment Treaty is not a self-contained closed legal system limited to provide for substantive material rules of direct applicability, but it has to be envisaged within a wider

3099. *Klöckner* v. *Cameroon*, *supra* note 748, Decision on Annulment (1985), para. 60.

3100. *Amco Asia* v. *Indonesia*, *supra* note 408, Decision on Annulment (16 May 1986), para. 20. The *ad hoc* Committee constituted in *Amco* stated that "the Convention authorizes an ICSID tribunal to apply rules of international law only to fill up lacunae in the applicable domestic law".

3101. "If there are no relevant host-state laws on a particular matter, a search must be made for the relevant international laws" (*Amco Asia* v. *Indonesia*, *supra* note 408, Resubmitted Case, Award (31 March 1990), para. 40).

3102. "It is certainly well settled that international law may fill lacunae when national law lacks rules on certain issues (so called complementary function)" (*Autopista* v. *Bolivia*, *supra* note 2716, Award (23 September 2003), para. 102).

3103. *Ioan Micula* et al. v. *Romania* (2008), *supra* note 102: "[P]ursuant to Article 42 (2) of the [ICSID] Convention the Tribunal will certainly apply residually international law if the other applicable rules are silent or obscure or are eventually determined not to apply ratione temporis" (Decision on Jurisdiction and Admissibility (24 September 2008), para. 151). See Gaillard and Banifatemi, *supra* note 20, p. 230.

3104. *Enron* v. *Argentina*, *supra* note 451, Award (22 May 2007), para. 207.

juridical context in which rules from other sources are integrated through implied incorporation methods, or by direct reference to certain supplementary rules, whether of international law character or of domestic law nature" [3105].

These cases make clear that tribunals use a variety of techniques in order to apply international law on a supplementary basis. Jan Bischoff notes that it is inevitable that tribunals applying international law in a supplementary manner "rather cherry-pick and mix legal considerations" from national and international law, "instead of conducting a clear legal analysis" [3106]. The matter requires a rigorous examination as will be attempted in the ensuing pages. The following differentiations must be made.

1. Supplementation by considering the convergence of international law and domestic law

Several arbitral tribunals use the technique of pointing out convergences between national and international law in drafting their reasons. The technique is no different than those used in many national courts. A survey undertaken by the International Law Association's Committee on International Law in National Courts shows that, on occasion, domestic courts apply international law to confirm what that national law already mirrors from it [3107].

In *Adriano Gardella* v. *Côte d'Ivoire* [3108] and *LETCO* v. *Liberia* [3109], the tribunals held that the host States' laws were applicable and found that no divergence existed with international law in the matters under discussion. In *CMS* v. *Argentina* (2005), the Tribunal wrote that

> "indeed there is here a close interaction between the [Argentinean] legislation and the regulations governing the gas privatization, the License and the international law, as embodied in the Treaty and

3105. *AAPL* v. *Sri Lanka*, *supra* note 453, Final Award (27 June 1990), 4 *ICSID Reports*, p. 250, p. 257.

3106. Bischoff, *supra* note 15, p. 757.

3107. G. Guillaume, "The Work of the Committee on International Law in National Courts of the International Law Association", *International Law Forum du droit international*, Vol. 3 (2001), p. 39.

3108. *Gardella* v. *Côte d'Ivoire*, *supra* note 1083, Award (29 August 1977), para. 4.3.

3109. *LETCO* v. *Liberia*, *supra* note 456, Award (31 March 1986), 2 *ICSID Reports*, p. 343.

customary international law. All of these rules are inseparable and will, to the extent justified, be applied by the tribunal"[3110].

The case *BG Group* v. *Argentina* (2007) is also illustrative in this regard[3111].

International tribunals likewise often find that there is no contradiction between national law and international law. In *LG&E Energy Corp.* v. *Argentina* (2006), the Arbitral Tribunal held:

> "International law overrides domestic law when there is a contradiction since a State cannot justify non-compliance of its international obligations by asserting the provisions of its domestic law. . . . If this contradiction does not exist [which was the situation for the Tribunal in this case], it is not an easy task to establish the relationship between international law and domestic law."[3112]

In turn, national law can be applied when international law is silent. In the SCC Rules case *Eastern Sugar BV* v. *Czech Republic* (2007), the Tribunal applied Czech law after determining that international law was silent on the matter of damages, writing that

> "[t]he Arbitral Tribunal believes that it should apply the statutory interest provided by the applicable law, which is Czech law, which on this point does not conflict with International Law"[3113].

In the Iran-United States Claims Tribunal case *American Bell International Inc.* v. *Government of the Islamic Republic of Iran* et al., Judge Mosk wrote that

> "[a]s a practical matter, in many cases the choice of whether to utilize public international law, general principles of law, municipal law (past or present) or some other law will not affect the result"[3114].

3110. *CMS* v. *Argentina*, *supra* note 84, Award (12 May 2005), para. 117.

3111. *BG Group* v. *Argentina*, *supra* note 310, Award (24 December 2007). See also *Occidental* v. *Ecuador*, *supra* note 571, Final Award (1 July 2004), para. 93.

3112. *LG&E* v. *Argentina*, *supra* note 448, Decision on Liability (3 October 2006), paras. 94-95 (applying ICSID Convention, Art. 42 (1), second sentence).

3113. *Eastern Sugar* v. *Czech Republic*, fn. 166, Partial Award, paras. 196, 373. In *Jan Oostergetel and Theodora Laurentius* v. *Slovak Republic*, it was ruled that: "Whenever the BIT is silent on an issue, the Tribunal will resort to either municipal or international law depending on the nature of the issue in question." See this and other cases in Kjos, *supra* note 2296, p. 259.

3114. *American Bell International Inc.* v. *Government of the Islamic Republic of Iran et al.*, Interlocutory Award (11 June 1984), Concurring and Dissenting Opinion by

Other examples emerge from *Benjamin R. Isaiah* v. *Bank Mellat* (1983) [3115] and *Morrison-Knudsen Pacific Limited* v. *Ministry of Roads and Transportation (MORT) and Iran* (1984) [3116].

According to Hege Elisabeth Kjos, the consistency between modern national and international law, which is "both unsurprising and desirable" [3117], is often neglected in scholarship. In this regard, the US Supreme Court Justice O'Connor stated in *Roper* v. *Simmons* (2005) that "we should not be surprised to find congruence between domestic and international values . . . expressed in international law or in the domestic laws of individual countries" [3118].

2. *Supplementation by incorporating international law within domestic law*

Potential conflicts between international and municipal law disappear when tribunals note the incorporation of international law within domestic law [3119]. In *BG Group* v. *Argentina*, the Tribunal wrote:

> "[T]he challenge of discerning the role that international law ought to play in the settlement of this dispute, vis-à-vis domestic law, disappears if one were to take into account that the BIT and underlying principles of international law, as 'the supreme law of the land', are incorporated into Argentine domestic law, superseding conflicting domestic statutes." [3120]

R. M. Mosk, 6 IUSCTR, p. 74, p. 98. See also *Harnischfeger* v. *Ministry*, *supra* note 2447, Award (26 April 1985), Dissenting Opinion of Judge R. M. Mosk, 8 IUSCTR, p. 119, 140-141; *Aminoil*, *supra* note 1059, Award (1982), para. 10; *PSEG* v. *Turkey*, *supra* note 523, Award (19 January 2007), para. 249.

3115. Restitutionary theories such as unjust enrichment and *enrichissement sans cause* are found in the laws of many nations. See J. Dawson, *Unjust Enrichment: A Comparative Analysis*, Boston, Little, Brown & Co., 1951. In international law unjust enrichment is an important element of State responsibility, vid. *Isaiah* v. *Mellat*, *supra* note 2435, at sec. IV.

3116. "Nothing in Iranian law has been called to the Tribunal's attention that contradicts this general legal principle." *Morrison-Knudsen* v. *Iran*, *supra* note 2453, Award (13 July 1984). Other cases: *Dic* v. *Tehran*, *supra* note 1987, at sec. B (1); *RN Pomeroy* v. *Iran*, Award (8 June 1983), at Section V (1) and Concurring Opinion of Judge R. M. Mosk; *Oil Field* v. *Iran*, *supra* note 2442, Interlocutory Award (9 December 1982), pp. 361-362; *Bendone-DeRossi Int'l* v. *Iran*, Award No. 352-375-1 (11 March 1988), Concurring Opinion of H. M. Holtzmann (at Section II) and Concurring Opinion of Judge A. Noori.

3117. Kjos, *supra* note 2296, p. 271.

3118. *Roper* v. *Simmons*, 125 S.Ct. 1183, 1216 (2005), dissenting opinion of J. O'Connor.

3119. Blackaby *et al.*, *supra* note 255, p. 468.

3120. *BG Group* v. *Argentina*, *supra* note 310, Final Award, para. 97. See also *Siemens* v. *Argentina*, *supra* note 531, Award (2007), paras. 78-79.

3. *Supplementation by* renvoi *to international law*

In *Wena* v. *Egypt*, the treaty in question contained a "without prejudice clause" in favor of the relevant treaty provisions. According to the *Wena ad hoc* Annulment Committee, this amounted to a kind of *renvoi* to international law by the very law of the host State [3121].

As seen in the previous chapter, Article 42 (1) of the ICSID Convention alludes to the "whole law" of the host State, but its second sentence makes clear that the provision would not inevitably lead that law to be applied to the substance of the claim. Therefore, if a law other than that of the host State is more connected to the dispute, the conflict of laws rules of the host State would likely dictate its application. In the assumption that *dépeçage* is recognized, different laws could apply to diverse aspects of the claim [3122].

4. *Supplementation by considering a lacuna in domestic law*

In *SPP* v. *Egypt* [3123], the Tribunal reasoned those lacunae (or gaps) within the chosen domestic law implied that the parties had not chosen an applicable law in the sense of Article 42 (1) of the ICSID Convention. As such, the proper law to be applied was international law in accordance with Article 42 (1) (2) of the Convention [3124]. As stated by Christoph Schreuer, the Tribunal did not end with the lacuna: they put the national law under the scrutiny and control of the international law instead [3125].

3121. *Wena Hotels* v. *Egypt*, *supra* note 601, Decision on Annulment (2002), para. 42. See also the Argentine cases: *CMS* v. *Argentina*, *supra* note 84, Award (12 May 2005), paras. 119-120; *Azurix* v. *Argentina*, *supra* note 327, Award (2006), para. 65; *LG&E* v. *Argentina*, *supra* note 448, Decision on Liability (3 October 2006), paras. 90-91; *Siemens* v. *Argentina*, *supra* note 531, Award (6 February 2007), para. 79; *Enron* v. *Argentina*, *supra* note 451, Award (22 May 2007), para. 208; *Sempra* v. *Argentina*, *supra* note 451, Award (28 September 2007), paras. 237-238. Schreuer *et al.*, *supra* note 102, p. 582.

3122. The provision of Article 42 (1) gives arbitrators a great deal of discretion in deciding the applicable law. Bjorklund and Vanhonnaeker, *supra* note 13, p. 357.

3123. *SPP* v. *Egypt*, *supra* note 1085, Award (20 May 1992), para. 80.

3124. In the case of *SPP* v. *Egypt*, the Tribunal declared: "Finally, even accepting the Respondent's view that the Parties have implicitly agreed to apply Egyptian law, such an agreement cannot entirely exclude the direct applicability of international law in certain situations. The law of the ARE [Arab Republic of Egypt], like all municipal legal systems, is not complete or exhaustive, and where a lacuna occurs it cannot be said that there is agreement as to the application of a rule of law which, *ex hypothesi*, does not exist. In such case, it must be said that there is 'absence of agreement' and, consequently, the second sentence of Article 42 (1) would come into play" (*SPP* v. *Egypt*, *supra* note 1085, Award (20 May 1992), para. 80).

3125. Schreuer *et al.*, *supra* note 102, p. 585 ff. The dissenting opinion, however, expressed that domestic systems have their own devices to close perceived gaps. *SPP* v. *Egypt*, *supra* note 1085, Dissenting Opinion (20 May 1992), 3 *ICSID Reports*, p. 249, 321.

The *Liberian Eastern Timber Corporation* v. *Government of the Republic of Liberia* (1986) case is also illustrative in this regard. In that case, the ICSID Tribunal stated:

> "The primary source of Liberian law and the basic document from which all other sources of law emanate is the Liberian Constitution; other sources include treaties, statutes and what may be called 'residual law'. . . . In the absence of any relevant constitutional or statutory provisions, residual law will be applied." [3126]

According to this decision, before determining the existence of a lacunae in the national law, the tribunal should in principle look to statutory and case law within the national jurisdiction in question, in addition to considering its own arbitral mechanism for filling the lacunae. It is important to note here that the absence of a remedy does not necessarily represent a gap in the domestic law to be applied – it may reflect a conscious decision by national legislators to avoid regulating a certain matter or to regulate it differently. As such, within these types of cases the application of public international law will not always be appropriate [3127].

5. *Choice of law and the supplementary role of international law*

In their exercise of party autonomy, the parties may decide to accord international law a supplementary role. In *AGIP SpA* v. *People's Republic of the Congo* (1979), the ICSID Tribunal recognized the parties' choice in this regard, understanding that it permitted the Tribunal to apply the philosophy that "principles of international law can be made either to fill a lacuna in Congolese law, or to make any necessary additions to it" [3128].

In that case, the Tribunal used the terms "supplement", "addition" and "compete" to describe the relationship between international law

3126. *LETCO* v. *Liberia*, *supra* note 456, Award (31 March 1986), rectified 10 June 1986, 26 ILM, p. 647, 665 (1987).

3127. Accordingly, absent true lacunae in the national legal order, the gap-filling role of international law should preferably be limited to ancillary questions of law; it should not create causes of action as such. Otherwise, the claimant would get more than it "bargained for" when agreeing to the application of national law. Also, nowadays, most national legal systems are so advanced that the question of lacunae will rarely occur. See Kjos, *supra* note 2296, p. 194.

3128. *AGIP* v. *Congo*, *supra* note 454, Award (30 November 1979), para. 82.

and the host State's law. This terminology is particularly vague and imprecise. Nevertheless, the circumstances of that case permitted the Tribunal to conclude that the claim would have been upheld even if the host State's action had been found legal under the Congolese law [3129].

F. Corrective application of international law or national law

As previously discussed, national laws possess formidable tools for correcting the harsh application of their rules. In this vein, Jan Paulsson believes that investment tribunals must give full effect to their mandate of applying national law, when selected. This objective must be fulfilled to the extent that they – much as courts of first and last instance – should strike down "unlawful laws" without reference to international law by broadly construing the concept of national law [3130].

Notwithstanding the existence of a treaty, if the matter could be decided in accordance with the local law, then the host State could simply pass legislation preventing the application of a particular part of the treaty [3131]. This situation is unacceptable to foreign investors.

According to the 1969 Vienna Convention on the Law of Treaties (VCLT), treaties are "governed by international law" and must be interpreted in light of "any relevant rules of international law applicable" [3132]. In this regard, the Annulment Committee in the *Vivendi* v. *Argentina* case held that:

3129. Express stipulations by parties for the application of such a "system of concurrent law" were also typically seen as giving international law a gap-filling and/or regulatory role in relation to the specified national law. Thus, in *AGIP* v. *Congo* (*supra* note 454, Award (30 November 1979), paras. 323-324), the Tribunal observed that the provision quoted earlier, according to which Congolese law supplemented by international law would be applicable, meant "at the very least, that recourse to principles of international law can be made either to fill a lacuna in Congolese law, or to make any necessary additions to it" (Parra, *supra* note 510, p. 182). Schreuer notes that in *AAPL* v. *Sri Lanka* the parties made an implicit choice of law in the BIT and hence of international law in general, in Schreuer *et al.*, *supra* note 102, p. 581.

3130. J. Paulsson, "Unlawful Laws and the Authority of International Tribunals", Lalive Lecture, Geneva, 27 May 2009, *ICSID Review: Foreign Investment Law Journal*, Vol. 23, No. 2 (2008), p. 215.

3131. Blackaby *et al.*, *supra* note 255, pp. 466-467. In the *CDSE* v. *Costa Rica* case, the Tribunal stated: "To the extent that there may be any inconsistency between the two bodies of law, the rules of public international law must prevail. Were this not so in relation to takings of property, the protection of international law would be denied to the foreign investor and the purpose of the ICSID Convention would, in this respect, be frustrated" (*CDSE* v. *Costa Rica*, *supra* note 455, Final Award (17 February 2000), para. 64). See similarly in *Enron* v. *Argentina*, *supra* note 451, Decision on Jurisdiction (14 January 2004), paras. 206-209; *LG&E* v. *Argentina*, *supra* note 448, Decision on Liability (3 October 2006), para. 98.

3132. VCLT, *supra* note 470, Articles 2 (1) *(a)* and 31 (3) *(c)*.

> "[I]n respect of a claim based upon a substantive provision of that BIT . . . the inquiry which the ICSID tribunal is required to undertake is one governed by the ICSID Convention, by the BIT and by applicable international law. Such an inquiry is neither in principle determined, nor precluded, by any issue of municipal law." [3133]

According to Zachary Douglas, treaties are creations of international law and operate within the international legal system. As decided in *Georges Pinson (France* v. *Mexico)* [3134], "[e]very international convention must be deemed tacitly to refer to general principles of international law for all questions which it does not itself resolve in express terms and in a different way" [3135].

The substantive standards in investment treaties are *lex specialis* and, as such, are a primary source from which to determine the applicable law. Since these treaties are international law instruments, the VCLT applies in their interpretation, which must be made in light of "any relevant rules of international law applicable" [3136].

Moreover, the standard by which to assess the legality of the host State's conduct can be found within international law. In this regard, Article 3 of the ILC's Draft Articles on State Responsibility provides that the "characterisation of an act of a State as internationally wrongful is governed by international law" [3137].

3133. *Vivendi* v. *Argentina*, *supra* note 456, Decision on Annulment (3 July 2002), para. 102. See also *AAPL* v. *Sri Lanka*, *supra* note 453, Final Award (27 June 1990), paras. 20-21. See Ferguson Reed and Paulsson, *supra* note 1147, p. 73.

3134. *Georges Pinson (France)* v. *Mexico*, Decision No. 1 (19 October 1928), 5 RIAA, p. 327.

3135. Douglas, *supra* note 39, p. 85. Umpire Plumley stated in this regard in *Aroa Mines* in respect of the Protocol of 14 February 1903 establishing the British-Venezuelan Mixed Claims Commission:

"International law is not in terms invoked in these protocols, neither is it renounced. But in the judgment of the umpire, since it is part of the law of the land of both governments, and since it is the only definitive rule between nations, it is the law of this tribunal interwoven in every line, word, and syllable of the protocols, defining their meaning, and illuminating the text; restraining, impelling, and directing every act thereunder . . . Since this is an international tribunal established by the agreement of nations there can be no other law, in the opinion of the umpire, for its government than the law of nations; and it is, indeed, scarcely necessary to say that the protocols are to be interpreted and this tribunal governed by that law, for there is no other; and that justice and equity are invoked and are to be paramount is not in conflict with this position, for international law is assumed to conform to justice and to be inspired by the principles of equity." (*Ibid.*, pp. 85-86)

3136. Article 31 (3) *(c)*.

3137. Article 3 of the ILC Draft Articles on State Responsibility, *supra* note 433, also states: "Such characterization is not affected by the characterization of the same act as lawful by internal law", Ferguson Reed and Paulsson, *supra* note 1147, p. 73.

Ole Spiermann explains that if investors are affected in a way that runs contrary to the principle of *pacta sunt servanda* when it comes to treaty interpretation and national law does not provide an adequate remedy, an arbitral tribunal is likely to apply a law other than national law. The aim of *pacta sunt servanda* is not to render the national law of the host State inapplicable, nor to bring simple breaches of contract beyond the confines of this system, but merely to put the parties on an equal footing by regulating the powers of the host State [3138]. In short, *pacta sunt servanda* thus serves as an overarching standard against which all aspects of national law may be assessed, both procedural and substantive.

Sometimes, however, tribunals unduly twist the balance in favor of the application of international law. In this regard, Douglas criticizes the *Aucoven* v. *Venezuela* decision for having mistakenly applied international law as a "corrective" source of rules [3139]. In that case, the Tribunal found Venezuelan *force majeure* rules applicable to the merits of the dispute but maintained that its application could be corrected if international law were violated [3140]. According to Douglas, Venezuelan law should have been applied unless it was demonstrated that the doctrine of *force majeure* under Venezuelan administrative law violated an obligation of general international law regarding the treatment of foreign nationals [3141].

This provision was relied on in *Vivendi* v. *Argentina*, *supra* note 456, Decision on Annulment (3 July 2022), paras. 95-96. See also: *Azurix* v. *Argentina*, *supra* note 327, Award (2006), para. 67.

3138. Spiermann, *supra* note 979, pp. 94-95.

3139. *Autopista* v. *Bolivia*, *supra* note 2716, Award (23 September 2003), 10 *ICSID Reports* 309, pp. 131-132.

3140. The Tribunal's reasoning on this point expressly relied upon the first edition of Schreuer's commentary, vid. Schreuer *et al.*, *supra* note 102, p. 585.

3141. "For instance, if the relevant provision of Venezuelan administrative law provided that, in administrative contracts with foreign investors, force majeure could be invoked by a Venezuelan State party where a supervening event rendered performance 'inconvenient' rather than 'impossible', it might well be the case that such a provision would constitute a per se violation of the international minimum standard due to its discriminatory nature. But this role for international law is not tantamount to asking whether international law 'imposes a different standard': this is clear from the Tribunal's citation of the ILC's Draft Articles on State Responsibility and international precedents on force majeure in international law. Even if Article 23 of the ILC's Draft Articles on *force majeure* stipulated a different test for the invocation of the doctrine than that envisaged by Venezuelan administrative law, this would not compel the application of the former in preference to the latter. Article 23 of the ILC's Draft Articles on force majeure is a 'circumstance' which can be relied upon by a State to preclude its secondary responsibility for the breach of an international obligation. Here the claim was not founded upon an international obligation. Article 23 does not purport

If national law violates international law rules, tribunals must not uphold discriminatory or arbitrary action by host States or bad faith breaches of the State's undertakings which amount to a denial of justice (even if they conform to the law of the host State). In short, tribunals may not apply the law of the host State if it would violate international law rules, such as the minimum standards for the protection of aliens and their property [3142].

G. Direct application of public international law

In situations in which the relevant international norm grants investors a higher degree of protection, international law applies directly. Kjos notes that when this is the case, it is not entirely appropriate to refer to the application of international law as "supervening". Rather, international law should apply directly [3143].

International law can also be applied by itself if the appropriate rule is found in this ambit. According to this view, where the claim in question is international in nature, national law will not apply on a primary basis [3144]. National law applies when the "essential basis" has a national character, as is often the case with contract claims. In these situations, international law will only be applied in a supervening fashion when in conflict with domestic law [3145].

H. Combined application of national and international law

As seen, bilateral investment treaties may or may not contain applicable law provisions. When they do, they frequently mention both international law and domestic law, without indicating which prevails or how each one should be applied [3146]. Whether or not the investment

---

to regulate the circumstances where a party may be released from the performance of its obligations under an administrative contract." Douglas, *supra* note 39, p. 132.

3142. See Schreuer *et al.*, *supra* note 102, pp. 585-586.

3143. Kjos, *supra* note 2296, pp. 210-211.

3144. *Ibid.*, p. 170.

3145. *Ibid.*, p. 211.

3146. For instance, Article 8 of the United Kingdom-Argentina BIT states: "The arbitral tribunal shall decide the dispute in accordance with the provisions of this Agreement, the laws of the Contracting Party involved in the dispute, including its rules on conflicts of laws, the terms of any specific agreement concluded in relation to such an investment and the applicable principles of international law." Agreement between the Government of the United Kingdom of Great Britain and Northern Ireland and the Government of the Republic of Argentina for the Promotion and Protection of Investments, signed on 11 December 1990, entered into force on 19 February 1993.

treaty specifies the applicable law, it is clear that public international law has a "controlling role" [3147]. As decided in the *CME* v. *Czech Republic* (2001/03) case, "[t]o the extent that there is a conflict between national law and international law, the arbitral tribunal shall apply international law" [3148].

Also, when the parties agreed upon the combined application of national and international law in an investment contract, international law can apply in a supervening way. For instance, in the three Libyan oil cases, the choice of law clauses were identical and specified that "[t]his Concession shall be governed by and interpreted in accordance with the principles of law of Libya common to the principles of international law" [3149].

I. Can minimum public international law standards be waived?

Given that instruments like the ICSID Convention (and Art. 42 (1) in particular) give prominence to the principle of party autonomy, the parties may in principle choose the sole application of national laws [3150].

However, international tribunals may not disregard questions of international law and must consider their eventual prevalence. As several writers have argued, the traditional procedure of diplomatic protection may not be replaced or discarded using the ICSID Convention in favor of a mechanism that ignores internationally guaranteed minimum standards. Moreover, it would be difficult to reconcile how awards that disregard international law would fall into the general obligation to recognize and enforce awards under Article 54 (1) of the Convention [3151].

Calvo Clauses that have been designed to waive substantive international law standards have not been successful when invoked before international tribunals, as seen in Chapter III. This must cast grave doubt on the ability of a choice of law clause to exclude international minimum standards due to the mere omission of a reference to international law.

3147. Blackaby *et al.*, *supra* note 255, p. 465.
3148. *CME* v. *Czech Republic*, UNCITRAL Final Award (14 March 2003), para. 91.
3149. *BP* v. *Libya*, *supra* note 1019, Award (1973), para. 1; *Liamco*, *supra* note 946, Award (1977), paras. 122-123; *Texaco* v. *Libya*, *supra* note 119, Award (1977), para. 23.
3150. See Spiermann, *supra* note 979, p. 100.
3151. Schreuer *et al.*, *supra* note 102, pp. 586-587.

In addition, it is highly unlikely that parties intend to make a choice of law to the total exclusion of international law including the international minimum standards [3152].

In addition to investment treaties, arbitral rules may also provide guidance regarding the supervening application of international law to a contract [3153]. For instance, in accordance with Article 42 of the ICSID Convention, where the parties have not agreed on an applicable law, "the Tribunal shall apply the law of the Contracting State party to the dispute (including its rules on the conflict of laws) and such rules of international law as may be applicable" [3154].

Hege Elisabeth Kjos notes that international law should be applied in a supervening way particularly for internationalized tribunals on the basis that they operate within the international legal field [3155].

This is not always the case when it comes to territorialized tribunals. Article 35 (1) of the 2010 UNCITRAL Arbitration Rules provides that, failing designation by the parties, the Tribunal "shall apply the law which it determines to be appropriate". As seen in Chapter XVIII, the reference to "law" within Article 35 (1) has been interpreted to exclude "rules of law". "Rules of law" in this context are generally understood to also include public international law.

3152. *Ibid.*, p. 586.

3153. Blackaby *et al.*, *supra* note 255, pp. 464-465.

3154. "An attempt to restrict the applicability of international law to filling gaps in the host State's law was defeated" (*History of the ICSID Convention*, *supra* note 1078, II-2, pp. 802-804). "Although some mention was made of a principle of priority for domestic law which was to be 'of primary importance' and would be applied 'in the first place' (*ibid.*, II-1, p. 571; II-2, p. 800), a suggestion to insert the word 'first' into the text was not adopted" (*ibid.*, p. 804). "It was made clear that international law would prevail where the host State's domestic law violated international law, for instance, through a subsequent change of its own law to the detriment of the investor" (*ibid.*, II-1, pp. 570-571; II-2, p. 985). "The Chairman's explanation of the vote which retained the reference to international law (*ibid.*, p. 804) pointed out that international law would come into play both in the case of a lacuna in domestic law and in the case of any inconsistency between the two" (*ibid.*, p. 804). See Schreuer *et al.*, *supra* note 102, pp. 617-618.

3155. See Kjos, *supra* note 2296, p. 196. Lauterpacht notes that notwithstanding the silence of the first sentence of Article 42 (1) of the ICSID Convention on the question of the applicability of international law, the competence of the tribunal to pass upon such questions without express reference thereto in the relevant proper law clause is inherent in its very status as a tribunal set up to dispose of issues under international investment contracts and in deliberate substitution for alternative modes of international protection, in "The World Bank Convention on the Settlement of International Investment Disputes", *Recueil d'Etudes de Droit International en Hommage à Paul Guggenheim*, Geneva, Tribune, 1968, pp. 658.

J. Controversy regarding the ICSID Convention absence of choice provision

1. Introduction

Where the parties have not chosen an applicable law, the relationship between national and international law becomes "complex", as reflected in the second sentence of Article 42 (1) of the ICSID Convention.

A wide range of interpretations of this provision are currently in competition. Many writers consider international law to have a supplemental and corrective role, while others argue that it should be applied on its own. Even regarding the supplemental and corrective powers, commentators have come to markedly divergent conclusions depending on whether they emphasize the importance of domestic law or of international law [3156].

The matter received significant attention after two decisions emerged during the mid-1980s: the *Klöckner* and *Amco* v. *Indonesia* cases [3157]. At the time, it was widely accepted that Article 42 (1) should play a corrective role. However, among the cases registered in the first twenty years of the Convention, few actually applied international law in a supervening way. Several tribunals merely stated that domestic law was not in conflict with international law [3158], as was the case in the *LETCO* v. *Liberia* award, for instance. This decision referred to Article 42 (1) as providing

> "that, in the absence of any express choice of law by the parties, the Tribunal must apply a system of concurrent law. The law of the Contracting State is recognized as paramount within its own territory but is nevertheless subjected to control by international law" [3159].

Article 42 (1) of the ICSID Convention uses the words "such rules of international law as may be applicable". From this drafting, it should

---

3156. Schreuer *et al.*, *supra* note 102, p. 626.

3157. Parra, *supra* note 510, p. 180.

3158. There was a glaring exception to such restraint in the *SPP* award. See *ibid.*, p. 182.

3159. The Tribunal, after noting that "[t]he role of international law as a 'regulator' of national systems of law has been much discussed", declared itself "satisfied that the rules and principles of Liberian law which it has taken into account are in conformity with generally accepted principles of public international law governing the validity of contracts and the remedies for their breach" (*LETCO* v. *Liberia*, *supra* note 456, Award (31 March 1986), para. 358).

be interpreted that not *all* international law rules must be applied – only *relevant* international law rules [3160]. Interpretations vary on when this will be the case.

2. The interpretation in early cases

In early ICSID cases, particularly from the 1980s with some others following thereafter [3161], international law exercised a supplementary or corrective role only when there was a lacuna within domestic law, or where international law was inconsistent with the applicable national law.

In a landmark early decision in 1985, the ICSID *ad hoc* Annulment Committee in the *Klöckner* case [3162] held the following:

> "Article 42 of the Washington Convention certainly provides that 'in the absence of agreement between the parties, the Tribunal shall apply the law of the Contracting State party to the dispute . . . and such principles of international law as may be applicable'. This gives these principles . . . a dual role, that is, complementary (in the case of a 'lacuna' in the law of the State), or corrective, should the State's law not conform on all points to the principles of international law." [3163]

3160. As observed by the *LG&E* Tribunal, this reading of Article 42 (1) is corroborated by the French version of the provision: with reference to the rules of international law and, particularly, to the language "as may be applicable", found in Article 42 (1) of the ICSID Convention, the Tribunal holds the view that it should not be understood as if it were in some way conditioning application of international law. Rather, it should be understood as making reference, within international law, to the competent rules to govern the dispute at issue. This interpretation could find support in the ICSID Convention's French version that refers to the rules of international law *en la matière*, *LG&E* v. *Argentina*, *supra* note 448, Decision on Liability (3 October 2006), para. 88. *En la matière* can be translated in English as "on the matter" or "on the subject". See Fouret, Gerbay and Alvarez, *supra* note 70, p. 358.

3161. *Klöckner* v. *Cameroon*, *supra* note 748, Decision on Annulment (1985); *Amco Asia* v. *Indonesia*, *supra* note 408, Decision on Annulment (16 May 1986); *LETCO* v. *Liberia*, *supra* note 456, Award (31 March 1986), rectified (14 May 1986); *Southern Pacific* v. *Egypt*, *supra* note 128, Award (20 May 1992); *CDSE* v. *Costa Rica*, *supra* note 455, Award (17 February 2000). See criticisms in Douglas, *supra* note 39, p. 130.

3162. *Klöckner* v. *Cameroon*, *supra* note 748; *Amco Asia* v. *Indonesia*, *supra* note 408. The decision thus confirms the supplemental and corrective functions of international law while emphasizing that an award may not be based on international law alone. See Schreuer *et al.*, *supra* note 102, p. 621. See also M. Sasson, "The Applicable Law and the ICSID Convention", in C. Baltag (ed.), *ICSID Convention after 50 Years: Unsettled Issues*, The Hague, Kluwer Law International, 2016, p. 275.

3163. *Klöckner* v. *Cameroon*, *supra* note 748, Decision on Annulment (1985), para. 69.

In turn, in *Amco* v. *Indonesia*, in 1986 the *ad hoc* Annulment Committee wrote:

> "[W]here there are applicable host-state laws, they must be checked against international laws, which will prevail in case of conflict. Thus, international law is fully applicable and to classify its role as 'only supplemental and corrective' seems a distinction without a difference." [3164]

International law lays down standards by which to judge actions taken by host States in relation to contracts with foreign investors. These standards lead to a two-step analysis: first of national law and then of international law. These do not have distinct spheres of application; if domestic law has not been exhausted prior to the application of international law, it must be applied. The approach is vertical in the sense that the State is seen as a sovereign that reigns over private subjects (including investors) but whose powers are circumscribed by international law [3165].

This interpretation has been upheld in the *travaux préparatoires* of the ICSID Convention, although it does not clearly emerge from the written text [3166]. Where the contract does not contain a choice of law clause, the horizontal approach entitles tribunals to apply public international law directly. As such, it is not necessary for the tribunal to first establish *(a)* the investor's rights under municipal law or *(b)* the gap that exists within municipal law, or that *(c)* municipal law violates international law. However, the investor can nevertheless base their claims upon municipal law if it contains more favorable terms [3167].

3164. ILR 580, p. 594, para. 40. See also *Amco Asia* v. *Indonesia*, *supra* note 408, Decision on Annulment (16 May 1986), 12 YB Comm. Arb. (1987), pp. 129-148, para. 186.

3165. Spiermann, *supra* note 979, pp. 96-98. This is what Spiermann refers to as *pacta sunt servanda* as a rationale of applicable law (Vertical Approach). Contrastingly, the horizontal approach reflects a notion of equality – both the State and the investor are placed on an equal footing. Public international law is taken as a proper law in some respects regarding minimum standards of protection. This is in the words of Spiermann the horizontal approach, prevailing view today, analogous to the private international law doctrine of *dépeçage*. An early example of this approach is the 1958 *Aramco* case, *supra* note 1004. It applied general principles of law as part of the proper law of contract. It relates the question of in which system of systems to situate the relationship with the investor, with general principles of law being open to such a choice in the exact same manner as systems of national law. Internationalization took the form of general principles of law, as distinct from public international law, possibly to not sound to eccentric if the Tribunal held that contracts were subject directly to public international law.

3166. Sasson, *supra* note 3162, pp. 294-295.

3167. Bischoff, *supra* note 15, pp. 756-757.

Outside the ICSID mechanism, in *CME* v. *Czech Republic* (2003), the UNCITRAL Tribunal wrote that there is "a strict inter-relationship of domestic and international law requiring an arbitral tribunal to follow a certain ranking when applying the law applicable to an investment treaty" [3168]. This ranking is unconvincing [3169]. As stated in *Methanex* v. *United States* (2005), "a tribunal has an independent duty to apply imperative principles of law or *jus cogens* and not to give effect to parties' choices of law that are inconsistent with such principles" [3170]. Therefore, only in these *jus cogens* situations should international law prevail over the parties' choices.

3. *Reisman's alternative view*

Michael Reisman proposed an alternative view regarding how to determine which rules of international law must be applied in a particular dispute and, more importantly, how such norms interact with host State law [3171].

According to Reisman, if the law of the host State addresses the contentious issue directly or indirectly, it should apply even if it diverges from international law. Only in the presence of a "veritable collision" or a "violation of something fundamental to international law" should international law apply. The appropriate question to ask does not concern the consistency between host State law and international law, "but whether applying the Contracting State's law would constitute a violation of something fundamental to international law" [3172].

Reisman argues that an ICSID tribunal may apply international law in the absence of the parties' choice in the following situations: *(i)* where the parties have so agreed (during the proceedings); *(ii)* where the law of the host State calls for the application of public international law; *(iii)* where the matter is directly regulated by an applicable treaty; and *(iv)* where the host State has violated a peremptory public international law norm [3173].

3168. *CME Czech Republic BV* v. *The Czech Republic*, UNCITRAL, Final Award (14 March 2003), para. 410.

3169. Spiermann, *supra* note 979, p. 106.

3170. See *supra* note 795.

3171. Fouret, Gerbay and Alvarez, *supra* note 70, p. 358.

3172. W. M. Reismann, "The Regime for Lacunae in the ICSID Choice of Law Provision and the Question of Its Threshold", *ICSID Review: Foreign Investment Law Journal*, Vol. 15, No. 2 (2000), p. 375.

3173. *Ibid.*, p. 380. He clarified his position in a subsequent article written with Arsanjani. They referred specifically to point iii above: "international law applies where there is a treaty between the State parties to the dispute. A BIT will be *eo ipso*

Within these strict parameters, international law rarely comes into play [3174].

4. Pragmatism

After the *Klöckner* and *Amco* v. *Indonesia* cases, ICSID tribunals began to depart from the approach of first applying the host State law and then international law in a supplementary or corrective manner.

In *Wena* v. *Egypt*, the *ad hoc* Annulment Committee held that the second sentence of Article 42 (1) of the ICSID Convention "allowed for both legal orders to have a role", for "the law of the host State [. . . to] be applied in conjunction with international law if this is justified" or for "international law [. . . to] be applied by itself if the appropriate rule is found in this other ambit" [3175].

This decision recognized that the BIT had been selected by the parties as "the primary source of applicable law for this arbitration", however, it "was a terse document that did not contain all the applicable rules" [3176].

In 2005, the Tribunal in *CMS* v. *Argentina* advocated in favor of this "more pragmatic and less doctrinaire approach . . . allowing for the application of both domestic law and international law if the specific facts of the dispute so justify" [3177].

---

applicable law regarding breaches of protections therein established, even if it does not contain an explicit provision on the applicable law. Thus, the second sentence of Article 42 (1) will not be applicable when there is a BIT governing the dispute, in which case being a treaty 'it would have to be interpreted in accordance with international law'. According to this interpretation, Article 42 (1), second sentence, receives a limited application, since it would be excluded in all the cases where the dispute arose out of a BIT". See Sasson, *supra* note 3162, pp. 275-276.

3174. From a different perspective, Prosper Weil considers that under the second sentence of Article 42 (1), international law always gains the upper hand and ultimately prevails, on the grounds that international law can be applied both via its incorporation into domestic law and via its applicability to correct deficiencies or contrariness in the domestic law, in P. Weil, "The State, the Foreign Investor, and International Law: The No Longer Stormy Relationship of a Ménage À Trois", *ICSID Review: Foreign Investment Law Journal*, Vol. 15, No. 2 (2000), p. 401, 409.

3175. *Wena Hotels* v. *Egypt*, *supra* note 601, Decision on Annulment (2002).

3176. *Ibid.*, para. 79.

3177. *CMS* v. *Argentina*, *supra* note 84, Award (12 May 2005). This approach was followed by *Sempra* v. *Argentina*, *supra* note 451, Award (28 September 2007), paras. 236 and 240. See Parra, *supra* note 510, pp. 305-306. See also Ferguson Reed and Paulsson, *supra* note 1147, p. 73. In *Goetz* v. *Burundi* (1999), *supra* note 93, the ICSID Tribunal expressed that the matter "has received divergent responses, abundantly commented on in academic writings: hierarchal relationships according to some, domestic law applying first of all but being overborne where it contradicts international law; according to others, relationships based on subsidiarity, with international law being called upon only to fill lacunae or to settle uncertainties in national law; according

Several scholars have also argued in favor of this logic. According to Emmanuel Gaillard and Yas Banifatemi, Article 42 (1) grants arbitrators the freedom to apply the law that they consider most appropriate, whether national or international. ICSID tribunals enjoy a great deal of latitude in determining the applicability of international law [3178]. This was the position taken by the Tribunal in the *Wena* v. *Egypt* case [3179].

5. *A "Broches approach"*

Monique Sasson has criticized Gaillard and Banifatemi's viewpoint as "misguided", pointing out that it ignores the *travaux préparatoires* [3180]. Instead, Sasson argues in favor of what she calls the "Broches approach", due to the important role played by Aron Broches in the drafting of the ICSID Convention [3181].

Sasson points out that the ICSID Convention departs from prior codification efforts in several significant ways [3182]. Party autonomy

---

to others again, complementary relationships, with domestic law and international law each having its own sphere of application" (ICSID Case No. ARB/95/3, Award – comprising the Parties' Settlement Agreement, 10 February 1999, para. 97).

3178. An analysis of the wording of Article 42 can be found in Gaillard and Banifatemi, *supra* note 2414, pp. 406 and 409. See also Bjorklund and Vanhonnaeker, *supra* note 13, p. 368.

3179. Gaillard represented Wena Hotels in *Wena Hotels* v. *Egypt*, *supra* note 601. The flexibility that the parties and the arbitrators enjoy as to the applicable law can be placed in the context of a global development whereby States seek to stimulate and attract international commercial arbitration as a form of dispute resolution, and thereby also commercial activity, such as foreign investment. Further, "the primary applicability of the law of the host State is often perceived by capital – importing States as a symbolic guarantee that their law – which they assume to be more favorable – would be given maximum effect", Gaillard and Banifatemi, *supra* note 2414, p. 380.

3180. The discussion that preceded the adoption of Article 42 (1) clearly shows that the States opposed the attribution of such freedom to arbitral tribunals. To enter into international treaties is an "attribute of State sovereignty". See Sasson, *supra* note 3162, p. 299.

3181. *Ibid.*, p. 276. Schreuer also pays particular attention to the drafting history of the ICSID Convention and Broches' interventions in this regard, in Schreuer *et al.*, *supra* note 102, p. 618.

3182. Sasson, *supra* note 3162, pp. 299-300:

> "In the Abs-Shawcross Draft Convention on Investment Abroad (1959), Article VI, the applicability of municipal law, only to the extent that it is more favorable than international or treaty law, is in significant contrast with the role of municipal law in the subsequent ICSID Convention. In Harvard Draft Convention on the International Responsibility of States for Injuries to Aliens (1961), Article 2, though it does not expressly identify the law applicable to the merits, states that with regard to the determination of the responsibility of the State, international law must prevail. The article echoes principles later incorporated in the ILC's Articles on State Responsibility. Again, municipal law cannot be invoked unless it is more favorable to the investor. In the Organisation for Economic Cooperation and Development, Draft Convention on the Protection of Foreign Property (1967),

is recognized under the Convention and, where the parties have not chosen an applicable law, the Convention specifies that municipal law or international law may be applied where relevant. *The travaux préparatoires* reveal the intention of the drafters to narrow the scope of the arbitrators' discretion to determine the applicable law. As such, international law will only be applied on an exceptional basis [3183].

According to Broches, the fact that national law is mentioned before international law in the second sentence of Article 42 (1) of the ICSID Convention does not denote their hierarchical order. Rather, the wording of the second sentence of Article 42 (1) reflects the fact that the investment has been made within a national jurisdiction and, absent an agreement to the contrary, domestic law should govern any potential dispute [3184].

In his own words, Broches argues that:

> "International law will be then applied when agreed by the parties; or when the law governing the dispute *calls* for the application of international law; or where the subject-matter or issue is directly regulated by international law, for instance by the applicable treaty; or where the applicable law or action taken

---

Article 8, there is no provision on applicable law, but it is clarified that if there are provisions more favorable to the investor, these should be applicable, without any mention of whether they are national or international rules. However, municipal law again does not play any role unless it is more favorable."

3183. . Paragraph 40 of Report of the Executive Directors of the IBRD on the ICSID Convention. See more in Sasson, *supra* note 3162, p. 281. See also *History of the ICSID Convention*, *supra* note 1078, II-2, pp. 802-803.

3184. *Ibid.*, pp. 390-391:

> "This could have been expressed as well, and in fact it was so expressed in an earlier draft, by saying that a Tribunal should apply such rules of national and international law as may be applicable. This draft ran, however, into very strong opposition on the part of many developing countries, including those who were not opposed to the application of international law. This group felt that the applicable national law would of necessity be the law of the host country, since that is where the investment is made. It has to be admitted that in most cases this result would be reached in any event by the application of conflict rules. Broches point that the first sentence of 42 (1) referring to the parties' choice of law does not exclude the country law's conflict rules. The first sentence of the article does not mention conflict rules, whereas they are expressly mentioned in the second. Since the first sentence alludes of rules of law, which may not be the rules of a national system at all, a reference to conflict rules would have been wholly inappropriate. Their express mention in the second sentence, was motivated by a desire to remove any possible ambiguity."

under that law violates international law. Here, international law exercises its corrective role." [3185]

6. An "integrationist approach"

Andrea Bjorklund and Lukas Vanhonnaeker also warn about the danger of granting arbitral tribunals excessive discretionary powers. They point to the *Venezuela Holdings* v. *Venezuela* decision, in which the Annulment Committee dealt with a broadly drafted choice of law clause [3186]. The Committee found that there are limitations to the tribunals' discretion to determine the applicable law and held that it is "obvious that in an appropriate case the resolution of a disputed issue under international law can itself entail the application of national law, simply because that is what the international rule requires" [3187].

According to Bjorklund and Vanhonnaeker, the Tribunal in *Venezuela Holdings* v. *Venezuela* failed to recognize the limitations of arbitrators' discretionary powers and that their corrective powers must be exercised in accordance with choice of law rules [3188]. Nonetheless, Bjorklund and Vanhonnaeker recognized that "despite some criticism and potential for pitfalls, the discretionary approach remains dominant" [3189].

In the same vein, years ago James Crawford advocated in favor of an integrationist approach, attempting to conciliate the differing positions in this field. On the one hand, a host State cannot rely on its own law to justify the violation of its international obligations. On the other hand,

3185. *Ibid.*, pp. 392-394:

> "The major question whether rules or, for that matter, principles of international law can be directly applied to a dispute between a State and a non-State party is clearly answered in the affirmative by the text of the Convention. If the intention had been merely to refer to the rules of international law which were applicable as part of the law of the State party to the dispute, the text could have dealt with them in the same manner as with the conflict rules and could have stated that 'the Tribunal shall apply the law of the Contracting State party to the dispute (including its rules on the conflict of laws and its rules of international law)'."

3186. *Venezuela Holdings* v. *Venezuela, supra* note 110, Decision on Annulment (9 March 2017), paras. 153-189.

3187. *Ibid.*, para. 181.

3188. "In addition, the ad hoc Committee was absolutely correct to note that the choice of international law was the rule of decision does not preclude the application of municipal law where appropriate. Furthermore, it has been argued that this approach contradicts the intention of the drafters of the ICSID Convention as expressed in the instrument's *travaux préparatoires*", Fouret, Gerbay and Alvarez, *supra* note 70, pp. 364-365.

3189. *Ibid.*, pp. 364-365.

a foreign investment "is, in the very first place and by definition, a transaction occurring in the host State and governed by its laws" [3190].

This integrationist viewpoint is also "pragmatic" and reflects prevailing ICSID practice. Within the integrationist approach, Schreuer explains that in focusing upon the facts of the case, tribunals will identify the various legal issues before them and place them within their proper legal context. Tribunals will then apply international law to certain issues and domestic law to others. In making this decision, tribunals will not have complete discretion in selecting between international and domestic law; they will have to identify the questions to which each legal system will apply [3191].

K. *Uniform law for supplementary and corrective purposes?*

In an influential scholarly work, Spiermann stated that:

> "Transnational law in the form of trade usages, the UNIDROIT Principles, or a *lex mercatoria*, may find sympathy with an arbitral tribunal resolving a dispute between a state and a foreign investor, perhaps to a higher degree than in international commercial arbitration in general." [3192]

Schreuer provides a different perspective, arguing that a comparative search of the applicable law is less useful where the host State's

---

3190. Crawford, *supra* note 484, p. 352. In investment arbitration, lack of restrictions as to the application of national and international law takes on added significance in light of the concurrent relevance of both sources of law to the investor-State relationship. See Kjos, *supra* note 2296, p. 296.

3191. Schreuer *et al.*, *supra* note 102, p. 630. Schreuer summarizes the current practice as follows (p. 626):

> "1. A tribunal applying the second sentence of Art. 42(1) may not restrict itself to applying either the host State's law or international law but must examine the legal questions at issue under both systems.
> 2. A decision which can be based on the host State's domestic law need not be sustained by reference to general principles of law.
> 3. A tribunal may render a decision based on the host State's domestic law, even if it finds no positive support in international law as long as it is not prohibited by any rule of international law.
> 4. A tribunal may not render a decision on the basis of the host State's domestic law which is in violation of a mandatory rule of international law.
> A claim which cannot be sustained on the basis of the host State's domestic law must be upheld if it has an independent basis in international law."

3192. According to Spiermann, given that the investment arbitration is already being internationalized in certain respects due to the principle of *pacta sunt servanda*, it must be considered whether other aspects of the investment relationship should be subjected to law other than national law, Spiermann, *supra* note 979, pp. 106-107.

domestic law offers a clear rule to one of the issues raised in the dispute. Furthermore, comparative searches do not guarantee that minimum standards of protection will be observed [3193].

Schreuer's position stated above assumes that public international law provides comprehensive rules for investment protection. On the contrary, several chapters of this work have demonstrated that public international law typically only provides broad standards and rules that are often subject to contradictory interpretations by tribunals. Comparative law, and particularly uniform law, can provide assistance in determining the scope of the standards to be applied when dealing with matters such as the interpretation of investment contracts. For instance, the UNIDROIT Principles comprehensively tackle issues related to the parties' legitimate expectations when entering into contractual relationships. As such, these principles can prove useful for supplementary purposes to interpret the broad standards provided in investment treaties, such as fair and equitable treatment or legitimate expectations in relation to investment contracts.

Furthermore, uniform law can serve a corrective purpose in relation to the domestic laws of the host State. If a solution provided for by local law is anachronistic or ill-suited to an international contract, the application of a neutral and balanced text like the UNIDROIT Principles can guide the adjudicator in exercising flexibility in their interpretive task, as authorized by several private international law and arbitral rules.

Andrea Carlevaris notes that trade usages appear unrelated to the general principles of commercial law and to an analysis of their role in international investment claims. However, certain commentary advocates in favor of a broad notion of trade usages, considering them as rules of conduct that complement the legal relationship and applicable regardless of the parties' express intention. According to this position, the distinction between implied terms to the contract and normative principles becomes blurred and trade usages thus apply, as do the general principles of commercial law, "without limits *ratione personae* (the practices established between the parties) and *ratione materiae* (the particular sector of trade concerned)" [3194].

3193. It will be difficult to argue that there is a general principle of law which is at variance with the host States law. Moreover, general principles of law do not necessarily set mandatory minimum standards which must be complied with. See Schreuer *et al.*, *supra* note 102, p. 620.

3194. Carlevaris, *supra* note 770, p. 210.

It is noteworthy that Article 21 (2) of the ICC Rules provides that "[t] he arbitral tribunal shall take account of the provisions of the contract, if any, between the parties and of any relevant trade usages". As pointed out by Carlevaris, the words "if any" and "any" were added to the 2012 revision of these rules to take into account situations in which no contract underlying the dispute exists, as is typically the case in investor-State disputes involving only treaty claims [3195].

Uniform law has, undoubtedly, an enormous – often underexplored – potential for supplemental and corrective purposes in relation to international investment claims issues not only emerging from contracts but also deriving from treaties.

3195. *Ibid.*, p. 209.

CHAPTER XXI

PUBLIC POLICY AND INVESTMENT ARBITRATION

A. Introduction

Public policy has been characterized as the *enfant terrible* of international legal relationships [3196] and by an old 1824 English case as an "unruly horse" (*Richardson* v. *Melish*). Like the Himalayas, its summit remains surrounded by clouds and its contours can only be vaguely perceived by the observer [3197].

Public policy as a source of international law is indeed a highly contested notion, and no consensus has been reached regarding its relevance and applicability [3198]. There has also been a lack of effective communication between scholars and practitioners, further complicating this concept [3199]. Most legal systems do not even have a statutory definition of public policy [3200], contributing to the confusion. Public policy is rendered even more obscure by the imprecision, diversity and confusion of the vocabulary typically used [3201]. Significant divergences exist in public policy nomenclature across civil and common law [3202],

3196. O. Kahn-Freund (ed.), *General Problems of Private International Law*, Leiden, A. W. Sijthoff, 1974, p. 174.

3197. C. G. J. Morse and M. Rubino-Sammartano (eds.), *Public Policy in Transnational Relationships*, Boston/Deventer, Kluwer Law and Taxation Publishers, 1991, p. 5 (preface).

3198. Morse, *supra* note 1303, p. 9.

3199. L. A. Mistelis, "Mandatory Rules in International Arbitration: Too Much Too Early or Two Little Too Late?", in G. A. Bermann and L. A. Mistelis (eds.), *Mandatory Rules in International Arbitration*, New York, JurisNet, 2010, p. 291 (concluding chapter).

3200. Only very few jurisdictions have codified a definition of public policy; Tunisia ("the fundamental choices of the Tunisian legal system"); United Arab Emirates (only regarding domestic public policy, but courts sometimes refer to it to define public policy in the international domain as well); United States of America (Art. 3540 of the Louisiana codification defines a fundamental policy as a policy that "reflects objectives or gives effect to essential public or societal institutions beyond the allocation of rights and obligations of parties to a contract at issue"). See D. Girsberger, T. Kadner Graziano and J. L. Neels (eds.), *Choice of Law in International Commercial Contracts: Global Perspectives on the Hague Principles*, Oxford, Oxford University Press, 2021, p. 110. Australia also defines statutorily public policy. See further in IBA Subcommittee on Recognition and Enforcement of Arbitral Awards, Report on the Public Policy Exception in the New York Convention, 2015, p. 2.

3201. Lalive, *supra* note 1646, p. 260, para. 3.

3202. According to the IBA report, "[t]hese principles seem, however, to be differently expressed by courts (and scholars) depending on whether they are in civil

and even within each of these legal systems [3203]. Disagreements exist to the unfortunate point that public policy has been characterized as a "catch-all" notion [3204] or a chameleon-like abstraction [3205] to be used in a variety of contexts and purposes [3206].

B. Notion of public policy

Public policy responds to the idea of the supremacy of the community over the individual [3207]. It protects political, social and economic institutions – for instance, freedom of competition – in addition to more vulnerable parties such as workers and consumers.

Whether public policy principles originate in private or public law should make no difference. It is the weight and intensity of public policy norms that matter most. The following question is central: does public policy express "essential principles of morality or justice" [3208]?

The notion of *ordre public*, included in Article 6 of the 1804 French Civil Code, was thereafter extended to other civil codes. This concept of *ordre public* in civil law is understood as "public policy" in the common law [3209]. The German Civil Code uses the terms "moral", "public good" and "good mores" to refer to this notion. German case law consi-

law or common law jurisdictions. In the first group, the definitions of public policy generally refer to the basic principles or values upon which the foundation of society rests, without precisely naming them. In the second group, on the other hand, the definition often refers to more precisely identified, yet very broad, values, such as justice, fairness or morality" (IBA Report on Public Policy Exception, *supra* note 3200, p. 6).

3203. See criticisms of the terminology and the confusion it creates in H. Alvarez, "Guiado por una mano invisible. El orden público al amparo del artículo 11 del Tratado de Libre Comercio" (Guided by an Invisible Hand Public Policy under Chapter 11 of the North American Free Trade Agreement), *Revista Peruana de Arbitraje*, No. 1 (2005), p. 15.

3204. H. Van Houtte, "From a National to a European Public Policy", in J. A. R. Nafziger and S. C. Symeonides (eds.), *Justice in a Multistate World: Essays in Honor of Arthur T. von Mehren*, New York, Transnational Publishers, 2002, p. 841.

3205. Craig, Park and Paulsson, *supra* note 837, p. 504.

3206. In the words of Juenger, nobody has defined this vague and elusive concept. Like pornography, one only knows it when seen. See Juenger, *supra* note 1201, p. 200.

3207. J. Carbonnier, *Derecho Civil*, Vol. 2, trans. M. M. Zorrilla Ruíz, Barcelona, Editorial Bosch, 1971, p. 266.

3208. Mann poses an example from private international law: "If, for instance, English law subjects the contracts of moneylenders to special rules, these clearly cannot be eliminated by submitting the contracts to a foreign law. But if a moneylender's contract is made in India where it is not subject to the restrictions imposed by English law, would it be invalid in England in case its terms run counter to the policy underlying the English legislation about moneylending? The answer should be negative", in Mann, *supra* note 1757, p. 129.

3209. Van Houtte, *supra* note 3204, p. 842.

ders all to be englobed under the encompassing concept of public policy[3010].

C. Public policy and private international law

1. Origins

The notion of *statuta odiosa*, developed during the Middle Ages, holds that a foreign law must be rejected when incompatible with the local court's system. Later, in the second half of the seventeenth century, Ulrick Huber advocated against the applicability of the legal doctrine of *comitas* or judicial collaboration in transborder transactions when its result could wrong the local State or its citizens.

The modern doctrine of public policy in private international law emerges from the writings of US jurist Joseph Story in 1834 and the French jurist Jean-Jacques Foelix in 1843. Subsequently, Friedrich von Savigny and Pasquale Mancini wrote on the topic, although their opinions on the theoretical grounds of public policy differed[3210]. Notwithstanding, public policy was established as one of the techniques that may be used by adjudicators in order to make the conflict of laws system operative.

As expressed by Paul Lagarde[3211], public policy would have developed in a very different way had the scholars of the time advocated for the direct application of the "better law", referred to by Magister Aldricus and the canon lawyers in the Middle Ages and defended in modern times by Friedrich Juenger[3212]. According to the "better law" theory, there is no place for public policy nor for conflicts of laws in general. Instead, the *ius commune*, *lex mercatoria* or (in modern times) the uniform law should be applied.

Mancini helped develop a different technique, further advanced by Charles Brocher toward the end of the nineteenth century[3213]. According to this approach, certain aspects of the law of the forum are fundamental and must always be applied in the jurisdiction concerned. Public policy is thus treated as a direct factor in determining the applicable law. In

3210. See Kegel, *supra* note 1264, p. 8.

3211. Lagarde, *supra* note 1458, pp. 3-5.

3212. See his general position in Lagarde, *ibid.*, pp. 3-5. The book is a revised version of a prior Hague Academy publication based on his lectures therein.

3213. M. Rubino-Sammartano, "Italy", in C. G. J. Morse and M. Rubino-Sammartano (eds.), *Public Policy in Transnational Relationships*, Deventer/Boston, Kluwer Law and Taxation Publishers, 1991, p. 13.

this positive aspect, public policy rules are also called *lois de police* in French.

Public policy has a negative facet as well, which has been developed particularly under the influence of Savigny. This aspect refers to public policy – *stricto sensu* – as an exception to the choice of law mechanism. This negative aspect repeals the legal rule that would apply in accordance with the conflict of laws technique when offensive to basic postulates of the local law.

2. Facets of the modern concept of international public policy

As a result of the developments described above, public policy has two facets in the international context.

The first precludes the use of the applicable law as determined by the conflict of laws rule if the result would be "manifestly incompatible" with the public policy of the forum. From this first standpoint, public policy serves as a "barrier" or a "shield" that bars the application of the law that would otherwise be applicable under the conflicts rules.

The other facet comprises "overriding mandatory rules" of the forum that must be applied irrespective of the applicable law as determined by the conflict of laws rule. In this second facet, public policy is manifested through "mandatory rules" applied directly to the international case, without any consideration of the conflict of laws rules that may point to a different result. Many State laws contain these types of provisions that function as a "sword" and apply directly to transborder issues, without regard for the intent of the parties or any other conflict of laws rule [3214].

3214. "The distinction is well known in Europe and Latin America. Australia and New Zealand – which legal systems are based on the common law – distinguish in their private international law system between overriding mandatory rules and public policy. However, the lawmakers of these countries have not further defined either of such categories", Girsberger, Graziano and Neels, *supra* note 3200, p. 103. The situation in the United States is quite different. In its statutory texts or court decisions, the term "overriding mandatory rules" does not appear. Further, the term is not commonly used in academic literature. Instead, the term "public policy" is used "to limit the effect of party autonomy, whether it is the public policy of the forum or of the law that would have applied in the absence of choice" (*ibid.*, p. 104). In Africa, there exists much diversity on this topic, due to the influence of the colonial legal system. For instance, "Tunisia and Egypt have been particularly influenced by the French law; Angola and Mozambique have been influenced by Portuguese law, while English common law has influenced the former British colonies such as Gambia, Ghana, Kenya, Malawi, Nigeria, Sierra Leone, Tanzania, Uganda, Zambia, and, in part, South Africa. In front of this diversity, attempts to find a common denominator are found within the framework of OHADA" (*ibid.*, p. 101). In Asia, a sophisticated system regarding public policy has been developed by various States. The same can be said, but to a lesser extent, regarding overriding mandatory rules. For instance, "South Korea and Vietnam have

These two facets of public policy as a shield and a sword have been called "two sides of the same coin" [3215]. Both aspects are contemplated in diverse legal systems and are generally included within the broad umbrella of public policy [3216].

3. *Domestic and international public policy*

Domestic public policy is a defense mechanism permitting the adjudicator to refrain from applying contractual arrangements contradicting it. As such, domestic public policy can be understood to have a corrective function [3217].

The situation is different in private international law, where domestic public policy will not necessarily prevail, as decided by the Cour de cassation in the famous 1950 *Messageries Maritimes* case [3218]. That case involved an international loan made in Canadian dollars, which were exchangeable for gold at a guaranteed rate. A Canadian law enacted after the conclusion of the contract devalued the currency and prohibited "gold clauses" without distinguishing between internal and international payments. The Court ignored this domestic regulation and declared that "the parties to such a contract were entitled to agree, even against the mandatory rules of a municipal law governing their contract, a gold value clause valid under a French law of 25 June 1928 in keeping with the French concept of international public policy". With its decision, the Court developed a different rule regarding gold clauses in international contracts – a sort of *ius gentium* – that was to exist in parallel to domestic law [3219].

Three leading Supreme Court cases in the United States also recognized the distinction between domestic and international public policy

---

adopted very detailed private international law statutes, whose general provisions and provisions on party choice of law largely correspond to those of the Hague Principles, including rules on public policy and overriding mandatory provisions" (*ibid.*, p. 102).

3215. J. Harris Q. C. and A. Dickinson, "Article 11, Overriding Mandatory Rules and Public Policy (Ordre Public)", in D. Girsberger, T. Kadner Graziano and J. L. Neels (eds.), *Choice of Law in International Commercial Contracts: Global Perspectives on the Hague Principles*, Oxford, Oxford University Press, 2021, p. 112. The same expression is found in Principios sobre la elección del Derecho aplicable en materia de contratos comerciales internacionales (Spanish version), The Hague, Hague Conference on Private International Law, 2016, p. 75.

3216. On the interplay of the different conflicts systems (unilateral, multilateral) and the role of public policy and mandatory rules in them, see Muir Watt, *supra* note 1252, pp. 278-280.

3217. Van Houtte, *supra* note 3204, p. 842.

3218. *Messageries Maritimes Case*, Cour de cassation (21 June 1950).

3219. Lalive, *supra* note 1646, p. 274, para. 55.

(*The Bremen* v. *Zapata Offshore Co.*, *Scherk* v. *Alberto-Culver Co.* and *Mitsubishi Motor Corp.* v. *Soles Chrysler-Plymouth Inc.*) [3220]. In these cases, instead of imposing a domestic public policy rule, tribunals required the creation of a substantive rule in accordance with the necessities and particular context of international commerce [3221].

The concept of international public policy is found – using this terminology – in Articles 1514 and 1520 (5) of the French Civil Procedural Code (amended by Art. 2 of the Decree 2011-48 of 13 January 2011), in Article 1096 *(f)* of the 1986 Portuguese Civil Procedural Code, as well as in the legislation of Algeria, Lebanon and Paraguay, to cite a few examples. Legislation in Romania and Tunisia also refer to "public policy as it is understood in private international law" [3222].

4. A "manifest" contravention of public policy

The US Restatement (Second) Conflict of Laws refers to "fundamental" and "substantial" violations of public policy [3223]. A leading English case dealing with this issue stated that:

> "It has to be shown that there is some element of illegality or that the enforcement of the award would be clearly injurious to the public good or, possibly, that enforcement would be wholly offensive to the ordinarily reasonable and fully informed member of the public on whose behalf the powers of the State are exercised." [3224]

All the Hague Conventions of Private International Law after 1955 use the word "manifest" to allude to the infringement of public policy, thus highlighting its restrictive character in the international field [3225]. In this way, they implicitly embrace the terminology "international public

---

3220. More recent cases confirm this position: *Shearson/American Express, Inc.* v. *McMahon* (8 June 1987); *Rodríguez de Quijas* v. *Shearson/American Express, Inc.* (15 May 1989). See ILA Interim Report on Public Policy, *supra* note 1583, p. 13. See also para. 187 of the Restatement (Second) Conflict of Laws, and para. 1-301 of the UCC.

3221. Lalive, *supra* note 1646, p. 275.

3222. Some legislation refers to public policy (or public order) and good morals, for example Japan, Libya, Oman, Qatar, United Arab Emirates and Yemen. See ILA Interim Report on Public Policy, *supra* note 1583, pp. 11-12.

3223. Para. 187 comment g (1971) of the Restatement (Second) Conflict of Laws.

3224. *Deutsche* v. *Ras Al Khaimah*, *supra* note 2274, paras. 769, 779.

3225. As stated by Jayme, *supra* note 894, p. 229.

policy" [3226]. The word "manifestly" has also been used by Article 16 of the Rome Convention of 1980, current Article 21 of Rome I, Article 18 of the Mexico Convention and other recent Inter-American instruments. The Hague Principles adopt the expression as well in its Article 11. The Commentary to the Hague Principles notes this expression's emphasis that where there is any doubt regarding the compatibility of the chosen law with the law of the forum, tribunals must nonetheless apply the law chosen by the parties [3227].

From a terminological stance, it is perhaps preferable to use the term "manifest" when referring to the incompatibility of the chosen law and the law of the forum. Other terms – such as "international public policy" or "truly international public policy" – are overly broad and insufficiently descriptive [3228].

When drafting the Hague Principles, a key consideration for the Working Group was restricting State interference with party autonomy. The drafters concluded that it is impossible to lay down precise guidelines on this matter, except in regard to the restrictive nature of public policy as an exception to party autonomy [3229]. The OAS Guide in the Americas follows the same approach [3230].

The distinction between public policy and international public policy is also recognized by resolutions and reports of the International Law Association (ILA) [3231] and of the International Bar Association (IBA) [3232], both specifically related to arbitration. In a report, the ILA included in its definition of "international public policy" the principles of universal application, comprising fundamental rules of natural law, principles of universal justice, *jus cogens* in public international law and the general principles of morality accepted by what are referred to as "civilised nations" [3233].

3226. See Rubino-Sammartano and Morse, *supra* note 3197, p. 20.

3227. Available at https://assets.hcch.net/docs/21356f80-f371-4769-af20-a5e70646554b.pdf, accessed 17 May 2022, p. 79.

3228. See Part Seventeen of the OAS Guide, *supra* note 1309.

3229. Consolidated Version of Preparatory Work leading to the Draft Hague Principles on the Choice of Law in International Contracts, Permanent Bureau, 2012, http://www.hcch.net/upload/wop/contracts_2012pd01e.pdf, accessed 17 May 2022, p. 32.

3230. See Part Seventeen of the OAS Guide, *supra* note 1309.

3231. A. Sheppard, "Mandatory Rules in International Commercial Arbitration: An English Law Perspective", in G. A. Bermann and L. A. Mistelis (eds.), *supra* note 3199, p. 174 (chap. 6).

3232. Both the Interim Report (see ILA Interim Report on Public Policy, *supra* note 1583, pp. 4-6) and Resolution 2/2002 dictated consequently. See also IBA Report on Public Policy Exception, *supra* note 3200, pp. 4-5.

3233. ILA Interim Report on Public Policy, *supra* note 1583, pp. 6-7.

The Final ILA Report on the matter conveys that some instruments include the term "manifestly" in reference to provisions or laws that run contrary to public policy wording [3234]. The report does not include the word "manifestly" in its recommendation. The public policy violation must usually be relatively obvious or clear, but scrutiny of the facts of the case may be justified in some circumstances [3235]. In this sense, "the court should undertake a reassessment of the facts only when there is a strong prima facie argument of violation of international public policy" [3236]. Further, the ILA Final Report states that "[i]f any part of the award which violates international public policy can be separated from any part which does not, that part which does not violate international public policy may be recognised or enforced" [3237]. The report notes that this separation criteria would not be inconsistent with the provisions and objectives of the New York Convention and the UNCITRAL Model Law [3238]. It also stresses that this approach has even been adopted by several courts [3239].

The matter of public policy and arbitration and its particular nuances will be addressed further in this chapter.

5. *Public policy as an exceptional escape clause*

Harold Gutteridge has argued that public policy is a serious menace to cooperation in matters related to private international law. An expansive interpretation of the principle of public policy can swallow the application of a foreign rule. Courts and tribunals have applied public policy principles in a contradictory manner, further complicating the matter [3240].

Lagarde proposes to resolve this issue via the following formula: in the absence of a special link with the forum, if the *lex fori* regulates the

---

3234. For example, the 1979 Montevideo Convention, the 2001 EC Regulation and the draft Hague Convention, in P. Mayer and A. Sheppard, "Final ILA Report on Public Policy as a Bar to Enforcement of International Arbitral Awards", *Arbitration International*, Vol. 19, No. 2 (2003), p. 252.

3235. *Ibid.*, pp. 252-253.

3236. *Ibid.*, p. 262.

3237. Recommendation 1 *(h)*.

3238. Mayer and Sheppard, *supra* note 3234, p. 258.

3239. For example, in *Laminoirs-Trefileries-Cableries de Lens SA v. Southwire Co.*, US District Court for the Northern District of Georgia, 484 F. Supp. 1063 (18 February 1980); *JJ Agio Industries (P) Ltd.* v. *Texuna International Ltd.*, 2 HKLR 391 (1992); *Societé European Gas Turbines SA* v. *Westman International Ltd.*, 2 Rev. Arb., p. 359 (1994), in Mayer and Sheppard, *supra* note 3234, p. 258.

3240. Juenger, *supra* note 1201, p. 258.

matter more strictly than the typical foreign law, this average should serve as a basis for comparison when assessing a manifest public policy incompatibility [3241].

The old English case *Richardson* v. *Mellish* (1824) suggested that public policy was "a very unruly horse, and when once you get astride it you never know where it will carry you. It may lead you from sound law. It is never argued at all, but when other points fail" [3242]. In *Enderby Town Football Club Ltd.* v. *The Football Association Ltd.* (1971), Lord Denning stated that "[w]ith a good man in the saddle, the unruly horse can be kept in control" [3243]. In the end, it is up to courts to determine the line between international harmony and local consciences [3244].

Moreover, public policy is often used as an "escape clause" to introduce "back door" rules contrary to those indicated by the conflict system [3245]. For this reason, Frank Visher asks whether it would not be more honest to simply admit an ample escape clause as a corrective mechanism to achieve appropriate solutions in particular cases [3246]. For instance, Europe has admitted the concept of alternative connections as a conflict of laws technique [3247], or a general exception clause for particular situations [3248], which ensures that public policy does not act beyond its proper function [3249].

3241. Lagarde, *supra* note 1458, p. 45.

3242. ILA Interim Report on Public Policy, *supra* note 1583, p. 35.

3243. *Ibid.*, p. 35.

3244. Khan-Freund, *supra* note 1256, p. 111.

3245. Juenger, *supra* note 1201, p. 258.

3246. Visher, *supra* note 1200, p. 106.

3247. See Reimann, *supra* note 1457, p. 114. Also G. P. Callies, "Coherence and Consistency in European Consumer Contract Law: A Progress Report, The European Commission's Action Plan COM, 2003, 68 final and the Green Paper on the Modernisation of the 1980 Rome Convention COM, 2002, 654 Final", *German Law Journal*, Vol. 4, No. 4 (2003), p. 333.

3248. In this sense, the 1987 Swiss Private International Law Act provides in its Article 15 an escape clause. The rule states the following: "As an exception, the law referred to by this Act is not applicable if, considering all the circumstances, it is apparent that the case has only a very loose connection with that law and that the case has a much closer connection with another law" (official translation available at https://www.fedlex.admin.ch/eli/cc/1988/1776_1776_1776/en, accessed 29 September 2022). This escape clause is also provided in Article 8, paragraph 3, of the Convention on the Applicable Law to Sales Contracts of 1987. The North American Restatement follows a broader formula: "Unless there is a more significant relationship with another State" as an escape valve to the result produced by the conflictual mechanism.

3249. B. Audit, "Le Caractère Fonctionnel de la Règle de Conflit", *Recueil des cours*, Vol. 186 (1984), pp. 349-350.

6. Nationality of international public policy?

When it comes to conflict of law, public policy protects against the consequences of admitting *in abstracto* the possible application of foreign laws through neutral conflict rules, which has been described as a "jump into the dark" [3250].

The main role of public policy is to offer a neutral mechanism to scrutinize the law that is determined through conflict of laws rules. Therefore, it is used to correct the blindness of the conflict system regarding the substantive content of the law that would be applicable within a particular case. Public policy obliges the adjudicator to evaluate the result and examine its compatibility in accordance with the *lex fori* [3251]. The forum ultimately controls the applicable law [3252].

In this regard, it has been said that international public policy is ultimately national and not international and that, as a result, the distinction is artificial. The term "international" is merely used when public policy operates within private international law [3253]. Already in 1929, the PCIJ, in the *Serbian Loans* case, established that, in the international context, the very definition of public policy depends on each country and, particularly, on the prevailing opinion of the legal concept at a given moment [3254]. The same has been said by the Paris Court of Appeal in 1965 and by the Belgian Court of Cassation [3255].

Article 1502 (5) of the French Code of Civil Procedure (currently Art. 1520 (5) due to an amendment made by Article 2 of Decree 2011-48), expressly mentions the "international public order". Well-known commentators argue that this represents "the French conception of international public order" [3256].

3250. Rubino-Sammartano and Morse, *supra* note 3197, p. 8.

3251. Visher, *supra* note 1200, p. 100.

3252. *Ibid.*, p. 139.

3253. The term "international public policy" is a "red herring" because it tends to confuse the casual observer into thinking that it invokes supranational elements. In fact, as demonstrated by two great twentieth-century scholars, Pieter Sanders and Pierre Lalive, the term "international public policy" is used to mean the international, as opposed to the internal, public policy *(ordre publique)* applied by national courts. See M. Hunter and G. Conde e Silva, "Transnational Public Policy and its Application in Investment Arbitrations", *Journal of World Investment & Trade*, Vol. 4 (2003), p. 378.

3254. The PCIJ stated that "[t]he law which may be held by the Court to be . . . applicable to the obligation in the case, may in a particular territory be rendered inoperative by a municipal law of this territory, that is to say, by legislation enacting a public policy the application of which is unavoidable even though the contract has been concluded under the auspices of some foreign law" (*Serbian Loans*, *supra* note 978).

3255. Van Houtte, *supra* note 3204, p. 844 and decisions therein cited.

3256. See ILA Interim Report on Public Policy, *supra* note 1583, p. 6.

In Portugal, Article 1096 *(f)* of the 1986 Code of Civil Procedure makes an express reference to the "Portuguese" international public policy. Several courts have also recognized the distinction, like the Swiss court in the *Omnium de Traitement et de Valorisation* (*OTV*) case [3257]. The nationality of public policy is approached differently in arbitration, which in principle contains no *lex fori* regarding the applicable substantive law, as will be discussed below in this same chapter.

7. "Regional" public policy

There is still a reference to an "inter-national" law, despite the fact that several non-State organizations are recognized as subjects of international law [3258] with legislative capacity. This is the case, for instance, of the European Union.

A particular public policy emerges from shared fundamental values, such as the ones emerging of regional integration [3259]. Several important issues arise related to this "regional" public policy. If regional regulatory powers are not exclusively granted to the head of the nation-States in the region but are instead distributed across various bodies at the regional level, it is difficult to understand why the conflict rules should always refer to the private law of a State [3260]. It also becomes difficult to understand why the concept of public policy should be limited to being taken from local rights alone.

For instance, the European Convention on Human Rights generates a regional public policy [3261], as declared by the European Court of Justice in the renowned *Krombach* (C-7/98) case of 2000. The European Union has mandatory rules regarding antitrust and concerning the free movement of persons and goods, as recognized in *Eco Swiss China Time* v. *Benetton* (1999) in relation to Article 85 of the Treaty of Rome

3257. See *Omnium de Traitement et de Valorisation SA (OTV)* v. *Hilmarton Ltd.*, EWCA (24 May 1999).

3258. *Ibid.*, p. 4.

3259. The matter has arguments in favor and against. See D. P. Fernández Arroyo, "El Derecho Internacional Privado en el MERCOSUR: ¿Hacia un Sistema Institucional?", in Universidad Complutense de Madrid (ed.), *El derecho internacional privado interamericano en el umbral del siglo XXI : sextas jornadas de profesores de derecho internacional privado : Segovia, 1 y 2 de Diciembre de 1995*, Madrid, Departamento de Derecho Internacional Público y de Derecho Internacional Privado de la Universidad Complutense de Madrid, 1995 (republished by EurolexSL, 1997), pp. 180-183.

3260. *Ibid.*, p. 6.

3261. See Jayme, *supra* note 894, p. 231. See also Loussouarn, Bourel and Vareilles-Sommières, *supra* note 1203, p. 54.

and other antitrust issues. In 2000, the European Court of Justice in the *Ingmar GB Ltd.* v. *Eaton Leonard Technologies Inc.* case (C-381/98) determined that certain provisions of community law may also be characterized as imperative [3262].

Moreover, in the European Union, a regional court such as the European Court in Luxembourg may feel entitled to tell the courts of that Member State which EU legal norms they should regard as *ordre public* and which they should not [3263].

Article 3.4 of Rome I addresses this issue specifically, stating:

> "Where all other elements relevant to the situation at the time of the choice are located in one or more Member States, the parties' choice of applicable law other than that of a Member State shall not prejudice the application of provisions of Community law, where appropriate as implemented in the Member State of the forum, which cannot be derogated from by agreement."

There is no analogous provision that addresses regional public policy in the Hague Principles, the Mexico Convention or any other regulatory text in the Americas. Perhaps this is because within this region, there is no supranational law similar to that within the EU. For instance, the intergovernmental law that emanates from the MERCOSUR organs must be incorporated into the domestic legal systems of its member States, just like that of any other treaty.

Regional public policy has been recognized in arbitral practice, such as in ICC Cases No. 6197 of 1995 and No. 4132 of 1983 [3264].

The MERCOSUR Permanent Revision Tribunal also recognizes the legitimacy of regional public policy. In its Advisory Opinion

---

3262. The European Union continues to amplify mandatory rules in common market in search of harmonization of regional legal order, particularly the internal market. See Sheppard, *supra* note 3231, p. 201.

3263. G. A. Bermann, "Introduction: The Origin and Operation of Mandatory Rules", *Mandatory Rules in International Arbitration*, JurisNet LLC New York, 2010, p. 5. See also G. A. Bermann, "Mandatory Rules of Law in International Arbitration", in F. Ferrari and S. Kröll (eds.), *Conflict of Laws in International Commercial Arbitration*, New York, NYU Center for Transnational Litigation and Commercial Law / Juris, 2019, p. 517.

3264. The case *Thales Air Defense* v. *GIE* is striking. Euromissile and La SA EADS France, Paris Court of Appeal, Decision (18 November 1994). In this case, the arbitrators decided not to apply a European peremptory norm on competition law. The Court of Appeal, taking the transnational vision to the maximum, said simply that it could not analyze that point under the public order complaint because that would mean getting to the bottom of the matter.

No. 1/2007, the Tribunal refers to the challenge that legislators face with respect to mandatory restrictions. It reads (in Spanish) as follows:

> "In universal and regional circles, it is often fervently advocated, with ever greater impetus, about the need for mandatory restrictions to also be harmonized, for the sake of a more effective integration of the different legal systems, and as such should be the goal of the negotiators and legislators of the MERCOSUR countries. These should aim for mandatory restrictions to be not only exceptional – so as not to detract from the principle of party autonomy, one of the pillars of modern contracting – but fundamentally, that solutions are homogeneous, as in the European Union with its various mandatory directives that concern international contracting." [3265]

The majority view in this MERCOSUR decision held that mandatory rules correspond fundamentally to two types of interests that must be protected. First, they seek to safeguard the so-called public policy of direction – that is, the authority of the State to intervene in matters affecting its sovereignty or economic activity, in addition to regulations such as those relating to currency or the defense of competition.

Second, each State typically creates its own public policy of protection in order to safeguard the rights of weaker parties in contractual relationships, such as consumers. This protection is established based on the understanding that there are scenarios in which the parties have not entered into the contractual relationship freely but under the influence of other factors. Thus, the scope of the State's public policy of direction or protection acts as an exceptional limitation upon party autonomy where necessary, and within the specific parameters created by the State. The Tribunal ultimately held that, where appropriate, specific abuses or violations of mandatory rules or principles will be ruled on by the intervening national judge [3266].

3265. Permanent Court of Review, Advisory Opinion No. 1/2007, "Norte SA Imp. Exp. w/Northia Laboratories Corporation, Commercial, Industrial, Financial, Real Estate and Agricultural s/Indemnification for Damages and Losses and Loss of Profit", petition filed by the Supreme Court of Justice of Republic of Paraguay, regarding the case file of the Court of First Instance in the Civil and Commercial Court of the First Court of the jurisdiction of Asunción, https://www.tprmercosur.org/pt/opi_consultivas.htm, accessed 17 May 2022.

3266. Permanent Tribunal of Review of MERCOSUR, Advisory Opinion No. 1 of 2007, https://www.mercosur.int/quienes-somos/solucion-controversias/opiniones-consultivas, accessed 9 June 2022.

Another important question arises regarding whether regional public policy is essentially a matter of "national" public policy. In 1998, the Austrian Supreme Court held in two cases that EU law was directly applicable to the Member States and, given its supremacy, should automatically be considered a part of Austrian national public policy (although some might consider this to be a minority view) [3267].

8. Transnational (or truly international) public policy

Transnational (or truly international) public policy is a creature of doctrinal writings, linked to the broader project of advocating for a *lex mercatoria* in international transactions [3268]. Transnational public policy is a child of liberal arbitration advocates such as Philippe Fouchard, Berthold Goldman and Pierre Lalive, who lived, studied and worked in several countries and developed a strong cosmopolitan appreciation for different legal cultures and traditions. Transnational public policy thus emerges as the underpinning legal justification for the construction of a transnational legal order, which transcends national boundaries and legal traditions [3269].

Lalive's writings have been particularly influential in spreading this concept. He advocated in favor of the recognition of a theory of a "truly transnational" public policy in relation to the most fundamental interests of humanity, such as the prohibition of slavery, respect for human rights, prohibitions against bribery, money laundering, drug trafficking, terrorism and stolen goods, and bans on human and organ trafficking [3270].

Lalive invokes several precedents that favor the notion of a truly transnational public policy. In the mid-twentieth century, under the impulse of Paul Lerebours-Pigeonnière, the Cour de cassation referenced the idea of a truly transnational public policy made up of principles of universal justice capable of conforming to a sort of *ius gentium* or common cosmopolitan law [3271]. Moreover, a 1958 ICJ decision between

3267. ILA Interim Report on Public Policy, *supra* note 1583, cases cited at p. 20.

3268. See J. Kleinheisterkamp, "The Myth of Transnational Public Policy in International Arbitration", *American Journal of Comparative Law*, in press; *apud* S. Brekoulakis, "Transnational Public Policy", in T. Schultz and F. Ortino (eds.), *The Oxford Handbook of International Arbitration*, Oxford, Oxford University Press, 2020, p. 122.

3269. *Ibid.*, p. 122.

3270. Lalive, *supra* note 1646, p. 286.

3271. See *ibid.*, p. 276, para. 62.

the Netherlands and Sweden stated that the latter country cannot invoke public policy according to the Swedish interpretation of this concept alone but must also take into account the practices and ideas of other civilized nations [3272]. Following this logic, Hersch Lauterpacht stated that public policy was a general principle of law in accordance with Article 38 of the ICJ Statute [3273].

French commentary and case law emerging from the Paris Court of Appeals (for instance, the *Fougerolle* [3274] and *European Gas Turbines* cases [3275]) and Cour de cassation (the *Hilmarton* case [3276]) confirm that public policy must be of universal application [3277]. If it is not universal, it must at least be common to several countries [3278], be international [3279] or recognized within the majority of States in the international community [3280].

The 1958 *Ragazzoni/Sethia* case is one of the leading English cases dealing with this issue and has inspired the idea that public policy must be universal [3281]. This idea was once again revisited in the 2000 *Kuwait Airways* case [3282]. The Swiss Federal Tribunal has also recognized this theory in several cases [3283].

Typically, the interests protected by transnational public policy are also contemplated within international treaties, which renders it moot to inquire whether such interests are safeguarded within the instruments

3272. Van Houtte, *supra* note 3204, pp. 845-846.
3273. Khan-Freund, *supra* note 1256, p. 28.
3274. *Fougerolle* v. *Procofrances*, Paris Court of Appeals (25 May 1990), Rev. crit. DIP (1990), p. 753.
3275. *European Gas Turbines SA* v. *Westman International Ltd.*, Cour d'Appel, Paris, not indicated (30 September 1993), 20 YB Comm. Arb. (1995), pp. 198-207.
3276. *Société Hilmarton Ltd.* v. *Société Omnium de traitement et de valorization (OTV)*, Cour de cassation 1st Cív., Case No. 92-15.137 (23 March 1994), in *Revista Brasileira de Arbitragem*, Vol. 5, No. 18 (2008).
3277. *Fougerolle* v. *Procofrances*, *supra* note 3274, p. 753.
3278. Lagarde, *supra* note 1458, p. 59.
3279. *Republique de Cote d'Ivoire* v. *Norbert Beyrard*, Rev. Arb. 685 (12 January 1993).
3280. *European Gas Turbines* v. *Westman*, *supra* note 3275.
3281. Lalive, *supra* note 1646, p. 280, para. 75.
3282. *Kuwait Airways Corp.* v. *Iraqi Airways Co. (No. 6)*, UK House of Lords (16 May 2002), para. 29, https://publications.parliament.uk/pa/ld200102/ldjudgmt/jd020516/kuwait-1.htm, accessed 17 May 2022. See Brekoulakis, *supra* note 3268, p. 124.
3283. *Les Emirats Arabes Unis, Royaume d'Arabie Saoudite and others* v. *Westland Helicopters Limited*, cited in *Bull. ASA 404* (19 April 1994), p. 221; see also *State agency A and State-owned bank B* v. *Consultant X*, Tribunal Fédéral, First Civil Chamber, 4P 115/1994 (30 December 1994), 21 YB Comm. Arb. (1996), pp. 172-80. Swiss Supreme Court, 4P.278/2005 (8 March 2006), *ASA Bulletin*, Vol. 24 (2006), pp. 172-180.

as such or whether they are safeguarded by the principles themselves. For example, the Agreement of the International Monetary Fund (Bretton Woods Agreement) expressly provides that the mere choice of another law within the contract cannot modify the applicability of foreign exchange regulations (Art. VIII (2) *(b)*).

Nevertheless, international instruments will not always offer an alternative to national laws in this way. The Universal Declaration of Human Rights, for example, lacks the force of a diplomatic treaty and, as such, is not an alternative source acting similarly to national laws. The situation is different in countries that have signed human rights treaties, such as the European Convention of 1950 or the United Nations Convention of 1966, as these texts have also been adopted by the respective national laws of the States, where they may be enforced [3284].

Moreover, when it comes to initiatives to combat bribery, the UN Convention against Corruption is the only legally binding universal instrument that exists on the matter [3285]. Other universal instruments have been created by private organizations such as the International Chamber of Commerce Rules of Conduct and Recommendations to Combat Extortion and Bribery [3286].

Lalive recognizes that there are comparatively few opportunities for the international arbitrator to apply the concept of transnational public policy, and bribery serves as a prime example [3287]. In any case, Lalive recommends that arbitrators exercise great caution in the application of their "creative powers" [3288].

Doubts remain whether it is convenient to establish a new category of transnational public policy, to be distinguished from international public policy [3289]. As argued by José Alvarez, the notion of transnational public policy has been criticized for being uncertain and unpredictable,

---

3284. Lagarde, *supra* note 1458, pp. 48-50.

3285. UN Convention against Corruption, https://www.unodc.org/unodc/es/treaties/CAC/, accessed 17 May 2022.

3286. ICC Rules of Conduct and Recommendations to Combat Extortion and Bribery, https://iccwbo.org/publication/icc-rules-of-conduct-and-recommendations-to-combat-extortion-and-bribery-2005-edition/, accessed 17 May 2022.

3287. See Lalive, *supra* note 1646, p. 286. para. 99. Brekoulakis adds the example of good faith, *supra* note 3268, p. 149.

3288. See Lalive, *supra* note 1646, p. 287.

3289. In this regard, Kessedjian points out that international public policy is different from the transnational one since it's State law. It consists of rules included in international conventions that are in force, that are mandatory and that the parties cannot derogate, in "Transnational Public Policy", in A. Jan Van den Berg (ed.), *International Arbitration 2006: Back to Basics?* (ICCA Congress Series, No. 13), The Hague, Kluwer Law International, 2007, pp. 859-860.

in addition to lacking a clear definition in terms of its parameters, substance and application [3290]. In turn, Michael Reisman warns against the "almost unlimited and protean potential" of transnational public policy, the application of which could lead to great uncertainty. By applying transnational public policy, international arbitrators relieve themselves of the burden of showing that the policy in question has become customary within international law, allowing them to act upon their own preferences instead [3291].

D. Public policy and public international law

Public international law is generally recognized as existing on a horizontal plane [3292]. However, certain of its norms have a superior status to others. These peremptory norms of international law, or *jus cogens* norms, are according to Article 53 of the Vienna Convention on the Law of Treaties "accepted and recognized by the international community of States as a whole from which no derogation is permitted" [3293].

From Article 53 emerge three basic elements of *jus cogens*. First, they are norms of general international law. Second, *jus cogens* norms are accepted and recognized by the international community of States as a whole, and third their derogation is not permitted.

An ILC report on *jus cogens* adds other elements that are not explicitly mentioned in Article 53 but are generally accepted in practice and scholarly writings. First, *jus cogens* norms are universally applicable. Second, *jus cogens* norms are superior to other norms of international law. Finally, *jus cogens* norms serve to protect fundamental values of the international community [3294].

3290. K. M. Curtin, "Redefining Public Policy in International Arbitration of Mandatory Laws", *Defense Counsel Journal*, Vol. 64 (1997), pp. 279, 282; Alvarez, *supra* note 3203, p. 31.

3291. W. M. Reisman, "Law, International Public Policy (So-called) and Arbitral Choice in International Commercial Arbitration", in A. Jan Van den Berg (ed.), *supra* note 3289, pp. 853-856.

3292. ILC Fragmentation Report, *supra* note 106, p. 166, para. 324.

3293. VCLT, *supra* note 470. Also Report of the Proceedings of the Committee of the Whole, 21 May 1968, UN Doc. A/Conf. 39/11, pp. 471-472; Vienna Convention on the Law of Treaties Between States and International Organizations or Between International Organizations, 21 March 1986, *supra* note 475, Article 53.

3294. ILC First Report on *Jus Cogens*, *supra* note 154, accessed 9 June 2022. This has been recently reaffirmed by UN General Assembly, ILC, Peremptory Norms of General International Law (*jus cogens*), Conclusion 2 [3], https://t.co/Hr74lL2tQh, accessed 9 June 2022, p. 1.

The *jus cogens* norms invalidate norms that conflict with them, whether emerging from treaty law or customary law [3295]. For instance, Article 103 of the UN Charter provides that

> "[i]n the event of a conflict between the obligations of the Members of the United Nations under the present Charter and their obligations under any other international agreement, their obligations under the present Charter shall prevail" [3296].

This provision is interpreted to mean that the United Nations' mandate of maintaining peace and security and protecting human rights forms part of international public policy and, as a result, all other treaty regimes must abide by the same [3297]. Consequently, United Nations member States, for instance, must comply with the UN Security Council's resolutions regardless of their treaty obligations [3298]. The *Nicaragua* case followed this logic; the ICJ emphasized the predominance of obligations under the Charter over other treaty obligations [3299].

The ILC report on *jus cogens* traces the roots of the theory of non-derogable norms to Roman law [3300], but notes that the adoption of the

3295. ILC Fragmentation Report, *supra* note 106, fn. 93, p. 166, para. 324, and p. 185, para. 367. Also the Restatement of the Law, Third, Foreign Relations Law of the United States, Case Citation, Rules and Principles, Part 1 – International Law and its Relation to United States Law, Chapter 1 – International Law: Character and Sources, The American Law Institute, 1987, p. 5.

3296. "Article 103 does not say that the Charter prevails, but refers to obligations under the Charter. Apart from the rights and obligations in the Charter itself, this also covers duties based on binding decisions by United Nations bodies. The most important case is that of Article 25 that obliges Member States to accept and carry out resolutions of the Security Council that have been adopted under Chapter VII of the Charter. Even if the primacy of Security Council decisions under Article 103 is not expressly spelled out in the Charter, it has been widely accepted in practice as well as in doctrine" (ILC Fragmentation Report, *supra* note 106, pp. 168-169).

3297. *Ibid.*, p. 21, para. 35. The Canadian Model Investment Treaty provides the following: "Nothing in this Agreement shall be construed . . . to prevent any Party from taking action in pursuance of its obligations under the United Nations Charter for the maintenance of international peace and security" (Canadian Model Investment Treaty, 2004, Art. 10 (4) *(c)*, p. 14).

3298. Presumably, Charter obligations would also prevail over inconsistent customary international law. The hierarchical effect of Charter obligations is not the invalidity or suspension of the conflicting obligation, but its non-enforceability in the immediate case. See D. F. Donovan, "Investment Treaty Arbitration", in G. A. Bermann and L. A. Mistelis (eds.), *supra* note 3199, p. 279.

3299. *Military and Paramilitary Activities in and against Nicaragua (Nicaragua* v. *United States of America)*, Jurisdiction and Admissibility, *ICJ Reports 1984*, p. 440, para. 107; ILC Fragmentation Report, *supra* note 106, p. 180.

3300. ILC First Report on *Jus Cogens*, *supra* note 154, p. 22.

Covenant of the League of Nations and a number of its provisions that reflect the principle of peremptoriness played a significant role in consolidating the notion in international law [3301]. An individual opinion of Judge Schücking in the *Oscar Chinn* case before the PCIJ in 1934 explicitly refers to *jus cogens*, admitting that the "doctrine of international law in regard to questions of this kind is not very highly developed". He concludes, however, that

> "it is possible to create a *jus cogens*, the effect of which would be that, once States have agreed on certain rules of law, and have also given an undertaking that these rules may not be altered by some only of their number, any act adopted in contravention of that undertaking would be automatically void" [3302].

Jus cogens was also invoked in an arbitral award under the French-Mexican Claims Commission, in the *Pablo Najera* case, in reference to the acceptance of the idea that there are, as a matter of principle, rules from which no derogation is permitted [3303].

In the 1930s Alfred Verdross wrote an influential article on the matter [3304] that later inspired the work of the Commission and the final text of the Vienna Convention on the Law of Treaties (VCLT) regarding the issue. This convention served to solidify the concept of *jus cogens* as part of the body of international law [3305]. Article 53 of the VCLT refers to the question, as well as other provisions such as Article 64 (emergence of new peremptory norms) and Article 66, subparagraph *(a)* (disputes concerning the interpretation and application of Arts. 53 and 64).

Sir Humphrey Waldock, the last Special Rapporteur for the VCLT, proposed a text on *jus cogens*, noting in the commentary of the provision that the concept is controversial, but the

> "view that in the last analysis there is no international public order – no rule from which States cannot at their own free will contract out – has become increasingly difficult to sustain".

3301. *Ibid.*, p. 13.

3302. Separate Opinion of Judge Schücking in the *Oscar Chinn* case, Judgment of 12 December 1934, PCIJ, Ser. A/B, No. 63, p. 65, para. 148.

3303. *Pablo Najera (France)* v. *United Mexican States*, Decision No. 30-A (19 October 1928), 5 RIAA, p. 466, paras. 470 and 472.

3304. A. Verdross, "Forbidden Treaties in International Law", *American Journal of International Law*, Vol. 31 (1937), p. 572.

3305. ILC First Report on *Jus Cogens*, *supra* note 154, p. 15.

He also cautions that rules having the character of *jus cogens* are the exception rather than the rule [3306].

After the VCLT, references to *jus cogens* by States and tribunals increased manyfold. By 2016, the ICJ had made, since its 1969 adoption of the VCLT, eleven explicit references to *jus cogens* in majority judgments or orders [3307]. The ICJ sometimes refers to *jus cogens* as "obligations *erga omnes*" [3308], and other times as "intransgressible principles of international customary law" [3309]. In addition, by 2016 there were seventy-eight express mentions of *jus cogens* in individual opinions of the members of the Court [3310].

In 2019, after five years of intense discussions, the ILC adopted a complete set of Draft Conclusions on Peremptory Norms of General International Law *(jus cogens)*. In its final wording, Conclusion 3 conveys the "[g]eneral nature of peremptory norms of general international law *(jus cogens)*": peremptory norms of general international law *(jus cogens)* that reflect and protect fundamental values of the international community are hierarchically superior to other rules of international law and are universally applicable.

According to the Special Rapporteur Dire Tladi:

> "Sometimes, the Commission . . . has decided to 'depart' from the text of the Vienna Convention and follow more closely

3306. Second Report on the Law of Treaties, by Mr Sir Humphrey Waldock, Special Rapporteur, *Yearbook of the International Law Commission*, Vol. 2 (1963), A/CN.4/156, p. 36, 89. *Ibid.*, Article 13, pp. 52-53. The term *jus cogens* first appeared in the Third Report of Sir Gerald Fitzmaurice, which was the eighth report on the law of treaties overall. See Third Report on the Law of Treaties by Mr G. G. Fitzmaurice, Special Rapporteur, A/CN. 4/115 and Corr. 1, under the title "Legality of the Object", *Yearbook of the International Law Commission*, Vol. 2 (1958), pp. 26–27.

3307. For instance, in *Case Concerning Application of the Convention on the Prevention and Punishment of the Crime of Genocide* (*Bosnia and Herzegovina* v. *Serbia and Montenegro*), Judgment (26 February 2007), *ICJ Reports 2007*, p. 43, paras. 147-184; *Accordance with International Law of The Unilateral Declaration of Independence in Respect of Kosovo*, Advisory Opinion (22 July 2010), *ICJ Reports 2010*, p. 403; *Germany* v. *Italy: Greece intervening*, *supra* note 294, p. 99, paras. 92 *et seq.*; *Questions Relating to the Obligation to Prosecute or Extradite (Belgium* v. *Senegal)*, Judgment (20 July 2012), *ICJ Reports 2012*, p. 422, paras. 99-100; *Application of the Convention on the Prevention and Punishment of the Crime of Genocide (Croatia* v. *Serbia)*, Judgment (3 February 2015), *ICJ Reports 2015*, p. 3, para. 87.

3308. *Barcelona Traction*, *supra* note 24, *South West Africa (Second Phase)*, *supra* note 957, para. 33; *East Timor (Portugal* v. *Australia)*, *ICJ Reports 1995*, para. 29; *Legal Consequences of the Construction of a Wall in the Occupied Palestinian Territory*, Advisory Opinion, *ICJ Reports 2004*, p. 136, paras. 155-157; *Legal Consequences of the Separation of the Chagos Archipelago from Mauritius in 1965*, Advisory Opinion, *ICJ Reports 2019*, p. 156, para. 180.

3309. *Legality of the Threat*, Advisory Opinion, *supra* note 1179, paras. 79 and 83.

3310. ILC First Report on *Jus Cogens*, *supra* note 154, p. 26.

> the practice. This was the case with the characteristics. The Vienna Convention does not mention 'hierarchical superiority', 'universal applicability', or 'fundamental values'. Although these characteristics are not included in the Vienna Convention, they are not inconsistent with it. They have emerged from the implementation and application of Article 53 and have become part of the fabric of the definition of *jus cogens*." [3311]

As noted by Patricia Galvão Teles, while it is true that the text of Article 53 of the VCLT does not refer specifically to fundamental values, *jus cogens* norms have some special characteristics that distinguish them from other rules of international law – hence their superiority. They are characterized not by coming from a special or superior formal source but rather because they protect the values of the international community as a whole. Therefore, the superiority comes from "a prohibition of derogation, the invalidity of rules that derogate from them, and the possibility of modifying such norms only by subsequent norms having the character of *jus cogens*" [3312].

Alain Pellet and Daniel Müller also note that *jus cogens* is not a "new" category of formal sources of international law:

> "It describes a particular quality of certain *norms*, usually of a customary nature, the existence of which is proven by an 'intensified *opinio juris*' which has to be established by following the same method as that relevant for demonstrating the existence of an 'ordinary' customary rule."

As a consequence, a treaty is void if at the time of its conclusion it conflicts with a peremptory norm of general international law; a peremptory norm can only be modified by a subsequent norm of general international law having the same character, and serious breaches to these norms entail special consequences in addition to the usual obligations resulting from an internationally wrongful act [3313].

3311. See P. Galvão Teles, "Peremptory Norms of General International Law *(Jus Cogens)* and the Fundamental Values of the International Community", in D. Tladi (ed.), *Developments in International Law*, Vol. 75, Leiden/Boston, Brill Nijhoff, 2021, p. 62.

3312. *Ibid.*, pp. 45-46.

3313. "However, this does not contradict the principle that the various sources of international law are not in a hierarchical position with regard to one another – but rather means that some norms, parts of a still rudimentary international public order, are, intrinsically, because of their content, superior to all others (whatever their source). According to Sir Ian Brownlie's often-quoted formula: 'The vehicle does not often leave the garage', and its legal stature is still partly uncertain", Pellet and Müller, *supra* note 239, p. 938.

However, several issues attracted fierce debate and disagreement within the Commission and even the General Assembly [3314]. Robert Kolb recalls strong opposition occurring in reaction to the notion that peremptory norms reflect and protect the fundamental values of the international community and are universally applicable and hierarchically superior [3315]. Uncertainties emerge if there is a hierarchical superiority of peremptory norms: the doctrine of *jus cogens* becomes tantamount to a doctrine of constitutional law norms. Then, something like the definition of a material constitution of the international community has to be established. In this understanding, *jus cogens* becomes a body of substantive rules of international law distinguished from all other rules [3316]. However, those who defend this position were never able to provide a precise list of such norms, and even when they are proposed, the list is not exhaustive. Moreover, argues Kolb, not only is the lack of proper identification of the norms a problem but also the lack of identification of the precise peremptory content of each norm [3317].

Further, another ILC report, referring to the fragmentation of international law, notes that it is a difficult challenge to determine which norm prevails between "conflicting *jus cogens* norms – for example the question of the right to use force in order to realize the right of self-determination". At this point, "it cannot be presumed that the doctrine

3314. The commentary on Draft Conclusion 3 states, among other things, that it provides a general orientation, recognizing that according to some views "such 'characteristics' have an insufficient basis in international law, unnecessarily conflate the identification and effects of these norms, and risk being viewed as additional criteria for determining whether a specific peremptory norm of general international law *(jus cogens)* exists". Commentaries to Draft Conclusion 3 of the Draft Conclusions on Peremptory Norms, in Report of the ILC, Seventy-First Session, 2019, https://legal.un.org/ilc/reports/2019/english/a_74_10_advance.pdf, accessed 9 June 2022, p. 150.

3315. R. Kolb, "Peremptory Norms as a Legal Technique Rather than Substantive Super-Norms", in D. Tladi (ed.), *Developments in International Law*, Vol. 75, Leiden/Boston, Brill Nijhoff, 2021, p. 1. "This conception hinges upon the idea that peremptory norms are the expression of a material public order of the international community" (*ibid.*, p. 22).

3316. *Ibid.*, p. 27, on a material public order of the international community. "It gives rise to the conception that no 'exception' whatsoever can be accepted in respect of such norms, neither derogation, nor non-application, nor inferiority of any type. The main elements of this substantive view of vertical collision of norms are: *(i)* fundamental values; *(ii)* giving rise to a public order of the international community *(iii)* hierarchical superiority of the norms flowing from the latter; *(iv)* from where various effects of those norms flow, ranging from nullity of the contrary norm to aggravated responsibility and amongst others and amongst others. If one goes to the core of the matter, the substantive view can be reduced to two elements: values and hierarchy" (*ibid.*, p. 22).

3317. Kolb, *supra* note 3315, p. 28.

of *jus cogens* could itself resolve such conflicts: there is no hierarchy between *jus cogens* norms *inter se*" [3318].

Perhaps the root of these divergences lies in the different theories that have been advanced to explain the peremptory nature of *jus cogens* norms. Natural law and positivism are the two main schools of thought behind the concept [3319].

According to ILC Reporter Dire Tladi, natural law generally assumes the idea of higher norms, whether derived from divinity, reason or some other source of morality as a basis for *jus cogens*. The problem here is who determines these norms. In practice, international law relies on the opinions of scholars, judges or officials, which often diverge. This position also runs against the text of Article 53 of the VCLT. By providing that peremptory norms may only be modified by other peremptory norms, these provisions recognize that norms of *jus cogens* are not "immutable", which is a hallmark of natural law. Moreover, Article 53 contains the requirement that peremptory norms be "recognized by the international community of States" – suggesting a role for the "will" of States in their emergence [3320].

Per the same report by Tladi, from a positivist stance, international law is only made by the consent of States, and thus norms can only achieve *jus cogens* status once consented to by them. But this position seems at odds with the idea of a higher set of norms from which no derogation even by the consent of States is permissible [3321].

Unsurprisingly, both approaches appear in judicial practice. The ICJ, for example, at times appears to endorse the natural law approach to *jus cogens*, while at other times relies on positivist and consent-based thinking [3322]. The case law of other courts and tribunals is equally

---

3318. ILC Fragmentation Report, *supra* note 106, pp. 168-169.

3319. According to the report, "a caveat is necessary here: there is no natural law theory to *jus cogens*, just as there is no positive law theory to *jus cogens*; there are, rather, natural law theories and positivist theories. However, time and space do not permit a detailed account of each – at any rate a theoretical treatise is not the objective here. Instead, broad brushstrokes of each school of thought are provided" (*ibid.*, p. 30).

3320. ILC First Report on *Jus Cogens*, *supra* note 154, pp. 30-32.

3321. Moreover, it is difficult to understand, if States have the free will to make any rules, why some rules cannot be derogated from by consent. Even if there were a way to address the question of emergence of peremptory rules through consent – or consensus – it is not clear why those States that have joined in the consensus could not later withdraw their consent, thus damaging the consensus. See ILC First Report on *Jus Cogens*, p. 32.

3322. Individual opinions of the judges of the Court have been similarly diverse. Many such opinions have expressed *jus cogens* as a rejection of positivism and an embrace of the immutable, natural law approach while others have advanced a positive law approach to *jus cogens*. See *ibid.*, p. 33.

inconclusive on the matter [3323], which has led to scholarly opinions that the binding and peremptory force of *jus cogens* is perhaps best understood as an interaction between natural law and positivism [3324]. Further developments must, however, unfold in public international law to achieve greater clarity on this matter and its practical impact.

On a final note on this topic, evidently *jus cogens* or public policy in accordance with public international law applies not only within this discipline but also in private international legal relationships. Later in this chapter the matter will be addressed regarding, in particular, foreign investment claims.

E. Mandatory rules

1. A sword

Public policy, as a shield, prevents the application of foreign rules that would otherwise govern in accordance with the conflicts mechanism. But in another facet, public policy also acts as a sword, consisting of mandatory norms with respect to matters such as antitrust, consumer law and transportation that cannot be discarded by the will of the parties [3325].

Mandatory rules that are relevant internationally apply directly in an international case irrespective of the law that would govern according to either the parties' choice of law or conflict of laws rules. These international mandatory rules limit party autonomy. In other words, the parties cannot circumvent them through contractual agreement.

There is also a difference in terminology with respect to mandatory rules that are relevant internationally. For instance, French law refers to *lois de police* or *règles de droit impératives*. The French expression *lois de police* was apparently used for the first time by Jean Bouhier, who lived between 1673 and 1746 [3326]. The 1804 Code Civil adopted the expression in its Article 3 (1).

3323. *Ibid.*, p. 34.
3324. *Ibid.*, p. 37.
3325. Commentary by Giuliano and Lagarde to Article 7 (2) of the Rome Convention on Applicable law (1980), in Giuliano and Lagarde, *supra* note 1290, pp. 26-28. There is no authoritative and exhaustive list of mandatory laws, but there is some agreement on the kinds of municipal laws usually considered imperative. They are those having to do with foreign exchange controls, environmental regulation, competition law, securities laws, company law, embargoes, blockades or boycotts and, sometimes, those laws that protect parties deemed to be in an inferior bargaining position. See A. K. Bjorklund, "Investment Arbitration", in G. A. Bermann and L. A. Mistelis (eds.), *supra* note 3199, pp. 239-240 (chap. 8).
3326. Rubino-Sammartano and Morse, *supra* note 3197, p. 10.

This notion was popularized in France by Phocion Francescakis some decades ago under the expression *lois d'application immediate*[3327]. The concept of "laws of immediate application" is close to that of mandatory rules, in the sense that it concerns material or substantive rules primarily intended to govern international transactions directly. However, the "laws of immediate application" do not originate as local rules that require extraterritorial application in specific cases but rather are norms designed to govern international cases directly.

Comparative law also incorporates other terms related to mandatory rules such as "self-limiting clauses" in laws *(norme autolimitate)*[3328], "spatially conditioned internal rules", "localized rules" and *norme di applicazione necesaria*[3329] in Italian law[3330], all of which pertain to the positive aspect of public policy "as a sword".

After centuries of referring to illegality or public policy, the term "mandatory rules" was introduced relatively recently within the common law tradition in England via the promulgation of the Unfair Contract Terms Act of 1977 and the Sale of Goods Act of 1979[3331]. The term "mandatory rules" includes mandatory laws in both the domestic and international spheres[3332].

One of the difficulties with identifying mandatory rules is that legislators typically do not indicate that a rule itself is mandatory[3333]. As a result, the adjudicator must do it pragmatically[3334]. This was the approach adopted by the House of Lords in *Boissevain* v. *Weil* (1950)[3335].

Mandatory rules do not take any particular form and can be found in any number of instruments. These rules may be set forth in economic or public policy laws, or in instruments designed to protect weaker parties in contractual relationships. For the purposes of facilitating international commerce and creating greater certainty with respect to international commercial contracts, it may be useful for mandatory rules

3327. The roots lie in Savigny's doctrine, Visher, *supra* note 1200, p. 153, when he spoke of "strictly positive laws", Juenger, *supra* note 1201, p. 201.

3328. Khan-Freund, *supra* note 1256, p. 95.

3329. Rubino-Sammartano and Morse, *supra* note 3197, p. 16.

3330. See other expressions in European legal systems in European Principles of Contract Law (PECL), comment on Article 1:103, https://www.jus.uio.no/lm/eu.contract.principles.parts.1.to.3.2002/portrait.pdf, accessed 17 May 2022.

3331. Sheppard, *supra* note 3231, pp. 176-177.

3332. See *ibid.*, p. 177. See the parallel with French law (*ibid.*, p. 174, para. 4).

3333. Visher, *supra* note 1200 pp. 154-155.

3334. See Fernández Arroyo, *supra* note 3259, p. 295. Adjudicators must attempt "to gauge the strength and depth of the attachment of the legal system in question to the values that the rule of law is thought to embody", Bermann, *supra* note 3263, p. 518.

3335. See Rubino-Sammartano and Morse, *supra* note 3197, p. 17.

to be codified or legislated. Codification would help avoid surprising parties to international contracts with a mandatory rule that is unwritten and not well known. It has also been said that

> "[i]t is not necessary that an overriding mandatory provision should take a particular form (i.e., it need not be a provision of a constitutional instrument or statute), or that its overriding, mandatory character should be expressly stated" [3336].

According to Bernard Audit, the development of mandatory rules is a result of the growing expansion of public law [3337]. On a positive note, Pierre Mayer stresses that mandatory rules contribute harmonizing legal solutions since their application does not depend on the adjudicator's discretion but on the purposes of the *lois de police* [3338]. This contention holds as long as their reach is not abusive, and the adjudicator considers it illegitimate [3339]. There must be a close connection and the consequences of the application of these regulations to the States involved must be measured. In this regard, Article 190, paragraph 2, of the Swiss Private International Law Act provides: "In deciding whether such a provision is to be taken into consideration, one shall consider its aim and the consequences of its application, in order to reach a decision that is appropriate having regard to the Swiss conception of law" [3340].

Since there is no harmonization of internationally relevant mandatory rules in comparative law, differing decisions still arise under similar circumstances [3341].

3336. "General Comparative Report", *supra* note 1330, p. 111.

3337. Audit, *supra* note 3249, p. 365.

3338. "Yet, there is a suggestion . . . that, while a rule might well be mandatory in the sense of displacing the 'otherwise applicable law' (as identified through the ordinary play of conflict of laws rules), it may nevertheless be one around which the parties may still be permitted to contract or one whose advantages the party meant to benefit from the mandatory rule may waive. It seems to me useful to leave very much open the possibility that a rule of law may be mandatory in the sense of being applicable, notwithstanding 'the otherwise applicable law,' but nevertheless subject to being derogated from by parties who clearly enough express that intention", Bermann, *supra* note 3263, p. 3.

3339. Mayer and Heuzé, *supra* note 1506, p. 86. Thereon, Hay points out that the Rome Convention, for example, aims, on the one hand, to ensure the protection of the expectations of the parties; and, on the other, to safeguard interests that States may have in protecting "weak parties" such as the consumer and the employee. These interests can be of the forum or of a third State. See Hay, *supra* note 1456, p. 396.

3340. F. Visher, "New Tendencies in European Conflict of Laws and the Influence of the US Doctrine: A Short Survey", in J. A. R. Nafziger and S. C. Symeonides (eds.), *Justice in a Multistate World: Essays in Honor of Arthur T. von Mehren*, New York, Transnational Publishers, 2002, p. 462.

3341. L. A. Mistelis, "Delocalization and its Relevance in Post-award Review", chapter 8 in F. Bachand and F. Gélinas (eds.), *The UNCITRAL Model Law after Twenty-*

2. Mandatory rules in private international law instruments

Various modern private international law instruments, including all the Hague Conference conventions on choice of law matters drafted over the past few decades, contain a distinction between public policy and mandatory rules [3342].

The Rome Convention uses the expression "mandatory rules" (Art. 7) [3343], while Rome I alludes to "provisions that cannot be derogated from by agreement" in reference to employment contracts (Art. 8.1) and "overriding mandatory provisions" (Art. 9) that are "regarded as crucial by a country for safeguarding its public interests, such as its political, social or economic organization". Recital 37 of Rome I indicates that the latter should be construed more restrictively [3344].

The Mexico Convention refers expressly to this issue in Article 11, paragraph 1, by indicating that "the provisions of the law of the forum shall necessarily be applied when they are mandatory requirements".

The Hague Principles similarly include the term "mandatory rules". Article 11.1 states: "These Principles shall not prevent a court from applying overriding mandatory provisions of the law of the forum which apply irrespective of the law chosen by the parties."

This issue was the subject of intense debate in the meetings of the Hague Conference Working Group; its members expressed some concerns regarding the detailed definition of "mandatory rules" or other equivalent terms adopted by pre-existing international instruments. Consequently, the proposal to include a definition was rejected [3345].

Five Years: Global Perspectives on International Commercial Arbitration, New York, Juris, 2013, originally published in Queen Mary School of Law Legal Studies Research Paper No. 144/2013, http://ssrn.com/abstract=2262257, accessed 18 May 2022, see p. 179.

3342. For instance, Articles 16-17 of the 1978 Hague Agency Convention, Articles 17-18 of the 1986 Hague Sales Convention and Article 11 of the Hague Convention on the Law Applicable to Certain Rights in Respect of Securities held with an Intermediary. Texts available at https://www.hcch.net/en/instruments/conventions, accessed 18 May 2022.

3343. A decision of the House of Lords of 1958 *(Ragazzoni/Sethia Case)* is usually mentioned as a precedent to this norm, in which the mandatory law that prohibited the export of jute to South Africa was taken into account in a contract governed by English law. It should be noted that, paradoxically, England did not adopt Article 7 (1); however, nothing would prevent the English judge from contemplating this situation. See Briggs, *supra* note 1198, p. 47.

3344. See Comment 37 of the "recitals" of the Rome I Regulation. According to Sheppard, this combines the European and American traditions, in Mistelis, *supra* note 3199, pp. 293-294.

3345. Second Meeting of the Working Group on Choice of Law in International Contracts, 15-17 November 2010, https://assets.hcch.net/docs/6580f1b8-86d2-4c74-bc79-b933ea0376cf.pdf, accessed 18 May 2022, pp. 3-4.

As explained in the Hague Principles, there is no required form for mandatory rules. Mandatory rules need not be provisions of a constitutional instrument or law and need not expressly state their mandatory or overriding character [3346]. However, two requisite characteristics serve "to emphasize the importance of the provision within the relevant legal system and to narrow the category". First, mandatory rules must be mandatory in nature, in the sense that parties may not derogate from them. Second, mandatory rules must be "overriding", in the sense that a court must apply them [3347].

The Hague Principles make clear that the impact of overriding mandatory rules is limited; the application of the law that would otherwise apply is constrained only to the extent of its incompatibility with the mandatory rule in question. The mandatory rule does not invalidate the rest of the applicable law, which "must be applied to the greatest possible extent consistently with the overriding mandatory provisions" [3348].

3. *Mandatory rules of a foreign State*

Some modern bodies of law authorize the adjudicator to consider the mandatory rules of another legal system not referred to by their conflict of laws rules. This authority is granted by the 1978 Hague Agency Convention (Art. 16), which inspired the Rome Convention and Article 9.3 of Rome I, which provides:

> "Effect may be given to the overriding mandatory provisions of the law of the country where the obligations arising out of the contract have to be or have been performed, in so far as those overriding mandatory provisions render the performance of the contract unlawful. In considering whether to give effect to those provisions, regard shall be had to their nature and purpose and to the consequences of their application or non-application."

Article 9.3 of Rome I may have its roots in adjudication. In a 1966 decision from the Netherlands, it was stated that

> "although the law applicable to contracts of an international character can, as a matter of principle, only be that which the

3346. Commentary 11.17.
3347. Commentary 11.16.
3348. Commentary 11.18.

parties themselves have chosen, it may be that, for a foreign State, the observance of certain of its rules, even outside its own territory, is of such importance that the courts must take account of them, and hence apply them in preference to the law of another State which may have been chosen by the parties to govern their contract" [3349].

Nevertheless, European case law on the issue is quite limited. More recently, in 2016 the European Court of Justice held that Article 9 (3) of Rome I does not prevent a court of a Member State from taking into consideration the overriding mandatory provisions of the law of another Member State (other than the place of performance) as matters of fact (that is, considering them indirectly) [3350].

Article 11 of the Mexico Convention also leaves it to the discretion of the forum "to decide when it applies the mandatory provisions of the law of another State with which the contract has close ties [connections]".

Similarly, Article 11.2 of the Hague Principles provides that "[t]he law of the forum determines when a court may or must apply or take into account overriding mandatory provisions of another law". This flexible and open approach leaves it to the forum to determine whether the overriding mandatory rules of a third State may be applied. Current practice and State opinions with regard to the usefulness of provisions of this type vary widely. The Hague Principles seek to accommodate this diversity by deferring the matter to the private international law of the forum [3351].

A recent comparative study detected differences between the "application" and the "taking into account" of overriding mandatory provisions of third States. These two scenarios may vary considerably, as do their requirements and consequences [3352]. Different provisions in national and international instruments do not require that these mandatory rules be applied directly. Rather, these provisions must simply be given "effect" or "taken into account" by adjudicators [3353].

3349. A. V. M. Struycken, *Alnati Case*, Netherlands Supreme Court (13 May 1966), Rev. crit. DIP 56, p. 522.

3350. *Hellenic Republic* v. *Nikiforidis*, Case C-135/1, 5 ECJ (19 October 2016).

3351. Commentary 11.19.

3352. "General Comparative Report", *supra* note 1330, p. 108.

3353. K. Siehr, "Mandatory Rules of Third States from Ole Lando to Contemporary European Private International Law", *European Review of Private Law*, Vol. 28, No. 3 (2020), p. 513.

F. Public policy and arbitration

1. In general

In arbitration, public policy is also a highly controversial matter and considered to be one of its most difficult questions [3354]. Due to the mobile character of arbitration, and because arbitrators are not judges or State officials, no law of the forum (or *lex fori*) exists [3355].

The *lex fori* contains private international law provisions related, for instance, to characterization, connecting factors and public policy [3356]. Now, since there is no local forum and foreign law in international arbitration, all national laws must be considered to exist on the same footing [3357] and no national law is granted a privileged status [3358]. Moreover, when arbitrators choose to apply non-State law, in exercising their discretion, their selection also implicates the application of public policy elements that exist independently from national laws [3359].

Arbitrators cannot ignore international public policy on the ground, or under the pretext that it does not exist within an organ of the State.

3354. M. Blessing, "Mandatory Rules of Law versus Party Autonomy in International Arbitration", *Journal of International Arbitration*, Vol. 14 (1997), pp. 58-59; also M. Blessing, *Impact of the Extraterritorial Application of Mandatory Rules of Law on International Contracts* (Swiss Commercial Law Series, ed. N. P. Vogt, No. 9), Basel / Frankfurt am Main, Helbing und Lichtenhahn, 1999. See ILA Interim Report on Public Policy, *supra* note 1583, p. 18.

3355. "When parties chose an arbitral situs, they almost certainly had no regard to the content – even mandatory content – of the situs' substantive law, particularly if they inserted a choice of law provision designating some other law as substantively applicable", Bermann, *supra* note 11, p. 314.

3356. Lalive, *supra* note 1646, p. 271.

3357. Statement like this are usually found on commentaries on arbitration. Born considers these overstatements. He says that "[w]here the law of the arbitral seat dictates the application of particular rules by a locally-seated arbitral tribunal through local mandatory laws that by their terms apply to an issue, and where no international treaty or rule of law precludes application of those rules of national law, then the arbitral tribunal is obligated to apply those mandatory rules; that is the consequence, under applicable conflicts rules, of the arbitration being seated within the relevant state", Born, *supra* note 2273, p. 2919. He has a point, but in several cases, awards annulled in their seat have been enforced in other jurisdictions. See *Pabalk Ticaret Limited Sirketi* v. *Norsolor SA*, Rev. Arb., p. 431 (1985), note B. Goldman; *Société Hilmarton Ltd.* v. *Société Omnium de Traitement et de Valorisation (OTV)*, JDI (1994), pp. 701 *et seq.*, particularly p. 702, note E. Gaillard; in *République Arabe d'Egypte* v. *Société Chromalloy Aero Services*, cited in Clay, *supra* note 2363, p. 159, among other decisions in this direction. See also F. Mantilla-Serrano, in García Represa *et al.*, *supra* note 1579, pp. 110-111. See more recently Bermann, *supra* note 11, pp. 315.

3358. Y. Derains, "Possible Conflict of Laws Rules and the Rules Applicable to the Substance of the Dispute", in P. Sanders (ed.), *UNCITRAL's Project for a Model Law on International Commercial Arbitration* (ICCA Congress Series, No. 2), Lausanne, Kluwer Law International, 1984, pp. 175-176.

3359. See ICC Case No. 3267 of 1980, cited by Lagarde, *supra* note 1458, p. 51.

On the one hand, arbitrators must strive to render valid and enforceable awards. On the other hand, arbitrators are legally and morally bound to consider relevant international public policy in order to meet the "legitimate" expectations of the parties. Arbitrators cannot be expected to establish or validate a manifest violation of public policy [3360].

The key question is not whether arbitrators should contemplate mandatory rules – or international public policy in general – but rather how arbitrators should determine what should be considered a mandatory rule or public policy for the purposes of each particular dispute [3361].

In this matter, there is also terminological chaos within arbitration. Article 1.3 of the UNCITRAL Arbitration Rules refers to "law applicable to the arbitration from which the parties cannot derogate". Alan Redfern and Martin Hunter use the expressions "mandatory rules" and "public policy" throughout their work [3362]. Lawrence Craig, William Park and Jan Paulsson use the terminology "contracts against *bonos mores*" [3363].

The terms "public order", "good morals" and "public policy" usually appear within arbitral awards. In specific reference to arbitration, the Final Report and Resolution 2/2002 of the ILA Committee on International Arbitration included the expression "international public policy", which distinguished between "procedural public policy" and "substantive public policy" [3364].

Recommendation 1 *(e)* of the ILA Final Report considers the prohibition of the abuse of rights, *pacta sunt servanda*, the prohibition against uncompensated expropriation, the prohibition against discrimination, the prohibition of activities that are *contra bonos mores* and the proscription against piracy, terrorism, genocide, slavery, smuggling, drug trafficking and pedophilia as examples of substantive fundamental principles [3365].

An example of a fundamental procedural principle is the requirement that tribunals be impartial. Other examples include the requirement that the issuance of the award not be induced or affected by fraud, corruption or the breach of the rules of natural justice, and the requirement that the parties be on an equal footing in the appointment of the tribunal, among others. The Committee that drafted the ILA Final

3360. Lalive, *supra* note 1646, pp. 272-273, para. 48.
3361. Sheppard, *supra* note 3231, pp. 172-173.
3362. Blackaby *et al.*, *supra* note 255, pp. 353-414.
3363. Craig, Park and Paulsson, *supra* note 837, p. 64.
3364. Mayer and Sheppard, *supra* note 3234, p. 253.
3365. *Ibid.*, pp. 253-255.

Report highlighted that "procedural public policy rules overlap with the requirements of due process, prescribed in Article V (1) *(b)* of the New York Convention" [3366].

In turn, according to an IBA Report, "alleged violations of procedural public policy appear to be slightly more likely to result in denial of enforcement of a foreign award than alleged violations of substantive public policy" [3367].

The challenge of applying public policy within arbitration is linked to the sovereign reserve made by States that can control arbitration both in the seat of the proceedings as well as in the enforcement stage. This challenge can be addressed by applying a more restrictive international public policy in this context [3368]. Arbitration has its own procedural and substantive public policy [3369] that exists independently from judicial proceedings [3370].

2. *International public policy in arbitration*

As a shield, international public policy in this setting dictates that arbitrators should proscribe bribes and the trafficking of arms, drugs or people [3371], regardless of the provisions included within local laws. ICC Case No. 1110 of 1963 is instructive in this regard, wherein single arbitrator Judge Lagergren decided that he would not preside over the dispute because the object of the contract was the bribery of government officials [3372], which he understood to be a gross violation of public morals and international public policy – even an "international evil". Judge Lagergren thus refused jurisdiction on the basis that the

---

3366. *Ibid.*, pp. 255-256.

3367. IBA Report on Public Policy Exception, *supra* note 3200, p. 14.

3368. ILA Interim Report on Public Policy, *supra* note 1583, p. 13; Carbonneau refers to the restrictive approach taken by successive cases in France and the United States, in Carbonneau, *supra* note 1469, pp. 32-33.

3369. The Recommendation 1 *(c)* of the Final ILA Report on Public Policy, approved by Resolution ILA 2/2002, gives a citizenship letter, as it were, from a forum of great descent, to the terms "procedural international public policy" and "substantial international public policy". See Mayer and Sheppard, *supra* note 3234, p. 253; Mistelis makes the figure of international procedural public order coincide essentially with that of due process, Mistelis, *supra* note 3199, p. 295.

3370. I. Suárez Anzorena, "La acumulación de arbitrajes: ¿acumulación de problemas?", in F. Mantilla-Serrano (ed.), *Arbitraje Internacional, Tensiones actuales*, Bogotá, Legis, Comité Colombiano de Arbitraje, 2007, p. 332.

3371. Van Houtte, *supra* note 3204, p. 846.

3372. Lagarde, *supra* note 1458, pp. 63-64. The case is from 1963, published in 1964. In this case, the arbitrator declared himself without jurisdiction. The alternative approach is to invalidate the contract and state that, notwithstanding, the arbitral tribunal has jurisdiction (ICC 2930/1982, *supra* note 2378).

parties "had forfeited any right to ask for assistance of the machinery of justice in settling their disputes"[3373].

In 1989, the Institute of International Law adopted a resolution in this regard, which states that "[i]n no case shall an arbitrator violate principles of international public policy as to which a broad consensus has emerged in the international community"[3374].

Since the arbitrators do not deliver justice on behalf of any State, they will be guided in their work by principles that can be extracted from comparative law or from instruments such as the 1997 OECD Convention on Combating Bribery of Foreign Public Officials in International Business Transactions[3375].

This instrument shows that the international community has developed precise rules related to combating bribery that can be applied by arbitrators as transnational public policy. These rules mainly refer to the definition of reprehensible conduct and to the inadmissibility of certain defenses that are frequently invoked. Thus, arbitrators that are presented with the argument that bribes made to a public official were minimal, or that there is a generalized practice of corruption in the State in question, may conclude that within the international community "[the] bribery of foreign public servants in order to obtain or maintain business is a crime regardless of the value or result of the bribery, the perception of local customs or the tolerance of bribery by local authorities"[3376].

When applied in this way, public policy is not negative, but positive – that is, it directly and positively influences arbitrators' decisions when matters of contractual morality or fundamental interests of commerce are involved[3377]. Arbitrators cannot apply norms that contradict these fundamental values.

3373. See ICC Award No. 1110 of 1963 by Gunnar Lagergren, ICA 1996, p. 11, para. 20. The Paris Court of Appeal, in another decision rendered on 25 May 2021, found that corruption does not need to be established in order to find breach of international public policy. Paris Court of Appeal, 25 May 2021, No. 18/18708.

3374. Institut de Droit International, Session of Santiago de Compostela, 1989, Arbitration Between States, State Enterprises, or State Entities, and Foreign Enterprises, 18th ed., https://www.idi-iil.org/app/uploads/2017/06/1989_comp_01_en.pdf, accessed 18 May 2022, Article 2.

3375. Convention to Combat the Bribery of Foreign Public Servants in International Business Transactions, November 21, 1997, Annex on the "agreed common elements of criminal legislation and related measures", point 3. The Convention is available at https://www.oecd.org/daf/anti-bribery/ConvCombatBribery_ENG.pdf, accessed 18 May 2022.

3376. Gaillard, *supra* note 836, p. 145.

3377. Lalive, *supra* note 1646, p. 313.

Loukas Mistelis describes a consensus in doctrinal writings that arbitration does not develop *sans loi* or *contra legem* [3378]. It is difficult to determine the basis to apply public policy in this context. It is clear that arbitrators must deploy their best efforts to deliver enforceable awards, even though this may be done merely by speculation on where the decision will be enforced. In this regard, the doctrine of transnational public policy and generally accepted public policy rules can bring sanity and sobriety to a field rife with uncertainty [3379].

A particular problem arises in contracts with the State when the law changes during the term of the contract and thus fundamentally alters its content: there are precedents in commercial arbitrations in which such changes that unilaterally affect the contract have been rejected by invoking international public policy, as in the ICC Case No. 1803 of 1972, *Société des Grands Travaux de Marseille and East Pakistan Industrial Development Corporation*, regarding a presidential order from Bangladesh that pretended to terminate the contractual obligations of the State company [3380]. As an alternative, a provision freezing the rights of the contracting State could have been included in the contract, which guaranteed that regulatory changes would not be made during the term of the agreement. Likewise, sophisticated long-term contracts usually admit the possibility of legislative changes and define financial consequences for the parties. Similarly, a change in the law of the contracting State can be accepted, but only so long as it is in accordance with the law of the co-contracting party. An alternative is to accept the change in the law, so long as it is in accordance with non-national rules such as general principles, equity, and so on. This occurred in an investment context in the three cases concerning the nationalization of the Libyan oil concessions during the 1970s (the *BP* v. *Libya* award, the *Texaco* v. *Libya* award and the *Liamco* award), referred to in Chapter VIII.

3378. Mistelis, *supra* note 3199, p. 306, para. 443. See also e.g. *Sapphire*, *supra* note 1013, reprinted in *International and Comparative Law Quarterly*, Vol. 13 (1964), p. 1012 ("[c]ontrary to a State judge, who is bound to conform to the conflict law rules of the State in whose name he metes out justice, the arbitrator is not bound by such rules"), in Mistelis, *supra* note 3199, p. 306, para. 443.

3379. Mistelis, *ibid.*, p. 308.

3380. Other cases may also be mentioned, such as *Setenave* v. *Settebello*, Case No. 723 of The Netherlands Arbitration Institute, and *Aminoil*, *supra* note 1059. See J. A. Moreno Rodríguez, "Orden Público y Arbitraje: Algunos llamativos pronunciamientos recientes en Europa y el MERCOSUR", *Revista Electrónica Lima Arbitration* (2007), fn. 88.

Invoking international or transnational public policy should not represent a problem if the parties have adopted international law directly through a selection clause, or if they have done so indirectly by opting for ICSID arbitration without mentioning a choice of law. There tends to be support within both international arbitration practice and arbitration literature for the recognition of at least some so-called international or "transnational" imperative principles [3381].

Specifically in reference to arbitration, Emmanuel Gaillard observes that courts appear reluctant to privilege the application of the *lois de police* of a State if they do not correspond to a norm generally recognized by the international community regarding the provisions of the law chosen by the parties. This is true irrespective of the forcefulness of the policy that the *lois de police* claim to reflect. ICC Case No. 7047 of 1994 illustrates this view [3382].

3. *Mandatory rules in arbitration*

As a sword in the arbitration context, in a well-known ICC case the application of *lois de police* was favored where it would have a direct impact on the performance of the contract (ICC Case No. 1399) [3383].

Now, a choice of law issue arises of whether the parties are able to displace the mandatory rules of their chosen law. As noted by George Bermann, this matter is controversial as is the application of mandatory legal norms other than the law chosen by the parties [3384]. Some scholars consider the mandatory rules of the seat applicable because if parties that have consented to an arbitral seat fail to comply with its mandatory rules, courts of that jurisdiction can annul the award. In response, Bermann argues that "an arbitral tribunal should have pause before disregarding the parties' choice of law in favour of the mandatory law of the arbitral situs". This is because, as he explains, the mandatory law of the seat could be objectionable from a substantive point of view. For instance, a mandatory law of the seat that undermines the international arbitration institution as a whole might be considered objectionable in this regard [3385].

3381. Bermann, *supra* note 3263, p. 21.
3382. ICC Case No. 7047 (28 February 1994), see Gaillard, *supra* note 836, p. 143.
3383. See Mistelis, *supra* note 3199, p. 298.
3384. Bermann, *supra* note 11, pp. 312-313.
3385. *Ibid.*, p. 313.

Furthermore, the selection of an arbitral seat relates principally to the selection of a legal framework for the conduct of the proceedings or, in short, a procedural *lex arbitri*. It is unreasonable to expect that the parties should be bound by that jurisdiction's mandatory rules on substantive matters. In short, "parties almost certainly had no regard, in choosing the situs, to the content – even mandatory content – of the situs' substantive law, particularly if they inserted a choice of law provision designating some other law as substantively applicable" [3386].

In principle, applying the laws of a third jurisdiction undermines the value of autonomy and the notion of international arbitration. However, arbitrators have a public role and function to fulfill, and cannot turn a blind eye to the values that underly truly imperative norms, irrespective of their source. The political role of the tribunal is thus enhanced in investment arbitrations [3387].

In a well-known arbitral case, it was decided that the public policy of a third State and the location of the headquarters or the seat of incorporation of a business entity must be considered when it comes to determining incapacity or establishing the party's authority to enter into an agreement. This is because lack of capacity is grounds to deny enforcement of an award [3388].

Even though commentators support the possibility of applying the public policy of a third country, they also point out that this rarely occurs in practice [3389]. The CJEU has only recently ruled on this issue in the 2016 *Hellenic Republic* v. *Nikiforidis* case. The Court stated that "a court of the forum is precluded from applying mandatory rules of a 'third country', unless this third country is where the obligations arising out of the contract had to be or have been performed" [3390].

The case for arbitral tribunals giving effect to the mandatory law of a third country is stronger than for national judges. Since international arbitrators owe no allegiance to the substantive law of a jurisdiction, they enjoy a greater freedom when it comes to applying the mandatory rules of law of third countries [3391]. This may most often be the case

---

3386. *Ibid.*, pp. 313-314.
3387. Bermann, *supra* note 3263, p. 11.
3388. *Videocon Power Limited, Rep.* v. *Tamil Nadu Electricity Board*, Madras High Court, ARBLR 399 Madras (9 December 2004). See also Sheppard, *supra* note 3231, p. 203.
3389. Bermann, *supra* note 3263, pp. 522-523.
3390. *Hellenic Republic* v. *Nikiforidis*, Case C-135/15, ECLI:EU:C:2016:774, 2016. See Bermann, *supra* note 3263, p. 522.
3391. Bermann, *supra* note 3263, p. 523.

regarding the mandatory rules of the potential place of enforcement of the award. If these mandatory rules can be identified in advance, arbitrators would be "foolish" to disregard them [3392].

4. Public policy and enforcement of awards

Public policy as a ground for refusing to recognize or enforce foreign awards is provided for in Article V (2) of the New York Convention and in Article 36 of the UNCITRAL Model Law.

However, problems occur when judges assimilate local "mandatory" rules and the international public policy of the forum without further examination or reflection, which can lead to the annulment of or refusal to recognize the arbitral award without any substantive reason [3393]. Fortunately, adjudicators typically interpret this point quite restrictively [3394]. In several States, courts have a policy to give effect to arbitral awards to the greatest extent possible, rather than providing incentives to resort to litigation before its courts [3395].

According to an ILA Report, "many courts have expressed a policy favouring enforcement" as in the case *Eco Swiss China Time* v. *Benetton* (1999). In that case, the European Court of Justice stated:

> "[I]t is in the interest of efficient arbitration proceedings that review of arbitration awards should be limited in scope and that annulment of or refusal to recognise an award should be possible only in exceptional circumstances."

The ILA Report has endorsed that policy and recommends that "enforcement should be refused only in exceptional circumstances" [3396].

Bermann has pointed out that discussions on this topic are mainly doctrinal or academic [3397]. However, domestic courts "have had occasion to consider withholding recognition or enforcement of awards on public

3392. *Ibid.*, p. 524.

3393. Lalive, *supra* note 1646, p. 313, para. 6.

3394. See IBA Report on Public Policy Exception, *supra* note 3200, p. 12.

3395. R. J. Caivano, "El Rol del Poder Judicial en el Arbitraje Comercial Internacional", in OAS, *Arbitragem Comercial Internacional. Reconocimiento y Ejecución de Laudos Arbitrales Extranjeros*, São Paulo, Editorial LTr, 1998, p. 157.

3396. Mayer and Sheppard, *supra* note 3234, pp. 250-253. The public policy exception to enforcement should, according to the majority of the Committee, be restricted "to the greatest extent possible". However, some members of the Committee – mainly from developing countries – did not share this view but considered that "[s]tate courts should be entitled to protect the State from perverse and/or prejudiced awards, and there should be no attempt to restrict the scope of public policy".

3397. Bermann, *supra* note 14, p. 60.

policy grounds" [3398]. For instance, in the *Ogden Entertainment Services Inc.* v. *Eijo, Néstor E.* case, the Argentine Court "refused to enforce an award that had imposed on the prevailing party costs that greatly exceeded the value of the award itself that had been rendered in favor of the prevailing party. Enforcement under these circumstances was found to violate public policy because it vitiated access to justice" [3399]. A similar conclusion was reached in the *Subway Franchise Systems of Canada Ltd.* v. *Laitch* case, wherein a Canadian court rejected a foreign award because the award afforded a party double recovery [3400]. Furthermore, in the *Nisan Albert Gad* v. *David Simon Tov* case, an Israeli court "refused to enforce a foreign award that in turn enforced an agreement to bribe public officials, even though the conduct had all taken place in a jurisdiction that tolerates the bribery of public officials" [3401].

The New York Convention refers to the public policy "of that country". The negotiators of the Convention did not, therefore, surreptitiously seek to harmonize public policy or establish a common international standard, despite the fact that the Drafting Committee referenced certain terms alluding to the requirement of a clear incompatibility with public policy or fundamental principles of law. The inclusion of these terms would obviously have led to a broader conception of public policy approaching a universal standard; however, these terms were ultimately not adopted in the final text [3402].

The ILA Final Report has also opined on the matter, writing that "the drafters of the various international conventions and the UNCITRAL Model Law did not seek to prescribe a universal standard of public policy". The only exception to this is the 1999 OHADA Uniform Arbitration Law, which states that enforcement shall be refused if the "award is manifestly contrary to a rule of international public policy of the Member States". In a similar sense, the European Court of Justice might develop a common public policy amid the members of the European community [3403].

3398. *Ibid.*, p. 60.

3399. *Ogden Entertainment Services Inc.* v. *Eijo*, Néstor E, National Commercial Court of Appeals, Buenos Aires, Chamber E (20 September 2004), cited in *La Ley*, Vol. 2005-B, p. 21.

3400. *Subway Franchise Systems of Canada Ltd.* v. *Laitch*, SKQB 249, 206 ACWS (3d) 655 (2011).

3401. *Nisan Albert Gad* v. *David Simon Tov*, Case No. 2103/03, Jerusalem District Court, 2003.

3402. ILA Interim Report on Public Policy, *supra* note 1583, p. 8.

3403. Mayer and Sheppard, *supra* note 3234, p. 254.

Despite the fact that few harmonization efforts have been made, the ILA Final Report found that the majority of State courts applied a restrictive approach when interpreting and relying on the notion of public policy. The Committee highlighted that this "has resulted in a notable consistency of decisions amongst courts of different countries and legal traditions" [3404].

5. The Hague Principles and public policy in arbitration

The question of public policy in arbitration was one of the "most sensitive" issues addressed in the drafting of the Hague Principles [3405]. The guidelines offered in Article 11.5 of the Hague Principles do not "confer any additional powers on arbitral tribunals" and do not "purport to give those tribunals an unlimited and unfettered discretion to depart from the law" that is applicable in principle. On the contrary, tribunals might be required to take public policy and mandatory rules into account and determine the extent to which they must prevail over other rules in the specific case [3406].

> "As seen before, according to Article 11 of the Hague Principles, arbitrators may, on an exceptional basis, apply two categories of restrictions on the application of the law chosen by the parties: overriding mandatory provisions, and public policy (*ordre public*). These two categories are dealt with in separate provisions in recent national and international instruments. In line with their restrictive approach, the Hague Principles also emphasize the exceptional character of both public policy and overriding mandatory provisions in the context of arbitration." [3407]

3404. *Ibid.*

3405. Consolidated version, http://www.hcch.net/upload/wop/contracts_2012pd01e.pdf, accessed 18 May 2022.

3406. Similarly, Giuliano and Lagarde, referring to Article 16 of the Rome Convention, explained that: "Public policy is only to be taken into account where a certain provision of the specified law, if applied in an actual case, would lead to consequences contrary to the public policy *(ordre public)* of the forum. It may therefore happen that a foreign law, which might in the abstract be held to be contrary to the public policy of the forum, could nevertheless be applied, if the actual result of its being applied does not in itself offend the public policy of the forum", in Giuliano and Lagarde, *supra* note 1290, p. 38.

3407. Principles on Choice of Law in International Commercial Contracts, The Hague Conference on Private International Law, Permanent Bureau, Netherlands, 2015, p. 73, available at https://www.hcch.net/, accessed 18 May 2022. The OAS Guide follows the Hague Principles on this topic in its Part 17, VI, see *supra* note 1284.

G. Public policy in investment arbitration

1. In general

The terminology used in reference to public policy in investment arbitration is also not homogeneous. For instance, Christoph Schreuer refers to "peremptory rules of international law" and "international public policy" [3408]. He also alludes to "mandatory rules of international law" that must be observed, such as the prohibition of the denial of justice, the discriminatory taking of property and the arbitrary repudiation of contractual undertakings. These apply independently of any choice of law and are the public order framework within which such transactions operate. This framework is not open to the disposition of the parties [3409].

Since it draws upon the classical party-driven model of arbitration, it has been said that no rethinking is required for international arbitration investment-related issues [3410] regarding, for instance, public policy. However, many caveats must be made to this statement, as will be discussed in this section.

Public policy issues may become relevant in several matters related to international investment arbitration [3411], including incidental issues that may arise regarding norms governing access to information, environmental laws or foreign exchange control regulations. Public policy matters may also relate to subjective non-arbitrability (or incapacity of the State to arbitrate), the absence of special powers by the signatory of an arbitration agreement, immunity from jurisdiction and contracts in violation of a United Nations resolution or embargo, among others [3412].

3408. Schreuer *et al.*, *supra* note 102, p. 566.

3409. *Ibid.*, p. 587, para. 115.

3410. D. F. Donovan and A. K. A. Greenawalt, "Mitsubishi After Twenty Years: Mandatory Rules before Courts and International Arbitrators", L. A. Mistelis and J. Lew (eds.), *Pervasive Problems in International Arbitration*, The Hague, Kluwer Law International, 2006, pp. 53-54.

3411. Investment claims include a concept of public policy that operates at the international level amid "general principles of law", Z. Douglas, "The Plea of Illegality in Investment Treaty Arbitration", *ICSID Review: Foreign Investment Law Journal*, Vol. 29 (2014), p. 169. When addressing the rules that are applicable to an international investment dispute based on a treaty, Richard Kreindler refers to "principles of international law, including transnational public policy", in "Competence-Competence in the Face of Illegality in Contracts and Arbitration Agreements", *Recueil des cours*, Vol. 361 (2013), p. 218.

3412. See Hunter and Conde e Silva, *supra* note 3253, pp. 369-370.

Moreover, some investment arbitrations are contract-based rather than treaty-based. In these cases, the transaction will be subject not only to the *lex causae* but potentially to the mandatory laws of third countries as well [3413]. The following pages will consider these scenarios in particular.

Another issue relates to the possibility for arbitrators to disregard laws in a national system that violate superior domestic laws, which often occurs due to the impugned law's conflict with a constitution. According to Paulsson, "[i]nternational courts and tribunals must have at least equally great authority if their duty to apply the national law is to have its full meaning" [3414]. Even though international tribunals have no national *lex fori*, their members routinely deal with the interpretation and application of national norms. When doing so, they must not become paralyzed by declarations or decisions of the State, its legislature or its judiciary. If the State, for instance, violates its own fundamental laws, in the words of Paulsson,

> "an international tribunal empowered to apply that national law should not give effect to them – and is under no obligation to wait for the national courts (if ever) to make such a determination; the international tribunal's authority to determine and apply that national law is plenary. . . . When the tribunal does so, it is proper for it to refuse to recognize unlawful laws" [3415].

3413. "Moreover, respondent States may interpose counterclaims or setoffs in an investment arbitration that, in the view of those States at least, implicate their own mandatory rules of law", Bjorklund, *supra* note 3325, p. 22, fn. 55.

3414. Paulsson, *supra* note 3130, p. 224.

3415. *Ibid.*, p. 224. At p. 232:

> "We should naturally consider the effect of the application of national corrective norms on perceptions of the legitimacy of international adjudication. It may be argued, on the one hand, that national sentiment could be offended when international adjudicators presume to apply national norms understandable only to those who are part of the national community. Certainly it is likely that the government of the day, and its supporters of the day, will take umbrage. But on the other hand, as long as international adjudicators are mandated to apply the national law (which is after all something which *ex hypothesi* the relevant State insisted on when committing to international jurisdiction), they simply cannot do so selectively; the difficult questions are precisely the ones likely to be important. In the long run, when a government has overreached, when it has cowed legislators or judges, when it has followed a practice of weakening the judiciary, even citizens of the country whose law is in question may come to see the international tribunal as a defender of enduring national values."

2. International or transnational public policy in investment arbitration

Martin Hunter and Gui Conde highlight that many arbitrators do not realize, or at least do not mention expressly, that they are applying international or transnational public policy principles in their decisions, as was the case in *SD Myers* v. *Canada*[3416]. Nuances of these terms have been addressed earlier in this chapter. Here, both expressions will be used interchangeably.

In investment arbitration, only international or transnational public policy ought to be relevant[3417]. Host States may not rely on their national public policy to override a rule or principle of international or transnational public policy. This is because, by its very nature, transnational or international public policy is based on internationally and commonly recognized principles "that must be accepted without question"[3418].

Matters involving the application of transnational or international public policy often relate to corruption or fraud, which have both been addressed in ICSID cases[3419]. In the *World Duty Free* v. *Kenya* decision, the Tribunal stated that it would

> "have been minded to decline in the present case to recognize any local custom in Kenya purporting to validate bribery committed by the Claimant in violation of international public policy"[3420].

3416. "If the Tribunal had been told that it had in fact applied no less than six principles of transnational public policy in its First Partial Award (on liability), the individual arbitrators would no doubt have been astonished", Hunter and Conde e Silva, *supra* note 3253, p. 370).

3417. Mistelis, *supra* note 3199, p. 304.

3418. Hunter and Conde e Silva, *supra* note 3253, p. 374.

3419. "If any theoretical justification is needed for this matter, it can be found in the fact that the Convention is rooted in international law which, in a wider sense, is the *lex fori* of ICSID arbitration", Schreuer *et al.*, *supra* note 102, p. 566.

3420. See *World Duty Free* v. *Kenya*, *supra* note 1081, Award (4 October 2006), paras. 158 and 172. In *Niko Resources* v. *Bangladesh*, the Tribunal followed the *World Duty Free* v. *Kenya*, stating "The Tribunal therefore accepts without further development that the prohibition of bribery forms part of international public policy" (ICSID Case No. ARB/10/18, Decision on Jurisdiction, 19 August 2013, paras. 431-433). The Tribunal also ruled that "[a] contract in conflict with international public policy cannot be given effect by arbitrators" (*ibid.*, para. 434). In *Unión Fenosa Gas* v. *Egypt*, the Tribunal concluded that "the effect of international public policy [implies that] proven corruption by the Claimant in procuring the [sale and purchase agreement] would be fatal to the Claimant's claims . . . as regards jurisdiction, admissibility and the merits" (*Unión Fenosa Gas, SA* v. *Arab Republic of Egypt*, ICSID Case No. ARB/14/4, Award (31 August 2018), para. 7.48). This statement was endorsed by Mark Clodfelter in his Dissenting Opinion: "I fully concur with the majority's determination that such corruption, if proven, would, under the [t]reaty and as a matter of international public policy under international law, defeat jurisdiction over the claims, deny their

In the *Inceysa* case brought against El Salvador [3421], the Tribunal recurred to the notion of "international public policy" to refuse jurisdiction on a dispute arising from a contract obtained through fraud committed in the bidding process. According to the Tribunal:

> "International public policy consists of a series of fundamental principles that constitute the very essence of the State, and its essential function is to preserve the values of the international legal system against actions contrary to it." [3422]

The Tribunal also stated that "respect for the law is a matter of public policy not only in El Salvador, but in any civilized country . . . there is a meta-positive provision that prohibits attributing effects to an act done illegally" [3423].

Donald Donovan notes that the Tribunal was not entirely clear in this decision and applied international public policy as one of several "general principles of law" such as good faith and the prohibition against unjust enrichment. In Donovan's opinion, reliance on these principles would have sufficed to support the conclusion that the Tribunal ultimately arrived at [3424].

As it has been stated, in the *World Duty Free* v. *Kenya* case, the Tribunal addressed corruption issues by applying international public policy. Interestingly, those matters could have been resolved by recurring to either (or both) English and Kenyan law, each of which were applicable to the case. As in the *Inceysa* case, the issues could have been decided by invoking the laws applicable to the contract rather

admissibility, and render them unmeritorious" (*ibid.*, Dissenting Opinion of Marc Clodfelter, para. 3).

3421. See *Inceysa*, *supra* note 1079, Award (2 August 2006).

3422. *Ibid.*, para. 145.

3423. *Ibid.*, para. 248.

3424. Donovan, *supra* note 3298, pp. 289-290. J.-M. Marcoux, "Transnational Public Policy as an International Practice in Investment Arbitration", *Journal of International Dispute Settlement*, Vol. 10, No. 3 (2019):

> "Interestingly, some decisions seem to suggest that tribunals themselves have an obligation not to protect investments that are contrary to transnational public policy. Rather than imposing a direct obligation on foreign investors to establish an investment that conforms with transnational public policy, such an approach suggests that the obligation to comply with transnational public policy ultimately rests on the tribunal itself. For example, the Tribunal in *Inceysa v. El Salvador* suggested that 'not to exclude Inceysa's investment from the protection of the [bilateral investment treaty] would be a violation of international public policy, which this Tribunal cannot allow' [*Inceysa*, *supra* note 1079, Award (2 August 2006), para. 252]. This and other examples seem to suggest that a violation of transnational public policy does not occur when the investor adopts a conduct contrary to the doctrine, but when protection is granted to an illegal investment."

than to the notion of international public policy, which the Tribunal resorted to despite not identifying a gap in the applicable governing legal regimes. According to Donovan,

> "[h]ence, the place of the doctrine in international investment arbitration and, indeed, any need for it, remains to be established" [3425].

Certain rules of public international law present additional challenges. While it is difficult to conceive of a setting where an investment treaty conflicts with a *jus cogens*, the UN Charter obligations present an interesting scenario [3426]. For instance, if the UN Security Council passed a resolution seizing individual assets for funding piracy on the high seas, the affected party cannot succeed in an investment arbitration claiming damages against the State. In this situation, the UN resolution will prevail over the bilateral investment treaty. However, as stated by Donovan, *jus cogens* norms and Charter obligations "are not mandatory rules in the meaningful sense". They are part of international law, which is the legal order governing the treaty [3427].

Public policy has also been invoked by investment treaty tribunals dealing with jurisdictional issues. In *Banro* v. *Congo* [3428], the Tribunal referred to international public policy considerations that prohibit an investor from abusing the investor-State dispute settlement system [3429]. Also, in *Maffezini* v. *Spain* [3430], the Tribunal analyzed whether public policy considerations would limit the operation of the most-favored-nation clause, and thus extend a BIT between Argentina and Spain to a BIT between Chile and Spain. The Tribunal found public policy considerations applicable against the most-favored-nation clause, particularly regarding its claim for treaty shopping. The decision was followed in the case *Siemens* v. *Argentina* [3431]. Further, in *Liman Caspian Oil* v. *Kazakhstan*, the Tribunal referred to the invalidating effect of a violation of public policy in the following statement:

3425. Donovan, *supra* note 3298, pp. 288-290.

3426. See, on this topic, Schreuer *et al.*, *supra* note 102, p. 566.

3427. Donovan, *supra* note 3298, p. 279.

3428. See *Banro American Resources, Inc. and Société Aurifère du Kivu et du Maniema SARL* v. *Democratic Republic of the Congo*, ICSID Case No. ARB/98/7, Award (1 September 2000).

3429. Brekoulakis, *supra* note 3268, p. 143.

3430. See *Maffezini* v. *Spain*, *supra* note 456, Decision of the Tribunal on Objections to Jurisdiction (25 January 2000), para. 64.

3431. *Siemens* v. *Argentina*, *supra* note 531, Decision on Jurisdiction (3 August 2004), para. 120.

"[T]here are situations in which a transaction is to be considered as automatically invalid from the very beginning. A violation of international public policy is such a case in which an investment is invalid without a legal action for invalidation and without a court declaration of invalidity having to be issued." [3432]

Despite these precedents, the use of public policy in treaty interpretation still has its problems, as made clear in *Wintershall* v. *Argentina* [3433] and *Plama* v. *Bulgaria* [3434]. The origin of public policy considerations to limit most-favored-nation clauses is unclear. Furthermore, it is questionable whether public policy allows a tribunal to read important qualifications and implicit policy objectives into international treaties. Neither Article 31 nor Article 32 of the VCLT include public policy as a primary or supplementary tool for interpreting treaties [3435].

Moreover, in *Plama* v. *Bulgaria* the Tribunal referred to "the basic notion of international public policy", without further examining the legal nature of this notion [3436]. The same can be said in respect of *Vladislav Kim* v. *Uzbekistan* [3437], *Unión Fenosa Gas* v. *Egypt* [3438], and *Churchill Mining* v. *Indonesia* [3439].

3432. *Liman Caspian Oil BV and NCL Dutch Investment BV* v. *Republic of Kazakhstan*, ICSID Case No. ARB/07/14, Award (22 June 2010), para. 193.

3433. *Wintershall* v. *Argentina*, *supra* note 2037, para. 182.

3434. *Plama* v. *Bulgaria*, *supra* note 1370, Decision on Jurisdiction (8 February 2005), para. 221.

3435. Brekoulakis, *supra* note 3268, pp. 143-145.

3436. Marcoux, *supra* note 3424, fn. 32. The Tribunal wrote that "[i]t would also be contrary to the basic notion of international public policy - that a contract obtained by wrongful means (fraudulent misrepresentation) should not be enforced by a tribunal" (*Plama* v. *Bulgaria*, *supra* note 1370, Award (2008), para. 143).

3437. The Tribunal "agree[d] that such an international public policy exists and is present implicitly in [bilateral investment treaties]" (*Vladislav Kim and others* v. *Republic of Uzbekistan*, ICSID Case No. ARB/13/6, Decision on Jurisdiction, 8 March 2017, para. 593).

3438. Here, the Tribunal addressed the "effect of international public policy", without seeking to find any legal basis to back such an affirmation. See *Unión Fenosa Gas* v. *Egypt*, *supra* note 3420, Award (31 August 2018), para. 7.48.

3439. The absence of a proper explanation by the Tribunal in *Churchill Mining* v. *Indonesia* was even cited in the Application for Annulment, challenging the proposition that "claims arising from rights based on fraud or forgery which the claimant deliberately or unreasonably ignored are inadmissible as a matter of international public policy" (ICSID Case Nos. ARB/12/14 and 12/40, Award, 6 December 2016, para. 508). Other awards also relied upon transnational public policy, such as in *Fraport AG Frankfurt Airport Services Worldwide* v. *Republic of the Philippines*, ICSID Case No. ARB/03/25, Dissenting Opinion of Bernardo M. Cremades (16 August 2007), p. 23; *Metal-Tech Ltd.* v. *Republic of Uzbekistan* (*Metal-Tech td* v. *Republic of Uzbekistan*, ICSID Case No. ARB/10/3, Award (4 October 2013), para. 292; *Blusun SA, J.-P. Lecorcier and M. Stein* v. *Italian Republic*, ICSID Case No. ARB/14/3, Award (27 December 2016), para. 264.

In sum, these uncertainties put into question whether transnational public policy in fact has a place in international investment arbitration [3440], at least in relation to treaty claims.

3. Mandatory rules of the host State

State courts apply overriding mandatory rules of their forum to international relationships. By contrast, in the context of investment arbitration a mandatory municipal law cannot prevail over international law applicable under the relevant investment treaty [3441]. Investment treaties also typically contain substantive investment protections regarding fair and equitable treatment, full protection and security, freedom of transfer, prohibition of expropriation, and non-discrimination. These treaty obligations are imposed upon signatory States and cannot be overridden by national law [3442].

In *CME* v. *Czech Republic* (2003), the host State argued that the "Tribunal must apply any Czech laws of mandatory nature" [3443]. The Tribunal did not accept this argument [3444]. However, as decided by the Tribunal in *Metalclad* v. *Mexico* (2000), in accordance with the ICSID Additional Facility Rules, "[a] State party to a treaty may not invoke the provisions of its internal law as justification for its failure to perform the treaty" [3445]. The *Kaiser* v. *Jamaica* case was decided following a similar logic [3446].

3440. The point is made by Donovan, *supra* note 3298, p. 286.

3441. Bjorklund, *supra* note 3325, p. 234. However, as Bischoff points out, referring to the cf. *Noble Ventures* v. *Romania* case, *supra* note 1090, "[j]ust because the host State has violated a rule under municipal law, this does not warrant a remedy under international law"; Bischoff, *supra* note 15, p. 757.

3442. Donovan, *supra* note 3298, p. 277.

3443. *CME* v. *Czech Republic*, UNCITRAL, Final Award (14 March 2003), para. 398.

3444. With a dissenting opinion of Arbitrator Hándl, who criticized his colleagues for "non-respecting of the provisions of the Czech Law that are of mandatory character e.g. the Media Law or the Administrative Proceedings Code" (*CME* v. *Czech Republic*, UNCITRAL, Partial Award Dissenting Opinion by J. Hándl (13 September 2001), pp. 22). See also *AAPL* v. *Sri Lanka*, *supra* note 453, Award, Dissenting Opinion of Asante (15 June 1990), p. 577.

3445. *Metalclad* v. *Mexico*, *supra* note 327, Award (30 August 2000), para. 70 (referring to Article 27 of the VCLT); see also *Total* v. *Argentina*, *supra* note 16, para. 40, section 2.3 (on the superior nature of international law *vis-à-vis* national law).

3446. Here, the choice of law agreement purported to exclude any rule which threw doubt upon the authority or the ability of the Government to enter agreements between the Parties. This is, according to Schreuer, a difficult question. "Much will depend on whether the domestic provision is seen to affect the State's capacity to contract resulting in the agreement's nullity or whether it is seen as a simple prohibition not affecting the agreement's validity. In case of doubt, the latter solution, upholding the validity of the agreement, is to be preferred, especially where the investor has relied in

On occasion, arbitral tribunals have applied, or *in dicta* supported the application of, international law in a supervening manner despite an agreement made by the parties regarding the application of national law alone. The *Aucoven* v. *Venezuela*[3447], *Caratube* v. *Kazakhstan*[3448] and *Methanex* v. *USA*[3449] cases serve as examples. In the *Methanex* v. *USA* case, the Arbitral Tribunal that had been constituted in accordance with NAFTA[3450] stated that it had a "duty to apply imperative principles of law or *jus cogens* and not to give effect to parties' choices of law that are inconsistent with such principles"[3451].

Several writers have raised doubts regarding the applicability of the mandatory rules' doctrine in investment-related contexts. After embarking on an analysis of arbitral practice (rather than theory), Donovan and Alexander Greenawalt concluded that there have been virtually no cases where the application of a mandatory rule was needed to justify a decision other than what would have been found by applying the law chosen by the parties[3452]. In the situations they discussed, mandatory rules were never applied to override the parties' choice.

Importantly, the chosen law itself will sometimes require tribunals to consider the rules of another system. Other times, such in situations of *force majeure*, national law has not been chosen but constitutes an underlying fact of the case. The conflict of laws rules of the chosen law, if not excluded, may also lead to the application of mandatory rules of another legal system[3453]. In addition, the tribunal may also consider the mandatory rules of a third country where necessary. For instance, the mandatory rules related to performance may be considered in situations where an export or import ban exists.

When it comes to the ICSID Convention, the domestic legal system of the home State cannot in itself provide standards for public policy. A

good faith on the host State's capacity to contract. Nevertheless, provisions of this kind in domestic law should be a cause of concern and should be investigated thoroughly before relying on a contractual clause purporting to exclude them", Schreuer *et al.*, *supra* note 102, p. 565, paras. 46-47.

3447. *Autopista* v. *Bolivia*, *supra* note 2716, Award (23 September 2003).

3448. "[T]he Tribunal finds that it cannot disregard, but must take into account international law, in particular mandatory rules of international law, when deciding the dispute" (*Caratube* v. *Kazakhstan*, *supra* note 16, para. 290).

3449. *Methanex* v. *USA*, *supra* note 527, Award (3 August 2005).

3450. *Ibid.*

3451. *Methanex* v. *USA*, *supra* note 527, Final Award, Part IV, Ch. C, Final Award (3 August 2005), p. 11, paras. 24-26, cited in Bermann, *supra* note 3263, p. 528.

3452. Donovan and Greenawalt, *supra* note 3410, p. 54.

3453. *Ibid.*, pp. 47-50.

State that invokes its own *ordre public* contrary to what it agreed upon regarding the application of another system is simply breaching its commitment concerning the selection of the chosen law [3454]. The *ordre public* of another State in which an ICSID award might potentially be enforced is irrelevant in principle, since Articles 53 and 54 of the ICSID Convention do not provide an *ordre public* exception to the obligation to recognize and enforce awards [3455].

4. Regional public policy in investment arbitration

According to Henri Alvarez, some groups of States (generally those that ratify substantively similar treaties or the same regional treaty) may find themselves more extensively linked to public policy values emerging therefrom. Thus, a regional public policy could be developed, for instance, within the European Union or NAFTA [3456].

The European Court of Justice considered certain provisions of EU law "as a matter of public policy within the meaning of the New York Convention" [3457]. According to Bischoff,

> "[i]t could be thus argued that an award based on a choice of law agreement that excludes the application of mandatory provisions of EU law may not be enforced in the European Union" [3458].

The ICSID Tribunal in *AES* v. *Hungary* (2010) addressed this issue specifically [3459]. Hungary argued that EU competition law should be considered as part of the applicable law or should be taken into account in relation to the Energy Charter Treaty providing for the arbitrator's jurisdiction. The Tribunal resolved any potential clash between the applicable laws by deciding that the respondent's acts would be assessed under the ECT as the applicable law and that EU law would be taken into account as a relevant fact [3460].

3454. For instance, a State, after having consented to the subjection of a loan agreement to French law, could not argue that the obligation to pay interest is contrary to the public policy of its religiously inspired domestic law. See Schreuer *et al.*, *supra* note 102, p. 566, para. 48.

3455. See *ibid.*, p. 566.

3456. Álvarez, *supra* note 3203, p. 34.

3457. *Eco Swiss China Time Ltd.* v. *Benetton International NV*, Case C-126/97, E.C.R. I-3055 (1 June 1999), para. 39.

3458. Bischoff, *supra* note 15, pp. 768-769.

3459. *Summit Generation* v. *Hungary*, *supra* note 607, Award (2010).

3460. *Ibid.*, paras. 7.2.1-7.2.5 and 7.6.12.

Another example of how an ICSID tribunal took into account – while not strictly applying – national and European Union law was illustrated in the *Maffezini* v. *Spain* (2000) case [3461]. In dismissing the investor's claim, the arbitrators found that Spain had "done no more in this respect than insist on the strict observance of the EEC and Spanish law applicable to the industry in question" [3462].

5. A "foreign investments public policy"?

Alvarez sees potential for public policy to be developed more specifically in international economic or investment-related matters. In this regard, he mentions a Paris Court of Appeals decision holding that rules related to public control over foreign investment express, via peremptory norms, the idea that an international economic public policy exists. This is because these rules aim to preserve, in the public interest, the balance between economic and financial relations with the rest of the world by controlling the movement of capital across borders (*Courreges Design* v. *Andre Courreges*, 1990) [3463]. This matter has not, however, received widespread scholarly attention.

3461. *Maffezini* v. *Spain*, *supra* note 456, Award (13 November 2000).
3462. *Ibid.*, p. 24, para. 71.
3463. Álvarez, *supra* note 3203, p. 34.

CHAPTER XXII

CONCLUDING REMARKS

The modern international investment claims regime faces several proposals for reform. Some corners of academia, governments and even the European Union direct their criticism toward the current practice of arbitration, arguing that the installation of permanent international tribunals staffed by State-appointed adjudicators (as is the case, for example, with the International Court of Justice) will improve the current dispute resolution mechanism. Several critics of the international investment system envision these courts functioning as at least an appellate body, thereby ensuring – according to them – jurisprudential uniformity in contrast to the contradictory award precedents that currently coexist in several substantive areas of the foreign investment legal regime.

However, a core issue remains unaddressed in most of these reform discussions: the nature of the substantive law applicable to foreign investments. An adjudicator, whoever and however appointed, is limited in their ability to produce reliable precedent in the absence of an appropriate substantive regulatory framework.

The preceding chapters took no position regarding the question of the optimal dispute resolution mechanism or the avenues of reform for international investment claims, and instead focused on the critical matter of the applicable substantive law.

Given that there is no realistic hope for the negotiation, much less the ratification, of a universal instrument to comprehensively deal with this matter, focus can and must shift to current evolution in relevant areas of law related to foreign investments.

Impressive developments in public and private international law, and in international arbitration, already exist today that, taken as a whole, are conducive to a more appropriate handling of the substantive law applicable to foreign investments. However, better interdisciplinary dialogue is needed. Private and international private law provide adequate answers to many of the problems that have led to contradiction in several foreign investment matters. Arbitration itself provides tools that favor an integrative dialogue in disputes resolved through the arbitral process.

In its birth, public international law borrowed legal concepts from ancient Roman private law thanks to the academic work of jurists such as Hugo Grotius, Francisco de Vitoria, Alberico Gentile and Emer de Vattel, who in the seventeenth century devised justifications for protecting the economic interests of Western Europe resulting from its investments in its fledgling colonies. Certain minimum standards of protection were eventually consolidated over time, thanks to their adoption in numerous treaties of "Friendship, Commerce and Navigation" and through the creation of special international tribunals or "mixed claims commissions" that resolved international investment disputes and gradually created a rudimentary case law as a result.

However, the treaties – and customary international law in general at that time – were sparing with respect to minimum standards of protection. To fill the gap, the public international law theorists and special tribunals of the time resorted to the law then common in Europe: the Roman private law that had taken root over the centuries, and which continued to nourish the various new branches emerging from it. The doctrine and jurisprudence at the time frequently used concepts entrenched in Roman law and progressively developing after the Middle and Modern Ages, such as good faith, estoppel, strict performance and unjust enrichment. The decisions that emerged therefrom became recognized as established rules within public international law. Thus, for centuries, private law has shaped public international law. What better than the *ratio scripta* [3464] – which is how Roman law was applied – to fill the gaps in an incipient discipline such as this? Its suitability was reinforced by Rome's strong protection of the right to property, recognition of appropriate compensation for damages and defense of the sanctity of contracts; in other words, all the ingredients desired by those who advocated meaningful legal protection of European economic interests across the full breadth of their colonial empires.

This mechanism was called into question in the Americas toward the end of the nineteenth century as independence movements spread in the region. It was one thing for Europeans to impose their own law on their colonies, but it was quite another for independent countries to be forced to accept such an imposition. That new tension gave rise to the so-called "Calvo Doctrine", which advocated applying the national laws of the countries receiving foreign investment and the judicial supremacy not of international tribunals but of national courts. Critics observed that

3464. Literally, "written reasons".

this doctrine contravened safeguards needed for foreign investment to flourish, since host countries could alter protection standards – as they have in fact done repeatedly through changes in their regulations – and consequently leave those ventures at the mercy of domestic political vicissitudes and judgments by local courts frequently shaped by the sensibility that "in my backyard, my rules prevail".

As the colonialist yoke began to yield in other regions, the tensions of this debate transferred to the League of Nations and then to the United Nations. Still, neither in these nor in other institutions that attempted to do so – for example, the Organization for Economic Cooperation and Development – was a consensus reached on what course should be pursued nor, even less, on a comprehensive substantive law corpus on the field of international investments. At most, the United Nations managed to approve "soft law" instruments such as a document on the responsibility of States for unlawful acts, with "secondary obligations" for non-compliance (e.g., reparation for damages and other penalties provided for under public international law). In other words, this document dealt with the consequences of not complying with "primary obligations" but failed to address regulating them due to the absolute lack of consensus within the United Nations.

Thus, to this day there is no corpus of norms dealing with the substantive law applicable to foreign investments. The international customary law developed through the centuries in doctrine and by international tribunals therefore survives until even today, despite the Calvo Doctrine's efforts to dethrone it. Public international law gradually became imbued with private law and its principles, which were recognized and accepted over time by international tribunals and doctrinal works. It is true that there have been treaties throughout the centuries, such as those of "Friendship, Commerce and Navigation", which included minimum standards formulas for the protection of foreign investment. However, due to the abstract nature of some of those formulas and gaps in several others, international tribunals and doctrine needed to supplement them with ingredients found mostly in private law and its principles. The signing of bilateral and multilateral investment treaties helped formalize several of these broad standards of protection developed by customary international law, and even went further in some cases, for example by arguably [3465] incorporating

3465. As seen in Chap. XIV, there is some dispute as to whether it is basically the same formula introduced under another label or whether it is the same or something altogether different.

principle of fair and equitable treatment into the minimum standard of protection. However, there is still an absence of a corpus regulating or "establishing" the manner in which those broad standards are applied, which largely explains the controversies they have given rise to and even the contradictory pronouncements made by arbitration tribunals.

These treaties, as well as investment laws and contracts of recent decades, have increasingly favored the use of arbitration, and the broad powers granted to arbitrators in terms of determining the applicable substantive law continues to contribute to the development of the content of those broad standards.

Especially toward the middle of the twentieth century, the contribution of arbitration tribunals was particularly fruitful for the consolidation of principles, such as those recognized in well-known Middle East oil cases, and even led to the development of other sources of public international law in relation to investments, such as custom and *opinio juris* or the writings of notable publicists – in turn enriched by private, private international, and uniform law.

In the pages of this book, the developments of comparative law and its various techniques have received particular attention, although the various methods employed by those who make the comparisons remain controversial, which in turn generates disparities in the answers proposed to the problems posed by foreign investment claims.

In recent times, private international law has benefited from countless global, regional and national efforts to improve it. These endeavors are generating numerous hard law instruments (such as treaties and statutes) and soft law texts (such as guides, model laws and restatements or "principles" – as they call themselves), which tend to break with the "localizing" conflict of laws orthodoxy in international cases. They have tapped a series of resources, such as those that enable judges to be flexible when the localizing mechanism leads to unfair or inequitable results, thereby making it possible to expand the application of uniform law texts, for example the CISG. In this latter sense, the UNIDROIT Principles have become a powerful tool with potentially beneficial consequences not only in international commerce but also in the field of foreign investments, by providing formulas such as those relating to *force majeure* and unforeseeable circumstances that may arise in such contexts.

Likewise, other "conflict of law" developments in current private international law, when properly understood, provide formidable tools for dealing with recurrent foreign investment-related problems.

However, this option that is insufficiently exploited due to the lack of a fruitful interdisciplinary dialogue that would make it possible to take advantage of the many potential benefits. Foreign investment claims may involve conflict of laws discussions relating, for example, to capacity, non-contractual liability, property law and even complex issues relating to financial instruments and guarantees. Recent progress in private international law on these issues, such as that made under the lead of organizations like UNIDROIT, UNCITRAL and the Hague Conference on Private International Law, may have a marked impact on the fate of many foreign investment disputes, so it is critical that they be handled appropriately.

Worth stressing, too, is the fact that the public-private distinction so vaunted by academia has been notoriously thinned, impacting foreign investment arbitrations in which private law issues are frequently addressed. This situation typically occurs in cases related to contractual breaches, but it also happens in many others in which public law is unable to provide satisfactory answers.

In addition to the above developments in public and private international law, arbitration also experienced impressive progress in the second half of the twentieth century, with milestones such as the so-called New York Convention of 1958 on the Recognition and Enforcement of Foreign Arbitral Awards, the 1974 UNCITRAL Arbitration Rules and its amendments, the UNCITRAL Model Law of 1985 and its amendment, and the legislative modernization initiatives derived from those instruments worldwide: the New York Convention has been ratified by more than 160 countries, and a significant number of countries on five continents have amended their laws to bring them into line with the UNCITRAL model. The same is true of the rules of procedure of arbitration institutions, the content of which is strongly impacted by the UNCITRAL model, as is the case, for example, with the rules of the Permanent Court of Arbitration based in The Hague, which has been registering an increasing number of investment arbitration cases as a result of treaties or international contracts that are now concluded subject to them.

To the abovementioned growth must be added the "revolution" brought about by the International Centre for Settlement of Investment Disputes (ICSID) since its establishment in 1965, and its peculiar self-sufficient system not subject to the scrutiny of national courts. This also impacts arbitral discretion in applying the substantive law – again, interdisciplinary tools may provide unvaluable assistance for this task.

ICSID became the leading mechanism recurred to by investors, which in turn has generated an impressive number of precedents in recent decades.

Both the ICSID rules and those of other arbitration mechanisms contain sparse but highly important provisions on the law applicable to the merits of disputes submitted in accordance with them, including rules related to their choice or lack of selection, as well as criteria governing their flexible application, if pertinent, and to public policy. These rules also allow for the possibility of opting for an equity or *ex aequo et bono* arbitration mechanism.

Despite their brevity, these provisions potentially entail weighing multiple issues of public international law, private international law, uniform law, and private law in general. The absence of a corpus or body of comprehensive substantive norms in foreign investment matters makes it imperative to resort, depending on the context, to answers provided by the aforementioned disciplines, which reaffirms the compelling need for a fruitful interdisciplinary dialogue to cast their diverse lights on this field. Hopefully, this book has made a case in favor of that necessity.

PUBLICATIONS DE L'ACADÉMIE
DE DROIT INTERNATIONAL
DE LA HAYE

PUBLICATIONS OF THE
HAGUE ACADEMY OF INTERNATIONAL
LAW

RECUEIL DES COURS

Depuis 1923, les plus grands noms du droit international ont professé à l'Académie de droit international de La Haye. Tous les tomes du *Recueil* qui ont été publiés depuis cette date sont disponibles, chaque tome étant, depuis les tout premiers, régulièrement réimprimé sous sa forme originale.

Depuis 2008, certains cours font l'objet d'une édition en livres de poche.

En outre, toute la collection existe en version électronique. Tous les ouvrages parus à ce jour ont été mis en ligne et peuvent être consultés moyennant un des abonnements proposés, qui offrent un éventail de tarifs et de possibilités.

INDEX

A ce jour, il a paru sept index généraux. Ils couvrent les tomes suivants:

1 à 101	(1923-1960)	379 pages	ISBN 978-90-218-9948-0
102 à 125	(1961-1968)	204 pages	ISBN 978-90-286-0643-2
126 à 151	(1969-1976)	280 pages	ISBN 978-90-286-0630-2
152 à 178	(1976-1982)	416 pages	ISBN 978-0-7923-2955-8
179 à 200	(1983-1986)	260 pages	ISBN 978-90-411-0110-5
201 à 250	(1987-1994)	448 pages	ISBN 978-90-04-13700-4
251 à 300	(1995-2002)	580 pages	ISBN 978-90-04-15387-7

A partir du tome 210 il a été décidé de publier un index complet qui couvrira chaque fois dix tomes du *Recueil des cours*. Le dernier index paru couvre les tomes suivants:

311 à 320 (2004-2006) 392 pages Tome 320A ISBN 978-90-04-19695-7

COLLOQUES

L'Académie organise également des colloques dont les débats sont publiés. Les derniers volumes parus de ces colloques portent les titres suivants: *Le règlement pacifique des différends internationaux en Europe: perspectives d'avenir* (1990); *Le développement du rôle du Conseil de sécurité* (1992); *La Convention sur l'interdiction et l'élimination des armes chimiques: une percée dans l'entreprise multilatérale du désarmement* (1994); *Actualité de la Conférence de La Haye de 1907, Deuxième Conférence de la Paix* (2007).

CENTRE D'ÉTUDE ET DE RECHERCHE

Les travaux scientifiques du Centre d'étude et de recherche de droit international et de relations internationales de l'Académie de droit international de La Haye, dont les sujets sont choisis par le Curatorium de l'Académie, faisaient l'objet, depuis la session de 1985, d'une publication dans laquelle les directeurs d'études dressaient le bilan des recherches du Centre qu'ils avaient dirigé. Cette série a été arrêtée et la dernière brochure parue porte le titre suivant: *Les règles et les institutions du droit international humanitaire à l'épreuve des conflits armés récents*. Néanmoins, lorsque les travaux du Centre se révèlent particulièrement intéressants et originaux, les rapports des directeurs et les articles rédigés par les chercheurs font l'objet d'un ouvrage collectif.

Les demandes de renseignements ou de catalogues et les commandes doivent être adressées à

MARTINUS NIJHOFF PUBLISHERS

B.P. 9000, 2300 PA Leyde Pays-Bas **http://www.brill.nl**

COLLECTED COURSES

Since 1923 the top names in international law have taught at The Hague Academy of International Law. All the volumes of the *Collected Courses* which have been published since 1923 are available, as, since the very first volume, they are reprinted regularly in their original format.

Since 2008, certain courses have been the subject of a pocketbook edition.

In addition, the total collection now exists in electronic form. All works already published have been put "on line" and can be consulted under one of the proposed subscription methods, which offer a range of tariffs and possibilities.

INDEXES

Up till now seven General Indexes have been published. They cover the following volumes:

1 to 101	(1923-1960)	379 pages	ISBN 978-90-218-9948-0
102 to 125	(1961-1968)	204 pages	ISBN 978-90-286-0643-2
126 to 151	(1969-1976)	280 pages	ISBN 978-90-286-0630-2
152 to 178	(1976-1982)	416 pages	ISBN 978-0-7923-2955-8
179 to 200	(1983-1986)	260 pages	ISBN 978-90-411-0110-5
201 to 250	(1987-1994)	448 pages	ISBN 978-90-04-13700-4
251 to 300	(1995-2002)	580 pages	ISBN 978-90-04-15387-7

From Volume 210 onwards it has been decided to publish a full index covering, each time, ten volumes of the *Collected Courses*. The latest Index published covers the following volumes:

311 to 320 (2004-2006) 392 pages Volume 320A ISBN 978-90-04-19695-7

WORKSHOPS

The Academy publishes the discussions from the Workshops which it organises. The latest titles of the Workshops already published are as follows: *The Peaceful Settlement of International Disputes in Europe: Future Prospects* (1990) ; *The Development of the Role of the Security Council* (1992); *The Convention on the Prohibition and Elimination of Chemical Weapons: A Breakthrough in Multilateral Disarmament* (1994); *Topicality of the 1907 Hague Conference, the Second Peace Conference* (2007).

CENTRE FOR STUDIES AND RESEARCH

The scientific works of the Centre for Studies and Research in International Law and International Relations of The Hague Academy of International Law, the subjects of which are chosen by the Curatorium of the Academy, have been published, since the Centre's 1985 session, in a publication in which the Directors of Studies reported on the state of research of the Centre under their direction. This series has been discontinued and the title of the latest booklet published is as follows: *Rules and Institutions of International Humanitarian Law Put to the Test of Recent Armed Conflicts.* Nevertheless, when the work of the Centre has been of particular interest and originality, the reports of the Directors of Studies together with the articles by the researchers form the subject of a collection published by the Academy.

Requests for information, catalogues and orders for publications must be addressed to

MARTINUS NIJHOFF PUBLISHERS

P.O. Box 9000, 2300 PA Leiden The Netherlands **http://www.brill.nl**

TABLE PAR TOME DES COURS PUBLIÉS CES DERNIÈRES ANNÉES

INDEX BY VOLUME OF THE COURSES PUBLISHED THESE LAST YEARS

Tome/Volume 358 (2011)

Brand, R. A.: Transaction Planning Using Rules on Jurisdiction and the Recognition and Enforcement of Judgments, 9-262.
Hafner, G.: The Emancipation of the Individual from the State under International Law, 263-454.
(ISBN 978-90-04-22732-3)

Tome/Volume 359 (2012)

Opertti Badán, D.: Conflit de lois et droit uniforme dans le droit international privé contemporain: dilemme ou convergence? (conférence inaugurale), 9-86.
Chen Weizuo: La nouvelle codification du droit international privé chinois, 87-234.
Kohler, Ch.: L'autonomie de la volonté en droit international privé: un principe universel entre libéralisme et étatisme, 285-478.
(ISBN 978-90-04-25541-8)

Tome/Volume 360 (2012)

Basedow, J.: The Law of Open Societies — Private Ordering and Public Regulation of International Relations. General Course on Private International Law, 9-516.
(ISBN 978-90-04-25550-0)

Tome/Volume 361 (2012)

Pinto, M. C. W.: The Common Heritage of Mankind: Then and Now, 9-130.
Kreindler, R.: Competence-Competence in the Face of Illegality in Contracts and Arbitration Agreements, 131-482. (ISBN 978-90-04-25552-4)

Tome/Volume 362 (2012)

Arsanjani, M. H.: The United Nations and International Law-Making (Opening Lecture), 9-40.
Alland, D.: L'interprétation du droit international public, 41-394.
(ISBN 978-90-04-25554-8)

Tome/Volume 363 (2012)

Sur, S.: La créativité du droit international. Cours général de droit international public, 9-332.
Turp, D.: La contribution du droit international au maintien de la diversité culturelle, 333-454. (ISBN 978-90-04-25556-2)

Tome/Volume 364 (2012)

Gaja, G.: The Protection of General Interests in the International Community. General Course on Public International Law (2011), 9-186.
Glenn, H. P.: La conciliation des lois. Cours général de droit international privé (2011), 187-470. (ISBN 978-90-04-25557-9)

Tome/Volume 365 (2013)

Crawford, J.: Chance, Order, Change: The Course of International Law. General Course on Public International Law, 9-390. (ISBN 978-90-04-25560-9)

Tome/Volume 366 (2013)

Hayton, D.: "Trusts" in Private International Law, 9-98.
Hobér, K.: Res Judicata and Lis Pendens in International Arbitration, 99-406.
(ISBN 978-90-04-26395-6)

Tome/Volume 367 (2013)

Kolb, R.: L'article 103 de la Charte des Nations Unies, 9-252.
Nascimbene, B.: Le droit de la nationalité et le droit des organisations d'intégration régionales. Vers de nouveaux statuts de résidents?, 253-454.
(ISBN 978-90-04-26793-0)

Tome/Volume 368 (2013)

Caflisch, L: Frontières nationales, limites et délimitations. — Quelle importance aujourd'hui? (conférence inaugurale), 9-46.
Benvenisti, E.: The International Law of Global Governance, 47-280.
Park, K. G.: La protection des personnes en cas de catastrophes, 281-456.
(ISBN 978-90-04-26795-4)

Tome/Volume 369 (2013)

Kronke, H.: Transnational Commercial Law and Conflict of Laws: Institutional Co-operation and Substantive Complementarity (Opening Lecture), 9-42.
Ortiz Ahlf, L.: The Human Rights of Undocumented Migrants, 43-160.
Kono, T.: Efficiency in Private International Law, 161-360.
Yusuf, A. A.: Pan-Africanism and International Law, 361-512.
(ISBN 978-90-04-26797-8)

Tome/Volume 370 (2013)

Dominicé, Ch.: La société internationale à la recherche de son équilibre. Cours général de droit international public, 9-392.
(ISBN 978-90-04-26799-2)

Tome/Volume 371 (2014)

Lagarde, P.: La méthode de la reconnaissance est-elle l'avenir du droit international privé?, 9-42.
Charlesworth, H.: Democracy and International Law, 43-152.
de Vareilles-Sommières, P.: L'exception d'ordre public et la régularité substantielle internationale de la loi étrangère, 153-272.
Yanagihara, M.: Significance of the History of the Law of Nations in Europe and East Asia, 273-435.
(ISBN 978-90-04-28936-9)

Tome/Volume 372 (2014)

Bucher, A.: La compétence universelle civile, 9-128.
Cordero-Moss, G.: Limitations on Party Autonomy in International Commercial Arbitration, 129-326.
Sinjela, M.: Intellectual Property: Cross-Border Recognition of Rights and National Development, 327-394.
Dolzer, R.: International Co-operation in Energy Affairs, 395-504.
(ISBN 978-90-04-28937-6)

Tome/Volume 373 (2014)

Cachard, O.: Le transport international aérien de passagers, 9-216.
Audit, M.: Bioéthique et droit international privé, 217-447.
(ISBN 978-90-04-28938-3)

Tome/Volume 374 (2014)

Struycken, A. V. M.: Arbitration and State Contract, 9-52.
Corten, O., La rébellion et le droit international: le principe de neutralité en tension, 53-312.
Parra, A.: The Convention and Centre for Settlement of Investment Disputes, 313-410. (ISBN 978-90-04-29764-7)

Tome/Volume 375 (2014)

Jayme, E.: Narrative Norms in Private International Law – The Example of Art Law, 9-52.
De Boer, Th. M.: Choice of Law in Arbitration Proceedings, 53-88.
Frigo, M.: Circulation des biens culturels, détermination de la loi applicable et méthodes de règlement des litiges, 89-474. (ISBN 978-90-04-29766-1)

Tome/Volume 376 (2014)

Cançado Trindade, A. A.: The Contribution of Latin American Legal Doctrine to the Progressive Development of International Law, 9-92.
Gray, C.: The Limits of Force, 93-198.
Najurieta, M. S.: L'adoption internationale des mineurs et les droits de l'enfant, 199-494. (ISBN 978-90-04-29768-5)

Tome/Volume 377 (2015)

Kassir, W. J.: Le renvoi en droit international privé – technique de dialogue entre les cultures juridiques, 9-120.
Noodt Taquela, M. B.: Applying the Most Favourable Treaty or Domestic Rules to Facilitate Private International Law Co-operation, 121-318.
Tuzmukhamedov, B.: Legal Dimensions of Arms Control Agreements, An Introductory Overview, 319-468.
(ISBN 978-90-04-29770-8)

Tome/Volume 378 (2015)

Iwasawa, Y.: Domestic Application of International Law, 9-262.
Carrascosa Gonzalez, J.: The Internet – Privacy and Rights relating to Personality, 263-486. (ISBN 978-90-04-32125-0)

Tome/Volume 379 (2015)

Lowe, V.: The Limits of the Law.
Boele-Woelki, K.: Party Autonomy in Litigation and Arbitration in View of The Hague Principles on Choice of Law in International Commercial Contracts.
Fresnedo de Aguirre, C.: Public Policy: Common Principles in the American States.
Ben Achour, R.: Changements anticonstitutionnels de gouvernement et droit international.
(ISBN 978-90-04-32127-4)

Tome/Volume 380 (2015)

Van Loon, J. H. A.: The Global Horizon of Private International Law.
Pougoué, P.-G.: L'arbitrage dans l'espace OHADA.
Kruger, T.: The Quest for Legal Certainty in International Civil Cases.
(ISBN 978-90-04-32131-1)

Tome/Volume 381 (2015)

Jayme, E.: Les langues et le droit international privé, 11-39.
Bermann, G.: Arbitrage and Private International Law. General Course on Private International Law (2015), 41-484.
(ISBN 978-90-04-33828-9)

Tome/Volume 382 (2015)

Cooper, D., and C. Kuner: Data Protection Law and International Dispute Resolution, 9-174.
Jia, B. B.: International Case Law in the Development of International Law, 175-397.
(ISBN 978-90-04-33830-2)

Tome/Volume 383 (2016)

Bennouna, M.: Le droit international entre la lettre et l'esprit, 9-231.
Iovane, M.: L'influence de la multiplication des juridictions internationales sur l'application du droit international, 233-446.
(ISBN 978-90-04-34648-2)

Tome/Volume 384 (2016)

Symeonides, S. C.: Private International Law Idealism, Pragmatism, Eclecticism, 9-385. (ISBN 978-90-04-35131-8)

Tome/Volume 385 (2016)

Berman, Sir F.: Why Do we Need a Law of Treaties?, 9-31.
Marrella, F.: Protection internationale des droits de l'homme et activités des sociétés transnationales, 33-435.(ISBN 978-90-04-35132-5)

Tome/Volume 386 (2016)

Murphy, S. D.: International Law relating to Islands, 9-266.
Cataldi, G.: La mise en œuvre des décisions des tribunaux internationaux dans l'ordre interne, 267-428. (ISBN 978-90-04-35133-2)

Tome/Volume 387 (2016)

Lequette, Y.: Les mutations du droit international privé: vers un changement de paradigme?, 9-644. (ISBN 978-90-04-36118-8)

Tome/Volume 388 (2016)

Bonell, M. J.: The Law Governing International Commercial Contracts: Hard Law versus Soft Law, 9-48.
Hess, B.: The Private-Public Divide in International Dispute Resolution, 49-266.
(ISBN 978-90-04-36120-1)

Tome/Volume 389 (2017)

Muir Watt, H.: Discours sur les méthodes du droit international privé (des formes juridiques de l'inter-altérité). Cours général de droit international privé, 9-410. (ISBN 978-90-04-36122-5)

Tome/Volume 390 (2017)

Rau, A. S.: The Allocation of Power between Arbitral Tribunals and State Courts, 9-396. (ISBN 978-90-04-36475-2)

Tome/Volume 391 (2017)

Cançado Trindade, A. A.: Les tribunaux internationaux et leur mission commune de réalisation de la justice : développements, état actuel et perspectives, Conférence spéciale (2017), 9-101.

Mariño Menéndez, F. M. : The Prohibition of Torture in Public International Law, 103-185.

Swinarski, C.: Effets pour l'individu des régimes de protection de droit international, 187-369.

Cot, J.-P.: L'éthique du procès international (leçon inaugurale), 371-384. (ISBN 978-90-04-37781-3)

Tome/Volume 392 (2017)

Novak, F.: The System of Reparations in the Jurisprudence of the Inter-American Court of Human Rights, 9-203.

Nolte, G.: Treaties and their Practice – Symptoms of their Rise or Decline, 205-397. (ISBN 978-90-04-39273-1)

Tome/Volume 393 (2017)

Tiburcio, C.: The Current Practice of International Co-Operation in Civil Matters, 9-310.

Ruiz De Santiago, J.: Aspects juridiques des mouvements forcés de personnes, 311-468. (ISBN 978-90-04-39274-8)

Tome/Volume 394 (2017)

Kostin, A. A.: International Commercial Arbitration, with Special Focus on Russia, 9-86.

Cuniberti, G.: Le fondement de l'effet des jugements étrangers, 87-283. (ISBN 978-90-04-39275-5)

Tome/Volume 395 (2018)

Salerno, F.: The Identity and Continuity of Personal Status in Contemporary Private International Law, 9-198.

Chinkin, C. M.: United Nations Accountability for Violations of International Human Rights Law, 199-320. (ISBN 978-90-04-40710-7)

Tome/Volume 396 (2018)

Jacquet, J.-M.: Droit international privé et arbitrage commercial international, 9-36.

Brown Weiss, E.: Establishing Norms in a Kaleidoscopic World. General Course on Public International Law, 37-415. (ISBN 978-90-04-41002-2)

Tome/Volume 397 (2018)

D'Avout, L.: L'entreprise et les conflits internationaux de lois, 9-612. (ISBN 978-90-04-41221-7)

Tome/Volume 398 (2018)

Treves, T.: The Expansion of International Law, General Course on Public International Law (2015), 9-398. (ISBN 978-90-04-41224-8)

Tome/Volume 399 (2018)

Kanehara, A.: Reassessment of the Acts of the State in the Law of State Responsibility, 9-266.

Buxbaum, H. L.: Public Regulation and Private Enforcement in a Global Economy: Strategies for Managing Conflict, 267-442. (ISBN 978-90-04-41670-3)

Tome/Volume 400 (2018)

Chedly, L.: L'efficacité de l'arbitrage commercial international, 9-624. (ISBN 978-90-04-42388-6)

Tome/Volume 401 (2019)

Wood, P.: Extraterritorial Enforcement of Regulatory Laws, 9-126.

Nishitani, Yuko: Identité culturelle en droit international privé de la famille, 127-450. (ISBN 978-90-04-42389-3)

Tome/Volume 402 (2019)

Kinsch, P.: Le rôle du politique en droit international privé. Cours général de droit international privé, 9-384.

Dasser, F.: "Soft Law" in International Commercial Arbitration, 385-596. (ISBN 978-90-04-42392-3)

Tome/Volume 403 (2019)

Daudet, Y.: 1919-2019, le flux du multilatéralisme, 9-48.

Kessedjian, C.: Le tiers impartial et indépendant en droit international, juge, arbitre, médiateur, conciliateur, 49-643. (ISBN 978-90-04-42468-5)

Tome/Volume 404 (2019)

Rajamani, L.: Innovation and Experimentation in the International Climate Change Regime, 9-234.

Sorel, J.-M.: Quelle normativité pour le droit des relations monétaires et financières internationales?, 235-403. (ISBN 978-90-04-43142-3)

Tome/Volume 405 (2019)

Paulsson, J.: Issues arising from Findings of Denial of Justice, 9-74.

Brunée, J.: Procedure and Substance in International Environmental Law, 75-240. (ISBN 978-90-04-43300-7)

Tome/Volume 406 (2019)

Bundy, R.: The Practice of International Law, Inaugural Lecture, 9-26.
Gama, L.: Les principes d'UNIDROIT et la loi régissant les contrats de commerce, 27-343.

(ISBN 978-90-04-43611-4)

Tome/Volume 407 (2020)

Wouters, J.: Le statut juridique des standards publics et privés dans les relations économiques internationales, 9-122.
Maljean-Dubois, S.: Le droit international de la biodiversité, 123-538.

(ISBN 978-90-04-43643-5)

Tome/Volume 408 (2020)

Cançado Trindade, A. A.: Reflections on the Realization of Justice in the Era of Contemporary International Tribunals, 9-88.
González, C.: Party Autonomy in International Family Law, 89-361.

(ISBN 978-90-04-44504-8)

Tome/Volume 409 (2020)

Shany, Y: The Extraterritorial Application of International Human Rights Law, 9-152.
Besson, S.: La *due diligence* en droit international, 153-398.

(ISBN 978-90-04-44505-5)

Tome/Volume 410 (2020)

Koh, H. H.: American Schools of International Law, 9-93.
Peters, A.: Animals in International Law, 95-544.

(ISBN 978-90-04-44897-1)

Tome/Volume 411 (2020)

Cahin, G: Reconstrution et construction de l'Etat en droit international, 9-573.

(ISBN 978-90-04-44898-8)

Tome/Volume 412 (2020)

Momtaz, D: La hiérarchisation de l'ordre juridique international, cours général de droit international public, 9-252.
Grammaticaki-Alexiou, A.: Best Interests of the Child in Private International Law, 253-434.

(ISBN 978-90-04-44899-5)

Tome/Volume 413 (2021)

Ferrari, F.: Forum Shopping Despite Unification of Law, 9-290.

(ISBN 978-90-04-46100-0)

Tome/Volume 414 (2021)

Pellet, A.: Le droit international à la lumière de la pratique: l'introuvable théorie de la réalité. Cours général de droit international public, 9-547.

(ISBN 978-90-04-46547-3)

Tome/Volume 415 (2021)

Trooboff, P. D.: Globalization, Personal Jurisdiction and the Internet. Responding to the Challenge of adapting settled Principles and Precedents. General Course of Private International Law, 9-321. (ISBN 978-90-04-46730-9)

Tome/Volume 416 (2021)

Wolfrum, R: Solidarity and Community Interests: Driving Forces for the Interpretation and Development of International Law. General Course on Public International Law, 9-479. (ISBN 978-90-04-46827-6)

Tome/Volume 417 (2021)

d'Argent, P.: Les obligations internationales, 9-210.

Schabas, W. A.: Relationships Between International Criminal Law and Other Branches of International Law, 211-392. (ISBN 978-90-04-47239-6)

Tome/Volume 418 (2021)

Bollée, S.: Les pouvoirs inhérents des arbitres internationaux, 9-224.

Tladi, D.: The Extraterritorial Use of Force against Non-State Actors, 225-360. (ISBN 978-90-04-50380-9)

Tome/Volume 419 (2021)

Kolb, R.: Le droit international comme corps de «droit privé» et de «droit public». Cours général de droit international public, 9-668. (ISBN 978-90-04-50381-6)

Tome/Volume 420 (2021)

Perrakis, S.: La protection internationale au profit des personnes vulnérables en droit international des droits de l'homme, 9-497. (ISBN 978-90-04-50382-3)

Tome/Volume 421 (2021)

Estrella Faria, J. A.: La protection des biens culturels d'intérêt religieux en droit international public et en droit international privé, 9-333. (ISBN 978-90-04-50829-3)

Tome/Volume 422 (2021)

Karayanni, M.: The Private International Law of Class Actions: A Functional approach, 9-248.

Mahmoudi, S.: Self-Defence and "Unwilling or Unable" States, 249-399. (ISBN 978-90-04-50830-9)

Tome/Volume 423 (2022)

Kinnear, M.: The Growth, Challenges and Future Prospects for Investment Dispute Settlement, 9-36.

Weller, M.: "Mutual Trust": A Suitable Foundation for Private International Law in Regional Integration Communities and Beyond?, 37-378. (ISBN 978-90-04-51411-9)

LES LIVRES DE POCHE DE L'ACADÉMIE

(Par ordre chronologique de parution)

1
Gaillard, E. : Aspects philosophiques du droit de l'arbitrage international, 2008, 252 pages. (ISBN 978-90-04-17148-0)

2
Schrijver, N. : The Evolution of Sustainable Development in International Law : Inception, Meaning and Status, 2008, 276 pages. (ISBN 978-90-04-17407-8)

3
Moura Vicente, D. : La propriété intellectuelle en droit international privé, 2009, 516 pages.
(ISBN 978-90-04-17907-3)

4
Decaux, E. : Les formes contemporaines de l'esclavage, 2009, 272 pages.
(ISBN 978-90-04-17908-0)

5
McLachlan, C. : Lis Pendens in International Litigation, 2009, 492 pages.
(ISBN 978-90-04-17909-7)

6
Carbone, S. M. : Conflits de lois en droit maritime, 2010, 312 pages.
(ISBN 978-90-04-18688-0)

7
Boele-Woelki, K. : Unifying and Harmonizing Substantive Law and the Role of Conflict of Laws, 2010, 288 pages.
(ISBN 978-90-04-18683-5)

8
Onuma, Y. : A Transcivilizational Perspective in International Law, 2010, 492 pages.
(ISBN 978-90-04-18689-7)

9
Bucher, A. : La dimension sociale du droit international privé. Cours général, 2011, 552 pages. (ISBN 978-90-04-20917-6)

10
Thürer, D. : International Humanitarian Law : Theory, Practice, Context, 2011, 504 pages. (ISBN 978-90-04-17910-3)

11
Alvarez, J. E. : The Public International Law Regime Governing International Investment, 2011, 504 pages.
(ISBN 978-90-04-18682-8)

12
Wang, G. : Radiating Impact of WTO on Its Members' Legal System : The Chinese Perspective, 2011, 384 pages.
(ISBN 978-90-04-21854-3)

13
Bogdan, M. : Private International Law as Component of the Law of the Forum, 2012, 360 pages. (ISBN 978-90-04-22634-0)

14

Davey, W. J.: Non-discrimination in the World Trade Organization: The Rules and Exceptions, 2012, 360 pages. (ISBN 978-90-04-23314-0)

15

Xue Hanqin: Chinese Contemporary Perspectives on International Law — History, Culture and International Law, 2012, 288 pages. (ISBN 978-90-04-23613-4)

16

Reisman, W. M.: The Quest for World Order and Human Dignity in the Twenty-first Century: Constitutive Process and Individual Commitment. General Course on Public International Law, 2012, 504 pages. (ISBN 978-90-04-23615-8)

17

Dugard, J.: The Secession of States and Their Recognition in the Wake of Kosovo, 2013, 312 pages. (ISBN 978-90-04-25748-1)

18

Gannagé, L.: Les méthodes du droit international privé à l'épreuve des conflits de cultures, 2013, 372 pages. (ISBN 978-90-04-25750-4)

19

Kohler, Ch.: L'autonomie de la volonté en droit international privé : un principe universel entre libéralisme et étatisme, 2013, 288 pages. (ISBN 978-90-04-25752-8)

20

Kreindler, R.: Competence-Competence in the Face of Illegality in Contracts and Arbitration Agreements, 2013, 504 pages. (ISBN 978-90-04-25754-2)

21

Crawford, J.: Chance, Order, Change: The Course of International Law. General Course on Public International Law, 2014, 540 pages. (ISBN 978-90-04-26808-1)

22

Brand, R. A.: Transaction Planning Using Rules on Jurisdiction and the Recognition and Enforcement of Judgments, 2014, 360 pages. (ISBN 978-90-04-26810-4)

23

Kolb, R.: L'article 103 de la Charte des Nations Unies, 2014, 416 pages. (ISBN 978-90-04-27836-3)

24

Benvenisti, E.: The Law of Global Governance, 2014, 336 pages. (ISBN 978-90-04-27911-7)

25

Yusuf, A. A.: Pan-Africanism and International Law, 2014, 288 pages. (ISBN 978-90-04-28504-0)

26

Kono, T.: Efficiency in Private International Law, 2014, 216 pages. (ISBN 978-90-04-28506-4)

27
Cachard, O., Le transport international aérien de passagers, 2015, 292 pages.
(ISBN 978-90-04-29773-9)

28
Corten, O. : La rébellion et le droit international, 2015, 376 pages.
(ISBN 978-90-04-29775-3)

29
Frigo, M., Circulation des biens culturels, détermination de la loi applicable et méthodes de règlement des litiges, 2016, 552 pages.
(ISBN 978-90-04-32129-8)

30
Bermann, G. A., International Arbitration and Private International Law, 2017, 648 pages.
(ISBN 978-90-04-34825-7)

31
Bennouna, M., Le droit international entre la lettre et l'esprit, 2017, 304 pages. (ISBN 978-90-04-34846-2)

32
Murphy, S., International Law relating to Islands, 376 pages.
(ISBN 978-90-04-36154-6)

33
Hess, B., The Private-Public Law Divide in International Dispute Resolution, 328 pages.
(ISBN 978-90-04-38490-3)

34
Rau, A. : The Allocation of Power between Arbitral Tribunals and State Courts, 2018, 608 pages.
(ISBN 978-90-04-38891-8)

35
Muir Watt, H. : Discours sur les méthodes du droit international privé (des formes juridiques de l'inter-altérité, 2019, 608 pages. (ISBN 978-90-04-39558-9)

36
Nolte, G. : Treaties and Their Practice – Symptoms of Their Rise or Decline, 2018, 288 pages.
(ISBN 978-90-04-39456-8)

37
Cuniberti, G. : Le fondement de l'effet des jugements étrangers, 2019, 288 pages.
(ISBN 978-90-04-41180-7)

38
D'Avout, L. : L'entreprise et les conflits internationaux de lois, 875 pages.
(ISBN 978-90-04-41668-0)

39
Brown Weiss, E. : Establishing Norms in a Kaleidoscopic World, 528 pages.
(ISBN 978-90-04-42200-1)

40
Brunnée, J. : Procedure and Substance in International Environmental Law, 2020, 240 pages.
(ISBN 978-90-04-44437-9)

41

Rajamani, L.: Innovation and Experimentation in the International Climate Change Regime, 2020, 336 pages.
(ISBN 978-90-04-44439-3)

42

Kessedjian, C.: Le tiers impartial et indépendant en droit international, juge, arbitre, médiateur, conciliateur, 2020, 832 pages. (ISBN 978-90-04-44880-3)

43

Maljean-Dubois, S.: Le droit international de la biodiversité, 2021, 590 pages.
(ISBN 978-90-04-46287-8)

44

Dasser, F.: "Soft Law" in International Commercial Arbitration, 2021, 300 pages.
(ISBN 978-90-04-46289-2)

45

Peters, A.: Animals in International Law, 2021, 641 pages.
(ISBN 978-90-04-46624-1)

46

Besson, S.: La *due diligence* en droit international, 2021, 363 pages.
(ISBN 978-90-04-46626-5)

47

Ferrari, F.: Forum Shopping Despite Unification of Law, 2021, 446 pages.
(ISBN 978-90-04-46626-5)

48

Wolfrum, R.: Solidarity and Community Interests: Driving Forces for the Interpretation and Development of International Law, 2021, 663 pages.
(ISBN 978-90-04-50832-3)

49

Kolb, R.: Le droit international comme corps de «droit privé» et de «droit public», 2022, 976 pages.
(ISBN 978-90-04-51836-0)

50

Tladi, D.: The Extraterritorial Use of Force against Non-State Actors, 2022, 208 pages.
(ISBN 978-90-04-52147-6)

51

Schabas, W. A.: Relationships between International Criminal Law and Other Branches of International Law, 2022, 272 pages.
(ISBN 978-90-04-52149-0)

52

Bollée, S.: Les pouvoirs inhérents des arbitres internationaux, 2023, 306 pages.
(ISBN 978-90-04-67848-4)

53

Laghmani, S.: Islam et droit international, 2023, 168 pages.
(ISBN 978-90-04-67850-7)

429 - 23 (II)/04-23